EVIDENCE LAW

A Student's Guide to the Law of Evidence as Applied in American Trials

Second Edition

By

Roger C. Park
James Edgar Hervey Chair of Litigation
University of California—Hastings College of the Law

David P. Leonard
Professor of Law, William M. Rains Fellow
Loyola Law School, Los Angeles

Steven H. Goldberg
Professor of Law
Pace University School of Law

HORNBOOK SERIES®

THOMSON
™
WEST

Mat #40098897

Hornbook Series, *WESTLAW* and West Group are trademarks registered in the U.S. Patent and Trademark Office.

COPYRIGHT © 1998 WEST GROUP
© 2004 West, a Thomson business
      610 Opperman Drive
      P.O. Box 64526
      St. Paul, MN 55164–0526
      1–800–328–9352

Printed in the United States of America

ISBN 0–314–14401–3

 TEXT IS PRINTED ON 10% POST CONSUMER RECYCLED PAPER

To Suzanne
R.C.P.

To Susan, Matthew, and Adam
D.P.L.

For Julia
and
In memory of Barbara
S.H.G.

*

Preface to the Second Edition

In the six years since the first edition of this "lawyer's treatise designed specifically for law students," the law of evidence has continued to evolve. There have been changes in the Federal Rules of Evidence, some of substantial significance, others simply efforts at clarification. Judicial decisions have, as always, added nuance to already established doctrine. Those rule and interpretation changes pale, however, beside two blockbuster changes in the law of evidence.

First, there have been important developments in the treatment of expert testimony, as the courts and rule makers have wrestled with the revolution started by the Supreme Court's 1993 decision in *Daubert v. Merrell Dow Pharmaceuticals*. Some of the post-*Daubert* questions we anticipated in the first edition have been answered by Supreme Court decisions and by amendments to the Federal Rules of Evidence. Chapter Ten discusses these changes, highlights some of the specific areas of expert testimony that have been affected, anticipates some of the still unanswered questions raised by the *Daubert* approach, and compares that approach, as it has grown in the federal system, to the still important *Frye* approach to expert testimony.

The Court's 2004 decision in *Crawford v. Washington* made a sharp departure from earlier confrontation cases, holding that "testimonial" statements, even if they fall within firmly rooted exceptions to the hearsay rule, are inadmissible against criminal defendants unless the out-of-court declarant is unavailable and the defendant previously had an opportunity to cross-examine the declarant about the statement. The decision, discussed in Chapter Seven, may leave more questions than it answers. The Court leaves open the definition of a "testimonial" statement and suggests that in the future it may decide that "non-testimonial" statements do not implicate the confrontation clause, their admissibility depending solely upon the law of hearsay.

We have, in this edition, kept faith with the advocate's approach to evidence. As the first edition was an adaptation of the TRIAL OBJECTIONS HANDBOOK, this edition continues to rely for its approach on that practitioner manual's focus on the notion that evidence law is something lawyers must employ quickly and concisely in the courtroom. We have been gratified by our students' responses to learning the language of the courtroom from that perspective and have been reinforced in our resolve to present the law of evidence as much as possible through example and with a constant eye to context.

In addition to the debt we owe our Evidence and Trial Objections students for comments and suggestions that have made this edition closer to our ideal, we would not have been able to complete it without the hard work and dedication of our research assistants, Jone Tran and John-Paul Buchanan at University of California, Hastings, Sabrina Cao-Garcia at Loyola Law School, and Sarah Courtman at Pace Law School.

ROGER C. PARK
San Francisco, California

DAVID P. LEONARD
Los Angeles, California

STEVEN H. GOLDBERG
White Plains, New York

June, 2004

Preface to the First Edition

This is a lawyer's treatise designed specifically for law students. It is an adaptation of the TRIAL OBJECTIONS HANDBOOK, a work for practitioners that provided a concise description of the law of evidence from the perspective of the advocate who had to offer and oppose it, rather than from the perspective of the judge who had to rule on it. Where possible, the HANDBOOK discussed evidence issues in the language of the courtroom—full of examples and arguments in context as spoken by trial lawyers. In preparing this version for students, we have kept the advocate's perspective and have tried to be true to the notion that lawyers must employ evidence rules quickly and concisely in the courtroom.

We have been mindful that law students do not have the courtroom experience of practicing lawyers. The first four chapters on the operation of the courtroom have been added to give law students a sense of the context and environment that has so much influence on individual evidence rulings. In addition, we have expanded discussions of major cases and doctrines beyond that presented in the Handbook.

We hope this approach will enhance the student's understanding of the law of evidence in action. Wherever possible, we have employed examples to give the student a feel for the context in which the particular evidence problem might arise and for the language used by lawyers and judges in resolving it. We have also discussed the rationales and purposes of particular rules, believing that effective advocacy often means persuading the decision-maker that the result sought is beneficial as a matter of policy.

If law students come away from this hornbook with a sense of how to speak the language of evidence in the courtroom, as well as with an understanding of the law of evidence, we will have fulfilled our desire to help beginning trial lawyers on their way.

For able research on the practitioner's edition, we wish to thank Mark Dunn, Julia Erickson, Tom Holm, and Brendan Randall, graduates of the University of Minnesota law school. Julia Erickson deserves special recognition for editorial contributions. Only her untimely death prevented us from inviting her to participate in this edition. Two trial lawyers, John Sands and Peter Wold, gave selflessly of their time and made perceptive comments on the practitioner's edition.

Students in the Trial Objections courses at Minnesota and Hastings and in Evidence classes at Pace offered helpful suggestions and spotted errors in earlier versions. Christine Cupino, Loyola Law School class of 1999, Gene Sitnitsky, Loyola Law School class of 2000, Melanie Slaughter, Pace University Law School Class of 1998, and Russell Stein, UC Hastings Class of 1999, provided helpful research assistance on the student edition. We also owe thanks to Stephen Lothrop, head of Faculty Support at UC Hastings, for his diligent and careful work.

Roger Park owes his largest debt to his wife and best friend, Suzanne Park—not only for her love and support and her large if not endless patience, but also for her tireless proofreading, editing, and counseling on both editions. Her organizational abilities alone made it possible to miss deadlines by much smaller margins than would otherwise have been the case.

ROGER C. PARK
San Francisco, California

DAVID P. LEONARD
Los Angeles, California

STEVEN H. GOLDBERG
White Plains, New York

June, 1998

WESTLAW® Overview

Evidence Law, A Student's Guide to the Law of Evidence as Applied in American Trials, by Roger C. Park, David P. Leonard and Steven H. Goldberg, offers a detailed and comprehensive treatment of basic rules, principles and issues relating to evidence. To supplement the information contained in this book, you can access Westlaw, a computer-assisted legal research service of West Group. Westlaw contains a broad array of legal research resources, including case law, statutes, expert commentary, current developments and various other types of information.

Learning how to use these materials effectively will enhance your legal research abilities. To help you coordinate the information in the book with your Westlaw research, this volume contains an appendix listing Westlaw databases, search techniques and sample problems.

The instructions and features described in this Westlaw overview are based on accessing Westlaw via westlaw.com® at **www.westlaw.com**.

THE PUBLISHER

*

Summary of Contents

——————

*

Table of Contents

The Subsequent Remedial Measures Rule [FRE 407]

Exceptions That Apply Only if the Declarant Is Unavailable [FRE 804]

*

EVIDENCE LAW

A Student's Guide to the Law of Evidence as Applied in American Trials

Second Edition

*

Chapter 1

PRESENTING EVIDENCE AT TRIAL: AN OVERVIEW

Table of Sections

§ 1.01 The Adversarial Trial

The justice system in the United States is based upon the common law trial—a contest waged by at least two opposing parties before a neutral decision-maker in a court of law. Inherited from the English common law tradition, the trial is the theoretical centerpiece of adversary justice—a system of dispute resolution in which the parties control the gathering, preparation, and presentation of information for decision by a relatively passive neutral. Of course, trial itself is only the tip of a very large iceberg. Barely half of our societal grievances ripen into disputes and an infinitesimal percentage of those disputes end up in court filings.[1] Less than 10 percent of those court filings ever end up in trial.[2] Adversarial justice, nevertheless, pervades our dispute resolution culture, influencing even some of the forms of what is popularly described as Alternative Dispute Resolution. Trial results cast a long

---

1. Richard E. Miller & Austin Sarat, *Grievances, Claims, and Disputes: Assessing the Adversary Culture*, 15 Law & Soc'y Rev. 525 (1980–81).

2. These and other related statistics are available at the Department of Justice Website. http://www.ojp.usdoj.gov/bjs/civil.htm (August 19, 2003).

shadow over other stages of litigation and methods of dispute resolution, because actors use them as guides to settlement.

Adversarial justice is at once more complex and simpler than finding the truth, determining what "really happened", or achieving results that seem equitable to everyone. It is a system of dispute resolution that is sufficient to order a society—good enough to keep us from resolving our differences by other less systematic, less predictable, less reliable, and ultimately less peaceful methods. Although the validity of the system depends, at one level, upon our belief that the common law trial will help us discover what really happened, it depends equally upon our belief that our less-than-perfect process is the best available in light of a myriad of societal values.

We accept individual results that may be a less-than-perfect reflection of what actually happened, not only because we know that perfect re-creation is impossible, but because our dispute resolution incorporates other values of importance. Our interest in determining what really happened in a criminal matter, for example, must co-exist with our judgment that it is better to mistakenly leave at liberty someone who ought to be incarcerated than it is to mistakenly incarcerate someone who ought to be left at liberty. In civil disputes, equity must co-exist with society's interest in stability, so we affirm the status quo (the possession of the property, the cost of repairing an injury, etc.) even though the case for change in a particular dispute is equally as strong as the case for the status quo. Our interest in the truth co-exists with privileges such as those that encourage privacy (communication between spouses) and confidential relations (lawyer/client, physician/patient, priest/penitent, etc.); with our desire to make sure that parties have their say and with our desire to reach peaceful settlements.

The idea that justice will emerge when people with opposing interests gather, shape, and present information to a neutral decision-maker has not been accepted universally. Predecessors to modern rational systems—the ordeal, trial by battle—depended at least in theory upon divine intervention. Today, other societies seek justice in systems other than the adversary system. Active-judge or "inquisitorial" systems distrust any process in which interested parties control the generation and presentation of information. Continental systems, for example, often depend more upon neutrals than upon adversaries for development of evidence and questioning of witnesses, especially in criminal cases. (Civil cases on the continent are often party-controlled.) There is a lively dispute about whether tendentious presentations by partisans are preferable to a more active fact-finder—one who, though officially neutral, might be subject to prejudgment and less satisfactory to parties eager to have their "day in court."[3]

3. *See, e.g.,* Mirjan Damaska, Evidence Law Adrift, 74–124 (1997); Joan L. Dwyer, *Fair Play the Inquisitorial Way: A Review of the Administrative Appeals Tribunal's Use of Inquisitorial Procedures*, 22 J. NAALJ 81, (Spring, 2002); Oscar G. Chase, *American "Exceptionalism" and Comparative Procedure*, 50 Am. J. Comp. L. 277 (Spring, 2002).

The adversarial system, coupled with the institution of jury trial, has a profound impact on American rules of evidence. To counteract adversarial bias in the selection and presentation of evidence, we have evidence rules that seek to prevent adversaries from sweeping good evidence under the rug and preferring unreliable alternatives. For example, the hearsay rule partly serves to prevent adversaries from offering polished-up hearsay reports in lieu of shaky live witnesses. The supposed naïveté of the lay jury is the justification for many other rules that seek to protect against prejudice and misuse of evidence. Furthermore, the bifurcated court used in jury trials makes the system of exclusionary rules more workable, because the judge can exclude evidence without the jury ever hearing of it.

§ 1.02   Stages of a Common Law Trial

Lawyers dominate the American trial process. They interview witnesses and gather information; they shape the client's legal posture; they prepare the pleadings; they conduct the formal discovery; they prepare the witnesses; and they oversee the production of exhibits that will convey information to the fact-finder. At trial, they have a role in choosing the fact-finder; they speak to the fact-finder about the case before the evidence is presented; and they sum it up afterwards. During presentation of evidence to the fact-finder, it is the lawyer who examines the witnesses and limits the information that the opponent can present. Lawyers even assist the judge in determining the law that will be applied to the evidence presented to the fact-finder.

Rules and statutes about the conduct of a common law trial vary from jurisdiction to jurisdiction, but the general structure is the same. The Federal Rules of Civil Procedure and the Federal Rules of Evidence provide a general outline for the conduct of trials in the federal courts and in most states, although there are differences in the various jurisdictions, some of which remain dear to a jurisdiction's lawyers and judges.

Today, many trials involve multiple parties on one or both sides. Any of the parties may bear the burden of persuasion on one or another of the issues to be decided by the fact-finder. The common law trial reduced to a minimum, however, assumes that there are two parties who disagree about an issue the law is competent to decide. Usually, the party who wants to change the status quo brings the lawsuit, is called the plaintiff or prosecution, and bears the burden of persuasion on the issue about which the parties disagree. The party who wants to maintain the status quo must answer the suit and bears no burden of persuasion in order to maintain the status quo.[4]

We employ this minimum model—two opposing parties, one issue for which the plaintiff, or prosecution in criminal cases, bears the burden of persuasion—in examining the conduct of the common law trial.

---

4. *See* **Ch. 4** for a full discussion of burdens and presumptions.

Pre-trial

Pre-trial discovery, motions, and hearings have come to dominate our adversary system. There is often more adversarial activity before trial than during. Many more disputes are resolved in the pre-trial period than following a full trial. Although most of the substantial number of rules, procedures, and activities of pre-trial litigation are beyond the scope of this book, many important evidentiary issues are raised, considered, and sometimes decided during pre-trial hearings.[5]

Jury Selection

When one of the parties demands a jury trial, jury selection is the first trial activity. Much of the law about the conduct of a trial, particularly the law of evidence, is based upon assumptions about how jurors think and act as fact-finders, even though many trials are conducted with the judge as fact-finder.

The group of prospective jurors first brought to the courtroom is called the venire. Members of the venire are questioned in court to determine their qualifications to sit as jurors on the case at hand. The process is called *voir dire*. In most federal courtrooms, the questioning is done by the judge, with the lawyers having the right to submit questions for the judge to ask. In many state courts, the lawyers are allowed to question the prospective jurors, either as a group or individually. The right of parties to question prospective jurors through their lawyers, rather than through the judge, is one of those differences between the federal system and the states that many lawyers hold dear.

The venire is reduced to the proper number of jurors and alternates through a series of challenges made by the lawyers for the parties. (A judge may remove a prospective juror *sua sponte*, but judges rarely do so.) A challenge for cause may be asserted against any prospective juror. A cause challenge will be sustained if the judge finds that the juror either does not meet the statutory qualifications for jury service or because responses made during *voir dire* demonstrate that the person will not hear the matter impartially. A party may exercise a peremptory challenge for any reason and to any prospective juror. The right to exercise peremptory challenges is limited, as to reason, only by the United States Constitution[6] and, as to number, only by the statutes or rules of the various jurisdictions. Generally, more peremptory challenges are permitted in criminal cases than in civil. The number in criminal cases often varies with the seriousness of the charge.

Opening Statements

Once the jurors and alternates have been sworn in, the lawyers have an opportunity to make opening statements. Often mischaracterized in the media as opening arguments, opening statements are limited to a

---

5. *See* §§ **2.02, 2.06**.

6. *See, e.g.,* Batson v. Kentucky, 476 U.S. 79 (1986) (restricting exercise of peremptory challenges based solely upon race).

description of the evidence the lawyer expects to present to the jury in support of the client's theory of the case. The lawyer may describe the evidence in a persuasive manner, but is prohibited from drawing inferences or asking the jury to reach conclusions about the described evidence. Although argument is supposed to be restricted to summation, many courts are less than strict in enforcing the prohibition against argument in an opening statement.[7]

The party with the burden of persuasion—the plaintiff or prosecutor in our model—has the opportunity to make the first opening statement. In many jurisdictions, the defendant may reserve making an opening statement until after the plaintiff's case-in-chief. As a matter of practice, this is now rare, most defendants seizing the opportunity to address the jurors immediately following the plaintiff.

Plaintiff's Case-in-Chief

The plaintiff calls witnesses to testify (subject to cross-examination) and produces tangible evidence in support of the plaintiff's cause of action. Witnesses are first examined by the plaintiff and then cross-examined by the defendant. When the plaintiff has produced all the evidence in support of the plaintiff's case, the plaintiff rests. The testimony from the witnesses and the exhibits offered in the plaintiff's case-in-chief must be sufficient to support a jury finding in favor of the plaintiff for every proposition for which the plaintiff bears the burden of persuasion. If it is not, the judge will grant a defense motion for judgment as a matter of law. The plaintiff's obligation to produce evidence sufficient to avoid a judgment as a matter of law at the end of the plaintiff's case (sometimes referred to as a *prima facie* case) is called the burden of production. It is sometimes also described as the burden of going forward or the burden of producing evidence.[8]

Defendant's Case-in-Chief

If the judge has denied a defense motion for judgment as a matter of law (because the plaintiff produced sufficient evidence to support a finding for plaintiff) it is the defendant's turn to proceed.

Despite the judge's determination that the plaintiff has presented a *prima facie* case, the defendant might choose not to present any evidence, believing that while the evidence is sufficient to support a finding for the plaintiff, it is not sufficient to obtain that finding. If the defendant believes it will prevail with the jury without presenting evidence of its own, the defendant rests and argues to the jury based upon the evidence in the plaintiff's case-in-chief, including evidence elicited on cross-examination of plaintiff's witnesses. This tactic—admittedly rare in civil cases—is possible because of the important difference between the burden of producing evidence and the burden of persuasion.

---

7. For the various objections to Opening Statements, *see* Roger C. Park, Trial Objections Handbook, ch. 10 (2d Ed.2001).

8. *See* § **4.06**.

The burden of producing evidence is satisfied if the plaintiff's evidence meets the bare minimum needed to support a jury verdict for the plaintiff, while the burden of persuasion is carried only when the evidence is powerful enough actually to persuade the jury to find for the plaintiff.

In the usual case, the defendant presents the testimony of witnesses and offers exhibits in roughly the same fashion as was done in the plaintiff's case-in-chief. The defendant's evidence may be offered to establish the defendant's positive contentions (the defendant was somewhere else, the defendant has legal title to the property, etc.) or may be offered to discredit the plaintiff's witnesses or counter the plaintiff's evidence. When the defendant has presented all of the evidence relating to the plaintiff's claim, or any affirmative defenses the defendant may have to that claim, the defendant rests.

Plaintiff's Rebuttal and Defendant's Surrebuttal

The plaintiff has an opportunity, after the defendant has rested, to offer witnesses and exhibits to rebut matters or discredit witnesses put forth during the defendant's case-in-chief. The plaintiff may not, however, present evidence that does not in some way qualify or otherwise relate to the evidence or witnesses produced in the defendant's case-in-chief. For example, if the defendant presents testimony that tends to discredit the testimony of the plaintiff's second witness, the plaintiff may present rebuttal testimony that credits the plaintiff's second witness or that witness' testimony. The plaintiff may not present rebuttal testimony, however, that credits testimony given by plaintiff's third witness, because that witness or that witness' testimony was not attacked in the defendant's case-in-chief.[9]

When the plaintiff's rebuttal case is concluded, the defendant has an opportunity for surrebuttal (or rejoinder). The defendant's surrebuttal case is limited to qualifying or otherwise responding to the evidence produced in the plaintiff's rebuttal case.

The trial judge may allow a departure from the ordinary practice of keeping rebuttal within the scope of the defendant's case and surrebuttal within the scope of rebuttal if circumstances and fairness warrant.

Motions for Judgment as a Matter of Law or Judgment of Acquittal

When there is no more rebuttal testimony from either side, and both sides have rested, one or both parties in a civil action may move for a judgment as a matter of law. The motion asks the judge to rule that on all of the evidence presented in the trial, no reasonable jury could find in favor of the other party. The motion is often different from the defen-

---

9. Our model does not assume a counter-claim by the defendant. If the defendant asserts a counter-claim, the defendant presents that claim in the defendant's case-in-chief and the plaintiff presents evidence on that claim during the plaintiff's rebuttal case.

dant's motion for judgment as a matter of law at the end of the plaintiff's case-in-chief for failure to make a *prima facie* case. Even if the plaintiff has met the burden of production, the judge may enter judgment for the defendant as a matter of law, if a reasonable jury could not conclude, based on all of the evidence from both sides, that the plaintiff has met the burden of persuasion. The judge will not grant the motion merely because the judge, if sitting without a jury, might find in favor or the moving party. The judge must be willing to say that no reasonable jury could reach any other conclusion. In a criminal case, only the defense may move the judge to take the decision away from the jurors and enter a judgment of acquittal.

Closing Arguments (Summation)

After all of the evidence has been presented to the jury, the lawyers have an opportunity to address the jurors. Closing argument is the lawyer's opportunity to sum up the case, to explain why the evidence presented to the jurors, combined with the law they will hear from the judge, mandates conclusions that lead inexorably to a verdict for the lawyer's client.

In the federal system and in many state jurisdictions, the party with the burden of persuasion is given the first and last word to the jury. The plaintiff makes the first closing argument, the defendant makes the second, and the plaintiff is then allowed a rebuttal to respond to arguments made by the defendant. Various jurisdictions employ different rules concerning the order of summation.

Jury Instructions

After the lawyers have made their closing arguments, the judge instructs the jurors on the law that is applicable to the case before them. These instructions are usually worked out with the lawyers in an instruction conference held sometime before the closing arguments, so that the lawyers may use the legal principles as a framework for arguing their cases to the jurors. In a few jurisdictions, judges instruct juries on the law before the lawyers make their closing arguments, but the predominant method is to the contrary.[10]

Jury Deliberations, Verdict Forms, and Verdicts

When the judge finishes instructing on the law, the jurors retire to the jury room to deliberate alone, separated from contact with all outside influences. They take with them into the jury room the verdict form agreed to by the lawyers and the judge and, usually, all of the tangible evidence introduced at trial.

---

10. Our model does not include the situation in which the defendant asserts affirmative defenses for which the defendant carries the burden of production—insanity in a criminal case, for example. If there is an affirmative defense for which the defendant has the burden of producing evidence, the judge will include the law about the affirmative defense in the instructions only if the defendant has produced sufficient evidence to raise the issue with the jury.

In most jurisdictions, the jurors' first task is to select one of their members as a foreperson to lead the discussion and communicate, if necessary, with the court. (In a few jurisdictions, the court appoints the jury foreperson before the beginning of testimony.)

In most criminal cases, in most jurisdictions, a jury verdict must be unanimous. Jurisdictions differ as to whether civil verdicts require unanimity or might be reached by some kind of a majority—often three quarters or five sixths of the jurors are required to join in the verdict.

Verdict forms in criminal cases are general, giving the jurors options of "guilty" or "not guilty" on the various charges being considered. Verdict forms in civil cases vary. Many jurisdictions provide options of a general verdict form, a special verdict form, or a verdict form that requires the jurors to answer specific interrogatories.

If the jury reaches a verdict, the foreperson completes the verdict form, signs it, and delivers it to the judge.

After the verdict has been read, a party may request that the judge poll the jurors, asking each juror individually and in open court whether the verdict read is that juror's verdict. If the number of jurors needed to return a verdict affirm that the verdict read is their verdict, the judge enters judgment accordingly, unless the judge is asked to consider post-trial motions for judgment notwithstanding the verdict or for a new trial.[11]

§ 1.03 Evidence in a Common Law Trial—Overview

Evidence has many meanings in common parlance and more than one meaning as lawyers use the term. We commonly say, in response to someone's assertion of some proposition, "show me the evidence." It is a way of saying, "prove it." The great evidence teacher, Irving Younger, was fond of using the various meanings lawyers employ for "evidence" in describing the process of bringing information about a disputed event to the attention of jurors: "Evidence is admissible in evidence in accordance with the law of evidence."

The first "evidence" is the entire collection of perceptions and objects available about and from the event at issue—the totality of the information the lawyer might gather during the process of interviewing witnesses and engaging in formal discovery. It is the representation, by word or object, of all the information about what happened, whether it is legally important or not. It is the starting point for the lawyer, the haystack of information in which the lawyer may find the needle(s) of information that will support the client's cause of action. The process of finding out everything that happened, without any prejudgment about its importance at trial, is a critical step for the lawyer. If the lawyer prejudges too severely which pieces of information about the event will be important, something crucial almost always goes undiscovered.

---

11. These motions are not available to the government in a criminal case.

The second "evidence" is that portion of the perceptions about and objects from the event that support the client's position at trial and that the lawyers present to the jury through witnesses and exhibits. These are the needles of trial evidence that the lawyer found in the haystack of initial information. It is what the jurors consider in deciding what happened.[12] Most of this is *viva voce* evidence—from the mouths of witnesses—but tangible evidence also plays a significant role in jury decision making. Tangible evidence includes both "real" and demonstrative evidence. "Real" evidence is an object that played a role in the events at issue, for example, the knife found at a crime scene, a written contract, or nurses' notes about the progress of a hospital patient. Demonstrative evidence is an object that although it played no role in the events at issue, illustrates something about those events—a map, diagram, model, photograph, or the like.

The third "evidence" is the body of rules that determines which parts of the first kind of "evidence"—all of the perceptions about and objects from the event—may become the second kind of "evidence"— what is presented to the trier of fact for consideration in deciding what happened. This third kind of "evidence"—the Law of Evidence—is a subset of the law of procedure. Unlike the law of property, or torts, or contracts, evidence law does not define relationships and determine substantive rights between people. Evidence law, in the words of the drafters of the Federal Rules of Evidence, exists "to secure fairness in administration, elimination of unjustifiable expense and delay . . . to the end that truth may be ascertained and proceedings justly determined."[13]

The common law of evidence evolved over the centuries, as did most other law, appellate case by appellate case. But, it grew, also, through constant usage by lawyers and trial rulings about evidence by judges. Although there was no shortage of evidence cases in the appellate courts, the evidence questions raised on appeal represented an infinitesimal percentage of the evidence issues decided by trial judges and an even smaller percentage of the evidence issues considered by trial lawyers in the heat of trial.

Evidence law in the United States was relatively homogeneous, despite the plethora of jurisdictions and the lack of opportunity for appellate courts to decide the great variety of evidence issues that arose hundreds of thousand times a day in tens of thousand courtrooms around the country. The law of evidence evolved in the fashion of a language, influenced as much by the usage of lawyers and the on-the-spot rulings of judges in courtrooms as by appellate opinions.[14] As a

---

12. *See* Scott W. Howe, *Untangling Competing Conceptions of "Evidence,"* 30 Loy. L.A. L. Rev. 1199 (1997) (stating that jurors consider substantially more than what judges instruct is "evidence"); *See also* Paul F. Kirgis, *The Problem Of The Expert Juror*, 75 Temple L. Rev. 493 (Fall, 2002).

13. Fed. R. Evid. 102 (1996).

14. *See* Ronald J. Allen, *The Simpson Affair, Reform of the Criminal Justice Process, and Magic Bullets*, 67 U. Colo. L. Rev. 989, 995 (the common law, like natural languages, is a grown order rather than a made order).

result, the words that lawyers used in talking about evidence in the various jurisdictions were remarkably similar, even though the accents were different. A trial lawyer, familiar with one jurisdiction's law of evidence, might try a case in a different jurisdiction, confident that a general familiarity with the language of the courtroom would be sufficient to deal with most of the evidence questions that might arise during an average trial day. That is not to say that evidence law did not vary significantly among the jurisdictions, but those major areas of difference were often statutory or the subject of an important appellate decision in the jurisdiction, relatively easy to find and assimilate.

Although the language of the courtroom was more similar than different throughout the United States, the differences were strongly held. Various attempts to codify evidence law were defeated by apathy and procedural conservatism,[15] until the enactment of the Federal Rules of Evidence in 1975.

The Federal Rules of Evidence reduce the way lawyers and judges talk about evidence to about sixty relatively short rules. Though they constitute the law of evidence only in the federal system, their influence has been much wider. Most jurisdictions have now codified their common law of evidence, and most of the codifications are similar in organization and substance to the Federal Rules of Evidence. Even in New York, the largest remaining common law evidence jurisdiction, the evidence spoken in state courtrooms is almost identical to that spoken in federal courtrooms.

The common law system of adversary justice depends upon the lawyers to find, produce, and refine the evidence. Judges have the power to call witnesses and to exclude evidence on their own motion, but they rarely do so.

To be an effective evidence advocate in court, the lawyer must have a firm grasp of the legal theory of the case, an ear for the nature of evidence being offered, and an almost automatic understanding of the law of evidence—a speaking facility for the language of the courtroom.

Relevance is the first consideration for any evidence and is often important in arguing other rules of exclusion, particularly hearsay. Without a clear understanding of the elements of the claim and defense, the trial lawyer is not equipped to handle questions of relevancy.

Knowing the law of evidence, or where to find it, is not enough to be an effective evidence advocate in the courtroom. Evidence at trial comes as fast as every question and answer. The lawyer's primary task is to pay attention to the substance of the testimony, not its admissibility. To deal effectively with admissibility, the lawyer must learn the language of the courtroom—must be able to anticipate when a question is objectionable

---

15. *See* Roger C. Park, *A Subject Matter Approach to Hearsay Reform,* 86 Mich. L. Rev. 52, 53 at n.11–13 (1987) (concerning the failure of the 1942 Model Code of Evidence and the 1953 Uniform Rules of Evidence to achieve significant support). The 1966 California Evidence Code was the first major enactment of an evidence code within the United States. *Id.*

or an answer should be struck and make an instant fact based legal argument for why evidence law does not allow the evidence. There is a rhythm to the admission and exclusion of evidence that the evidence advocate must master in order to make the law of evidence work for the lawyer's client.

§ 1.04   Admission and Exclusion of Evidence; Preliminary Questions of Fact [FRE 104]

A trial judge's most frequent, if not most important, role in jury trials is to rule on evidence questions. For every question of substantive law a judge must decide in a trial, there are hundreds of evidence questions presented. Some evidence issues are sufficiently foreseeable and important for lawyers to present by motion and to brief. Many of the most important evidence issues, issues that are often outcome determinative, are handled at pre-trial hearings. The great volume of evidence questions, however, are raised unexpectedly during the heat of trial. One lawyer asks a question. The other lawyer stands and says, "objection," followed by a one or two word label for the evidence issue—leading, hearsay, best evidence, or some similar reference to a rule of exclusion. The judge says "sustained" or "overruled." The question of evidence law was raised, discussed, and decided in about twenty seconds. Occasionally one of the lawyers will ask permission to argue the matter to the judge. It might take a minute or two before that question of evidence law has been handled. It is not surprising, therefore, that the common law of evidence placed an uncommon amount of discretion in the trial judge, and that appellate courts afforded substantial deference to the trial judge's evidence rulings. There was too much happening, too fast, for any other result. More importantly, it was happening in the midst of an intellectual contest in which context was of critical importance to the decision—a context apparent to the trial judge, but unlikely to be apparent in the cold transcript available to the appellate bench.

The extraordinary discretion that the common law lodged with the trial judge found its way into the Federal Rules. The Federal Rules of Evidence codified more than they changed the common law, so most evidentiary objections under the Rules still involve questions that depend for resolution on an understanding of the context. In addition, some of the Rules place explicit discretion with the trial judge to determine specific issues.[16]

16. *See generally*, David P. Leonard, *Appellate Review of Evidentiary Rulings*, 70 N.C. L. Rev. 1155 (1992) (discussing the use of discretion in Rules 608 and 611); David P. Leonard, *Power and Responsibility in Evidence Law*, 63 S. Cal. L. Rev. 937 (1990) (discussing the extent to which the Federal Rules of Evidence grant discretion to the trial court); Jon R. Waltz, *Judicial Discretion in the Admission of Evidence Under the Federal Rules of Evidence*, 79 Nw. U. L. Rev. 1097 (1984) (discussing discretion in evidence law). The Federal Rules of Evidence are replete with opportunities for the trial judge to exercise her discretion in evidentiary matters. *See e.g.*, Fed. R. Evid. 104; United States v. Mark, 943 F.2d 444 (4th Cir. 1991) (Construing Rule 105, the trial court, *sua sponte*, gave limiting instruction as to evidence of uncharged misconduct. The trial court has discretion to protect a party from its own oversight.); Fed. R. Evid. 201 (court may take judicial

Rule 608(b), for example, makes it discretionary with the trial judge whether a lawyer may attack the credibility of a witness, by asking that witness, on cross-examination, about specific instances of the witness' conduct that demonstrate untruthfulness. Rule 102 charges the trial judge with the duty to exercise discretion to ensure that "the truth may be ascertained and the proceedings justly determined." Rule 403 invokes the judge's discretion to exclude admittedly relevant testimony if it carries "the danger of unfair prejudice, confusion of the issues, or misleading the jury." Rule 611 gives the judge discretion to modify the order and the mode of interrogation and presentation. It allows the judge to change the normal conduct of the trial, if the judge believes it will aid in ascertaining the truth, save time, or protect witnesses. Rule 614 gives the judge the power to examine witnesses called by the parties or to call and examine the judge's own witnesses.

What does the judge do when a lawyer raises an issue of admissibility by lodging an objection to a question put to a witness or an exhibit that is being offered?

Rule 104(a) places the obligation on the judge to decide whether evidence that is objected to by one of the lawyers is admissible. The judge is not bound by the rules of evidence, except for privileges, in making the decision.[17] The standard the judge employs to determine whether the evidence objected to is admissible is the civil standard—more probably true than not true. If, for example, the question is whether a witness is qualified to testify as an expert, the judge hears the qualifications of the witness, any discrediting or qualifying information from the opponent, and then decides whether the witness is more likely an expert than not. Besides the qualification of witnesses, the existence of a privilege, the voluntariness of a confession, and the applicability of a hearsay exception are indicative of the kinds of questions that usually are decided by the trial judge under Rule 104(a).

Example

Plaintiff sues defendant for speeding, running a red light, and smashing his blue Miata sports car into plaintiff's car. Defendant admits being involved in the accident, but denies speeding and running the red light. Plaintiff calls a witness who was a back seat passenger in another car driving along the same road the defendant was traveling. At what is established as being about two minutes before the accident, the passenger in the front seat of the car said something.

Plaintiff's lawyer: What did he say?

Defense lawyer: Objection, hearsay.

Plaintiff's lawyer: Your honor, may we approach?

---

notice of adjudicative facts); Fed. R. Evid. 403.

17. *See* **Ch. 8** for a discussion of evidentiary privileges.

[At sidebar] The witness will say that the passenger in the front seat said: "That blue Miata sports car just passed us going about 90. That big guy driving it is going to hit someone." It is either within the present sense impression exception or the excited utterance exception to the rule against hearsay.

The passenger's statement is hearsay—an out of court statement offered to prove the truth of what is asserted in the statement—and is inadmissible unless it qualifies under one of the two exceptions to the rule against hearsay for which the plaintiff's lawyer has argued. Rule 104(a) designates the judge as the one to determine whether the statement qualifies under either the present sense impression exception or the excited utterance exception to the rule against hearsay.

In order to admit the passenger's statement as a present sense impression, the judge must find the preliminary fact that it was "a statement describing . . . an event . . . while the declarant was perceiving the event . . . or immediately thereafter."[18] In order to admit the passenger's statement as an excited utterance, the judge must find the preliminary fact that the statement related to a "startling event" made while the passenger was "under the stress of excitement caused by the event."[19] The judge will admit the statement upon finding either the preliminary facts required for a present sense impression or the preliminary facts required for an excited utterance to exist more likely than not. The judge will exclude the statement upon finding it more likely than not that neither preliminary fact existed. It is the judge, rather than the jury, who decides these "facts," even though the jury is normally the fact finder in a trial.

The judge's responsibility to apply the civil standard and to be the fact finder of the preliminary facts under Rule 104(a) exists even in those cases in which the jurors will consider the same question. Moreover, the judge applies the civil standard even in those cases in which the jurors will decide the same question by applying a more rigorous standard. In a criminal conspiracy prosecution, for example, the jury must decide beyond a reasonable doubt whether the defendant was a conspirator. The judge, however, must admit the statement of another claiming the defendant was a conspirator, if the judge finds it more likely than not that the person making the statement was actually a co-conspirator.[20] The judge, of course, may not contaminate the jury's deliberation

18. Fed. R. Evid. 803(1).

19. Fed. R. Evid. 803(2).

20. Fed. R. Evid. 801(d)(2)(E); Bourjaily v. United States, 483 U.S. 171 (1987); *See, e.g.,* United States v. Elam, 678 F.2d 1234 (5th Cir. 1982) (where the trial judge determines that the requisite foundation has been established for the introduction of conspirator statements, no jury instruction is necessary and none should be given. The jury should not know that judge has decided the issue of conspiracy for the purposes of evidence lest the jury think the issue has been finally decided for all other purposes as well.); United States v. Barksdale–Contreras, 972 F.2d 111 (5th Cir. 1992) (statements of coconspirators were admissible even though a defendant was acquitted of conspiracy, given the different standards applicable to admissibility and guilt determinations).

on the conspiracy issue by telling the jurors that the judge has already decided the question, albeit using a different standard.

Why have the judge involved in this preliminary fact finding under Rule 104(a)? Why not have the judge admit the statement and then instruct the jurors: If you find either that the passenger was excited when making the statement or was describing an event as it was happening you may consider the statement in deciding the case. If you do not find one of those two preliminary facts to exist; you must decide the case without considering the passenger's statement?

Rule 104(a) takes this fact finding from the jury and gives it to the judge in order to safeguard operation of the rules of evidence—many of which exist because we are fearful that jurors will not process certain information in the way the law deems appropriate. If the jurors had to determine whether the witness was either describing an event as it took place or was sufficiently excited to allow the hearsay statement into evidence, they would be in an untenable position. If they found neither of the preliminary facts to exist, they would have to ignore relevant evidence they had already heard. Asking people who typically are not lawyers and who serve for only one case to uphold technical rules of evidence, rather than consider relevant evidence in the one case that they have to decide, asks too much. Human nature dictates that the jurors will not follow the court's instruction to ignore the passenger's important out-of-court statement, even if they do not believe the passenger was describing an ongoing event or was excited when speaking.

It is particularly important for the judge to make this kind of fact finding because Rule 104(a) contemplates that the decision maker should be able to consider inadmissible evidence in making the determination of whether the preliminary facts needed for admissibility exist.

Example

Same sports car accident as described in the above example, except that the front seat passenger does not say anything about the speeding car as it passes, but rather, says something as their car comes upon the scene of the accident. The witness is the back seat passenger in the car.

Plaintiff's lawyer: What did he say?

Defense lawyer: Objection, hearsay.

[At sidebar]
Plaintiff's lawyer: The witness will say that the passenger in the front seat said: "When I saw that blue Miata sports car speed past us, at 90, I thought to myself, the big guy driving that car is going to hit someone." It is either within the present sense impression exception or the excited utterance exception to the rule against hearsay.

Defense lawyer:	Your honor, that statement is not a present sense impression, because it neither describes nor explains the event of the speeding sports car. That it relates to that event of seeing the speeding sports car would be all right if this was an excited utterance, but there is no evidence that the declarant was under the stress of excitement when making the statement.[21]
Judge:	Well, it is not a present sense impression, so let's find out whether the witness was excited.
Defense lawyer:	This witness testified at a deposition in this matter that the front seat passenger made the statement in a calm voice and with no sign of excitement.
Judge:	[To plaintiff's lawyer.] That doesn't sound like excitement to me. Is that what happened?
Plaintiff's lawyer:	I have an affidavit from the person who talked to the front seat passenger when he was dropped off. Here's what the passenger said: "I'm calm now, but when I saw the accident, the sight of that speeding car came into my head. The accident scene made my heart race. I was so excited, I don't know how I got out any words. I told the guys in the car about the premonition I had when I saw the speeding car. I don't know how I kept my voice so calm when I told them. I've never been so upset." That sounds like excitement to me.
Defense lawyer:	Judge, that affidavit is not admissible evidence. And even if the person making the affidavit were here, the conversation about being upset would be inadmissible hearsay.
Judge:	When I am deciding something preliminary to the admission of evidence under 104(a), I don't have to follow the rules of evidence. I am going to consider the affidavit. Based on what it says, I find that what the front seat passenger said to the others in the car when they passed the accident was an excited utterance and admissible as an exception to the rule against hearsay.

The judge not only may consider inadmissible evidence in finding Rule 104(a) preliminary facts; the judge may also assess the credibility of

---

21. The statement relates to the event of the sports car speeding. Although an excited utterance may be a statement "relating to" a startling event, a present sense impression may only "describe or explain" an event while or immediately after perceiving it. *See* §§ **7.11, 7.12**

witnesses in making the determination. The judge, normally, has no role in determining the credibility of witnesses. Once evidence has been admitted, the jurors alone determine whether the witnesses are credible and, therefore, whether they ought to give weight to the witness' testimony. But Rule 104(a) recognizes that a judge often will be unable to determine the existence of a preliminary fact without believing one witness and disbelieving another. In the example above, what if, rather than a single affidavit, there had been two witnesses with opposite versions of the passenger's statement about being excited by the accident? In order to determine the preliminary fact of whether the passenger was excited, the judge would have to hear the two witnesses outside the presence of the jury, believe one, and disbelieve the other.

Although Rule 104(a) makes the judge the primary keeper of the evidence rules, there is one evidence rule for which there is often no risk of jury non-enforcement—the rule that "evidence which is not relevant is not admissible."[22] Rule 104(b) creates an exception, albeit in unfortunately complex terms, to the 104(a) rule that the judge decides questions preliminary to the admissibility of evidence:

> When the relevancy of evidence depends upon the fulfillment of a condition of fact, the court shall admit it upon, or subject to, the introduction of evidence sufficient to support a finding of the fulfillment of the condition.

This is often described as "conditional relevancy."[23] When the relevance of the evidence depends upon the existence of some other fact, the judge alone does not determine the existence of that other fact. The judge involves the jury, because the preliminary fact finding needed to determine relevance will not put the jurors in the untenable position of choosing between an evidence rule for which they have little understanding and almost no stake, and reaching a decision using all of the relevant information. This is apparent if we look at the prior example, assuming that the front seat passenger had not included the color and make of the sports car in the statement.

---

22.   Fed. R. Evid. 402.

23.   Some commentators have questioned the logic of the concept of "conditional relevancy." In a case in which defendant's negligence depends upon proof that the defendant was driving over the speed limit, they would contend that evidence a car was speeding is relevant, without any evidence that the defendant was driving the car. They would argue that evidence a car was speeding increases to some degree the probability that the defendant was driving a speeding car and is, therefore, relevant in the Rule 401 sense—i.e., its relevance is not "conditioned" on proof that the defendant was driving. *See, e.g.,* 1 John H. Wigmore, Evidence in Trials at Common Law § 14.1 (Peter Tillers rev. 1983); Ronald J. Allen, *The Myth of Conditional Relevancy,* 25 Loy. L.A.L. Rev. 871 (1992); Vaughan C. Ball, *The Myth of Conditional Relevancy,* 14 Ga. L. Rev. 435 (1980); Richard D. Friedman, Conditional Probative Value: Neoclassicism Without Myth, 93 Mich. L. Rev. 439 (1994). Though the scholarship in the area is intriguing and clever, it has yet to have much impact on the way courts view the subject. We, therefore, will use the traditional concept of conditional relevancy as set forth in the Rules and the Advisory Committee Note.

Example

Plaintiff's lawyer: What did he say?

Defense lawyer: Objection, hearsay.

[At sidebar]
Plaintiff's lawyer: The witness will say that the passenger in the front seat said: "That sports car just passed us going about 90." It is admissible either as a present sense impression or as an excited utterance.

Judge: [Having decided that the circumstances establish the preliminary fact that it is more likely than not that the passenger was describing an event as it was being perceived.] Present sense impression. The hearsay objection is overruled.

Defense lawyer: It may be a present sense impression, your honor, but it isn't relevant. There is no evidence that the sports car the declarant saw was the defendant's.

The defense lawyer's relevance objection raises a question of "conditional relevancy" that the judge will handle under 104(b), rather than under 104(a).

That the speeding sports car belonged to the defendant is the "condition of fact" upon which the relevance of the passenger's statement depends. The jurors can decide that question without being put in the untenable position of ignoring important information, in the event that they find the preliminary fact that it was the defendant's sports car does not exist. If the jurors do not find that the speeding sports car was the defendant's, they will naturally ignore the passenger's statement. Rule 104(b) requires the judge to overrule the relevance objection and to let the jury decide the existence of the preliminary fact, unless no reasonable jury could reach such a conclusion. If there is not enough evidence to support a jury finding that it was the defendant's sports car that the passenger saw, the judge will sustain the objection and exclude the statement.

Example

Defense lawyer: Judge, there is not enough evidence "to support a finding"[24] that the car the passenger saw belonged to the defendant.

Judge: I agree. The only evidence the sports car belonged to the defendant is the coincidence that the accident and the sighting were on the same road. Need more to support a jury finding that it is more likely than not it was the defendant's car the passenger saw.

---

24. Fed.R.Evid. 104(b).

Plaintiff's lawyer:	Your honor, I have another witness who saw the sports car. He was sitting right next to the declarant. Unfortunately, he cannot be here to testify for two days. When he testifies, he will say that the sports car was a blue Miata, driven by a big man with long black hair, both characteristics of the defendant. I ask that you allow the back seat passenger to testify to what the front seat passenger said and allow me to show the relevance—to "connect it up"—when the driver testifies.
Judge:	Rules 104(b) and 611(a) give me discretion to allow this testimony now and to withdraw it from the jurors' consideration, if you do not connect it up. Given the flow of the case, I think it is important for this evidence to come out at this time.

[Two days later the driver testifies.]

Plaintiff's lawyer:	Did you see the sports car that the passenger said was "going about 90?"
Witness:	Yes.
Plaintiff's lawyer:	Please describe it.
Witness:	It was a blue Miata with a big guy behind the wheel.
Plaintiff's lawyer:	Could you see the driver's face?
Witness:	No, all I could see was that he was big man with long black hair.
Defense lawyer:	Sidebar, your honor?

[At the sidebar]

Defense lawyer:	Your honor, I renew my objection that the passenger's statement is not relevant because the fact has not been established that the car was the defendant's. I am prepared to bring in a witness who will testify that he was speeding in his blue Miata on the same road at the same time that the passenger saw the speeding sports car. My client will testify that he was not speeding.
Judge:	Let me stop you, counsel. Even if you produce those witnesses, and even if I believe it is more likely than not that the speeding sports car the

passenger saw belonged to the other witness, I have to admit the passenger's statement and leave it to the jury to decide whose sports car the passenger saw. There is plenty of evidence to support a jury finding that the passenger saw the defendant's car. It was on the same road as the accident. The car was the same color and make as the defendant's and it was driven by someone the same size and with the same hair color and style as the defendant.

Defense lawyer: But your honor, what about my evidence that there was another car there and my client's testimony that he was not speeding?

Judge: Whether those witnesses—or any witnesses, for that matter—are to be believed is the sole province of the jurors. There is enough evidence here if the jurors believe it, and if they reject any evidence that might lead to a contrary judgment, for the jurors to conclude that it is more likely than not that the car the passenger saw belonged to the defendant. Your relevance objection is overruled. Argue it to the jury.

But what happens if the information suggesting that the car the passenger saw speeding was not admissible evidence from the driver, but rather, inadmissible evidence? Suppose the only connection between the car the passenger saw speeding and the car at the accident is the front seat passenger's statement, made after passing the scene of the accident and in an unexcited state. The witness, the passenger in the back seat, could tell the judge that the front seat passenger said, "That car back there was the same one we saw speeding earlier." The statement is inadmissible hearsay. When the judge was making a 104(a) determination about whether the declarant was excited, the judge could use inadmissible information to make the determination. When the judge is making a 104(b) judgment, the judge is not deciding whether the judge believes, based on whatever information the judge has, that the preliminary fact more likely than not exists. Under 104 (b) the judge is deciding whether there will be "introduction of evidence *sufficient to support a finding*"[25] by the jury.

Both logic and authority[26] suggest that the judge may not use inadmissible evidence in deciding whether there is sufficient evidence to

25. Fed. R. Evid. 104(b) (emphasis added).

26. In re Japanese Elec. Prod. Antitrust Litig., 723 F.2d 238, 285 (3d Cir. 1983), *rev'd on other grounds*, 475 U.S. 574 (1986) (" [T]he evidence required to establish a prima facie case that the evidence is what the proponent claims it to be must itself be admissible."); United States v. Casto, 889 F.2d 562 (5th Cir. 1989); United States v. Blackwell, 694 F.2d 1325 (D.C. Cir. 1982).

support a jury finding. The judge could not possibly use inadmissible information to make a decision that there is information to "support a jury finding" and then tell the plaintiff's lawyer, who must establish the preliminary fact that the car was the defendant's, to "argue it to the jury." There would be no evidence from which to argue.

Authentication of documents and other tangible items is a common exception to the general proposition that the judge alone decides questions of evidence admissibility. Authentication generally is treated as a matter of "conditional relevance" under Rule 901(a). Rule 1008, delineating the fact-finding functions of judge and jury for the authentication of documents is to the same effect.[27]

Example

Plaintiff sues defendant to enforce a written contract. Defendant claims there was no contract. To prevail, plaintiff must prove the existence of the contract and its terms. During its case-in-chief, plaintiff offers a copy of the contract, claiming that the original is in the possession of the defendant. The defendant, claiming there never was an original, objects to the copy, because it is not the original document required by Rule 1005. If the judge admits the copy under Rule 104(a), believing that it is more likely than not that there was an original, the judge will have effectively taken the only issue in the case—the existence of a written contract—away from the jury. The judge does not do that. Instead, the judge hears the plaintiff's evidence in favor of existence and any evidence the defendant offers to show non-existence and then applies the same test as is applied to a request for a judgment as a matter of law. Unless the judge can say that no reasonable jury could ever find that the contract existed, the judge admits the contract and leaves it to the jury to decide whether plaintiff can establish it is more likely than not that the original contract existed.

§ 1.05 Examination of Witnesses—To Lead or Not to Lead [FRE 611]

Examining witnesses is the lawyer's most common task during trial. The lawyer's skill in asking questions can have as much influence on the evidence that is admitted as can the law of evidence. Moreover, the lawyer's skill in asking questions can have a significant influence upon how the jurors assess the evidence that is admitted.

The form of a question asked of a witness can vary from a completely open question that asks for a narrative response—"What happened next?"—to a completely closed question that leads the witness directly to the answer—"You next opened the window, didn't you?" Most of the

---

27. *See* **Ch. 11**.

questions that lawyers ask are in between—more directive than "what happened," but less suggestive than a question that contains the answer.

"What did you see?" is a less open question (more directive) than "What happened next?" because it limits the range of the witness' possible responses. What the witness smelled, thought, heard, felt, or was told by another are not proper responses. "What did you see behind the door?" is an even more directive question—narrowing the inquiry to a particular place—though still not so directive that it leads the witness to the answer. "Did you see a cat behind the door?" is so directive that it suggests the answer to the witness, even though the words of the question, alone, do not tell the witness whether the lawyer wants an answer of "yes" or "no". "You saw a cat behind the door, didn't you?" is beyond suggestive, almost demanding a positive response from the witness.

Most good trial lawyers believe that witnesses are more credible when important information comes from the witness' mouth, rather than from a mere affirmation by the witness of what the lawyer says. Conversely, a witness is more easily controlled and less likely to make a favorable impression on jurors when the witness is restricted to a one word response—such as "yes" or "no." As a result, good trial lawyers ask mostly open questions on direct examination of friendly witnesses and mostly leading questions on cross-examination of witnesses called by the opponent.

A question is leading when its words or its context suggest the answer to the witness.

This is a leading question, isn't it?

Is this a leading question?

A question is not leading just because it is one that can be answered "yes" or "no," though that is often a clue that the question may be leading. "Could you tell whether the driver was dead?" calls for a "yes" or a "no" answer, when asked of a person who saw an unconscious person pinned behind the steering wheel of a smashed car. It may not be leading, because the answer—the witness either could or could not tell—is not suggested by the words and may not be suggested by the context of the question.

Rule 611(c) reflects the trial lawyer's advocacy wisdom in establishing the evidence law for the norms of direct and cross-examination of witnesses at trial.

> (c) Leading questions. Leading questions should not be used on the direct examination of a witness except as may be necessary to develop the witness' testimony. Ordinarily leading questions should be permitted on cross-examination. When a party calls a hostile witness, an adverse party, or a witness identified with an adverse party, interrogation may be by leading questions.

By discouraging the use of leading questions during direct examination, the Rule forces the lawyer to ask questions that encourage the witness, rather than the lawyer, to tell the jurors what happened. This provides the jurors with a reasonable opportunity to assess the witness' credibility. By allowing leading questions on cross-examination, the Rule provides the cross-examiner, who is trying to identify specific weaknesses in the witness' testimony, with control of the organization and the flow of the inquiry. This provides the jurors with a reasonable opportunity to follow the inconsistencies the cross-examiner wants to explore.

The trial lawyer's wisdom and the rule of evidence—do not lead on direct, lead on cross—both grow out of the common law theory of adversary justice. One lawyer has the opportunity to prepare the witness and shape the delivery of the information from the witness to the jury. That lawyer does not need to suggest answers to the witness and, because the witness is friendly, should not be able to give the witness verbal cues when the witness is in front of the jurors. The other lawyer did not have an opportunity to prepare the witness and is charged with discrediting the witness' testimony. That lawyer, with whom the witness has no interest in cooperating, needs to control the inquiry in order to identify the problems with the witness' testimony.

There are some common exceptions to the general rule of trial craft and evidence that a lawyer should not lead on direct and should lead on cross. They arise out of the same approach to the adversary system of examination as the rule itself and are expressed in Rule 611(c).

On direct examination, leading questions are permitted "as may be necessary to develop the witness' testimony."[28] A child witness who freezes on the witness stand or who is not articulate is an obvious example.[29] If the normal direct examination method of examination proves ineffective in bringing the witness' testimony to the jurors, leading questions will often be permitted. This is consistent with the overall approach of modern evidence law, which is to treat rules about the form of questions as rules of preference, allowing the evidence to be presented in an inferior form and trusting the trier of fact to give it the proper weight. The jurors will have seen that open-ended questions were ineffective in eliciting information from the witness and will, therefore, have the information necessary to evaluate the use of the leading questions.

Transitional and preliminary questions are less dramatic but more common examples of the permissible use of leading questions on direct examination. When such questions will elicit facts that are not in dispute, they allow the lawyer "to develop the witness' testimony" more expeditiously without the risk that the lawyer will suggest answers to the witness on anything of consequence.

"Was there another meeting on June 13?" is a typical transition question that takes the witness to a new topic. In some cases there is no

---

28. Fed. R. Evid. 611(c).

29. *See e.g.,* Rotolo v. United States, 404 F.2d 316, 317 (5th Cir.1968); United States v. Wright, 119 F.3d 630 (8th Cir. 1997).

other way to turn to a new topic, in others it would take four or five more open questions to arrive at the same place.

"You live right next door to the defendant, don't you?" is a leading question that will be permitted if it is preliminary and not in dispute. The fact, necessary to explain why the witness knows something about the defendant could be elicited by a number of non-leading questions: "Where do you live?" Who lives next door to the east?" But why bother? Over the course of a trial with a number of witnesses and many preliminary facts, direct examinations without leading questions on preliminary matters would consume more time than necessary or desirable.

Direct examination of witnesses who are not cooperative may often be conducted by using leading questions. This is most often the "adverse party or a witness identified with an adverse party," though it may be a witness who is "hostile" without being necessarily aligned with the adverse party.[30]

On cross-examination, leading questions may not be allowed, if the witness is one who might be favorable to the cross-examiner. The cross-examiner's client, called for adverse testimony or a witness who is identified with the cross-examiner's client are common examples.[31]

Whether a witness is hostile, identified with the adverse party, or is for some other reason so situated that the normal method of examination should not be followed is a question for the judge to decide.[32] There are many more circumstances of examination, witnesses, and relationships than the law of evidence can conveniently categorize. A witness called by a party may not wish to testify because the witness has been threatened, because the witness is fearful that some interest of the witness' may be compromised, or just because the witness does not like the party. Rule 611(a) handles the inevitable uncertainty of witnesses by placing the control of the mode and order of interrogation and presentation within the discretion of the trial judge—a discretion that is virtually never overturned on appeal.

Rule 611. Mode and Order of Interrogation and Presentation

(a) Control by court. The court shall exercise reasonable control over the mode and order of interrogating witnesses and presenting evidence so as to (1) make the interrogation and presentation effective for the ascertainment of the truth, (2) avoid needless consumption of time, and (3) protect witnesses from harassment or undue embarrassment.

30. Fed. R. Evid. 611(c).

31. *See* Deshpande v. Ferguson Bros. Constr. Co., 611 So.2d 877, 878–79 (Miss. 1992) (defense may not ask leading questions in cross-examining a witness called by the plaintiff, but employed by the defendant).

32. *See, e.g.,* Fed. R. Evid. 611(c); United States v. Degraffenried, 339 F.3d 576 (7th Cir. 2003); United States v. Archdale, 229 F.3d 861 (9th Cir. 2000); United States v. Collins, 321 F.3d 691 (8th Cir. 2003); Flannery Props. v. Byrne, 216 F.3d 1087, 2000 Colo. J. C.A.R. 2996 (10th Cir. 2000).

Sometimes judges refuse the request to have a witness declared hostile or otherwise uncooperative,[33] and the lawyer must patiently try to extract the testimony with open-ended questions. Moreover, a lawyer who persists in asking improper leading questions in bad faith or in apparent defiance of the court is likely to find the examination terminated by the court.[34]

§ 1.06   Direct Examination

Direct examination is the examination conducted by the party calling the witness, whether the witness is friendly or not. Most direct examinations, however, are of friendly witnesses whom the lawyer would like the jurors to believe and who have more than one matter of importance to tell the jurors.

If a lawyer has a poised, articulate, and persuasive witness with knowledge of an important sequence of events, it is tempting to give the witness an opportunity to tell the jurors the story without interruption. After the witness has testified to name, address, and brief introductory information about standing on the corner when two cars collided in the intersection, the lawyer might try to give the witness the opportunity to narrate.

Example

Direct examiner: Tell the jurors, in your own words, what happened.

Witness: I was standing on the corner waiting to catch the bus I take to work every day. It was a nice day, though the weather report said it was going to rain. Rush hour traffic was pretty much over. There were not many people waiting for the bus. Just before the bus arrived, I saw a Chevrolet speed through the intersection—must have been going forty miles an hour—and smash into a Ford. The Ford got hit so hard it rolled over and landed on its roof. It was awful. The woman standing next to me said, "Did you see that? That idiot tried to beat the yellow light." I heard the driver of the Ford screaming, so I ran over to see if I could help. The driver was stuck behind the wheel. There was nothing I could do by myself, so I went to the phone and called for help.

33. In the criminal trial of the Chicago Eight for conspiracy to riot during the 1968 Democratic National Convention, Judge Julius Hoffman refused to declare Mayor Richard Daly a hostile witness though it was clear he did not like nor did he wish to cooperate with the defendants. *See* David Dellinger, The Conspiracy Trial 386–89 (J. Clavir & J. Spitzer eds. 1970).

34. *See* United States v. Clinical Leasing Service, Inc., 982 F.2d 900, 905 (5th Cir.1992) (district court did not abuse discretion in terminating direct examination because of blatant and excessive leading questions).

Trial lawyers often disagree about the persuasive merits of a narrative that leaves the shape of the direct examination to the predilections of the witness, rather than the questions of the lawyer. The persuasive value of an uninterrupted story can be undermined by cluttering the narrative with information that is not important (the weather forecast), by omitting information that may be important (the color of the light for the Ford when it entered the intersection), and by leaving the impression that all of the information given is of equal importance. On the other hand, the narrative response, followed by questions searching for detail, provides an opportunity for the lawyer to present the same information to the jury twice. The lawyer is able to provide emphasis, add detail, and have the witness tell, again, a story with which the jurors are already familiar, by following the narrative with questions such as: Where were you standing when you first saw the Chevrolet? Which of the traffic lights could you see? When did the Ford enter the intersection? What color was the light for the Ford when it started into the intersection?

Rule 611 leaves it within the judge's discretion whether a lawyer may conduct a direct examination using questions that call for a narrative from the witness. It is such a common issue at trial that judges develop individual tendencies to generally favor or disfavor the narrative. A narrative response may be more expeditious, generally, but it carries the potential for presenting information to the jurors that is not admissible under the rules of evidence. The lack of questions from the direct examiner makes it difficult for the opposing lawyer to object to the inadmissible material.

When a lawyer objects to a question that calls for a narrative response, the judge's general tendency to allow or disallow the narrative will be moderated by the nature of the narrative requested, the risk of inadmissible information in the particular circumstance, and the representation of the lawyers about what they expect and fear in the testimony. If the judge decides to allow the narrative and then discovers that the fear of inadmissible information was valid, the judge is free to stop the narrative and require the direct examiner to provide better direction for the examination through more specific questions.

Leading questions—at the other end of the question continuum from those that ask for a narrative response—provide another common problem in the mode of direct examination, but more for the lawyers than for the judge. Unlike questions that call for a narrative response, the normal rule about leading questions is set out in Rule 611(c). The judicial response to leading question objections, therefore, is more predictable and less dependent upon individual judicial preference than judicial responses to questions that call for a narrative response.

Lawyers, on the other hand, often have difficulty conducting a direct examination without using leading questions in violation of the Rule. Because direct examination is the lawyer's opportunity to present the client's story in as compelling a fashion as possible, the lawyer is eager to make sure the jurors hear all of the important detail of the client's entire story, and in the most persuasive words. The poised, articulate, and persuasive witness who knows all about a sequence of events that we posited in discussing narrative responses is, in fact, rare. More often than not, the lawyer, who knows the story, the right words, and the courtroom so well, is tempted to tell the story through the questions rather than through the witness' answers.

Example

Direct examiner:	You saw the defendant's Chevrolet enter the intersection at the end of the yellow light, didn't you?
Witness:	Yes.
Direct examiner:	When the Chevrolet entered the intersection, it was traveling about forty miles per hour, isn't that right?
Witness:	Yes.
Direct examiner:	It smashed into the plaintiff's Ford at that speed, didn't it?
Witness:	Yes.
Direct examiner	The Chevrolet smashed into the driver's side of the Ford, isn't that right?
Witness:	Yes.
Direct examiner:	The Ford had just entered the intersection with a green light, hadn't it?
Witness:	Yes.
Direct examiner:	The impact rolled the Ford over and pinned the poor plaintiff in under the steering wheel, didn't it?
Witness:	Yes.
Direct examiner:	You heard the witness cry out, saw blood all over the place, and could see the bone sticking out of the plaintiff's arm, couldn't you?
Witness:	Yes.

The jurors hear all of the facts, with the words the lawyer wants, but the examination is improper under Rule 611, and not very effective, to boot. The jurors have not heard anything from the witness except a witless "yes" that seems programmed. Each question suggested the answer to the witness and was, therefore, leading.

To present testimony effectively through the words of the witness and to avoid the natural temptation to lead the witness into telling the story as the lawyer would, many direct examiners try to begin their questions with the "who, what, where, when, why, and how" of the reporter's liturgy. It is difficult to make such a question leading and it provides the witness an opportunity to tell the story.

Rule 611(c) contains an exception to the normal prohibition against using leading questions in a direct examination. The direct examiner may use leading questions to move the testimony along smoothly and efficiently—in the words of the Rule "to develop the witness' testimony." Sometimes this can mean leading a young child or other witness who has difficulty in testifying. Its most common use, however, is to allow the direct examiner to lead a friendly witness as to preliminary or non-controversial matters and as a means of easy transition from one subject area or time to another, while asking non-leading questions in areas where the answer is important.

Example

Direct examiner:	Were you at the corner of Third and Sheridan at 3:00 p.m. on August 1 of last year? [Leading, but preliminary.]
Witness:	Yes.
Direct examiner:	Did you witness a collision? [Leading, but unless controverted, proper as a preliminary question.]
Witness:	Yes.
Direct examiner:	What did you see?
Witness:	I saw a Chevrolet race through an intersection trying to make a yellow light and slam into a Ford.
Direct examiner:	How fast was the Chevrolet going when it slammed into the Ford?
Witness:	Over the speed limit—at least forty miles per hour.
Direct examiner:	Where was the Ford when the Chevrolet ran though the red light and slammed into it?
Witness:	It had just entered the intersection, not even half way through.

Direct examiner:	What color was the light for the Ford when it entered the intersection?
Witness:	Green.
Direct examiner:	What happened when the Chevrolet slammed into the Ford?
Witness:	It hit the Ford hard enough to roll it over. The Ford came to rest on its top.
Direct examiner:	When things came to rest, did you go over to the Ford? [Leading, but transitional.]
Witness:	Yes.
Direct examiner:	Why did you go over to the Ford?
Witness:	I heard the driver screaming and I went over to see if I could help.
Direct examiner:	What did you see when you got there?
Witness:	The driver was pinned beneath the steering wheel. There was blood all over the place. I could see the upper bone in the driver's arm sticking out through the skin. It was awful.

Rule 611(c) recognizes that some witnesses called on direct examination will not be friendly, but rather, witnesses that would normally appear in the opponent's case—witnesses the lawyer did not prepare and who would normally be subject to cross-examination by the lawyer. The adverse party or witnesses identified with an adverse party are common examples. When such a witness is called, the direct examiner is usually allowed to proceed through the use of leading questions, in the fashion of a cross-examination.

§ 1.07 Refreshing Recollection [FRE 612]

Witnesses forget. It is often a long time between the event to which someone might have been a witness and the trial in which that person must testify. For someone who is not experienced in trials and familiar with the courtroom, the witness box can be a frightening place, not particularly conducive to recollection.

Refreshing the recollection of a witness is most often accomplished by showing the witness a document that will remind the witness of the forgotten information, but any question or device that will jog the witness' memory may be used, including a leading question. Rule 611(c) specifically provides for judicial discretion to allow leading questions on direct examination "to develop the witness' testimony."

Although a failure of memory can happen to any witness, it is, ironically, people familiar with trials and courtrooms who most often are in need of having their recollections refreshed. Witnesses who regularly perform similar tasks and are asked to testify in court about many of them often have difficulty sorting out the proper event months or years after it occurred. Police officers, who investigate hundreds of incidents and make written reports, are common examples.

The officer who investigated the collision between the Chevrolet and the Ford is likely to have investigated a hundred accidents between the time of the collision and the time of the trial of the Ford driver's claim against the driver of the Chevrolet. At trial, the officer is not likely to have a current detailed recollection of finding broken headlamp glass near where the Ford entered the intersection. The officer may not recall the headlamp damage to the Chevrolet or that the glass found in the intersection matched that of the Chevrolet headlamp.

If the direct examiner can establish the officer's lack of current recollection, the examiner will be able to use the officer's notes, a leading question, or any other device the judge will allow to refresh that recollection. The device used to refresh recollection need not be admissible evidence. It will neither be offered into evidence by the direct examiner nor admitted by the judge.[35]

Example

Direct examiner:	Officer, were you called to investigate an automobile collision between a Chevrolet and a Ford at the corner of Third and Sheridan on August 1st of last year?
Witness:	Yes.
Direct examiner:	What did you find at the scene of the collision?
Witness:	I'm sorry counsel, I investigate a lot of accidents in a year. I don't remember the details of this one.

Having demonstrated that the witness has no current recollection of the facts, the direct examiner must find out whether there is anything that will refresh that recollection and bring the once known information back up. If the officer wrote a report detailing where the glass was found, the damage to the Chevrolet, and the match, the direct examiner might use the report as a device to refresh the officer's recollection.

---

35. *See, e.g.,* State v. Schultz, 392 N.W.2d 305, 307 (Minn.App.1986) (recognizing that the use of an accident report to refresh a police officer's memory while testifying to facts within his knowledge permitted although the report was inadmissible under state statute); *See e.g.,* United States v. Weller, 238 F.3d 1215 (10th Cir. 2001) ("Anything may be used to refresh a witness' recollection, even inadmissible evidence.").

Direct examiner: Did you make a report of your investigation of the collision at Third and Sheridan on August 1 of last year?

Witness: Yes.

Direct examiner: Would reviewing that report refresh your recollection about what you found at the scene of the collision?

Witness: Yes, I am sure that it would.

Once the officer has demonstrated lack of current memory and has said that something would assist in calling the information up, the direct examiner may show the item to the officer. After the officer has looked at the report, the direct examiner must determine whether it has, in fact, refreshed the officer's recollection.

Direct examiner: Officer, does the report refresh your recollection about what you found at the scene of the collision?

Witness: Yes, it does.

The direct examiner has now completed the foundation needed to repeat the question about what was found at the scene of the collision. Before asking the question, however, the lawyer must retrieve the report from the officer. The report may be used to refresh the officer's recollection, but it may not, upon this foundation, be used as a substitute for the officer's current recollection. (Use of the report, itself, if it does not refresh the officer's current recollection, raises hearsay issues. The use of a report as a substitute for a witness' failure of current recollection is called Past Recollection Recorded, which is discussed at § 7.15 and compared with refreshed recollection.)

The same kind of foundation must be demonstrated regardless of the device being used to refresh the witness' recollection. Showing the officer the glass collected from the intersection might refresh the officer's recollection as well as the report that says, "I found headlamp glass in the southeastern quadrant of the intersection." A leading question, "Did you find headlamp glass in the intersection?" might be equally as useful and much quicker than either the report or the glass. Just as with the use of the report, the object (the glass particles) or the leading question may only be presented after the direct examiner has shown that the officer cannot remember and that the device used will revive the memory. Some judges believe that the direct examiner should ask permission before using a leading question to refresh a witness' recollection, so that the opponent and the judge will have the same kind of notice as when the witness is shown the report.

Example

Direct examiner:	Officer, were you called to investigate an automobile collision between a Chevrolet and a Ford at the corner of Third and Sheridan on August 1st of last year?
Witness:	Yes.
Direct examiner:	What did you find at the scene of the collision?
Witness:	I'm sorry counsel, I investigate a lot of accidents in a year. I don't remember the details of this one.
Direct examiner:	May we approach?
Judge:	You may.
Direct examiner:	[At the bench.] Your honor, I am going to ask this witness a leading question about a fact set out in his written report to see if that will refresh his recollection. His report says that he found broken glass in the southeast quadrant of the intersection. That will be the subject of the leading question.

The direct examiner may wish to use the leading question instead of the report, if the report contains material that the direct examiner would rather not have before the jury. If the officer uses the report to refresh recollection during the trial, Rule 612 entitles the adverse party to have the report produced, to introduce into evidence those portions of the report that relate to the refreshed recollection, and to use the report to cross-examine the witness.

§ 1.08 Cross-examination

Cross-examination is the interrogation of a witness by a lawyer other than the lawyer who called the witness to testify. In most instances, cross-examination is of a witness whom the other side prepared and who has offered testimony harmful to the cause of the cross-examining lawyer's client. Neither preparation by the other side nor harmful testimony, however, is required. After one lawyer has called a witness and conducted a direct examination, the subsequent examination is called cross-examination, even if the witness is friendly toward the cross-examiner. The usual purpose of cross-examination, however, is to discredit the witness or to diminish the impact, in some way, of the witness' testimony.

The facts that might diminish a witness' testimony are often not facts that the witness is eager to divulge or that the lawyer calling the witness for direct examination wants the jurors to hear. The cross-examiner, therefore, usually employs leading questions to focus the examination on the witness' uncertainty, a previous contrary statement made by the witness, additional facts that raise questions about the witness' direct testimony, or other factors that discredit the witness or raise questions about the direct testimony. The leading question ensures that the jurors hear the discrediting or doubt-raising information, because it comes from the lawyer's mouth. It is in the question put to the witness. It does not depend upon the witness' willingness to volunteer it. Leading questions also help the lawyer to control the witness and to limit the witness' response to an affirmation or denial of the cross-examiner's assertion.

Consider, again, the accident witness who, in the direct examination example, left the jurors with the impression that the witness saw clearly what happened. If at the time of the collision, the witness was preoccupied studying a memorandum for the first meeting of the day at work, that is information the witness is unlikely to offer. If the cross-examiner could not ask leading questions of the witness, the examination would probably not elicit the pre-occupation and not allow the lawyer to present information to the jurors that might cast some doubt on the witness' attentiveness.

Examples

A non-leading examination would reveal only the innocuous.

Cross-examiner: What were you doing just before seeing the accident?

Witness: Waiting for the bus.

If, on the other hand, the cross-examiner states the answer, which the witness does not want to offer, as a part of the question, the truthful witness will affirm the fact when confronted with it.

Cross-examiner: Just before seeing the accident, you were reading a memorandum for work, isn't that right?

Witness: Yes.

Cross-examiner: The memorandum was about a meeting to be held as soon as you arrived at work, wasn't it?

Witness: Yes.

Cross-examiner: That was an important meeting?

Witness: Yes.

Non-leading questions about the witness' estimate of the speed of the Chevrolet would be unlikely to elicit that the witness was not certain about the speed, was not experienced at judging the speed of cars, and was not in a position to see that the light for the Chevrolet was yellow.

Cross-examiner:	How do you know the Chevrolet was going forty miles per hour?
Witness:	It was right in front of me and going a lot faster than cars normally travel on this road.
Cross-examiner:	How fast do cars normally travel on that road?
Witness:	About the speed limit during rush hour.
Cross-examiner:	How do you know what color the light was for the Chevrolet?
Witness:	I could see it.

Leading questions, on the other hand, put the "answer" into the question. This allows the cross-examiner to "testify" (by asking the questions) to the witness' uncertainty about the exact speed, to the witness' lack of experience estimating the speed of passing cars, and to facts suggesting the witness did not actually see that the light was yellow for the Chevrolet.

Cross-examiner:	You said that the Chevrolet was going forty miles per hour, isn't that right?
Witness:	Yes.
Cross-examiner:	Could have been thirty-eight, couldn't it?
Witness:	Yes. [The Cross-examiner does not care what the witness answers. If the witness answers, "no," the Cross-examiner will argue that the witness is too precise to be credible on what is necessarily an estimate.]
Cross-examiner:	You were not looking at the speedometer, were you?
Witness:	No.
Cross-examiner:	You did not have some other kind of timing device at the time?
Witness:	No.
Cross-examiner:	You have no experience watching cars pass by you at different speeds and then comparing their times against a timing device, do you?
Witness:	No.

Cross-examiner:	There were no other cars driving in the same direction as the Chevrolet, so you could draw a comparison when you estimated the Chevy's speed, were there?
Witness:	No.
Cross-examiner:	Now, you know the light for the Ford was green when it entered the intersection?
Witness:	Yes.
Cross-examiner:	The traffic lights at the intersection have those black hoods that shield the light color from cars approaching from the side, don't they?
Witness:	Yes.
Cross-examiner:	You were facing the Ford's light directly, weren't you?
Witness:	Yes.
Cross-examiner:	So that black hood that shields the light color from those approaching from the side didn't interfere with your ability to see that the Ford's light was green, did it?
Witness:	No.

Leading questions may not be appropriate for every cross-examination. Rule 611 provides that "ordinarily leading questions should be permitted on cross-examination." When the witness is not prepared by and is not friendly to the direct examiner, the cross-examiner may not be allowed to lead the witness. This is the other side of the Rule 611(c) coin that allows a direct examiner to lead certain unfriendly witnesses. The cross-examiner's own client, witnesses closely identified with that client, and neutral witnesses from whom the potential cross-examiner is as eager to elicit information as the direct examiner are examples of witnesses for whom leading questions during cross-examination might not be appropriate. The judge has the discretion, but is not required, to prohibit leading questions if the examination is a cross-examination procedurally, but a direct examination in substance.

§ 1.09 Scope of Cross-examination and Other Subsequent Examinations [FRE 611(b)]

Rule 611(b), Scope of Cross-examination, limits cross-examination "to the subject matter of the direct examination and matters affecting the credibility of the witness." The Rule is based upon the same general assumption about the normal progress of a trial as is the rule that limits the plaintiff's rebuttal case to matters raised in the defendant's case-in-chief and the defendant's surrebuttal case to matters raised in the plaintiff's rebuttal case.

As a general proposition, lawyers are allowed to conduct subsequent interrogations of a witness until everything the witness can offer is before the jury. The direct examiner's subsequent examinations of the witness are called redirect examinations and the cross-examiner's subsequent examinations of the witness are called re-cross examinations. How many layers of redirect and re-cross are necessary to present the full testimony to the jurors is entirely within the discretion of the trial judge.[36]

The language of Rule 611(b) addresses only cross-examination, but the principle expressed in the Rule—that the subsequent examination is limited to the subject matter of the preceding examination—is usually applied to redirect examinations, as well as to cross and re-cross examinations. The judge's discretion, pursuant to Rule 611(a), to promote the orderly presentation of evidence by restricting redirect examination to the scope of the cross-examination can, of course, be exercised in the other direction. The judge can allow the proponent on redirect to repair omissions in the direct examination, by allowing questions that go beyond the scope of the cross-examination.

A few jurisdictions do not follow the principle that a subsequent examination must relate to the subject matter of the preceding examination or to the credibility of the witness. Known as "wide open" cross-examination jurisdictions, they allow a cross-examiner to ask about any relevant matter within the witness' knowledge.[37] In most jurisdictions, however, the lawyers must pay attention to the scope of examination in determining what questions they may ask in a subsequent examination.

36. Martin v. State, 775 A.2d 385 (Md. App. 2001) (Judge has discretion regarding the scope of cross examination.); United States v. Speight, 75 Fed.Appx. 802, 806 (2003) (same).

37. *See, e.g.,* People v. Milbratz, 751 N.E.2d 650 (Ill.App.2d Dist.2001) ("Cross examination is generally limited in scope to the subject matter of the direct examination of the witness and to matters affecting the credibility of the witness. However, courts should liberally construe this limitation to allow inquiry into whatever subject tends to explain, discredit, or destroy the witness's testimony."); Dubreuil v. Witt, 781 A.2d 503 (Conn.App.2001) (Cross is limited to scope of direct but "a question on cross-examination is within the scope of the direct examination if it is intended to rebut, impeach, modify, or explain any of the witness's direct testimony. A party who initiates discussion of an issue, whether on di-

rect or cross-examination, is said to have opened the door to inquiry by the opposing party, and cannot later object when the opposing party so questions the witness."); Stotler v. State, 834 So.2d 940 (Fla.App. 4th Dist.2003) ("When the direct examination opens a general subject, the cross-examination may go into any phase, and may not be restricted to mere parts or to the specific facts developed by the direct examination. Cross-examination should always be allowed relative to the details of an event or transaction a portion only of which has been testified to on direct examination. Cross-examination is not confined to the identical details testified to in chief, but extends to its entire subject matter, and to all matters that may modify, supplement, contradict, rebut or make clearer the facts testified to in chief."); *see also* State v. McCall, 549 N.W.2d 418 (Wis.1996).

Example

If the lawyer for the driver of the Ford calls the investigating officer to testify only about the location of the Chevrolet headlamp glass in the intersection, the Chevrolet driver's lawyer can cross-examine the witness on the time of arrival at the scene; whether there was evidence that others had been in the intersection and moved the glass; whether the officer had measured accurately to locate the position of the glass; and the like—all within the scope of the direct.

If the officer happens to have more information—information the direct examiner elected not to present, for whatever reason—the cross-examiner might want to ask the following questions:

Q: Did the driver of the Ford say to you, "I should have been watching more carefully?"

Q: Isn't it true that the yellow light on the traffic signal at Third and Sheridan lasts for seven seconds?

Q: Officer, didn't you happen to see, quite by coincidence, the driver of the Ford about a month after the accident throwing a ball with the arm that was supposed to be broken?

If the direct examiner objects to these questions, which of them will be allowed will depend upon the judge's view of whether the question is within the subject matter of the direct examination.

It is difficult to state with precision a test for distinguishing between examination that does or does not go beyond the scope of the direct. A test sometimes cited says that in exercising discretion, the judge may permit cross-examination "as to all matters reasonably related to the issues put in dispute by . . . testimony on direct."[38]

If the judge believes that the subject matter of the direct examination, in the above example, was the location of broken headlamp glass, all of the additional questions are beyond the scope of the direct examination. If, on the other hand, the judge believes that the subject matter of the direct examination was the officer's investigation of the accident, some of the additional questions will be within the scope of the direct. The questions about the Ford driver's statement of fault and about the length of the yellow light at the intersection are probably part of the officer's investigation. The question about the officer's inadvertent observation of the plaintiff's use of a supposedly injured arm is probably beyond the scope of any characterization of the direct examination.

If the throwing incident is beyond the scope, that does not mean the defendant's lawyer may not ask the officer about it. The scope of examination issue is not whether the cross-examiner may ask about the throwing incident, but when and how. Rule 611(b) provides that the "court may, in the exercise of discretion, permit inquiry into additional

---

38. United States v. Vasquez, 858 F.2d 1387, 1392 (9th Cir. 1988) (*quoting* United States v. Miranda–Uriarte, 649 F.2d 1345, 1353 (9th Cir. 1981); United States v. Green, 648 F.2d 587, 594 (9th Cir. 1981)). Allowing cross examination beyond the scope of direct is addressed to the discretion of the trial judge. Fed. R. Evid. 611(b).

matters as if on direct examination." The judge has discretion to allow the question during cross-examination or to require the defendant to wait and present the officer during the cross-examiner's case.

Judicial discretion on scope of the examination issues is likely to turn on questions of convenience for the witness, the length of the examination that the lawyer wants to conduct, how severely the examination will interfere with the orderly presentation of the proponent's case-in-chief, and similar factors that influence the orderly presentation of evidence—the flow of the trial.

§ 1.10 "Opening the Door," "Curative Admissibility," "Fighting Fire With Fire"

The theory of adversary justice and the notion that a trial should progress through a series of moves and related counter-moves are responsible, together, for the trial phenomena known as "opening the door," "curative admissibility," and "fighting fire with fire." These phrases are sometimes considered by courts and commentators to be merely different ways to colorfully express a single idea: that a party is allowed to do something or to present evidence that ordinarily would be improper only because the other party did it first. While each of the phrases describes a situation in which "evening up" is an important consideration, there are differences that affect the possible consequences when the action of one party, be it appropriate or inappropriate, "opens the door" to reaction by the opponent.

"Curative admissibility," coined by Wigmore,[39] is the narrowest of the terms. It applies only to the circumstance in which one party's presentation of inadmissible evidence causes a problem that the judge will cure by allowing the other party to present inadmissible evidence. "Fighting fire with fire," McCormick's phrase,[40] is a broader concept. It includes "curative admissibility," but it also includes an otherwise improper action—such as an argumentative opening statement—that a party might take in response to the other party's initial improper action. "Opening the door" is the broadest of the terms. It describes what the initial party does that leads to "curative admissibility" and that prompts the other party to "fight fire with fire." But it also describes what happens when the initiating party offers admissible evidence and, as a result, the other party may offer previously inadmissible evidence.

It is worth noting that the three terms describe different actors. The party who begins the process by doing something "opens the door." In certain circumstances, that initial action will cause the judge to allow otherwise inadmissible evidence to go to the fact finder as an act of "curative admissibility." "Fighting fire with fire" describes what the responding party does in response to the initial action. The focus on the

39. *See* David Leonard the New Wigmore: A Treatise on Evidence Selected Rules of Limited Admissibility § 6.7 (2000). (Curative Admissibility).

40. *See* 1 McCormick on Evidence § 57 (4th ed. John W. Strong ed. 1994) (Fighting Fire With Fire: Inadmissible Evidence as Opening the Door).

different actors can be helpful in sorting out the various situations that appear similar in some respects, but are analytically different.

A judicial determination that one party's action "opens the door" to action by the other party—action that could not be taken "but for" the door opening—is a universal precondition to rebuttal. The action, however, may vary widely from offering competent, admissible evidence to making an improper argument to a jury. Whether and what kind of retaliation will be permitted depends in part on which door was "opened," what was used to "open the door," and what the opponent did to avoid the draft.

The following examples represent three different door openings: 1) presenting competent evidence that increases the issues before the jury and makes otherwise inadmissible counter evidence admissible, 2) presenting inadmissible evidence that creates a problem that can be cured only by allowing other inadmissible evidence, and 3) taking inappropriate trial action that justifies retaliatory inappropriate action.

Example—"Opening the door" with admissible evidence

During a prosecution for possession and distribution of cocaine, the prosecution wants to elicit that the arresting agent set up the buy from the defendant because she had received word from U.S. Customs that he was a major drug dealer. Defendant's hearsay objection is sustained. The court rejects the prosecution's argument that the statement is offered to show the agent's state of mind, saying that the agent's state of mind is not relevant.[41]

In his case-in-chief, the defendant claims that the agent framed him, because she held a grudge against him. He produces evidence of the grudge.

In rebuttal, the prosecution should be able to call the agent and elicit the hearsay testimony that was not admissible in the government's case-in-chief. The defendant has "opened the door" to the testimony by making the agent's motive (state of mind) relevant.

Expanding the issues is a common explanation for the phenomenon of "opening the door."[42] It happens so regularly in some contexts, that those situations have been codified. Rules 404 and 608 are examples of "opening the door" to otherwise inadmissible evidence by expanding the issues. Rule 404(a) prohibits offering evidence of a character trait to prove that someone acted in conformity with that trait. The prosecution, therefore, may not offer evidence that the defendant is someone with a long criminal history. Rule 404(a)(1), however, permits a criminal defendant to offer evidence of good character to show that the defendant did not do the action charged. If the defendant chooses to offer such evidence, the same rule "opens the door" for the prosecution to offer the

---

41. United States v. Hernandez, 750 F.2d 1256 (5th Cir. 1985).

42. *See,* Clark v. State, 629 A.2d 1239 (Md. 1993) (discussing the distinction be- tween opening the door and curative admissibility); State v. Lessley, 601 N.W.2d 521 (Neb. 1999); State v. Farthing, 751 A.2d 123 (N.J.Super. 2000).

defendant's long criminal history. Similarly, Rule 608(a) prohibits a party from offering proof of a witness' character for truthfulness. If, however, the other party offers evidence that the witness has a reputation for being an untruthful person, that party "opens the door" to the otherwise prohibited testimony about the witness' character for truthfulness.

Waiver is another common explanation for situations in which the action of one party "opens the door" to retaliatory evidence from the other party—evidence that would not be admissible, but for the door opening. In *State v. Banks*,[43] a prosecution for child molestation, defendant made an adamant and expansive denial: "As God is my witness, I have never had sexual contact with my daughter or with any child under the age of 18 years old." The *Banks* Court held that the denial constituted a waiver of the jurisdiction's statute prohibiting evidence of specific instances of sexual activity by either victims or defendants.[44] The defendant had "opened the door" to the prosecution's otherwise inadmissible evidence from two minor girls of their prior sexual activity with the defendant.

The "opening the door" concept is complex. Although expansion of the issues and waiver are common reasons for the door to be opened to otherwise inadmissible evidence, the door may be opened because the opponent holds some right. In *Government of Virgin Islands v. Jacobs*,[45] a rape victim's direct testimony that she was a virgin before the rape "opened the door" to cross-examination in which the defense was allowed to confront the witness with impeachment evidence of prior sexual conduct. The questions, not normally permitted by Rule 412, were allowed not because the government waived anything, but because of the defendant's constitutional right of confrontation.[46]

Example—"Opening the door" with inadmissible evidence

Defendant presents a witness who testifies that the plaintiff has a reputation for being untruthful.

Plaintiff calls a witness in plaintiff's rebuttal case who is prepared to testify to three separate and compelling instances in which the plaintiff was truthful, in an attempt to undercut the untruthful reputation presented in defendant's case-in-chief.

Rule 608(b) specifically prohibits testimony about specific instances of conduct for the purpose of attacking or supporting a witness'

---

43. 593 N.E.2d 346, 349 (Ohio App. 1991).

44. *Id.*

45. 634 F.Supp. 933 (D.V.I.1986).

46. *Id.* at 940. *But see* United States v. Duran, 886 F.2d 167 (8th Cir. 1989) (In sexual abuse trial, defendant's confrontation right not sufficient to allow cross-examination question about the identity of the father of a child the victim testified she had while living with defendant's family. *Jacobs* distinguished because the response to the cross-examination question about the father of the child would not go to the credibility of the witness.); *see also* United States v. Eagle Thunder, 893 F.2d 950 (8th Cir. 1990).

credibility. The rebuttal witness' testimony, therefore, will be inadmissible, if defendant objects.

Defendant does not object to the rebuttal witness' testimony about the three specific instances of truthfulness, but during its surrebuttal case, calls a witness who will testify to two separate and compelling instances in which the plaintiff was untruthful.

The same provision of Rule 608(b) that would have prohibited the rebuttal witness' testimony, had the defendant objected, prohibits the surrebuttal witness' testimony, unless the plaintiff "opened the door" for the surrebuttal testimony by offering specific instances of truthful conduct during the rebuttal case. The trial judge is likely—but may not be required—to allow the defendant to present a witness who will "even up" the specific instance evidence available to the jury.

If the judge allows the defendant's inadmissible specific conduct evidence, it is because it is the only way to cure the problem caused by the plaintiff's inadmissible specific conduct evidence. The basis for the court's discretion to admit inadmissible evidence to cure other inadmissible evidence is not obvious. The early cases upholding trial court decisions to allow retaliatory inadmissible evidence consider it a matter of simple fairness.[47] This common law rule that gives the judge discretion to use fairness as the standard for admitting inadmissible evidence to "cure" other inadmissible evidence apparently was not superseded by the Federal Rules of Evidence. The advisory committee's note to Rule 611(a) suggests that many of the common law rules giving judges discretion to make trials fair are embodied in the judge's obligation to "make the interrogation and presentation effective for the ascertainment of the truth."[48] When and under what circumstances the judge should use what one court has described as a "nebulous and nodus so-called doctrine"[49] to admit otherwise inadmissible evidence is not so clear from jurisdiction to jurisdiction. "Evening up" is the goal, and "fairness" the mechanism in almost every jurisdiction, but the methods for obtaining the goal and for being fair differ.

Some courts will not allow inadmissible "curative" evidence from a party who has objected to the initial party's inadmissible evidence.[50]

---

47. *See, e.g.,* Bogk v. Gassert, 149 U.S. 17 (1893) ("manifestly unfair" to allow one party's inadmissible version of a conversation without allowing the other party to give its equally inadmissible version of the conversation.)

48. Rule 611(a). The advisory committee's note states:

The ultimate responsibility for the effective working of the adversary system rests with the judge.

 * * *

Item (1) restates in broad terms the power and obligation of the judge as developed under common law principles. It covers ... questions arising during the course of a trial which can be solved only by the judge's common sense and fairness in view of the particular circumstances.

49. Daniels v. Dillinger, 445 S.W.2d 410, 415 (Mo. App. 1969).

50. *See, e.g., id.* (*citing* Wigmore for the proposition that "curative admissibility" should not be applied when an objection has been made to the original evidence because the objection will protect the party.)

Other courts take the opposite position and will not allow inadmissible "curative" evidence from a party who seeks "to introduce whatever incompetent evidence it desires by the simple expedient of failing to object to the introduction of incompetent evidence by the opposing party."[51]

Few courts will allow bootstrapping. A party may not cross-examine on a subject beyond the scope of direct examination, elicit a response that is inadmissible, and then offer inadmissible evidence to "cure" the inadmissible evidence elicited on cross-examination.[52]

One federal court has stated succinctly the contours of the "curative admissibility" doctrine:

"Under the doctrine of curative admissibility 'the introduction of inadmissible evidence by one party allows an opponent, in the court's discretion, to introduce evidence on the same issue to rebut any false impression that might have resulted from the earlier admission.' '"'However, the rule 'does not permit the introduction of evidence that is related to a different issue or is irrelevant to the evidence previously admitted.' "[53]

Some jurisdictions enumerate circumstances under which the judge must allow "curative admissibility."[54] Other jurisdictions leave "curative admissibility" to the discretion of the judge, if the proper circumstances exist. *Clark v. State*,[55] is an example of the kind of preconditions imposed in some jurisdictions. A judge has discretion to permit curative admissibility of inadmissible evidence if:

(1) prejudicial inadmissible evidence was admitted without timely objection or timely motion to strike;

(2) the failure to object or move to strike was not shown to be an intentional or tactical decision in order to admit the "curative evidence;"

(3) the inadmissible evidence is highly prejudicial and a motion to strike the previously admitted evidence and a cautionary instruction would not cure its prejudicial effect;

51. Busch v. Busch Const., Inc., 262 N.W.2d 377, 387 (Minn. 1977).

52. *See e.g.,* United States v. Pantone, 609 F.2d 675, 681 (3d Cir. 1979); United States v. Millard, 139 F.3d 1200 (8th Cir. 1998) (government argued that it was not error for the trial court to permit it to use inadmissible character evidence [past bad acts used to show criminal propensity] because defendant had "invited the error" by referring to those prior convictions first. The appellate court disagreed because the government had actually the been the first party to mention the prior convictions which were not properly admitted into evidence. *See also* State v. Gowan, 13 P.3d 376

(Mont.2002); Roberts v. State, 29 S.W.3d 596 (Tex.App. 2000).

53. Nguyen v. Southwest Leasing & Rental, Inc., 282 F.3d 1061 (9th Cir. 2002) (internal citations and quotations omitted).

54. *Busch, supra* note 50.

In order to be entitled as a matter of right to present rebutting evidence on an evidentiary fact: (a) the original evidence must be inadmissible and prejudicial, (b) the rebuttal evidence must be similarly inadmissible, and (c) the rebuttal evidence must be limited to the same evidentiary fact as the original inadmissible evidence. *Id.*; *See also* State v. Vandeweaghe, 827 A.2d 1028 (N.J.2003).

55. 629 A.2d 1239 (Md.1993).

(4) the "curative" inadmissible evidence goes no further than neutralizing previously admitted inadmissible prejudicial evidence without injecting additional issues in the case and does not allow the curing party to gain a tactical advantage from the failure to object to inadmissible evidence;

(5) the curative inadmissible evidence is of the same character as the previously admitted inadmissible evidence; and

(6) the probative value of the otherwise inadmissible curative evidence outweighs the danger of "confusion of the issues or misleading the jury or . . . considerations of undue delay, waste of time [etc.]" See Fed. R. Evid. 403.

Basically, these rules can be distilled into a rather simple maxim which can be characterized by McCormick's cliché "fighting fire with fire."[56]

McCormick used "fighting fire with fire" to describe what Wigmore called "curative admissibility,"[57] but the phrase is useful to describe a kind of "evening up" that is common in trial courts, but does not necessarily involve "opening the door" with inadmissible evidence or curing a problem with inadmissible evidence. The closing arguments from *United States v. Young*,[58] present a too common example of improper argument by counsel.

Example—"Opening the door" and "fighting fire with fire" through improper trial activity

In a prosecution for mail fraud, the defendant's lawyer begins his closing argument by saying that the prosecution has unfairly presented the defendant and that from the beginning the prosecution's statements were designed to unfairly poison the minds of the jurors. The defense lawyer goes on to intimate that the prosecution deliberately withheld exculpatory evidence. He charges the prosecution with acting reprehensibly in attempting to cast a false light on respondent's activities, pointing to the prosecutor's table and saying: "I submit to you that there's not a person in this courtroom including those sitting at this table who think the defendant intended to defraud anyone." The defendant, he says, is "the only one in this whole affair that has acted with honor and with integrity."

The prosecutor does not object to defense counsel's summation, but rather, improperly presents his own views about the guilt of the defendant. He says, "I think defense counsel said that not anyone

---

56. *Id.* at 1246.

57. 1 McCormick, *supra* note 39, § 57.

58. 470 U.S. 1 (1985); *See also* United States v. Brown, 327 F.3d 867 (9th Cir. 2003) (government's improper use of propensity evidence on closing argument coupled with trial court's failure to rule on defense's objection, offer curative instruction or admonish the government was reversible error); United States v. Carter, 236 F.3d 777 (6th Cir.2001) (It was reversible error for prosecution to respond to defense counsel's improper argument with an improper argument of his own, including repeatedly accusing the defense attorney of lying and of telling "a colossal lie".) *Id.* at 791.

sitting at this table thinks that Mr. Young intended to defraud anyone. Well, I was sitting there and I think he did. I think he got 85 cents a barrel for every one of those 117,250.91 barrels he hauled and every bit of the money they made on that he got one percent of. So, I think he did. If we are allowed to give our personal impressions since it was asked of me. I don't know what you call that; I call it fraud." The prosecutor finished his closing by giving his opinion about the defendant's honor and integrity. "I don't know whether you call it honor and integrity, I don't call it that. If you feel you should acquit him for that it's your pleasure. I don't think you're doing your job as jurors in finding facts as opposed to the law that this Judge is going to instruct you. If you think that's honor and integrity then stand up here in this courtroom and say that's honor and integrity. I don't believe it."

The *Young* Court expressed concern for the "all too common occurrence in criminal trials—the defense counsel argues improperly, provoking the prosecutor to respond in kind, and the trial judge takes no corrective action."[59] It asserted that "two improper arguments—two apparent wrongs—do not make for a right result" and made it clear that courts "have not intended" by any means to encourage the practice of zealous counsel's going "out of bounds" in the manner of defense counsel here, or to encourage prosecutors to respond to the "invitation."[60] The Court went on to say that the prosecutor should have objected, rather than "fight fire with fire" and that "invited responses" might be diminished if trial courts would take prompt action. But it let the conviction stand.

Misconduct in argument is not restricted to criminal cases.[61] Examples of judges using their discretion to even things up by allowing aggrieved counsel to "fight fire with fire" after the other lawyer has done something improper are as common across all litigation as the *Young* Court thought true of criminal cases.

§ 1.11 Documents in Context [FRE 106]

Rule 106, Remainder of Related Writings or Recorded Statements, is another example of judicial discretion as the major factor in managing the proper flow of evidence at trial. The Rule allows the judge, upon

---

59. *Young*, 470 U.S. 1 at 11.

60. *Id.*

61. *See, e.g.,* Findlay v. Griffin, 484 S.E.2d 80 (Ga. App. 1997); Amador v. Lea's Auto Sales & Leasing, Inc., 916 S.W.2d 845 (Mo. App. 1996); Harrison v. Purdy Bros. Trucking Co., 312 F.3d 346 (8th Cir. 2002) (Plaintiff's attorney closing argument contained "the defendants in the case finally fessed up" and "these defendants have not been willing to do [justice]". The trial court issued curative instructions. The circuit affirmed the trial court in "all respects") *Id.* at 353, 354; Hemmings v. Tidyman's Inc., 285 F.3d 1174 (9th Cir. 2002) (Plaintiff's counsel said in his closing argument " '[Tidyman's has] not corrected any of these discriminatory policies and they knew that they should because this is not the first time they have been sued. I have sued them before in 1994, so they had subjective policies which had disparate impact on all women, including plaintiffs, and that proves our case because they did not have a business necessity for doing it, and there were ways to fix it.' ") *Id.* at 1192.

motion by the other party, to require the proponent of a portion of a document or recording to offer the remainder of the document or recording at the same time. It is a matter of fairness. Depositions are the most common example. If a statement on page 3 is qualified by another statement on page 100, the judge might not allow the statement from page 3 to be admitted without the qualifying statement from page 100.

The Rule allows the same result when the proponent offers an entire document and its full context will not be understood without consideration of some other document, as, for example, when a letter purporting to be an acceptance is offered. If determining whether the letter is really an acceptance requires that the jurors see the offering letter at the same time, the judge might require the latter to be admitted with the former.

The Rule does not mean that if a party wants to offer a portion of a document the party must introduce the entire document, or when offering one document, all other related documents must be offered as well. There are reasons of emphasis, admissibility, and time economy, among other considerations, that might lead a party to introduce only a portion of a document or only one of a series of documents. The other side is often fully protected by the right to inquire about or offer the remainder of the document or related documents on cross-examination or through later examination of a different witness. When that is the case, the judge is not likely to compel a party to interrupt the flow if its case to offer the entire document or related documents.

Rule 106, a codification of the common law rule of completeness, allows the judge, upon complaint that admission of a portion of a document or a single document will be prejudicial, to require introduction of the entire document or related documents.

There is disagreement in the Federal circuits as to whether Rule 106 is merely a Rule about the order of proof,[62] or whether it authorizes admission of otherwise inadmissible evidence to demonstrate the context of a document or a portion of a document, in order to avoid misleading jurors.[63] In the 1988 case of *Beech Aircraft Corp. v. Rainey*,[64] a case better known for its discussion of the meaning of "factual findings" in the public records exception to the hearsay rule,[65] the Supreme Court discussed the common law Rule of Completeness as it was codified in Rule

62. United States v. Woolbright, 831 F.2d 1390, 1395 (8th Cir. 1987) (Rule 106 addresses only order of proof); United States Football League v. National Football League, 842 F.2d 1335, 1375–76 (2d Cir. 1988); United States v. Terry, 702 F.2d 299 (2d Cir. 1983) (holding that Fed. R. Evid. 106 does not compel introduction of evidence otherwise inadmissible); United States v. Gallagher, 57 Fed. Appx. 622, 629 (6th Cir. 2003) (holding that Fed. R. Evid. 106 *cannot* be used to make otherwise inadmissible evidence admissible).

63. United States v. Sutton, 801 F.2d 1346 (D.C. Cir. 1986) (holding Fed. R. Evid.

106 "can adequately fulfill its function only by permitting the admission of some otherwise inadmissible evidence when the court finds in fairness that the proffered evidence should be considered contemporaneously. A contrary construction raises the specter of distorted and misleading trials, and creates difficulties for both litigants and the trial court.") *Id.* at 1368. *See also* United States v. Houlihan, 92 F.3d 1271 (1st Cir. 1996).

64. 488 U.S. 153 (1988).

65. *See* § **7.29**.

106. The Court's discussion suggests that the rule allows the admission of an otherwise inadmissible portion of a document, if it is necessary to demonstrate the context of the admissible portion of the document offered by the opposing party.

In *Rainey*, the defendant called the plaintiff, husband of the deceased Navy pilot as an adverse witness and asked him about a portion of a letter he sent to the Navy concerning his wife's airplane accident. The plaintiff, a pilot himself, had written to the Navy expressing his opinion that the crash was a result of a power failure in the airplane. The portion of the letter that the defense elicited on direct examination of the adverse party made three points, suggesting the crash was the result of something other than a power failure. It said the plaintiff's wife had attempted to cancel the flight, partly because her student was tired and emotionally drained; that "unnecessary pressure" was placed on them to proceed with the flight; and that the plaintiff's wife or her student had abruptly initiated a hard right turn when the other aircraft unexpectedly came into view. On cross-examination, the plaintiff's lawyer attempted to ask about the remainder of the letter, which made clear the plaintiff's position that the crash was the result of power failure. The trial court would not allow the cross-examination on grounds that the testimony would constitute an opinion of a non-expert.

The Court of Appeals reversed and remanded for new trial because the trial court's refusal to allow the plaintiff to testify to the rest of the letter misled the jury as to the plaintiff's position. Even though the letter itself had not been offered, the Court of Appeals held that the rule of completeness as to documents as codified in Rule 106 applied. It held that the trial court had abused its discretion in not allowing examination about the remainder of the letter.

The Supreme Court found the "concerns underlying Rule 106" to be relevant and agreed with the Court of Appeals that the trial court abused its discretion in not permitting questions about the remainder of the letter:

The common-law "rule of completeness," which underlies Federal Rule of Evidence 106, was designed to prevent exactly the type of prejudice of which Rainey complains. In its aspect relevant to this litigation, the rule of completeness was stated succinctly by Wigmore: "[T]he opponent, against whom a part of an utterance has been put in, may in his turn complement it by putting in the remainder, in order to secure for the tribunal a complete understanding of the total tenor and effect of the utterance." 7 J. Wigmore, Evidence in Trials at Common Law § 2113, p. 653 (J. Chadbourn rev. 1978).[66]

§ 1.12   Judicial Notice of Adjudicative Facts [FRE 201]

The witness testified that at eleven o'clock at night, by the light of a full moon, he saw the defendant kill a man in the middle of a field some

66. 488 U.S. at 171.

hundred and fifty feet away. But the moon was not full on August 29, 1857, the night of the killing. It was barely past the first quarter. How would Abraham Lincoln, the lawyer for the defendant, prove the moon was not full, so that he could argue to the jurors that the supposed eyewitness was not believable? He might call as a witness someone who remembered looking up at the moon at eleven on August 29, 1857 and who could recall it was barely past first quarter. But who remembers the moon on a particular night? And why should the jurors believe one amateur stargazer over another? He might call an astronomer as an expert witness, if one were easily available in the pre-Civil War frontier of Illinois and if the Court would recognize the area of expertise. Lincoln chose, instead, to ask the sheriff to bring him a copy of the almanac for 1857. The Court took judicial notice of the moon phase information in the almanac.[67] By asking the Court to take judicial notice, Lincoln was taking advantage of a shortcut in proof that the common law had developed to reduce the time and expense required in proving something certain beyond argument.[68]

Judicial notice can be a powerful tool with which a lawyer can prove a fact that is not easily demonstrated through the traditional means of calling a witness, but which is a fact that "everyone knows" or is "beyond argument."

Rule 201 permits a lawyer to establish an "adjudicative fact"[69] that is "not subject to reasonable dispute"[70] merely by asking the Court to take judicial notice of it. If a fact is one "generally known within the territorial jurisdiction of the trial court" or is one capable of determination "by resort to sources whose accuracy cannot reasonably be questioned"[71] the judge may take judicial notice of it, even if no lawyer asks for it.[72] If a lawyer does ask a court to take judicial notice and supplies the trial court with the "necessary information," the judge must take judicial notice of the fact.[73]

In a civil case, a judicially noticed fact may be more powerful than a fact presented through the testimony of a witness. While jurors may refuse to accept what a witness says as fact, the judge instructs civil jurors that they must accept the judicially noticed fact as conclusive.[74] Judges may not instruct criminal jurors to accept anything offered against an accused, so the Rule requires judges in criminal cases to instruct jurors that they may, but are not required, to accept the judicially noticed fact.[75]

Rule 201 is limited to judicial notice of adjudicative facts as substitutes for presenting evidence to a fact-finder through witnesses and

67. Albert A. Woldman, Lawyer Lincoln 123 (1996).

68. For a thorough discussion of the history and rationale behind the development of common law judicial notice, see 2 McCormick, *supra* note 39 § 328.

69. Fed. R. Evid. 201(a).

70. Fed. R. Evid. 201(b).

71. *Id.*

72. Fed. R. Evid. 201(c).

73. Fed. R. Evid. 201(d).

74. Fed. R. Evid. 201(g).

75. *Id.*

exhibits. "Adjudicative facts"—"simply the facts of the particular case"[76] —and "legislative facts" are two terms coined by Professor Kenneth Davis to help to understand the two different functions of the court or agency—adjudication and law making.[77] "Adjudicative facts" are the "facts that normally go to the jury in a jury case."[78] Professor Davis' definition, though arguably too narrow by its limitation to the parties, is repeated with approval by the advisory committee.

> When a court or an agency find facts concerning the immediate parties—who did what, where, when, how, and with what motive or intent—the court or agency is performing an adjudicative function, and the facts are conveniently called adjudicative facts....[79]

"Legislative facts," on the other hand, are those that a court uses in the law making process. Courts are often required to interpret a statute or to define the limits of a common law rule. Such decisions often turn on policy, which, in turn, depends upon acceptance of some social, economic, or other hypothesis the court must adopt as "fact" to reach a decision.

The oldest and simplest basis for judicial notice is that the adjudicative fact to be established is one that is so universally known that there is no argument about it.[80] As Florida courts have said, "What everybody knows the courts are assumed to know...."[81] For example, "everybody knows" that the Grand Canyon is in the United States; the Eiffel Tower is in Paris, France; and George Washington was the first President of the United States.

That "everybody knows," of course, has never actually been the test[82] and is not a requirement under Rule 201. A court may take judicial notice of a fact that is only "generally known" and that general knowledge need be only "within the territorial jurisdiction of the trial court."[83] The fact that the Chicago Cubs last won the World Series in 1908 and are never likely to win it again is probably not as well known as the fact that George Washington was the first President of the United States. The Cubs' almost century-long failure to win baseball's greatest prize might be, nevertheless, the subject of judicial notice in a court sitting on Chicago's north side—even if no one else in the country knows or cares when the Cubs last were supreme. ("Are never likely to win it again" is probably an opinion rather than a fact, except to the most dispirited of rabid Cub fans. See **§ 10.01** for a discussion of the lack of a clear dividing line between fact and opinion.)

76. Advisory committee note, FRE 201(a).

77. Kenneth C. Davis, *An Approach to Problems of Evidence in the Administrative Process*, 55 Harv. L. Rev. 364, 404–407 (1942).

78. Kenneth C. Davis, 2 Administrative Law Treatise 353 (1958).

79. *Id.*

80. McCormick, *supra*, note 39 at § 329.

81. St. Lucie County Bank & Trust Co. v. Aylin, 114 So. 438, 440 (Fla. 1927); United States v. American Nat'l Bank, 255 F.2d 504, 508 (5th Cir. 1958); *See also* In re Buszta's Estate, 186 N.Y.S.2d 192, 193 (Sur. 1959).

82. McCormick, *supra*, note 76.

83. Fed. R. Evid. 201(b).

Even a fact that is *not* "generally known within the territorial jurisdiction of the trial court" (or anywhere else, for that matter) may be judicially noticed. A court in New Mexico, for example, might take judicial notice that the Cubs last won the world series in 1908—four years before New Mexico became a state—because the fact is "capable of accurate and ready determination by resort to sources whose accuracy cannot reasonably be questioned."[84] Sometimes referred to as "almanac-type facts," these facts are often ones that "nobody knows" except through resort to the "sources." The Encyclopedia of Baseball, for example, might suffice as a source for the Cubs' near-century of despair.[85]

Judicial notice of an adjudicative fact that is critically important to a case "may be taken at any stage of a proceeding,"[86] even if no lawyer requests it.[87] When the plaintiff in the oft cited case of *Varcoe v. Lee*[88] forgot to prove that Mission Street was in a business district (in order to establish that speed in excess of fifteen miles per hour constituted negligence per se), the judge was free, nevertheless, to instruct the jury that Mission Street was in San Francisco's business district.

A party against whom a fact is judicially noticed is entitled "to be heard as to the propriety of taking judicial notice and the tenor of the matter noticed."[89] While this will often be easy to accommodate when one party asks for notice during a trial, it may not be so simple when the trial judge takes notice of a fact inadvertently, as in *Varcoe v. Lee*, or when it is an appellate court that takes the notice. The rule recognizes the problem and allows the party to be heard after judicial notice has been taken.[90]

Judicial notice of such standard reference material as when the Cubs last won the World Series is not particularly remarkable,[91] but

---

84. *Id.*

85. *Compare* Smith v. Pro Football, Inc., 593 F.2d 1173 (D.C.Cir. 1978). In defending the use of the use of Encyclopedia of Pro Football to notice when the Minnesota Vikings selected a player in the pro football draft, MacKinnon, C.J., a former All–American football player at the University of Minnesota, said:

> The majority complains of reference to facts disclosed in the Encyclopedia of Pro Football and to matters of common knowledge that can be readily verified by reference to encyclopedias, books and other publications of established authenticity. This however is clearly permissible and may be done for the first time on appeal as is recognized by the Federal Rules of Evidence, Rule 201(f) which states: "Judicial notice may be taken at any stage of the proceedings."

Id. at 1213, fn. 71 (MacKinnon, C.J., concurring and dissenting).

86. Fed. R. Evid. 201(f).

87. Fed. R. Evid. 201(c).

88. 181 P. 223 (Cal.1919).

89. Fed. R. Evid. 201(e).

90. *Id.*

91. *See, e.g.,* George v. Hilaire Farm Nursing Home, 622 F.Supp. 1349, 1354 (S.D.N.Y. 1985) (judicial notice of dates from a calendar); Hays v. National Elec. Contractors Ass'n, Inc., 781 F.2d 1321, 1324 (9th Cir. 1985) (judicial notice of American Automobile Association map of Alameda County); In re Marriage of Aud, 491 N.E.2d 894 (Ill.App. 1986) (statistics prepared by the United States Bureau of Census were the proper subject of judicial notice); Estate of Torres v. Terhune, 2002 WL 32107987 (E.D.Cal. 2002) (records and reports of an administrative body); Kraft Foods Holdings, Inc. v. Helm, 2002 WL 31473843 (N.D.Ill. 2002) (copies of trademark registrations); United States v. Cout-

what about Abraham Lincoln's use of the almanac to show that the moon was just past the first phase on August 29, 1857? The almanac writer did not spend every night walking outside to look up and record the phase of the moon—charting history, as it were. The phases of the moon were undoubtedly derived from the work of an astronomer who used a scientific principle to produce the information. In spite of the almanac, should the judge have required Lincoln to bring in the astronomer for cross-examination?

The first time expert opinion was offered in court about ballistics, radar, genetic testing, and the like, lawyers undoubtedly produced substantial testimony in an effort to persuade the judge of the validity of the underlying scientific principles.[92] As the underlying scientific principles became well accepted, trial courts no longer required elaborate proof of the validity of the science, but rather took judicial notice of the validity of the theory and required evidence only of the particular application or of the qualifications of the particular expert. Appellate courts in various jurisdictions have at one time or another decided that the forensic science of "ballistics" can assist in the identification of the gun from which a bullet was fired,[93] that the speed of an approaching car can be measured by a radar gun,[94] and that genetic markers can be used to establish parentage.[95] Although many scientific principles have become so well accepted that they are judicially noticed, the process to reach that status is often difficult during the period in which the science is being developed.[96]

When a court takes judicial notice of the scientific principle underlying radar, for example, it is not clear whether that judicial notice is of an

---

chavlis, 260 F.3d 1149, 1154 (9th Cir. 2001) (judicial notice of a map "in determining whether a defendant known to have driven from one location to another passed through a particular jurisdiction."); Ibarra v. Sunset Scavenger Co., 2003 WL 21244096 (N.D.Cal. 2003) ("statistics published by the Equal Employment Opportunity Commission which indicate the composition of the workforce in Oakland, San Jose and San Francisco by race and job category"); Scotty's Contr. & Stone, Inc. v. United States, 326 F.3d 785 (6th Cir. 2003) (a page of a brief submitted in a different case).

92. *See* **Ch. 10**.

93. Oliver Wendell Holmes, when he served on the Massachusetts Supreme Judicial Court, is credited by David Faigman, et al, Modern Scientific Evidence § 23–1.2 (1997) with the first decision admitting modern firearms identification—Commonwealth v. Best, 62 N.E. 748 (Mass.1902).

94. *See, e.g.,* People v. Magri, 147 N.E.2d 728 (N.Y. 1958) (no longer be necessary to require expert testimony in each case as to the nature, function or scientific

principles underlying stationary radar); People v. Knight, 530 N.E.2d 1273 (N.Y. 1988) (no longer necessary to require expert testimony as to scientific principles underlying <u>moving</u> radar).

95. *Compare* Clark v. Jeter, 486 U.S. 456 (1988) (Court ordered blood test to determine parentage accepted as a matter of course); In re Request for Judicial Assistance, 1997 WL 1052017 (D.Conn. 1997) (same); United States v. Floyd, 81 F.3d 1517 (10th Cir. 1996) (Same; trial court ordered blood test and used results to conclude defendant was not the biological father of the child in question).

96. DNA testing, for example, is now widely accepted by courts. *See e.g.* Tuan Anh Nguyen v. INS, 533 U.S. 53, 80 (2001) ("Modern DNA testing, in addition to providing accuracy unmatched by other methods of establishing a biological link, essentially negates the evidentiary significance of the passage of time."); Weinstein, *The Nation's Death Penalty Foes Mark a Milestone Crime: Arizona convict freed on DNA tests is said to be the 100th known condemned U.S. prisoner to be exonerated since execu-*

"adjudicative" or a "legislative fact." It is of some moment because "legislative facts," unlike "adjudicative facts," are not governed by Rule 201.

"Legislative facts" are often central to a court's determination of a legal issue, but the "legislative fact" is not always identified as something of which the court is taking judicial notice. A "legislative fact," unlike an "adjudicative fact," is often not "generally known," cannot be found in a source "whose accuracy cannot reasonably be questioned," and is not something the parties necessarily had an opportunity to address.

The scientific principles underlying radar, ballistics, DNA and the like seem to be "adjudicative facts" to the extent that they constitute evidence that without the judicial notice would normally go to a jury for its consideration. On the other hand, the scientific principle underlying radar is an hypothesis not unlike the social or economic hypotheses that are usually characterized as "legislative facts." The difference is that our belief in science allows us a greater certainty about the truth of the hypothesis.

In re Sealed Case[97] presents a clear example of "legislative fact." In trying to secure notes of conversations between a White House aide and the aide's lawyer, a prosecutor argued that the lawyer-client privilege did not survive the death of the White House aide. While recognizing the Supreme Court's earlier finding of a "legislative fact"—that the provision of legal advice "can only be safely and readily availed of when free from the consequences or apprehension of disclosure"[98]—the District of Columbia Court of Appeals found its own "legislative fact," though it did not denominate it as such. To support departing from the long established rule that the client's need to be "free from the consequence or apprehension of disclosure" required that the privilege survive the death of the client, the court said: "[I]t is surely true that the risk of post-death revelation will typically trouble the client less than pre-death revelation."[99]

The "fact" that post-death disclosure of privileged information will trouble the client less than pre-death disclosure is as subject to quarrel as is the "fact" that legal advice cannot exist without confidentiality in the first instance.[100] Both propositions are more properly characterized as "hypotheses" than "fact," but they are noticed and treated as facts by courts that are engaged in the law making, as opposed to the fact finding, process.

tions resumed, L.A. Times, Apr. 10, 2002, at A16.

97. 124 F.3d 230 (D.C. Cir. 1997), *rev'd sub nom*. Swidler & Berlin v. United States, 524 U.S. 399. (1998). The Supreme Court expressed doubt about the validity of the lower court's conclusions concerning the likely effect of the loss of privilege. *Id*. at 407-408.

98. Hunt v. Blackburn, 128 U.S. 464, 470 (1888).

99. 124 F.3d at 233.

100. *See* David Louisell, *Confidentiality, Conformity, and Confusion: Privileges in Federal Court Today,* 31 Tul. L. Rev. 101, 112 (1956) for an argument that the effect of disclosure is speculative and cannot be proven scientifically.

While the individual judge's "knowledge" of an hypothesis that the judge will notice as a "legislative fact" in support of legal reasoning is inevitable, the individual judge's "knowledge" of an "adjudicative fact" is neither necessary nor sufficient for judicial notice under Rule 201. A judge who does not know the Chicago Cubs from the fuzzy, brown four-footed creatures in the zoo will take judicial notice of the last year the Chicago Cubs won the World Series when shown the Encyclopedia of Baseball. But if that same judge should happen to know the ages of the children of the Cubs' current manager, the judge is not entitled to take judicial notice of them.

The adjudicative facts most trial lawyers will be concerned about in substituting for the testimony of witnesses may be called to the court's attention in any number of ways. The most common is: "Your honor, I ask the court to take judicial notice that the Chicago Cubs last won a World Series in 1908 and that the Boston Red Sox have been forlorn for almost as long, last winning the World Series in 1918."

Chapter 2

PROCEDURES FOR OFFERING
AND OPPOSING EVIDENCE IN
A COMMON LAW TRIAL

Table of Sections

§ 2.01 Lawyers as Evidence Police

The lawyers, who are primarily responsible for the content of an adversary system common law trial, have the privilege and the obligation to determine which evidence rules will be enforced and which will not—at least in the first instance. The trial judge may on a rare occasion exclude information *sua sponte*—when the United States Constitution prohibits the evidence, for example—but the lawyers are ordinarily responsible for rooting out inadmissible evidence.

Information offered by a proponent that does not meet the requirements of the evidence rules usually will be admitted as evidence, unless the opponent objects to it. Often the opponent knows the information is not admissible, but has no tactical or strategic reason to exclude it. Other times, both parties may have an equal interest in having the information before the jurors. Sometimes the opponent will be unaware that the information can be excluded. Occasionally the opponent will not be quick enough with an objection to keep it from the jurors' ears, and not interested in emphasizing the information by asking the judge to strike it and tell the jurors to disregard it.

Rule 103(a)(1) recognizes the importance of the lawyer as the enforcer of evidence law, by requiring an objection before admission of evidence can be appealed, unless the admission amounts to plain error.[1]

Lawyers enforce evidence law in two different ways. Some evidence issues are sufficiently obvious before trial and critical enough to the way the trial will proceed to be researched, briefed, and argued to the judge in the fashion of any major matter of law. This method of enforcing evidence law demands the same skills and effort as the presentation of any other legal position. Most evidence issues, however, pop up unexpectedly at trial. They require the trial lawyer to hear the issue in the examiner's question; recognize the applicable evidence law; gain the judge's attention, while quieting the witness; object precisely; and be prepared to argue evidence theory and its applicability to the facts presented—all in less than half a minute.

§ 2.02   Motions in Limine

A motion in limine is a common method for raising evidentiary matters of a substantial or highly prejudicial nature, the resolution of which will influence the conduct of and streamline the trial. This anticipatory motion, usually made in writing before the beginning of the trial, gives the lawyers an opportunity to ensure that objectionable and particularly prejudicial information will never be offered in front of, and, therefore, never heard by the jurors. Although the motion is most often used to exclude evidence, it also can provide a mechanism for a lawyer planning to offer controversial evidence to obtain a pre-trial ruling on admissibility.

Lawyers should be sure to obtain a clear ruling from the judge on the motion in limine and should make certain that the motion and the ruling are entered into the trial record. The record and the lawyer's understanding of the rationale for the judge's decision are important for the trial of the case as well as for any possible appeal. Denial of a motion in limine does not mean, necessarily, that the judge will exclude or admit the evidence in question at trial. In many cases, the judge will deny a motion in limine, not because the motion is wrong on the merits, but because a ruling is not possible without hearing the proffered evidence in the context of other evidence. Admission of a critical hearsay statement, for example, may depend upon the facts surrounding the utterance-facts that will not be apparent until the testimony of the person who heard the statement. Similarly, before trial a judge may not be confident enough of the context or of other evidence to exclude evidence for which it is claimed the prejudicial effect substantially outweighs the probative value.

If the denial of a motion in limine to exclude evidence is merely a postponement, the moving lawyer will make the objection at trial. A moving lawyer losing a motion to admit evidence will, similarly, offer the evidence at trial.

---

1.   On plain error, *see* § **12.04.**

If the denial of a motion in limine is not a postponement, but a ruling on the merits, the losing lawyer faces a quandary. The lawyer is tempted not to object at trial in order to avoid emphasizing the evidence in front of the jury. The problem is that jurisdictions have been split on whether a matter determined on the merits in limine is preserved for appeal. The lawyer who failed to object again at trial ran a risk that the matter decided in limine would not be preserved.

The 2000 amendment to FRE 103 attempted to remove the risk in the Federal system by adding: "Once the court makes a definitive ruling on the record admitting or excluding evidence, either at or before trial, a party need not renew an objection or offer of proof to preserve a claim of error for appeal." Whether it will eliminate the risk remains to be seen, for it is hard to predict when an appellate court will regard a ruling as "definitive." The easy cases for the lawyer concerned with making an objection at trial are those in which the trial court is clear that it has "reserved its ruling or indicated that the ruling is provisional"[2] and those in which "the court makes a definitive ruling on the record admitting or excluding evidence."[3] The potential problem arises in those cases in which the court indicates that the ruling is definitive but the record is less than clear. The lawyer can attempt to ensure there are no unpleasant surprises, by insisting upon a hearing record that includes the judge's specific ruling and affirmation that it is definitive, or not.[4] If the in limine ruling is definitive and the judge does not change course at trial on the issue as a result of a party's departure from the pre-trial representations, the lawyer need not object to preserve the matter for appeal even in the face of the judge's invitation to renew the objection.[5] If, on the other hand, the court has made a definitive pre-trial ruling, there is "nothing in the amendment prohibits the court from revisiting its decision when the evidence is offered."[6] In that event, "objection must be made when the evidence is offered to preserve the claim of error for appeal."[7]

Defense lawyers in criminal cases are sometimes forced to make hard choices at trial if the judge has made a pretrial ruling that prior convictions will be admissible to impeach their clients. The Supreme Court ruled in *Luce v. United States*[8] that an in limine denial of a motion to prohibit the prosecution from impeaching the defendant with prior criminal convictions is forfeited unless the lawyer calls the defendant to testify and the defendant is impeached with the criminal convictions.[9]

2. Advisory Committee Note to 2000 Amendment, Fed. R. Evid. 103.

3. Fed. R. Evid. 103.

4. Anticipating the problem, the Advisory Committee Note to 2000 Amendment Fed. R. Evid. 103 suggest that the amendment "imposes the obligation on counsel to clarify whether an in limine ... ruling is definitive when there is doubt on that point."

5. United States v. Gajo, 290 F.3d 922 (7th Cir. 2002) (where definitive pre-trial ruling admitted evidence if the claimed

foundation could be produced at trial and foundation was produced at trial, matter preserved for appeal even though defense counsel responded "no" when district judge inquired at trial whether defense wished to make an objection).

6. Advisory Committee Note to 2000 Amendment, Fed. R. Evid. 103.

7. *Id.*

8. 469 U.S. 38 (1984).

9. The Advisory Committee, in discussing the 2000 amendment of FRE 103, spe-

The high price for preserving the appeal—risking that the jury will be overly influenced by a defendant's prior convictions—was made even higher by the Court's recent decision in *Ohler v. United States*.[10] Lawyers solving the *Luce* dilemma by having the defendant testify in order to preserve the appeal often had the defendant testify to those convictions during direct examination. The idea was that by having the defendant testify during direct examination about the prior convictions the prosecution was sure to ask about on cross-examination, the defendant could at least avoid the appearance of hiding something. As predicted in the first edition of this text, the *Ohler* Court held that the defendant waived her pre-trial objection to the government's impeachment use of a prior drug conviction when she testified to the conviction on direct examination.[11] *Luce* and *Ohler* are non-constitutional rulings and a number of state jurisdictions have agreed with *Ohler* dissent that the rules are "unfair."[12]

§ 2.03 Objections and Motions to Strike at Trial [FRE 103]

The lawyer's choices about and the procedure for making objections at trial can have an important influence on the outcome of the trial, as well as on whether evidence issues are preserved for appeal. The constant tension between the tactics that will be most effective at trial and the steps necessary to create a good record for appeal are never more apparent than when a lawyer is objecting to evidence.

The ability to appeal an evidentiary ruling can be waived by any number of actions or inaction. Failure to object constitutes a waiver.[13] Waiver also may result from an objection that is untimely,[14] an objection that is not sufficiently specific,[15] or an objection that is made on the

cifically stated that the amendment was not "intended to affect the rule set forth in [Luce] and its progeny."

10. 529 U.S. 753, 754 (2000).

11. *Id.*

12. *See e.g.,* State v. Keiser, 807 A.2d 378 (Vt. 2002); State v. Cross, 110 Wash. App. 1031, 2002 WL 234832 at *2 (Wash. Ct. App. 2002) (Holding "Even if we were inclined to agree with the general holding in *Ohler*, that rule is contrary to established precedent in this state."); Zola v. Kelley, 826 A.2d 589, 592 (N.H. 2003) (Holding "[b]ecause preservation is a procedural issue, we are not bound by the Supreme Court's holding in *Ohler*. We therefore look to our own jurisprudence." And furthermore, "in general, a definitive ruling by the trial court on a motion in limine sufficiently preserves for appellate review the particular issue presented to the trial court. We concluded that this satisfies the require-

ment that a party must make a contemporaneous and specific objection at trial to preserve an issue for appellate review. . . .")

13. United States v. Weed, 689 F.2d 752, 756 (7th Cir.1982); Khanh Phuong Nguyen v. United States, 539 U.S. 69 (2003) (Court reiterates that the failure to object at trial ordinarily constitutes a waiver).

14. In some courts, a timely objection requires objection during the opponent's opening statement if the proposed evidence is mentioned. *See* Reagan v. Brock, 628 F.2d 721, 723 (1st Cir. 1980); Bewley v. Allright Carpark, Inc., 617 S.W.2d 547, 552 (Mo. App. 1981); Evans v. Andraschko, 70 Fed. Appx. 533, 535 (10th Cir. 2003); United States v. Carter, 42 Fed. Appx. 418, 425 (10th Cir. 2002); Diefenbach v. Sheridan Transp., 229 F.3d 27 (1st Cir. 2000).

15. *See* § **2.04**; *See also* Diefenbach v. Sheridan Transp., 229 F.3d 27, 29 (1st Cir. 2000).

wrong ground.[16] The purpose for requiring a timely objection that states the proper specific ground is to give the trial judge an opportunity to correct the error and to prevent a wasted trial. Moreover, it gives the proponent an opportunity to withdraw the matter and rely on other evidence or to cure the problem by laying a further foundation.[17] The plain error rule occasionally will preserve an evidentiary matter for appeal, irrespective of anything that may have occurred at trial,[18] but the trial lawyer cannot afford to rely on the chance that plain error will save a mistake in evidence advocacy. The effective evidence advocate must combine knowledge of the substance of the case with fluency in the language of the courtroom in order to make the most difficult judgment—whether to object to inadmissible evidence—and then to object in a timely and proper fashion.

Most accomplished trial lawyers relieve the tension between protecting the record and conducting the best possible trial by objecting to evidence only when the question is objectionable *and* the answer will be harmful to the objecting party's case. The lawyer who makes too many objections may be seen as an obstructionist who is trying to conceal information. Moreover, overruled objections can be harmful to the case. The jurors may give the admitted evidence more weight than it would otherwise receive, because attention has been drawn to it by the objection.

Sometimes failure to make a valid objection is sound because the opponent's evidence will open the door to devastating evidence that would not otherwise be admissible.

Technical objections to foundation may backfire. If the lawyer knows that the opposing party can lay the foundation, then the objection should ordinarily be withheld. Otherwise, the lawyer appears to be obstructing the trial for no reason. Moreover, the opponent's evidence may be more persuasive if the full foundation has been laid. The same principle applies to certain objections to the form of questions, such as objections to questions that are vague or over-broad. The re-phrased question may elicit testimony that is more persuasive than what would have been brought forth by the original testimony.

Technical objections, on the other hand, may break the flow of a cross-examiner's effective examination, and give the direct examiner's friendly witness time to think about what is coming next. Occasionally, a direct examiner will not be very adept. Posing technical objections may make it impossible for such an examiner to complete the direct examination, let alone make it persuasive.

---

16. United States v. Johnson, 722 F.2d 407, 409 (8th Cir. 1983); Ralston v. Plogger, 476 N.E.2d 1378, 1384 (Ill.App. 1985); United States v. Farag, 41 Fed. Appx. 338, (10th Cir. 2002); Int'l Land Acquisitions, Inc. v. Fausto, 39 Fed. Appx. 751, 756 (3d Cir. 2002); United States v. Causwell, 10 Fed. Appx. 80, (4th Cir. 2001).

17. *See* United States v. Del Llano, 354 F.2d 844, 847–48 (2d Cir. 1965); 1 Weinstein's Federal Evidence § 103.02[2] (2d ed. Joseph M. McLaughlin ed. 1997).

18. *See* § **12.04** (discussing the plain error doctrine).

The lawyer with a strong or sympathetic jury case should generally be less eager to make objections. The trial judge may err in sustaining the objection, thereby giving the opponent an appeal point with which to overturn the verdict.

Careful preparation and knowledge of the judge's individual predilections can help the lawyer to prepare for the quick give and take of trial evidence. Judges have vastly different attitudes about the admission and exclusion of evidence. Some give lawyers much more leeway than do others. Since most of the Rules rest upon the judge's discretion, the lawyer's conduct must be adjusted to take into account whether the judge is free and easy in receiving evidence, or extremely technical-minded about excluding it. Some judges, for example, have a strict attitude toward asking questions in proper form, and will frequently sustain objections to leading questions or to questions that call for a narrative response. Others are impatient with attorneys who make such objections and are likely to give the jury the impression that the objecting attorney is wasting everyone's time. Because a trial judge's rulings on matters of form almost never create reversible error, the individual judge's attitude is determinative.

Consideration of the potential objections to be made at trial is an important part of the lawyer's trial preparation, given the risk that error will be waived by failing to object, and the counter-danger that over-objecting will try the patience of the judge and the jurors. The lawyer should be able to anticipate and identify most of the opponent's damaging evidence before trial and should outline the legal grounds for exclusion and consider the language which will be most effective in persuading the judge without offending the jurors.

No lawyer, however, can anticipate every potential piece of damaging, but inadmissible, evidence the opponent might offer. In the heat of trial, the jurors might hear such evidence because the witness responds to the question either before the objecting lawyer can object or before the judge can instruct the witness not to answer. If that happens, the objecting lawyer must move, immediately, to have the question and answer stricken from the record and the jurors instructed to disregard them, in order to protect the record and preserve the matter for appeal.

Example

Proponent:	What happened next?
Witness:	My wife told me it was the same car that had been cruising around our house the day before.
Opponent:	Objection! Hearsay, irrelevant and prejudicial. I move to strike the answer, your Honor.
Judge:	Motion granted, the answer is stricken.
Opponent:	Move to instruct the jury to disregard.

Judge: The jury will disregard the witness' answer to
                          the question.

The separate motion for an instruction may not be necessary.
Judges will often anticipate and instruct the jurors to disregard at the
same time as striking the testimony.

Judge: Motion granted. The answer is stricken and the jury is
instructed to disregard it.

The same motion to strike and for an instruction to disregard will
protect the record if a witness volunteers damaging, inadmissible information without a question being posed; makes a non-responsive answer
to a proper question; or has testified on direct, but is unavailable for
cross-examination due to death, sickness, refusal to testify further, or
some similar reason.

Whether a lawyer should make the motion to strike and for an
instruction to disregard is subject to the same tactical considerations as
whether the lawyer should object to evidence in the first instance. When
jurors have already heard the information, there is the added consideration that a motion to strike and an instruction from the judge to
disregard will only emphasize the information and ensure that the jurors
will not forget it. The more prejudicial the information, the more likely
the lawyer will want to preserve the point for appeal and will move to
strike and for an instruction to the jury to disregard.

In some cases, the information may be so prejudicial that the lawyer
will consider moving for a mistrial. Whether that is a wise course
requires the lawyer to make a sophisticated analysis of, among other
things, whether the case will try better a second time; if it is a criminal
case, whether double jeopardy might bar a second trial; how the jurors
are likely to decide the case, if the judge instructs them to disregard the
prejudicial evidence and they take it to heart; and the cost to the client
of delay and appeal.

§ 2.04   How to Phrase an Objection

It is not possible to give a formula of words that will work in every
courtroom for all objections. Much depends upon the particular judge.
When preparing a case to be tried before an unfamiliar judge, the
attorney should try to learn the unwritten customs of the trial judge by
talking to other lawyers or by sitting in the courtroom. Knowledge of the
judge will tell the lawyer whether the judge is likely to rule on a general
objection or will require articulation of a specific basis. If the judge
requires a specific basis, the lawyer will learn whether it may be
expressed by description, or whether a rule number is required. In courts
where the judge prefers a description, the lawyer will learn whether the
judge expects a short legal description, such as "hearsay" or "document
has not been properly authenticated," or will allow longer objections
aimed at letting the jurors know why the particular question is "unfair."

"Objection, your honor, the question calls for a hearsay response, depriving the jurors of the opportunity to hear the truth from the person who actually made the observation" will tell the jurors more about the reason for the lawyer's objection than does "Objection, hearsay." Many judges will not allow the lawyer to justify the objection to the jurors[19] for fear that the justification will persuade the jurors not to consider a type of evidence that the law of evidence has determined is entitled to consideration.

Although no two judges treat evidence issues in precisely the same fashion, the language of the courtroom has developed some general conventions of articulation that will work in most situations.

A lawyer who, upon hearing an objectionable question, stands and says, "Objection, your honor," and then states the precise reason for the objection, such as "hearsay," "leading," "calls for a narrative response," and the like will be on safe ground in most courtrooms. Anything more general runs the risk of not preserving the objection for appeal.

Rule 103, Rulings on Evidence concerns preserving evidence matters for appeal and Rule 103(a)(1), Objection, requires that "timely objection or motion to strike appears of record, stating the specific ground of objection, if the specific ground was not apparent from the context."[20]

The Rules' requirement of something more than a general objection to preserve the matter for appeal has made almost extinct the once common practice in some courtrooms of not allowing lawyers to say anything more than "objection," unless asked to give a reason by the judge.[21] Because general objections will not preserve the issue for appeal, virtually all judges allow an objecting lawyer to articulate the specific reason.

Some reasons often used by lawyers are not sufficient to preserve an issue for appeal. They are general objections, even though the lawyer has said something more than just "Objection."

The time-honored objection "Irrelevant, immaterial and incompetent," despite its length remains a general objection that is not sufficient to preserve error, except, perhaps, when the only objection is that the evidence is irrelevant under Rule 401.[22]

---

19. *See* People v. Simpson, No. BA097211, 1995 WL 294282 (Cal. Super. Trans. Apr. 26, 1995) for Judge Ito's attempt, in a nationally televised case, to keep the lawyers from communicating to the jurors through their objections. "Speaking objections are forbidden. The proper procedure is to notify the court of the objection by standing and stating, 'Objection.' The court will then ask for a statement of the specific legal ground(s). Counsel may not expand beyond that specific and precise statement without leave of court"; United States v. Valenzuela, 17 F.3d 397 (9th Cir. 1994); Auscape Int'l v. National Geographic Soc'y, 2002 WL 31014829 (S.D.N.Y. 2002); United States v. Galin, 222 F.3d 1123 (9th Cir. 2000).

20. Fed. R. Evid. 103(a)(1).

21. *See e.g.,* United States v. Yeager, 331 F.3d 1216, 1223 (11th Cir. 2003).

22. 1 Weinstein's Federal Evidence § 103.12[1] (2d ed 1997); *See e.g.,* United States v. Mejia, 909 F.2d 242, 246 (7th Cir. 1990).

A "no foundation" objection without explanation as to the nature of the failure is not a "specific ground" that will satisfy Rule 103(a)(1).[23] The objection could refer to a variety reasons for exclusion. It could refer, for example, to failure to lay a foundation establishing the authenticity of a document, a foundation for a hearsay exception, or a foundation showing the existence of personal knowledge.

That a general objection usually will not preserve a matter for appeal does not mean that a lawyer should never lodge a general objection. When a lawyer hears a question that will lead to dubious evidence, but the lawyer cannot think of the specific ground for objection, a general objection is better than nothing at all.

"Objection" alone, or "objection" followed by a stock phrase such as "prejudicial," "no foundation," "not a proper question," or even "that can't be asked," will preserve the point for appeal, if the appellate court finds that the specific ground is "apparent from the context."[24] Moreover, the general objection may cause the evidence to be excluded at trial, because the trial judge may appreciate the specific ground for the objection, even if the objecting lawyer does not. The judge's exclusion of the evidence will be upheld on appeal if there was any ground to support it.[25] Ironically, when the general objection is sustained at trial, the objecting lawyer may be in a better position on appeal than if a specific objection had been made on the wrong ground and sustained by the judge.[26]

When a general objection is made and sustained, the attorney offering the evidence should consider asking that the ground for objection be specified. This is particularly true when the lawyer is unsure how to proceed to get the testimony into evidence in the face of the objection. Many objections can be obviated by changing the form of the question or

23. *See e.g.,* McKnight By & Through Ludwig v. Johnson Controls, 36 F.3d 1396 (8th Cir. 1994); United States v. Moore, 923 F.2d 910, 914–915 (1st Cir. 1991).

24. Fed. R. Evid. 103(a); *but see* United States v. Moore, 923 F.2d 910, 914–915 (1st Cir. 1991) ("merely uttering word 'foundation' was not sufficient objection to introduction of computer records that defendant contended on appeal were inadmissible under Fed. R. Evid. 803(6) because government's foundation evidence did not indicate sufficient trustworthiness."); United States v. Diaz, 300 F.3d 66, 75 (1st Cir. 2002) ("Objection, *Daubert*" held insufficient to apprise the District Court to which of "an array of expert witness issues" counsel was referring where *"Daubert"* requires the court to look to Fed. R. Evid. 702 which includes "the qualifications of the witness, the relevance of the proffered testimony, the adequacy of the facts or data underlying an opinion, the scientific reliability of the witness's methodology, and the reliability of the witness's application of that methodology to the facts."). For the question of waiv-

er versus forfeiture see the commentary to Rule 103.

25. Reddin v. Robinson Prop. Group, 239 F.3d 756 (5th Cir. 2001); Killgore v. Agtrans, Inc., 208 F.3d 226 (10th Cir. 2000); Gee v. Shepherd, 210 F.3d 389 (10th Cir. 2000); Pittman v. ANR Freight Sys., 47 Fed. Appx. 266, (6th Cir. 2002); Jodoin v. Toyota Motor Corp., 284 F.3d 272 (1st Cir. 2002).

26. Although in most cases an objection sustained on the wrong ground, when a proper ground exists, will not be reversed on appeal, commentators have suggested the result might be different if the proponent of the evidence could have cured the problem upon a proper objection, had it been made. *See* 1 Weinstein's Federal Evidence, *supra* note 14, at ¶ 103.12[4]; Edmund M. Morgan, Basic Problems of State and Federal Evidence 48 (5th ed. 1976); 1 McCormick on Evidence § 52 at 131 (4th ed. John W. Strong ed. 1994).

by bringing out the evidence in another fashion. Inexperienced lawyers, however, sometimes give up from confusion or embarrassment and lose the benefit of admissible testimony, because of problems with the form in which it is being elicited. In cases like this, the lawyer should *not* issue the request for clarification as a challenge to the trial judge ("Judge, why specifically did you sustain the objection?"), but should respectfully ask the court's help.

Examples

Requesting that counsel give a specific ground.

Proponent:	Dr. Green, when did you first see the patient?
Witness:	[Refers to notes before answering.]
Opponent:	Objection.
Judge:	Sustained.
Proponent:	[Confused] Your honor, may I request that counsel state a specific ground for objection, so that I can ask the question in a proper form?
Judge:	What is the basis for the objection?
Opponent:	No foundation.
Proponent:	Your honor, that is still a general objection. Counsel should specify what type of foundational objection is being made.
Opponent:	No foundation has been laid for the witness's use of the notes to refresh memory or as past recollection recorded.

Asking the trial judge for help.

Proponent:	Mr. Green, would you indicate on the diagram where you were standing at the time of the collision?
Opponent:	Objection, no foundation.
Judge:	Sustained.
Proponent:	[Having been stymied in this fashion on several similar questions] Your Honor, may I approach the bench?
Judge:	Yes.

Proponent: Your Honor, I am having problems here. I think that the witness's testimony would be admissible if I could put the questions in the proper form. Could you give me some guidance about how to proceed? [Or simply, "Could you give me some help here, judge?"]

The words to articulate various specific grounds for objections may not be susceptible to formula, but ought to be chosen in mind of the two reasons that underlie the requirement of specificity. Hearing the specific ground for an objection allows the judge to make an intelligent ruling and provides the proponent of the evidence with an opportunity to cure the defect.

In jurisdictions in which the rules of evidence have been codified, the requirement of specificity can often be met by referring to rule numbers.[27] This is particularly true when there is no universally recognized catch phrase that describes the objection.

Examples

"Objection! The question asks about statements made during mediation. Those are excluded under Rule 408."

"Objection! Rule 407. That change was a subsequent remedial measure."

"Objection! Rule 403. Prejudicial, confusing, and a waste of time."

In other instances, the words describing the objection may be so familiar as to render reference to the rule number superfluous or pedantic.

"Objection! Hearsay. [No need to refer to Rule 801(c).]

"Objection! Attorney-client privilege. [No point in referring to Rule 501.]

When evidence is admissible in part and objectionable in part—for example, when the medical history portion of a hospital record is admissible, but the portion of the history that contains plaintiff's description of the accident is not—the objecting lawyer must identify the portion of the offered or expected testimony that is objectionable. If the ground for objection is not applicable to the entire statement or document, the court can overrule the objection.[28]

---

27. *See* Jack Pope & Charles E. Hampton, *Presenting and Excluding Evidence*, 9 Tex. Tech L. Rev. 403 (1978). Even when rule numbers would be more precise, however, use of them is not required to preserve error. "Any expression which pointedly discloses the vulnerable quality of the proof or the character of the incompetency is sufficient.... [However,] care must be taken that the objection strike at the very heart of the infirmity." *Id.* at 445. *See also* Mason Ladd, *Objections, Motions and Foun-* *dation Testimony*, 43 Cornell L.Q. 543, 550–51 (1958); *but see* United States v. David, 96 F.3d 1477, 1480 (D.C. Cir. 1996) (The federal rules "therefore, do not require a pinpoint citation to a provision of the Rules or relevant precedent for every objection; what they do require is enough specificity to alert the district court and opposing counsel to the basis for the objection.").

28. *See e.g.*, United States v. Holland, 880 F.2d 1091, 1094 (9th Cir. 1989) (Defendant's blanket objection to the admission of

In many instances, there are multiple grounds for objection to a single item of evidence. The objecting lawyer should raise *all* the legal grounds that apply. To make the grounds clear for the judge and to avoid confusion in the record, the grounds can be numbered as they are stated. Identifying multiple grounds not only avoids the risk of choosing the wrong ground, but one of several correct grounds may be more persuasive to the judge than others.

It is necessary to enumerate all specific grounds in order to be sure of preserving the objection on appeal. An objection that specifies the wrong ground is as bad as an insufficient general objection. If the trial judge overrules the objection on the specific ground stated, the appellate court will affirm, even if the evidence would be excludable on other grounds, unless that other ground is plain from the context.[29]

§ 2.05   Timing of Objections

The most perplexing problem for the lawyer learning the language of the courtroom is the speed with which it must be spoken. In a sense, the law of evidence has a very short life, from the time of an objectionable question until the witness answers. If the lawyer does not spot the evidence issue as the question is asked and voice the objection in that brief pause between question and answer, the law of evidence might have no effect. Courts have held that objections raised after the answer is given are not adequate, unless the answer was given so quickly that objection could not possibly be interposed.[30] Some trial judges are strict about requiring the objection before the answer, at least when the objection concerns a matter of form.

Example

Proponent: Did Mr. Brown's vehicle cross the centerline?

Witness: Yes.

Opponent: Objection, leading question.

Judge: Asked and answered, counsel. Next question.

Despite the best efforts of the objecting lawyer and the judge, there are a variety of reasons why a witness' inadmissible testimony may be heard by the jurors, before the operation of the law of evidence can avoid the problem. The witness might offer testimony without a question being posed. The witness might answer so quickly that there is no time to

a tape, parts of which were admissible, does not preserve an objection to the court's failure to redact the tape and admit only those parts which were relevant where defense had not made the distinction.); United States v. Ball, 35 F.3d 572 (9th Cir. 1994)

29.   United States v. Johnson, 722 F.2d 407, 409 (8th Cir. 1983); Ralston v. Plogger,

476 N.E.2d 1378, 1384 (Ill.App. 1985); United States v. Evans, 883 F.2d 496, 499 (6th Cir. 1989); United States v. Sandifer, 188 F.3d 992, 995 (8th Cir.1999).

30.   Am. Jur. 2d *Trial* § 403 (2003); 1 McCormick, *supra* note 18, § 52.

interpose an objection. The basis for an objection might not be apparent in the question, becoming obvious only with the witness' answer. The witness might respond to an unobjectionable question with a non-responsive answer. The witness might respond to the question, despite a timely objection, before the judge has an opportunity to rule. The judge might sustain an objection, but the witness might answer, anyway. To preserve the point for appeal in any of these situations, the lawyer must make sure the objection is of record and must make a motion to strike the testimony and for an instruction to the jurors to disregard it.

The motion to strike the testimony and for an instruction to the jurors to disregard might not actually cure the harm, as it relates to the outcome of the trial. It might even aggravate it by calling attention to the matter. But if the lawyer's judgment is that the client's cause will be better served by preserving the appeal point than it will be hurt by the added emphasis, the lawyer must make the motion.

There will be times when a lawyer anticipates objectionable evidence and wants to interpose the objection immediately, to avoid any danger that the jurors will hear the prejudicial and inadmissible information, because it comes out before the operation of the law of evidence prohibits it. Some trial judges will treat objections to preliminary questions as premature. For instance, if the examiner asks whether the witness has an opinion and the other lawyer objects because the opinion will be inadmissible, the trial judge might treat the objection as untimely until the witness has actually been asked to state the opinion. Similarly, some trial judges treat objections to questions about conversations as premature until the witness has actually been asked to state the contents of the conversation. If the court takes this tack, the objecting lawyer should be careful to renew the objection in order to exclude the evidence. The problem might not be with the nature of the objection, but only with its timing.

Example

Prosecutor:	Did you have a conversation with the victim?
Defense lawyer:	Objection—hearsay.
Judge:	Overruled. He hasn't asked what was said.
Witness:	Yes.
Prosecutor:	What did the victim say?
Defense lawyer:	Objection, hearsay.
Judge:	Sustained.

The defense lawyer might be making the early objection to avoid the common problem of a witness who does not respond to the first question with a "yes" or "no," but with a recitation of the conversation. If that is the case, the lawyer should ask the judge who overrules the objection to instruct the witness to answer precisely.

Example

Prosecutor:	Did you have a conversation with the victim?
Defense lawyer:	Objection—hearsay.
Judge:	Overruled. He hasn't asked what was said.
Defense lawyer:	Will your honor please caution the witness to answer "yes" or "no" and not to testify to the contents of the conversation?

A similar timing problem can arise when an exhibit is being marked, authenticated, and then offered into evidence. When the proponent begins the process by having the exhibit marked for identification, there is no question posed and, therefore, nothing about which to object. The handling of an exhibit can be cumbersome and can lead to the exhibit being seen by the jurors before it is admitted into evidence. If it is an exhibit the opponent expects to exclude, and even the mention of it might be prejudicial, the lawyer should raise the issue at the earliest possible time.

Example

Proponent:	Your honor, may I have an exhibit marked for identification.
Judge:	[Assents by nodding the head and pointing toward the clerk who will mark the exhibit.]
Opponent:	May we approach the bench?

Or

Objection, may we approach?

The request for a sidebar conference without the objection is likely to let the judge know that there is an evidentiary issue surrounding the exhibit. The judge will probably respond by asking the lawyers to approach for a discussion outside the hearing of the jurors. If the judge does not understand or does not agree to the sidebar, the lawyer will have to expand the request and let the judge know specifically that the lawyer wishes to lodge an objection outside of the hearing of the jurors.

An objection to the marking of an exhibit cannot be sustained—even if the judge is not going to allow its admission—because the exhibit must be marked for the record to be complete. The judge may, nevertheless, entertain the argument over admission, at the time the exhibit is being marked, particularly if the objection is one that can be settled without the judge first hearing the foundation testimony. By asking for the sidebar conference when the proponent first asks to have the exhibit marked, the objecting lawyer avoids making the objection in front of the jury, is not responsible for squelching the natural anticipation that jurors feel when they are about to see an exhibit, and avoids the jurors seeing the exhibit through inadvertent display.

§ 2.06 Sidebar Conferences (Bench Conferences); Excusing the Jury

Rule 103(c), Hearing of the jury, explicitly encourages lawyers and judges to use all available means "to prevent inadmissible evidence from being suggested to the jury by any means."

Pretrial conferences—before the jurors are even empanelled—and hearings conducted outside the presence of the jurors, when lengthy offers of proof are made by the question and answer method, are often employed to keep jurors from learning information that, ultimately, will be ruled inadmissible. Although many judges try to encourage settling as many evidence issues as possible in pre-trial conferences, particularly issues surrounding tangible exhibits, the sidebar conference is still the most common device employed to further the ends of Rule 103(c). Much as lawyers anticipate and attempt to handle evidence matters before trial with motions in limine, there are always matters that arise at trial that should be discussed outside the presence of the jurors.

The sidebar (or bench) conference is an effective device for furthering the goals of Rule 103(c) and keeping matters from the jurors. The problem for the trial lawyer, and for the judge, to some extent, is that the jurors sit around bored—and maybe resentful about being left out—while the lawyers and the judge thrash out evidence law problems.

Lawyers may ask for a sidebar at anytime, but granting the request is within the discretion of the judge. Refusal to allow a sidebar is unlikely to be cause for a reversal, unless as a result, a party is denied the opportunity to make an offer of proof, or the jurors receive information so prejudicial that the side requesting the sidebar is denied a fair trial. When a lawyer wants a sidebar conference outside the hearing of the jurors to make an objection, to argue about an objection, or to make an offer of proof regarding evidence that the judge has ruled inadmissible, the lawyer requests a hearing. "Sidebar, your honor?" "May we approach?" "May we approach the bench, your honor?" "Bench conference, your honor?" are various ways a lawyer might signal the judge that the lawyer wishes to discuss a matter outside of the hearing of the jurors, but without excusing the jurors from the courtroom.

Judges, aware of jurors' impatience with discussions in their presence to which they are not privy, do not grant every request for a sidebar. Generalization about how any judge will handle requests for a sidebar is impossible, but there are some general clues to the exercise of judicial discretion.

Lawyers who want to make every objection at the bench are unlikely to be welcome at the bench for that purpose after their goal becomes apparent to the judge.

Lawyers who wish to argue every objection, irrespective of the importance of the proposed evidence or the rectitude of the argument, are unlikely to be welcome at the bench when the pattern becomes apparent.

When a real dispute about evidence is apparent, sidebars will almost always be granted.

"Offer of proof, your honor?" will almost always result in a sidebar conference, because it is specifically mentioned in Rule 103(c). If the offer is to be made by questioning a witness, the jurors will be excused, but often the offer can be made by narrative at the bench, without the disruption of removing the jurors from the courtroom.

When a question asks about character, criminal convictions, specific acts, or other matters that might have a prejudicial effect if they are heard by the jurors and not admitted into evidence, a request for a sidebar, following an objection made without stating a specific ground, is likely to be granted.

When the judge can tell from the context of a request for a sidebar that the articulation of an objection and a ruling might cause the jurors to give extraordinary weight to evidence they have heard or to speculate about excluded evidence, the request is likely to be granted.

During sidebar conferences, whether requested by the lawyers or initiated by the judge, the lawyer should be sure that the conference is conducted in the kind of hushed tones that will not be heard by the jurors *and that the conference is on the record*. Without the court reporter present to record the bench conference, anything said or done at the conference is beyond appellate review.

§ 2.07 Continuing Objections

The requirement that objections be specific, both as to the legal grounds and to the part of the evidence objected to, can require a lawyer to object to each one of a series of questions posed to a witness on the same topic. Because such repeated objections can antagonize both judge and jury, the objecting lawyer might want to request a continuing objection to a line of questioning.

When the objection is first raised and overruled by the judge, the lawyer may ask for a continuing objection that will obviate the need constantly to interrupt the examination in order to preserve the record.

Example

Proponent:	How many incidents did you discuss with the deceased?
Witness:	Seven.

Proponent:	Do you remember what the deceased said about the incident of March 2, 1998?
Witness:	Yes.
Proponent:	What did the deceased say about that incident?
Opponent:	Objection, hearsay.
Judge:	Overruled.
Opponent:	Your honor, if counsel is going to ask what the deceased said about all seven encounters, may I have a continuing hearsay objection to what the deceased said?
Judge:	You may.

The lawyer asking for the continuing objection must obtain the judge's consent on the record, in order for the continuing objection to preserve the issue for appeal.

If the testimony that is the subject of a continuing objection is likely to be critical to the outcome, the lawyer should take care in relying upon a continuing objection. If the ground for objection to a later question differs from the ground upon which the continuing objection is granted, the issue for the later question will not be preserved, because the continuing objection to the question will not have stated the proper specific ground for exclusion. It is often difficult to determine where the continuing objection should end, and differences of opinion on that point could result in the failure to preserve error.

At the end of a witness' testimony, for which a continuing objection has been taken, the objecting lawyer should renew the objection for the record, move to strike the entire line of testimony, and move to have the jurors instructed to disregard it.

§ 2.08   Voir Dire to Lay the Foundation for an Objection

There will be times when a lawyer believes that certain testimony will be improper, that the foundation is lacking for an exhibit, or that a witness is not qualified to testify, but the basis for the objection is not apparent from the questions posed by the direct examiner. When such a circumstance first becomes apparent to the lawyer, it is appropriate to object and to ask permission of the court to "take the witness on voir dire." The objecting lawyer is asking the judge to interrupt the direct examination and to allow a limited cross-examination for the purpose of laying the foundation for the objection. There are times when the lawyer will ask or the judge may prefer that the voir dire is conducted outside the hearing of the jurors, but more often, the jurors will hear the examination. A typical example is when a proponent has apparently qualified a witness as an expert, and the objecting lawyer has additional information that might change the judge's willingness to accept the witness as an expert in the field designated by the direct examiner.

Example

Proponent:	Your honor, plaintiff submits that Dr. Wissard is qualified as an expert in the design and and operation of radial tires.
Opponent:	Objection, your honor. May I take the witness on voir dire?
Judge:	You may.
Opponent:	Dr. Wissard, isn't it true that your Ph.D is from Western Atlantic University?
Witness:	Yes.
Opponent:	Western Atlantic University is a correspondence school located above a hardware store, isn't that right?
Witness:	Well, yes. But it is a good school.
Opponent:	Dr. Wissard, you have never designed a radial tire, have you?
Witness:	No.
Opponent:	Dr. Wissard, you have never run tests comparing the operation of the defendant's radial tires to those of other manufacturers, have you?
Witness:	No. But I have read the literature.
Opponent:	Your honor, defense believes that Dr. Wissard is not qualified as an expert in the design and operation of radial tires and objects to the court accepting him as an expert witness in that field.

The judge might disqualify the witness, believing that the points raised in the voir dire disqualify the witness from testifying to an expert opinion. On the other hand, the judge might believe that the points raised on voir dire affect the weight of the expert's testimony, but are insufficient to disqualify the witness as an expert. In the latter case, the judge is likely to say something like: "Counsel, the issues you have raised concerning the witness' education and experience go to weight. You may argue them to the jurors, but the court accepts Dr. Wissard as an expert in the design and operation of radial tires."

§ 2.09 Motion for Limiting Instruction [FRE 105]

Valid objections to evidence will often be overruled because the evidence is admissible in part, or for a limited purpose. A portion of an exhibit may be admissible while other portions are not. Where there are multiple parties on one side, evidence may be admissible against one party, but not against another. In any of these situations, the objecting lawyer must take steps to prevent prejudicial evidence from being used improperly by the jurors.

A motion for a limiting instruction might be the only precaution available to the lawyer who has not been able to persuade the judge to invoke remedies that will keep the information from the jurors.[31] If the lawyer believes the jurors are more likely to heed the judge's instruction than to be influenced by the emphasis that the specific instruction might give to the evidence, the lawyer should make the motion as soon as the evidence is presented.[32] The motion should be restated at the completion of the case, for inclusion in the judge's instructions to the jurors.

Example

Cross-examiner:	Isn't it true that you previously said the light was green for the Chevrolet?
Direct examiner:	Objection, hearsay.
Cross-examiner:	Impeachment, your honor.
Judge:	Overruled.
Direct examiner:	Your honor, I request an instruction to the jurors regarding the limited use of the witness' answer.
Judge:	Members of the jury. An out of court statement by a witness is not admissible in evidence to prove the contents of the statement. It may, however, be admitted as it bears on the credibility of the witness. You may consider the answer you hear from the witness only as it bears on the witness' credibility.

---

31. Oral testimony that is admissible for one purpose, but not for another may be excluded if the prejudice resulting from the inadmissible purpose substantially outweighs the probative value of the admissible purpose. Fed. R. Evid. 403. Some exhibits can have the inadmissible information redacted without ruining the proper use of the exhibit. However, other evidence might be so prejudicial that the party against whom it is not admissible will be entitled to a severance.

32. Many lawyers believe that an instruction to use something for one purpose and not for another is impossible to state and equally difficult to do. The lawyer who asks for a limiting instruction should be prepared to say something in closing argument to turn the emphasis to the lawyer's advantage. If no such argument is apparent to the lawyer, a motion for a limiting instruction might hurt more than it will help.

Cross-examiner: You may answer.

Witness: Yes.

The judge might well wait until after the witness' answer to give the limiting instruction. The instruction at the end of the trial might be general with respect to using evidence only for the purpose offered or specific with respect to a piece of evidence when requested by the lawyer who asked for the limiting instruction.

§ 2.10   Offer of Proof

Rule 103(a)(2) provides for offers of proof. When an objection to evidence is sustained, the issue will not be preserved for appeal unless the proponent makes sure that the "substance of the evidence was made known to the court by offer or was apparent from the context within which questions were asked." Rulings sustaining objections to the form of the question or lack of foundation do not call for an offer of proof, because the examiner should simply proceed by asking the question in a different fashion or presenting the additional information that will complete the foundation. It is only when the judge has sustained an objection that excludes evidence and the lawyer cannot cure the problem, that an offer of proof is needed.

An offer of proof will further two of the examiner's goals. It will comply with Rule 103(a)(2), making it possible for an appellate court to evaluate the effect of the exclusion of the evidence on the proponent's case and, therefore, not invoke the common response that the trial judge's error does not justify reversal, because the error was harmless.[33] A solid demonstration of the importance of the evidence to the proponent's case might, also, persuade the trial judge to reconsider the ruling and admit the evidence. Even if the context within which the questions are asked gives the trial judge sufficient knowledge of the substance of the evidence to preserve the point for appeal,[34] the proponent of the evidence might wish to make an offer of proof, in hopes the judge will be persuaded to reverse the ruling and admit the evidence.

There are two usual forms of offer, both of which are conducted outside the hearing of the jurors, to comply with the mandate of Rule 103(c) to keep inadmissible evidence from being presented to the jurors. The narrative form—in which the lawyer who wants to offer the evidence tells the judge and the other lawyer what testimony would be produced from which witnesses—is usually conducted at sidebar. The question and answer form—in which the proponent puts the witness on

33. *See* United States v. Adams, 271 F.3d 1236, 1241–43 (10th Cir. 2001); United States v. Peak, 856 F.2d 825 (7th Cir. 1988); United States v. Jackson, 208 F.3d 633 (7th Cir. 2000).

34. *See* Fed. R. Evid. 103(a)(2); Fed. R. Evid. 103 Commentary: *Offer of proof. See*

also United States v. Rettenberger, 344 F.3d 702, 706 (7th Cir. 2003) ("An offer of proof is unnecessary if the substance of the excluded testimony may be found in the record.").

the stand and conducts the proposed examination—is usually conducted in the courtroom, after the jurors have been excused.

Before making any offer of proof, the proponent should be certain of the grounds for the objection so that the grounds may be addressed in the offer. If the specific ground is not clear, or if the court has sustained a general objection, the proponent should request the court to ask objecting counsel to state the specific grounds.

The showing required in an offer of proof in order to persuade a trial judge to admit the evidence is the same as is needed to persuade an appellate court to reverse, if the trial judge does not admit the evidence:

A pertinent question was asked of a witness who could have provided an answer.

What the answer would have been.[35]

Why the testimony was relevant.

How the testimony would benefit the proponent's case.

Why the evidence should be admitted under the rules of evidence.[36]

The offer of proof must be precise. Where more than one piece of testimony or more than one tangible item are the subjects of an offer, the lawyer must handle each piece as if it were a separate offer of proof. If the lawyer does not differentiate the bases and arguments for each piece, there is a risk of losing the point on appeal, even though some of the evidence should have been admitted, because one of the pieces was properly excluded.[37]

When the proponent of excluded evidence makes an offer of proof at sidebar, that lawyer should ask the judge to excuse the witness. In the event the offer persuades the judge to admit the evidence, the witness will not have heard the offer and will not be able to tailor the testimony to be consistent with the offer. When a cross-examiner is making an offer of proof, it is even more important that the lawyer make sure the witness is excused so that the offer does not tip the witness to the direction of the cross-examination.

35. *See e.g.,* Mason v. Southern Ill. Univ. at Carbondale, 233 F.3d 1036 (7th Cir. 2000); Phillips v. Hillcrest Med. Ctr., 244 F.3d 790, (10th Cir. 2001).

36. The lawyer should state all grounds on which the evidence is admissible. This is particularly important when dealing with hearsay objections. *See* Huff v. White Motor Corp., 609 F.2d 286, 290 (7th Cir. 1979) (after hearsay objection, proponent should have alerted trial court to the statement against interest exception in order to preserve error on that ground); "Even where the new theory of admissibility serves the same purpose as the one used at trial—such as substituting one hearsay exception for another—the fact remains that each theory of admissibility has its own unique proof requirements. The party who proffers the evidence must show by a preponderance that the applicable admissibility requirements are met and were in fact established at trial." Fed. R. Evid. 103 Commentary. *See e.g.,* Shepard v. United States, 290 U.S. 96 (1933) (the leading case for the proposition that all possible exceptions to the hearsay doctrine should be interposed in defending against objection lest the appellate court decline to review exceptions other than the one argued at trial).

37. For a complete treatment of offers of proof for the trial lawyer, see Roger C. Park, Trial Objections Handbook (2d Edition) §§ 1.9–1.14) (West Group).

An offer of proof should do more than enumerate, if it is to be effective. It should inform the trial judge as to the exact nature of the testimony, the specific relation of the evidence to the claim or defense in the proponent's case, the evidence rule under which the evidence is admissible, the argument for its application, and the prejudice the proponent's case will suffer if the evidence is excluded.

Example

Defense lawyer:	What did she say she saw?
Plaintiff lawyer:	Objection, your honor, hearsay.
Judge:	Sustained.
Defense lawyer:	Offer of proof, your honor.
Judge:	Approach.
Defense lawyer:	[At sidebar, after plaintiff lawyer has requested that the judge ask the witness to stand down from the witness chair so the offer of proof is not overhead.]
	Your honor, if allowed to answer the question about what she heard, the words used by the man who saw the accident will demonstrate why the testimony is admissible under two different exceptions to the rule against hearsay.
	If allowed, the witness will testify that the man said, "Oh my God, my God. Did you see that? Did you see that? That blue car sped right through that red light and slammed into the white car. Is anybody hurt? What should we do? Can we call someone? Oh, my God."
	The words, themselves, indicate that the man was very excited and that the statement was made immediately after he saw the accident. That makes the statement admissible under two separate exceptions to the hearsay rule: the excited utterance exception and the present sense impression exception.
	This is the only available evidence we have to demonstrate that the plaintiff here, not the defendant, caused this accident.

In the rare case in which a trial judge will not allow an offer of proof to be made, error will be preserved if the lawyer puts the offer of proof in writing and requests that it be entered into the record before the close of trial.[38]

38. An offer of proof will not preserve a matter for appeal if it is not on the record. If the judge refuses to hear an offer of proof, the written offer (with copies given to opposing counsel, the judge, the clerk, and the court reporter) is likely to preserve the matter for appeal.

Chapter 3

OBJECTIONS TO THE FORM
OF THE QUESTION OR
THE ANSWER

Table of Sections

---

§ 3.01 The Rules of the Game

Objections to the form of the question or answer are rules about the conduct of the trial, rather than about the validity of various kinds of evidence. They relate not to what was asked or answered, but rather, how it was done. They are, in short, rules of the game. As a result, most good trial lawyers avoid making such objections, unless they believe that the objection will influence the effectiveness with which either the examiner or the witness is able to relate to the jurors. The trial lawyer uses the objections to the form of the question to influence the flow of the information to the jurors. As with presentation of any material, "how" the information is presented to the jurors can often be as influential as "what" the information is. Aside from issues of witness credibility, the effectiveness of presentation (or lack of it) can determine whether the information ever reaches the jurors ears or eyes. Just because something is said or shown does not mean it is heard or seen. Trial results come from what is heard and seen.

Objections to the form of the question or answer ask the judge to exercise the discretion provided by Rule 611 to control the mode of questioning witnesses. They invoke the universal understanding that lawyers and judges have about the language of the courtroom. Because the particular dialect of the trial judge determines almost entirely whether objections to form are sustained or ignored, the trial lawyer is well advised to be familiar with the judge's predilections about questions and answers that touch only on the "how" and not the "what" of the examination of witnesses. Except in the most egregious case (amounting to denial of a fair trial) the last word on how the evidence will be educed belongs to the trial judge.

There are many objections to form and more than a few ways to express each of them. This chapter contains some of the more common objections to form and the manner in which they are expressed.

§ 3.02 "Objection, Leading"

Leading questions are prohibited on direct examination, except for those questions that are preliminary, transitional, about non-controversial matters, or asked of an uncooperative witness or a witness designated in Rule 611(c).

A question is leading when its words or its context suggest the answer to the witness.

Q: You were in the hallway when the shot was fired, weren't you?

A complete discussion of the importance of leading questions in defining direct and cross-examination is found at **§ 1.03**.

§ 3.03 "Objection, Calls for a Narrative"

Judges prohibit questions that call for an extensive narrative response, when they foresee that the narrative may make it impossible for the opponent to interpose a timely objection, with the result that the jurors will hear inadmissible and prejudicial evidence that will not be susceptible to cure by an instruction to disregard. Although some judges are sticklers about the objection, even if those dangers do not appear imminent, narratives are tolerated, if not encouraged, in some courtrooms because they often speed up a trial. The lawyer who wants to be successful in objecting to a question that calls for a narrative response should be prepared to illustrate the problem or the extremely prejudicial nature of the possible answer.

Some questions that call for a narrative are more likely to carry the dangers of the narrative response than are others. "What happened next?" is a question without limitation, except for the time of beginning. "Will you please tell us how the collision occurred?" is limited to a specific event and asks for a description. Either may be allowed or prohibited in the face of an objection that the question calls for a narrative, but the latter might carry less danger that the jurors will hear inadmissible evidence than the former, because the subject matter of the latter is known. "Will you please tell us what you know about the collision," though limited to a specific event, might carry a greater danger that the opponent cannot interpose a timely objection concerning the source of the witness' knowledge. The answer might well contain inadmissible evidence such as hearsay or opinion that the opponent cannot reasonably anticipate.

More than any other objection, the objection that a question calls for a narrative is a matter of feel and understanding of the trial judge's preferences, and Rule 611 gives the judge ample room to exercise judgment as to the most appropriate response in each situation.

§ 3.04   "Move to Strike, The Answer Is Not Responsive"

Witnesses often give narrative responses to questions that do not fairly call for a narrative and occasionally give specific answers that are not responsive to the question asked. The opposing lawyer should move to strike these answers and request an instruction to the jurors to disregard them. Although some judges maintain that the motion to strike a non-responsive answer belongs only to the lawyer asking the question, the better view is that either lawyer may make such a motion. The mistaken notion that the motion to strike as non-responsive belongs only to the questioner may have its origin in the fact that it is almost always the cross-examiner who gets a non-responsive answer and wants it stricken.

The cross-examiner uses leading questions to control what the witness can tell the jurors. Witnesses often attempt to thwart that control and offer an excuse or an explanation at the same time as their assent to a cross-examination question that does not put them or their testimony in a favorable light.

Example

Cross-examiner:	During your direct testimony you said that the Ford had the green light when it entered the intersection, didn't you?
Witness:	Yes.
Cross-examiner:	Two days after the accident you signed a statement under oath that the Chevrolet had the green light, didn't you?
Witness:	I was confused.
Cross-examiner:	Move to strike, your honor, as non-responsive, [and maybe add] and will your honor instruct the witness to answer the questions that are asked?
Judge:	The response is stricken; jurors, you are to disregard the witness' previous answer; [and

maybe, if the witness has been evasive and non-responsive to a series of cross-examination questions] and, witness, you should listen to the question and answer only what is asked. If there are explanations required, you may be asked about them on redirect examination.

The cross-examiner is using the motion to strike the non-responsive answer not so much to keep the information from the jurors, as to gain help in controlling the witness and in keeping the witness' answers to one word—"yes" or "no." Further, while the "explanation" will undoubtedly be part of the redirect examination, it may appear to be more of an after-the-fact excuse than an at-the-time reason for the difference between the testimony and the statement under oath.

A direct examiner may, also, receive non-responsive answers, but is not as likely as the cross-examiner to want the non-responsive answer stricken. The non-responsive answer is likely to be the answer to the next question or inadmissible evidence that the direct examiner cannot otherwise present to the jurors. The opponent, who will probably not object if the non-responsive answer results from a witness' innocent anticipation of the next question, will want the answer stricken if it is inadmissible evidence, if it constitutes a narrative, or if the issue of admissibility will turn on further information.

Example

Direct examiner:	Did you see what happened?
Witness:	I saw the Chevy speed into the intersection at the end of a yellow light and smash into the Ford.

The responsive answer to the question, "Did you see what happened," would be "yes." Neither lawyer, however, is likely to object that the answer is non-responsive, because it is a proper answer to the next question: "What did you see?"

Example

Direct examiner:	What happened at the intersection of Third and Sheridan?
Witness:	The Chevy sped into the intersection on a yellow light and smashed into the Ford. The driver of the Chevy was drunk.
Opponent:	Move to strike that portion of the answer following "smashed into the Ford" as non-responsive and for an instruction to the jurors to disregard it.

The question did not ask for the witness' opinion about the condition of the driver of the Chevy. The part of the response that contains that opinion is non-responsive. The witness' opinion that the Chevy driver was drunk may be admissible, if the direct examiner can demonstrate that the opinion is the result of the witness' rational perception. The opponent should be entitled, however, to have the testimony struck, until the foundation for the opinion has been shown. The judge should strike the non-responsive testimony, even though it is the opponent, not the questioner, making the motion. Most judges will.

§ 3.05   "Objection, Assumes Facts Not in Evidence"

"When did you stop beating your wife?" as the first question to a witness on cross-examination, is the classic example of a question that assumes facts not in evidence. The first assumed fact is that the witness beat his wife. The second assumed fact is that he stopped.

A question that assumes facts not in evidence is particularly unfair on cross-examination. The assumed fact in the question is usually inadmissible or unavailable. Because the cross-examiner can place the fact into a leading question, there is some danger the jurors will remember the information, but not the source. In order to answer properly, the witness must make an explanation about why the assumed fact is untrue, when the form of the question does not call for an explanation. The process may make the witness appear evasive, when it is the form of the question, not the witness that is responsible for the explanation. If the direct examiner does not protect the witness by objecting to the question that assumes a fact not in evidence, the witness may seem less credible to the jurors.

Example

Plaintiff's witness in a wrongful death action came upon the accident at 12:30 in the morning. The witness was driving home from a dinner club after seeing the late show. There has been no evidence that the witness was drunk, or even drinking.

Cross-examiner: What time was it when you were driving drunk on the loop highway?

Witness: I wasn't drunk.

Cross-examiner: You don't know what time it was?

Witness: Yes, but I wasn't drunk.

Cross-examiner: You had been drinking, isn't that right?

Witness: No.

Cross-examiner: You didn't have wine with dinner?

Witness: Well, yes, but that was one glass at 7:30 in the evening.

By asking the first question, assuming the fact not in evidence—that the driver was drunk—the cross-examiner raises questions about the witness' ability to observe, because of alcohol consumption. The witness, trying to counter the assumed fact, ends up looking less than fully credible. If the direct examiner protects the witness by objecting, the witness' credibility will not be damaged.

Cross-examiner: What time was it when you were driving drunk on the loop highway?

Direct examiner: Objection, your honor. The question assumes a fact not in evidence.

Judge: Sustained.

Direct examiner: Will your honor instruct the jury that there is no basis in fact for the cross-examiner's assertion that the witness was drunk.

Judge: Yes. Members of the jury, there has been no showing that this witness was under the influence of alcohol.

The direct examiner can, also, ask questions that assume facts not in evidence, though the opponent may not be as eager to object as when such a question is asked on cross-examination. When the direct examiner asks a question that assumes a fact not in evidence, the jurors, who have not heard the assumed fact, may be confused by the question and may not hear or understand the answer. In that circumstance, the opponent is unlikely to object and give the direct examiner an opportunity to dispel the confusion.

Example

The plaintiff's first witness is a person who saw the collision between the Ford and the Chevrolet. The person is called to the witness stand, takes the oath, and then gives name, address, and occupation.

Plaintiff's lawyer: Where were you when the collision occurred?

Witness: On the corner of Third and Sheridan.

Jurors: [What collision? When? How many cars? Not much chance they will hear the witness' answer while they are trying to figure out what this is all about.]

Defense lawyer: [Does nothing and hopes the direct examiner does not remember to get back to the collision so that the jurors know what the witness is talking about.]

A direct examination question that assumes facts not in evidence is used sometimes as a means of leading a witness or of filling in facts that may not otherwise be available. The opponent will object if the evidence is important and unavailable.

Example

Police officer-witness testifies to arriving at the scene of a shooting and conducting an investigation, including the taking of photographs of the scene after the body had been removed. The pictures show some objects and some distance relationships that suggest the defendant was the shooter.

Prosecutor: After the body had been removed and everything was put back in place, did you take pictures?

Defense lawyer: Objection, your honor, assumes facts not in evidence.

In this case, where the objects and their locations are important, the picture will not be admitted, showing the objects and their relationships, unless the prosecution can show that things were moved away and replaced with great precision, when the body was moved. If care was not taken, if there were a number of officers moving things, so that no one person can say where everything was, the prosecution will not be able to make that showing. If the defense lawyer fails to object to the question that assumes the fact that "everything was put back in place," the prosecution will put valuable evidence before the jurors that would be unavailable otherwise.

Some questions that assume facts not in evidence are permissible on direct. If the fact assumed is a natural consequence of a previous answer, most judges will allow the question as a convenient way to move the testimony along.

Example

Direct examiner: Where did you go?

Witness: Into the bedroom.

Direct examiner: What did you see?

Witness: There was a body on the bed.

The question, "What did you see" assumes a fact not in evidence—that the witness saw something. Seeing something when one enters a room is a natural consequence of being in the room, absent some evidence of the unusual, such as that the room was dark, the witness was blind, or the witness' eyes were shut.

Direct examiners who are unaware that most judges will allow a question that assumes a fact of natural consequence often try to cure the problem of the assumed fact by adding an awkward and disingenuous, "if anything" somewhere in the question. "What did you see, if anything" or "what, if anything, did you see." The questions still assume that when people are wherever they are, they see things. For those concerned that some judge may disfavor a question that assumes a fact of natural consequence, an easier and less awkward sounding approach is to lead the witness with a transition question.

Example

Direct examiner: Did you see anything when you went into the bedroom? [Leading, but transitional or preliminary.]

Witness: Yes.

Direct examiner: What did you see? [No longer assumes a fact not in evidence.]

The objection that a question assumes a fact not in evidence should not be confused with the cross-examination question that asks about a specific fact not brought out during direct examination, but that is, nevertheless, within its scope. A cross-examination that brings out new facts is both proper and common.

Example

A police officer testifies on direct examination about the investigation conducted at the crime scene, but says nothing about fingerprints because none were found. The defense wishes the jury to know that the police did check for fingerprints and that the defendant's prints were not found at the scene.

Defense lawyer: You checked for fingerprints at the scene, didn't you?

Prosecutor: Objection. Assumes a fact not in evidence.

Judge: Overruled. You may answer.

Police officer: Yes.

Defense lawyer: When you checked for prints, you did not find my client's fingerprints at the scene of the crime did you?

Prosecutor: Objection. Assumes a fact not in evidence.

Judge: Overruled. You may answer.

Police officer: No.

Notice that had the second question, "When you checked for prints, you did not find my client's fingerprints at the scene of the crime did you?" been asked first, it would have improperly assumed a fact not in evidence. It would have *assumed* that the police "checked for prints"—a fact not brought out during direct examination and, without the first question, not brought out during cross-examination, either.

§ 3.06   "Objection, Argumentative"

An argumentative question is one that makes an argument to the jurors rather than posing a question to the witness.

Examples

Cross-examiner: Isn't that preposterous?

or

Cross-examiner: Do you expect the jury to believe that you drove twenty miles home and back during the most important business day of the year solely to get your handkerchief?

"Objection, argumentative," is the direct examiner's response to either question.

The argumentative objection often is made when counsel is harassing a witness. The harassment, however, is not the basis for the argumentative objection. The essential feature of the objection is that counsel is making an argument that should be saved for the summation. In the summation, counsel is free to draw inferences from the testimony, to characterize it as believable or ridiculous, to point out inconsistencies and improbabilities. Ordinarily, the questioning process should be limited to drawing information from the witnesses about what they observed. It should not be used to argue the believability of the testimony or the wisdom of drawing particular inferences from it.

§ 3.07   "Objection, Counsel Is Harassing the Witness"

This objection is not really about a particular question, but rather, about the cross-examiner's approach to the witness. The problem is often not the form of the question, but rather, the way the examiner is treating the witness. Cross-examination can be embarrassing, insulting, and unpleasant for the witness and still be permissible, if the questions are pertinent and not cumulative. But the cross-examiner may not make it ugly. In addition to using the kinds of questions that have an unfair form—argumentative, assume facts, and the like—harassment might include yelling at a witness, cutting off the witness' answer unreasonably, and getting up into the witness' face. Give or take a little, the objection is the equivalent of saying to the judge: "Please stop that lawyer from beating up my witness, enough is enough." Whether the objection is sustained will depend upon the judge's sensibilities.

§ 3.08 "Objection, Compound Question"

Cross-examiner:	As you approached the intersection, did you look down, change the radio station, and then look up and for the first time notice the oncoming car?
Opponent:	Objection, compound question.

§ 3.09 "Objection, Vague" (or Ambiguous or Confusing)

Ambiguity is objectionable:

Q. Your wife works downtown?

A. Yes.

Q. When does she get home?

Objection. Vague as to date.

So are questions that are confusing:

Direct examiner:	Did you turn left or right or not?
Opponent:	Objection, confusing.

Occasionally a question is so incomprehensible that a mere objection that the question is vague does not do the situation justice. Consider the following question and imaginative objection taken from an actual trial transcript.

Direct examiner:	When he went, had you gone and she, if she wanted to and were able, for the time being excluding all the restraints on her not to go, gone also, would he have brought you, meaning you and she, with him to the station?
Opponent:	Objection. That question should be taken out and shot.

§ 3.10 "Objection, Misstates the Evidence"

After a witness testifies on direct examination to hearing the fire truck make a noise like a foghorn, the following cross-examination occurs:

Cross-examiner:	When you first heard the fire truck siren, where were you?
Opponent:	Objection, misstates the evidence.

On cross-examination, the question that misstates the evidence can operate in the same fashion and with the same dangers as the question that assumes a fact not in evidence.

Questions that are compound, vague, or misstate the evidence exemplify the kind of question that can confuse the witness because of the form, producing answers that do not reflect what the witness knows or wants to say. While any of them might be asked as easily on direct examination as on cross-examination, they are most likely to draw objection on cross-examination. The direct examiner, who called the witness, makes the objection to protect the witness from appearing less than fully credible on cross-examination. The cross-examiner, upon hearing direct examination question that will confuse the witness, is usually pleased and unlikely to object. The unintelligible question on direct examination carries its own penalty.

§ 3.11 "Objection, Asked and Answered"; "Objection, Cumulative"

These objections both invoke the judge's discretion to prohibit questions that create a "needless consumption of time" under Rule 611 or constitute a "needless presentation of cumulative evidence" under Rule 403. They usually occur, however, in different circumstances.

The "asked and answered" objection is usually made by the direct examiner when a cross-examiner has asked the same question, or different questions about the same subject, a number of times. It is one of a number of objections that a direct-examiner uses to protect the witness from an unfair cross-examination.

Example

Cross-examiner:	You were drunk when you walked into that room, weren't you?
Witness:	No.
Cross-examiner:	You had consumed so much alcohol you didn't know where you were, isn't that right?
Direct examiner:	Objection, your honor, asked and answered.
Judge:	This is cross-examination, counselor. Overruled.
Witness:	No.
Cross-examiner:	Isn't it true that you had so much to drink that you were not even aware of what was going on?
Direct examiner:	Objection, your honor, asked and answered.
Judge:	Sustained. Move along, counsel.

The "cumulative" objection is usually made by the cross-examiner when a direct examiner has tried to drive a point home by having the witness or a succession of witnesses testify to the same thing a number of different times.

Example

Direct examiner: What did you see at the intersection?

Witness: I saw the Chevrolet speed into the intersection and slam into a Ford that was entering the intersection on a green light.

Direct examiner: What color was the light for the Ford when it was entering the intersection?

Cross-examiner: Objection, cumulative.

Judge: Overruled.

Witness: It was green.

[A number of intervening questions about other observations during the collision and the aftermath.]

Direct examiner: Now what color was the light for the Ford when it entered the intersection?

Cross-examiner: Objection, cumulative.

Judge: Sustained.

Repeating questions on both cross and direct examinations is subject to the judge's tolerance for allowing lawyers to do things that they believe will help persuade the jurors and to the judge's patience with the pace of the trial at the time the objection is made. As a result, cross-examiners may often be allowed a couple of questions on the same subject and direct examiners are likely to be able to present important facts at least twice. When the repetition becomes obvious or the judge becomes irritated, the objection will be sustained the first time it is made.

§ 3.12   "Objection, Improper Opinion" (Calls for Speculation, or Too General)

Lay opinions rationally based upon perception and expert opinions[1] are admissible, but it does not follow that all opinion is admissible.

If a particular perception does not justify the opinion—that is, if it is not rationally based—the witness may not testify to the inference.

---

1.   *See* **Ch. 10**.

Direct examiner:	What was his condition?
Witness:	He was stoned on marijuana.
Cross-examiner:	Objection, improper opinion.
Judge:	Sustained. [If the witness not only perceived the activity, but also perceived the use of marijuana preceding the activity, the opinion *might* be allowed.]
Cross-examiner:	Move to strike.

If an opinion is speculative because it is not based on perception, it is not admissible.

Direct examiner:	Where was the cow when you arrived?
Witness:	On the roof of the building.
Direct examiner:	How did it get there?
Cross-examiner:	Objection, calls for speculation.
Judge:	Sustained.

If an opinion is too broad to be helpful or can be communicated easily in more concrete terms, it may be inadmissible.

Direct examiner:	What was he doing?
Witness:	He was acting silly.
Cross-examiner:	Objection, too broad.
Judge:	Sustained.
Cross-examiner:	Move to strike.

§ 3.13   "Objection, The Document Speaks for Itself"

Direct examiner:	I'm handing you what has been received in evidence as plaintiff's exhibit A. Are you familiar with it?
Witness:	Yes.
Direct examiner:	What is it?
Witness:	It's a memorandum telling the marketing department that . . .
Cross-examiner:	Objection, your honor, the document speaks for itself.

Having a witness read a document received in evidence is often the most effective way to present the information to the jury and is proper under most circumstances. Paraphrasing the document, however, can be misleading and confusing and violate Rule 403. Moreover, a paraphrase constitutes an opinion about the emphasis intended by the author of the document that, in the absence of some expertise needed for the interpretation, is not likely to be "helpful" to a jury capable of reading for itself.

§ 3.14   "Objection, Lack of Personal Knowledge"

Direct examiner: Where was Mr. Jones at 8:00 p.m. on July 12?

Cross-examiner: Objection, no showing of personal knowledge.

It may be that the witness does not know where Jones was, but it is more likely that the witness does know and the lawyer has used bad form in asking. Rule 602 provides that "[a] witness may not testify to a matter unless evidence is introduced sufficient to support a finding that the witness has personal knowledge of the matter." Had the lawyer first laid a personal knowledge foundation, there would have been no problem with the question. As it stands in the example, the judge should sustain the objection unless the direct examiner promises to establish the witness' personal knowledge.

The personal knowledge requirement is sometimes confused with the hearsay objection, because the witness' knowledge is sometimes based on what the witness heard. But the two objections are not the same. While the witness might be prepared to provide information based on what the witness heard—in which case either a hearsay or no personal knowledge objection would suffice—it may also be that the witness heard nothing and is merely engaged in speculation. If the answer is based on speculation, only the personal knowledge objection is appropriate.

§ 3.15   One Non–Objection—"Self–Serving"

"Objection, self-serving" is heard in many courtrooms. The form problem here is not with the question, but with the objection. As with "Incompetent, irrelevant, and immaterial," "self serving" is not a sufficient objection to preserve a matter for appeal. Although the "self serving" objection is often made in situations that are unlikely to produce reversible error, there are times when it will be made instead of a specific objection that would preserve an important issue for appeal.

Most evidence is "self serving." The adversary assumption is that each side presents evidence that will serve its purpose and hurt the other side. Far from being inadmissible, "self-serving" evidence is the whole idea.

There are two problems a lawyer might encounter by using the "self serving" objection. It might signal to the judge that the lawyer does not really understand the law of evidence. More importantly, it might substitute for an objection, which, if made, would preserve an important point for appeal, where the "self serving" objection may not.

The temptation to make the "self serving" objection may arise because "self serving" often describes the analytic problem with a piece of evidence, even though it does not describe the specific evidentiary problem. The specific evidentiary problem, however, is necessary to allow the judge to avoid the error by an exclusionary ruling or to allow the opponent to cure the problem or rely on other evidence.

Example

In a contest between two people who shared a house over the ownership of a painting that was assumed to be of minimal value when purchased and now is valued at $1,000,000, plaintiff calls a person who was a regular guest at the house.

Plaintiff's lawyer: Have you ever seen what has been received in evidence as Plaintiff's exhibit #1?

Witness: Yes.

Plaintiff's lawyer: Under what circumstances?

Witness: In plaintiff's bedroom. I saw it on the wall and asked plaintiff about it.

Plaintiff's lawyer: What did the plaintiff say?

Defense lawyer: Objection, self-serving.

Judge: Overruled.

Witness: The plaintiff said: "It's my favorite possession. I paid $20 dollars for it. Now it's worth a million.

The plaintiff's out-of-court statement offered to prove that the plaintiff owns the painting is hearsay. When offered by the other side, it would be an admission, not hearsay. When the party making the statement offers it, "self-serving" may be the idea, but hearsay is the specific objection that will exclude the statement.

Example

A personal injury action by automobile driver against trucking company, following a collision between driver's automobile and company's truck.

The company requires its drivers to file an accident report with the company after every incident. The statement is made immediately after the accident, if the driver is able. The statements are kept in an accident file and are reviewed regularly by the company in assessing the adequacy of its insurance, the progress of its training programs, and the position it should take in any lawsuit resulting from the incident. The report in this particular case includes the driver's recitation of the plaintiff's statement to the driver immediately after the accident: "It was my fault; I wasn't watching." The driver is no longer available to testify, so the company offers the report as a business record.

Defense lawyer:	[After laying the traditional business records foundation through the company record custodian]. Defense offers the report of the same date as the event as Defense exhibit #1.]
Plaintiff's lawyer:	Objection, self-serving.
Judge:	Overruled.

The self-serving objection will probably not preserve the matter for appeal. There is a substantial chance that the hearsay report does not fall within the business records exception to the rule against hearsay, because it does not satisfy the trustworthiness requirement of Rule 803(6). While the theory for failure to fall within the business records exception—prepared for litigation—is something akin to self-serving, hearsay is the specific objection that will keep the report from being admitted and preserve the matter for appeal.[2]

2. *See* Palmer v. Hoffman, 318 U.S. 109 (1943).

Chapter 4

BURDENS AND PRESUMPTIONS

Table of Sections

---

§ 4.01 Introduction

Few legal terms related to the law of evidence have engendered as much confusion as those to be considered in this brief chapter.[1] Perhaps this is partly because the entire subject of burdens of proof and presumptions is not clearly associated with any particular area of the law. The lion's share of evidence law, after all, is concerned with admissibility of particular classes of evidence, not with the *effect* evidence has under given circumstances. Thus, evidence law does not determine which party has a "burden of proof" with respect to a particular issue, nor is the *level* of that burden a function of the types of rules we normally associate

---

1. Referring to the confusion surrounding the term "burden of proof," one renowned evidence scholar wrote:

Under our law the term burden of proof has been used to express two rather different ideas, and as might be expected this usage has led to a jumble. Incisive thinkers have framed a more particularized vocabulary, duly segregating the ideas, but have not managed to get their vocabulary into universal use.

John M. Maguire, Evidence: Common Sense and Common Law 175 (1947). Wigmore wrote of the "lamentable ambiguity of phrase and confusion of terminology under which our law has so long suffered." 9 John H. Wigmore, Evidence in Trials at Common Law § 2485, at 283 (James H. Chadbourn rev. 1981). McCormick's handbook calls the term presumption "the slipperiest member of the family of legal terms, except its first cousin, 'burden of proof.'" 2 McCormick on Evidence § 342, at 433 (5th ed. John W. Strong ed. 1999).

with "evidence law." The same can be said for presumptions, which concern not particular classes of evidence, but the effect certain evidence is to have if certain conditions are satisfied.

One must approach the subject with at least three understandings: (1) courts often describe issues involving burdens of proof and presumptions using variable and ill-defined terms; (2) courts often use the same term to mean different things and do not indicate clearly which meaning is intended in a particular context; and (3) even where courts have reached consensus about the meaning of certain terms, some key unresolved questions remain. With these admonitions in mind, we approach this chapter with the modest goals of setting forth some basic principles and pointing out where some of the land mines are buried.

Although questions of "burden of proof" apply to bench trials as well as jury trials, throughout the discussion we will assume that the case is being tried to a jury.

§ 4.02 "Burden of Proof": Two Meanings

The term "burden of proof" is an umbrella term that's used to refer to both the burden of *persuasion* and the burden of *production*.[2] The burden of persuasion concerns the final decision of the jury or other trier of fact, and involves two distinct things: the determination of the *quantum of evidence* (or standard of proof) required to establish an ultimate question of fact, and the *allocation of the risk* that the factfinder will not be persuaded to that prescribed degree of certainty.

The burden of production does not deal with proof in the sense of ultimate persuasion. It is of concern only to the trial judge, and its effect is expended before the case is submitted to the jury. This subcategory of "burden of proof" comes into play when one party claims that the other party has not offered sufficient evidence even to merit continuing with the case as to that issue or claim, and that the judge must grant a preemptive motion at that point. This concept is sometimes referred to as the burden of producing evidence, or the burden of "going forward," though the term burden of production will generally be used here.

§ 4.03 Burden of Persuasion

The burden of persuasion concerns the ultimate question in the trial: legally satisfactory proof of all elements of a claim or defense.[3] Two key questions related to the "burden of persuasion" must therefore be addressed any time a claim is made or a defense raised. First, to what degree must the factfinder be persuaded in order for the claim or defense

---

2. *See* James B. Thayer, A Preliminary Treatise on Evidence at the Common Law 355 (1898); Larry L. Teply & Ralph U. Whitten, Civil Procedure 828 (1994).

3. *See* Cal. Evid. Code § 115 (1966) (using term "burden of proof" and stating

that the concept "means the obligation of a party to establish by a requisite degree of belief concerning a fact in the mind of the trier of fact or the court").

to be "proven?" Second, which party must meet that burden of persuasion?

Before turning to those questions, it is necessary to stress that at law, claims or defenses are only "proven" if the factfinder believes that *each element* of the claim has been established by the requisite degree of proof. Thus, in a civil action for battery, the jury cannot find the defendant liable unless it believes that plaintiff has established each element of the claim (volitional act, unlawful intent to contact, and harmful or offensive contact)[4] by the prescribed degree of proof. If the jury is sufficiently persuaded that defendant acted volitionally and with unlawful intent, but concludes that no contact occurred, it must find for the defendant. The same principle holds in criminal cases, and indeed more strongly; proof of each element beyond a reasonable doubt is constitutionally mandated before a person may be convicted of a crime.[5]

§ 4.04 Burden of Persuasion—Defining Burdens of Persuasion: Standards of Proof

Standards of proof exist "to instruct the factfinder concerning the degree of confidence our society thinks he should have in the correctness of factual conclusions for a particular type of adjudication."[6] Substantive law prescribes the various levels of proof that must be offered to establish particular claims or defenses—levels of confidence the factfinder must have in the correctness of the propositions at issue. Three degrees of proof are common. The first is best denoted "more likely than not," though the terms "greater weight of the evidence" and "preponderance of the evidence" are frequently used as well.[7] This is the least demanding burden to satisfy, as it requires the factfinder's mind be tipped only slightly in favor of the party with the burden. It is applied to the vast majority of civil claims and defenses. Thus, in a negligence case, plaintiff must offer enough evidence as to duty, breach, cause in fact, proximate cause, and damages to cause the jurors' minds to be tipped just slightly in favor of the existence of each element. The easiest way to understand this burden is to see it as one of risk: if after considering all the evidence, the jurors either believe some element has not been proven by this amount, or are in "equipoise" (they cannot decide either way),

4. *See* Restatement (Second) of Torts § 18 (1965).

5. In re Winship, 397 U.S. 358, 364 (1970) ("[T]he Due Process clause protects the accused against conviction except upon proof beyond a reasonable doubt of every fact necessary to constitute the crime with which he is charged.").

6. *Id.* at 370 (Harlan, J., concurring).

7. *See* Larry L. Teply & Ralph U. Whitten, Civil Procedure 828 (1994) ("In civil actions, the burden of persuasion is usually described as a requirement that there must be a *preponderance of evidence,* or that the *greater weight of the evidence*

must exist in favor of the party having the burden of persuasion. . . .") (emphasis in original). These terms can be misleading because they suggest that the jury need only be convinced of the truth of a proposition by the greater weight of the *evidence actually produced at the trial*. This quantum of evidence might not be sufficient, however, to persuade the jurors that the proposition is "more likely than not" true. *See* Norman Dorsen & Daniel A. Rezneck, *In re Gault and the Future of Juvenile Law,* Fam. L.Q. 1, 26–27 (Dec. 1967) (making similar point), quoted approvingly in *Winship,* 397 U.S. at 367–68.

the party with the burden of persuasion (here, plaintiff) must lose. This is why the burden of persuasion is sometimes referred to as the "risk of nonpersuasion."[8]

At the other end of the spectrum, the most onerous burden imposed by the law is that of proof "beyond a reasonable doubt," the standard applicable to criminal cases.[9] Defining the term reasonable doubt is of course difficult, and indeed there has been some debate about whether it is appropriate even to attempt to define the concept in an instruction to the jury.[10] Pattern instructions can give the flavor of "reasonable doubt,"[11] and jurisdictions have attempted to state their own definitions,[12] but in the end, the term is almost wholly subjective. Despite this lack of precision, courts scrutinize jury instructions on reasonable doubt with great care,[13] making it particularly important to frame instructions in accordance with existing statutory and judicial standards. In some jurisdictions, in fact, courts have approved of tendering no instruction defining reasonable doubt, or of instructions stating only a very general definition.[14] And in *Victor v. Nebraska*,[15] the Supreme Court approved of such an approach, holding that the Constitution does not prohibit trial courts from defining reasonable doubt nor does it require them to do so. As long as the court instructs the jury of the necessity that the prosecution prove defendant's guilt beyond a reasonable doubt, the Court held, no particular form of instruction is required.

A middle ground lies between "preponderance of the evidence" and

---

8. *See, e.g.*, Fed. R. Evid. 301 (referring to the "burden of proof in the sense of the risk of nonpersuasion"); 9 John H. Wigmore, Evidence in Trials at Common Law § 2485 (James H. Chadbourn rev. 1981).

9. *Winship*, 397 U.S. at 364.

10. *See, e.g.*, Henry A. Diamond, Note, Reasonable Doubt: To Define or Not to Define, 90 Colum. L. Rev. 1716 (1990); Note, *Reasonable Doubt: An Argument Against Definition*, 108 Harv. L. Rev. 1955 (1995).

11. *See, e.g.*, Kevin F. O'Malley et al., Federal Jury Practice and Instructions § 12.10 (5th ed. 2000):

It is not required that the government prove guilt beyond all possible doubt. The test is one of reasonable doubt. A reasonable doubt is a doubt based upon reason and common sense—the kind of doubt that would make a reasonable person hesitate to act. Proof beyond a reasonable doubt must, therefore, be proof of such a convincing character that a reasonable person would not hesitate to rely and act upon it in the most important of his or her own affairs.

12. *See, e.g.*, Cal. Penal Code § 1096 (West 1985) (Reasonable doubt "is not a mere possible doubt; because everything re-

lated to human affairs is open to some possible or imaginary doubt. It is that state of the case, which, after the entire comparison and consideration of all the evidence, leaves the minds of jurors in that condition that they cannot say they feel an abiding conviction of the truth of the charge).

13. *See, e.g.*, United States v. Campbell, 874 F.2d 838, 842–43 (1st Cir.1989) (error to give instruction repeatedly using term "fair doubt"; such a term could impose a lower burden on the prosecution); Lanigan v. Maloney, 853 F.2d 40, 48 (1st Cir.1988) (holding instruction stating that beyond a reasonable doubt meant "to a degree of moral certainty" constitutionally defective as potentially lightening prosecution's burden).

14. *See, e.g.*, United States v. Jorge, 865 F.2d 6, 10 (1st Cir.1989) (Defendant claimed error in not giving instruction which contained no definition of reasonable doubt; while court affirmed conviction, it stated that "it may be prudent on the part of a trial court to consider seriously a defendant's request to define the concept only minimally, or not at all").

15. 511 U.S. 1 (1994).

"beyond a reasonable doubt." In some contexts,[16] proof must be "clear and convincing." That term, of course, is no more easily defined than the others, but it certainly falls between the extremes.[17]

§ 4.05　Burden of Persuasion—Allocating the Burden of Persuasion Between the Parties

Once the quantum of proof is defined, it remains to determine which party must "carry" that burden—which party must lose unless the jury finds that the burden has been met. This, too, is a matter of substantive rather than evidence law, and is affected by several factors. As one commentator has written:

> (1) *Caution* and *convenience* often result in the burden of proof being placed upon the party seeking change. (2) *Policy* may dictate charging one side or the other with a particular element as a means of encouraging or discouraging a given kind of litigation.... (3) *Fairness* may suggest placing the burden of an element upon the party within whose control the evidence lies.... (4) *Probabilities* may be estimated and the burden placed upon the party who will benefit by a departure from the supposed norm.[18]

Though each of these factors affect the allocation of the burden of persuasion, no one factor controls the determination. Instead, the courts appear to accord the various factors different levels of importance in different situations. As Wigmore wrote, "[t]he truth is that there is not and cannot be any one general solvent for all cases. It is merely a question of policy and fairness based on experience in the different situations."[19] Often, however, the burden is placed on the party who wishes to disturb the status quo by asserting a claim for relief, or a party

---

16. For example, it is common for courts to hold that certain elements of a fraud case must be proved by clear and convincing evidence. *See, e.g.,* Kungys v. United States, 485 U.S. 759, 789 (1988) (under statute applicable to naturalization of citizens, proof of materiality of representation—that it was predictably capable of affecting decision to grant citizenship—must be shown by clear, unequivocal, and convincing evidence). Some jurisdictions provide that punitive damages cannot be awarded unless the jury makes the requisite finding by clear and convincing evidence. *See, e.g.,* Cal. Civ. Code § 3294 (West Supp. 1997) (punitive damages available if "it is proven by clear and convincing evidence that the defendant has been guilty of oppression, fraud, or malice"). *See also* Addington v. Texas, 441 U.S. 418, 431 (1979) (applying standard to civil commitment); Rosenbloom v. Metromedia, 403 U.S. 29, 52 (1971) (libel).

17. One state defines clear and convincing evidence as evidence that "leads you to a firm belief or conviction that the allegations are true. This is a higher standard of proof than proof by the greater weight of the evidence. The evidence presented need not be undisputed to be clear and convincing." N.D. Jury Instructions Civ. No. 41 (1991).

18. 1 Michael H. Graham, Handbook of Federal Evidence § 301.2, at 138 (4th ed. 1996) (emphasis in original). Wigmore listed several factors courts consider in allocating burden of persuasion: (1) the burden is on the party having the burden of pleading; (2) the burden is on the party to whose case the fact is essential; (3) the burden is on the party assumed to have "*peculiar means of knowledge*" of the facts. 9 John H. Wigmore, Evidence in Trials at Common Law § 2486 (James H. Chadbourn rev. 1981) (emphasis in original). Morgan offered a similar list. Edmund M. Morgan, *Some Observations Concerning Presumptions*, 44 Harv. L. Rev. 906, 910–11 (1931).

19. 9 Wigmore, *supra* note 18 § 2486, at 291.

asserting an affirmative defense to a claim.[20] Thus, in a negligence case, the plaintiff has the burden of persuasion as to the elements of the prima facie case. Because the burden of persuasion is preponderance of the evidence, this means that if, after all deliberations have concluded, the jury either believes by a preponderance of the evidence that any or all elements have not been satisfied, or believes the evidence as to any or all elements is equally balanced, the jury must find for the defendant. By the same token, defendant has the burden of persuasion as to any affirmative defenses, such as contributory (or comparative) negligence. Unless the jury believes by a preponderance of the evidence that sufficient evidence has been offered to satisfy each element of the defense, it must find for the plaintiff on that issue.

The general principles just described apply regardless of the quantum of proof necessary to meet a burden of persuasion. So, in a criminal case, the prosecution bears the burden as to all essential elements of the crime.[21] The law regarding defenses is somewhat uncertain, however. There is no constitutional barrier against imposing a burden of persuasion on defendant as to certain excuses or justifications, including insanity, intoxication, and self-defense.[22] However, it is likely that principles of due process impose some limits on the gravity of the burden defendant must meet. It has been held, for example, that if the burden of proving insanity is placed on the defendant, defendant's burden cannot be greater than a preponderance of the evidence.[23] Moreover, about half the states place the burden on the prosecution to prove the defendant's sanity beyond a reasonable doubt.[24]

Once the law has placed the burden of persuasion on a party, that burden rarely shifts during the trial. In criminal cases, even in the face of overwhelming evidence of guilt, the state may never shift to the defendant the burden of persuasion as to any elements of the crime. The same is true in civil cases, with rare exceptions. One common exception holds that where two parties each acted negligently but only one caused the injury in question, the court may shift to each defendant the burden

---

20. *See, e.g.,* Cal. Evid. Code § 500 (1966) ("Except as otherwise provided by law, a party has the burden of proof as to each fact the existence or nonexistence of which is essential to the claim for relief or defense that he is asserting.").

21. In re Winship, 397 U.S. 358 (1970). *See* 1 Wayne R. LaFave & Austin W. Scott, Jr., Substantive Criminal Law § 1.8(b) (1986).

22. *Id. See also* Medina v. California, 505 U.S. 437 (1992) (state may presume defendant competent to stand trial and require defendant to prove incompetence by preponderance of the evidence); Buzynski v. Oliver, 538 F.2d 6 (1st Cir.1976) (Maine rule requiring defendant to persuade jury of insanity by preponderance of the evidence did not deny due process).

23. Although the Supreme Court held in Leland v. Oregon, 343 U.S. 790 (1952) that a state may require a defendant to prove insanity beyond a reasonable doubt, the continuing validity of the decision is unclear. In Mullaney v. Wilbur, 421 U.S. 684 (1975), the Court held that the prosecution has the burden of overcoming a mitigating defense of heat of passion on sudden provocation beyond a reasonable doubt. And in Cooper v. Oklahoma, 517 U.S. 348 (1996), the Court held that an Oklahoma law providing that defendant is presumed competent to stand trial unless defendant proves incompetence by clear and convincing evidence violates due process.

24. *See* 1 LaFave & Scott, *supra* note 21 § 4.5.

of showing that her conduct was not the cause in fact of the injury.[25] In some jurisdictions, the operation of a presumption can cause the burden of persuasion to shift.[26] Except in the case of these few exceptions, the burden of persuasion stays put.

§ 4.06 Burden of Production

The term "burden of proof" also includes the burden of production, a concept entirely different from the burden of persuasion. The burden of production does not define or assign the ultimate burden of convincing the jury. Instead, it is a function of the division of responsibilities between the judge and the jury; it refers to the judge's power to prevent a party from reaching the jury at all or as to particular elements of a claim or defense. The burden of production pinpoints, at key moments in the trial, whether a particular party is subject to a peremptory motion if that party does not produce further evidence to support its claim or defense. Put more simply, the party who bears the burden of production at any given point in the trial, if subjected to a motion to dismiss, a motion for directed verdict, or similar challenge, must satisfy the judge that the party has offered sufficient evidence to merit submission of the case to the jury.[27] If that party does not convince the judge, the judge will declare that party's claim or defense unproven. Generally speaking, but not always, the burden of producing evidence begins with the party on whom the burden of persuasion falls.[28]

Because this concept is more easily understood by example than by definition, several examples follow.

Examples

P sues D for negligence following a collision between their two cars. At trial, P rests after producing evidence showing only that the two cars collided at an intersection, and that as a result of the collision, P suffered property damage and personal injury. D moves for a directed verdict. The court should grant the motion. In a negligence case, plaintiff has the burden of persuasion as to all elements of the prima facie case (roughly speaking, duty, breach, cause in fact,

25. *See, e.g.,* Summers v. Tice, 199 P.2d 1 (Cal.1948) (where two negligent hunters each fired the direction of the plaintiff but only one shot caused the significant harm, burden of proof shifted to each defendant to prove that his shot did not cause that harm).

26. *See* § **4.10** (describing effect of Morgan–McCormick approach to presumptions).

27. *See* Cal. Evid. Code § 110 (1966) (defining burden of producing evidence as "the obligation of a party to introduce evidence sufficient to avoid a ruling against him on an issue"). *See also* 9 John H. Wigmore, Evidence in Trials at Common Law § 2487, at 293 (James H. Chadbourn rev. 1981) (explaining concept).

28. *See* Cal. Evid. Code § 550 (1966) ("The burden of producing evidence as to a particular fact is initially on the party with the burden of proof as to that fact"). That this generalization is not always true is illustrated by the rule in some states that a criminal defendant who wishes to rely on the defense of insanity must both plead and initially produce evidence tending to prove insanity, but that the prosecution bears the ultimate burden of persuading the jury that the defendant was sane. *See* 1 Wayne R. LaFave & Austin W. Scott, Jr., Substantive Criminal Law § 4.5 (1986).

proximate cause, and damages). Plaintiff also has the burden of production as to each element. Because P failed to offer any evidence that the collision between the cars resulted from D's breach of a duty of reasonable care, P has not met the burden of production as to those elements. To allow the case to go forward would be to permit the jury to render a verdict based on speculation rather than evidence. This would be improper.

In the automobile collision case discussed in the previous example, P offers evidence sufficient to meet the burden of producing evidence as to all elements of the prima facie negligence case. D's answer to P's complaint alleged that the accident was partly P's fault, and that accordingly, P's recovery, if any, should be reduced by the proportion of fault attributable to P's conduct. At trial, D offers no evidence to support the comparative negligence claim.[29] If P moves to dismiss D's comparative negligence defense, the court must grant the motion. D had both a burden of persuasion and a burden of production as to the elements of the defense. Because D failed to produce any such evidence, the court must not permit the claim to go to the jury.

Following a barroom brawl, the state brings criminal charges against D for assault and battery. At trial, the prosecution fails to call a witness to testify that D was present in the bar at the time of the altercation. If D moves for a directed verdict at the close of the prosecution's case-in-chief, the court will grant the motion because the prosecution has failed to offer any evidence to support its contention that the person on trial was one of the participants in the brawl.

Unlike the burden of persuasion, the burden of producing evidence can shift back and forth during the trial. A party cannot cause the burden of production to shift to the opponent merely by offering evidence sufficient to meet the burden. However, the burden will shift to the opponent if the party who had the burden offers evidence strong enough to require a peremptory finding in favor of that party.[30]

The operation of the burden of production can be illustrated graphically:[31]

---

29. In addition, it will be assumed that D did not produce any evidence to support the claim during cross-examination of P's witnesses.

30. *See also* Larry L. Teply & Ralph U. Whitten, Civil Procedure 829 (1994) (making similar point).

31. This diagram can be found in Richard H. Field, Benjamin Kaplan, & Kevin M. Clermont, Civil Procedure: Materials For a Basic Course 672 (7th ed. 1997). It, in turn, is based on a diagram in 9 Wigmore, *supra* note 27 § 2487, at 298.

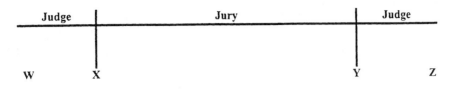

Now imagine the following case: P brings a negligence action against D following an intersection collision between their two cars. P claims D ran a red light, causing the collision. P has the burden of production as to evidence of D's negligence—in this case, that D ran a red light. At the commencement of trial, consider P's evidence to be at point W. Were P to offer no evidence of D's violation, the judge would grant D's motion for directed verdict. There being no basis for a jury finding that D was negligent (no reasonable jury could find, based on the evidence, that D was negligent) the judge's responsibility is to take the case from the jury.

Suppose, however, that P and P's friend, who was a passenger in the car, testify that P had the green light. This will likely meet P's burden of production on that issue, which moves P's evidence into the points between X and Y in the diagram. Should D move for a directed verdict at the close of P's case, the court will deny the motion because P has made out a case sufficient to reach the jury. Note that at this point, P is entitled only to reach the jury. The burden of production has not shifted to D. Even if D rested without offering any evidence to rebut the inference of negligence created by P's evidence, the judge would still let the jury decide the negligence issue. This makes very good sense. Particularly because P had an interest in the outcome, and because P's witness was an acquaintance who might have been biased in P's favor, the jury could rationally decide the case either way. This weighing of credibility is not for the judge; the judge's only role is to assess whether the evidence, if credible, could lead a rational jury to find for P on the negligence issue. If so, the case goes to the jury. This is the most common situation; the burden of production has not shifted, but has remained with P. And of course, P still has the burden of persuasion, which means convincing the jury that D was "more likely than not" negligent.

Suppose, however, that in addition to the testimony noted above, P calls a police officer who lays the foundation for admission of a videotape produced by a police camera mounted near the intersection for monitoring of traffic. The tape displays the date and time of the accident, and clearly shows P and D entering the intersection simultaneously, with the green light in P's favor. At this point, P has most likely produced sufficient evidence to move the evidence past point Y, and the burden of production will shift to D. Unless D offers evidence refuting D's illegal entry into the intersection, the court would almost certainly grant a directed verdict for P on the issue of D's negligence.[32] If D offers

32. *See* 2 McCormick on Evidence § 338, at 420–21 (5th ed. John W. Strong ed. 1999):

sufficient evidence to meet a burden of production on that issue, such evidence will have moved the case back between points X and Y, once again making a jury issue. On the facts, it is almost inconceivable that D could offer sufficient evidence to move the case back past point X; evidence already adduced by P remains before the jury, along with D's evidence of non-negligence.

An additional question is raised at this point: What does it take to "meet" a burden of producing evidence? For obvious reasons, this question has no quantifiable answer. As the previous discussion indicates, to satisfy the burden of production does not mean a party must offer enough evidence to *require* the jury to render a verdict in its favor on the issue. The party must merely offer evidence sufficient to *justify* a reasonable jury in rendering a verdict in its favor. Thus, if a directed verdict or similar motion is made against a party who has the burden of production, the court may grant the motion only if it finds that it would be unreasonable for the jury to decide in favor of the party with the burden.[33] If a verdict in favor of the party with the burden would be reasonable, it must deny the motion. The court does not become the factfinder on a motion to dismiss or for a directed verdict; it merely decides whether only one verdict would be reasonable.

How much evidence, then, is enough? This is where no clear answer can be given. To say that "more than a scintilla" is required,[34] of course,

---

We have seen something of the mechanics of the process of "proceeding" or "going forward" with evidence, viewed from the point of view of the *first* party who is stimulated to produce proof under threat of a ruling foreclosing a finding in her favor. She may in respect to a particular issue pass through three states of judicial hospitality: (a) where if she stops she will be thrown out of court; (b) where if she stops and her adversary does nothing, her reception will be left to the jury; and (c) where if she stops and her adversary does nothing, her victory (so far as it depends on having the inference she desires drawn) is at once proclaimed. Whenever the first producer has presented evidence sufficient to get her to the third stage and the burden of producing evidence can truly be said to have shifted, her adversary may in turn pass through the same three stages. Her evidence again may be (a) insufficient to warrant a finding in her favor, (b) sufficient to warrant a finding, or (c) irresistible, if unrebutted.

33. One federal court wrote, in the similar context of a motion for judgment notwithstanding the verdict, that "if there is substantial evidence opposed to the [motion], that is evidence of such quality and weight that reasonable and fair-minded men in the exercise of impartial judgment might reach different conclusions, the [motion] should be denied." Boeing Co. v. Shipman, 411 F.2d 365, 374 (5th Cir.1969).

34. *See* 2 McCormick on Evidence, *supra* note 32 § 338, at 416–17 ("A 'scintilla' of evidence will not suffice. The evidence must be such that a reasonable person could draw from it the inference of the existence of the particular fact to be proved. . . .") The caselaw contains many similar expressions. *See, e.g.*, United States v. Groessel, 440 F.2d 602, 606 (5th Cir. 1971) (the burden of going forward means producing "more than a scintilla" of evidence; failure to do so means party is not entitled to have issue submitted to the jury). The Supreme Court has also used the term. In one case, it held that if the defendant in a civil case moves for summary judgment or directed verdict based on lack of proof of a material fact,

the judge must ask himself not whether he thinks the evidence unmistakably favors one side or the other but whether a fair-minded jury could return a verdict for the plaintiff on the evidence presented. The mere existence of a scintilla of evidence in support of the plaintiff's position will be insufficient; there must be evidence on which the jury could reasonably find for the plaintiff.

is only to utter an abstract expression, and the same is true of other similar phrases.[35] The decision can only be made in the context of each case, taking into account the state of the evidence at the time the motion is made.

More precision than this is rather difficult, though some guidance can be offered. First, most courts require that the party with the burden of production must offer some affirmative evidence of the propositions it is charged with proving—that reliance on the jury's disbelieving adverse witnesses is not enough. In *Chesapeake & O. Ry. Co. v. Martin*,[36] for example, plaintiff brought an action to recover damages for alleged misdelivery of a carload of potatoes. A crucial issue concerned the reasonableness of an eight-day delay in delivery. Plaintiff called an experienced witness who testified that forty-eight hours was a reasonable time for delivery, and this witness's testimony stood unimpeached. Nevertheless, the trial court allowed this issue to go to the jury. The Supreme Court held:

> We recognize the general rule . . . that the question of the credibility of witnesses is one for the jury alone; but this does not mean that the jury is at liberty, under the guise of passing upon the credibility of a witness, to disregard his testimony, when from no reasonable point of view is it open to doubt. The complete testimony of the agent . . . discloses no lack of candor on his part. It was not shaken by cross-examination; indeed, upon this point there was no cross-examination. Its accuracy was not controverted by proof or circumstances, directly or inferentially; and it is difficult to see why, if inaccurate, it readily could not have been shown to be so.[37]

The Court acknowledged that the witness was an employee of the party that called him, but held that "[i]n the circumstances . . . , we are of opinion that this was not enough to take the question to the jury. . . ."[38]

Another case illustrates the point. In *Dyer v. MacDougall*,[39] plaintiff brought a four-count complaint for libel and slander. Unfortunately, plaintiff could offer no affirmative evidence that defendant had made

Anderson v. Liberty Lobby, Inc., 477 U.S. 242, 252 (1986). *See also* Rodney L. Bean & Sean P. McGinley, *West Virginia's Very Own* Celotex *Trilogy: A Series of Recent Opinions By the Supreme Court of Appeals of West Virginia Reveals that the Rumors of Rule 56's Death Were Greatly Exaggerated*, 98 W. Va. L. Rev. 571, 597 (1996) (to defeat a motion for summary judgment, party "must demonstrate the ability to produce enough competent evidence at trial to enable a finding in his or her favor. A mere 'scintilla of evidence' will not suffice, nor will evidence which is 'conjectural,' 'problematic,' 'merely colorable,' or 'not significantly probative.' ") (footnotes omitted).

35. *See* Laura G. Kniaz, *Animal Liberation and the Law: Animals Board the Underground Railroad*, 43 Buff. L. Rev. 765, 834 n.273 (1995) ("Across jurisdictions, the quantum of evidence required to satisfy a [criminal] defendant's burden of production have included the following standards: some evidence, more than a scintilla, slight evidence, evidence to support, some credible evidence, and evidence sufficient to raise a reasonable doubt") (citing 1 Paul H. Robinson, Criminal Law Defenses § 4(c), at 35–36 (1984)).

36. 283 U.S. 209 (1931).

37. *Id.* at 216.

38. *Id.*

39. 201 F.2d 265 (2d Cir.1952).

these statements, and defendant moved for summary judgment, supporting the motion with several affidavits and a deposition, all of which
denied that the statements were ever made. Plaintiff's response to the
motion was supported by affidavits, the contents of which would be
inadmissible at trial. Ultimately, the court granted summary judgment
as to two counts, on the ground that plaintiff would have no evidence
that the statements alleged in those counts were made, except the
testimony of witnesses all of whom would deny their utterance.

On appeal from the dismissal of the two counts, plaintiff argued that
he should be able to go to trial even without affirmative evidence
because the jury would be entitled to disbelieve the evidence that no
defamatory utterances had been made, and find, in fact, that the
opposite was true. In other words, plaintiff wished to rely solely on the
demeanor of the witnesses, and perhaps the plausibility of their testimony, to establish the truth of his claims. The Court of Appeals for the
Second Circuit, Judge Hand writing for the majority, affirmed. In the
court's view, failure to grant summary judgment under these circumstances would eviscerate the effectiveness of motions of this kind, as a
party could always claim that a jury could find in her favor because it
believed the opposing witnesses were lying and that the opposite of what
they testify is true. The court was particularly struck by plaintiff's
failure to exercise an opportunity to depose several witnesses prior to
trial. *Dyer* thus tells us that satisfying a burden of production at trial
means offering some affirmative evidence to support the allegations of
the complaint.[40]

The rule in *Dyer* is followed by most courts,[41] although a few cases
suggest that a witness's demeanor and the content of the witness's
testimony can, in some instances, suffice to meet a burden of production.[42] Moreover, in *Dyer* itself, Judge Frank offered a persuasive argument that demeanor could, in some cases, suffice to allow a party to
reach the jury:

40. *See also* Teply & Whitten, *supra* note 30, at 829 ("To satisfy the burden of production, a party must ordinarily intro-duce some affirmative evidence that the fact in question has occurred"). Although *Dyer* arose in the summary judgment con-text, rather than on a motion for directed verdict, the standards to be applied by the trial judge are essentially the same. *See id.* at 786.

41. "[T]here is virtual unanimity among the courts that have addressed the issue that a fact finder may not base its finding of fact on disbelief of a witness. The party with the burden of proof must intro-duce affirmative evidence to sustain its bur-den." J. Palmer Lockard, *Summary Judg-ment in Pennsylvania: Time for Another Look at Credibility Issues*, 35 Duq. L. Rev. 625, 682 (1997).

42. *See, e.g.,* In re Melnick, 360 F.2d 918, 920 (2d Cir.1966) (in bankruptcy pro-

ceeding in which debtor had burden of proving he did not knowingly and fraudu-lently make a false oath as to a material matter, referee entitled to disbelieve debt-or's testimony); Morrison v. Lefevre, 592 F.Supp. 1052, 1065 (S.D.N.Y.1984) (in civil rights action against prison officials arising from alleged planting of contraband, testi-mony of three defendants who "found" con-traband established that one of them plant-ed it, even though they did not so testify; court held that "[t]he stories told by the three officers and their demeanor on the stand strongly support the inference that they were responsible for 'planting' and then 'discovering the vial of florescent fluid. As Judge Learned Hand observed in Dyer v. MacDougall, ... a witness' implausible de-nials can lead a court to infer the true state of affairs...."); In re Bebar, 315 F.Supp. 841 (E.D.N.Y.1970) (similar). Note that be-cause none of these cases involved jury tri-

One can imagine a case in which a man would suffer a grave injustice, if it were the invariable rule that a plaintiff can never win a case when (1) he can offer only the oral testimony of the defendant, the one available witness, which is flatly and unswervingly against the plaintiff but (2) the jury (in a jury trial) or the judge (in a judge trial) is thoroughly convinced by the witness' demeanor that he is an unmitigated liar. On that account, I would oppose such a rule.[43]

In several opinions issued in 1986, the Supreme Court signaled its strong support for the judge's power to grant summary judgment against the party who had the burden of production.[44] Though the Court may not have wished to increase plaintiffs' burden on summary judgment substantially,[45] the cases do demonstrate the Court's commitment to the trial court's close analysis of the allegations and proof, and the need for the plaintiff to rely on meaningful evidence to support its claims.

als, the propriety of directed verdicts was not in issue. Nevertheless, the courts' actions demonstrate a willingness to accept that a proposition may be sufficiently established even in the absence of affirmative evidence.

Some scholars have supported such an argument. *See, e.g.*, Richard D. Friedman, *Route Analysis of Credibility and Hearsay*, 96 Yale L.J. 667, 742 n.134 (1987) ("Indeed, it may be that in some cases a factfinder may find a proposition to be true solely on the basis of a witness' demeanor in testifying to the contrary of that proposition"); Edmund Morgan, *Admissions*, 12 Wash. L. Rev. 181, 185–86 (1937). *See also* Olin Guy Wellborn, III, *Demeanor*, 76 Cornell L. Rev. 1075, 1102 (1991) (distinguishing between relying on demeanor and relying on the content of the testimony itself to establish facts contrary to the witness' testimony).

43. *Dyer*, 201 F.2d at 272 (Frank, J., concurring). Judge Frank believed that the case at hand was not such a case, because in the relevant counts, plaintiff claimed to have been slandered in his absence and in the presence of only two other persons, both of whom would deny the slander. Thus, "only plaintiff's own suit serves to publicize the alleged slander." *Id.* In his majority opinion, Judge Hand also pointed out that plaintiff had failed to avail himself of the opportunity to depose the witnesses prior to trial. *Id.* at 267.

44. Anderson v. Liberty Lobby, Inc., 477 U.S. 242 (1986) (in libel action where plaintiffs were required to demonstrate actual malice, trial court properly granted summary judgment for defendants where defendants produced affidavit of author-employee detailing quality of research and variety of sources used in the articles; even

though plaintiffs submitted affidavits demonstrating numerous inaccuracies in the stories and that several of defendants' sources were unreliable, the trial court must consider the heavy burden on plaintiffs of showing actual malice, and plaintiffs' showing was insufficient to defeat motion); Celotex Corp. v. Catrett, 477 U.S. 317 (1986) (in wrongful death action alleging exposure to asbestos manufactured by defendant, district court properly granted summary judgment where plaintiff was unable to produce evidence of exposure to defendant's products; after adequate time for discovery, party with burden of proof must be able to make showing sufficient to establish the existence of the element, and in the absence of such a showing, defendant was not obligated to come forward with materials outside the pleadings to negate plaintiff's claim); Matsushita Electric Industrial Co. v. Zenith Radio Corp., 475 U.S. 574 (1986) (in antitrust action alleging conspiracy to raise, fix, and maintain artificially high prices for television sets in Japan and artificially low prices for sets in United States, district court properly granted summary judgment for defendant on ground plaintiffs did not raise genuine issue of material fact; in antitrust action, plaintiff must present evidence showing that inference of conspiracy is reasonable, and the nature of predatory pricing conspiracies is such that defendants had no plausible motive to engage in conspiracy charged in complaint).

45. *See* Eastman Kodak Co. v. Image Technical Servs., Inc., 504 U.S. 451, 468–69 (1992) (*Matsushita* did not introduce special burden on plaintiffs in antitrust cases, but economic theory relied upon by plaintiffs in proving violation must not be "senseless").

Because of the similarity of the standard for granting summary judgment and directed verdict,[46] these cases lend considerable support to the same conclusion in regard to motions for directed verdict. Thus, meeting a burden of production in modern civil litigation almost certainly means offering affirmative evidence to support one's claims.

A series of examples can illuminate somewhat further the problem of when a party has met a burden of production. Suppose the crops on P's farm are destroyed by a toxic chemical seeping onto the land through the soil. P sues D, the operator of a nearby business that uses the chemical in its manufacturing process. There is no dispute that P's crops were destroyed by exposure to the type of chemical used by D. The question is whether D was the source of the chemical, or whether it came from one of several other businesses located near P's farm that also use the chemical. Suppose P offers the following evidence to prove that D was the source of the chemical that destroyed the crops:

1. Testimony that P's crops were destroyed within several months after D began using the chemical in question.

2. Testimony of an expert that given the relative locations of P's farm and D's business, it would have been possible for a liquid leaking out of D's plant to migrate through the soil and underground streams to P's farm, destroying the crops.

3. Testimony of the same expert that given the relative locations of the other businesses and the flow of groundwater in the area, only one other business could have been the source of the chemical.

4. Testimony from a safety engineer at the other plant that her routine inspections of the plant's equipment revealed no leakage of toxins for several months before P's crops were destroyed.

If P only offers the evidence described in 1. above, and D moves for a directed verdict, the court almost certainly should grant it. Though it is not utterly irrational to causally relate the destruction of P's crops with D's beginning to use the chemical in its business, the fallacy of *post hoc ergo propter hoc* applies to remind us that a temporal correspondence between two events does not mean the first event caused the second. For the court to allow the jury to render a verdict for P on such speculative evidence almost certainly would be incorrect. P has not met the burden of production on the issue of causation.[47]

The evidence described in 2. above is also speculative. Though if it is credible, it shows that D could have been the source of the chemical that destroyed P's crops, it still does not present any basis for distinguishing

---

46. *See supra* note 40.

47. A directed verdict for D might be justified for another reason. Given that P has failed to offer any evidence linking D with the harm except D's admitted use of the chemical, and given that the chemical is used by other businesses in the area, it seems appropriate to place on P the burden of presenting evidence distinguishing D from the other businesses, and forcing P to bear the consequences of an ill-prepared case. *See, e.g.,* Smith v. Rapid Transit, Inc., 58 N.E.2d 754 (Mass.1945) (plaintiff's testimony that bus causing her to strike a parked car was a "great big, long, wide affair," and that defendant's buses were the only ones authorized to operate on that street at that time of night was insufficient

D from any of the other nearby businesses that use the chemical. Without any effort to demonstrate that the locations of the other businesses made it unlikely that they could have been the source of the chemical, the jury would again be speculating about the validity of the evidence for P's case. An appellate court would likely affirm a directed verdict for D.

The evidence described in 3. above is more helpful in one sense: if it is valid, it narrows the universe of reasonably probable sources of pollution to two, of which D is one. But P still has not offered any evidence that would support a rational conclusion that it was D, rather than the other business, that polluted P's land. Once again, it is likely that an appellate court would affirm a directed verdict for D.

The evidence described in 4. above, if credible, begins to distinguish D's business from the only other reasonably probable source of the toxic chemical. Though P has not presented positive evidence that D was the source of the toxin, P's evidence can be sufficient to support a rational inference that no other source was likely responsible. Still, the evidence only creates a negative inference; P has failed to call any witness or offer any other evidence suggesting that D *did* release the chemical at issue. As a result, it is likely that an appellate court would affirm a ruling either way on D's motion for directed verdict.

Some further possibilities, also based on the toxic chemical example, are also instructive about the quantum of proof necessary to satisfy a burden of production. First, assume that P offers all of the evidence described above, and that the court denies D's motion for directed verdict. Now, D calls an Environmental Protection Agency enforcement officer whose job is to inspect plants that use toxic chemicals. The witness testifies that she inspected D's plant during the period when the chemical was destroying P's crops. Among other things, she took soil samples from the land surrounding the plant, and water samples from the underground stream that flows onto P's property. None of these samples revealed the presence of the chemical. If D renews its motion for directed verdict, what should the court do? The state of the evidence appears to be overwhelmingly against P. No positive evidence connects D with the damage, and some evidence shows that D was not he source. In such a case, the risk of inferential error is likely too great to justify allowing the jury to decide for P. Though it is always possible that P's allegations are true, a directed verdict would likely be required.[48]

As discussed above, failure to offer evidence sufficient to meet a burden of production will result in the granting of a peremptory motion, generally leading to the dismissal of a claim or defense. Of course, the court has discretion to grant the party's motion to reopen its case to

to overcome defendant's motion for directed verdict; plaintiff's failure to develop any further evidence, such as testimony from bystanders or bus passengers, might have motivated court to affirm judgment for defendant).

48. *Cf.* Pennsylvania R. Co. v. Chamberlain, 288 U.S. 333 (1933). Plaintiff brought suit against a railroad to recover for the death of a brakeman struck by train cars. Plaintiff claimed that the accident was caused by the violent collision of one string of cars with the string on which the de-

offer additional evidence if it believes that the interests of justice would be served by doing so.

§ 4.07 Presumptions; Introduction

The word "presumption" has perhaps suffered from more misuse and inconsistent use than any other evidentiary term. The next several sections will distinguish true presumptions from other devices and concepts, and will then explain how presumptions operate. Throughout, it will be the conventional wisdom that is presented.[49] Despite the articulation of arguments that there is no need for a distinct law of presumptions,[50] courts and commentators continue to use the term, and the language of presumptions is likely to be with us for the foreseeable future.

§ 4.08 Presumptions; Presumptions Defined and Distinguished From Other Devices

A presumption is a rule providing that proof of a designated fact has a predetermined effect in establishing the existence of another fact. It

ceased was riding. At trial, three employees riding on the other string of cars testified that no collision occurred, and they were corroborated by all other employees in a position to see the event. The only witness favorable to plaintiff on this issue testified to hearing a loud crash and to seeing the two strings of cars together shortly afterward. The witness was standing 900 feet from where the deceased's body was found, and his angle of vision to the possible crash was such that he would not have been able to determine whether the two strings of cars were actually in contact. The district court directed a verdict for defendant. The Court of Appeals reversed, but the Supreme Court reinstated the judgment for defendant. The Court held that the testimony of plaintiff's witness was "wholly circumstantial, and the inferences which might otherwise be drawn from it were shown to be utterly erroneous unless all of petitioner's witnesses were willful perjurers." *Id.* at 338. The Court held that the evidence did not even raise a conflict: "It, of course, is true, generally, that where there is a direct conflict of testimony upon a matter of fact, the question must be left to the jury to determine, without regard to the number of witnesses upon either side. But here there really is no conflict in the testimony as to the facts. The witnesses for petitioner flatly testified that there was no collision between the nine-car and the two-car strings. [Plaintiff's witness] did not say there was such a collision. What he said was that he heard a 'loud crash,' which did not cause him at once to turn, but that shortly thereafter he

did turn and saw the two strings of cars moving together with the deceased no longer in sight...." *Id.* at 338–39.

49. *See, e.g.,* Fleming James, Jr. et al., Civil Procedure § 7.17 (4th ed. 1992); 2 McCormick on Evidence § 342 (5th ed. John W. Strong ed. 1999).

50. *See, e.g.,* Ronald J. Allen, *Presumptions, Inference and Burden of Proof in Federal Civil Actions—An Anatomy of Unnecessary Ambiguity and a Proposal for Reform,* 76 Nw. U.L. Rev. 892 (1982); Ronald J. Allen, *Presumptions in Civil Actions Reconsidered,* 66 Iowa L. Rev. 843 (1981) (arguing that presumption concept is artificial and should be replaced by a direct approach allocating burdens of proof and allowing careful judicial comment on evidence, and that where proof adduced at trial is sufficiently strong to require shifting or reassigning a burden of persuasion, this can be done by means of a "conditional imperative"); Edward W. Cleary, *Presuming and Pleading: An Essay on Juristic Immaturity,* 12 Stan. L. Rev. 5 (1959) (suggesting elimination of concept of presumptions that transfer burden of proof). *But see* Kenneth S. Broun, *The Unfulfillable Promise of One Rule for All Presumptions,* 62 N.C. L. Rev. 697 (1984) (recognizing validity of argument that courts should discuss propriety of allocating burdens rather than technical application of presumptions, but noting that presumption concept is unlikely to be displaced and that "conditional imperative" suffers from same difficulties as current presumption language).

thus expresses a legal relationship between certain facts (what we will call the "foundational" or "basic" facts) proved by a party and certain other facts (what we will call the "presumed facts").[51]

A "true" presumption is rebuttable by evidence to the contrary of the presumed facts. When it is not rebutted, it is deemed conclusive in the sense that the jury will be informed that the fact at issue is proven. It is not that the law no longer demands that the underlying (presumed) fact be proven, but that the presumed fact should be deemed proven in the absence of contrary evidence.

A few examples will clarify the nature of true (rebuttable) presumptions.

Examples

A presumption states that a letter properly addressed, stamped, and deposited in an appropriate receptacle is presumed to have been received in the ordinary course of the mail.[52] Unless the presumption created by this rule is rebutted, the properly addressed, stamped, and deposited letter will be deemed to have been received in what is considered to be the ordinary amount of time needed in that delivery area.

A presumption states that money delivered to another person is presumed to have been due to that person.[53] Unless the presumption is rebutted, if delivery is proven, the money will be deemed to have been owed to the person to whom it was delivered.

A presumption provides that a writing is presumed to have been accurately dated.[54] Unless the presumption is rebutted, the writing in question will be deemed accurately dated.

Note that if a true presumption is not rebutted, the factfinder might be required to make a factual conclusion that does not accord with reality. The properly addressed, stamped, and mailed letter might actually not have been received in what is considered to be the ordinary course of the mail. The money delivered might have been a gift rather than payment of a debt. The writing might have been dated incorrectly. Nevertheless, this is the essential effect of presumptions, and the thing that separates them from mere inferences; if not rebutted, they will require a factual finding even if that finding is contrary to reality.

Just as several reasons support the law's determination to assign a burden of persuasion to one party or another, presumptions are also created for a variety of reasons. Among them are *fairness*—to "correct

---

51. *See* Cal. Evid. Code § 600(a) (1966) ("A presumption is an assumption of fact that the law requires to be made from another fact or group of facts found or otherwise established in the action"). McCormick's handbook states that "a presumption is a standardized practice, under which certain facts are held to call for uniform treatment with respect to their effect as proof of other facts." 2 McCormick on Evidence § 342, at 433 (5th ed. John W. Strong ed. 1999).

52. *See* Legille v. Dann, 544 F.2d 1 (D.C.Cir.1976).

53. *See* Cal. Evid. Code § 631 (1966).

54. *See* Cal. Evid. Code § 640 (1966).

an imbalance resulting from one party's superior access to the proof."[55] Some presumptions are supported by reasons of *substantive policy*—to encourage or discourage certain "primary" (non-litigation) behavior, or to effectuate a goal of the law.[56] Some presumptions are created simply to *resolve issues* otherwise difficult to resolve because of the absence of proof.[57] The most common reason for creating presumptions, however, is simply the *facilitation of the litigation process* by resolving matters in accordance with *high probability*. In other words, most presumptions are created for situations in which the presumed fact is very likely to be true. This both streamlines the process of proof of the fact and avoids the factfinding distortion that might occur were the jury to decide that the fact is not true.[58]

Individual presumptions often exist for a combination of reasons. For example, the common presumption that a person not heard from in a certain period of years is dead[59] does indeed facilitate proof of the person's death where the risk of error is slight, but it also does more. It reflects a social policy that the affairs of people who have been missing for a period of years should be wrapped up without the necessity of burdensome (and often practically unavailable) proof. Similarly, the presumption that a ceremonial marriage is valid[60] both facilitates proof that a marriage is lawful and effectuates a policy that the marriage of people who go through a marriage ceremony should not be subject to question except in unusual cases. Also, the common presumption that the official actions by public officers were regularly and legally performed[61] exists because the probability of regular and legal performance is high, because it is often difficult for a public official who conducts a great deal of repetitive business to remember exactly how the act at issue was performed, and because people should be confident that officials perform their duties correctly. Even the presumption of receipt of mail in the regular course is supported by more than probability; the presumption also facilities proof where, as is often true, the postal

55. 2 McCormick on Evidence, *supra* note 51 § 343, at 437. An example would be the presumption that as between connecting carriers of goods, damage occurred while the goods were in the possession of the last carrier. *Id*. at n.4, citing Chicago & Northwestern Ry. Co. v. C.C. Whitnack Produce Co., 258 U.S. 369 (1922).

56. A common example is the presumptions of the death of a person not heard from for a specified period of years, which serves the goal of settling issues of title and of estates. *See, e.g.*, Cal. Evid. Code § 667 (1966).

57. 2 McCormick on Evidence, *supra* note 51 § 343, at 438 (giving as an example presumptions resolving questions of who survived longest in a common disaster). Presumptions in Title VII employment discrimination cases are an important contem-

porary example. *See, e.g.*, Price Waterhouse v. Hopkins, 490 U.S. 228 (1989) (holding that once plaintiff proved that firm's failure to promote her to partner was motivated in part by her gender, burden of persuasion was placed on defendant to demonstrate lack of unlawful discrimination).

58. 2 McCormick on Evidence, *supra* note 51 at 437–38. For an illustrative list of such presumptions, *see* Cal. Evid. Code §§ 630–647 (1966).

59. *See, e.g.*, Cal. Evid. Code § 667 (1966) (five years); Green v. Royal Neighbors of America, 73 P.2d 1 (Kan.1937) (seven years).

60. *See, e.g.*, Cal. Evid. Code § 663 (1966).

61. *See* Cal. Evid. Code § 664 (1966).

worker cannot be expected to remember delivering a particular piece of mail at a particular time.

Further support for the multi-faceted rationale for presumptions is provided by the existence of some presumptions in situations in which a logical inference would be difficult to draw—or, more precisely, where the probative value of the evidence is very slight. For example, the presumption that the driver of an automobile was the agent of the owner exists where a rational inference is possible, but the probative value of the inference is often sufficiently slight that, in the absence of an agency presumption, the plaintiff will likely face dismissal of the claim against the owner. If presumptions only existed in situations where the probability of the presumed fact is high, the agency presumption would not exist.

True presumptions must be distinguished from other concepts, including the permissive inference and the "conclusive presumption."[62] A permissive inference is a factual conclusion that the factfinder *may*, but is not required to, draw from another fact or group of facts.[63] An inference is based on simple everyday logic—the factfinder's application of everyday experience to determine the likelihood that a given fact is true. Thus, one may infer that a person whose usual practice is to fasten the automobile seat belt did so on the relevant occasion. Similarly, one may infer that marks on a person's body matching the teeth of a particular dog living next door were made by the dog.

Note that inferences are not always accurate. The driver might not have worn the seat belt on the occasion in question; the dog might not have bitten the person. But in each case, it is logical to assume, given the facts stated, that the events happened as initially indicated. In each case the court would not require the jury to reach a given conclusion; unless the evidence was so one-sided as to require the conclusion, the jury will be permitted to draw the inference but will not be compelled to do so. These types of inferences, then, are purely permissive in nature.

True presumptions must also be distinguished from so called "conclusive presumptions" or "irrebuttable presumptions." These devices are not actually presumptions at all, even though they operate in a mandatory fashion and even though they express a relationship between certain basic facts and a presumed fact. Instead, they are rules of law that change the nature of the facts needed to be proven. A few examples will demonstrate the nature of "conclusive presumptions."

Examples

A statute states that except as provided in a separate statute, "the child of a wife cohabiting with her husband, who is not impotent or

---

62. Another concept to be distinguished is the so-called "permissive presumption," a term the United States Supreme Court has used in the context of criminal cases, which raise special issues regarding presumptions. *See* § **4.12.**

63. *See* Cal. Evid. Code § 600(b) (1966) ("An inference is a deduction of fact that may logically and reasonably be drawn from another fact or group of facts found or otherwise established in the action").

sterile, is conclusively presumed to be a child of the marriage."[64] This statute means that the biological facts are no longer important to the law. If a husband and wife are cohabiting, and if the husband is not impotent or sterile, the child is presumed to be the child of the marriage. Unless an exception applies, no evidence to the contrary would be admissible.

A statute provides that "[t]he facts recited in a written instrument are conclusively presumed to be true as between the parties thereto, or their successors in interest; but this rule does not apply to the recital of a consideration."[65] What this rule means is that unless the issue concerns consideration, all that matters is the facts recited in the written instrument. The law is no longer concerned about the "true" facts, and proof of those facts will not be heard.

A criminal statute provides that "[a] defendant who does not plead not guilty by reason of insanity shall be conclusively presumed to have been sane at the time of the commission of the offense charged...."[66] As a result of this rule, even a person who fails to meet the test for insanity under that state's law would be considered sane for purposes of the trial if she did not plead not guilty by reason of insanity.

"Conclusive presumptions" are not evidentiary devices. They are not evidence rules at all. They are new rules of substantive law. In virtually every case, they exist because of a policy-based determination that the existence of certain facts should establish a factual issue and that society would not be served by permitting contrary evidence. In the examples given above, this is easiest to understand with respect to the presumption of paternity. This presumption represents a legislative judgment that the legitimacy of children born under the specified circumstances should not be subject to challenge. In all likelihood, such a presumption is created in order to protect such children from ridicule or from the domestic battles of their now-estranged parents. Thus, while other legal issues concerning custody and support must still be resolved in circumstances involving paternity, the father's initial responsibility for the child will be beyond question. The presumption thus establishes a new substantive rule: that a child born to a married woman cohabiting with her husband, who is not impotent or sterile, is entitled to inherit from the mother's husband whether or not the child is the biological child of the husband.

§ 4.09   Presumptions; Causing Presumptions to Take Effect

A presumption does not come into being in a given case until the party seeking to employ it has "proven" its foundational facts. Proof involves two steps. First, the party seeking to take advantage of the

---

64. Cal. Fam. Code § 7540 (1994). *See also* In re Findlay, 170 N.E. 471, 473 (N.Y. 1930).

65. Cal. Evid. Code § 622 (1966).

66. Cal. Penal Code § 1016 (1985).

presumption must offer evidence sufficient to meet a burden of production as to each foundational fact. It is up to the trial court to determine whether this has occurred. Unless the opponent offers evidence that overwhelmingly rebuts those facts, the party using the presumption is entitled to reach the jury for a determination of the existence of those facts. The second step is the jury's decision whether the foundational facts are indeed true. If the proponent passes both steps, the presumption comes into being. It will then have conclusive effect in the litigation unless the presumption is "rebutted."

A simple example will illustrate how presumptions come into being. Suppose P, a second-floor tenant in D's apartment building, suffers a fall on a dark stairway leading to the second floor. P sues D, the building's owner, claiming that D failed to maintain the stairway in a reasonably safe condition because several of its lights did not work. To prove notice to D of the stairway's condition, P wishes to prove that two weeks before the accident, she mailed a letter to D, who lived in the building, informing D that several of the lights in the stairway no longer worked.[67] At trial, P testifies that she addressed the letter properly, placed a first-class stamp on it, and took it to a United States Postal Service receptacle around the corner from the apartment building. P also offers testimony that letters sent from one address to another in the city normally arrive within two days.

As described, the testimony offered by P is sufficient to meet a burden of production as to each foundational fact necessary to raise the common presumption that a letter properly addressed, stamped, and mailed was received in the ordinary course of the mail. In the absence of substantial contrary evidence concerning those facts,[68] the court will instruct the jury that if it finds that those facts are true,[69] it must find that D received the letter well before the accident.

§ 4.10   Presumptions; Rebutting Presumptions

How does one go about "rebutting" a presumption? The simple answer is by offering evidence attacking either its foundational (basic) facts or the presumed fact. The reality is somewhat more complicated.

A party against whom a presumption would operate actually has several choices. The party may:

---

67. Notice to D of the defect would make D's failure to repair the condition more likely unreasonable.

68. To prevent the issue from going to the jury, D will have to offer evidence not merely strong enough to meet a burden of production as to the nonexistence of the foundational facts, but so strong as to require that finding. This will not often occur, though one might imagine that if D asks the court to take judicial notice that there was a nationwide postal strike stopping all mail delivery during the entire relevant period, the court would hold that P did not notify D of the alleged defect in the manner to which P testified.

69. We are assuming at this point that D does not offer evidence attacking *receipt* of the letter. For discussion of what happens if D does offer evidence attacking the presumed fact, *see* § **4.10**.

1. offer no evidence challenging the existence of either the foundational facts or the presumed fact;

2. offer evidence challenging the existence of only the foundational fact;

3. offer evidence challenging the existence of only the presumed fact; or

4. offer evidence challenging the existence of both the foundational and presumed fact.

To illustrate the consequences of these choices, the hypothetical discussed in the previous section, involving P's letter to D warning of the darkness of the stairway, will be used.

Challenging Neither Foundational Nor Presumed Facts

Suppose first that D chooses not to offer evidence challenging either the foundational facts (addressing, stamping, depositing) or the presumed fact (D's receipt of the letter well before the plaintiff's accident). In this situation, the court will simply instruct the jury that if it finds the foundational facts to be true, it *must* find that D received the letter in the ordinary course (about two days after P mailed it). Of course, P has the burden of persuasion as to these facts, because they form part of the basis of P's prima facie negligence case against D.[70] And P also has the burden of producing evidence of those facts.[71] But as long as P's evidence is sufficient to meet her burden of production, the question of the existence of the foundational facts will be for the jury. If the jury is even slightly more persuaded of the existence of the foundational facts than of their nonexistence, P will have met the burden of persuasion, and the jury must find that D received the letter well before the accident (thus making D more likely negligent in failing to take precautionary steps).

In the absence of evidence from D of the nonexistence of either the foundational or presumed facts, there are two possible outcomes: (1) In most instances, P will only have to meet a burden of production as to the existence of the foundational facts. This means that the court will merely leave the question of the foundational facts to the jury. This is the likely result in our hypothetical, where P's evidence, though compelling on the surface, comes from a witness (P) with an interest in the outcome of the case. Thus, it would not be irrational for the jury to disbelieve P, and find that the foundational facts are not true. (2) In some cases, the evidence of the existence of the foundational facts will be so strong as to compel a finding of their existence, and thus of the presumed fact. So, in the hypothetical case, assume that P's evidence of each of the foundational facts includes testimony from unimpeached, disinterested witnesses.[72] In such a case, P would be entitled either to a directed verdict

---

70. *See* § 4.05.

71. *See id.*

72. For example, suppose P claims to have sent the letter by registered mail. To establish mailing to the correct address, P

as to an element of the case, or a binding jury instruction requiring the jurors to make a certain factual finding.[73]

Challenging Only Foundational Facts

If D chooses only to challenge the existence of the foundational (basic) facts, the consequences are similar. Suppose, then, that D testifies that there is no United States Postal Service mailbox around the corner from the apartment building, or that P was on vacation out of state for more than a week beginning on the day P claims to have mailed the letter. In this instance, the court will almost certainly allow the jury to determine whether the foundational facts exist, and instruct the jury that if it finds that the facts do indeed exist, it *must* find that the letter was received in the ordinary course. Because D has done nothing to challenge the existence of the presumed fact—his receipt of the letter—the presumption will come into play and mandate a finding of receipt if proper addressing, stamping, and mailing are proven by the preponderance of the evidence.[74]

Challenging Only Presumed Fact

There is a long-standing debate about what happens when the party against whom the presumption would operate challenges the existence of the presumed fact.[75] To take our hypothetical as the starting point, suppose D does not challenge P's proper addressing, stamping, and mailing of the letter, but offers testimony to support a contention that he never received the letter. For example, D might testify that he picked up and read his mail diligently each day from the date on which P claims to have mailed the letter until the date of the accident, and that he never saw the letter. What happens to the presumption now? There are two distinct views, each associated with respected evidence scholars.

(1) The Thayer–Wigmore "bursting bubble" theory. If presumptions are nothing more than devices that facilitate proof and help to ensure that the correct factual conclusions are reached where the risk of error is very slight,[76] presumptions should have no effect once "rebutted" with

offers in evidence a telephone book listing D's address and a postal receipt showing that the letter, addressed to the same address, was deposited in the post office on a date two weeks before the accident.

73. *See, e.g.,* Chesapeake & O. Ry. Co. v. Martin, 283 U.S. 209 (1931) (where question concerned reasonableness of eight-day delay in delivery, trial court erred in failing to direct verdict on basis of witness's unimpeached, uncontradicted testimony that forty-eight hours was a reasonable time; even though witness was employed by party calling him, this was not enough to raise a jury question). In the hypothetical case, the most likely outcome would be a jury instruction telling the jurors to assume that D received the letter more than a week in

advance of the accident. Such notice, in turn, would increase the likelihood that the jury would find D to have been negligent in failing to remedy the danger before the accident.

74. In light of D's testimony attacking the foundational facts, there is virtually no chance that the court will instruct the jury to find that the foundational facts are true.

75. "The problem of the effect of a presumption when met by proof rebutting the presumed fact has literally plagued the courts and legal scholars." 2 McCormick on Evidence § 344, at 445 (5th ed. John W. Strong ed. 1999).

76. For discussion of the purposes of presumptions, *see* § **4.08**.

evidence challenging the presumed fact. This was the view of the Missouri court, which in 1906 wrote that presumptions are "like bats of the law flitting in the twilight, but disappearing in the sunshine of actual facts."[77] This position also gave rise to the "bursting bubble" theory of presumptions, usually associated with Thayer,[78] and supported by Wigmore[79] (though the positions of both authors were actually somewhat different from the pure "bursting bubble" theory).[80] The theory holds that a presumption does no more than shift to the opponent the burden of producing evidence, not the burden of persuasion. And when the opponent offers evidence sufficient to meet that burden of production, the presumption disappears from the case entirely. In other words, a presumption has spent its currency once proof is offered sufficient to meet a burden of production as to the nonexistence of the presumed fact—that is, sufficient to support a finding that the presumed fact is not true.

Under the "bursting bubble" theory, the disappearance of the presumption means that the jury should not be apprised about the presumption.[81] However, note the state of the evidence in our hypothetical: P has offered evidence concerning proper addressing, stamping, and mailing a warning letter. D has offered evidence that he never received the letter. If there had never been a presumption in the case, the jury would simply apply its sense of logic and experience and determine, as a matter of permissive inference, whether P mailed and D received a letter concerning the dark stairway. It would hardly be unreasonable to reach such a conclusion, nor would it be unreasonable in some cases to conclude that D did not receive any such letter. The same procedure applies under the "bursting bubble" theory; the question of D's receipt of a letter from P is simply left to the jury as a matter of logical inference. This being the case, there is no more reason to instruct the

---

77. Mackowik v. Kansas City, St. Joseph & Council Bluffs R. Co., 94 S.W. 256, 262 (Mo.1906).

78. James B. Thayer, A Preliminary Treatise on Evidence at the Common Law ch. 8 (1898).

79. 9 John H. Wigmore, Evidence in Trials at Common Law § 2491(2) (James H. Chadbourn rev. 1981).

80. Thayer was not so unequivocal about the disappearance of presumptions upon the admission of evidence contradicting the presumed fact. *See* 2 McCormick on Evidence, *supra* note 75 § 344, at 445 n.7; 21 Charles A. Wright & Kenneth W. Graham, Jr., Federal Practice and Procedure: Evidence § 5122 (1977). As Wright and Graham state,

> neither Thayer nor Wigmore advocated the "bursting bubble" theory of presumptions, the notion that the judge was required to direct a verdict against the plaintiff once the presumption was rebutted, unless there was an underly-

ing inference sufficient to take the case to the jury.... In fact, what both Thayer and Wigmore seem to have believed was that a presumption vanished in the face of rebuttal only in the sense that the proponent was no longer entitled to a directed verdict; both Thayer and Wigmore seem to have assumed that the case would still go to the jury unless the evidence in rebuttal was such that no reasonable juror could find the nonexistence of the presumed fact.

Id. at 573 n.86, citing Thayer, *supra* note 78, at 336–37; James B. Thayer, *Presumptions and the Law of Evidence,* 3 Harv. L. Rev. 141, 165 (1889); 9 Wigmore, *supra* note 79 §§ 2487, 2491, 2493, 2494, 2498.

81. 2 McCormick on Evidence, *supra* note 75 § 344, at 445–46 (*citing* Orient Ins. Co. v. Cox, 238 S.W.2d 757 (Ark.1951); Ammundson v. Tinholt, 36 N.W.2d 521 (Minn. 1949)).

jury about applying its reasoning powers to this evidence than there is with respect to any other disputed fact; the jury will simply decide, guided by argument of counsel.[82]

Even under the "bursting bubble" theory of presumptions, it is possible that the evidence offered by the party against whom the presumption would operate is so strong as to require a directed verdict or partial directed verdict in the absence of further evidence from the opponent. Such a result would be rather unlikely in our hypothetical case because the simple inference of receipt from proper mailing is so strong. But suppose instead that the presumption on which a party seeks to rely is artificial, in the sense that it gives rise only to a weak logical inference. For example, suppose the jurisdiction in which the case is tried adheres to the presumption that the driver of a vehicle owned by another is the agent of the owner. P, a pedestrian, is struck in a crosswalk by a dry cleaning delivery truck driven by X. It is firmly established that D owns the dry cleaning business and the truck, and that X is employed by D as a delivery driver. Suppose, however, that D calls X, who testifies that she was on her way to a midnight poker game when the accident occurred, and that P is unable to do anything to impeach the witness. This evidence almost certainly would do more than meet a burden of production. Rather, it is likely so strong as to require a directed verdict for D. Thus, even under the "bursting bubble" theory of presumptions, it is possible for the party against whom the presumption operates to rebut the presumption with evidence sufficient to meet a burden of production (which would leave the factual matter for the jury), but also to rebut the presumption with evidence so compelling as to require a directed verdict for that party.

(2) The Morgan–McCormick theory. Morgan, McCormick, and some other legal scholars reject the notion that presumptions are so fragile as to disappear when evidence is offered to rebut the existence of the presumed fact. They have emphasized that presumptions are more than simple procedural devices for the facilitation of proof, but also exist for reasons of policy.[83] As McCormick's handbook explains:

> Presumptions . . . have been created for policy reasons that are similar to and may be just as strong as those that govern the allocation of the burdens of proof prior to the introduction of evidence. These policy considerations may persist despite the existence of proof rebutting the presumed fact.[84]

These scholars believe that the "bursting bubble" theory gives too "slight and evanescent" an effect to presumptions.[85] Thus, they reject

---

82. Under Supreme Court Standard 107, it is permissible for the trial court to instruct the jury as to the permissive inference. The validity of the procedure is questionable given the large number of inferences possible in any given case and the fact that the trial judge gives no instruction as to the vast majority of them.

83. *See* § 4.08.

84. 2 McCormick on Evidence, *supra* note 75 § 344, at 446–47.

85. Edmund M. Morgan & John M. Maguire, *Looking Backward and Forward at Evidence*, 50 Harv. L. Rev. 909, 913 (1937).

the view that presumptions disappear on the presentation of evidence sufficient to support the non-existence of the presumed fact.[86] Instead, they assert that once a presumption is raised by proof of the foundational facts, the *burden of persuasion* as to the existence of the presumed fact shifts to the opponent.[87] To use the landlord-tenant hypothetical, if the jury finds that P properly addressed, stamped, and mailed the letter sufficiently in advance of the accident, D must now prove it is more likely than not that he never received the letter or suffer a finding that he did.

The battle between the Thayer–Wigmore and Morgan–McCormick views of presumptions is exemplified dramatically in Title VII employment discrimination cases. Even though the cases speak in the language of burdens rather than that of presumptions, pressing considerations of policy bear heavily on the process of proof, and the Court has dealt with the question of whether "prima facie" evidence offered by the employee shifts the burden of persuasion or only of production to the employer on the issue of discrimination. For a time, the Supreme Court's decisions might have supported a shifting of the burden of persuasion (consistent with the Morgan–McCormick theory of presumptions).[88] It now seems clear, however, that only the burden of production shifts to the employer.[89]

86. *See* Edmund M. Morgan, Some Problems of Proof 74–81 (1956); Edward W. Cleary, *Presuming and Pleading: An Essay on Juristic Immaturity*, 12 Stan. L. Rev. 5, 18 (1957); Alfred L. Gausewitz, *Presumptions in a One-Rule World*, 5 Vand. L. Rev. 324, 342 (1952); Morgan & Maguire, *supra* note 85, at 913.

87. McCormick agreed with Morgan in rejecting the Thayer–Wigmore theory, though he tended to emphasize the usefulness of jury instructions as a way to assure that presumptions retain their effectiveness even in the face of evidence challenging the presumed fact. He argued that the jury should be instructed about the existence of the presumption and about its power to make a factual finding consistent with the presumption even in the face of evidence challenging the presumed fact. Charles T. McCormick, Handbook on the Law of Evidence §§ 311, 316 (1954).

88. In McDonnell Douglas Corp. v. Green, 411 U.S. 792 (1973), the Supreme Court held that employee has the burden of proving by a preponderance of the evidence a "prima facie case" of discrimination. Upon such proof, the burden shifts to the employer "to articulate some legitimate, nondiscriminatory reason for the employee's rejection." *Id.* at 802. If the employer succeeds, the employee then has an opportunity to prove by a preponderance of the evidence that the employer's alleged reasons were pretextual. *Id.* at 804. Some

years later, in Price Waterhouse v. Hopkins, 490 U.S. 228 (1989), the Court held that once the employee shows that her gender played a part in the decision not to promote her to partnership, the employer had the burden of persuasion on the issue whether decision was unlawfully discriminatory.

89. In Texas Dept. of Community Affairs v. Burdine, 450 U.S. 248, (1981), the Court held that where the employee proves a prima facie case of discrimination, the employer bore only the burden of explaining clearly the nondiscriminatory reasons for its actions, and did not have burden of persuasion on issue of nondiscriminatory intent. The Court held that "[t]he ultimate burden of persuading the trier of fact that the defendant intentionally discriminated against the plaintiff remains at all times with the plaintiff." *Id.* at 253. *See also* Reeves v. Sanderson Plumbing Products, Inc., 530 U.S. 133 (2000) (in age discrimination action, employee's prima facie evidence of discrimination may shift to employer "intermediate evidentiary burden" to produce evidence sufficient to support nondiscriminatory explanation for its action, but once it does so, presumptions disappear; plaintiff retains burden of proving that the employer intentionally discriminated against plaintiff; in case at bar, plaintiff offered sufficient evidence for jury to find that employer intentionally discriminated, thus supporting verdict for employee); St. Mary's Honor

Because the burden of persuasion shifts under the Morgan–McCormick theory once the proponent offers sufficient evidence to meet a burden of production as the existence of the foundational (basic) facts, a jury instruction is needed in most situations. There are several possibilities, each described and then followed by an example of an instruction based on the hypothetical slip-and-fall case:[90]

Examples

Description: If the proponent's evidence of the existence of the foundational facts is sufficient only to meet a burden of production, and the opponent's evidence of the nonexistence of the presumed fact is sufficient only to meet a burden of production, the court must instruct the jury that if it finds the foundational facts to be true, it must find the presumed fact to be true unless the opponent persuades the jury that it is more likely than not that the presumed fact is not true.

Application: If you find that the letter described by P was correctly addressed, stamped, and mailed two weeks before the accident, then you must find that D received the letter approximately two days after it was mailed unless D persuades you that it is more likely than not that he did not receive any such letter during the time in question.

Description: If the proponent's evidence of the existence of the foundational facts compels a finding of their existence, but the opponent's evidence concerning the nonexistence of the presumed fact is only strong enough to meet a burden of production, the court must instruct the jury that it must find the presumed fact to be true unless the opponent persuades the jury that it is more likely than not that the presumed fact is not true.

Application: I instruct you to find that P correctly addressed, stamped, and mailed to D two weeks before to the accident a letter as described in P's testimony. You must therefore find that D received the letter approximately two days later unless D persuades you that it is more likely than not that he did not receive the letter during the time in question.

Description: Regardless of whether the proponent's evidence of the existence of the foundational facts compels or merely allows a finding of their existence, if the opponent's evidence of the nonexis-

---

Center v. Hicks, 509 U.S. 502 (1993) (in race discrimination case where trier of fact rejected employer's asserted nondiscriminatory reason for demoting employee, employee was not entitled to judgment as matter of law); Wards Cove Packing Co. v. Atonio, 490 U.S. 642 (1989) (where employee offers statistical evidence to show disparate impact, only the burden of producing evidence of non-discriminatory purpose shifts to employer).

90. The examples are of instructions that do not directly mention the term "presumption" or instruct the jury to "presume" any facts. Other forms of instruction, including forms that address the matter in terms of presumptions, are possible. For extended discussion of alternative forms of jury instruction in the context of presumptions, *see* 2 McCormick on Evidence, *supra* note 75 § 344, at 450–52.

tence of the presumed fact is so strong as to compel a finding of their nonexistence, the court need not mention a presumption, and need only instruct the jury that the presumed fact is not true.

Application: I instruct you to find that D never received from P during the time in question a letter describing the condition of the stairway.

(3) Compromise positions. As is often the case with long-standing academic debates, there is more than a thread of validity to each position. The reality is that most presumptions are overwhelmingly based in probability, and have little or no fairness or policy purpose, while some have deeper substantive than probability-based roots, and some are almost entirely policy-based. Because of this, there is no reason to treat all presumptions in the same way. A theoretically simple approach is to treat probability-based presumptions under the Thayer–Wigmore theory, and to treat presumptions created largely for substantive reasons under the Morgan–McCormick view. This, in fact, is the approach of the California Evidence Code,[91] and it is eminently sensible in some cases.[92] The problem with the California approach arises from the nature of presumptions. Though some are entirely or overwhelmingly based on one consideration (generally probability, fairness, or policy), most exist for a mixture of reasons the relative importance of which is often not determinable. Different courts are likely to assign different levels of importance to the various factors, and thus treat the same presumptions differently.[93] Unless a legislature were to decide exactly how each presumption is to be treated,[94] the risk of inconsistency among courts is unavoidable.

If, then, the language of presumptions is to be maintained, there does not appear to be a perfect solution to determining their effect where the opponent offers evidence contesting the existence of the presumed fact. Though neither the Thayer–Wigmore nor the Morgan–McCormick approach operates satisfactorily in all cases, these approaches at least offer some degree of consistency and predictability. Middle-ground approaches such as that of the California Evidence Code are finer-tuned, but will often lead to less consistent and predictable results.

91. The California Evidence Code divides presumptions into those affecting only the burden of production (§§ 630–647), and those affecting the burden of persuasion (denoted burden of "proof") (§§ 660–670).

92. An approach based on similar principles, but which required the opposite conclusions, was that taken by the original version of the Uniform Rules of Evidence. Uniform Rule 14 (1953) provided that if a presumption has "probative value" (if it gives rise to a reasonable inference as to the presumed fact), it shifts the burden of persuasion, but that if the presumption does not have probative value, it shifts only the burden of production and disappears when sufficient contrary proof is offered. The drafters of the Uniform Rules eventually abandoned this approach in favor of a Morgan–McCormick position (all presumptions shift the burden of persuasion). Unif. R. Evid. 301 (1986).

93. *See* 2 McCormick on Evidence, *supra* note 75 § 344, at 454–55.

94. Note that although the California Evidence Code divides presumptions into two categories, its list is hardly exhaustive of all presumptions that can be found in the massive California Code, many of which are codified in Codes other than the Evidence Code.

Challenging Both the Foundational and the Presumed Facts

If the jurisdiction follows the "bursting bubble" theory of presumptions, this situation creates no additional complications. Once the opponent offers evidence sufficient to satisfy a burden of production as to the presumed fact, regardless of the evidence offered concerning the foundational (basic) facts, the presumption simply disappears, leaving the jury to decide the question as a matter of permissive inference.[95]

In a jurisdiction employing the Morgan–McCormick theory of presumptions, the matter is considerably more complicated. The court must consider the evidence offered on both sides concerning both the foundational (basic) facts and the presumed fact. An unadopted Federal Rule of Evidence attempted to set forth the possibilities, and what the trial court must communicate to the jury:

> When evidence as to the existence of the basic facts is such that reasonable minds would not necessarily agree whether their existence is more probable than not and any evidence as to the nonexistence of the presumed fact is such that they would not necessarily agree that its nonexistence is more probable than not, the judge shall submit the matter to the jury with an instruction to find in favor of the existence of the presumed fact if they find from the evidence that the existence of the basic facts is more probable than not and unless they find the nonexistence of the presumed fact more probable than not, otherwise to find against the existence of the presumed fact.[96]

It is highly unlikely that jurors would understand the complex set of instructions mandated by this approach. As one author has written, the complexity of the proposed rule is "[t]he strongest single argument in favor of [the existing Federal Rule] and against the Morgan approach.... It is ventured to say that not only does such an instruction, if understood, by its very structure result in a greater burden of persuasion being placed upon the party opposing the presumption than if the identical burden of persuasion had been initially placed, but that there is not one juror in a hundred able to understand the instruction as presented at trial."[97]

§ 4.11 Presumptions; The Problem of Conflicting Presumptions

What should a court do when two presumptions appear to be raised by the facts of a case, and the presumptions would require inconsistent factual findings? *Atkinson v. Hall*,[98] a paternity case, provides an illustration. To summarize a complicated set of facts, plaintiff claimed that

---

95. Of course, the opponent's evidence as to the nonexistence of the presumed fact might be so strong as to require a directed verdict or partial directed verdict.

96. Proposed Fed. R. Evid. 303(c), 46 F.R.D. (paper edition) 161, 214 (1969).

97. 1 Michael H. Graham, Handbook of Federal Evidence § 301.13, at 164 (4th ed. 1996).

98. 556 A.2d 651 (Me.1989).

the father of her child, which defendant denied. The child
al months after plaintiff married another man, though the
less than a year after the child was born.

es relied on presumptions. Blood tests performed on the
ed a 98.27 percent probability that he was the father. A
e provided that when blood tests show a 97 percent or
probability of paternity, a presumption of paternity is created
that can only be rebutted by "clear and convincing evidence." Plaintiff
asked the court to instruct the jury in accordance with this presumption.
Defendant relied on a different statutory presumption that a child born
during a lawful marriage is presumed to be the child of the husband
unless the party claiming otherwise proves the husband's nonpaternity
beyond a reasonable doubt. The trial court ignored both presumptions
and instructed the jury that plaintiff had the burden of proving paternity
by a preponderance of the evidence.

The Maine Supreme Court affirmed. Maine evidence law provided
that when two presumptions conflict, the court shall apply the presumption that is founded on weightier considerations of policy and logic, and
that if neither satisfies this test, both presumptions are to be disregarded. The court examined the two presumptions raised by the facts, and
noted that the presumption of paternity from the blood tests was based
on weightier considerations of logic, but that the presumption of legitimacy from marriage was supported by weightier considerations of policy
("to minimize official intrusion into marital and family relations"[99]). The
Court determined that the legitimacy presumption was at least as
weighty as the paternity presumption, and hence that the trial judge did
not prejudice the plaintiff's case by discarding both presumptions and
sending the case to the jury with instructions that the plaintiff bore the
burden of persuasion.

Many cases of conflicting presumptions have involved the validity of
a second marriage. One presumption is that a ceremonial marriage is
valid; another is that a person's original married status continued. In
these cases, a court could disregard both presumptions and leave the
question of the validity of the second marriage to the jury. Apparently,
however, many courts do not disregard the conflicting presumptions in
these cases, but hold that the presumption of the validity of a marriage
is stronger, and validate the second marriage.[100]

No single approach to the conflicting presumptions problem can be
ventured. Thayer believed that in such cases, both presumptions should
be ignored and the jury left to weigh the logical inferences arising from
the foundational facts.[101] In some circumstances, this seems to be the
most appropriate course of action. In other cases, particularly where one

99. *Id.* at 653.

100. *See* 2 McCormick on Evidence § 344, at 449 (5th ed. John W. Strong ed. 1999) (*citing* cases).

101. Thayer, A Preliminary Treatise on Evidence at the Common Law 346 (1898). Wigmore agreed. 9 John H. Wigmore, Evidence in Trials at Common Law § 2493 (James H. Chadbourn rev. 1981).

of the presumptions is considerably more grounded in substantive policy than the other, perhaps it is better to give effect to the policy-based presumption, but to stress to the jury that it should examine the facts closely to determine whether the presumption has been rebutted.[102] Many courts have followed this type of approach, seeking to give effect to the "weightier" presumption.[103] Among the facts to be considered, of course, are the foundational facts supporting the other presumption, which may still be considered as a matter of logical inference. Such an approach, however, suffers from the familiar problem of lack of predictability. Courts are likely to view particular presumptions differently, leading to different analyses in similar cases. Other approaches to this difficult problem have also been considered,[104] though none perfectly resolves all cases.

§ 4.12 Presumptions; Presumptions in Criminal Cases

In the landmark case of *In re Winship*,[105] the United States Supreme Court held that the Due Process clause demands that a criminal defendant be convicted only "upon proof beyond a reasonable doubt of every fact necessary to constitute the crime with which he is charged."[106] In *Ulster County v. Allen*[107] and *Sandstrom v. Montana*,[108] the Court made clear that this requirement has left little or no room for the operation of true (mandatory) presumptions in criminal cases.

In *Ulster County*, four defendants were charged with illegal possession of handguns (among other items). Two of the handguns were found in the front of the car in a handbag belonging to one defendant, who was 16 years old. A New York statute provided that a firearm in an automobile is presumed to be possessed illegally by all occupants. The Supreme Court attempted to set forth clearly the difference between permissive devices and mandatory devices, and their treatment under the Constitution:

> Inferences and presumptions are a staple of our adversary system of factfinding. It is often necessary for the trier of fact to determine the existence of an item of the crime—that is, an "ultimate" or "elemental" fact—from the existence of one or more "evidentiary" or "basic" facts.... The value of these evidentiary devices, and their validity under the Due Process Clause, vary from case to case, however, depending on the strength of the connection between the particular basic and elemental facts involved and on the degree to which the device curtails the factfinder's freedom to assess the evidence independently. Nonetheless, in criminal cases, the ultimate

---

102. Morgan favored giving effect to the presumption founded on stronger considerations of policy. Morgan, *Some Observations Concerning Presumptions*, 44 Harv. L. Rev. 906, 932 n.41 (1931).

103. *See* 2 McCormick on Evidence, *supra* note 100 § 344, at 449.

104. *See id.*

105. 397 U.S. 358 (1970).

106. *Id.* at 364.

107. 442 U.S. 140 (1979).

108. 442 U.S. 510 (1979). For a brief summary of the cases leading up to *Ulster County* and *Sandstrom, see* 2 McCormick on Evidence, *supra* note 100 § 347.

device's constitutional validity remains constant: the
not undermine the factfinder's responsibility at trial,
idence adduced by the State, to find the ultimate facts
asonable doubt.[109]

uestion is whether the device, as applied, undercut the
le to determine guilt beyond a reasonable doubt based on
evidence. A device that operates in a mandatory fashion—one that
requires the jury to reach a certain factual finding based on the presence
of certain foundational facts—will usually do so, while one that operates
permissively—allowing the jury to reach conclusions it deems appropriate under the circumstances—will not. As the Court wrote:

> Because this permissive presumption leaves the trier of fact free to
> credit or reject the inference and does not shift the burden of proof,
> it affects the application of the "beyond a reasonable doubt" stan-
> dard only if, under the facts of the case, there is no rational way the
> trier could make the connection permitted by the inference. For only
> in that situation is there any risk that an explanation of the
> permissible inference to a jury, or its use by a jury, has caused the
> presumptively rational factfinder to make an erroneous factual
> determination.[110]

Note that the Court spoke in terms of "mandatory presumptions"
and "permissive presumptions." This usage can easily confuse the reader accustomed to thinking of "presumptions" as mandatory devices and
"inferences" as permissive devices. Nevertheless, for criminal cases, the
Court has chosen this terminology, dividing presumptions into permissive and mandatory types, and holding that the former is constitutional[111] while the latter is normally not.[112] As applied to the facts of the case
before it, the Court scrutinized not simply the language of the presumption, but the way in which the trial court instructed the jury about the
presumption. Analyzing the facts, the Court held that the device did not
operate in a mandatory fashion because the court instructed the jury
using permissive language.[113] This left only the question whether there

---

109. *Ulster County*, 442 U.S. at 156.

110. *Id.* at 157.

111. As the language quoted in text indicates, a permissive "presumption" will only be constitutionally infirm if the "pre-sumption" allows a finding of fact where a rational inference is not even permissible. Such a situation would be unusual.

112. The Court's language left open the possibility that a mandatory presump-tion would be constitutional where the ba-sic (foundational) facts, standing alone, would be sufficient to support the inference of guilt beyond a reasonable doubt. *Id.* at 167. It has been suggested that such a presumption would always be unconstitu-

tional. *See, e.g.,* Ronald L. Allen & Lee Ann DeGrazia, *The Constitutional Requirement of Proof Beyond Reasonable Doubt in Crimi-nal Cases: A Comment Upon Incipient Chaos in the Lower Courts,* 20 Am. Crim. L. Rev. 1, 12 (1982). It is indeed difficult to visualize a mandatory presumption that could survive the *Ulster County* test.

113. *Id.* at 160–65. The trial court in-structed the jury about the presumption but stated that it "need not be rebutted by affirmative proof or affirmative evidence but may be rebutted by any evidence or lack of evidence in the case." *Id.* at 161 n.20.

was a rational basis for a finding of guilt beyond a reasonable doubt, which the Court held did exist.[114]

In *Sandstrom v. Montana*,[115] a homicide prosecution, the Court dealt with a presumption that a person intends the ordinary consequences of his voluntary acts. Defendant claimed that the degree of the offense should be reduced because he suffered from a personality disorder that was aggravated by his intoxication. The Supreme Court reversed defendant's conviction, holding that as applied in jury instructions, the jury could have believed that the presumption was mandatory or shifted the burden of persuasion on the intent issue to the defendant. Even if the trial court's instruction was subject to interpretation as creating a permissive "presumption," the Court held that the instruction was unconstitutional because it could also have been interpreted as mandatory or as imposing on the defendant the burden of persuasion as to intent.[116]

In 1985, the Court revisited the subject in *Francis v. Franklin*.[117] Defendant, convicted of murder during a prison escape, sought federal habeas corpus relief. The only contested issue at trial was intent. Defendant claimed constitutional error in the trial court's jury instruction (1) that "[t]he acts of a person of sound mind and discretion are presumed to be the product of the person's will, but the presumption may be rebutted"; and (2) that a "person of sound mind and discretion is presumed to intend the natural and probable consequences of his acts but the presumption may be rebutted." The Court examined whether the instructions were unconstitutional because they relieved the state of the burden of proving defendant's guilt by creating a mandatory presumption of intent upon proof of other elements, and held that the instructions were in fact unconstitutional.

Even though the Georgia Supreme Court had interpreted the offending language as creating no more than a permissive inference, the Court held that a reasonable juror could have understood the charge as creating a mandatory presumption shifting the burden of persuasion on the element of intent once the state had proved the underlying acts. The words of the charge were stated as a command; even though the court instructed the jury that the presumption could be rebutted, the jurors reasonably could have understood that they must find intent unless defendant persuaded them to the contrary. Though any ambiguity in the instructions can be cured by the particular context, in this case neither the instruction concerning the presumption of innocence nor an instruction telling the jury that a person will not be presumed to act with criminal intention was sufficient. As the Court explained, "a reasonable juror could ... have thought that, although intent must be proved beyond a reasonable doubt, proof of the firing of the gun and its ordinary consequences constituted proof of intent beyond a reasonable doubt unless the defendant persuaded the jury otherwise."[118] Nor was the error

114. *Id*. at 167.
115. 442 U.S. 510 (1979).
116. *Id*. at 516–19.

117. 471 U.S. 307 (1985).
118. *Id*. at 319.

cured by a later instruction that "[a] person will not be presumed to act with criminal intention," because a reasonable juror could have understood the instruction to refer to a different element of the crime than intent. Even if not, the Court held, jurors might resolve the apparent conflict between this instruction and the invalid instructions "by choosing to abide by the mandatory presumption and ignore the prohibition of presumption."[119]

Finally, while not addressing the question whether this type of error could ever be harmless, the Court let stand the determination of the Court of Appeals that it was not harmless in this case.[120]

Although there remains much uncertainty even after *Ulster County*, *Sandstrom*, and *Francis*,[121] the cases do seem to establish certain propositions. True (mandatory) presumptions are almost always unconstitutional as applied in criminal cases against the defendant. Counsel must scrutinize not only the language of the device itself, but the way in which it is explained to the jury and any other instructions that might have cured any defect, because even a presumption that appears mandatory on its face can be saved, under the circumstances, by an instruction that unambiguously leaves the matter to the jury's judgment as a matter of logical inference. A "permissive presumption," on the other hand, will be constitutional if a reasonable person could conclude that it is more likely than not that the "presumed" fact rationally follows from the foundational facts.[122]

§ 4.13 Presumptions; The Federal Rules of Evidence and Presumptions

The Federal Rules of Evidence only address the subject of presumptions in civil cases. Rule 301 provides the basic rule:

> In all civil actions and proceedings not otherwise provided for by Act of Congress or by these rules, a presumption imposes on the party against whom it is directed the burden of going forward with evidence to rebut or meet the presumption, but does not shift to such party the burden of proof in the sense of the risk of nonpersua-

---

119. *Id.* at 322.

120. *Id.* at 325–26.

121. *See* 1 Michael H. Graham, Handbook of Federal Evidence § 303.4, at 186–93 (4th ed. 1996). For discussion of the use of presumptions against the criminal defendant, *see* Ronald J. Allen, *Structuring Jury Decisionmaking in Criminal Cases: A Unified Constitutional Approach to Evidentiary Devices*, 94 Harv. L. Rev. 321 (1980); Charles R. Nesson, *Rationality, Presumptions, and Judicial Comment: A Response to Professor Allen*, 94 Harv. L. Rev. 1574 (1981); Stephen Saltzburg, *Burdens of Persuasion in Criminal Cases: Harmonizing*

the Views of the Justices, 20 Am. Crim. L. Rev. 393 (1983).

122. Special problems are also created by the use of affirmative defenses in criminal cases. The Supreme Court has held that there are limits to the state's ability to create affirmative defenses, holding that such defenses are permissible as long as they do not simply negative an element of the crime. Patterson v. New York, 432 U.S. 197, 210 (1977). Determining when that is the case is a difficult question of interpretation; the law needs further development. For further discussion of affirmative defenses in this context, *see* 2 McCormick on Evidence, *supra* note 100 § 348.

sion, which remains throughout the trial upon the party on whom it was originally cast.[123]

At first glance, it appears that the language of Rule 301 adopts the pure "bursting bubble" theory of presumptions, and some authorities have so stated.[124] Once a presumption goes into effect, it shifts to the opponent only the burden of going forward, not the burden of persuasion. However, the language and legislative history of Rule 301 leave some room for doubt as to the drafters' intent. While it is clear that the drafters rejected the Morgan–McCormick view, but it is not so clear that they opted for full adoption of the "bursting bubble" theory, either. At one point, for example, the Conference Committee report states that "[i]f the adverse party does offer evidence contradicting the presumed fact, the court cannot instruct the jury that it may *presume* the existence of the presumed fact from proof of the basic facts. The court may, however, instruct the jury that it may infer the existence of the presumed fact from proof of the basic facts."[125] This appears to suggest that some remnant of the presumption may in fact outlive the admission of evidence contradicting the presumed fact. The authors of one treatise have argued that the Rule in fact adopt aspects of the Morgan–McCormick and "true" Thayer–Wigmore theories.[126]

Whatever the actual approach of Rule 301, it is undercut to some degree by Rule 302, which provides that "the effect of a presumption respecting a fact which is an element of a claim or defense as to which State law supplies the rule of decision" is to be decided in accordance with state law. Thus, in cases brought in federal court by virtue of diversity of citizenship, Rule 301 generally will not determine the effect of a presumption. Instead, the parties must look to the state's law.

As noted above, the Federal Rules do not address presumptions in criminal cases. The Advisory Committee proposed such a rule,[127] but Congress declined to adopt it. In federal criminal cases, therefore, the

---

123. Fed. R. Evid. 301.

124. *See, e.g.*, 1 Michael H. Graham, Handbook of Federal Evidence § 301.12, at 158 (4th ed. 1996). *See also* In re Yoder Co., 758 F.2d 1114, 1120 (6th Cir.1985) (stating that most commentators take the position that Rule 301 embodies the "bursting bubble" approach).

125. H.R. Fed. Rules of Evidence, Conf. Rep. No. 1597, 93d Cong., 2d Sess., at 5 (1974); 1974 U.S. Code Cong. & Ad. News 7098, 7099 (emphasis in original).

126. 21 Charles A. Wright & Kenneth W. Graham, Jr., Federal Practice and Procedure (Evidence) § 5122 (1977). The authors state:

Rule 301 ... creates a presumption that is neither Thayer–Wigmore nor Morgan–McCormick. Since the effect of Rule 301

is to increase the number of cases that are decided by the jury rather than the judge, it leans toward the Morgan–McCormick point of view. On the other hand, the mandatory effect of the Rule 301 presumption is limited to taking the case to the jury; thereafter, it has only such effect as the jury chooses to give it. In this respect, the Rule may be said to resemble the true Thayer–Wigmore theory. Since the Rule contemplates telling the jury about the presumption in most cases, it adopts a policy advanced by Professor McCormick.... The Rule 301 presumption operates only against the judge; insofar as the jury is concerned it is simply an authorized inference.

Id. at 572–73. For discussion the actual views of Thayer and Wigmore, *see* § **4.10**.

127. Proposed Fed. R. Evid. 303.

law of presumptions will be governed by judicial interpretation of the Constitution's demands, as discussed in a previous section.[128]

128. *See* § **4.12.**

Chapter 5

RELEVANCY AND ITS LIMITS

Table of Sections

GENERAL CONCEPTS OF RELEVANCY [FRE 401–403]

CHARACTER AND OTHER MISCONDUCT EVIDENCE

THE SUBSEQUENT REMEDIAL MEASURES RULE [FRE 407]

THE OFFERS IN COMPROMISE RULE (SETTLEMENT NEGOTIATIONS AND AGREEMENTS) [FRE 408]

OTHER OBJECTIONS BASED ON RELEVANCY AND ITS LIMITS

GENERAL CONCEPTS OF RELEVANCY [FRE 401–403]

§ 5.01　The Minimal Relevancy Requirement of Rule 401

Federal Rules of Evidence 401, 402, and 403 establish general principles of relevancy and general limits on the admission of relevant evidence. They are supplemented in many situations by more specific rules, such as those governing character evidence.[1]

Rule 401 provides that an item of evidence is relevant if it has "any tendency to make the existence of any fact that is of consequence to the determination of the action more probable or less probable than it would be without the evidence."[2] Rule 402 sets forth the general rule that relevant evidence is admissible except as otherwise provided by rule, statute, or constitution.[3] The rule also states that irrelevant evidence is not admissible. Rule 403 provides that even if relevant, evidence may be excluded if its probative value is substantially outweighed by considerations of unfair prejudice, waste of time, or confusion of issues.[4]

Rule 401 adopts a very broad concept of relevancy. Almost anything that a rational lawyer would attempt to offer into evidence would be "relevant" within the meaning of Rule 401 because it would have some minimal effect on the probability that a particular proposition of consequence to the case is true or false.[5] In a personal injury case, the fact that the defendant had a fight with his wife on the morning of the accident that is the subject of the suit might be minimally probative of a

1. Fed. R. Evid. 404–415.

2. Fed. R. Evid. 401.

3. Fed. R. Evid. 402. For an expansive interpretation of this part of Rule 402, *see* Edward J. Imwinkelried, *Federal Rule of Evidence 402: The Second Revolution*, 6 Rev. Litig. 129 (1987) (arguing that the first sentence of Rule 402 abolishes common law rules, such as the *Frye* test, that Congress failed to codify in the Federal Rules of Evidence). The Supreme Court offered substantial support for this expansive interpretation of the Rules by ruling that the drafters did indeed intend to abolish the more restrictive *Frye* test for admissibility of novel scientific evidence, and replace that test with a standard of relevancy and reliability. Daubert v. Merrell Dow Pharmaceuticals, 509 U.S. 579 (1993). *See* **Ch. 10.**

4. Fed. R. Evid. 403.

5. *See* Fed. R. Evid. 401 advisory committee's note (evidence is relevant if it makes the existence of a fact " 'more probable or less probable than it would be without the evidence' "). *See, e.g.*, United States v. Casares–Cardenas, 14 F.3d 1283, 1287 (8th Cir.1994) (in conspiracy case, evidence that woman with same surname as co-defendant was captured with defendant during case-related illegal entry was relevant, even though it did not conclusively show link to co-defendant); Conway v. Chemical Leaman Tank Lines, Inc., 525 F.2d 927, 930 (5th Cir.1976) (Rule 401's definition of relevant is "generous" and includes background information); International Merger & Acquisition Consultants, Inc. v. Armac Enters., 531 F.2d 821, 823 (7th Cir.1976) (Rule 401 provides "rather liberal standard" of relevancy); David Crump, *On the Uses of Irrelevant Evidence*, 34 Hous. L. Rev. 1, 6 (1997) ("the relevancy 'standard' in Rule 401 is no standard at all, because it indiscriminately admits every arguable proposition no matter how low its probative value").

fact at issue (perhaps he was not paying attention to his driving because he was thinking about domestic problems). Yet though "relevant" within the meaning of 401, the court would almost certainly exclude the evidence as a waste of time (and possibly for reasons of unfair prejudice) under Rule 403.[6]

§ 5.02 Logical and Legal Relevancy

The term *logically relevant* has sometimes been used to refer to evidence that has any tendency in logic to establish a proposition, while *legally relevant* has sometimes been used to refer to evidence whose probative value is great enough to justify the delay, expense, prejudice, or confusion that is involved in considering it.[7] The Federal Rules of Evidence do not use these terms, but the concept of "logical relevancy" is in effect embodied in Rule 401, while evidence that previously might have been called "logically relevant but not legally relevant" could now be described as "relevant under Rule 401 but not admissible because of Rule 403."[8]

§ 5.03 Relevancy and Materiality; Dealing with Evidence Offered on a Conceded Issue

Relevancy is sometimes contrasted with *materiality*. While those two terms probably have as many meanings as they do users, the following distinction is as common as any. Evidence is irrelevant if it has no tendency in logic to establish the fact that the proponent asserts the evidence will help prove. Evidence is immaterial when, although it has a tendency in logic to establish the fact that it is offered to prove, that fact is not in issue.[9] For example, the fact might have been removed as an issue because of an admission in the pleadings.

To apply this terminology, imagine a slander case in which plaintiff alleges that defendant falsely called plaintiff a thief. If defendant offers evidence that plaintiff was seen on the street corner selling new gold watches for five dollars apiece, that evidence is relevant to show that the slanderous statement was true. However, if the defense of truth had been eliminated from the case because defendant admitted in the plead-

---

6. *See* Fed. R. Evid. 403 advisory committee's note.

7. *See, e.g.,* Cotton v. United States, 361 F.2d 673, 676 (8th Cir.1966) (although evidence that some people who pass counterfeit bills are innocent is logically relevant in counterfeiting trial, evidence is not legally relevant because it is potentially confusing). *See also* 1A John H. Wigmore, Evidence in Trials at Common Law § 28 (Peter Tillers rev. 1983) (stating that the standard for "legal relevancy" is higher than that for logical relevancy). To avoid creating confusion, we will eschew the term "legal relevancy" and instead discuss the precise principle under which logically rele-

vant evidence might be excluded in a given situation.

8. *See* Fed. R. Evid. 401, 403 advisory committee's note.

9. *See, e.g.,* 1 John H. Wigmore, Evidence In Trials at Common Law § 2, at 18 (Peter Tillers rev. 1983) (explaining distinction between materiality and relevancy); United States v. Williams, 545 F.2d 47, 50 (8th Cir.1976) (evidence concerning state insurance statutes and regulations relevant to insurance agent's knowledge of law, but inadmissible in mail fraud prosecution against insurance purchaser because agent's knowledge of law not a material issue).

ings that the statement was false, then the evidence, though relevant, would be "immaterial" because it would have no bearing on any issue to be tried.

The federal rules do not use the term "immaterial." Evidence that previously would have been described as "immaterial" is now "irrelevant" within the meaning of Federal Rule of Evidence 401 if, in the language of the Rule, it is not "of consequence" to the determination of the action.[10] Suppose, for example, that in a prosecution for forgery of a check, defendant admits signing another person's name to the check, but wishes to offer evidence that a week later, she "covered" the check with her own money. This evidence would be irrelevant—not "of consequence"—because it would not affect her guilt of the crime; evidence of later remorse has no bearing on defendant's state of mind at the time she forged the check.[11]

Where evidence is offered on an issue of consequence to the case, but which has been conceded, the Federal Rules take a somewhat different position. For example, suppose that in a personal injury case, plaintiff alleges that defendant's negligent driving caused permanent disability. Plaintiff makes no claim for punitive damages. Defendant, knowing that the evidence of negligence is overwhelming, and wishing to avoid exposing the jury to damaging details of her conduct, admits negligence but disputes the amount of damages.[12] At trial, plaintiff offers evidence that the defendant was intoxicated at the time of the accident. Assuming that the evidence of intoxication has no bearing on any issue other than that of liability, which has been conceded, some jurists using pre-Federal Rules terminology would have excluded the evidence as irrelevant,[13] and a number of states would do the same today under their own codes.[14] The federal rules, however, would treat such evidence as relevant but exclude it as a waste of time or prejudicial under Rule 403.[15]

---

10. *See* Fed. R. Evid. 401 advisory committee's note; 2 Weinstein's Federal Evidence § 401.04[3] (2d ed. Joseph M. McLaughlin ed. 1997).

11. Repayment is not a defense to a forgery charge. *See* United States v. Wilson, 28 C.M.R. 844, 850, 1959 WL 3562 (A.F.B.R. 1959) (military law); People v. Morris, 92 P.2d 644, 645 (Cal.App.1939). *See also* 37 C.J.S., Forgery § 41 (1943).

12. For results in cases in which this tactic has been used, *see* Annotation, *Admission of Liability as Affecting Admissibility of Evidence as to the Circumstances of Accident on Issue of Damages in a Tort Action for Personal Injury, Wrongful Death, or Property Damage*, 80 A.L.R.2d 1224 (1961); Jarvis v. Hall, 210 N.E.2d 414 (Ohio App.1964) (where defendant admits liability, evidence that defendant was driving while drunk inadmissible).

13. *See, e.g.,* 9 John H. Wigmore, Evidence in Trials at Common Law § 2591, at

824 (James H. Chadbourn rev. 1981) ("A fact that is judicially admitted [e.g., by being admitted in the pleadings] *needs* no evidence from the party benefiting by the admission. But his evidence, if he chooses to offer it, *may* even be *excluded;* first, because it is now immaterial to the issues ..." [emphasis in original]).

14. *See, e.g.,* Cal. Evid. Code § 210 (West 1966) ("Relevant evidence" means evidence ... having any tendency in reason to prove or disprove any *disputed fact* that is of consequence to the "determination of the action") (emphasis added).

15. Fed. R. Evid. 401 advisory committee's note ("[t]he fact to which the evidence is directed need not be in dispute. While situations will arise which call for the exclusion of evidence offered to prove a point conceded by the opponent, the ruling should be made on the basis of such considerations as waste of time and undue prejudice ..., rather than under any general

The importance of the Federal Rules' broad concept of relevance in relation to issues conceded by one party was made clear by the Supreme Court in *Old Chief v. United States*.[16] In *Old Chief*, defendant was charged with being a felon in possession of a firearm, assault with a deadly weapon, and using a firearm in connection with a crime. He had previously been convicted of assault causing serious bodily injury, a felony that put him within the ambit of a federal statute prohibiting certain felons from possessing firearms. Prior to trial, defendant moved to prevent the government from mentioning any details of the prior conviction, except to state that he had been convicted of a crime punishable by imprisonment in excess of a year. In return, defendant offered to stipulate to the offense. The prosecutor refused the stipulation, arguing that he had a right to prove the essential facts of the case in his own way, despite defendant's offer to stipulate to one of the elements of the offense. The court denied defendant's motion, and at trial, the prosecutor introduced the record of conviction, which revealed defendant's prior conviction, including the nature of the crime and the sentence he received. Defendant was convicted, and the Ninth Circuit affirmed. In a 5–4 decision, the Supreme Court reversed. Though the Court rejected defendant's argument that the name of the prior offense was irrelevant,[17] it held that the trial court was obligated to grant defendant's motion pursuant to Rule 403.

Several aspects of the Court's discussion of Rules 402 and 403 have broad application.[18] In its discussion of relevance principles, the Court spoke broadly, emphasizing that "beyond the power of conventional evidence to support allegations and give life to the moral underpinnings of law's claims, there lies the need for evidence in all its particularity to satisfy the jurors' expectations about what proper proof should be."[19] As the Court explained:

> Unlike an abstract premise, whose force depends on going precisely to a particular step in a course of reasoning, a piece of evidence may address any number of separate elements, striking hard just because it shows so much at once; ... Thus, the prosecution may fairly seek to place its evidence before the jurors, as much to tell a story of guiltiness as to support an inference of guilt, to convince the jurors that a guilty verdict would be morally reasonable as much as to point to the discrete elements of a defendant's legal fault.[20]

requirement that evidence is admissible only if directed to matters in dispute").

16. 519 U.S. 172 (1997).

17. *Id.* at 178–79. The Court held that the nature of the conviction "was a step on one evidentiary route to the ultimate fact, since it served to place Old Chief within a particular sub-class of offenders for whom firearms possession is outlawed by [the relevant federal statute]. A documentary record of the conviction for that named offense was thus relevant evidence in making Old's

Chief's ... status more probable than it would have been without the evidence." *Id.* The Court made clear that the availability of alternative means of proving the prior crime did not render the proof offered by the prosecutor irrelevant. *Id.* at 179.

18. For consideration of the Court's discussion of Rule 403, *see* § **5.04**.

19. *Id.* at 188.

20. *Id.* at 187–88.

This reasoning, in part, is what gives rise to the adage that the prosecution is entitled to prove its case by evidence of its own choice—that defendant has no right to "stipulate or admit his way out of the full evidentiary force of the case as the government chooses to present it."[21] Aphorizing that "a syllogism is not a story," the Court wrote that the prosecution is entitled to the benefit of a colorful story with descriptive richness.[22] This led the Court to state a principle that, if carried to its logical extreme, would revolutionize the law of relevancy: in ruling on the admissibility of evidence, the court should take into account the prosecution's need to establish the "human significance" of a crime and to awaken a juror's "obligation to sit in judgment."[23] This suggests that the prosecution is entitled to offer evidence to show more than what is strictly necessary for logical inference when the extra evidence is needed to insure that the jury does not nullify substantive law and does not require greater certainty than proof beyond a reasonable doubt. The Court also noted, less adventurously, that in some cases the absence of proof can cause the jury to draw unfair inferences unfavorable to the prosecution.[24]

Nevertheless, the Court held that these principles had virtually no application in the case at bar, where the fact to be proved was the defendant's legal status, a decision to be rendered apart from the concrete facts of the present case but merely on the basis of some prior adjudicated events. As the Court stated, "[p]roving status without telling exactly why that status was imposed leaves no gap in the story of a defendant's subsequent criminality, and its demonstration by stipulation or admission neither displaces a chapter from a continuous sequence of conventional evidence nor comes across as an officious substitution, to confuse or offend or provoke reproach."[25] Here, then, the evidence the prosecution wished to offer carries the unfairly prejudicial risk that the jury will convict defendant because of his apparently bad character or simply to prevent him from committing future crimes regardless of his guilt in the present case. At the same time, the evidence has no greater probative value than the defendant's offered stipulation, which would have been "seemingly conclusive evidence" of an essential element of the crime.[26] Thus, in this situation, "the only reasonable conclusion was that the risk of unfair prejudice did substantially outweigh the discounted

---

21. *Id.* at 186–87. For example, in a pornography case, the prosecution would ordinarily be entitled to display the allegedly pornographic material to the jury, even if the defendant was willing to concede that the material was pornographic and wanted merely to dispute the element of possession. *See* Parr v. United States, 255 F.2d 86, 88 (5th Cir.1958) (*cited* favorably in *Old Chief*).

22. *Id.* at 189. *See also* Blue Cross and Blue Shield of New Jersey, Inc. v. Philip Morris, Inc., 138 F.Supp.2d 357, 369–70 (E.D.N.Y. 2001) (Weinstein, J.) (after *Old Chief*, relevance must be considered with eye toward whether the evidence contributes background to the story of the case, not merely to whether it is logically relevant).

23. *Old Chief*, at 519 U.S. at 187–88.

24. *Id.* at 188–89.

25. *Id.* at 190–91.

26. *Id.* at 186.

probative value of the record of conviction, and it was an abuse of discretion to admit the record when an admission was available."[27]

§ 5.04   Rule 403: The Universal Fall–Back Objection

Evidence that is otherwise admissible under the rules is still subject to the Federal Rule of Evidence 403 balancing test and can still be excluded if its reception would be too unfairly prejudicial, too misleading, or waste too much time.[28] (The sole exception to the Rule 403 balancing test is evidence that impeaches a witness with a conviction for a crime of dishonesty, in which instance Rule 609 mandates admission without balancing.[29]) Rule 403 thus provides an almost universal "fall-back" argument for the attorney seeking the exclusion of evidence. The rule applies equally to all parties in both civil and criminal cases.[30] Rule 403 also provides a basis for arguing, when evidence is admissible for one purpose but inadmissible for another, that the evidence should be excluded in its entirety because of the danger that the jury will not follow a limiting instruction.[31]

The task of balancing probative value against the enumerated dangers in Rule 403 is hardly a precise one. Neither the rule itself nor its accompanying commentary offers specific guidelines for the judge. The court must consider the dangers not in the abstract, but in the precise context of the case at hand.[32]

27. *Id.* at 191. The Court left open the possibility that the error was harmless. *Id.* at 192 n.11. For a similar issue in a civil context, *see* Briggs v. Dalkon Shield, 174 F.R.D. 369, 375 (D. Md.1997) (in action against IUD manufacturer, plaintiff was not required to accept defendant's stipulation to all elements of her case except causation and damages; stipulation would change focus of trial from evidence against defendant's product to defendant's claim that plaintiff's injuries were caused by sexually transmitted disease rather than IUD).

28. 2 Weinstein's Federal Evidence § 403.02[1][a] (2d ed. Joseph M. McLaughlin ed. 1997). *See, e.g.,* Trevino v. Gates, 99 F.3d 911, 922 (9th Cir.1996) (though jury could consider suffering of plaintiff's child as element of damages in suit based on killing of father by Los Angeles Police Department officers, it was nonetheless proper to prevent 5-year-old child from testifying; she had not been born at time of father's death and could contribute little to an understanding of her past or future suffering); United States v. Hicks, 103 F.3d 837, 842–44 (9th Cir.1996) (held, trial court did not abuse discretion in carjacking prosecution by admitting evidence of uncharged rape and murder of occupants; evidence went to "force and violence" element of carjacking offense); United States v. Merriweather, 78 F.3d 1070, 1077 (6th Cir.1996) (even

though evidence of unrelated drug crime relevant to intent and identity, Rule 403 requires exclusion where prosecution had better means of proof).

29. *See* **Ch. 9**. On the doctrine of limited admissibility, see § **2.09**.

30. One author has argued that in criminal cases, Rule 403 is unconstitutional because it prescribes a balancing test that places the major risk of erroneous decision-making on the defendant. D. Craig Lewis, *Proof and Prejudice: A Constitutional Challenge to the Treatment of Prejudicial Evidence in Federal Criminal Cases*, 64 Wash. L. Rev. 289 (1989). The author proposes revising the standard as applied to evidence offered against the defendant, requiring the prosecution to demonstrate that the probative value of its evidence substantially outweighs the danger of unfair prejudice (the opposite of the current standard).

31. *See, e.g.,* United States v. Beasley, 809 F.2d 1273, 1278–80 (7th Cir. 1987) (although evidence of prior drug offenses admissible to show intent in narcotics prosecution, trial court erred in admitting evidence without considering prejudicial effect because it was inadmissible to show defendant acted in conformity with prior conduct).

32. For discussion of the meaning and operation of the rule, *see* Victor J. Gold,

In the *Old Chief* case,[33] the Supreme Court attempted to clarify the trial court's task in applying Rule 403. The Court held that on objection, the trial judge should decide whether the questioned evidence raises a danger of unfair prejudice. If such a danger exists, the judge must "take account of the full evidentiary context of the case as the court understands it when the ruling must be made."[34] In particular, the judge should consider not just the evidence itself, but also the probative value and risk of prejudice of any available substitutes for that evidence. The Court continued:

> If an alternative were found to have substantially the same or greater probative value but a lower danger of unfair prejudice, sound judicial discretion would discount the value of the item first offered and exclude it if its discounted probative value were substantially outweighed by unfairly prejudicial risk.... The judge would have to make these calculations with an appreciation of the offering party's need for evidentiary richness and narrative integrity in presenting a case, and the mere fact that two pieces of evidence might go to the same point would not, of course, necessarily mean that only one of them might come in. It would only mean that a judge applying Rule 403 could reasonable apply some discount to the probative value of an item of evidence when faced with less risky alternative proof going to the same point.[35]

Among the alternatives a court might consider are verbal testimony in lieu of an exhibit, using a stipulation in lieu of verbal testimony, using pre-autopsy photos in lieu of post-autopsy photos, and using still illustrations in lieu of computer animations. The court may also tell lawyers to instruct witnesses to avoid true but inflammatory characterizations, though this approach has obvious dangers of making witness testimony seem artificial and of requiring witnesses to self-censor their most comfortable way of speaking.[36]

Limiting Judicial Discretion to Exclude Prejudicial Evidence, 18 U.C. Davis L. Rev. 59 (1984); Victor J. Gold, *Federal Rule of Evidence 403: Observations on the Nature of Unfairly Prejudicial Evidence*, 58 Wash. L. Rev. 497 (1983); Edward J. Imwinkelried, *The Meaning of Probative Value and Prejudice in Federal Rule of Evidence 403: Can Rule 403 Be Used to Resurrect the Common Law of Evidence?*, 41 Vand. L. Rev. 879 (1988).

33. Old Chief v. United States, 519 U.S. 172 (1997). For discussion of the Court's relevance analysis, *see* § **5.03**.

34. *Id*. at 182.

35. *Id*. at 182–83.

36. On instructing witnesses to rephrase testimony to avoid prejudicial characterizations, *see* United States v. Neill, 166 F.3d 943, 946 (9th Cir.1999) (even though defendant's residence in work release center was relevant because he was absent from the center on the night of the crime, it was error to allow witnesses to refer to the work release center in testimony because that reference revealed that defendant had a prior conviction; government should have prepared witnesses to testify using the phrase "Residential Program" instead of "Work Release Center"). (In authors' opinion, this decision might cause lawyers to rehearse their witnesses too much, overly reducing spontaneity and making it more difficult for the jury to judge demeanor. *Cf.* Bruce A. Green, *"The Whole Truth?": How Rules of Evidence Make Lawyers Deceitful*, 25 Loyola L.A. L. Rev. 699 (1992).

Following are examples of the operation of Rule 403:

Examples

Emotional appeal. Plaintiff offers a day-in-the-life film that not only depicts the plaintiff's daily activities, but also shows plaintiff in sentimental scenes with plaintiff's family. Rule 403 gives the trial judge discretion to edit out the portions of the film that are likely to have an undue emotional appeal.[37]

Waste of time, confusion. The plaintiff in a personal injury action offers evidence about defects in shotgun shells manufactured by defendant corporation at a plant other than the one that manufactured the shell that injured the plaintiff. The evidence has some probative value, but evaluating it would require extensive examination of differences between the two plants, which would entail dangers of confusing the jury and wasting resources. Rule 403 gives the trial judge authority to exclude.[38]

Ineffectiveness of limiting instruction. At a trial of D for murder by poison, where D claims that V, the alleged victim, took her own life, the prosecution offers evidence that before her death, V accused D of poisoning her. The prosecution claims that the statement, though inadmissible to prove the truth of what it asserted, should be

37. *See* Grimes v. Employers Mut. Liab. Ins. Co., 73 F.R.D. 607, 610, 612 (D.Alaska 1977). *Compare* Nichols v. American Nat. Ins. Co., 154 F.3d 875, 885 (8th Cir.1998) (where plaintiff claimed emotional distress from sexual harassment, court violated Rule 403 by admitting evidence that plaintiff had an abortion eight years earlier, even if the abortion could have provided an alternative explanation for emotional distress because the abortion was contrary to plaintiff's Catholic beliefs). *See also* State v. Smith, 857 S.W.2d 1 (Tenn. 1993) (no error in allowing witness to describe crime scene as victim lying in a "pool of blood"); Moreno v. State, 858 S.W.2d 453, 465–66 (Tex.Crim.App.1993) (in murder prosecution, trial court erroneously admitted contents of deceased victim's wallet, including photographs of friends, and a love poem written by his girlfriend; despite the "infinitesimally incremental" probative value of evidence, admission constitutes harmless error due to overwhelming evidence of defendant's guilt).

38. *See* Classen v. Remington Arms Co., 379 N.W.2d 133, 136 (Minn.App.1985) (interpreting Minn. R. Evid. 403, based on Fed. R. Evid. 403). *See also* United States v. McVeigh, 153 F.3d 1166, 1189 (10th Cir. 1998) (on review of conviction of Timothy McVeigh for bombing federal building in Oklahoma City, held, trial court did not err in excluding defense evidence that members of a survivalist group had discussed bombing targets including federal building; pro-

bative value in suggesting possible alternative suspects was weak and evidence could have led to confusion and speculation); Strauss v. Springer, 817 F.Supp. 1211, 1222–23 (E.D.Pa.1992) (in civil action for excessive use of force by police officer, plaintiff's expert offered testimony based on a review of internal police investigations of shootings by other police officers, to show custom of indifference to use of excessive force; held, other shootings evidence excluded as confusing to jury). *But cf.* United States v. Blackburn, 992 F.2d 666, 668–69 (7th Cir.1993) (held, in prosecution for bank robbery, district court did not abuse its discretion by allowing government to introduce testimony of exotic dancer that defendant gave her approximately one hundred one-dollar bills as birthday present shortly after robbery, despite fact that government admitted to court that the one-dollar bills were not the same bills as those taken from bank; moreover, though defendant's character may have been impugned by evidence that he frequented bar where the exotic dancer worked, testimony regarding defendant's patronage of bar supplied background narrative material linking him to the dancer). *See generally* United States v. Thomas, 86 F.3d 647, 652–54 (7th Cir. 1996) (in cocaine conspiracy case, evidence that defendants belonged to same Mafia Insane Vice Lords gang held admissible to illuminate relationship, but evidence of death threats by third parties should have been excluded as prejudicial).

admitted for the limited purpose of showing that V was not in a suicidal state of mind.[39] In this situation, an instruction to the jury to consider the evidence only to prove V's state of mind, and not to prove that D poisoned V, would almost certainly be ineffective. The low probative value of the evidence for this limited purpose, combined with the great potential for prejudice against D, calls for exclusion of the evidence under Rule 403.

Although Rule 403 gives the trial judge the discretion to exclude evidence on grounds that it will prejudice, confuse, or mislead the jury, one limitation should be noted. The trial judge must still respect the jury's role in assessing the credibility of witnesses and cannot exclude evidence on grounds that the testifying witness is unreliable. Weighing probative value against unfair prejudice under Rule 403 means accepting the accuracy of the witness's testimony and then assessing the probative value of the inferences to be drawn from it; the judge is not supposed to decide whether or not the witness is believable.[40]

Finally, it is not enough for the court to find that one of the enumerated dangers simply outweighs the probative value of the evidence; the danger must *substantially* outweigh the probative value. Thus, the greater the probative value of the evidence, the more difficult it will be to exclude it under this rule. And the converse is also true. If the probative value of the evidence is slight, the degree of danger necessary to satisfy the rule's standard need not be particularly great.

CHARACTER AND OTHER MISCONDUCT EVIDENCE

§ 5.05 The Prohibition on Use of Character to Show Conduct: In General [FRE 404(a)]

A definition of the character evidence rule is a helpful starting point in grasping both its limits and its breadth, though the generalities of the definition can only establish a starting point, not provide an invariable test for the decision of particular cases. In general, the rule against character evidence prohibits the reception of evidence illuminating a person's general disposition, when that evidence is offered to show action in conformity with that disposition on a particular occasion.[41] The rule is

39. *See* Shepard v. United States, 290 U.S. 96 (1933).

40. *See* Ballou v. Henri Studios, Inc., 656 F.2d 1147, 1154 (5th Cir.1981) (trial court erred in excluding results of blood alcohol test on ground that it did not find results credible).

41. *Compare* Fed. R. Evid. 404(a), which states that, with enumerated exceptions, "evidence of a person's character or a trait of character is not admissible for the purpose of proving action in conformity therewith on a particular occasion...." *See generally* Bonilla v. Yamaha Motors Corp., 955 F.2d 150 (1st Cir.1992) (held, in case

where personal injury plaintiff sued for design defect in motorcycle, trial court committed reversible error by admitting evidence of prior speeding offenses in support of defendant's claim that speeding was cause of accident; evidence not admissible either to show a predisposition to speed or to impeach plaintiff's denial of having a speeding record; to allow impeachment in this fashion would create a situation in which otherwise inadmissible evidence would inevitably come in (either because plaintiff admitted the prior speeding offenses, or because plaintiff denied them and they were received to impeach).

subject to exceptions that will be discussed later. See §§ **5.06–5.15.** At this point, we will examine the contours and limits of the general rule itself.[42]

Before considering how and when the rule operates, it is necessary to attempt to define "character." Interestingly, neither the language of Federal Rule 404 nor the official commentary to the rule define the term. However, in distinguishing "character" from "habit," the drafters wrote:

> Character is a generalized description of one's disposition, or of one's disposition in respect to a general trait, such as honesty, temperance, or peacefulness.... If we speak of character for care, we think of the person's tendency to act prudently in all the varying situations of life, in business, family life, in handling automobiles and in walking across the street.[43]

This description begins to explain the meaning of character, but does not complete the story. Not all general tendencies constitute character. For example, a stroke victim's propensity to forget would not be seen as a trait of character, but as a medical condition. And despite the Advisory Committee's reference to "temperance" as a character trait, one could argue that intemperate use of alcohol is a medical condition rather than a character trait—though admittedly this view has not achieved acceptance.[44] To constitute a character trait, one would think (though this is not settled) that the tendency must arise in some reasonable degree from the person's *moral* being—from traits over which the person has a substantial element of choice, and which cause observers to regard the person more favorably or less favorably upon learning of the individual's behavior.[45] This principle becomes more obvious when one observes the

42. For general discussion of the character evidence rules, *see* H. Richard Uviller, *Evidence of Character to Prove Conduct: Illusion, Illogic, and Injustice in the Courtroom,* 130 U. Pa. L. Rev. 845 (1982); Richard C. Wydick, *Character Evidence: A Guided Tour of the Grotesque Structure,* 21 U.C. Davis L. Rev. 123 (1987).

43. Fed. R. Evid. 406 advisory committee's note (quoting Charles T. McCormick, Handbook of the Law of Evidence § 162 at 340 (1954)).

44. *See* Reyes v. Missouri Pacific R. Co., 589 F.2d 791, 794 (5th Cir.1979) (evidence of plaintiff's "character trait of drinking to excess" to prove that he was drunk on night of accident inadmissible because it did not fall into any exceptions in Fed. R. Evid. 404(a)); 1 McCormick on Evidence § 195, at 686 (5th ed. John W. Strong ed. 1999) (describing "temperance" as a character trait). *See also* Quinto v. City and Borough of Juneau, 664 P.2d 630, 634 (Alaska App.1983) (in prosecution for driving while intoxicated, testimony that defendant had a community reputation for being

"a cautious, sober individual" should not have been excluded because it demonstrated a relevant trait of character). One court took note of an Air Force regulation that apparently attempted to distinguish between character-based and medically-based causes of excessive alcohol consumption of alcohol; Rowe v. United States, 167 Ct.Cl. 468 (1964) (citing Air Force regulation giving authority to discharge personnel for "unfitness" on grounds including "evidence of habits or traits of character manifested by ... chronic alcoholism" not caused by psychiatric disease).

45. Unfortunately, the legal literature reflects little effort to define character. Wigmore defined character as "the actual moral or psychical disposition or sum of traits...." 1A John H. Wigmore, Evidence in Trials at Common Law § 52, at 1148 (Peter Tillers rev. 1983). Elsewhere, however, he did not appear to confine the concept of character to aspects of the person that reflect her moral qualities. For example, he defined "character or disposition" as simply

examples listed in the drafters' notes to the Federal Rule. The drafters list "honesty, temperance, [and] peacefulness" in one place,[46] and use the terms "violent disposition" and "honesty" in another.[47]

While the statement of the prohibition offered here is necessarily general, it does provide guidelines to some of the principal features of the rule against character evidence:

1. The rule applies not only to evidence of reputation, but also to any evidence that illuminates character. Reputation is not character, but only one way of showing character. (One's reputation, after all, might be deserved or undeserved.) Evidence of a person's specific deeds, whether good or bad, is also character evidence if offered to show a person's general disposition as described above.

2. The rule only applies, however, to evidence offered to show a person's general disposition. When, for example, evidence of a prior bad act is offered not to show general disposition, but something other than general disposition, such as motive or opportunity to commit a crime, *see* **§ 5.16,** the ban on character evidence does not apply. Moreover, the ban does not apply when the trait shown by the evidence is too narrow and specific to be considered a trait of character. There is a varying and hard-to-define line between general character-based disposition, which embraces such traits as honesty, peacefulness, and the like, and specific disposition, which embraces evidence of "habit", evidence of modus operandi, and evidence of other relatively narrow tendencies of a person. *See generally* **§ 5.30**. Evidence of general disposition or proclivities is "character evidence" that falls under the ban; evidence of specific or narrow disposition is not "character evidence." The distinction, like many troublesome legal distinctions, is one of degree.

3. The rule bans only character evidence that is offered for the purpose of showing action in conformity with character on a

"a fixed trait or the sum of traits." *Id.* § 55, at 1159. The Model Code of Evidence offered a similarly broad definition of character as "the aggregate of a person's traits, including those relating to care or skill and their opposites." Model Code of Evidence, Rule 304 (1942). The authors of one treatise have noted the difficulty of defining character:

> The Evidence Rules do not define "character." That may seem quite justifiable; doesn't everyone know what the word means in this context? Perhaps. But suppose the prosecution in a criminal case offers evidence that the accused is a "professional gambler" or that the victim of an attempted rape was a "virgin." Is this evidence barred by Rule 404(a) when offered as circumstantial evidence

of conduct? Or take a civil case in which it is proposed to prove that the defendant was "clumsy" or "colorblind" or "accident prone" or a "wealthy playboy." Are any or all of these evidence of "character"? Consider also testimony that the accused was "a member of the Mafia" or a "skillful practitioner of the martial arts" offered to show a motive for a murder or the ability to commit it or the identity of the perpetrator.

22 Charles A. Wright & Kenneth W. Graham, Jr., Federal Practice and Procedure (Evidence) § 5233, at 349–50 (1978).

46. Fed. R. Evid. 406 advisory committee's note.

47. Fed. R. Evid. 404 advisory committee's note.

particular occasion—or, as it is sometimes put, character evidence is barred only when it is offered *circumstantially* to prove out-of-court behavior. When character is the ultimate issue, as in a defamation case in which truth is the defense, then the ban against character evidence does not operate because the evidence is not offered to show action in conformity with character, but to show character as an end in itself. *See* § **5.29**.

The principles set forth above may be represented diagrammatically. Suppose that "E" in the diagram set forth below represents the testimony of a witness offered at trial. "C" represents a general character-based disposition of the person whom the testimony concerns, such as the disposition to generosity or lack of generosity, to violence or nonviolence, to care or carelessness, or to obey the law generally. "A" represents an act of that person that is sought to be proven at trial.

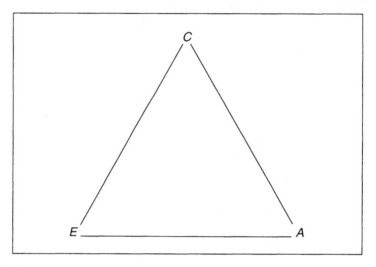

Evidence (E) falls within the character evidence ban only if it is offered to show a person's *general disposition* (C) en route to showing a specific act (A). If the evidence is offered to show general disposition without any further inference to a specific act (as is the case when character is the ultimate issue, *see* § **5.29**) then the character evidence ban does not apply. If the testimony leads to an inference that the act occurred *without the necessity* of any intermediate inference about general disposition, then the character evidence ban also does not apply. Examples of such testimony include testimony about habit (plaintiff always fastened his seat belt), modus operandi (defendant had previously robbed banks using an identical threatening note), or motive (defendant had debts from illegal gambling, and therefore had a motive to embezzle). Such testimony leads to an inference that the subsequent act was more likely to have occurred (the person was more likely to have fastened his seat belt, robbed the bank, or embezzled the money) without the necessity of drawing any inference about the person's general disposition or character. In other words, it is possible to go from

"E" to "A" on the diagram without the necessity of a trip through "C." The ban on character evidence prohibits only the use of the route E–C–A; it does not prohibit a trip from E to C when C is the ultimate issue and no trip to A is necessary; and it does not prohibit a trip from E to A if that can be done without going through C. If evidence offered to prove a specific act tends to make the doing of the act more likely both because it throws light upon general disposition and because it shows something else, such as motive, then the doctrine of limited admissibility applies and the evidence will ordinarily be admitted with a limiting instruction. *See* § **2.09.** However, the limits of Rule 403 and its common law analogues apply here as elsewhere; if the value of the evidence, when considered for its legitimate purpose, is substantially outweighed by dangers of prejudice, confusion, or waste of time, then it may be excluded even though, in theory, it would be acceptable if its use were restricted to one purpose.

Purposes of the Rule Excluding Character Evidence

It has long been accepted that character evidence is relevant in the minimal sense of having some tendency to make a fact of consequence more likely or less likely than would be the case without the evidence.[48] The fact that a defendant had previously robbed banks makes it somewhat more likely that the defendant is guilty of the bank robbery charged in the present case. That is, we are generally willing to accept that a person who has robbed banks possesses a general disposition toward this type of criminal behavior. Of course, the evidence is certainly not conclusive, but it does possess some probative value. Similarly, the opinion testimony of a close acquaintance of the defendant that defendant is the type of person who would rob banks is probative of defendant's relevant character trait and is circumstantial evidence of behavior. The same can be said for testimony concerning defendant's community reputation as a bank-robbing type of person. Yet, in contrast to some European systems, all of the evidence just discussed, whether in the form of specific instances of conduct, opinion, or reputation, is inadmissible if offered to show defendant's disposition to rob banks.

The reason most commonly given for the character ban is that the trier of fact would be unduly prejudiced by the information[49] and might

---

48. As Wigmore wrote, "[a] defendant's character, then, as indicating the probability of his doing or not doing the act charged, is essentially relevant." 1A Wigmore, *supra* note 45 § 55, at 1157 (emphasis in original). *See also* John Jay McKelvey, Handbook of the Law of Evidence § 108, at 149 (1898) ("Where the question is whether X. did or did not do a certain act, his character, if proved, might throw a strong light upon the issue, and justify an inference as to the act charged"); James B. Thayer, A Preliminary Treatise on Evidence at the Common Law 525 (1898)

("Undoubtedly, as a mere matter of reason, it often affords a good basis of inference").

49. *See, e.g.,* Michelson v. United States, 335 U.S. 469 (1948). Justice Jackson wrote:

The inquiry [into character] is not rejected because character is irrelevant; on the contrary, it is said to weigh too much with the jury and to so overpersuade them as to prejudge one with a bad general record and deny him a fair opportunity to defend against a particular charge. The overriding policy of excluding such evidence, despite its ad-

either overestimate the value of the evidence as proof that the defendant committed the crime charged[50] or decide to punish the defendant for being a bad person (or for the past misconduct) even if the trier was not convinced that the defendant was guilty of the crime charged.

Unfair prejudice is not the only concern, however. Commentators have long stressed at least two other reasons to exclude evidence of other acts. First is simple fairness and surprise: the supposed unfairness of surprising the actor with such evidence. This consideration overlaps with that of unfair prejudice, but encompasses basic fairness concerns as well. Though surprise is less of a concern under modern rules,[51] it can still be a concern in some situations. Second is the fear of over-complicating the issues of the trial, leading to confusion and distraction of the jury and undue lengthening of the trial. The danger of over-complication of issues is very real. As one writer has noted, "particularly if there is a dispute about whether the defendant committed the other acts, introduction of evidence concerning those acts could be time-consuming and distract the factfinder from the central issues in the case."[52] Thus, in some situa-

mitted probative value, is the practical experience that its disallowance tends to prevent confusion of issues, unfair surprise, and undue prejudice.

Id. at 475–76 (footnote omitted). *See also* 1 John H. Wigmore, Evidence in Trials at Common Law § 58.2 at 1212 (Peter Tillers rev.1983) (evidence of other acts is excluded, "not because it has no appreciable probative value, but because it has too much. The natural and inevitable tendency of the tribunal—whether judge or jury—is to give excessive weight to the vicious record of crime thus exhibited, and either to allow it to bear too strongly on the present charge, or to take the proof of it as justifying a condemnation irrespective of guilt of the present charge").

50. Empirical research suggests that "trait theory" is flawed. Trait theory relies on the notion that people possess relatively stable, general traits that manifest themselves consistently and predictably across situations. Today the more dominant theory, interactionism, posits that behavior in a given situation is governed both by a person's general tendencies and by the similarity of the situation to others the person has faced. Even with a large amount of data (an amount no trial court would presently allow), prediction is extremely difficult. For reviews of the psychological literature, *see* Susan M. Davies, *Evidence of Character to Prove Conduct: A Reassessment of Relevancy*, 27 Crim. L. Bull. 504 (1991); David P. Leonard, *The Use of Character to Prove Conduct: Rationality and Catharsis in the Law of Evidence*, 58 U. Colo. L. Rev. 1 (1986–87); Miguel Angel Mendez, *The Law of Evidence and the Search for a Stable*

Personality, 45 Emory L.J. 221 (1996); Miguel Angel Mendez, *California's New Law on Character Evidence: Evidence Code Section 352 and the Impact of Recent Psychological Studies*, 31 UCLA L. Rev. 1003 (1984); Andrew E. Taslitz, *Myself Alone: Individualizing Justice Through Psychological Character Evidence*, 52 Md. L. Rev. 1 (1993). *See also* Michael R. Gottfredson & Travis Hirschi, A General Theory of Crime 85–91 (1990) (developing a new type of propensity-based theory, arguing that criminality is linked to lack of self-control and appreciation for long-term consequences of committing the crime; authors find much evidence of different crimes committed by criminals rather than specialization in particular crimes).

51. The drafters of the Federal Rules of Evidence did not include "surprise" as among the dangers against which probative value should be measured when determining whether to exclude relevant evidence. The Advisory Committee appeared to believe that danger of surprise can be reduced by notice requirements and other procedural devices, and that its impact can be evaluated under the heading of "unfair prejudice." *See* Fed. R. Evid. 403 advisory committee's note. An amendment to Federal Rule 404(b), in fact, requires that in criminal cases, the prosecution provide the defendant notice of its intent to introduce evidence of the defendant's other acts, and of the general nature of the evidence it intends to offer. Fed. R. Evid. 404(b).

52. Richard B. Kuhns, *The Propensity to Misunderstand the Character of Specific Acts Evidence*, 66 Iowa L. Rev. 777, 777 (1981).

tions, the character evidence rule promotes adjudicative efficiency by preventing the tribunal from pursuing side issues about whether other crimes or acts were in fact committed.

Another justification for the character rule is aspirational. The principle that guards against trial by character is deeply embedded in English and American history and practice. The rule thus represents a substantive value about how people *should* behave in relation to each other. It tells us that in making formal judgments that affect a person's life or freedom, some kinds of considerations should be out of bounds. To be sure, we use evidence of character in our daily lives when deciding such diverse matters whether to hire an individual as a caretaker for our children or whom to entrust with a bank deposit. Nobody would deign to tell us we should not do so, and any effort to regulate our behavior to prevent us from considering such qualities would fail utterly. Moreover, we can live comfortably with inaccuracy in this realm of private behavior. If it turns out that the information we received about the person's past behavior or general character is simply wrong, the error will usually cause only a relatively small degree of harm (though at times, the harm can be great, as in marriage or employment decisions). It would thus be both impracticable and of little actual value to try to regulate the use of character evidence in the private dealings of daily life. Decisions made in the courtroom are fundamentally different. In that public forum established for the formal resolution of disputes about past events, we are forced to adjudicate facts; we can seldom avoid making concrete and largely final decisions about events. In this context, the harms that can be engendered by character-based decision-making can be extremely costly for several reasons. First, even though we are aware that "truth" can never be determined with certainty, factfinding error can be very costly. Naturally, error can have significant impact on the parties, whose financial well being, freedom, and even life will depend upon the outcome. To the extent admission of character evidence creates a significant risk of inferential error, decisions based upon it can be highly dubious. Not only do judgments based on erroneous factfinding affect the parties in the case before the court, but they erode public confidence in the civil and criminal justice systems, creating a very real risk of disorder. Second, and regardless of the accuracy of character evidence in a given situation, its use in formal adjudication violates the common aspiration that people should not be judged based upon their characters. The trial can and should be a model for formal decision making. The types of evidence we find acceptable in that setting should represent our best, not our most base, instincts about how we *ought* to behave. If we believe that we should avoid decision based on character, then the trial process should reinforce that belief through regulation of character evidence. As such, it can model the kind of decision-making to which we aspire.

It would have been possible to leave the question of character evidence to the discretion of the trial court, under some general guideline such as that provided by Rule 403. However, the common law had built up a structure of specific rules dealing with this species of evidence, and the drafters of the Federal Rules decided to follow the common law tradition in almost all respects. The result is a series of familiar, but complicated and sometimes arbitrary, rules governing the reception of the evidence. In a leading case, the Supreme Court stated that much of the law is "archaic, paradoxical and full of compromises and compensations by which an irrational advantage to one side is offset by a poorly reasoned counter-privilege to the other." Nonetheless, the Court said, the system had proven workable if clumsy, and to "pull one misshapen stone out of the grotesque structure is more likely simply to upset its present balance between adverse interests than to establish a rational edifice."[53]

§ 5.06 Exceptions to the Rule Against Using Character Evidence to Show Conduct [FRE 404(a)(1)–(3)]

The rule against using character evidence to prove conduct is subject to exceptions. Before examining these exceptions, however, we should emphasize that most of the litigation concerning character evidence does not deal with the scope of the exceptions, but rather with whether the character evidence rule applies at all. The rule has limited scope, applying only to evidence of general disposition offered for the purpose of showing action in conformity with disposition. Evidence of other crimes, wrongs, and acts is often received, not under an *exception* to the character evidence rule, but under the theory that the character evidence rule simply does not apply, because the evidence is being received for some purpose other than showing conduct in conformity with character. *See* § **5.16**.

The character evidence rule, limited as it is, has long been subject to three exceptions, recognized both at the common law and under the Federal Rules. Recently, a new exception was added to the Federal Rules. Thus, there are now four exceptions:

1. The defendant in a criminal case is permitted to offer character evidence, and if the defendant opens the door by offering this evidence, the prosecution may rebut it with contradictory character evidence. *See* §§ **5.07–5.08.**

2. With limits, the defendant and the prosecution may offer relevant evidence about the character of the victim of a crime. For example, in a homicide case in which the defendant claims that the alleged victim was the first aggressor, the defendant is allowed to call witnesses to testify that the victim had a violent character. When the defendant makes this attack, the prosecution may rebut by supporting the victim's character or by attacking the defendant's character for the same trait. *See* § **5.09.**

---

53. Michelson v. United States, 335 U.S. 469, 486 (1948).

3. Any party in a civil or criminal case may attack the character of a witness for truthfulness. After the witness's character for truthfulness has been attacked, it may be supported. *See* § **5.11**.

4. Recently, a new exception to the general rule against character to prove conduct was added to the Federal Rules. This exception allows evidence of other similar misconduct of the defendant in prosecutions for sexual assault and child molestation, and for civil actions arising from such misconduct. This controversial exception, which has also been enacted in some states, will be discussed in § **5.10**.

§ 5.07   Exceptions to the Rule Against Using Character Evidence to Show Conduct [FRE 404(a)(1)–(3)]—Evidence of Defendant's Good Character in Criminal Cases [FRE 404(a)(1)]

Both the common law and the Federal Rules recognize an exception to the rules against character evidence for defendants who wish to offer witnesses to attest to their good character.[54] In this respect the defense has an advantage over the prosecution. The defense has an absolute right to offer character evidence as part of defendant's case in chief; the prosecution may offer character evidence only if the defendant "opens the door." The reason for different treatment is unclear. One reason might be that because our system has a built-in preference for freeing the guilty over convicting the innocent, the dangers inherent in bad character offered against the criminal defendant are considerably greater than the possible inferential error invited by the defendant's use of good character evidence to prove innocence. Perhaps the exception is just a merciful dispensation to the defendant, or a compensation for other features of a criminal trial that throw the balance in favor of the prosecution. Certainly the danger that a person who has led an unblemished life might become enmeshed in a web of incriminating circumstantial evidence through pure coincidence leads to the natural feeling there should be some way to show the jury what the person is really like, and some way for one's friends to help in an hour of need. For that matter, there may in fact be a difference in the probative force of evidence of good and bad character, on the theory that proof of good character is considerably more probative of behavior on a particular occasion than is evidence of bad character.[55] From a more cynical perspective, the rule allowing defendants to present character evidence is likely to favor

---

54. *See* Fed. R. Evid. 404(a); Michelson v. United States, 335 U.S. 469, 476 (1948) (describing common law rule); David P. Leonard, *The Use of Character to Prove Conduct: Rationality and Catharsis in the Law of Evidence,* 58 U. Colo. L. Rev. 1 (1986–87) (reviewing common law and Federal Rule); Richard Uviller, *Evidence of Character to Prove Conduct: Illusion, Illogic, and Injustice in the Courtroom,* 130 U. Pa. L. Rev. 845 (1982) (reviewing entire structure of character evidence rules); Richard C. Wydick, *Character Evidence: A Guided Tour of the Grotesque Structure,* 21 U.C. Davis L. Rev. 123 (1987) (similar).

55. *See* 22 Charles A. Wright & Kenneth W. Graham, Jr., Federal Practice and Procedure (Evidence) § 5236, at 380–81 (1978).

persons who have status and connections, and this may have given the rule additional appeal to lawmakers who themselves would be able to present character witnesses if accused of crime.

Whatever the reason, it is well established that the defendant in a criminal case may offer evidence of good character. There are limits, however, on the form that the evidence may take. While evidence of actual good deeds by the defendant—for example, acts of honesty and kindness—might in reality be the most persuasive evidence of character, it is universally excluded. Specific acts are not admissible to show character, though to a limited extent the defendant's attorney is entitled to introduce some "background" about such matters as the defendant's occupation, education, family, and military service.[56] Instead, at common law, character evidence had to take the relatively colorless form of evidence about community reputation. Under the Federal Rules, the permissible form of evidence has been expanded to include a knowledgeable witness's opinion of the defendant's character. *(See* § **5.12** on methods of proving character.) Originally, reputation in the community was considered more probative than specific acts, representing as it did the community's collected wisdom, discussed and relied upon, about a lifetime of activity.[57] In modern society, where transient populations and breakdowns of community ties make it more difficult to derive reliable reputation testimony, evidence of specific acts is probably a better indicator of true character. Nonetheless, the limitation to reputation and opinion testimony is still a rational one, because restricting the testimony to that form saves time and avoids collateral conflicts about whether specific good or bad deeds actually took place.

A great deal of ink has been spilled discussing the question of what aspects of the defendant's character may be the subject of testimony. In general, the testimony has to concern a "pertinent" trait of character.[58] Thus, a defendant charged with a crime of dishonesty may not offer testimony about his character for peacefulness, but is limited to providing testimony about traits relating to honesty.[59] What about testimony about an extremely general trait, such as the defendant's proclivity to obey the law? Some common law courts permitted witnesses to testify about the defendant's reputation as a law-abiding person; others have required more specificity.[60] The exception for defense character evidence in the Federal Rules of Evidence refers to a the admissibility of a "pertinent trait of character"[61] and the advisory committee's note states

---

56. *See* State v. Stokes, 523 P.2d 364, 366 (Kan.1974) ("background information" and "biographical data" such as "place of birth, education, length of residence in the community, length of marriage, size of family, occupation, place of employment, service in armed forces and receipt of honorable discharge" not considered character evidence entitling prosecution to respond with evidence of bad character; defendant "entitled to let the jury know who he is").

57. *See* 5 John H. Wigmore, Evidence in Trials at Common Law § 1610, at 582 (James H. Chadbourn rev. 1974).

58. *See* Fed. R. Evid. 404(a)(1).

59. *See* 22 Wright & Graham, *supra* note 55 § 5236, at 385.

60. *See* 1A John H. Wigmore, Evidence in Trials at Common Law § 59 nn.1–2 (Peter Tillers rev. 1983).

61. Fed. R. Evid. 404(a)(1).

that proof is limited to "pertinent traits of character, rather than character generally,"[62] so it would appear that under the Federal Rule specific traits, such as honesty and nonviolence, are admissible, but general testimony that a person has "good character" is not.

§ 5.08 Exceptions to the Rule Against Using Character Evidence to Show Conduct [FRE 404(a)(1)–(3)]—Rebuttal by the Government of Defendant's Character Evidence [FRE 404(a)(1)]

There are two ways in which the defendant may open the door to attack by the prosecution on his or her character. The first is by producing favorable evidence about his or her own character, or, in some jurisdictions, attacking the alleged victim's character, thereby implicitly inviting comparison between the defendant's character and that of the victim.[63] Any of these situations may be called placing one's character *as a defendant* in controversy. The second is by taking the stand as a witness. This may be called placing one's character *as a witness* in controversy. The defendant in a particular case may do one without doing the other, or may do both or neither. The two forms of placing character in controversy lead to different consequences. By placing one's character *as a defendant* in question, the defendant opens the door to prosecution evidence about character traits relevant to the crime charged. When testifying, the defendant's character *as a witness* is in question, and the prosecution is permitted a different form of attack. Principally, this attack consists of introducing the prior convictions of the defendant that bear upon the defendant's credibility as a witness, though it may also take the form of putting on character witnesses who derogate the defendant's character for truthfulness. This attack on defendant's character *as a witness* is described elsewhere, under the rubric of witness impeachment. *See* **Ch. 7**. The present section describes how the prosecution may attack the defendant's character *as a defendant.*

When the defendant offers character witnesses who attest to the defendant's good character, the defendant has opened the door to rebuttal by the prosecution. Although it is often said that by offering character evidence the defendant has put his or her "character in issue," this phrase is technically incorrect. Character does not become an ultimate issue, in the sense that term is used in **§ 5.29**, merely because the defendant has offered character evidence. The ultimate issue is still whether the defendant committed the crime charged, not whether the defendant had a good or bad character. Character is merely an evidentiary fact that bears upon this issue.

---

62. Fed. R. Evid. 404 advisory committee's note.

63. An amendment to the Federal Rule of Evidence 404(a)(1) in 2000 provides that if the defendant offers evidence of a trait of the alleged victim's character, the prosecution may respond with evidence of the same trait in the defendant. This is true even if the defendant has not first offered evidence of her good character. For discussion of this rule, *see* **§ 5.09.**

Once the defendant has opened the door, the prosecution may offer character evidence of its own, and it may do so in one of two ways. First, the prosecution may call its own witnesses to offer evidence of defendant's character. Like the defendant's witnesses, such testimony must be in the form of reputation or opinion. Second, the prosecution may cross-examine defendant's character witnesses, and such cross-examination may include questions about specific instances of defendant's conduct that bear on the traits of character to which the witness testified on direct examination.[64]

This second form of attack is likely to be the most potent. The defendant's character witnesses must testify in the form of opinion and reputation, and may not describe specific good deeds of the defendant; but on cross-examination the prosecution may elicit testimony about bad acts or prior crimes that the defendant is believed to have committed. For example, in *Michelson v. United States*,[65] the defendant's character witnesses testified favorably about his reputation for honesty and truthfulness and for being a law-abiding citizen. On cross-examination, the prosecutor asked certain of the character witnesses the following questions:

"Did you ever hear that Mr. Michelson on March 4, 1927 was convicted of a violation of the trademark law in New York City in regard to watches?"

"Did you ever hear that on October 11th, 1920, the defendant, Solomon Michelson, was arrested for receiving stolen goods?"

One of these questions concerned a 20-year-old conviction; the other concerned an arrest which, so far as appeared, did not even result in conviction. Both involved specific acts, not general testimony about reputation or opinion. Nonetheless, the Supreme Court affirmed the conviction, indicating that the questions were proper.[66]

The theory on which the prosecution's questions were permitted in *Michelson* was that they were pertinent, not to the question of whether the defendant had actually committed the prior acts, but to the question

---

64. *See* Fed. R. Evid. 404(a)(1), 405(a). *See also* United States v. Holt, 170 F.3d 698, 701 (7th Cir.1999) (where part-time police officer charged with conspiring to transfer an automatic weapon called a character witness to testify about his good reputation for being a law-abiding person, court did not err in allowing prosecution to ask the witness about defendant's non-payment of child support and about sexual harassment allegations against defendant); United States v. Smith–Bowman, 76 F.3d 634, 636 (5th Cir.1996) (permissible to ask defendant's character witness whether he had heard that defendant, a Red Cross official, had used her Red Cross VISA card (a) to pay for a motel room for a rendezvous with her boyfriend and (b) to buy jewelry for herself); SEC v. Peters, 978 F.2d 1162,

1171–73 (10th Cir.1992) (trial court committed reversible error by allowing defendant to present impressive array of "good character witnesses" while refusing to allow SEC to cross-examine witnesses about sworn charges and past lawsuits against defendant for fraud and insider trading).

65. 335 U.S. 469 (1948).

66. The advisory committee's note to Rule 405(a) endorses *Michelson* and implies that the same questions would still be permissible. For cases presenting a different point of view about cross-examination on arrest records, *see* Commonwealth v. Scott, 436 A.2d 607 (Pa.1981); People v. Roberts, 479 N.E.2d 386 (Ill.App.1985); Kruse v. State, 483 So.2d 1383 (Fla.App.1986).

whether the character witnesses were actually knowledgeable about the defendant's reputation. If they had not heard about the arrest and conviction, the character witnesses were not fully knowledgeable; if they had heard, then one might question their criteria for good reputation.

The presentation of character evidence by the defense therefore opens the door to potentially very harmful questioning of the character witnesses about prior acts of the defendant, whether or not they resulted in conviction. However, there are significant limitations upon the prosecutor's freedom in using evidence of this nature. First, the prosecutor can only ask the questions, and must take the witness's answer. *Extrinsic evidence of the defendant's prior conduct is not admissible.* If the witness denies having heard of the prior conduct, the prosecution may not produce other witnesses to prove that the defendant in fact engaged in the character-destroying conduct.[67] Second, the prosecutor must have a good faith basis for asking the question. That is, the prosecutor cannot simply manufacture questions about prior convictions, arrests, or bad acts, but must actually have information indicating that these events occurred.[68] Third, because the misconduct is only admissible to impeach the character witness, it cannot be secret misconduct known only to the prosecutor. In the case of an opinion character witness, it must be misconduct that the witness reasonably could be expected to know about; in the case of a reputation witness, it must be misconduct that would have wings in the community.[69] Finally, the prosecution should refrain from asking hypothetical questions about whether the witness would testify differently if she assumed the defendant to be guilty of the charged crime.[70]

If the prosecutor questions character witnesses about prior acts of the defendant, the defendant is entitled to a limiting instruction describ-

---

67. *See* Fed. R. Evid. 405(b), and advisory committee's note thereto.

68. Michelson v. United States, 335 U.S. 469, 481 n. 18 (1948); 1 McCormick on Evidence § 191, at 677 (5th ed. John W. Strong ed. 1999); United States v. Wells, 525 F.2d 974 (5th Cir.1976); United States v. Beno, 324 F.2d 582 (2d Cir.1963); State v. Keul, 5 N.W.2d 849 (Iowa 1942). Logically speaking, the prosecution should be permitted to ask defendant's reputation witnesses about the arrest as long as there is a good faith belief that rumors were circulating through the community that the arrest had occurred, even if such rumors were untrue. (If rumors were circulating, and the witnesses had not heard them, the jury might question the witnesses' knowledge; if the witnesses had heard the rumors but nevertheless testified favorably about defendant's reputation, the jury might question the witnesses' judgment.) The Court recognized this illogical aspect of the rule, but retained the common law requirement of a good faith belief that the arrest actually

occurred, in order to prevent undue prejudice to the defendant. *Michelson*, 335 U.S. at 481 n.18.

69. *See* United States v. Monteleone, 77 F.3d 1086, 1090 (8th Cir.1996) (question about whether character witness had heard that defendant perjured himself before grand jury improper since witness would not know what had happened in secret grand jury proceedings).

70. United States v. Guzman, 167 F.3d 1350, 1352–53 (11th Cir.1999) (error, although harmless, to allow prosecution to question character witness with a hypothetical question asking whether witness's opinion would change if defendant was guilty of the crime charged); United States v. Mason, 993 F.2d 406 (4th Cir.1993) (court erred in allowing prosecutor to cross-examine character witness about whether witness would change mind if defendant was guilty of instant crime).

ing the way in which the jury is supposed to use the evidence.[71] Because the concept under which the evidence is admitted is a complicated one, the instruction is necessarily a hard one to understand and apply, but it should nevertheless be requested by the defense, if only to preserve the point on appeal if the instruction is not given. The instruction should state that the jury is not to assume that the incidents asked about actually took place, but use the evidence only to test the witness's standard for evaluating the reputation of the defendant.[72]

§ 5.09 Exceptions to the Rule Against Using Character Evidence to Show Conduct [FRE 404(a)(1)–(3)]—Character of the Victim in Criminal Cases [FRE 404(a)(2), 412]

The prosecution or defense will sometimes seek to offer evidence about the character of the victim in a criminal case. Such evidence is, of course, not admissible to show that the victim was a bad person who deserved to be a victim, but it may be admissible if it is relevant to a legal defense of the accused. Though it is possible for the issue to arise in other contexts,[73] the most common situations in which victim character is offered are homicide cases, in which the defendant claims that the victim was the first aggressor (and hence that the defendant should be acquitted on grounds of self-defense),[74] and rape cases, in which the defendant claims that the victim consented to the sexual act, and seeks to introduce evidence of her prior sexual conduct to show a proclivity to consent.

Homicide Cases

A defendant raising the claim of self-defense may seek to introduce evidence that the victim had a violent or turbulent character in order to persuade the trier that the victim was the first aggressor. Similarly, the prosecution may seek to introduce evidence of the victim's peaceable character to show that victim did not attack the defendant.

---

71. *See* Fed. R. Evid. 105.

72. One example of this instruction was given by the trial court in the *Michelson* case. The instruction stated:

> I instruct the jury that what is happening now is this: the defendant has called character witnesses, and the basis for the evidence given by those character witnesses is the reputation of the defendant in the community, and since the defendant tenders the issue of his reputation the prosecution may ask the witness if she has heard of various incidents in his career. I say to you that regardless of her answer you are not to assume that the incidents asked about actually took place. All that is happening is that this witness's standard of opinion

of the character or reputation of the defendant is being tested.

Michelson v. United States, 335 U.S. 469, 472 n. 3 (1948).

73. *See* 1A John H. Wigmore, Evidence in Trials at Common Law § 63 n.1 (Peter Tillers rev. 1983), suggesting that under the Federal Rule "in an embezzlement case, an accused might be allowed to put in the propensity of a victim to defraud insurers in order to show that the victim rather than the accused removed certain money from a safe."

74. Evidence of the victim's propensity toward violence would also be relevant in an assault and battery prosecution in which the defendant claims self-defense. *See* "Other Criminal Cases" discussion, *infra*.

In cases in which the victim's violent character was known to the defendant, the rule against character evidence erects no obstacle, and no exception is needed in order to make the evidence admissible. The evidence would be admissible, even in the absence of an exception to the character evidence rule, on grounds that it is not offered as evidence to show action in conformity with character; instead, it is being used to show the reasonableness of the defendant's belief in the necessity for violent resistance.[75] If the defendant believed that the victim had violent propensities, then that belief might form the basis for a claim that defendant's conduct was reasonable, whether or not the victim actually had that character, and whether or not the victim acted in conformity with it. The admissibility of evidence of the victim's violent character, when that character was known to the defendant prior to the incident, is clearly established.[76]

An exception to the rule against character evidence is needed when the defendant offers evidence of the victim's violent character, for the purpose of showing that the victim was the first aggressor, rather than for the purpose of showing defendant's belief in the victim's aggressiveness. Most jurisdictions, and the Federal Rules, provide for such an exception.[77] By use of reputation evidence or, in jurisdictions following the Federal Rules, by opinion testimony as well, the defendant may show that the victim had a violent character. In jurisdictions following the Federal Rules, specific instances of conduct are not admissible for this purpose, if the sole reason is to show that the victim had a general

---

75. In terms of the diagram in § 5.05, the use of the evidence does not require either an inference from E to C (it is not necessary that the victim have actually had a violent character, so long as the defendant believed it to be so) or a trip from C to A (it is not necessary that the victim have acted in conformity with character for the evidence to be probative of the defendant's subjective belief).

76. 1A Wigmore, *supra* note 73 § 63, at 1369; Smith v. State, 606 So.2d 641, 642–43 (Fla.App.1992) (trial court erred by excluding evidence of victim's specific acts of violence against defendant, his family and others, when defendant knew about the attacks and defendant pleaded self-defense); State v. Miranda, 405 A.2d 622 (Conn. 1978); People v. Lynch, 470 N.E.2d 1018 (Ill.1984); State v. Jacoby, 260 N.W.2d 828 (Iowa 1977).

Specific violent acts may be offered to bolster the accused's testimony that the victim bragged to the accused about her own past violent acts, even if the accused did not have other knowledge of those acts. In United States v. James, 169 F.3d 1210 (9th Cir.1999), defendant was accused of aiding and abetting manslaughter. She claimed self-defense, asserting that her acts were a reasonable response to the threat of attack by a person she believed to be very dangerous. The decedent had bragged to the accused about various atrocities he had committed. Some of his stories sounded far-fetched and fanciful, and the jury could have believed either that the accused invented them or that the decedent told the stories in a way that made them not readily believable. The jury, in fact, asked the court whether there were records to prove decedent committed those acts, but even though some of the stories could have been substantiated by court documents, the judge declined to answer the question and excluded the documents on the ground that only those specific instances known to the accused were admissible. The Ninth Circuit reversed, holding that the court should have admitted the evidence to corroborate the accused's testimony. The court's theory was that the fact that the decedent actually committed the acts made it more likely that he told the accused about them, and did so in a convincing and believable fashion. This, in turn, supported the accused's self-defense claim. The Ninth Circuit's theory is solid as applied to the facts of the case.

77. *See* Fed. R. Evid. 404(a)(2); 1A Wigmore, *supra* note 73 § 63.

disposition toward violence.[78] Of course, specific acts of violence by the victim are admissible if they are relevant for some other purpose, such as showing motive or a specific disposition to act violently toward a specific person. Thus, a husband's prior acts of beating his wife while intoxicated are admissible when offered to show, not that the husband was a generally violent person, but that he had a specific propensity to beat his wife, and hence that the wife acted in self-defense.[79]

Once the defendant has opened the door by attacking the victim's character for peacefulness, or has otherwise offered testimony to support the claim that the victim was the first aggressor, the prosecution may support the victim's character with evidence that the victim had a peaceable disposition. In some circumstances, the character of a victim can be supported even if the defense has not attacked it with evidence of bad character. Under the Federal Rules of Evidence, the prosecution can also offer evidence of the good character of the victim if, in a homicide case, the defendant has offered evidence that the victim was the first aggressor.[80] The defendant need not have supported the claim with character evidence; the right of the prosecution to support character is triggered by any evidence that the victim was the first aggressor, whether the evidence takes the form of character evidence or of testimony about what the victim did during the encounter that forms the basis for the prosecution.

In some jurisdictions, including the federal courts, when the defendant attacks the character of the alleged victim, the prosecution may respond by offering evidence of the same trait of the defendant's character.[81]

Rape Cases

At common law, some courts admitted evidence of a woman's character for chastity, in the form of either reputation testimony or specific acts testimony, to show that she had a propensity to consent, and therefore that she consented on a particular occasion.[82] This approach deterred the pursuit of rape complaints because of the victims' fear of abuse and degradation in the courtroom. Moreover, its premise

---

78. Fed. R. Evid. 405(a); United States v. Keiser, 57 F.3d 847, 856–57 (9th Cir. 1995) (though relevant, character evidence of the victim was properly excluded under Rule 405; defendant had shot victim but claimed it was done in self-defense; defense wanted to proffer evidence that in lobby outside courtroom, victim pointed to the defendant's brother and told his family and friends that he was "the fucker's brother" and to remember his face); United States v. Waloke, 962 F.2d 824, 830 (8th Cir.1992) (although evidence of victim's reputation for violence after drinking was properly allowed, danger of unfair prejudice and "collateral mini trials" warranted excluding ev-

idence in assault case of specific violent acts by victim).

79. See, e.g., United States v. McIntire, 461 F.2d 1092, 1092–93 (5th Cir.1972); White v. State, 717 S.W.2d 784 (Ark.1986); Worthington v. State, 405 N.E.2d 913 (Ind. 1980).

80. See Fed. R. Evid. 404 (a)(2).

81. See Fed. R. Evid. 401(a)(1), as amended December 1, 2000.

82. See 1A Wigmore, supra note 73 § 62; People v. Allen, 124 N.E. 329 (Ill. 1919); Graham v. State, 67 S.W.2d 296 (Tex.Crim.App.1933); Fry v. Commonwealth, 177 S.E. 860 (Va.1935).

that consent on one occasion with one partner is worthy evidence of consent on another is untenable in an age in which "one can presume that a woman will freely choose her partners, picking some and rejecting others, in line with highly personal standards not susceptible of generalization."[83] As part of a reform effort supported by the women's movement and by law enforcement officials, almost all state legislatures and Congress adopted "rape shield" legislation in the 1970s that limited the use of evidence of prior sexual conduct in sexual assault cases.[84]

Rape shield legislation differs from state to state, but all statutes have at least one common feature: evidence of reputation and sexual behavior is not admissible purely for purpose of showing unchaste character, as the basis for a further inference that the complainant consented to sex on the occasion in question. The statutes generally do allow prior sexual behavior to be admitted for certain limited purposes. Two widely recognized examples of admissible behavior are (a) the complainant's prior sexual behavior with the defendant, as opposed to behavior with other persons, and (b) evidence of the complainant's sexual behavior with other persons, when offered for purposes of explaining the physical consequences of the alleged rape—e.g., injury, the presence of semen, pregnancy, or venereal disease.[85] But the defendant may not present evidence of disease, pregnancy, or semen where the prosecution has not benefited from the evidence and has done nothing to open the door.[86] Other examples of admissible behavior, though not universally recognized, are instances in which the evidence is offered to show a motive for fabrication by the complainant[87] or to show other behavior so nearly identical to the behavior on the occasion in question

83. Vivian Berger, *Man's Trial, Women's Tribulation: Rape Cases in the Courtroom,* 77 Colum. L. Rev. 1, 56 (1977).

84. For a thorough and insightful review of this legislation, *see* Harriett R. Galvin, *Shielding Rape Victims in the State and Federal Courts: A Proposal for the Second Decade,* 70 Minn. L. Rev. 763 (1986). Professor Galvin reports that 48 states and the federal government have adopted reform legislation. *Id.* at 808. *See also* Ann Althouse, *Thelma and Louise and the Law: Do Rape Shield Rules Matter?,* 25 Loy. L.A. L. Rev. 757 (1992).

85. *See, e.g.,* Fed. R. Evid. 412; Mich. Comp. Laws Ann. § 750.520j (West Supp. 1987); Mass. Ann. Laws ch 233, § 21B (1986); Minn. R. Evid. 404(c).

86. *See* United States v. White Buffalo, 84 F.3d 1052, 1054 (8th Cir.1996) (where government made no effort to introduce semen evidence, defendant was not entitled to present evidence of rape complainant's prior consensual intercourse solely to impeach her by showing that she falsely told a hospital doctor that she had not had consensual intercourse within 72 hours of the rape). If the prosecution seeks to prove rape by putting in evidence that, for example,

the complainant became pregnant, it is only fair to allow the defense to rebut by showing that another man could have caused the pregnancy. But the defense is not entitled to put in evidence of disease, pregnancy, or semen where the prosecution has not benefited from the evidence and has done nothing to open the door.

87. *See* Md. Code Ann. art 27, § 461A (1996). *See also* Olden v. Kentucky, 488 U.S. 227 (1988) (unconstitutional to prevent defendant from cross-examining accuser about fact that she lived with male friend R., when R. saw accuser disembarking from defendant's car after alleged rape, and defense was based on claim that accuser fabricated rape in order to protect relationship with R.); United States v. Platero, 72 F.3d 806, 814–16 (10th Cir.1995) (trial court erred in not allowing evidence of victim's affair with her co-worker, to whom victim reported the rape; defense alleged that victim engaged in consensual intercourse and that she had fabricated the rape to protect her relationship with the co-worker; issue whether affair had occurred was for jury, not trial judge, to decide).

that it leads to a reliable inference of consent.[88] The statutes generally also have a procedural element, providing for hearings in limine on the issue of admissibility, and in some cases providing for in camera hearings to protect the woman's privacy.[89] Indeed, some statutes do little more than set up a procedural mechanism for pretrial decision and call attention to the problem, providing only some general standard of admissibility, such as weighing prejudice against probative value.[90] Others attempt a more radical approach to exclusion by providing that the evidence may be received only for specific purposes.[91] The more radical statutes have sometimes been challenged on grounds that they deny due process by preventing defendants from presenting legitimate exculpatory evidence.[92]

Exclusion of the sexual conduct of a rape victim can raise constitutional issues. In *Olden v. Kentucky*,[93] the Supreme Court held that cutting off the defense attempt to cross-examine the alleged victim about her affair with another witness violated the defendant's right to confrontation. *Olden* was a sexual assault case in which defendant claimed consent. After the incident, defendant drove complainant to the house of his half-brother, Bill Russell. The defense wanted to cross-examine the complainant about an alleged affair she was having with Bill Russell; the defense theory was that the complainant had fabricated her claim of sexual assault to protect her relationship with Bill Russell, who had seen her get out of defendant's car and may have been suspicious. The trial judge excluded the evidence concerning the affair. The Supreme Court held that the evidence was admissible.

Several factors favor admissibility in *Olden*. Complainant's alleged boyfriend saw her get out of defendant's car. Her motive to fabricate a sexual assault to explain why she was with defendant was greater than it would have been had she reported the assault to the police before her boyfriend knew about it. Also, although the court did not use this argument, the prosecution arguably lost its right to object to the evidence after it elicited from the complainant on direct examination that she lived with her mother, when in fact she lived with Bill Russell. These facts tend to make *Olden* somewhat special, though not unique. Normally, the court's refusal to allow free cross-examination of a rape victim

---

88. *See* Minn. R. Evid. 404(c).

89. *See* 23 Charles A. Wright & Kenneth W. Graham, Jr., Federal Practice and Procedure (Evidence) § 5391 (1980). *But cf.* United States v. Platero, 72 F.3d 806, 813 (10th Cir.1995) (held, issue whether rape victim had prior sexual relationship was for the jury, not the judge, to decide under amended Rule 412).

90. *See, e.g.,* R.I. Gen. Laws § 11–37–13 (1981) (providing for notice to court and discussion of admissibility "out of hearing of jury").

91. *See* Fed. R. Evid. 412.

92. *See, e.g.,* State v. Jalo, 557 P.2d 1359 (Or.App.1976) (unconstitutional to ex-

clude evidence of child complainant's prior sexual conduct when adult defendant claimed that she had falsely accused him because he told her that he was going to inform her parents of her sexual conduct with his son and others); Commonwealth v. Black, 487 A.2d 396 (Pa.Super.1985) (unconstitutional to exclude sexual behavior evidence that shows bias). *See also* Clifford S. Fishman, *Consent, Credibility, and the Constitution: Evidence Relating to a Sex Offense Complainant's Past Sexual Behavior*, 44 Cath. U.L. Rev. 709 (1995).

93. 488 U.S. 227 (1988).

about current sexual partners will not violate the defendant's constitutional right to confrontation. But *Olden* does show that at times, the Constitution requires that the court allow criminal defendants to offer evidence that otherwise would be excluded by rape shield laws.

The defendant's right to jury trial may also limit the operation of rape shield statutes. In *United States v. Platero,*[94] the trial judge excluded evidence on the ground that he did not believe an alleged affair between the victim and the defendant had taken place. The Court of Appeals held that the defendant's right to jury trial guaranteed him the right to have a jury decide that factual issue. Under this approach, the rape shield rule still has force because the defendant must show that sexual conduct, if it occurred, fits one of the exceptions to the rule, but the testimony that the alleged victim did in fact engage in sexual conduct with another person must be assumed to be true in making that determination.

Many jurisdictions provide a protection analogous to the rape shield statutes for plaintiffs and others involved in civil sexual harassment cases. For example, Federal Rule 412(b)(2) excludes evidence of sexual predisposition or sexual behavior of an alleged victim unless "its probative value substantially outweighs the danger of harm to any victim and of unfair prejudice to any party."[95]

Other Criminal Cases

Under the Federal Rules of Evidence, and subject to the limitation for rape cases, the defendant is allowed to offer evidence of a "pertinent trait" of the victim's character.[96] Suppose, for example, defendant is charged with assault and battery, and claims self-defense, asserting that the victim attacked first. Because the case is not a homicide prosecution, the exception previously discussed relating to homicide cases does not apply, but the rule nevertheless permits the defendant to offer character evidence to show the victim's violent character, and thus the likelihood that the victim was the first aggressor.[97]

An important difference from the homicide exception is that, as with her own character, the defendant holds the key to the admissibility of character evidence of the victim in these cases. If defendant does not offer evidence of the victim's character to prove the victim's behavior on the occasion in question, the prosecution may not do so. Of course, the

---

94. 72 F.3d 806 (10th Cir.1995).

95. *See* Rodriguez–Hernandez v. Miranda–Velez, 132 F.3d 848, 855 (1st Cir. 1998), where the substantive issue was whether plaintiff was fired for refusing sexual advances or for poor job performance. The trial court excluded much of the defendant's proffered sexual behavior evidence under Rule 412's reverse–403 balancing test set forth in the text, but admitted testimony concerning an affair that allegedly distracted plaintiff from her work to such a degree that it impaired her work performance. The First Circuit affirmed, finding no abuse of discretion.

96. Fed. R. Evid. 404(a)(2).

97. *See, e.g.,* United States v. Perez–Casillas, 607 F.Supp. 88 (D.Puerto Rico 1985) (in prosecution of police officers for perjury and conspiracy in killing two individuals, evidence that victims had reputation for violence and aggression admissible to prove alleged victims were first aggressors in confrontation that led to their deaths).

rule permits the prosecution to "rebut" defendant's character evidence, and in those circumstances the rule works identically with that governing the defendant's character. In examining its own witnesses, the prosecution is limited to evidence of reputation and opinion, but in cross-examining defendant's witnesses, the prosecution may inquire about relevant specific instances of conduct.

The key threshold question is what traits of the victim's character are "pertinent" to the defendant's claims. Obviously, a general tendency toward violence would be pertinent to the defendant's claim that the victim attacked first. But just as discussed above, such evidence would not be admissible to prove the subtly different self-defense claim based on the defendant's *belief* that the victim was violent, and thus to explain why *defendant* attacked first. In many criminal cases, the victim's character simply will not be pertinent to any issue. It is difficult to imagine, for example, how the victim's character could be relevant in prosecutions for robbery, burglary, or fraud. Unless the defendant can convince the court that a particular character trait is pertinent to her defense, this exception will not apply.

§ 5.10 Exceptions to the Rule Against Using Character Evidence to Show Conduct [FRE 404(a)(1)–3]—Character of Defendant in Sexual Assault and Child Molestation Cases [FRE 413–415]

In the trial of a defendant charged with a sex crime, there are three ways in which evidence of similar crimes committed by the defendant might come to light. First, the other crimes might be offered for a non-character purpose such as showing motive, plan, or preparation, or identifying the defendant as the perpetrator by showing that he committed prior "signature" crimes using the same modus operandi.[98] When offered on these grounds, the other crime evidence is not character evidence, and no exception to the character ban is needed, though of course the judge must weigh the danger that it will be used for the forbidden character purpose against its probative value for a permitted other purpose.

Second, if defendant testifies, evidence that defendant was *convicted* of other sex crimes might be offered to impeach his character for truthfulness as a witness.[99] Third, in some jurisdictions including the

98. *See* § **5.24**; David P. Bryden & Roger C. Park, *"Other Crimes" Evidence in Sex Offense Cases*, 78 Minn. L. Rev. 529, 540–56 (1994).

99. *See* § **9.09.** The evidence is highly prejudicial and of minimal probative value when offered under this theory alone. Theoretically, it is relevant because the commission of a prior sex crime casts a shadow on the witness's character for truthfulness. However, evidence of prior sex crimes shows much more about the defendant's propensity to commit other sex crimes than it does about his propensity to tell the truth. Though if the evidence is admitted, the judge will instruct the jury to use it only to assess credibility, there is a danger that the jury will use it for its common sense value even. For a social science study indicating the inefficacy of this type of limiting instruction, *see* Roselle L. Wissler & Michael J. Saks, *On the Inefficacy of Limiting Instructions: When Jurors Use Prior Conviction Evidence to Decide on Guilt*, 9

federal courts, the other crimes might be offered as evidence of a propensity to commit sex crimes under an exception to the rule against character evidence. The first two routes to admission are covered in other sections; the third is the subject of this section.

In 1994 federal crime legislation was enacted that included three new evidence rules making evidence of other sexual misconduct admissible "on any matter to which it is relevant." Specifically, evidence of other sexual assaults is now admissible in prosecutions for sexual assault,[100] evidence of other acts of child molestation is now admissible in prosecutions for child molestation,[101] and the same types of misconduct are admissible in civil actions arising out of alleged sexual assault and child molestation.[102] Though case law will be needed to clarify the rules in many respects, it is clear that Congress intended to allow juries in these types of cases to employ the character reasoning forbidden by longstanding rules. In a prosecution for rape, for example, it will now be permissible for the government to offer evidence of other rapes or sexual assaults committed by the defendant, in order to establish defendant's character-based propensity to commit such crimes, and thus, the likelihood that defendant committed the charged offense. There is no requirement of special similarity; the crime need only be of the same general type currently charged. Thus, even a dissimilar rape is admissible in a rape case, and a dissimilar act of child molestation is admissible in a child molestation case.

The general admissibility of this evidence does not render futile all attacks upon it. Certainly, Congress did not intend to abolish the trial judge's discretion to exclude the evidence when its probative value is substantially outweighed by the danger of unfair prejudice.[103] Though the

---

Law & Hum. Behav. 37 (1985). Nonetheless, some courts will admit the evidence. *See* cases cited in Bryden & Park, *supra* note 98, at 534–37.

100. Fed. R. Evid. 413.

101. Fed. R. Evid. 414.

102. Fed. R. Evid. 415.

103. *See* United States v. LeMay, 260 F.3d 1018, 1025–27 (9th Cir.2001) (Rule 414 does not deprive defendant of constitutional rights by allowing propensity evidence to be admitted in child sex abuse case; however, it is not a complete blank check for admissibility of propensity evidence because court may still exclude such evidence under Rule 403 if its prejudicial effect substantially outweighs its probative value); United States v. Castillo, 140 F.3d 874 (10th Cir.1998) (Rule 414, as qualified by Rule 403, does not violate equal protection or due process; case remanded with instructions to articulate on the record why probative value was not substantially outweighed by danger of unfair prejudice); United States v. Enjady, 134 F.3d 1427

(10th Cir.1998) (trial court has authority, pursuant to Rule 403, to exclude evidence otherwise admissible under Rule 413; so understood, the rule survives constitutional due process and equal protection challenges); United States v. Larson, 112 F.3d 600, 605 (2d Cir.1997) (Rule 403 applies to evidence covered by Rule 414, but history of Rule 414 was taken into account as a positive factor in deciding to admit similar acts that occurred 16–20 years before trial; drafters of Rule 414 intended its temporal scope to be broad); United States v. LeCompte, 131 F.3d 767, 769 (8th Cir.1997) (held, on pretrial appeal, reversible error to exclude similar 8-year-old instance of child sex abuse; Rule 403 balancing must be conducted with due regard for the "strong legislative judgment that evidence of prior sexual offenses should ordinarily be admissible"); United States v. Guardia, 955 F.Supp. 115, 117 (D.N.M.1997) ("A common sense reading of Rule 403 ... indicates that since it applies only to evidence otherwise admissible, it applies to evidence otherwise admissible under Rule 413";

defendant will no longer be able to argue that the evidence is unfairly prejudicial in that it invites the jury to convict based upon the belief that he is the kind of person who would commit such a crime, the court may still exclude the evidence on the basis that the jury will convict based on emotional grounds, that it will overvalue the evidence, or on other bases.[104]

In addition, not all character evidence will be admissible under the new rules. Only specific instances of conduct are allowed, and, as noted above, the rules limit the prosecution to evidence of the same type of misconduct. Thus, acts of child molestation generally will not be admissible in prosecutions for rape.[105]

One can expect a number of states to follow the lead of the federal government and provide for admission of this kind of evidence. California, for example, enacted similar legislation in 1995,[106] and other states are sure to follow.[107] Whether the new rules will work a significant change in actual practice is unclear.[108] Many states have long followed

court limited number of witnesses prosecution permitted to call to present evidence under Rule 413); Frank v. County of Hudson, 924 F.Supp. 620, 624 (D.N.J.1996) ("evidence proffered under [Rules 413 to 415] must still be shown to be relevant, probative and 'legally relevant' under FRE 403"; because probative value of questioned evidence was slight and potential for prejudice was high, court granted protective order against its use). *See also* David J. Karp, *Evidence of Propensity and Probability in Sex Offense Cases and Other Cases*, 70 Chi.-Kent L. Rev. 15, 19 (1994) (statement of author of legislation that "[t]he general standards of the rules of evidence would apply to evidence offered under these rules, including ... the authority of the court to exclude relevant evidence under Rule 403").

104. One issue left open by the new rules is whether the evidence is admissible against a non-human defendant. *See* Cleveland v. KFC Nat. Mgmt. Co., 948 F.Supp. 62, 65–66 (N.D.Ga.1996) (where Title VII party defendant was corporate employer, Rule 415 nevertheless applies to admit relevant sexual acts of defendant's manager despite language in rule referring to "a party's" other sex offenses).

105. *See* Fed. R. Evid. 413(a) ("In a criminal case in which the defendant is accused of an offense of sexual assault, evidence of the defendant's commission of another offense or offenses of sexual assault is admissible...."); Fed. R. Evid. 414(a) ("In a criminal case in which the defendant is accused of an offense of child molestation, evidence of the defendant's commission of another offense or offenses of child molestation is admissible....").

106. Cal. Evid. Code § 1108 (West Supp. 1997).

107. *See, e.g.,* Ind. St. Ann. § 35–37–4–15 (1994) (allowing similar crimes evidence in prosecutions for child molestation and incest if probative value of evidence is not substantially outweighed by danger of unfair prejudice); *cf.* Mo. Rev. Stat. § 566.025 (1995) (in prosecutions for some crimes against minors, allowing evidence of other crimes against minors to show propensity to commit such crimes).

108. The new rules have engendered substantial commentary, much of it critical. Among the many works criticizing the rules are Katharine K. Baker, *Once a Rapist? Motivational Evidence and Relevancy in Rape Law*, 110 Harv. L. Rev. 563 (1997); Craig R. Callen, *Proving the Case: Simpson, Fuhrman, Grice, and Character Evidence*, 67 U. Colo. L. Rev. 777 (1996); James J. Duane, *The New Federal Rules of Evidence on Prior Acts of Accused Sex Offenders: A Poorly Drafted Version of a Very Bad Idea*, 157 F.R.D. 95 (1994); Karen M. Fingar, *And Justice For All: The Admissibility of Uncharged Sexual Misconduct Evidence Under the Recent Amendment to the Federal Rules of Evidence*, 5 S. Cal. Rev. L. & Women's Stud. 501 (1996); Stephen R. Henley, *Caveat Criminale: The Impact of the New Military Rules of Evidence in Sexual Offense and Child Molestation Cases*, Army Law. 82 (March, 1996); Edward J. Imwinkelried, *Some Comments About Mr. David Karp's Remarks on Propensity Evidence*, 70 Chi.-Kent L. Rev. 37 (1994); Edward J. Imwinkelried, *Undertaking the Task of Reforming the American Character Evidence Prohibi-*

lenient rules of admissibility of such evidence in sexually related crimes, sometimes on the theory that the evidence is not "character" as used in those cases. *See* § **5.24**.

§ 5.11   Exceptions to the Rule Against Using Character Evidence to Show Conduct [FRE 404(a)(1)–(3)]—Character of Witnesses

Another exception to the rule against using character to show action in conformity involves the firmly rooted rule allowing the impeachment of the credibility of witnesses by showing their prior convictions or by offering testimony about their bad character for truthfulness. For a discussion of this topic, see the sections on impeachment of witnesses in Chapter 9.

§ 5.12   Methods of Showing Character: Evidence of Reputation, Opinion, and Specific Acts [FRE 405]

As the previous discussion indicates, the rules governing the admissibility of character evidence to prove conduct specify the *form* of character evidence that may be offered. Though the rules are technical

tion: The Importance of Getting the Experiment Off on the Right Foot, 22 Fordham Urb. L.J. 285 (1995); David P. Leonard, *The Federal Rules of Evidence and the Political Process*, 22 Fordham Urb. L.J. 305 (1995); James S. Liebman, *Proposed Evidence Rules 413 to 415—Some Problems and Recommendations*, 20 U. Dayton L. Rev. 753 (1995); Louis M. Natali, Jr. & R. Stephen Stigall, *"Are You Going to Arraign His Whole Life?": How Sexual Propensity Evidence Violates the Due Process Clause*, 28 Loy. U. Chi. L.J. 1 (1996); Jeffrey G. Pickett, *The Presumption of Innocence Imperiled: The New Federal Rules of Evidence 413–415 and the Use of Other Sexual–Offense Evidence in Washington*, 70 Wash. L. Rev. 883 (1995); Mark A. Sheft, *Federal Rule of Evidence 413: A Dangerous New Frontier*, 33 Am. Crim. L. Rev. 57 (1995); Anne Elsberry Kyl, Note, *The Propriety of Propensity: The Effects and Operation of New Federal Rulers of Evidence 413 and 414*, 37 Ariz. L. Rev. 659 (1995); Lisa M. Segal, Note, *The Admissibility of Uncharged Misconduct Evidence in Sex Offense Cases: New Federal Rules of Evidence Codify the Lustful Disposition Exception*, 29 Suffolk U.L. Rev. 515 (1995). In 1995, the American Bar Association adopted a resolution opposing the substance of the new rules. *See* Myrna S. Raeder, *American Bar Association Criminal Justice Section Report to the House of Delegates*, reprinted in 22 Fordham Urb. L.J. 343 (1995). The Judicial Conference, given an opportunity to comment on the proposed rules before they became effective, suggested revisions to "clarify drafting ambiguities and eliminate constitutional infirmities." Report of the Judicial Conference of the United States on the Admission of Character Evidence in Certain Sexual Misconduct Cases 1 (Feb. 1995).

There has been some commentary favorable to aspects of the new rules. *See, e.g.,* Bryden & Park, *supra* note 98 (proposing a limited exception to the character bar in sexual assault cases involving acquaintances); Karen M. Fingar, *And Justice for All: The Admissibility of Uncharged Sexual Misconduct Evidence Under the Recent Amendment to the Federal Rules of Evidence*, 5 S. Cal. Rev. L. & Women's Stud. 501 (1996); Norman M. Garland, *Some Thoughts on the Sexual Misconduct Amendments to the Federal Rules of Evidence*, 22 Fordham Urb. L.J. 355 (1995) (supporting the policy of the new rules though sharply criticizing the drafting); Roger C. Park, *The Crime Bill of 1994 and the Law of Character Evidence: Congress Was Right About Consent Defense Cases*, 22 Fordham Urb. L.J. 271 (1995) (supporting the new rules in cases in which the accused raises a consent defense); Andrew E. Taslitz, *Patriarchal Stories I: Cultural Rape Narratives in the Courtroom*, 5 S. Cal. Rev. L. & Women's Stud. 387, 494–96 (1996) (favoring limited change while criticizing the new rules).

(and arcane), lawyers must take care to offer the evidence in its permissible form.

The most general rule is that the character of a person is ordinarily not provable through specific instances of a person's conduct,[109] but only through reputation or opinion. While reputation and opinion testimony may not carry as much flavor as specific act testimony, it is much less time-consuming and less likely to distract the jury with confusing collateral issues.

The common law rule restricted evidence of character to testimony about reputation, which was thought to represent the accumulated wisdom of the community, and hence to be more reliable than the mere opinion of any particular person. This restriction was too hobbling; because of the transitory conditions of modern society, it is more difficult to acquire a broad, reliable reputation. At any rate, "reputation" evidence often merely represented the witness's opinion in disguise. The Federal Rules take a broader view, and allow the testimony to be given in the form of either reputation or opinion.[110]

Reputation and Hearsay

Evidence of reputation, when used to show character, is evidence of out-of-court statements offered for the truth of the matter asserted, and hence is hearsay. (Reputation, after all, is what the community *says* about a person.) However, the Federal Rules provide a special hearsay exception applicable to reputation testimony.[111] At common law, whether implicitly or explicitly, reputation for character was also treated as falling within a hearsay exception, so the question was not whether the evidence was hearsay, but whether it was admissible under the rules governing character evidence.

Reputation in the Community or in the Workplace

Some common law cases restricted reputation evidence to evidence about a person's reputation in the community in which he or she lived, thereby preventing testimony about the person's reputation in the place of work.[112] As a hard-and-fast rule, this view never had much to recommend it; sometimes reputation at the place of work was more pertinent

---

109. The exception to this rule occurs when character is an ultimate issue. *See* § **5.29.**

110. Fed. R. Evid. 405(a).

111. Fed. R. Evid. 803(21). It should be noted that this exception does not guarantee the admission of all reputation evidence that meets the requirements of the exception, but only takes care of any hearsay objection that might be made to the testimony. The reputation-for-character evidence, even though not hearsay, must still fall into a category in which character evidence is admissible in order to be received. *See* Fed. R. Evid. 404(a). *Compare* United States v. Reveles, 1993 WL 135864, at *6

(A.F.C.M.R.1993), *aff'd.,* 41 M.J. 388 (1995) (trial court properly excluded bartender's testimony as to victim's reputation for intemperance, because reputation based upon group of patrons at Officers' Club bar, not a "recognized community"; Rule 404(d) of Military Rules of Evidence defines reputation as the "estimation in which a person is generally held in the community").

112. *See* Williams v. United States, 168 U.S. 382 (1897) (reputation at place of work excluded, on grounds that it existed only among a limited number of people in a particular building).

than reputation in the neighborhood. As one early source put it, when a schoolmaster is accused of beating schoolchildren, which reputation is more convincing, that of the schoolroom or that among his neighbors?[113] With the advent of suburbia and the apartment complex, and the modern separation of job and home, the view has become even less defensible, since a person may often have closer acquaintances in the place of work than in the place of residence. The Federal Rules accordingly provide for the admission of reputation evidence either "in the community" or "among associates."[114]

Personal Knowledge Requirement

When character evidence is offered in the form of reputation, the witness must have personal knowledge of reputation. The witness usually will also know the person whose reputation is the subject of testimony, but it is personal knowledge of reputation, not directly of the person's character, that is required. When the witness is testifying about his or her own opinion of a person's character (as is permitted in jurisdictions following the Federal Rules), he or she must have personal knowledge of the person about whom the opinion has been formed and enough experience with that person to justify entertaining an opinion; but it is not necessary for the opinion witness to know the reputation of the subject.

The reputation knowledge must be acquired by having heard the reputation discussed with a sufficient number of people, though the number is not precisely quantifiable.[115] A witness who reports reputation secondhand (that is, who reports what one other person says about reputation) is reporting hearsay that does not fall under an exception.

Can an investigator acquire knowledge of reputation specifically for purposes of a case, and then testify about reputation? Despite early cases to the contrary, the prevailing view appears to be that the investigators can acquire reputation knowledge for purposes of a particular case.[116] The partisanship of the investigator may throw some doubt upon the veracity of the evidence, but this is true of any facts discovered by an investigator, and of course the investigator is subject to cross-examination concerning his or her testimony about reputation. If the investigation was thorough and the investigator testifies truthfully, then the

---

113. Keener v. State, 18 Ga. 194, 221 (1855), excerpted in 5 John H. Wigmore, Evidence in Trials at Common Law § 1616, at 591 (James H. Chadbourn rev. 1974).

114. Fed. R. Evid. 803(21).

115. There is no precise number or percentage of people in a community who must discuss their opinion of a person for that opinion to be a "reputation." It is clear that it need not be a majority, See 5 Wigmore, supra note 113 § 1613; Girch v. State, 177 N.W. 798 (Neb.1920) (witness who heard 15 to 20 people in a community

of 200 say that defendant had a bad reputation for truth competent to testify as to that reputation). Cf. United States v. Neff, 343 F.Supp. 978, 982 (E.D.Pa.1972) (witness talked to "seven or eight people" about defendant; problem with testimony was that they did not know defendant, not that number was insufficient).

116. See 3 John H. Wigmore, Evidence in Trials at Common Law § 692 (James H. Chadbourn rev. 1970).

investigator's work product is as reliable as any testimony of a resident of the community.

Absence of Bad Reputation

The witness who testifies to having never heard anything about the reputation of the subject may be demonstrating a lack of personal knowledge about reputation. The testimony should not be received in this exact form. However, the witness who testifies to being acquainted with people who know the defendant, and is in a position to hear derogatory statements if any were made, is permitted to testify about not having heard anything unfavorable. The mere fact that a person who was in a position to hear unfavorable comments has never heard them, despite having been privy to conversations concerning the person whose reputation is the subject of testimony, is itself evidence of good character. Acts of misconduct are more a topic of conversation among one's associates than acts of ordinary rectitude, and the law recognizes that the person who has led an unstained life may show that to be so through the testimony of a witness who has "never heard anything against" the person.[117]

§ 5.13   Methods of Showing Character: Evidence of Reputation, Opinion, and Specific Acts [FRE 405]— Laying the Foundation for Character Evidence: Examples

The Federal Rules of Evidence permit character evidence to be presented either in opinion form or reputation form. Most pre-Rules common law jurisdictions allowed only reputation testimony.[118]

Example (Reputation)

Q.   Do you know Mr. Smith [the defendant]?

A.   Yes

Q.   Is he here in the courtroom today?

A.   Yes.

Q.   Where is he sitting?

---

117. *See, e.g.,* Deschenes v. United States, 224 F.2d 688, 691 (10th Cir.1955) ("silence speaks in his favor and the fact that a character witness has never heard ill said of the defendant is evidence within itself of a good reputation"); State v. Foster, 665 S.W.2d 348 (Mo.App.1984); State v. Floyd, 289 S.E.2d 139 (N.C.App.1982); 5 Wigmore, *supra* note 79 § 1614. An interesting example of this problem arose in the celebrated murder trial of Harvard Medical College Professor John Webster in 1849. One of Webster's character witnesses testified that he had been defendant's neighbor for 15 years but had never heard his character for violence or inhumanity discussed.

He was permitted to testify that he had "never heard any acts of violence, or inhumanity, imputed to him." Testimony of John G. Palfrey, Stone, Report of the Trial of Professor John W. Webster 145 (1850). *Cf.* SEC v. Peters, 978 F.2d 1162, 1171–73 (10th Cir.1992) (trial court erred by excluding "have you heard" cross-examination questions about defendant's prior misconduct to an opinion character witness for the defense).

118. *See* 5 John H. Wigmore, Evidence in Trials at Common Law § 1610 (James H. Chadbourn rev. 1974).

A.　Right next to you, on your left.

COUNSEL: Let the record reflect that the witness has identified Mr. Smith.

Q.　How long have you known Mr. Smith?

A.　Four years.

Q.　During that period, how often did you see him?

A.　Every day during the weekends, then sometimes during the week.

Q.　What is the nature of your association with him?

A.　We are next-door neighbors.

Q.　Anything else?

A.　We served on the homeowners' association together, both on the Board of Directors for two years.

Q.　Did you know other people who knew him?

A.　Yes.

Q.　How many?

A.　Dozens. He is very well known.

Q.　Did you discuss with these people, or hear discussed, the defendant's reputation for being a [law-abiding] [truthful] [peaceable and nonviolent] person?

A.　Yes.

Q.　What is his reputation for being a [law-abiding] [truthful] [peaceable and nonviolent] person?

A.　It is excellent, the best.[119]

Example (Opinion)

Q.　Do you know Mr. Smith [the defendant]?

A.　Yes.

Q.　Is he here in the courtroom today?

A.　Yes.

Q.　Where is he sitting?

A.　Right next to you, on your left.

COUNSEL: Let the record reflect that the witness has identified Mr. Smith.

Q.　How long have you known Mr. Smith?

A.　Four years.

---

119. Note that in this example, the witness testifies to knowing Mr. Smith personally. This is not necessary for a reputation witness. It is common for such a wit-ness to be quite familiar with a person's community reputation without knowing the individual personally.

Q.   During that period, how often did you see him?

A.   Every day during the weekends, then sometimes during the week.

Q.   What is the nature of your association with him?

A.   We are next-door neighbors.

Q.   Anything else?

A.   We served on the homeowners' association together, both on the Board of Directors for two years.

Q.   Did you know him well enough to form an opinion as to his character for [truth and veracity] [being a law-abiding person] [being a peaceable and nonviolent person]?

A.   Yes, certainly.

Q.   What is your opinion?

A.   He is an extremely [truthful and honest] [law-abiding] [peaceable and nonviolent] person.

§ 5.14   Character Evidence in Civil Cases—In General

The Federal Rules of Evidence do not permit the use of character evidence in civil cases, except insofar as it may be used to impeach the credibility of witnesses.[120] The rule makers reasoned that character evidence is of slight probative value and may be very prejudicial. They recognized that the same could be said of character evidence in criminal cases, but stated the criminal rule was "deeply imbedded in our jurisprudence," while the admissibility of character evidence in civil cases was not, and "those espousing change [in civil cases] have not met the burden of persuasion."[121] Nevertheless, there is a dissenting view that the provision in Rule 404(a) allowing the "accused" to put in character evidence applies to a party in a civil action who is accused of crime-like conduct, such as a police officer in a federal civil rights action accused of killing a person,[122] or a defendant in a wrongful death action who has been accused of intentionally killing the victim.

---

120. *See* Fed. R. Evid. 404(a), which creates exceptions only for impeaching witnesses and for evidence offered for and against an "accused" person.

121. Fed. R. Evid. 404 advisory committee's note.

122. *See* 22 Charles A. Wright & Kenneth W. Graham, Jr., Federal Practice and Procedure (Evidence) § 5236, at 386–89 (1978) which, though conceding that apparently the word "accused" was intended to refer to the defendant in a criminal case, argues that the word could be construed to embrace as well the party in a civil action who is accused of a criminal act. *See also* Perrin v. Anderson, 784 F.2d 1040, 1044–45 (10th Cir.1986) (victim character evidence would be admissible in a civil case in which defendant accused of unlawful killing; however, because plaintiff's evidence constituted specific instances of conduct rather than opinion or reputation, such evidence was inadmissible). *But see*, for a well-reasoned opinion excluding defense character evidence in a civil case, *see* S.E.C. v. Towers Financial Corp., 966 F.Supp. 203, 204 (S.D.N.Y.1997) (defendant in civil action alleging fraudulent pyramid scheme not entitled to offer character evidence; Magistrate Judge Andrew J. Peck noting that the words "accused" and "prosecution" in the Rule indicate that it applies only to criminal cases).

The rule against use of character evidence in civil cases must be understood in light of the limited nature of the character evidence ban. As noted in § **5.05,** the ban applies only to evidence of general disposition, when offered to show conduct in conformity with that disposition. It does not prohibit the use of habit evidence. *See* § **5.30.** Nor does it prohibit the use of evidence of prior acts when offered for the purpose of showing something other than character, such as motive, opportunity, preparation, plan, or the like. *See* § **5.16.** Also, it does not prohibit the use of evidence of character when the evidence is not used to show action in conformity with character, as is the case when character is the ultimate issue. *See* § **5.29.** Moreover, the rule is subject to an exception, applicable in civil as well as criminal cases, permitting the impeachment of a witness by evidence of prior bad acts reflecting on the witness's honesty, by criminal convictions, or by opinion and reputation evidence concerning the witness's character for truthfulness. *See* **Ch. 7.** It is also subject to Rule 415, which permits the use of evidence of specific instances of misconduct in civil actions involving allegations of rape or child molestation. *See* § **5.10**.

Rule 412, the federal "rape shield" rule, now applies in modified form to civil cases. As amended in 1994, the rule generally excludes evidence offered to prove that an alleged victim engaged in other sexual behavior and evidence of the alleged victim's sexual predisposition.[123] However, the rule further provides that in civil cases, "evidence offered to prove the sexual behavior or sexual predisposition of any alleged victim is admissible if it is otherwise admissible under these rules and its probative value substantially outweighs the danger of harm to any victim and of unfair prejudice to any party."[124] Further, evidence of an alleged victim's reputation is admissible only if the alleged victim has placed that reputation in controversy.[125]

Not all jurisdictions follow the restrictive position of the Federal Rules concerning the use of character evidence in civil cases. In some jurisdictions, a party is permitted to offer evidence of good character in a civil case, in response to an allegation of criminal conduct or conduct involving moral turpitude. Once this evidence has been offered and received, the opposing party may meet it with evidence of bad character.[126]

§ 5.15 Character Evidence in Civil Cases—Other Claims, Other Frauds

A character evidence problem can arise in civil cases in situations in which a litigant wishes to prove that a civil plaintiff is "claim-minded."[127]

---

123. Fed. R. Evid. 412(a).

124. Fed. R. Evid. 412(b)(2).

125. *Id.*

126. *See generally* 1A John H. Wigmore, Evidence in Trials at Common Law §§ 65–67 (Peter Tillers rev. 1983).

127. *See generally* 3A John H. Wigmore, Evidence in Trials at Common Law § 963, at 808 (James H. Chadbourn rev. 1970) (courts divided on admissibility of evidence); 1 McCormick on Evidence § 196 (5th ed. John W. Strong ed. 1999) (admissibility of party's prior actions or defenses).

For example, a defendant in a personal injury case might offer evidence that on one or more other occasions the plaintiff claimed to have been injured while boarding a bus. When offered to show that the plaintiff is litigious, it is character evidence that may prejudice the jury. Evidence of other claims is usually rejected.[128] However, it can be received if there is a showing of a distinct pattern of making false claims.[129] When such a showing is made, the evidence is not offered as character evidence to show a general disposition to make such claims, but is admitted under Rule 404(b) as evidence of intent, plan, or modus operandi.[130]

Civil cases in which a claim or defense turns on fraud can also raise potential character evidence problems. For example, the alleged victim of a misrepresentation by a real estate broker might wish to show that the broker made similar misrepresentations to other clients. In such instances, the party claiming fraud is usually allowed to put in evidence of similar past frauds by the opposing party.[131] This evidence would not be admissible if it were relevant only to show the bad character of a human adversary. However, it usually comes in for its bearing on some other issue that is at least semantically distinct, such as intent, knowledge, or lack of mistake or accident.[132]

§ 5.16 Evidence of Other Crimes, Wrongs, or Acts When Used for a Purpose Other Than Showing Action in Conformity With Character—In General [FRE 404(b)]

Suppose a defendant charged with bank robbery raises the defense of alibi. As part of its proof, the prosecution seeks to show that the defendant robbed a convenience store a year before the bank robbery. The inferential process most likely set in motion by this evidence is the following:

EVIDENCE: The defendant committed one armed robbery.

---

128. *See, e.g.,* Lowenthal v. Mortimer, 270 P.2d 942, 945 (Cal.App.1954) (plaintiff's fifteen prior lawsuits inadmissible, prejudicial); 1 McCormick on Evidence, *supra* note 127 § 196, at 692–93 (evidence usually excluded when offered to show plaintiff is chronic litigant).

129. *See, e.g.,* Hemphill v. Washington Metropolitan Area Transit Authority, 982 F.2d 572 (D.C. Cir.1993) (per curiam) (in personal injury action, trial court improperly gave "claims-minded plaintiff" instruction where defendant failed to show plaintiff's prior claims were false); Sessmer v. Commonwealth, 103 S.W.2d 647, 649 (Ky. 1937) (prior unfounded claims admissible in disbarment proceeding for blackmailing physician with frivolous claim); 1 McCormick on Evidence, *supra* note 127 § 196, at 693 (party's previous similar claims admissible if fraudulent).

130. *See* Fed. R. Evid. 404(b).

131. *See, e.g.,* Edgar v. Fred Jones Lincoln–Mercury, 524 F.2d 162, 167 (10th Cir. 1975) (similar past conduct in tampering with odometer to falsify mileage on second-hand cars); 1 McCormick on Evidence, *supra* note 127 § 197, at 695 (evidence of similar frauds frequently admitted).

132. *See, e.g., Edgar,* 524 F.2d at 167 (past tampering with odometer admissible to show intent); Dial v. Travelers Indem. Co., 780 F.2d 520, 523–24 (5th Cir.1986) (plaintiff's association with two other intentionally set fires also destroying insured property admissible to show intent or plan); 1 McCormick on Evidence, *supra* note 127 § 197 (past frauds admissible to demonstrate intent, knowledge, lack of accident, or plan or scheme).

INFERENCE: The defendant is the type of person who commits armed robberies.

CONCLUSION: It is more likely that the defendant is guilty of the present crime than would otherwise be the case.

When offered on this reasoning, the evidence would be barred by the rule against character evidence.[133] First, it is evidence of a general disposition offered to show conduct in conformity with that disposition, and hence is barred by the general rule against character evidence. *See* § **5.05.** Second, even if one of the exceptions to the rule against use of character evidence to show conduct applied—for example, even if the defendant had opened the door to evidence about character traits by putting on witnesses who testified that the defendant was honest and law-abiding—the evidence about the prior convenience store robbery would still be inadmissible, because it is evidence of a specific act offered to prove character, and character may only be proven by reputation and opinion testimony. *See* § **5.15.**

How is it, then, that specific acts and specific prior crimes are often admitted in criminal cases (and sometimes in civil cases)? Of course, when the defendant testifies, prior convictions may be admitted, subject to restrictions, for the purpose of impeaching credibility. *See* § **5.11** and **Ch. 9.** Yet even when the defendant does not testify, and even when prior conduct has not led to a conviction, other instances of defendant's misconduct may be admissible, not to show a defect in credibility, but as substantive evidence of guilt. The theory of admission is that the evidence is not offered to show character, but to show something else—either a trait of personality that is too narrow to be called character, or something that is not a trait of personality at all. The Federal Rules of Evidence provide for admission under the following formula in Rule 404(b):

> Evidence of other crimes, wrongs, or acts is not admissible to prove the character of a person in order to show that he acted in conformity therewith. It may, however, be admissible for other purposes, such as proof of motive, opportunity, intent, preparation, plan, knowledge, identity, or absence of mistake or accident.[134]

The list of purposes for which other crimes may be offered is a time-honored (though non-exclusive) one. Similar lists appeared in decisions and treatises long before the adoption of the Federal Rules of Evidence.[135]

---

133. Fed. R. Evid. 404(a). *See, e.g.,* United States v. Brown, 71 F.3d 1158, 1162 (5th Cir.1995) (in drug sale case, held error to admit, under Rule 404(b) to show identity, evidence that the defendant had previously been convicted of possession of cocaine with intent to distribute since prior conviction was only relevant to show bad character); United States v. Phillips, 599 F.2d 134 (6th Cir.1979) (prior bank robberies inadmissible when no showing of similarity of plan). For a case that, in the authors' opinion, violates this principle, *see* State v. Smith, 707 P.2d 289, 297 (Ariz. 1985) (robbery of other convenience stores admissible in prosecution for robbing convenience store).

134. Fed. R. Evid. 404(b).

135. H. Richard Uviller, *Evidence of Character to Prove Conduct: Illusion, Illog-*

Suppose, therefore, that in the previous bank robbery hypothetical, the evidence suggests that the crime was committed by an individual wearing a clown mask and who handed the teller a note claiming to be Robin Hood, saying all the money would be given away to the "poor people on the streets," and instructing the teller to empty the drawer of all small bills. The prosecution wishes to prove that on several other occasions, defendant robbed banks in the same town using precisely the same method. Though the evidence would be inadmissible if offered to prove defendant's general character for unlawful behavior and thus her guilt of the present crime, it would likely be admissible to prove her *identity* as the bank robber on the following reasoning:

EVIDENCE: Defendant robbed other banks using exactly the same method.

INFERENCE: Defendant is a bank robber who uses that distinctive method to commit the crime.

CONCLUSION: Defendant is the person who committed the crime at issue.

Note that this reasoning does not involve an inference of or from a general disposition to commit crime, or even to rob banks. It is offered to establish defendant's identity as the bank robber solely through reasoning that does not require an inference that defendant possesses a general character trait. This does not mean the jury will not employ the forbidden reasoning; in many instances the danger that this will occur even with a limiting instruction is sufficiently great to merit exclusion.[136] But in the absence of too great a danger of that eventuality (and assuming exclusion is not required for other reasons), the evidence would almost certainly be admissible.

The admissibility of other crimes and acts has been a hotly and exhaustively debated and litigated subject, and it is perhaps the most commonly asserted ground for appeal in criminal cases. Federal Rule 404(b) has generated more reported appellate litigation than any other subsection of the rules.[137]

In such litigious terrain, one might expect to find well-trodden paths furnished with helpful guideposts, and perhaps even a paved way to the most common destinations. To the contrary—the terrain is so vast, inconsistent, and full of different starting points that judges who travel it must find a way to their destinations mainly through a sense of what

---

ic, and Injustice in the Courtroom, 130 U. Pa. L. Rev. 845, 877 (1982):

> The entire list, obviously, arrived—complete—down the chute of history. A virtually identical version can be found in a famous decision of the New York Court of Appeals written in the second year of this century, and several earlier treatises recite a comparable catalogue. The origins are doubtless obscure in the mists antedating the great treatises.

(Footnotes omitted.)

136. For an excellent analysis and critique of the rule, particularly noting that the rule does not avoid all propensity inferences, *see* Richard B. Kuhns, *The Propensity to Misunderstand the Character of Specific Acts Evidence*, 66 Iowa L. Rev. 777 (1981).

137. *See* 2 Jack B. Weinstein & Margaret A. Berger, Weinstein's Evidence ¶ 404[08] (1984); 22 Charles A. Wright & Kenneth W. Graham, Jr., Federal Practice and Procedure: Evidence § 5239 (1979).

is fit for the particular case, with the language of case law and treatises serving more as soothing incantations than as guideposts. The ultimate question presented (when is specific past human conduct a reliable predictor of present action?) is so difficult, so susceptible to differences of opinion, and so dependent upon the peculiar facts of the individual case, that it is unlikely that any set of hard-and-fast rules will provide exact answers.

The decided cases do, however, provide some general guidelines. If the evidence is relevant only to show character, then its use is prohibited by Rule 404(a), Rule 404(b), and by the Rules' common law antecedents. If the evidence is relevant for some other purpose—and, as noted, the list in 404(b) is merely a list of examples, not an exhaustive list—then the probative value of the evidence must be balanced against its prejudicial effect, as well as the danger of waste of time and confusion.[138] In other words, even if the evidence falls into one of the categories listed in Rule 404(b), it must still withstand scrutiny under Rule 403. Among the considerations that bear upon the Rule 403 determination are whether the prior crime has the capacity to arouse horror or sympathy or to invoke a desire to punish; the remoteness in time of the evidence of other crimes and bad acts; and whether the fact sought to be proven by the uncharged crime is really in dispute and, if so, whether it might be proven with other evidence.[139] Another factor mentioned by some courts is the strength of the evidence (aside from evidence of uncharged crimes or collateral bad acts) that is available against the defendant. If the evidence directly concerning the charged crime is very powerful, then the incremental probative value of the other crimes evidence is less, and there is therefore (under this line of reasoning) less reason for admitting it.[140] As the Supreme Court made clear in *Old Chief v. United States*,[141] the trial court must consider the *context* in which evidence is offered, which includes the other evidence available to prove the fact.[142] The basic task is one of balancing, and as the advisory committee's note to Rule 404(b) states, the rule offers no mechanical solution.

It is also necessary for the court to consider the quantum of evidence that the defendant in fact committed the other misconduct which the prosecution offered. The Supreme Court has held that there

---

138. Fed. R. Evid. 404 advisory committee's note to subdivision (b); 2 Weinstein's Federal Evidence § 404.07[4] (2d Ed. Joseph M. McLaughlin ed. 1997).

139. *See* 1 McCormick on Evidence § 190, at 672–73 (5th ed. John W. Strong ed. 1999).

140. United States v. Beechum, 582 F.2d 898 (5th Cir.1978). One may question whether this is a proper consideration, since it seems to suggest that when the proof of the charged crime is weak, evidence the prejudicial effect of which would otherwise outweigh its probative value should be admitted, thus putting the defendant with a

good case on the facts of the particular crime charged in a worse position than one who is clearly guilty of the particular crime charged. Perhaps, however, in some cases the weighing of this factor can be justified on the ground that the other crimes evidence is simply a waste of time when the immediate evidence is overwhelming.

141. 519 U.S. 172 (1997).

142. *Id*. at 184 ("what counts as the Rule 403 'probative value' of an item of evidence, as distinct from its Rule 401 'relevance,' may be calculated by comparing evidentiary alternatives"). For discussion of *Old Chief, see* § **5.03**.

need only be evidence sufficient to support a finding by a preponderance of the evidence that defendant committed the act, but not all states follow this permissive rule. *See* § **5.28**.

It should be noted that the evidence of other crimes, wrongs, or acts is not limited to evidence of convictions. Crimes or wrongs that did not result in conviction may be admissible if they are offered for a proper purpose. Indeed, most courts hold that even a crime that resulted in an acquittal may be admissible, provided that its commission is established in the present proceeding in accordance with the rules about quantum of proof that are in force in the jurisdiction. *See* § **5.28**. It should also be noted that the rules do not require that the other crimes, wrongs, or acts have occurred prior to the events at issue in the case. Uncharged misconduct that occurs *after* the events at issue may also be admissible. For example, a defendant who used a distinctive modus operandi in a series of murders was charged with the murder that was first in time, but was identified as the murderer partly by evidence that he was linked with subsequent murders having a similar method.[143]

As a convenient shorthand, this book will refer to evidence of other crimes, wrongs and acts as *uncharged misconduct* evidence.[144] The term *uncharged* refers to the fact that the other misconduct is not charged in the present case; it does not mean that the person was never charged with the misconduct, since prior convictions can be one form of uncharged misconduct evidence. The term *misconduct* correctly emphasizes that the evidence offered need not be evidence of a crime, but may be evidence of some form of non-criminal misconduct. The term is not absolutely precise, for though the evidence will usually in practice be evidence of misconduct offered to show the commission of a crime, in theory (and occasionally also in practice) it might be evidence of a good act offered to show the commission of another good act. (The same principle applies to the latter as to the former; prior good acts are not admissible for an inference of good character en route to an inference of action in conformity with good character, but they may be admissible to show conduct if that can be done without relying upon an inference about character.)

§ 5.17   Specific Purposes for Which Uncharged Misconduct Evidence May Be Offered

This section will offer examples of particular purposes for which other crimes evidence may be admitted. As Rule 404(b) suggests, the list of specific purposes is not exhaustive; evidence of uncharged misconduct may be admissible for other reasons not listed. In addition, the purposes listed below often overlap. For example, evidence that is offered to show intent may also show a common plan; evidence that is offered to show identity often does so by showing modus operandi. The proponent of the

---

143. Rex v. Smith, [1914–15] All E.R. Rep. 262, the celebrated "Brides in the Bath" case described at § **5.19** was just such a case of the use of subsequent acts to prove an earlier crime.

144. In this respect, we have followed the usage of Edward J. Imwinkelried, Unchanged Misconduct Evidence (rev.ed.1998).

uncharged misconduct evidence must specify the 404(b) purpose under which the evidence falls.[145]

It is also important to recognize that the various possible purposes for which the evidence might be offered are not all of the same order. A close examination of the list in Rule 404(b) reveals that most of the potential uses of uncharged misconduct evidence are merely circumstantial evidence of other facts that must be proven to establish a claim or defense (ultimate facts). For example, motive, opportunity, preparation, and plan are not ultimate facts, but only facts that, if shown to exist, offer circumstantial support to the existence or nonexistence of ultimate facts. Intent and identity, on the other hand, are usually ultimate facts; unless these facts can be established, the facts necessary to sustain the charge will not have been proven. Knowledge is often in this category of ultimate facts as well.[146] Because relevance issues often arise with respect to uncharged misconduct evidence, counsel must not only identify the *immediate* purpose for which the evidence is offered, but also the *ultimate* fact such evidence tends to prove. While a person's conduct might well establish an evidentiary fact, unless that fact is relevant to an ultimate issue in the case, the evidence should be rejected. Suppose, for example, that in a prosecution for receiving stolen goods knowing them to be stolen, defendant admits knowingly possessing the goods but claims they were not stolen. If the prosecution offers evidence of other instances in which defendant received stolen goods, it is important to inquire why such evidence is relevant. If offered on a modus operandi theory to prove identity (that defendant was the person who possessed the goods), defendant should argue that the evidence should be rejected because identity is not a contested issue.[147] If offered to prove plan as a means to show intent, defendant should also argue for exclusion because defendant admits knowingly possessing the goods. Counsel should be prepared in advance to make and meet relevance arguments whenever the admissibility of uncharged misconduct evidence is at issue.

§ 5.18 Specific Purposes for Which Uncharged Misconduct Evidence May Be Offered—Motive

The uncharged misconduct may be received to show a motive for the charged crime. Though motive is not itself an issue in a criminal

---

145. *See* United States v. Sampson, 980 F.2d 883, 888 (3d Cir.1992) (prosecution may not list the "litany" of 404(b) exceptions without specifying which one(s) apply).

146. For example, in a prosecution for receiving stolen goods, it is not sufficient that the prosecution prove that defendant received goods and that the goods were stolen; the prosecution must also prove that defendant *knew* the goods were stolen. Without proof of this fact, defendant will prevail. For discussion of the use of uncharged misconduct evidence to prove knowledge, *see* § **5.21**.

147. Technically, the evidence would be relevant under Fed. R. Evid. 401, but should be rejected under Rule 403. *See* § **5.04**. Some courts have held, however, that even if defendant does not contest the existence of an element of the crime, the prosecution may still offer evidence to prove that element. *See, e.g.,* United States v. Bastanipour, 41 F.3d 1178, 1183 (7th Cir. 1994); United States v. Gilliam, 994 F.2d 97, 102 (2d Cir.1993). Even so, when an issue is undisputed, defendant can argue that the probative value of the uncharged misconduct evidence is slight when compared with the danger of unfair prejudice.

prosecution, motive can be relevant to an ultimate issue such as criminal intent or the identity of the perpetrator. Motive can also be relevant in a civil case, for example to prove the predicate for the award of punitive damages.

To take a simple example of motive, if a murder defendant and another person previously committed a crime together, and the defendant knew that the other person was prepared to testify against him in a prosecution for the other crime, then the defendant would have a motive for murdering the other person, and the prior crime—though perhaps not all of its details—would be admissible for that purpose.[148] In such a case, motive could be offered to prove that defendant committed the crime (if defendant denies involvement), or that the killing was intentional (if defendant admits killing the victim but asserts lack of criminal intent). Similarly, some courts have admitted evidence of a defendant's drug addiction as showing a motive for a crime of theft, on grounds that the addiction would create an extraordinary need for money.[149] This, in

---

148. *See* United States v. Clark, 988 F.2d 1459, 1465 (6th Cir.1993) (evidence of defendant's car theft activities admissible to show his motive for killing his brother-in-law and former employee, who told FBI about defendant's illegal acts); United States v. McKinney, 954 F.2d 471, 480–81 (7th Cir.1992) (evidence that victim had botched a drug transaction 20 months before the charged conspiracy to commit murder admissible to establish motive); United States v. Dunn, 946 F.2d 615, 617–18 (9th Cir.1991) (evidence that defendant had been dealing cocaine on evening of gun offense admissible to show defendant's motive for threatening security guard with gun); United States v. Felix–Gutierrez, 940 F.2d 1200, 1207 (9th Cir.1991) (prior drug trafficking offenses admissible to prove motive for charged offense of accessory after the fact to kidnapping, torture, and murder of DEA agent). *But see* United States v. Murray, 103 F.3d 310, 316–18 (3d Cir.1997) (held, reversible error to admit evidence of prior murder by defendant charged with drug-related murder; court noted lack of evidence that prior murder was part of some criminal scheme or committed in some distinctive fashion; dubious character of witness who purported to have knowledge of prior murder may have influenced court, though court did not expressly allude to that consideration as a basis for its decision).

Evidence of the uncharged crime can provide a motive for murder in a variety of ways. *See, e.g.,* United States v. Santiago, 46 F.3d 885, 889 (9th Cir.1995) (held, evidence of defendant's dealings with the prison gang "the Mexican Mafia" was properly admitted to explain motive in killing an inmate with whom defendant was not ac-

quainted); State v. King, 468 S.E.2d 232, 239 (N.C.1996) (held, evidence proving defendant involved in drug operations was properly admitted in defendant's trial for first-degree murder and assault with a deadly weapon since prosecution's theory was that defendant threatened to murder victim because of his belief that victim had robbed one of defendant's "lieutenants" in his drug organization). *Cf.,* United States v. Harvey, 526 F.2d 529 (2d Cir.1975) (boy's statements implicating defendant in crime jointly committed by boy and defendant admissible to show defendant murdered boy).

149. United States v. Robinson, 956 F.2d 1388, 1396–97 (7th Cir.1992) (evidence of defendant's prior imprisonment admissible to show that raising money for his family was motive for charged cocaine distribution); United States v. Saniti, 604 F.2d 603 (9th Cir.1979); Archie v. State, 224 S.E.2d 64 (Ga.App.1976). *Cf.* United States v. Cunningham, 103 F.3d 553, 556–57 (7th Cir. 1996) (Posner, J.) (in case in which nurse allegedly replaced Demerol with saline solution in syringes, thus depriving patients of pain medication, evidence of nurse's addiction admissible to show motive; Judge Posner concedes that "motive" overlaps with "propensity"). *But see* United States v. Swan, 250 F.3d 495, 501 (7th Cir.2001) (in RICO prosecution of city alderman who allegedly created "ghost jobs" for himself and others, trial court abused discretion by admitting evidence of defendant's gambling to show motive to steal; "most people want money for a variety of reasons"; case might have been different had prosecution been able to show large, pressing gambling debt; error not reversible because of strength of other evidence).

turn, would generally tend to establish defendant's identity as the perpetrator. In an unusual case, the court admitted evidence that a doctor had patients perform fellatio while he wrote them prescriptions for Quaalude; the uncharged misconduct was received to show that the doctor was motivated by something other than a desire to provide legitimate medical treatment.[150] In a celebrated case growing out of the Watergate scandal, evidence of the break-in in the office of Daniel Ellsberg's psychiatrist was admitted to show a motive for a subsequent cover-up by Nixon administration officials Haldeman and Erlichman. Among other things, the court pointed out that the payment of money to one of the Watergate burglars, E. Howard Hunt, could have been motivated partly by a desire to conceal evidence of the Ellsberg break-in.[151]

Sometimes evidence of prior assaults is admitted in an assault case under the rubric of "motive." If the defendant has previously assaulted the same person, then these courts allow the prior assault to be used as evidence that the defendant disliked the person, providing a motive for a subsequent assault. Such evidence could be admissible to prove that defendant committed the crime,[152] or that the killing was intentional rather than the result of an accident.[153] Acts showing enmity toward a racial group can also be used as evidence of subsequent discrimination.[154] Similarly, enmity toward an opponent in corporate politics may be shown by similar acts against another.[155] Also, in an incest or statutory

150. United States v. Potter, 616 F.2d 384 (9th Cir.1979). *Cf.*, United States v. Cunningham, 103 F.3d 553, 556–57 (7th Cir.1996) (Posner, J.) (in case in which nurse allegedly replaced Demerol with saline solution in syringes, thus depriving patients of pain medication, evidence of nurse's addiction admissible to show motive, Judge Posner conceded that "motives" derived from a taste for engaging in a crime or compulsion to do it, as here, "overlap" with propensity).

151. United States v. Haldeman, 559 F.2d 31, 88–91 (D.C.Cir.1976).

152. *See* State v. Green, 652 P.2d 697, 700–01 (Kan.1982) (in prosecution for murdering wife, evidence of several prior violent altercations between defendant and wife, for one of which defendant had been convicted of battery, admissible to show relationship of parties giving rise to motive and intent and thus defendant's identity as killer). Normally, prior assaults upon the murder victim are admissible under Rule 404(b), for example to show hostility that gives a motive for the murder. Sometimes, however, the courts will exclude assaults that are remote in time. For an unusually restrictive attitude toward this sort of evidence, *see* Spencer v. State, 703 N.E.2d 1053, 1055–56 (Ind.1999), where the court, while recognizing that normally the prior assaults would be admissible as showing something other than character, held that it was error, though harmless, to admit assaults occurring three years before the alleged murder because they were too remote. The court indicated, however, that the trial court acted properly in admitting evidence of an attack that occurred only two years before the murder.

153. State v. Hedger, 811 P.2d 1170, 1173–74 (Kan.1991) (in prosecution for murdering wife where defendant claimed he shot her accidentally, evidence of two prior violent incidents between defendant and wife admissible to prove "ongoing relationship between the parties").

154. *See* Johnson v. Hugo's Skateway, 949 F.2d 1338, 1345–46 (4th Cir.1991), *aff'd in relevant part*, 974 F.2d 1408 (4th Cir. 1992) (failure to abide by prior consent decree's nondiscrimination requirements, including failure to obey requirement that sign be posted on premises stating policy of equal access to persons of all races, admissible in case alleging defendant caused racially biased arrest of plaintiff).

155. *See* Duckworth v. Ford, 83 F.3d 999, 1001–02 (8th Cir.1996) (held, in civil suit based on premise that superior retaliated against employee for supporting rival, judgment against same defendant in favor

rape case, some courts admit the defendant's prior unlawful sex acts, when committed with the same person as the person involved in the charged crime, to show motive, on the theory that the prior acts show a passion for illicit relations with that particular person.[156] Some courts admit evidence of sexual misconduct toward a third person if it sprang from the same motive as the charged misconduct.[157] As will be discussed later, some courts have stretched even further to admit evidence of other misconduct in sexual misconduct cases. Applying theories such as these to particular cases often blurs the line between evidence offered to show a general bad character and evidence legitimately offered to show motive. Opponents of such evidence should be prepared to argue either that the line has been crossed, or that even if the evidence *in theory* is relevant to a purpose other than character, the jury is unlikely to use it in that permissible way.[158]

§ 5.19 Specific Purposes for Which Uncharged Misconduct Evidence May Be Offered—Modus Operandi

Evidence that the defendant was involved in prior crimes accomplished by a distinctively similar method is often admissible for several purposes. "Modus operandi" is not specifically listed in Rule 404(b) as one of the "other purposes" for which evidence of uncharged crimes and acts may be admitted. As discussed previously, this does not matter; the list of purposes in the rule is not exclusive. In any event, Rule 404(b) does list "identity" as a purpose, and most often, evidence showing modus operandi is offered to identify the defendant as a perpetrator of the crime.[159] At other times it may be relevant to such matters as intent or lack of mistake or accident, which are also listed as permissible purposes in Rule 404(b).[160] Of course, if the probative value of the evidence under the modus operandi theory is substantially outweighed by the danger of unfair prejudice, the court will exclude the evidence. A

or another employee based on same theory admissible to show motive and intent).

156. *See* State v. DeLong, 505 A.2d 803 (Me.1986) (father's prior sexual relations with same daughter admissible in incest case); Commonwealth v. Machado, 162 N.E.2d 71, 72–73 (Mass.1959) (evidence of intercourse with same victim admissible if not too remote in time); Collins v. State, 669 S.W.2d 505 (Ark.App.1984) (evidence of previous sexual overtures toward victim admissible in sexual abuse case).

157. *See* Heyne v. Caruso, 69 F.3d 1475, 1478–81 (9th Cir.1995) (defendant's acts of sexual harassment against other employees admissible to show that, in firing plaintiff, defendant was motivated by desire to retaliate because plaintiff had refused his sexual advance); United States v. Aramony, 88 F.3d 1369, 1376–78 (4th Cir.1996) (in prosecution of former CEO of United Way

of America, where prosecution's theory was that defendant had defrauded United Way in order to obtain sexual pleasure at no cost to himself, evidence of the defendant's sexual advances and activities with other United Way employees was relevant and admissible to show motive for charged crimes, even though crimes involved expenditures on other women).

158. For a general analysis of the "motive" theory for admission of uncharged misconduct evidence, with particular attention to the distinction, if any between "motive" and "character" in particular types of cases, see David P. Leonard, *Character and Motive in Evidence Law*, 34 Loy. L.A. L. Rev. 439 (2001).

159. *See, e.g.*, State v. Williams, 670 P.2d 1348, 1352 (Kan.1983).

160. *See, e.g.* United States v. Woods, 484 F.2d 127 (4th Cir.1973).

defendant's tendency to use a distinctive modus operandi is too narrow a tendency to be considered a trait of character, and evidence of it is therefore not excluded by Rule 404.

In one of the most celebrated examples of the use of uncharged misconduct evidence, the "Brides in the Bath" case, the evidence was used both to show that a crime had been committed (in particular, that the death of the defendant's wife had been the result of a crime rather than an accident) and that the defendant was the perpetrator. The defendant, under a false name, married a woman who had inherited a small trust fund.[161] After the couple had made out joint wills, the wife was found drowned in the bathtub. The defendant soon thereafter married another woman under another name in another county; she also made out a will to him (and named him the beneficiary of a life insurance policy), and also drowned in the bathtub in similar circumstances. A third wife died in the same fashion, after making out an appropriate will and taking out insurance, only one day after having gone through the marriage ceremony with the defendant. In the trial for the murder of the first victim, the issue turned upon the admissibility of the second and third drownings. The evidence against the defendant was otherwise scant: there was no proof he was with the victim at the time of the drowning; the victim had previously consulted a doctor about seizures, which might account for an accidental drowning; and there was no sign of violence or of a struggle. The crucial issue concerned admissibility of the evidence of greatest importance to the prosecution: the strikingly similar other drownings.[162] The evidence was admitted, and the defendant, protesting to the end that he was an innocent victim of coincidence, was convicted and hanged.[163]

It has sometimes been said that evidence of modus operandi must be extremely distinctive, so as to amount to the equivalent of the defendant's signature. The degree to which courts have been willing to require this amount of similarity has varied. Sometimes uncharged crime evidence is admitted even though the degree of similarity is minimal—in one case, for example, the only similarity noted by the court between the uncharged crimes and the charged crime was that the crimes all involved robberies of similar convenience stores.[164] Other courts have taken a stricter view. For example, the Fifth Circuit has held that the similarities between two bank robberies were not great enough to justify

161. Rex v. Smith, [1914–15] All E.R. Rep. 265. Technically, the defendant did not legally marry any of the victims with whom he went through the marriage ceremony; he was already married, a fact that he did not reveal to the victims.

162. One observer has written that "throughout the trial the atmosphere of the court was not, 'is this man innocent or guilty' but 'is there sufficient evidence in law to convict this undoubtedly guilty man.' "? E. Marjoribanks, For the Defense: The Life of Sir Edward Marshall Hall 312 (1931).

163. For a comparable case, *see* United States v. Woods, 484 F.2d 127 (4th Cir. 1973) (defendant's child mysteriously died, possibly smothered; evidence that nine other children in defendant's care had each suffered twenty or more episodes of cyanosis (blue coloration due to lack of oxygen) held admissible).

164. State v. Smith, 707 P.2d 289, 297 (Ariz.1985). *Cf.* People v. Massey, 16 Cal. Rptr. 402 (App.1961) (evidence of similar burglary admitted, though similarities hardly enough to justify analogy to "signature").

admission of the second robbery in a trial for the first, despite similarities in time of day (late afternoon), disguise (gloves and stocking masks), weapons (revolvers), and location of bank (outlying, on a highway).[165] The court may have been influenced partly by the fact that the earlier robbery was committed by a single person, while the later one involved multiple robbers. Nevertheless, even the supposedly distinctive factors could describe many typical bank robberies. Another case displaying a strict attitude is *Sutphin v. Commonwealth*.[166] In *Sutphin*, defendant was charged with burglary. Entry during the charged burglary had been accomplished by throwing a cinder block through a glass door. The trial court admitted evidence that earlier in the same day, the defendant had used a brick to break a glass door and enter another establishment. The appellate court reversed on grounds that the similarities between the two crimes were not great enough; breaking in with a cinder block, brick, or similar object was not distinctive enough to justify admission under a modus operandi rationale. Of course, the less similarity there is between the uncharged misconduct and the charged crime, the more likely the evidence is more properly characterized as impermissible character evidence; and, even where the evidence in theory is relevant for the non-character purpose, the greater the chance the defendant will be unfairly prejudiced by the jury's employing the evidence for its forbidden (character) purpose.[167]

Another potential problem with the modus operandi theory for admission of uncharged misconduct evidence arises with respect to what has been called the "doctrine of chances." As Wigmore described the theory, the relevance of similar misconduct

> derives purely from the point of view of the doctrine of chances—the instinctive recognition of that logical process which eliminates the element of innocent intent by multiplying instances of the same result until it is perceived that this element cannot explain them all. Without formulating any accurate test, and without attempting by

---

165. United States v. Myers, 550 F.2d 1036 (5th Cir.1977).

166. 337 S.E.2d 897 (Va.App.1985).

167. *See also* United States v. Murray, 103 F.3d 310, 316–18 (3d Cir.1997) (trial court committed reversible error by admitting evidence of prior murder by defendant charged with drug-related murder; the court noted lack of evidence that prior murder was part of same scheme or committed in same distinctive fashion; dubious character of witness who purported to have knowledge of prior murder might have influenced court as well, though court did not expressly allude to that consideration as a basis for its decision); United States v. Carrillo, 981 F.2d 772 (5th Cir.1993) (held, prior sales of drugs in balloon not sufficiently distinctive to satisfy modus operandi requirements in case where defendant charged with sale of drugs in balloon). *But see* United States v. Smith, 103 F.3d 600,

603–04 (7th Cir.1996) (held, similarities between two bank robberies justified admitting evidence of other robbery to show identity through modus operandi; court listed several similarities, the most distinctive of which was that both robbers held a knife vertically when entering bank) (authors' note: *query* appropriateness of court's listing fact that both robberies were "committed by young white males with slender builds"; such evidence goes only to whether defendant was guilty of other robbery, a matter not in dispute, and not to the *modus* of the robberies); United States v. Sanchez, 988 F.2d 1384, 1393–94 (5th Cir.1993) (evidence of subsequent offense of drugs sold in pink balloons admissible to counter defendant's misidentification defense because act was sufficiently similar to charged crime to qualify as modus operandi evidence).

numerous instances to secure absolute certainty of inference, the mind applies this rough and instinctive process of reasoning, namely that an unusual and abnormal element might perhaps be present in one instance, but that the oftener similar instances occur with similar results, the less likely is the abnormal element likely to be the true explanation of them.[168]

To put it more simply, the doctrine of chances asks us to inquire how likely it is that the defendant would be involved innocently in so many similar acts. In the "Brides in the Bath" case,[169] for example, how likely is it that so many of defendant's wives would have died in such a similar manner unless defendant had killed them? Though applicable to the "modus operandi" theory for admissibility of uncharged misconduct evidence, the "doctrine of chances" has also been applied to a number of other admissibility routes described here.[170] The reasoning behind the theory seems compelling, and has been embraced quite broadly.[171] No doubt, it helps us to understand the small likelihood of innocence in many cases. But the reasoning can also be dangerously misleading, and potentially violative of the character prohibition.[172] The tendency to "round up the usual suspects"[173] can often lead to undue suspicion of people who have been guilty of similar crimes in the past but who were not involved in the crime under consideration. In some cases, "it is not so unlikely that an innocent person would be repeatedly charged falsely."[174] The doctrine should therefore be used with care to avoid possible inferential error.

§ 5.20   Specific Purposes for Which Uncharged Misconduct Evidence May Be Offered—Opportunity

Evidence of uncharged misconduct may be used to show that the defendant had the opportunity to commit the charged offense. For

168. 2 John H. Wigmore, Evidence in Trials at Common Law § 302 (James H. Chadbourn rev. 1979).

169. Rex v. Smith, [1914–15] All E.R. Rep. 265. *See supra* notes 161–63 and accompanying text.

170. For a careful review of some of the many potential uses of "doctrine of chances" reasoning in a class of cases, *see* Mark Cammack, *Using the Doctrine of Chances to Prove Actus Reus in Child Abuse and Acquaintance Rape: People v. Ewoldt Reconsidered*, 29 U.C. Davis L. Rev. 355 (1996).

171. *See, e.g.,* Edward J. Imwinkelried, *The Evolution of the Use of the Doctrine of Chances as Theory of Admissibility for Similar Fact Evidence*, 22 Anglo–Am. L. Rev. 73 (1993).

172. Paul F. Rothstein, *Intellectual Coherence in an Evidence Code*, 28 Loy. L.A. L. Rev. 1259, 1260–64 (1995) (arguing that

the doctrine relies on prohibited propensity reasoning). *But see* Myrna S. Raeder, *The Admissibility of Prior Acts of Domestic Violence:* People v. Simpson *and Beyond*, 69 S. Cal. L. Rev. 1463, 1491 & n.152 (1996) (questioning Rothstein's position). *See also* Edward J. Imwinkelried, *The Use of Evidence of an Accused's Uncharged Misconduct to Prove Mens Rea: The Doctrines that Threaten to Engulf the Character Evidence Prohibition*, 130 Mil. L. Rev. 41, 54–56 (1990) (characterizing "doctrine of chances" reasoning as non-character reasoning).

173. For the most famous use of the phrase, *see* "Casablanca" (Warner Bros. 1942). In the movie's climactic scene, after the hero has killed a Nazi officer, a police officer lets the hero go and orders another officer to "round up the usual suspects" to hold responsible for the killing.

174. Rothstein, *supra* note 172, at 1263.

example, evidence that the defendant had previously stolen a key to the premises that were later burglarized would be admissible, in a trial for the burglary, to show opportunity.[175] Other examples include evidence that the defendant had, shortly before the crime, escaped from prison in the vicinity of the crime charged;[176] this evidence shows opportunity (the defendant was free in the area of the crime) as well as motive (a fugitive has a motive to commit crimes to obtain the means of avoiding capture, especially since obtaining funds and transportation by legitimate means may be more difficult for a fugitive than for other persons). The fact that the defendant was previously seen in an area where the defendant had no right to be also shows access and therefore opportunity.[177] Prior criminal activity that puts defendant in contact with an organization or mechanism for committing the prior crime may also be admissible to prove opportunity.[178]

Defense counsel faced with a claim that a prior crime is relevant to opportunity should seek to avoid prejudice by pointing out other ways in which the prosecution could prove that the defendant had access to the area in which the crime was committed, by stipulating to access, or by offering ways in which the evidence could be received in a redacted fashion. Doing so could prevent the prejudice likely to occur in situations such as that of the prison break just discussed; it is not very difficult to prove access to the area in which the crime was committed without mentioning that defendant was present there as a result of the escape. *See §§* **5.34.**

§ 5.21 Specific Purposes for Which Uncharged Misconduct Evidence May Be Offered—Knowledge

Another purpose for which uncharged crimes evidence may be admitted is to show guilty knowledge. In fact, this is one of the oldest uses of uncharged misconduct evidence.[179] One who tries to deduct a

---

175. *See, e.g.,* State v. Uthe, 542 N.W.2d 810, 814 (Iowa 1996) (in prosecution for forgery of checks from a stolen checkbook, Evidence that defendant forged another check from same checkbook a few days after last charged forgery admissible to show possession of checkbook and therefore opportunity to commit earlier forgeries; opportunity tended to prove defendant's identity as perpetrator).

176. United States v. Stover, 565 F.2d 1010 (8th Cir.1977) (escape from prison, to show presence in area).

177. *See* United States v. DeJohn, 638 F.2d 1048 (7th Cir.1981) (testimony about defendant's presence and taking of checks at other times in mailbox area of YMCA admissible to show access).

178. *See, e.g.,* United States v. Robinson, 956 F.2d 1388, 1395–96 (7th Cir.1992) (marijuana distribution conspiracy in the 1970s admissible to show opportunity in

prosecution for cocaine distribution, where nearly identical organizational scheme was used for both offenses; prior offense Evidence also relevant to establish intent and motive). *But see* United States v. Hill, 953 F.2d 452 (9th Cir.1991) (evidence that co-conspirator used small amounts of cocaine five years earlier inadmissible even though it explained why co-conspirator approached defendant about financing drug transaction).

179. The most common use of other misconduct evidence in the English cases through the nineteenth century was to prove that a person possessed a particular kind of guilty knowledge that would constitute an element of a crime or tort. Many of the cases were prosecutions for forgery and uttering of forged instruments, where, to prove the uttering charge, it was necessary to demonstrate that the defendant knew the instrument was forged. *See, e.g.,* Rex v.

roommate as a dependent cannot claim good faith if the Internal Revenue Service warned her against doing the same thing in a previous year, and evidence of the spurious deduction that led to the warning would be admissible even though it necessarily suggests a prior crime. Similarly, if a defendant found in possession of a quantity of heroin claimed that he did not know that the substance was heroin, then evidence that he had previously used or sold heroin would be admissible to show guilty knowledge.[180] Even if defendant previously had been charged with possession of heroin and had been *acquitted*, evidence of the prior trial might be admissible on the theory that defendant became familiar with the appearance of heroin through the prior experience.[181] Similarly, where a person is charged with committing a crime using a sophisticated technique or device, evidence that defendant had at another time committed a similar crime using the same method would be admissible to prove defendant knew how to use such a device or method, and thus might have been involved in the crime.[182] In many cases, the

Whiley, 168 Eng. Rep. 589 (1804), also reported at 127 Eng. Rep. 393 (1804) as Rex v. Wylie. Such evidence was also admitted in fraud cases, where it was necessary to demonstrate not only the defendant's intent to defraud, but also quite often, as a necessary part of this, that the defendant knew the true nature of the item she sought to transfer to the alleged victim. *See, e.g.,* Regina v. Roebuck, 7 Cox C.C. 126 (1856). Courts also admitted evidence of other misconduct to prove guilty knowledge in prosecutions for receiving stolen goods, where defendant's knowledge that the goods in question were stolen was an essential element of the charge. *See, e.g.,* Rex v. Davis, 172 Eng. Rep. 1196 (1833). Early American case authority, which relied heavily on English law, was very similar. *See* Samuel March Phillipps, A Treatise on the Law of Evidence 137 (John A. Dunlap ed. 1816); Thomas Starkie, A Practical Treatise on the Law of Evidence 378 (Theron Metcalf ed. 1826). For a discussion of the reasoning behind and application of the "knowledge" theory for the admission of uncharged misconduct evidence, *see* David P. Leonard, *The Use of Uncharged Misconduct Evidence to Prove Knowledge,* 81 Neb. L. Rev. 115 (2002).

180. *See* United States v. Beckman, 298 F.3d 788, 794 (9th Cir.2002) (where self-proclaimed leader of drug smuggling ring testified as government witness against one of his couriers, evidence of courier's prior border crossing admissible to show that courier knew drugs were hidden on his vehicle and to show relationship of parties, explaining why courier was trusted with such a valuable load). *See also* United States v. Osum, 943 F.2d 1394, 1403–04 (5th Cir.1991) (subsequent fraudulent

claims of injury from bus accidents admissible against bus driver charged with fraudulent claim, when bus driver claimed that he was genuinely injured and had not known that codefendants were making false claims); United States v. Obiuwevbi, 962 F.2d 1236, 1240–41 (7th Cir.1992) (evidence that defendant withdrew large amounts of money five times in the previous five years before making trips to Nigeria admissible "other acts" evidence to show knowledge and intent in present prosecution for violation of currency reporting requirement); In re Korean Air Lines Disaster of Sept. 1, 1983, 932 F.2d 1475, 1483–84 (D.C. Cir. 1991) (in suit arising from shooting down of flight over Soviet airspace, evidence of prior instances of airline's commercial flights straying into Soviet airspace properly admitted to show knowledge of consequences of straying and to rebut certain defense evidence). *See generally* 2 Weinstein's Federal Evidence § 404.08[2] (2d ed. Joseph M. McLaughlin ed. 1997).

181. *See* United States v. Rocha, 553 F.2d 615 (9th Cir.1977) (where defendant was charged with possession of marijuana with intent to distribute and defendant claimed he thought the sacks he was loading onto a truck contained furniture, evidence of prior acquittal for possession of marijuana was properly admitted to prove knowledge). *See also* 22 Charles A. Wright & Kenneth W. Graham, Jr., Federal Practice and Procedure (Evidence) § 5245, at 505 (1979).

182. *See, e.g.,* United States v. Jones, 982 F.2d 380, 382 (9th Cir.1992) (where defendant charged with conspiracy involving large drug smuggling operation, evidence that defendant had been involved in

evidence could also be characterized as proving opportunity; the categories overlap significantly.[183]

Not all cases in which evidence is ostensibly offered to show guilty knowledge are so easy. For example, suppose the search of a vehicle reveals a suitcase full of heroin in the trunk. The owner of the vehicle claims never to have seen the contents of the suitcase at all, asserting that the offending suitcase belonged to a passenger who told the vehicle owner nothing about its contents. Here, evidence that the vehicle owner had previously been involved in drug dealings would seem to be evidence of character; it shows "knowledge" only through the inferential route of showing that the defendant has propensity to possess quantities of drugs, and hence that he is more likely to have been guilty on this particular occasion. The evidence does not show something narrower than character (such as familiarity with the physical characteristics of a drug). In terms of the diagram set forth in § 5.05, it is necessary to take the forbidden inferential route through general propensity in order to reach the desired conclusion. Nonetheless, courts have not always drawn such fine distinctions, particularly in drug cases, and the evidence is sometimes admitted to show knowledge of the presence of a drug even when there is no claim that the defendant was naive about the drug's characteristics.[184] Such cases blur the line between character and non-character uses of uncharged misconduct evidence.

§ 5.22 Specific Purposes for Which Uncharged Misconduct Evidence May Be Offered—Intent; Absence of Mistake or Accident

Evidence of uncharged misconduct is sometimes relevant to show that the defendant had the requisite intent to commit the crime charged—for example, the intent to steal in a larceny case, or the intent

similar operations in previous years was admissible to prove, *inter alia*, defendant's knowledge and intent with regard to the present scheme).

183. *See, e.g.*, State v. Campbell, 367 N.W.2d 454 (Minn.1985) (evidence of prior criminal act of using mace admissible to show defendant's knowledge of the use of mace and to show that defendant had opportunity to use the substance).

184. *See* State v. Garza, 735 P.2d 1089 (Idaho App.1987) (held, defendant's large money transactions with person shown to be drug dealer was evidence that he knew of existence of marijuana in residence he shared with his wife). *But see* United States v. Garcia–Orozco, 997 F.2d 1302, 1303–04 (9th Cir.1993) (prior incident in which defendant, a passenger in car, fled car containing hidden drugs not admissible to show knowledge in subsequent case in which defendant prosecuted for importing drugs); United States v. Harrison–Philpot, 978 F.2d 1520, 1527 (9th Cir.1992) (tape recording or drug negotiations between defendant and undercover agent admissible to show defendant's knowledge of drug distribution ring when defendant claimed drugs were for personal use only); United States v. Bakke, 942 F.2d 977, 980–83 (6th Cir. 1991) (held, reversible error to admit evidence of unrelated subsequent drug transaction involving defendant accused of being member of drug conspiracy; only issue was membership in conspiracy, not knowledge or intent). *But cf.* United States v. Beasley, 809 F.2d 1273 (7th Cir.1987) (Easterbrook, J.) (denying proposition that any drug offense can be used to show intent to commit another drug offense, and remanding for reconsideration of admission of other crimes evidence in case in which defendant was alleged to have fraudulently obtained prescriptions from physician to obtain drugs for sale).

to kill in a murder case. This use of the evidence differs from use to show motive, in that it seeks not to show the reason why the defendant might have committed the crime, but the existence of the state of mind that is a prerequisite for the commission of the crime. The category does, however, overlap with some of the other categories listed, since intent may be shown by demonstrating a similar modus operandi[185] or by showing the absence of mistake or accident.

Sometimes the use of uncharged misconduct evidence to show intent can be non-controversial. The defendant's claim that he shot his wife on sudden impulse is less plausible if, on the way to shooting his wife, the defendant shot his wife's lover.[186] Yet in other circumstances the showing of intent is very close to a showing of character. To show that a defendant intended to kill, one might argue that prior killings by the defendant of unrelated persons throw light upon intent. And so they do, but only by showing that the defendant has a violent, murderous character—exactly the sort of inferential process that is prohibited by the first sentence of Federal Rule of Evidence 404(b), which forbids admission of other bad acts to prove a person's character, and from that, an inference that the person acted in conformity with that character trait on the occasion in question.[187] Some opinions recognize this principle, and restrict the use of this type of evidence,[188] while others tend to

185. *Modus operandi* and *intent* are not parallel categories, but describe different matters: modus operandi describes the nature of the circumstantial evidence (similarity of method) that causes us to infer guilt by inferring intent or identity, whereas intent describes not the evidence, but the ultimate inference that is sought to be drawn from the evidence.

186. *Compare* State v. Shackford, 506 A.2d 315 (N.H.1986) (defendant accused of stabbing and killing a stranger in a shopping center; held, evidence that shortly before he attacked the victim, he accosted and threatened another woman was admissible on issues of premeditation and intent).

187. *See* Chrysler Intern. Corp. v. Chemaly, 280 F.3d 1358 (11th Cir.2002) (defendant's fraudulent alteration of bills of lading in way unrelated to fraud alleged in present action not admissible to show motive or intent; the two frauds were significantly different).

188. *See* State v. Robtoy, 653 P.2d 284, 292 (Wash.1982) (prior unrelated murder inadmissible to show premeditation; jury "could well have interpreted the evidence of the prior killing as proof that Robtoy acted in conformity therewith on this occasion"). For an example of a restrictive attitude toward admitting evidence to show intent under Federal Rule 404(b), *see* Sparks v. Gilley Trucking Co., 992 F.2d 50, 52 (4th Cir.1993). The plaintiff was injured when

he lost control of his Corvette while driving up a mountain road and struck a tree. He sued the defendant for negligence, alleging that its truck had run his car off the road. At trial, the defendant argued that the plaintiff had been racing another car and thus had been contributorily negligent. In support of this contention, the defendant offered evidence that the plaintiff had received six speeding tickets in the preceding three years. The district court admitted evidence of the speeding tickets under Rule 404(b) "to show intent, preparation, plan or motive to race or speed on the day in question." The Fourth Circuit held that the evidence of the tickets virtually presented speeding as the plaintiff's character trait and, hence, was inadmissible. The court noted that the Circuit had approved the admission of such evidence when *intent to commit a crime* was at issue. However, in this case, the defendant merely sought to prove the plaintiff was negligent, and "proof of negligence does not require a showing of intent or plan." *See also* Hynes v. Coughlin, 79 F.3d 285, 290–92 (2d Cir. 1996) (where prison inmate denied kicking guard, error to admit evidence of inmate's prior assaults and threats against prison staff because intent not in issue).

The dangers of the "intent" theory of admissibility under Rule 404(b) are discussed in Edward J. Imwinkelried, *The Use of Evidence of an Accused's Uncharged Misconduct to Prove Mens Rea: The Doctrines Which Threaten to Engulf the Character*

ignore the principle or show a rather lenient attitude toward admitting evidence to show intent under Rule 404(b).[189]

Because intent is often proven by showing the commission of similar crimes, one finds statements in opinions that the similarities must be marked, or that the crimes must show the same intent, or even that they must show the same physical elements.[190] These requirements make sense if the only basis for showing intent is the inference that the defendant had the state of mind to commit that sort of crime—that is, if intent evidence is offered as a sort of narrow character evidence, in which the defendant has a behavioral tendency that is deemed not to constitute a trait of character. Yet in appropriate cases, intent may be shown even by producing evidence of a quite different crime. For example, if the defendant claims that he robbed a bank with X because of duress, proof that the defendant shortly afterward committed another crime with X under circumstances in which duress was obviously absent throws reflected light upon the claim of duress, without committing the sin of defaming the defendant's character in general.[191]

Evidence Prohibition, 51 Ohio St. L.J. 575 (1990).

189. For a case that appears to ignore the principle, *see* State v. Harris, 726 P.2d 943 (Or.App.1986) (prior assaultive behavior with rifle, unrelated to present incident, admissible to show intent to kill in murder case). For an example of a lenient attitude toward admitting evidence to show intent under Rule 404(b), *see* United States v. Neely, 980 F.2d 1074 (7th Cir.1992). The trial court admitted evidence of a prior insurance fraud scheme involving breaking up cars when the instant case involved faking automobile accidents. The Seventh Circuit held that the evidence was admissible even though the defendant claimed intent was not an issue. *See also* United States v. Long, 86 F.3d 81, 82–85 (7th Cir.1996) (defendant, charged with possession of crack cocaine with intent to distribute, claimed cocaine found in his car belonged to another person; held, evidence that defendant on another occasion had traded crack cocaine for goods admissible; court states that uncharged crime need not be a "duplicate" of the charged crime to be admissible, an understatement in view of the lack of similarity between the two crimes).

Some cases display a receptive attitude toward evidence of prior drug offenses to show intent. *See* United States v. Butler, 102 F.3d 1191, 1195–96 (11th Cir.1997) (held, in an opinion citing cases on both sides, evidence of personal drug use more than three years before an unrelated prosecution for distribution conspiracy is admissible to prove intent); United States v. Moore, 98 F.3d 347, 350 (8th Cir.1996) (Lo-

ken, J.) (a "mere presence" defense to a drug charge puts intent in issue, so other drug offenses are admissible to show intent); United States v. Perkins, 94 F.3d 429, 433–34 (8th Cir.1996) (prior contact of defendant with crack cocaine admissible to show his knowledge and intent); United States v. Broussard, 80 F.3d 1025, 1039–40 (5th Cir.1996) (no abuse of discretion to admit prior drug offenses, despite remoteness in time as to one defendant and lack of similarity as to another); United States v. Bermea, 30 F.3d 1539, 1562 (5th Cir.1994) (noting general receptiveness toward drug offenses as 404(b) evidence). *But see* United States v. Beasley, 809 F.2d 1273, 1279–81 (7th Cir.1987) (Easterbrook, J.) (one drug offense not always admissible to prove another, even when intent is in issue; remanded for on-the-record 404(b) balancing).

190. *See* United States v. Haywood, 280 F.3d 715, 721 (6th Cir.2002) (held, in 2–1 decision, that district court abused discretion in allowing evidence of subsequent offense of mere possession of cocaine to be introduced to show intent in case charging possession of cocaine with intent to distribute; "Haywood's possession of a small quantity of crack cocaine for personal use on one occasion, sheds no light on whether he intended to distribute crack cocaine in his possession on another occasion nearly five months earlier"); (United States v. Beechum, 582 F.2d 898 (5th Cir.1978) (abandoning same physical element requirement, but retaining same intent requirement).

191. *See* United States v. Daniels, 948 F.2d 1033, 1035 (6th Cir.1991) (defendant's request to acquaintance to call in bomb

The difficulties inherent in the separation of intent and character evidence are displayed in the well-known case of *United States v. Beechum*.[192] Beechum, a substitute letter carrier, was accused of unlawfully possessing a silver dollar that he knew to be stolen from the mail. To establish that Beechum intentionally and unlawfully possessed the silver dollar, the prosecution introduced evidence that two Sears credit cards were found in Beechum's wallet when he was arrested. Neither card was issued to Beechum, neither was signed, and both were mailed some ten months earlier to addresses on routes Beechum had serviced. Beechum claimed that the silver dollar fell out of the mailbox as he was raking out the mail and that he planned to turn it in. The fact that he kept the credit cards suggested he intended to keep the silver dollar. The crucial question was whether the inference of intent derived from a forbidden inference about character, or whether the evidence can be viewed as something other than character evidence. An en banc majority of the Fifth Circuit viewed the evidence as related to intent, not character, and held it to be admissible. According to the majority, the evidence would show a larcenous state of mind even in the absence of proof that the credit cards had been stolen from the mail. A forceful dissent charged that the court's concept of intent was really propensity in disguise, and that the evidence was inadmissible character evidence. The case illustrates the very thin line between permissible and impermissible uses of uncharged misconduct evidence. There is no obviously "correct" answer; different courts employ different reasoning.

In addition to "intent," Rule 404(b) lists "absence of mistake or accident" as one of the permissible purposes for which evidence of uncharged crimes may be offered. This seems to be merely a way of stating a subcategory of the intent category, since the defense of mistake or accident is a defense based on the absence of criminal intent.[193] Examples of using uncharged misconduct to rebut a claim of mistake or accident include cases in which the defendant claims that a death caused by him was accidental,[194] that sexual touching of a child was inadver-

---

threat against employer admissible against defendant in case in which defendant, a striking worker, was charged with shooting at bus belonging to employer; prior act showed specific intent to do harm to employer during strike); United States v. Hearst, 563 F.2d 1331 (9th Cir.1977) (subsequent criminal activity of Patricia Hearst admissible to show her intent at time of original bank robbery, thus rebutting duress defense). *Cf.* United States v. Tan, 254 F.3d 1204, 1210–11 (10th Cir.2001) (in prosecution of drunk driver for second degree murder, prior drunk driving convictions were offered for proper purpose of showing intent because the jury could infer that because of the prior convictions, defendant was "especially aware of the problems and risks associated with drunk driving" rather than for the "impermissible purpose of proving . . . a propensity to drive drunk";

on remand, trial judge must conduct new Rule 403 balancing).

192.   582 F.2d 898 (5th Cir.1978).

193.   *See, e.g.,* United States v. Pless, 79 F.3d 1217, 1220 (D.C. Cir.1996) (bank fraud prosecution alleging that defendant owned corporation which held bank accounts at two different financial institutions, and to obtain more expendable funds, defendant overdrew the accounts in both banks, hiding overdrafts by cross-depositing checks in the two banks; held, trial court properly received evidence of defendant's failure to pay corporate, employment withholding, and personal federal taxes to rebut defendant's defense that he believed that those overdrafts would be treated as loans).

194.   *See* United States v. Harris, 661 F.2d 138 (10th Cir.1981) (prior battering of child admissible to show death, which fa-

tent,[195] that property was destroyed by accident, rather than by arson,[196] or that illegal dumping of waste was inadvertent.[197]

§ 5.23 Specific Purposes for Which Uncharged Misconduct Evidence May Be Offered—Preparation

Evidence of uncharged crimes may be admissible to show preparation for the charged crime. For example, the prosecution may show that the defendant stole a car (the uncharged crime) to use as a getaway car for the charged crime, or that the defendant broke into a store to steal tools to use in the charged burglary.[198] In these cases, preparation is

ther claimed occurred because he tripped while holding child, was not accidental). *Cf.*, Kopf v. Skyrm, 993 F.2d 374, 380–81 (4th Cir.1993) (in civil litigation claiming excessive force by defendant police officer, allegedly in retaliation for plaintiff's attack on defendant's police dog, trial court erred by excluding evidence of prior incident in which defendant shot and killed a fleeing burglary suspect after the suspect killed another police dog); United States v. Marion, 977 F.2d 1284, 1288 (8th Cir.1992) (prosecution may refute defendant's argument that failure to appear to serve sentence was mistake with evidence that defendant previously failed to appear in court and fled the state).

195. *Cf.* Findley v. State, 577 P.2d 867 (Nev.1978).

196. *See* Hammann v. Hartford Accident & Indem. Co., 620 F.2d 588 (6th Cir. 1980) (prior incendiary fires on plaintiff's property, in conjunction with evidence that plaintiff had concealed information about fires from insurance company, admissible to show arson).

197. *See* United States v. Paccione, 949 F.2d 1183, 1198–99 (2d Cir.1991) (evidence of attempt to bribe state officials who called buried garbage to defendant's attention, admissible in mail fraud RICO prosecution arising from illegal dumping of garbage in illicit landfill, to show that dumping was not accidental or mistaken).

On the issue of intent generally, *see also* United States v. Hadley, 918 F.2d 848 (9th Cir.1990). Hadley, a teacher, was accused of sexually abusing a male student. Evidence of similar acts with other students was admitted by the trial judge on the issue of intent. Hadley argued that the acts were inadmissible because he did not contend that he lacked intent, but instead denied participation in the acts charged. The Ninth Circuit held that the evidence was admissible because the government still had the burden of proof on intent whether the defendant relied on that defense or not.

On the use of prior drug-related acts to show intent, *see* United States v. Parziale, 947 F.2d 123 (5th Cir.1991). In *Parziale*, defendant was the pilot of a stolen amphibious aircraft that flew from Louisiana to Montego Bay, Jamaica, and then attempted to make a return trip. He took off from Montego Bay but crashed at sea. Though the defendant was rescued the aircraft was not, and its contents were lost. The government sought to put in prior acts of the defendant to show intent. The other crime was an attempt to smuggle four and one-half pounds of marijuana into the country from Jamaica on a prior occasion. On the prior occasion, he had carried the marijuana in his clothing. The court held that the evidence was admissible because it showed intent, not character. It rejected the argument that uncharged misconduct evidence was inadmissible because the defendant had not put intent in issue. It held that in a conspiracy case the mere entry of a not guilty plea raises the issue of intent sufficiently to justify the admission of uncharged misconduct evidence.

198. *See* Lewis v. United States, 771 F.2d 454, 456 (10th Cir.1985) (defendant broke into one establishment to steal cutting torch and oxygen for use in second burglary; prior crime admissible in trial for second). *But cf.* People v. Zackowitz, 172 N.E. 466 (N.Y.1930) (Cardozo, J.), where the defendant whose wife had been insulted by a bystander, went home and returned with a pistol, which he used to shoot the bystander. The prosecution sought to introduce evidence that defendant had other weapons in his home, in rebuttal of defendant's claim that he shot the bystander in self-defense after an altercation started upon his return to the scene. In dictum, Justice Cardozo distinguished a hypothetical case in which the defendant purchased the weapons in preparation for the particular crime; had that been the case, the evidence would have been admissible.

offered to prove the ultimate fact of identity—that defendant in fact participated in the charged crimes. Preparation can also be relevant to the ultimate issue of intent. For example, if in a murder prosecution defendant claims lack of premeditation, evidence that she broke into a gun store prior to the killing and stole what would become the murder weapon would tend to prove premeditation. The "preparation" theory overlaps other categories including "plan" and "opportunity."

§ 5.24   Specific Purposes for Which Uncharged Misconduct Evidence May Be Offered—Other Acts of Sexual Misconduct

Prior sex acts may be admissible either under an *exception* to the ban against character evidence, or as *falling outside* the ban because they show something other than character. When they are admissible under an exception such as those contained in Federal Rules 413–415, no limiting instruction need be given and the proponent may argue that the subject has the character of a rapist or child molester. The exception is discussed in a previous section.[199] Evidence of other sex offenses in cases involving charges of rape, sexual assault, child abuse, or incest may be admissible under the traditional theories described above. Thus, prior sexual contact with a particular person may be received on the theory that it shows motive, because it shows sexual passion for that person; or prior rapes of unrelated persons, committed in a particularly distinctive way, may be admitted on grounds that they show a particular modus operandi. Nonetheless, sex crimes deserve special treatment here, because some courts have shown a greater willingness to admit evidence of uncharged misconduct in cases involving sexual offenses.

It seems to be generally recognized that other offenses and prior sexual acts with the same victim are often admissible. For example, when a defendant is accused of incest, other acts of incest with the same child are admissible, not as showing character but as showing an inclination to engage in sexual activity with that particular victim.[200] Where defendant denies that any crime occurred, evidence of other sexual misconduct with the same victim has been admitted to prove that the charged crime was in fact committed.[201] When the uncharged crimes

---

199. *See* § 5.10.

200. *See, e.g.*, State v. DeLong, 505 A.2d 803 (Me.1986) (father's prior acts with same daughter admissible in prosecution for incest); Commonwealth v. Machado, 162 N.E.2d 71, 73 (Mass.1959) (broad statement that when defendant is charged with illicit sexual intercourse, evidence of similar crimes against the same victim, if not too remote in time, is admissible as " 'relevant to show the probable existence of the same passion or emotion at the time in issue' "); State v. Cameron, 349 S.E.2d 327, 331 (N.C.App.1986) (trial court admitted evidence of prior sexual acts with same victim;

on appeal, court notes that in sexual offense cases, state's courts have "liberally permitted the introduction of evidence of prior sexual acts committed by the defendant upon the same prosecuting witness"); Brown v. State, 736 P.2d 1110 (Wyo.1987) (testimony of victim and her half-sister implicating defendant in prior sexual abuse was properly admitted); 1 McCormick on Evidence § 190, at 668–69 (5th ed. John W. Strong ed. 1999).

201. *See, e.g.*, People v. Ewoldt, 27 Cal. Rptr.2d 646, 867 P.2d 757 (1994) (in prosecution for child molestation, evidence of similar misconduct with victims was admis-

evidence relates to sexual acts with other persons, the evidence is, of course, admissible if the prior acts show a distinctive pattern that amounts to a modus operandi.[202]

Some courts have shown an inclination to go further, admitting, for example, prior acts of rape to rebut a consent defense, even when the only clear commonality between different incidents was the forced nature of the intercourse. For example, in *Carey v. State*,[203] the court took a broad view of the admissibility of prior crimes in rape cases involving defense of consent. It held that two prior assaults (one sexual assault and one mugging), one resulting in acquittal and other resulting in dismissal of charges, were admissible on the issue of consent, stating that "in cases involving sexual misconduct prior conduct consisting of bad acts is of increased pertinency," and:

> In an instance such as this, when the accused denies the use of force and claims consent, evidence which contradicts his denials of previous use of force in sexual encounters is of assistance to the trier of fact in evaluating his testimony with respect to motive, knowledge and intent in resolving the issue of fact and in evaluating his credibility.

Cases liberally admitting this evidence are difficult to reconcile with the general rule against character evidence.

Some jurisdictions have admitted other acts of sexual misconduct to show "lustful disposition" or "depraved sexual instinct" in cases involving sex crimes against children.[204] Other courts have rejected the theory.[205] Of course, in jurisdictions that have followed the recent federal

---

sible to prove design or plan, which in turn is admissible to prove that the defendant in fact engaged in the alleged criminal conduct); Brown v. State, 817 P.2d 429, 433–35 (Wyo.1991) (in prosecution for sexual abuse of two stepdaughters where defendant claimed the charges were fabricated, evidence of prior sexual misconduct between defendant and stepdaughters was admissible to prove course of conduct and motive; court held motive was important to case given defendant's claim of fabrication).

202. State v. Coen, 382 N.W.2d 703, 705–08 (Iowa App.1985) (prior offense admitted when similar modus operandi of flattening tire, then asking to fix it and get ride with woman in order to rape her); State v. Bennett, 672 P.2d 772 (Wash.App.1983) (defendant had enticed teenage runaways into exchanging sex for food and shelter; prior conduct with unrelated runaways admitted in statutory rape case as showing plan to take advantage of runaways).

203. 715 P.2d 244, 248 (Wyo.1986). *See also* United States v. Sneezer, 983 F.2d 920, 924 (9th Cir.1992) (broad standard); State v. Crocker, 409 N.W.2d 840 (Minn.1987) (rape of adult; court upholds admission of

other sexual assaults, including sex offense against seven-year-old girl, with no showing of similarity except that all the crimes were "opportunistic" assaults); State v. DeBaere, 356 N.W.2d 301, 305 (Minn.1984) (enunciating and applying a broad test for admissibility). For a case taking a more restrictive approach, *see* State v. Saltarelli, 655 P.2d 697 (Wash.1982) (held, in rape case with consent defense, that evidence of a prior attempted rape of another woman four and a half years earlier was not admissible to show motive or intent to rape).

204. *See, e.g.,* State v. Tobin, 602 A.2d 528 (R.I.1992) ("lewd disposition" exception to rule against character evidence recognized in case in which evidence of prior acts involved same victim); State v. Raye, 326 S.E.2d 333, 335 (N.C.App.1985). *See generally* Edward J. Imwinkelried, Uncharged Misconduct Evidence § 4:14 (rev. ed.1998).

205. *See, e.g.,* Lannan v. State, 600 N.E.2d 1334 (Ind.1992) (overruling Indiana "depraved sexual instinct" exception to character evidence rule). *But see* Ind. Code 35–37–4–15 (1993) (legislative reinstate-

example and created specific rules admitting prior acts of sexual assault and child molestation, it is not necessary to develop such a specific (and dubious) theory for admission of such evidence; it is admissible under an exception to the ban on character evidence.

§ 5.25   Specific Purposes for Which Uncharged Misconduct Evidence May Be Offered—Common Plan or Scheme

Evidence of uncharged misconduct may also be admissible to show a common plan or scheme leading to the charged crime. This route to admission or exclusion of uncharged misconduct evidence has proven especially challenging for the courts, and diverse views prevail.

Where a person commits several acts in pursuit of a single, pre-established goal, the theory operates in a straightforward and uncontroversial manner. Thus, if the defendant is trying to reconstitute a gun collection previously owned by his father, evidence that defendant committed one burglary in which one gun was recaptured would be admissible to show the defendant's involvement in another burglary in which another was recaptured.[206]

Note that in applying this reasoning, there is no need for a great degree of similarity in the *manner* in which the person committed the various acts. In the gun collection situation, for example, the evidence would be admissible even if the first gun was obtained by using a passkey to obtain entry to an apartment, while the second was obtained by using a hatchet to break down the door of a house in broad daylight. Indeed, defendant need not have obtained the guns in both cases by means of burglary. If, for example, the first gun was obtained by burglary, and the charged crime by fraud, evidence of the burglary would likely still be admissible.

It is important to distinguish the use of uncharged misconduct to prove common plan or scheme from its use to prove modus operandi. There is, of course, some overlap between the theories.[207] Some cases fall into both categories. The man who makes a practice of marrying women of means and then drowning them in the bathtub may be said to have

---

ment of Indiana exception). Some of these courts have construed the Federal Rules of Evidence as precluding the reception of evidence of a "lustful disposition" or "depraved sexual instinct" theory. *See, e.g.,* Getz v. State, 538 A.2d 726, 733–34 (Del. 1988) ("[t]he sexual gratification exception proceeds upon the assumption that a defendant's propensity for satisfying sexual needs is so unique that it is relevant to his guilt. The exception thus equates character disposition with evidence of guilt contrary to the clear prohibition of DRE Rule 404(b)").

206. *See* State v. Wallace, 431 A.2d 613 (Me.1981).

207. In fact, federal modus operandi cases sometimes use the phrase "common plan" because "plan" is listed as one of the specific purposes for which uncharged misconduct evidence may be offered, while "modus operandi" is not. There is no need to try to force the modus operandi cases into the common plan category, however, since the Rule 404(b) list of permissible purposes for which other misconduct evidence may be offered is not exclusive, and hence modus operandi evidence may be admissible even though not specifically listed.

both a modus operandi (bathtub drowning) and a plan (to acquire wealth by marrying and murdering). In others, the plan theory applies though the modus operandi theory does not. That is true of the gun case in which the guns were obtained using different means. Another example is provided by the film *Kind Hearts and Coronets* (EAL/GFD 1949), in which a character plotted to acquire a title by killing off the eight people (all eight were played by Alec Guinness) with a superior claim. Each of the bizarre killings was different, but each was in pursuit of the same goal. They showed a common plan but not a common method. In still other cases, modus operandi theory applies though there is no common scheme. A defendant may have committed multiple crimes with a distinctive method without planning more than one crime at a time. For example, a person may have committed two unconnected spite killings at different times and places, having no idea that the occasion for the second killing would arise at the time of the first, but finding it convenient to use exactly the same distinctive method when the occasion did arise.

The most controversial common scheme or plan cases are those in which the evidence fails to establish a single, persistent plan leading to a clear goal and covering both the uncharged acts and the crime for which the person is on trial. It is in these situations that the cases are most diverse and difficult to categorize. Some courts hold that the evidence is inadmissible unless the charged and uncharged acts are linked by a single plan.[208] Some are very liberal in finding a common plan in similar offenses. For example, prior acts of accepting kickbacks from different persons have been admitted to show a common scheme to use one's position to get kickbacks;[209] other activity involving drug offenses has been admitted liberally in some cases on the theory that selling drugs is a continuous business involving a common plan.[210] As Weinstein and Berger have stated, "The cases reveal a continuum ranging from situations close to the common design, to cases where the boundaries of the

---

208. *See* United States v. Varoudakis, 233 F.3d 113, 124 (1st Cir.2000) (evidence of car fire set by defendant not admissible in case charging defendant with arson of restaurant; there was no link showing a common plan, and the fact that both crimes arose from a common motive of financial gain did not save the evidence from exclusion as character evidence); United States v. Mejia–Uribe, 75 F.3d 395, 398–99 (8th Cir.1996) (in trial for possession of cocaine with intent to distribute, trial court erred in admitting evidence of defendant's 17-year-old drug conviction; the two different crimes were not linked as such to be considered part of one common scheme, because the earlier crime involved a single sale whereas the charged crime involved large scale, ongoing operations).

209. Commonwealth v. Schoening, 396 N.E.2d 1004, 1009 (Mass.1979) (held, evidence that defendant took kickbacks on two other occasions, even if from a different party, is admissible to show motive, plan, common scheme—"The defendant's use of his position to guarantee contracts to particular firms and thus to guarantee kickbacks to himself provided the common or general scheme underlying all three transactions"). *But see* United States v. O'Connor, 580 F.2d 38, 42 (2d Cir.1978) (bribes taken from third parties not sufficiently probative of "definite project" of committing present crime).

210. *See* United States v. Carson, 702 F.2d 351, 368–69 (2d Cir.1983). *But see* United States v. Beasley, 809 F.2d 1273 (7th Cir.1987) (Easterbrook, J.) (denying proposition that any drug offense can be used to prove another drug offense).

scheme are astonishingly wider."[211] The very expansive interpretation of "plan," a theory one commentator has called the "spurious plan,"[212] does not require a single, coherent scheme on the actor's part. Instead, the actor's thinking is "this worked before, therefore I'll do it again." This type of "plan" case threatens to undermine the character evidence ban because it relies on the same basic concept as the modus operandi cases, but without requiring proof of a distinctive method.[213] Under this theory, virtually any time a person is charged with a crime, evidence that she has committed a similar type of crime on another occasion would be admissible. It is difficult to square the theory with the rule that forbids character evidence to prove conduct on a particular occasion.

The different approaches to these controversial cases are exemplified by recent authority from the California courts. In *People v. Tassell*,[214] the California Supreme Court held that common design or plan could not be established by evidence of even extremely similar misconduct unless all of the acts were part of a single, continuing conception or plot. A decade later, in *People v. Ewoldt*,[215] the court overruled *Tassell*, holding that *Tassell* had failed to recognize that evidence of similar misconduct could be relevant to prove not only intent or identity, but a common scheme or plan, which in turn is relevant to prove that the defendant engaged in the charged offense. The court announced a new, far less restrictive rule that "evidence of a defendant's uncharged misconduct is relevant where the uncharged misconduct and the charged offense are sufficiently similar to support the inference that they are manifestations of a common design or plan."[216] The validity of the respective views has been the subject of spirited debate.[217]

§ 5.26   Specific Purposes for Which Uncharged Misconduct Evidence May Be Offered—Identity

Under Federal Rule of Evidence 404(b), another purpose for which uncharged misconduct evidence may be offered is to show the identity of the person who committed a certain act. For example, the fact that

---

211. 2 Weinstein's Federal Evidence § 404.08[5][b], at 404–123 to 404–125 (2d ed. Joseph M. McLaughlin ed. 1997) (footnote omitted).

212. Edward J. Imwinkelried, Uncharged Misconduct Evidence § 3:24 (rev. ed.1998).

213. *See, e.g.*, United States v. Powers, 978 F.2d 354, 361–62 (7th Cir.1992) (prior convictions for bank robbery and attempted bank robbery admissible as "plan" evidence when in all instances, perpetrator wore wide-brimmed hat, dark glasses, a business suit, had a mustache, and carried a briefcase; modus operandi concept could not have been used because of lack of sufficient distinctiveness).

214. 679 P.2d 1 (Cal.1984).

215. 867 P.2d 757 (Cal.1994).

216. *Id.* at 769.

217. *See, e.g.*, Mark Cammack, *Using the Doctrine of Chances to Prove Actus Reus in Child Abuse and Acquaintance Rape:* People v. Ewoldt *Reconsidered*, 29 U.C. Davis L. Rev. 355 (1996); Edward J. Imwinkelried, *Using a Contextual Construction to Resolve the Dispute Over the Meaning of the Term "Plan" in Federal Rule of Evidence 404(b)*, 43 U. Kan. L. Rev. 1005 (1995); Miguel A. Mendez & Edward J. Imwinkelried, People v. Ewoldt: *The California Supreme Court's About–Face on the Plan Theory for Admitting Evidence of an Accused's Uncharged Misconduct*, 28 Loy. L. A. L. Rev. 473 (1995); Jeannie Mayre Mar, Note and Comment, *Washington's Expansion of the "Plan" Exception After State v. Lough*, 71 Wash. L. Rev. 845 (1996).

Lizzie Borden had attempted, on a false pretense, to buy a deadly poison on the day before her parents were hacked to death with a hatchet was offered to identify her as the perpetrator, on the theory that her original plan was to poison the parents.[218] Like intent, identity is usually an ultimate fact rather than merely a fact offered to prove an ultimate fact. In a criminal case, for example, the prosecution must prove not only that a crime was committed, but that it was the defendant who committed it. Sometimes, other misconduct evidence tends to prove another fact, and from that, identity. Most commonly, the uncharged misconduct evidence tends to prove identity by means of modus operandi.[219] For another example, uncharged misconduct might be offered to prove that defendant had a motive, and thus that she was the person who committed the crime.[220]

Sometimes, the uncharged misconduct evidence proves identity more directly. For example, evidence that defendant threatened prospective prosecution witnesses or attempted to bribe a witness or juror tends to evidence a consciousness of guilt, which serves to identify the defendant as the perpetrator of the crime in question.[221]

Of course, there must be limits to the degree to which evidence of uncharged misconduct can be admissible to prove identity. Otherwise, whenever there was an issue whether the defendant was the person who committed the crime charged, the door would open to evidence of other crimes by the defendant. The mere fact that the defendant committed prior robberies, for example, does have some probative value in identifying the defendant as the one who committed the robbery involved in the instant case; all else being equal, a person who has robbed before is part

---

218. In the actual Lizzie Borden case, the court excluded the evidence of her prior attempt to buy poison; this result, which was never the subject of appeal because Borden was acquitted, has been soundly criticized by Wigmore and other authorities. *See* Robert Sullivan, Goodbye Lizzie Borden 142–43, 194–98 (1974).

219. *See, e.g.*, United States v. Tai, 994 F.2d 1204, 1208 (7th Cir.1993) (in prosecution of extortion scheme, evidence of threats against others and assaults by defendant's employee admissible to show defendant's identity); *see also* State v. Rehberg, 919 S.W.2d 543, 548–50 (Mo.App. 1995) (where defendant charged with stealing plumbing equipment by placing it in an opened lamp box, sealing the box with tape and later purchasing the box, paying only for the lamp, evidence that defendant had been stealing equipment in such a manner for the past four years was held admissible since the crimes were so nearly identical and the methodology so distinctive that it showed a signature; United States v. Hamilton, 684 F.2d 380, 384 (6th Cir.1982) (prior crime with similar modus operandi admissible on issue of identity of defendant

charged with circulating altered currency); Commonwealth v. Madyun, 458 N.E.2d 745 (Mass.App.1983) (subsequent rapes by defendant admissible to prove identify, when there were "striking similarities in the unconnected crimes and the subject crime"); State v. Williams, 670 P.2d 1348, 1352 (Kan.1983). *Cf.* United States v. Williams, 994 F.2d 1287, 1288 (8th Cir.1993) (in prosecution for drug distribution, evidence that defendant "showed up" during a later drug deal admissible to show his identity); State v. Speer, 501 N.W.2d 429 434 (Wis.1993) (held, in burglary prosecution, trial court properly admitted evidence of defendant's prior burglary conviction to establish identity; both burglaries occurred during daylight at houses with "For Sale" signs posted nearby).

220. *See* § **5.18**.

221. *See, e.g.*, United States v. Meling, 47 F.3d 1546, 1557 (9th Cir.1995) (in prosecution for product tampering, evidence that defendant threatened his father-in-law and uncle to intimidate them into withholding information from the FBI admissible to demonstrate consciousness of guilt).

of a population that is more likely to commit robbery than the general population. Yet to allow that reasoning to prevail would be to admit character evidence. It seems clear from the structure of Rule 404(b) that, while evidence of uncharged crimes is admissible to prove identity if the chain of reasoning can bypass inferences about the general character of the defendant, it is not admissible if identity is sought to be proven by showing the defendant to have a bad character and to have acted in conformity with that bad character. To hold otherwise would vitiate the first sentence of Rule 404(b).[222]

§ 5.27　Res Gestae; Background; Complete Story Principle

Sometimes incidental crimes are admitted simply because the testimony of witnesses would be unduly hamstrung by attempting to avoid reference to them, and the incidental crimes have no particular prejudicial effect. This would be true, for example, if a witness mentioned that the defendant and his cohorts smoked some marijuana while negotiating a cocaine sale, or that the defendant stole an (uncharged) item from B at the same time that a (charged) item was stolen from A. The concept behind admissibility is that the witness should be permitted to tell the story in a natural fashion. The trier should get the full flavor of the events that occurred at the time of the crime; and the evidence is being admitted for this purpose, not for the purpose of saying anything about the character of the defendant. This route of admissibility is sometimes designated as *res gestae*, though perhaps it would be better to avoid the vagueness of the Latin term and refer to the "complete story" principle.[223]

Though evidence often should be admitted under this theory if it helps provide the trier with a complete picture, it is also necessary to exercise great care to avoid prejudice. The less probative value the

---

222. Fed. R. Evid. 404(b). *Cf.* 1 McCormick on Evidence § 190, at 668 (5th ed. John W. Strong ed. 1999).

223. *See* United States v. Rivera (Reynaldo Vazquez), 83 F.3d 542, 546 (1st Cir. 1996) (Coffin, J.) (in case charging carjacking, not error to admit evidence that defendant raped victim during carjacking; it might help explain, inter alia, why she heard but did not see firearm); United States v. Richards, 967 F.2d 1189, 1193–94 (8th Cir.1992) (evidence of incriminating items seized from trunk at the same time officers seized firearms is admissible as part of the res gestae of the firearms possession), citing United States v. Moore, 735 F.2d 289, 292 (8th Cir.1984) (per curiam) (res gestae exception to Rule 404(b) permits "introduction of evidence of other criminal activity" occurring at the time and place of arrest "for the purpose of providing the context in which the crime occurred"); Atkins v. Singletary, 965 F.2d 952, 960 (11th Cir.1992)

(evidence of confession to uncharged sexual battery admissible as part of the res gestae of the charged homicide); United States v. Dudley, 941 F.2d 260, 262–63 (4th Cir.1991) (no error in allowing evidence of uncharged offense as part of the "res gestae"; "The jury is entitled to know the setting of a case. It cannot be expected to make its decision in a void—without knowledge of the time, place and circumstances of the acts which form the basis of the charge"); State v. Price, 598 P.2d 985, 987 (Ariz. 1979) (in trial for aiding and abetting sale of heroin, evidence that defendant asked for a "taste" of substance admissible, *inter alia*, under "complete story" theory); Hurns v. State, 616 So.2d 313, 321 (Miss. 1993) (in prosecution for murder of inmate, evidence of sexual assaults admissible to show "complete story" of defendant's "total domination over all the inmates").

evidence has in establishing the full story, and the more likely the evidence is to cause unfair prejudice, the more likely the court should exclude the evidence under Rule 403.[224]

§ 5.28 Quantum of Proof Required for Evidence of Uncharged Misconduct

Evidence of uncharged misconduct may include not only evidence of prior convictions, but also evidence of crimes or misconduct that did not result in conviction, including, in proper cases, crimes that resulted in an acquittal. This result is not illogical; the issue in the present case is not whether the person was guilty of the uncharged offense beyond a reasonable doubt, but whether all the evidence in the present case, including the uncharged offense, demonstrates proof of the charged offense beyond a reasonable doubt.[225]

The fact that the prior misconduct need not have resulted in conviction does not, of course, mean that no proof that the prior misconduct occurred is required. Some courts require that the prosecution, as a preliminary matter, convince the judge by a preponderance of the evidence or even by clear and convincing evidence that the defendant committed the crime.[226] Until the United States Supreme Court unanimously held in *Huddleston v. United States*[227] that this line of authority does not state the rule under the Federal Rules of Evidence, a substantial number of lower federal courts followed a similar practice.[228]

224. *See* United States v. Hill, 953 F.2d 452, 457 (9th Cir.1991) (doctrine allowing introduction of other crimes where it is inextricably intertwined with charged crime should be applied narrowly to avoid overly broad, so-called res gestae exception); United States v. Vizcarra–Martinez, 66 F.3d 1006, 1012–13 (9th Cir.1995) (evidence of defendant's possession of small "personal-use" amount of methamphetamine when arrested should not have been admitted under aegis of complete story principle in case where defendant charged with more serious crime of possessing substance knowing it would be used to manufacture methamphetamine). *Cf.* United States v. Forcelle, 86 F.3d 838, 842 (8th Cir.1996) (where defendant charged with illegally obtaining corporate funds to purchase drag racing chassis and make home improvements, trial court improperly admitted evidence that defendant stole platinum from corporation, since it was distinct from the charged crimes; however, trial court properly admitted evidence of defendant's home improvements since such activity could be construed to be intertwined with the charged crimes).

225. *See* People v. Massey, 16 Cal. Rptr. 402 (App.1961) (evidence about alleged burglary, of which defendant had

been acquitted, admitted in trial for another burglary; similar modus operandi); Dowling v. United States, 493 U.S. 342, 348–50 (1990) (held, not violation of double jeopardy to use conduct resulting in acquittal as other crime evidence).

226. Holmes v. State, 394 N.W.2d 818, 822 (Minn.App.1986); Ali v. United States, 520 A.2d 306, 310 & n. 4 (D.C.1987).

227. 485 U.S. 681 (1988). *See also* United States v. Anderson, 933 F.2d 1261, 1267–74 (5th Cir.1991), *aff'd*, 976 F.2d 927 (5th Cir.1992) (proponent need show only that a reasonable jury could conclude that defendant committed the prior acts; remanding for on-record determination of whether standard of proof for preliminary facts was met.

228. Prior to *Huddleston*, several circuits followed this rule. *See, e.g.,* United States v. Leight, 818 F.2d 1297, 1302 (7th Cir.1987); United States v. Weber, 818 F.2d 14 (8th Cir.1987); United States v. Vaccaro, 816 F.2d 443, 452 (9th Cir.1987). For a summary of the pre-*Huddleston* practice in the various circuits, *see Huddleston* at 685 n. 2.

Huddleston was a case in which the defendant was accused of selling stolen goods in interstate commerce. The charge was based on defendant's sale of 5,000 blank video cassette tapes at a price below the cost of manufacture. The defendant did not deny selling the tapes, but did deny knowing that they were stolen. As evidence of the defendant's guilty knowledge, the government offered, and the trial judge received, evidence that the defendant had at other times sold large quantities of stolen or apparently stolen consumer goods for extremely low prices.

The Court rejected the argument that the government was required to make a preliminary showing by a preponderance of the evidence that the defendant had committed the prior similar acts. Instead, it held that all that was required was a showing of evidence sufficient to allow a reasonable jury to conclude that the defendant had committed the prior acts. The decision was based upon the Court's view that the admissibility of the evidence was governed by the "conditional relevancy" theory embodied in Federal Rule of Evidence 104(b), which provides that when "the relevancy of evidence depends upon the fulfillment of a condition of fact," the court shall admit it if there is evidence sufficient to support a finding that the condition has been fulfilled. In sending the evidence to the jury, the court should inform the jury of its obligation to consider the evidence only if it decides (by a preponderance of the evidence) that the fact at issue is true.

In the authors' opinion, Rule 104(b) does not really answer the question confronted by the Court. By its reference to "sufficient" evidence, the Rule implicitly incorporates reference to an unstated, externally established burden of persuasion; what is "sufficient" to support a reasonable verdict when the burden of persuasion is a mere preponderance of the evidence may not be "sufficient" when the burden is proof beyond a reasonable doubt. While Rule 104(b) may be enough to suggest that the judge should defer to the jury in a jury trial, it is not enough to state exactly what the level of deference should be. If common law principles otherwise require that the jury be convinced by an extraordinary quantum of proof, then the judgment of what is "sufficient" must be altered accordingly.

In addition, the Court arguably did not give sufficient consideration to the problem of prejudice. Any time a jury is informed of a person's other misconduct—particularly serious criminal activities—there is a very real danger that the jury will employ the evidence for its improper (character) purpose and not for the more narrow purpose for which it might properly be considered. The standard adopted by the court takes a significant amount of filtering power out of the hands of the judge; it stands to reason that in the vast majority of cases, the prosecution can offer at least some evidence to support the defendant's participation in the uncharged misconduct, and courts will generally find this evidence "sufficient to support a finding" that defendant was in fact involved.[229]

---

229. In a footnote, the Court rejected defendant's contention that in performing the Rule 403 balance, the court must find that the prejudicial impact of the evidence

The court's ability to control the jury's very natural (though impermissible) tendency to employ the evidence for the wrong reason is quite limited. Moreover, if defendant decides seriously to contest her commission of the uncharged misconduct, the trial on the charged activities will often be sidetracked along a time-consuming and confusing course. This, too, creates the risk of injustice.

The Supreme Court has spoken for the federal system. It is likely, though, that some states will continue to adhere to a stricter standard of proof, even where the Federal Rules of Evidence have been used as a model for corresponding state rules.

In states in which a more demanding standard is applied, it is appropriate to consider all of the charged and uncharged misconduct together in deciding whether the standard has been met. Even if the defendant's commission of a prior crime, *when considered by itself*, has not been established by clear and convincing evidence, the suspicious prior circumstances, when taken together with the circumstances of the charged crime, may be enough to prove the charged crime beyond a reasonable doubt. For example, it might be impossible to establish by clear and convincing evidence that the defendant had drowned his previous wife in the bathtub when the facts of that transaction are considered in isolation, but when the facts are considered in conjunction with evidence that the defendant drowned his second wife in the bath, the two crimes corroborate each other and ought to be considered together.[230]

§ 5.29 Character as an Ultimate Issue [FRE 405(b)]

Evidence of a party's character is not admissible, under the general rule, to show action in conformity with character. In such cases, character is not the ultimate issue; it is merely an evidentiary fact that is offered to prove something else (the action in conformity). Sometimes,

outweighs its probative value unless the court concludes by a preponderance of the evidence that the defendant committed the uncharged act. The Court conceded, however, that "the strength of the evidence establishing the similar act is one of the factors the court may consider when conducting the Rule 403 balancing." 485 U.S. at 689 n.6.

230. *Cf.* Rex v. Smith, [1914–15] All E.R. Rep. 265. For a case that apparently ignores this principle, *see* Tucker v. State, 412 P.2d 970 (Nev.1966), a case that suggests, if nothing else, that the rules of character evidence are not just dressed-up common sense. In May, 1957, Tucker phoned the police station and asked someone to come to the Tucker home in North Las Vegas. When the police arrived, they noticed that Tucker had been drinking. Tucker led them to the dining room where one Kaylor was laying dead on the floor, having been shot several times. Tucker explained that he had awakened and found Kaylor there. No one was ever charged with the crime. In October, 1963, Tucker again called the police. He had again been drinking. He led police to a dead man on the living room sofa. the man had been shot. Tucker explained that he had awakened and found the man dead on the couch. He was convicted of second-degree murder, with the evidence of the Kaylor killing being admitted over objection. The Nevada Supreme Court reversed, reasoning that there was nothing in the record to establish that Tucker killed Kaylor. It announced a rule that before evidence of a collateral offense is admissible for any purpose, the prosecution must first establish by plain, clear, and convincing evidence that the defendant committed that offense.

however, character is not offered to prove any action; character itself is an ultimate issue (in the language of the Federal Rule, character is itself "an essential element of a charge, claim, or defense"[231]). The substantive law makes the rights and liabilities of the parties turn on a trait of character. When that is the case, character evidence is freely admissible. In fact, the character evidence need not be in the form of reputation and opinion testimony; evidence of specific instances of conduct is also admissible.[232]

Examples

The fitness of a parent, in custody litigation.[233]

The predisposition of a defendant, when the defendant relies upon the entrapment defense. For example, if the defendant claims that he was entrapped by the government into selling drugs, the government may freely introduce prior drug sales to show that the defendant was predisposed.

The relevant trait of character that forms the basis for a defamation action, when truth is raised as a defense. For example, if the defendant called the plaintiff a thief, and in a defamation action admits making the statement but claims that it was true, the defendant is free to produce evidence showing the plaintiff to be a thief. (There are limits to the principle. Suppose D published an article that alleged that P stole a car on a certain date. If P sues for libel and D asserts truth as a defense, evidence to show that P stole the car would of course be admissible. However, evidence of P's general reputation as a car thief, or the opinion of one who knows P that P is the kind of person who steals cars, would not be admissible to prove truth because even though P's character is to some extent "in issue," the evidence would be offered as circumstantial evidence of P's conduct, for which purpose it is not admissible.)

After *Robinson v. California*,[234] modern legislators have avoided explicitly attempting to make the possession of a trait of character itself a crime. But they do sometimes make a pattern of bad acts an element of an aggravated offense, as in enactments that make it an additional offense to commit crimes as part of racketeering enterprises or in furtherance of gang activities. Because the jury must determine whether defendant is guilty of the offense, evidence of other crimes is freely admitted in cases in which the other crimes establish an element of a substantive offense. Such statutes may become as great a threat to

231. Fed. R. Evid. 405(b).

232. *See* Fed. R. Evid. 405(b); 2 Weinstein's Federal Evidence §§ 404.03[2], 405.05[4] (2d ed. Joseph M. McLaughlin ed. 1997); United States v. Sonntag, 684 F.2d 781 (11th Cir.1982); Crumpton v. Confederation Life Ins. Co., 672 F.2d 1248 (5th Cir.1982).

233. *See* 1A John H. Wigmore, Evidence in Trials at Common Law § 69.1 (Peter Tillers rev. 1983).

234. 370 U.S. 660 (1962) (unconstitutional to criminalize mere status of being addicted).

traditional ideas about trying the defendant only for the offense charged as are the more overt assaults on the character evidence rule.[235]

§ 5.30   Character and Habit [FRE 406]

In most jurisdictions, character evidence is not admissible in civil cases as circumstantial evidence of conduct, and it is admissible in criminal cases only under prescribed exceptions. However, evidence of *habit* is freely admissible. The distinction between character and habit is largely a matter of degree. In describing the distinction, the advisory committee to the Federal Rules of Evidence quoted McCormick's classic definition:

> Character and habit are close akin. Character is a generalized description of one's disposition, or of one's disposition in respect to a general trait, such as honesty, temperance, or peacefulness. "Habit," in modern usage, both lay and psychological, is more specific. It describes one's regular response to a repeated specific situation. If we speak of character for care, we think of the person's tendency to act prudently in all the varying situations of life, in business, family life, in handling automobiles and in walking across the street. A habit, on the other hand, is the person's regular practice of meeting a particular kind of situation with a specific type of conduct, such as the habit of going down a particular stairway two stairs at a time, or of giving the hand-signal for a left turn, or of alighting from railway cars while they are moving. The doing of the habitual acts may become semi-automatic.[236]

The rules provide not only for the admission of habit evidence about human beings, but also for admission of evidence of the *routine practice* of a corporation or other organization. In contrast to the earlier practice of some jurisdictions, the Federal Rules contain no requirement that habit or routine practice be corroborated by other evidence; it can itself

---

235.   *See* United States v. Tse, 135 F.3d 200 (1st Cir.1998) (in case charging attempted murder/conspiracy to commit murder in aid of a racketeering enterprise, no error to admit subsequent offense of attempting to smuggle aliens into the United States); People v. Gardeley, 59 Cal.Rptr.2d 356, 927 P.2d 713, 722 (1996), as modified on denial of reh'g (1997) (allowing testimony by an expert on "criminal gang activity" about a pattern of criminal conduct in order to support a "gang enhancement" of robbery and attempted murder charges). *Cf.* Old Chief v. United States, 519 U.S. 172 (1997) (prosecution under federal "felon with a firearm" statute; though Court held that jury should not learn of nature of the prior felony, its opinion poses no obstacle to telling jury that the defendant was convicted of an unspecified qualifying felony in order to establish that element of the offense).

236.   Fed. R. Evid. 406 advisory committee's note (quoting Charles T. McCormick, McCormick on Evidence § 162, at 340 (1954)). *See also* Jones v. Southern Pac. R.R., 962 F.2d 447, 449 (5th Cir.1992) (habit evidence is superior to character evidence "because the uniformity of one's response to habit is far greater than the consistency with which one's conduct conforms to character"). *Cf.* Mobil Exploration & Producing U.S., Inc. v. Cajun Const. Servs., Inc., 45 F.3d 96, 100 (5th Cir.1995) (in suit claiming supplier had short-loaded its deliveries of limestone, trial court erroneously excluded evidence of supplier's method of loading its trucks; supplier's method of loading amounted to habit under Fed. R. Evid. 406 because the same procedure was used with such regularity as to amount to a routine business practice).

be sufficient to prove the doing of an act. Nor is there any rule that habit evidence is admissible only if eyewitness testimony is not available. One's habit—say, a habit of using seat belts—is admissible under the Federal Rules whether or not eyewitnesses are also available who could testify that the person wore the seat belt on the occasion in question.

Examples of habit or routine practice include a doctor's regular practice of advising patients of risks of joint replacement surgery, to show that the advice was given on a particular occasion involving ankle replacement surgery;[237] a bar's regular practice of serving intoxicated persons, to support the inference that it did so on a particular occasion;[238] a drinker's habit of getting drunk at a particular social club nearly every weekend, to show intoxication at the time of a hit-and-run accident;[239] a railroad crew's practice of not blowing a whistle at a particular crossing,[240] or of operating a switch engine without a flagman in the street;[241] an undercover agent's routine practice of marking and sealing illicit drugs seized during an investigation, to show that the practice was followed on a particular occasion;[242] a nurse's routine practice of taking blood samples;[243] a business's routine practice of stamping mail with sufficient postage and sending it with a proper return address;[244] and a hospital's routine practices concerning the presentation and signing of medical malpractice arbitration forms.[245]

In general, habit evidence has tended to be evidence of responses, often semi-automatic, to relatively narrow specific situations. The evidence is sometimes rejected on grounds that the conduct is not sufficiently regular or that the trait in question is actually a trait of character.[246] On the other hand, where the need is great enough and the

---

237. Bloskas v. Murray, 646 P.2d 907, 911 (Colo.1982). *See also* Meyer v. United States, 464 F.Supp. 317, 321 (D.Colo.1979) (dentist's practice of informing patients of the risks involved in extraction of third molars).

238. Tommy's Elbow Room, Inc. v. Kavorkian, 727 P.2d 1038 (Alaska 1986).

239. State v. Radziwil, 563 A.2d 856, 861 (N.J.Super.1989), *affirmed*, 582 A.2d 1003 (1990). *See also* Loughan v. Firestone Tire & Rubber Co., 749 F.2d 1519, 1522–24 (11th Cir.1985) (worker's habit of bringing cooler of beer to work on back of truck and drinking from it while working admissible as evidence of drunkenness on a particular occasion).

240. Bradfield v. Illinois Central Gulf R.R., 505 N.E.2d 331 (Ill.1987).

241. Williams v. Union Pac. R.R., 465 P.2d 975 (Kan.1970).

242. State v. Van Sickle, 434 A.2d 31 (Me.1981).

243. State v. Shelton, 176 N.W.2d 159, 161–62 (Iowa 1970).

244. Swink & Co. v. Carroll McEntee & McGinley, Inc., 584 S.W.2d 393 (Ark. 1979).

245. McKinstry v. Valley Obstetrics–Gynecology Clinic, P.C., 405 N.W.2d 88 (Mich.1987).

246. *See* Estate of Keys v. City of Harvey, 1996 WL 34422, at *2 (N.D.Ill.1996) (in wrongful death action stemming from killing by police sergeant, records of the sergeant's disciplinary and personnel files inadmissible under Fed. R. Evid. 406; records could only show a tendency to react violently to challenges to his authority, not conduct semi-automatic in nature; the degree of "specificity and frequency" of the action distinguishes habit evidence from impermissible character evidence); Jones v. Southern Pac. R.R., 962 F.2d 447, 450 (5th Cir.1992) (evidence of nine violations in 29-year career as railroad engineer not admissible to prove habit of driving negligently); DeMatteo v. Simon, 812 P.2d 361, 362–63 (N.M.App.1991) (defendant's post-accident driving record not admissible to show a habit of negligence); Stapleton v. Great Lakes Chem. Corp., 616 So.2d 1311, 1317–

testimony convincing, some courts have treated rather broad traits as being "habit" traits.[247] There is much room for disagreement about just how much specificity is enough to establish habit.[248]

Habit evidence is often offered in civil cases to show a careful or careless habit. (In such instances, the evidence must actually demonstrate a habit, and not just a general tendency toward care or its opposite.) It should be noted, however, that although use of the habit concept is one way of justifying the receipt of other acts evidence in civil cases, it is not the only way. As already discussed, in both civil and criminal cases, evidence of uncharged misconduct (or of good conduct) may be admitted for one of the other purposes listed in Rule 404(b), as long as it is not offered for an inference about character. Thus, in a civil case in which a fire insurance company offers a defense of arson, the company may wish to offer evidence that other property belonging to the defendant had been destroyed by the defendant's arson. The commission of arson can hardly be regular enough to be considered a "habit," but if a distinctive modus operandi was involved, or if the arson was part of a common scheme or plan, it would be admissible under the principles of Rule 404(b).[249] *See* §§ **5.19.**

18 (La.App.1993), *vacated in part on other grounds,* 627 So.2d 1358 (1993) (harmless error for trial court to admit testimony of defendant's good driving record and awards for safe driving as habit evidence); Smith v. State, 601 So.2d 201 (Ala.Crim.App.1992) (picking up prostitutes in certain area is not habit); *Cf.* Neuren v. Adduci, Mastriani, Meeks & Schill, 43 F.3d 1507 (D.C.Cir. 1995) (in an employment discrimination case, defendant's evidence that the plaintiff had experienced similar work-related problems, such as tardiness, on another job was inadmissible character evidence; court made no allusion to the "habit" theory of admissibility); State v. Lagasse, 410 A.2d 537, 542 (Me.1980) ("The tendency of a person to engage in violent acts while under the influence of intoxicating liquor does not establish 'the regular response to a repeated specific situation' necessary to constitute habit under M. R. Evid. 406"); Henry v. Cline, 626 S.W.2d 958 (Ark.1982) (testimony that witness had seen party drive on a road a dozen times and that party was speeding half the time not sufficient to establish habit; behavior not "nearly or completely involuntary"); Ritchey v. Murray, 625 S.W.2d 476 (Ark.1981) (tendency of driver to weave across centerline when reaching for chewing tobacco or delivering newspapers not sufficiently regular to constitute habit; no evidence that driver was delivering newspapers on occasion in question).

247. *See, e.g.,* Derring v. State, 619 S.W.2d 644 (Ark.1981) (regularity, reliabili-ty, and promptness of supposed victim admissible as habit evidence to show he would not have disappeared without foul play; query whether some of the traits described as habit should really be considered character).

248. *Compare* Loughan v. Firestone Tire & Rubber Co., 749 F.2d 1519, 1522–24 (11th Cir.1985) (evidence that employee regularly drank on the job from cooler of beer he carried on his truck was admitted at trial for purposes of showing that employee was impaired at time of accident; held, showing of regularity was sufficient to establish habit under Rule 406, and evidence was admissible despite absence of direct evidence that employee drank on day of accident) *with* Reyes v. Missouri Pac. R.R., 589 F.2d 791 (5th Cir.1979) (four prior convictions for intoxication held *inadmissible* to show action in conformity; evidence was evidence of character, not habit, and hence forbidden). *See* 1 McCormick on Evidence § 195, at 687 n.8 (5th ed. John W. Strong ed. 1999) (probative force of habitual intoxication to prove intoxication on particular occasion depends on regularity of details of characteristic behavior).

249. *Cf.* Hammann v. Hartford Accident & Indem. Co., 620 F.2d 588 (6th Cir. 1980) (prior incendiary fires on plaintiff's property admissible). *See also* Gail A. Randall, Note, *Product Liability Litigation: Impact I of Federal Rule of Evidence 404(b) Upon Admissibility Standards of Prior Accident Evidence,* 61 Wash U.L.Q. 799 (1983).

§ 5.31 Procedural Aspects of Character and Other Crimes Evidence

Because of its potentially inflammatory nature, procedural safeguards are sometimes used to prevent the jury from learning about character evidence before it has been formally admitted, from using character evidence for an improper purpose, and from receiving more details than absolutely necessary. The following sections deal with those safeguards.

§ 5.32 Procedural Aspects of Character and Other Crimes Evidence—Notice; Motions in Limine; Voir Dire Hearings

As we have discussed, character evidence is potentially inflammatory. For this reason, procedural safeguards are sometimes used to prevent the jury from learning about character evidence before it has been admitted formally, from using character evidence for an improper purpose, and from receiving more details than absolutely necessary.

Since December, 1991, the Federal Rules of Evidence have required that the prosecution provide notice of intent to offer uncharged misconduct evidence. Fed. R. Evid. 404(b) states that "upon request by the accused, the prosecution in a criminal case shall provide reasonable notice in advance of trial, or during trial if the court excuses pretrial notice on good cause shown, of the general nature of any such evidence [of other crimes, wrongs, or acts] it intends to introduce at trial." No such requirement is imposed on the defendant in criminal cases, or on either party in civil actions.

Some states require that the prosecutor notify defense counsel prior to trial of intent to use uncharged misconduct evidence. For example, the Minnesota Rules of Criminal Procedure require the prosecution to disclose any additional offenses that may be offered in evidence at trial,[250] and the admissibility of the prior offenses may be explored at the "omnibus hearing" prior to trial. Several states also provide for notice and pretrial hearings on uncharged misconduct evidence.[251]

When the defendant learns of the possibility that the prosecution will use uncharged misconduct evidence, a motion in limine may be used to attempt to obtain a pretrial ruling on admissibility, so that an effective response can be planned against potentially very damaging evidence. The motion may be particularly useful, for example, when the prosecution does not plan to offer extrinsic evidence of other acts, but to cross-examine the defendant about them, because this may influence the defendant's decision whether to take the stand. The trial judge is under no obligation, however, to decide the issue prior to trial, even where

---

250. Minn. R. Crim. Proc. 7.05.

251. *See* Fla. Stat. Ann. § 90.404 (West 1979); Alaska R. Evid. 404; Vt. R. Crim. Proc. 26(c).

delaying a ruling until the issue arises during trial may put the defendant in a bind.[252]

In any event, the defendant, upon request, is entitled to a hearing outside the presence of the jury to determine the admissibility of other crimes evidence.[253] The hearing may occur prior to trial, during trial with the jury excused, at the sidebar, or in chambers.

§ 5.33 Procedural Aspects of Character and Other Crimes Evidence—Limiting Instructions

When evidence that is offered for a limited purpose, such as showing motive or intent, also reflects upon a defendant's character, the defendant is entitled to an instruction informing the jury of the limited purpose of the evidence. Often, the limiting instruction is likely to have little practical significance. An example of this sort of limiting instruction is contained in the account of the trial of Smith in the "Brides in the Bath" case. According to the account by Marjoribanks:

> The judge, however, admitted the evidence [that other wives of the defendant had been found drowned in the bath], warning the jury that they must not use it to infer that the prisoner was a man of bad character and infamous acts, likely to have committed the murder, but to help them to decide whether the death of Miss Mundy was accidental or designed by the prisoner.[254]

A juror, or anyone for that matter, would need a remarkably compartmentalized mind to be able to use the evidence solely on the issue of whether the defendant "designed" to kill his wife, and not whether the defendant was "likely to" have committed the murder. Yet even in these circumstances it might be worthwhile to seek a limiting instruction, if only to preserve a point for appeal.

In addition, limiting instructions can be made more effective than the one given in the "Brides" case, and counsel should be prepared to offer the court alternative language that better communicates to the jury the purpose for which the evidence may be considered and that for which it is not admissible.[255] Where they are effective, limiting instructions may be worth reiteration in final argument. One such case was the Seddon trial, in which Mr. and Mrs. Seddon were accused of poisoning a lodger, Miss Barrow. One of the motives was supposed to be acquiring a sum of about £300 which Miss Barrow supposedly kept in a lockbox in the house, and which disappeared after her death. There was strong evi-

---

252. *See* United States v. Lutz, 621 F.2d 940 (9th Cir.1980).

253. *See* Fed. R. Evid. 104(c); United States v. Beechum, 582 F.2d 898 (5th Cir. 1978).

254. E. Marjoribanks, For the Defense: The Life of Sir Edward Marshall Hall 324 (1931).

255. For discussion of the factors that make jury instructions difficult to under-

stand and of ways to improve their comprehensibility, *see* Amiram Elwork, Bruce D. Sales & James J. Alfini, Making Jury Instructions Understandable (1983); Robert P. Charrow & Veda R. Charrow, *Making Legal Language Understandable: A Psycholinguistic Study of Jury Instructions*, 79 Colum. L. Rev. 1306 (1979); Peter Meijes Tiersma, *Reforming the Language of Jury Instructions*, 22 Hofstra L. Rev. 37 (1993).

dence that the Seddons had taken the money and other possessions of Miss Barrow, but the evidence that they had poisoned her was less convincing. The evidence that they stole her money was, of course, admissible as evidence providing a motive for the murder. Marshall Hall's closing argument pointed out the limited purpose for which the evidence could be used:

> [This] is one of those curious cases where, by reason of the fact that it is necessary in law to prove a motive for the poisoning, for the object of providing a motive, this man and this woman have been exposed to merciless cross-examination on the suggestion that they were thieves. In no other circumstances would that have been possible. If this man had been charged with any other crime, he could never have been cross-examined, nor could the woman have been cross-examined, as my learned friend the Attorney–General frankly admitted, to carry out the suggestion that they had robbed this woman. We are not trying these people on a charge of robbery. You will have to take the greatest care in this case that you do not allow the prejudice which has been brought into it to influence you unduly.... The only possible thing in which the matter might be dangerous, so far as your honest deliberations are concerned, is that you might think that the proposition is, "We have cross-examined these people to show they are thieves. If you think they are thieves therefore you must think they are murderers." It is a fallacy. It is a proposition which will not hold water in a Court. It has nothing to do with the question we have to deal with.[256]

In general, a limiting instruction should inform the jury that the only purpose of the evidence is to shed light on the defendant's possible motive (or intent, or whatever forms the basis for admission), and that it may not be used as evidence that the defendant had a bad character and was likely to commit crimes of the nature charged.[257]

Another situation in which a limiting instruction is appropriate is that in which the prosecution has cross-examined a defense character witness about uncharged misconduct by the defendant, in order to impeach the witness's knowledge of the defendant's reputation. This topic is discussed in **§ 5.08.** One form of limiting instruction, suggested by a well-known guide, reads as follows:

> The attorney for the government now proposes to ask certain questions on cross examination of this witness as to certain alleged events in the defendant's past.

---

256. F. Young, Trial of the Seddons 281–82 (1914). Similarly, in the O.J. Simpson criminal trial, defense attorney Johnnie Cochran quoted the court's limiting instruction about the use of evidence of the defendant's prior physical abuse of one of the murder victims, and said, "So this isn't about character assassination of O.J. Simpson, as you might think at first blush. This is about Mr. Darden [one of the prosecutors] trying to conjure up a motive for you." State v. Simpson, 1995 WL 686429, at *35 (Cal. Super. Trans.).

257. *Cf.* United States v. Adcock, 558 F.2d 397, 401 (8th Cir.1977).

I caution you that these questions will be permitted solely for the limited purpose of testing the testimony of this witness that [*he*] [*she*] was familiar with the reputation of Defendant _____ in the community. The answers to these questions are to be considered by you only for the purpose of testing the credibility of this witness. The questions and answers in this area are not to be considered as any evidence that the defendant committed the crime[*s*] charged in this indictment.[258]

While the instruction is technically accurate, defense counsel should request that the forbidden purpose be more specifically described, by telling the jury that "Regardless of Mr. _____'s answer you are not to assume that the incidents asked about actually took place. All that is happening is that this witness's standard of opinion of the reputation of the defendant is being tested."[259]

§ 5.34 Procedural Aspects of Character and Other Crimes Evidence—Partial Exclusion; Redaction; Limited Inquiry

The fact that evidence of uncharged misconduct is relevant to some permissible purpose, such as demonstrating motive or opportunity, does not mean that the full facts concerning the uncharged misconduct must be admitted. The court can sometimes limit inquiry or exclude evidence in part to avoid prejudice. In *United States v. Sims*,[260] for example, the defendant's failure to return to a halfway house was offered to identify him as one of the robbers of a savings bank. The trial court admitted the evidence, but in neutered form. In affirming the conviction, the court noted approvingly the care with which the trial court had attempted to avoid prejudice:

> Sims is correct in his assertion that the jury may have inferred from his residency in the halfway house that he had previously been involved in some other criminal activity. However, the trial judge carefully confined the jury's consideration of this matter and thus mitigated any possible prejudice. The testimony was limited to a showing that Sims was a resident of the halfway house, was required to return, and had failed to return on the day of the robbery. There was absolutely no mention made of any of Sims' prior criminal activity. Additionally, there was no testimony that only convicted criminals resided at the halfway house.[261]

258. Kevin F. O'Malley *et al.*, Federal Jury Practice and Instructions § 11.15 (5th ed. 2000).

259. This was part of the instructions given by the trial judge, and implicitly approved by the Supreme Court, in Michelson v. United States, 335 U.S. 469, 473 n. 3 (1948).

260. 617 F.2d 1371, 1378–79 (9th Cir. 1980). *See also* United States v. Beasley, 809 F.2d 1273 (7th Cir.1987) (Easterbrook, J.) (trial court criticized for allowing evidence of missing witness's addiction and hospitalization, possibly because witness had obtained drugs from defendant; it would have been sufficient to tell jury that witness was missing through no fault of the prosecution).

261. 617 F.2d at 1378–79.

THE SUBSEQUENT REMEDIAL MEASURES
RULE [FRE 407]

§ 5.35 The Subsequent Remedial Measures Rule: Definition and Rationale

Under the subsequent remedial measures rule, evidence that after an accident the defendant made repairs or took other remedial measures that, if taken before the accident, would have made the accident less likely to occur, is not admissible to prove negligence or other culpable conduct.

Example

Plaintiff, who slipped and fell on defendant's stairs, alleges that defendant was negligent in not providing a handrail and in allowing the stairs to become slick and worn. After the accident, defendant added an abrasive surface and a handrail to the stairs in question. Evidence of the defendant's subsequent improvements is not admissible to prove that defendant was negligent at the time of the accident.

A typical formulation of the subsequent remedial measures rule may be found in Federal Rule of Evidence 407. A majority of states have adopted rules based on Federal Rule 407, and even those states that have yet to adopt an evidence code or have addressed the subsequent remedial measures problem with different statutory language usually follow the policy of the Federal Rule.[262] This Rule, which codifies conventional doctrine, provides that:

When, after an injury or harm allegedly caused by an event, measures are taken which, if taken previously, would have made the event less likely to occur, evidence of the subsequent measures is not admissible to prove negligence, culpable conduct, a defect in a product, a defect in a product's design, or a need for a warning or instruction. This rule does not require the exclusion of evidence of subsequent measures when offered for another purpose, such as proving ownership, control, or feasibility of precautionary measures, if controverted, or, impeachment.

The subsequent remedial measures rule is often applied in cases in which a defendant made physical repairs after an accident. It is not, however, limited to evidence of repairs or physical improvements. Any remedial measure that would have made the accident less likely to occur falls under the scope of the rule. For example, if a defendant fired a careless employee who caused an accident, the termination of the employee is a remedial measure that is inadmissible to prove negligence. A change in manufacturing procedures, in training of employees, or in the

---

262. Only Rhode Island has rejected the policy of the Federal Rule in favor of a rule freely admitting evidence of subsequent remedial measures. R.I. R. Evid. 407. For a review of the states' provisions, *see* David P. Leonard, The New Wigmore: A Treatise on Evidence: Selected Rules of Limited Admissibility §§ 2.3.4, 2.5 (rev. ed.2002).

design of a product can also be a remedial measure within the meaning of the rule. A manufacturer's recall letter to product purchasers can qualify. So, too, can a hospital's post-accident self-evaluative study made to find ways to improve patient care.[263]

The primary purpose of the remedial measures rule is to encourage defendants to make needed improvements or repairs by removing the danger that evidence of improvements or repairs will be used against them in litigation. Though the real-world validity of this rationale has not been sufficiently tested, it is generally assumed that the absence of an exclusionary rule might discourage the taking of precautionary measures and thus increase overall societal harm.

The rule also has secondary purposes. One purpose is to exclude evidence of doubtful relevancy or that even if relevant, has very low probative value. Even so, the conventional view is that subsequent remedial measures are relevant as an implied recognition of responsibility or fault.[264] Thus, in the example given above, it is likely that at least one motivation behind defendant's improvement of the stairway was defendant's belief that the stairway was not sufficiently safe at the time of the accident. Because as the owner of the stairs, defendant is likely in a position to know if the stairs are safe, defendant's conduct is relevant.[265] But the fact that, with hindsight, a defendant decided to take additional precautionary measures often does not provide the jury with much assistance in deciding whether the defendant was negligent at the time of the accident. As one court put it, it is fallacious to assume that "because the world gets wiser as it gets older, therefore it was foolish before."[266]

Another purpose of the rule is to promote fairness to the repairing party. To put it simply, it seems unfair to punish a party that engaged in

---

263. *See generally id.* § 5.6.1.

264. Wigmore wrote:

The opponent's conduct in taking precautions to prevent an apprehended injury, or to remedy one already inflicted, may sometimes indicate a consciousness of wrong, in respect either to the party's identity as the wrongdoer or to his culpability in doing the act.

2 John H. Wigmore, Evidence in Trials at Common Law § 282, at 146 (James H. Chadbourn rev. 1979). It is often said that the conduct constitutes an implied "admission" of fault, *see* Fed. R. Evid. 407 advisory committee's note, but we do not use that term here in order to avoid confusion with the hearsay rule. To be an admission, the conduct must constitute a "statement," which is defined in this context as assertive conduct. Fed. R. Evid. 801(a) (defining a "statement" as "(1) an oral or written as-

sertion or (2) nonverbal conduct of a person, if it is intended by the person as an assertion"). Because people generally do not undertake subsequent remedial measures in order to *assert* their belief in the dangerousness of the condition, their conduct is not assertive and thus not hearsay. As such, the admissions rule, which exempts statements of parties from the definition, is not implicated.

265. The existence of alternative explanations for defendant's conduct (such as that defendant improved the stairs merely in order to make them more attractive) does not make the evidence irrelevant for its offered purpose unless under the circumstances it would be irrational for the jury to conclude that defendant was motivated at least in part by a belief in the stairway's danger. *See* Leonard, *supra* note 262 § 2.2.

266. Hart v. Lancashire & Yorkshire Ry. Co., 21 L.T.R. (N.S.) 261, 263 (1869).

useful, accident-prevention conduct by turning that conduct against it in subsequent litigation.[267]

§ 5.36   Remedial Measures Evidence That Falls Outside the Rule

The subsequent remedial measures rule excludes evidence of safety measures only when the evidence is offered for one of the forbidden purposes—e.g., showing negligence through an inference that the conduct reflects the actor's belief that the pre-measures condition was unreasonably dangerous. If the evidence is offered for any other purpose or through any other reasoning, it falls outside the scope of the rule and will not be excluded unless other evidence rules so require. If evidence of remedial measures is relevant both to the issue of negligence and to some other issue, such as whether the measures were feasible, then the trial judge must make a Rule 403 determination whether the probative value of the evidence when offered for its permissible purpose is substantially outweighed by its possible prejudicial effect. If the trial judge admits the evidence, the objecting party has the right to a limiting instruction informing the jury that the testimony may not be used as evidence of negligence.[268]

The following sections contain a nonexclusive list of other purposes for which the evidence may be offered. The list cannot be exclusive because subsequent remedial measures evidence is admissible when it is offered for any purpose other than showing negligence, culpable conduct, or other fact specifically mentioned in the rule, by means of reasoning involving an implied recognition of responsibility.[269] Therefore, the purposes listed in the following sections are only examples.

Before turning to the particular purposes, several preliminary issues must be considered. First, subsequent remedial measures evidence will only be admissible for these purposes if the issue on which the evidence is offered is "controverted." Most states follow the same rule. Generally, courts have held that the controversion requirement applies to all alternate uses of subsequent remedial measures evidence, whether or not

---

267. *See* 2 Christopher B. Mueller & Laird C. Kirkpatrick, Federal Evidence § 127, at 26 (2d ed. 1994); 23 Charles A. Wright & Kenneth W. Graham, Jr., Federal Practice and Procedure (Evidence) § 5282, at 96 (1980).

268. *See* Fed. R. Evid. 105 (providing that on request, the court "shall restrict the evidence to its proper scope and instruct the jury accordingly").

269. For example, some courts have held that remedial measures by third parties fall outside the rule. *See* Buchanna v. Diehl Machine, Inc., 98 F.3d 366, 370 (8th Cir. 1996) (Rule 407 does not preclude evidence of remedial measures by nonparties, since admitting such evidence does not de-

ter safety measures); TLT–Babcock, Inc. v. Emerson Elec. Co., 33 F.3d 397, 399 (4th Cir.1994) (held, evidence of subsequent remedial measures properly admitted when performed by third parties). *But see* In re Air Crash Disaster, 86 F.3d 498, 528–30 (6th Cir.1996) (held, defendant Northwest not entitled to put in evidence of its own safety improvements on aircraft to show that manufacturer's original version was unsafe; Rule 407 is not limited to remedial measures by party who originally manufactured product). For discussion of whether the acts of non-parties are covered by the exclusionary principle, see David P. Leonard, The New Wigmore: Selected Rules of Limited Admissibility § 2.6.3 (rev. ed.2002).

the purpose at issue is listed in the rule. This is a wise position, as there is no principled reason to risk discouraging repair conduct and potential prejudice to the defendant when the evidence is offered on an undisputed point.[270]

There is also a question whether the subsequent remedial measures rule only excludes evidence of action taken *after the accident at issue occurred*. State rules that track original Federal Rule 407 provide for exclusion when measures are taken "after an event." Suppose plaintiff is injured in an automobile accident and brings a product liability action against the automobile's manufacturer alleging defective design of the braking system. Plaintiff learns that after she bought the car, but *before* the accident occurred, defendant altered the design of its braking system in a way that would have prevented the plaintiff's accident. Plaintiff argues that the exclusionary rule should not apply because the "event" at issue was the accident, and the design change was made before the accident. Although the literal language of the rule supports the plaintiff, some courts have held that the exclusionary rule can apply even if the remedial measure was not taken after the accident at issue.[271] Others, perhaps a majority, have held that for the exclusionary rule to apply, the remedial conduct must have been undertaken after the accident that gave rise to the action.[272]

If the primary purpose of the rule is to encourage remedial measures, thus reducing accidents, it is difficult to discern why it should matter whether or not the accident in question has occurred at the time the remedial measure is taken. Especially if *some* accident has already occurred, or where the occurrence of accidents is a reasonably foreseeable event, application of the rule would encourage parties to take remedial measures without concern that doing so will be used against them. It is true that applying the rule to cases such as this will result in

270. The credibility of witnesses is always "controverted" in the sense that the jury will weigh the value of each witness's testimony.

271. *See, e.g.,* Mills v. Beech Aircraft Corp., 886 F.2d 758, 763 (5th Cir.1989) (rejecting claim that rule only applies to measures taken in response to accident at issue); Petree v. Victor Fluid Power, Inc., 831 F.2d 1191, 1197–98 (3d Cir.1987) (in product liability action, trial court properly excluded evidence that after defendant sold machine at issue, but before plaintiff suffered injury, defendant added warning decal to machine; court rested decision on policy purpose of the rule, holding that the policy is "equally as supportive of exclusion of safety measures taken before someone is injured by a newly manufactured product....").

272. *See, e.g.,* Roberts v. Harnischfeger Corp., 901 F.2d 42, 44 n. 1 (5th Cir.1989) (Federal Rule 407 inapplicable where change in policy concerning equipment sold along with a crane occurred one month before accident); Chase v. General Motors Corp., 856 F.2d 17, 21–22 (4th Cir.1988) (rule inapplicable where automobile manufacturer changed brake design occurred after sale of car at issue but before accident occurred); Arceneaux v. Texaco, Inc., 623 F.2d 924, 928 (5th Cir.1980) (Federal Rule 407 inapplicable where accident occurred after design change; but trial court did not err in excluding evidence because it was irrelevant under circumstances of case). *Cf.* Foster v. Ford Motor Co., 621 F.2d 715, 720–21 (5th Cir.1980) (in wrongful death action against truck manufacturer, trial court excluded evidence of redesign of trucks manufactured after truck in question but before accident; court was uncertain whether general exclusionary rule applies in products liability cases and whether "after the event" language in Federal Rule 407 applies to manufacture of product or accident involving it).

a loss of relevant evidence in some cases, but if the policy behind the rule is to prevail, it is difficult to identify a meaningful distinction between post-accident measures and pre-accident measures. On the other hand, there is little evidence that the exclusionary rule is needed in defective product cases, as a means of encouraging the taking of remedial measures. It does not seem very likely that a product manufacturer would forgo the remedial measure solely to avoid liability in the instant case. Rather, it seems more likely that the manufacturer would take the measure in order to avoid future mishaps.[273]

A 1997 amendment to Federal Rule 407 makes clear that the rule only applies to remedial measures taken after the event at issue in the case.[274] The evidence could still be excluded under Rule 403, however.[275]

§ 5.37 Remedial Measures Evidence That Falls Outside the Rule—Evidence Offered to Show Ownership or Control

Evidence of subsequent remedial measures is admissible when it is offered, not to show negligence, but to show that the defendant owned or controlled the instrumentality of injury.

Example

Plaintiff is injured by a truck driven by a construction worker. A dispute arises about whether the truck was owned by the worker who was driving it or by the construction company that employed the worker. Evidence that the company subsequently had the truck repaired would be admissible to show the company's ownership and control of the truck.

A typical case of the use of remedial measures to show control is *Huxol v. Nickell*.[276] The plaintiff in *Huxol* sought to recover for injuries sustained when he fell into a hole at a construction site. The general contractor and the subcontractor each took the position that the other was responsible for safety measures at the site. This opened the door to

---

273. For discussion of the lack of empirical support for the incentive effects of the exclusionary rule, *see* Leonard, *supra* note 269 § 2.4.1.

274. As amended, Rule 407 provides for exclusion only if the remedial measures were taken "after an injury or harm allegedly caused by an event." For detailed discussion of the "after an event" problem, *see id.* § 5.6.4.

275. *See* Bogosian v. Mercedes–Benz of North America, Inc., 104 F.3d 472, 480–81 (1st Cir.1997) (though Rule 407 does not apply to post-manufacture, pre-accident design modifications, such evidence may still be excluded under Rule 403.

276. 473 P.2d 90 (Kan.1970). *See also* Clausen v. Sea–3, Inc., 21 F.3d 1181, 1191 (1st Cir.1994) (held, in personal injury suit,

admission of evidence of subsequent remedial measures undertaken on ramp where plaintiff slipped and fell was not plain error; control over the ramp was an unresolved issue in the case, evidence was admissible for limited purpose of showing that defendant controlled ramp area at time of accident); Eoff v. Hal & Charlie Peterson Found., 811 S.W.2d 187, 197 (Tex.App. 1991) (excluding evidence of sign subsequently placed in hospital emergency room notifying patients that physicians were not employees of hospital, where ownership of emergency room was uncontroverted, and where agency and control were issues in establishing liability).

the admission of evidence that, after the accident, the general contractor erected a barrier around the hole.[277]

Note that when subsequent remedial measures evidence is used to prove ownership or control, the reasoning by which the evidence is relevant to that issue still depends on acceptance of the proposition that the repair conduct evidences the party's belief that the condition at the time of the accident was unsafe. However, because the actor's belief is not offered to prove that the condition was unsafe but only to prove that the condition was under the actor's control, the evidence is not excluded by the rule. In a case such as *Huxol*, the evidence is offered to prove the existence of a *duty*, not whether that duty was *breached*. Nevertheless, the permissible reasoning is only subtly different from the forbidden "negligence or culpable conduct" reasoning. For that reason, counsel should be prepared to request a limiting instruction, or, in cases raising serious questions of unfair prejudice from the jury's improper use of the evidence, to ask that the evidence be excluded under the probative value/unfair prejudice rule.

§ 5.38 Remedial Measures Evidence That Falls Outside the Rule—Evidence Offered to Impeach a Witness

Evidence of remedial measures is sometimes admitted on the theory that it is being received not to show negligence, but to impeach a witness.[278]

Example

After falling down a flight of stairs, plaintiff sues the owner of the stairs, claiming that the owner negligently maintained the stairs, allowing them to become slick and worn. At trial, defendant testifies that the stairs had an "excellent" surface at the time of plaintiff's fall and that the surface would "never need to be replaced." This testimony opens the door to evidence that, shortly after the accident, defendant covered the stairs with a more abrasive surface.[279] In

---

277. *See also* Wallner v. Kitchens of Sara Lee, Inc., 419 F.2d 1028 (7th Cir.1969) (employee of company that installed conveyor unit at defendant's plant fell on slippery floor near conveyor and suffered injury when caught hand in machine as he tried to break his fall; held, evidence that after accident, defendant installed metal guard on conveyor, added drain lines, and took other steps that would have prevented injuries admissible to prove defendant was responsible for repair and daily maintenance of conveyor, where there was dispute concerning who was responsible for maintenance).

278. *See, e.g.,* Dollar v. Long Mfg., N.C., Inc., 561 F.2d 613, 618 (5th Cir.1977) (although letter warning of dangers of product was subsequent remedial measure, it

should have been received to impeach the trial testimony of the expert who wrote it); Rimkus v. Northwest Colo. Ski Corp., 706 F.2d 1060, 1065 (10th Cir.1983) (alternative holding) (evidence that rocks on which plaintiff was injured while skiing were subsequently marked with bamboo poles admissible to impeach defense witness who testified that rocks were visible for 200 feet).

279. *See* Pierce v. J.C. Penney Co., 334 P.2d 117 (Cal.App.1959) (plaintiff alleged that fall on steps in defendant's store occurred because abrasive strip on step was worn, making step too slippery; evidence that after the accident, manager authorized installation of new abrasive slips on stairs

theory, the testimony is not offered to show defendant's negligence at the time of the injury, but to impeach defendant's credibility as a witness by showing that defendant engaged in conduct that is inconsistent with her testimony or that defendant attempted to mislead the jury with the testimony. Thus, the evidence impeaches the witness by a type of impeachment by contradiction; the witness's own prior behavior evidences facts different from those to which the witness has testified, casting doubt on the credibility of the witness's testimony.

The rule that evidence of subsequent remedial measures can be used for impeachment purposes opens large potential gaps in the exclusionary rule. For one thing, if interpreted too broadly, this route to admissibility of subsequent remedial measures evidence threatens to destroy the exclusionary principle. To be sure, the evidence should be admissible when defendant has taken unfair advantage by presenting testimony that creates a misleading impression. That is true when defendant testifies as in the example above, or has volunteered that she never made any changes to the instrumentality of the accident after its occurrence. In such instances, plaintiff should be permitted to offer evidence to neutralize defendant's unfair advantage. But suppose defendant merely testifies that the instrumentality was safe or in "normal condition" at the time of the accident.[280] Does this open the door to evidence of the subsequent remedial measure? If it does, the exclusionary effect of the rule is narrow indeed, for one should expect just this kind of testimony from a party accused of negligence. Forcing the defendant to deny danger (and thus invite evidence of the subsequent remedial measure) or forgo evidence to support that defense (and risk an inference that her lack of denial constitutes an admission of danger), places defendant in an untenable position.[281] In the end, the admissibility of the evidence under this kind of impeachment theory must be decided in the context of each case.

Another risk created by allowing "impeachment" use of subsequent remedial measures evidence is one of abuse by the plaintiff rather than the defendant. In some cases, plaintiff's counsel might be able to maneuver the defendant's witnesses into saying something that could be "impeached" by evidence of subsequent measures when the main goal is

---

admissible to impeach manager's testimony that steps were neither worn nor slippery).

280. *See* Wilkinson v. Carnival Cruise Lines, Inc., 920 F.2d 1560, 1568–69 (11th Cir.1991) (reversible error to admit for impeachment purposes evidence that cruise ship line kept sliding glass door locked in open position after accident; ship's officer testified that the door appeared to be in normal condition on the day of the accident and appeared to have been properly maintained but did not testify that the line had exercised "all reasonable care" in maintaining the door, or that the door was the "safest" or in the "best" condition).

281. *See* Kelly v. Crown Equipment Co., 970 F.2d 1273 (3d Cir.1992). Defendant's expert testified that design of forklift involved in accident was excellent and proper. The court held that this testimony was not contradicted by the design alteration made after the accident because "alteration did not compel the conclusion that the first design was defective." *Id.* at 1278. *See also* Flaminio v. Honda Motor Co., Ltd., 733 F.2d 463, 468 (7th Cir.1984) (making similar point).

not truly to impeach, but to place the subsequent measures before the jury as evidence of negligence. For example, in *Daggett v. Atchison, Topeka, & Santa Fe Ry. Co.*,[282] a case arising from a train-auto collision, the plaintiffs succeeded in introducing evidence that the railroad had installed new signals after the accident and that the railroad had changed the speed limit for trains going through the intersection. The evidence of the new speed limit was introduced after the engineer who was operating the train at the time of the accident testified, during adverse examination by the plaintiff, that the speed limit "is 90" in the area. Over objection by the defense, the plaintiff was permitted to ask "Well, Mr. Benton, the restriction now is 50 miles an hour, isn't it?" The California Supreme Court sustained this line of questioning on grounds that it impeached the credibility of the engineer. The court also sustained the reception of the evidence about the new signals on impeachment grounds. The evidence impeached the testimony of a defense expert that the signal in use at the time of the accident was the "safest type of signal."

Whenever subsequent remedial measures evidence is offered to impeach, the court should weigh the impeachment value of the evidence against its possible prejudicial effect (i.e., the possibility that the jury will use the testimony as evidence of negligence). In some situations, the evidence should be excluded.[283]

Example

In a wrongful death action based upon a fall down a stairway, the defendant-landowner is questioned during a deposition about the condition of the stairway. In response to a question by plaintiff's attorney, the owner answers that the stairway is now in the same condition that existed at the time of the accident. In fact, a handrail

282. 313 P.2d 557 (Cal.1957). *See* Blythe v. Sears, Roebuck & Co., 586 So.2d 861, 864–65 (Ala.1991) (evidence of subsequent remedial measures may be introduced to impeach testimony when witness testifies in superlative that the condition was "the safest" or "the best"; but evidence is admissible to impeach only if testimony sought to be impeached is initiated by defendant, the witness authorized or directed the remedial measures, the evidence is offered for a material purpose, evidence is relevant to issue at hand, and the prejudicial effect does not substantially outweigh the probative value). For a narrow interpretation of the impeachment exception to Rule 407, *see* Harrison v. Sears, Roebuck & Co., 981 F.2d 25 (1st Cir.1992). Harrison claimed to have been injured by a joint-planer manufactured by the defendants. An in-house expert testified for a defendant that there was no hazardous area on the joint-planer where the plaintiff's hand could unintentionally make contact with the cut-

ter head. The trial judge refused to allow the plaintiff to impeach the witness with evidence that the witness had later made a design change that closed up the aperture through which the plaintiff's finger allegedly came into contact with the blade. The First Circuit upheld the decision on appeal, indicating that the impeachment use had to be strictly limited because of Rule 407.

283. *See, e.g.,* Stecyk v. Bell helicopter Textron, Inc., 295 F.3d 408 (3d Cir.2002) (admission of subsequent remedial measures evidence to impeach expert witnesses must be limited to prevent the impeachment use of the evidence from swallowing the exclusionary rule; here, defense claim that improvement would have been difficult to install and was not suited to a military environment was not sufficient to justify admitting evidence that defendant later made the improvement, as other material was available with which to cross-examine the witnesses).

had been added after the plaintiff's fall. Subsequently, defendant notifies plaintiff that this answer was incorrect, claiming that the witness had misunderstood the question. In view of the negligible impeachment value of the witness' inaccurate deposition answer, the trial judge would have discretion to exclude evidence about the witness' inaccurate answer to the deposition question. The impeachment value of the evidence is substantially outweighed by the prejudice that would result from revealing the remedial measure.[284]

§ 5.39 Remedial Measures Evidence That Falls Outside the Rule—Evidence Offered to Explain Exhibit Illustrating Scene of Accident

In appropriate situations, evidence revealing that safety measures were taken after an accident will be admissible because it is offered, not to show negligence, but to prevent the jury from being confused by an exhibit that depicts the scene of the accident after the measures were put into place.

Example

In an action to recover for injuries caused by falling down stairs, plaintiff claims defendant was negligent in maintaining stairs that were slick and worn, and that had no handrail. At trial, defendant introduces a photograph of the stairs to show that the stairs were not slick and worn. The photograph shows a handrail that was installed after the accident. The plaintiff is entitled to point out that the handrail was installed after the accident, in order to give the jury an accurate picture of the condition of the stairs at the time of the accident. (The same principle would apply if the jury had taken a view of the scene of the accident.)

In such a case, the evidence that the handrail was installed after the accident is admissible on the theory that it is not being used to prove "negligence or culpable conduct," but merely to prevent the jury from being confused about the condition of the stairs at the time of the accident. The defendant is entitled to a limiting instruction telling the jury not to use the testimony as evidence of negligence.

Can the plaintiff open this avenue of admissibility by offering a photograph that shows subsequent repairs and then offering evidence that the repairs were made after the accident? Clearly this should not be permitted in cases in which the plaintiff's photograph does not serve to give the jury a clearer understanding of the physical facts at the time of the accident than could otherwise be obtained.[285] However, the issue

284. *See* Hanson v. Roe, 373 N.W.2d 366 (Minn.App.1985). *See also* Agostinho v. Fairbanks Clinic Partnership, 821 P.2d 714, 716–17 (Alaska 1991) (trial court committed reversible error by failing to balance probative value against potential prejudice before determining whether to admit evidence of subsequent sanding and salting to impeach defense witness's testimony that walks did not appear to be icy when plaintiff fell).

285. *See* Gignoux v. St. Louis Public Serv. Co., 180 S.W.2d 784, 785–87 (Mo.App. 1944), and cases cited therein.

should be resolved, not by an absolute rule excluding photographs showing repairs when they are offered by plaintiffs, but by a flexible rule that weighs whether the evidence is needed for some purpose other than showing negligence. If, for example, a photograph of the scene taken after the repairs were made is the only means available to help the jury visualize how the accident occurred, then the photograph should be admitted, with a limiting instruction, even if it unavoidably shows the existence of repairs.[286] If, however, the condition of the scene at the time of the accident can be satisfactorily illustrated in some other fashion, then the photograph should be excluded. For example, if plaintiff has access to photographs or other evidence that adequately illustrates the scene without revealing that safety measures have been taken after the accident, then a photograph showing the safety measures should be excluded. Similarly, if, without distorting the condition of the scene at the time of the accident, the photograph could be cropped so that it does not show the subsequent repairs, then the photo should be cropped to avoid prejudice.

§ 5.40 Remedial Measures Evidence That Falls Outside the Rule—Evidence Offered to Show Feasibility of Precautionary Measures

Although evidence of subsequent remedial measures is not admissible to show negligence or culpable conduct, it is admissible to show that the remedial measures were feasible, if feasibility is controverted.

Example

Plaintiff was injured while operating a drill press in defendant's plant. Plaintiff claims that the drill press should have been protected by a finger guard. Defendant asserts that installing a finger guard was not feasible; the workers would not have been able to operate the drill press properly because a finger guard would have interfered with their access to it. Evidence that the defendant subsequently installed a finger guard would be admissible to show feasibility.

Most claims that remedial measures were not feasible do not involve claims that it would have been physically impossible to take the proposed safety measure. Rather, the defendant will concede that safety measures were physically possible, but claim that they would be so costly or burdensome that they were not required by ordinary prudence. In such circumstances, evidence of remedial measures is admissible on the issue of feasibility. For example, in *Whitehead v. St. Joe Lead Co.*,[287] the court stated that evidence showing that after plaintiff's injury, defendant had affixed warning labels to its product should be received as evidence that

286. *See, e.g.,* Lebrecht v. Bethlehem Steel Corp., 402 F.2d 585, 592 (2d Cir.1968) (plaintiff entitled to put in photo of site of accident, even though it showed planking added as safety improvement; photo illustrated conditions at time of accident and jury was instructed to ignore the added planking).

287. 729 F.2d 238, 247 n. 6 (3d Cir. 1984).

warnings were not too costly, and hence that precautions were feasible under the circumstances.

Obviously, the question of feasibility overlaps with the question of "negligence or culpable conduct" to some extent. The evidence ultimately leads to the same conclusion on the same issue as it would if offered for the forbidden purpose. There is a thin line between offering evidence of the subsequent remedial measure to prove that it was feasible to take those steps (and thus that defendant had a duty to take them), and offering the evidence to prove that defendant was aware of the danger (and thus had a duty to correct it sooner). Ultimately, the court must determine whether the evidence has much probative value on the issue of feasibility, and whether the jury is likely to understand and abide by a limiting instruction.

The federal rule makers included a provision that subsequent repairs evidence is inadmissible when the issue of feasibility is not "controverted." Suppose defendant claims that it was not negligent because the safety measures were so costly that the prudent person would not undertake them. In that instance, feasibility is controverted and the rule permits the admission of evidence to rebut the claim that the measures were impracticable because too costly. In other situations, however, it is possible to deny negligence without controverting feasibility. For example, when the defendant claims that the lack of safety devices was not the cause of the plaintiff's injury, or that the need for safety devices could not have been foreseen at the time of the accident, then it is possible to defend against a negligence claim without "controverting" the feasibility of safety devices. The defendant should also be able to avoid controverting the issue of feasibility by conceding that additional safety measures were economically feasible, while maintaining that its original measures were adequate and acceptable.[288]

The scope of the exclusionary rule will also be affected by the definition of "feasibility" applied by the courts. Although a number of cases have excluded evidence despite an argument that the evidence should be admitted to show feasibility, others have taken a very broad view of the admissibility of evidence on the issue of feasibility. For example, in *Anderson v. Malloy*,[289] the defendant did not contend that

---

288. *See* Grenada Steel Indus. v. Alabama Oxygen Co., 695 F.2d 883, 888 (5th Cir.1983), which notes that while it is true that feasibility may "almost always" be in question in design defect cases, that is not always so; sometimes the manufacturer does not claim that another design was impracticable, but "only that it adopted an acceptable one."

289. 700 F.2d 1208, 1213 (8th Cir. 1983). For a case that takes a similarly broad view of feasibility, *see* Lewis v. Cotton Belt Route–Saint Louis Southwestern Ry., 576 N.E.2d 918, 929–30 (Ill.App.1991) (allowing evidence that injured lone worker

was replaced by a worker plus a spotter, to impeach and controvert defense witness's testimony that using a spotter was not feasible, although witness apparently used the word "feasible" to mean "not necessary under the circumstances" rather than "impossible"). *See also* Wilkinson v. Hyatt Corp., 1993 WL 121287, at *2–3 (E.D.La. 1993) (plaintiff may introduce evidence of subsequent security changes when report by defendant's expert witness stated defendant should not be expected to do what society itself cannot do, to prevent all crime); Ross v. Black & Decker, Inc., 977 F.2d 1178, 1184 (7th Cir.1992) (defendant's

additional safety measures would have been too costly, but merely claimed that they would have been superfluous. The principal plaintiff had been raped by a stranger while alone in a room in a motel owned by the defendants. She had opened the door in response to a knock by the assailant, who spoke to her in a muffled voice that she thought was her husband's. She claimed that the motel should have installed peepholes and chain locks on the doors, and sought to introduce evidence that after the rape the defendants did install these devices. The trial judge excluded the evidence, and on appeal, the Eighth Circuit reversed, holding that the evidence was admissible.

The Eighth Circuit alluded to certain testimony by defendant Malloy, one of the owners of the motel. Plaintiffs had called Malloy as an adverse witness. He testified that he had talked to the village police chief about security measures for the hotel. According to his testimony, the officer had told him that because the motel had six-foot picture windows right next to the doors (through which the guests could look to see who was knocking) peepholes were unnecessary. Also, chains would be "false security." In the view of the Eighth Circuit, this testimony raised an issue of the "feasibility" of peepholes and chains. The court held that "feasible" means not only "possible," but also "capable of being utilized ... or dealt with successfully." For the defense witness to say that peepholes and chains would only provide a false sense of security was to say that they could not be "utilized successfully," and hence to challenge the feasibility of the security measure.

The dissenting opinion by Judge Gibson questioned the majority's definition of feasibility. To him, a claim that a safety measure was not feasible had to be a claim that adopting the safety measure would be impossible or overly costly. Here, the defendants did not claim that the safety measures would not be feasible, only that they would not be desirable.

The *Anderson* majority takes a very broad view of the concept of feasibility, making it more difficult for a defendant to claim that its failure to use certain safety measures was not negligent without at the same time opening the door to an assertion that the defendant has challenged the feasibility of the safety measures, and hence that evidence of subsequent use of the measures is admissible. If the defendant claims that the reasonable person would not have used the safety measures because they were impracticable or too costly, then defendant has challenged feasibility under the *Whitehead* line of cases previously discussed. If the defendant claims that a reasonable person would not have used the safety measures because they were not necessary, then defendant has challenged feasibility under the *Anderson* case.

"tactical error" in failing to stipulate feasibility of remedial measures makes post-manufacture remedial measures admissible). On feasibility in general, *see* Southland Enter., Inc. v. United States, 24 Cl.Ct. 596, 603 (1991) (allowing evidence that the Park Service redesigned road well after plaintiff completed construction, where parties contested feasibility).

Other courts have taken a much narrower view than that taken in the *Anderson* case, and have held that a defendant can maintain that safety measures were not necessary without putting feasibility into issue. In *Tuer v. McDonald*,[290] an opinion that gives a very full treatment of the problem, the highest court of Maryland noted the definition used in *Anderson v. Malloy*, but preferred a different approach for the case before it. In the court's view, the word "feasible" should be taken to refer not to whether a measure was advisable but to whether the measure was practicable. Under that approach, a defendant can contest the safety or wisdom of an improvement without raising an issue of "feasibility" that opens the door to subsequent remedial measures evidence. Similarly, in *Gauthier v. AMF, Inc.*,[291] the defendant conceded that the safety devices in question were technologically and economically feasible, but argued it had been justified in deciding that the questionable benefit of the device did not outweigh such factors as the consumer frustration that would arise from the inconvenience caused by it. The court held that this position did not constitute a challenge to the feasibility of the safety devices, and hence did not open the door to evidence that they had been installed later.[292]

§ 5.41 Remedial Measures Evidence That Falls Outside the Rule—Evidence Offered to Show Causation of Accident

Some courts have allowed plaintiff to offer evidence of subsequent remedial measures to prove that defendant's negligence was a cause of the injury or harm. In *Kuhn v. Illinois C. R.R.*,[293] for example, plaintiff alleged that his property was damaged by emissions from smokestacks on defendant's roundhouse. To prove causation, plaintiff was allowed to

290. 701 A.2d 1101 (Md. 1997). Plaintiff sued for medical malpractice, alleging that defendants should have continued administering Heparin, an anti-coagulant, in the hours before the decedent's scheduled surgery. The hospital changed its procedure after the surgery. Despite defense testimony that it would have been "unsafe" to continue administering the anti-coagulant, the court held that "feasibility" had not been raised as an issue, noting that the testimony did not "constitute an assertion that restarting of the Heparin was not feasible. It was feasible but, in [the view they held prior to the change in procedure], not advisable."

291. 788 F.2d 634, 637–38 (9th Cir. 1986), *amended on denial of reh'g*, 805 F.2d 337 (9th Cir. 1986).

292. *See also* Phar–Mor, Inc. v. Goff, 594 So.2d 1213, 1218 (Ala.1992) (excluding photographs of baskets in store, stacked a different way after plaintiff's slip-and-fall accident; feasibility of stacking baskets different was not controverted); In re Joint Eastern Dist. and Southern Dist. Asbestos Litigation, 995 F.2d 343, 345 (2d Cir.1993) (holding feasibility "not an open sesame whose mere invocation parts Rule 407 and ushers in evidence of subsequent repairs and remedies.... [T]o read it that casually will cause the exception to engulf the rule..."); Flaminio v. Honda Motor Co., 733 F.2d 463, 468 (7th Cir.1984) (in product liability action against motorcycle manufacturer alleging that motorcycle was defective because of a "wobble" at high speed, defendants did not controvert feasibility of eliminating wobble; "[t]heir argument was that there is a tradeoff between wobble and 'weave,' and that in designing the model on which Flaminio was injured Japanese Honda had decided that weave was the greater danger because it occurs at high speeds and because the Gold Wing model ... was designed for high speeds. The feasibility, as distinct from the net advantages, of reducing the danger of wobble was not in issue").

293. 111 Ill.App. 323 (1903).

offer evidence that after the smokestacks were heightened, the damages ceased. Even though admission risked unfair prejudice to defendant, the evidence in *Kuhn* appears to have been highly probative of causation.[294]

§ 5.42 Remedial Measures Evidence That Falls Outside the Rule—Evidence Offered to Support or Defend Against Award of Punitive Damages

There are circumstances in which evidence of subsequent remedial measures can be relevant and admissible either to demonstrate the appropriateness of punitive damages or show that the party's behavior does not justify such an award.

Plaintiff may present evidence of subsequent remedial measures when the subsequent measure itself constitutes the predicate for an award of punitive damages. In *Northern Indiana Public Service Co. v. G.V.K. Corp.*,[295] for example, plaintiffs brought suit against a public utility following an explosion that occurred while the utility was excavating property. While preparing to excavate, a government biologist with whom plaintiffs were working asked defendant NIPSCO where the utilities were located on the property. NIPSCO responded by placing yellow flags over an active gas line. The employee who did so knew there were actually four active pipelines, however. Plaintiffs avoided the flagged pipeline but caused an explosion when they struck an unmarked line. Aside from the basic damage claim, plaintiffs sued NIPSCO for fraud, alleging that after the explosion, the company sent an employee back to the property to move the existing flags and place a second row of flags marking an active pipeline. Over defendant's objection, the court permitted plaintiffs to present evidence of this post-accident activity. Though the evidence would not be admissible to prove liability for the initial damage to the property, the measures were the very act that arguably justified an award of punitive damages.[296]

Defendant, on the other hand, may wish to present evidence of subsequent remedial measures as factual support for an argument that punitive damages are not appropriate. This might be appropriate when, for example, defendant seeks to prove that it acted in good faith. A subsequent remedial measure is relevant to the party's good faith at the time of the accident because it tends to show that the party did not mean to cause harm or otherwise act with a state of mind that can support an award of punitive damages.[297]

294. *See also* George v. Morgan Construction Co., 389 F.Supp. 253, 264 (D.Pa. 1975) (evidence of post accident change in mill design admissible to prove, *inter alia*, that condition at time of accident was a proximate cause of accident).

295. 713 N.E.2d 842 (Ind. App.1999).

296. *Id.* at 849–50. The court also held that the evidence was admissible to impeach NIPSCO's account of the events before the accident and to prove the feasibility of precautionary measures. *Id.* at 849.

297. *See, e.g.,* Swinton v. Potomac Corp., 270 F.3d 794 (9th Cir.2001) (approving general principle of admissibility for this purpose, but holding that trial court's exclusion was justified under the circumstances).

§ 5.43   Remedial Measures Evidence That Falls Outside the Rule—Evidence Offered in Strict Liability Cases

Before the 1997 amendments, the applicability of Federal Rule of Evidence 407 in strict liability cases was a matter of dispute. By its terms, Rule 407 only prohibited the use of remedial measures to show "negligence or culpable conduct." A minority of the courts that interpreted Rule 407 took the position that because "negligence or culpable conduct" is not an issue in a strict liability action, the rule did not apply.[298] They reasoned that the policy of Rule 407 did not require that it be extended to strict liability cases, since the typical defendant in a strict liability case is a mass producer of goods that will not forgo making improvements, and thereby risk innumerable lawsuits, merely to prevent evidence from being introduced in a lawsuit commenced prior to the improvement.[299]

Other courts disagreed, holding that Rule 407 did apply to strict liability actions.[300] For example, in *Gauthier v. AMF, Inc.*,[301] the court

[298]. *See* Herndon v. Seven Bar Flying Serv., 716 F.2d 1322, 1331 (10th Cir.1983); Robbins v. Farmers Union Grain Terminal Assn., 552 F.2d 788, 792–93 (8th Cir.1977). *Accord* Unterburger v. Snow Co., 630 F.2d 599, 603 (8th Cir.1980). The Eighth Circuit modified its position in the subsequent case of DeLuryea v. Winthrop Labs., 697 F.2d 222 (8th Cir.1983). In *DeLuryea*, the plaintiff sued for damages allegedly suffered as a result of tissue damage and drug dependence caused by the drug Talwin. The trial judge admitted evidence of a change in warnings concerning Talwin's side effects that defendants had issued after plaintiff stopped taking Talwin. The court noted that cases admitting remedial measures evidence in strict liability actions had been based on the theory that proof of negligence or culpable conduct is not required in a strict liability action because the issue is the product's defect rather than the manufacturer's conduct. Here, however, where the product was unavoidably unsafe (all prescription drugs are capable of doing harm if misused), the issue turned upon whether the manufacturer had failed to give "reasonable and adequate warnings" of dangers that were "reasonably foreseeable." This standard was similar to a negligence standard. *Id.* at 227–28. Therefore, the evidence of subsequent alterations in the warnings was offered for purposes of showing "negligence or culpable conduct" within the meaning of Rule 407, and should have been excluded. *Accord* Werner v. Upjohn Co., 628 F.2d 848, 858 (4th Cir.1980). Recently, the Eighth Circuit further modified its position in Burke v. Deere & Co., 6 F.3d 497, 506–07 (8th Cir.1993). In *Burke*, a

strict liability case, the court held that the district court abused its discretion by admitting evidence of subsequent remedial measures on the issue of punitive damages. The court reasoned that the evidence was admitted as ostensibly relevant to the defendant's state of mind relating to the imposition of a punitive award; the evidence of subsequent remedial measures was used, therefore, to show the defendant's "culpable conduct in connection with the event" and, hence, fell within the prohibitions of Rule 407.

[299]. *See* Robbins v. Farmers Union Grain Terminal Assn., 552 F.2d 788, 792–93 (8th Cir.1977). The California Supreme Court reached the same conclusion in applying California's subsequent remedial measures rule. Ault v. International Harvester, 528 P.2d 1148 (Cal.1974).

[300]. *See* Raymond v. Raymond Corp., 938 F.2d 1518, 1522 (1st Cir.1991) (explicitly holding for the first time that Rule 407 applies to strict liability cases; noting that the majority of sister circuits apply the rule to strict liability cases); *see also* Wood v. Morbark Indus., Inc., 70 F.3d 1201, 1206–07 (11th Cir.1995) (Rule 407 applies in strict products liability cases when plaintiff alleges that a product is defective because the design is unreasonably dangerous); Gauthier v. AMF, Inc., 788 F.2d 634 (9th Cir.1986), *amended on denial of reh'g*, 805 F.2d 337 (9th Cir.1986); Flaminio v. Honda Motor Co., 733 F.2d 463 (7th Cir.1984); Grenada Steel Indus. v. Alabama Oxygen Co., 695 F.2d 883 (5th Cir.1983); Josephs v. Harris Corp., 677 F.2d 985, 990 (3d Cir.

took issue with the public policy basis for decisions holding that Rule 407 did not apply, saying that "it is precisely the large manufacturers who are defendants in many product liability suits who are most likely to know about Rule 407 and be affected by the decision whether to apply it."[302] The court also apparently considered a strict liability claim that the defendant had marketed a defective product to be a claim of "culpable conduct" that fell within the language of original Rule 407.[303] The court noted that nearly all the circuits that had reached the issue had decided that Rule 407 applies to strict liability cases.[304]

In 1997, Rule 407 was amended, making clear that the exclusionary provision does in fact apply in all three main kinds of product liability cases (manufacturing defect, design defect, and failure to warn cases).[305]

§ 5.44   Practice Considerations

The subsequent remedial measures rule has sometimes been characterized as ineffective because evidence of repairs is so commonly admissible to prove ownership, control, or feasibility, or for impeachment. Nevertheless, precautions can be taken to preserve the objection or to mitigate the effect of admission of the evidence.

Defense counsel should consider giving specific pretrial notice to plaintiff that the feasibility of remedial measures is not controverted. Removing feasibility from contention eliminates one common way of placing into evidence the fact that defendant took remedial measures after an accident.

In preparing defense witnesses, counsel who wish to preserve the objection should bear in mind that testimony of defense witnesses may open the door to evidence of remedial measures. This can occur if the witness testifies that a given way of preventing an accident is not practical (even though the measure was later taken), if the witness states that the safety measures in effect at the time of the accident were the best available, or if the witness states or implies that conditions have not changed since the accident. Testimony of this nature opens the door to use of remedial measures evidence to show feasibility or to impeach the witness. Defense counsel should object to exhibits, such as photographs, that show the existence of remedial measures. The court should be asked to crop photographs so that repairs or safety measures are not

---

1982); Cann v. Ford Motor Co., 658 F.2d 54 (2d Cir.1981); Werner v. Upjohn Co., 628 F.2d 848 (4th Cir.1980); Bauman v. Volkswagenwerk Aktiengesellschaft, 621 F.2d 230 (6th Cir.1980). For a discussion of the arguments that admitting subsequent remedial measures evidence in strict liability cases chills product improvement, *see* 2 Richard A. Givens, Manual of Federal Practice § 7.11, at 271–73 (Shepard's/McGraw–Hill 4th ed. 1991).

301. 788 F.2d 634 (9th Cir.1986), *amended on denial of reh'g,* 805 F.2d 337 (9th Cir.1986).

302. *Id.* at 637.

303. *Id.* at 636–37.

304. *Id.* at 636, and authorities cited therein.

305. As amended, Federal Rule 407 provides for exclusion of evidence of subsequent remedial measures to prove "negligence, culpable conduct, a defect in a product, a defect in a product's design, or a need for a warning or instruction."

shown. When this is not practical, counsel should point out that evidence about the condition of the premises could be presented in another fashion—for example, by use of drawings or diagrams or by oral testimony. If other evidence of the condition of the premises has already been introduced by plaintiff, defense counsel should argue that reception of the photograph showing the safety measure is redundant and prejudicial.

Counsel should be prepared to argue that even if evidence of remedial measures fits one of the categories for which it is admissible, such as impeachment or showing feasibility, its value for this purpose is substantially outweighed by Federal Rule of Evidence 403 considerations—prejudice, confusion, and waste of time. In making this argument, it is helpful to point out that the fact the evidence is ostensibly offered to prove could be proven in some other fashion, or that other evidence on the point has been introduced and evidence showing safety measures is merely cumulative. When evidence is offered on a feasibility theory, counsel can point out that defendant does not dispute the practicability of the safety measure, but only claims that the measures in effect at the time of the accident were adequate.

If the court overrules an objection to evidence of safety measures, defense counsel should request a limiting instruction. The instruction will be most effective if it explains the policy of the rule to the jury. For example, if repairs appear on a photograph offered to show the condition of the premises, the court could be requested to give the following instruction:

> Members of the jury, you should disregard the fact that safety measures were taken after the accident. The law provides that repairs cannot be used as evidence against the defendant, because the making of repairs and improvements is something to be encouraged and supported.

If evidence of subsequent repairs has been offered and received, the defendant may wish to deal with the evidence in final argument. Defense counsel can point out that the law does not require perfection. The defendant's concern for safety caused it to make improvements after the accident, but the fact that improvements were made does not mean that the defendant was careless before.

§ 5.45   Form of Objection

At trial, when opposing counsel asks a question or offers an exhibit that would reveal the existence of safety measures taken after an accident, the objection may be made as follows:

> Objection! Plaintiff is offering evidence of remedial measures taken after the accident.

If the objection is overruled, counsel should request a limiting instruction:

> Your Honor, I request a limiting instruction telling the jury that evidence that [name of defendant] took additional precautions after

the accident may not be used as evidence of negligence at the time of the accident.

Whatever the practical value of the limiting instruction in convincing the jury, it should be requested to preserve the issue for appeal. Counsel should also request that the judge, in the final instructions, explain the reason for the remedial measures rule. Compare the instruction described in § **5.54**.

Even if objection is made and sustained at trial, the jury may infer the existence of remedial measures from the nature of the questions asked by plaintiff's counsel prior to the objection. When evidence of remedial measure is likely to cause serious prejudice to the defendant, defense counsel should consider making a pretrial motion asking the court's assistance in preventing the jury from learning, directly or indirectly, of the remedial measures.

Example (Motion in Limine)

The defendant respectfully moves the Court to instruct the plaintiff's counsel to refrain from offering any evidence that, subsequent to the accident that is the subject of this suit, the defendant modified the design of any of its snowblower models or other products to incorporate control devices that would stop the engine from running when the user left the operator's position.

The defendant also moves that the Court instruct plaintiff's counsel to refrain from asking any question, making any statement, offering any exhibit, or otherwise indicating to the jury, directly or by innuendo, that these design changes in the defendant's product were planned, discussed, or made after the accident in which plaintiff was injured. Defendant further moves that plaintiff's counsel be instructed to caution every witness called by them to refrain from any direct or indirect reference to design changes in defendant's product after the accident.

This motion is made on the ground that evidence of the design change would be evidence of a remedial measure offered in violation of Rule 407. The defendant concedes and will stipulate that the design change adding the above described control devices was feasible. Because feasibility is not controverted, there is no legitimate basis for offering evidence of the design change. If the design change becomes known to the jury, the defendant will be prejudiced even if the court were to sustain an objection and instruct the jury not to consider the evidence.

If the trial judge denies the motion in limine, on the ground that events at trial may open the door to remedial measures evidence, defense counsel may request that the court admonish the plaintiff not to introduce evidence of remedial measures without first clearing such evidence with the court in a conference held out of the hearing of the jury.[306]

306. This was the procedure employed by the trial court, and noted with approval by the appellate court, in Rimkus v. North- west Colo. Ski Corp., 706 F.2d 1060, 1065 (10th Cir.1983).

THE OFFERS IN COMPROMISE RULE (SETTLEMENT NEGOTIATIONS AND AGREEMENTS) [FRE 408]

§ 5.46 Exclusion of Evidence of Settlement Agreements and Settlement Offers

A settlement offer or settlement agreement is generally inadmissible to prove the validity or invalidity of a claim or its value. This exclusionary rule applies not only to settlements or settlement efforts between the parties to the litigation in which the evidence is offered, but also to settlements between a party and a nonparty.

Examples

Offer of settlement to opposing party. Plaintiff, a condominium homeowners' association, sued defendant, a general contractor, claiming damages for allegedly defective work on the condominium's heating system. Defendant offered a substantial settlement. Plaintiff declined the offer. At trial, plaintiff seeks to introduce testimony about defendant's offer, arguing that the size of defendant's offer is evidence that defendant was conscious that the work was in fact defective. The evidence is inadmissible.

Completed settlement with a nonparty. Plaintiff, a motorcyclist, sues defendant, a motorcycle manufacturer, after being injured in a motorcycle accident in which plaintiff's motorcycle collided with a car. In a previous settlement, plaintiff had received a payment from the driver of the car and released the driver from liability. At trial, defendant offers plaintiff's settlement agreement with the third party into evidence, on the theory that the agreement is evidence that plaintiff believed that the accident was caused by the car driver, not by any defect in the motorcycle. The agreement is inadmissible if offered solely to show the plaintiff's belief that the claim against the motorcycle manufacturer is invalid,[307] though it may be admissible if offered for another purpose. For example, if the driver testifies as a witness,[308] or remains as a party in the case under a Mary Carter agreement,[309] the prior settlement may be admissible to show the bias of a witness or to explain trial conduct.

Settlement offers and settlement agreements, when offered as evidence of liability or nonliability on the underlying claim, are inadmissible

---

307. *See* McInnis v. A.M.F., Inc., 765 F.2d 240 (1st Cir.1985). The court in *McInnis* noted that the jury's verdict could be reduced by the amount of the payment received in the settlement.

308. *See* § **5.52**.

309. *See* General Motors Corp. v. Simmons, 558 S.W.2d 855, 857 (Tex.1977) (evidence of agreement admissible because it gave settling parties an interest in the outcome that might affect their testimony or conduct). There has been extensive case law concerning both the validity and the admissibility of Mary Carter and similar types of agreements. For review of the problems raised by these agreements, *see* David P. Leonard, The New Wigmore: A Treatise on Evidence: Selected Rules of Limited Admissibility §§ 3.7.4–3.7.5 (rev. ed.2002).

both at common law and under the Federal Rules.[310] Federal Rule of Evidence 408 states, in relevant part:

> Evidence of (1) furnishing or offering or promising to furnish, or (2) accepting or offering or promising to accept, a valuable consideration in compromising or attempting to compromise a claim which was disputed as to either validity or amount, is not admissible to prove liability for or invalidity of the claim or its amount.[311]

Rule 408 has proven very influential. Many states have adopted language substantively identical or nearly identical to the Federal Rule, and a number of others have followed most aspects of the rule. No states reject the basic premise that evidence of compromises or compromise offers should be excluded when offered to prove validity or invalidity of a claim or defense.[312]

Several theories have been advanced in support of the exclusionary rule. One theory is that the evidence is simply irrelevant; an offer of settlement is not probative of the validity of the underlying claim, because the offeror may only have been seeking peace, rather than admitting that his or her legal position was weak.[313] While this theory may be valid in some situations, it does not explain a blanket rule of exclusion; an offer of settlement for more than the cost of litigation has some probative value as an indication of the party's belief in the strength or weakness of its legal position. For example, an offer to settle for 90 per cent of the other person's claim would certainly suggest that the offeror believed he or she had a weak case. A sounder basis for a blanket rule of exclusion is public policy: evidence of settlement offers is excluded in order to encourage settlement, in the belief that settlement of disputes serves the useful function of relieving court congestion and bringing peace to litigants. Whether the rule serves this purpose, or whether offers would be made even in the absence of an exclusionary rule, remains unclear. Nevertheless, the policy rationale is the most commonly cited reason for the rule.[314] The rule also tends to discourage tricky pretrial tactics, such as inveigling the other party into making an offer solely for the purpose of acquiring evidence at trial.[315] Finally, the rule

310. For a full discussion of common law theories under which settlement evidence was excluded, *see* Esser v. Brophey, 3 N.W.2d 3 (Minn.1942). *See also* Leonard, *supra* note 309 § 3.3.

311. Fed. R. Evid. 408. The rule may not apply in criminal cases. *See* Manko v. United States, 87 F.3d 50, 54–55 (2d Cir. 1996) (in tax fraud prosecution, not error to admit evidence of defendant's prior settlement with IRS; Rule 408 not applicable in criminal cases).

312. For examination of state provisions, *see* Leonard, *supra* note 309 § 3.6.

313. *See id.* § 3.3.2.

314. For full discussion of the policy rationale, *see id.* §§ 3.3.3, 3.4.

315. *See* Fed. R. Evid. 408 advisory committee's note; George M. Bell, *Admissions Arising Out of Compromise—Are They Irrelevant?* 31 Tex. L. Rev. 239, 241–42 (1953). *See also* Pierce v. F.R. Tripler & Co., 955 F.2d 820 (2d Cir.1992) (plaintiff in age discrimination case entitled, under circumstances, to have fact that defendant offered him job during subsequent settlement negotiations excluded; court rejects argument that policy of Rule 408 does not support exclusion when offeror of settlement seeks to have evidence admitted, on grounds that free admission of such offers would result in rash of disqualification of counsel motions, because counsel would need to be witness in order to prove making of offer and settlement purpose of offer, and

arises from considerations of fairness—from a desire not to punish a party who acts in a socially useful way by seeking to resolve disputes without the necessity of trial.[316]

§ 5.47   Exclusion of Statements Made During Settlement Negotiations: Common Law and Federal Rule Approaches

At common law, offers of settlement and settlement agreements were inadmissible, but statements made during settlement negotiations were admissible.[317] For example, if a party or party's representative made an admission of fault during negotiations, that admission could be received into evidence, although the offer of settlement itself was inadmissible.[318] This result was consistent with the view, advocated by Wigmore,[319] that the true reason for excluding settlement offers was that they were not probative of the fault of the offeror, who might be making an offer solely for the purpose of buying peace. A statement admitting fault was clearly relevant and hence was not excluded. Because statements in conjunction with settlement offers were often admitted at common law, counsel often sought to protect clients by noting during settlement negotiations that all statements were made hypothetically, or "without prejudice," or for purposes of discussion only.[320]

Contemporary law has taken the opposite position, holding that statements of fact made in connection with compromise discussions are generally inadmissible. This position is most consistent with the policy rationale for the rule excluding offers of compromise. Achieving compromise requires candor; if parties were aware that their opponents would be permitted to offer into evidence portions of the compromise discussions, they would be less likely to begin compromise discussions, or, even if they did enter into such discussions, they might be less forthcoming. The fairness rationale for the compromise rule also demands exclusion of

counsel who plans to be witness must often withdraw under rules of professional responsibility; language of Rule 408 itself does not support exception for evidence proffered by maker of settlement offer).

316. *See* Leonard, *supra* note 309 § 3.3.4.

317. For discussion of evolution in the treatment of statements of fact made in connection with compromise discussions, *see* David P. Leonard, The New Wigmore: A Treatise on Evidence: Selected Rules of Limited Admissibility § 3.5.2 (rev. ed.2002). The earliest case admitting statements of fact in connection with compromise discussions appears to have been Waldridge v. Kennison, 1 Esp. 143, 170 Eng. Rep. 306 (1794), in which defendant's admission during settlement negotiation that certain document was in his handwriting admissible. The court stated that admission not con-

nected with merits of case and that facts easily could be proved by other evidence). The rule represented by *Waldridge* was not followed by all earlier courts, however. *See Leonard, supra* this note § 3.3.4, at 3:47 & n.8.

318. *See* 2 McCormick on Evidence § 266 (5th ed. John W. Strong ed. 1999); Albert Hanson Lumber Co. v. United States, 261 U.S. 581, 588–89 (1923).

319. *See* 4 John H. Wigmore, Evidence in Trials at Common Law § 1061 (James H. Chadbourn rev. 1972).

320. By analogy to contract law, common law courts were willing to treat an unaccepted offer as having no effect, Evidential or otherwise, if it was made "without prejudice." *See id.* § 1061, at 35. The contract rationale for the exclusionary rule never took hold in the United States. *See* Leonard, *supra* note 317 § 3.3.1.

statements of fact made in the course of compromise discussions. It is unfair to punish a candid party genuinely seeking compromise by admitting such statements.

The Federal Rules of Evidence follow this rationale, excluding both compromise offers and statements made during negotiations. Rule 408[321] expressly states that "Evidence of conduct or statements made in compromise negotiations is ... not admissible." The drafters of the Rules reasoned that uninhibited freedom of expression was necessary to facilitate settlement. A good example of the operation of the Federal Rule may be found in *Ramada Development Co. v. Rauch,*[322] an action in which Ramada sued for the balance due under a construction contract with Rauch. Rauch claimed defects in Ramada's construction of the project. Ramada retained an architect to study the alleged defects, and to prepare a report to be used as a tool in attempting settlement. The report was submitted to Rauch during settlement negotiations. There was no pretrial agreement between the parties about whether the report would be admissible or not. At trial, Rauch offered the architect's report as evidence because it confirmed the existence of many of the alleged defects. The trial judge excluded it on grounds that it was inadmissible under Rule 408. The Third Circuit upheld the exclusion.

Not all documentary evidence exchanged during compromise negotiations will be protected even by the expansive approach of Rule 408. Rule 408 expressly provides that it "does not require the exclusion of any evidence otherwise discoverable merely because it is presented in the course of compromise negotiations." The purpose of this provision is to prevent parties from immunizing pre-existing documents by turning them over to the opposing party during negotiations. For example, a party cannot turn over its business records during negotiations and later claim that the opposing party could not use them at trial because of Rule 408. The opposing party would be entitled to use the discovery rules to obtain the records and then would be entitled to introduce them at trial. The case of *Ramada Development Co. v. Rauch,* discussed in the previous paragraph, is distinguishable from the situation in which the party seeks to immunize pre-existing documents. The Rauch court held that Rule 408's exception for documents "otherwise discoverable" did not apply to cases in which the document would *not have existed but for the negotiations.* In such cases, negotiations are not being used to frustrate discovery by making existing documents unreachable.

§ 5.48   Settlement Evidence That Is Admissible Despite the Rule of Exclusion

Settlement evidence is sometimes admissible despite the rule of exclusion. First, the rule of exclusion applies only to offers of compromise and statements made in seeking compromise of disputed claims.[323]

---

321. For the full text of Rule 408, *see* **App. A.**

322. 644 F.2d 1097, 1106 (5th Cir. 1981).

323. Of course, the rule also applies to

Second, the rule of exclusion does not apply when the evidence is offered for any purpose other than to prove the validity or invalidity of the claim at issue in the case. If offered for any other purpose, it is potentially admissible.

§ 5.49   Settlement Evidence That Is Admissible Despite the Rule of Exclusion—Settlement of an Undisputed Claim

The purpose of Federal Rule of Evidence 408, and of many of its common law cognates, is to promote compromise when claims are genuinely disputed. The rulemakers did not intend to protect defendants who do not genuinely contest claims but who merely seek an extension of time or a discount for the nuisance value of litigation. Rule 408 provides no protection to the debtor who tells his creditor, "You'll have to take 50 cents on the dollar on what I owe you—if you don't like it, sue me." Such statements are admissible because they do not reveal any dispute; the debtor's reference to "what I owe you" demonstrates that she is not seeking compromise, but merely avoidance of part of a proper obligation. Rule 408 specifically provides that the rule of exclusion only applies to claims that are "disputed as to either validity or amount." The rulemakers reasoned that the policy considerations that favor settlement negotiations are not applicable to a debtor who seeks to get a creditor to settle an admittedly due amount for lesser sum.

Note that the rule *does* apply if the claim is disputed as to *either* validity or amount. In tort actions, and in contract actions not involving a debt for a sum certain, the amount of the claim will almost always be disputed even if its validity is not. Thus, if counsel for a personal injury defendant says "O.K., there's no doubt about liability, but your damages demand is too high. Let's try to arrive at a reasonable figure for damages," the statement is not admissible because, though liability is conceded, the plaintiff's damage claims are not.

The common law rule about settlement offers is consistent with this aspect of Rule 408. To be affected by the rule of exclusion, the offer had to be an offer of compromise, not a concession that the full amount was due. Thus, for example, when the sales representative of an herbicide manufacturer told a farmer whose crop had been damaged by the herbicide that the company would pay for the damage, the statement was held admissible on grounds that it was not an offer of compromise.[324] Of course, there is a gray area between offers of compromise and noncompromise offers, and an admission of liability accompanied by an offer to pay for damage can still be an offer of compromise if there is an express or implicit dispute about the amount of the damages.

completed compromises, as the language of Rule 408 makes clear. *See also* David P. Leonard, The New Wigmore: A Treatise on Evidence: Selected Rules of Limited Admissibility § 3.7.1(a) (rev. ed.2002).

324. Perzinski v. Chevron Chem. Co., 503 F.2d 654, 658 (7th Cir.1974).

Example

Demand for full payment of claim. Plaintiff, a retail store, brings a breach of contract action against a manufacturer for failure to deliver a popular toy in time for the holiday giving season. Plaintiff's letter to defendant, written after the scheduled delivery date had passed, setting forth its estimate of lost sales and demanding "full payment," is not an offer in compromise and is therefore not excluded by the compromise rule.

§ 5.50   Settlement Evidence That Is Admissible Despite the Rule of Exclusion—Discussions Constituting Business Negotiations Rather Than Negotiations to Compromise a Legal Dispute

The compromise rule does not exclude evidence of discussions that took place in the context of business negotiations rather than a legal dispute, nor does it apply to other situations that, in the court's view, fall short of "compromise negotiation."[325]

Sometimes it is difficult to determine whether the parties were actually disputing a question of liability, or were engaged in other types of communication such as business negotiations. It is not possible to resolve cases such as these with a simple rule but several factors can affect the decision whether to treat the discussions as compromise negotiations.[326] The most important of these is the timing of the discussions at issue. Certainly, communications can be excluded pursuant to the rule even if no formal claim has been made at the time they took place. In addition, the mere fact that all of the events that might give rise to liability have occurred prior to the discussions does not necessarily mean that the discussions fall within the rule and must be excluded. However, if the discussions occurred before it was apparent to the parties that there was a genuine dispute, the discussions likely do not constitute an effort to compromise a disputed claim and are probably admissible.[327] Some courts have gone quite far, holding that discussions

---

325. *See* S.A. Healy Co. v. Milwaukee Metro. Sewerage Dist., 50 F.3d 476, 480 (7th Cir.1995) (Posner, J.) (plaintiff, who had made a request or "claim" to city for adjustment of payment as provided in its contract with city, sought to introduce evidence that city engineer had remarked that plaintiff's "claim" probably had merit; held, engineer's statement admissible over a Rule 408 objection because no dispute had arisen at time of statement; a claim is not a dispute until it has been rejected); Sage Realty Corp. v. Insurance Co. of N. Am., 34 F.3d 124, 128 (2d Cir.1994) (letter presenting party's version of obligations under lease not a statement made in settlement negotiations and hence admissible); Davidson v. Prince, 813 P.2d 1225, 1232 (Utah App. 1991) (plaintiff's letter to defendant's insur-

ance company describing circumstances of injury and demanding compensation not an "offer in compromise"; narrow interpretation of rule).

326. For extended discussion of this issue, *see* David P. Leonard, The New Wigmore: A Treatise on Evidence: Selected Rules of Limited Admissibility § 3.7.5 (rev. ed.2002).

327. *See* Crues v. KFC Corp., 768 F.2d 230 (8th Cir.1985) (in fraud action by food franchisee, evidence that defendant offered to convert franchise from one type to another was properly admitted because, *inter alia*, conversation occurred more than three years before the filing of the action, when it was not clear that any disputed claim existed). *But see* Schlossman & Gunkelman, Inc.

constitute business communications if they take place before litigation had been threatened,[328] though this is unlikely to become the majority position.[329]

The difficulty of distinguishing between business negotiations and compromise negotiations is illustrated by *Aaron v. Marcove*.[330] Aaron sued to partition property he and Marcove owned as tenants in common. Part of the property was leased to a company which formerly had been owned by Aaron and Marcove. Three years before the litigation commenced, Aaron sold his share of the company to Marcove. The issue was whether the company occupied the premises under a long-term lease or as a tenant at will. Aaron and Marcove tried for some time to reach compromise to disentangle their business interests before giving up and turning to litigation. At trial, Aaron offered a letter Marcove wrote to Aaron's attorney denying the existence of a lease to the company. This position was contrary to the position Marcove took at trial. On appeal, the court held that admission of the letter was proper because the letter was written during a period when the parties were negotiating a long-term lease, not the settlement of the controversy about whether a lease existed at all. In other words, the court characterized the letter as part of business discussions rather than discussions aimed at compromising the claim at issue in the trial. *Aaron* is a close call, and certainly could have gone either way.

Example

Business discussions rather than negotiations to compromise disputed claim. Plaintiff and defendant, two partners in a retail clothing business, have a difference of opinion about whether their store should change its focus from middle-aged customers to younger buyers. As their differences increase, the partners begin to consider dissolving their partnership. At one point, the two discuss the value of the business, and agree that it is in the range of $2 million. A year

v. Tallman, 593 N.W.2d 374 (N.D.1999) (even though dispute was in its early stages, it was apparent to the parties at the time of their correspondence that a potential dispute was brewing over what proved to be a large real estate commission).

328. *See* Big O Tire Dealers, Inc. v. Goodyear Tire & Rubber Co., 561 F.2d 1365, 1368 (10th Cir.1977) (because discussions took place before litigation had been threatened in trademark dispute, they were not subject to exclusion under Rule 408; decision might be justified on ground that there were indications defendant was using the negotiations to buy time and take advantage of trademark during pendency of the talks and possible litigation).

329. *See* Affiliated Mfrs., Inc. v. Aluminum Co. of America, 56 F.3d 521 (3d Cir. 1995), for example, Affiliated argued that for there to be a "dispute" within the meaning of Rule 408, there must have been at least "a threat or contemplation of litigation, that goes beyond conduct or statements made to resolve differences of opinion as to the validity or amount of a claim." *Id*. at 526. Affiliated relied on several cases, including *Big O*. The court held that if *Big O* stands for the proposition that Rule 408 applies only if there has been a threat of litigation, the case is too restrictive. *Id*. at 527. Rule 408 is invoked, the court held, "where an actual dispute or a difference of opinion exists, rather than when discussions crystallize to the point of threatened litigation." *Id. See also* Alpex Computer Corp. v. Nintendo Co., 770 F.Supp. 161 (S.D.N.Y.1991) (also rejecting had rejected such a narrow reading of exclusionary scope of Rule 408).

330. 685 P.2d 268 (Colo. App.1984).

later, the two partners end up in litigation when they are unable to resolve their differences. At trial, to prove the business was worth $2 million in total, plaintiff wishes to present evidence of their prior discussion. The trial judge would be operating within her discretion in admitting the evidence on the ground that at the time of the prior discussion, the parties' differences probably did not reach the point of a "disputed claim" that would fall within the compromise rule.

§ 5.51   Settlement Evidence That Is Admissible Despite the Rule of Exclusion—Compromise or Behavior During Compromise Discussions as the Subject of the Action

The compromise rule does not apply in a suit to enforce the terms of the settlement contract itself. This result is required if the law is to be able to enforce the terms of agreements reached after an allegedly successful effort to compromise a disputed claim. Similarly, the exclusionary rule does not apply when the present action is based upon allegedly tortious conduct that occurred during discussions to compromise a disputed claim.

Examples

Compromise as subject of the action. Plaintiff, who suffered injuries when she was struck in a crosswalk by Defendant's vehicle, brings a breach of contract action against Defendant claiming that Defendant failed to pay damages agreed to pursuant to a compromise settlement of the claim. The compromise agreement is the subject of the action, and is therefore not excluded by the compromise rule.

Behavior during compromise negotiations as basis of action. Plaintiff brings a claim for intentional infliction of emotional distress against an insurance company after the insurance company, without a valid reason, threatens to withhold disability benefits. The insurance company's letters to plaintiff containing those threats, written during discussions for compromise of plaintiff's disability claim, were not offered to prove liability under the insurance policy, but as part of the conduct that caused emotional distress.[331] Therefore, they are not excluded by the compromise rule.

§ 5.52   Settlement Evidence That Is Admissible Despite the Rule of Exclusion—Evidence Offered to Impeach a Witness or for Other Purposes

Federal Rule of Evidence 408 prohibits use of statements made during compromise negotiations when the purpose is to show the validity or invalidity of the plaintiff's claim, but not when the evidence is offered for another purpose. When a party offers evidence of a settlement offer or completed settlement for the purpose of showing the *bias of a witness,*

---

331. *See* Fletcher v. Western National Life Ins. Co., 89 Cal.Rptr. 78, 90 (1970).

it is not offered to show the validity or invalidity of the underlying claim, and hence is admissible. For example, if the plaintiff has settled with one of the codefendants, and that codefendant testifies in the case, the settlement may be introduced into evidence because the payment to the codefendant may have influenced the testimony.[332] Of course, the impeachment value of the evidence must be weighed against its prejudicial effect, and in cases where impeachment value is slight, counsel opposing the offer should argue that the evidence should be excluded on Rule 403 grounds. In addition, a fair settlement arguably has little impeachment value because the recipient of the settlement is not getting paid anything more than he or she lost.[333] In any event, the party objecting to the testimony is entitled to a limiting instruction to the effect that the evidence may only be used for its bearing on the credibility of the witness, and not as evidence of liability.

Evidence of statements made during settlement negotiations is sometimes offered on the theory that the statements are being used for *impeachment of a witness with inconsistent statements,* and not to prove the validity or invalidity of the underlying claim. For example, if the plaintiff's accountant submits information about lost profits for a settlement conference, the defendant may later seek to use the document if the accountant testifies at trial inconsistently with the representations made in the document. The literal language of Rule 408 suggests that the evidence should be admitted because it is not offered directly on the issue of the claim's validity, but merely for the purpose of showing that a witness is not reliable. Yet use of evidence of statements made during settlement negotiations for impeachment purposes would impede the frank and free discussion that the rulemakers sought to promote. A difference of opinion has arisen about the admissibility of such statements.[334] Of course, counsel can always argue that the impeachment

---

332. *Cf.* John McShain, Inc. v. Cessna Aircraft Co., 563 F.2d 632 (3d Cir.1977) (not error to receive evidence of plaintiff's pretrial settlement with third party, where expert associated with third party testified in favor of plaintiff). *See also* Johnson v. Hugo's Skateway, 949 F.2d 1338, 1345–46 (4th Cir.1991), *superceded on other grounds at* 974 F.2d 1408 (4th Cir.1992) (evidence of prior consent decree admissible; evidence was not offered to show validity of claim that resulted in consent decree, but to show later racial bias by showing that provisions of decree, such as posting sign on premises announcing policy of equal access to all races, were not followed; requirements, such as posting equal access sign, admissible in case alleging defendant caused racially biased arrest of plaintiff); Reichenbach v. Smith, 528 F.2d 1072, 1075 (5th Cir.1976).

333. *Cf.* Paster v. Pennsylvania R.R., 43 F.2d 908, 911 (2d Cir.1930) (Hand, J.).

334. *See* Stainton v. Tarantino, 637 F.Supp. 1051 (E.D.Pa.1986) (holding evidence admissible for impeachment); Wayne D. Brazil, *Protecting the Confidentiality of Settlement Negotiations,* 39 Hastings L.J. 955, 978 (1988) (arguing that because perfect consistency is almost impossible, allowing use of prior statements somewhat inconsistent with trial testimony would undercut exclusionary rule). *See also* Davidson v. Prince, 813 P.2d 1225, 1233 n. 9 (Utah App.1991) (even if statements are part of offer in compromise, they are admissible to impeach maker's inconsistent trial testimony) (alternative holding). In the authors' opinion, the holding in *Davidson* might undermine the goal of encouraging settlement. Of course, the cautious lawyer can avoid the danger by measures such as getting a stipulation before entering negotiations or stating that factual assertions are "hypothetical" or "without prejudice." Nonlawyers negotiating on their own behalf will probably be the people most hurt by decisions such as *Davidson.*

value of the evidence is outweighed, under Rule 403, by its prejudicial effect.[335]

Evidence of statements made during settlement negotiations may be introduced for a variety of other purposes that do not involve use of the evidence to prove or disprove the validity of the underlying claim. These include use of the evidence to negate a claim of unnecessary delay, to show that defendants engaged in dilatory negotiations that prevented plaintiffs from mitigating their damages,[336] to show that a party engaged in an unfair labor practice during the settlement negotiations, or to prove an effort to obstruct a criminal investigation or prosecution.[337]

Examples

Impeachment by prior inconsistent statement. Vehicles driven by plaintiff and defendant collided in an intersection controlled by traffic signals. Plaintiff was injured and his car damaged. At the scene, each claimed the other was responsible, but the two discussed a possible compromise of their dispute. During the discussion, plaintiff said he "might have edged out a little into the intersection before my light turned green." At trial, however, plaintiff testifies that he did not proceed into the intersection until the light turned green. Defendant wishes to present evidence of plaintiff's statement about edging out into the intersection before the light turned green. Though there is some controversy about the matter, some courts would admit the statement as a prior inconsistent statement to impeach plaintiff's credibility. (Under Federal Rule of Evidence 801(d)(1)(A), the statement is not admissible to prove that plaintiff actually edged into the intersection because he did not make the statement under oath, subject to the penalty of perjury, at a trial, hearing, or in a deposition.)

Showing bias of witness. Plaintiff and W, a passenger in plaintiff's vehicle, are injured when plaintiff's vehicle is involved in a collision with defendant's vehicle. At trial, W testifies that defendant's car ran the red light and struck plaintiff's car. Defendant wishes to present evidence that previously, W had made a claim against plaintiff, and that plaintiff had paid W in settlement of the claim.

For a further analysis of inconsistent statements made during settlement negotiations for impeachment, *see* the discussion of Rule 408 in ABA Section on Litigation, Emerging Problems Under the Federal Rules of Evidence 61 (2d ed. 1991) (see Appendix II of West's Federal Rules of Evidence pamphlet); Michael H. Graham, Handbook of Federal Evidence § 408.1 (4th ed. 1996); 1 Stephen A. Saltzburg, Michael M. Martin & Daniel J. Capra, Federal Rules of Evidence Manual 512–13 (6th ed. 1994). As these sources indicate, courts and commentators are divided on the appropriateness of allowing this use of statements made during settlement negotiations.

335. For a more detailed examination of the strengths and weaknesses of the different impeachment theories under which compromise evidence might be offered, *see* David P. Leonard, The New Wigmore: Selected Rules of Limited Admissibility § 3.8.2 (rev. ed.2002). One other such theory is that the evidence is admissible to impeach *by contradiction. Id.*

336. Urico v. Parnell Oil Co., 708 F.2d 852 (1st Cir.1983).

337. For discussion of alternate routes to admissibility, *see* Leonard, *supra* note 335 §§ 3.8.3–3.8.5.

This evidence is most likely admissible to demonstrate that W might have been biased toward plaintiff, causing W to shade her testimony in plaintiff's favor.

§ 5.53 Practice Considerations

In the few jurisdictions that follow the common law rule, statements of fact made during settlement negotiations are admissible when offered by the opposing party, though settlement offers are not. Counsel who wish to discuss the facts of a case during negotiations should either make clear during settlement negotiations that any statements of fact are made without prejudice for the purpose of achieving settlement or obtain an agreement with opposing counsel that statements made during negotiations will not be offered in evidence. In the absence of an express agreement, factual statements should be made hypothetically, or counsel should note that statements are being made "without prejudice."

Because the Federal Rules of Evidence expressly provide protection for statements of fact as well as for offers, such precautions might not seem necessary in jurisdictions that follow the Federal Rules. However, an express agreement not to offer statements during negotiations as evidence or a statement that negotiations are "without prejudice" does no harm, and may serve a function even under the Federal Rules. For example, in *S. Leo Harmonay, Inc. v. Binks Mfg. Co.*,[338] plaintiff's attorney sent defendant a letter that stated: "In accordance with our prior discussions and without prejudice to our clients' respective legal positions, I am taking the liberty of setting forth below a summary of the damages suffered by Harmonay . . . ."

Defendant offered the letter in evidence at trial in order to impeach the testimony of one of plaintiff's witnesses. In deciding that Rule 408 barred admission of the letter, the court noted that the words *without prejudice*, were no longer absolutely dispositive. However, it stated that the words "may still be evidence of the intent of the speaker which we may rely upon to determine whether the statement was made 'in compromise.'" Thus, use of the phrase *without prejudice*, which cost nothing, seems to have contributed to a decision in favor of excluding the evidence, even under the Federal Rules.

Because the exclusionary rule only applies to discussions aimed at compromising disputed claims,[339] and because in hindsight it can sometimes be questionable whether certain communications were of this type, counsel who wish to take advantage of Rule 408 should clarify the nature of the negotiation at the time the negotiation takes place in order to lay the foundation for invoking the rule.

§ 5.54 Form of Objection; Request for Limiting Instruction

At trial, the objection may be made as follows:

338. 597 F.Supp. 1014, 1023 (S.D.N.Y. 1984), *aff'd*, 762 F.2d 990 (2d Cir.1985).

339. *See* § 5.46.

Objection! The question calls for testimony about [a settlement offer] [an offer in compromise] [a statement made during settlement negotiations].

If the objection is overruled on grounds that the evidence is offered for some purpose other than showing the validity or invalidity of the claim, then the objecting party should request a limiting instruction. For example, in instances where the basis for admission is that the evidence shows the bias of a witness, counsel could request the following instruction:

> Your Honor, I request that a limiting instruction be given informing the jury that this evidence may be used only for the purpose of assessing credibility, and that it may not be used as evidence that the plaintiff's claim is valid or that the defendant is liable.

If the evidence is admitted for a limited purpose, counsel should request a further instruction at the close of the case explaining the policy of the rule against use of settlement offers. For example, counsel might request the following instruction:

> Members of the jury, evidence that a settlement offer was made was admitted for the limited purpose of assisting you in assessing the credibility of a witness. You should not use this evidence as proof of the validity of plaintiff's claim or as evidence that defendant is liable. The settlement of cases before trial is something that the law seeks to encourage and promote. For that reason, the law protects persons who make settlement offers by providing that a settlement offer may not be used at trial as evidence that the person making the offer is legally liable. Otherwise, people would hesitate to make offers and the chances of settlement would be reduced.

OTHER OBJECTIONS BASED ON RELEVANCY AND ITS LIMITS

§ 5.55 Evidence of Payment of Medical and Similar Expenses [FRE 409]

Suppose that after a traffic accident, one of the parties offers to pay the hospital expenses of the other. If the offer is part of an offer to settle the case, then the evidence would be inadmissible under Rule 408.[340] But even if the offer or payment is made without settlement in mind, Rule 409 makes the evidence inadmissible. Under Rule 409, evidence of furnishing or offering or promising to pay medical, hospital, or similar expenses occasioned by an injury is not admissible to prove liability for the injury.[341]

There are several rationales for the rule.[342] The primary rationale is one of policy—that humane acts should be encouraged, not punished.

---

340. Fed. R. Evid. 408.

341. Fed. R. Evid. 409.

342. *See* David P. Leonard, The New Wigmore: A Treatise on Evidence: Selected Rules of Limited Admissibility § 4.4 (rev. ed.2002).

Another purpose is one of relevancy—that a payment of medical expenses is often not an expression of belief in fault, but merely an expression of human kindness.[343] As with evidence of subsequent remedial measures and compromise, there is also the consideration of fairness—that it would be unfair to use a party's humanitarian behavior against her at trial.[344]

Though the general rule of exclusion is followed almost universally,[345] the rule has attracted little attention. Either it has rarely been invoked to exclude evidence, or the rule is so clear that it has not created the interpretive problems that beget reported decisions.

The rule does not apply to statements made in conjunction with payment of medical expenses.[346] Thus, the party who pays medical expenses and apologizes for an accident or admits fault is likely to be faced with the apology in court.[347] This aspect of the rule contrasts with Rule 408, which covers not only offers in compromise but statements in conjunction with the offers.[348] The rationale for the difference is that offers in compromise come as part of settlement negotiations and statements of fact are an indispensable part of such negotiations. The nonnegotiator who does the good deed of paying medical expenses could do the deed just as effectively without commenting on the events that led to the injury, and hence is stripped of the protection that belongs to the negotiator on grounds that beneficial conduct is not being deterred by receiving evidence of the statements.[349]

Though the rule generally does not exclude statements of fact, there is a general social trend toward encouraging expressions of apology. Supported by research into the social value of such expressions,[350] and

---

343. Fed. R. Evid. 409 advisory committee's note. *See also* 2 Weinstein's Federal Evidence § 409.02, at 409–4 (2d ed. Joseph M. McLaughlin ed. 1997) (traditional theory: offer to pay medical costs usually made from humane impulses, not admission of liability; and also stating policy rationale).

344. *See* 2 Christopher B. Mueller & Laird C. Kirkpatrick, Federal Evidence § 139, at 114 (1994) ("it would be unseemly to receive evidence that one who felt responsible had paid such expenses in a responsible manner, if he objected to the evidence"); 23 Charles A. Wright & Kenneth W. Graham, Jr., Federal Practice and Procedure (Evidence) § 5321, at 298 (1980) (it is "considered unfair to pervert a generous act into a confession of fault").

345. Nearly half of the states have adopted the language of Rule 409 verbatim, and several have adopted rules with only minor differences. Though other states have enacted rules somewhat less similar in structure to Rule 409, these rules are likely to have the same scope as Rule 409. *See* Leonard, *supra* note 342 § 4.7.

346. Fed. R. Evid. 409 advisory committee's note.

347. *See, e.g.,* Sims v. Sowle, 395 P.2d 133, 135 (Or.1964) (defendant's apology to plaintiff accompanying offer to pay medical expenses admissible); Weinstein's Federal Evidence, *supra* note 317 § 409.03[3] (admissions of liability accompanying offer of assistance admissible if severable from offer).

348. Fed. R. Evid. 408.

349. Fed. R. Evid. 409 advisory committee's note. For more detailed discussion of the admission of statements of fact made in connection with payment of medical expenses, see Leonard, *supra* note 342 § 4.6.2.

350. A great deal of "therapeutic jurisprudence" scholarship has been published in recent years. *See, e.g.,* The Passions of the Law (Susan A. Bandes ed. 1999); Practicing Therapeutic Jurisprudence: Law as a Helping Profession (Dennis P. Stolle et al., ed. 2000); Laura E. Little, *Negotiating the Tangle of Law and Emotion*, 86 Cornell L.

concerned that current evidence rules discourage people from apologizing or expressing regret over accidents that injure others, a few states have enacted laws specifically forbidding the use of such statements. In Massachusetts, for example, "[s]tatements, writings, or benevolent gestures expressing sympathy or a general sense of benevolence relating to the pain, suffering, or death of a person involved in an accident and made to such person or to the family of such person" are not admissible as admissions of liability in civil cases.[351] Though these statutes typically do not exclude statements of fault,[352] recall that if such a statement is made in the context of an effort to compromise a disputed claim, it will be excluded by the compromise rule.

As with evidence of subsequent remedial measures and compromise, evidence concerning payment of medical expenses is admissible if offered for purposes other than to prove an implied recognition of responsibility. For example, the evidence might be offered to prove control of an instrumentality, identity of the apparatus causing the injury, or defendant's status as an employer or principal of the person who caused the injury.[353]

§ 5.56 Plea Bargaining Statements; Withdrawn Guilty Pleas; Pleas of Nolo Contendere [FRE 410]

Under Federal Rule of Evidence 410, statements made during plea bargaining with an attorney for the prosecuting authority are inadmissible.[354] The primary purpose of the rule is to encourage full disclosure during negotiations for a plea.[355] In this sense, the rule is analogous to the rule covering statements of fact made in the course of compromise discussions.

A withdrawn guilty plea is also inadmissible.[356] The permission to withdraw must have been granted for a reason—such as involuntariness, lack of true understanding of the nature of the charges or the consequences of conviction, or the denial of assistance of counsel—and whatever reason is good enough to permit withdrawal is considered good enough to keep the plea out of evidence.[357] The rule is thus based

Rev. 974 (2001); Symposium, *The Role of Forgiveness in the Law*, 27 Fordham Urb. L.J. 1351 (2000).

351. Mass. Ann. Laws ch. 233, § 23D. *See also* Cal. Evid. Code § 1160; Fla. Stat. § 90.4026; Tex. Civ. Prac. & Rem. Code § 18.061. For discussion of the various proposals, *see* Jonathan R. Cohen, Legislating Apology: The Pros and Cons, 70 U. Cin. L. Rev. 819, 830–833 (2002).

352. *See, e.g.,* Cal. Evid. Code § 1160 ("A statement of fault, however, which is part of, or in addition to, [the expression of sympathy or other benevolence] shall not be inadmissible pursuant to this section").

353. *See id.* § 4.13.

354. Fed. R. Evid. 410(4).

355. Fed. R. Evid. 410 advisory committee's note.

356. Fed. R. Evid. 410. *But cf.* United States v. Greene, 995 F.2d 793, 798 (8th Cir.1993) (held, defendant not entitled to introduce evidence that he had rejected favorable plea agreement; defendant argued that his rejection of agreement was evidence of "consciousness of innocence").

357. Fed. R. Evid. 410 advisory committee's note (citing Kercheval v. United States, 274 U.S. 220 (1927)) (admitting withdrawn guilty plea would undermine purpose of allowing defendant to withdraw plea); 2 McCormick on Evidence § 257 (5th ed. John W. Strong ed. 1999) (where plea

strongly in considerations of fairness.[358] Its primary purpose, however, is to encourage the settlement of criminal cases, which is necessary in order to prevent the criminal justice system from collapsing under the weight of contested trials.[359]

Like any other statement of a party, a guilty plea not withdrawn is admissible as an admission.[360] However, where the plea is to a minor traffic offense—especially where the "plea" is made by mail—the inference that the statement shows consciousness of guilt may be too weak to permit it to be received in evidence. Persons accused of traffic violations often make such pleas simply for convenience, to avoid going to court. Though such pleas are usually not excluded by the rule, their use as evidence of guilt may be misleading.[361] Nevertheless, the party pleading guilty will usually have the opportunity to explain to the fact finder why he or she did so, potentially minimizing the misunderstanding that could result from admission of the evidence.

A plea of nolo contendere is not admissible in either a civil or criminal suit.[362] The trial judge who allowed the plea—which cannot be made as of right[363]—determined in allowing the plea that this consequence should not attach to the conviction.[364] Indeed, in many cases the most compelling motivation to utilize the nolo contendere plea is precisely to dispose of the case without creating adverse evidence for subsequent civil or criminal litigation.[365]

Unlike the federal rules governing evidence of subsequent remedial measures, compromise evidence, and evidence of payment of medical

withdrawn to correct injustice, admission would undermine effectiveness of remedy).

358. *See* David P. Leonard, The New Wigmore: A Treatise on Evidence: Selected Rules of Limited Admissibility § 5.4.2 (rev. ed.2002). Another rationale for the exclusionary rule are prevention of unfair prejudice. *Id.* § 5.4.3.

359. *See id.* § 5.4.4.

360. *See, e.g.,* Taylor v. Whitley, 933 F.2d 325, 327 (5th Cir.1991) (guilty plea is an admission that defendant committed charged offense); Jacobs v. Goodspeed, 429 A.2d 915, 917 (1980) (plea of guilty to following too closely admissible as admission in negligence action); Teitelbaum Furs, Inc. v. Dominion Ins. Co., 375 P.2d 439, 441, 25 Cal.Rptr. 559 561 (1962) (guilty plea admissible in civil action as admission).

361. *See, e.g.,* Hannah v. Ike Topper Structural Steel Co., 201 N.E.2d 63, 65 (Ohio App. 1963) (plea of guilty to failing to yield signed on form attached to traffic ticket inadmissible; cost of defense and inconvenience of court appearances compared to fine motivating factor for plea); 2 McCormick on Evidence, *supra* note 357 § 257, at 145–46 (recognition that collateral consequences as opposed to guilt often control-

ling factor in traffic violation guilty pleas has led to some tendency to exclude plea); *But see* Duvall v. Borough of Oxford, 1992 WL 59163, at *4 n. 6 (E.D.Pa.1992) (rejecting argument that guilty plea to underage drinking charge should be inadmissible as an admission because "like traffic violations, this charge is regularly 'admitted' even when false, because the costs of contest outweigh the punishment"); Ando v. Woodberry, 168 N.E.2d 520, 521, 203 N.Y.S.2d 74, 76 (N.Y. 1960) (plea of guilty to failing to signal and making improper turn admissible in negligence action; plea was made in court, however, so inconvenience explanation not available).

362. Fed. R. Evid. 410(2).

363. *See* Fed. R. Crim. Proc. 11(b).

364. 1 McCormick on Evidence, *supra* note 357 § 257, at 145–46 & n.31 (judge assumedly considers admissibility of plea as factor in deciding whether to permit plea of nolo contenders).

365. For discussion of the application of the exclusionary rule to pleas of nolo contendere, *see* Leonard, *supra* note 358 § 5.8.3. Many states do not permit the entry of nolo pleas. *See id.* § 5.2.3.

expenses, Rule 410 generally does not allow the use of plea evidence to impeach.[366] Some state codes expressly permit such use.[367]

In *United States v. Mezzanatto*,[368] the Supreme Court issued an important decision concerning waiver of the protections of the rule. The Court held that a person may waive protection of the rule. Defendant was arrested on narcotics charges. Shortly after his arrest, defendant and his attorney met with the prosecutor to discuss cooperation. The prosecutor informed defendant that he would not continue with the discussion unless defendant agreed that any statements he made during the meeting could be used to impeach his testimony by contradiction should he testify at trial. After consultation with his attorney, defendant agreed to the prosecutor's terms, and then made evasive and false statements during the discussion. The prosecutor terminated the meeting on the basis that defendant was not being truthful, and when defendant testified inconsistently with certain statements he made during the session, the prosecutor offered the prior statements into evidence to impeach his credibility. The Supreme Court held that the trial court's admission of the evidence was proper, relying primarily on the theory that a criminal defendant may waive many rights by voluntary agreement. Defendant argued that the disparity of bargaining power makes such agreements "inherently unfair and coercive." In response, the Court acknowledged that the plea bargaining process exerts pressure on defendants to plead guilty and that there is potential for prosecutorial abuse. But, the Court wrote, such potential for abuse "is an insufficient basis for foreclosing negotiation altogether.... Instead, the appropriate response to [defendant's] predictions of abuse is to permit case-by-case inquiries into whether waiver agreements are the product of fraud or coercion."[369]

The scope of *Mezzanatto* is not yet clear. Justice Thomas' opinion for the Court strongly hinted that *any* of the protections of Rule 410 could be waived, but three concurring Justices distanced themselves from this position, and there were two dissenters. Certainly, any "waiver" of rights accorded by Rule 410 must be knowing and voluntary.[370] In addition, prosecutorial overreaching might invalidate an agreement.[371] But defense counsel should not underestimate the scope of waivers

366. *See id.* § 5.10.

367. *See id.*

368. 513 U.S. 196 (1995).

369. *Id.* at 210.

370. *See* United States v. Krilich, 159 F.3d 1020, 1021 (7th Cir.1998) (for a waiver to be valid, a party must be aware of the right being abandoned as well as the consequences of abandoning it.

371. *See* United States v. Duffy, 133 F.Supp.2d 213 (E.D.N.Y.2001) (prosecutor would not enter into plea discussions until defendant agreed to make a proffer of facts, describe the assistance he could provide in the prosecution of other individuals, and sign a standard, non-negotiable agreement providing, *inter alia*, that any statements he made in his proffer would be admissible "as substantive evidence to rebut any evidence offered or elicited, or factual assertions made, by or on behalf of [defendant] at any stage of a criminal prosecution" should plea negotiations not succeed; held, prosecutor's use of defendant's proffer statements at his trial violated his Sixth Amendment right to make a defense and to effective assistance of counsel; unlike the waiver in *Mezzanatto*, the standard agreement essentially prevented defendant from making a meaningful defense).

Mezzanatto will permit. Though the Supreme Court is unlikely to permit waiver of the defendant's constitutional right to exculpatory evidence relevant either to guilt or punishment under *Brady v. Maryland*,[372] many rights under Rule 410 are waivable. Recently, for example, the Supreme Court held that the Constitution does not require prosecutors to disclose, prior to entering into a binding plea agreement with the defendant, information that would assist the defendant in impeaching the credibility of informants or other witnesses before entering into a binding plea agreement with a defendant.[373]

Mezzanatto was decided largely as a matter of statutory interpretation. For that reason, the states are free to interpret their own rules as they deem just.

Even in the absence of waiver, statements made to prosecutors in hopes of obtaining lenience can fall outside the protection of the rule. The Eighth Circuit has held that revelations of incriminating information by the defendant, made during preliminary discussions with the prosecutor about the benefits of cooperation, did not occur during the "course of plea discussions" and hence did not qualify for protection.[374]

§ 5.57 Evidence of Liability Insurance [FRE 411]

Federal Rule of Evidence 411 prohibits evidence of the presence or absence of liability insurance, when offered on the issue whether the insured party acted negligently or wrongfully.[375] The general rule is followed almost universally. Some states have adopted language identical or virtually identical to Federal Rule 411; others have codified somewhat different versions of the rule. The few remaining common law states also tend to follow the general principles of Rule 411.[376]

The rule has three rationales. First, the relevance of insurance to the issue of liability is questionable. While it is conceivable that a person who buys insurance will act carelessly because there is less risk of economic loss, it is also possible that those who buy insurance are more careful by nature.[377] Second, the evidence about insurance has obvious potential for prejudice. If the jury finds out that a defendant is insured, it might be more likely to hold the party liable because of the presence of a deep pocket. If the jury finds out that a defendant is not insured, then

---

372. 373 U.S. 83 (1963).

373. United States v. Ruiz, 536 U.S. 622 (2002).

374. United States v. Morgan, 91 F.3d 1193, 1196 (8th Cir.1996) (interpreting Rule 410's counterpart in Fed. R. Crim. Proc. 11(e)(6)(D)).

375. Fed. R. Evid. 411. *See, e.g.,* Rozark Farms, Inc. v. Ozark Border Elec. Coop., 849 F.2d 306, 309 (8th Cir.1988) (defendant's attorney asked plaintiff "And was this property damage insured by you?"; question abandoned after objection; trial

judge did not rule on objection or give curative instruction; held, reversible error).

376. For discussion of state law, *see* David P. Leonard, The New Wigmore: A Treatise on Evidence: Selected Rules of Limited Admissibility § 6.6 (rev. ed. 2002). Interestingly, Louisiana appears to reject the general exclusionary rule. *See id.* at 6:80. In light of Louisiana's direct action statute permitting the liability insurer to be made a party to the action, an exclusionary rule would serve little purpose.

377. *See* Fed. R. Evid. 411 advisory committee's note.

the jury may make a finding of nonliability because it is afraid that a contrary verdict will bring financial ruin.[378] Similarly, if it finds out that a plaintiff is not insured for a loss such as destruction of property by fire, then the jury might make a lawless assignment of liability because of a defendant's greater resources.[379] Finally, the rule is occasionally supported by a policy rationale—that excluding evidence of liability insurance encourages people to carry such insurance.[380]

Of course, in many situations jurors will assume that parties are insured in the absence of evidence. For example, jurors will ordinarily assume some level of insurance when a case involves an automobile accident or destruction of property by fire. In this situation, it can be argued that revealing the true state of affairs when there is no insurance merely counteracts prejudice caused by this erroneous assumption, rather than injecting prejudice. This argument, however, cannot be accepted in jurisdictions following the Federal Rules of Evidence, because it is contrary to the plain language of Rule 411. In other jurisdictions, the argument has had scant success.[381] The uninsured party can, however, request an instruction that at least suggests the possibility of no insurance. For example, the instruction could state:

> There has been no evidence in this case about whether [the party] was covered by liability insurance. The reason is that the law does not permit evidence of the absence or presence of liability insurance to be presented to you. The evidence is inadmissible because you are not supposed to consider insurance one way or the other in this case. When deciding the case, you should put out of your mind the possibility that the loss in this case was covered, or was not covered, by liability insurance.

Although evidence of liability insurance is inadmissible when offered to show negligence or wrongful conduct, it is admissible when offered for another purpose. For example, it is admissible to show agency, ownership, or control[382] or to show the bias or prejudice of a witness.[383] Thus,

---

378. On the other hand, there is the possibility that the jury might wish to punish a party who, contrary to law, fails to carry automobile liability insurance.

379. See Fed. R. Evid. 411 advisory committee's note. *See also* Falkowski v. Johnson, 148 F.R.D. 132, 136 (D.Del.1993) (plaintiff's statements in closing argument implying that defendant's employer would pay personal injury damages constitutes reversible error).

380. *See, e.g.,* 2 Weinstein's Federal Evidence § 411.02[2] (2d ed. Joseph M. McLaughlin ed. 1997) (the exclusionary rule "seeks to implement a general policy favoring insurance. Both insurers and insured are, in effect, encouraged to enter into contracts of insurance with the implied promise that they will not, as a result of their forethought, have what they believe to be

the somewhat harmful inference of carelessness used against them"). Weinstein's text also states the prejudice rationale. *See id.* § 411.02[1].

381. 1 McCormick on Evidence § 201 (5th ed. John W. Strong ed. 1999) (few courts will allow defendant to demonstrate lack of insurance; instruction on insurance suggested).

382. Fed. R. Evid. 411. *See, e.g.,* Hunziker v. Scheidemantle, 543 F.2d 489, 495 n. 10 (3d Cir.1976) (insurance admissible to prove agency relationship between owner and pilot of aircraft which crashed in wrongful death action by survivors of passenger); Newell v. Harold Shaffer Leasing Co., 489 F.2d 103, 110 (5th Cir.1974) (plaintiff's car damaged in accident with truck; draft from insurance company to plaintiff for amount of damages naming defendant

when there is a dispute about whether landlord or tenant is responsible for the maintenance of an office building's elevator, evidence that the tenant maintained liability insurance on the elevator would be admissible. Similarly, when an insurance investigator testifies, evidence that the investigator works for the insurer of one of the parties is often admitted to show the witness's possible bias.[384] Some trial judges, however, will seek to eliminate possible prejudice by requiring that the reference to the insurer be removed. For example, the judge might require that the investigator be asked whether he or she is an investigator for the defense, without mention of the insurance company. Defense counsel should ask for a ruling before the question is asked.

Rule 411 sets forth certain purposes for which evidence of insurance may be received.[385] This list, however, is not exclusive. Insurance evidence is admissible for any relevant purpose not specifically prohibited by Rule 411, that is, on any issue other than showing that the insured acted negligently or otherwise wrongfully.[386] Thus, for example, evidence of insurance sometimes comes in incidentally in the impeachment of a witness's credibility, even if the impeachment is based on grounds other than the listed purpose of showing bias. If a witness has filed a claim of loss that is inconsistent with the witness's in-court testimony, it is permissible to impeach the witness with the prior inconsistent statement.[387] Of course, if liability insurance is itself an essential element of a claim or defense, evidence of the insurance must be admitted.[388]

The fact that insurance evidence circumstantially tends to prove something other than negligence or wrongful conduct does not automatically make it admissible. As with other evidence that is admissible for one purpose but not for another, the trial judge must weigh the danger

as insured, admissible to show ownership); Dobbins v. Crain Bros., 432 F.Supp. 1060, 1069 MD Pa 1976), *aff'd in part, revd in part,* 567 F.2d 559 (3d Cir.1977) (defendant's insurance coverage on barge admissible to prove ownership).

383. Fed. R. Evid. 411. *See, e.g.,* Charter v. Chleborad, 551 F.2d 246, 248 (8th Cir.1977) (plaintiff not permitted to show impeachment witness for defense employed by same insurance company representing defendant; held, reversible error).

384. *See, e.g.,* Ouachita Natl. Bank v. Tosco Corp., 686 F.2d 1291 (8th Cir.1982), *modified on rehg,* 716 F.2d 485 (8th Cir. 1983) (en banc) (defendant could inform jury of insurance coverage when it intended to call insurance adjuster as witness); Filloon v. Stenseth, 498 N.W.2d 353, 355 (N.D. 1993) (held, in tort action arising from automobile-bicycle accident, trial court committed reversible error in automatically barring evidence that key witness also worked for driver's insurance carrier; trial court should have admitted evidence under state's Rule 411, subject to probativeness

versus prejudice balancing under state's Rule 403); 1 Stephen A. Saltzburg, Michael M. Martin & Daniel J. Capra, Federal Rules of Evidence Manual 553 (6th ed. 1994) (where insurance adjuster testifies, permissible to demonstrate relationship between witness and employer).

385. The purposes are agency, ownership, control, and bias or prejudice of a witness. Fed. R. Evid. 411.

386. For extended discussion of permissible uses of liability insurance evidence, *see* Leonard, *supra* note 376 §§ 6.9–6.15.

387. *See* Rozark Farms, Inc. v. Ozark Border Elec. Co–op., 849 F.2d 306, 309 & n. 2 (8th Cir.1988) (dictum) (stating that an amount set forth on a proof of loss form can be used to impeach testimony by insured that greater loss was suffered, and noting that it is not always possible to avoid reference to insurance in the process of this impeachment).

388. *See* Leonard, *supra* note 376 § 6.11.

of prejudice against the probative value of the evidence in deciding whether to admit it.[389] When the court determines that admission is justified, it should issue a limiting instruction informing the jury of the limited purposes for which the evidence is admitted.

If the trial judge sustains an objection to the interjection of insurance, counsel should typically[request a mistrial and then, if the request is denied, request a curative instruction telling the jury to ignore the evidence. These steps will protect the right to reversal on appeal. Of course, they may not be tactically wise in every situation. Getting a mistrial from the trial judge is no victory when the present jury is favorable.

In jurisdictions that allow substantial questioning of jurors on voir dire, insurance is sometimes brought in through the back door by questions to the jurors. For example, the plaintiff in a personal injury case might be permitted to ask jurors whether they work for an insurance company or whether they own stock in a liability insurance company.[390] In such jurisdictions, counsel may still be able to object successfully if the questions become too pointed. For example, one can argue that asking about employment with a specific insurance company is too suggestive, and that a question about general insurance employment is sufficient. Commentators have also suggested that the information about insurance be obtained from the venire by questionnaire prior to assignment to any particular case, but this solution does not appear to have been widely adopted.[391] In any event, the court must seek an appropriate balance between the conflicting rights to an unbiased jury and the avoidance of prejudice to the insured party.[392]

§ 5.58 Collateral Source Rule

A number of jurisdictions provide that the defendant's liability for damages caused by an injury is not diminished by the fact that the plaintiff has collected partial compensation from a collateral source.[393]

---

389. *See, e.g.,* Posttape Assocs. v. Eastman Kodak Co., 537 F.2d 751, 757–58 (3d Cir.1976) (trial court erred in excluding as prejudicial otherwise admissible evidence of plaintiff's insurance; evidence not prejudicial).

390. Drickersen v. Drickersen, 604 P.2d 1082, 1084–85 (Alaska 1979) (attorney entitled to ask prospective jurors if they had interest in, or connection with, any insurance company); 2 Weinstein's Federal Evidence, *supra* note 380 § 411.04[4] (jury panel may be questioned concerning interest in, or connection with, insurance company involved in litigation).

391. *See* Boos, *Recent Decisions, Practice and Procedure—Under What Circumstances May Counsel Ask Jurors Regarding Their Interest in Insurance Companies on Trial of a Case Against an Insured Defen-*

dant, 43 Mich. L. Rev. 621, 623 (1944) (give every member of jury panel questionnaire concerning relations with insurance companies); *Recent Cases, Jury—Competency of Jurors—Questioning Jurors on Voir Dire as to Their Connections with Insurance Company,* 52 Harv. L. Rev. 166, 166 (1938) (examine entire jury panel concerning connections to insurance companies before trial of any cases during term).

392. For further discussion of the problem of revealing evidence of liability insurance during jury selection, *see* Leonard, *supra* note 376 § 6.7.4.

393. *See, e.g.,* Gypsum Carrier, Inc. v. Handelsman, 307 F.2d 525, 535 (9th Cir. 1962) (benefits to injured seaman under compensation plan not deductible from Jones Act recovery; federal courts generally follow collateral source rule); Helfend v.

For example, under this rule, the plaintiff whose hospital bills were paid by health insurance is still entitled to recover the amount paid to the hospital from the party whose negligence caused the injury.[394] The rationale behind the collateral source rule is that the wrongdoer should not benefit from the injured person's expenditures or relationships that may exist between the injured person and third parties.[395]

The collateral source rule is not really a rule of evidence, but a rule of substantive law that causes certain evidence to be irrelevant.[396] If the substantive law does not allow collateral payments to diminish recovery, evidence of collateral payments should be excluded as irrelevant.[397]

In recent years, however, the collateral source rule has come under attack. Many scholars have argued the rationale of the collateral source rule is outdated. Some have argued that the rule stymies what would otherwise be an economically sensible form of loss spreading.[398] In

Southern California Rapid Transit Dist., 465 P.2d 61, 63 (Cal.1970) (compensation for injuries received from source independent of tortfeasor may not be deducted from damages injured party would otherwise recover); Wilson v. Hoffman Group, Inc., 546 N.E.2d 524, 530 (Ill.1989) (benefits received by injured party from source independent of and collateral to tortfeasor will not diminish damages); Restatement (Second) of Torts § 920A (1979) ("Payments made to or benefits conferred on the injured party from other sources are not credited against the tortfeasor's liability although they cover all or a part of the harm for which the tortfeasor is liable").

Alabama's recent tort reform yielded a statute that allows admission of evidence that an outside source has paid or will pay or reimburse a plaintiff for certain medical or hospital expenses. Ala. Code § 12–21–45 (1995). An Alabama district court has found the statute inapplicable in federal diversity cases (Killian v. Melser, 792 F.Supp. 1217 (N.D.Ala.1992)) and has noted that, in the absence of an authoritative ruling by the Alabama Supreme Court, many state trial courts apparently allow the evidence accompanied by an instruction that the jury "may consider" it.

394. See, e.g., Carter v. United States, 982 F.2d 1141, 1145 (7th Cir.1992) (veterans' benefits not considered collateral source payments); Berg v. United States, 806 F.2d 978, 985–86 (10th Cir.1986) (Medicare benefits for injuries suffered at veterans' hospital could not be deducted from damages against federal government under Federal Torts Claim Act, 28 U.S.C § 2671, for medical malpractice); Helfend, 465 P.2d at 69 (defendant could not mitigate damages by medical insurance payments to injured plaintiff); Restatement (Second) of

Torts § 902A comment c (1979) (collateral benefits from insurance policies not subtracted from plaintiff's recovery).

395. See, e.g., Wilson, 546 N.E.2d at 524 (wrongdoer should not benefit from injured party's expenditures or take advantage of contacts or other relations between injured party and third parties); Greenwood v. Hildebrand, 515 A.2d 963, 968 (Pa.Super.1986) (wrongdoer should not receive benefit of fortuitous existence of collateral remedy).

396. As a rule of substantive law, one would expect that federal courts in diversity cases would be required to follow the state's collateral source rule. See Erie R. Co. v. Tompkins, 304 U.S. 64 (1938); Bradford v. Bruno's Inc., 94 F.3d 621 (11th Cir.1996), (Alabama's statutory modification of its common law collateral source rule was substantive law that must be applied in federal diversity action); In re Air Crash Disaster Near Chicago, Illinois, on May 25, 1979, 803 F.2d 304, 308 (7th Cir.1986) (holding that federal court in diversity case must apply collateral source rule of state whose law governs case).

397. See Jones on Evidence: Civil and Criminal § 4.48, at 480–81 (Spencer A. Gard 6th ed. 1972) (evidence of plaintiff's financial condition including receipts of benefits from collateral sources inadmissible as irrelevant to issue of compensatory damages).

398. See, e.g., John G. Fleming, The Collateral Source Rule and Loss Allocation in Tort Law, 54 Calif. L. Rev. 1478, 1547 (1966) (moral postulates yielding to modern economic value system; "question is not so much whether a wrongdoer deserves to be relieved as which of several competing 'risk

addition, the proliferation of medical malpractice suits and the rising cost of insurance led the American Medical Association to campaign for a variety of tort reforms including abolition of the collateral source rule.[399] In recent years, several jurisdictions have modified or abolished the collateral source rule in medical malpractice cases.[400] Although such laws have been attacked on both equal protection and due process grounds, the courts generally have held them constitutional.[401]

§ 5.59   Other Accidents, When Offered by Personal Injury Plaintiffs

A personal injury plaintiff may seek to introduce evidence of similar accidents involving the defendant's property or product. For example, in a slip-and-fall case involving a fall on a carpet on defendant's premises, the plaintiff might offer evidence that other customers had previously fallen on the same carpet, to support a claim that the carpet was loose.[402] Such evidence is relevant if the conditions under which the other accidents occurred were sufficiently similar to the accident at issue to make it more likely either that the prior accidents were caused by the same defect or that the prior accidents would have given a reasonable property owner notice of a possible defect. Whether the evidence will in fact be admissible in a given case turns on a Federal Rule of Evidence

communities' should bear the loss"). Fleming argues that the collateral source rule is no longer justified in light of the high cost of shifting the loss to the tortfeasor from some form of collectivized risk-bearing regime which has already paid for the loss and could absorb it as well or even better than the tortfeasor. *Id.* at 1547–48.

399. *See* Banks McDowell, *The Collateral Source Rule—The American Medical Association and Tort Reform*, 24 Washburn L.J. 205, 215–16 (1985).

400. *See* Bernier v. Burris, 497 N.E.2d 763, 774–75 (Ill.1986) (listing state laws modifying or abrogating collateral source rule in medical malpractice cases permitting recovery to be reduced by amounts received from private or public sources).

401. *See, e.g.,* Marsh v. Green, 782 So.2d 223, 230–31 (Ala. 2000) (statute abrogating collateral source rule does not violate equal protection or due process rights); Fein v. Permanente Med. Group, 695 P.2d 665, 685–86 (Cal.1985) (statute allowing defendant to introduce evidence of collateral payments to injured party in medical malpractice suit does not violate due process or equal protection); *Bernier*, 497 N.E.2d at 775 (provision allowing judgment in medical malpractice cases to be reduced by up to 50 per cent for benefits received from collateral sources does not violate due process). *See generally*, McDowell, *supra* note

399, at 215–19 (discussing general reform movement and constitutional challenges to abrogation of rule).

402. *See, e.g.,* Beck v. City of Pittsburgh, 89 F.3d 966, 973–75 (3d Cir.1996) (error to exclude other complaints against police officer to show defendant city's tolerance of excessive force); Tait v. Armor Elevator Co., 958 F.2d 563, 568–69 (3d Cir. 1992) (excluding evidence of prior accidents in other elevators in same elevator bank, where plaintiff failed to substantiate argument that accidents arose from similar cause); Wyatt v. Otis Elevator Co., 921 F.2d 1224, 1228 (11th Cir.1991) (allowing evidence of prior accidents involving failure of elevator doors to reverse and detract; discussion in court of other types of elevator accidents cured by jury instruction); Robitaille v. Netoco Community Theatres, 25 N.E.2d 749, 751 (Mass.1940) (held, reversible error to admit evidence of other fall two or three weeks earlier in same spot; no sufficient showing of similar conditions or similar conduct by victims of fall); Gable v. Kroger Co., 410 S.E.2d 701 (W.Va.1991) (excluding evidence of two previous slip-and-fall accidents, where neither accident occurred in same area of store or arose from a similar problem). *Cf.* Bitsos v. Red Owl Stores, Inc., 459 F.2d 656, 659–60 (8th Cir. 1972) (earlier falls on steps; admissible to demonstrate presence of foreign substance on steps).

403 balancing of probative value against prejudice, confusion, and waste of time, with a measure of discretion accorded to the trial judge.[403]

In exercising discretion, the trial judge should consider whether a convincing showing of similar conditions has been made.[404] Also, the trial judge should consider whether the prior accidents are offered merely to show that a condition was dangerous—something that could be shown by other evidence with less waste of time or danger of prejudice—or whether the evidence is also relevant to the issue whether the defendant was on notice of the existence of the dangerous condition. If the evidence is relevant to notice, then the requirement of similar conditions is applied less strictly. All that is required is that the prior accident be similar enough to alert the defendant to the danger.[405]

When the evidence of other accidents is offered to show the carelessness of a human being, rather than merely to show the dangerousness of a thing, then the rules against character evidence come into play. The evidence is admissible only if it can be received under Rule 404(b) as probative of something other than a propensity to be negligent. *See* § 5.14.

§ 5.60   Absence of Other Accidents, When Offered by Personal Injury Defendants

Just as the plaintiff may wish to offer evidence of prior accidents to establish the dangerousness of a condition or notice to the defendant of possible danger, the defendant may wish to offer evidence that *no* accidents had occurred in the manner plaintiff claimed, even though the conditions had remained essentially unchanged. While some jurisdictions forbid receipt of such evidence,[406] most appear to recognize that evidence

---

403. *See, e.g.,* Simon v. Kennebunkport, 417 A.2d 982, 986 (Me.1980) (Me. R. Evid. 403 abolishes former Maine rule of exclusion and leaves admissibility of prior falls on same sidewalk to discretion of trial judge).

404. *See, e.g., id.* (error to exclude evidence of earlier falls; as many as one hundred people fell under similar circumstances. *See also* Drabik v. Stanley–Bostitch, Inc., 997 F.2d 496, 508 (8th Cir. 1993) ("for other accidents evidence to be admissible, the proponent of the evidence must show that the facts and circumstances of the other incident are substantially similar to the case at bar"); Lolie v. Ohio Brass Co., 502 F.2d 741, 745 (7th Cir.1974) (evidence that other metal clips failed inadmissible; no offer of proof that other clips were comparable to clips in issue).

405. *See, e.g.,* Exum v. General Elec. Co., 819 F.2d 1158, 1159–60 (D.C.Cir.1987) (prior accident in which fast food employee burned by appliance; court states that high-

er degree of similarity is required when issue is dangerousness than when issue is notice); Gardner v. Southern Ry. Sys., 675 F.2d 949, 952 (7th Cir.1982) (prior railroad collision, to show notice of hazard at grade crossing; court indicates that it is appropriate to relax requirement of similar conditions when purpose is to show notice); City of Taylorville v. Stafford, 63 N.E. 624–25 (Ill.1902) (other people stumbled on sidewalk; admissible to show notice of dangerous condition). *See also* Four Corners Helicopters, Inc. v. Turbomeca, S.A., 979 F.2d 1434 (10th Cir.1992) (held, other failures of helicopter screws admissible to show notice; where issue is notice, lesser showing of similarity is sufficient); Cooper v. Firestone Tire & Rubber Co., 945 F.2d 1103, 1105 (9th Cir.1991) (noting that the circuits are split concerning whether evidence of similar accidents is admissible when relevant to witness credibility).

406. *See, e.g.,* Jones v. Pak–Mor Mfg. Co., 700 P.2d 819, 821 (Ariz.1985) (stating a categorical rule in Arizona forbidding re-

of the absence of accidents can be relevant in various types of actions including basic negligence and product liability cases.[407] As with evidence of prior accidents, the issue is first one of relevance, and then of balancing the probative value of the evidence against its potential to cause undue prejudice or to confuse the jury. At times, the evidence should be excluded, particularly because of its tendency to confuse the jury. In other cases, however, the evidence has substantial probative value. Where, for example, a condition has remained static for a number of years and nobody has suffered an injury, plaintiff's claim that the condition represents an undue danger is particularly weak. Depriving the jury of the evidence of the lack of accidents in such a case would be misleading.

The authorities have generally supported admission, and this appears to be the modern trend.[408] At least one authority suggested, in fact, that evidence of favorable safety history carries more probative value than plaintiff's evidence of prior accidents.[409]

---

ceipt of evidence of the absence of prior accidents to prove lack of defect, lack of danger, or similar issues); Paulison v. Chicago, M., St. P. and P. R.R., Inc., 392 N.E.2d 960, 965–66 (Ill.App.1979) (in wrongful death action against railroad for failure to provide automatic gates at crossing, evidence of only three minor accidents in prior fifteen years not admissible to prove lack of danger; prior Illinois authority had held such evidence admissible only to prove lack of notice, which was not an issue in this case).

407. *See, e.g.,* Benson v. Honda Motor Co., Ltd., 32 Cal.Rptr.2d 322, 325–28 (Cal. App.1994) (in product liability action alleging both negligence and failure to warn, manufacturer may offer evidence of absence of similar prior accidents); Carbin v. National Super Markets, Inc., 823 S.W.2d 93 (Mo.App.1991) (in negligence action by gro-

cery store customer alleging injury from striking eye on display rack, held, defendant may offer evidence that manager was not aware of any prior similar accidents in the store; evidence admissible to prove store lacked knowledge, or reason to know, of dangerous condition); Reiger v. Toby Enterprises, 609 P.2d 402, 404 (Or.App.1980) (in product liability action by employee of meat processing plant against manufacturer of meat slicer for hand injuries, evidence of absence of prior accidents admissible to prove product not unreasonably dangerous).

408. *See, e.g.,* 1 McCormick on Evidence § 200, at 708–10 (5th ed. John W. Strong ed. 1999); 2 John H. Wigmore, Evidence in Trials at Common Law §§ 443–44, at 528–32 (James H. Chadbourn rev. 1979).

409. Clarence Morris, Studies in the Law of Torts 87–89 (1952).

Chapter 6

COMPETENCY

Table of Sections

---

§ 6.01   Rules of Competency in General [FRE 601]

Rules of competency are rules that disqualify a witness from testifying. Usually the ground of disqualification is that the witness has some personal defect that will prevent the testimony from being accurate. Some competency rules, however, are based upon considerations of extrinsic policy. Rules rendering jurors incompetent to impeach their own verdicts, for example, are based on a desire for stability and an end to litigation, not upon concerns about accuracy of testimony.[1]

The common-law rules of incompetency, which persisted in many jurisdictions until the middle of the nineteenth century or later, are to the modern lawyer bizarre and arbitrary. On grounds of preventing perjury, parties and others with an interest in a lawsuit were prohibited from testifying.[2] A criminal defendant, for example, could not testify in his or her own behalf, though the rule was mitigated in many jurisdictions by allowing an unsworn statement that did not amount to "testimony."[3] One spouse could not testify on behalf of the other.[4] A convicted felon could not testify at all.[5]

Rules of this nature are contrary to the modern approach to trials, which is to allow evidence to come in for what it is worth, and to trust the trier of fact to recognize its impurities and separate the grain from the chaff. For the most part, the rules of incompetency have given way to

---

1. *See* Fed. R. Evid. 606(b) advisory committee's note.

2. 2 John H. Wigmore, Evidence in Trials at Common Law § 577, at 817 (James H. Chadbourn rev. 1979).

3. *See id.* § 579, at 826–27.

4. *See id.* § 600, at 856.

5. *See id.* § 519, at 725.

rules allowing witnesses to testify, subject to being impeached by the same facts (*e.g.*, bias, convictions) that would previously have made the witness incompetent.[6]

Some of the ancient rules of incompetency, however, persist in qualified form. Some states maintain rules against testimony by children or the insane, unless they can be shown to be of sufficient understanding.[7] Others maintain "dead man's statutes" that prevent interested survivors from testifying in their suits against a dead person's estate.[8] Some of the rules of competency—those prohibiting testimony by judges and jurors—have not been affected by the modern trend, because they rest on a basis other than that of protecting the trier from inaccurate evidence.[9] Finally, a new sort of incompetency rule seems to be taking hold in states that have barred the reception of testimony by a witness whose memory has been hypnotically refreshed.[10]

Rule 601 provides that "[e]very person is competent to be a witness except as otherwise provided in these rules." When state law provides the rule of decision, however, the state competency law governs in federal court.[11] As a practical matter, it is rare that a judge finds, pursuant to Rule 104(a), that a witness is incompetent. The competency bar is very low. Considerations that might affect competency—a child's inability to distinguish between the truth and a lie, a person's inability to perceive well, a failure of memory, and the like—are more appropriately matters of weight and credibility for the jury.[12] When a witness of questionable competency is offered, a lawyer might be well advised to object even if the objection is likely to fail in the end. The judge will allow the lawyer to conduct a voir dire examination on competency that may help the lawyer to develop facts that can be used to impeach the witness when the witness is allowed to testify.

§ 6.02   Incompetency of Insane Person

The Federal Rules of Evidence do not disqualify an insane person. The insanity may be shown to impeach, but may not be used to keep the witness off the stand.[13] Some state jurisdictions still allow objections to testimony to be based on the insanity of the witness.[14] Where incompetency by virtue of mental illness is a ground for objection, however, the objection will not succeed simply on a showing that the proposed witness

---

6. *See* Fed. R. Evid. 601 advisory committee's note.

7. *See* § 6.03 *infra.*

8. *See* § 6.04 *infra.*

9. *See* § 6.05 *infra.*

10. *See* § 6.07 *infra.*

11. Fed. R. Evid. 601.

12. Fed. R. Evid. 601 advisory committee's note, citing citing 2 Wigmore §§ 501, 509.

13. Fed. R. Evid. 601 advisory committee's note.

14. *See, e.g.*, Mich. R. Evid. 601 (witness must have mental capacity or sense of obligation to testify truthfully and understandably); Ohio R. Evid. 601(A) (persons of unsound mind incapable of receiving just impressions or relating them truthfully not competent); Tex. R. Evid. 601(a)(1) (persons insane at time offered as witness or when event occurred about which they are offered to testify are incompetent); Ga. Code O.C.G.A. § 24–9–7 (2002); Code of Ala. § 12–21–165 (2003).

is mentally ill. Typically, the state will provide that the insane person may testify if able to understand the duty to tell the truth, or able to express thought in an understandable manner, or both.[15]

§ 6.03   Incompetency of Child

The Federal Rules of Evidence do not contain restrictions on testimony of child witnesses.[16] Many states, however, do have restrictions at least in theory on the testimony of children, and in those federal cases in which state law provides the substantive rule of decision the state law applies.[17]

Typically, a state statute on incompetency of children will provide that a child under a certain age is incompetent unless shown to understand the duty to tell the truth and to be of sufficient understanding to be able to testify accurately.[18] In recent years, concern for prevention of child abuse has led to relaxation of competency requirements in some states.[19] Minnesota's statute, for example, now provides that a child under ten years is competent unless shown to lack the capacity to remember facts correctly or to testify truthfully, a reversal of the prior burden of persuasion on competency.[20]

§ 6.04   Dead Man's Statute

The dead man's statute is a rule of evidence that, broadly speaking, prohibits an adverse party from testifying against a dead person's estate

---

15. *See, e.g.,* Mich. R. Evid. 601 (witness must have mental capacity or sense of obligation to testify truthfully and understandably); Minn. Stat. Ann. § 595.02(1)(f) (West 1988) (persons of unsound mind not competent if they lack capacity to remember or to relate facts truthfully); N.C. R. Evid. 601(b) (witness disqualified if incapable of testifying in understandable manner or incapable of understanding duty to tell truth).

16. *See* Fed. R. Evid. 601; 3 Weinstein's Federal Evidence § 601 App.102[8] (2d ed. Joseph M. McLaughlin ed. 1997) (Rule 601 codified judicial practice in federal courts against indiscriminately disqualifying witnesses based on age).

17. Fed. R. Evid. 609; State v. Warden, 891 P.2d 1074 (Kan.1995) (trial court properly allowed autistic child witness to testify through a "facilitator" who guided witness' hands while he typed; but since child was capable of signing "yes" or "no," he should have been required to make those responses independently of facilitator; moreover, facilitator should generally be prevented from hearing questions asked to child in order to ensure that answer comes from child, not facilitator). *Compare* In re Basilio T., 5 Cal.

Rptr.2d 450, 456 (Cal. App. 1992) (Cal. Evid. Code §§ 700–701 (1966) provide that regardless of age, witness is competent as long as he or she has "the capacity to observe, sufficient intelligence, adequate memory, the ability to communicate, and an appreciation of the obligation to speak the truth." Id. at 457 n 7; State v. Roman, 622 A.2d 96, 100 (Me.1993) (holding that "[a] child of any age is presumed competent to testify as a witness unless disqualified under [Maine] Rule 601(b)" as incapable of expressing herself, of understanding duty to tell truth, or lacking "reasonable ability" to perceive or remember the issue).

18. *See, e.g.,* Ohio R. Evid. 601(A) (children under ten years old, who appear incapable of perceiving facts correctly or of relating them truthfully incompetent); Sizemore v. State, 416 S.E.2d 500, 502 (Ga. 1992) (Ga. Code Ann. § 249–9–5 excepts children who are victims of crime from competency challenge based on allegations that child does not understand nature of oath).

19. John E.B. Myers, Child Witness Law and Practice § 3.11, at 73–74 (1987).

20. Minn. Stat. Ann. § 595.02(1)(*l*) (West 2002).

about transactions or conversations with the dead person.[21] The theory behind the statute is that it is unfair to allow the party to give self-serving testimony when the lips of the dead person are sealed.[22] There are competing values and not all states have adopted a dead man's statute. Those jurisdictions with dead man's statutes have given primary consideration to the risk that unscrupulous people will take advantage of the death of others to make false claims against their estates. Those jurisdictions that have rejected the notion have given primary consideration to the risk that honest creditors will not be able to prove up legitimate debts of the decedent. The differences among dead man's statutes are so substantial that it is difficult to generalize about them, and of course it is essential to consult the local statute and case law.

The Federal Rules of Evidence do not recognize the dead man's statute.[23] There is no prohibition against the testimony in federal cases, unless state substantive law governs and the state maintains a dead man's statute. Under the federal rules, the danger of self-serving perjury is something that goes to the weight of the testimony, not its admissibility.[24]

§ 6.05 Testimony by Judge or Juror [FRE 606]

The Federal Rules of Evidence contain an absolute prohibition against testimony by a judge in a case over which the judge is presiding.[25] No objection is necessary to preserve the error. To save the lawyer from the awkwardness of challenging the presiding judge, the rules provide for an automatic objection.[26] Occasionally a judge will do the equivalent of testifying by making a comment from the bench based on personal knowledge. Unless the statement concerns a matter that is an appropriate subject for judicial notice,[27] this conduct is objectionable.[28]

The Federal Rules also provide that jurors may not testify in cases in which they are sitting.[29] When a juror is called to testify, it is necessary to make an objection in order to preserve error. The lawyer

---

21. *See* 1 McCormick on Evidence § 65 (4th ed. John W. Strong ed. 1992).

22. *See id.* at 105–107.

23. Fed. R. Evid. 601 advisory committee's note.

24. *Id.*

25. Fed. R. Evid. 605.

26. *Id.* & advisory committee's note.

27. *See* Fed. R. Evid. 201(b) defines a judicially noticeable fact as "one not subject to reasonable dispute in that it is either (1) generally known with the territorial jurisdiction of the trial court or (2) capable of accurate and ready determination by resort to sources whose accuracy cannot reasonably be questioned."

28. *See, e.g.,* Fox v. City of West Palm Beach, 383 F.2d 189, 191 (5th Cir. 1967)

(judge's frequent statements based on own extrajudicial experience reversible error); 3 Weinstein's Federal Evidence § 605.07[1] (2d ed. Joseph M. McLaughlin ed. 1997) (judge may not introduce personal experience under guise of judicial notice); United States v. Jones, 29 F.3d 1549, 1553 (11th Cir. 1994)(explaining that the effect of judicially noticing a fact is like precluding the opposing party from introducing evidence to the contrary and is essentially a directed verdict against that party as to the noticed fact); Fawcett v. State, 697 A.2d 385 (Del. 1997) (Judge may not take judicial notice of an element of the crime with which the defendant is charged).

29. Fed. R. Evid. 606(a).

must be given an opportunity, however, to make the objection outside the hearing of the jury.[30]

The long-respected doctrine that jurors may not be heard to impeach the verdict is carried forward in the Federal Rules.[31] This means that after verdict, jurors may not testify that the verdict was produced by an unlawful method, such as a coin toss or by agreeing to write down numbers and accept the average as the figure for recovery.[32] They may testify, however, that there was a mistake in reporting the actual verdict.[33] The Federal Rules do provide that jurors may testify about the introduction of extraneous prejudicial information or improper outside influence.[34] Thus, jurors would be able to testify that one of the jurors brought a newspaper describing the case into the jury room, or that a juror was bribed.[35] The Supreme Court has interpreted the exception for outside influence narrowly, holding in *Tanner v. United States*,[36] that

30. *Id.*

31. *See* Fed. R. Evid. 606(b).

32. *Id.*; *see, e.g.*, United States v. Straach, 987 F.2d 232, 242 (5th Cir. 1993) (defendant not entitled to mistrial when two jurors signed statements that they believed defendant's innocence throughout the jury deliberations, but were "pressured" into accepting a verdict of guilty); Dallas v. Arave, 984 F.2d 292, 296 (9th Cir. 1993) (trial court properly denied defendant's motions to supplement the record with jurors' testimony that by finding the defendant guilty of voluntary manslaughter, they found the defendant initially acted in self-defense); Williams v. Price, 343 F.3d 223 (3d Cir. 2003) (explaining the "no impeachment" rule and its development); Solis v. Cockrell, 342 F.3d 392 (5th Cir. 2003) (juror's belief that inmate had reputation for stealing, learned while living near inmate, was not an extreme situation sufficient to presume bias.); Fullwood v. Lee, 290 F.3d 663 (4th Cir. 2002) (Evidentiary hearing required on whether juror had been improperly influenced by her husband and whether the jury improperly learned of a previous death sentence for the same murder.); Hartley *ex rel.* Hartley v. Guthmann, 532 N.W.2d 331, 335–36 (Neb. 1995) (Brochure discussing detrimental effects of smoking on fetus in suit alleging malpractice during birth is sufficient evidence of juror misconduct).

33. Latino v. Crane Rental Co., 630 N.E.2d 591 (Mass. 1994) (trial judge suspecting variation in verdicts properly inquired whether jury agreed on special verdicts announced in open court by limiting questions to what jury decided, not why); State v. Williquette, 526 N.W.2d 144, 145 (Wis. 1995) (after discharge, jurors competent to testify to clerical error in jury verdict).

34. Fed. R. Evid. 606(b); United States v. Walker, 1 F.3d 423 (6th Cir. 1993) (Trial court erred in failing to hold hearing on impact on jurors of inadmissible taped depositions inadvertently sent to jury room with other exhibits); Powell v. Allstate Ins. Co., 652 So.2d 354, 357 (Fla. 1995) (juror allegations that all white jury made racial jokes about black plaintiffs during deliberations); Castaneda *ex rel.* Correll v. Pederson, 518 N.W.2d 246, 252–253 (Wis. 1994) (juror's misconduct in researching and reporting average malpractice award); Williams v. Price, 343 F.3d 223 (3d Cir. 2003) (Hearing required on issue of whether juror lied during voir dire.); *but see* United States v. Klee, 494 F.2d 394, 396 (9th Cir. 1974) (denying motion for new trial even though jurors discussed the case during breaks and expressed premature opinions about the defendant's guilt) and Belmontes v. Woodford, 350 F.3d 861 (9th Cir. 2003) (juror misconduct must be so prejudicial as to have denied petitioner a fair trial).

35. Fed. R. Evid. 606(b) advisory committee's note (citing Mattox v. United States, 146 U.S. 140 (1892)). *See also* United States v. Swinton, 75 F.3d 374, 381 (8th Cir.1996) (juror revelation that defendant had a criminal record is "extraneous prejudicial information"); Haugh v. Jones & Laughlin Steel Corp., 949 F.2d 914, 916–919 (7th Cir. 1991) (new trial proper where marshal told jurors they would be locked up until they reached a verdict, but trial court was wrong to ask juror whether consent to verdict was result of agreement or desire to go home).

36. 483 U.S. 107 (1987).

jurors could not testify about other jurors' use of alcohol or drugs during the trial.[37]

§ 6.06   Witness Has Not Taken Oath [FRE 603]

Occasionally a witness who does not want to testify will simply refuse to take the oath. Other witnesses may refuse to take an oath on religious grounds. The federal rules and most state codes permit the witness to take either an oath or affirmation.[38] The affirmation omits the word "swear" and references to "God" from the oath. A witness might be asked, for example, "Do you affirm that the evidence you shall give is the truth, the whole truth, and nothing but the truth?" A witness who refuses to take the oath or affirmation is not eligible to testify.[39] The trial judge should be willing to tailor the affirmation to avoid scruples of the witness, so long as the witness is willing to agree to tell the truth under penalty of perjury.[40]

§ 6.07   Hypnotically Refreshed Testimony

Hypnotically refreshed memory has been the subject of concern in the courts, because though it is often useful in developing leads for investigation and carries the promise of otherwise unavailable testimony, it carries, also, great danger of inaccuracy. The hypnotized person is highly suggestible, can easily be influenced by unintentional cues from

37. *Id.* at 121–25. *See also* United States v. Griffith, 17 F.3d 865 (6th Cir.) cert. denied, 513 U.S. 850 (1994) (juror attempt to discuss case with deputy marshal not an extraneous influence); United States v. Martinez–Moncivais, 14 F.3d 1030, 1036 (5th Cir. 1994) (that two jurors mentioned that if defendant were innocent he would have testified was not improper external influence); Sassounian v. Roe, 230 F.3d 1097 (9th Cir. 2000) (Jurors' consideration of excluded evidence they overheard from sidebar of terrorist phone call claiming responsibility for assassination in question was misconduct having "substantial and injurious effect" on sentence.); United States v. Davis, 177 F.3d 552 (6th Cir. 1999) (No presumption of prejudice will arise from the bare fact that improper contact with the jury occurred.); State v. Cherry, 20 S.W.3d 354 (Ark. 2000) (New first-degree murder trial properly granted when jurors concluded appellee's guilt before deliberations and discussed those conclusions with other jurors).

38. *See* Fed. R. Evid. 603; Gregory P. Joseph, Stephen A. Saltzburg & Trial Evid. Comm., ABA, Evidence in America: The Federal Rules in the States § 37.2, at 1 (1987) (at least 31 states follow Rule 603 or comparable rule).'

39. *See* Fed. R. Evid. 603; United States v. Fowler, 605 F.2d 181, 185 (5th Cir. 1979) (court did not err in refusing to allow defendant to testify after he refused to swear or affirm that he would tell truth); United States v. Allen J., 127 F.3d 1292 (10th Cir. 1997) ("Fed. R. Evid. 603 requires every witness to declare he or she will testify truthfully. In addition to confirming for the court the victim understood the oath, the initial questioning of the victim also served 'to awaken the witness' conscience and impress the witness' mind with the duty to [testify truthfully],' as required by Rule 603.").

40. *See* Fed. R. Evid. 603 advisory committee's note ("The rule is designed to afford the flexibility required in dealing with religious adults, atheists, conscientious objectors, mental defectives, and children. Affirmation is simply a solemn undertaking to tell the truth; no special verbal formula is required. As is true generally, affirmation is recognized by federal law."); United States v. Ward, 989 F.2d 1015, 1020 (9th Cir. 1993) (Witness should be allowed to replace the word "truth" with the phrase "fully integrated honesty before taking the oath."); Lawson v. Washington, 296 F.3d 799, 809 (9th Cir. 2002) (discussing oaths in general); Gordon v. Idaho, 778 F.2d 1397, 1400 (9th Cir. 1985) (any statement indicating that witness is impressed with duty to tell truth and understands that she is subject to penalty of perjury, sufficient).

the hypnotist,[41] and is likely to manufacture false memory or confabulate true memory in a way that is undetectable either to the hypnotist or to the subject.[42] Moreover, the subject's memory tends to harden after hypnosis, creating an artificially high level of certainty.[43]

The potential value and the potential danger of hypnotically refreshed testimony has led to an inconsistent history in the courts. The testimony was considered *per se* inadmissible[44] until 1968, when, following the Maryland Supreme Court decision in *Harding v. State*,[45] most jurisdictions changed course and held the testimony to be *per se* admissible. Beginning in the 1980's courts began to move toward a middle ground between *per se* inadmissibility and *per se* admissibility.[46] Today only North Dakota[47], Oregon[48], Wyoming[49], and Tennessee[50] consider the testimony *per se* admissible in at least some situations.[51] While no jurisdiction considers the testimony *per se* inadmissible in all cases, some severely restrict the testimony.[52] Some jurisdictions admit hypnotically

41. *See, e.g.*, State ex rel. Collins v. Superior Court, 644 P.2d 1266, 1269–70 (Ariz. 1982) (common characteristic of subject under hypnosis is hyper-suggestibility); Emily E. Smith–Lee, *Note: Recovered Memories Of Childhood Abuse: Should Long–Buried Memories Be Admissible Testimony?*, 37 B.C. L. Rev 591, 595–96 (May 1996) ("Courts have recognized three primary dangers associated with hypnosis: the danger of suggestibility; the possibility that the subject will "confabulate," or fill in the gaps of his or her story, in order to present a more coherent picture of an event; and the danger that the subject will experience an increased, often unjustified, confidence in the truth of his or her story.); Joseph A. Spadaro, *NOTE: An Elusive Search for the Truth: The Admissibility of Repressed and Recovered Memories in Light of Daubert v. Merrell Dow Pharmaceuticals, Inc.*, 30 Conn. L. Rev. 1147 (Spring 1998).

42. *See, e.g.*, State v. Hurd, 432 A.2d 86, 92–93 (N.J. 1981) (quoting Martin T. Orne, *The Use and Misuse of Hypnosis in Court*, 27 Int'l J. Clinical & Experimental Hypnosis 311, 317–18 (1979)) (subject under hypnosis experiences need to fill gaps in memory and may create facts; impossible to distinguish truth from fiction without independent verification); *See also* Rock v. Arkansas, 483 U.S. 44, 59–60 (1987).

43. *Id.* at 93–94, citing *Orne, supra* note 42, at 318–20 (subject tends to be incapable of distinguishing prior memory from hypnotic recall and to have strong subjective confidence in validity of post-hypnotic recall); *See also* Rock v. Arkansas, at 60; Love v. Freeman, 1999 WL 671939 (4th Cir. 1999); Alcala v. Woodford, 334 F.3d 862, 876 (9th Cir. 2003).

44. People v. Ebanks, 49 P. 1049, 1053 (Cal. 1897) ("The law of the United States does not recognize hypnotism."), *overruled on other grounds*; People v. Flannelly, 60 P. 670 (Cal. 1900).

45. 246 A.2d 302 (Md.App. 1968).

46. Roark v. Kentucky, 90 S.W.3d 24, 29 (Ky. 2002)(containing an exhaustive history of hypnotically refreshed testimony in the courts).

47. State v. Brown, 337 N.W.2d 138 (N.D. 1983) (A previously hypnotized witness is not incompetent to testify. Hypnotically refreshed recall is admissible with the jury determining the weight of that testimony.).

48. ORS § 136.675 (2001) (Hypnotically refreshed testimony may be offered <u>in a criminal proceeding</u> so long as the entire session was recorded and that recording made available to all parties.); State v. Jorgensen, 492 P.2d 312 (Or.App. 1971).

49. Haselhuhn v. State, 727 P.2d 280 (Wyo. 1986).

50. State v. Glebock, 616 S.W.2d 897 (Tenn. Crim. App. 1981).

51. Borawick v. Shay, 68 F.3d 597, 604 (2d Cir. 1995) (describing the rule).

52. State v. Coon, 974 P.2d 386 (Alaska 1999)(Applies *Daubert* analysis in overruling Contreras v. State, 718 P.2d 129 in which court, based on *Frye* analysis held testimony per se inadmissible); Schall v. Lockheed Missiles & Space Co., 37 Cal. App.4th 1485 (1995)(In civil cases, refreshed testimony is per se inadmissible except for testimony about events recalled and related to others before hypnosis); Mersch v. City of Dallas, 207 F.3d 732, 735, 736 (5th Cir. 2000) (Per se inadmissible in

refreshed testimony if the proponent can establish that procedural safeguards were followed.[53] These safeguards can include a requirement that the hypnotist has certain qualifications, the witness's recollection of the event before hypnosis be recorded, the hypnotic sessions be recorded, and only the hypnotist and the subject be present.[54] Other jurisdictions consider whether the "totality of the circumstances" suggest admitting the testimony.[55] The "totality of the circumstances" test appears to be

only one instance, where "a hypnotized subject identifies for the first time a person he has reason to believe is already under suspicion" regardless of the procedural safeguards employed in the hypnotic session.); People v. Zayas, 131 Ill.2d 284 (Ill. 1989); State v. Tuttle, 780 P.2d 1203(Utah 1989).

53. *See, e.g.*, White v. Ieyoub, 25 F.3d 245, 248 n.13 (5th Cir. 1994) (preferable that hypnosis be performed by professional, independent hypnotist with little knowledge of case and that the session be recorded); Sprynczynatyk v. General Motors Corp., 771 F.2d 1112, 1122–23 & n. 14 (8th Cir. 1985), *cert. denied*, 475 U.S. 1046 (1986) (hypnotically refreshed testimony admissible if certain safeguards followed); Borawick v. Shay, 842 F.Supp. 1501, 1505, 1508 (D. Conn. 1994) (court excluded testimony on post-hypnotic memories where hypnotist held no educational degree, served apprenticeship abroad researching "faith healers," and spent time as a "stage hypnotist"); Haislip v. Roberts, 788 F.Supp. 482, 486 (D. Kan. 1992), *affd*, 992 F.2d 1085 (10th Cir. 1993) (hypnotically refreshed testimony is not per se inadmissible, as long as proper safeguards protect the reliability of the testimony; opponent of testimony must show hypnosis accounts for differences in witness's pre-and post-hypnotic statements); State v. Lopez, 887 P.2d 538, 540 (Ariz. 1994) (hypnotized police officers could not testify despite concurring pre-hypnosis reports where there were no records of safeguards used during hypnosis); State v. Hurd, 432 A.2d 86, 95–97 (N.J. 1981) (hypnotically refreshed testimony admissible only if certain safeguards followed); People v. Lozado, 620 N.Y.S.2d 32, 33 (N.Y. App. Div. 1994) (where eyewitness descriptions of perpetrator remained consistent before and after hypnosis and police could not have suggested defendant was perpetrator, state "established by clear and convincing evidence that the hypnosis had virtually no effect on the witnesses' pre-hypnotic recollection"); State v. Evans, 450 S.E.2d 47, 51 (S.C. 1994) (post-hypnotic testimony admissible if shown to be independent of the dangers associated with hypnosis, consistent with pre-hypnotic statements, and corroborated by circumstantial evidence; *See*

e.g., United States ex rel. Wilson v. Peters, 60 F.Supp.2d 777, 784 (N.D. Ill. 1999); ("The Seventh Circuit has declined to require adherence to any specific guidelines, but it has often suggested that adherence to the following standard practices during hypnosis be followed: 1) The session should be conducted by a licensed psychiatrist or psychologist trained in hypnosis, 2) the professional should be independent of either party, 3) any information given the hypnotist should be written down so that it can be examined later, 4) a pre-hypnotic recording should be made of what the subject recollects, 5) the session should be recorded, and 6) only the hypnotist should be present. These guidelines are similar to the safeguards used by the majority of courts to have considered this issue."); State v. Choinacki, 734 A.2d 324 (N.J.Super.1999)); State v. Medrano, 86 S.W.3d 369, 372 (Tex. App. 2002) (trial court should scrutinize "(1) the level of training in the clinical uses and forensic applications of hypnosis by the person performing the hypnosis; (2) the hypnotist's independence from law enforcement investigators, prosecution, and defense; (3) the existence of a record of any information given or known by the hypnotist concerning the case prior to the hypnosis session; (4) the existence of a written or recorded account of the facts as the hypnosis subject remembers them prior to undergoing hypnosis; (5) the creation of recordings of all contacts between the hypnotist and the subject; the presence of persons other than the hypnotist and the subject during any phase of the hypnosis session, as well as the location of the session; (6) the appropriateness of the induction and memory retrieval techniques used; the appropriateness of using hypnosis for the kind of memory loss involved; (7) the existence of any evidence to corroborate the hypnotically-enhanced testimony; (8) the presence or absence of overt or subtle cuing or suggestion of answers during the hypnotic session.").

54. *See, e.g., Sprynczynatyk*, 771 F.2d at 1123 n. 14; *Hurd*, 432 A.2d at 96–97.

55. Alabama advocates a case-by-case inquiry informed by a 403—like balancing test. *See* Martin v. State, 839 So.2d 665

gaining adherents in the federal circuits[56] even though there is no specific prohibition against hypnotically refreshed testimony in the Federal Rules of Evidence and prohibiting the testimony is arguably in conflict with the spirit of the notion in Rule 601 that "[e]very person is competent." In applying the "totality of the circumstances" test, the courts often balance the probative value and the prejudicial effect of hypnotic testimony.[57] The courts have bottomed their decisions on various theories including the defendant's fifth and sixth amendment rights of self-defense and confrontation,[58] witness competence following hypnosis,[59] and the scientific validity (or invalidity) of hypnosis under *Frye* or *Daubert*.[60]

In *Borawick v. Shay*, the Second Circuit considered "the circumstances under which an alleged victim of sexual abuse may testify as to memories of abuse following therapeutic hypnosis"[61] by reference to *Daubert*. Rejecting both *per se* admissibility and inadmissibility, it recommended that the trial court conduct a full pre-trial evidentiary hearing at which it could weigh all of "the factors in favor and against the reliability of the hypnosis procedure in the exercise of its discretion whether to admit the post-hypnotic testimony."[62] The burden of proof should be on the proponent of the refreshed testimony and among other things that the trial court might consider important, it should pay specific intention to: 1) "the purpose of the hypnosis" and even if the purpose was therapeutic, rather than investigative, to be wary of "the possibility that the subject may have received subtle suggestions from

---

(Ala. Ct. Crim. App. 2001) ("The fact that a witness has been hypnotized before testifying does not, per se, disqualify the witness. In considering hypnotically enhanced testimony, a court must conduct a balanced inquiry to determine if the testimony has a basis that is independent of the dangers associated with hypnosis. The inquiry should determine whether the witness's memory and ability to testify from it were distorted by an earlier hypnosis. The admissibility of such testimony is to be evaluated on a case-by-case basis, and the probative value of the testimony is to be weighed against its possible prejudicial effect."); Roark v. Commonwealth, 90 S.W.3d 24, 35 (Ky. 2002) (Uses a hybrid test including guidelines under which hypnosis must take place and balancing of probative value and prejudicial impact, with burden on proponent of testimony); Mersch v. City of Dallas, 207 F.3d 732, 735, 736 (5th Cir. 2000) (Courts are required to "evaluate such testimony on a case by case basis." But, still per se inadmissible where "a hypnotized subject identifies for the first time a person he has reason to believe is already under suspicion" regardless of the procedural safeguards employed in the hypnotic session.).

56. Mersch v. City of Dallas, 207 F.3d 732, 735, 736 (5th Cir. 2000); Borawick v. Shay 68 F.3d 597, 598 (2d Cir. 1995); Armstrong v. Young, 34 F.3d 421 (7th Cir. 1994); *See e.g.*, Roark v. Commonwealth, 90 S.W.3d 24, 35 (Ky. 2002); Lozado v. Superintendent, 2001 WL 1160592 (S.D.N.Y. 2001).

57. *See e.g.*, Martin v. State, 839 So.2d 665 (Ala. Ct. Crim. App. 2001).

58. See e.g., Rock v. Arkansas, 483 U.S. 44 (1987); Bundy v. Florida, 479 U.S. 894 (1986); Mancuso v. Olivarez, 292 F.3d 939 (9th Cir. 2002) (hypnotically refreshed testimony does not violate confrontation clause).

59. *See e.g.*, Franklin v. Stevenson, 987 P.2d 22 (Utah 1999).

60. People v. Zayas, 131 Ill.2d 284 (Ill. 1989) (Relying on *Frye*, the court held testimony related to post-hypnotic recall per se inadmissible and that proponent of testimony of a previously hypnotized witness bore the burden of proving that all testimony was related to matters recalled prior to hypnosis.).

61. 68 F.3d 597, 598 (2d Cir. 1995).

62. *Id.* at 608–609

the therapist that abuse or trauma could be at the root" of the condition; 2) whether the witness received suggestions from the therapist or others before or during hypnosis; 3) the "presence or absence of a permanent record", with an audio or videotaped session being preferred; 4) whether the hypnotist was qualified in psychology or psychiatry; 5) whether corroborating evidence of the hypnotically refreshed memories existed; 6) how suggestible is the subject to hypnotic suggestions; and 7) expert evidence as to the reliability of the specific hypnosis procedures used in the case.[63]

New Hampshire v. Hungerford,[64] is an example of a state court taking a *Daubert*-like approach. The New Hampshire Supreme Court concluded that recovered memory was not generally accepted by the psychological community, that it is a phenomenon unfamiliar to the average juror, and that to be admissible, the trial judge must be persuaded of its validity, partly as a matter of competence and partly as a matter of expert scientific evidence. The proponent of recovered memory in a sex crime case must show "a reasonable likelihood that the recovered memory is as accurate as ordinary human memory." The Court identified eight relevant factors for the trial judge to consider: 1) the level of peer review and publication on the phenomenon of recovered memory, 2) whether the phenomenon has been generally accepted in the psychological community, 3) whether it can be and has been empirically tested, 4) the potential or known rate of false recovered memories, 5) the age of the complainant at the time the memories were made, 6) the length of time between the event and the recovery of the memory, 7) the presence or absence of objective, verifiable corroboration of the event, and 8) the circumstances attending the witness' recovery of memory.[65]

Concern about the reliability of recovered memory has been sufficiently great so that the United States Supreme Court has suggested that even a criminal defendant's constitutional right to testify might not include testimony based upon irresponsible hypnotically refreshed testimony. In *Rock v. Arkansas,*[66] the accused in a murder case had undergone hypnosis to help remember the events on the night of the fatal shooting. The trial judge excluded the hypnotically refreshed testimony. In holding that the rigid Arkansas rule absolutely excluding such testimony violated the constitutional right to testify in one's own defense,[67] the Court left open the possibility that a more narrowly prescribed rule excluding hypnotically refreshed testimony taken without adequate precautions would be constitutional.[68]

63. *Id.*

64. 697 A.2d 916 (N.H.1997).

65. *Id.* at 925.

66. 483 U.S. 44 (1987).

67. *Id.* at 57–58.

68. *Id.* at 61.

Chapter 7

THE HEARSAY RULE AND ITS EXCEPTIONS

Table of Sections

THE DEFINITION OF HEARSAY [FRE 801]

EXCEPTIONS TO THE HEARSAY RULE

EXCEPTIONS THAT APPLY WHETHER OR NOT THE DECLARANT IS AVAILABLE [FRE 803]

EXCEPTIONS THAT APPLY ONLY IF THE DECLARANT IS UNAVAILABLE [FRE 804]

OTHER HEARSAY ISSUES

THE DEFINITION OF HEARSAY [FRE 801]

§ 7.01   Definition of Hearsay; Out-of-Court Statements That Are Not Hearsay

Why is hearsay excluded? There are many answers to that question, and this text is not the place to canvass them all.[1] One answer is sufficient for most purposes: hearsay is excluded because the out-of-court declarant has not been subjected to the test of cross-examination. The absence of cross-examination creates an unacceptable danger that the trier of fact will give too much value to the declarant's statement.

There is no need to cross-examine the out-of-court declarant when the trier of fact can use the declarant's out-of-court statement without relying on the declarant's credibility—that is, without relying on the sincerity, perception, memory, or narrative ability of the declarant. For example, when the out-of-court statement "Help me!" is offered solely for the purpose of showing that the declarant was alive at the time of making the statement, the trier is not being asked to rely upon the declarant's credibility. Nothing is lost by the fact that the out-of-court declarant was not subjected to cross-examination. What is important is that the statement was made, not the credibility of the person making it. Hence, the hearsay rule does not exclude the statement. In fact, the statement would not be considered hearsay at all. The same would be true even if the statement had been "I'm alive!" The relevance of the statement derives from its having been made, not by its contents.

---

1. For a critical examination of the standard explanation for excluding hearsay, and a suggestion that other reasons for excluding hearsay may also be important, see Roger C. Park, *A Subject Matter Approach to Hearsay Reform*, 86 Mich. L. Rev. 51 (1987). For other analyses of the basis and theory of the hearsay rule, see Craig R. Callen, *Hearsay and Informal Reasoning*, 47 Vand. L. Rev. 43 (1994); Richard D. Friedman, *Toward a Partial Economic, Game–Theoretic Analysis of Hearsay*, 76 Minn. L. Rev. 723 (1992); Eleanor Swift, *A Foundation Fact Approach to Hearsay*, 75 Cal. L. Rev. 1339 (1987); Glen Weissenberger, *Reconstructing the Definition of Hearsay*, 57 Ohio St. L.J. 1525 (1996).

Some jurisdictions follow a *declarant-oriented definition* of hearsay. Under this definition, an out-of-court statement is hearsay if its use by a trier of fact will require reliance upon the credibility of the declarant.[2] However, the Federal Rules of Evidence and most common law jurisdictions follow the more familiar *assertion-oriented definition*. Under this definition, a statement is not hearsay unless it is being offered to show the truth of the matter asserted in the statement.[3] Usually, when a statement is not offered to show the truth of an assertion contained within the statement, the trier is not being asked to rely upon the credibility of the declarant, and therefore there is no reason to treat the statement as hearsay.[4] This is not always the case,[5] but it is usually so, and perhaps the existence of the exceptional situations in which it is not so do not justify departing from this familiar definition.[6]

Utterances that are not hearsay under the assertion-oriented definition generally fall into one of the following three categories:

2. *See* Laurence H. Tribe, *Triangulating Hearsay*, 87 Harv. L. Rev. 957, 959 (1974). Tribe explains that four factors are usually identified as affecting the declarant's credibility: *perception* (the accuracy of the declarant's perception of the event); *memory* (the accuracy of the declarant's recollection of the event); *narration* or *ambiguity* (the comprehensibility of the declarant's statement about the event); and *sincerity* (the honesty of declarant in making the statement). A statement or conduct will be hearsay under a declarant-oriented definition of hearsay if its usefulness to the trier of fact is affected by any of these four factors as they relate to the declarant or actor. *See also* Paul Bergman, *Ambiguity: The Hidden Hearsay Danger Almost Nobody Talks About*, 75 Ky. L.J. 841 (1987). For an example of a declarant-centered definition in action, see Regina v. Kearley, [1992] 2 All E.R. 345 (HL (E)) (intercepted attempts to buy drugs not admissible against alleged drug dealer whose premises were raided by police).

3. Fed. R. Evid. 801 (c).

4. The sentence begins with "usually" because a few statements that are not offered to prove the truth of what they assert nevertheless involve a degree of reliance on credibility. This is true of statements offered as circumstantial evidence of the declarant's state of mind, such as those set forth later in this section. For an explanation, see Roger C. Park, *McCormick on Evidence and the Concept of Hearsay: A Critical Analysis Followed by Suggestions to Law Teachers*, 65 Minn. L. Rev. 423, 427–31 (1981).

5. For example, statements offered for their falsity are clearly not offered for the truth of the assertion, but they often rely on the credibility of the witness. Suppose that X is charged with robbery in Boston and X's wife tells police that on the date in question X was with her in Denver, even though her statement is demonstrably false. The prosecution offers the wife's statement against X for the inference that she lied because she knew X was guilty. Because the wife's statement is not offered for its truth, it is not hearsay; yet in order to accept the inference of X's guilt, the factfinder must rely on the wife's memory, perception, and narrative ability. *See also* Anderson v. United States, 417 U.S. 211, 219–20 (1974) (admitting testimony about false statements made by defendant's associate); Park, *McCormick on Evidence and the Concept of Hearsay, supra* note 4, at 424–41.

6. *See* Roger C. Park, *"I Didn't Tell Them Anything About You": Implied Assertions as Hearsay Under the Federal Rules of Evidence*, 74 Minn. L. Rev. 783 (1990). *See also* Gray v. Genlyte Group Inc., 289 F.3d 128 (1st Cir.2002) (Boudin, J.) (plaintiff, who alleged emotional damages as a result of sexual taunting by J.H., offered evidence that coworker had told her that J.H. had severely beaten coworker's wife, on theory that it explained severity of her own emotional reactions to harassment by J.H.; held, trial judge acted within discretion in ruling that plaintiff was limited to testifying that co-worker had made statement to her that made her more afraid of J.H.; trial judge entitled to decide that reference to physical injuries of co-worker's wife was too prejudicial).

Statements Offered to Show Their Effect on the Hearer or Reader

If a statement is not offered for the truth of what it asserts, but to show its effect upon the hearer or reader of the statement, then it is not hearsay.

Examples

The out-of-court statement, "Do it or I'll kill you," offered to show that the hearer acted under duress.[7]

"Please don't step in that ketchup," to show that the listener had been warned.[8]

"The sponge count came out wrong" to show that the surgeon, upon hearing this statement in the operating room, was negligent in not checking for a sponge in the patient's body.[9]

"Dr. Salinsky is incompetent," to show that a hospital was negligent in hiring Dr. Salinsky after being told of Dr. Salinsky's incompetence.[10]

"There's somebody poking around in your neighbor's garage," offered to explain the hearer's reason for checking out the garage of her absent neighbor.

Sometimes both the truth of the matter asserted and the effect on the hearer are relevant to issues in a lawsuit. When a statement has this

---

7. *See* United States v. Williams, 952 F.2d 1504 (6th Cir.1991) (declarants' statements to alleged victim suggesting adverse economic consequences to victim if victim did not cooperate not hearsay because offered to show effect on victim's state of mind, i.e., victim's fear and the reasonableness of that fear); Martinez v. McCaughtry, 951 F.2d 130 (7th Cir.1991) (threats and verbal abuse by defendant's brother toward third person admissible to show why defendant, who was present, shot third person); United States v. Herrera, 600 F.2d 502, 504 (5th Cir.1979); Subramaniam v. Public Prosecutor, 100 Solicitor's Journal 566 (Privy Council, Malaya, 1956) (threats to show duress).

8. *See* Safeway Stores, Inc. v. Combs, 273 F.2d 295, 296 (5th Cir.1960). *But cf.* United States v. Sallins, 993 F.2d 344, 346 (3d Cir.1993) (police radio dispatch call alerting officers to whereabouts of black male suspect wearing black clothes and carrying gun held inadmissible hearsay even when statement offered to explain officers' reasons for suspecting defendant and not for its truth; officers' conduct could be explained through other non-hearsay testimony; moreover, in closing arguments prosecutor used statement for its truth).

9. *See* Smedra v. Stanek, 187 F.2d 892, 894 (10th Cir.1951).

10. Johnson v. Misericordia Community Hosp., 294 N.W.2d 501, 515–16 (Wis.App. 1980). *See also* United States v. Calhoon, 97 F.3d 518, 533–34 (11th Cir.1996) (Schwarzer, J.) (held, corporate outside counsel's advice that defendant's method of collapsing advertising into single account was improper was admissible over hearsay objection because not offered to show truth, but merely to show that defendant was on notice that he had reason to question propriety of his action; evidence was relevant to question whether he had knowingly filed false Medicare claims); Matter of the Marriage of Fromdahl, 840 P.2d 683, 690 (Or. 1992) (held, in custody case where mother alleged to be insane, polygraph examiner's reports whose contents were known to the mother, saying father had sexually abused children admissible to show that mother's belief in father's abuse was not an insane delusion). *Compare* Rotolo v. Digital Equipment Corp., 150 F.3d 223, 225 (2d Cir.1998) (held, reversible error to admit videotape of experts discussing danger that keyboards could cause repetitive stress injury to be played at trial, in absence of evidence that defendant should have known about it).

sort of double relevancy, a limiting instruction should be given to the effect that the statement should not be used for its truth.[11] For example, suppose a mechanic tells a customer, "the brakes on your car are bad." This statement is not hearsay when offered to show that the customer had notice that the brakes were bad, but is hearsay when offered to show that the brakes were, in fact, bad. A limiting instruction should be given.

A limiting instruction is not always a sufficient protection when a statement has both a permissible nonhearsay use and a forbidden hearsay use. The trial judge must weigh the statement's probative value for its permitted use against the danger that the jury will use it for the forbidden purpose, and should consider redaction or exclusion if the danger of prejudice is unacceptably high. For example, consider the use of statements made to a police officer to explain the officer's subsequent conduct:

1. A houseguest at the mansion of a suspected murderer tells an investigating police officer that he heard thumps on the wall the night before. The investigator looks in the bushes near the wall and finds a bloody glove. The statement should be admitted to explain the officer's conduct, especially if the officer is accused of planting the bloody glove. The statement explains why the officer was searching in the bushes and the need for that explanation outweighs the danger that the jury will misuse the statement by accepting it for the truth of what it asserts.

2. A dispatcher's call tells the officer of a hit-and-run at Larkin and Turk and describes the suspect. The officer proceeds to Larkin and Turk and measures skidmarks. The description of the suspect should be excluded because it is not needed to explain the officer's conduct. The officer's conduct can be explained simply by allowing her to testify that she received a call from the dispatcher and, in response, went to Larkin and Turk. It is not necessary to quote the contents of the call.

3. The officer receives a call from the dispatcher, then proceeds to the scene to arrest a suspect who meets the description given in the call. Here a stronger case can be made that the contents should be described in order to explain the officer's conduct, but the better view is that the evidence should be excluded because of the danger of misuse.[12]

11. *See* Fed. R. Evid. 105. For a discussion of limiting instructions, see § **2.09.**

12. *See* United States v. Sallins, 993 F.2d 344, 346–47 (3d Cir.1993) (police radio dispatch call alerting officers to whereabouts of black male suspect wearing black clothes and carrying gun held inadmissible hearsay even when statement offered to explain officers' reasons for suspecting defendant and not for its truth; officers' conduct could be explained through "testimony that he acted 'upon information received' or words to that effect"; moreover, in closing arguments, prosecutor used statement for its truth). *Compare* Vincelette v. Metropolitan Life Ins. Co., 968 P.2d 275, 277 (Mt. 1998) (held, prejudicial error to admit testimony that officer had received word that plaintiff had fallen on carpet because she was drunk; statement about drunkenness not necessary for nonhearsay purpose of showing why engineer investigated fall); United States v. Mancillas, 580 F.2d 1301,

Legally Operative Language

Legally operative language is language that itself establishes a new legal relationship or that establishes a new legal relationship if uttered with a certain intent. It is considered not to be an assertion, and hence is not hearsay. It is not offered for what it says, but for what it does. In essence, the words uttered or written are not a statement about something, but are the thing itself. They create a legal right, duty, power, privilege, or other legal relationship. Legally operative language is often characterized as a "verbal act"[13] or a "verbal part of an act,"[14] though these terms have been avoided in this text because they are indeterminate and because they suggest that speech explaining or substituting for conduct is generally not hearsay.[15]

Examples

"Take this as a gift," to show a gift.[16]

"This is a loan," to show a loan.

"I offer you $3000 a carload for your widgets," to show a contract offer.[17]

"This is my property," to show adverse possession.[18]

"We guarantee the loan," to prove a guarantee.[19]

Legally operative language is not hearsay even if it sets forth the exact proposition to be proved. Thus, "I am making you an offer of $3000 a carload" is not hearsay when offered to show the making of an

---

1309–10 (7th Cir.1978) (excluding statement on grounds of prejudice).

Sometimes evidence that police disregarded statements by out-of-court declarants that incriminated persons other than the accused will be admissible to show the state of mind of the police in "rushing to judgment" and twisting evidence to favor the hypothesis that the defendant was guilty. But where the evidence has only a weak bearing on the state of mind of the investigating officer, and where the most likely use of it would be for the truth of the matter asserted, it may be excluded. See United States v. Sesay, 313 F.3d 591, 598–600 (D.C. Cir.2002) (Edwards, J.), a case in which the defendant wanted to put into evidence a police report that stated that witnesses had claimed someone else had been seen in possession of the gun in question at the time that defendant was later charged with possessing it. The government claimed it had checked with the witnesses and that the police report contained a mistaken rumor. The appellate court upheld the exclusion of the police report, saying that to use the report to support the defense contention that the police had "lied and manipulated the evidence in a manner designed to strengthen the case against [defendant]" would required that the jury rely upon the truth of the matter asserted in the report's double hearsay.

13. *See, e.g.*, 2 Michael H. Graham, Handbook of Federal Evidence § 801.5, at 208–14 (4th ed. 1996).

14. *See* 6 John H. Wigmore, Evidence in Trials at Common Law § 1772 (James H. Chadbourn rev. 1976).

15. *See* Park, *McCormick on Evidence and the Concept of Hearsay, supra* note 4, at 441–49.

16. *See* 6 Wigmore, *supra* note 14, § 1777.

17. *Cf.* California Trucking Assn. v. Brotherhood of Teamsters, 679 F.2d 1275, 1291–92 n. 20 (9th Cir.1981) (holding evidence of contract rejection admissible as nonhearsay).

18. *See* 6 Wigmore, *supra* note 14, § 1778.

19. *See* Ries Biologicals, Inc. v. Bank of Santa Fe, 780 F.2d 888, 890 (10th Cir. 1986); NLRB v. H. Koch & Sons, 578 F.2d 1287, 1290–91 (9th Cir.1978); see generally 2 McCormick on Evidence § 249 (4th ed. John W. Strong ed. 1992).

offer of $3000 a carload. Superficially, the utterance seems to be a statement "offered for the truth of the matter asserted" within the meaning of the assertion-oriented definition. Commentators have reconciled the result with the definition by saying that the statement is not an "assertion" or that it is not offered for its truth because it cannot be false.[20] Another way to view the problem is to recognize that if the courts were to exclude legally operative language as hearsay, they would render virtually impossible the proof of claims recognized by substantive law. Thus, if the court refuses to allow a party seeking to prove the existence of an oral contract to testify that she said "I am making you an offer of $3000 a carload," the only way to prove the contract would be by circumstantial evidence of the behavior of the parties, something that would be virtually impossible, given that the action itself probably arose because at least one of the parties acted as though there was no contract.[21] One commentator has argued that "words need not be hearsay when they have important performative aspects and are offered to prove other acts, events, or conditions in the world."[22] Whatever the explanation, the nonhearsay status of legally operative language is established beyond dispute.[23]

Legally operative language is nonhearsay only when it is offered to show the legal relationship that it creates. If it is offered to show something else, then it might be hearsay. For example, language in a pleading (a complaint or answer in a civil case) is not hearsay if it is offered only to show what the issues are in a lawsuit. When used for purposes of defining issues and limiting proof, the language in pleadings is legally operative. Thus, an allegation of negligence in a complaint would not be hearsay when offered to show that the issue of negligence had been raised, but it would be hearsay when offered to show that the defendant was in fact negligent.

Circumstantial (Indirect) Evidence of Declarant's State of Mind

Within this category are utterances that are considered not to be hearsay because they can be used to show the declarant's own state of mind without accepting the truth of what is asserted in the utterance.[24]

---

20. *See* Jack H. Friedenthal & Michael Singer, The Law of Evidence 83–84 (1985); E. Kimball, Programmed Material on Problems in Evidence 273 (1978); Creaghe v. Iowa Home Mut. Cas. Co., 323 F.2d 981 (10th Cir.1963).

21. *See* David P. Leonard, *Rules of Evidence and Substantive Policy*, 25 Loy. L.A. L. Rev. 797, 804–07 (1992).

22. Christopher B. Mueller, *Incoming Drug Calls and Performative Words: They's Not Just Talking About It, Baron Parke!*, 16 Miss. C.L. Rev. 117, 117 (1995).

23. *See, e.g.*, United States v. DiMaria, 727 F.2d 265, 270 n. 4 (2d Cir.1984).

24. *See, e.g.*, Fun–Damental Too, Ltd. v. Gemmy Industries Corp., 111 F.3d 993, 1003–1004 (2d Cir.1997) (held, complaints by customers who erroneously thought "currency cans" were the same product as "toilet banks" not hearsay when offered as evidence that defendant's packaging caused declarants to confuse its product with plaintiff's product). *See also* United States v. Newell, 315 F.3d 510, 523 (5th Cir.2002) (accountant's notes concerning rumors of fake expenses was admissible to show reason why accountant confronted defendant).

These statements would technically be hearsay under a strict application of the declarant-oriented definition, but they are not hearsay under the assertion-oriented definition.[25]

Examples

"My husband beats me," offered to show that the declarant hated her husband. One can believe that declarant hated the husband without believing the truth of the matter asserted, that is, without believing that the husband actually beat the declarant. In fact, a false accusation might be more persuasive evidence of the declarant's hatred than a true one would be.[26]

"Daddy tried to kill me," to show the declarant's fear of her father, as evidence in a custody dispute that being with the father was not in the best interest of the child.[27]

A false alibi, offered to show that the person providing the alibi was trying to cover up for the beneficiary of the alibi, and hence that the beneficiary was guilty of a crime. E.g., the defendant's wife tells police that her husband was with her on the day of the crime, and the prosecution offers her statement in evidence, knowing that it can prove that it is a fabrication. Her statement is not offered to show its truth; indeed, the prosecution's whole theory is based upon the supposition that it is false.[28]

In an apparent application of the principle that circumstantial evidence of declarant's state of mind is not hearsay under the assertion-centered definition of the Federal Rules of Evidence, a number of cases have admitted drug ledgers into evidence on the theory that they were not being offered for the truth of anything asserted in the ledger, but merely to show that drug activity was taking place on the premises.[29] The theory under which this evidence is received is arguably wrong, since the ledgers could be viewed as assertions that quantities of drugs or money changed hands. If the ledgers make that general assertion, then they are being offered for the truth of that assertion when used to show drug activity.

---

25. For discussion of the distinction between the declarant-oriented and assertion-oriented definitions of hearsay, see discussion earlier in this section.

26. *Cf.* Loetsch v. New York City Omnibus Corp., 291 N.Y. 308, 311, 52 N.E.2d 448, 449 (1943) (holding admissible, in husband's wrongful death action against streetcar company, wife's testamentary statement accusing husband of cruelty to show that wife would not have given husband full comfort and support had she survived).

27. *See* Betts v. Betts, 473 P.2d 403, 407–09 (Wash.App.1970).

28. *Cf.* Anderson v. United States, 417 U.S. 211, 219–20 (1974). Statements of this nature do involve some reliance upon the credibility of the declarant, see Park, *McCormick on Evidence and the Concept of Hearsay*, *supra* note 4, at 426, but this reliance has generally been ignored.

29. *See, e.g.*, United States v. Huguez–Ibarra, 954 F.2d 546, 552–53 (9th Cir.1992) (no need for government to lay a foundation for admission of drug ledgers as co-conspirator statements because ledgers were only being admitted to show that the type of activities charged in the indictment were being carried out in the residence); United States v. Alvarez, 960 F.2d 830 (9th Cir. 1992) (pay/owe sheet not hearsay when used to show that drug deals had occurred in apartment). See also cases cited in Park, *Implied Assertions*, *supra* note 6, at 817 n.220.

Another example of cases offered as circumstantial evidence of the declarant's state of mind are cases in which evidence of intercepted telephone calls is used to show that the premises were being used for an illegal purpose. One example of this type of case arises when the police raid a suspected bookmaker and receive calls asking to place bets, or raid a suspected drug dealer and receive calls from persons who want to buy drugs. Most courts have treated these calls as admissible on ground that they are not hearsay, despite the existence of some conceivable hearsay dangers.[30] Under the assertion definition of hearsay, it can be argued that a call asking to place a bet is not an "assertion," but a question or command.[31]

In another class of cases, verbal utterances have been received solely as circumstantial evidence of contact or association between two people, or between a person and a thing. The typical example is the instance in which, while searching a person who is in custody, the police find the name and telephone number of another person. The evidence is offered to show that the two are acquainted. Applying the assertion definition, the court is likely to say either that the name and number were not offered to prove what they were asserting (that a certain person had a certain number) or that they were not offered assertively at all, but rather as circumstantial evidence of association.[32] Thus, the following utterances have been deemed not to be hearsay under the assertion definition: (1) an address book, when used to show that the holder knew the people listed therein; (2) a receipt for rent or goods, to show linkage between a person named in the receipt and the premises or goods; (3) a letter addressed to the defendant at a certain street address, to link the defendant with the house at that address; (4) a name mentioned in conversation, when used to show that the defendant knew the person named; (5) car papers, when used to show a link between the car and

---

30. *See id.* (collecting cases).

31. One area of controversy concerns whether a statement should be classified as hearsay if offered for an unintended implication of the statement. For an analysis of this issue, see Paul R. Rice, *Should Unintended Implications of Speech Be Considered Nonhearsay? The Assertive/Nonassertive Distinction Under Rule 801(a) of the Federal Rules of Evidence*, 65 Temp. L. Rev. 529 (1992).

32. An interesting example of this type of case is United States v. Arteaga, 117 F.3d 388 (9th Cir.1997). Defendants were charged with involvement in a scheme of drug money laundering. One defendant (Arteaga) allegedly used Western Union to wire drug money from Alaska to another defendant (Arrango–Laverde), who was in California. The prosecution offered evidence of Western Union "to-send-money" forms, used by Western Union on the sending end, and "to-receive-money" forms, issued on the receiving end. Copies of two "to-send-money" forms were found in defendant's apartment. They listed the recipient as "Linda Arce," allegedly an alias of Arrango–Laverde. The trial court instructed the jury that it was not permitted to consider the forms to prove the truth of the matters asserted. On appeal, the court explained the nonhearsay use of the evidence, stating that the piece of paper found in Arteaga's possession is evidence that he had knowledge necessary to commit the criminal acts. Since the name Linda Arce was an alias, proven by independent evidence to have been used by Laverde in a drug conspiracy, it is unlikely that anyone not involved in that conspiracy would have had knowledge of, or reason to use, that name. In other words, ... the pieces of paper provided strong circumstantial evidence that the defendant had the knowledge necessary to commit the act, and, therefore, that he likely did commit the act. *Id.* at 398.

those named in the papers. These utterances are not offered for the truth of anything they assert, but to show something else.[33]

Pre-death statements by a person who later became a homicide victim, describing threats or abuse by the person later accused of the homicide, may also be offered as circumstantial evidence of the declarant's state of mind. The issue often boils down to whether the victim's state of mind is relevant and, if so, whether the relevance of the evidence for the permitted purpose of showing state of mind outweighs any prejudice that may result from use of the statement to show the truth of the matter asserted. The statements are often admitted where:

(1) they are needed to show hostility between the victim and the accused,

(2) the accused advances a defense of self-defense and the victim's fear is used to show that the victim was unlikely to be the first attacker, or

(3) the defense is suicide and the statement shows a will to live.[34]

33. *See* Park, *Implied Assertions supra* note 6, at 817–23 (collecting cases). For cases taking the concept to its limit, *see* United States v. Alvarez, 960 F.2d 830 (9th Cir.1992) (inscription "Garnika, Spain" on pistol not hearsay when offered to prove that pistol came from Spain); United States v. Snow, 517 F.2d 441 (9th Cir.1975) (red tape on briefcase bearing defendant's name is not hearsay because it is a "mechanical trace" and thus a type of circumstantial evidence designed to show the occurrence or non-occurrence of a certain act in the past; query applicability of circumstantial evidence concept here, where a label placed with intent to say, "this is Snow's briefcase" was offered to show that in fact it was Snow's briefcase); People v. Cox, 135 Cal. Rptr.2d 272, 304–306 (2003) (in murder trial, evidence that another person gave police accurate directions to an area where murder victim's body was found was admissible as nonhearsay circumstantial evidence of the declarant's knowledge of the murder). *But see* Payne v. Janasz, 711 F.2d 1305, 1313–14 (6th Cir.1983) (habeas corpus proceeding; deputy's testimony that on the day after the police raid, he saw two pearl-handled pistols in an evidence bag marked with an evidence tag stating "10001 Cedar Avenue" constituted hearsay because it was offered to show sheriff's possession of the pistols and the Sheriff's office's method of handling guns; admission did not violate defendant's confrontation rights, however); United States v. Vigneau, 187 F.3d 70, 74–75 (1st Cir.1999) (held, Western Union sender forms listing defendant as sender of money orders inadmissible hearsay when offered to show that defendant was in fact sender; court indicates result would have been different had Western Union required identification from senders, because then there would have been adequate foundation for admitting the sender form as the admission of a party-opponent).

34. For a full discussion that is still relevant under the Federal Rules of Evidence, *see* United States v. Brown, 490 F.2d 758, 763–64 (D.C. Cir.1973). *Compare* United States v. Day, 591 F.2d 861 (D.C. Cir. 1978) (statement that defendant was out to get declarant not admissible, but declarant's slip of paper containing defendant's phone number admissible as circumstantial evidence of association). For a case using the hostility theory, see Rufo v. Simpson, 103 Cal.Rptr.2d 492 (Cal.App.2001) (in civil wrongful death action against O.J. Simpson for damages caused by double murder, appellate court affirms trial court decision admitting statements by victim Nicole Brown Simpson saying that defendant had abused her, stalked her, and threatened to kill her; held, statements were admissible to show her state of mind of fear and hostility toward Simpson; evidence of Nicole Brown Simpson's state of mind valuable because it helped resolve disputed issues about the pre-murder interaction between the victim and the defendant; plaintiffs claimed that defendant was motivated to commit murder because he had been rejected by Nicole Brown Simpson and because she had slighted him at their daughter's dance recital on the night of the murder; defendant denied being rejected or slighted).

§ 7.02 Nonverbal Conduct as Hearsay

Nonverbal conduct can sometimes amount to a statement offered for the truth of what it asserts. For example, when a person points at another in response to the question "who did it?," the pointing amounts to an assertion that the person pointed at was the perpetrator. If done out of court, and offered into evidence to show who did do the act, the pointing would be hearsay.

Under the Federal Rules of Evidence,[35] whether nonverbal conduct is hearsay depends upon whether it was intended as an assertion, and if so, whether it is being offered to prove the truth of the matter asserted. If nonverbal conduct was not intended as an assertion, then it is not hearsay, even if its use in evidence requires the trier of fact to rely upon the credibility of the declarant.

Examples

In response to a question about who saw the accident, declarant raises his or her hand. The hand-raising gesture is assertive, and if offered to show that declarant saw the accident, would be hearsay.

To prove that it was raining, the proponent offers into evidence the fact that the witness saw pedestrians walking about with open umbrellas. Because the pedestrians did not intend to make a statement by opening the umbrellas, the evidence is not hearsay, even though its value depends upon the assumption that the pedestrians believed it was raining and were correct in that belief.

As evidence of innocence, defendant offers testimony that after the crime a third person fled the jurisdiction. The purpose of the offer is to show that the third person committed the crime. The testimony is not hearsay, because the third person's act of fleeing was not intended as an assertion; the person was merely trying to escape, not to assert guilt. Note that the evidence is categorized as nonhearsay despite the fact that its value depends upon inferences about the state of mind of the third person (that the fleeing was based upon belief in self-guilt, and that the belief was accurate). The fact that it would be helpful to put the third person on the stand to explore the reasons for the conduct was not considered by the rule makers to be a sufficient reason to classify the conduct as hearsay.[36]

The rule makers thought that because the trier does not rely upon the sincerity of the declarant when drawing inferences from nonassertive conduct, the conduct should be treated as nonhearsay. The existence of other dangers, they felt, should affect the weight accorded to the evidence, not its admissibility.[37]

---

35. *See* Fed. R. Evid. 801(a).

36. *See* John M. Maguire, *The Hearsay System, Around and Through the Thicket*, 14 Vand. L. Rev. 741, 766 (1961). For an argument that such statements should be considered hearsay, see Ted Finman, *Implied Assertions as Hearsay: Some Criticisms Of the Uniform Rules of Evidence*, 14 Stan. L. Rev. 682, 687–88 (1962).

37. *See* Fed. R. Evid. 801(a) advisory committee's note (citing Judson F. Falknor, *The "Hear–Say" Rule as a "See–Do" Rule*,

In the example just given, it is conceivable, though unlikely, that the third person's reason for fleeing was actually to draw suspicion away from someone else. Where there is a dispute about whether conduct was intended as an assertion, the trial judge decides the question of intent as a preliminary question of fact under Rule 104(a). The opponent of the evidence has the burden of proving that the conduct was intended as an assertion.[38]

§ 7.03 Prior Statements of Witnesses

The mere fact that a person is on the witness stand does not automatically mean that that person's out-of-court statements become admissible. To put it another way, the hearsay rule sometimes operates to exclude statements made out of court even when the declarant has testified under cross-examination in the very action in which the out-of-court statements were offered. The hearsay rule, in other words, applies even when the witness and the declarant are the same person. Yet there are many ways in which the witness/declarant's statement may become admissible. First, of course, it may fall under one of the traditional hearsay exceptions. Second, it may be admissible on the theory that it is not offered to prove the truth of the matter asserted, but to accredit or discredit the witness. Third, it may fall under one of the special categories of nonhearsay created by the Federal Rules of Evidence—categories applicable to prior inconsistent statements, prior consistent statements, and prior statements of identification.[39]

§ 7.04 Prior Statements of Witnesses—Prior Inconsistent Statements [FRE 801(d)(1)(A)]

Under the Federal Rules of Evidence, there are two separate bases for receiving the prior inconsistent statement of a witness despite a hearsay objection.[40] The first is Rule 801(d)(1)(A), which provides:

> A statement is not hearsay if. . . . [t]he declarant testifies at the trial or hearing and is subject to cross-examination concerning the statement, and the statement is. . . . inconsistent with the declarant's testimony, and was given under oath subject to the penalty of perjury at a trial, hearing, or other proceeding, or in a deposition.[41]

33 Rocky Mt. L. Rev. 133 (1960); *see also* Finman, *supra* note 36, at 691–93 (discussing reliance as a substitute for cross-examination). For criticism of the advisory committee's view, see 2 Michael H. Graham, Handbook of Federal Evidence § 801.3 (4th ed. 1996).

38. *See* Fed. R. Evid. 801 (a) advisory committee's note.

39. *See* Fed. R. Evid. 801(d)(1).

40. Of course, the statement can also be received if it falls under an exception to the hearsay rule. The statement in text applies to prior inconsistent statements that do not fall under any of the enumerated exceptions.

41. Fed. R. Evid. 801(d)(1)(A). Not all "proceedings" qualify under this rule. For example, an affidavit taken under oath administered by an IRS special agent in an investigative interview is not a statement made in a "proceeding" within the meaning of this rule. United States v. Williams, 272 F.3d 845 (7th Cir. 2001), as amended on clarification (Feb. 11, 2002).

If the prior inconsistent statement falls under Rule 801(d)(1)(A), then it is admissible as substantive evidence (to prove the truth of the matter asserted).

Rule 801(d)(1)(A) is not the only route of admissibility, however. Many inconsistent statements are routinely admitted even though they do not meet the requirements of Rule 801(d)(1)(A). For example, witness statements taken by police officers or insurance investigators are not made under oath or at a "proceeding," but nonetheless are routinely admitted. They are received under the second theory of admission, a traditional theory that was available at common law long before the advent of the Federal Rules. The theory is that prior inconsistent statements offered *solely to impeach* are not offered to prove the truth of the matter asserted, and hence are not hearsay within the traditional definition stated in Rule 801(c). For example, suppose that the prior statement, "The light was red," is offered to impeach a witness who has testified at trial that the light was green. The statement is considered not to be hearsay because it is offered to impeach credibility. The fact that the declarant said different things at different times reflects poorly on the declarant's credibility, whether the original statement was true or not.

One consequence of receiving the prior inconsistent statement under the common law theory, rather than under Rule 801(d)(1)(A), is that the opponent is entitled to a limiting instruction. The limiting instruction informs the jury that it may use the statement for its bearing on the credibility of the witness, but not as evidence of the truth of the matter asserted. Another consequence, perhaps one with more impact than the limiting instruction, flows from the concept that the evidence may not be used to prove its truth. Thus the prior statement, because it is not substantive evidence, may not be used to overcome a motion for a directed verdict. If elements A, B, and C are essential elements of the plaintiff's case, and the only evidence that plaintiff has on element C is the prior inconsistent statement of a witness who now testifies to Not–C, then the defendant is entitled to a directed verdict. The only admissible evidence on the point is the witness's courtroom testimony affirming Not–C; the only purpose for which the prior statement may be used is to impeach the testimony; even if the impeachment is complete, there is still no evidence affirming C. In this manifestation, the rule has an impact even in nonjury trials.[42] If the only evidence to support the verdict in a nonjury trial is evidence of a prior inconsistent statement that can be used only to impeach, then there is no admissible evidence to support the verdict and the trial judge's verdict in favor of the plaintiff must be overturned.

A final consequence of the need to rely upon the common law theory in cases in which 801(d)(1)(A) does not apply is that evidence should

---

42. Normally, the impact of the hearsay rule is minimal in nonjury trials, because of the rule that even when the trial judge errs in admitting hearsay, the trial judge's verdict will stand if there is enough admissible evidence to support the verdict. *See* 1 McCormick on Evidence § 60, at 238 (4th ed. John W. Strong ed. 1992).

sometimes be excluded on grounds that the limiting instruction would be ineffective. If the theory that the evidence is not received to prove its truth is taken seriously, then the evidence should be excluded under Rule 403 when the danger that it will be used for the truth outweighs its probative value for impeachment. The proponent should not be able to put on a witness known to be worthless merely to get in a prior inconsistent statement, in hopes that the jury will ignore the limiting instruction and accept the prior statement as true. For example, when a prosecutor knows that the witness will deny any knowledge of a criminal transaction, the prosecutor should not be able to call the witness and put in a prior statement incriminating the defendant, because the statement cannot possibly help the prosecution if used properly (if the jury believes that the witness is not credible, what does the witness contribute?), and can only be helpful if the jury ignores the limiting instruction and puts the statement to a forbidden use, that is, only if the jury accepts the statement as true, as substantive evidence of guilt.[43]

§ 7.05   Prior Statements of Witnesses—Prior Consistent Statements [FRE 801(d)(1)(B)]

Suppose a witness testifies that the light was red, and the proponent of the witness wishes to put into evidence the witness's prior out-of-court statement that the light was red. The Federal Rules of Evidence do not require that the prior statement have been made under oath or at a proceeding in order for it to qualify as substantive evidence, but Rule 801(d)(1)(B) does require that the prior consistent statement be "offered to rebut an express or implied charge against the declarant of recent fabrication or improper influence or motive"[44] in order to be admissible under that provision. If it qualifies, the statement is admissible as non-hearsay to prove the truth of the matter asserted.

The statement in Rule 801(d)(1)(B) concerning admissibility of prior consistent statements offered to rebut a charge of fabrication or impropriety sometimes leads to the assumption that unless the prior consistent statement is offered to rebut a charge of fabrication or impropriety, it is not admissible. That is not the case. Just as in the case of the prior

---

43. *See* United States v. Hogan, 763 F.2d 697 (5th Cir.), *modified* 771 F.2d 82 (5th Cir.1985) (government called witness it knew would testify favorably toward defendants, then offered prior inconsistent statements of witness and called several other witnesses to contradict him; because none of this impeaching matter was substantively admissible, and because government's primary purpose in calling witness was to place impeaching matter before the jury, court should not have permitted government to call witness) (modification did not affect issue under consideration here). *See also* Michael H. Graham, *Employing Inconsistent Statements for Impeachment and as Substantive Evidence: A Critical Review*

and Proposed Amendments of Federal Rules of Evidence 801(d)(1)(A), 613, and 607, 75 Mich. L. Rev. 1565, 1613–15 (1977).

44. Fed. R. Evid. 801(d)(1)(B). *See also* Gaines v. Walker, 986 F.2d 1438, 1444 (D.C.Cir.1993) (held, in civil rights action, plaintiff's cross-examination of defendant police officer regarding supposed omission in latter's police report is implied claim of fabrication; district court abused discretion in preventing defendant from rebutting fabrication claim by introducing actual police report as evidence of prior consistent statement). *See also* § **9.12** for a discussion of rehabilitation of witnesses through the introduction of prior consistent statements.

inconsistent statement, a common law theory of admissibility is available, as long as the statement is relevant to the declarant's credibility.[45] One instance in which a prior consistent statement is relevant to the declarant's credibility (even in the absence of a charge of fabrication or impropriety) is the instance in which the declarant made a "prompt complaint" of a crime such as rape. Were the jury not informed that the declarant made a complaint near the time of the occurrence, it might draw inferences against the declarant's credibility even without attack by opposing counsel. Thus the evidence can be received as not offered for the truth of the matter asserted, but only for its bearing on the declarant's credibility.[46] This limitation on its use has relatively trivial consequences. It can lead to a truly unintelligible limiting instruction, telling the jury not to use the prior statement that the light was red as evidence of the truth of the matter asserted (that the light was red), but only for its bearing on the witness's credibility (in testifying that the light was red). The only effect of treating a prior consistent statement as substantive evidence under Rule 801(d)(1)(B), instead of as evidence not offered for its truth under the common law theory, is to eliminate the need for the limiting instruction.[47]

A prior statement is not useful to rebut a claim of fabrication, undue influence or improper motive if the statement was made at a time when the witness was affected by the same motive or influence that now is alleged to bias the trial testimony. For example, when a witness is attacked at trial on grounds that the witness is bending his or her testimony in return for leniency from the prosecution, a prior statement made after the witness had acquired the hopes for leniency has no real probative weight and should be excluded by the trial judge. (The same result could be obtained without the hearsay rule, on grounds that the

---

45. The Minnesota rule explicitly allows for admission of prior consistent statements that are "helpful to the trier of fact in evaluation the declarant's credibility as a witness." Minn. R. Evid. 801(d)(1)(B).

46. *See* Roger C. Park, *McCormick on Evidence and the Concept of Hearsay: A Critical Analysis Followed by Suggestions to Law Teachers*, 65 Minn. L. Rev. 441 (1981). The prompt complaint rule (also referred to as the "fresh complaint" rule) is explored in the following cases: Nitz v. State, 720 P.2d 55, 62–63 (Alaska App.1986); People v. Bailey, 532 N.E.2d 587, 590 (Ill.App.1988); State v. Hesse, 281 N.W.2d 491, 492 (Minn. 1979); State v. Campbell, 705 P.2d 694, 702 (Or.1985); Commonwealth v. Stohr, 522 A.2d 589, 592–93 (Pa.Super.1987); State v. Murray, 375 S.E.2d 405, 410 (W.Va.1988); State v. Golden, 336 S.E.2d 198, 203 (W.Va. 1985). The prompt complaint rule is distinct from Fed. R. Evid. 801(d)(1)(C) under which prior identification of the assailant is admissible as nonhearsay. *See* § 7.06. For commentary on the prompt complaint rule see Michael H. Graham, *The Cry of Rape: The Prompt Complaint Doctrine and the Federal Rules of Evidence*, 19 Willamette L. Rev. 489 (1983).

47. In contrast to the prior inconsistent statement, the fact that a prior consistent statement is not substantively admissible under Rule 801(d)(1)(B) (but is instead admitted under the common law theory that it is not offered to prove its truth) cannot lead to a directed verdict or the overturning of a judgment on appeal. The witness has testified in court to the existence of the element that was the subject of the out-of-court statement. The in-court testimony provides the basis for overcoming the directed verdict motion or for supporting the nonjury trier's verdict on appeal. The prior statement merely bolsters credibility for the trier.

prior statement is cumulative and a waste of time, and hence subject to exclusion under Rules 403 and 611.[48])

The Supreme Court addressed the issue of the admissibility of prior consistent statements in its 1995 decision in *Tome v. United States*.[49] In *Tome*, the defendant was charged with sexual abuse of his four-year-old daughter. He and the child's mother were divorced and had joint custody. The child made out-of-court statements indicating that she had been abused by her father. The defense argued that the statements were concocted to prevent the father from sharing custody.

The child, who was six and a half at the time of trial, testified and was cross-examined. For the most part, her direct testimony consisted of one-and two-word answers to a series of leading questions. On cross-examination, the child was reluctant to answer questions, seemed to lose concentration, and sometimes took as long as forty-five seconds to answer a question.[50]

After the child testified, the government put on six witnesses who testified to prior statements by the child describing sexual assaults by her father. A babysitter testified that the child told her she didn't want to return to her father because he "gets drunk and thinks I'm his wife." The mother testified to details she overheard the child describe. A social worker and three pediatricians also testified about details that the child had told them.[51] The statements were offered by the government as prior consistent statements under Rule 801(d)(1)(B). The trial court admitted the statements and the Tenth Circuit affirmed, accepting the theory that the statements were all admissible under the rule.

The Supreme Court reversed, holding that the prior consistent statements are only admissible under Rule 801(d)(1)(B) if they were made before the charged recent fabrication or improper influence or motive. These conditions are not established here.[52] Aside from precedent, the court offered a policy justification for its holding—that "if the rules were to permit the introduction of prior statements as substantive evidence to rebut every implicit charge that a witness's in-court testimony results from recent fabrication or improper influence or motive, the whole emphasis of the trial would shift to the out-of-court statements, not the in-court ones." The Court suggested that the case before it was an example, because the government was permitted to present a "parade of sympathetic and credible witnesses" who repeated the child's out-of-court statements.

---

48. *Cf.* Mills v. Scully, 826 F.2d 1192, 1196 (2d Cir.1987) (noting that prior statements may be excluded as cumulative).

49. 513 U.S. 150 (1995).

50. *Id.* at 153.

51. *Id.*

52. *Id. Cf.* United States v. Prieto, 232 F.3d 816 (11th Cir.2000) (government sought to enhance credibility of accomplice who was cooperating with government by introducing consistent statements made to police between time accomplice was arrested and a month later, when accomplice signed cooperation agreement; court holds that whether statements were made before motive to fabricate arose was question of fact for district court and that appellate court must defer to district court, which decided to admit the evidence; query whether it is realistic to suppose that accomplice was free of motive to help self when making statements to police after arrest, in absence of specific showing otherwise, which was absent here).

For the federal courts, *Tome* settled the question of whether, when a statement is offered under Rule 801(d)(1)(B), the trial judge has discretion to admit pre-motive statements to bolster the witness. The majority endorsed a *per se* rule that the statements must be excluded unless they were made before the motive to fabricate or improper influence arose. Note, however, that *Tome* involved statements offered under Rule 801(d)(1)(B), which allows prior consistent statements to be offered not only to bolster credibility, but as substantive evidence to show the truth of the matter asserted. The Court did not directly address the question whether prior consistent statements might sometimes be admissible on the theory that they fall outside the hearsay ban because they are offered to show something other than the truth of the matter asserted. For example, suppose an elderly witness testifies about the details of a transaction, and is impeached by cross-examination that touches on problems of forgetting as well as on the witness's motive to help the proponent. The elderly witness's prior statements made soon after the transaction would arguably be admissible to show that the witness's memory was accurate. Just as a prior inconsistent statement might be admitted for a purpose other than showing its truth, so might a prior consistent statement. If so, then the *Tome* pre-motive requirement might not apply to those consistent statements. *Tome* expressly states that its "holding is confined to the requirements for admissibility under Rule 801(d)(1)(B),"[53] so one might infer that the ruling does not cover the use of prior consistent statements to rehabilitate the witness when the proponent does not rely on that rule but instead offers the statement on the theory that it is not being offered to prove the truth. However, there is language elsewhere in *Tome* that suggests that the Court might have believed that Rule 801(d)(1)(B) was the only route through which prior consistent statements could be received to combat impeachment. For example, the Court states that "Prior consistent statements may not be admitted to counter all forms of impeachment or to bolster the witness merely because she has been discredited."[54]

§ 7.06 Prior Statements of Witnesses—Prior Identification Statements [FRE 801(d)(1)(C)]

Under the Federal Rules of Evidence, a witness's prior statement of identification is not hearsay and is admissible under Rule 801(d)(1)(C).[55] Prior identification is often more reliable than identification made at trial, because at trial "suggestions of others and the circumstances of the trial may have intervened to create a fancied recognition in the witness's

---

53. *Id.* at 167.

54. *Id.* at 157. For a full analysis, see Norman M. Garland & Romy Schneider, *Prior Consistent Statements As Evidence in the United States and Canada*, 2 S.W. U.J.L. & Trade Am. 451 (1995). *See also* United States v. Gluzman, 154 F.3d 49, 51 (2d Cir.1998) (prior consistent statements may be admissible for rehabilitation with-

out making use of Rule 801(d)(1)(B) and without making *Tome* showing that statement was made prior to motive to fabricate).

55. Fed. R. Evid. 801(d)(1)(C). *See* People v. Johnson, 701 P.2d 620, 622 (Colo. App.1985).

mind."[56] The prior identification does not have to have been made close to the time of the occurrence; an identification from a photo display or a line-up made several days or weeks after the crime is just as admissible as a victim's identification at the scene of the crime.[57]

As with other prior witness statements governed by Rule 801(d)(1), prior identification statements are admissible only if the witness testifies in court and is subject to cross-examination on the statement.[58] A witness's identification can be admitted at trial either through that witness or through the testimony of another witness who observed the out-of-court identification.[59] For instance, a witness who identified the defendant from a photo display can testify to that fact, and the testimony can be corroborated by the police officer who observed the identification.[60] In addition, testimony about the prior identification will be admissible even though the witness is not able to make an identification in court.[61] Furthermore, under the Federal Rules of Evidence, if the witness cannot remember, or perhaps even denies, having made the out-of-court identification, another witness can testify to the prior identification.[62]

Admission of an out-of-court identification is independent of the restrictions of 801(d)(1)(A) and 801(d)(1)(B).[63] Thus, even if the out-of-court identification is inconsistent with the in-court identification, the former will be admitted and no allegation of fabrication is required for its admission. The out-of-court identification statement, thus, may be admitted before the in-court identification takes place.

The hearsay rule is not the only basis for objecting to identification evidence. When the police have used a suggestive identification procedure, defense counsel can challenge the admissibility of the identification on due process grounds. Identifications can also be challenged on grounds that the sixth amendment right to counsel was violated because of absence of counsel at a line-up or show-up.

56. Gilbert v. California, 388 U.S. 263, 272 n. 3 (1967) (quoting People v. Gould, 354 P.2d 865, 867, 7 Cal.Rptr. 273, 275 (Cal.1960) (overruled on other grounds by People v. Cuevas, 48 Cal.Rptr.2d 135, 906 P.2d 1290 (1995)); *see also* United States v. Barbati, 284 F.Supp. 409, 413 (E.D.N.Y. 1968) (noting that in-court identifications are generally "an almost worthless formality"); *see generally* Annotation, *Admissibility of Evidence as to Extra–Judicial or Pretrial Identification of Accused*, 71 A.L.R.2d 449 (1960 & Later Case Service).

57. *See* 5 Weinstein's Federal Evidence § 801.13[3], at 801–35 (2d ed. Joseph M. McLaughlin ed. 1997).

58. Fed. R. Evid. 801(d)(1); *see* United States v. Owens, 484 U.S. 554, 561–64 (1988).

59. *See* Thomas A. Mauet, *Prior Identification in Criminal Cases: Hearsay and Confrontation Issues*, 24 Ariz. L. Rev. 29, 43–49 (1982).

60. *See* United States v. Elemy, 656 F.2d 507, 508 (9th Cir.1981); United States v. Miller, 381 F.2d 529, 538 (2d Cir.1967).

61. *See* United States v. DiTommaso, 817 F.2d 201, 212–14 (2d Cir.1987); United States v. Lewis, 565 F.2d 1248, 1252 (2d Cir.1977).

62. *See* United States v. Owens, 484 U.S. 554 (1988); United States v. O'Malley, 796 F.2d 891, 899 (7th Cir.1986); United States v. Jarrad, 754 F.2d 1451, 1456 (9th Cir.1985).

63. *See* United States v. Lewis, 565 F.2d 1248, 1251–52 (2d Cir.1977).

§ 7.07 Admissions of a Party–Opponent [FRE 801(d)(2)(A)–(D)]

Admissions of a party-opponent are deemed nonhearsay by Federal Rule of Evidence 801(d)(2). The theory behind saying that admissions are not hearsay at all, as opposed to saying that they are hearsay that falls within an exception, is rather abstruse and perhaps over-refined. The advisory committee evidently accepted the following line of reasoning: The exceptions to the hearsay rule apply to admit hearsay when surrounding circumstances provide guarantees of reliability. There are no guarantees of reliability in the case of an admission. Therefore, admissions do not qualify for an exception to the hearsay rule. Nevertheless, admissions have been received into evidence since time immemorial. If they do not qualify as an exception, then they must have been received because they are not hearsay at all.[64]

If admissions are not reliable, why are they allowed into evidence? The standard view is that simple notions of fairness are involved and requiring a party to be stuck with his or her own statement is just. As Morgan said, "A party can hardly object that he had no opportunity to cross-examine himself or that he is unworthy of credence save when speaking under sanction of an oath."[65] One might add that while there is no requirement that the admission be against interest or that the party be available to rebut it, these two features are usually present. The first gives added reliability to the admission, the second compensates for lack of cross-examination at the time. Since the two features are usually present, perhaps the virtues of having a simple rule justify not trying to make exceptions for the rare cases in which the features are not present.

If the hearsay ban is seen solely as a rule protecting the jury from its own shortcomings, then it is hard to justify some aspects of admissions doctrine. However, the hearsay ban should also be seen in its adversarial context, what is, in the context of a system in which the parties control the gathering and presentation of proof.[66]

The rule against hearsay has a beneficial effect on evidence gathering and evidence presentation by the parties. It encourages adversaries to present live witnesses, and helps avoid angle-shooting maneuvers, such as the manufacture of hearsay with an eye to litigation or encouraging unpresentable witnesses to make themselves inaccessible. While

---

64. *See* Fed. R. Evid. 801(d)(2) advisory committee's note ("Admission by a party-opponent are excluded from the category of hearsay on the theory that their admissibility in evidence is the result of the adversary system rather than satisfaction of the conditions of the hearsay rule"). For commentary on the rationale of the admissions rule, see Roger C. Park, *The Rationale of Personal Admissions*, 21 Ind. L. Rev. 509 (1988); *see also* Edmund M. Morgan, Basic Problems of Evidence 265 (1962); Edmund M. Morgan, *Admissions as an Exception to the Hearsay Rule*, 30 Yale L.J. 355 (1921); John S. Strahorn, *A Reconsideration of the*

Hearsay Rule and Admissions, 85 U. Pa. L. Rev. 484, 493, 569–88 (1937); 5 Weinstein's Federal Evidence § 801.20[1] (2d ed. Joseph M. McLaughlin ed. 1997) (discussing theory of the rule on admissions); United States v. United Shoe Machinery Corp., 89 F.Supp. 349, 352 (D.Mass.1950) (stating that admissions are outside the hearsay rule).

65. Morgan, Basic Problems, *supra* note 64, at 231.

66. *See, e.g.*, Mirjan R. Damaska, Evidence Law Adrift 79–81 (1997).

these dangers exist in the case of hearsay generally, in the case of admissions there is not much danger that adversarial conduct will prevent the trier from getting better evidence. To the extent that a statement of a party helps the opponent, its utility is probably not poisoned by hard-to-penetrate machinations, nor will its admission encourage undesirable practices. Put another way, the admission of a party opponent is the opposite of a party's affidavit offered on behalf of the affiant; the danger of encouraging the substitution of fine-tuned hearsay for spontaneous evidence is simply not present.[67]

The federal approach to admissions is found in Fed. R. Evid. 801(d)(2), which provides that a statement is not hearsay if

> [t]he statement is offered against a party[68] and is (A) the party's own statement in either an individual or a representative capacity or (B) a statement of which the party has manifested an adoption or belief in its truth, or (C) a statement by a person authorized by the party to make a statement concerning the subject, or (D) a statement by the party's agent or servant concerning a matter within the scope of the agency or employment, made during the existence of the relationship, or (E) a statement by a coconspirator of a party during the course and in furtherance of the conspiracy.

As applied to individual admissions, the Federal Rule is very broad. It means that any statement by a party, offered by an opponent, overcomes the hearsay hurdle. Use of the admission may encounter some other obstacle, such as privilege, but the admission is not hearsay. It does not matter whether the statement was against interest when made.[69] Nor does the statement have to be made based upon personal knowledge.[70] Furthermore, the opinion rule is no obstacle.[71]

Examples

"It wasn't my fault—the brakes went out." (not against interest when made, but admissible if offered by the opposing party)

---

67. In light of this argument, one author of this text is not sure he still agrees with every point he made in Park, *The Rationale of Personal Admissions, supra* note 64.

68. The quoted language apparently does not allow admissions to be used against successors in interest. *See* 2 McCormick on Evidence § 260, at 171–72 (4th ed. John W. Strong ed. 1992). *But cf.* Hilao v. Estate of Marcos, 103 F.3d 767, 775 (9th Cir.1996) (in class action by torture victims against estate of dictator, held, torturer's statements admissible against estate as admission of agents; no reference to problem that Fed. R. Evid. 801(d)(2) does not provide for admissions to be used against successors in interest).

69. *See* People v. Meier, 954 P.2d 1068, 1070 (Colo.1998) (admission need not be

against interest when made to be admissible); Russell v. United Parcel Serv., Inc., 666 F.2d 1188, 1190 (8th Cir.1981); 2 McCormick, *supra* note 68 § 254.

70. *See* United States v. Lindemann, 85 F.3d 1232, 1237–39 (7th Cir.1996) (held, not necessary to show declarant's personal knowledge as part of foundation for admission of co-conspirator's statement); Mahlandt v. Wild Canid Survival & Research Center, Inc., 588 F.2d 626, 630–31 (8th Cir.1978); *see also* United States v. Haldeman, 559 F.2d 31, 110 (D.C.Cir.1976) (stating that opinion rule and lack of firsthand knowledge do not bar admissions under co-conspirator exception to hearsay rule).

71. *See* Russell v. United Parcel Serv., Inc., 666 F.2d 1188, 1190 (8th Cir.1981); Owens v. Atchison, Topeka & Santa Fe Ry. Co., 393 F.2d 77, 79 (5th Cir.1968).

"It was all my fault." (opinion, but still admissible)

"My wolf bit a little girl." (admissible even if no personal knowledge)[72]

Admissions by Silence

An admission by silence occurs when a party hears a statement and fails to deny it, in circumstances in which the party would naturally deny the statement were it untrue. By failing to deny the statement, the party adopts it.

Examples

After an accident involving Driver A and Driver B, Driver A accuses Driver B of crossing the centerline. Driver B hangs his head and says nothing. Driver B has adopted Driver A's statement as his own admission, assuming the absence of circumstances (such as severe injury, or fear of provoking an attack) that would inhibit him from answering.

Defendant's girlfriend mentions to a visitor, in front of defendant, that they have "sacks" of money in the house. If defendant doesn't say anything, he has adopted her statement.[73]

Sometimes a statement is not an admission by silence by reason of the defendant's reliance on the Fifth Amendment. The clearest example is when the defendant relies on *Miranda* rights during custodial interrogation.[74] The principle that invocation of the right to remain silent cannot be used against the defendant has also been held to apply even to implicit invocation of the right during noncustodial police interrogation.[75] It is permissible, however, to use prearrest silence as an admission if the defendant would have spoken had he been innocent.[76]

---

72. *See* Mahlandt v. Wild Canid Survival & Research Center, Inc., 588 F.2d 626, 630–31 (8th Cir.1978) (no requirement of personal knowledge).

73. *See* United States v. Hoosier, 542 F.2d 687 (6th Cir.1976). *See also* United States v. Schaff, 948 F.2d 501, 505 (9th Cir.1991). There, the defendant's sister was being questioned by police officers in the presence of defendant. His failure to contradict her was held to be an admission by silence of the statements she made, such as the statement that she had made entries in a suspicious notebook at his direction.

74. Miranda v. Arizona, 384 U.S. 436 (1966). *See also* Dickerson v. United States, 530 U.S. 428 (2000) (affirming constitutional status of *Miranda* warnings).

75. *See* United States v. Burson, 952 F.2d 1196, 1200 (10th Cir.1991) (defendant's adamant attitude in refusing to answer investigator's questions constituted invocation of right to remain silent, even

though defendant did not specifically mention constitutional rights); Coppola v. Powell, 878 F.2d 1562, 1567–69 (1st Cir.1989) (noncustodial statement, "[I]f you think I'm going to confess to you, you're crazy" by street-smart defendant who new right against self-incrimination; held, use of this silence in prosecutor's case in chief violated defendant's Fifth Amendment rights).

76. United States v. Oplinger, 150 F.3d 1061, 1065–67 (9th Cir.1998) (held, when under no government compulsion to speak, prosecution's use of defendant's noncustodial silence did not violate right against self-incrimination; defendant remained silent during a meeting at which employers inquired into defendant's scheme to convert bank funds to his own use); United States v. Zanabria, 74 F.3d 590, 593 (5th Cir.1996) (defendant claimed duress, caused by unidentified third party's threats against defendant's daughter, as reason for possession of cocaine; held permissible for prosecutor

Agency Admissions

The Federal Rules of Evidence remove some of the common law restrictions on the admissibility of agency admissions. In many common law jurisdictions, the statement of an agent was not admissible against the principal unless the agent was authorized to speak for the principal.[77] This rule was sometimes expressed by saying that the agent had to be a "speaking agent." Under the "speaking agent" rule, if a truck driver admitted fault after an accident, the driver's admission was not admissible against the trucking company, because the truck driver was only authorized to drive trucks, not to speak for the company. In contrast, the Federal Rules provide that an agent's admission is admissible if *either* (a) the agent was authorized to speak for the principal,[78] or (b) the agent was speaking about a matter within the scope of his employment.[79] Under this approach, the truck driver's admission of fault would be admissible against the trucking company.[80] However, a driver's statement about something outside his job responsibilities, such as a statement about the safety of elevators at the company's main office, would not be admissible against the company.[81]

to use defendant's prearrest silence regarding such threats to rebut defendant's duress defense). *Cf.* Jenkins v. Anderson, 447 U.S. 231, 235–238 (1980) (held, not a violation of the Fifth Amendment to cross-examine defendant about prearrest silence or to comment on it during closing argument).

77. Kelly v. Diesel Const. Div. of Carl A. Morse, Inc., 315 N.E.2d 751, 358 N.Y.S.2d 685 (1974) (elevator accident, allegedly due to overcrowding; superintendent's statement to inspector that there were 22 men on the elevator not admissible against superintendent's principal because superintendent was not authorized to speak on the subject); 4 John H. Wigmore, Evidence in Trials at Common Law § 1078 (James H. Chadbourn rev. 1982). *See also* United States v. Sokolow, 91 F.3d 396, 402–03 (3d Cir.1996) (held, changes made to documents by insurance company formed by defendant were not made with the defendant's consent and thus not an admission by an agent of the party-opponent); United States v. Brandon, 50 F.3d 464 (7th Cir. 1995) (attorney responding to subpoena is an agent of the client "so long as important policies concerning effective assistance or the counsel of one's choosing are preserved") (citing United States v. Harris, 914 F.2d 927 (7th Cir.1990)).

78. Fed. R. Evid. 801(d)(2)(C). *See* United States v. Reilly, 33 F.3d 1396, 1412–15 (3d Cir.1994) (in scheme to dump ash into the ocean, radiotelegram from non-employee instructing captain of ship to travel to Sri Lanka with 500 tons of ash admissible against the defendant on ground

that defendant authorized non-employee to make statements regarding that particular topic).

79. Fed. R. Evid. 801(d)(2)(D). A statement of an agent who is not speaking about a matter within the scope of employment can nonetheless be admitted if it is adopted by another agent whose job duties do embrace the subject matter covered by the statement. *See* Sea–Land Service, Inc. v. Lozen Intern., LLC., 285 F.3d 808, 821 (9th Cir.2002) (employee adopted another employee's statement by forwarding it by email with the preface, "Yikes, Pls note the rail screwed us up....") (alternative holding).

80. Woodman v. Haemonetics Corp., 51 F.3d 1087 (1st Cir.1995) (held, in a case in which plaintiff claimed to have been terminated because of age, that a statement made by plaintiff's supervisor, after the supervisor attended a management discussion of terminations, that "these damn people" in higher management wanted younger employees, was admissible against the company as the admission of an agent; even if the declarant was merely a "first-line" supervisor with no authority to make final termination decisions, the statement was still within the scope of her employment, and it was not necessary that she be acting at the instance of her employer for her statement to qualify as an agent's admission).

81. *See, e.g.,* Williams v. Pharmacia, Inc., 137 F.3d 944, 949 (7th Cir.1998) (held, error, though harmless, to allow plaintiff in sex discrimination case to put in evidence

The common law requirement that the agent be authorized to speak could be construed to mean that statements of the agent *to* the principal were not admissible against the principal.[82] Thus, if a company authorized one of its officers to conduct an internal investigation, the officer's report of the investigation would not be admissible. The Federal Rules contain no such restriction on the admissibility of internal reports. Of course, the lawyer attempting to acquire an internal report may encounter work product or privilege objections, but the hearsay rule will pose no obstacle to admission.

Who is an agent for the purposes of the rule? The most common approach to answering this question involves looking to the substantive law of agency, borrowing from it distinctions between "agents" and "independent contractors," and treating statements by "independent contractors" as inadmissible. This includes statements of outside experts who testified in prior litigation. They are normally considered to be independent contractors whose statements are not admissions of those who employ them.[83] The general rule is that an agent is one "employed by a master to perform service in his affairs whose physical conduct in the performance of the service is controlled or is subject to the right to control by the master."[84] An independent contractor "is a person who contracts with another to do something for him but who is not controlled

---

that other female employees had complained about boss's conduct and about boss's failure to act on complaints; matter was not within the scope of employment and hence did not qualify as an agency admission); In re Air Crash Disaster, 86 F.3d 498, 536 (6th Cir.1996) (held, airline maintenance employee's out-of-court statement about what airline vice president said on inspecting crash site not admissible as agent's admission because it was not part of job of maintenance employees to investigate or report on accidents); Wilkinson v. Carnival Cruise Lines, 920 F.2d 1560, 1564–67 (11th Cir.1991) (trial court erred in admitting statement of cruise line steward about condition of sliding doors on passenger deck; the statement did not qualify as an agent's admission because the steward did not have responsibility for doors and was not authorized to be in area where the doors were located) (collecting cases); Precision Piping and Instruments, Inc. v. E.I. Dupont de Nemours and Co., 951 F.2d 613, 617–18 (4th Cir.1991) (in antitrust action, trial court properly excluded statement of employee of rival company, where employee's statement concerned company's decision not to deal with plaintiff and where employee, who was responsible for engineering matters, had influence over which contractors were used but no actual authority to hire or discharge them; held, the statement was not within the scope of employment of the employee of an opponent).

82. *See* Morgan, Basic Problems, *supra* note 64, at 236–37 ("an agent whose duty is to make statements to the principal or master cannot be said to be representing or speaking for him in performing that duty"; hence statements to principal not admissible because of common law "speaking agent" requirement).

83. *See* Kirk v. Raymark Industries, Inc., 61 F.3d 147, 163 & n. 20 (3d Cir.1995) (testimony of expert witness for party in one case is not admissible in later unrelated case as admission of party because expert is not necessarily either an "agent authorized to speak on [the party's] behalf" or an agent speaking about a matter within the scope of employment). *See also* American Eagle Ins. Co. v. Thompson, 85 F.3d 327, 332–33 (8th Cir.1996) (common-law master-servant doctrine provides definition of "agent" for purposes of Fed. R. Evid. 801(d)(2)(D); under facts presented, insurance agent was not "agent" of insurance company for purposes of rule); United States v. Wiedyk, 71 F.3d 602, 606 (6th Cir.1995); Sanford v. Johns–Manville Sales Corp., 923 F.2d 1142, 1149–50 (5th Cir. 1991) (held, plaintiffs failed to prove that a doctor testifying as an expert for the defendants was an agent of the defendants since he was merely an independent contractor and not under the control of the defendants).

84. Restatement (2d) of Agency § 2(2).

by the other nor subject to the other's right to control with respect to his physical conduct in the performance of the undertaking."[85]

Normally, the question whether a person is an agent is the same as whether the person is an employee. However, the two concepts can sometimes be different, as in the case of a person who is an agent for a particular purpose, or the person whose status has technically changed to ex-employee but who continues to perform the same duties under the same restraints.[86]

A number of courts have admitted statement by interpreters as statements of agents of the person speaking, even when the person speaking did not hire the interpreter. Thus, when the opposing party spoke through an interpreter, the opponent's statement was admissible as the personal admission of a party opponent, while the interpreter's translation was admissible as the statement of an agent.[87] In many situations, this expansive interpretation of the concept of agency is unnecessary, since the interpreter's statement would be admissible as the interpreter's present sense impression of the statement just made by the opponent.[88]

Courts are split on whether admissions by government agents are admissible against the government. Though Rule 801(d)(2) is silent on the issue and, if literally interpreted, would admit the evidence, some federal authority follows earlier law and excludes it.[89] In 1993, the Third

85. *Id.* at § 2(3).

86. *See* United States v. Chappell, 698 F.2d 308, 311 (7th Cir.1983) (held, statement by defendant's accountant, who was no longer on defendant's general payroll but still acting as company's accountant, admissible under Rule 801(d)(2)(D). For an example of the opposite situation, deeming a person an early ex-employee for purposes of evidence law, see Young v. James Green Management, Inc., 327 F.3d 616 (7th Cir. 2003) (held, resignation letter in which employee charged employer with racial discrimination was not a statement of an agent about a matter within the scope of employment; policy of rule did not apply because writer was no longer inhibited by relationship with employer from making statements that would harm the employer).

87. *See, e.g.,* United States v. Nazemian, 948 F.2d 522 (9th Cir.1991).

88. *See generally* DCS Sanitation Mgmt., Inc. v. Occupational Safety & Health Rev. Com'n, 82 F.3d 812, 814–16 (8th Cir.1996) (hearsay-within-hearsay problem in which one level of alleged hearsay was out-of-court translator's rendition of declarant's statements from Spanish to English; court describes various approaches to translators' statements and admits the evidence). For an opinion that simply sweeps away the second layer of hearsay,

see Correa v. Superior Court, 117 Cal. Rptr.2d 27, 29 (Cal.2002) (simultaneous translation into English of a statement made in another language does not create second level of hearsay; a "generally unbiased and adequately skilled translator simply serves as a 'language conduit' ").

89. *See* cases cited in Christopher B. Mueller & Laird C. Kirkpatrick, Evidence § 904, at 34–35 (1995); Murrey v. United States, 73 F.3d 1448, 1455 (7th Cir.1996) (Posner, J.) (held, statement by Secretary of Veterans Affairs that poor care at VA hospital had contributed to death of patient admissible in malpractice suit by patient's estate against government). *Cf.* United States v. Rioux, 97 F.3d 648, 660–61 (2d Cir.1996) (held, statements of defendant sheriff's subordinates admissible as agency admissions in prosecution of sheriff for extortion; agency relationship existed even if sheriff did not control daily tasks of declarants). For an example of the traditional view, see United States v. Durrani, 659 F.Supp. 1183, 1185 (D. Conn. 1987), which follows the pre-Federal Rules case of United States v. Santos, 372 F.2d 177, 180 (2d Cir.1967) in holding that admissions are not admissible against the government. The reasoning of *Santos* is hard to summarize, but seems to turn on the hard-to-grasp concept that because the government represents all, none

Circuit addressed the issue of whether a police informant may serve as an agent of the law enforcement officer for the purposes of Rule 801(d)(2)(D). In *Lippay v. Christos,*[90] the plaintiff sued the defendant police officer under § 1983 for malicious prosecution. At trial, the district court admitted, as an agency admission, testimony by the plaintiff's witness regarding out-of-court statements allegedly made by the defendant's police informant. The Third Circuit held that the informant was not an agent within the meaning of Rule 801(d)(2)(D). In reaching this conclusion, the court interpreted the term "agent" using federal common-law principles of agency law, reasoning that an agency relationship is established only where the party-opponent personally directed the declarant's work on a continuing basis. The court declined to adopt a per se rule that an informant can never serve as an agent of a police officer within the meaning of the rule; rather, the court merely held that in the instant case, the plaintiff failed to establish that the informant was an employee directly controlled by the defendant.

Under the 1997 amendments to Federal Rule 801(d)(2),[91] the contents of an alleged agency statement must be considered in deciding whether the agency or employment relationship existed and whether the statement falls within the scope of the agency or employment. However, independent evidence must also be offered on that point to justify the court's finding; the statement will not alone support its own admissibility. This is a limitation on the general approach of Rule 104(a), under which judges are not bound by the rules of evidence in deciding whether foundation facts have been established. Thus, the judge could find that the foundation has been laid for admitting a statement as a present sense impression by relying solely on the statement itself,[92] whereas in determining whether a person was an agent for the purpose of the admission exemption, the judge is to consider the statement, but cannot base a finding of agency on the statement alone.

are its agents. For criticism of the traditional view, see Edward J. Imwinkelried, *Of Evidence and Equal Protection: The Unconstitutionality of Excluding Government Agents' Statements Offered as Vicarious Admissions Against the Prosecution,* 71 Minn. L. Rev. 269 (1986).

90. 996 F.2d 1490, 1497 (3d Cir.1993), *aff'd without opinion,* 61 F.3d 895 (3d Cir. 1995)

91. *See* § 7.08. The purpose of the amendment was to clear up a question left open by Bourjaily v. United States, 483 U.S. 171, 174 (1987), which involved "bootstrap-ping" in laying the foundation for the co-conspirator exemption. The Advisory Committee decided to apply the clarification to all admissions, however, not merely to co-conspirator statements.

92. *See* Booth v. State, 508 A.2d 976, 981–82 (Md. 1986) (telephonic statement held to have laid its own foundation; extensive discussion); United States v. Campbell, 782 F.Supp. 1258, 1259–61 (N.D. Ill.1991) (call to 911 dispatcher, from declarant who stated that he was in a store that had "just" been scene of shooting, admissible as present sense impression under Rule 803(1) or as excited utterance under Rule 803(2)).

§ 7.08　Admissions of a Co-conspirator [FRE 801(d)(2)(E)]

The statements of a member[93] of a conspiracy are admissible against the co-conspirators.[94] The prevailing view appears to be that statements made before the defendant against whom they are offered joined the conspiracy are nonetheless admissible against that defendant.[95] The co-conspirator rule applies whether or not conspiracy is one of the charged offenses,[96] and applies in both civil and criminal cases.[97] There is a division of authority about whether statements of an alleged co-conspirator may be admitted against the defendant even if the district court decides to acquit the alleged co-conspirator of the conspiracy charge.[98]

Under the Federal Rules of Evidence, and in most states, the statements must have been made in *furtherance of* the conspiracy and during the course of the conspiracy.[99] To be *in furtherance*, a statement must advance the main objectives of the conspiracy.[100] The *furtherance* requirement means that idle chatter or bragging about the conspiracy, or about the members of it, is not admissible.[101] Sometimes statements

---

93. The declarant must be a co-conspirator at the time the statement is made. Fed. R. Evid. 801(d)(2)(E). *See also* United States v. Abrahamson, 568 F.2d 604, 606 (8th Cir.1978) (statements made to co-conspirator by unidentified informant not admissible); United States v. Lum, 466 F.Supp. 328, 335 (D.Del.1979) (preconspiracy statements are outside the rule); *cf.* State v. Stanley, 753 P.2d 182, 185 (Ariz.App. 1988). *Cf.* United States v. Monteleone, 257 F.3d 210, 221–22 (2d Cir.2001) (held, despite requirement that declarant be member of conspiracy and that statement be in furtherance of conspiracy in order to qualify for admission under the rule, statement of informant who was secretly cooperating at time of making out-of-court statement was admissible; "the status as a co-conspirator of one who is passing information to the government turns on whether his efforts as an agent of the government supplant his efforts as an agent of his co-conspirators"; in case at bar, declarant was still trying to help conspiracy succeed even though he was exchanging information with the government).

However, statements made by a co-conspirator during the conspiracy are admissible against conspirators who join after the statement was made. United States v. United States Gypsum Co., 333 U.S. 364, 393 (1948). For criticism of this rule, see 5 Weinstein's Federal Evidence § 801.33[2], at 801–62 to 801–63 (2d ed. Joseph M. McLaughlin ed. 1997).

94. *See generally* Ethyl R. Alston, Annotation, *Admissibility of Statement of Co-conspirator Under Rule 801(d)(2)(E) of Federal Rules of Evidence*, 44 A.L.R. Fed. 627 (1979).

95. *See* United States v. Goldberg, 105 F.3d 770, 775 (1st Cir.1997) (held, a late-

joining conspirator takes the conspiracy as he finds it, and statements admissible against other conspirators are admissible against the late joiner even though made before he joined; problems with doctrine acknowledged but precedent followed); United States v. U.S. Gypsum Co., 333 U.S. 364, 393 (1948). For criticism of this rule, see 4 Jack B. Weinstein & Margaret M. Berger, Weinstein's Evidence ¶ 801(d)(2)(E)[01], at 801–247 to 801–253 (1988).

96. United States v. Stratton, 779 F.2d 820, 829 (2d Cir.1985).

97. Filco v. Amana Refrigeration, Inc., 709 F.2d 1257, 1267 (9th Cir.1983); SEC v. Tome, 638 F.Supp. 629, 633–36 (S.D.N.Y. 1986).

98. *See* United States v. Peralta, 941 F.2d 1003, 1005–1008 (9th Cir.1991), as amended on denial of reh'g (Oct. 31, 1991) (collecting cases).

99. Fed. R. Evid. 801(d)(2)(E); *see* United States v. Tombrello, 666 F.2d 485, 490 (11th Cir.1982).

100. 5 Weinstein's Federal Evidence, *supra* note 93 § 801.34; United States v. Hamilton, 689 F.2d 1262, 1269–70 (6th Cir. 1982 ("need not actually further the conspiracy . . . enough that they be intended to promote the conspiratorial objectives"). *See* United States v. Watchmaker, 761 F.2d 1459, 1472 (11th Cir.1985) (recognizing that "[s]tatements made to a non-conspirator in order to induce him to become part of a conspiracy come within the exception as furthering the purposes of the conspiracy"); United States v. Gibbs, 739 F.2d 838, 846 (3d Cir.1984) (statements to induce continued participation).

101. *See* United States v. Means, 695 F.2d 811, 818 (5th Cir.1983) (holding that

about who is a member of the conspiracy may be in furtherance of the conspiracy, as, for example, when their purpose is to induce another person to participate by showing the range and power of the conspiracy. Though the reliability of such statements may be in question, some courts have admitted them.[102]

The *course of* requirement means that the statement must have been made before the conspiracy has terminated.[103] Under federal law, a conspirator's participation in the conspiracy normally terminates with his or her arrest for the offense,[104] and, therefore, statements made by the arrestee to jailhouse informers are *not in the course of the conspiracy* and are not admissible against other co-conspirators.[105] Statements made after arrest may be admissible in some states if, for instance, their purpose is to cover up the conspiracy;[106] in federal court, statements

statement was "mere idle conversation" and should have been excluded); City of Tuscaloosa v. Harcros Chemicals, Inc., 158 F.3d 548, 558–59 (11th Cir.1998) (statements made over drinks on and golf course that did not solicit participation in or otherwise further conspiracy were not admissible as co-conspirator statements); *cf.* United States v. Guerro, 693 F.2d 10, 12 (1st Cir. 1982) (holding comments not idle and therefore conversation admissible); United States v. Piccolo, 696 F.2d 1162, 1169 (6th Cir.1983) (holding statement not "mere conversation").

Idle chatter is sometimes found admissible under the "against penal interest" provision of Fed. R. Evid. 804(b)(3), or the state-of-mind exception to the hearsay rule. *See, e.g.*, United States v. Paone, 782 F.2d 386, 390–91 (2d Cir.1986).

102. *See* United States v. Patton, 594 F.2d 444, 447 (5th Cir.1979) (statements identifying participants could be "intended to affect future dealings between the parties"); United States v. Dorn, 561 F.2d 1252, 1256–57 (7th Cir.1977) (overruled on other grounds by United States v. Read, 658 F.2d 1225 (7th Cir.1981) (holding admissible statement enlisting co-conspirators).

103. The termination of a conspiracy is sometimes defined as occurring after the time of the last "overt" act of the conspirators. *See* United States v. Lewis, 759 F.2d 1316, 1346–48 (8th Cir.1985) (citing Fiswick v. United States, 329 U.S. 211, 216 (1946)); United States v. Barnes, 586 F.2d 1052, 1059 (5th Cir.1978); United States v. Sisto, 534 F.2d 616, 622 n. 7 (5th Cir.1976).

104. Wong Sun v. United States, 371 U.S. 471, 490 (1963) ("out-of-court declaration made after arrest may not be used against one of the declarant's partners in crime"); United States v. Postal, 589 F.2d 862, 888 (5th Cir.1979).

105. United States v. Alonzo, 991 F.2d 1422, 1427 (8th Cir.1993) (in narcotics pros-

ecution, trial court committed reversible error by admitting arrested co-conspirator's statement that he still owed defendant, his "source," money); United States v. Taylor, 802 F.2d 1108, 1117 (9th Cir.1986); *cf.* United States v. Guerro, 693 F.2d 10, 12 (1st Cir.1982) (noting each case is decided on its facts, where defendant, arrested for unrelated crime, continued to be involved in conspiracy, co-conspirator statement admissible); United States v. Smith, 623 F.2d 627, 631 (9th Cir.1980) (conspiracy ended as to co-conspirator when he turned informer); United States v. Smith, 578 F.2d 1227, 1233 (8th Cir.1978) (statements of arrested co-conspirator acting as informant not admissible); United States v. Williams, 548 F.2d 228, 232 (8th Cir.1977).

106. *See* R.A. Horton, Annotation, *Admissibility of Statements of Coconspirator Made after Termination of Conspiracy and Outside Accused's Presence*, 4 A.L.R.3d 671, at § 15(b)(1965); People v. Meagher 388 N.E.2d 801, 805 (Ill.App.1979) (subsequent efforts at concealment are part of conspiracy if proximate in time); Reed v. People, 402 P.2d 68, 71 (Colo.1965) (holding admissible statements made while trying to cover up crime); *cf.* Romani v. State, 528 So.2d 15, 23 (Fla.App.1988) (holding that meetings of conspirators after murder to arrange payments were during the course of the conspiracy); State v. Elam, 328 N.W.2d 314, 319 (Iowa 1982); State v. Clevenger, 733 S.W.2d 782, 784–85 (Mo.App.1987).

For the federal rule regarding concealment activities, see Grunewald v. United States, 353 U.S. 391, 405–06 (1957) (statements made during concealment phase are admissible under co-conspirator exception if concealment is "done in furtherance of main criminal objectives of the conspiracy"). *See also* Dutton v. Evans, 400 U.S. 74, 81 (1970) (contrasting broader Georgia exception for concealment with federal *Kru-*

made after arrest may be admissible if their purpose is to further a continuing conspiracy and not merely to cover up a dead one.[107] Some courts have held that once the defendant is arrested, ending his or her participation in the conspiracy, statements made after the defendant's arrest by other co-conspirators are not admissible against the defendant.[108]

The co-conspirator doctrine has led to some complex procedural doctrine. Among the questions that have arisen are:

1. Who decides whether the doctrine applies—the judge or the jury?

2. What is the quantum of proof for the foundational requirements for the doctrine? That is, does the existence of a conspiracy, and membership in the conspiracy, need to be proven beyond a

---

lewitch rule); Krulewitch v. United States, 336 U.S. 440 (1949) (rejecting concealment as part of conspiracy); *cf.* Mares v. United States, 383 F.2d 805, 810 (10th Cir.1967) ("acting in concert to conceal the crime and avoid detection" is activity in course of conspiracy).

107. *See* United States v. Emuegbunam, 268 F.3d 377 (6th Cir.2001) (arrested co-conspirator #1 decided to cooperate with authorities and made monitored call to co-conspirator #2, who made statements incriminating co-conspirator #3, the defendant against whom the statement was later offered in evidence; held, statement was made in course of and in furtherance of conspiracy because co-conspirators #2 and #3 were still at large and capable of achieving goals of conspiracy); United States v. Williams, 87 F.3d 249, 253–54 (8th Cir. 1996) (arrest of conspirator does not end conspiracy where other conspirator continued illegal acts and arrested conspirator's statements were aimed at furthering the conspiracy).

108. *See* United States v. Smith, 578 F.2d 1227, 1233 & n. 12 (8th Cir.1978); United States v. Mardian, 546 F.2d 973, 978 n. 5 (D.C.Cir.1976) (stating that if the defendant had withdrawn from the conspiracy, "the declarations of co-conspirators uttered after the date of his withdrawal would not be admissible against him") (citing Lutwak v. United States, 344 U.S. 604, 617–18 (1953)). *But see* United States v. Williams, 87 F.3d 249, 253–54 (8th Cir.1996) (arrest of conspirator does not end conspiracy where other conspirator continued illegal acts and arrested conspirator's statements were aimed at furthering the conspiracy); United States v. Taylor, 802 F.2d 1108, 1117 (9th Cir.1986) (statements made by an unarrested coconspirator after the arrest of a conspirator can be introduced against the

arrested conspirator); United States v. Saavedra, 684 F.2d 1293, 1298 (9th Cir. 1982); United States v. Killian, 639 F.2d 206, 209 (5th Cir.1981) (stating that "a member of a conspiracy continues to be responsible for acts committed by coconspirators even after the former's arrest unless he has withdrawn from the conspiracy"); United States v. Wentz, 456 F.2d 634, 637 (9th Cir.1972) ("unarrested coconspirator still operating in furtherance of the conspiracy may say and do things which may be introduced against the arrested one if the conspiracy is still in operation"); United States v. Marques, 600 F.2d 742, 750 n. 4 (9th Cir.1979).

When a conspirator legitimately withdraws from the conspiracy, his or her post-withdrawal statements are not admissible against the remaining conspirators. *Cf.* United States v. Smith, 578 F.2d 1227, 1233 (8th Cir. 1978). Legitimate withdrawal requires "affirmative action to defeat or disavow the purpose of the conspiracy ... [m]ere cessation of the activity in furtherance of the conspiracy does not constitute withdrawal." United States v. Garrett, 720 F.2d 705, 714 (D.C.Cir.1983); *see also* United States v. Hamilton, 689 F.2d 1262, 1268 (6th Cir.1982) (without affirmative action to withdraw or terminate it, conspiracy is presumed to continue).

The arrest of some of the co-conspirators does not necessarily end the whole conspiracy. United States v. Ammar, 714 F.2d 238, 253 (3d Cir.1983); *cf.* United States v. Gullett, 713 F.2d 1203, 1212–13 (6th Cir.1983) (finding error in admission of recording from meeting held between two co-conspirators to discuss primarily concealment was not "in course" of conspiracy because two other co-conspirators had already been arrested and others were under grand jury investigation).

reasonable doubt before the doctrine applies, or is some lesser amount of proof, such as proof by a preponderance of the evidence, sufficient?

3. Is "bootstrapping" allowed, so that for purposes of deciding whether the defendant was a member of the conspiracy to determine the application of the co-conspirator rule, the judge may take into account the very statements that are sought to be admitted under the rule? For example, if the defendant's alleged co-conspirator said out of court that the defendant was a member of the conspiracy, can that statement be used to show the defendant's membership as a foundation for the doctrine?

1. Who decides?

In the federal system, the judge decides whether the requirements for the co-conspirator rule have been satisfied.[109] The judge must make a preliminary determination that the foundation has been laid. Of course, the prosecutor may request that the out-of-court statements be admitted provisionally, subject to being "linked up" with evidence laying the foundation for the rule. If the linkage evidence is not supplied, then the judge must strike the earlier evidence, or perhaps even grant a mistrial if the prejudice cannot be cured.[110] Whether the judge makes the determination before admitting any evidence of statements or whether the statements are admitted subject to a later foundation, it is still the judge who determines whether the requirements of the co-conspirator rule have been met.

Some states allow the jury to decide. Under this approach, the statements are admitted and the jury is instructed to disregard them if it fails to find that there was a conspiracy, that the defendant was a member, and that the statement was made in the course of and in furtherance of the conspiracy.[111] Even in the states where the jury

---

109. Bourjaily v. United States, 483 U.S. 171, 175 (1987) (existence of a conspiracy and defendant's involvement in it are preliminary questions of fact that the court must resolve pursuant to Rule 104(a)).

110. *See* United States v. Grassi, 616 F.2d 1295, 1300–01 (5th Cir.1980); United States v. Lyles, 593 F.2d 182, 194 (2d Cir. 1979). *See also* 2 Michael H. Graham, Handbook of Federal Evidence § 801.25, at 336–38 (4th ed. 1996) (discussing order of proof issues). *Cf.* People v. Montoya, 753 P.2d 729, 734 (Colo.1988) (en banc) (discussing order of proof).

111. *See, e.g.,* Cal. Evid. Code § 1223 (West 1966); Fla. Stat. Ann. § 90.803(18)(e) (West Supp. 1997); see *also* People v. Smith, 231 Cal.Rptr. 897, 905–06 (Cal.App. 1986) (disapproved of on other grounds by People v. Bacigalupo, 2 Cal.Rptr.2d 335 (1991) (noting requirement that jury make preliminary finding of conspiracy); State v.

Morales, 460 So.2d 410, 413 (Fla.App.1984) (discussing the "Apollo instruction" which defense counsel can request to be given to the jury "that the conspiracy and each member's participation in it must be established by independent evidence," and noting that despite the instruction, the trial court has the responsibility for determining the admissibility of hearsay evidence); Eaton v. State, 438 So.2d 822, 824 (Fla.1983) (discussing the "Apollo instruction"); Commonwealth v. Beckett, 373 366 N.E.2d 1252, 1259 (Mass.1977) (stating that "jury must be instructed that, before they may consider the statements of one coconspirator against another, they must make definite findings on the same questions which the judge must pass on before he may permit the jury to consider whether that evidence may be used against all"); People v. H., 449 N.Y.S.2d 605, 609 n. 1 (N.Y.Sup. 1982) (indicating that jury must be in-

decides, the judge must exclude the statement if no reasonable jury could decide that the foundational requirement had been met.

2.   What is the quantum of proof?

In the federal system, the prosecution must show the judge by a preponderance of the evidence that the foundational requirements have been met.[112] This is in accordance with the standard generally applied to preliminary fact determinations under Rule 104(a). In some state jurisdictions, a different standard of proof may apply.[113] In states where the jury essentially decides the admissibility of a co-conspirator statement, all that the judge must do is determine that there is evidence sufficient to support a finding by the jury.[114]

3.   Is "bootstrapping" permissible?

Suppose the statement of A is offered against alleged co-conspirator B, and the hearsay issue to be decided is whether the statement is admissible under the co-conspirator rule. May the statement itself be considered in making this determination? Before the enactment of the Federal Rules of Evidence and for many years afterwards, many federal courts answered "no" to this question. They required that the existence of the conspiracy, and B's part in it, be shown by "independent evidence," exclusive of the co-conspirator statement, as part of the foundation for the hearsay statement.[115] The Supreme Court abandoned this requirement in 1987 in *Bourjaily v. United States*,[116] referring to Rule

structed to make preliminary finding of conspiracy before using co-conspirator's statements); People v. Pontani, 306 N.Y.S.2d 240, 241 (App.Div.1969) (approving a similar charge).

For an argument that having the jury make the preliminary fact determination makes more sense in the context of the co-conspirator exception than in other contexts, see John Kaplan, *Of Mabrus and Zorgs*, 66 Cal. L. Rev. 987, 997–98 (1978). Kaplan's argument is that, at least in the case where the preliminary fact issue is whether the defendant was a member of the conspiracy, that we should not be overly disturbed by the relegation of the preliminary fact determination to the jury, since the jury will surely not act on the evidence without determining that the fact exists, since the jury must determine that the defendant is a member of the conspiracy in order to convict. This is true, but from the standpoint of those who believe that the peril of hearsay is that the jury cannot properly evaluate it, then the contemplation of the jury possibly using hearsay to determine whether a hearsay exception applies should still be disturbing.

For an argument that it is preferable for the judge to make the preliminary determinations of admissibility, see Christopher B. Mueller, *The Federal Coconspirator Exception: Action, Assertion, and Hearsay*, 12 Hofstra L. Rev. 323, 365–70 (1984).

112. Bourjaily v. United States, 483 U.S. 171, 175–76 (1987); United States v. Chaney, 662 F.2d 1148 1153 (5th Cir.1981); United States v. Shelton, 669 F.2d 446, 465 (7th Cir.1982).

113. *See, e.g.*, McDowell v. State, 746 P.2d 149, 150 (Nev.1987) (slight evidence of conspiracy required before statement is admitted); State v. Lassiter, 354 S.E.2d 595, 601 (W.Va.1987) (fair preponderance standard); Burke v. State, 746 P.2d 852, 855 (Wyo.1987) (requiring prima facie evidence "sufficient ... to permit the trial court to reasonably infer that a conspiracy existed").

114. *See supra* note 111 and accompanying text.

115. *See* United States v. Simpson, 709 F.2d 903, 909 (5th Cir.1983); United States v. Dean, 666 F.2d 174, 179 (5th Cir.1982); United States v. Lyles, 593 F.2d 182, 194 (2d Cir.1979); United States v. Chaney 662 F.2d 1148, 1153 (5th Cir.1981); United States v. James, 590 F.2d 575, 581, 588 (5th Cir.) (en banc 1979); United States v. Martorano, 561 F.2d 406, 406 (1st Cir.1977) (canvassing other circuits); *see generally* John J. Michalik, Annotation, *Necessity and Sufficiency of Independent Evidence of Conspiracy to Allow Admission of Extrajudicial Statements of Co–Conspirators*, 46 A.L.R.3d 1148 (1973).

116. 483 U.S. 171, 176–81 (1987).

104(a) and noting that otherwise inadmissible evidence may be used by the judge in making preliminary fact determinations.

In *Bourjaily*, the Court left open the question whether the co-conspirator's statement could be the only basis for a trial court finding that the defendant was a member of the conspiracy; in the case before it there was other evidence in addition to the statement. A 1997 amendment to the Rule resolves the issue by making clear that while the court shall consider the contents of the co-conspirator's statement in deciding whether the foundation for the doctrine has been laid, the proponent must also produce independent evidence.[117] The amendment codifies the result reached by most of the circuits.[118] Some states also still embrace the independent evidence requirement, requiring that the trial judge not consider the statement as part of the evidence that the defendant was a member of the conspiracy.[119]

117. Fed. R. Evid. 801(d)(2). This rule also makes this concept applicable to the issue of the declarant's authority under the authorized admissions rule and the agency or employment relationship and their scope under the agency admissions rule. As amended, the Rule reads as follows:

(2) Admissions by party-opponent. The statement is offered against a party and is (A) the party's own statement, in either an individual or representative capacity or (B) a statement of which the party has manifested an adoption or belief in its truth, or (C) a statement by a person authorized by the party to make a statement concerning the subject, or (D) a statement by the party's agent or servant concerning a matter within the scope of the agency or employment, made during the existence of the relationship, or (E) a statement by a coconspirator of a party during the course and in furtherance of the conspiracy. The contents of the statement shall be considered but are not alone sufficient to establish the declarant's authority under subdivision (C), the agency or employment relationship and scope thereof under subdivision (D), or the existence of the conspiracy and the participation therein of the declarant and the party against whom the statement is offered under subdivision (E).

For a discussion of the wisdom of certain amendments to the co-conspirator rule, see James Joseph Duane, *Some Thoughts on How the Hearsay Exception for Conspirators' Statements Should—and Should Not—Be Amended*, 165 F.R.D. 299 (1996).

118. *See, e.g.*, United States v. Castaneda, 16 F.3d 1504, 1507 (9th Cir.1994) (foundation for co-conspirator statement must include "fairly incriminating" independent evidence, aside from proffered statement, showing defendant to be a member of the conspiracy); United States v. Sepulveda, 15 F.3d 1161, 1181–82 (1st Cir. 1993); United States v. Gambino, 926 F.2d 1355, 1361 n. 5 (3d Cir.1991); United States v. Garbett, 867 F.2d 1132, 1134 (8th Cir. 1989); United States v. Silverman, 861 F.2d 571, 577 (9th Cir.1988); United States v. Zambrana, 841 F.2d 1320, 1344–45 (7th Cir. 1988); United States v. Daly, 842 F.2d 1380, 1386 (2d Cir.1988).

119. *See, e.g.*, State v. Edwards, 536 So.2d 288, 294 (Fla.App.1988) (specifically rejecting the rule of Bourjaily and requiring independent evidence); People v. Woodland Oil Co., 396 N.W.2d 541, 544 (Mich.App. 1986) (requiring independent evidence); State v. Scanlon, 268 N.W.2d 63, 64 (Minn. 1978) (requiring "independent prima facie proof"); State v. Riggins, 519 N.E.2d 397, 403 (Ohio App. 1986); *see also* State v. Frederickson, 739 S.W.2d 708, 711 n. 3 (Mo.1987) (en banc) (recognizing Bourjaily and noting that Missouri law probably requires some independent evidence in addition to the co-conspirator statement); State v. Florie, 411 N.W.2d 689, 696 (Iowa 1987) (requiring some independent proof in addition to the statement); People v. Montoya, 753 P.2d 729, 734–36 (Colo.1988) (en banc) (statement can be considered in determining admissibility, but "cannot be the sole basis for establishing" admissibility).

Confrontation Issues

Even if a statement fits under the co-conspirator rule, the defendant may still claim that his or her right to confrontation was violated. This claim is unlikely to succeed in federal court because the Supreme Court has held that neither a showing that the declarant is unavailable nor a particularized showing of reliability is necessary if a statement meets the requirements of the co-conspirator rule.[120] The argument may still be available under the confrontation clause of state constitutions, however.[121]

EXCEPTIONS TO THE HEARSAY RULE

§ 7.09　Exceptions to the Hearsay Rule—Introduction

Under the traditional common law approach to hearsay, the question whether the hearsay rule barred the reception of a statement could be reduced to two questions:

1. Was the statement being offered for the truth of the matter asserted? If not, it was not hearsay, and the hearsay rule posed no obstacle.

2. If the statement was hearsay, did it fall under an exception?

The Federal Rules of Evidence complicated this system of organization.[122] Instead of treating admissions and statements of co-conspirators as statements that are hearsay but admissible under exceptions to the hearsay rule, they treated them as statements that were not hearsay at all even though offered to prove the truth of the matter asserted. Some commentators have referred to them as "exemptions" or "exclusions" from the hearsay rule, as opposed to "exceptions." The advisory committee's reason for adopting this approach has been explained in an earlier section.[123] Whether or not one agrees with this approach, the Federal Rules have become so pervasive that it makes sense to follow the committee's organizing principles. Therefore, under the Federal Rules

---

120. Bourjaily v. United States, 483 U.S. 171, 181–84 (1987); United States v. Inadi 475 U.S. 387, 399–400 (1986) (unavailability is not a necessary condition to admission of extrajudicial co-conspirator's statement). *See* United States v. Paris, 827 F.2d 395, 400 (9th Cir.1987) (stating that after *Bourjaily*, "Sixth Amendment requirements for admitting coconspirator statements [are] 'identical' to those of Rule 801(d)(2)(E)"). *Cf.* Dutton v. Evans, 400 U.S. 74, 78 (1970) (upholding admission of evidence under state co-conspirator exception against confrontation clause challenge). For fuller discussion of the confrontation clause and co-conspirator statements, see § 7.67.

121. *Cf.* Arnold v. State, 751 P.2d 494, 504–05 (Alaska App.1988) (listing four indi-

cators of reliability to be established before hearsay is admitted under the co-conspirator doctrine, based on United States and Alaskan constitutions); Nunez v. People, 737 P.2d 422, 424–26 (Colo.1987) (en banc) (citing the two-step formulation from Ohio v. Roberts, 448 U.S. 56 (1980).

122. *See* James W. McElhaney, *Hidden Rules*, A.B.A.J., May 1989, at 92.

123. *See* § 7.07. For a critical examination of the advisory committee's approach to admissions, and suggested justifications for treating admissions as exceptions to the hearsay rule, see Roger C. Park, *The Rationale of Personal Admissions*, 21 Ind. L. Rev. 509 (1988).

the following questions should be asked in determining whether an out-of-court statement is barred by the hearsay rule:

1. Is the statement offered to prove the truth of the matter asserted? If not, it is not hearsay under the definition of Rule 801(c), and the hearsay rule poses no obstacle to receiving it.

2. If the statement is offered to prove the truth of the matter asserted, does it nonetheless fit into one of the special categories of nonhearsay described in Rule 801(d), such as admissions, statements of coconspirators, and prior statements of witnesses? If so, it is likewise not hearsay.

3. If the statement is hearsay within the definition of Rule 801(c), and does not fall into any of the special categories of nonhearsay described in Rule 801(d), does it nevertheless fit one of the exceptions described in Rules 803 and 804, so that it is admissible even though it is hearsay?

The preceding sections of this chapter have dealt with the first two questions. The remainder of this chapter is devoted to the third question: whether an out-of-court statement fits an exception to the hearsay rule.

EXCEPTIONS THAT APPLY WHETHER OR NOT THE DECLARANT IS AVAILABLE [FRE 803]

§ 7.10   Generally

The Federal Rules of Evidence divide the exceptions to the hearsay rule into two categories, those that apply only when the declarant is unavailable (Rule 804 exceptions), and those that apply whether or not the declarant is available (Rule 803 exceptions). By far the larger number of exceptions fall into the latter category, permitting hearsay to be offered whether or not the declarant's testimony can be obtained. The only exceptions that require unavailability are the exceptions for dying declarations,[124] for statements against interest[125] for former testimony,[126] for statements of personal and family history,[127] and for statements made by a declarant whose unavailability was either procured by or acquiesced in by the party against whom they are offered.[128] Although one might expect a more widespread use of the idea that the declarant should be called if available,[129] the more than twenty exceptions in Rule 803 do not contain this requirement, so that one can put into evidence excited utterances, business records, statements for medical diagnosis or treatment, and many other statements even if one has failed to call a declarant who is sitting in the back of the courtroom.

124. *See* § **7.51**.
125. *See* § **7.52**.
126. *See* § **7.47**.
127. *See* § **7.35**.
128. *See* § **7.55**.

129. *See generally* Daniel Stewart, Jr., *Perception, Memory, and Hearsay: A Criticism of Present Law and the Proposed Federal Rules of Evidence*, 1 Utah L. Rev. 1 (1970).

§ 7.11 The Present Sense Impression Exception [FRE 803(1)]

Federal Rule of Evidence 803(1) provides a hearsay exception for "[a] statement describing or explaining an event or condition made while the declarant was perceiving the event or condition, or immediately thereafter."[130] Examples of utterances falling under 803(1) include the following:

"I can't seem to turn the wheel," offered to show that the declarant, who was then attempting to do so, could not turn the wheel.[131]

"There's a mouse in the bottle," offered to show that declarant, who was then looking in the bottle, saw a mouse.[132]

"The license number of that car was FJY 644," offered to show that the license number was in fact FJY 644.[133] (The statement need not be made exactly at the time of observing the event; substantial contemporaneity is all that is required.)[134]

The rationale of the present sense impression exception is that (1) there is no substantial danger that defects in the declarant's memory will affect the value of the statement, (2) the declarant would not have had much time to fabricate before making the statement, and (3) in many cases, the person to whom the statement was addressed would have been in a position to check its accuracy; hence, declarant would speak with care.

When determining whether to admit a statement as a present sense impression, the trial judge must determine, as a preliminary question under Fed. R. Evid. 104(a), whether the statement was made at the time of the event or immediately afterward. The contents of the statement being offered may be used for this purpose. In other words, it is permissible to "bootstrap" by using the utterance to lay its own foundation, as in a case where the declarants made the statement over the telephone and there is no way to know whether it was made contemporaneously with the event other than examining the contents of the statement itself.[135] The word "immediately" in Rule 803(1) is not defined, and

---

130. Fed. R. Evid. 803(1).

131. *See* Fratzke v. Meyer, 398 N.W.2d 200, 204 (Iowa App.1986) (statement by boy just before being struck by car, "Hurry up there is a car coming," admissible as present sense impression).

132. *See* Hall v. De Saussure, 297 S.W.2d 81, 89–90 (Tenn.App.1956) (doctor's statement while looking at x-ray, "He certainly did take a big chunk out of your spine," held admissible as present sense impression).

133. *See* State v. Smith, 285 So.2d 240, 244–45 (La.1973) (slip of paper on which bystander wrote license number of robbery getaway car offered to prove the license number of the car admissible as present sense impression or excited utterance).

134. *See* Fed. R. Evid. 803(1) advisory committee's note; *see also* United States v. Peacock, 654 F.2d 339, 350 (5th Cir.1981) (statements made by declarant immediately after phone conversation describing the conversation admissible under 803(1); the underlying conversation was admissible as the statement of a coconspirator.)

135. United States v. Campbell, 782 F.Supp. 1258, 1259–61 (N.D. Ill.1991) (call to 911 dispatcher by declarant who had stated that he was in store that had "just" been scene of shooting was admissible as a present sense impression under Rule 803(1) or as an excited utterance under Rule

one court has held that the immediacy requirement was satisfied even though the statement might have been made as long as twenty-three minutes after the event.[136] Another has suggested, however, that fifteen or more minutes after the event is too long.[137] In deciding whether a given period satisfies the requirement of contemporaneity under 803(1), the trial judge should take into account the rationale of 803(1), and decide whether the lapse of time provided an opportunity, under the circumstances, for fabrication or memory loss.[138] The question whether the lapse of time also eliminated the opportunity for the person who heard the declarant's statement to observe what the declarant was describing is also relevant. Although independent observation is not an absolute requirement for admission as a present sense impression,[139] one of the justifications for the exception is that the person to whom declarant addressed the statement would often have a chance to check on the validity of the statement by observing the same thing, and therefore the declarant would have a motive to be accurate. Where a lapse of time has removed this opportunity for independent observation by the addressee, the court may consider that fact in deciding whether to find that the statement was made "immediately" after the event.[140]

A statement offered as a present sense impression is not admissible unless the proponent demonstrates that the declarant had personal knowledge. For example, in *Bemis v. Edwards*,[141] the court rejected the argument that statements made in a 911 call were admissible as a present sense impression, stating that the proponent had failed to show that the declarant had firsthand knowledge. It noted that in fact the declarant's statement contained an affirmative indication that he lacked

803(2)); State v. Jones, 532 A.2d 169, 172 (Md.1987) (anonymous CB transmissions, purported to be from truck drivers, about their observations of errant police cruiser, making statements such as "Look at Smoky Bear southbound with no lights on," admissible without independent evidence that statements made contemporaneously with witnessing conditions); Booth v. State, 508 A.2d 976, 985 (Md.1986) (statements about persons present while declarant was talking on telephone admissible as present sense impressions). *Compare* United States v. Cain, 587 F.2d 678, 681 (5th Cir.1979) (CB transmission about identification of persons walking near abandoned stolen truck does not satisfy immediacy requirement because circumstantial evidence indicated substantial lapse of time between truck's abandonment and statement).

136. United States v. Blakey, 607 F.2d 779, 785–86 (7th Cir.1979) (overruling on other grounds recognized by United States v. Harty, 930 F.2d 1257 (7th Cir.1991)).

137. Hilyer v. Howat Concrete Co., 578 F.2d 422, 426 n. 7 (D.C.Cir.1978).

138. *See* Fed. R. Evid. 803(1) advisory committee's note; *see also* Houston Oxygen

Co. v. Davis, 161 S.W.2d 474, 476–77 (Tex. Com.App.1942); 4 Christopher B. Mueller & Laird C. Kirkpatrick, Federal Evidence § 438, at 483–85 (1992).

139. For discussion of the corroboration issue, see Jon R. Waltz, *The Present Sense Impression Exception to the Rule Against Hearsay: Origins and Attributes*, 66 Iowa L. Rev. 869, 898 (1981) (stating that corroboration by an equally percipient witness should not be required, and that the event itself and the circumstances surrounding it event will often supply adequate information regarding the accuracy of the statement).

140. *See* United States v. Ruiz, 249 F.3d 643 (7th Cir.2001) (held, whether remote hearer of present sense impression statement was in a position to verify the statement goes to weight of statement but not admissibility); 5 Weinstein's Federal Evidence § 803.03[2] (2d ed. Joseph M. McLaughlin ed. 1997).

141. 45 F.3d 1369, 1373–74 (9th Cir. 1995).

firsthand knowledge of the events described. The court stated that the proponent has the burden of proving by a preponderance of the evidence that the declarant had firsthand knowledge. (In the authors' opinion, the requirement of proof by a "preponderance" may be correct when the exception being applied is the present sense impression exception, since the exception by its terms requires a preliminary showing that the declarant personally sensed the matter being described. However, the "preponderance" test cannot be generalized to other instances in which a showing of personal knowledge is required. As to that more general requirement of a showing of firsthand knowledge, the Advisory Committee's Note to Rule 602 indicates that the appropriate standard is whether there is *evidence sufficient to support a finding* of personal knowledge, not the higher standard of proof by a preponderance of the evidence.)

Where the challenged statement expressly or implicitly shows that the declarant was speaking from first-hand knowledge, that requirement is satisfied, without need of further proof of first-hand knowledge.[142]

§ 7.12   The Excited Utterance Exception [FRE 803(2)]

Federal Rule of Evidence 803(2) provides an exception for "a statement relating to a startling event or condition made while the declarant was under the stress of excitement caused by the event or condition."

A core example of an excited utterance is a statement concerning a startling event or condition made while the event or condition is occurring or immediately thereafter. For example, a statement such as "My God! The car is on fire!", made while looking at the burning car and offered to show that the car is on fire, would fit comfortably within the exception. A more difficult example is a statement such as "He's the one who did it!", offered to prove that the person referred to did the act, and made upon seeing the person at some later time. In this second example, because of the lapse of time between the act to which the statement refers and the statement itself, one must determine whether the excited utterance exception should apply even though the declarant was not under the stress of excitement caused by the startling event itself. If the declarant was not suffering the stress of excitement caused by *any* startling event or condition, the exception obviously should not apply. On the other hand, if the court finds in our example that seeing the person referred to was itself a startling event, and that the declarant spoke while suffering from the stress of excitement caused by the new event, the excited utterance exception should apply.[143]

142. *See* First State Bank of Denton v. Maryland Cas. Co., 918 F.2d 38 (5th Cir. 1990) (statement of person answering telephone, that this was the Millses' residence but Mr. Mills was not at home, admissible where declarant apparently looked for Mills before making statement).

143. *See* United States v. Napier, 518 F.2d 316, 317–18 (9th Cir.1975) (brain damaged victim said "he killed me!" when shown photograph of defendant long after event; court upholds admission as excited utterance); *but cf.* People v. Grubbs, 492 N.Y.S.2d 377 (1985) (testimony that claimant recoiled when she first saw defendant in identification lineup held inadmissible, with no explicit hearsay analysis; dissenting opinion cites *Napier* and states that evidence should have been admitted as excited utterance).

The rationale of this exception is that excited utterances are reliable because excitement suspends the capacity to fabricate. This reliability theory has been questioned on grounds that excitement, while it suspends fabrication, may also weaken the ability to perceive and report the event accurately. Despite convincing experimental support for this criticism,[144] the rule makers decided to retain the exception, basically on grounds that it was well established in precedent.[145]

The question whether the declarant was under the stress of excitement at the time the utterance was made is a question for the judge to determine under Rule 104(a). In deciding the question, all of the circumstances can be taken into account, including the contents of the utterance itself.[146] In other words, the fact that the utterance contains words like "My God!" can be used by the trial judge as evidence on the preliminary determination of fact about excitement. As is the case with other preliminary determinations of fact under Rule 104(a), the judge is not bound by the rules of evidence (except privilege) in making a determination whether a factual foundation has been laid for admission of an utterance under a hearsay exception.[147]

The exception for excited utterances is closely akin to the exception for present sense impressions.[148] There are, however, three differences between the two exceptions:

1. The excited utterance exception has no specific time limit,[149] while the present sense impression statement must be made while observing the event or "immediately" thereafter.

144. *See* Daniel Stewart, Jr., *Perception, Memory, and Hearsay: A Criticism of Present Law and the Proposed Federal Rules of Evidence*, 1 Utah L. Rev. 1, 27–29 (1970), and authorities cited therein; Robert M. Hutchins & Donald Slesinger, *Some Observations on the Law of Evidence: Spontaneous Exclamations*, 28 Colum. L. Rev. 432, 437–39 (1928).

145. *See* Fed. R. Evid. 803(2) advisory committee's note.

146. *See* United States v. Brown, 254 F.3d 454, 459–60 (3d Cir.2001) (held, court could use excited utterance itself to establish that foundation requirement of startling event was satisfied). When the declarant is an unidentified bystander, courts sometimes do not admit the statement as proof of the event due to insufficient proof of firsthand knowledge. *See* Fed. R. Evid. 803(1) advisory committee's note; *see also* Garrett v. Howden, 387 P.2d 874, 876–78 (N.M.1963) (not an abuse of discretion to reject testimony of unidentified bystander concerning speed of car prior to collision). *But cf.* United States v. Medico, 557 F.2d 309, 315–16 (2d Cir.1977). In the *Medico* case, an unidentified bystander described the license plate number of a getaway car,

and testimony about the bystander's statement was admitted at trial. The trial judge, Judge Jack Weinstein, admitted the evidence under the residual exception created by Rule 804(b)(5). The Court of Appeals opinion notes that the statement fits the requirements of the present sense impression exception, and speculates that Judge Weinstein may have avoided that exception because of caveats about unidentified bystanders set forth in the advisory committee's note to Rule 803(1). It then examines admissibility under Rule 804(b)(5), since that was the rule that the trial judge used, and decides that the statement is admissible under that exception.

147. See Fed. R. Evid. 803(2) advisory committee's note; *see also* United States v. Obayagbona, 627 F.Supp. 329, 338–39 (E.D.N.Y.1985); United States v. Phelps, 572 F.Supp. 262, 265–66 (E.D.Ky.1983).

148. *See* § 7.11.

149. *See* United States v. Rivera, 43 F.3d 1291 (9th Cir.1995) (held, not an abuse of discretion for district court to admit as excited utterance testimony that victim said at least half an hour after event that the defendant raped and threatened

2. The present sense impression exception does not require that the declarant be excited.

3. The excited utterance need only "relate to" the exciting event; the present sense impression must "describe or explain" the event. The excited utterance can embrace a broader subject matter. For example, a statement by a bystander "That has been on the floor for a couple of hours" would be admissible under the excited utterance exception even though it does not describe the exciting event (someone falling on the substance on the floor.)[150] Hence, the advisory committee suggests, the quoted statement would not qualify as a present sense impression.

§ 7.13   Statements About the Declarant's Present State of Mind or Body [FRE 803(3)]

Federal Rule of Evidence 803(3) provides an exception for a statement of the declarant's then existing state of mind, emotion, sensation, or physical condition (such as intent, plan, motive, design, mental feeling, pain, and bodily health), but not including a statement of memory or belief to prove the fact remembered or believed unless it relates to the execution, revocation, identification, or terms of declarant's will.[151]

Examples

"My back hurts" (to show pain)

"I hate him" (to show hatred)

"I'll kill him" (to show intent to kill)

"I'm going to my uncle's house" (to show intent to go to the uncle's house)

---

the victim; in determining whether a statement was made under stress of excitement, court should consider not only lapse of time but declarant's age, characteristics of the event, and subject matter of the statements). *See also* Simpson v. Wal–Mart Stores, 744 A.2d 625, 628–29 (N.H.1999) (neither lapse of time nor fact that statement came in response to question prevents it from qualifying as an excited utterance if excitement persisted).

150. *See* Fed. R. Evid. 803(2) advisory committee's note.

151. Fed. R. Evid. 803(3). *See* United States v. Tokars, 95 F.3d 1520, 1535–36 (11th Cir.1996) (in prosecution of husband for murdering wife, wife's statements to other persons about her intent to divorce husband and take away his money admissible to show her state of mind, which was probably manifested to him in some way,

thus giving him a motive to kill); United States v. DiNome, 954 F.2d 839, 846 (2d Cir.1992) (held, murder victim's statement prior to crime that he was going to see a lawyer about his suspicion that his competitor was dealing in stolen cars admissible under Fed. R. Evid. 803(3) to show victim-declarant's intent and hence to show competitor's motive to murder declarant to keep him quiet; statement was not made in the presence of competitor, but court evidently assumed that competitor might have heard of statement or of similar conduct by declarant); United States v. Veltmann, 6 F.3d 1483, 1494–95 (11th Cir.1993) (held, in arson-murder prosecution, trial court erred by excluding witness's videotaped deposition testimony on prior alleged suicide threats by murder victim; testimony was admissible in light of relevance to defense that victim had committed suicide).

The rationale behind this exception is that the declarant's defects of memory will not affect the validity of the statement, because there has been no lapse of time between the condition being described and the description of it.[152] Also, there is a diminished danger of fabrication because there has been less time to fabricate in many instances— although, of course, in some cases, such as that of a personal injury plaintiff saying "my back hurts," there may be a preexisting motive to fabricate.[153]

The exception for statements of present state of mind includes statements of present intent to do a future act, offered to show that the declarant did the future act. In the leading case on the subject, *Mutual Life Insurance Co. v. Hillmon*,[154] the declarant's statement that he was going to Colorado with Hillmon was held admissible to show that he had in fact done so.

However, the exception does not cover statements of present state of mind that are statements of memory or belief offered to show the fact remembered or believed. For example, the statement, "I remember that it was X who attacked me yesterday" is not covered by exception. For example, the statement, "I remember that it was X who attacked me yesterday" is not covered by the exception.[155] Such statements of memory or belief are inadmissible unless they "relate to the execution, revocation, identification, or terms of declarant's will."[156]

A potential objection arises whenever a statement expressly or implicitly describes the intent of some person other than the declarant. Suppose that the statement "I'm going out with Harry" is offered against Harry to prove that the declarant, a murder victim, did go out with Harry, who is charged with her murder. This statement shows the intent of the declarant to go out with Harry, but it also relies upon her memory about what Harry himself said about Harry's plans; the statement would have little evidentiary value unless Harry had said he was going to go out with her. During the congressional process, the House Committee on the Judiciary issued a report asserting that Rule 803(3) should be construed "so as to render statements of intent by a declarant admissible only to prove his future conduct, not the future conduct of

---

152. *Cf.* Fed. R. Evid. 803(3) advisory committee's note (arguably incorporating rationale of present sense impression exception). For an analysis of the concepts underlying the exception, see Glen Weissenberger, *Hearsay Puzzles: An Essay on Federal Evidence Rule 803(3)*, 64 Temp. L. Rev. 145 (1991).

153. United States v. Veltmann, 6 F.3d 1483, 1494–95 (11th Cir.1993). Unlike the Federal Rule, the California rules governing statements of mental or physical state explicitly provide for exclusion "if the statement was made under circumstances such as to indicate its lack of trustworthiness." Cal. Evid. Code § 1252 (1966).

154. 145 U.S. 285, 295–300 (1892).

155. *See, e.g.*, United States v. Neely, 980 F.2d 1074, 1082 (7th Cir.1992) (trial court properly excluded defendant's letter denying any involvement with fraudulent schemes written two and one-half weeks after defendant received letter from government witness detailing defendant's role in insurance fraud scheme); United States v. Soghanalian, 777 F.Supp. 17 (S.D.Fla.1991) (self-exculpatory statement by defendant who did not testify at trial, made hours after plane arrived in Iraq with illegal cargo, that arms in cargo were supposed to have been off-loaded in Switzerland, was not made admissible by Rule 803(3) because it was a statement of memory or belief offered to prove the fact remembered or believed).

156. Fed. R. Evid. 803(3), final clause.

another person."[157] In a jurisdiction that follows the view set forth in the House Report, a statement like "X and I are going to rob a bank" would be inadmissible when offered against X to show that X participated in the robbery—unless, of course, some other basis for receiving the statement could be found, such as the rule receiving statements of co-conspirators. The statement "I'm going out with Harry" is more problematic. It is arguably admissible even if one accepts the view in the House Report. The theory of admission would be that it is offered not to show Harry's intent, but for the limited purpose of showing declarant's intent to go out with Harry should Harry come. Under this theory the defense would be entitled to a limiting instruction to the effect that the statement could be used to show that the declarant was planning to go out with Harry but not that Harry was planning to go out with the declarant. Courts have generally favored the reception of these statements despite the danger that the jury would use them to show another's intent.[158]

Moreover, one can argue that the House Report does not set forth the proper way to interpret Rule 803(3). To accept the House Report's view would be to reject the common law foundation for Rule 803(3). The leading Supreme Court case, *Mutual Life Insurance Co. v. Hillmon*,[159]

· **157.** Fed. R. Evid. 803(3) advisory committee note.

158. *See* United States v. Astorga–Torres, 682 F.2d 1331 (9th Cir.1982) (statement by inmate that he intended to bring two guards to site of drug transaction; "Ambriz's statement was properly admitted not as proof that in fact he did bring guards with him to Tulare . . . but as evidence that he had the intent to do so, from which evidence inferences could properly be drawn by jury"; admissible for this purpose against defendants other than declarant; trial court gave limiting instruction); United States v. Pheaster, 544 F.2d 353, 374–80 (9th Cir.1976) (canvassing arguments, and deciding in favor of admission; trial court gave limiting instruction; Federal Rules were not applicable to case); United States v. Houlihan, 871 F.Supp. 1495 (D. Mass. 1994) (applying expansive interpretation of Rule 803(3)). For a leading case from a non-Rules jurisdiction, see People v. Alcalde, 148 P.2d 627 (Cal.1944) (decedent's statement that she was going out with a certain person admitted in that person's murder trial; however, court gave limiting instruction "that the evidence was admitted for the limited purpose of showing the decedent's intention"). The California Supreme Court reaffirmed the *Alcalde* rule in People v. Jones, 54 Cal.Rptr.2d 42, 50–51 (1996) (held, murder victim's statement to her daughter that she was going to another city with defendant, and that the daughter should call her aunt if declarant did not

return, was admissible against defendant; court held that Cal. Evid. Code § 1250 (state of mind exception) was intended in part to codify *Alcalde* rule). For a narrow interpretation of Fed. R. Evid. 803(3), *see* United States v. Jenkins, 579 F.2d 840, 843 (4th Cir.1978) ("Congress directed only that [Rule 803(3)] be construed to confine the doctrine in *Hillmon* so that statements of intent by declarant would be admissible only to prove the Declarant's future conduct, not the future conduct of others"; statement is dictum, however). *See generally* Diane Kiesel, Comment, *One Person's Thoughts, Another Person's Acts: How the Federal Circuit Courts Interpret the* Hillmon *Doctrine*, 33 Cath. U.L. Rev. 699 (1984).

Some courts will only admit these statements if there is independent evidence of the other person's participation. Generally, such evidence consists of testimony showing that the defendant acted consistently with the declarant's statement. *See* United States v. Badalamenti, 794 F.2d 821, 825–26 (2d Cir.1986) (admitting statement); United States v. Cicale, 691 F.2d 95, 103–04 (2d Cir.1982) (admitting statement); United States v. Delvecchio, 816 F.2d 859, 863 (2d Cir.1987) (held, trial court should have excluded statement because there was not independent evidence linking defendant to the other person's expression; error was harmless, however).

159. 145 U.S. 285, 288 & 295–300 (1892) (admitting statement "I expect to

was a case in which the declarant spoke not only about the declarant's own intent but about the intent of another (though the statement was admitted solely to prove the intentions of the declarant), and the advisory committee noted the Hillmon case favorably.[160] Though the House Report suggests a different legislative intent,[161] it is only the report of one House, not a statute adopted by Congress, and courts that have given a generous scope to the exception cannot be said to be ignoring any clear statement of uniform legislative intent.[162]

§ 7.14 Statements for Medical Diagnosis or Treatment [FRE 803(4)]

Federal Rule of Evidence 803(4) creates an exception for:

statements made for purposes of medical diagnosis or treatment and describing medical history, or past or present symptoms, pain, or sensations, or the inception or general character of the cause or external source thereof insofar as reasonably pertinent to diagnosis or treatment.

Rule 803(4) creates a relatively broad exception. In contrast with the common law rules of some jurisdictions, note the following features of Rule 803(4):

1. The Rule does not require that the statement be made to someone who is going to provide treatment. For example, statements made to forensic physicians whose only function is to provide testimony fall within the ambit of the Rule because of the Rule's reference to "diagnosis." This result seems inconsistent with the rationale of the exception (that persons who make statements for treatment will be careful to be accurate, since their health depends upon it). However, the advisory committee reasoned that pre-Rule courts would have allowed a non-treating expert to describe the patient's statements anyway, in order to bolster his or her credibility by showing a basis for the diagnosis. The theory was that the statements are admissible not for the truth of the matter asserted, but to show that the doctor was

leave Wichita on or about March the 5th, with a certain Mr. Hillmon" for the truth of the matter asserted).

160. *See* Fed. R. Evid. 803(3) advisory committee's note.

161. *See* House Comm. on the Judiciary, H.R. Rep. No. 650, 93d Cong., 1st Sess. 5 (1973).

162. Nevertheless, it is worth noting that the party in Hillmon against whom the evidence was offered, though objecting to the statement's admission for any purpose, would not have objected to the statement being used to prove Hillmon's intentions, once the statement was found admissible to prove the declarant's intention. The issue is whether a body found at Crooked Creek was that of Hillmon. To the extent the statement was offered to show the body might have been that of Walters, the declarant, it also increases the likelihood that the body was that of Hillmon. Thus, once Walters' statement was admitted, the opponent logically would have *wanted* the reference to Hillmon to be heard by the jury. The same would not be true in the case of the person who announces that she intends to go out with Harry. It is unlikely that there would be any real issue as to the declarant's having gone out; the real question would be with whom. To the extent the statement mentions the defendant, defendant will obviously object to its admission to prove his intention to go out with the declarant.

diligent in forming the diagnosis. If admissible under this theory, then a limiting instruction would be appropriate. As the advisory committee pointed out, the limiting instruction would be rather difficult to follow.[163] One could handle this problem by deciding that this type of credibility bolstering is not permissible because the jury could not follow the limiting instruction. Instead, the advisory committee elected to remove the need for the limiting instruction by providing that the statements made to the forensic expert are admissible without limit, on the same basis as statements made to a treating physician.[164] Doctor-to-patient statements generally are not covered by this rule,[165] though they often may be admissible under another exception.

2. The Rule does not require that the statement be made to a *physician*. As long as it is made for purposes of obtaining diagnosis or treatment, it could be made to anyone—an ambulance attendant, a nurse, or even a family member.[166]

3. The statement need not even be made by the person who was injured or who suffers from the condition being treated or diagnosed. For example, if a mother brings in a child and describes the child's accident from her firsthand knowledge, her statement falls under the Rule.[167]

---

163. Fed. R. Evid. 803(4) advisory committee's note.

164. *Id. See also* United States v. Whitted, 994 F.2d 444, 446–47 (8th Cir. 1993), reh'g granted and opinion vacated on other grounds, (Aug. 2, 1993) and on reh'g on other grounds, 11 F.3d 782 (8th Cir. 1993) (trial court acted within its discretion by allowing government doctor retained solely as a trial witness to repeat statements made by alleged child victim of sex abuse). *But cf.* United States v. Armstrong, 36 M.J. 311, 313–14 (C.M.A.1993) (held, statements made by child sex abuse victim during interview with psychologist and trial counsel inadmissible because statements were made by victim to trial counsel in preparation for trial, not by victim to doctor for purposes of medical treatment).11 F.3d 782, 785 (8th Cir.1993) (trial court properly admitted government doctor solely retained as a trial witness to repeat statements made by alleged child victim of sex abuse).

165. Bombard v. Fort Wayne Newspapers, Inc., 92 F.3d 560, 564 (7th Cir.1996) (doctor's statement to patient recommending course of treatment not admissible under Rule 803(4), which was not designed to cover statements by the person providing the medical attention).

166. Fed. R. Evid. 803(4) advisory committee's note. *See also* Davignon v. Clemmey, 322 F.3d 1 (1st Cir.2003) (held, statement to social worker in effort to enlist help in addressing mental health issues fell under medical treatment exception); United States v. Armstrong, 36 M.J. 311, 314 (C.M.A. 1993) (held, statements made by child sex abuse victim during interview with psychologist and trial counsel inadmissible because statements were made by victim to trial counsel in preparation for trial, not by victim to doctor for purposes of medical treatment).

167. *See* Lovejoy v. United States, 92 F.3d 628, 631–32 (8th Cir.1996) (mother's statement to care provider on behalf of handicapped child describing abuse of child witnessed by mother admissible under exception); United States v. Yazzie, 59 F.3d 807, 812 (9th Cir.1995) (held, parent's note declaring "Step-dad brainwashed" victim and "I ask help, please" deemed admissible in child sex abuse case because the statement were apparently made to aid medical treatment of child). Weinstein explains that as the relationship between the affected person and the declarant becomes less close, the statement will be less reliable and courts might exclude under Rule 403 balancing test. 5 Weinstein's Federal Evidence § 803.09[3], at 803–43 (2d ed. Joseph M. McLaughlin ed. 1997).

4.   The Rule is not limited to statements of present symptoms. If made for purposes of medical diagnosis or treatment, statements of past symptoms ("My back has been hurting for three years") are admissible. So are statements about the cause of an injury ("I drank a beer that had a mouse in it") if reasonably pertinent to diagnosis or treatment. However, a statement that "I got hit by a car that went through a red light" would not be admissible in full because the statement about the red light is not pertinent to diagnosis or treatment.[168] A statement such as "I slipped on a banana peel" is problematic; the fact that the patient slipped on a banana peel arguably tends to rebut the theory that the patient had a balance disorder or was intoxicated, and hence is relevant to diagnosis and treatment. However, one can argue that the statement should be redacted so that only the portion saying that the declarant "slipped" is admissible.[169]

A number of courts have used Federal Rule 803(4) as a basis for admitting the statements of sexual assault victims to physicians who have examined them after the assault, including statements identifying the perpetrator or describing the details of the incident. One justification has been that the physician must treat the whole patient, psychologically as well as physically, and that what the perpetrator said to the victim and the identity of the perpetrator can be relevant to treatment in the broader sense.[170]

168. *See* Fed. R. Evid. 803(4) advisory committee's note.

169. *See* United States v. Pollard, 790 F.2d 1309, 1313–14 (7th Cir.1986) (reversible error to exclude portion of medical record relating to cause, though portion relating to fault clearly inadmissible); Roberts v. Hollocher, 664 F.2d 200, 204–05 (8th Cir. 1981) (excluding portion of hospital report, based on patient's statements, that said the patient's injuries were "consistent with excessive force" because statement was a "a conclusion going to fault rather than the cause of the condition and does not serve to promote diagnosis or treatment"). Statements regarding identity of individual responsible for injuries or condition are seldom pertinent to treatment or diagnosis. United States v. Iron Shell, 633 F.2d 77, 84 (8th Cir.1980). However, statements by child abuse victim that abuser is member of victim's immediate household are reasonably pertinent to treatment and therefore admissible. The key is the need for psychological treatment. *See* United States v. Renville, 779 F.2d 430, 436–38 (8th Cir.1985); *Iron Shell*, 633 F.2d at 82–85.

170. *See* United States v. Norman T., 129 F.3d 1099, 1105–06 (10th Cir.1997) (applying Rule 803(4) to statements of five-year-old to physician and nurse, rejecting defense argument that a child that young does not understand the need for accuracy in reporting to medical personnel; child's statement accusing defendant of digital penetration considered reasonably pertinent to diagnosis or treatment); United States v. Cherry, 938 F.2d 748, 756–57 (7th Cir.1991) (in case arising from sexual abuse on military base, court concluded that district court did not abuse discretion in admitting statements of victim to doctor in which victim said to doctor, "He held my arms so I couldn't do anything. He laid me on the floor and had intercourse with me. He said not to tell anyone"); United States v. Moreno, 36 M.J. 107, 120 (C.M.A. 1992) (statement of teenager hospitalized for suicide attempt, that depression was partly due to sexual activity with his stepfather, admissible under exception); Eleanor Swift, *The Hearsay Rule at Work: Has It Been Abolished De Facto by Judicial Decision?*, 76 Minn. L. Rev. 473, 498 (1992) (describing permissive decisions which use hearsay exceptions (excited utterances, statement for diagnosis or treatment, and residual hearsay exception) to admit out-of-court statements made by child victims of sexual abuse). *Cf.* White v. Illinois, 502 U.S. 346 (1992) (no violation of confrontation clause for Illinois to take broad view of its medical diagnosis exception). *Compare* Ring v. Er-

The exception for statements made for diagnosis or treatment is only one possible route for admission of statements relevant to medical condition. Some statements admissible under this exception are also admissible under other exceptions. For example, the statement, "my leg hurts" is probably admissible under Rule 803(3) as a statement of then existing physical condition. The same statement might also be admissible as a present sense impression under Rule 803(1) or, if made under the stress of excitement caused by a startling event, under Rule 803(2) as an excited utterance.

Statements of patients that are described in hospital records raise the special problem of hearsay within hearsay. To be admissible under the Rules, each statement must fall within an exception to the hearsay rule.[171] The patient's statement is admissible under Rule 803(4), and the statement of the person who records the patient's statement is admissible under the business records exception.[172] If either statement is not relevant to diagnosis or treatment, its opponents may challenge its admissibility.[173]

Another possible route for admitting statements related to medical care is the special hearsay exception applicable to expert witnesses. Under Rule 703, in forming their opinions experts may rely upon hearsay that is not otherwise admissible in evidence, so long as the hearsay is the type of data upon which experts in the field reasonably rely in forming their professional opinions.[174] Thus, experts may rely upon the statements of patients and their families in making a diagnosis and testifying to an expert opinion based upon the hearsay. However, there is case law supporting the position that Rule 703, while it may allow an expert to rely upon hearsay, does not necessarily allow the expert to repeat the hearsay statements.[175] Thus, according to some

ickson, 983 F.2d 818, 819–20 (8th Cir.1992) (held, admission of videotaped interview between alleged child victim of sexual abuse and physician violated defendant's rights under the confrontation clause; government failed to establish reliability of victim's statement where victim's mother, not victim, sought medical treatment, where victim did not realize she spoke with a doctor, and where victim's statements lacked "particularized guarantees of trustworthiness"); State v. Haslam, 663 A.2d 902, 908 (R.I. 1995) (held, a prior statement by a counselor, who testified that a minor patient had previously identified the defendant as her molester, was inadmissible as a prior consistent statement because the prior statement was not made before the motive to lie arose).

For an especially expansive interpretation of the medical treatment exception in sex abuse cases, see United States v. Yazzie, 59 F.3d 807, 812 (9th Cir.1995) (held, although statements assigning blame for an injury are not normally admissible under the medical treatment exception, they are admissible in sexual abuse cases because the physician must treat emotional as well as physical injuries; in this case, a parent's note declaring "Step-dad brainwashed" victim and "I ask help, please" was apparently made to aid medical treatment of child). See also United States v. Tome, 61 F.3d 1446 (10th Cir.1995) (10th Circuit decision following Supreme Court reversal and remand) (held, sexual abuse victim's out-of-court statements to three pediatricians identifying her father as her abuser were properly admitted under Fed. R. Evid. 803(4) as reasonably pertinent to the victim's treatment or diagnosis).

171. Fed. R. Evid. 805.

172. See Fed. R. Evid. 803(6).

173. See § 7.27.

174. See § 10.08.

175. See, e.g., Rose Hall, Ltd. v. Chase Manhattan Overseas Banking Corp., 576 F.Supp. 107, 158 (D.Del.1983), affd, 740

courts, while the expert may rely on the hearsay in forming an opinion, the hearsay is not itself rendered admissible in evidence.

§ 7.15   Past Recollection Recorded [FRE 803(5)]

Federal Rule of Evidence 803(5) provides a hearsay exception for:

A memorandum or record concerning a matter about which a witness once had knowledge but has insufficient recollection to enable the witness to testify fully and accurately, shown to have been made or adopted by the witness when the matter was fresh in the witness' memory and to reflect that knowledge correctly. If admitted, the memorandum or record may be read into evidence but may not itself be received as an exhibit unless offered by an adverse party.

This exception allows a writing or recording to be received for the truth of its contents.[176] The rationale for Rule 803(5) is threefold: (1) *necessity*—the witness has insufficient memory to testify fully and accurately; (2) *trustworthiness*—the memorandum or report was made while the matter was fresh in the witness's memory and was embodied in a writing or recording;[177] and (3) *opportunity for cross-examination of the witness*—a witness who made or adopted the memorandum is available for testimony.

The foundational requirements of the past recollection recorded exception must be satisfied before a writing or recording may be received as substantive evidence.[178] Rule 803(5) requires that: (1) the witness once

F.2d 958 (3d Cir. 1984) (holding that while expert on value of land could base opinion partly on information gleaned from telephone conversation with surveyor, the expert could not repeat the contents of the conversation); State v. Towne, 453 A.2d 1133 (Vt.1982) (excluding testimony by expert witness that he had talked to author of learned treatise and that author agreed with him). *See also* Gacy v. Welborn, 994 F.2d 305, 315–16 (7th Cir. 1993) (trial court properly excluded as hearsay testimony by psychiatrists and psychologists repeating murder defendant's comments, but allowed experts to paraphrase defendant's remarks). *See generally* Ronald L. Carlson, *Experts, Judges, and Commentators: The Underlying Debate About an Expert's Underlying Data*, 47 Mercer L. Rev. 481 (1996); Ronald L. Carlson, *Policing the Bases of Modern Expert Testimony*, 39 Vand. L. Rev. 577, 584 & n.23 (1986); Ronald L. Carlson, *Collision Course in Expert Testimony: Limitations on Affirmative Introduction of Underlying Data*, 36 U. Fla. L. Rev. 234 (1984).

176. *See, e.g.,* 5 Weinstein's Federal Evidence § 803.10[1] (2d ed. Joseph M. McLaughlin ed. 1997).

177. Note that the witness does not have to make the record. A record adopted while the matter was fresh in the witness's mind may be admissible under Rule 803(5). Moreover, the advisory comments to Rule 803(5) state that multiple person involvement in the process of observing and recording is entirely consistent with the exception. Fed. R. Evid. 803(5) advisory committee's note.

178. *See, e.g.,* United States v. Riccardi, 174 F.2d 883 (3d Cir.1949). The Third Circuit stated:

[W]hether the record is directly admitted into evidence, or indirectly by the permissive parroting of the witness, it is nevertheless a substitute for his memory and is offered for the truth of its contents. It assumes a distinct significance as an independent probative force, and is therefore ordinarily required to meet certain standards. These requirements are [necessary because] the court is ... determining whether the writing may be safely received as a substitute for the witness's memory and for the truth of the matter asserted.

Id. at 887–88 (footnotes omitted).

had sufficient personal knowledge of the underlying events to meet the personal knowledge requirement of Rule 602 if testifying about these matters; (2) the record was made when the matter was fresh in the witness's memory; (3) the record accurately reflects the witness's knowledge;[179] (4) the witness cannot testify from present memory[180] (counsel must lay the foundation showing lack of present memory because if the witness has a present memory of the facts recited in the record, the witness's memory is considered superior to the hearsay record);[181] and (5) the testifying witness "made or adopted" the record. The "made or adopted" requirement of Rule 803(5) would seem to require that the person whose recollection has been recorded either make the record or examine and approve it. However, that interpretation of the rule has not been universal.[182]

179. *See* United States v. Edwards, 539 F.2d 689 (9th Cir.1976) (concluding that declarant's intoxication at time he made statement bears heavily on weight to be given statement, but not on its admissibility where declarant testified that he believed the statement accurately reflected his recollection at the time it was made, statement was signed and acknowledged by declarant, and government agent who was present at the interview testified that declarant's answers were "fairly detailed narrations"). *Cf.* United States v. Porter, 986 F.2d 1014, 1017 (6th Cir.1993) (at trial, defendant's girlfriend repudiated her prior statement implicating defendant, claiming she was confused and on drugs when statement was made; held, statement admissible because, among other things, witness signed and made corrections to statement immediately after events giving rise to prosecution). One court has held that a record that fails to meet the trustworthiness requirement of the business records exception can be admitted under the recorded recollection exception. Parker v. Reda, 327 F.3d 211 (2d Cir.2003) (record made by prison official about use-of-force incident in which he was involved was admissible under recorded recollection exception even though not sufficiently reliable to be admitted as a business record; difference in treatment justified because person making the record is available for cross-examination in case of recorded recollection).

Rule 803(5) attempts to ensure that the witness accurately recorded his knowledge when the witness remembered what he perceived. 5 Weinstein's Federal Evidence, *supra* note 176 § 803.10[4[c], at 803–52 to 803–53. A witness who does not remember the facts recorded cannot be cross-examined about his or her perception and, thus, direct testimony about what the witness perceived cannot be obtained. A criminal defendant may claim that the confrontation clause is violated if the witness has no recollection about the underlying event because the witness's perception cannot adequately be tested by cross-examination. *See* California v. Green, 399 U.S. 149, 155 (1970) (recognizing that hearsay exceptions and the confrontation clause are not necessarily congruent and expressing doubts about the constitutionality of the overlap between hearsay exceptions and the Sixth Amendment); *But see* United States v. Kelly, 349 F.2d 720, 770 (2d Cir.1965) (stating that virtually all of the hearsay exceptions, including the past recollection recorded, do not involve any deprivation of the defendant's right of confrontation under the sixth amendment).

180. *See, e.g.,* United States v. Felix–Jerez, 667 F.2d 1297, 1300 (9th Cir.1982) (error to admit marshal's written statement based on his notes of an interview with defendant where there was no showing marshal had insufficient recollection to testify); United States v. Judon, 567 F.2d 1289, 1294 (5th Cir.1978) (error to admit statement under Rule 803(5) where there was no showing of witness's insufficient recollection). Thus, the proponent of a recorded recollection must show that the witness's memory was not refreshed by the record.

181. *See* Meder v. Everest & Jennings, Inc., 637 F.2d 1182, 1185–86 (8th Cir.1981) (police report that contained information officer did not personally know but obtained from someone else constituted hearsay within hearsay and was not admissible under Rule 803(5)).

182. *See* Meder v. Everest & Jennings, Inc., 637 F.2d 1182, 1185–86 (8th Cir.1981) (police report containing information officer did not personally know but obtained from someone else constituted hearsay within hearsay and was not admissible under Rule

Counsel opposing the admission of a past recollection recorded should challenge the memorandum's foundation under Rule 803(5). Once counsel establishes a document's foundation under Rule 803(5), it may be read into evidence but cannot be received as an exhibit or sent to the jury unless offered by the opposing party.[183] The rationale for limiting the admission of a recorded recollection is that the memorandum is a substitute for oral testimony, and offering the memorandum into evidence may encourage the jury to give it undue emphasis in relation to other oral testimony.[184]

Establishing the Foundation for a Past Recollection Recorded

Suppose a case in which counsel's witness is expected to testify about the contents of a warehouse, but on the stand the witness cannot remember everything that was in the warehouse. Counsel attempts to proceed as follows with a list of what was in the warehouse:

Q: I show you plaintiff's Exhibit 1. What is it?

A: A list of the items in the warehouse.

Q: Now, please tell us what was in the warehouse.

A: [Witness reads list]

This procedure is objectionable and the witness should not be permitted to read from the list because the foundational requirements of Rule 803(5) have not been satisfied.

To present the testimony in admissible form:

1.   After showing the witness the list, have the witness testify that the witness's memory is not refreshed. Although the witness's recollection must be impaired, it need not be wholly exhausted before the record is admissible as evidence.[185] If the witness's

---

803(5)). However, that interpretation of the rule has not been universally followed. *See* Boehmer v. LeBoeuf, 650 A.2d 1336 (Me. 1994), which, in interpreting a Maine rule identical in wording to Fed. R. Evid. 803(5), stated that a person whose recollection is recorded by another in a "jointly produced past recollection recorded" need not have physically adopted or verified the record in order for the exception to apply. Under the facts of the case before it, however, the court held that the trial court did not abuse its discretion in excluding an investigator's notes of a child witness's recollection of the accident made two months after the accident, because it was reasonable for the court to find that there had not been a sufficient showing that the notes were accurate when made.

183. *See, e.g.*, United States v. Ray, 768 F.2d 991, 995 (8th Cir.1985) (recognizing transcript of defendant's prior attor-

ney's statement was properly admitted under Rule 803(5), but holding admission of transcript as an exhibit constituted reversible error where the statement was the only evidence on a crucial element of the charged offense).

184. *See* Jack R. Jelsema *et al.*, Comment, *Hearsay Under the Proposed Federal Rules: A Discretionary Approach*, 15 Wayne L. Rev. 1077, 1139 (1969).

185. A judge should admit pertinent portions of a recorded recollection which fail to refresh the witness's present memory. *See, e.g.*, United States v. Williams, 571 F.2d 344 (6th Cir.1978) (admitting statement made to government agent with where witness's memory sufficient to testify generally about his conversations with defendant but did not recall whether defendant told him how the defendant acquired the forged government checks); United States v. Senak, 527 F.2d 129, 137–38 (7th

memory is refreshed, take the list back and proceed to question the witness about the items in the warehouse. Testimony of a witness who can recollect the events recited in the record does not have to satisfy Rule 803(5) because the witness is testifying from present memory and is not putting the contents of a hearsay record into evidence.

2. After showing the witness the list, have the witness testify:

    a. The witness made or adopted the list;

    b. The list was made when the witness's memory of the warehouse's contents was fresh. Many factors affect whether the matter was sufficiently fresh to guarantee the memory's trustworthiness: time when list was made, quality of memory in the list, and whether the list was made before litigation commenced. Under Rule 803(5), courts have discretion to expand the concept of "freshness";[186]

    c. The list was accurate when made;

    d. The witness does not now remember what was in the warehouse. Although the witness cannot remember the warehouse's contents, the witness can remember being careful in making the list of items. The witness must testify either that the witness recalls making an accurate list or that, although the witness does not specifically recollect the witness's state of mind when making the list, the witness would not have made it unless it were correct.[187]

Now, the list may be read into evidence but is not received as an exhibit unless offered by the adverse party.

Refreshing Memory

The technique of refreshing a witness's memory[188] is sometimes confused with the hearsay exception for past recollection recorded. The Third Circuit described the distinction between refreshing memory and past recollection recorded in *United States v. Riccardi*:[189]

Cir.1975) (admitting statement made to FBI agent where witness told part of conversation and cannot remember the rest); Fortier v. Dona Anna Plaza Partners, 747 F.2d 1324, 1332 (10th Cir.1984) (admitting subsurface report referred to by an expert witness in a negligent construction case as the recorded recollection of an expert witness as it enabled the expert to testify fully and accurately).

186. *See, e.g.*, United States v. Patterson, 678 F.2d 774, 778 (9th Cir.1982) (holding trial judge's finding, that witness's memory was fresh at the time he testified before grand jury about his conversation with defendant although 10 months elapsed between the conversation and grand jury appearance, did not abuse the broad discretion intended by Rule 803(5)); see 5 Weinstein's Federal Evidence, *supra* note 176 § 803.10[4][b], at 803–51 to 803–52.

187. *See, e.g.*, 3 John H. Wigmore, Evidence in Trials at Common Law § 747 (James H. Chadbourn rev. 1970) (stating that "the witness must be able now to assert that the record accurately represented (the witness's) knowledge at the time . . . the witness [must] affirm that [he] knew it to be true at the time").

188. *See* § 1.06.

189. 174 F.2d 883 (3d Cir.1949).

The primary difference between the two classifications is the ability of the witness to testify from present knowledge; where the witness's memory is revived, and he presently recollects the facts and swears to them, he is obviously in a different position from the witness who cannot directly state the facts from present memory and who must ask the court to accept a writing for the truth of its contents because he is willing to swear, for one reason or another, that its contents are true.[190]

One of the consequences of the concept that documents used to refresh memory are not evidence is that otherwise inadmissible documents may be used to refresh memory. For example, if a state statute provides that accident reports are inadmissible, counsel can still use the accident report to refresh the memory of a witness on the stand.[191] Because the report is not being used as evidence, and the witness is on the stand at the trial or hearing, the hearsay rule is not implicated.

The differences between refreshing memory and using a writing as past recollection recorded are:

1. Counsel can use anything to stimulate or refresh the witness's memory, regardless of whether the thing was prepared by the witness or somebody else. The stimulant need not be a writing; it may be anything that might help to jog the witness's memory.

2. The witness's memory must actually be refreshed before the witness can testify; the witness must testify independently from memory because the witness cannot read from a writing on the witness stand without first satisfying Rule 803(5).

3. A writing or recording used to refresh the witness's memory is not admissible into evidence, unless the opponent offers it.

4. The witness does not have to testify that the document is accurate because the document is only being used to awaken the witness's memory, not as evidence (note: if counsel uses the witness's notes to refresh memory and the notes differ from the witness's testimony, opposing counsel can use the notes to impeach the witness under Rule 612).

§ 7.16   The Business Records Exception [FRE 803(6)]

Federal Rule of Evidence 803(6) creates an exception for

[a] memorandum, report, record, or data compilation, in any form, of acts, events, conditions, opinions, or diagnoses, made at or near the time by, or from information transmitted by, a person with knowledge, if kept in the course of a regularly conducted business

---

190. *Id.* at 886 (footnote omitted). *See* United States v. Rinke, 778 F.2d 581, 587–88 (10th Cir.1985) (holding trial judge properly permitted witness to use notes of telephone conversations with defendants to refresh his memory while testifying).

191. *See, e.g.,* State v. Schultz, 392 N.W.2d 305, 307 (Minn.App.1986) (recognizing that use of accident report to refresh a police officer's memory while testifying to facts within his knowledge permitted although report inadmissible under state statute).

activity, and if it was the regular practice of that business activity to make the memorandum, report, record, or data compilation, all as shown by the testimony of the custodian or other qualified witness, or by certification that complies with Rule 902(11), Rule 902(12), or a statute permitting certification, unless the source of information or the method or circumstances of preparation indicate lack of trustworthiness. The term "business" as used in this paragraph includes business, institution, association, profession, occupation, and calling of every kind, whether or not conducted for profit.[192]

The rationale of the business records exception is that there is a motive to be accurate for the sake of the business; that regularity breeds habits of precision; that systematic checking is likely, and careless employees may be fired. Furthermore, it would be impractical to have each employee who participated in the creation of a business record testify in court.[193]

§ 7.17   The Business Records Exception [FRE 803(6)]— Regular Practice of the Business

Part of laying the foundation for a business record is showing that the record was made in the course of a regularly conducted business activity and that it was the regular practice of that business activity to make the record.[194] Occasionally, a record made in the course of business will be rejected on the ground that the proponent failed to demonstrate that it was the "regular practice" to make such records. For example, in *United States v. Freidin*,[195] the defendant, a tax partner in a large

192. Note that the quoted language includes "opinions" and "diagnoses." Despite this language, opinions in business records are sometimes excluded. *See* § **7.24.** *See also* Vance v. Peters, 97 F.3d 987, 995 (7th Cir.1996). A female prison inmate brought a civil suit to recover for damages allegedly caused by excessive force by guard. The finding of the employee review officer, signed by the warden, that the guard had used excessive force was held inadmissible even though the requirements of Rule 803(6) were met. The court held that Rule 403 required exclusion because the jury should make up its own mind. (In the authors' view, the decision deprives plaintiff of valuable evidence by persons quite capable of forming a judgment on the subject, and who are unlikely to make such a finding unless it was true. Note also the possible application of the public records exception (Fed. R. Evid. 803(8)) and the agency admissions rule (Fed. R. Evid. 801(d)(2)).

193. Fed. R. Evid. 803(6) advisory committee's note; 2 McCormick on Evidence § 286 (4th ed. John W. Strong ed.

1992); United States v. Snyder, 787 F.2d 1429 (10th Cir.1986).

194. *See* Fed. R. Evid. 803(6) advisory committee's note; *see also* 2 McCormick on Evidence, *supra* note 193 § 288 (4th ed. John W. Strong ed. 1992); United States v. Chatman, 994 F.2d 1510, 1516 (10th Cir. 1993) (trial court properly admitted records of calls made from cellular phone when records routinely printed for billing purposes).

195. 849 F.2d 716 (2d Cir.1988). For examples of records held admissible, see Malek v. Federal Ins. Co., 994 F.2d 49, 53 (2d Cir.1993) (social worker's case notes admissible); United States v. Linn, 880 F.2d 209, 216 (9th Cir.1989) (computer printout of telephone call admissible); United States v. Versaint, 849 F.2d 827, 831–32 (3d Cir. 1988) (police report admissible); United States v. Catabran, 836 F.2d 453, 457 (9th Cir.1988) (computer printouts of accounting data admissible); City of Idaho Falls v. Beco Constr. Co., 850 P.2d 165, 172–73 (Idaho 1993) (computer printout summary of labor and equipment costs admissible).

accounting firm, was charged with filing false income tax returns and making a false statement to the IRS in connection with those returns. The defendant received a substantial fee from a client, which he allegedly deposited in his personal account at his firm without reporting the fee on his income taxes. During his IRS audit, he claimed to have turned over the fee to his firm. One of the crucial pieces of government evidence was an internal office memorandum of the accounting firm memorializing Freidin's directive to place the fee in his own personal account. The memo, which was prepared by the secretary to the controller, stated that Freidin had given her a check for $22,000 and told her that it was to go into his personal account. There was no testimony at trial that it was the regular practice of the business to make such memoranda. Instead the testimony was that only the partners' secretaries normally made directives about depositing money in personal accounts, and only at the direction of a partner. Rejecting the argument that the record need not be a routine record if it was made in the regular course of business, the court found this record to be an "isolated document" and held that it should have been excluded on grounds that it was not the regular practice of the business to make this type of record. The court acknowledged that it was taking a narrow view of the "regular practice" requirement and noted the existence of authority taking a broader view.[196]

§ 7.18 The Business Records Exception [FRE 803(6)]— Authentication With and Without a Testifying Witness

The federal rules are liberal, allowing the custodian or other qualified witness to lay the foundation for a business record. The witness need not have made the record or have custody of it, but must be able to testify that the record is made as a regularly conducted business activity, that it is the practice of that business to make that type of record, that the source of the information was a person with knowledge, and that the record was made at or near the time of the event.[197]

196. *See also* United States v. Wells, 262 F.3d 455, 462–63 (5th Cir.2001) (held, witness should not have been permitted to testify from memory about the contents of destroyed drug ledgers; foundation elements, such as showing records were kept in course of regularly conducted business, were missing); Pierce v. Atchison Topeka and Santa Fe Ry. Co., 110 F.3d 431 (7th Cir.1997) (not abuse of discretion to exclude memo marked "to file" summarizing corporate executive's discussions with plaintiff about release of ADEA claim; district court was justified in excluding document, even though executive testified that he regularly maintained personnel records and drafted memos recording "unique" dealings with employees; district court had concluded that memo was not regular or routine because it recorded an "unusual incident" that had "litigation potential"); United States v. Davis, 571 F.2d 1354, 1359 (5th Cir.1978) (error to admit form indicating Colt had manufactured and shipped gun to Georgia when Colt did not make such records as a regular practice). *But see* 4 Jack B. Weinstein & Margaret M. Berger, Weinstein's Evidence ¶ 803(06)[03], at 803–182 (1987) (arguing that if made in regular course of business and trustworthy, lack of routineness should not preclude admission despite "regular practice" language of rule).

197. *See* 2 McCormick on Evidence § 292 (4th ed. John W. Strong ed. 1992).

Applying a rule identical to Federal Rule 803(6), the Minnesota Supreme Court has allowed a witness who was not an employee of the business to lay the foundation for a business record. The record in question was an Underwriters' Laboratory report, and the witness laying the foundation demonstrated that he was familiar with the operations and procedures employed by the organization for product certification.[198] Some courts have gone further, allowing records of a business to be sponsored by outsiders who merely relied on the records in their own separate business.[199]

The 2000 amendments to the Federal Rules of Evidence allow the proponent to authenticate business records without producing a foundation witness. The proponent may do so by producing an affidavit from a person with knowledge averring that the record was made at or near the time of the occurrence, from information transmitted by a person with knowledge, kept in the regular course of business by a business whose regular practice it was to make the record.[200]

---

198. National Tea Co. v. Tyler Refrigeration Co., 339 N.W.2d 59, 61–62 (Minn. 1983); *But see* Karme v. Commissioner, 673 F.2d 1062, 1064 (9th Cir.1982) (records not admissible since government agent not a custodian or qualified witness capable of testifying that bank records were kept as regularly conducted business activity).

199. *See* MRT Const. Inc. v. Hardrives, Inc., 158 F.3d 478, 483 (9th Cir.1998) (Lay, J.) (client could lay foundation for bills of law firm if client relied on accuracy of bills in client's own business); United States v. Duncan, 919 F.2d 981 (5th Cir.1990) (insurance company representative could lay foundation for hospital records contained within insurance company records where insurance company routinely relied on hospital records). *But see* NLRB v. First Termite Control Co., 646 F.2d 424 (9th Cir. 1981) (NLRB sought to introduce a carrier's freight bill for transportation of lumber through an employee of the buyer of the lumber for the purpose of establishing the lumber's origin; held, freight bill not admissible under the business records exception because the witness knew nothing about how the carrier prepared the freight bill and the company employing the witness did not rely upon or use the information concerning the lumber's origin). *See also* Cameron v. Otto Bock Orthopedic Indus., 43 F.3d 14 (1st Cir.1994) (Boudin, J.). Plaintiff alleged that he had been injured by a defective artificial leg manufactured by the defendant. In upholding the trial judge's rulings on admissibility, the Court of Appeals held (1) that pre-accident "product failure reports" sent by prosthetists to defendant were admissible as nonhearsay evidence of

notice of defect, but (2) that post-accident "product failure reports" were inadmissible hearsay that did not fall under the business records exception. The reports had been prepared by prosthetists based partly upon reports from patients. The court remarked that "[w]hile the reports may be part of the business records of Otto Bock in a colloquial sense, that does not render admissible information contained in the records whose source is a non-party to the business. Under Fed. R. Evid. 803(6), the report must be made by a person acting 'in the course of a regularly conducted business activity.' It is quite clear that the prosthetists' patients are not part of Otto Bock's business." Cameron, 43 F.3d at 16.

200. *See* Fed. R. Evid. 803(6), 902(11), and 902(12), as amended effective December 1, 2000. *Compare* Calif. Evid. Code § 1562 (on laying foundation for business records by affidavit). Even before the federal amendments, Federal Rule 104(a), which allows trial judges to consider otherwise inadmissible hearsay in making preliminary determinations about whether foundation facts have been established, might have been read to allow a trial judge to permit the foundation for a business record to be established by affidavits. At least one court, however, declined to take that route on the facts before it. *See* Kolmes v. World Fibers Corp., 107 F.3d 1534 (Fed. Cir.1997) (affidavits not sufficient to lay foundation for business record because opponent needed opportunity to cross-examine sponsoring witness; moreover, consultant to business could not sponsor records because of lack of familiarity with record-keeping procedures).

§ 7.19 The Business Records Exception [FRE 803(6)]— The Business Duty Requirement

In the leading pre-Rules case of *Johnson v. Lutz*,[201] the plaintiff in a wrongful death action offered a police officer's report of the accident involved. The police officer had not been present at the accident; his report was based on statements by third persons about what had happened.

The New York statute purported to eliminate any requirement of personal knowledge. Nevertheless, the New York court held that the business records exception does not apply to third-party hearsay from someone who has no business duty to report.

The Advisory Committee for the Federal Rules of Evidence reached the same conclusion. *Johnson v. Lutz* was specifically cited and approved by the committee, which wrote that "[i]f . . . the supplier of the information does not act in the regular course [of business], an essential link is broken; the assurance of accuracy does not extend to the information [supplied]."[202]

In the years since the Federal Rules became effective, the courts have tended to water down the business duty requirement by holding that information provided by customers of the business is admissible if the business made an effort to verify its accuracy.[203] Where there was no such effort, however, the courts have tended to exclude the evidence.[204]

201. 170 N.E. 517 (N.Y.1930).

202. Fed. R. Evid. 803(6) advisory committee's note; *see* Ramrattan v. Burger King Corp., 656 F.Supp. 522, 529 (D.Md. 1987) (court excluded bystander's statement to police at site of auto accident because bystander was not acting in the regular course of business).

For an interesting case excluding testimony based on police records on grounds that the police records contained hearsay from declarants who were under no business duty, see People v. Hernandez, 63 Cal. Rptr.2d 769 (Cal.App.1997). Defendant was prosecuted for rape of two different victims committed in the same general area within a one-month period. The court allowed the prosecution to present the testimony of a police expert that she had searched the San Diego police department's "Sherlock" database for similar crimes, using search criteria such as "suspect not black" and "stranger rape" to identify similar cases. She reported that the only two rapes for an 18–month period in Beats 125 and 114 that had characteristics like those of the charged rapes were the charged rapes themselves. The prosecutor argued to the jury that the lack of evidence of similar crimes in the area before the defendant moved in or after his arrest pointed to the defendant. The court reversed defendant's conviction on hearsay grounds, saying that the "Sherlock" database did not qualify for the business records exception because it contained information from victims and witnesses who had no official duty to observe and report the relevant facts.

203. *See, e.g.*, United States v. Sokolow, 91 F.3d 396, 403–04 (3d Cir.1996) (insurance company documents containing unpaid insurance claims admissible under business records exception, even though some of the people documenting the information were not under a business duty, because insurance company had standard practice of verifying information); United States v. Emenogha, 1 F.3d 473, 482 (7th Cir.1993) (trial court properly admitted Currency Transaction Reports to rebut defendant's claim that an impostor used his name; obtaining identification before commencing transaction was a regular business practice and bank employees testified as eyewitnesses to the transactions with defendant).

204. *See* United States v. Vigneau, 187 F.3d 70, 74–75 (1st Cir.1999) (Western Union sender forms listing defendant as sender of money orders not admissible as business record of Western Union because sender under no business duty; Western Union did not require identification from

Of course, if the statement contained within the business record is admissible under another hearsay exception, then the business record exception and the other exception can combine to provide a route of admission.[205] For example, in *Kelly v. Wasserman*,[206] the New York courts held that an entry in the records of the welfare department by a caseworker who had talked to one of the parties to a lawsuit was admissible. The entry stated that the defendant had promised to allow the plaintiff to live rent-free in an apartment plaintiff had conveyed to him. The caseworker's statement was a business record, and the defendant's statement was the admission of a party.[207]

§ 7.20   The Business Records Exception [FRE 803(6)]— Transmitted by a Person With Knowledge

Strict personal knowledge is not required when admission is sought under the business records exception. For example, when a ledger entry made by a bookkeeper is offered, it is not necessary that the bookkeeper have personal knowledge of the underlying transactions represented by the entry. However, the rule does require *either* personal knowledge or that the information have been transmitted by a person with knowledge.[208] Several layers of hearsay can be involved without transgressing this rule, so long as the foundation is laid showing that the original source was a person with knowledge. For example, if employee one observes the transaction, reports it in the regular course of business to employee two, who transmits the information to employee three in the regular course, then the record comes from information that has been transmitted by a person with knowledge and is admissible.[209]

senders); United States v. McIntyre, 997 F.2d 687, 700–01 (10th Cir.1993) (motel arrival and departure log inadmissible as business record when guest supplied relevant information, employee only recorded it, and motel had no specific policy asking guests to show identification; receiving evidence was not plain error, however); Stahl v. State, 686 N.E.2d 89, 92 (Ind.1997) (affidavit executed for bank by customer in which customer averred that he had not authorized anyone to use his ATM card inadmissible in prosecution of person who withdrew money from customer's account using card; customer under no business duty).

205. *See* Fed. R. Evid. 805 (hearsay within hearsay admissible if each statement falls within an exception); *see e.g.*, United States v. Baker, 693 F.2d 183 (D.C.Cir. 1982).

206. 158 N.E.2d 241 (1959).

207. *See also* In re Fleet, Inc., 95 Bankr. 319, 330–31 (E.D.Pa.1989) (records admissible since OCA record was business record and statements within record were admissions of party opponents).

208. For an example of a case in which plaintiff failed to satisfy the rule, see Petrocelli v. Gallison, 679 F.2d 286, 289–91 (1st Cir.1982). There, the plaintiff offered a hospital record that stated that plaintiff had suffered a severed nerve in earlier surgery at another hospital. The source of knowledge was not apparent from the record and it appeared unlikely that the physician or nurses at the second hospital would have personally observed the injury. The evidence was excluded for failure to show that the information was transmitted by a person with knowledge. *See also* Ricciardi v. Children's Hosp. Medical Center, 811 F.2d 18, 21–23 (1st Cir.1987) (handwritten notation, not by doctor with personal knowledge of operation, inadmissible to show what happened during operation).

209. *See* 2 McCormick on Evidence § 290 (4th ed. John W. Strong ed. 1992); United States v. Baker, 693 F.2d 183, 188 (D.C.Cir.1982) (discussing double hearsay problem in employment context).

Issues involving transmission by a person with knowledge have become more complicated with the advent of computerized record-keeping.[210] Today, businesses of all sizes make extensive use of spreadsheets, databases, and other complex software, and locating the source of a particular item within a record is a considerably more daunting task than with handwritten ledgers. Indeed, even defining a "record" is complicated by the way computers store information and the fact that human input—often by a person with no knowledge of the data's accuracy—is necessary in order to retrieve information in a form that can be interpreted by a factfinder. As a result, while computerized record-keeping can be (and generally is) very accurate, some attention must be paid to the way in which the information presented to the court has been prepared, entered into the computer's storage system, and retrieved. One should not simply assume that because information was retrieved for trial from a computerized spreadsheet, database, or the like, it is reliable. The careful lawyer must always remain a skeptic.[211]

§ 7.21   The Business Records Exception [FRE 803(6)]—At or Near the Time

Federal Rule of Evidence 803(6) requires that the business record be made "at or near the time" of the event recorded. Thus, for example, where a telex describing bank deposits was made two years after the deposits, it did not satisfy this requirement of substantial contemporaneity.[212]

§ 7.22   The Business Records Exception [FRE 803(6)]— Lack of Trustworthiness

The final clause of Federal Rule 803(6) provides that even if a record otherwise qualifies as a business record, it can be excluded by the trial judge when "the source of information or the method or circumstances of preparation indicate lack of trustworthiness."

Probably the most common examples of records excluded for lack of trustworthiness are those that were prepared in anticipation of litigation.[213] However, occasionally other records are found that lack the requisite trustworthiness.[214]

---

210. For discussion of authentication of computer-generated records, see § **11.11**.

211. *See* Rudolph J. Peritz, *Computer Data and Reliability: A Call for the Authentication of Business Records Under the Federal Rules of Evidence*, 80 Nw. U.L. Rev. 956 (1986) (suggesting expanded foundation for admission of computerized business records).

212. United States v. Kim, 595 F.2d 755, 760–63 (D.C.Cir.1979); *cf.* Gulf South Machine, Inc. v. Kearney & Trecker Corp., 756 F.2d 377, 381 (5th Cir.1985) (logbook of machine malfunctions admissible where

similar books kept for other machines and entries logged within 24 hours of problem).

213. *See* § **7.23**.

214. *See* Pan–Islamic Trade Corp. v. Exxon Corp., 632 F.2d 539, 560 (5th Cir. 1980) (excluding record prepared originally as partisan document for presentation to Algerian oil agency); Schaps v. Bally's Park Place, Inc., 58 Bankr. 581, 583 (E.D.Pa. 1986), judgment aff'd 815 F.2d 693 (3d Cir. 1987) and judgment aff'd 815 F.2d 695 (3d Cir.1987) (books and records of debtor inadmissible because they were not submitted by the regular custodian and party admit-

The mere fact that a business record is self-serving does not mean that it will be excluded as untrustworthy. For example, a record showing that a department store customer owes money on a credit card is, when offered by the department store in a collection action, a self-serving statement. Yet if it was prepared in the regular course of business, not for litigation, and if the other requirements of the rule are met, it would be admitted routinely.[215]

§ 7.23   The Business Records Exception [FRE 803(6)]— Statements Prepared for Litigation

In another leading pre-Rules case, *Palmer v. Hoffman*,[216] the United States Supreme Court interpreted the federal business records statute to exclude from evidence a report prepared for a railroad by an engineer describing an accident in which the engineer had been involved. The Court held that statements prepared by parties in anticipation of litigation were not admissible under the exception, even if the business made a regular practice of collecting such reports. Searching for a way to exclude the report, the Court said that the railroad was in the railroad business, not the accident-reporting business, and therefore the accident report was not a business record.

The Advisory Committee for the Federal Rules of Evidence spoke approvingly of *Palmer v. Hoffman* in its note, but it did not adopt the Court's reasoning. Instead, it provided generally that the business records exception would not apply when the circumstances of preparation "indicate lack of trustworthiness." The mere fact that the record was prepared in anticipation of litigation might not always mean that it was untrustworthy, though the advisory committee seems to have expected that usually this would be the case.[217]

One example of a statement prepared for litigation that nevertheless qualifies as a business record is described in *Yates v. Bair Transport, Inc.*[218] There, reports to an insurance company concerning the plaintiff's injuries and prepared by doctors retained by the insurance company were admitted. The reports were offered by the plaintiff, not the company, and the court found the fact that they had been prepared for a company whose interests would be harmed if they were favorable to

ted that the records were not kept in business like manner, thus the records were untrustworthy).

215. *See* Matador Drilling Co. v. Post, 662 F.2d 1190, 1198–99 (5th Cir.1981) (plaintiff's daily drilling records admissible despite claim that they were self-serving); Downing v. Overhead Door Corp., 707 P.2d 1027, 1031 (Colo.App.1985) (error to exclude insurance adjuster's report even though it was claimed to be prejudicial and self-serving).

216. 318 U.S. 109, 111–15 (1943).

217. *See* Fed. R. Evid. 803(6) advisory committee's note.

218. 249 F.Supp. 681, 688–92 (S.D.N.Y.1965); *See also* State v. Therriault, 485 A.2d 986, 994–95 (Me.1984) (police report prepared in anticipation of litigation admissible when offered by other party). *But see* United States v. Blackburn, 992 F.2d 666, 670 (7th Cir.1993) (report prepared for FBI was not admissible under Rule 803(6) as a record of regularly conducted business activity; report was specially prepared at FBI's behest, with knowledge that any information it supplied would be used in an ongoing criminal investigation).

plaintiff to be a sufficient guarantee of trustworthiness when they were offered by plaintiff. The court, however, did not permit the plaintiff to offer reports prepared by doctors he retained.

As discussed previously,[219] computerized business records can sometimes present special foundational problems. One should not lose sight of the fact that reports prepared for litigation from computers can be no less self-serving than any other types of records. Both proponents and opponents of such reports should be prepared to consider carefully the foundational issues raised by computer-based records.

§ 7.24 The Business Records Exception [FRE 803(6)]— Special Problems With Hospital Records

Hospitals are businesses under the business records exception, whether they are for-profit or nonprofit institutions. However, that they are businesses does not automatically mean that everything in their records is admissible.

Hearsay Within Hearsay in Hospital Records

Sometimes hospital records contain hearsay within hearsay. For example, the hospital record might repeat what the plaintiff told the doctor, nurse, or other hospital employee. Suppose, for example, that the hospital record contains a statement by plaintiff describing the plaintiff's symptoms and the cause of plaintiff's injury.

If the record is offered in favor of the plaintiff, then a hearsay within hearsay problem arises because the plaintiff was under no business duty to the hospital, hence the business records exception does not cover the plaintiff's statement. The plaintiff's statement may, however, be covered by another exception, such as the Federal Rule of Evidence 803(4) exception for statements for medical diagnosis or treatment.[220] This exception would apply if the plaintiff's statements repeated within the record were reasonably pertinent to diagnosis or treatment. Statements by the plaintiff that his leg hurt or that he had been hit by a car would fit the exception. A statement by the plaintiff that the car that hit him went through a red light would not qualify.[221]

219. *See* § **7.20.**

220. *See* § **7.14.** *See also* Elmer v. Tenneco Resins, Inc., 698 F.Supp. 535, 543–45 (D.Del.1988) (medical records containing plaintiff's statements regarding 1952 surgery admissible).

221. *See* Merrow v. Bofferding, 581 N.W.2d 696, 701–03 (Mich.1998) (plaintiff claimed injury occurred after door's glass broke as he was using his hand to stop door from closing on young child; hospital record stated that plaintiff put his arm through plate glass window after "fight with his girlfriend"; held, though hospital record fits business record exception, hearsay-within-hearsay in record must be shown to fit

another exception; reference to fight with girlfriend had no medical relevance and was not admissible under Rule 803(4); statement also not admissible to impeach or as admission of a party because of inadequate foundation showing that plaintiff was the person who made the statement). *Cf.* Cook v. Hoppin, 783 F.2d 684, 689–90 (7th Cir. 1986). In that case the court held that the trial judge committed reversible error by admitting a statement in a hospital record that an injury had been caused by a "shoving or wrestling match." The anonymous source of the statement was not under any business duty to make it, so Rule 803(6) did not apply to it; Rule 803(4) could not be

If the record is offered against the plaintiff, then there is no problem with fitting the plaintiff's statement into a hearsay exception—it is the admission of a party opponent. However, the record that repeats the plaintiff's statement—the out-of-court declaration of the doctor or nurse asserting that the plaintiff made the statement—must also fit within an exception to be admissible. The obvious candidate is the business records exception. That exception will work for statements that are pertinent to diagnosis or treatment, such as statements that the plaintiff's leg hurt or that the plaintiff had been hit by a car, since the foundation showing that it is the regular practice of the hospital to make such records can be laid. However, the foundational requirements might not be met in cases in which the hospital employee-declarant recorded something that had no direct connection with medical treatment, such as a statement that the plaintiff had been hit by a car that went through a red light.[222] Hospitals do not regularly record assessments of whether the patient was the victim of a traffic law violation, and a hospital that did would be creating records that might be excluded under the final "lack of trustworthiness" clause of the business records rule. That the patient was injured by a car violating the law is not closely connected with the hospital's business; the hospital employee has no particular reason to record any such statements accurately. Thus, that part of the record would be excluded for lack of trustworthiness.

Diagnoses in Hospital Records

The business records exception specifically provides for the reception of "opinions" and "diagnoses" that are contained in hospital records. This provision would appear to undermine a series of pre-Rule cases that excluded hospital records containing expert opinions on grounds that the expert should be subject to cross-examination and the qualifications should be explored.[223] However, courts have sometimes found another

used as a basis for receiving the evidence because Rule 803(4) does not apply to "statements relating to fault which are not relevant to diagnosis or treatment." *See also* Brown v. St. Paul City Ry. Co., 62 N.W.2d 688, 695–96 (Minn.1954) (statement in hospital record that plaintiff's injury occurred when she fell from a step after streetcar door "was closed suddenly in her face" held inadmissible).

222. *See* Williams v. Alexander, 129 N.E.2d 417, 418–20 (N.Y.1955) (hospital record offered against plaintiff stated that plaintiff said "he was crossing the street and an automobile ran into another automobile that was at a standstill, causing the standing car to run into him"; trial court reversed for admitting statement on the grounds that it is not the business of the hospital to determine how the accident occurred). *See also* Wagner v. Thomas J. Obert Enterprises, 396 N.W.2d 223, 228 (Minn.1986) (excluding hospital record con-

taining plaintiff's version of accident when offered by defendant on basis that such a record lacks trustworthiness).

223. For examples of pre-Rules cases excluding medical opinions, see Raycraft v. Duluth, Missabe & Iron Range Ry. Co., 472 F.2d 27, 31 (8th Cir.1973) (stating that lack of opportunity to cross-examine expert medical witness may indicate lack of trustworthiness); England v. United States, 174 F.2d 466, 468 (5th Cir.1949) (excluding reports containing doctor's individual opinions about defendant's mental capacity); Mullican v. United States, 252 F.2d 398, 404 (5th Cir.1958) (hospital records concerning defendant's mental condition ruled expert opinions and excluded due to lack of opportunity to cross-examine). For post-Rules cases admitting diagnosis from hospital records, see Norton v. Colyer, 828 F.2d 384, 386–87 (6th Cir.1987) (medical records concerning plaintiff's alleged drug abuse as hospital diagnosis admissible under 803(6));

way to exclude diagnoses or opinions in medical records. For example, in *Fowler v. Carrollton Public Library*,[224] the plaintiff offered hospital records on the issue of damages. The records contained a statement that plaintiff had been hospitalized for three days with a diagnosis of "transient global amnesia." They were offered by plaintiff on the theory that the hospitalization was caused by the stress of mistreatment on the job. The court of appeals reversed on other grounds, and went on to discuss the issue to give guidance on retrial. It wrote that

> the district court here abused its discretion in admitting medical records from Fowler's brief hospital stay with no accompanying expert explanation of their significance. The fact of hospitalization in establishing pain and suffering is equivocal, at best, because no expert witness appeared to support Fowler's subjective belief that her "transient global amnesia" was caused by stress at work. The court sustained an objection preventing Fowler from testifying as a layman to the causal connection. This court as well as the jury remains completely unenlightened by the record evidence as to the cause and nature of transient global amnesia. The records could lead only to unwarranted speculation by the jury and inferences in favor of Fowler, and their prejudicial impact manifestly outweighed the benefit of verifying such uncontested facts as the hospitalization. This court has held, in a 1983 case, that where a plaintiff attempted to prove that racially motivated harassment proximately caused a fatal heart condition, speculation will not suffice. *Hamilton v. Rodgers*, 791 F.2d at 444–45. So should it be on retrial.

Though the court did not make specific reference to Rule 403 in its decision, perhaps this case could be viewed as one in which the record got over the hearsay ban by reason of Rule 803(6), only to run afoul of Rule 403 because, without the help of an expert to explain it, it was confusing and misleading.[225]

Another case excluding a diagnosis in a hospital record is *Petrocelli v. Gallison*.[226] In *Petrocelli*, the plaintiff's medical record, created for his second hernia surgery, contained a statement that in his first hernia surgery, the plaintiff's ilioinguinal nerve had been severed. The plaintiff was suing the physician who had allegedly severed the nerve. It was not clear where the statement in the medical record had come from; the plaintiff himself might have told the recordkeeper that the nerve had been severed in prior surgery. The court upheld the trial judge's exclu-

---

Pieters v. B–Right Trucking, Inc., 669 F.Supp. 1463, 1464–66 (N.D.Ind.1987) (hospital record of blood alcohol level admissible); Manko v. United States, 636 F.Supp. 1419, 1425 (W.D.Mo.1986) (medical diagnosis admissible under 803(6)).

224. 799 F.2d 976, 983 (5th Cir.1986).

225. *See also* Lovell v. Beavers, 987 S.W.2d 660 (Ark.1999) (because of potential for jury confusion, trial judge has discretion under Rule 403 to exclude unexplained medical records even if the records meet the requirements of the business records exception); Nauni v. State, 670 P.2d 126, 131 (Okla.Crim.App.1983) (excluding psychiatric opinions and diagnosis in hospital record under Rule 403 when doctors were not available for cross-examination, to clarify otherwise speculative and subjective process).

226. 679 F.2d 286, 289–91 (1st Cir. 1982).

sion of the record, noting that there was no foundation showing that the information had been transmitted by a "person with knowledge" as required by Rule 803(6). The court recognized that Rule 803(4) theory had not been advanced as a basis for letting in hearsay within hearsay if the source of information was the patient himself, but since the Rule 803(4) theory had not been advanced at trial it refused to allow it to be used on appeal.[227]

§ 7.25 The Business Records Exception [FRE 803(6)]— Police Records as Business Records

As a regularly conducted activity, the police qualify as a "business" within the meaning of the business records rule. Moreover, unlike Federal Rule of Evidence 803(8), Rule 803(6) contains no express prohibition of use of police records against a criminal defendant. However, the difference in language may have been inadvertent. It seems unlikely that Congress intended to exclude police records from use under Rule 803(8), while allowing them to be routinely admitted under Rule 803(6). For this reason, some courts have refused to allow them to be used against criminal defendants under either Rule,[228] though not all courts have reached this conclusion.[229] One could justify exclusion in terms of the language of Rule 803(6), by saying that when suspicion has focused upon a particular person, a police report incriminating that person is subject to dangers of bias that disqualify it under the final "trustworthiness" clause of the business records exception.

227. *Id*: *see also* Ricciardi v. Children's Hosp. Medical Center, 811 F.2d 18, 21–23 (1st Cir.1987) (handwritten note by doctor with no knowledge of operation inadmissible).

228. One leading case on the subject is United States v. Oates, 560 F.2d 45, 78 (2d Cir.1977), *on remand* 445 F.Supp. 351 (E.D.N.Y.), *aff'd without opinion*, 591 F.2d 1332 (2d Cir.1978). The Oates court reversed a conviction because the trial judge had admitted a laboratory report identifying a substance as heroin without requiring testimony of the chemist who performed the analysis. The court reasoned that the congressional intent not to allow law enforcement reports to be used against the defendant in criminal cases under Rules 803(8)(B) and (C) required that they be excluded when offered as business records under Rule 803(6). *See also* United States v. Cain, 615 F.2d 380, 382 (5th Cir.1980) (per curiam) (reversible error to receive prison escape report under 803(6); United States v. Ruffin, 575 F.2d 346, 356 (2d Cir.1978) (error, though harmless, to receive IRS investigator's file note describing phone call by defendant). However, in dicta the *Oates* court suggested that law enforcement records are not admissible under any

of the other hearsay exceptions. For discussion of the admissibility of police reports, see § **7.28**. This position has not been accepted generally. *See* United States v. Picciandra, 788 F.2d 39, 44 (1st Cir.1986) (DEA agent's report admissible against defendant under Rule 803(5)); United States v. Metzger, 778 F.2d 1195, 1201 (6th Cir. 1985) (certificate that defendant had not registered a destructive device or paid tax on one was admissible under Rule 803(10)); United States v. Neff, 615 F.2d 1235, 1241 (9th Cir.1980) (IRS certificate admissible under Rule 803(10)); United States v. Sawyer, 607 F.2d 1190, 1193 (7th Cir.1979) (reports excluded under Rule 803(8)(B) may be received under Rule 803(5)). *Cf.* United States v. Blackburn, 992 F.2d 666, 672 (7th Cir.1993) (report prepared for FBI investigation admissible under Rule 803(24) (now Rule 807) although inadmissible under Rule 803(6).

229. Some courts have also held that where the author testifies, Rule 803(8)(C) does not require exclusion of reports that satisfy Rule 803(6). *See, e.g.*, United States v. Sokolow, 91 F.3d 396, 404–05 (3d Cir. 1996); United States v. Hayes, 861 F.2d 1225, 1230 (10th Cir.1988); United States v. King, 613 F.2d 670, 672–73 (7th Cir. 1980).

§ 7.26 The Business Records Exception [FRE 803(6)]— Absence of Entry in Business Record [FRE 803(7)]

Federal Rule of Evidence 803(7) provides for admission of testimony about absence of an entry in a business record. The proponent must lay the foundation by showing that the record involved was kept in the regular course of business, from information transmitted by persons with knowledge, and that it was the regular practice of the business to make entries such as the one missing in this case. The foundation must also show that an adequate search was made for the missing record. Examples of the use of this provision include testimony about the absence of records of orders for fishing reels, to show that the orders had not been received;[230] the absence of records showing receipt of money, to show that the money was not received;[231] and the absence of any record of an offer to donate property, to show that no such offer was made.[232]

§ 7.27 The Public Records Exception [FRE 803(8)]

Federal Rule of Evidence 803(8), the public records exception, is one of the most complicated portions of Rule 803. The exception is divided into three sections, each of which covers a slightly different type of public record.

Part (A) of the Rule covers records and reports setting forth the activities of an office or agency. It applies to both civil and criminal cases. Any party, whether plaintiff, prosecution, or defendant, whether governmental or nongovernmental, can take advantage of the exception.[233]

Examples of matters falling under part (A) include payroll documents, personnel records, records of receipts and disbursements, and so forth.[234] More exotic examples include a report of the Department of Commerce about the usual ease of expediting defense deliveries, offered to show approval of a "jawboning" policy that gave defense orders informal priority,[235] and a report of the Center for Disease Control to show the existence of vaccine-induced polio cases,[236] though one might argue that these reports would fit more readily under part (B) or (C) of the Rule than part (A).

230. Fury Imports, Inc. v. Shakespeare Co., 554 F.2d 1376, 1381 (5th Cir.1977).

231. United States v. Zeidman, 540 F.2d 314, 319 (7th Cir.1976).

232. United States v. 34.60 Acres of Land, More or Less, In the County of Camden, 642 F.2d 788, 790 (5th Cir.1981).

233. Glen Weissenberger, Weissenberger's Federal Evidence § 803.42, at 495 (2d ed. 1995).

234. *See* e.g., Major v. Treen, 574 F.Supp. 325, 330 n. 6 (E.D.La.1983) (records of joint committee and subcommittee sessions of Louisiana legislature admissible under 803(8)(A)); Needham v. United States, 564 F.Supp. 419, 421–22 (W.D.Okla. 1983) (IRS computer printout of mailing admissible under 803(8)(A)).

235. Eastern Air Lines, Inc. v. McDonnell Douglas Corp., 532 F.2d 957, 983 n. 79 (5th Cir.1976).

236. Givens v. Lederle, 556 F.2d 1341, 1346 (5th Cir.1977).

Part (B) of the Rule covers matters observed pursuant to a duty imposed by law when there is also a duty to report. The rule contains an exception, however, applicable to criminal cases. Read literally, it prohibits use by any party in a criminal case, whether government or defense, of police or law enforcement reports. There is case authority, however, which supports the use of 803(8)(B) reports by a criminal defendant.[237] The rule permits either party in criminal cases to use the public records exception when the report is not a law enforcement report.[238] And in civil cases, reports falling within Part (B) of the rule can be offered by either party.

Examples of matters falling under part (B) include weather records, maps, a court reporter's transcript, an officer's letter describing the circumstances of a refusal to accept induction, a federal "warrant of deportation," routine INS records, and a police property receipt for a weapon.[239]

Part (C) of the Rule covers findings resulting from an investigation made pursuant to legal authority. It applies both in civil and criminal cases, but only the defendant may take advantage of the exception in criminal cases. Apparently the rule makers made a judgment that in fairness the government ought not to be able to suppress its own prior findings, but that the defendant is entitled to confront an accuser in a criminal case.[240]

Examples of findings falling under part (C) include a Coast Guard report containing conclusions about the causes of the grounding of an oil tanker, a report by state police authorities containing factual information and opinions about certain racial disturbances, administrative findings about sex discrimination or employment discrimination, and FAA findings about the safety of the plane that injured the plaintiff.[241]

---

237. *See* United States v. Smith, 521 F.2d 957, 968 (D.C.Cir.1975) (permitting defense use of police report despite literal language of Rule 803(8)(B)).

238. *See* 2 McCormick on Evidence § 296 (4th ed. John W. Strong ed. 1992).

239. *See* Fed. R. Evid. 803(8) advisory committee's note; United States v. Contreras, 63 F.3d 852, 857 (9th Cir. 1995) (warrant of deportation); United States v. Agustino–Hernandez, 14 F.3d 42, 43 (11th Cir. 1994) (routine INS records); United States v. Brown, 9 F.3d 907, 910–11 (11th Cir. 1993) (police property receipt for a weapon); United States v. Torres, 733 F.2d 449, 455 n. 5 (7th Cir.1984) (tribal rolls establishing defendants as American Indians admissible under 803(8)(B)); United States v. Grady, 544 F.2d 598 (2d Cir. 1976) (police records which routinely log serial numbers of guns recovered in Ireland admissible under 803(8)(B)).

240. *See* 2 McCormick on Evidence, *supra* note 238 § 296.

241. *See* In re Complaint of Nautilus Motor Tanker Co., Ltd., 85 F.3d 105 (3d Cir.1996) (Coast Guard report concerning grounding of oil tanker); Clark v. Clabaugh, 20 F.3d 1290, 1294–95 (3d Cir.1994) (Pennsylvania State Police report about circumstances surrounding certain civil disturbances); Chandler v. Roudebush, 425 U.S. 840, 863 n. 39 (1976) (administrative findings regarding claims of discrimination generally admissible under 803(8)(C); Melville v. American Home Assurance Co., 443 F.Supp. 1064, 1110–13 (E.D.Pa.1977) (FAA directives concerning safety of plane admissible), *rev'd on other grounds*, 584 F.2d 1306 (3d Cir.1978); 3 Stephen A. Saltzburg, Michael M. Martin & Daniel J. Capra, Federal Rules of Evidence Manual 1422–26 (6th ed. 1994).

Like the business records exception embodied in Rule 803(6), the public records exception allows the court to exclude evidence otherwise satisfying any part of the rule if the court finds that "the sources of information or other circumstances indicate lack of trustworthiness." This is an important part of the rule; the opponent of a party offering a public record should be prepared to demonstrate lack of trustworthiness, and the offering party should be prepared to defend the report's accuracy.

The rationale for the public records exception is (1) government officials are considered trustworthy, (2) the legal duty to be accurate is thought to provide incentive to be careful, and (3) the exception is considered necessary because public officials handle many matters and may forget facts important to the determination of the suit.[242]

Many public records are also business records, since the government is a business within the meaning of the business records exception. However, the public records exception serves an important function because it covers matters that are not recorded with regularity. For example, a civil defense official might only once record observations about nuclear damage, but the recorded observations would be public records.[243] Also, records based on information received from a person who had no duty to the public office are admissible when they qualify as "factual findings" under part (C) of Rule 803(8). For example, a hearing officer's findings would be admissible even if based on testimony from persons who were not public employees and who had no duty to report. In contrast, business records must be based on information received from persons with a business duty.[244]

---

242. *See* Fed. R. Evid. 803(8) advisory committee's note; 2 McCormick on Evidence, *supra* note 238 § 295. Note that the burden of proof is on the party opposing the introduction of public records to overcome their presumed trustworthiness. *See* Montiel v. City of Los Angeles, 2 F.3d 335, 341 (9th Cir.1993) (in § 1983 action, district court erred by failing to presume the trustworthiness of the Report of the Independent Commission on the Los Angeles Police Department (Christopher Commission Report) and by not shifting the burden of establishing the report's untrustworthiness to the defendant city). *Compare* Curtis v. M & S Petroleum, Inc., 174 F.3d 661, 673 (5th Cir.1999) (upholding trial judge's Rule 403 exclusion of state agency reports indicating that a refinery was not equipped to handle certain hazardous substances and that it did not have proper permits; there was a danger that the government report would be given too much weight; other evidence on the same point was not available).

243. *See, e.g.,* United States v. Versaint, 849 F.2d 827, 831 n. 9 (3d Cir.1988) (police report admissible under 803(8), thus not necessary to determine if report would

meet 803(6) requirements of reliability and regularity); United States v. Harris, 446 F.2d 129, 131 (7th Cir.1971) (letter from state hospital stating that defendant had failed to appear for alternative service admissible).

244. For a case that could be read as stating broadly that Rule 803(8)(C) cannot be a vehicle for findings based upon hearsay from a declarant who was not under a public duty, see Miller v. Field, 35 F.3d 1088 (6th Cir.1994). *Miller* was a federal civil rights case arising from an alleged prison rape. The court held that public records must contain either factual findings from firsthand knowledge of the report's preparer or conclusions derived from those facts. Hence, it ruled, state police reports setting forth witness statements and conclusions of investigators were inadmissible. While *Miller* reaches the right result on its facts, it goes too far in its statement of the limits on Rule 803(8)(C). Under that rule, when a public official actually makes "findings" pursuant to an investigation required by law (as opposed to merely recording information without evaluating it), then those

Finally, the public record has long been admissible without the need of a foundation witness. If it meets the self-authentication requirements of Rule 902 (which makes certified copies and like documents self-authenticating), then the foundation for the public records hearsay exception will usually be adequate, because the record will show on its face that it meets the requirements of Rule 803(8).[245] In contrast, in the absence of a stipulation to foundation, it has traditionally been necessary for the proponent of a business record to call a foundation witness. However, with the 2000 amendments to the Federal Rules, it is now possible to sponsor business records with affidavits instead of a live witness,[246] so this difference between public records and business records is now a matter of the form of the paperwork supporting the record.

§ 7.28   The Public Records Exception [FRE 803(8)]—Police Records

The public records exception contains specific language prohibiting the use of law enforcement records in most criminal cases.[247] Yet there are still some bases for arguing that certain law enforcement records are admissible against the defendant in criminal cases.

First, a law enforcement record could be offered not as a public record, but as a business record. There is no doubt that law enforcement agencies are businesses within the meaning of the business records rule. The rule is not restricted to profit-making private activity, but applies to any regularly conducted activity, whether it is public, charitable, or otherwise.[248]

However, the legislative intent of the public records exception indicates a strong purpose to prevent the police officer's report from taking his or her place on the witness stand. Apparently Congress simply overlooked the fact that police reports and other law enforcement records would also qualify as business records. Because of the intent to exclude law enforcement records when offered under the public records exception, some courts have held that they are likewise not admissible as

findings are admissible unless shown to be untrustworthy. Passages of the *Miller* opinion could be read to say that findings based upon statements from declarants who are not under a public duty are simply inadmissible, whether or not they are shown to be untrustworthy. Under that reasoning, findings by hearing officers conducting administrative hearings would be inadmissible whenever based on hearing testimony by persons not under a public duty, a result that seems clearly inconsistent with the intent of the rule makers and the examples given in the Advisory Committee's Note.

245. *See* Zambito v. Blair, 610 F.2d 1192, 1198 (4th Cir.1979) (certified "Order Finding Probable Cause" admissible under Rules 902(1) and 803(8)(A)); United States v. Hart, 673 F.Supp. 932, 934 n. 2 (N.D.Ind. 1987) (government exhibit self-authenticating under 902(1) and admissible under 803(8)). Note also that Rule 803(8) does not require record to be created contemporaneously with the event recorded, as in 803(6). *See* Weissenberger, *supra* note 233 § 803.41, at 426–26.

246. *See* § **7.18**, supra.

247. *See* Fed. R. Evid. 803(8)(B), (C).

248. *See* Fed. Rules of Evidence, H.R. Conf. Rep. No. 1597, 93d Cong., 2d Sess. 11 (1974).

business records, though other courts have reached the contrary conclusion.[249]

Second, some recent case law has supported the admission of law enforcement records under Rule 803(5), the exception for past recollection recorded. This result has been justified on grounds that Congress, in excluding law enforcement records, was concerned about the danger that the defendant would lose the right to cross-examine the officer who made the report. This danger is not present when the past recollection recorded exception is used, because under that exception the person who made or adopted the record must testify in order to lay the foundation for the admission of the report.[250]

Third, courts have allowed law enforcement records into evidence under other exceptions, including Rule 803(10) (the exception for evidence of absence of a public record),[251] and Rule 803(24) (one of the former residual hearsay exceptions, now contained in Rule 807).[252]

Finally, some courts have created an exception for routine, non-adversarial law enforcement reports. Rule 803(8) does not specifically distinguish between routine reports of objective facts, such as records of serial numbers, or fingerprint records, and reports prepared during an investigation that incriminate a particular defendant. However, a number of courts have made a distinction of this nature. They have used words such as "routine," "non-adversarial," "ministerial," "objective," and "non-evaluative" to describe law enforcement records deemed admissible against the defendant despite the restrictions of Rule 803(8).[253] Typically, these courts have reasoned that routine non-adversarial reports are not subject to the same dangers of bias and clouded perception

249. *See* § **7.25.**

250. *See* United States v. Picciandra, 788 F.2d 39, 44 (1st Cir.1986) (DEA agent's report was admissible against criminal defendants under Rule 803(5)); United States v. Sawyer, 607 F.2d 1190, 1193 (7th Cir. 1979) (reports excluded under Rule 803(8)(B) may be received under Rule 803(5)).

251. *See, e.g.*, United States v. Metzger, 778 F.2d 1195, 1201 (6th Cir.1985) (certificate that defendant had not registered a destructive device or paid tax on one admissible under 803(10) even if record kept by law enforcement official); United States v. Neff, 615 F.2d 1235, 1241 (9th Cir.1980) (IRS certificate admissible under 803(10)); United States v. Yakobov, 712 F.2d 20, 25 (2d Cir.1983) (upon a proper showing of diligent search, ATF certificate stating that there was no record that defendant had applied for or received a firearms license would be admissible).

252. *See, e.g.*, United States v. Blackburn, 992 F.2d 666, 672 (7th Cir.1993) (re-

port prepared for FBI investigation admissible under Rule 803(24)).

253. *See* United States v. Wiley, 979 F.2d 365, 369 (5th Cir.1992) (in action for passing counterfeit IRS obligations, reports indicating that IRS agents investigated and froze third-party's account admissible under public records hearsay exception because law enforcement actions occurred within "routine, non-adversarial setting"); United States v. Puente, 826 F.2d 1415, 1417–18 (5th Cir.1987) (held, Customs Service records of license plates of cars crossing from Mexico to United States admissible under 803(8), even though Customs officers are law enforcement officers; 803(8)(B) does not apply to routine, objective factual observations); United States v. Wilmer, 799 F.2d 495, 500–01 (9th Cir. 1986) (1987) (calibration certificate for breathalyzer admissible); United States v. Gilbert, 774 F.2d 962, 964–65 (9th Cir. 1985) (report on location of latent print admissible; court notes non-evaluative, routine, nonadversarial nature of report).

as are other police reports.[254] To put it another way, in these cases the cross-examination is most unlikely to yield information that would be helpful to the defendant. In some limited circumstances, routine police activities, such as the recording of serial numbers, might be considered "activities of the office" and hence under part (A).[255]

§ 7.29 The Public Records Exception [FRE 803(8)]—The Concept of "Factual Findings"

Part (C) of Federal Rule of Evidence 803(8) permits the admission, in civil suits and against the government in criminal cases, of reports containing "factual findings" derived from investigations made under authority of law.

Before *Beech Aircraft v. Rainey*,[256] there was a conflict of authority in the federal courts on the question whether opinions contained in Rule 803(8)(C) reports were also admissible. For example, the Second Circuit excluded an FDA finding that a drug was dangerous on grounds that it was a medical opinion, not a factual finding.[257] However, the Sixth Circuit admitted a finding by an administrative law judge that a tow boat captain had not been negligent, saying that "[a]lthough a finding that [the captain's] actions were reasonable is somewhat conclusory, we do not believe that such a label is controlling.... In our view a finding that amounts to an inference drawn from subsidiary findings is admissible under Rule 803(8)(C)."[258]

In *Beech Aircraft v. Rainey*, the United States Supreme Court came down on the side of free admission of opinions. *Beech Aircraft* was a wrongful death action against an aircraft manufacturer by the survivors of two naval aviators who had been killed in a crash during a training exercise. A naval investigator had issued a JAG report describing the surrounding facts and also offering the opinion that the most probable cause of the crash was pilot error. The Court held that the opinion was admissible, interpreting Rule 803(8)(C) to permit reception of opinions contained in investigative reports so long as the reports also contain factual findings.[259]

254. *See* United States v. Gilbert, 774 F.2d 962, 965 (9th Cir.1985).

255. *Cf.* United States v. Grady, 544 F.2d 598, 604 (2d Cir.1976) (police records of routine nature, such as recording of serial numbers, are admissible under 803(8); in putting limits on admissibility of police records, Congress did not have this sort of routine function in mind); United States v. Orozco, 590 F.2d 789, 793–94 (9th Cir.1979) (computer cards recording vehicle license plate numbers admissible under 803(8)).

256. 488 U.S. 153 (1988).

257. Lindsay v. Ortho Pharmaceutical Corp., 637 F.2d 87, 94 (2d Cir.1980); *see also* Matthews v. Ashland Chemical, Inc., 770 F.2d 1303, 1309–10 (5th Cir.1985)

(memo outlining future inquiries into safety measures and offering opinions on expected results inadmissible under 803(8)(C)).

258. *See* Complaint of Paducah Towing Co., Inc., 692 F.2d 412, 420 (6th Cir.1982); *see also* Kehm v. Procter & Gamble Mfg. Co., 724 F.2d 613, 619–20 (8th Cir.1983) (reports analyzing statistical relationship between tampon use and toxic shock syndrome admissible); Zenith Radio Corp. v. Matsushita Elec. Indus. Co., 505 F.Supp. 1125, 1145 (E.D.Pa.1980) (factual findings as used in the Rule encompass evaluative reports of public agencies).

259. 488 U.S. 153 (1988). *See* Goodman v. Pennsylvania Turnpike Com'n, 293 F.3d 655 (3d Cir.2002) (held, Budget and

The mere fact that conclusions can be admitted under Rule 803(8) does not mean that they *must* be admitted. Conclusions may still be excluded if shown to be untrustworthy, prejudicial, confusing, or a waste of time. Exclusion may be grounded either on the trustworthiness proviso of Rule 803(8) or under the general discretion granted by Rule 403.[260]

Note that even in a jurisdiction that excludes the public record from direct admission because it contains opinions and not findings, the record still might be the basis upon which an expert could rely in forming his or her opinion under Rule 703, which allows experts to rely upon data not admissible in evidence.[261]

Finance Committee Report criticizing political partisanship in appointments to state office admissible as Rule 803(8)(C) record in case in which plaintiff claimed he had been denied a promotion for political reasons); Ake v. General Motors Corp., 942 F.Supp. 869, 877 (W.D.N.Y.1996) (tentative "findings" of National Highway Traffic Safety Administration excluded under Rule 803(8)'s trustworthiness proviso; they might have been changed after public hearing); Distaff, Inc. v. Springfield Contracting Corp., 984 F.2d 108, 111–12 (4th Cir.1993) (held, report by naval investigator about cause of fire admissible, even though Navy refused to permit him to testify subject to cross-examination). Note that the evidence may still be inadmissible if there is reason to suspect it lacks trustworthiness. *See* Nipper v. Snipes, 7 F.3d 415, 417 (4th Cir. 1993) (held, judicial findings of fact are not "public records" within the meaning of Rule 803(8)); Cortes v. Maxus Exploration Co., 977 F.2d 195, 201 (5th Cir.1992) (held, trial judge did not err in excluding conclusory EEOC document containing determination that plaintiff had not been sexually harassed; though government reports are presumptively reliable under Rule 803(8) in the absence of an affirmative showing of untrustworthiness by the opponent, here the danger of prejudice substantially outweighed the probative value, justifying exclusion under Rule 403); Kemper Architects v. McFall, Konkel, 843 P.2d 1178, 1188 (Wyo.1992) (held, trial court properly excluded exhibit prepared by Army Corps of Engineers under state's version of Rule 803(8)(C); exhibit lacked indicia of trustworthiness because it contained multiple hearsay-within-hearsay statements, impermissible legal conclusions, and appeared to have been prepared with a view towards possible litigation); 5 Weinstein's Federal Evidence § 803.13[4][b], at 803–93 to 803–94 (2d Ed. Joseph M. McLaughlin ed. 1997).

260. *See* United States v. Jackson–Randolph, 282 F.3d 369 (6th Cir.2002)

(held, lack of trustworthiness precluded hearing examiner from relying on accomplice testimony in reaching findings); U.S. Steel, LLC v. Tieco, Inc., 261 F.3d 1275 (11th Cir.2001) (held, statement of facts in prior judicial opinion, drafted for prior judge by proponent of evidence in self-serving fashion, is inadmissible hearsay not fitting under any exception); Lathem v. Department of Children and Youth Services, 172 F.3d 786, 791 (11th Cir.1999) (held, trial judge had discretion under Rule 403 to exclude EEOC no-cause determination in gender discrimination case after finding that agency had not made a complete investigation); Ake v. General Motors Corp., 942 F.Supp. 869, 879 (W.D.N.Y. 1996) (tentative "findings" of National Highway Traffic Safety Administration excluded under Rule 803(8)'s trustworthiness proviso; they might have been changed after public hearing); Kemper Architects, P.C. v. McFall, Konkel & Kimball Consulting Engineers, Inc., 843 P.2d 1178 (Wyo.1992) (held, trial court properly excluded exhibit prepared by Army Corps of Engineers under state's version of Federal Rule 803(8)(C); exhibit lacked indicia of trustworthiness because it contained multiple hearsay-within-hearsay, impermissible legal conclusions, and appeared to have been prepared with a view toward possible litigation). *But see* Blake v. Pellegrino, 329 F.3d 43 (1st Cir.2003) (trial judge erred in striking cause of death from death certificate on ground it was inaccurate; trustworthiness proviso of Rule 803(8)(C) does not allow judge to strike hearsay merely because judge finds it unpersuasive; in this context, the proviso refers to matters such as manner in which death certificate was completed, the sources of information utilized, and credentials of the person completing it, and how the record was maintained, not to whether the judge found the conclusion credible).

261. *See* **§ 10.08;** Smith v. Isuzu Motors Ltd., 137 F.3d 859, 862–63 (5th Cir.

Because there is no "business duty" requirement in Rule 803(8)(C), the official making the factual finding may use trustworthy hearsay from persons outside the government.[262]

There is a division of authority on the issues of whether Rule 803(8)(C) may be used to admit prior convictions or judicial findings of fact. A persuasive argument can be made that the rule applies only to administrative findings, and that judicial findings are covered by other exceptions. For discussion, see § 7.40.

§ 7.30   Absence of Public Record or Entry [FRE 803(10)]

Federal Rule of Evidence 803(10) provides an exception for evidence that data was not contained in a public record, provided that certification or testimony shows that a diligent search was made.

Examples of the operation of this exception include reception of a certificate from the IRS reciting its failure to find income tax returns, as evidence of failure to file,[263] and use of a certificate from the Navy reciting failure to find a record of registration, to show that a vehicle was not registered.[264]

At common law, evidence of a diligent search through public records was admissible to show the absence of a record, but some courts would not allow the search to be established by a certificate from a public official reciting that the diligent search had been made.[265] Rule 803(10) cures that omission.

The opponent of the record can seek to rebut the claim that a diligent search occurred. Because the certification provision allows the substitution of a certificate for the person who did the search, this can be difficult unless the opponent has affirmative witnesses. However, in some instances lack of diligence may appear from the face of the certificate, as when the certificate uses incorrect names or contains other mistakes.[266]

The public records exception, Rule 803(8), prohibits use of police and other law enforcement records as evidence against criminal defendants. Rule 803(10) does not contain any such prohibition, and there is sub-

1998) (excluding National Highway Traffic Safety Administration staff memos on grounds that the memos did not reflect "factual findings" of the agency, but rather the views of individual staff members, which the agency later declined to adopt).

262. *See, e.g.,* Union Pacific Railroad Co. v. Kirby Inland Marine, Inc., 296 F.3d 671 (8th Cir.2002) (in case in which river barge towboat collided with an allegedly defective railroad bridge, district court did not abuse discretion in admitting a Coast Guard order to alter the bridge; the fact that Coast Guard investigators relied on hearsay did not make the report untrustworthy).

263. *See* United States v. Cepeda Penes, 577 F.2d 754, 761 (1st Cir.1978) (certificate from computer check showing defendant had not filed tax returns admissible under Rule 803(10)).

264. United States v. Martinez, 700 F.2d 1358, 1364–65 (11th Cir.1983) (under Rule 803(10), no error to admit naval certificate concluding that vessel was not registered).

265. 5 John H. Wigmore, Evidence in Trials at Common Law § 1678 (James H. Chadbourn rev. 1974).

266. *See* United States v. Yakobov, 712 F.2d 20 (2d Cir.1983).

stantial authority for allowing evidence of the absence of a law enforcement record to be used against a criminal defendant. For example, in *United States v. Yakobov*,[267] the Second Circuit ruled that upon a proper showing of diligent search, an ATF certificate stating that there was no record that defendant had applied for or received a firearms license would be admissible, even though the record was a law enforcement record.[268]

§ 7.31 Records of Vital Statistics; Death Certificates [FRE 803(9)]

Federal Rule of Evidence 803(9) provides a hearsay exception for "[r]ecords or data compilations, in any form, of births, fetal deaths, deaths, or marriages, if the report thereof was made to a public office pursuant to requirements of law."

This exception allows official records of birth, death, and marriage to be received in evidence even if someone other than a public official prepares the records.[269] Thus, a death certificate is admissible whether it is prepared by a private doctor, mortician, or public coroner; a marriage certificate is admissible whether it was prepared by a judge or by a minister. In the absence of Rule 803(9), these records might be considered admissible under a generous reading of Rule 803(8)(B) (the public records exception), but the present exception resolves any doubt about whether the private status of the record-makers affects admissibility.

Many states also have statutes providing for the admission of death certificates. These statutes often provide that death certificates are prima facie evidence of the facts stated in them.[270]

Death certificates have been offered in evidence in a wide variety of situations.[271] These include the prosecution's offer of a death certificate to show the victim in a murder case died of gunshot wounds;[272] an insurance defense counsel's offer, in a suit to recover on a life insurance

---

267. *Id.* at 25.

268. *See also* United States v. Metzger, 778 F.2d 1195, 1201 (6th Cir.1985) (held, certificate that defendant had not registered a destructive device or paid tax on it was admissible under 803(10) even if record kept by law enforcement official); United States v. Neff, 615 F.2d 1235, 1241 (9th Cir.1980) (IRS certificate admissible under Rule 803(10)).

269. *See, e.g.*, 5 Weinstein's Federal Evidence § 803.14[1], at 803–102 (2d Ed. Joseph M. McLauglin ed. 1997).

270. D.E. Evins, Annotation, *Official Death Certificate as Evidence of Cause of Death in Civil or Criminal Action*, 21 A.L.R. 3d 418, 422 n.5 (1968 & Supp. 1996). If a narrow state statute predates the adoption of a state version of Rule 803(9), Rule 803(9) supersedes the statute or at least expands the limits of admissibility-provided

the state supreme court adopted Rule 803(9) under an enabling act that renders prior inconsistent statutes ineffective after implementation of Rule 803(9).

271. *See generally id.* (discussing the admissibility of death certificates in wrongful death actions, actions on life insurance policies, will contests, personal injury actions, actions to recover property, and criminal homicide prosecutions).

272. *See, e.g.*, Stevens v. Bordenkircher, 746 F.2d 342 (6th Cir.1984). *But see* 2 Michael H. Graham, Handbook of Federal Evidence § 803.10, at 519 (4th ed. 1996) (stating that if a record concerning cause of death is offered against a criminal defendant, it should not be received because admission would violate the policy of Rule 803(8)).

policy, of a statement that the cause of death was suicide;[273] the government's offer of death certificates in a tax case to show that the death of two taxpayers was not simultaneous, and therefore one inherited from the other;[274] and a plaintiff's offer, in an asbestosis wrongful death action, of a death certificate to show that plaintiff's decedent died of adenocarcinoma of the lung.[275]

The reception of statements from death certificates may raise dangers of unreliability. For example, a death certificate may contain assertions based on hearsay or speculation by a record-maker who does not have firsthand knowledge of the facts stated in the certificate; or a lay coroner may express a medical opinion in the certificate that only a qualified expert could state with confidence. In these situations, cross-examination of the person who prepared the death certificate would be useful. Counsel faced with an unreliable statement in a death certificate could object on several possible grounds:

1. An objection might assert that the certificate contains statements not based on personal knowledge or contains hearsay within hearsay. Courts often confound the personal knowledge objection and the problem of hearsay within hearsay. (For a distinction between the two, see **7.58**.) The advisory committee's comments to Rule 803 state that neither Rule 803 nor Rule 804 dispenses with the requirement of personal knowledge.[276] Thus, when a death certificate describes something that the coroner clearly did not observe, the personal knowledge objection should prevent reception of the evidence.[277]

---

273. For cases excluding such statements, see Security Life Ins. Co. v. Blitch, 270 S.E.2d 349, 352 (Ga.App.1980) (holding trial court did not err in deleting "homicide" from death certificate before receiving certificate in double indemnity insurance recovery case); Hestad v. Pennsylvania Life Ins. Co., 204 N.W.2d 433, 436 (Minn.1973) (indicating courts should redact portion of death certificate saying that suicide or accident was cause of death). In Hestad, the Minnesota Supreme Court stated:

[D]eath certificates are not admissible to show the manner in which the death occurs, such as by accident or suicide, but may be admitted only to show the immediate cause of death, which, in this case, was carbon monoxide poisoning. Statements as to the manner of death in a death certificate constitute conclusions and hearsay.

Id. Accord State v. Jurgens, 424 N.W.2d 546, 552 (Minn.App.1988) (dictum).

274. See, e.g., Vaughn v. United States, 536 F.Supp. 498 (W.D.Va.1982). In Vaughn, an assailant shot and killed a father and daughter in their home. Id. at 500. According to the death certificate, the father died at home and the daughter died

about an hour later at the hospital. Id. The court admitted the certificate as evidence that the deaths were not simultaneous, and thus the daughter's estate owed additional taxes because she inherited money from her father upon his death. Id. at 501–02.

275. See, e.g., Burton v. Johns–Manville Corp., 613 F.Supp. 91 (W.D.Pa.1985). In Burton, the district court explains why a death certificate stating that the decedent died of adenocarcinoma of the lung was admitted in an asbestos case. The court applied a Pennsylvania statute making a death certificate prima facie evidence of its contents. Id. at 93 n.2. The court also noted that, in any event, reception of the death certificate did not harm the defendant because a medical expert with firsthand knowledge was cross-examined about the cause of death.

276. Fed. R. Evid. 803 advisory committee's note (paragraph 3, preceding discussion of Rule 803(1)).

277. See Bowman v. Redding & Co., 449 F.2d 956, 961 (D.C.Cir.1971) (statement in death certificate describing how decedent's fall occurred inadmissible); State v. Gould, 704 P.2d 20 (Mont.1985) (admis-

2. Where the death certificate expresses an expert opinion, an objection may claim that the declarant was not qualified as an expert, or at least that the declarant should be produced for cross-examination about qualifications.[278] When the record-maker is not a qualified medical expert and the certificate is admitted, counsel can argue that the medical conclusions stated in it are insufficient to get the opponent past a directed verdict.[279]

3. Where the death certificate contains extraneous matter, counsel can argue that Rule 803(9)'s prerequisite that the record be made "pursuant to requirements of law" is not satisfied as to the extraneous matter, because its inclusion is not required by law. Similarly, where the argument for admission rests on a state statute that admits death certificates as prima facie evidence of the "facts" stated in them, some courts have redacted the certificates to exclude matters deemed to be opinion or speculation rather than fact.[280]

When an unreliable death certificate is offered in a criminal case, the confrontation clause furnishes another basis for objection. In a

sion of portion of death certificate containing statement that decedent was in a pick-up truck which left roadway and over-turned, ejecting decedent, was error because statement was based on hearsay; error harmless under circumstances). *But see* Shell v. Parrish, 448 F.2d 528, 531 (6th Cir.1971) (statement in death certificate that "victim fell in ditch" admissible). One eminent authority has suggested, however, that, in accordance with prior precedent, courts should admit such statements for what they are worth. 5 Weinstein's Federal Evidence, *supra* note 269 § 803.14[4], at 803–107.

A number of cases exclude statements in death certificates on personal knowledge or hearsay within hearsay grounds. *Gould* was a negligent homicide case in which the victim was a passenger in the defendant's car. The victim's death certificate contained the statement, "Decedent was passenger in a pick-up truck which left the roadway and over-turned. She was ejected from the vehicle." State v. Gould, 704 P.2d 20 (Mont. 1985). The court held that the trial court erred in admitting that portion of the certificate. The testimony of the coroner who prepared the certificate established that the statement was based on hearsay. The error was harmless, however, because the death certificate merely confirmed in an insignificant way conclusions already established by other evidence. *Id.* at 30. Note that the court found the certificate should have been redacted even though both Montana Rule 803(9) and a Montana statute providing that the certificate was prima facie evidence

of cause of death were applicable. The court construed the rule and the statutes not to require the admissions such as the one in *Gould. But see* Shell v. Parrish, 448 F.2d 528, 531 (6th Cir.1971) (statement in death certificate that "victim fell in ditch" admissible).

278. *See, e.g.,* Charleston Nat. Bank v. Hennessy, 404 F.2d 539, 542 (5th Cir.1968) (holding lay coroner's opinion that decedent "apparently had heart attack" would not be admissible if offered in live testimony and statement did not become admissible because included in official death certificate).

279. *See* De Courcy v. Trustees of Westminster Presbyterian Church, Inc., 134 N.W.2d 326, 328–29 (Minn.1965) (holding death certificate prepared by nonexpert insufficient substitute for expert testimony regarding cause of death, and concluding trial court should have directed verdict for defendant hospital where death allegedly occurred as a result of fracture caused by hospital's negligence).

280. *See* Carswell v. State, 320 S.E.2d 249, 253 (Ga.App.1984) (excluding statement that "auto struck pedestrian"). *See also* Lockwood v. Travelers Ins. Co., 498 P.2d 947, 952 (Colo.1972) (error to admit death certificate containing conclusory statement that death resulted from accident rather than suicide or homicide); People v. Fiddler, 258 N.E.2d 359, 361 (Ill.1970) (coroner's statement about cause of death not a "fact" within meaning of state statute making facts in death certificates admissible).

leading federal case, *Stevens v. Bordenkircher*,[281] the Sixth Circuit Court of Appeals held that the reception of a death certificate of questionable reliability in lieu of live testimony violated the confrontation clause. *Stevens* was a habeas case arising from a state court murder conviction. One of the issues at trial was whether the alleged victim was murdered or simply disappeared. The state claimed that bones found in a sawdust pile were those of the victim. The state's principal evidence of murder consisted of the testimony of a highly questionable witness who described alleged inculpatory statements the codefendants made to him. The state also introduced a death certificate that identified the body recovered from the sawdust pile as the victim's, stated that gunshot wounds to the thorax caused the victim's death, and noted the approximate date of death. This information, on the surface, corroborated the story of the state's chief witness. Although the coroner who prepared the death certificate had been subpoenaed, the prosecutor released him from the subpoena as a personal favor and, over objection, produced the death certificate instead. The death certificate purported to be an autopsy that revealed the identity of the body, the cause of death, and the approximate date of death. The state court trial resulted in the petitioner's conviction. At the federal evidentiary hearing on the habeas motion, the coroner stated that only fifteen pounds of bones remained when he examined the body. The coroner also admitted that he did not find any metallic fragments or other evidence of gunshot death, and that he obtained the information stated in the certificate from the police. The Sixth Circuit held that receiving the death certificate under these circumstances violated the petitioner's constitutional right to confrontation. Citing the Supreme Court's decision in *Ohio v. Roberts*,[282] the court

281.   746 F.2d 342 (6th Cir.1984). *But see* Manocchio v. Moran, 919 F.2d 770, 772 (1st Cir.1990). There, the medical examiner's autopsy report contained the following statement: "The decedent was beaten by assailants in a parking lot on Mineral Springs Avenue, North Providence, on November 2, 1980 at approximately 1:00 A.M.—He was taken to Roger Williams General Hospital where he died at 1:47 A.M.—Manner of death: Homicide." The First Circuit accepted the proposition that Rule 803(9) was not a "firmly rooted" hearsay exception and hence that hearsay admitted under it should be subjected to special scrutiny for trustworthiness when challenged on 6th Amendment grounds. Nevertheless, the court found that the record before it had sufficient indicia of reliability to survive 6th Amendment scrutiny.

For a case raising similar confrontation issues in the context of medical records, see Pickett v. Bowen, 626 F.Supp. 81, 83–85 (M.D.Ala.1985) (holding medical record describing ruptured hymen inadmissible in child sexual abuse case as confrontation clause violation; examining doctor testified

at habeas hearing to facts that, if brought out on cross, would have shown vagina's condition required 3–5 minutes of manipulation, not merely one touch as described in child's testimony).

282.   448 U.S. 56 (1980). The *Roberts* Court established a two-pronged test for determining whether the introduction of hearsay violates the confrontation clause. The first prong of the *Roberts* test requires that the prosecution produce the hearsay declarant or demonstrate that the declarant is unavailable. *Id.* at 65. This requirement, however, is not absolute: it only applies in the "usual" case and the prosecution need not demonstrate unavailability if the utility of confrontation is "remote." *Id.* at 65 n.7. The second prong of the *Roberts* test requires that the hearsay have "adequate 'indicia of reliability.'" *Id.* at 65. In some cases, this prong requires "a showing of particularized guarantees of trustworthiness." *Id.* at 66 & n.9. The Supreme Court, however, apparently recognized the need for certainty in criminal trials and provided more specific guidance. The Court indicated that courts should defer to established

concluded that the death certificate's assertions lacked the required indicia of trustworthiness, and also noted that the death certificate's maker was available for cross-examination but was excused by the prosecutor.[283]

§ 7.32   Learned Treatise Exception [FRE 803(18)]

Federal Rule of Evidence 803(18) provides a generous exception for learned treatises and other expert publications. The exception allows the introduction of passages from books, scholarly journals, technical magazines, and other published works on any science or art, once a foundation has been established that the work is a reliable authority.

The exception is based on the theory that most learned publications are reliable enough to be helpful. The author has no bias or interest in any particular case. In addition the author realizes that the work will be read and evaluated by other members of the same profession. Thus the author is highly motivated to be accurate and complete.[284]

The federal rule makes substantial changes in the common law. The common law theory was that learned treatises were admissible solely for purposes of impeaching experts.[285] In some jurisdictions, the expert could not be impeached with the treatise unless the expert had testified that he or she had relied upon the treatise in preparing an expert opinion. This theory was based upon the view that the treatise was not being used to prove the truth of what it asserted, but only to show that the expert was unreliable. For example, suppose a case in which plaintiff's expert testified that a patient's spleen should be removed only if severely damaged. Suppose also that the defense attorney has in hand a treatise

hearsay exceptions by stating reliability can be inferred "without more" where evidence falls within a "firmly rooted" hearsay exception. *Id.* at 66. For extended discussion of the Supreme Court's analysis of hearsay and the confrontation clause, see §§ **7.66– 7.68**.

Cf., Manocchio v. Moran, 919 F.2d 770 (1st Cir.1990) (although finding no confrontation violation under the circumstances, court finds *Roberts* requires a finding of adequate "indicia of reliability" and because Rule 803(9) is not "firmly rooted," the government must show "particularized guarantees of trustworthiness").

283.   It should be noted that since *Stevens* was decided in 1984, the Supreme Court has interpreted *Roberts* rather narrowly. Under the Court's current analysis, if Montana's broad interpretation of the hearsay exception is "firmly rooted," no further confrontation analysis would be required.

284.   Fed. R. Evid. 803(18) advisory committee's note; 2 McCormick on Evidence § 321 (4th ed. John W. Strong ed.

1992); *see also* Schneider v. Revici, 817 F.2d 987, 991 (2d Cir.1987).

285.   *See generally* 2 McCormick on Evidence, *supra* note 284 § 321; *see also* Brown v. United States, 419 F.2d 337, 341 (8th Cir.1969) (medical treatises may be used in cross-examination "but are not admissible to prove the probative facts of opinions in the treatise"); United States v. One Device, 160 F.2d 194, 198–99 (10th Cir.1947) (medical books and treatises are not admissible to prove the truth of the statements they contain); Annotation, *Medical Treatises; Rule of Inadmissibility*, 84 A.L.R.2d 1341 (1962). Courts refused to recognize the exception primarily because the author was not subject to cross-examination and was not under oath, and because of the difficulty in determining whether the author was an authority in the field. Also courts expressed concern that jurors would become confused and that trials might devolve into conflicts between authors that jurors would not be equipped to resolve fairly. *See* 2 McCormick on Evidence, *supra* note 284 § 321; Annotation, *supra* this note, at 1347.

stating that the spleen should be removed whenever it has suffered the slightest trauma. The defense attorney could ask the opposing expert whether the expert had relied on the treatise. If the expert claimed reliance on the treatise in preparing the opinion, then the attorney could read the damaging passage to the jury or require the expert to do so.[286] The theory was not that the treatise was being admitted under a hearsay exception, but that it was not hearsay at all. The treatise was not being used to prove the truth of anything that it asserted, but to show that the expert was untrustworthy or careless because the expert claimed to have relied upon an unsupportive treatise.

The impeachment of an expert who claims to have relied upon a treatise can be highly impressive. Wellman's classic work on cross-examination contains a pungent example from his own experience. Wellman was examining an adverse medical expert. He reported that he asked the expert whether anyone agreed with the expert's diagnosis, and the expert testified that Ericson on the Spine agreed with him. Wellman asked who Ericson was, and the expert answered patronizingly that Ericson was probably one of the most famous surgeons that England has ever produced. Wellman then posed the following question:

> *Wellman*: "Well, how is it that a man, whose time is so much occupied as you have told us yours is, has leisure enough to look up medical authorities to see if they agree with him?"

To which he got the dream answer:

> *Doctor* [fairly beaming on counsel]: "Well, Mr. Wellman, to tell you the truth, I have often heard of you, and I half suspected that you would ask me some such foolish question; so this morning after my breakfast, and before starting for court, I took down from my library my copy of Ericson's book, and found that he agreed entirely with my diagnosis in this case."

Wellman then reached under the counsel table and took out his own copy of "Ericson on the Spine" and asked the doctor to find the place at which Ericson agreed with him. The doctor said "I have not time to do it now." Wellman responded "Time!—why, there is all the time in the world." The witness sat in pained silence until excused by the trial judge.[287]

This form of impeachment can still be used under the Federal Rules. If the witness will say that he or she has relied on a treatise, then the impeachment will be very successful if the treatise does not support the witness's position. Undoubtedly there are lawyers who encounter such

286. *See* Carter Prods., Inc. v. FTC, 201 F.2d 446, 449 (9th Cir.1953) (noting that many courts hold that learned treatises cannot be used in cross-examination unless witness has relied on treatise in forming opinion, and citing authority); Ullrich v. Chicago City Ry. Co., 106 N.E. 828, 829 (Ill.1914) (scientific books not admissible to impeach witness unless witness has relied upon that particular work in forming opinion); Percoco's Case, 173 N.E. 515, 516 (Mass.1930) (error to admit medical books when expert, though stating he had read the books, was not shown to have relied on them in forming opinion).

287. Francis L. Wellman, The Art of Cross–Examination 69–70 (1923).

witnesses, just as there are poker players who draw royal flushes. But most experts will not fall into this trap. They will deny relying upon the disagreeable treatise, perhaps upon any treatise. The problem with the common law rule was that the expert could always short-circuit the cross-examination by denying reliance on the treatise in forming the opinion.[288]

Some common law courts allowed broader use of the treatise to impeach. Even if the expert was not willing to testify that the expert had relied upon the treatise, the treatise could be used in evidence if the expert was at least willing to concede that the treatise was a reliable authority in the field.[289] This approach, however, still allowed the expert witness to block cross-examination simply by refusing to concede that the treatise was authoritative.[290]

The common law position was not completely uniform. Some courts were far more liberal in allowing cross-examination on treatises. Some allowed it even when the opposing expert neither relied on the work nor recognized it as an authority, on grounds that the cross-examination was still a valuable way to test the expert's knowledge, credibility, and accuracy.[291] But many courts imposed restrictions that severely hampered the use of learned treatises.

Liberalization in the Federal Rules

The federal rule makers thought that the learned treatise ought to be admissible if its reliability was established by any means, whether or not the opposing expert conceded that it was authoritative. The rule makers said that the testing of professional knowledge was incomplete without exploration of the witness's knowledge of, and attitude toward, established treatises in the field.[292]

Because of the danger that the treatise, even if reliable in itself, might be misleading and confusing without the guidance of an expert, the rule makers did require that an expert be available and that the treatise be shown to the expert on the stand.[293] The expert is not

---

288. *See* Percoco's Case, 173 N.E. 515, 516 (Mass.1930); De Haan v. Winter, 241 N.W. 923, 925 (Mich.1932) ("If a medical witness refers to a textbook as his authority, then the book may be used to contradict him").

289. *See, e.g.,* Shaw v. Duncan, 194 F.2d 779, 783 (10th Cir.1952) (error to exclude cross-examination upon treatise when witness testified he had read the treatise in question); Lawrence v. Nutter, 203 F.2d 540, 543 (4th Cir.1953) (error to exclude cross-examination of witnesses from treatise recognized by witnesses as authority).

290. Hastings v. Chrysler Corp., 77 N.Y.S.2d 524, 527 (1948) ("If the expert witness does not concede the authoritativeness of the literature attempted to be resorted to, it may not be used on cross-

examination"); *see also* Nutter, 203 F.2d at 543.

291. *See* Atlanta Corp. v. Olesen, 124 F.Supp. 482, 488 (S.D.Cal.1954) (reading portions of medical texts proper method to test knowledge, accuracy, and credibility of expert witness, and to determine if expert agreed with the text); Reilly v. Pinkus, 338 U.S. 269, 275–76 (1949) (prejudicial error not to allow cross-examination concerning statements in medical texts to test expert's testimony).

292. Fed. R. Evid. 803(18) advisory committee's note.

293. *Id.; see* Tart v. McGann, 697 F.2d 75, 78 (2d Cir.1982) (medical literature admissible as long as called to the attention of expert witness and established as authorita-

required to actually explain the treatise, but the expert is available if either party wishes to ask questions about it.[294]

§ 7.33 Learned Treatise Exception [FRE 803(18)]—Foundation for Use of Learned Treatise

Established as Reliable Authority

The treatise must be shown to be authoritative. This can be done in a number of ways.[295] The treatise may be established as reliable authority through the testimony of the proponent's own expert witness.[296] Or the opposing expert can be used to establish that the work is authoritative when the opponent's expert is willing to concede the point. Even a grudging concession that the treatise is "somewhat" authoritative may be enough to support admission.[297] Or the treatise can be established as authoritative through judicial notice.[298] It seems that this would rarely be appropriate, but Judge Weinstein suggests that

> In a medical malpractice case ... if plaintiff cannot get an expert to testify on the standard of care, it is equally unlikely that an expert will testify about authoritative treatises. If defendant's experts refuse to concede the qualifications of a particular work, the trial judge should be liberal in allowing other proof of the treatise's authoritativeness so long as it indicates that the book is recognized by the medical professional. For example, reading lists used in medical school courses or postgraduate seminars might be admissible as market reports or commercial publications and a court might

tive); Schneider v. Revici, 817 F.2d 987, 991 (2d Cir.1987).

294. Note this also helps reduce the danger of passages of learned treatises being taken out of context. *See* 5 Weinstein's Federal Evidence § 803.23[1] (2d ed. Joseph M. McLaughlin ed. 1997).

295. *See* Fed. R. Evid. 803(18) advisory committee's note; see also Johnson v. William C. Ellis & Sons Iron Works, 609 F.2d 820, 822 (5th Cir.1980) (treatises may be established as reliable authority by either testimony or admission of an expert witness, or by other expert testimony, or by judicial notice).

296. *See* Burgess v. Premier Corp., 727 F.2d 826, 834 (9th Cir.1984) (books on cattle investment offered by proponent's expert witness admissible where expert testified that author was the pre-eminent industry expert).

297. *See* Allen v. Safeco Ins. Co., 782 F.2d 1517, 1519–20 (11th Cir.1986) (opposing expert testified that fire investigation magazine was "somewhat" authoritative

and that he had used it himself; authority of magazine sufficiently established; no error by trial judge in admitting evidence); Dawson v. Chrysler Corp., 630 F.2d 950, 961 (3d Cir.1980) (reports inferentially conceded by opposing experts as authoritative properly established). The trial judge, of course, always has discretion under Rule 403 to exclude prejudicial or confusing evidence. For a decision that, on unusual facts, appears to go beyond the rule by requiring that a testifying expert *rely* upon the learned treatise, see Conde v. Velsicol Chem. Corp., 804 F.Supp. 972, 990 (S.D.Ohio 1992) (in products liability action, scholarly article alleging manipulation of health data by defendant corporation inadmissible when plaintiffs failed to show any expert relied on it and article author did not testify at trial; however, letter to editor, in medical journal, discrediting study upon which defense relied admissible).

298. *See* Hemingway v. Ochsner Clinic, 608 F.2d 1040, 1047 (5th Cir.1979) (medical text written by registered nurses could not be established by judicial notice).

take judicial notice of books admitted in the course of other litigation.[299]

A learned treatise might be admitted conditionally, with the expert laying the foundation after it has already been used in cross-examination.[300] However, if the expert being cross-examined says that the treatise is worthless and if there has been no prior testimony establishing that it is authoritative, the judge ought to be reluctant to admit it conditionally.[301] In any event, when there is a controversy about whether the treatise is a reliable authority, the issue is a preliminary question of fact for the trial judge to resolve in determining whether the evidence is admissible.[302]

Shown to Expert

The treatise must be shown to an expert, either one's own expert or the opponent's, on the witness stand. Even if the authoritative nature of the treatise is established by judicial notice, as opposed to expert testimony, it is still necessary that an expert witness testify in order for the excerpt from the treatise to be admissible. The reason for this requirement is that the trier ought to have the aid of an expert in interpreting the treatise, however authoritative it may be.[303]

Limitation: Treatise Is Not an Exhibit

Federal Rule of Evidence 803(18) provides, "If admitted, the statements may be read into evidence but may not be received as exhibits." The advisory committee wrote:

> The rule avoids the danger of misunderstanding and misapplication by limiting the use of treatises as substantive evidence to situations in which an expert is on the stand and available to explain and assist in the application of the treatise if desired. The limitation upon receiving the publication itself physically in evidence, contained in the last sentence, is designed to further this policy.[304]

299. Weinstein goes on to note that the finding of authoritativeness goes only to admissibility; it is up to the jury to decide what weight to give to the treatise. 5 Weinstein's Federal Evidence § 803.23[14], at 803–122 to 803–123 (2d ed. Joseph M. McLauglin ed. 1997) (footnotes omitted).

300. Cf. Fed. R. Evid. 104(b); see Maggipinto v. Reichman, 481 F.Supp. 547, 550–52 (E.D.Pa.1979) (treatise used for impeachment purposes properly excluded for substantive purposes where treatise not offered and established as reliable authority).

301. See Dawsey v. Olin Corp., 782 F.2d 1254, 1263–64 (5th Cir.1986) (no error in prohibiting use of government publication in cross-examination where no experts testified that publication was reliable authority and one testified that it was unreliable).

302. See Fed. R. Evid. 104 (a).

303. See Fed. R. Evid. 803(18) advisory committee's note; see also 2 McCormick on Evidence § 321, at 352 (4th ed. John W. Strong ed. 1992) (the restriction is "designed to ensure that materials are used only under the sponsorship of an expert who can assist the fact finder and explain how to apply the materials").

304. Fed. R. Evid. 803(18) advisory committee's note; see also Dartez v. Fibreboard Corp., 765 F.2d 456, 465 (5th Cir. 1985):

> The reason for the Rule's restrictions on the use of learned treatises is to avoid the possibility that the jury will misunderstand and misapply the technical language within such an article if they are allowed to consider the publication itself

In other words, the lawyer or witness can read a passage from the treatise to the jury once the foundation has been established, but the jurors cannot take the treatise into the jury room and read it themselves.

§ 7.34   Ancient Documents [FRE 803(16)]

The exception for statements in ancient documents is recognized both at common law and under the Federal Rules.[305] It applies to allow the reception of documents that have been in existence for a certain period of time—20 years under the federal rules. Common law exceptions often contained a requirement that the document be found in a place where it would naturally be expected to be found.[306] The Federal Rule simply affirms that the document must be authentic.[307] Courts appear to admit evidence under Federal Rule of Evidence 803(16) as long as it is properly authenticated under Rule 901.[308] It is at least arguable, however, that the burden of proof for admission under 803(16) is different than that for authenticating evidence under 901. Under Rule 803(16) the document must be shown to be authentic by a preponderance of the evidence;[309] under Rule 901 evidence sufficient to support a finding would have been enough.[310] Of course, one of the ways to show that a document is authentic under the Federal Rules is to show that it was found where it would most likely be if authentic, and that it is in a condition that raises no suspicion as to its authenticity.[311]

An example of the operation of the rule appears in *In re Rhode Island Asbestos Cases*.[312] In that case, plaintiff offered records of an asbestos company that were prepared more than 20 years before the action. Noting the age of the documents and the fact that their origin

instead of receiving the information through the testimony of an expert in the field.

305. *See generally* 5 Weinstein's Federal Evidence § 803.21 (2d ed. Joseph M. McLaughlin ed. 1997); 2 McCormick on Evidence § 323 (4th ed. John W. Strong ed. 1992).

306. *See, e.g.,* Sinkora v. Wlach, 35 N.W.2d 40, 47–48 (1948) (66-year-old passport found where expected admissible); Tillman v. Lincoln Warehouse Corp., 423 N.Y.S.2d 151, 153 (1979) (30-year-old inventory shown to have come from proper custody admissible).

307. Fed. R. Evid. 803(16). *See also* United States v. Stelmokas, 100 F.3d 302, 312 (3d Cir.1996) (held, Nazi and Soviet records showing Stelmokas membership in Lithuanian unit that murdered Jews admissible as ancient documents despite allegations of policy of spoliation and forgery by such authorities; Holocaust experts vouched for authenticity of documents).

308. *See, e.g.,* DeWeerth v. Baldinger, 658 F.Supp. 688, 695 n. 12 (S.D.N.Y.1987)

("The relevant exhibits, specifically the 1943 photograph . . . have been in existence 20 years or more and thus contain hearsay admissible under the ancient documents exception of Fed. R. Evid. 803(16)"); Dartez v. Fibreboard Corp., 765 F.2d 456, 464 (5th Cir.1985) ("The authentication requirement is governed by the standards set forth in Fed. R. Evid. 901(a)").

309. It is arguable that the foundation for any hearsay exception must be shown by a preponderance. *See* Bourjaily v. United States, 483 U.S. 171, 175–76 (1987) (holding that the preliminary facts necessary to establish the foundation for evidence under 801(d)(2)(E) must be proven by a preponderance of the evidence).

310. *See* Fed. R. Evid. 901(a); the requirement of authentication is satisfied by "evidence sufficient to support a finding that the matter in question is what its proponent claims."

311. *See* Fed. R. Evid. 901(b)(8).

312. 11 Fed. R. Evid. Serv. (Callaghan) 444 (D.R.I.1982).

and storage had been adequately accounted for, the court admitted them under the ancient documents exception.[313]

Another modern case admitting an ancient document as an exception to the hearsay rule is *Fulmer v. Connors*.[314] In *Fulmer*, the court admitted cash books and time and payment books of a company to establish that certain wages were paid in 1941. The books were over 20 years old, had been found as expected in the company's records, and did not appear suspect.[315]

For a case in which the exception did not apply because of problems of showing that the document was authentic, see *Dartez v. Fibreboard Corp.*[316] *Dartez* involved intracompany correspondence about employees possibly injured by exposure to asbestos. The plaintiff failed to introduce evidence that the documents came from the company's records, and the court considered that the requirement of authentication had not been satisfied because the documents were not found in the expected place. While finding the documents in the expected place is not an invariable requirement (they can be authenticated by other means, so long as they are shown to be what they purport to be), the absence of other admissible evidence to authenticate the documents in this case made the failure to make that showing fatal.[317]

The use of an ancient document to prove the truth of its assertion involves hearsay dangers. The maker of the document might have been insincere or deficient in some other way. However, the age of the document at least provides assurance that it was not prepared in a self-serving manner with the present controversy in mind. Also, there is a special need for the hearsay, because memories of persons who lived at the time may have faded, or it might be difficult to find other evidence. Finally, the fact that the document is in writing at least removes dangers that the in-court witness might have misunderstood the hearsay statement or manufactured it.[318]

§ 7.35 Family History Exceptions and Related Matters [FRE 803(19), 804(b)(4)]

Classroom teachers sometimes startle students by asking them whether asking a witness "How old are you?" is objectionable. The witness has no personal knowledge, at least not of the exact date of birth. The witness's knowledge is derived from the statements of others, and those statements are out-of-court statements that are offered for the

---

313. *Id.* at 447. *See also* United States v. Stelmokas, 100 F.3d 302, 312 (3d Cir. 1996) (held, Nazi and Soviet records showing Stelmokas membership in Lithuanian unit that murdered Jews admissible as ancient documents despite allegations of policy of spoliation and forgery by such authorities; Holocaust experts vouched for authenticity of documents).

314. 665 F.Supp. 1472 (N.D.Ala.1987).

315. *Id.* at 149.

316. 765 F.2d 456 (5th Cir. 1985).

317. *Id.* at 464–65.

318. *See* 5 Weinstein's Federal Evidence, *supra* note 305 § 803.21[1]; 2 McCormick on Evidence, *supra* note 305 § 323, at 358; Roger C. Park, *A Subject Matter Approach to Hearsay Reform*, 86 Mich. L. Rev. 51, 71–73 (1987).

truth of the matter asserted. So the rules requiring personal knowledge and banning hearsay seem to stand in the way of this everyday testimony.[319]

The question is not entirely a silly classroom exercise. Sometimes a fact such as age can be a crucial fact in the litigation. This is the case, for example, when the defendant is accused of a sexual crime that can only be committed against a victim who is underage.[320] Ideally one might want to require the best evidence available, such as a birth certificate or even the testimony of someone present at the birth. However, that degree of strictness has not usually been observed. The testimony of a witness about the witness's own age is admissible in evidence, both at common law[321] and under the Federal Rules of Evidence.[322] The hearsay exceptions governing statements about family history cover not only testimony about name and birthdate, but also about adoption, marriage, divorce, legitimacy, family relationship (by blood, marriage, or adoption), ancestry, and similar facts of personal or family history. They apply not only to testimony by the witness on the stand about the witness's own family history, but also about the family history of others.

The modern family history exceptions are descendants of the common law pedigree exception. The pedigree exception is one of the first established exceptions to the hearsay rule. Chief Justice John Marshall listed it in 1813 as one of the four exceptions "said to be as old as the [hearsay] rule itself."[323]

319. For an example of taking this idea to its logical extreme, see Mary Morton, Note, *The Hearsay Rule and Epistemological Suicide*, 74 Geo. L.J. 1301 (1986) (when witness testifies that the witness saw a chair, the testimony is hearsay because the witness only knows what a chair is by having been told by others).

320. *See* Government of Virgin Islands v. Joseph, 765 F.2d 394, 397 n. 5 (3d Cir. 1985) (held, victim may testify about her own age over hearsay objection). Of course, where age is a crucial fact, the party seeking to prove the person's age will have an incentive to offer stronger evidence of the victim's age. In cases such as *Joseph*, for example, the jury might well discount the victim's own testimony.

321. *See* 5 John H. Wigmore, Evidence in Trials at Common Law § 1493 (James H. Chadbourn rev. 1974); United States v. Austrew, 202 F.Supp. 816, 822 (D.Md. 1962). However, common law courts were occasionally quite strict. *See* Pickering v. Peskind, 183 N.E. 301, 305–06 (1930) (plaintiff not allowed to testify about own birthdate, as told to her by her grandmother); National Aid Life Assn. v. Wiles, 41 P.2d 655 (1935) (daughter of insured not allowed to testify to family reputation about insured's age). The latter case can perhaps be explained on policy grounds as a case in

which age was crucial, the statements were self-serving, and better evidence should have been available.

322. *See* Government of Virgin Islands v. Joseph, 765 F.2d 394, 397 n. 5 (3d Cir. 1985) (held, victim may testify about her own age over hearsay objection).

323. Mima Queen & Child, Petitioners for Freedom v. Hepburn, 11 U.S. (7 Cranch) 290, 296 (1813) (Marshall, J.):

To this rule there are some exceptions which are said to be as old as the rule itself. These are cases of pedigree, of prescription, of custom, and in some cases of boundary. There are also matters of general and public history, which may be received without that full proof which is necessary for the establishment of a private fact.

The *Mima Queen* case was a petition for freedom by persons held in slavery. Chief Justice Marshall refused to extend the pedigree exception to allow reception of evidence that the petitioners' ancestors had been free, holding that hearsay evidence on this subject should be excluded, and stating that "this Court is not inclined to extend the exceptions further than they have already been carried." *Id*. at 297. An able dissent by

We have referred to "family history exceptions." The Federal Rules of Evidence actually contain four separate exceptions dealing with family history.

The first is the exception created by Rule 803(19) for reputation about family history. It allows a witness to testify about reputation with regard to marriage, birth, and similar facts of personal or family history. The reputation must be either among the family members, among associates, or in the community. The foundation for the testimony is similar to the foundation laid for reputation as to character. For example, the basic foundation for showing through a witness that Julie Curran is the daughter of James Curran could be laid as follows:

Example of Foundation

Did you know James Curran?

How long did you know him?

What was the nature of your association with him?

Do you know Julie Curran?

How long have you known her?

What is the nature of your association with her?

Do you know other persons who have known both James and Julie Curran?

Who are those other persons?

What is their relationship to James and Julie Curran?

[The reputation sources can be members of the family, the community, or other associations, such as co-workers.]

Have you talked to those persons about the family relationship of Julie Curran and James Curran?

Are you familiar with the reputation for family relationship of John Curran and Julie Curran among those persons?

What is that reputation?

When proceeding under this exception, there is no need to show that the declarants (the persons making the statements that collectively make up the reputation) are unavailable. However, it is necessary to show the existence of general reputation. The fact that the witness has been told

---

Justice Duvall argued that hearsay evidence was admissible

[u]pon the same principle, upon which it is admitted to prove a custom, pedigree and the boundaries of land;—because from the antiquity of the transactions to which these subjects may have reference, it is impossible to produce living testimony. To exclude hearsay in such cases, would leave the party interested without remedy.... It appears to me that the reason for admitting hearsay evidence upon a question of freedom is much stronger than in cases of pedigree or in controversies relative to the boundaries of land. It will be universally admitted that the right to freedom is more important than the right of property.

by one person that X was the child of Y does not constitute a reputation.[324]

An exception for statements of family history is recognized by Federal Rule of Evidence 804(b)(4). This exception covers oral or written statements about birth, marriage, adoption, and the like. It does not require a showing of reputation. The statement of one person is enough. However, either that one person must be the person whose family history is sought to be proven (e.g., the statement of declarant about where she was born)[325] or the statement must be that of someone related by blood or marriage or otherwise "so intimately associated with the other's family as to be likely to have accurate information concerning the matter declared."[326] Moreover, the declarant must be unavailable. In contrast, the reputation-based family history exception, Rule 803(19), does not require any showing of unavailability.

The common law version of the exception for statements of family history required that the statement be made *ante litem motam*, that is, before the controversy arose. Once the controversy arose, the danger of fabricated evidence was considered to be too great.[327] This requirement was intentionally omitted from the Federal Rule. The advisory committee considered that this and other motives to fabricate should go to weight, not to admissibility.[328]

The third family history exception recognized by the Federal Rules of Evidence relates to family records, such as statements in family Bibles or on tombstones.[329] The fourth relates to judgments of family history.[330] These exceptions are described in separate sections of this hornbook.[331]

§ 7.36 Market Reports and Commercial Publications [FRE 803(17)]

Federal Rule of Evidence 803(17) recognizes a hearsay exception for market reports and commercial publications. The exception applies to stock market quotations, telephone directories, business directories, commercial compilations, lists, tabulations, and similar publications. The rule requires that the compilations be published and that they be generally used and relied upon by the public or by persons in particular occupations.

The rationale of the exception is that there is ordinarily no motive to deceive and that reliance upon the publications by the public or by business users is an assurance of trustworthiness. In any event, it would usually not be feasible to call all of the people involved in making a

---

324. *See* § **7.35**.

325. For examples of statements involving place of birth, decided under the common law precursors to the federal exceptions, see 5 Wigmore, *supra* note 321 § 1501.

326. *See* Fed. R. Evid. 804(b)(4) and advisory committee's note.

327. *See* 5 Wigmore, *supra* note 321, at § 1483.

328. *See* Fed. R. Evid. 804(b)(4) advisory committee's note.

329. *See* Fed. R. Evid. 803(13).

330. *See* Fed. R. Evid. 803(23).

331. *See* §§ **7.35** and **7.43**.

compilation, so if the information is to be received at trial at all, it must be received in its published form.[332]

The exception overlaps with the business records exception to some extent. Often the foundation for reception as a business record could be laid in the case of a commercial publication. For example, in *United States v. Grossman*,[333] the defendant was charged with knowingly receiving stolen property. The property in question was 300 stolen Colibri cigarette lighters. At trial, a Colibri catalog was admitted to prove the retail price and to show that the lighters in evidence were the same models as those listed in the invoice of a stolen shipment. The court held that the catalog was admissible under the business records exception. In the view of the court, a sufficient foundation had been established through the testimony of a witness who was a purchasing agent for Colibri Corporation. The court went on to note that the trial judge could have admitted the catalog as a commercial publication under Rule 803(17), because "the catalog was a published compilation generally used and relied upon by retailers of Colibri lighters."[334] The exception specifically requires both that the report be published and that it be generally relied upon. There is some authority for a third requirement, that the report concern objective facts not requiring interpretation or analysis.[335]

Reports that fail to meet both these requirements may nonetheless be used by experts in forming opinions if they meet the reasonable reliance requirements of Rule 703.[336]

§ 7.37   Reputation Concerning Boundaries, Land Customs, and General History [FRE 803(20)]

Rule 803(20) of the Federal Rules of Evidence creates what amounts to two exceptions. The first is an exception for reputation in the community as to boundaries or customs affecting lands. As to this exception, the Rule specifically requires that the reputation arise before the controversy, though it does not require that the reputation be ancient.[337] The second is an exception for reputation in the community as to events of general history. As to this exception, the Rule does not specifically require either that the reputation be ancient or that it arise before the controversy. However, the Rule's reference to general "history" may cause courts to infer that the information must be non-contemporary. For example, in *State ex rel. Abrams v. Ocean Club, Inc.*,[338] the court refused to admit, under the exception, a club's relatively contemporaneous reputation for being anti-Semitic as evidence of dis-

332. *See* 5 Weinstein's Federal Evidence § 803.22[1], at 803–115 (2d Ed. Joseph M. McLaughlin ed. 1997).

333. 614 F.2d 295, 296–97 (1st Cir. 1980).

334. *Id*. at 297.

335. *See* White Indus. v. Cessna Aircraft Co., 611 F.Supp. 1049 (W.D.Mo.1985) (rejecting prospectus filed with SEC as evidence, and noting both publication require-

ment and requirement that the publication concern objective facts).

336. *See* § **10.08**.

337. *See* Fed. R. Evid. 803(19)-(21) advisory committee's note (stating "The reputation is required to antedate the controversy, though not to be ancient").

338. 602 F.Supp. 489 (E.D.N.Y.1984).

crimination, on grounds that the reputation should be either ancient or at least not likely to be provable with living witnesses. This interpretation is supported by the reason that the advisory committee gave for not requiring, in the second part of the rule, that the reputation arise before the controversy—that "the historical character of the subject matter dispenses with any need that the reputation antedate the controversy with respect to which it is offered."

Like other reputation evidence, the supposed guarantee of trustworthiness for this type of evidence is that the community will have discussed and scrutinized the matter carefully, so that its conclusion is likely to be reliable.[339] It has been said that to be probative the reputation must concern "such facts as have been of interest to all members of the community as such, and therefore have been so likely to receive general and intelligent discussion and examination by competent persons, so that the community's received opinion on the subject cannot be supposed to have reached the condition of definite decision until the matter had gone, in public relief, beyond the stage of controversy and had become settled with fair finality.[340]

In both parts of the exception, the reputation involved must be community reputation, not merely the word of one person or reputation among a narrow slice of the community. This requirement was examined in *Ute Indian Tribe v. Utah*,[341] in which the court held that the reputation in the non-Indian community about tribal boundaries was admissible, but noted that it would be given little probative weight in the bench trial because of the adverse attitude of the non-Indian community to the Indian community.

As to most events of history, the "general history" part of the exception is not needed. Most historical events are offered not as adjudicative facts, which relate to the issues of who did what in the particular lawsuit, but as legislative facts, which relate to how to interpret law or what the law should be. Legislative fact issues may be resolved by judicial notice. That is, even if there is a reasonable dispute about the accuracy of a legislative fact, a court may resolve the dispute without taking testimony, by referring to whatever sources the court deems reliable.[342] Even as to adjudicative facts, many historical facts are

339. Fed. R. Evid. 803(19)-(21) advisory committee's note; Ute Indian Tribe v. Utah, 521 F.Supp. 1072 (D.Utah 1981), *revd on other grounds* 773 F.2d 1087 (10th Cir. 1985).

340. 5 John H. Wigmore, Evidence in Trials at Common Law § 1598, at 564–65 (James H. Chadbourn rev. 1974); *see also id.* §§ 1583–1597.

341. 521 F.Supp. 1072 (D.Utah 1981), *rev'd. on other grounds* 773 F.2d 1087 (10th Cir.1985).

342. Kenneth C. Davis, Administrative Law Treatise 296 (3d ed. 1972):

The cardinal distinction which more than any other governs the use of extra-record facts by courts and agencies is the distinction between legislative facts and adjudicative facts. When a court or an agency finds facts concerning the immediate parties—who did what, where, when, how and with what motive or intent—the court or agency is performing an adjudicative function, and the facts are conveniently called adjudicative facts. When a court or agency develops law or policy, it is acting legislatively. The courts have created the common law through judicial legislation, and the

generally known within the territorial jurisdiction of the trial court or capable of accurate and ready determination by resort to sources whose accuracy cannot reasonably be questioned, and hence are judicially noticeable under Rule 201(b).

The "general history" aspect of the exception is little used. Facts of general history are likely to be derived from information that qualifies for another hearsay exception, such as the exceptions for ancient documents, learned treatises, and business records, or to be a proper subject for judicial notice, as is the case when the historical fact is being used for lawmaking or law interpretation.[343]

The exception was used, or at least alluded to as one possible basis for receiving evidence, in Pan American World Airways v. Aetna Casualty & Surety Co.[344] This case involved insurance claims arising out of the hijacking of a Pan Am jet by persons aligned with the Palestine Liberation Organization. To allocate the insurance liability between the "all risk" and the "war risk" carriers, the court had to consider facts about the nature of the PLO and the Middle East conflict. It noted that in hearing the case it had generally taken a liberal view of the admissibility of hearsay, on grounds that it would have to consider hearsay or be in the dark about many issues. It alluded to the predecessor common law general history exception, as exemplified by what was then Proposed Rule 803(20), and to judicial notice as possible bases for admitting the evidence.

§ 7.38 Use of Prior Convictions to Prove the Convicted Person Committed the Acts Charged and Related Matters [FRE 803(22)]

Records of prior convictions can be offered for a variety of reasons.

Examples

1. The judgment of conviction can be offered for impeachment of a witness in a civil or criminal case, as an attack on the witness's character for truth and veracity. This use of the prior conviction is discussed in the section of this Hornbook that deals with impeachment of witnesses under Federal Rule of Evidence 609(a)(2).

facts which inform the tribunal's legislative judgment are called legislative facts.... The exceedingly practical difference between legislative and adjudicative facts is that, apart from facts properly noticed, the tribunal's findings of adjudicative facts must be supported by evidence, but findings or assumptions of legislative facts need not be, frequently are not, and sometimes cannot be supported by evidence.

(Footnotes omitted.)

343. *See* 5 Weinstein's Federal Evidence § 803.26[3] (2d ed. Joseph M. McLaughlin ed. 1997) (noting that there has always been a dearth of authority under the exception, and that under the Federal Rules there is probably less need of the exception than before because of the learned treatise exception).

344. 368 F.Supp. 1098 (S.D.N.Y.1973) (although Federal Rule 803(20) was not in effect at the time of this case, the court alluded to the proposed version of the rule).

2. The judgment of conviction can be offered as circumstantial evidence of another crime that the convicted person is alleged to have committed. For example, suppose that the prior conviction is a conviction for distributing cocaine. It is offered as evidence in a subsequent case arising from a separate occurrence. In the new case, the defendant is charged with possessing cocaine with intent to distribute. The defendant claims that the cocaine possessed in the second case was for the defendant's own personal use, and that he or she had no intent to distribute. Most courts would admit the prior conviction as evidence of intent to distribute. (For that matter, most would admit evidence of prior sales of cocaine that did not lead to conviction on the same theory.) This hornbook discusses this basis for receiving prior convictions in the sections of the character evidence chapter that deal with admissibility of other crimes, wrongs, and acts under Rule 404(b). *See* **Ch. 5**.

3. A judgment of conviction may be offered because a fact determined in a criminal case is in issue in a subsequent civil action that arises from the same transaction or occurrence. The convicted defendant is seeking to relitigate in the civil case a fact necessarily determined in the criminal case. The prior conviction is being used to establish, in the civil case, one of the very facts that was at issue in the criminal case. This way of using prior convictions is the subject of the present section.

One example of this third type of proffer of a prior conviction occurs when, in a personal injury action, plaintiff offers evidence that defendant was convicted of driving under the influence, the conviction arises from the accident that caused the plaintiff's injury, and the conviction is offered to show that defendant was driving under the influence at the time of the accident.[345] Another example is the action to recover on a fire insurance claim, where the defendant insurance company offers evidence that the claimant was convicted of arson in the burning of the property that forms the basis for the claim.[346]

The use of records of convictions to establish facts essential to the conviction has undergone dramatic changes in modern law. Until relatively recently, the general rule was that the prior conviction was not even *admissible* in evidence.[347] In recent decades, the courts have moved toward treating these convictions not only as admissible (but rebuttable) evidence, but as being *conclusive* on the facts established in the first case

---

345. *See, e.g.,* Scott v. Robertson, 583 P.2d 188 (Alaska 1978) (held, drunken driving conviction admissible in subsequent civil action, and conclusive on issue of whether defendant was driving when intoxicated). For cases adopting a more restrictive view, see W.E. Shipley, Annotation, *Conviction or Acquittal as Evidence of the Facts on Which It was Based in Civil Action,* 18 A.L.R.2d 1287 (1951).

346. *See, e.g.,* Schindler v. Royal Ins. Co., 179 N.E. 711 (N.Y.1932) (insurer allowed to introduce conviction for making fraudulent insurance claim, not preclusive but admissible as evidence).

347. *See* Shipley Annotation, *supra* note 345, for numerous citations to cases supporting the traditional view.

under the principles of collateral estoppel. We will turn first to this strongest use of the prior conviction.

§ 7.39 Use of Prior Convictions to Prove the Convicted Person Committed the Acts Charged and Related Matters [FRE 803(22)]—Principles of Collateral Estoppel and the Prior Conviction

Historical Doctrine

The offering of a prior conviction as rebuttable evidence must be distinguished from the offering of a prior conviction as precluding relitigation under the principles of collateral estoppel, or to use a term favored by many modern proceduralists, under the principles of issue preclusion.[348] Take, for example, the case in which a convicted arsonist brings a civil action to recover on a fire insurance policy. If the prior conviction is merely admissible in evidence, then the plaintiff is entitled to present countervailing evidence and to go to the jury on the issue of whether the fire was caused by the plaintiff's arson. If the prior conviction has preclusive effect because of the doctrine of collateral estoppel, then the arson cannot be contested at trial and the insurance company is entitled to summary judgment on the issue.

The traditional reason for declining to give collateral estoppel effect to a prior conviction is the doctrine of mutuality. In the arson example, the insurer would not have been bound by a decision in the criminal case in favor of the alleged arsonist because it was not a party.[349] (It would not be fair to bind the insurer with the results of a case in which it was not represented. In any event, it could not be bound by an acquittal, which is merely a decision that there was a reasonable doubt, not a decision that the accused did not commit arson. When the standard of proof changes from proof beyond a reasonable doubt to some lower requirement, then collateral estoppel does not apply if the party against whom it is sought to be used is the beneficiary of a more favorable standard of proof in the second action.[350]) Under the doctrine of mutuality of estoppel, if the first judgment went in favor of the insurance company, then the convicted arsonist would not be bound in the second case. A person who had not been a party to the prior lawsuit was neither bound by the prior suit nor permitted to take advantage of any determinations made in the prior action.[351]

348. Fleming James, Geoffrey Hazard & John Leubsdorf, Civil Procedure § 11.3 (4th ed. 1992) (stating that the "effect traditionally known as collateral estoppel now is called issue preclusion.").

349. See, e.g., Show–World Center v. Walsh, 438 F.Supp. 642 (S.D.N.Y.1977); Restatement (Second) of Judgments § 34(3) (1980). For exceptions to the rule that nonparties are not bound by a judgment, see id. §§ 34–61 (codifying privity exceptions); Teitelbaum Furs, Inc. v. Dominion Ins. Co.,

375 P.2d 439, 25 Cal.Rptr. 559, (Cal. 1962) (en banc; Traynor, J.) (closely held corporations collaterally estopped from recovering alleged insurance loss after president convicted of crimes arising from false insurance claims based on same loss).

350. See Restatement (Second) of Judgments § 28(4) (1980) and cases cited in Reporter's Note thereto.

351. James, Hazard & Leubsdorf, supra note 348, § 11.25.

The traditional mutuality rule was based on the notion that it was unfair to allow someone to take advantage of findings in an action in which that person was not a party, since that person was not bound by any adverse determination. The doctrine's appeal to notions of equal treatment was based on an oversimplification. It treated persons equally when in fact they were in quite different situations. It treated the party who had an opportunity to litigate in the first action in the same way that it treated a nonparty who had no opportunity.

The mutuality rule never appealed to scholars. Bentham said that the rule was more appropriate to the gaming table than the law court.[352] Other scholars have maintained his attack upon the doctrine, and the courts seem to have listened. They made repeated incursions on the mutuality doctrine. It became riddled with exceptions, and then itself became the exception. The prevailing modern view is that if a party had a full and fair opportunity to litigate in the first action, that party ought generally to be bound in subsequent litigation, in the absence of special circumstances.[353]

The once-prevalent ban on prior criminal convictions as collateral estoppel in subsequent civil cases was a specific application of the mutuality doctrine, though other considerations, such as the absence of discovery in criminal actions and procedural differences between criminal and civil cases, may also have had an impact.[354]

Issue Preclusion Where Mutuality Exists

Cases in which a criminal action is followed by a civil suit by the government are simpler than those in which the civil litigant is a private party, because they do not present the same problems of mutuality. The same parties are present in both actions. An example of issue preclusion in a case not raising mutuality problems is *United States v. Killough*.[355]

---

352. 7 Works of Jeremy Bentham 171 (U. Bowring ed. 1843), as quoted in Brainerd Currie, Mutuality of Collateral Estoppel.—Limits of the Bernhard Doctrine, 9 Stan. L. Rev. 281, 284 (1957):

> Another curious rule is, that, as a judgment is not evidence against a stranger, the contrary judgment shall not be evidence for him. If the rule itself is a curious one, the reason given for it is still more so:—"nobody can take benefit by a verdict, who had not been prejudiced by it, had it gone contrary": a maxim which one would suppose to have found its way from the gaming table to the bench.

353. *See, e.g.,* Parklane Hosiery Co. v. Shore, 439 U.S. 322 (1979) (permitting offensive issue preclusion in favor of plaintiffs seeking to take advantage of determination in prior action, brought by SEC, that defendant had issued a materially misleading and false proxy statement); Restatement (Second) of judgments § 29 (1980).

354. *See* Gray v. Genlyte Group, Inc., 289 F.3d 128 (1st Cir.2002) (Boudin, J.) (misdemeanor conviction for using offensive and disorderly acts or language in accosting or annoying member of opposite sex not admissible in civil sexual harassment trial to prove seriousness of harassing conduct; conviction prejudicial because it would be possible to be convicted under the statute without committing serious harassment). *Cf.* Annotation, *Conviction or Acquittal as Evidence of the Facts on Which it was Based in Civil Action*, 18 A.L.R.2d 1287, 1291–98 (1951) (describing reasons given by common law courts, both for not giving preclusive effect and for excluding evidence of the conviction); Scott v. Robertson, 583 P.2d 188 (Alaska 1978) (describing reasons for cautious attitude in course of adopting much more adventuresome one).

355. 848 F.2d 1523 (11th Cir.1988).

Killough was a civil action in which the United States sued to recover money lost to contractors who had worked on disaster relief in the wake of Hurricane Frederic in 1979. The contractors had submitted fraudulently inflated invoices for mobile home set-ups. They had been involved in a scheme under which they would pay kickbacks to officials, and then would inflate the amount charged the government to recoup the kickbacks. The officials and the defrauding contractors were convicted after a guilty plea of conspiracy to defraud the United States.

The government sued the contractors and two officials. It filed a motion for partial summary judgment, claiming that preclusive effect should be given to the guilty pleas. The trial court granted summary judgment on all issues except damages. On appeal, the court noted that "when an issue is resolved in favor of the United States in a criminal prosecution, that issue may not be contested by the same defendant in a subsequent civil suit brought by the government." The prior judgment was not merely evidence of guilt, it conclusively established guilt.[356] On the general question of preclusion when there are successive suits by the government to impose a criminal penalty and then recover the proceeds of crime, the *Killough* case represents established law. There appears to be general agreement under modern law that when the government seeks to recover the proceeds of a crime, the prior conviction precludes relitigation.[357]

Issue Preclusion Despite Lack of Mutuality

In *Killough*, the parties were the same in both cases, so the dangers of unfair preclusion were reduced.[358] Cases in which a third party seeks to obtain preclusive effect from a criminal conviction are more difficult. However, the trend seems to be in favor of preclusion even when mutuality is lacking, that is, even when the conviction is sought to be used by a third party, not by the government. The preclusion is most likely to be granted in cases in which the convicted party is seeking to benefit from the crime, as in cases in which the arsonist sues for the proceeds of the fire insurance policy[359] or the murderer sues as the

---

356. *See id.* at 1528 and cases cited therein. The prior judgment was conclusive on the guilt of the defendants and on the fact that they had paid at least $577,400 in kickbacks. *Id.*

357. *See* Hiroshi Motomura, *Using Judgments As Evidence*, 70 Minn. L. Rev. 979, 990 & n.39 (1986).

358. Arguably, there was a problem of unequal treatment because had the defendants been acquitted in the first action, the government would not necessarily have been bound. *See* United States v. Killough, 848 F.2d 1523 (11th Cir.1988). However, some of the other problems that arise when the parties are different were missing in *Killough*. There was no danger of unforeseeability of the second action, and there

was no danger that the first action was influenced by sympathy for a now-absent party.

359. *See* Eagle, Star & British Dominions Ins. Co. v. Heller, 140 S.E. 314 (Va. 1927) (after conviction for arson, arsonist barred from recovering on policy). *Compare* Breeland v. Security Ins. Co., 421 F.2d 918 (5th Cir.1969) (held, under Louisiana law applicable in diversity case, prior criminal conviction for fraud in reporting value of fire loss precludes civil suit and justifies summary judgment). *See generally* Jonathan C. Thau, *Collateral Estoppel and the Reliability of Criminal Determinations: Theoretical, Practical, and Strategic Implications for Criminal and Civil Litigation,* 70 Geo. L.J. 1079 (1982).

beneficiary of the life insurance policy.[360] There is also ample authority for allowing a victim of crime to use preclusion to recover from the perpetrator the proceeds of the crime.[361] In other situations, the law is more muddled, but the trend seems to be toward greater and greater use of the doctrine of preclusion, at least when there was a full and fair opportunity to litigate in the first action and the loser in that action cannot point to any obvious defect in the proceeding.[362]

An example of the modern trend toward allowing issue preclusion even though mutuality is lacking is *Scott v. Robertson*.[363] There, the plaintiff in a personal injury action arising from an automobile accident had been convicted of drunken driving in the very accident that gave rise to the civil action. The Alaska court expressed the view that the defendants in the civil action should be permitted not only to introduce the conviction into evidence, but to have it be given preclusive effect on the issue whether the plaintiff had been driving while intoxicated at the time of the accident. The court was willing to do this despite the absence of mutuality (the party seeking to take advantage of preclusion in the second action was not a party in the first action, and hence could not have been bound by any result of the first action). It noted that the prior conviction was for a relatively serious offense, punishable by a year's incarceration for the first offense, and that the defendant had in fact had a full and fair trial at the first hearing. It noted that its result might have been different had defendant lacked some significant procedural right, such as the right to jury trial.[364]

Though the trend seems to be toward preclusion, the result reached by cases like *Scott* is by no means firmly established. There are likely to continue to be jurisdictions that give prior convictions lesser effect, with a good deal of local variation in a field that is in so much flux.[365]

360. *See* Travelers Ins. Co. v. Thompson, 163 N.W.2d 289 (Minn.1968) (held, husband's conviction for murdering wife preclusive in his later action to recover proceeds from her life insurance policy).

361. *See* Hancock v. Dodson, 958 F.2d 1367 (6th Cir.1992) (guilty plea to misdemeanor is admissible as admission of a party opponent, even though final judgment following guilty plea is not admissible under language of Rule 803(22); court leaves open possibility that plea could be excluded under Rule 403 in case in which plea to misdemeanor was made under conditions that suggest its untrustworthiness); Motomura, *supra* note 357, at 990.

362. *See* Restatement (Second) of Judgments § 85(2)(a) comment e (1980) thereto, and authorities cited in comment e. Section 85(2)(a) provides, "A judgment in favor of the prosecuting authority is preclusive in favor of a third person in a civil action ... [a]gainst the defendant in the criminal prosecution as stated in § 29."

Section 29 provides generally that a party precluded from relitigating an issue with an opposing party is precluded against third parties, with certain exceptions designed to protect public policy or avoid unfairness. Most of the exceptions, for example, the exception for cases in which the party seeking to use preclusion could have effected joinder in the first action, see § 29(3), would appear not to be applicable in the usual criminal case. However, the exception for cases in which there are procedural opportunities in the second action that might have significantly affected the outcome, see § 29(2) and comment d, might apply in some cases involving criminal convictions (*e.g.*, the traffic court conviction followed by the million dollar civil action).

363. 583 P.2d 188 (Alaska 1978).

364. *Id.* at 193.

365. *See, e.g.*, Brown v. Green, 738 F.2d 202 (7th Cir.1984) (under Illinois law, where defendant is convicted on the merits

When considering whether a conviction has preclusive effect, one of the traditional requirements of collateral estoppel should be borne in mind. The doctrine of collateral estoppel traditionally applies only to issues that were actually litigated and determined in a prior action. This traditional requirement has also undergone some erosion. Where followed, however, the requirement of actual litigation imposes a severe limit upon the preclusive effect of prior convictions. It would mean not only that prior convictions resulting from a plea of nolo contendere are not preclusive, but also that prior convictions resulting from a guilty plea are not preclusive. The *Killough* case, described above, seems to represent the current trend in the federal courts, at least in cases in which the government brings a civil action after having prevailed in a criminal action. In *Killough*, the prior convictions were treated as preclusive even though they arose from guilty pleas, not from actual litigation. The defendants were precluded from contesting the facts that they had admitted in the guilty pleas. They were not even allowed to put in evidence explaining why they made the pleas.[366] There is, however, authority to the contrary.[367] The traditional view was well stated by Judge Traynor:

> A plea of guilty is admissible in a subsequent civil action on the independent ground that it is an admission. It would not serve the policy underlying collateral estoppel, however, to make such a plea conclusive. "The rule [of collateral estoppel] is based upon the sound public policy of limiting litigation by preventing a party who has had one fair trial on an issue from again drawing it into controversy." ... "This policy must be considered together with the policy that a party shall not be deprived of a fair adversary proceeding in which fully to present his case." ... When a plea of guilty has been entered in the prior action, no issues have been "drawn into controversy" by a "full presentation" of the case. It may reflect only a compromise or a belief that paying a fine is more advantageous than litigation. Considerations of fairness to civil litigants and regard for the expeditious administration of criminal justice ... combine to prohibit the application of collateral estoppel against a party who, having pleaded guilty to a criminal charge, seeks for the first time to litigate his cause in a civil action.[368]

at trial, conviction not preclusive, but evidence surrounding prior conviction admissible in subsequent civil proceeding as prima facie evidence of facts on which conviction based; citing, *inter alia*, Thornton v. Paul, 384 N.E.2d 335 (Ill.1978). *See also* Aetna Cas. & Surety Co. v. Niziolek, 481 N.E.2d 1356 (Mass.1985) (under Massachusetts law, insured who was conviction at trial of burning property to collect insurance proceeds was collaterally estopped from relitigating issues in civil action; but conviction of second defendant of arson, entered on guilty plea, did not collaterally estop that party from litigating issues in later civil action, though conviction was admissible in evidence).

366. *See* United States v. Killough, 848 F.2d 1523, 1528 (11th Cir.1988) (trial judge did not abuse discretion in excluding the evidence).

367. *See* David L. Shapiro, *Should a Guilty Plea have Preclusive Effect?*, 70 Iowa L. Rev. 27 (1984).

368. Teitelbaum Furs, Inc. v. Dominion Ins. Co., 375 P.2d 439, 441 (Cal.1962) (dictum) (citations omitted).

§ 7.40   Use of Prior Convictions to Prove the Convicted Person Committed the Acts Charged and Related Matters [FRE 803(22)]—Use of Prior Convictions as Evidence

Even if a prior conviction is not preclusive under the doctrine of collateral estoppel, it might still be admissible as evidence of the facts necessary to support the judgment.[369] Though rebuttable, it is likely to be persuasive.

Traditionally, courts have not favored this use of the prior conviction. They have cited some of the same concerns about lack of mutuality that have impeded acceptance of the prior conviction as collateral estoppel. They have also expressed concern that the evidence would be too powerful, that jurors would tend to treat it as conclusive even if told not to do so.[370] Finally (and perhaps least important) the prior conviction is technically hearsay. When offered to prove guilt of the prior crime or to establish a fact essential to the judgment, the record of prior conviction is hearsay. It is the unsworn, uncross-examined statement of the trier of fact that the accused committed the crime charged. For the answer to the question whether the judgment is admissible to prove the truth of what it asserts, we must turn to the hearsay exception covering judgments of prior convictions, the federal version of which is Federal Rule of Evidence 803(22).[371]

Although Rule 803(22) technically addresses only the hearsay problem, leaving open the possibility of exclusion of a prior conviction on Rule 403 grounds if the jury is likely to be over-influenced by it, in practice the prior conviction that meets the requirements of Rule 803(22) is likely to be admitted.

Under Rule 803(22), the prior conviction must have been for a crime punishable by death or imprisonment for more than a year.[372] Note, however, that when a prior conviction results from a guilty plea, the

---

369. For an example of a prior conviction that was admissible but not given preclusive effect, see Brown v. Green, 738 F.2d 202 (7th Cir.1984). Brown v. Green arose in federal court in a state that did not give preclusive effect to prior convictions. The federal court applied state preclusion law but admitted the conviction as rebuttable evidence under Fed. R. Evid. 803(22).

370. For a useful discussion of the rationale for the traditional view, by a court that departs from it drastically, see Scott v. Robertson, 583 P.2d 188 (Alaska 1978).

371. The use of prior convictions solely to impeach the credibility of a witness is not affected by Rule 803(22). If a prior conviction-satisfies the requirements of Rule 609, then it is not required separately to satisfy the requirements of Rule 803(22). For example, Rule 803(22)'s provision that only convictions for crimes punishable by

more than a year are admissible is not applicable when the conviction is for a crime of dishonesty within the meaning of Rule 609(a)(2). In such an instance, even though the conviction is still hearsay and even though it is being offered to prove the truth of the matter asserted, Rule 609 itself creates an exception that supplements the exception created in Rule 803(22).

372. Some courts have allowed convictions for lesser crimes to be admitted under Rule 803(8) despite the apparent intent of this rule. See Stroud v. Cook, 931 F.Supp. 733, 736 (D.Nev.1996) (misdemeanor conviction that did not qualify under Rule 803(22) was admissible as public record under Rule 803(8) (alternative holding). Accord, United States v. Loera, 923 F.2d 725, 730 (9th Cir.1991).

guilty plea may be independently admissible as the admission of a party-opponent.[373] However, guilty pleas to very minor offenses, such as traffic offenses, might not be very probative on the issue of guilt, because of the possibility that the defendant merely wanted to dispose of the problem without bothersome proceedings. Yet when the defendant had a real chance to contest the proceedings, the willingness to plead guilty seems at least relevant, and explanations can always be weighed by the trier of fact.

On the other hand, Rule 803(22), which specifically provides an exception for evidence of a final judgment entered after a trial *or upon a plea of guilty*, so long as the crime is punishable by a year or more, could be construed to carry a negative implication. What would be the point of excluding the prior conviction resulting from the plea of guilty if the guilty plea itself could come in?[374]

The public records exception contains a provision allowing "factual findings" to be admitted if "made pursuant to authority granted by law" and if offered in a civil action or against the government in a criminal case. May a misdemeanor conviction that does not satisfy the punishment requirement of Rule 803(22) nonetheless be admitted under the public records exception? The language of Rule 803(8) seems literally to apply, but the better view is that if the punishment requirement of Rule 803(22) is not satisfied, Rule 803(8) is not available as a backdoor alternative. The rule makers considered the requirements needed for admission of convictions when drafting the more specific rule, Rule 803(22), and they decided that minor convictions should not be admissible to show the commission of the underlying offense. It would be peculiar to allow the broader rule, Rule 803(8), which was drafted without an eye to the problem of evidentiary use of criminal convictions, to be used as a way of getting around this intended limit. Despite the force of this argument, however, there is a division of authority about whether Rule 803(8) may be used to receive misdemeanor convictions.[375]

---

373. Guilty pleas to very minor offenses, such as traffic offenses, may not be highly probative on the issue of guilt, because of the possibility that the defendant merely wanted to dispose of the problem without bothersome proceedings. Yet there are undoubtedly some cases in which a guilty plea to even a minor traffic offense has substantial probative value. In addition, when the defendant had a real chance to contest the proceedings, the willingness to plead guilty seems at least relevant, and explanations can always be weighed by the trier of fact. *See* Ando v. Woodberry, 168 N.E.2d 520 (1960) (rejecting argument that guilty plea to traffic offense should be inadmissible because people who believe themselves innocent often plead guilty merely to avoid expenditure of time and expense of trial). *See also* Jay M. Zitter, Annotation, *Admissibility of Traffic Conviction in Later State Civil Trial*, 73 A.L.R. 4th 691 (1990) (reviewing cases).

374. For differing views on the subject, see 5 Weinstein's Federal Evidence § 803.28[2], at 803–130 (2d ed. Joseph M. McLaughlin ed. 1997) (evidence of guilty pleas in cases punishable by less than a year should not be admissible under other exceptions); Hinshaw v. Keith, 645 F.Supp. 180 (D.Me.1986) (expressly disagreeing with Weinstein, and holding that guilty plea to leaving scene of accident was admissible in subsequent civil case); McCormick v. United States, 539 F.Supp. 1179, 1183 (D.Colo.1982) (guilty plea to traffic light violation admissible in subsequent civil action).

375. *See* Stroud v. Cook, 931 F.Supp. 733, 736 (D. Nev.1996) (held, misdemeanor conviction that did not qualify under Rule

The limits of rule 803(22) apply when a prior conviction is used for some purpose other than impeachment of a witness—for example, when the conviction is sought to be used as evidence of criminal conduct in a subsequent tort action by the victim of the crime to recover damages from the perpetrator. The limits do not apply when a prior conviction is offered under Rule 609 to impeach a witness. That rule is itself a hearsay exception as well as an exception to the character evidence prohibition, and convictions admissible under Rule 609 will encounter no separate hearsay rule obstacle. Thus, a conviction for a misdemeanor crime of dishonesty is admissible under Rule 609 even though it does not meet the requirements of Rule 803(8).[376] Rule 803(22), by its express terms, does not apply to guilty verdicts that are the result of pleas of nolo contendere, but only to verdicts that follow a trial or guilty plea. The rule preserves the traditional characteristics of a nolo plea, which was created essentially to avoid some of the consequences of an admission of guilt but to allow the case to be disposed of without trial.[377]

§ 7.41   Records of Religious Organizations [FRE 803(11)]

Federal Rule of Evidence 803(11) creates an exception for regularly kept records of religious organizations. These records may be used to show births, marriages, divorces, deaths, legitimacy, ancestry, relationship by blood or marriage, or other similar facts of personal or family history.

803(22) nevertheless admissible as public record under Rule 803(8)) (alternative holding); *cf.* United States v. Wilson, 690 F.2d 1267, 1275 n. 2 (9th Cir.1982) (court states that Judgment and Commitment Order relating to the conviction for which defendant, now being prosecuted for escape, was being held at time of escape is admissible under public records exception; in authors' opinion, the *Wilson* precedent does not apply to situations in which the conviction is offered to prove the facts necessary to sustain the conviction, because all that was necessary in *Wilson* was to prove that he had been convicted and committed, not that he was actually guilty of the underlying crime of counterfeiting for which he had been committed at the time of the escape). *But c.f.* Nipper v. Snipes, 7 F.3d 415, 417 (4th Cir.1993) (held, Rule 803(8)(C) does not apply to judicial findings of fact).

For a thoughtful discussion in the analogous context of civil judgments, see Herrick v. Garvey, 298 F.3d 1184 (10th Cir.2002). An earlier district court decision found as a fact that a certain corporation had transferred ownership of its aircraft business to another company. The plaintiff offered the prior finding of fact as evidence to prove the truth of the matter. The court held that the finding was properly excluded as hearsay. Rule 803(8)(C) did not apply for three reasons. First, that rule only applies to "investigations made pursuant to authority granted by law," and a judge is not an investigator. Second, the Advisory Committee Note to Rule 803(8)(C) indicates that the intent of the drafters was to cover findings of fact by executive orders, not by judges. Third, the hearsay exceptions for judgments, Rules 803(22) and 803(23), would be rendered redundant by holding that Rule 803(8)(C) provides a "blanket ground" for admission of prior judgments.

376.   Fed. R. Evid. 609(a)(2). *See* Martin v. National R.R. Passenger Corp., 1998 WL 575183 (S.D.N.Y. 1998) (evidence of defendant's prior convictions of the "crimen falsi" misdemeanors of fraudulent accosting and criminal impersonation admissible under Rule 609(b)).

377.   *See* advisory committee's notes to Fed. R. Evid. 803(22) and 410. This result is consistent with prior decisions under the Clayton Act, to the effect that guilty pleas are admissible in subsequent litigation, but nolo pleas are not. *See, e.g.,* General Elec. Co. v. San Antonio, 334 F.2d 480, 484–87 (5th Cir.1964).

Most of this information would be admissible under the business records exception. A religious organization would be a "business" within the meaning of Rule 803(6), which covers institutions and callings of every kind, whether or not conducted for profit. However, the advisory committee decided to supplement the business records exception with the present exception because the business records exception requires that persons contributing to an entry be part of the business or activity (the "business duty" requirement).[378] Were the business records exception the only exception available, many but not all of the records admissible under the present exception would still be admissible. For example, a baptismal certificate could be used to show the fact of baptism, but the business records exception might not provide a basis for using the baptismal certificate to show the date of birth, since that information would have been contributed by the parents or by someone else not under a "business duty" to the religious organization.[379] The committee's decision to extend the present exception beyond the business records exception was based upon the unlikelihood that false information would be furnished in conjunction with an occasion such as baptism.[380]

Recent federal litigation on the exception has centered on attempts by taxpayers to use church-issued receipts or contribution statements as evidence of charitable contributions. The problem with using the exception for that purpose is that the offered evidence is not a statement of personal or family history similar to the examples listed in the rule. Both the Second Circuit and the Ninth Circuit have held that such evidence is not admissible under the present exception.[381] It is therefore necessary to lay a business record foundation for church records of this nature, showing that it was the regular practice of the church to make such records and that the records were kept in the regular course of the church's activities.

§ 7.42 Marriage, Baptismal, and Similar Certificates [FRE 803(12)]

Federal Rule of Evidence 803(12) provides an exception for marriage, baptismal, or similar certificates. The public records exception, Rule 803(8), covers the same ground when the issuer of the certificate is a public official. However, Rule 803(12) goes further in that it allows records prepared by clergy and other non-public officials who perform marriages and similar ceremonies to be admitted.

Rule 803(9), records of vital statistics, also covers some of the same ground as the present exception. For example, a certification of a marriage made to a public office would be admissible under Rule 803(9) as well as the present exception. However, the present exception covers

---

378. *See* § **7.19**.

379. *See* Fed. R. Evid. 803(11) advisory committee's note.

380. *Id.*

381. *See* Ruberto v. Commissioner, 774 F.2d 61 (2d Cir.1985); Hall v. Commissioner, 729 F.2d 632 (9th Cir.1984).

some matters not covered by Rule 803(9). Records of confirmation in a church, or of baptism, are not required to be reported to a public office, and hence are not admissible under Rule 803(9). They are admissible under the present exception, however.

The present exception differs from Rule 803(11) in that it does not require that the certificate be part of the internal record of the religious organization. It can, for example, be a certificate issued by a member of the clergy to the husband and wife after a marriage ceremony.

The present rule provides a hearsay exception, but does not state how the certificates covered are to be authenticated. The authentication requirements are governed by Rule 902(4).[382]

§ 7.43 Family Records [FRE 803(13)]

Federal Rule of Evidence 803(13) creates an exception for statements of fact concerning personal or family history contained in family Bibles, genealogies, charts, engravings on rings, inscriptions of family portraits, engravings on urns, crypts, tombstones, or the like. Examples of "statements concerning personal or family history" include statements about marriage, birth, death, ancestry, and the like.

The guarantee of trustworthiness presumed for the exception is the lack of motive to make a false statement and the likelihood that such statements would be screened by the family. It may not be necessary to make a showing of personal knowledge under the current exception, at least not if the family has accepted the record as valid.[383]

The exception is an ancient one that was long recognized at common law.[384] Related exceptions for family history, also of long lineage, are found in Rule 803(19) (reputation concerning personal or family history), Rule 803(23) (judgment as to personal, family, or general history, or boundaries), and Rule 804(b)(4) (statement of personal or family history).

§ 7.44 Records of Documents Affecting an Interest in Property [FRE 803(14)]

A record of a document affecting an interest in property, as proof of the contents of the original document, is excepted from the hearsay rule by Federal Rule of Evidence 803(14). The record must be the record of a public office, and a statute must authorize the recording of documents of that kind in that office. An example of the operation of this exception is

---

382. *See* **Ch. 11**.

383. For an extensive discussion of the exception at common law, see 5 John H. Wigmore, Evidence in Trials at Common Law §§ 1485–1497 (James H. Chadbourn rev. 1974).

384. For an early endorsement of the exception, see Whitelocke v. Baker, 13 Ves. 511, 514 (1804), quoted in 5 Wigmore, *supra* note 383 § 1482, at 373 (noting that statements of family history, including "descriptions upon monuments" and "descriptions in Bibles and registry books," are admitted "upon the principle that they are the natural effusions of a party who must know the truth, and who speaks upon an occasion when his mind stands in an even position, without any temptation to exceed or fall short of the truth").

the case in which a title record is offered to prove the contents of the record and its execution and delivery. If there is a local statute that authorizes the recording of title records and the recording of data about execution and delivery, then the evidence is admissible. The advisory committee's note indicates that personal knowledge of the recorder is not required:

> Under any theory of the admissibility of public records, the records would be receivable as evidence of the contents of the recorded document, else the recording process would be reduced to a nullity. When, however, the record is offered for the further purpose of proving execution and delivery, a problem of lack of first-hand knowledge by the recorder, not present as to contents, is presented.[385]

§ 7.45 Statements in Documents Affecting an Interest in Property [FRE 803(15)]

Federal Rule of Evidence 803(15) provides an exception for statements in documents affecting an interest in property. The statement must have been relevant to the purpose of the document. The exception does not apply if transactions concerning the property, which have occurred since the document was made, are not consistent with the truth of the statement in the document.

The exception covers recitals of fact in documents such as deeds. Examples are a recital that the parties granting title to the property constitute all of the heirs of the last record owner[386] or a recital that parties named in the deed are married to one another.[387]

EXCEPTIONS THAT APPLY ONLY IF THE DECLARANT IS UNAVAILABLE [FRE 804]

§ 7.46 Exceptions That Apply Only if Declarant Is Unavailable; Definition of Unavailability

The exceptions set forth in Rule 804 of the Federal Rules of Evidence apply only if the declarant is unavailable.[388] If the declarant is available, the law prefers live testimony over hearsay declarations. The proponent must produce the live witness instead of the witness's out-of-court statements.[389]

At first blush, this rule preferring live testimony would seem to be a sensible rule for all instances in which hearsay is offered. Why not require that the live witness be produced if available? Such a rule would give preference to the best evidence (live testimony), but would not stand

---

385. Fed. R. Evid. 803(14) advisory committee's note.

386. *See* Fed. R. Evid. 803(15) advisory committee's note.

387. *See* Compton v. Davis Oil Co., 607 F.Supp. 1221, 1228 (D.Wyo.1985).

388. Fed. R. Evid. 804(b).

389. Fed. R. Evid. 804(b) advisory committee's note.

in the way of admission of other evidence when the best was not available.

Though superficially attractive, this requirement would be too broad. It would be wasteful to require the testimony of every available declarant—for example, every declarant in the chain of information represented by a business record.[390] Also, sometimes hearsay is fully as reliable as in-court testimony. For example, a present sense impression statement made at the time of the event is probably more reliable than a witness's recollection, recited months afterward and after having been through preparation for litigation, about the same event.[391]

Undoubtedly historical accident has played a role in the assignment of exceptions to one category or the other.[392] Arguably, the statements covered by the exceptions in Rule 804 are more dangerous as substitutes for in-court testimony than are those covered by the Rule 803 exceptions. In addition, the situations represented by Rule 804 are often ones in which it is feasible to produce the witness if the witness is available.[393] It must be conceded, however, that there is a degree of arbitrariness in the division of exceptions between Rule 803 (unavailability immaterial) and Rule 804 (statement admissible only if witness is unavailable). For example, considered as a new matter, it would be hard to justify giving excited utterances (which are likely to be inaccurate because made under stress) preferred treatment over former testimony (which was subject to all of the safeguards of oath and cross-examination).[394] Yet that is what Federal Rules of Evidence 803 and 804 do.[395]

Definition of Unavailability

Death and disability are common causes of unavailability, but they are not the only ones.[396] Anything not the fault of the proponent, that as a practical matter prevents the witness from attending or testifying, constitutes unavailability.[397] If the witness is beyond the court's subpoena power and there is no other reasonable way to obtain the witness's testimony, the witness is unavailable.[398] If the witness appears and

---

390. Fed. R. Evid. 803(6) advisory committee's note.

391. *See* 2 McCormick on Evidence § 271, at 212 (4th ed. John W. Strong ed. 1992) (memory and sincerity dangers not present).

392. *See* Fed. R. Evid. 803, 804 advisory committee's notes.

393. Fed. R. Evid. 804(b) advisory committee's note.

394. *See* Robert M. Hutchins & Donald Slesinger, *Some Observations on the Law of Evidence*, 28 Colum. L. Rev. 432, 437 (1928) (excited utterances unreliable); Fed. R. Evid. 804(b)(1) advisory committee's note ("it may be argued that former testimony is the strongest hearsay and should be included under Rule 803").

395. *See* Fed. R. Evid. 803(2), 804(b)(1).

396. *See* Fed. R. Evid. 804(a)(4).

397. *See* Fed. R. Evid. 804(a); United States v. McGuire, 307 F.3d 1192 (9th Cir. 2002) (held, witness who was seven months pregnant was "unavailable" to testify at trial or deposition within meaning of Rule 804(a) because of dangers that stress of testimony raises for late term pregnancy); Kirk v. Raymark Indus., 61 F.3d 147 (Cowen, J.) (3d Cir. 1995) (held, expert who testified in prior case not "unavailable" merely because beyond subpoena power; proponent should have tried to contact expert and request his attendance at trial).

398. Fed. R. Evid. 804(a)(5). The mere fact that the witness is beyond the subpoena power is not enough; the Rule states that the proponent must be unable to obtain attendance by process or "other reasonable means." A proponent might have

invokes a privilege, the witness is unavailable.[399] If the witness appears, has no privilege, but refuses to testify after being ordered to do so, the witness is unavailable.[400] The witness is also unavailable if the witness appears and testifies to a failure of recollection about the subject matter.[401] Rule 804(a) is broadly designed to accommodate the faultless proponent, and it is only when the proponent has procured the unavailability of the witness or has not made proper efforts to subpoena the witness that the proponent will not be allowed to take advantage of the Rule.[402] In fact, when the proponent has procured the unavailability of the declarant, a new hearsay exception will admit the declarant's statement.[403]

Unavailability due to temporary illness poses a special problem. Here the trial judge could allow the witness to be heard in person by granting a continuance. Although trial judges have discretion in this area, a continuance should be granted in criminal cases where the witness is vital and the charge is serious.[404]

Requirement of Deposition

Suppose that a proponent can foresee that the declarant will not be present at trial. Should the proponent be required to depose the declarant, so that the opponent will have a chance for cross-examination during the deposition? The rule makers answered this question in the affirmative. In instances in which the declarant is not present at trial (as opposed to instances in which the declarant is present, but for some reason cannot or will not testify), the proponent of the hearsay testimony must show that reasonable efforts were made to obtain the declarant's testimony by deposition.[405] However, this requirement does not apply when the hearsay is in the form of former testimony admissible under Rule 804(b)(1).[406] Then, there is no reason to require a deposition

---

means other than subpoena when, for example, a state could request another state to furnish someone incarcerated in its prison system for testimony. Even if the incarcerated person were technically beyond the subpoena power, the state should make the effort to obtain the testimony by other means. *Cf.* Barber v. Page, 390 U.S. 719, 724–25 (1968) (held, violation of confrontation clause to use declarant's hearsay statement when state failed to make good faith effort to obtain cooperation of federal authorities in delivering declarant for testimony).

399. Fed. R. Evid. 804(a)(1).

400. Fed. R. Evid. 804(a)(2).

401. Fed. R. Evid. 804(a)(3).

402. *See* Fed. R. Evid. 804(a).

403. *See* § 7.55.

404. *See, e.g.,* United States v. Faison, 679 F.2d 292, 297 (3d Cir.1982) (trial court abused discretion in finding that key prosecution witness, who could not testify for at least four to five weeks because of surgery, was unavailable in prosecution for wire fraud and transporting stolen securities in interstate commerce). In *Faison,* the Third Circuit stated that

> In exercising discretion a trial judge must consider all relevant circumstances, including: the importance of the absent witness for the case; the nature and extent of cross-examination in the earlier testimony; the nature of the illness; the expected time of recovery; the reliability of the evidence of the probable duration of the illness; and any special circumstances counselling against delay.

Id.

405. Fed. R. Evid. 804(a)(5).

406. *Id.*

because the opportunity for cross-examination was provided at the prior proceeding during which the former testimony was taken.[407]

§ 7.47 The Former Testimony Exception and Related Matters [FRE 804(b)(1)]

A typical instance of the operation of the former testimony exception can arise after a case has been reversed on appeal and remanded for a new trial. If a witness at the first trial is unavailable for the second, then that witness's testimony is admissible under the exception.[408]

When the testimony is offered in the form of a transcript of the prior trial, there are two levels of hearsay. First, the transcript is the statement of the court reporter about what was said on the witness stand at the prior trial. The public records exception creates an exception for this statement.[409] Many jurisdictions have statutes that provide specific exceptions for statements of court reporters.[410] Second, the witness's testimony at the prior trial is also hearsay, at least under the federal definition.[411] The present exception applies to allow it to be received.

Former testimony often comes into evidence through some route other than this exception. For example, former testimony can be used to impeach a witness with a prior inconsistent statement. When the former testimony is used for impeachment of the witness who gave it, the present exception is not needed. Federal Rule of Evidence 801(d)(1)(A) provides the basis for receiving the testimony.[412] Similarly, former testi-

---

407. H.R. Rep. No. 650, 93d Cong., 1st Sess. 5 (1973), reprinted in 1974 U.S. Code Cong. & Admin. News 7075, 7088.

408. Fed. R. Evid. 804(b)(1).

409. Fed. R. Evid. 803(8)(B).

410. *See, e.g.,* N.C. Gen. Stat. § 8–85 (1996):

> Testimony taken and transcribed by a court reporter and certified by the reporter or by the judge who presided at the trial at which the testimony was given, may be offered in evidence in any court as the deposition of the witness whose testimony is so taken and transcribed, in the manner, and under the rules governing the introduction of depositions in civil actions.

California's Evidence Code provides for a public records exception in Cal. Evid. Code § 1291 (West 1966). The code also provides an arguably stronger exception for the transcript of a court reporter in Cal. Evid. Code § 273 (West 1966). Transcribed and certified reports as prima facie evidence: "The report of the official reporter, or official reporter pro tempore, of any court, duly appointed and sworn, when transcribed and certified as being a correct transcript of the testimony and proceedings in the case, is prima facie evidence of such testimony and proceedings." *See* also Fed. R. Civ. Proc. 80(c) Stenographic Report or Transcript as Evidence, which provides an exception for the federal courts: "Whenever the testimony of a witness at a trial or hearing which was stenographically reported is admissible in evidence at a later trial, it may be proved by the transcript thereof duly certified by the person who reported the testimony."

411. Under the Federal Rules, hearsay is "a statement, other than one made by the declarant while testifying at the trial or hearing, offered in evidence to prove the truth of the matter asserted." Fed. R. Evid. 801 (c). Excluded from this definition are prior statements by a witness at the same trial and admissions by party opponents. Fed. R. Evid. 801 (d). Wigmore felt that former testimony should also be excluded from the definition of hearsay. His rational was that since the testimony was subject to cross-examination in the first trial the primary purpose behind the hearsay rule was satisfied. 5 John H. Wigmore, Evidence in Trials at Common Law § 1370 (James H. Chadbourn rev. 1974).

412. *See* § **7.77.**

mony of the opposing party is admissible against that party under Rule 801(d)(2) without the need for laying the foundation for the current exception.[413] Also, deposition testimony can be admitted under Rule 32 of the Rules of Civil Procedure without the need for reliance upon this exception.[414] As long as the statements made in the deposition would be admissible under the rules of evidence if they had been made by a live witness at the present trial, and provided that the deposition is being used against a party who was present or represented at the deposition (or at least had adequate notice of the deposition to have been present or represented), then the statements made in the deposition can be offered as evidence under Rule 32. As in Federal Rule of Evidence 801(d)(2) concerning an admission of a party opponent, there is no requirement of witness unavailability when introducing the deposition of a party in the current case. However, there are requirements of witness unavailability

---

413. *See* § **7.07**.

414. Fed. R. Civ. Proc. 32(a) provides as follows:

(a) Use of Depositions. At the trial or upon the hearing of a motion or an interlocutory proceeding, any part or all of a deposition, so far as admissible under the rules of evidence applied as though the witness were then present and testifying, may be used against any party who was present or represented at the taking of the deposition or who had reasonable notice thereof, in accordance with any of the following provisions:

(1) Any deposition may be used by any party for the purpose of contradicting or impeaching the testimony of deponent as a witness, or for any other purpose permitted by the Federal Rules of Evidence.

(2) The deposition of a party or of anyone who at the time of taking the deposition was an officer, director, or managing agent, or a person designated under Rule 30(b)(6) or 31(a) to testify on behalf of a public or private corporation, partnership or association or governmental agency which is a party may be used by an adverse party for any purpose.

(3) The deposition of a witness, whether or not a party, may be used by any party for any purpose if the court finds: (A) that the witness is dead; or (B) that the witness is at a greater distance than 100 miles from the place of trial or hearing, or is out of the United States, unless it appears that the absence of the witness was procured by the party offering the deposition; or (C) that the witness is unable to attend or testify because of age, illness, infirmity, or

imprisonment; or (D) that the party offering the deposition has been unable to procure the attendance of the witness by subpoena; or (E) upon application and notice, that such exceptional circumstances exist as to make it desirable, in the interest of justice and with due regard to the importance of presenting the testimony of witnesses orally in open court, to allow the deposition to be used. (4) If only part of a deposition is offered in evidence by a party, an adverse party may require the offeror to introduce any other part which ought in fairness to be considered with the part introduced, and any party may introduce any other parts.

Substitution of parties pursuant to Rule 25 does not affect the right to use depositions previously taken; and, when an action has been brought in any court of the United States or of any State and another action involving the same subject matter is afterwards brought between the same parties or their representatives or successors in interest, all depositions lawfully taken and duly filed in the former action may be used in the latter as if originally taken therefor. A deposition previously taken may also be used as permitted by the Federal Rules of Evidence.

See Ueland v. United States, 291 F.3d 993 (7th Cir.2002) (held, Fed. R. Civ. P. 32(a)(3) supplements the former testimony exception of Fed. R. Evid. 804(b)(1), so that depositions of witnesses located more than 100 miles from the place of trial are admissible even if the witnesses are not available for testimony in the sense of being beyond the court's subpoena power).

similar to those in Federal Rule of Evidence 804(b)(1) when a party offers the deposition of a witness under Federal Rule of Civil Procedure 32(a)(3). Federal Rule of Civil Procedure 32(a)(3)(E) also allows a witness's deposition to be used under "exceptional circumstances" when it is "in the interest of justice." Though this rule potentially could allow in a great deal more evidence, even where the unavailability requirements have not been met, the courts have not read this exception broadly and it has had a rather limited effect in admitting otherwise objectionable evidence.[415]

The former testimony exception is based on the theory that cross-examination under oath at a prior proceeding is an adequate substitute for cross-examination in the current proceeding.[416] Because the absence of cross-examination is thought to be the principal reason for the exclusion of hearsay, one might expect that former testimony would be freely admissible. However, the exception has been hedged about with restrictions. These restrictions include those discussed in the following sections.

§ 7.48 The Former Testimony Exception and Related Matters [FRE 804(b)(1)]—Unavailability

Like the other Rule 804 exceptions, the former testimony exception does not apply unless the witness is unavailable. (For a discussion of the concept of unavailability, see § 7.46). Common law jurisdictions also required unavailability.[417]

§ 7.49 The Former Testimony Exception and Related Matters [FRE 804(b)(1)]—Identity of Parties

Some common law courts required that the party against whom the evidence is offered be the same in both actions.[418] This rule has been criticized on ground that it results in the exclusion of reliable evidence.[419] For example, in a case in which the issue is whether property was destroyed by arson, the alleged arsonist in a criminal trial who claims the fire was accidentally caused would have every incentive to cross-examine the witness vigorously. But if that witness became unavailable in a subsequent civil case involving another party (say, the person who allegedly benefited from the arson), the testimony would be inadmissible. Yet the testimony has almost all the safeguards of courtroom testimony,

415. *See* 8A Charles A. Wright & Arthur R. Miller, Federal Practice and Procedure: Civil §§ 2142, 2146, 2150 (2d ed. 1994).

416. *See* Fed. R. Evid. 804(b)(1) advisory committee's note; see also 5 Weinstein's Federal Evidence § 807.04[1][a] (2d ed. Joseph M. McLaughlin ed. 1997); 2 McCormick on Evidence § 301 (4th ed. John W. Strong ed. 1992).

417. *See, e.g.,* School Dist. of Pontiac v. Sachse, 264 N.W. 396, 397 (Mich.1936).

418. *See* School Dist. of Pontiac v. Sachse, 264 N.W. 396, 397 (Mich.1936) (court required party against whom testimony offered to be the same in prior and current actions). Some courts even required both parties to be the same in both actions; *see, e.g.,* Bulk Trans., Inc. v. Louisiana Pub. Serv. Commn., 209 So.2d 4, 6–7 (La.1968).

419. *See* 2 McCormick on Evidence § 303 (4th ed. John W. Strong ed. 1992).

and surely the jury could be trusted enough to treat it as being better than nothing.[420]

With this sort of problem in mind, the federal rule makers originally proposed that the exception be liberalized to provide that identity of parties was not necessary so long as the party in the first action had a similar motive to cross-examine as the party in the second action.[421] However, Congress rejected this attempt and the final version of Federal Rule of Evidence 804(b)(1) required that the party against whom the evidence is offered be the same as the party involved in the prior case or, in a civil case, either the same party or a predecessor in interest.[422] Thus, if the current action is a criminal prosecution and the government wishes to offer into evidence the testimony of a witness in a prior proceeding to which the defendant was not a party, that testimony is not admissible under this exception. The same would be true of prior testimony offered by the criminal defendant against the government if the government was not a party to the prior action. To put it more simply, former testimony is not admissible against the defendant in a criminal case if the defendant was not a party to the prior proceeding.[423] When the prior case was a civil case and the case in which the testimony is offered is a criminal case, some courts take the view that similarity of interest, rather than identity of parties, is the relevant test, at least where the testimony is offered against the government in the criminal case.[424] Given the language of Rule 804(b)(1), this conclusion is difficult to justify.

In a civil case, the question whether prior testimony is admissible against a party not represented in the earlier suit depends upon whether a "predecessor in interest" of that party was represented in the prior action.[425] In its core meaning, the term predecessor in interest describes someone who had a prior interest in property that is now subject to litigation or who was otherwise in privity with a party.[426] However, the

420. *See* Travelers Fire Ins. Co. v. Wright, 322 P.2d 417, 421–22 (Okla.1958) (allowing admission of former testimony given at criminal arson trial in subsequent civil action).

421. *See* Fed. R. Evid. 804(b) (1) (Supreme Court Proposed Draft 1973), reprinted in 2 James F. Bailey & Oscar M. Trelles, The Federal Rules of Evidence: Legislative Histories and Related Documents, Doc. 7, at 33 (1980).

422. *See* H.R. Rep. No. 650, 93d Cong., 1st Sess., 15 (1973), reprinted in 4 Bailey & Trelles, *supra* note 421, Doc. 13, at 15; *see also* 5 Weinstein's Federal Evidence § 807.04[4][a] (2d ed. Joseph M. McLaughlin ed. 1997).

423. Fed. R. Evid. 804(b)(1).

424. *See* United States v. McDonald, 837 F.2d 1287, 1291–93 (5th Cir.1988) (dictum), and see cases cited therein. *But see* United States v. Harenberg, 732 F.2d 1507,

1516 (10th Cir.1984) (depositions taken in prior civil action excluded in subsequent criminal case because the United States did not have an opportunity to cross-examine declarants in the civil depositions).

425. Fed. R. Evid. 804(b)(1); see generally 5 Weinstein's Federal Evidence, *supra* note 422 § 807.04[4][a], at 804–35; 2 McCormick on Evidence *supra* note 419 § 418.

426. In Lloyd v. American Export Lines, Inc., 580 F.2d 1179 (3d Cir.1978), Judge Stern, who concurred in the result but disagreed with the majority's interpretation of predecessor in interest in Rule 804(b)(1), noted that the commentators had defined predecessor in interest in terms of a privity relationship, and gave the following definition of privity:

"The term 'privity' denotes mutual or successive relationships to the same

term has been given an expansive meaning by some courts so that the exception has potentially much broader application in civil cases, where statements by predecessors in interest can fall under the exception, than in criminal cases. For example, in *Lloyd v. American Export Lines*,[427] the plaintiff, Roland Alvarez, brought a Jones Act claim against American Export Lines, Inc. Plaintiff, a merchant mariner, had been involved in a violent encounter with Lloyd, a fellow crew member on board the freighter on which both worked.[428] Plaintiff's theory of recovery was that American Export had failed to use due care in protecting him against Lloyd. He claimed that he had been harassed by Lloyd and had reported these prior incidents to superiors. Alvarez introduced testimony at trial that Lloyd, while intoxicated, made a vicious unprovoked attack upon him. The jury did not hear Lloyd's side of the story, although the defendant offered it in the form of a transcript of a Coast Guard hearing, as well as the report of the hearing examiner. The trial court excluded the evidence.

The Third Circuit held that the hearing examiner's report should have been admitted under the public records exception, see § **7.27**, and that the recorded testimony of Lloyd should have been admitted under 804(b)(1). It found that Lloyd's unavailability had been sufficiently established. On what it viewed as the "more difficult" question, the court decided that the Coast Guard, which had been a party in the prior hearing, was a "predecessor in interest" for purposes of Rule 804(b)(1), so the transcript of the hearing was admissible as former testimony. The same alleged misconduct was involved in both the Coast Guard hearing and Alvarez's civil action. The Coast Guard investigating officer at the prior hearing had sought to establish that Lloyd had been intoxicated, that he had started the fight with Alvarez, and that he had harassed Alvarez—all facts that Alvarez sought to establish in the later civil case. The court decided that because the Coast Guard and Alvarez had similar interests in the two cases and a similar motive to cross-examine, the predecessor in interest requirement was satisfied.[429]

The result is a very broad interpretation of that requirement, one that seems to make it essentially the same as the similar motive requirement. For that reason the decision seems contrary to legislative

---

rights of property, and privies are distributed into several classes, according to the manner of this relationship. Thus, there are privies in estate, as donor and donee, lessor and lessee, and joint tenants; privies in blood, as heir and ancestor, and co-parceners; privies in representation, as executor and testator, administrator and intestate; privies in law, where the law, without privity of blood or estate casts the land upon another, as by escheat."
The above passage quotes Metropolitan St. Ry. v. Gumby, 99 F. 192, 198 (2d Cir.1900), which is also quoted in 11 James A. Moore, Moore's Federal Practice § 807.04[02] (2d

ed. 1988). For a similar definition, see Black's Law Dictionary 1199 (6th ed. 1990).

427. 580 F.2d 1179, 1181–87 (3d Cir. 1978).

428. Lloyd, Alvarez's alleged attacker, brought the ongoing claim. Alvarez was impleaded by defendant. Lloyd then dropped out of the case.

429. *See also* Horne v. Owens–Corning Fiberglas Corp., 4 F.3d 276 (4th Cir.1993) (held, prior claimant in similar asbestos case was predecessor in interest because of similarity of motive to examine witnesses, even though the two parties had no relationship and were not in privity).

intent. Congress acted affirmatively to supplement the similar motive requirement with a requirement that the parties be either identical or a civil predecessor in interest. To read the predecessor in interest requirement to mean nothing more than that the parties have a similar motive renders this action by Congress meaningless.[430] During consideration of the Federal Rules, the House added the requirement either that the parties be identical or, in a civil case, that the party's predecessor in interest have had an opportunity for cross-examination. The House Committee on the Judiciary stated that the reason for the change was that "it is generally unfair to impose upon the party against whom the hearsay evidence is being offered responsibility for the manner in which the witness was previously handled by another party."[431] The Senate Committee on the Judiciary recommended approval of the House change, describing the difference between the original version containing only a similar motive requirement and the amended version as "not great."[432] The *Lloyd* case noted this language and stated, "We, too, fail to see a compelling difference between the two approaches."[433] It specifically rejected the idea that "this change in wording signaled a return to the common law approach to former testimony, requiring privity or a common property interest between the parties."[434] The Sixth Circuit has followed the *Lloyd* test, recognizing that it collapses the two criteria of predecessor in interest and similar motive to cross-examine into the same test, and approving of that result.[435]

430. *But see* 2 McCormick on Evidence, *supra* note 419 § 303, at 313, where the authors note the changing position of the treatise over time and ultimately opt for an "intermediate" position:

This state of legislative history has left little concrete guidance in determining congressional intent. Having taken the view in the 1978 Pocket Part that privity was required between the parties to satisfy the "predecessor in interest" requirement and the view in the 1984 Third Edition that the intention was to leave the Supreme Court version intact in civil cases, it is perhaps appropriate that this treatise now take an intermediate position. That, indeed, appears to be the proper course of action.

(Footnote omitted.) The authors then suggest that the rule be interpreted to "require[] the courts to insure fairness directly by seriously considering whether the prior cross-examination can be fairly held against the later party." *Id.* at 317.

431. H.R. Rep. No. 650, 93d Cong., 1st Sess. 15 (1973), reprinted in 4 Bailey & Trelles, *supra* note 421, Doc. 13, at 15.

432. S. Rep. No. 1277, 93d Cong., 2d Sess. 28 (1974), reprinted in 4 Bailey & Trelles, *supra* note 421, Doc. 15, at 28.

433. Lloyd v. American Export Lines, 580 F.2d 1179, 1185 (3d Cir.1978).

434. *Id.* at 1185 n.5. *See also* New England Mutual Life Ins. Co. v. Anderson, 888 F.2d 646 (10th Cir.1989) (court cites *Lloyd* case and apparently accepts its approach to predecessor in interest definition, but holds testimony in prior criminal trial against co-conspirator not admissible against civil party because, under circumstances, co-conspirator had no motive or interest in protecting innocence of party against whom testimony now offered).

435. *See* Murphy v. Owens–Illinois, Inc., 779 F.2d 340, 343 (6th Cir.1985); Dykes v. Ramark Indus., 801 F.2d 810, 815–16 (6th Cir.1986); *see also* Supermarket of Marlinton, Inc. v. Meadow Gold Dairies, Inc., 71 F.3d 119, 127–28 (4th Cir.1995) (in antitrust action alleging that certain dairies conspired to fix milk prices, trial court improperly excluded testimony of witness who testified against dairies in an earlier criminal trial; testimony should have been admitted because the dominant motive in both trials was to show that a conspiracy never occurred).

§ 7.50 The Former Testimony Exception and Related Matters [FRE 804(b)(1)]—Similar Motive to Cross-examine

Federal Rule of Evidence 804(b)(1) requires that the party in the prior action have had an "opportunity and similar motive to develop the testimony by direct, cross, or redirect examination." The similar motive can be lacking, for example, when the party in the first action had less to lose or different goals than in the second action. However, neither conceptual differences between the two actions nor development of additional ammunition for cross-examination between the two trials are enough to prevent admission of the prior testimony if the motives for cross-examination were essentially the same on the two occasions.[436]

The operation of the similar motive requirement is illustrated by the litigation over the deposition of Dr. Kenneth Wallace Smith, the deceased former medical director of Johns–Manville Corporation. The Smith deposition has nourished its own nest of cases on the former testimony exception.[437] Dr. Smith was a former medical director of a manufacturer of asbestos products with 20 years' experience. He was deposed in 1976 in a Pennsylvania state court case, and subsequently died. His deposition was later offered by plaintiffs in various asbestosis cases on issues such as the state of the art during the 1940s and 1950s. The reception it received depended upon the party against whom it was offered and the circumstances of the particular case. For example, in *Murphy v. Owens–Illinois, Inc.*,[438] the court upheld a trial judge's decision to exclude the deposition.[439] The party against whom the deposition was offered at trial had not been a party in the case in which the deposition was taken.[440] This in itself was not enough to support exclusion, in the view of the Sixth Circuit, since it took a generous view of the

436. *See* United States v. Miles, 290 F.3d 1341 (11th Cir.2002) (held, trial court did not abuse discretion in finding that defendant had similar motive to disprove connection with methamphetamine lab in second case as in first, even though broader conspiracy was alleged in second case); Supermarket of Marlinton, Inc. v. Meadow Gold Dairies, Inc., 71 F.3d 119, 127–28 (4th Cir.1995) (in antitrust action alleging that certain dairies conspired to fix milk prices, trial court improperly excluded testimony of witness who testified against dairies in an earlier criminal trial; testimony should have been admitted because the dominant motive in both trials was to show that a conspiracy never existed); United States v. Koon, 34 F.3d 1416, 1428 (9th Cir.1994) (held, defendants in federal civil rights/police brutality case arising from beating of Rodney King were not deprived of 6th Amendment right to confrontation by admission of videotaped trial testimony of witness against them in earlier state criminal trial; rule's requirements of similar motive and opportunity were satisfied despite fact that additional ammunition for cross-examination had been developed since first trial); Williams v. C.I.R., 999 F.2d 760, 764–66 (4th Cir.1993) (in action for tax deficiencies, transcript of testimony by government witness in defendant's prior criminal trial for possession of narcotics admissible where defendant failed to show how motive to cross-examine witness differed from prior trial and where transcript was only used to show commissioner's deficiency calculations were not arbitrary).

437. *See* Dykes v. Raymark Indus., 801 F.2d 810 (6th Cir.1986); Dartez v. Fibreboard Corp, 765 F.2d 456 (5th Cir. 1985); Murphy v. Owens–Illinois, Inc., 779 F.2d 340 (6th Cir.1985); Clay v. Johns–Manville Sales Corp., 722 F.2d 1289 (6th Cir.1983); In re Johns–Manville/Asbestosis Cases, 93 F.R.D. 853 (N.D.Ill.1982).

438. 779 F.2d 340 (6th Cir.1985).

439. *Id.* at 347.

440. *Id.* at 343.

requirement that the testimony be offered against a party who was represented or had a predecessor in interest in the prior litigation. If the prior litigant had a similar motive, then it qualified as a predecessor in interest. In this case the prior litigant did not have a similar motive.[441] The defendant corporations that were represented at the deposition did not have the same motive to prove a primitive state of the art during the 1940s and 1950s that the defendant against whom it was offered in the Murphy case did.[442] The reason was that the latter defendant, Owens–Illinois, had stopped manufacturing asbestos-containing products in 1958. The parties who took the deposition, Johns–Manville and Raybestos–Manhattan, had continued manufacturing until the 1960s and 1970s. They would possibly have harmed themselves if they had shown a primitive state of the art in the 1940s or 1950s, because that would have highlighted how much had been learned since then.[443] Owens–Illinois, on the other hand, would have wished to prove that the state of the art through 1958 was primitive, and had that company been able to examine Smith at his deposition, it would have sought to establish these facts. Therefore, Owens–Illinois would have conducted its examination of Smith much differently than Johns–Manville and Raybestos–Manhattan. In other cases where the difference in motive was not as pronounced, the Smith deposition has been admitted.[444]

The Supreme Court examined the "similar motive" requirement of the former testimony exception in *United States v. Salerno*.[445] *Salerno* was a case in which two grand jury witnesses had given testimony before the grand jury that was favorable to defendant. At trial, the grand jury witnesses claimed the right against self-incrimination and refused to testify. The defense sought to introduce their grand jury testimony under Rule 804(b)(1). The prosecution objected, arguing that at the grand jury stage its motive to cross-examine the witnesses was not similar to what its motive would have been at trial, and therefore that the "similar motive" requirement of the hearsay exception was not satisfied.

Speaking through Justice Thomas, an 8–1 majority of the Court concluded that the "plain language" of the rule supported the prosecution's contention. The defense had argued that adversarial fairness required that the evidence be admitted, contending that when witnesses testify favorably to the government at the grand jury stage, the government gives them immunity and obtains their trial testimony, but that when the witnesses testify unfavorably the government refuses to give immunity and objects to receiving their grand jury testimony. Justice

441. *Id.* at 347.

442. *Id.*

443. *Id.*

444. *See, e.g.*, Clay v. Johns–Manville Sales Corp., 722 F.2d 1289, 1295 (6th Cir. 1983) (where prior and current defendants had similar motive to cross-examine Smith regarding manufacturer's knowledge of hazards of asbestos in products liability cases, deposition was admissible); *see also* Dykes v. Raymark Indus., 801 F.2d 810, 817 (6th Cir.1986) (where objecting party failed to explain why motive and opportunity to cross-examine Smith differed in the first case, deposition was admissible in the second case).

445.   505 U.S. 317 (1992).

Thomas indicated that the concept of adversarial fairness did not justify carving an exception to the plain requirements of Rule 804(b)(1). The Court remanded the case for a determination as to whether the prosecutor did in fact have a similar motive to develop testimony at the grand jury stage. Justice Kennedy dissented, saying that the record of the particular case did show that the government had the opportunity and similar motive to develop the witness's testimony at the grand jury proceeding.

Whether the "similar motive" requirement of Rule 804(b)(1) has been satisfied is clearly a context-driven issue. Each case must be examined on its own facts, as small changes in legal theory, the line-up of parties, and other factors can affect the outcome. In each case, the parties must be prepared to demonstrate to the court the existence (or nonexistence) of a motive sufficiently similar to satisfy the Rule.

§ 7.51   The Dying Declarations Exception [FRE 804(b)(2)]

The theory behind the dying declarations exception is that one would not want to go to one's Maker with a lie upon one's lips. This has been questioned; some might feel freer to lie because they could escape earthly retribution. Also, the problems of memory, perception, and narrative mistakes may be amplified when a person is dying.[446] Nonetheless, this time-honored exception, one of the very oldest of hearsay exceptions, shows no signs of mortality itself.

There are several elements to the foundation for the exception, discussed in the ensuing sections.

Unavailability

As with the other Rule 804 exceptions, the declarant must be unavailable. Under the Federal Rule, it is possible for the declarant to be unavailable for some reason other than death.[447] For example, the declarant might have been shot at the same time and by the same person as the murder victim, named the perpetrator while believing that death was imminent, and then have recovered. If the declarant then refuses to testify, the requirements of the exception have been met.

---

446. Roger C. Park, *A Subject Matter Approach to Hearsay Reform*, 86 Mich. L. Rev. 51, 76–77 (1987) (noting these criticisms, but noting also that the circumstances under which these statements are made tends to decrease the dangers of fabrication by the declarant or in-court witness and that dangers of misreporting and improper influence on declarant through police interrogations are lessened); *see also* Fed. R. Evid. 804(b)(2) advisory committee's note; 2 McCormick on Evidence § 310 (4th ed. John W. Strong ed. 1992); 5 Weinstein's Federal Evidence § 807.05[1], at 804–42 to 804–43 (2d ed. Joseph M McLaughlin ed. 1997); Ralph Slovenko, *Deathbed Declarations*, 14 J. Psychiatry & L. 469 (1996).

447. *See* Fed. R. Evid. 804(b)(2) advisory committee's mote ("Unavailability is not limited to death"). Many courts previously only allowed the testimony if the declarant was dead. *See* State v. Carden, 183 S.E. 898, 903 (N.C.1936) (stating rule that declarant must have died before statement admissible).

Belief that Death Imminent

"Over the strong objections of the state prosecutors, Lincoln addressed the preacher: 'State whether you were with Grek Grafton shortly before he died and at the time he was expecting death, and if so, state what you heard, if you heard anything.' "[448]

Attorney Abe Lincoln may have been jumping ahead a bit in trying to lay the foundation and get in the evidence itself with one triple question, but his question incorporates a version of the most important element of the modern exception. The declarant must have been "expecting death," or, in the words of the Federal Rule, must have made the statement while believing that death was "imminent."[449] The victim's own statement about belief in imminent death may be used in laying the foundation, and it is perhaps the most common method.[450] Evidence that the victim was told of impending death,[451] or occasionally that the injury was so grievous that the imminence of death was obvious,[452] may also be used to lay the foundation.

Statement Concerns the Cause or Circumstances of Death

Suppose a declarant, knowing that death is imminent, makes the statement "Smith owes me $1000." The exception would not apply. The dying declaration must concern the cause and circumstances of the declarant's expected death.[453] This prevents dying persons from making

---

448. N.Y. Times, Feb. 10, 1989, at 25, col. 4 (excerpt from newly discovered Lincoln transcripts).

449. See Fed. R. Evid. 804(b)(2); see also Pfeil v. Rogers, 757 F.2d 850, 861 (7th Cir.1985) (affidavit containing statements of murder witness who later committed suicide not admissible, since statements were not made immediately before suicide and therefore were not made in contemplation of imminent death); United States v. Layton, 549 F.Supp. 903, 918 (N.D.Cal.1982) (tape-recorded statements of Jim Jones concerning the killing of Congressman Leo Ryan during the mass suicide at Jonestown inadmissible where there was no evidence showing Jones believed his own death was imminent and where statements would have nothing to do with the cause or circumstances of Jones death); State v. Penley, 347 S.E.2d 783, 789 (N.C.1986) (videotape of victim admissible where homicide victim's statements showed belief of imminent death); Boone v. State, 668 S.W.2d 17,20–21 (Ark.1984) (where child had vomited blood after beating and asked whether he was going to die, statements made by the child prior to assurances from his mother that he would live were admissible).

450. See Irving Younger, Hearsay: A Practical Guide Through the Thicket 158–59 (1988); see also Ferdinand S. Tinio, Annotation, *Statements of Declarant As Sufficiently Showing Consciousness of Impending Death to Justify Admission*, 53 A.L.R.3d

785 (1973); Annotation, *Opinion of Doctor or Other Attendant As to Declarants Consciousness of Imminent Death So As To Qualify His Statement as Dying Declaration*, 48 A.L.R.2d 733 (1956); Commonwealth v. Peyton, 62 A.2d 37, 40 (Pa.1948) (imminence of death established by nature of wound); 5 Weinstein's Federal Evidence, *supra* note 446 § 805.05[4][b], at 804–44 ("The declarant's belief in the imminence of death may be shown by the declarant's own statements, or through circumstantial evidence such as the nature of the wounds, opinions of declarant's physicians, the fact that declarant received last rites, and statements made in declarant's presence") (footnotes omitted).

451. See Shepard v. United States, 290 U.S. 96, 99–100 (1933) (requiring a positive statement from the declarant as to belief of imminent death); see 5 Weinstein's Federal Evidence, *supra* note 446 § 805.05[4][b], at 804–44; Annotation, *supra* note 450.

452. See, e.g., United States v. Mobley, 421 F.2d 345, 347 (5th Cir.1970) (wounds so severe that victim must have known death imminent); see also Commonwealth v. Peyton, 62 A.2d 37, 40 (Pa.1948) (severity of wounds indicated consciousness of imminent death).

453. Fed. R. Evid. 804(b)(2); 5 Weinstein's Federal Evidence, *supra* note 446 § 805.05[5][b], at 804–45, at 804–130; 2

self-serving statements designed to help their heirs. While the rule does not bar all such statements (e.g., a person dying from an accident might make a statement about the accident that was later helpful to heirs in a wrongful death action) it does bar statements that are irrelevant to the declarant's current predicament.[454]

Present Action Is a Civil Case or Homicide Prosecution

At common law, the dying declaration exception was limited to homicide prosecutions.[455] The federal rule makers extended its scope to civil actions. That leaves one area in which the federal exception does not apply—criminal prosecutions for matters other than homicide.[456] It is not clear why the exception was limited in this fashion. The danger of concocting dying declarations about matters other than death would seem to be met by the requirement that the declaration concern the circumstances and cause of death. Apparently the limitation was due to a general distrust of dying declarations, at least where criminal penalties are involved, and the influence of common law precedents.[457]

Personal Knowledge Required

As with most other hearsay exceptions, the dying declaration is admissible only to the extent that it would be admissible if the declarant were present and testifying.[458] Thus, the declarant who was shot while

McCormick on Evidence, *supra* note 446 § 311.

454. *See* Fed. R. Evid. 804(b)(2) advisory committee's note ("when the statement deals with matters other than the supposed death, its influence is believed to be sufficiently attenuated to justify the limitation"); United States v. Layton, 549 F.Supp. 903, 918 (N.D.Cal.1982) (statements made by Jim Jones regarding killing of congressman inadmissible because they did not concern the cause or circumstances of Jones's death, and because they were not clearly made with belief of imminent death); United States v. Sacasas, 381 F.2d 451, 454 (2d Cir.1967) (statement that co-indictee had nothing to do with bank robbery held inadmissible); 5 Weinstein's Federal Evidence, *supra* note 446 § 807.05[5][b], at 804–45 (noting that this requirement can result in keeping out some very helpful evidence and arguing for broad treatment of this requirement where "admission of the statement will help the jury in its task, i.e., whether it is sufficiently reliable and relevant to withstand exclusion because its probative value is substantially outweighed by the danger of prejudice to the party against whom it is offered"); Charles W. Quick, *Some Reflections on Dying Declarations*, 6 Howard L.J. 109, 116 (1960).

455. *See* 2 McCormick on Evidence, *supra* note 446 § 311; *see also* Annotation,

Admissibility of Dying Declarations in Civil Case, 47 A.L.R.2d 526 (1956).

456. Fed. R. Evid. 804(b)(2); 5 Weinstein's Federal Evidence, *supra* note 446 § 807.05[2], at 804–43.

457. *See* H.R. Rep. No. 650, 93d Cong., 1st Sess. 15 (1973), reprinted at 4 James F. Bailey & Oscar M. Trelles, The Federal Rules of Evidence: Legislative Histories and Related Documents, Doc. 13 at 15–16 (1980):

> The Committee did not consider dying declarations as among the most reliable forms of hearsay. Consequently, it amended the provision to limit their admissibility in criminal cases to homicide prosecutions, where exceptional need for the evidence is present. This is existing law. At the same time, the Committee approved the expansion to civil actions and proceedings where the stakes do not involve possible imprisonment, although noting that this could lead to forum shopping in some instances.

See also 2 McCormick on Evidence, *supra* note 446 § 283, at 328 ("The subsequent history of the rule is an object lesson in the use of precedents to preserve and fossilize judicial mistake of an earlier generation").

458. Generally the declarant must have the capacities required of any witness, that is, the declarant must be able to per-

sleeping, and who then states a suspicion about who did the shooting, has not made an admissible dying declaration because the declarant lacks personal knowledge.[459]

§ 7.52   The Declarations Against Interest Exception [FRE 804(b)(3)]

Federal Rule 804(b)(3) sets out an exception for declarations against interest. The exception is based on the theory that reasonable people usually do not make statements against their interest unless the statements are true.[460]

Admissions Rule Distinguished

The exception must be distinguished from the rule receiving admissions of party opponents:

1. The declaration against interest is admissible only if the person making the statement is unavailable–that is, dead, unable to testify because of mental or physical illness, unwilling to testify despite a court order, or not compellable for some other reason.[461]

   The admission of a party-opponent, by contrast, is admissible whether or not the declarant is available for testimony. Even if the declarant is sitting in the back of the courtroom when the statement is offered, the opponent can still offer the statement in lieu of live testimony. No one has an obligation to call the party-opponent.[462]

2. The declaration against interest is admissible whether or not the declarant is a party or the agent of a party.[463] The party admission is only admissible when the declarant is a party or the

---

ceive and relate facts, have personal knowledge of the facts testified to, and understand the obligation to tell the truth. *See* Boone v. State, 668 S.W.2d 17, 21 (Ark. 1984) ("In order to qualify as a dying declaration the statement must be made by a witness (1) who was a competent witness"); *see also* Annotation, *Admissibility in Criminal Trial of Dying Declarations Involving an Asserted Opinion or Conclusion*, 86 A.L.R.2d 905 (1962).

459. *See* Fed. R. Evid. 804(b) (2) advisory committee's note ("Continuation of a requirement of first-hand knowledge is assured by Rule 602"); 5 Weinstein's Federal Evidence, *supra* note 446 § 807.05[5][a], at 804–45; Shepard v. United States, 290 U.S. 96, 101 (1933) ("To let the declaration in, the inference must be permissible that there was knowledge or the opportunity for knowledge as to the acts that are declared"). *See also* United States v. Velent-

zas, No. 91 CR 38415, 1993 WL 37339 (E.D.N.Y. 1993) (denying government's motion in limine to admit murder victim's statements, after being shot repeatedly from car with tinted glass, that "Spiros [defendant] had done this to me" and victim's reply of "Spiros Velentzas" to police questions about who shot him; victim was talking to defendant on phone from defendant's travel agency, where victim had agreed to meet defendant, but victim lacked personal knowledge that defendant had him shot).

460.   Fed. R. Evid. 804(b)(3) advisory committee's note.

461.   Fed. R. Evid. 804(a), (b)(3); 5 John H. Wigmore, Evidence in Trials at Common Law § 1456 (James H. Chadbourn rev. 1974).

462.   Fed. R. Evid. 801(d)(2).

463.   Fed. R. Evid. 804(b)(3).

agent of a party, and then only when offered by the opposing party.[464]

3. A declaration against interest must have been against interest when made in order to be admissible.[465] The admission need not have been against interest. If a party made a statement at a time when the statement was self-serving, the opposing party is nonetheless entitled to have that statement received as a party admission at trial should it turn out to be to the advantage of the opposing party to do so.[466]

§ 7.53 The Declarations Against Interest Exception [FRE 804(b)(3)]—Types of Interest That Qualify

The declaration against interest must be against a certain type of interest in order to qualify for the exception. The common law judges constructed the following hierarchy of interests, with interests nearer the top of the list having a better chance of qualifying for the exception:

1. Pecuniary and proprietary interest (e.g., statements that admit a debt or concede another's property interest).

2. Tort or contract interest (statements that potentially expose the declarant to civil liability).

3. Penal interest (statements that expose the declarant to criminal liability).

4. Self-respect interest (statements that humiliate the declarant, but do not expose the declarant to liability).

Common law jurisdictions tended to admit statements in the first category, and perhaps the second, but not the third or fourth.[467] Thus, "I gave my diamond to my eldest daughter," "I owe Jarvik $100," "He has a right of way across my land," or "I am holding this as agent for Hardwick" would all be admissible as against declarant's interest, whereas the confession "I am Jack the Ripper" would not have been admissible at common law under the present exception.

At first impression this different treatment of statements against pecuniary/proprietary interest and statements against penal interest seems anomalous, even bizarre. Why should a statement that exposes the declarant to a prison term or worse be treated as less reliable than a statement that might only lead to a small money loss? The limitation is not as arbitrary as it appears at first glance, however. If the statement "I am Jack the Ripper" is offered *against the declarant*, then it does not need the help of the present exception to find its way into evidence. The

---

464. Fed. R. Evid. 801(d)(2).

465. Fed. R. Evid. 804(b)(3).

466. Fed. R. Evid. 801(d)(2) advisory committee's note.

467. *See, e.g.,* 5 John H. Wigmore, Evidence in Trials at Common Law § 1477 (3d ed 1940); Donnelly v. United States, 228 U.S. 243, 273 (1913) (declaration against penal interest as opposed to pecuniary interest inadmissible); G.M. McKelvey Co. v. General Cas. Co. of America, 142 N.E.2d 854, 856 (Ohio 1957) (rule limited to declarations against "pecuniary or proprietary interest").

admissions rule is an ample gateway. But when the statement "I am Jack the Ripper" is not offered to implicate the speaker who is a party to the action, but rather to exonerate another person, the present exception is needed. It is here that the common law judges shut the door.[468]

Why should the statement be admitted into evidence with open arms when it incriminates, but turned aside when it exonerates? The common law judges had a skeptical attitude founded on experience. They believed that persons accused of crime would be likely to find friends who would fabricate a confession by a declarant who had conveniently died or disappeared, and that gullible juries would be too ready to treat these concoctions as raising a reasonable doubt.[469] Even before the Federal Rules, there were dissenters from this skeptical attitude. Wigmore condemned it roundly, saying:

> This is the ancient rusty weapon that has always been brandished to oppose any reform in the rules of Evidence, viz., the argument of danger of abuse. This would be a good argument against admitting any witnesses at all, for it is notorious that some witnesses will lie and that it is difficult to avoid being deceived by their lies. The truth is that any rule which hampers an honest man in exonerating himself is a bad rule, even if it also hampers a villain in falsely passing for an innocent.[470]

The limitation has persisted stubbornly, however, though in a diminished form. The current Federal Rules do permit statements against penal interest to be received to exonerate the defendant in a criminal case, but only if they are clearly corroborated, and the courts have applied the rule as written.[471] In civil cases, however, declarations against penal interest are freely admissible without any requirement of corroboration.[472] The ancient distrust of the scheming prisoner is thus retained, but the criminal defendant has the opportunity to use the third-party confession to escape punishment if it is sufficiently corroborated by other evidence.[473]

---

468. For an analysis of the admissibility of statements tending to implicate someone other than the defendant, see David McCord, *"But Perry Mason Made It Look So Easy!" The Admissibility of Evidence Offered By a Criminal Defendant to Suggest that Someone Else is Guilty*, 63 Tenn. L. Rev. 917 (1996).

469. *See* Fed. R. Evid. 804(b)(3) advisory committee's note.

470. 5 Wigmore, *supra* note 467 § 1477.

471. Fed. R. Evid. 804(b)(3). *See also* United States v. Bahadar, 954 F.2d 821, 828–29 (2d Cir.1992) (statement made after arrest by alleged accomplice, admitting accomplice's guilt but attempting to exonerate proponent of statement, inadmissible as lacking in sufficient corroboration; declarant was "all over the place" in his stories

exonerating the accused); United States v. Arthur, 949 F.2d 211 (6th Cir.1991) (confession exonerating defendant was adequately against interest and corroborated, despite government argument that declarant had confessed to so many other crimes that the extra liability was insignificant; corroboration included similar confession of another person exonerating the accused, the fact that only two persons were involved in the robbery and the fact that the declarant had been filmed apparently casing the bank hours before the robbery).

472. *See id.*

473. As this edition went to press in spring, 2004, a proposed amendment to Rule 804(b)(3), not yet promulgated by the Supreme Court would provide:

> But in criminal cases a statement tending to expose the declarant to criminal

A proposed amendment to Rule 804(b)(3) would change the final sentence of the rule to read as follows:

> A statement tending to expose the declarant to criminal liability is admissible under this subdivision in the following circumstances only: (A) if offered in a civil case or to exculpate an accused in a criminal case, it is supported by corroborating circumstances that clearly indicate its trustworthiness, or (B) if offered to inculpate an accused, it is supported by particularized guarantees of trustworthiness.

The amendment would change the rule in two ways. First, it would require corroboration when a statement against penal interest is offered by either party in a civil case. Second, it codifies the constitutional doctrine that the statement must be supported by particularized guarantees of trustworthiness when offered by the prosecution in a criminal case. It does not, however, require corroboration when offered by the prosecution.[474]

There is one type of interest that will not suffice to support admission of a declaration against interest. A declaration that merely humiliates the declarant without exposing the declarant to legal liability will not suffice. For example, a shamefaced confession that the declarant has a secret vice will not suffice, in the absence of potential civil or criminal liability. The advisory committee originally proposed that self-degrading statements of this nature be received as declarations against interest, and the Supreme Court accepted this recommendation when it originally promulgated the Federal Rules of Evidence.[475] The House Committee on the Judiciary, however, eliminated the provision governing self-degrading statements. It stated that statements falling into this category did not have sufficient guarantees of reliability.[476] Despite the failure of the Federal Rules to embrace declarations against social interest, there is some state authority for including them within the exception,[477] and the commentary contains support for this extension of the traditional declaration against interest exception.[478]

Assuming the statement implicates one of the types of interest covered by the rule, the proponent must still persuade the court that the

---

liability is admissible under this subdivision in the following circumstances only:

if offered to exculpate an accused, it is supported by corroborating circumstances that clearly indicate its trustworthiness, or

if offered to inculpate the accused, it is supported by particularized guarantees of trustworthiness.

474. The proposed amendment has been released for public comment by the Standing Committee of the Judicial Conference. In the normal course of rule-making, it cannot become law before December 1, 2004.

475. H.R. Rep. No. 650, 93d Cong., 1st Sess. 16 (1973), reprinted in 1974 U.S. Code Cong. & Admin. News 7075, 7089.

476. *Id.*

477. *See, e.g.*, Cal. Evid. Code § 1230 (1966) (covering statements that "create[] . . . a risk of making [declarant] an object of hatred, ridicule, or social disgrace in the community").

478. *See, e.g.*, Edward J. Imwinkelried, *Declarations Against Social Interest: The (Still) Embarrassingly Neglected Hearsay Exception*, 69 S. Cal. L. Rev. 1427 (1996).

statement is "so far contrary" to that interest "that a reasonable person in the declarant's position would not have made the statement unless believing it to be true."[479] Though somewhat inelegantly, the rule establishes an objective test. The proponent must demonstrate that a reasonable person would not have made the statement unless that person believed it to be true. Whether the standard is satisfied in a given situation will depend on the context in which the statement was made. An inmate's statement taking responsibility for a stabbing might be highly credible if made while being questioned by prison authorities and having been informed of the right to remain silent. The same statement, however, might be less credible if made by a prison inmate to other inmates and outside the presence of authorities. In that situation, the desire to establish oneself in the inmate hierarchy might motivate a person to take responsibility for the stabbing even if the person is not responsible.

§ 7.54 The Declarations Against Interest Exception [FRE 804(b)(3)]—Statements That Are Only Partly Disserving

Questions sometimes arise about the status of statements that are partly disserving and partly self-serving or neutral. For example, in *United States v. Barrett*,[480] the court examined a case in which a man named Tilley had made an out-of-court statement to some card-playing acquaintances that implicated himself in a stamp theft conspiracy. Tilly also said that "Buzzy" was involved. When asked by his acquaintances whether he was referring to "Bucky [the defendant]" or "Buzzy," Tilley said, "No, Bucky wasn't involved. It was Buzzy." Naturally, the defendant wanted to use this out-of-court statement exonerating him as evidence in his defense. He argued that it was a statement against Tilley's interest because it implicated Tilley in crime.[481] The trial court excluded the statement on the ground that the relevant part—the part exonerating Bucky—was not against the declarant Tilley's interest. The first Circuit reversed, holding that the statement was admissible. It expressed the view that the whole statement was at least "arguably disserving" to Tilley, because knowing exactly who was involved showed an "insider's knowledge" that made Tilley's involvement more likely. The court also noted that the case law, "while far from settled," tended to grant a certain latitude to contextual statements.[482]

As the *Barrett* court noted, the treatment of neutral passages in otherwise disserving statements has been far from uniform. Many courts, fortified by Wigmore's approval, allowed the entire statement, including the neutral portion, into evidence, as if the utterance of one disserving thought had put the declarant in a truth-telling frame of

---

479. Fed. R. Evid. 804(b)(3).

480. 539 F.2d 244 (1st Cir.1976).

481. *Id.* at 249.

482. *Id.* at 252 (citing McCormick, Handbook of the Law of Evidence § 279(a) (2d ed.1972)).

mind.[483] And there was a contrary view, also amply supported, that would weed the garden, separating the disserving statements from those that are neutral or self-serving.[484]

The problem in *Barrett* is presented in a different form when the statement of a declarant implicates both the declarant and the defendant. In that situation, the declaration against interest exception is frequently not needed, because the statement will often be admissible as the admission of a co-conspirator.[485] Sometimes the co-conspirator route to admission, however, will not be available. For example, it would not be available if the statement was made after the conspiracy ended.[486] Then, the declaration against interest exception would furnish a possible basis for admission under the theory of *Barrett*, if the court were willing to accept "contextual latitude" and admit the statement implicating another person under the umbrella of the other, clearly disserving statement. Nothing in the Federal Rules of Evidence stands in the way of this approach. Indeed, after considering the issue, the Senate Judiciary Committee rejected a provision that would have prevented the use of confessions by others willing to inculpate the accused.[487]

In its 1994 decision in *Williamson v. United States*,[488] the Supreme Court addressed the application of the exception to statements that incriminate the defendant. In *Williamson*, the Court reviewed a drug crime conviction in which the trial court allowed the prosecution to use the post-arrest statements of an accomplice against the defendant. In the statements, the declarant admitted some involvement in the drug activity, but shifted the bulk of the blame to the defendant by implicating him as the person for whom the drugs were being delivered.

The Court held that each statement in a narrative must be considered separately, and that particular statements that do not individually inculpate the declarant are not admissible under Rule 804(b)(3), even if they are made within a broader narrative that is generally self-inculpatory. A district court may not assume that a statement is self-inculpatory just because the statement is part of a fuller confession, especially when, as in *Williamson*, the statement implicates someone else.

The Court maintained that this reading will not eviscerate the declaration against penal interest exception as it still allows admission of those statements which are truly self-inculpatory, rather than those that

483. *See, e.g.,* United States v. Goodlow, 500 F.2d 954, 956–57 (8th Cir.1974) (declarant's statements that he "was good for the crime" and defendant was not "good for it" must be considered together and are admissible); 5 John H. Wigmore, Evidence in Trials at Common Law § 1465 (James H. Chadbourn rev. 1974).

484. *See, e.g.,* United States v. Seyfried, 435 F.2d 696, 698 (7th Cir. 1970) (where statement is separable and one part is against declarant's interest and one is not, only part against interest is admissi-ble); United States v. Marquez, 462 F.2d 893, 895 (2d Cir.1972) (only proper to admit portion of statement against declarant's interest; portion exculpating another inadmissible).

485. *See* § 7.08.

486. Fed. R. Evid. 801(d)(2)(E).

487. S. Rep. No. 1277, 93d Cong., 2d Sess. 21, reprinted in 1974 U.S. Code Cong. & Admin. News 7051, 7068.

488. 512 U.S. 594 (1994).

merely attempt to shift blame or curry favor. The question under the rule is always whether the statement at issue is sufficiently against the declarant's penal interest under the rule's language, and this question can only be answered in light of all the surrounding circumstances.[489]

Statements made in custody that incriminate other people are often not against the individual interest of the declarant, as when they are motivated by the desire to shift blame. However, sometimes a statement that incriminates another person can also be against the interest of the declarant. Suppose that, under interrogation, a suspect admits that he has been living with another suspect. The admission may be genuinely incriminating of both the declarant and the other person.

Even if an accomplice statement fits within a jurisdiction's declaration against interest exception, it could still be excluded on the ground that receiving it would violate the right to confrontation under the Sixth Amendment.[490] The Court in *Williamson* did not find it necessary to reach the Sixth Amendment issue because it reversed on other grounds.[491] The Sixth Amendment issues are discussed in another section of this chapter.[492]

Sometimes the very same statement has self-serving and disserving aspects. For example, a statement of income in a tax return is self-serving insofar as it asserts that the declarant's income does not exceed a certain level, but disserving to the extent that it concedes that

---

489. For examples of cases applying *Williamson*, see Silverstein v. Chase, 260 F.3d 142 (2d Cir.2001) (held, reversible error to admit statements neutral as to declarant's interest contained in cancellation of indebtedness document even though main purpose of document was to relinquish declarant's interest); United States v. Mendoza, 85 F.3d 1347, 1351–52 (8th Cir. 1996) (held, statement by suspect caught with drug money implicating her boyfriend not admissible because she had nothing to lose by making statement and she may have been trying to curry favor); United States v. Costa, 31 F.3d 1073, 1077 (11th Cir.1994) (*Williamson* requires trial court to make fact-intensive inquiry of statements made during custodial interrogation to determine whether those statements are really against interest); *Cf.* American Automotive Accessories, Inc. v. Fishman, 991 F.Supp. 995 (N.D. Ill. 1998) (mere fact that statement by plaintiff's employee was facially self-incriminating was not enough to demonstrate that it was against interest where statement may have been made as part of effort to curry favor with plaintiff in obtaining negotiated settlement). *But see* First Nat. Bank of Louisville v. Lustig, 96 F.3d 1554, 1574 (5th Cir.1996) (held, no abuse of discretion in civil suit by bank against insurer involving coverage dispute in which key issue was whether loan officer employed by bank had

acted with intent to garner personal benefit or to harm bank by fraud; not error to admit evidence that loan officer pled guilty to bank fraud indictment that included factual references that would establish coverage under the bond; bank had worked with prosecutor in extraordinary way to add language to indictment that would help bank; query whether court sufficiently analyzed case to distinguish between against-interest, neutral, and self-serving aspects of the guilty plea).

490. In Lilly v. Virginia, 527 U.S. 116 (1999), a divided Supreme Court indicated that the mere fact that an accomplice's confession was partly against the declarant's interest does not insulate it from Confrontation Clause attack when it is offered to implicate the defendant. Four justices were ready to hold that accomplices' confessions that implicate a criminal defendant are not within a firmly rooted exception to the hearsay rule, but the other justices concurred on more limited grounds. *See* § **7.67.**

491. The Court's later decision in Crawford v. Washington, 124 S.Ct. 1354 (2004) makes clear that admission of the statement in *Williamson* would violate the confrontation clause. *See* § **7.67.**

492. *See* § **7.67.**

declarant had income up to a certain level. The sensible way to treat such statements is to receive them when they are offered to show facts that were against the declarant's interest when the statement was made—for example, to show that the income reached up to the level conceded in the return—but judicial treatment has not been uniform.[493]

Returning to *United States v. Barrett*, after *Williamson*, a court could still find that in its specific context, Tilley's statement that Buzzy rather than Bucky took part in the crime was self-inculpatory because it showed specific knowledge of the crime. This would make Tilley's entire statement against his interest, and thus admissible upon a showing of Tilley's unavailability.

§ 7.55   The Forfeiture by Wrongdoing Exception

In 1997, Rule of Evidence 804(b)(6) was added to the list of unavailability exceptions. The rule provides that the hearsay rule does not bar "a statement offered against a party that has engaged or acquiesced in wrongdoing that was intended to, and did, procure the unavailability of the declarant as a witness." The party forfeits not only the right to object on hearsay grounds, but also on confrontation grounds.

The exception is not based as much on the likely reliability of the statements that fall within its reach, as on the view that parties should not be able to deprive the fact-finder of the testimony of a witness by making the witness unavailable to testify. The most obvious application of the exception is to cases in which a criminal defendant arranges to murder a witness against him or to intimidate that person into refusing to testify. A party who would engage in such behavior based on such a motive arguably is not entitled to the protection of the hearsay rule, and the rule removes that protection. This is a rule of forfeiture, not of waiver. The party does not agree to forgo the exercise of a right; the rule withdraws that right because of the party's conduct.

The principle that a party may forfeit the protection of the hearsay rule by procuring the unavailability of an adverse witness was recognized at common law in many jurisdictions, including all federal circuits that had addressed the issue prior to the rule's enactment.[494] And the rule makes good sense. As one court stated, arranging the unavailability of a

---

493. *See, e.g.*, Ghelin v. Johnson, 243 N.W. 443, 446 (Minn. 1932) (declarant's statement on income tax return that he was unmarried was admissible as declaration against interest); Barrera v. Gonzalez, 341 S.W.2d 703, 705–06 (Tex.Civ.App.1960) (declarant's statement that he owed money not admissible because self-serving under circumstances; statement by declarant that he owed money to creditor amounted to assertion that declarant did not transfer real property to creditor in satisfaction of debt as creditor claimed); *but see, e.g.*, Veach's Admr. v. Louisville & I. Ry. Co., 228 S.W. 35, 37 (Ky.1921) (declarant's statement of income on tax return self-serving, even to prove income not less than amount stated); 2 McCormick on Evidence § 319, at 343 (4th ed. John W. Strong ed. 1992) (admissibility of statement as declaration against interest turns on perceived harm at time statement made).

494. *See, e.g.*, United States v. Houlihan, 92 F.3d 1271, 1278–81 (1st Cir.1996) (murder of declarant waives constitutional rights; defendant's responsibility for murder need only be shown by a preponderance of evidence).

witness who will testify against you "strikes at the heart of the system of justice itself."[495]

Before evidence of a statement will be admissible under this rule, the trial court must make the necessary factual finding pursuant to Rule 104(a). In doing so, the court may consider evidence not otherwise admissible.[496] Thus, if the question is whether the defendant murdered a missing declarant, the declarant's statement will not be admissible unless the trial court finds, by a preponderance of the evidence, that the defendant is responsible for the murder. It is important for courts to apply the rule cautiously, as its effect is to deprive a party of the constitutional right to confront the witnesses against her. This is particularly true with respect to situations in which the party did not directly procure the absence of the witness, but was only involved indirectly or tangentially.

What, exactly, does the rule mean when it states that an absent declarant's statement may be offered against a party who "acquiesced" in wrongdoing that procured with witness's absence? Is mere knowledge that someone else plans to procure the witness's unavailability sufficient? Is it enough that the party and the person who made the witness unavailable were both participants in a criminal conspiracy about which the witness would have testified? The rule is too new to have been interpreted definitively.[497]

OTHER HEARSAY ISSUES

§ 7.56 The Residual Exception to the Hearsay Rule

Federal Rule of Evidence 807 (formerly Rules 803(24) and 804(b)(5)[498]) creates a "residual" or "catchall" exceptions. The purpose of the exception is to "provide for treating new and presently unanticipated situations which demonstrate a trustworthiness within the spirit

495. United States v. Mastrangelo, 693 F.2d 269, 273 (2d Cir.1982).

496. *See* United States v. White, 116 F.3d 903, 914 (D.C. Cir.1997) (not error for trial judge, acting under Rule 104(a), to rely partly on hearsay in determining that defendants had forfeited hearsay objection by murdering hearsay declarant). *See also* Cotto v. Herbert, 331 F.3d 217 (2d Cir.2003) (trial judge reviewed an extensive hearsay record in finding that defendant had intimidated a witness into recanting testimony and hence had forfeited his right to object to evidence of what the witness said out of court).

497. In United States v. Cherry, 217 F.3d 811 (10th Cir.2000), five defendants were charged in a drug conspiracy. Much of the evidence against them was provided by a cooperating witness who was murdered prior to trial. Addressing the question of what constitutes "acquiescence" under

Rule 804(b)(6), the court held that "[a] defendant may be deemed to have waived his or her Confrontation Clause rights (and, a fortiori, hearsay objections) if a preponderance of the evidence establishes one of the following circumstances: (1) he or she participated directly in planning or procuring the declarant's unavailability through wrongdoing, ...; or (2) the wrongful procurement was in furtherance, within the scope, and reasonably foreseeable as a necessary or natural consequence of an ongoing conspiracy...." *Id.* at 820. The court remanded the case for determination whether the standard was satisfied.

498. Former Rules 803(24) and 804(b)(5) created two identical exceptions. These were consolidated and renumbered as Rule 807 in an amendment effective December 1, 1997. The change was purely technical and was not intended to affect the interpretation of the exception.

of the specifically stated exceptions," and to leave room "for growth and development of the law of evidence in the hearsay area."[499]

The main requirements of the residual exceptions can be expressed in three categories:[500]

1. The evidence must have "guarantees of trustworthiness" that are "equivalent" to those of the established exceptions.[501]

2. The evidence must be "more probative" on the point for which it is offered than any other evidence that can reasonably be obtained.[502]

---

499. Fed. R. Evid. 803(24) advisory committee's note. The advisory committee further noted that it would "be presumptuous to assume that all possible desirable exceptions to the hearsay rule have been catalogued and to pass the hearsay rule to oncoming generations as a closed system." This has not been interpreted to mean, however, that these exceptions are to be used to create whole new categories of exceptions. *See generally* 5 Weinstein's Federal Evidence § 803.30[4], at 803–148 (2d ed. Joseph M. McLaughlin ed. 1997). For criticism of the residual exceptions see Jon R. Waltz & James Beckley, *The Exception for Great Hearsay: Some Concerned Comments*, 1 Am. J. Trial Advoc. 123 (1977).

500. *See generally,* 5 Weinstein's Federal Evidence, *supra* note 499 § 803.30[2]; 2 McCormick on Evidence § 324 (4th ed. John W. Strong ed. 1992); United States v. Marchini, 797 F.2d 759, 762–64 (9th Cir. 1986) (discussing each of the requirements for admission under 804(b)(5)); FTC v. Amy Travel Serv., 875 F.2d 564, 576 (7th Cir. 1989) (discussing requirements of residual exception).

501. *See, e.g.,* United States v. Blackburn, 992 F.2d 666, 672 (7th Cir.1993) (held, computer printouts of electronic lensometer readings for lens of eyeglasses left by bank robber in stolen car are admissible under residual exception because test which produces readings used highly reliable method of analysis; further more, at time test was conducted, defendant was not even a suspect in the case); Polansky v. CNA Ins. Co., 852 F.2d 626, 631 (1st Cir. 1988) (proper to exclude letter written by representative of proponent which was self-serving and lacked guarantees of trustworthiness); United States v. Carlson, 547 F.2d 1346, 1354 (8th Cir.1976) (grand jury testimony was sufficiently trustworthy to be admitted where declarant was under oath and never recanted or expressed reservations about the accuracy of the testimony).

502. *See, e.g.,* United States v. Marchini, 797 F.2d 759, 764 (9th Cir.1986) (where unavailable declarant was the only person who could establish the link between drafting of supplier checks and their conversion to cash, thus demonstrating defendant's guilt in action for filing false tax returns, declarant's prior grand jury testimony was admissible under 804(b)(5)); Conoco, Inc. v. Department of Energy, 99 F.3d 387, 392 (Fed.Cir.1996) (purchase summaries prepared, long after the event, by nonparty purchaser of crude oil in response to Conoco's request for information for Department of Energy audit not admissible when offered under residual exception by Department of Energy because not more probative on point than other evidence that could be procured through reasonable efforts); United States v. Trenkler, 61 F.3d 45, 59 (1st Cir.1995) (held, error to admit, under residual exception, testimony that search of ATF database showed that, of bombs on record, only six resembled the one in case at bar and one of those six had been built by the defendant; insufficient showing of trustworthiness); Noble v. Alabama Dept. of Envtl. Management, 872 F.2d 361, 366 (11th Cir. 1989) (error to admit letter where proponent made no showing that reasonable efforts would not have brought writer to court to testify). *See, e.g.,* Larez v. City of Los Angeles, 946 F.2d 630, 641–44 (9th Cir.1991) (newspaper reports describing statements by defendant police chief satisfied trustworthiness requirement of 803(24) where independent reports were consistent with each other, but they did not satisfy the "more probative" requirement where reporters were available for testimony). One questions the continuing validity of the *Larez* dicta about trustworthiness after Idaho v. Wright, 497 U.S. 805 (1990) (*see* § **7.67**), which stated that the trustworthiness required by the confrontation clause must be found in the circumstances under which the statement was made, not in extrinsic corroboration of the statement.

3.   The opponent of the evidence must be given notice of intent to offer it prior to trial.[503]

There are also some makeweight provisions, such as the requirements that admitting the evidence be in the interest of justice and in accordance with the purposes of the Rules[504] and that the statement be offered as evidence of a "material" fact.[505]

The residual exception has been interpreted expansively by a number of courts. They have used the following techniques to expand the coverage of the exception:

Disregard of Notice Provision

The practicing bar objected to relaxation of the hearsay rule on the ground that if hearsay became freely admissible, trial lawyers would not know how to prepare for trial. In response to these concerns, Congress inserted in the rule language that clearly requires notice *before* trial— not during trial, even if such notice during the trial seems reasonable under the circumstances. However, most of the federal courts that have interpreted the provision have not enforced the requirement of pretrial notice. They have turned it instead into a rule against unfair surprise, and have admitted the evidence when the opposing party had a fair opportunity to meet it. In other words, the requirement of notice before trial, imposed by the plain language of the rule, has been watered down in most—but not all[506]—jurisdictions to allow notice during trial if the opponent is not prejudiced and if there is an excuse for not giving notice earlier.[507] This trend does not mean that notice never poses an obstacle,

503. This requirement has been watered down in many jurisdictions. *See infra.*

504. *See, e.g.,* Marsee v. United States Tobacco Co., 866 F.2d 319, 325 (10th Cir. 1989) (admission of reports establishing link between oral cancer and chewing tobacco not required in the interests of justice where expert testimony had previously established much of the same information); FTC v. Amy Travel Serv., 875 F.2d 564, 576 (7th Cir.1989) (admission of affidavits of injured consumers is in the interests of justice where "it would be cumbersome and unnecessarily expensive" to bring all consumers injured in a nationwide telemarketing scam to court to testify).

505. *See, e.g.,* FTC v., Amy Travel Service, Inc. 875 F.2d 564, 576 (7th Cir.1989) (affidavits probative on issue of whether consumers were injured in telemarketing scam were material); United States v. Carlson, 547 F.2d 1346, 1354 (8th Cir.1976) (grand jury testimony that showed defendant's "intent, knowledge, a common plan or scheme, and the absence of a mistake or accident" was relevant and material in criminal action for conspiracy to distribute cocaine). There is some question as to what "material" means as used in the residual exceptions. Some courts have held that it

means the same thing as "relevant" under Rule 401. *See, e.g.,* United States v. Muscato, 534 F.Supp. 969, 979 (E.D.N.Y.1982). Others suggest that it means more than mere relevance and is satisfied only by nontrivial matters. *See* United States v. Iaconetti, 406 F.Supp. 554, 559 (E.D.N.Y.1976).

Some appellate courts have required the district court to make detailed specific findings before admitting a statement under the residual exceptions. *See, e.g.,* Mutuelles Unies v. Kroll & Linstrom, 957 F.2d 707 (9th Cir.1992) (error not to make specific findings, but not unfairly prejudicial).

506. For strict interpretations of the notice requirement, *see, e.g.,* United States v. Cowley, 720 F.2d 1037, 1044–45 (9th Cir.1983); United States v. Ruffin, 575 F.2d 346, 357 (2d Cir.1978).

507. *See* Joseph W. Rand, Note, *The Residual Exceptions to the Federal Hearsay rule: The Futile and Misguided Attempt to Restrain Judicial Discretion,* 80 Geo. L.J. 873, 885–86 (1992) (collecting cases that have interpreted the notice requirement in a relaxed fashion). *See also* United States v. Carlson, 547 F.2d 1346 (8th Cir.1976) (court excused government from notice requirement where government's attorney

for courts will refuse to apply the exception when there is no excuse for not giving notice. It simply means that the obstacle can be overcome at the trial stage when the proponent has a good excuse. Moreover, it is possible that the trend will be reversed if the Supreme Court applies its evolving "plain meaning" philosophy to the notice provisions of the residual exception.[508]

Narrowing of "Point" on Which Evidence is Offered

In an attempt to insure that evidence is not admitted under the residual exception except in cases of special need, the rules require that the hearsay statement be "more probative on the point for which it is offered than any other evidence which the proponent can procure through reasonable efforts."[509] This provision would seem to mean, for example, that when the issue is whether a traffic light was red or green, hearsay statements are not admissible under the exception if witnesses with first-hand knowledge are available to testify about the color of the light.

Some courts, however, have taken a very liberal view of the provision. The "point" on which the evidence is relevant can sometimes be narrowed to such an extent that no other evidence addresses exactly that "point." The most extreme example of this narrowing of the "point" seems to be *United States v. Iaconetti*.[510] There, a hearsay statement was offered under the residual exception to resolve a conflict in testimony between witnesses with first-hand knowledge. The court admitted the statement, deciding, in effect, that it was the best evidence on the "point" of resolving the conflict of testimony. Other courts have been more circumspect in applying the requirement.[511]

Liberal Interpretation of "Trustworthiness" Requirement

The residual exceptions require that the hearsay statements have "guarantees of trustworthiness" that are "equivalent" to the established

first learned just before trial that its witness would refuse to testify; defendant did not request continuance); United States v. Leslie, 542 F.2d 285 (5th Cir.1976) (Furtado v. Bishop, 604 F.2d 80 (1st Cir.1979).

508. *See* Randolph N. Jonakait, *The Supreme Court, Plain Meaning, and the Changed rules of Evidence*, 68 Tex. L. Rev. 745, 762–64 (1990).

509. Fed. R. Evid. 807(B).

510. 406 F.Supp. 554 (E.D.N.Y.1976).

511. *See, e.g.*, Conoco Inc. v. Department of Energy, 99 F.3d 387, 392 (Fed. Cir.1996), as amended on reh'g in part, (Jan. 2, 1997) (purchase summaries prepared, long after the event, by nonparty purchaser of crude oil in response to Conoco's request for information for Department of Energy audit not admissible when offered under residual exception by Department of Energy because not more probative on point than any other evidence that could be procured through reasonable efforts); Larez v. City of Los Angeles, 946 F.2d 630, 641–44 (9th Cir.1991) (newspaper reports describing statements by defendant police chief satisfied trustworthiness requirement of residual exception where independent reports were consistent with each other, but they did not satisfy the "more probative" requirement where reporters were available to testify). The *Larez* dicta about using consistency of independent reports to show trustworthiness might be under a cloud after Idaho v. Wright, 497 U.S. 805 (1990), which stated that the trustworthiness required by the confrontation clause must be found in the circumstances under which the statement was made, not in extrinsic corroboration of the statement.

exceptions. Traditionally, the guarantees of trustworthiness that have supported the creation of hearsay exceptions have related to the circumstances in which the statements were made, and might be called intrinsic guarantees. For example, dying declarations are thought to be reliable because the circumstances (impending death) make lying unlikely. Similarly, the excited utterance exception is based in part on the theory that the circumstances limit a declarant's powers of fabrication. However, courts interpreting the residual exception have not always required intrinsic guarantees of trustworthiness. A number have admitted statements that had no such guarantees, but that seemed reliable because they were corroborated by extrinsic evidence.[512]

Possible Limit: "Near Miss" Hearsay

Despite a generally permissive trend in letting in evidence under the residual exception, there may be limits to how far the courts will go. When evidence almost, but not quite, fits under one of the established exceptions, some courts have been willing to conclude that Congress did not intend for the evidence to be admitted.[513] An example would be a nineteen-year-old document, which barely misses falling under the twenty-year minimum of the ancient documents exception to the hearsay rule. If the document has no other guarantees of trustworthiness except age, it should be excluded because Congress did not intent to admit documents merely on the basis of age unless they were twenty years old. This negative implication argument is sometimes called the "near miss" argument because it would mean that when a statement just misses qualifying under a specific hearsay exception, it also misses qualifying under the residual exception, at least when the proponent can point to no indicia of trustworthiness other than that supporting the specific exception.

Under the "near miss" concept, an argument can be made that the residual exception should never be applied to admit grand jury testimony. The residual exception, by its own terms, applies only to hearsay not "specifically covered" by other exceptions.

One could argue that all former testimony, including grand jury testimony, is "specifically covered" by Rule 804(b)(1), and further that Congress considered the question whether to admit former testimony when enacting that rule and decided not to allow it to be admitted except when the party harmed by it had the opportunity to cross-examine. However, despite endorsement of the "near miss" approach by a prominent judge,[514] the approach has not achieved general acceptance in its

---

512. See generally David A. Sonenshein, *The Residual Exceptions to the Federal Hearsay Rule: Two Exceptions in Search of a Rule*, 57 N.Y.U. L. Rev. 867 (1982).

513. *See generally, id. But see* United States v. Laster, 258 F.3d 525, 529–530 (6th Cir.2001) (over an interesting dissent, court accepted view that evidence not shown to satisfy requirements of a specific hearsay exception might be admissible under the residual exception; when the government failed to lay the proper foundation under the business records exception by not producing a sponsoring witness, the record was admissible under the residual exception).

514. *See* United States v. Dent, 984 F.2d 1453, 1465–66 (7th Cir.1993) (Easterbrook, J., concurring).

application to grand jury testimony and grand jury testimony has been admitted under the residual exception.[515]

Conclusion: Residual Exception Caselaw Shows Somewhat Receptive Attitude Toward Hearsay, but Courts Have Not Eviscerated Hearsay Ban

Although Congress apparently intended that the residual exceptions be applied only in a limited set of near-unique circumstances, some courts have been willing to apply them to ordinary hearsay that does not fit any other standard exceptions. The consensus of scholarly opinion seems to be that courts construing the residual exceptions have been quite liberal in finding evidence trustworthy enough to be received.[516]

Certainly there are some startlingly permissive cases. For example, in some jurisdictions it has become common for federal courts to admit grand jury testimony of absent witnesses, even though they may have a motive to lie, so long as the testimony is corroborated by other evidence.[517] Extension of this line of cases would seem to allow all grand jury testimony to come in as long as the other evidence against the defendant is good. However, the Supreme Court's 2004 decision in *Crawford v. Washington*[518] makes clear that admission of grand jury testimony against a criminal defendant violates the confrontation clause.

In child sex abuse prosecutions, prosecutors have increasingly turned to the residual exceptions, as well as to special state statutes admitting child hearsay. In *United States v. N.B.*,[519] for example, the court found that guarantees of trustworthiness were sufficient to admit under the residual exception a social worker-witness's testimony concerning the child-declarant's statements inculpating defendant in sexual abuse. The court held that in deciding whether statements are sufficiently trustworthy, a court should consider "the training and experience of the social worker; whether the child was interviewed using open-ended questions; the age of the child and whether the child used 'age-appropriate language' in discussing the abuse; the length of time between the incident of abuse and the making of the hearsay statement; and whether the child repeated the same facts consistently to adults."[520] In addition,

---

515. *See, e.g.*, United States v. Earles, 113 F.3d 796, 800 (8th Cir.1997) (grand jury testimony may be admitted under residual exception; court rejected near miss theory).

516. *See* Jeffrey Cole, *Residual Exceptions to the Hearsay Rule*, Litig. Mag., Fall 1989, at 26; Randolph N. Jonakait, *The Subversion of the Hearsay Rule: The Residual Hearsay Exceptions, Circumstantial Guarantees of Trustworthiness, and Grand Jury Testimony*, 36 Case W. Res. L. Rev. 431 (1986); Myrna S. Raeder, *The Effect of the Catchalls on Criminal Defendants: Little Red Riding Hood Meets the Hearsay Wolf*

and Is Devoured, 25 Loy. L.A. L. Rev. 925, 933 (1992); Sonenshein, *supra* note 512.

517. *See, e.g.*, United States v. Guinan, 836 F.2d 350 (7th Cir.1988) (overruling recognized by, United States v. Gomez–Lemos, 939 F.2d 326 (6th Cir.1991) (grand jury testimony by estranged wife admissible when corroborated by other evidence); Jonakait, *supra* note 516.

518. 124 S.Ct. 1354 (2004). For discussion of *Crawford*, see § **7.67**.

519. 59 F.3d 771, 776 (8th Cir.1995).

520. *Id.*

as the Supreme Court's decision in *Idaho v. Wright*[521] makes clear, the court must also consider whether admission of the child's statements would satisfy the requirements of the confrontation clause. *See* § **7.67**.

Some courts have been equally permissive in using the residual exception in civil cases.[522] If followed to the extent of their logic, the permissive residual exception cases could destroy the hearsay rule. Yet often the cases are merely examples of appellate courts upholding district court rulings under an abuse of discretion standard, leaving the district courts free to either admit or exclude, rather than requiring them to admit. In any event, there are decisions of equal status that are less permissive.[523]

§ 7.57 Miscellaneous Hearsay Exceptions

Statements of Recent Perception

The version of the Federal Rules of Evidence that was promulgated by the Supreme Court under its rulemaking power in 1973 had an exception for "statements of recent perception."[524] Congress prevented the Supreme Court's version of the rules from going into effect. By the time the Federal Rules of Evidence had been enacted as a statute by Congress in 1975, the exception had been removed completely.[525] The Supreme Court's version of the statement of recent perception provided an exception for

> A statement, not in response to the instigation of a person engaged in investigating, litigating, or settling a claim, which narrates, describes, or explains an event or condition recently perceived by the declarant, made in good faith, not in contemplation of pending or anticipated litigation in which he was interested, and while his recollection was clear.[526]

521. 497 U.S. 805 (1990).

522. *See, e.g.,* Turbyfill v. International Harvester Co., 486 F.Supp. 232 (E.D.Mich.1980) (employee's statement, helpful to employer, admitted against third party under residual exception).

523. *See* United States v. Gomez–Lemos, 939 F.2d 326 (6th Cir.1991) (reversing trial judge who admitted grand jury testimony under residual exception, noting that *Idaho v. Wright,* 497 U.S. 805 (1990) does not allow trustworthiness to be established by extrinsic corroboration); United States v. Fernandez, 892 F.2d 976, 980–84 (11th Cir. 1989) (refusing to admit grand jury testimony under the residual exceptions, and noting that the Eleventh Circuit has never done so).

524. *See* Fed. R. Evid. 804(b)(2) (Supreme Court Proposed Draft 1973), reprinted in 2 James F. Bailey & Oscar M. Trelles,

The Federal Rules of Evidence: Legislative Histories and Related Documents, Doc. 13, at 33 (1980); see also 5 Weinstein's Federal Evidence § 804App.01[3], at 804App.–12 (2d ed. Joseph M. McLaughlin ed. 1997).

525. *See* H.R. Rep. No. 650, 93d Cong., 1st Sess. 6 (1973), reprinted in 4 Bailey & Trelles, *supra* note 524, at 6; *see also* 5 Weinstein's Federal Evidence, *supra* note 524 § 804App.01[4], at 804App.–15; Kenneth E. Kraus, Comment, *The Recent Perception Exception to the Hearsay Rule–A Justifiable, Record,* 1985 Wis. L. Rev. 1525, 1543–44 (1985) (arguing for reconsideration of the exception).

526. *See* Fed. R. Evid. 804(b)(2) (Supreme Court Proposed Draft 1973), reprinted in 2 Bailey & Trelles, *supra* note 524, Doc. 7, at 33; *see also* 5 Weinstein's Federal Evidence, *supra* note 524 § 804App.01[3], at 804App.–12.

The Supreme Court's recent perception exception was one of the Rule 804 exceptions, which meant that the exception did not apply unless the declarant was unavailable.[527] Although Congress rejected the recent perception exception, versions of it have been adopted in some states[528] and as an option in the Uniform Rules.[529] The option provided in Uniform Rule 803(b)(5) is like the federal rule rejected by Congress, except that it applies only to civil cases.[530]

Although much of the territory covered by the recent perception exception is also covered by the residual exception and the present sense impression exception, it has a niche of its own. Unlike the residual exception, it allows the evidence to be received without notice, and does not require that it be the best evidence on the point.[531] Unlike the present sense impression exception, it does not require that the statement be made during or immediately after the event, though the event must be "recent" at the time of the statement.[532] The exception seems a useful supplement to the other hearsay exceptions. Because the declarant is unavailable, the choice is to hear the declarant's story in hearsay form or not at all. The protections of the recent perception exception, such as recency of perception, clarity of recollection, good faith, and unavailability of the declarant, seem sufficient.[533] Nevertheless, most states have not adopted this exception.

Statements of Deceased Persons

Since 1898, Massachusetts has had a statute making statements of decedents broadly admissible in civil actions. The current version of the statute reads as follows: "In any action or other civil judicial proceeding, a declaration of a deceased person shall not be inadmissible in evidence

527. *See id.*

528. *See, e.g.,* Haw. R. Evid. 804(b)(5):

Statement of recent perception. A statement, not in response to the instigation of a person engaged in investigating, litigating, or settling a claim, which narrates, describes, or explains an event or condition recently perceived by the declarant, made in good faith, not in contemplation of pending or anticipated litigation in which the declarant was interested, and while the declarant's recollection was clear....

See also Wis. Stat. Ann. § 908.045(2) (West 1993); Kraus Comment, *supra* note 525 at, 1527. For applications of the Wisconsin Rule *see, e.g.,* Kluever by Gonring v. Evangelical Reformed Immanuels Congregation, 422 N.W.2d 874, 876–78 (Wis.App.1988) (statement of injured worker regarding fall from ladder admissible even though made eight to ten weeks after the accident); State v. Kreuser, 280 N.W.2d 270, 274 (Wis. 1979) (out-of-court declarant's state-ment made within a day of the event reported admissible as recent perception).

529. *See* Unif. R. Evid. 803(b)(5).

530. The Uniform Rules had previously applied the exception to criminal cases as well. This practice was criticized by commentators. *See, e.g.,* Charles W. Quick, *Hearsay, Excitement, Necessity and the Uniform Rules: A Reappraisal of Rule 63(4),* 6 Wayne L. Rev. 204, 219–24 (1960).

531. *Cf.* Fed. R. Evid. 807; *see* § **7.56**.

532. *Cf.* Fed. R. Evid. 804(b)(3); *see* § **7.11**. *See, e.g.,* State v. Kreuser, 280 N.W.2d 270, 274 (Wis.1979) (out-of-court declarant's statement within one day of event described admissible); Kluever by Gonring v. Evangelical Reformed Immanuels Congregation, 422 N.W.2d 874, 876–78 (Wis.App.1988) (declarant's statement after eight to ten weeks held admissible as recent perception).

533. *See* Kraus Comment, *supra* note 525, at 1537.

as hearsay ... if the court finds that it was made in good faith and upon the personal knowledge of the declarant."[534]

The Massachusetts approach has not spread very widely, though a few states have enacted much more limited statutes for cases involving suits against the estates of decedents.[535] And in 1996, in the wake of the widely publicized murder trial of O.J. Simpson, California adopted a new hearsay exception covering statements of unavailable declarants that "purport[] to narrate, describe, or explain the infliction or threat of physical injury upon the declarant."[536] Though the rule contains a number of limitations,[537] it is potentially applicable to many types of civil and criminal cases.

Statements by Children Describing Abuse

A number of states have adopted statutory exceptions to the hearsay rule for statements by children about sexual or physical abuse.[538] Many of the statutes apply only when the child is either testifying and subject to cross, or unavailable so that the testimony must be received in hearsay form or not at all.[539] Typical definitions of unavailability include

534. *See* Mass. Ann. Laws ch. 233, § 65 (Law. Co-op 1986). For cases applying the Massachusetts rule see Cusher v. Turner, 495 N.E.2d 311, 316 (Mass.App.1986) (statements made by decedent in diary and tape recordings admissible); Fire Commr. v. Joseph, 498 N.E.2d 1368, 1370–71 (Mass. App.1986) (no error in not admitting decedent's statement where it was not made in good faith).

535. *See* 5 John H. Wigmore, Evidence in Trials at Common Law § 1576 (James H. Chadbourn rev. 1974 & Supp. 1996).

536. Cal. Evid. Code § 1370 (West 1997).

537. The statement must have been made at or near the time of the injury or threat; it must have been made under circumstances indicating its trustworthiness; and it must have been in writing, electronically recorded, or made to a law enforcement official. § 1370(a). In addition, the rule contains a provision requiring the proponent to make known its intention to offer the statement and its particulars "sufficiently in advance of the proceedings to provide the adverse party with a fair opportunity to prepare the meet the statement." § 1370(c).

538. *See generally* Michael H. Graham, *The Confrontation Clause, the Hearsay Rule and Child Sexual Abuse Prosecutions: The State of the Relationship*, 72 Minn. L. Rev. 523, 534–38 (1988); Jean L. Kelly, Comment, *Legislative Responses to Child Sexual Abuse Cases: The Hearsay Exception and the Videotape Deposition*, 34 Cath. U.L. Rev. 1021, 1035–41 (1985); Judy Yun, Note, *A*

Comprehensive Approach to Child Hearsay Statements in Sex Abuse Cases, 83 Colum. L. Rev. 1745 (1983).

539. *See, e.g.*, Minn. Stat. Ann. § 595.02(3) (West 1988):

An out-of-court statement made by a child under the age of ten years or a person who is mentally impaired ... alleging, explaining, denying, or describing any act of sexual contact or penetration performed with or on the child ... is admissible as substantive evidence if:

(a) the court or person authorized to receive evidence finds, in a hearing conducted outside of the presence of the jury, that the time, content, and circumstances of the statement and the reliability of the person to whom the statement is made provide sufficient indicia of reliability; and

(b) the child ... either:

(i) testifies at the proceedings; or

(ii) is unavailable as a witness and there is corroborative evidence of the act; and

(c) the proponent of the statement notifies the adverse party of the proponent's intention to offer the statement and the particulars of statement sufficiently in advance of the proceeding at which the proponent intends to offer the statement into evidence to provide the adverse party with a fair opportunity to prepare to meet the statement....

such things as the declarant's incompetence to testify.[540] Of course, many statements of children are admissible under conventional theories, such as the excited utterance,[541] the statement for medical diagnosis or treatment,[542] or one of the residual exceptions.[543]

§ 7.58 Hearsay Within Hearsay [FRE 805]

Sometimes the declarant's out-of-court statement will contain another out-of-court statement. For example, a hospital record might contain the patient's story about the cause of the injury. If the entry is offered to prove the cause of injury, the record has hearsay within hearsay. The first level of hearsay is the patient's oral statement to the record-maker about the cause of the injury. The second level is the record-maker's written statement in the hospital record describing what the patient said.

Federal Rule of Evidence 805, in accordance with prior law, provides that hearsay within hearsay is admissible if each level of hearsay falls under an exception to the hearsay rule.[544] In theory, out-of-court statements can be enclosed within each other ten deep if each statement is either not hearsay or falls under an exception.[545] A hearsay scholar who was extremely precise might point out that a nonhearsay statement contained within an admissible hearsay statement does not need Rule

For applications of this statute see State v. Dana, 422 N.W.2d 246, 248–50 (Minn.1988) (admissibility hearing sufficient; no error in admitting statements of two abused children); State v. Bellotti, 383 N.W.2d 308, 312–13 (Minn.App.1986) (statements of four-year-old sex abuse victim admissible).

540. See, e.g., Fed. R. Evid. 804(a)(4) (defining as unavailable a person who "is unable to be present or to testify at the hearing because of death or then existing physical or mental illness or infirmity"); Cal. Evid. Code § 240(a)(3) (West 1966) (same); Cal. Evid. Code § 240(c) (West 1966) (providing that witness can be found available due to physical or mental illness or infirmity if "[e]xpert testimony . . . establishes that physical or mental trauma resulting from an alleged crime has caused harm to a witness of sufficient severity that the witness is physically unable to testify or is unable to testify without suffering substantial trauma").

541. See, e.g., United States v. NB, 59 F.3d 771, 776 (8th Cir.1995) (discussed supra § **7.56**); United States v. Farley, 992 F.2d 1122, 1125–26 (10th Cir.1993) (trial court properly admitted testimony from child victim's mother as to victim's statements the morning after alleged sexual assault occurred when victim was still "under the stress of the event"); United States v.

Nick, 604 F.2d 1199, 1204 (9th Cir.1979) (statements of child admissible as excited utterances in sexual assault case).

542. Goldade v. State, 674 P.2d 721, 722–28 (Wyo.1983) (statements of child sex abuse victim to nurse and physician admissible under the "treatment and diagnosis" exception).

543. See, e.g., Doe v. United States, 976 F.2d 1071, 1074–78 (7th Cir.1992) (in Federal Torts Claim Act action alleging sexual abuse at government-owned center, three-year-old children's hearsay statements admissible under residual hearsay exception where essence of their story did not change despite the addition of varying details and where statements responded to questions by adults); United States v. Dorian, 803 F.2d 1439, 1446 (8th Cir.1986) (statement of child victim of sex abuse admissible under Rule 803(24)). See generally Graham, supra note 538, at 523.

544. See Fed. R. Evid. 805 advisory committee's note; 5 Weinstein's Federal Evidence § 805.02, at 805–4 (2d ed. Joseph M. McLaughlin ed. 1997); 2 McCormick on Evidence § 327.1 (4th ed. John W. Strong. ed. 1992).

545. See, e.g., United States v. Abell, 586 F.Supp. 1414, 1425 (D. Me. 1984) (three levels of statements, all admissible).

805 to be admitted at all, since it is not hearsay within hearsay.[546] In any event, it is clear that statements within statements are admissible so long as all statements in the chain are either nonhearsay or admissible under an exception.[547] Of course, each statement in the chain must be nonhearsay or fall within a hearsay exception for the chain to be admissible; it is not enough for one statement to fit if another does not.[548]

---

546. *See* 2 McCormick on Evidence, *supra* note 544, at §§ 323.1, at 369–709; *see also* United States v. Basey, 613 F.2d 198, 201 n. 1 (9th Cir.1979) (no double hearsay problem involved where first level statements were admissions or adoptive admissions, and second level fell under Rule 803(6)).

547. *See* Bondie v. Bic Corp., 947 F.2d 1531, 1533–34 (6th Cir.1991) (social worker's written report that child had told her she had started fire with matches, not cigarette lighter as claimed by plaintiff, admissible as hearsay within hearsay; social worker's report fit the business records exception and child's statement was the statement of a party-opponent); United States v. Diez, 515 F.2d 892, 895–96 n. 2 (5th Cir. 1975) (out-of-court statement offered to show declarant's state of mind, and falling under the hearsay exception of Fed. R. Evid. 803(3), admissible when contained within co-conspirator's out-of court statement, which Rule 801(d)(2)(E) classifies as nonhearsay).

548. *See* Pittman by Pittman v. Grayson, 149 F.3d 111, 123–24 (2d Cir. 1998) (plaintiff sued airliner after children were abducted by parent in domestic dispute, claiming airline knew that plaintiff had court order barring children from leaving country; held, statement by flight attendant on flight in question to news producer that airline personnel had helped "sneak" children out service entrance at airport was inadmissible against airline because declarant later told interviewer that this was "just a story that I have heard" and no showing was made that the hearsay-within-hearsay from declarant other than attendant fit an exception or exemption) (authors' comment: the original "sneak" statement standing alone would have qualified as an admission of a party opponent, and absence of personal knowledge would not have been a problem because a showing of personal knowledge is not required for party admissions under Rule 801(d)(2). However, the subsequent "just a story" statement expressly indicated that the original statement was based on statement of another, thus giving the court a basis for requiring a

foundation for the interior statement under Rule 805. It would seem a natural inference that the hearsay-within-hearsay statement also came from an airline employee, but the court nonetheless held that the foundation for that statement was insufficient); United States v. Sallins, 993 F.2d 344, 347 (3d Cir.1993) (held, police computer record detailing contents of a 911 call inadmissible; record itself falls within public records exception but government failed to show hearsay exception for statements made by person calling 911); Larez v. City of Los Angeles, 946 F.2d 630, 641–44 (9th Cir.1991) (held, where police chief was defendant, chief's statements to newspaper reporters were inadmissible hearsay where the reporters did not testify; the chief's statement was an admission, but the reporters' statements about what the chief said were inadmissible hearsay); Boren v. Sable, 887 F.2d 1032 (10th Cir.1989) (testimony of wife that her deceased husband told her that he had told his plant manager about a dangerous maintenance procedure was properly excluded since the first level of hearsay, the husband's out-of-court statement to his wife, did not fall under one of the hearsay exceptions); *see also* United States v. Reed, 887 F.2d 1398 (11th Cir.1989) (multiple hearsay admissible where each level either was nonhearsay or fell under an exception); Cedeck v. Hamiltonian Fed. Sav. & Loan Assn., 551 F.2d 1136, 1138 (8th Cir.1977) (where author of statement to supervisor unknown, the statement did not qualify as admission of party-opponent, thus plaintiff's testimony regarding the supervisor's relating that statement was inadmissible double hearsay). For a case that could be read as stating broadly that Rule 803(8)(C) cannot be a vehicle for findings based upon hearsay from a declarant who was not under a public duty, see Miller v. Field, 35 F.3d 1088 (6th Cir.1994). Miller was a federal civil rights case arising from an alleged prison rape. The court held that public records must contain either factual findings from firsthand knowledge of the report's preparer or conclusions derived from those facts. Hence, it ruled, state police reports setting forth witness statements and conclusions of investigators were inadmissible.

§ 7.59   Hearsay Within Hearsay [FRE 805]—Is Hearsay Within Hearsay Trustworthy?

Federal Rule of Evidence 805's liberal attitude toward hearsay within hearsay is in striking contrast to the requirements of trustworthiness that are set forth in many of the exceptions. Common sense tells us that hearsay within hearsay is likely to pose problems of reliability even if each statement fits an exception, and the Allport and Postman studies confirm what common sense tells us about multiple levels of hearsay.[549] Allport and Postman developed a series of experiments in which a subject viewed an illustration, and was asked to describe it to another subject, who described it to another subject, and so forth.[550] Allport and Postman noted that about 70 per cent of the information depicted in the illustration was lost after five or six mouth-to-mouth transmissions, even when the there was virtually no time interval between the statements. The most rapid loss came at the beginning, with the first one or two declarants.[551] The "level" (omission of details) and "sharpening" (selective reporting) effects noted were sometimes startling.[552] As the subjects struggled to assimilate what they had heard from others, they appear also to have added or changed vital details. For example, in more than half of the experiments the subjects erroneously "moved" a weapon (a straight razor blade) from the hand of the white person who held it in the illustration into the hand of a black antagonist during the telling of the story.[553]

Experiments like those performed by Allport and Postman could be used as a basis for arguing that the law should not allow endless levels of hearsay to come in, even if each layer meets an exception. However, one rarely runs into hearsay within hearsay stacked five times deep in litigation, because of the difficulty of fitting each statement into an exception and of showing that each declarant had personal knowledge.[554] Since in practice courts are dealing almost exclusively with one level of hearsay within hearsay, perhaps a rule of thumb that hearsay is admissi-

While *Miller* reaches the right result on its facts, it goes too far in its statement of the limits on Rule 803(8)(C). Under Rule 803(8)(C), when a public official actually makes "findings" pursuant to an investigation required by law (as opposed to merely recording information without evaluating it), those findings are admissible unless shown to be trustworthy. Passages of the *Miller* opinion could be read to say that findings based upon statements from declarants who are not under a public duty are simply inadmissible, whether or not they are shown to be untrustworthy. Under that reasoning, findings by hearing officers conducting administrative hearings would be inadmissible whenever based on hearing testimony by person not under a public duty, a result that seems clearly inconsistent with the intent of the rule makers and the examples given in the Advisory Committee's Note.

549. *See* Gordon W. Allport & Leo Postman, The Psychology of Rumor 75–76 (1947). *See also Comment, Hearsay Under the Proposed Federal Rules: A Discretionary Approach*, 15 Wayne L. Rev. 1077, 1231 (1969); *see also* Boren v. Sable, 887 F.2d 1032 (10th Cir.1989) (discussing dangers of multiple hearsay and exclusion of such evidence under Rule 403). United States v. Daniels, 572 F.2d 535, 539 (5th Cir.1978) (discussing the special problems double hearsay poses in a criminal trial).

550. Allport & Postman, *supra* note 549.

551. *Id.*

552. *Id.* at 75–98.

553. *Id.* at 111.

554. Personal knowledge is required for statements offered under most hearsay exceptions. *See* § **7.64**.

ble if each level fits an exception is the most simple and administrable approach.

In the case of the hospital record containing the account of the patient's injury, discussed in § 7.57, the record-keeper's statement would fall under the business records exception, if it was the regular practice of the hospital to make records of this sort of statement.[555] The patient's statement might be admissible either as an admission (if offered against the patient) or as a statement for purposes of diagnosis or treatment.[556]

§ 7.60   Hearsay Within Hearsay [FRE 805]—Illustrations

The late Irving Younger, whose unmatched talent for vivid illustration provided so many evidence learners with unforgettable memory aids, suggested that the hearsay-within-hearsay problem be visualized as follows:[557]

> A trial lawyer who has to deal with this problem every day in the hurly-burly circumstances of the courtroom might want to try the following device, which takes but an instant and is infallible....
>
> You or your opponent is offering a business record that consists of words. First, be satisfied that the business is a business, within the meaning of the business records statute, and that the record was routinely made in the regular course of business. That makes it a business record, which takes care of the first level of hearsay.
>
> Next, in your mind's eye, see the record come to life. Imagine it not as a record, but as the person who wrote the record. It takes the witness stand and it talks. It says from the witness stand whatever is written on it. If a real witness would be permitted to say that from the witness stand, then the record is admissible. If a real person on the stand would not be permitted to say it, then the record is not admissible.

Another common example of hearsay within hearsay is the trial or deposition transcript. The first level of hearsay is the witness's statement made at the prior trial or deposition. The second level is the court reporter's statement about what the witness said. The first level may or may not be admissible under the exception for former testimony or for depositions.[558] The second level (the court reporter) would be admissible

---

555. *See* § **7.17.**

556. *See* § **7.24** for a discussion of the different situations in which patient's statements in hospital records are admissible. For an example of a hospital record involving hearsay within hearsay, see Felice v. Long Island R.R., 426 F.2d 192, 197 (2d Cir.1970) (where patient's statement to nurse was admissible as a statement for the purpose of a medical diagnosis under

803(4), and nurse's entry of this statement was admissible as a business record under 803(6), entry was admissible as evidence of the cause of patient's injury).

557. Irving Younger, Hearsay: A Practical Guide Through the Thicket 127–28 (1988).

558. *See* § **7.47.**

under the public records exception and, in many jurisdictions, under specially tailored statutes.[559]

Another example of hearsay within hearsay that is nonetheless admissible is the out-of-court statement that shows the declarant's state of mind, contained within an out-of-court statement by a co-conspirator. For example, suppose that the co-conspirator made an out-of-court statement to an undercover agent who was pretending to be part of the conspiracy. In the out-of-court statement, the co-conspirator said that a parking lot attendant told him she was going to close the gates at 10:00. The co-conspirator is now dead. The statement of the dead co-conspirator is offered in evidence through the testimony of the undercover agent. The purpose of the testimony is to prove that the gates were closed at 10:00. Using Professor Younger's method, once the foundation for the co-conspirator exception has been laid, we imagine the co-conspirator has come alive and appeared on the witness stand to testify against the other conspirators. As a live witness, could he testify that the parking lot attendant told him that she was going to close the gates at 10:00? Yes, because under Federal Rule of Evidence 803(3) the statement of intent to do a future act is admissible as evidence that the future act was done. Each statement fits within an exception or exclusion to the hearsay rule and the evidence is admissible.

United States v. Diez provides another illustration.[560] The *Diez* court approved the admission of a statement of intent contained within a co-conspirator statement. The co-conspirator had given the agent an account of something that an IRS agent had told the co-conspirator. The court noted that the co-conspirator's statement was admissible under Rule 801(d)(2), and then noted:

> The fact that [coconspirator] DeGuzman's statement, like numerous others introduced at trial, relied on a statement by another person does not render the testimony inadmissible. [Internal Revenue Service] Agent Hunting's statement, reported to Agent Brock [the witness] by DeGuzman, was a statement of his intention to classify Palori as a dealer in real estate. The statement was received not to prove that Palori was or had been classified as a dealer, but rather to prove that Agent Hunting intended to regard him as one. The statement was thus a "statement of the declarant's then existing state of mind, emotion, sensation, or physical condition (such as intent, plan, motive, design, mental feeling, pain and bodily health)" and falls under the well-established exception to the hearsay rule for such statements. Fed. R. Evid. Rule 803(3).[561]

Statements within statements can also be admissible when an out-of-court statement that is hearsay fitting an exception contains another

559. *See* § **7.27**. *See also* Ramrattan v. Burger King Corp., 656 F.Supp. 522, 527–28 (D.Md.1987) (deposition properly excluded where, although deponent's statements in deposition would be admissible as admissions of party, statements included yet a third level of hearsay which did not meet any of the hearsay exceptions).

560. 515 F.2d 892 (5th Cir.1975).

561. *Id.* at 895–96 n.2.

out-of-court statement that is not hearsay at all. For example, in *Kulick v. Pocono Downs Racing Assn.*,[562] the plaintiff was seeking to prove that state officials were behind his ejection from the racetrack. He offered into evidence a statement by a racetrack employee that a state official had said that he should be ejected. The court noted that the racetrack employee's statement was admissible as the admission of a party-opponent. The statement-within-a-statement of the state official was admissible because it was not offered for the truth of anything asserted, but only to prove that a state official had made a statement that had the effect of contributing to plaintiff's ejection from the racetrack.[563]

§ 7.61 Hearsay Within Hearsay [FRE 805]—Present Sense Impressions as Double Hearsay

Litigators and judges sometimes overlook the possibility of making a Federal Rule of Evidence 805 argument for the admission of a present sense impression contained within a present sense impression. Suppose that Declarant A tells Declarant B the license number of a hit-and-run driver. Declarant B then tells Witness X, a police officer, the license number that the first declarant told him. If both statements were made on personal knowledge and were made at or soon after the event, then the joint operation of Rules 805 and 803(1) (the present sense impression exception) would seem to justify admitting the evidence. What Declarant A said ("The license number was 371 CUB") was Declarant A's statement of her present sense impression of the license number, made immediately after the event. What Declarant B said ("Declarant A told me that the license number was 371 CUB") is declarant B's statement of a present sense impression, from his sense of hearing, made immediately after the relevant event of hearing the other statement.[564]

There are some instances in which the theory outlined would not work because a foundation cannot be laid showing that the hearsay-within-hearsay declarant had personal knowledge. A present sense impression statement must be based upon personal knowledge.[565] Immediacy is also a requirement of the present sense impression hearsay exception.[566] In the car license hypothetical, suppose that Declarant A told Declarant B the license number over a CB radio. Neither Declarant B nor the in-court witness has any way of knowing whether Declarant A was reporting on personal knowledge immediately after the event. So no foundation could be laid showing personal knowledge or immediacy. An

562. 816 F.2d 895 (3d Cir.1987).

563. *Id.* at 897 & n.3; *see also* United States v. Basey, 613 F.2d 198, 201 n. 1 (9th Cir.1979) (no double hearsay problem involved where first level statements were admissions or adoptive statements, and second level fell under Rule 803(6)).

564. The courts have recognized a similar possibility where other hearsay exceptions are involved. *See, e.g.*, United States v. Rucker, 586 F.2d 899, 905–06 (2d Cir. 1978) (where both levels of hearsay fell under the exception for admissions of co-conspirators, Rule 801(d)(2)(E), evidence was admissible); *see also* United States v. Christian, 786 F.2d 203, 211–12 (6th Cir. 1986) (same).

565. *See* § **7.11**.

566. *See* § **7.11**.

example of this problem is shown in *United States v. Cain*,[567] a case in which a "CB'er" reported seeing an event, and the report of the "CB'er" was offered through a witness who heard the broadcast to prove the truth of the event observed by the "CB'er." The court held the evidence inadmissible, noting, "The distances and time lapses involved make it impossible to determine whether the declaration by the 'CB'er' was made immediately following the observation or not, but the chances that it was are slim. The exception to the hearsay rule found in Rule 803(1) is, therefore, inapplicable."[568] Suppose, however, that Declarant A said "I just this second saw the car speeding away and its license plate was 371 CUB," and Declarant B reported the statement to the in-court witness in exactly those words. If a specific claim of seeing the other car had been made, then the trial judge has authority to accept it as evidence of the existence of personal knowledge. Under Rule 104(a), which provides that in determining preliminary questions about the admissibility of evidence, the trial judge is not bound by the rules of evidence except those of privilege, the trial judge could consider hearsay in determining whether the personal knowledge requirement was satisfied.[569]

If the literal language of Rules 805 and 803(1) is followed, there would seem to be no obstacle to accepting the idea that the first level of hearsay, where the declarant reports what another person said immediately after the event, can be a present sense impression. If so, the second level would be admissible if it fit some exception or exclusion. Yet this argument seems to have been overlooked in some hotly contested cases. These cases arise from situations in which undercover agents were dealing with declarants through informer-intermediaries. One of the difficulties of drug investigations is that the targets do not want to meet new people, so it is difficult to get the targets to deal directly with undercover agents instead of dealing through persons whom they already know and perhaps trust. In any event, in each of the cases the informer had conversations over the telephone with the target while the agent was standing at the informer's shoulder. For one reason or another the informer did not testify at trial. The government's case would have benefited had the jury heard what the informer told the agent about what the defendant said over the phone, but the hearsay rule stood as an obstacle. In each case the trial prosecutor sought to solve the problem by putting into evidence the agent's contemporaneous instructions to the informer. The following excerpts from the transcripts illustrate the type

---

567. 587 F.2d 678 (5th Cir.1979), *revd on other grounds*, 615 F.2d 380 (5th Cir. 1980).

568. *Id.*; *see also* Wolf by Wolf v. Procter & Gamble Co., 555 F.Supp. 613, 620–21 (D.N.J.1982) (hearsay inadmissible under 803(1) and 803(6) where statements not recorded immediately).

569. *See* Bourjaily v. United States, 483 U.S. 171, 176–82 (1987) (held that court could consider the hearsay statements themselves in making Rule 104(a) preliminary fact determination); *see also* Fed. R. Evid. 104(a) advisory committee's note (" 'the judge should be empowered to hear any relevant evidence, such as affidavits or other reliable hearsay,' " quoting McCor-

of testimony elicited. In *United States v. Check*,[570] the government agent testified, inter alia:

> I instructed William Cali [the informer] that by no means did I intend to front any sum of money to Sandy Check [the defendant].... At that time I told William Cali I didn't particularly care whether or not Check was concerned about rats and not wanting to meet anyone new or about being busted by the man....

In *United States v. Figueroa*,[571] the agent's testimony included the following:

> Mike [the informer] had a conversation [over the telephone after having asked the hotel operator for a co-defendant's room] and Mike asked me, "Would it be all right if we did the two-kilogram deal one pound at a time?" And I told him to tell the people on the other end of the phone that that would be fine, we would deal one pound of cocaine at a time.... After Mike had a conversation with the other people on the phone, I told Mike that it would be all right if Leo [the defendant] sent his man down, Tommie, to count the money.

The trial judge in *Figueroa* made clear that the informer's phone call could be used to incriminate the defendant, stating that the informer had called "someone in the apartment who again gave his name as Leo, and they discussed the distribution of cocaine."[572]

In both cases the trial courts admitted the evidence, and in both cases the appellate courts reversed on hearsay grounds. Neither the trial nor appellate courts alluded to the possible theory that the informer's statement reporting what the target said was admissible as a present sense impression. Had that been so, then admissibility would have been no problem, because each level of hearsay would fit an exception. (The target's statements would be admissible as admissions or statements of co-conspirators.) In the Check case, the trial judge seems to have admitted the evidence on the theory that all prior statements of witnesses are admissible. The trial judge apparently accepted the view that if the agent's out-of-court statements were really his own, not merely an artifice to get into evidence another's statements, then they were admissible without limit because the agent was subject to cross-examination.[573] In *Figueroa*, the trial judge admitted the utterances as "verbal acts" through which the agent gave directions to the informer.[574]

The present sense impression theory that we have outlined would seem to be a better way of getting in the evidence, and the witness could have testified directly about what the informer said the target said without attempting the subterfuge of testifying only about the witness's

mick on Evidence § 53, at 135 (3d ed. Edward W. Cleary ed. 1984).

570. 582 F.2d 668, 671–73 (2d Cir. 1978).

571. 750 F.2d 232 (2d Cir.1984).

572. *Id.* at 241 (concurring opinion).

573. *See* the description of the trial court's theory in 582 F.2d at 678–79. Even under the trial judge's own theory, it appears that some of the statements should have been excluded.

574. 750 F.2d at 238–40.

own statements. However, perhaps the courts would be reluctant to do so because the in-court witness had no way to verify what the informer claimed the target said.[575] Although the drafters of Rule 803(1) did not expressly require that a present sense impression be verified by another equally percipient observer (e.g., by having the person who heard the present sense impression also testify that he or she observed the event about which the declarant spoke),[576] the probative value of the statement would certainly be enhanced were the witness reporting the out-of-court declarant's statement in a position to determine whether the declarant was telling the truth.[577]

§ 7.62   Out-of-Court Statements That Are Admissible in Part or for a Limited Purpose

Sometimes an out-of-court statement will be admissible for one purpose but not for another.[578] For example, an out-of-court statement giving a warning might be admissible to show that the person warned had notice, but not that the condition warned about in fact existed or was dangerous.[579] Or an out-of-court statement offered for impeachment

575. *See* Fed. R. Evid. 803(1) advisory committee's note (recognizing similarly that where the declarant is unidentified, cases "indicate hesitancy in upholding the statement alone as sufficient"); *see* generally 2 McCormick on Evidence § 271, at 214–15 (4th ed. John W. Strong ed. 1992) (discussing fact that 803(1) does not require corroboration).

576. *See* § **7.11**.

577. *See generally* Jon R. Waltz, *The Present Sense Impression Exception to the Rule Against Hearsay: Origins and Attributes*, 66 Iowa L. Rev. 869, 898 (1981); *see also* Booth v. State, 508 A.2d 976 (Md.1986) (rejecting a requirement of corroboration, though stating it may be used to determine the weight of the evidence).

578. *See generally* David P. Leonard, The New Wigmore: A Treatise on Evidence: Selected Rules of Limited Admissibility § 1.6.1 (rev. ed.2002); 1 Weinstein's Federal Evidence § 105.04[1] (2d ed. Joseph M. McLaughlin ed. 1997); 1 McCormick on Evidence § 59 (4th ed. John W. Strong ed. 1992). An out-of-court statement may also be admissible against one person but not another, as in the case of co-defendants. *See generally* Leonard, *supra* this note § 1.6.4; 1 Weinstein's Federal Evidence, *supra* this note § 105.06 and cases cited therein. Note also that in determining the admissibility of a hearsay statement under Rule 104, the judge may consider any evidence, including the proffered hearsay statement. *See* Fed. R. Evid. 104; Bourjaily v. United States, 483 U.S. 171, 176–80 (1987).

579. *See* § **7.01**; *see, e.g.*, Worsham v. A.H. Robins Co., 734 F.2d 676, 686–89 (11th Cir.1984) (hearsay reports of adverse reactions and references to other lawsuits admissible to show defendant had notice of a possible defect in the Dalkon Shield and of possible medical consequences, but not to prove that the reports were true); *see also* 2 McCormick on Evidence, *supra* note 578 § 250. *But see* United States v. Sallins, 993 F.2d 344, 346 (3d Cir.1993) (in criminal case against African–American defendant, government offered testimony concerning out-of-court statements contained within police radio call, stating there was a black male dressed in black with a gun at a particular location; district court admitted testimony for limited purpose of providing background as to why officers went to location and why they arrested defendant; appellate court reversed defendant's conviction, holding testimony inadmissible as hearsay; prosecution could have explained officers' actions with non-hearsay testimony; furthermore, any inference that radio call's contents were offered at trial for non-hearsay purpose was rebutted by fact that during closing arguments prosecutor used contents for truth asserted). *See also* United States v. Forrester, 60 F.3d 52 (2d Cir. 1995). In *Forrester*, the government offered testimony about statements made to an agent identifying the defendant as a drug kingpin on the theory that the evidence explained why the agent had omitted information incriminating the defendant from a report. The inference argued for was that because the agent already knew from other

purposes might be admissible to impeach, but not as substantive evidence of the truth of the matter stated.[580] The proponent should be sure to state the admissible purpose for which such evidence is offered unless it is perfectly obvious.[581]

If an out-of-court statement is admissible for one purpose but not for another, under Federal Rule of Evidence 105 the objecting party is entitled to a limiting instruction telling the jury the proper purpose and the forbidden purpose.[582] The request for a limiting instruction must be timely and must specifically identify the portions of the testimony to be limited.[583] Failure to request the limiting instruction will result in waiver of the right to assert error in the instructions on appeal.[584] The court may also issue limiting instructions sua sponte when the judge finds them necessary.[585] The most common limiting instruction is the instruc-

sources that the defendant was a drug kingpin, information to that effect was not noteworthy enough to go in the report. The court held that though the evidence was not hearsay when offered for that limited purpose, it nonetheless had to be excluded under Rule 403 because of danger that the jury would use out-of-court statements for the truth of matter asserted rather than for a limited nonhearsay purpose. It announced a four-part test for deciding whether to admit an out-of-court statement that is relevant to some other purpose other than its truth but that might be improperly used by the trier to prove the truth of its assertion. The four factors were whether the declaration addressed an important disputed issue in the trial, whether the declarant was knowledgeable and likely to be credited by the jury, whether the declarant is available for testimony, and whether curative or limiting instructions could effectively protect against prejudice. That four-part test is, obviously, a very substantial appellate court elaboration of Rule 403's list of factors to be considered.

580. *See* § **7.73**; *see, e.g.,* Kenny v. Southeastern Pa. Transp. Auth., 581 F.2d 351, 356 (3d Cir.1978) (evidence of remedial measure of installing lights in train station after rape of patron inadmissible to prove culpable conduct, but admissible to impeach transit authority's claim that all reasonable care was being exercised at the time of the incident).

581. *See* 1 McCormick on Evidence, *supra* note 578, at n.2 ("It seems, however, that the proponent, to complain of the judge's exclusion of evidence inadmissible in one aspect, must have stated the purpose for which it is competent, unless the admissible purpose is plainly apparent") (citations omitted).

582. *See* Fed. R. Evid. 105; Leonard, *supra* note 578 § 1.11; 1 Weinstein's Feder-

al Evidence, *supra* note 578 § 105.07 and cases cited therein; *see, e.g.,* United States v. Barron, 707 F.2d 125, 127–28 (5th Cir. 1983) (court gave limiting instructions to jury that evidence of prior dealings between witness and defendant admitted "for the sole purpose of showing plan, scheme, device on the part of the defendant, if any, toward those matters [at issue], and for that purpose only"). Note that some courts have narrowed this requirement at times by finding that a failure to issue the requested limiting instruction was harmless error. *See, e.g.,* Lubbock Feed Lots, Inc. v. Iowa Beef Processors, 630 F.2d 250, 265–66 (5th Cir.1980) (harmless error for court to have failed to give limiting instruction).

583. *See* Fed. R. Evid. 103(a)(1); United States v. Dozier, 672 F.2d 531, 543 (5th Cir.1982) ("If the defense, having lost the argument on general admissibility, desired a more precise limiting instruction on the extent to which the jury could consider such testimony it could and should have requested one"); United States v. Thirion, 813 F.2d 146, 155–56 (8th Cir.1987) (request denied where defendant did not specifically identify portion of testimony to be limited and where request was not specific or timely); see also 21 Charles A. Wright & Kenneth W. Graham, Jr., Federal Practice and Procedure (Evidence) § 5065, at 327 (1977).

584. Roth v. Black & Decker, United States, Inc., 737 F.2d 779, 782–83 (8th Cir. 1984) ("Black & Decker did not request a limiting instruction which may have been necessary under Rule 105 and 403 of the Federal Rules of Evidence ... not having requested such an instruction, Black & Decker cannot now claim that the district court erred").

585. *See* Leonard, *supra* note 578 § 1.11.1; 1 Weinstein's Federal Evidence,

tion that accompanies the prior inconsistent statement. One version of the instruction runs as follows:

> The testimony of a witness may be discredited or, as we sometimes say, impeached by showing that he or she previously made statements which are different than or inconsistent with his or her testimony here in court. The earlier inconsistent or contradictory statements are admissible only to discredit or impeach the credibility of the witness and not to establish the truth of these earlier statements made somewhere other than here during this trial. It is the province of the jury to determine the credibility of a witness who has made prior inconsistent or contradictory statements.[586]

If the danger that the jury will misuse the statement outweighs the probative value of the statement when used for its limited purpose, then the trial judge may exclude the entire statement under Rule 403.[587] A classic example of a case in which such exclusion would be proper is *Shepard v. United States*.[588] In that case, the defendant was accused of murdering his wife. The trial judge received testimony that shortly before her death, the wife had said, "Dr. Shepard has poisoned me."[589] On appeal, one of the theories of admission advanced by the prosecution was that the statement tended to negate any suicidal intent on the part of the wife. The Supreme Court recognized the theoretical validity of this ground, but held that the evidence should at any rate have been excluded because "the reverberating clang of those accusatory words would drown all weaker sounds."[590]

Sometimes an out-of-court statement can be redacted (edited) to remove inadmissible portions or avoid the danger that the jury will use the statement for an impermissible purpose. For example, the patient's account of who was at fault in an automobile accident can be removed

---

supra note 578 § 105.07[3] and cases cited therein.

586. Kevin F. O'Malley et al., Federal Jury Practice and Instructions § 15.06 (5th ed.2000).

587. *See* Fed. R. Evid. 105 advisory committee's note ("A close relationship exists between this rule and Rule 403 which ... [provides for] exclusion when 'probative value is substantially outweighed by the danger of unfair prejudice, confusion of the issues, or misleading the jury' "). Some commentators have questioned the effectiveness of limiting instructions in any case since a jury may well ignore the limiting instruction and use the admitted statement for an improper purpose. *See, e.g.*, Note, *The Limiting Instruction—Its Effectiveness and Effect*, 51 Minn. L. Rev. 264 (1966) (the limiting instructions discussed are different, but the argument is still applicable). Other commentators have argued that all relevant evidence should be admitted and limiting instructions should be preferred over exclu-

sion of evidence in all but the most extreme situations. *See* 1 Weinstein's Federal Evidence, *supra* note 578 § 105.03; 1 McCormick on Evidence, *supra* note 578 § 59, at 236; *see also* Petree v. Victor Fluid Power, Inc., 887 F.2d 34, 41–42 (3d Cir.1989) (not harmless error to exclude evidence of placement of safety decal on machine after accident where such evidence was offered to impeach expert testimony and limiting instructions could have been issued to assure jury considered evidence for only this purpose).

588. 290 U.S. 96 (1933).

589. *Id.* at 98.

590. *Id.* at 104; *cf.* United States v. Ingraham, 832 F.2d 229, 231–37 (1st Cir. 1987) (evidence of prior threatening letters and phone calls admissible for purpose of establishing identity of perpetrator, but inadmissible to show defendant's proclivities, where probative value outweighed danger of unfair prejudice).

from a hospital record, or references to the guilt of a codefendant might be removed from a confession.[591] The remaining portion of the statement would then be admissible.

§ 7.63 Attacking and Supporting the Credibility of a Hearsay Declarant [FRE 806]

Federal Rule of Evidence 806 provides that the credibility of a hearsay declarant can be attacked or supported as if the declarant were a witness.[592] In addition, it dispenses with foundational requirements for impeachment with prior inconsistent statements.[593] Rule 806 also allows a party to call the declarant as a witness, when this is possible, and to question the declarant as if on cross-examination when that declarant's hearsay statements are used against the party.[594]

To illustrate the operation of Rule 806, suppose that Declarant X makes an out-of-court statement that "the light was red." The statement is received at trial as an excited utterance. Obviously, the opponent ought to be able to put in evidence that at some other time declarant X said "the light was green," and the rule so provides. Once Declarant X's credibility has been attacked the proponent may offer any evidence to rehabilitate the declarant that would be admissible if X were a witness.[595]

Now, consider the situation in which Declarant X testified at a deposition that the light was red. The opponent had evidence that the declarant had at some other time stated that the light was green and had an opportunity to confront the declarant with the alleged prior statement and ask the declarant to explain or deny the statement. However, the opponent failed to use this opportunity and did not ask the declarant

591. *See, e.g.,* Richardson v. Marsh, 481 U.S. 200, 206–208 (1987) (confession of codefendant held admissible where all references to defendant redacted); Ramrattan v. Burger King Corp., 656 F.Supp. 522, 530 (D.Md.1987) (medical records admissible if plaintiff's statements regarding fault in an auto accident contained therein redacted). The court can, as in limiting instructions, order that information be redacted sua sponte. *See, e.g.,* Harris v. Upjohn Co., 115 F.R.D. 191, 192 (S.D.Ill.1987) (court could invoke Illinois physician-patient privilege and order patient names redacted from report offered into evidence at its discretion).

592. Fed. R. Evid. 806; *see generally* 5 Weinstein's Federal Evidence § 806.02 (2d ed. Joseph M. McLaughlin ed. 1997); 2 McCormick on Evidence § 327.2 (4th ed. John W. Strong ed. 1992). Note that Rule 806 also applies to nonhearsay statements under Rules 801(d)(2)(C), (D) and (E). *See also* Rules 608 and 609.

593. *See* Smith v. Fairman, 862 F.2d 630, 637–38 (7th Cir.1988):

    While the general rule is that a witness may be impeached by his prior inconsistent statements only after a proper foundation has been laid ... that rule has been dispensed with "where the witness is unavailable and hearsay evidence is offered to impeach the previously admitted hearsay evidence of the statements of the absent witness."

594. Fed. R. Evid. 806; *see also* United States v. Inadi, 475 U.S. 387, 397 (1986) ("if the party against whom a co-conspirator statement has been admitted calls the declarant as a witness, 'the party is entitled to examine him on the statement as if under cross-examination' ").

595. *See* 5 Weinstein's Federal Evidence, *supra* note 592 § 806.06; United States v. Lechoco, 542 F.2d 84, 88–89 (D.C.Cir.1976) (error to exclude evidence supporting credibility of out-of-court declarant where credibility has been impeached). Note that the inconsistent statement used to impeach the declarant can occur before or after the admitted hearsay statement. *See* Fed. R. Evid. 806 advisory committee's note.

anything about the prior statement during the deposition. Later the deposition is offered as evidence at trial because the declarant has become unavailable. Should the opponent be precluded from putting in the declarant's inconsistent statement, on grounds that the opponent failed to lay a foundation for it despite the opportunity to do so?[596] The drafters of Rule 806 answered this question in the negative. The rule specifically provides that "evidence of a statement or conduct by the declarant at any time, inconsistent with the declarant's hearsay statement, is not subject to any requirement that the declarant may have been afforded an opportunity to deny or explain."[597]

Rule 806 is not limited to impeachment by prior inconsistent statements. The hearsay declarant can be impeached by any method, including impeachment by prior convictions or by a showing of bias.[598]

As indicated, Rule 806 provides that the credibility of a hearsay declarant may be attacked by any evidence that would be admissible if declarant had testified as a witness. At the same time, Rule 608(b) bars extrinsic evidence of specific instances of conduct to attack credibility. What if the proponent seeks to attack the credibility of a hearsay declarant by offering specific instances of conduct? If the hearsay declarant had testified in person, the cross-examiner could have asked the witness about the specific instances on cross-examination, but could not have offered extrinsic evidence to prove those instances. This creates a tension between Rules 806 and 608(b). At least one court has opted to allow impeachment of a hearsay declarant with extrinsic evidence,[599] while another has held that the limitation of Rule 608(b) applies.[600]

---

596. For the in-court witness, Rule 612(b) provides that "[e]xtrinsic evidence of a prior inconsistent statement by a witness is not admissible unless the witness is afforded an opportunity to explain or deny the same and the opposite party is afforded an opportunity to interrogate the witness thereon, or the interests of justice otherwise require."

597. Fed. R. Evid. 806; *see also* Smith v. Fairman, 862 F.2d at 637–38. Wigmore supported a contrary position. He argued that a foundation should be required whenever an opportunity could have been provided to the declarant to explain or deny the inconsistency. Thus, different hearsay statements would be treated differently. For example, in a dying declaration there would very likely not be such an opportunity, but in prior testimony there would. *See* 3 John H. Wigmore, Evidence in Trials at Common Law §§ 1030–1035 (James H. Chadbourn rev. 1970). The Federal Rule treats all hearsay statements in the same way and is based upon the theory that finders of fact will be more likely to reach a just decision if they have all the relevant information. *See* 5 Weinstein's Federal Evidence, *supra* note 592 § 806.04[1].

598. *See* United States v. Becerra, 992 F.2d 960, 965 (9th Cir.1993) (held, in criminal case, district court improperly prevented defendant from attacking out-of-court declarant's credibility with evidence of declarant's prior statements, criminal convictions, and compensation as paid police informant); United States v. Bovain, 708 F.2d 606, 613–14 (11th Cir.1983) (evidence of declarant's prior narcotics and theft convictions held admissible to impeach out-of-court declarant's credibility); United States v. Lawson, 608 F.2d 1129, 1130 (6th Cir. 1979) (court did not err in admitting evidence of out-of-court declarant's felony convictions offered for impeachment purposes).

599. State v. Martisko, 566 S.E.2d 274 (W.Va.2002) (applying W. Va. R. Evid. 806).

600. United States v. Saada, 212 F.3d 210, 220 (3d Cir.2000) ("Fed. R. Evid. 806 does not modify Fed. R. Evid. 608(b)'s ban on extrinsic evidence of prior bad acts in the context of hearsay declarants, even when those declarant's are unavailable to testify").

§ 7.64 Requirement That the Hearsay Declarant Have Personal Knowledge

Suppose that a victim of poisoning tells all to the police just before dying. He says, "I know I am going to die. Dr. Blaeser poisoned me." The foundation for the hearsay exception for dying declarations has been satisfied because the declarant has manifested knowledge of the imminence of death. Yet absent additional facts the statement would not be admissible because the declarant did not have personal knowledge.[601] We do not know whether the declarant is merely speculating or whether, perhaps, the declarant is basing his accusation upon another's hearsay statement. An objection should be sustained.[602] The situation would be different, of course, had the declarant been shot in the chest. Then the trier could infer personal knowledge just from the circumstances. Probably the declarant had a view of the assailant, and the fact that the declarant has accused a particular person makes the likelihood even greater that the declarant had the view.[603]

The personal knowledge requirement applies to most out-of-court statements.[604] However, the requirement is not universal. For example, the admission of a party opponent need not have been made on personal knowledge in order to be admissible.[605] If a party says "my wolf bit a little girl" and the statement is offered against the party, then the statement is admissible even if the party can show that she was not present at the time of the alleged biting.[606] In fact, the Advisory Commit-

---

601. *See* 2 McCormick on Evidence § 313 (4th ed. John W. Strong ed. 1992) (personal knowledge requirement applies to dying declarations); 5 Weinstein's Federal Evidence § 807.05[5][a] (2d ed. Joseph M. McLaughlin ed. 1997); Shepard v. United States, 290 U.S. 96, 101 (1933) ("To let the declaration in, the inference must be permissible that there was knowledge or the opportunity for knowledge as to the acts that are declared").

602. *See e.g.*, Shepard v. United States, 290 U.S. at 101 (statement held inadmissible as a dying declaration on other grounds would almost certainly have failed to meet the personal knowledge requirement as well; the court noted this requirement without deciding whether this statement would meet it).

603. *See, e.g.*, Reese v. Bara, 479 F.Supp. 651, 655–56 (S.D.N.Y.1979) (woman stabbed in the abdomen would have been "a competent witness as to how she came by her stab wounds.").

604. *Cf.* 2 McCormick on Evidence, *supra* note 601 § 255, at 144–45.

605. *See id.* at 145.

[A] sufficient basis for generally dispensing with the requirement of firsthand knowledge qualification rests on the argument that admissions that become relevant in litigation usually concern some matter of substantial importance to declarants upon which they would likely have informed themselves. As a result, such admissions possess greater reliability than the general run of hearsay, even when not based on firsthand observation. Moreover, the possibility is substantial that the declarant may have come into possession of significant information not known to the opponent.

But see 5 Weinstein's Federal Evidence, *supra* note 601 § 801.29[3], at 801–57 (arguing that the statement "must be evaluated in light of the requirements that its probative value outweigh any dangers of prejudice or confusion and that its underlying basis has sufficient assurances of accuracy").

606. Mahlandt v. Wild Canid Survival & Research Center, Inc., 588 F.2d 626, 630–31 (8th Cir.1978) (admission by agent that wolf bit child held admissible without requirement of personal knowledge); Union Mutual Life Ins. Co. v. Chrysler Corp., 793 F.2d 1, 8–9 (1st Cir.1986) (letter containing admissions which was written by employee held admissible despite lack of personal knowledge); Freda F. Bein, *Parties' Admissions, Agents' Admissions: Hearsay Wolves in Sheep's Clothing*, 12 Hofstra L. Rev. 393 (1984) (arguing against result in Mahlandt

tee specifically noted that the admission rule was free of the personal knowledge requirement.[607] The business records exception is also free of the personal knowledge requirement in the sense that the witness need not have personal knowledge of the transaction recorded, though the information must have been transmitted by a person with knowledge.[608] Some of the other hearsay exceptions also expressly or implicitly dispense with the requirement that the hearsay declarant have personal knowledge. One such exception is Federal Rule of Evidence 803(8)(C), the exception for findings pursuant to investigation, which by its very nature contemplates that sometimes the declarant will make a finding about events that the declarant did not personally observe.[609] For example, in *Beech Aircraft v. Rainey*[610] the Supreme Court held admissible a naval investigator's conclusion about the cause of a fatal air crash. The investigator had not observed the crash nor did the investigator have personal knowledge of the basis for many of the facts and conclusions expressed in his report.[611] Another hearsay exception, the exception for statements of personal and family history in Rule 804(b)(4), expressly eschews any requirement of personal knowledge. It provides that statements concerning the declarant's own birth, adoption, marriage, family relationships, etc. are admissible "even though declarant had no means of acquiring personal knowledge of the matter stated."[612]

Where the hearsay exception requires that the declarant have spoken on personal knowledge, Federal Rule 602 applies. That rule provides that a lay witness "may not testify to a matter unless evidence is

case where agent's admissions are involved).

607. Fed. R. Evid. 801(d)(2) advisory committee's note ("The freedom which admissions have enjoyed from technical demands ... of the opinion rule and the rule requiring firsthand knowledge ... calls for generous treatment of this avenue to admissibility").

608. *See* United States v. Norton, 867 F.2d 1354, 136a (11th Cir.1989) (memorandum detailing telephone conversation prepared by one officer was admissible as business record through another officer who had no personal knowledge of its contents); United States v. Iredia, 866 F.2d 114, 119–20 (5th Cir.1989) (business record was admissible where witnesses who testified to the authenticity of the documents had no personal knowledge of "the record keeping practice and of the circumstances under which the objected to records were kept"); 5 Weinstein's Federal Evidence, *supra* note 601 § 803.11[1], at 803–61 to 803–64; 2 McCormick on Evidence, *supra* note 601 § 290. But note that the person initially gathering the information must have personal knowledge. *See* Meder v. Everest & Jennings, Inc., 637 F.2d 1182, 1186 (8th Cir.1981) (admission of police accident report was in error where officer could not

recall where he had obtained the information); Johnson v. Lutz, 170 N.E. 517 (N.Y. 1930).

609. *See* 2 McCormick on Evidence, *supra* note 601 § 296, at 291 ("As the name indicates, these reports embody the results of investigations and accordingly are often not the product of firsthand knowledge of the declarant ..."). Note that investigative reports have been restricted to investigations made pursuant to authority granted by law and to factual findings. *See* 5 Weinstein's Federal Evidence, *supra* note 601 § 803.13[4][a] (arguing for liberally construing the requirements of investigative reports and the exception for personal knowledge).

610. 488 U.S. 153 (1988).

611. *Id.* at 164–70; *see also* Wolf by Wolf v. Procter & Gamble Co., 555 F.Supp. 613, 625 (D.N.J.1982) (studies conducted by Centers for Disease Control and state health agencies admissible even if the authors did not have firsthand knowledge of the facts upon which findings were made).

612. Fed. R. Evid. 804(b)(4); *see generally* 5 Weinstein's Federal Evidence, *supra* note 601 § 807.07[2]; 2 McCormick on Evidence, *supra* note 601 § 322.

introduced sufficient to support a finding that the witness has personal knowledge of the matter." Under this standard, which tracks the standard contained in Rule 104(b) (the conditional relevancy rule), the trial court need not be convinced that the declarant had personal knowledge. The court need only find that there is evidence sufficient to support that conclusion (i.e., that it would not be unreasonable for the jury to conclude that the declarant had personal knowledge). Because this is not a very difficult standard to satisfy, the personal knowledge requirement will not often be a significant obstacle to the admission of hearsay under one of the exceptions.

§ 7.65   Hearsay Through the Mouth of an Expert

In the hands of a skillful trial lawyer, the expert can become a channel through which major fact evidence flows into the ears of jurors. Trial lawyers report that some trial judges allow experts to quote freely the statements of others in support of their opinions. For example, an expert on the causes and origins of fire might testify on the issue of arson. If the expert talked to eyewitnesses in the course of investigation, then the expert might be used as a conduit to put into evidence the narratives of those eyewitnesses without calling them to the stand.[613] Or the expert might be asked to describe the contents of reports of experiments done by others upon which the expert relied.[614] The supposed justification for this practice is Federal Rule of Evidence 703, which provides:

> The facts or data in the particular case upon which an expert bases an opinion or inference may be those perceived by or made known to the expert at or before the hearing. If of a type reasonably relied upon by experts in the particular field in forming opinions or inferences upon the subject, the facts or data need not be admissible in evidence.[615]

The problem with relying upon this Rule as authority for the proposition that experts can freely give hearsay testimony is that the rule only provides that experts may, within reason, rely upon otherwise inadmissible evidence in forming opinions. The Rule does not state that experts may freely repeat hearsay that they have heard while forming opinions.[616]

---

613.   *See* Stevens v. Cessna Aircraft, 634 F.Supp. 137, 142–43 (E.D.Pa.), *aff'd*, 806 F.2d 252 (3d Cir.1986) (expert's testimony regarding statements made to him during course of investigation held admissible); State v. Jones, 368 S.E.2d 844 (N.C. 1988) (expert's testimony as to contents of statements relied upon to form opinion held admissible).

614.   *See* Roger C. Park, *Confining the Expert: Rule 703(b) of the Rules of Evidence*, in The Bench and Bar of Minnesota 33–35 (March 1990).

615.   Fed. R. Evid. 703.

616.   *See* § **10.08**; *see generally* Ronald L. Carlson, *Collision Course in Expert Testimony: Limitations an Affirmative Introduction of Underlying Data*, 36 Univ. Fla. L. Rev. 234 (1984); *cf.* Stephen A. Saltzburg & Kenneth R. Redden, Federal Rules of Evidence Manual 671 (4th ed. 1986); Henry v. Brenner, 486 N.E.2d 934, 936–37 (Ill.App. 1985) (allowing expert to testify as to content of statements relied upon where jury given limiting instruction as to proper use of these statements). *But see* Paul R. Rice, *Inadmissible Evidence as a Basis For Expert Opinion Testimony: A Response to Professor Carlson*, 40 Vand. L. Rev. 583 (1987)

Testifying experts are permitted on direct examination to show that they did a careful job of preparing their opinions. To show diligence, it is often reasonable to allow experts to testify to the fact that a conversation took place, without revealing the content of the conversation. An expert might be allowed, for example, to state that the expert had conferred with another expert while forming an opinion, without expressly stating the opinion of the other expert.[617] However, when the expert begins to describe the content of conversations with other persons, the testimony is frequently objectionable.[618]

§ 7.66 Hearsay and the Right to Confrontation

Even if hearsay testimony meets the requirements of a hearsay exception, the criminal defendant still has a last resort. The defendant may argue that reception of the testimony would violate the confrontation clause.

The confrontation clause of the sixth amendment provides: "In all criminal prosecutions, the accused shall enjoy the right ... to be confronted with the witnesses against him...." The language of the amendment does not provide clear guidance about hearsay issues. It is susceptible to a variety of textually plausible interpretations. Under one possible interpretation, all hearsay declarants whose statements are offered by the prosecution would be considered "witnesses against" the defendant, and therefore the Constitution would require that the defendant be confronted with them at trial. This interpretation would lead to the exclusion of all hearsay, even hearsay that fell under an exception established at the time of the adoption of the amendment. Alternatively, one could interpret the amendment to require merely that the defendant be confronted with whatever witnesses the prosecution chose to produce at trial. Under this interpretation, trial witnesses could testify about hearsay declarations, and the confrontation clause would impose no limits upon the creation of new hearsay exceptions. It would merely require the presence of the defendant when evidence was presented to the trier of fact.[619] The amendment could also be construed so that

(arguing that admitting the expert's opinion without its basis is illogical because one cannot accept the truth of an opinion without implicitly accepting the facts upon which the opinion is based, and that depriving the jury of the basis of the opinion leads to undesirable blind deference to the witness; also arguing for adoption of a carefully tailored hearsay exception covering the basis of the expert's opinion).

617. *See* United States v. Rollins, 862 F.2d 1282, 1292–93 (7th Cir.1988) (experts testimony that he had conversations with others concerning the meaning of certain code-words used in illegal drug deals admissible where content of these conversations not revealed); Ronald L. Carlson, *Policing*

the Bases of Modern Expert Testimony, 39 Vand. L. Rev. 577, 584 & n.23 (1986).

618. See § **10.08** for a discussion of authorities on this point. If the statements of other experts are relevant to some proposition other than the truth of the matters asserted, such statements might be admissible for that purpose.

619. *See* Dutton v. Evans, 400 U.S. 74, 94 (1970) (Harlan, J, concurring); 5 John H. Wigmore, Evidence in Trials at Common Law § 1397, at 131, 134 (3d ed. 1940) (confrontation clause should be construed so that it merely requires cross-examination of witnesses who are required to testify in court by the hearsay rules in effect at the time of trial; nothing in the clause should

"witnesses against" the defendant referred only to persons who were available to testify. Under this interpretation, the prosecution would be required to produce declarants for cross-examination when possible, but the statements of unavailable declarants could be freely admitted.[620] Finally, one could interpret the clause to mean that the defendant has the right to confrontation whenever "testimonial" evidence is offered against him, but that the prosecution use of hearsay evidence that is not "testimonial" does not violate the confrontation clause. The Court's most recent confrontation decision is consistent with this final interpretation.[621]

§ 7.67 Hearsay and the Right to Confrontation—The *Roberts* Test and Beyond

The Supreme Court has never adopted either of the extreme interpretations of the confrontation clause. In an early case interpreting the clause, it rejected the absolute exclusion view by recognizing that dying declarations were admissible, despite the fact that the defendant had never confronted the declarant.[622] Four years later, however, it held that the confrontation clause could prevent legislative creation of a new hearsay exception. The court struck down a federal statute that permitted a third party's theft conviction to be used in a receiving stolen goods prosecution to prove that the goods were in fact stolen.[623] Subsequent cases steered between the two extremes of absolute exclusion of hearsay and absolute deference to hearsay exceptions. It is difficult to generalize about these cases, because they dealt with particular situations without establishing a general principle.[624] In the 1980 case of

---

be construed to inhibit revision and extension of hearsay exceptions).

620. *See* California v. Green, 399 U.S. 149, 174 (1970) (Harlan, J., concurring); Peter Westen, *The Future of Confrontation*, 77 Mich. L. Rev. 1185, 1188–89 (1979), Irving Younger, *Confrontation and Hearsay: A Look Backward, a Peek Forward*, 1 Hofstra L. Rev. 32 (1973).

621. Crawford v. Washington, 124 S.Ct. 1354 (2004).

622. Mattox v. United States, 156 U.S. 237, 243–44 (1895) (dictum). *See also* Kirby v. United States, 174 U.S. 47, 61 (1899) (dictum) ("the admission of dying declarations is an exception which arises from the necessity of the case. This exception was well established before the adoption of the Constitution, and was not intended to be abrogated").

623. Kirby v. United States, 174 U.S. 47 (1899). The actual statute made the conviction conclusive evidence that the goods were stolen, but the Court did not rest its decision on this ground. Instead, it made clear that merely admitting the third par-

ty's conviction into evidence was a violation of the confrontation clause. *Id.* at 55–56, 61.

624. *See* Pointer v. Texas, 380 U.S. 400 (1965) (introduction of testimony from preliminary hearing at which defendant was not represented, and at which he did not cross-examine, violates sixth amendment as applied to states); Douglas v. Alabama, 380 U.S. 415 (1965) (allowing prosecutor to, in effect, use accomplice's statement as evidence against defendant is unconstitutional in circumstances of case); Barber v. Page, 390 U.S. 719 (1968) (introducing declarant's former testimony against defendant, without sufficient attempt to produce declarant for trial, violates confrontation clause); Bruton v. United States, 391 U.S. 123 (1968) (admitting co-defendant's confession implicating both defendants violates confrontation clause, despite limiting instruction); California v. Green, 399 U.S. 149 (1970) (receiving witness's prior inconsistent statement as substantive evidence permissible under circumstances of case); Dutton v. Evans, 400 U.S. 74 (1970) (receiving co-conspirator's prior statement to cellmate permissible under circumstances of case).

Ohio v. Roberts,[625] however, the Court found majority support for an opinion that outlined a general approach to resolving confrontation issues. The *Roberts* Court established a two-pronged test for determining whether the introduction of hearsay violated the confrontation clause. The Court applied the test to all hearsay/confrontation clause cases for nearly a quarter century. Though the Court has abrogated the test for some categories of hearsay (including former testimony as in *Roberts*), the test arguably remains viable for others.[626]

The first prong of the *Roberts* test required that the prosecution produce the hearsay declarant or demonstrate that the declarant is unavailable.[627] This prong had exceptions, however: it only applied in the "usual" case;[628] the prosecution was not required to demonstrate unavailability in cases in which the utility of confrontation is "remote."[629]

The second prong of the *Roberts* test required that the hearsay have "adequate 'indicia of reliability.' "[630] In some cases, this prong required "a showing of particularized guarantees of trustworthiness." However, the Court appeared to recognize that the need for certainty in criminal trials required more specific guidance.[631] It indicated that deference should be given to established hearsay exceptions, saying that reliability could be inferred "without more" when evidence fell under a "firmly rooted" hearsay exception.[632]

Post-Roberts Cases on Statements of Co-conspirators

The Court has made clear that one hearsay exception to which it will give deference is the exception for admissions of co-conspirators. In *United States v. Inadi*, it held that, despite language in *Ohio v. Roberts*[633]

In a concurring opinion in California v. Green, 399 U.S. at 172–74 Justice Harlan advocated a general theory-that the confrontation clause required the production of available witnesses, but had no application when the witness was unavailable-but the majority did not adopt it and he soon afterward abandoned it himself. *See* Dutton v. Evans, 400 U.S. 74, 95–100 (1970) (Harlan, J, concurring). Justice Harlan changed his views because he had come to believe that requiring the production of available declarants in every case would be unduly inconvenient and of little utility. *Id.* His later view was that the confrontation clause should be construed only to guarantee the right to be present at trial and cross-examine the witnesses there presented. In flagrant cases, however, the misuse of hearsay might constitute a violation of due process. *Id.* at 98.

625.   448 U.S. 56 (1980).

626.   *See infra* note 657 and accompanying text.

627.   *Id.* at 65.

628.   "In the usual case (including cases where prior cross-examination has oc-

curred), the prosecution must either produce, or demonstrate the unavailability of, the declarant whose statement it wishes to use against the defendant." *Id.*

629.   *Id.* at 65, n.7.

630.   *Id.* at 65.

631.   *See, e.g., id.* at 66 (referring to the "need for certainty in the workaday world of criminal trials" as one reason why, in past cases, the Court had concluded that "certain hearsay exceptions rest upon such solid foundations that admission of virtually any evidence within them comports with the 'substance of the constitutional protection' ").

632.   *Id.* at 66. The Court indicated in a footnote that dying declarations fell under a "firmly rooted" hearsay exception, and implied that hearsay falling under the business records and public records exceptions would also pass confrontation clause scrutiny, at least where those exceptions were "properly administered." *Id.* at 66, n.8.

633.   448 U.S. 56 (1980).

about the necessity of producing an available declarant in the "usual" case, statements of co-conspirators may be used even when the declarant is available but not produced.[634] The Court reasoned that the purpose of a requirement that available declarants be produced is to get live testimony when possible because live testimony is usually the best evidence. However, in the case of co-conspirator statements, the out-of-court statement was better evidence than the declarant's in-court testimony would be. The statements, according to the Court, provide evidence "of the conspiracy's context" that "cannot be replicated," because "conspirators are likely to speak differently when talking to each other in furtherance of their illegal aims than when testifying on the witness stand."[635] It also suggested that the available witness could be called by the defense, so that "[p]resumably those declarants that neither side believes will be particularly helpful will not have been subpoenaed as witnesses."[636] While there are good answers to both of these arguments—and the dissenting Justices made them convincingly—the majority of the Supreme Court has not yet accepted them.

This reasoning about the unavailability rule is potentially applicable to other hearsay exceptions as well. Many out-of-court statements could be characterized as "better" than in-court testimony because they were made closer to the event and before the witness was influenced by preparation for litigation. So the Supreme Court's stated bases for receiving co-conspirator statements also provide a basis for arguing that other statements by available declarants should be received despite the confrontation clause.

The second prong in *Roberts*, the reliability prong, was also diluted in cases involving statements by co-conspirators. In the 1987 case of *Bourjaily v. United States*,[637] the majority gave short shrift to the defendant's argument that the prosecution had to make a particularized showing of reliability before a co-conspirator's statement could be received. The Court indicated that so long as the requirements of Federal Rule of Evidence 801(d)(2)(E) were satisfied, nothing further need be shown to surmount a confrontation clause challenge. It pointed out that *Roberts* had stated that no independent inquiry into reliability would be required so long as the out-of-court statement fell within a "firmly rooted" hearsay exception. Noting that the exception had repeatedly been recognized in its own case law since 1827, the Court described the exception as "firmly rooted."[638]

---

634. United States v. Inadi, 475 U.S. 387 (1986).

635. *Id.* at 395.

636. *Id.* at 397.

637. 483 U.S. 171 (1987).

638. In *Lilly v. Virginia*, 527 U.S. 116 (1999), the Court re-examined the application of the confrontation clause analysis to a confession by a nontestifying accomplice offered as a declaration against interest.

The confession contained some statements that were against the accomplice's own interest and others that incriminated only the defendant. The Virginia courts received the evidence as a declaration against interest, deeming it invulnerable to confrontation attack on the ground that the declaration against interest exception is "firmly rooted." The United States Supreme Court reversed. However, the Court was not able to muster a majority for any single theory. Four justices were ready to hold that "ac-

Although we have discussed confrontation clause doctrine in terms of the *Roberts* two-pronged test, that test does not, of course, provide answers for every case. For one thing, the Court's 2004 decision in *Crawford v. Washington*[639] abrogates the *Roberts* test for some confrontation cases. For others, it might make more sense to regard the Supreme Court's confrontation clause jurisprudence more as a set of responses to particular situations than as a product of some over-arching theory.[640]

Other Post-Roberts Confrontation Cases; "Firmly Rooted" Exceptions, Extrinsic Corroboration

In *Idaho v. Wright*.[641] the Court considered the nature of the indicia of trustworthiness required when evidence was admitted under a hearsay exception that was not firmly rooted. Defendant Laura Lee Wright was accused of helping Robert L. Giles in the sexual abuse of her two daughters. The evidentiary issue turned on the admissibility of statements by the younger daughter, who was two-and-one-half years old at the time of the crimes charged. The younger daughter had been questioned by a pediatrician after one of the children told an adult about abuse, and medical examinations revealed physical evidence of abuse. In response to questioning, she told the pediatrician that Giles had had sexual contact with her, and she volunteered that Giles had had sexual contact with the older sister. The trial judge found, and the parties agreed, that the younger daughter was "not capable of communicating to the jury," and hence the younger daughter did not testify. The trial judge admitted the pediatrician's testimony about the child's statements under Idaho Rule of Evidence 803(24), which is identical in relevant respects to Federal Rule 807. The Supreme Court held that admission of the statements to the pediatrician violated defendant's rights under the confrontation clause. No adequate indicia of reliability had been shown in the case. The pediatrician had conducted the interview in a suggestive manner. Reliability could not be inferred from corroborating evidence, such as the physical evidence of abuse. In what is perhaps the most significant part of its opinion, the Court's majority ruled that the relevant circumstances that can show particularized guarantees of trustworthiness are only those that surround the making of the statement;

complices' confessions that inculpate a criminal defendant are not within a firmly rooted exception to the hearsay rule as that concept has been defined in our Confrontation Clause jurisprudence." *Id*. at 134. hree other justices concurred in reversing the conviction but, were not willing to go so far as to say that a "genuinely self-inculpatory statement that also inculpates a codefendant" was constitutionally barred. *Id*. at 144–45. Justices Scalia and Thomas also concurred, noting in separate opinions that even under Justice Thomas's restrictive interpretation of the Clause, under which the confrontation right is "implicated by extrajudicial statements only insofar as they are contained in formalized testimonial material, such as affidavits, depositions, prior testimony, or confessions," the statement offered still did not pass muster. *Id*. at 143–45. Justice Thomas wrote that in his view, the confrontation clause does not impose a "blanket ban" on admission of accomplice statements that incriminate a defendant. *Id*.

639. 124 S.Ct. 1354 (2004).

640. For a useful and perceptive review, see Roger W. Kirst, *The Procedural Dimension of Confrontation Doctrine*, 66 Neb. L. Rev. 485 (1987).

641. 497 U.S. 805 (1990).

evidence corroborating the accuracy of the statement may not be considered.[642]

In *White v. Illinois*,[643] the Supreme Court seemed to swing toward limiting *Ohio v. Roberts* to former testimony situations. It stated flatly that *Roberts* "stands for the proposition that unavailability analysis is a necessary part of the Confrontation Clause inquiry *only when* the challenged out-of-court statements were made in the course of a prior judicial proceeding."[644] The defendant in *White* was convicted of sexually assaulting a four-year-old girl. Although the victim was available to testify, the Court upheld admission of her prior statements under the state law hearsay exceptions for spontaneous declarations and statements made in the course of receiving medical care. The Court took pains to explain how the statements involved in *White* were made in

642. For an example of a case in which the *Idaho v. Wright* standard was deemed to have been met, see McCafferty v. Leapley, 944 F.2d 445 (8th Cir.1991) (habeas from state prosecution; held, reception of child declarant's statements accusing defendant of sex abuse not a violation of confrontation clause under the circumstances, which included the following: the statements were explicit and consistent; the initial statement was given spontaneously in response to a nonleading question about how the child got a "hickey" mark on her neck; the child's knowledge of sexual matters was tape recorded; and the child had no motive to testify falsely against the defendant, for whom she still felt affection). *See also* Bugh v. Mitchell, 329 F.3d 496 (6th Cir.2003) (held, state did not violate confrontation rights by admitting prior consistent statement of four-year-old child about sexual abuse; child testified and was available for cross-examination); United States v. McKeeve, 131 F.3d 1, 9 (1st Cir.1997) (use of witness deposition taken in Britain against criminal defendant was not violation of Sixth Amendment where (1) witness was unavailable; (2) defendant's attorney was transported to Britain by government to participate in deposition; and (3) defendant was allowed to monitor the deposition telephonically and to communicate privately with counsel during the deposition); United States v. Ross, 33 F.3d 1507 (11th Cir.1994) (statute providing for admission of certified foreign business records does not violate confrontation clause; while the statutory exception was not "firmly rooted" because the statute did not require the custodian of the records to appear in court as a sponsoring witness, the statute nevertheless required sufficient guarantees of trustworthiness). For an example of a case which failed to meet the *Idaho v. Wright* standard, see Ring v. Erickson, 983 F.2d 818, 819–20 (8th Cir.1992) (admission of videotaped interview between child victim of alleged sexual abuse and social worker violated defendant's rights under the confrontation clause; Minnesota statute which created a special hearsay exception for child victims of sexual abuse was not a firmly rooted hearsay exception, and victim's statements lacked the requisite "particularized guarantees of trustworthiness").

Not surprisingly, some courts have interpreted the "intrinsic trustworthiness" requirement of *Idaho v. Wright* quite liberally. *See* United States v. Ellis, 951 F.2d 580, 582–84 (4th Cir.1991) (no violation of confrontation clause to admit statement of deceased accomplice because of the following guarantees of trustworthiness: (1) the statements were made before his own attorneys as well as government investigators; (2) the statements were made pursuant to a plea agreement that required the accomplice to be truthful; (3) the government agents were taking notes in front of the accomplice while the statements were being made; (4) the accomplice-declarant knew that his statements would be the subject of further investigation; and (5) the accomplice-declarant agreed to secretly record further conversations with the persons he had implicated, thus suggesting that he was willing to have the truthfulness of the statements tested). *See also* United States v. Canan, 48 F.3d 954 (6th Cir.1995) (held, over strong dissent by Judge Martin, that admission of accusatory videotaped statement taken by prosecution from accomplice 15 days before accomplice died of cancer did not violate confrontation clause, even though defendant was not given an opportunity to have attorney present or to cross-examine; fact that the declarant knew he was at death's door noted as factor supporting trustworthiness of his statements).

643. 502 U.S. 346 (1992).

644. *Id.* at 354 (emphasis added).

contexts that provided guarantees of trustworthiness that could not be recaptured in the courtroom. Hence, imposing an unavailability requirement that forced in-court testimony would not, in the Court's view, have substantially contributed to accuracy.[645]

In a concurring opinion, Justice Thomas, joined by Justice Scalia, argued for a fundamental change in interpretation of the confrontation clause. They argued that the Supreme Court's precedent had been wrong all along in assuming that all hearsay declarants are "witnesses against" a defendant within the meaning of the clause. They suggested a possible reformulation that they considered to be more faithful to the language and history of the clause than the Court's usual approach. Under their formulation, "[t]he federal constitutional right of confrontation extends to any witness who actually testifies at trial, but the Confrontation Clause is implicated by extrajudicial statements only insofar as they are contained in formalized testimonial materials, such as affidavits, depositions, prior testimony, or confessions."[646] As we will see, the Court later adopted the substance of the Thomas/Scalia view.

Crawford v. Washington: The Court Adopts a New Test for "Testimonial" Hearsay

The Court took a sharp turn in 2004 with its decision in *Crawford v. Washington*.[647] In *Crawford*, defendant Michael Crawford was charged with assault and attempted murder of a man he believed had tried to rape his wife Sylvia. The police interrogated both Michael and Sylvia, taking tape-recorded statements from each. In his statement, Crawford stated facts that would support a claim of self-defense. Sylvia's statement largely corroborated her husband's, but differed in several respects, most notably in its weaker support for the self-defense claim.[648] At trial, Sylvia did not testify because of Washington's adverse spousal testimony privilege, which bars a spouse from testifying without the other spouse's consent. The privilege does not apply when a statement satisfies a hearsay exception, however, and Sylvia's statement was self-incriminatory because it admitted that she had led her husband to Lee's apartment, which facilitated the assault.[649] Over defendant's confrontation objection, the court allowed the prosecution to play the tape of Sylvia's statement to the jury.

The Washington Court of Appeals reversed, applying a nine-factor test and determining that Sylvia's statement failed to contain sufficient particularized guarantees of trustworthiness required by the *Roberts*

---

645. For commentary on confrontation problems in child sexual abuse prosecutions, see Michael H. Graham, *The Confrontation Clause, the Hearsay Rule, and Child Sexual Abuse Prosecutions: The State of the Relationship*, 72 Minn. L. Rev. 523 (1988); Robert P. Mosteller, *Remaking Confrontation Clause and Hearsay Doctrine Under the Challenge of Child Sexual Abuse Prosecutions*, 1993 U. Ill. L. Rev. 691.

646. *Id.* at 365 (Thomas, J., dissenting).

647. 124 S.Ct. 1354 (2004).

648. Crawford stated that before he stabbed Lee, he thought he saw Lee reaching for a weapon. Sylvia's statement suggested that Lee reached for something only after Crawford had stabbed him. *Id.* at 1357.

649. *Id.* at 1358.

test. The Washington Supreme Court reinstated the conviction, holding that the statement bore sufficient guarantees of trustworthiness.

The Supreme Court once again reversed, holding that admission of Sylvia's statement violated Michael's confrontation rights. Writing for a majority of seven, Justice Scalia reviewed the history of the confrontation right from Roman times to the present. Placing primary emphasis on the state of the common law at the time of the sixth amendment's framing, Scalia wrote:

> First, the principal evil at which the Confrontation Clause was directed was the civil-law mode of criminal procedure, and particularly its use of *ex parte* examinations as evidence against the accused....

> Accordingly, we once again reject the view that the Confrontation Clause applies of its own force only to in-court testimony, and that its application to out-of-court statements introduced at trial depends upon "the law of Evidence for the time being." ... Leaving the regulation of out-of-court statements to the law of evidence would render the Confrontation Clause powerless to prevent even the most flagrant inquisitorial practices....

> The text of the Confrontation Clause reflects this focus. It applies to "witnesses" against the accused—in other words, those who "bear testimony." ... "Testimony," in turn, is typically "[a] solemn declaration or affirmation made for the purpose of establishing or proving some fact." ... An accuser who makes a formal statement to government officers bears testimony in a sense that a person who makes a casual remark to an acquaintance does not. The constitutional text, like the history underlying the common-law right of confrontation, thus reflects an especially acute concern with a specific type of out-of-court statement.[650]

Thus, the confrontation clause applies to "testimonial" statements. Though the Court declined to provide a precise definition of "testimonial,"[651] it held that the category included, "at a minimum ... prior testimony at a preliminary hearing, before a grand jury or at a former trial; and to police interrogations."[652]

The Court held that "[t]he historical record ... supports the proposition that the Framers would not have allowed admission of testimonial statements of a witness who did not appear at trial unless he was unavailable to testify, and the defendant had a prior opportunity for cross-examination."[653] Thus, the Court established a bright-line rule for

---

650. *Id.* at 1363–64.

651. The Court's distinction between "testimonial" and "non-testimonial" hearsay was the primary reason for the refusal of Chief Justice Rehnquist's and Justice O'Connor to join the majority. Rehnquist was concerned that the Court's failure to

articulate a definition of "testimonial" "casts a mantle of uncertainty over future criminal trials in both federal and state courts." *Id.* at 1374 (Rehnquist, C.J., concurring).

652. *Id.*

653. *Id.* at 1365.

"testimonial" hearsay offered against a criminal defendant: Such hearsay is only admissible if the declarant testifies at trial or is unavailable *and* the defendant had a prior opportunity to cross-examine the declarant. By so holding, the Court abolished the *Roberts* test in cases of "testimonial" hearsay.[654] Under *Roberts*, trustworthy hearsay could be admitted where the declarant was unavailable, even if the hearsay was testimonial. After *Crawford*, even a high degree of trustworthiness does not satisfy the confrontation clause. The Court said that "[d]ispensing with confrontation because testimony is obviously reliable is akin to dispensing with jury trial because a defendant is obviously guilty."[655]

Crawford is a key turning-point in the Court's confrontation clause jurisprudence. Now, even if hearsay fits within hearsay exceptions that admit "testimonial" statements, it will not be admissible against a criminal defendant unless the declarant is unavailable to testify and the defendant had a prior opportunity for cross-examination.[656] This will mean that grand jury statements will no longer be admissible against a criminal defendant because such statements are not subject to cross-examination. For the same reason, statements of others made during police interrogation will not be admissible. The *Crawford* decision also calls into question the validity of state child-hearsay exceptions, at least to the extent the child's statement is "testimonial" because it was made formally during police questioning. At the same time, the results of cases such as *Roberts* will not change, as long as the defendant had an opportunity to cross-examine the declarant at the preliminary hearing and as long as the declarant is either produced at trial or is unavailable. (Both of these conditions were satisfied in *Roberts*.)

When hearsay is not "testimonial," *Crawford* strongly suggests that the confrontation clause does not apply at all, and that the only barrier to admission is the hearsay rule. For example, the Court states in dictum that "[a]n off-hand, overheard remark might be unreliable evidence and thus a good candidate for exclusion under hearsay rules, but it bears little resemblance to the civil-law abuses the Confrontation Clause targeted."[657] However, the case before the Court did not actually involve nontestimonial hearsay, and the Court's language is arguably ambiguous on this point, leaving open some possibility that criminal defendants

---

654. The Court did not abrogate *Roberts* for non-testimonial hearsay, though dictum in the majority opinion suggests that the Court might in the future adopt the Thomas/Scalia view that the Confrontation Clause is simply inapplicable to non-testimonial hearsay. *Id*. at 1370 (suggesting that the Court's opinion "casts doubt" on its prior holding in *White* rejecting the Thomas/Scalia view). Further dictum in the case suggests that states would be permitted to exempt non-testimonial hearsay from Confrontation Clause scrutiny. *Id*. at 1374.

655. *Id*. at 1371.

656. The Court left open the possibility that statements satisfying the requirements of the dying declaration exception, even those that are "testimonial" in nature, might be admissible under the confrontation clause. *Id*. at 1367. The Court pointed to historical evidence that the exception was the only one recognized in criminal cases at common law, and wrote that "[i]f this exception must be accepted on historical grounds, it is *sui generis*." *Id*.

657. *Id*. at 1364.

could still invoke *Roberts* to exclude nontestimonial hearsay under the confrontation clause. The future is hardly predictable.

§ 7.68 Hearsay and the Right to Confrontation—The *Bruton* Case

One well-established subcategory of confrontation doctrine is the rule about co-defendant confessions created by *Bruton v. United States*.[658] *Bruton* was a case in which two co-defendants were tried together. The confession of one, implicating both, was received by the trial judge with instructions not to use it against the nonconfessing co-defendant. The Supreme Court held that this procedure violated the confrontation clause. The limiting instruction was not sufficient to eliminate danger that the jury would use the instruction against both defendants. The danger that the defendant would be convicted by the statement of one he could not cross-examine could have been avoided by severing the trials.

For a time, it appeared that the Supreme Court might be contemplating an exception to the *Bruton* rule for cases in which a co-defendant's confession "interlocked" with that of the defendant. However, a majority now appears to have settled upon the position that a co-defendant's interlocking confession is not admissible against the defendant, though the fact that the defendant has also confessed may make the error harmless because of the overpowering impact of the defendant's own confession.[659] On the other hand, a redacted confession of a co-defendant that does not mention the defendant by name and that has only an indirect, inferential incriminating effect may be received in a joint trial without violating the confrontation clause.[660]

A purely mechanical blanking out of names does not, however, always solve the *Bruton* problem. In *Gray v. Maryland*,[661] the Supreme Court held that redacting the confession of a nontestifying co-defendant by blanking out the name in a written exhibit or substituting the word "deletion" in oral testimony did not satisfy the requirements of *Bruton* because the jury would realize that the confession referred to defendant.

---

658.   391 U.S. 123 (1968). Despite *Bruton*, confessions of co-defendants are sometimes admitted as declarations against interest when the statement implicating the defendant was against the declarant's interest. *See* § 7.54.

659.   *See* Cruz v. New York, 481 U.S. 186 (1987) (held, reception of confession of codefendant which interlocks with defendant's own confession violates *Bruton*, at least when co-defendant's confession likely to have devastating effect at trial.) *Cf.* Lee v. Illinois, 476 U.S. 530 (1986) (held, confrontation clause bars reception of accomplice's partially interlocking confession implicating both accomplice and defendant).

660.   Richardson v. Marsh, 481 U.S. 200 (1987). *See* United States v. Washing-

ton, 952 F.2d 1402, 1406–07 (D.C.Cir.1991) (held, "where—as here—all references to the defendant in a codefendant's statement are replaced with indefinite pronouns or other general terms, the Confrontation Clause is not violated by the redacted statements's admission if, when viewed together with other evidence, the statement does not create an inevitable association with the defendant, and a proper limiting instruction is given").

661.   523 U.S. 185 (1998). For fuller discussion of the implications of *Gray*, see David P. Leonard, The New Wigmore: A Treatise on Evidence: Selected Rules of Limited Admissibility § 1.10 (rev. ed. 2002).

§ 7.69 Courtroom Expressions and Their Relationship to Hearsay Doctrine: Catch Phrases and Rules of Thumb

When arguing hearsay objections, advocates sometimes use catch phrases and rules of thumb that are hard to track down in works on the rules of evidence.[662]

§ 7.70 Courtroom Expressions and Their Relationship to Hearsay Doctrine: Catch Phrases and Rules of Thumb—"It's admissible because it was said in the presence of the defendant"

Advocates often say "it was said in the presence of the defendant" in response to a hearsay objection. Are all statements made in the presence of the defendant admissible? No, they are not. Are most of them admissible? Yes, they are. The response is a good one when the situation is right. Whether a statement was made in the presence of the defendant matters in two situations. First, the statement may be offered to show the effect on the hearer.[663] For example, if it is relevant, the statement may be offered to show that the defendant had notice or that the defendant had been warned. Such statements are not hearsay because they are not offered to prove the truth of the matter asserted. They are merely offered to show the impact of the statement on the state of mind of the hearer. Of course, when offered for this purpose it is necessary that the hearer have been present and have heard the statement. Second, the statement may be offered as an adoptive admission. For example, suppose that after an accident a bystander said to the defendant "it was all your fault." If the defendant said nothing in return, and if the circumstances were such that a person who was not responsible would be expected to deny the accusation, the statement would be admissible as an adoptive admission—the defendant's silence constitutes an adoption of the bystander's accusation.[664]

But the mere fact that a defendant is present does not automatically make the statement admissible. Sometimes the grounds for escaping the hearsay ban that have just been described—effect on hearer and adoptive admission—are not applicable. For example, suppose that the bystander told the defendant, "it's all your fault," and the defendant responded "no, it's not!" The effect on hearer theory does not make the statement admissible because the hearer's state of mind at that time is irrelevant to any of the issues in the personal injury action. The adoptive admission theory does not work because the defendant denied the accusation. In the situation described, the statement is inadmissible despite having been made in the presence of the defendant. If the state of mind is irrelevant and either the defendant denies the statement or the circum-

---

662. One such catch phrase that has implications for hearsay doctrine is the often invalid objection "self-serving." *See* § **3.15.**

663. *See* § **7.01.**

664. *See* § **7.07.**

stances are such that one would not expect a denial even if the statement was false, then the statement is inadmissible.

§ 7.71   Courtroom Expressions and Their Relationship to Hearsay Doctrine: Catch Phrases and Rules of Thumb—"It's part of the res gestae"

"The discredited shibboleth res gestae is no longer uttered in polite legal society, and we hope to lay its ghost to rest," said the Maryland Court of Appeals in 1988.[665] Probably no legal term has been the victim of such an intense eradication campaign. Wigmore long advocated that the phrase be put to death:

> The phrase "res gestae" has long been not only entirely useless, but even positively harmful. It is useless, because every rule of Evidence to which it has ever been applied exists as a part of some other well established principle and can be explained in the terms of that principle. It is harmful, because by its ambiguity it invites the confusion of one rule with another and thus creates uncertainty as to the limitations of both. It ought therefore wholly to be repudiated, as a vicious element in our legal phraseology. No rule of Evidence can be created or applied by the mere muttering of a shibboleth. There are words enough to describe the rules of Evidence. Even if there were no accepted name for one or another doctrine, any name would be preferable to an empty phrase so encouraging to looseness of thinking and uncertainty of decision.[666]

Morgan, Holmes, and Learned Hand also had unkind things to say about res gestae.[667]

Suppose an advocate makes a hearsay objection. The proponent of the evidence responds that the evidence is part of the res gestae. What answer can the objecting attorney make to this assertion? "There's no such thing as a res gestae exception" or "res gestae doesn't apply under the Federal Rules" are possibilities. If those do not work, then the advocate should attempt to identify the modern equivalent of the argu-

---

665. Cassidy v. State, 536 A.2d 666 (Md. App. 1988).

666. 6 John H. Wigmore, Evidence in Trials at Common Law § 1767, at 182 (3d ed. 1940).

667. Morgan wrote:

The marvelous capacity of a Latin phrase to serve as a substitute for reasoning, and the confusion of thought inevitably accompanying the use of inaccurate terminology, are nowhere better illustrated than in the decisions dealing with the admissibility of evidence as 'res gestae.' It is probable that this troublesome expression owes its existence and persistence in our law of evidence to an inclination of judges and lawyers to avoid the toilsome exertion of exact analysis and precise thinking. Certain it

is that since its introduction at the close of the eighteenth century, on account of its exasperating indefiniteness it has done nothing but bewilder and perplex.

Edmund M. Morgan, *A Suggested Classification of Utterances Admissible as Res Gestae*, 31 Yale L.J. 229 (1922). Holmes wrote that "[t]he man that uses that phrase (res gestae) shows that he has lost temporarily all power of analyzing ideas." Quoted in Cassidy v. State, 536 A.2d 666, 669 (Md. App. 1988). Learned Hand stated: "[A]s for 'res gestae' ... if it means anything but an unwillingness to think at all, what it covers cannot be put in less intelligible terms." United States v. Matot, 146 F.2d 197, 198 (2d Cir.1944).

ment being made and respond accordingly. For example, "this is not part of the res gestae because too much time had passed between the event and the statement" is appropriate if the phrase is being used as a stand-in for the present sense impression, or "he wasn't still under the stress of excitement" when the phrase seems to have been used to refer to the excited utterance exception.

§ 7.72 Courtroom Expressions and Their Relationship to Hearsay Doctrine: Catch Phrases and Rules of Thumb—"It's admissible because it shows state of mind"

The assertion that an out-of-court statement is admissible because it shows state of mind can mean either that the statement is offered to show the declarant's own state of mind, or that it is offered to show something about the state of mind of the hearer or reader of the statement.

A statement offered to show the state of mind of the hearer or reader of the statement is generally admissible on grounds that the statement is not being offered to prove the truth of the matter asserted, and hence is not hearsay.[668] An objection should still be sustained when the state of mind of the hearer or reader is not relevant to the case, or when the probative value of the statement in showing state of mind is outweighed by the danger that the jury will use the statement to prove the truth of what it asserts. For example, if the good faith of a police officer in making an investigation of a suspect is a bona fide issue, then evidence that the officer had been told by a reliable source that the suspect committed the crime under investigation is admissible. When, however, the only issue is the guilt of the suspect, not the state of mind of the officer, then what the officer was told about the suspect's guilt is inadmissible hearsay.[669]

An utterance offered to show the state of mind of the declarant is generally admissible under the hearsay exception for statements of present state of mind.[670] An objection should still be sustained, however, if the state of mind of the declarant is irrelevant, or though relevant, its probative value is outweighed by the danger that the jury will use the

---

668. *See* § **7.01**.

669. *See, e.g.,* United States v. Dean, 980 F.2d 1286, 1288–89 (9th Cir.1992) (trial judge committed reversible error in admitting out-of-court statement to police officer that defendant possessed weapon in his mobile home; since probable cause for search was not at issue, evidence had no relevance except for hearsay purpose of showing that defendant did in fact possess weapon); United States v. Hernandez, 750 F.2d 1256 (5th Cir.1985) (held, error to admit evidence that special agent had been told by United States Customs that defendant was a drug smuggler; agent's state of mind was not at issue); Spencer v. State, 703 N.E.2d 1053, 1056 (Ind.1999) (held, murder victim's statements about defendant's threats not admissible either as nonhearsay to show officer's reason for investigating or under state of mind exception to show victim's fear; but error in receiving the evidence was harmless in light of overwhelming evidence of guilt).

670. *See* Fed. R. Evid. 803(3); § **7.13**.

out-of-court statement for some purpose other than showing the declarant's state of mind.

An objection should also be sustained if the purpose of showing the declarant's state of mind is to show something about the past. In that case, the statement does not fit the hearsay exception for statements of present state of mind, because the hearsay exception does not cover statements of memory or belief offered to show the fact remembered or believed.[671]

Occasionally, the proponent will offer a statement to show a fact remembered or believed by the declarant, and assert that the statement is not hearsay at all because it is not offered to prove the truth of the matter asserted, but rather to show state of mind circumstantially.[672] For example, evidence that the declarant told a falsehood might be offered to show the guilty state of mind of the declarant, for purposes of showing that the declarant committed a crime in the past. Often such utterances will be admissible as the admission of a party opponent. When they are not (for example, when they are offered as evidence against someone other than the declarant), then their evidentiary status is problematic. Certainly offering a statement as a falsehood to show guilty state of mind does not seem to be offering it to prove the truth of what it asserts. On the other hand, the statement relies upon the belief of a person not subject to cross-examination, and has most of the infirmities of hearsay. Courts that have considered the admissibility of such statements under the Federal Rules of Evidence have reached divergent results.[673]

§ 7.73 Courtroom Expressions and Their Relationship to Hearsay Doctrine: Catch Phrases and Rules of Thumb—"It's admissible because it's only being offered to impeach"

The assertion "it's admissible because it's only being offered to impeach" is often a valid one. When an out-of-court statement is being offered as a prior inconsistent statement to impeach the person who made the statement, then it escapes the hearsay ban.[674] However, the word "impeach" is not a magic word that destroys the hearsay rule. When the statement of a declarant is used to impeach someone other than the declarant, then it is hearsay because it has no value for impeachment unless the trier first accepts the statement as proof of what it asserts.[675]

671. *See* Fed. R. Evid. 803(3).

672. *See* § **7.01**.

673. For an extended discussion, see Roger C. Park, *"I Didn't Tell Them Anything About You": Implied Assertions as Hearsay Under the Federal Rules of Evidence*, 74 Minn. L. Rev. 783, 802–10 (1990).

674. *See* § **7.04**.

675. *See* Bemis v. Edwards, 45 F.3d 1369, 1372 (9th Cir.1995) (inconsistent statement by another person not admissible to impeach police report of beating incident: "Whereas an inconsistent statement by a testifying witness can be used to impeach that witness's credibility, an inconsistent account by another source is offered to show an alternative view of the truth").

Examples

Mr. X testifies in court that "the light was red." Mr. X said to an investigator out of court that "the light was green." The out-of-court statement to the investigator is admissible to impeach. It has impeachment value whether or not one accepts the truth of what it asserts. The mere fact that the witness said different things at different times reflects poorly on the witness's credibility, without regard to the truth of what was said out of court.

Mr. X testifies on the stand "the light was red." Ms. Y said out of court "the light was green." The out-of-court statement of Ms. Y is offered to impeach Mr. X. The statement of Ms. Y is hearsay. It has no value in impeaching Mr. X unless one accepts the truth of the matter asserted in the statement.

§ 7.74 Courtroom Expressions and Their Relationship to Hearsay Doctrine: Catch Phrases and Rules of Thumb—"The statement is only offered to show that it was made"

This response to the hearsay objection is an abbreviated way of saying "The statement is only offered to show that it was made, not to prove the truth of any assertion in it." Of course, this is sometimes a valid point, for example, when the statement is legally operative language[676] or when it is offered to show its effect on the hearer or reader.[677] But the words "only offered to show that it was made" are not a magical incantation that allows anything to come into evidence. If the fact that the statement was made is relevant to the case only if one accepts the truth of the matter asserted in the statement, then the statement is hearsay. The statement is being offered to show its truth.

§ 7.75 Courtroom Expressions and Their Relationship to Hearsay Doctrine: Catch Phrases and Rules of Thumb—"A question can't possibly be hearsay"

The following excerpt from the transcript of a federal drug case illustrates this response to the hearsay objection. The prosecutor was trying to get the witness, an undercover agent, to describe what happened when the informant, in the presence of the agent, called a target to arrange a drug deal:[678]

Q: After this first telephone conversation about which you've just testified, were there any-further telephone conversations?

676. *See* § **7.01**.

677. *See* § **7.01**.

678. United States v. Figueroa, 750 F.2d 232, 233 (2d Cir.1984). The court of appeals reversed on grounds that this line of testimony should have been excluded.

However, the particular question that led to the assertion that "a question can't possibly be hearsay" was never answered in the trial court, so the court of appeals did not rule specifically on whether a question could ever be hearsay.

A: Yes.

Q: Will you explain how those came about?

A: There was a second telephone conversation. Mike [the informant] went to the phone. He dialed the number and he asked for room 638.

MR. SACHS: I object again to anything that Mike said on the grounds of hearsay. It is being offered for the truth of the things said. There is no way around that, your Honor.

THE COURT: No. Go ahead. What I'm interested in, you had the second phone call. What happened then?

THE WITNESS: Mike had a conversation and Mike asked me, "Would it be all right if we did the two-kilogram deal one pound at a time?" And I told him to tell the people on the other end of the phone that that would be fine, we would deal one pound of cocaine at a time.

THE COURT: This was a two-kilo deal, one kilo at a time?

THE WITNESS: One pound, of about four and a half pounds, at a time. So we deliver one pound at a time. And I told Mike to relay the message that that would be fine, that we could do one pound at a time.

THE COURT: All right.

Q: After these two telephone conversations, did there come a third telephone conversation?

A: Yes. The third telephone conversation—

Q: What room did Mike call?

A: He asked for—he called 638.

Q. And did he ask to speak to anybody?

A: Yes. He said "Hello" on the phone again.

Q. And can you describe what you heard-what you instructed him to say on the telephone?

A: I told—after the conversation, I told Mike—Mike asked me—

MR. SACHS: I object to what Mike asked him. That is hearsay once again.

MR. CHERTOFF: A question can't possibly be hearsay.

Mr. Chertoff's contention that "a question can't possibly be hearsay" is probably based upon the definition of hearsay as an assertion offered to prove the truth of the matter asserted. If an utterance is not an "assertion," it is not hearsay. The word "assertion" is not defined in the Federal Rules, and has received virtually no treatment in the case law. However, one usually does not think of a question as being an "assertion." There is some support for the position that only declarative sentences can be hearsay, a position that would exclude questions and imperative sentences from the hearsay definition.[679]

The proposition that "a question can't possibly be hearsay" does not make sense in all situations. A question such as "Why did you go so fast?," offered to show that the addressee was speeding, has no fewer dangers of insincerity than the declaration "you were going very fast." The same can be said of an imperative sentence such as "Throw that thief out of here!" when offered to show that the person referred to was a thief. The sentences just quoted contain implied assertions that the person was speeding or was a thief, and when offered to prove the truth of those implied assertions, they carry just as much of a danger of unreliability as a direct statement. Implied assertions are sometimes treated as hearsay, even under the Federal Rules of Evidence.[680]

§ 7.76 Hearsay in Relation to Other Objections

This chapter has dealt with the hearsay rule and its exceptions. Two important reminders are in order at this point.

First, other objections may be made even if the hearsay objection is overruled. The mere fact that an out-of-court statement satisfies the hearsay rule does not mean that it satisfies other exclusionary rules, such as the best evidence rule, the authentication rules, the rule against character evidence, and the rules of privilege.

Correspondingly, the hearsay ban is not satisfied just because some other evidence rule is satisfied. For example, the fact that evidence is admissible under Rule 404(b) as evidence of motive, plan, etc., does not mean that it can be offered in hearsay form without fitting it into some hearsay exception.

---

679. *See* Edward J. Imwinkelried, Paul C. Giannelli, Francis A. Gilligan & Frederic I. Lederer, Courtroom Criminal Evidence 1003 (3d ed. 1998) ("Because most assertive statements are declarative sentences, many trial judges use a rule of thumb that imperative, interrogative, and exclamatory sentences are not hearsay"; the authors would not follow the "rule of thumb" in all situations); Olin Guy Wellborn III, *The Definition of Hearsay in the Federal Rules of Evidence*, 61 Tex. L. Rev. 49, 72–73 (1982) (suggesting that this is at least a plausible, and perhaps the most plausible, interpretation of the word "assertion" in Rule 801(c)); United States v. Zenni, 492 F.Supp. 464, 466 n. 7 (E.D.Ky.1980) ("the utterance, 'Put $2 to win on Paul Revere in the third at Pimlico,' is a direction and not an assertion of any kind, and therefore can be neither true nor false").

680. *See* Lyle v. Koehler, 720 F.2d 426, 431–35 (6th Cir.1983) (Merritt, J.) (proof that X wrote letters to X's friends asking friends to set up a false alibi for X and Y is hearsay when offered against Y as evidence of Y's guilt). United States v. Reynolds, 715 F.2d 99 (3d Cir.1983) ("didn't tell them about you" is inadmissible hearsay when offered to show guilt of person addressed). Though the two cases cited did not deal specifically with the issue whether questions can ever be hearsay, their reasoning would lead to the conclusion that questions are hearsay when the questions contain implied assertions.

Chapter 8

EVIDENTIARY PRIVILEGES

Table of Sections

§ 8.01 The Origin and Policy of Privilege

Evidentiary privileges limit a party's ability to ask about certain communications that may be probative and to interrogate certain witnesses who may have important testimony to offer. These restrictions on the reach of the dispute resolution system exist because resolving disputes through discovery of the truth is not the only value cherished by society.

The lawyer-client, doctor-patient, husband-wife privileges and the privilege against self-incrimination are some of the more commonly known and more important evidentiary privileges. Unlike most evidentiary matters, the parties do not control decisions about the exercise of the privilege, the holders of the privilege do. Although the parties may suggest the existence of a privilege to a tribunal, because the values underlying the privilege do not relate to the dispute, only the holder of the privilege may decide to claim or to waive it.[1]

Husband-wife and lawyer-client privileges were the earliest to be recognized by the common law judges in England.[2] The earliest husband-wife privilege was of the kind that prevented a person from testifying at all, while the earliest lawyer-client privilege was of the kind that prevented testimony about communications. Until the early part of the 19th century, all privilege law in the United States was imported from the British common law and was created by the courts. In 1828, the New York legislature passed the first statute creating a privilege between doctor and patient.[3] From that time forward, the law of privilege has been a creature of the legislative process, except in the federal system, where the courts continue to be the creators of privilege.

The initial draft of the Federal Rules of Evidence included an attempt to codify the judicially created privileges applicable in the federal courts, but Congress rejected the proposal, leaving creation or rejection of privilege in the federal system to "reason and experience" as "interpreted by the courts."[4] Rule 501 provides that when a federal court is applying the substantive law of a state, it must apply the state's privilege rules and when applying federal substantive law, it must apply federal privilege law as interpreted in the light of reason and experience.[5] Thus, when the federal district court tries a personal injury diversity case, it applies state law; when it tries a federal antitrust case, it applies general federal common law.[6] Sometimes a case can involve both state and federal privileges, as when a state substantive claim is pendent upon a federal claim.[7]

There were various rationales and procedures for early common law privileges, but most modern privileges relate to professions and are supported by a utilitarian notion that the privilege will facilitate communication between the person in need of help and the professional able to provide it. Even the privileges that do not relate to the professions, such as the marital privileges, are justified by the instrumental concepts of preserving relationships and encouraging communications.

§ 8.02   The Difference Between Privilege and Professional Confidentiality

The professional privileges are often confused with the ethical requirements of the various professions to preserve the confidentiality of the professional relationship. Lawyers, doctors, and many other profes-

---

1. *See, e.g.,* Touma v. Touma, 357 A.2d 25 (N.J. Super. 1976) (marital communications privilege cannot be claimed by marriage counselor.)

2. 1 McCormick on Evidence § 75 (5th ed. John W. Strong ed. 1999).

3. N.Y. Rev. Stats. 1829, Vol. II, Part III, c. 7, tit. 3, art. 8 § 73.

4. Fed. R. Evid. 501.

5. *Id.*

6. H.R. Conf. Rep. No. 93–1597 (1974).

7. *See, e.g.,* FDIC v. Mercantile Nat'l Bank of Chicago, 84 F.R.D. 345, 349 (N.D. Ill. 1979) (state privilege did not bar discovery of information relevant to federal claim, even though also relevant to pendent state claim).

sionals have codes describing aspirations or propounding rules governing their conduct. Most such codes include confidentiality obligations. Even though the breach of those ethical confidentiality obligations might lead to professional discipline or loss of professional license, the professional codes do not provide a legal basis for the exclusion of evidence. Only the existence of a privilege will exclude a confidential communication from evidence.

The ethical obligations of confidentiality are usually broader than the privilege protecting communication between a professional and the client/patient/penitent. They are often designed to further goals other than or in addition to the utilitarian goals of the various privileges. The lawyer-client privilege, for example, only prohibits evidence in a judicial or other proceeding, and only protects communication between lawyer and client. The lawyer's ethical obligation of confidentiality, by contrast, applies in almost any situation and covers all information relating to the representation, whatever the source.[8] While the modern rationale for the privilege is to facilitate communication between client and lawyer, the ethical underpinning of the confidentiality requirement retains overtones of the original justification for the privilege, relating not to the needs of the client, but rather, to the profession's aspirations concerning its own status.

§ 8.03   The Lawyer–Client Privilege

Many states have statutes that deal with the lawyer-client privilege. However, cases interpreting these statutes often do not take a precise or technical view of the language of the statute. State Supreme Courts tend to treat their statutes as if they merely announced "this state has a lawyer-client privilege." They then derive the boundaries of the privilege from case law and treatises, without much attention to the exact language of the statute.[9] Thus, a statute that by its terms applies to all communications is likely to be interpreted to apply only to confidential communications. Common-law exceptions to the privilege, such as the exception for communications made in furtherance of fraud, are likely to be read into the statutes.[10]

Wigmore's definition of the privilege is frequently quoted and cited. He summarized the privilege as follows:

8. ABA Model Rules of Professional Responsibility 1.6, Comment.

9. Note, *Developments in the Law— Privileged Communications*, 98 Harv. L. Rev. 1450, 1458 (1985); Restatement (Third) of the Law Governing Lawyers § 68 ("Most states whose law of the privilege is embodied in a statute or evidence code have not interpreted these narrowly or technically but have shown great flexibility of interpretation.").

10. *See, e.g.*, State v. Montgomery, 499 So.2d 709, 711 (La. App. 1986) (court fol-

lowed common law rule that lawyer-client privilege extends to client's communications with lawyer's agents although statute only referred to communications with lawyer); Brown v. St. Paul City Ry. Co., 62 N.W.2d 688, 700–01 (Minn. 1954) (court endorsed Wigmore's definition of the lawyer-client privilege, including requirement that the communication be confidential, despite statute's unqualified language that appeared to apply to all communications).

(1) Where legal advice of any kind is sought (2) from a professional legal adviser in his capacity as such, (3) the communications relating to that purpose, (4) made in confidence (5) by the client, (6) are at his instance permanently protected (7) from disclosure by himself or by the legal adviser, (8) except the protection be waived.[11]

This definition is an accurate summary of the modern privilege, though two matters should perhaps be added. Communications from the lawyer to the client, as well as those by the client[12] to the lawyer are covered. Communications made through a representative of the lawyer or client are usually covered, as well as those involving the lawyer and client directly.[13] In addition, the definition does not describe some of the widely accepted exceptions to the privilege, such as the exception for communications made in furtherance of crime or fraud.

Another frequently quoted formulation of the privilege appears in an opinion by Judge Wyzanski:

The privilege applies only if (1) the asserted holder of the privilege is or sought to become a client; (2) the person to whom the communication was made (a) is a member of the bar of a court, or his subordinate and (b) in connection with this communication is acting as a lawyer; (3) the communication relates to a fact of which his lawyer was informed (a) by his client (b) without the presence of strangers (c) for the purpose of securing primarily either (i) an opinion on law or (ii) legal services or (iii) assistance in some legal proceeding, and not (d) for the purpose of committing a crime or tort; and (4) the privilege has been (a) claimed and (b) not waived by the client.[14]

A more recent attempt to restate the privilege appears in the tentative draft of an American Law Institute Restatement. Subject to exceptions, the Restatement's drafters provide that "[T]he attorney-client privilege may be invoked . . . with respect to

(1) a communication

(2) made between privileged persons

(3) in confidence

(4) for the purpose of obtaining or providing legal assistance for the client."[15]

---

11. 8 John H. Wigmore, Evidence in Trials at Common Law § 2291 (John T. McNaughton rev. 1961).

12. *See, e.g.,* Natta v. Hogan, 392 F.2d 686, 692–93 (10th Cir. 1968) (lawyer's letters to client privileged); Schwimmer v. United States, 232 F.2d 855, 863 (8th Cir. 1956) (purpose of lawyer-client privilege to promote communication by preventing disclosure of confidential information, requires protection of lawyer's communications to client); 8 Wigmore, *supra* note 11, § 2320 (seldom questioned that lawyer's communi-cations to client are privileged). *C.f.,* Mead Data Central, Inc. v. United States Dep't. of the Air Force, 566 F.2d 242, 254 (D.C. Cir. 1977) (privilege only extends to lawyer's communications to client if based on confidential information provided by client).

13. *See* § **8.05**.

14. United States v. United Shoe Machinery Corp., 89 F.Supp. 357, 358–59 (D. Mass. 1950).

15. Restatement, *supra* note 9, § 68.

"Privileged persons" are elsewhere defined as "the client (including a prospective client), the client's lawyer, communicating agents of either of them, and representing agents of the lawyer.[16]

The lawyer-client privilege seems originally to have been based upon the idea that the barrister was a gentleman of honor, and that a gentleman should not be forced to betray confidences.[17] Under this concept, the privilege was for the benefit of the lawyer and the lawyer had the authority to waive it.[18] This original concept has now generally been replaced by what is sometimes called the "utilitarian" rationale for the privilege. Under the "utilitarian" rationale, the purpose of the privilege is to encourage clients to confide in lawyers, so lawyers can provide full advice.[19]

Bentham made a slashing attack upon the utilitarian theory, saying that its only effect was to help the guilty to receive better advice; the innocent did not need the protection of the privilege, since they had nothing to hide.[20] But Bentham's attack, though powerful, is simplistic. Clients' cases are rarely all good or bad and even people who have a good cause may, also, have something the lawyer should know in order to prepare, but about which they are less than proud. The lawyer can give more realistic advice if the weak points of the client's case are known. Moreover, the more the lawyer knows of both the strengths and the weaknesses of the client's cause, the more likely the matter is to be settled in a way that saves time and expense for both the parties and for society at large.

In any event, abolition of the privilege would encourage misconduct. First, advocates would be more likely to call the opposing counsel to the stand as a litigation tactic, perhaps to sow dissension between lawyer and client or simply to disrupt the other party's case.[21] Second, a rule that allowed the opponent to force testimony would place the lawyer in the trilemma of committing perjury, hurting the client, or committing contempt. Dishonorable lawyers would prefer perjury, to keep the client's loyalty and business, and this would place honorable lawyers at a disadvantage. Despite these grounds for defending the privilege, even its supporters concede that the obstructing influence of the privilege on justice is plain and direct, while its benefits are conjectural and removed.[22]

Only communications, not acts and observations, are protected by the lawyer-client privilege. For example, suppose a client becomes a fugitive, and the lawyer is asked to reveal information about the client's physical appearance to aid in apprehension. Information about the

---

16. *Id.* § 70.

17. 8 Wigmore, *supra* note 11, § 2290.

18. *See id.* The privilege was "consideration for the oath and the honor of the lawyer." *Id.*

19. Upjohn Co. v. United States, 449 U.S. 383, 389 (1981); 8 Wigmore, *supra* note 11, § 2291.

20. 5 Jeremy Bentham, Rationale of Judicial Evidence 302–04 (1827).

21. Restatement, *supra* note 9, § 68.

22. 8 Wigmore, *supra* note 11, § 2291.

client's physical appearance is not privileged because it was not acquired through a communication. The lawyer can be forced to testify about the client's physical characteristics, dress, bearing, sobriety, mannerisms, and other matters that are non-communicative.[23]

A controversial application of this concept occurs when the lawyer is required to testify about the mental competency of a client. In *State v. Jensen*,[24] for example, the prosecution called defendant's lawyer in a prior trial to show that the defendant was mentally competent to stand trial. The defendant objected and the prior lawyer stated that he would be unable to divorce confidential information from expressions and other behavioral manifestations of the defendant. The trial court required the lawyer to testify. He testified that the defendant appeared normal during the prior representation and that he had discussed trial tactics with him.[25] The Minnesota Supreme Court ruled that there was no error in admitting the testimony, saying that a lawyer's observations of his client are "simply not communications."[26] Though it would appear that the lawyer's assessment of competency would at least partly be based on what the client communicated to the lawyer, the court ignored this aspect. The result (that lawyers may be required to testify about competency to stand trial) has been very widely accepted.[27] It has been suggested that these cases are really a special exception to the privilege founded on the necessity of getting testimony from the person best able to say whether the client was competent to cooperate in the client's defense.[28]

§ 8.04   The Lawyer–Client Privilege—The Requirement of Confidentiality

The lawyer-client privilege applies only to confidential communications. A communication may be considered non-confidential by reason of the presence of third parties.[29] Obviously, if the client says something to

23. *See, e.g.,* United States v. Kendrick, 331 F.2d 110, 113–14 (4th Cir. 1964) (complexion, demeanor, bearing, sobriety, dress, matters "observable by anyone" not privileged); 8 Wigmore, *supra* note 11, § 2306 (facts that another person would observe if present and not intended as a communication not privileged).

24. 174 N.W.2d 226 (Minn. 1970).

25. *See id.* at 228.

26. *See id.* at 230.

27. *See, e.g.,* Darrow v. Gunn, 594 F.2d 767, 774 (9th Cir. 1979) (state privilege protecting only "confidential communications" does not protect lawyer's observation and impressions of client's mental condition); United States v. Kendrick, 331 F.2d 110, 114 (4th Cir. 1964) (lawyer's testimony concerning client's cooperativeness and awareness at trial not privileged); Bishop v. Superior Court, 724 P.2d 23, 28–29 (Ariz.

1986) (lawyer's observations of defendant's ability to assist in defense not privileged). *But see* Gunther v. United States, 230 F.2d 222, 223–24 (D.C. Cir. 1956) (lawyer's testimony concerning client's competency violates privilege because it would lead to examination of facts underlying opinion, thereby opening door to inquiry of entire lawyer-client relationship).

28. *See* Restatement, *supra* note 9, § 68.

29. *See, e.g.,* United States v. Massachusetts Institute of Technology, 129 F.3d 681, 686 (1st Cir.1997) (Boudin, J.) (held, MIT lost privilege as to documents sought by IRS by sharing documents with Defense Contract Audit Agency as required by MIT's contracts with the agency); United States v. Cooper, 1991 WL 60371 (S.D.N.Y. 1991) (defendant waived lawyer-client privilege by making statement to lawyer in the

the lawyer at an open meeting of a corporation's shareholders, then the communication is not privileged because it is not intended to be confidential.

The presence of some third parties may not destroy the privilege. It is universally recognized that the lawyer's secretary or clerk can be present without destroying the privilege.[30] The cases also allow the presence of persons who are necessary for communication, such as translators, without any effect on the privilege.[31] Some cases have extended this principle to include other persons helpful to communication, such as an accountant trusted by the client to interpret financial data, or a close family member who aided the client.[32] The common-law cases are not wholly consistent on this point, but generally it seems that the privilege will be upheld if (1) the client reasonably believed that the discussion was confidential, and (2) the third person's presence was reasonably necessary in the furtherance of the consultation.[33] The unsettled nature of the law and the chance that the third person will be found unnecessary make it dangerous to allow the client to bring third persons to an interview, unless the necessity for having them present is clear.[34] The risk that it will abrogate the privilege is substantial. If the third person also has a privilege with the client and the communication is in furtherance of the service both the lawyer and the third person provide to the client, the circle of privilege is not broken.

---

presence of DEA agent standing five feet away and making no attempt to keep communication confidential); United States v. Melvin, 650 F.2d 641, 645–46 (5th Cir. 1981) (third person not part of defense team); United States v. Landof, 591 F.2d 36, 39 (9th Cir. 1978) (second lawyer not representing client or acting as agent of client's lawyer); In re Guardianship of Walling, 727 P.2d 586, 592 (Okla. 1986) (grandmother not necessary for transmission of communication); 8 John H. Wigmore, Evidence in Trials at Common Law § 2311 (John T. McNaughton rev. 1961) (presence of third person neither agent of client nor lawyer destroys privilege). *Cf.* In re Bieter Co. 16 F.3d 929 (8th Cir. 1994) (independent consultant hired by client was functional equivalent of client's employee for purposes of lawyer-client privilege; privilege applies therefore to communications between consultant and client's lawyer); United States v. Bigos, 459 F.2d 639, 643 (1st Cir.1972) (presence of client's father did not destroy privilege when circumstances indicated that parties still viewed communications as confidential). Disclosure to third parties of confidential written lawyer-client communications can also destroy the privilege.

30. *See, e.g.,* Taylor v. Taylor, 177 S.E. 582, 583 (Ga. 1934) (communications to lawyer's confidential secretary privileged); Sibley v. Waffle, 16 N.Y. 180, 183 (1857) (privilege protects communications to lawyer's clerk); 8 Wigmore, *supra* note 29, § 2310.

31. *See, e.g.,* United States v. Kovel, 296 F.2d 918, 921–22 (2d Cir. 1961) (privilege includes translators assisting lawyer to communicate with client).

32. *See, e.g., Kovel,* 296 F.2d at 921–22 (accountant who helped client by interpreting data for lawyer analogized to language translator; privilege upheld); Estate of Weinberg, 509 N.Y.S.2d 240, 242 (N.Y. Sur. Ct. 1986) (privilege covered daughter of client who aided in business).

33. *See, e.g.,* Restatement (Third) of the Law Governing Lawyers § 120, cmt. (Tent. Draft No. 2 1989) ("'[W]hether a client's communication in the presence of a third person is protected by the privilege depends upon whether the presence of the third person served to permit client and lawyer to communicate effectively or to permit client to understand or act upon the lawyer's advice'").

34. For examples of cases in which the third person was held to have destroyed confidentiality, *see supra* note 29.

Joint consultations present the possibility of unexpected loss of the privilege, if the parties to the joint consultation become adverse.[35] Suppose that X and Y consult a lawyer for purposes of forming a corporation. Then, as sometimes happens, they have a falling out and end up suing each other. While their original consultation was privileged as against any claim from others to produce its content in a judicial proceeding, neither party's communications with the lawyer are privileged in a dispute between the two clients. This result does not undermine the purpose of the privilege, that of encouraging disclosures to lawyers. The parties would not be inhibited about making disclosures during the joint consultation because neither would know who would profit or lose by later disclosure in a suit between them.[36] At any rate, they did not intend for the matter to be confidential between them and thus on the principle that the communication must be confidential the privilege falls.[37]

Suppose that, without the knowledge of the lawyer or the client, a third person overhears a lawyer-client communication, and that person is called to testify. In general, eavesdroppers are permitted to testify, even if the client and lawyer intended the communication to be confidential.[38] The client and lawyer are responsible for taking precautions. If they don't, or if they try but don't succeed, then the evidence is admissible in many jurisdictions.[39]

Even when third parties are not present at the time the communication is made, a communication may fall outside the lawyer-client privilege because the client intended for the lawyer to make the communication public at some later time. For example, if the client gave the lawyer information to be included in a public document, the communication is not privileged.[40]

§ 8.05　The Lawyer–Client Privilege—The Requirement of Communication to a Proper Person

The lawyer-client privilege applies only to communications between the client and the lawyer or the lawyer's representative. A client who seeks legal advice from someone who is not a lawyer is, of course, not

---

35. *See, e.g.,* Grand Trunk W. R. Co. v. H.W. Nelson Co., 116 F.2d 823, 835 (6th Cir. 1941) (communications made to lawyer when representing both parties not privileged in later dispute between parties); Emley v. Selepchak, 63 N.E.2d 919, 922 (Ohio App. 1945) (communications made to lawyer by two parties forming contract not privileged in suit for specific performance); 8 Wigmore, *supra* note 29, § 2312 (no privilege between joint clients because no secrecy existed between them at time of communication).

36. *Id.*

37. *Id.*

38. Clark v. State, 261 S.W.2d 339, 342 (Tex. Crim. App. 1953) (telephone operator who eavesdropped on conversation between lawyer and client could testify as to what she heard); 8 Wigmore, *supra* note 29, § 2326 (privilege does not cover third party overhearing communication with or without client's knowledge).

39. *See, e.g.,* Schwartz v. Wenger, 124 N.W.2d 489, 492 (Minn. 1963) (conversation overheard in the hallway of the courthouse admissible). *But see* discussion at § 8.11.

40. *See* United States v. White, 950 F.2d 426 (7th Cir. 1991) (information given to attorney for inclusion in bankruptcy schedule not confidential and hence not privileged).

entitled to the lawyer-client privilege, unless, perhaps, the client reasonably believed that person to be a lawyer.[41] Confidential communications with the non-lawyers employed by the lawyer—such as secretaries, investigators, paralegals, and clerks—are usually covered by the privilege, even if the lawyer is not present at the time of the communication.[42]

Experts in various areas, such as doctors, engineers, accountants, and others with specialized knowledge are often employed by a lawyer to assist in preparing particular aspects of the client's case. Whether conversations between the lawyer's client and these experts are covered by the lawyer-client privilege usually depends upon what the expert is being asked to do and by whom the expert is hired. In many jurisdictions, if the lawyer hires the expert and the expert's sole responsibility is to assist the lawyer in preparing the case, the communication between the client and the expert will be covered by the lawyer-client privilege.[43] There are two common circumstances in which the lawyer-client privilege may not cover the communication between the client and an expert assisting a lawyer to prepare the client's case. The first is when the expert is going to be a witness at trial. In that instance, the purpose of the communication between the client and the expert is to prepare the expert to testify, rather than to assist the lawyer in giving legal advice. The communication will not be privileged. The second is when the expert assisting the lawyer also has a separate professional relationship with the client. In that instance, there is some danger that the communication between client and expert will be viewed as one for the purpose of their professional relationship, rather than for the purpose of helping the lawyer to provide legal service. In that event, the communication is unlikely to be privileged, unless the relationship between the expert and the client is one that carries its own privilege. A lawyer is well advised,

---

41. *See, e.g.*, People v. Velasquez, 237 Cal.Rptr. 366, 371 (App. 1987) (client's communication not privileged because he did not talk to a lawyer or person he reasonably believed to be a lawyer); People v. Barker, 27 N.W. 539, 546 (Mich. 1886) (defendant's confession made to private detective falsely claiming to be a lawyer privileged); 8 John H. Wigmore, Evidence in Trials at Common Law § 2302 (John T. McNaughton rev. 1961) (client entitled to peace of mind, should not bear risk of deception or defective professional title). *Cf.*, Sample v. Frost, 10 Iowa 266, 267 (1859) (statements made to someone not yet admitted to bar not privileged).

42. *See, e.g.*, Hillary v. Minneapolis St. Ry. Co., 116 N.W. 933, 934 (Minn. 1908).

43. *See, e.g.*, United States v. Alvarez, 519 F.2d 1036, 1046 (3d Cir. 1975) (defendant's communications to psychiatrist retained by attorney privileged); City & County of San Francisco v. Superior Court, 231 P.2d 26, 31–32 (Cal. 1951) (client's communications to physician hired by attorney to help prepare for litigation privileged); Restatement (Third) of the Law Governing Lawyers § 120 (Tent. Draft No. 2, 1989):

> The privilege ... generally extends to client communications to an expert adviser retained by a lawyer, such as an accountant or a physician, to whom a client makes a communication for the purpose of providing a basis on which the expert adviser may consult with the client's lawyer on a technical or expert matter relevant to the representation. So long as such independent contractors or agents assist the lawyer in a confidential capacity in rendering legal assistance to the client, the privilege applies.

Cf. United States *ex rel.* Edney v. Smith, 425 F.Supp. 1038, 1054–55 (E.D.N.Y. 1976), *affd,* 556 F.2d 556 (2d Cir.1977) (under state law defendant waived privilege in relation to his communications to psychiatrist by raising insanity as defense).

therefore, not to employ an expert who has either a mixed purpose or a dual relationship, if the lawyer desires to make sure communications between the lawyer's client and the expert are privileged. Doctors present a common example. Even in a jurisdiction that does not have a doctor-patient privilege, communications between a client and a doctor, hired by the lawyer for the sole purpose of assisting the lawyer to prepare the case, are covered by the lawyer-client privilege.[44] But even in a jurisdiction that recognizes a doctor-patient privilege, a communication between a doctor and the lawyer's client is not covered by either privilege, if the doctor will be a witness at trial.

The requirement that the client's communication be with the lawyer or lawyer's representative also means that the client's pre-existing documents do not become privileged when the client transfers them to the lawyer.[45] Documents prepared by the client for some business or other purpose, therefore, do not become covered by the lawyer-client privilege when the client transfers them to the lawyer to assist in preparation of the client's case, even if the documents were originally created for a "secret" business or other purpose. The original communication—putting the thoughts or numbers on paper—was not for the purpose of communicating with a lawyer, but rather, for the business or other purpose. On the other hand, a client's recapitulation of business or some other dealings, written out for the lawyer, is covered by the lawyer-client privilege, even if the original dealings were not meant to be "secret."[46]

§ 8.06   The Lawyer–Client Privilege—The Requirement That the Purpose Be to Obtain Legal Advice or Service

The lawyer-client privilege applies only when the client seeks legal advice from the lawyer. But neither the formality of a lawyer-client retainer nor the condition of a professional environment is necessary for the communication to be covered by the privilege.[47] The communications

44. In re Grand Jury Proceedings v. United States (Nos. 91–5012, 91–5013, 91–5016), 947 F.2d 1188, 1190–9l (4th Cir. 1991) (when client consults accountant without consulting lawyer, no privilege attaches to matters discussed with accountant even if lawyer is later consulted; but when accountant is used as client's agent in communicating with lawyer, lawyer-client privilege attaches as to matters that client discussed with accountant).

45. *See, e.g.,* Colton v. United States, 306 F.2d 633, 639 (2d Cir. 1962) (pre-existing documents related to preparation and filing of tax returns, not prepared by client for purpose of communicating with lawyer not privileged); City of Philadelphia v. Westinghouse Elec. Corp., 205 F.Supp. 830, 831 (E.D. Pa. 1962) (client may not refuse

to disclose relevant information merely because she incorporated it into communication to lawyer); State ex rel. Dudek v. Circuit Court, 150 N.W.2d 387, 389 (Wis. 1967) (client cannot hide a pre-existing document be merely giving it to lawyer).

46. *See, e.g.,* Upjohn Co. v. United States, 449 U.S. 383, 395 (1981) (responses to lawyers' questionnaires used for providing legal advice to corporation privileged); *City of Philadelphia*, 205 F.Supp. at 831 (client cannot be compelled to testify as to what she said or wrote to lawyer).

47. *See, e.g.,* In re Dupont's Estate, 140 P.2d 866, 871–72 (Cal. App. 1943) (preliminary communications made by client seeking to contest will privileged, although lawyer refused employment; otherwise no person could safely consult lawyer for first

of a person who comes for a preliminary discussion and decides not to hire the lawyer is as covered as the communication between the lawyer and a client paying a million-dollar fee. Similarly, a communication about legal advice is as covered when conducted during a cocktail party as when conducted in the lawyer's office, so long as the person seeking the advice and the lawyer take measures to keep the communication confidential.

Communications made to a lawyer as a friend are not covered by the lawyer-client privilege, even if the friend is also a client.[48] If, for example, a friend's business lawyer receives a call in which the despondent friend discusses committing suicide and an issue arises in later litigation concerning whether the friend died a natural death, the conversation between friends is not privileged.[49]

A business in which the lawyer is, also, an executive or is regularly consulted for business as well as legal advice often presents the issue of the communication's purpose. Consider, for example, when a corporate vice president says in confidence to another corporate vice president who is, also, a lawyer: "We're thinking about acquiring IBM. What do you think?" If the question is asked to gain only business advice, it is not privileged.[50] If it is asked to gain legal advice, it is privileged, even if there is a secondary purpose to receive business advice.[51]

time); Taylor v. Sheldon, 173 N.E.2d 892, 895 (Ohio 1961) (communications made to lawyer by client seeking preparation of will privileged, even though lawyer chose not to prepare will); 8 John H. Wigmore, Evidence in Trials at Common Law § 2304 (John T. McNaughton rev. 1961) (preliminary communications made by person seeking legal counsel privileged whether person does not hire lawyer or lawyer declines employment). *Cf.*, McGrede v. Rembert Nat'l. Bank, 147 S.W.2d 580, 584 (Tex. Civ. App. 1941) (communications made after lawyer declines employment not privileged).

48. *See, e.g.*, Modern Woodmen of America v. Watkins, 132 F.2d 352, 354 (5th Cir. 1942) (communication of suicidal intent made to lawyer as friend not privileged); G & S Investments v. Belman, 700 P.2d 1358, 1364–65 (Ariz. App. 1984) (speaker's conversation with lawyer-friend about nature of speaker's interest in business partnership not privileged where speaker's purpose was to inform lawyer-friend that he was going to receive a bequest, rather than to get legal advice); 1 McCormick on Evidence § 88 (5th ed. John W. Strong ed. 1999) (communications made to lawyer as friend not privileged).

49. *See e.g.*, *Modern Woodmen*, 132 F.2d at 354.

50. *See, e.g.*, In re Grand Jury Investigation, 842 F.2d 1223, 1224–25 (11th Cir. 1987) (communications about income to

lawyer acting as tax return preparer not privileged because lawyer not giving legal advice; extensive citation of authority); United States v. Huberts, 637 F.2d 630, 640 (9th Cir. 1980) (lawyer who represented client in consignment sale of printing press, served as business agent and may not assert privilege); 1 McCormick, *supra* note 48, § 88, at 352–53 (consultations with lawyer as business advisor, banker, negotiator, or accountant not privileged). *See generally*, Scott N. Stone & Ronald S. Liebman, Testimonial Privileges § 1.38 (1983) (scope of lawyer-client privilege in relation to communications involving business advice).

51. *See, e.g.*, United States v. United Shoe Machinery Corp., 89 F.Supp. 357, 359 (D. Mass. 1950) (presence of relevant nonlegal considerations in communications primarily related to legal advice did not destroy privilege; "modern lawyer almost invariably advises his client upon not only what is permissible but also what is desirable"). *See also* Linde, P.C. v. Resolution Trust Corp., 5 F.3d 1508, 1514–15 (D.C. Cir. 1993) (attorney client privilege does not apply to communications between law firm and its insurer); Burroughs Wellcome Co. v. Barr Labs., Inc., 143 F.R.D. 611 (E.D.N.C. 1992) (attorney-client privilege does not protect nonlegal business advice).

The context of a communication that might be business or legal or both almost always will determine whether the communication will be covered by the lawyer-client privilege. If the question following the statement about acquiring IBM had been, "Will this give us a great market share, or what?" the conversation is probably to seek business not legal advice and, therefore, should not be privileged. If, on the other hand, the question had been, "Do we have an antitrust concern here?" there would be little doubt that the conversation was for the purpose of gaining legal advice and should be privileged. Notice, however, even if the question is about antitrust problems, if the communication is in the presence of others in the company, the privilege might not apply because the confidentiality requirement of the privilege might not have been met.[52]

§ 8.07 The Lawyer–Client Privilege—Failure of the Privilege to Cover Fact of Employment, Identity of Client, and Payment of Fees

Information about the fact of employment and the identity of the client is generally not covered by the privilege.[53] No special principle is needed, usually, to reach this result. The client's name is likely to appear in correspondence to third parties from the lawyer, on bills from the lawyer that are sent through the mail, and perhaps on pleadings in litigation in which adversaries are entitled to know against whom they are contending.[54] Because clients rarely expect their name and the fact that they have retained a lawyer to be confidential, the general principle of the lawyer-client privilege, protecting only material intended to be confidential, does not apply.[55]

There are a number of circumstances, however, in which a client might expect and even expressly ask for confidentiality. A whistle-blower with information about official corruption may want to hire a lawyer to convey the information to the proper authorities while keeping the whistle-blower's identity confidential to reduce the likelihood of retalia-

---

52. *See, e.g.,* Simon v. G.D. Searle & Co., 816 F.2d 397, 402–04 (8th Cir.1987) (communication of data to lawyer not privileged partly because data was business data, partly because it was shared with nonlawyer officers).

53. *See, e.g.,* United States v. Legal Services for New York City, 249 F.3d 1077 (D.C. Cir.2001) (faced with government audit, legal services grantee asserted that attorney-client privilege barred revelation of names of its clients; held, no privilege for fact of representation, even if government also sought information about general nature of cases that could be linked to clients' names); Alexiou v. United States, 39 F.3d 973, 976 (9th Cir. 1994) (attorney client privilege does not protect client from revelation of name, address, date, and amount of money paid to attorney in case in which

client paid attorney with counterfeit $100 bill; information would not constitute "last link" in chain of testimony necessary to convict client, and was therefore unprotected by the privilege); In re Grand Jury Investigation, 723 F.2d 447, 451 (6th Cir. 1983) (identity of client, with limited exceptions, not privileged); Colton v. United States, 306 F.2d 633, 637 (2d Cir. 1962) (identity of client and years of employment not privileged); People v. Adam, 280 N.E.2d 205, 207–08 (Ill.1972) (client's arrangement to meet and retention of lawyer not privileged).

54. *See* 1 Mccormick on Evidence § 90 (5th ed. John W. Strong ed. 1999).

55. *See* 8 John H. Wigmore, Evidence in Trials at Common Law § 2313 (John T. McNaughton rev. 1961).

tion or legal consequence.[56] A client may wish to use a lawyer to accomplish some personal mission, such as the anonymous payment of taxes, hoping that this will provide a basis for arguing against penalties, if the IRS ever discovers that the client has failed to pay taxes.[57] A client who has committed a crime, but who has not yet been identified by the authorities, may seek to have a lawyer engage in plea bargaining without revealing the client's identity.[58] Although courts have commonly recognized a limited exception to the general rule that client identity is not privileged, they have been divided over the exact nature of the exception.[59] The draft of the Restatement of the Law Governing Lawyers adopts the view that a client's identity is privileged whenever revealing the client's identity would necessarily reveal a confidential communication.[60]

The same general rule and exception that applies to the name of a client applies generally to information about a lawyer's fee. It is not

56. *See* In re Kozlov, 398 A.2d 882, 883 (N.J. 1979) (juror falsely testified that he neither knew nor was prejudiced against defendant). *See also* Stephan A. Saltzburg, *Communications Falling Within the Lawyer–client Privilege,* 66 Iowa L Rev. 811, 822–23 (1981) for a persuasive argument that if the privilege does not protect the client's identity in this situation, the authorities may be denied the information.

57. *See,* Baird v. Koerner, 279 F.2d 623, 626–27 (9th Cir. 1960). The lower federal courts have divided over the question of whether the attorney-client privilege and the attorney's ethical duty of confidentiality permit the attorney to refuse to disclose the client's identity when required by IRS regulations. *Id. Compare* United States v. Monnat, 853 F.Supp. 1301, 1302–04 (D. Kan. 1994) (privilege applicable) *with* United States v. Leventhal, 961 F.2d 936, 941 (11th Cir. 1992) (no privilege in such circumstances).

58. *See* Scott N. Stone & Ronald S. Liebman, Testimonial Privileges § 127 (1983); *Lawyer Refuses to Identify Hit–Run Driver,* 133 Chicago Daily L. Bull., Nov. 11, 1987, at 1, col. 5.

59. *See, e.g.,* In re Grand Jury Subpoenas Duces Tecum, 695 F.2d 363, 365 (9th Cir. 1982) (identity of client privileged where it would implicate client in very matter for which client sought legal advice); In re Grand Jury Proceedings, 680 F.2d 1026 (5th Cir. 1982) (identity of client privileged when "last link" of evidence necessary to incriminate client); NLRB v. Harvey, 349 F.2d 900, 905 (4th Cir. 1965) (identity of client privileged where it amounts to disclosure of otherwise confidential information). *See also* In re Grand Jury Subpoena Issued

to Gerson S. Horn, 976 F.2d 1314, 1315–18 (9th Cir. 1992) (identity of clients ordinarily not protected, but letters of consultation and retainer agreements protected); In re Grand Jury Proceedings, 946 F.2d 746 (11th Cir. 1991) (attorney was not required to disclose client's identity, even though government already knew client's reason for seeking legal advice). In re D'Alessio v. Gilberg, 617 N.Y.S.2d 484 (App.Div.1994) (name of hit-and-run driver represented by attorney in plea negotiations need not be revealed to civil litigant). *But see* United States v. Leventhal, 961 F.2d 936, 940–411 (5th Cir. 1992) (in suit to compel attorney to reveal client's identity on IRS Form 8300, held, identity of client and fact of payment were not protected by attorney client privilege; court noted that these facts ordinarily have nothing to do with legal advice, and information was not protected by the "last link" doctrine, which was said to apply to cases in which "disclosure of nonprivileged attorney-client communication also would reveal privileged information" (*id.*); thereby, court held that the cash-reporting statute itself created an exception to the attorney-client privilege (*id.*)); United States v. Monnat, 853 F.Supp. 1301, 1305 (D. Kan. 1994) (an attorney is bound to disclose client's identity in Form 8300 and may not advise client on how to avoid requirement, but should inform client regarding the statutory disclosure requirement). *See generally* In re Grand Jury Investigation, 723 F.2d 447, 451–54 (6th Cir. 1983) (discussing various limited exceptions to general rule that identity of client not privileged).

60. Restatement (Third) of the Law Governing Lawyers § 119, at 91–94, cmt. & illus. 7 (Tent. Draft No. 2, 1989) (identity of

privileged unless providing the fee information would divulge a confidential communication,[61] or providing the name of a third party who paid the fee would incriminate the client.[62]

§ 8.08   The Lawyer–Client Privilege—Duration of the Privilege Beyond the Life of the Client

The lawyer-client privilege has been held, generally, to survive the death of the client.[63] In the absence of implied or express consent from the client to reveal confidences after death, the lawyer should claim the privilege on behalf of the client. The principle of privilege survival does not apply in disputes over the disposition of a client's estate. Those claiming under the client's will and other claimants to an estate are entitled to have access to the confidential material, the privilege being impliedly waived in order to fulfill the client's testamentary intent.[64]

The long-standing principle of privilege survival came under attack in 1997, when an independent counsel appointed to investigate the President of the United States subpoenaed a lawyer's notes of a privileged communication between the lawyer and a former White House aide who had committed suicide shortly after the conversation. The trial court quashed the subpoena, but the appellate court reversed in a two to one panel decision, the majority stating that the principle of privilege survival was more presumed than decided in the common law.[65] Confronted with the United States Supreme Court's 1996 decision in *Jaffee*

client who anonymously paid back taxes through lawyer privileged because it would reveal confidential communication).

61. *See, e.g.*, In re Shargel, 742 F.2d 61, 62 (2d Cir. 1984) (fee information that government sought as evidence of unexplained wealth potentially derived from criminal activity not privileged); In re Osterhoudt, 722 F.2d 591, 594 (9th Cir. 1983) (fee information not privileged unless it would reveal substance of confidential communication); In re Slaughter, 694 F.2d 1258, 1260 (11th Cir. 1982) (fee information not privileged unless it would reveal identity of previously undisclosed client/suspect).

62. *See, e.g.*, In re Grand Jury Subpoenas, 803 F.2d 493, 498, *modified*, 817 F.2d 64 (9th Cir. 1987) (identity of third party who paid lawyer's fees for defendants in narcotics prosecution not privileged); Priest v. Hennessy, 409 N.E.2d 983, 987 (N.Y. 1980) (identity of third party who paid lawyer's fees for defendant's charged with prostitution not privileged). *But see* In re Grand Jury Proceedings, 517 F.2d 666, 671–73 (5th Cir. 1975) (identity of third party paying lawyer's fees for defendants in narcotics prosecution privileged because it would incriminate client under circumstances).

63. *See, e.g.*, United States v. Osborn, 561 F.2d 1334, 1340 (9th Cir. 1977) (privilege continues after client's death; case remanded for determination of whether communications privileged before death); 8 John H. Wigmore, Evidence in Trials at Common Law § 2323 (John T. McNaugton rev. 1961) (privilege continues even after death of client); 1 McCormick on Evidence § 94 (5th ed. John W. Strong ed. 1999) (privilege generally survives death of client).

64. Glover v. Patten, 165 U.S. 394, 406 (1897) (deceased's communications with lawyer concerning will not privileged in dispute between her daughters over construction of will). *See also* United States v. Osborn, 561 F.2d 1334, 1340 (9th Cir. 1977) (communications concerning will not privileged in dispute between testator's heirs, legatees, devisees, or other parties, all claiming under the will); 1 McCormick, *supra* note 63 § 94 (privilege does not apply in dispute between parties claiming under will); Wilcox v. Coons, 220 S.W.2d 15, 19 (Mo.1949) (deceased client's privilege may be waived by either grantees under deed or devisees under will).

65. In re Sealed Case, 124 F.3d 230 (D.C. Cir. 1997).

v. Redmond[66] explicitly rejecting a balancing test for the newly recognized federal therapist-patient, the majority tried to carve out a "discrete zone"[67] in which it thought a balancing test might be appropriate. The "discrete zone" it chose was all of criminal litigation. In *Swidler & Berlin v. United States*,[68] the Supreme Court acknowledged that the principle of survival had as often been presumed as decided, but rejected the appellate court's attempt to narrow the lawyer-client privilege by establishing a balancing test in criminal cases where the client was no longer alive. Proclaiming that "[k]nowing that communications will remain confidential even after death encourages the client to communicate fully and frankly with counsel," the Court refused to introduce "substantial uncertainty into the privilege's application."

§ 8.09 The Lawyer–Client Privilege—Application of the Privilege to the Corporate Client

A corporation consults with a lawyer through human agents, who are not usually the lawyer's clients in their individual capacities. Any number of corporate employees, from the CEO to the newest hire in the stockroom, might have occasion to communicate with the corporation's lawyer, but they are not entitled, in their individual capacities, to claim the protection of the lawyer-client privilege. The courts have held that a corporation may claim protection of the lawyer-client privilege for communications between its human agents and its lawyers, but they have not agreed as to which communications from which human agents are covered.

The "control group" test, first enunciated in *City of Philadelphia v. Westinghouse Electric Corp.*,[69] was at one time the majority rule in the federal courts.[70] It provided a privilege for communications from officers or employees in the upper echelon of the corporation—those employees in a position to control, or at least take a substantial part in, the decisions that the corporation might take upon the advice of the lawyer.

The "control group" test was criticized as being too narrow, and as failing to protect communications from lower-level employees who might possess information vital to the lawyer. Consequently, some courts accepted a broader view of the privilege under what became known as the "subject matter" test. The subject matter test protected communications to a corporation's lawyers by persons who were not part of the "control group" if (1) the employee made the communication at the direction of superiors, and (2) the subject of the communication concerned a matter within the scope of the employee's duties.[71]

66. 518 U.S. 1 (1996).

67. 124 F.3d 230 (D.C. Cir. 1997).

68. 524 U.S. 399 (1998).

69. 210 F.Supp. 483, 485 (E.D. Pa.1962).

70. *See* John E. Sexton, *A Post–Upjohn Consideration of the Corporate Lawyer-client Privilege*, 57 N.Y.U. L. Rev. 443, 451 (1982).

71. *See, e.g.*, Harper & Row Publishers, Inc. v. Decker, 423 F.2d 487, 491–92 (7th Cir. 1970).

In *Diversified Indus., Inc. v. Meredith*[72] the Eighth Circuit added another requirement to the "subject matter" test, placing the burden on the corporation to show that the communication was made for the purpose of securing legal advice.[73] This was an attempt to narrow the "subject matter" test, so that it did not become a routine mechanism by which corporations could place a protective shield over all employee communications, irrespective of the need for legal advice, by funneling them through the corporate lawyer to create the lawyer-client privilege.

When the United States Supreme Court granted certiorari in *Upjohn Co. v. United States*,[74] many observers expected it to establish a comprehensive approach to the lawyer-client privilege for corporate cases. The *Upjohn* Court rejected the "control group" test, but it is difficult to say exactly what else it did.

In *Upjohn*, the Internal Revenue Service attempted to subpoena the results of an investigation that had been conducted by the Upjohn Company's General Counsel following an independent audit that discovered suspicious payments by one of Upjohn's foreign subsidiaries. The internal investigation, aimed at discovering whether the payments were illegal bribes to foreign officials, included a questionnaire to corporate managers. The questionnaire, which went out over the signature of the Chairman of the corporation, stated that the General Counsel was conducting an investigation of questionable payments, and sought detailed information about such payments. The recipients of the questionnaire were told to treat the investigation as "highly confidential" and not to discuss it other than with employees who might be able to provide useful information. Responses were sent directly to the General Counsel. The General Counsel and outside counsel also interviewed the managers who received the questionnaire and thirty-three other officers and employees of Upjohn.[75]

In March 1976, the company voluntarily submitted a report to the SEC and the IRS that disclosed certain questionable payments. The IRS began an investigation to determine the tax consequences of the payments and subpoenaed the questionnaire answers and the interview notes.[76] The company refused to provide the material, citing the lawyer-client privilege and the work product doctrine.

The Court of Appeals, applying the "control group" test, ruled in favor of the government, saying that, "only the senior management,

---

72. 572 F.2d 596 (8th Cir.1977) (en banc).

73. The Diversified Industries court defined the test as follows:

[T]he lawyer-client privilege is applicable to an employee's communication if (1) the communication was made for the purpose of securing legal advice; (2) the employee making the communication did so at the direction of his corporate superior; (3) the superior made the request so that the corporation could secure legal advice; (4) the subject matter

of the communication is within the scope of the employee's corporate duties; and (5) the communication is not disseminated beyond those persons who, because of the corporate structure, need to know its contents.

Id.

74. 449 U.S. 383 (1981).

75. *Id.*

76. *See id.* at 387–88.

guiding and integrating the several operations, . . . can be said to possess an identity analogous to the corporation as a whole."[77]

The Supreme Court disagreed. It rejected the "control group" test, stating that a broader privilege was needed to encourage communications to corporate lawyers. The narrow "control group" approach would "limit the valuable efforts of corporate counsel to ensure their clients' compliance with the law."[78] The Court, however, declined to lay down a specific alternative rule.[79] Instead, it simply held that under the circumstances of the case, the communications to the corporate lawyer were privileged, enumerating some circumstances that influenced its judgment:

1. "The communications at issue were made by Upjohn employees to counsel for Upjohn acting as such, at the direction of corporate superiors in order to secure legal advice from counsel."[80]

2. "The communications concerned matters within the scope of the employees' corporate duties, and the employees themselves were sufficiently aware that they were being questioned in order that the corporation could obtain legal advice."[81]

3. "Pursuant to explicit instruction from the Chairman of the Board, the communications were considered 'highly confidential' when made and have been kept confidential by the company."[82]

In addition, the court may have been influenced by the fact that the information sought by the general counsel was not available from upper-level management.[83]

While *Upjohn* left open several issues (e.g., whether the privilege covers ex-employees whose information is sought by the lawyer), it suggests some guidelines that lawyers representing corporations should follow to ensure that information will be protected:

1. Make sure the corporation directs the employees to provide the information.

2. Ensure the employees know that the purpose of the inquiry is to obtain legal advice for the corporation.

3. Instruct the employees to keep the information strictly confidential.

4. Ask only for information that relates to matters within the scope of the employee's duties, as opposed to collecting information about unrelated matters.

The scope of the employee's duties appears to be the linchpin for the expansion of the group whose communication the Court is willing to protect by the corporate lawyer-client privilege. A clerical employee who

---

77. United States v. Upjohn Co., 600 F.2d 1223, 1226 (6th Cir. 1979), *rev'd*, 449 U.S. 383 (1981).

78. *Upjohn*, 449 U.S. at 392.

79. *See id.* at 386.

80. *Id.* at 394.

81. *Id.*

82. *Id.* at 395 (citation omitted).

83. *See id.* at 394.

witnessed an accident involving a company vehicle would apparently not be covered under *Upjohn*, while the driver of the vehicle might be.

Upjohn might cause unintended mischief, if other courts follow the decision in *Baxter Travenol Laboratories, Inc. v. Lemay.*[84] In a remarkable extension of the *Upjohn* rationale, *Baxter* suggests that an outside witness's statement to corporate counsel may become privileged, simply by putting the witness on the payroll. Baxter hired, as a litigation consultant, a person who had previously worked for Lemay. The litigation consultant's job was to provide Baxter's lawyer with information about Lemay's alleged misuse of Baxter's proprietary information.[85] The court upheld Baxter's assertion that the confidential communications of the "litigation consultant" were protected by the privilege, finding that nearly all of the features of *Upjohn* were present.[86] The effect of *Baxter* is to allow a corporation to hire an informant from the other side and then blanket the "espionage" with the lawyer-client privilege.

Upjohn does not demand the *Baxter* result. It could have been distinguished easily on grounds that the employees in *Upjohn* were communicating about matters within the scope of the duties they performed for the corporation claiming the privilege. Baxter's "litigation consultant" communicated about matters concerning employment for Lemay, another corporation, and one that had no interest in Baxter's privilege.

It is worth noting that, although *Upjohn* and its progeny create a broad corporate lawyer-client privilege, they do not prevent the opposing party from seeking the same information from other sources. The lawyer-client privilege covers only confidential communications between lawyer and client, and not the underlying data upon which those communications were based.[87] The IRS in *Upjohn*, for example, was free to depose Upjohn's employees to ask them what they knew about illegal payments; it was only precluded from gathering what they had told corporate counsel about illegal payments.[88]

The *Upjohn* case is not, of course, binding on state courts, and a few have refused to follow it. They are free to follow the control group test or some other test for application of the privilege in the corporate context.[89]

The client of corporate counsel is, of course, the corporation. Officers and employees who provide information to corporate counsel are normally not protected if the corporation decides to waive the privilege.

---

84. 89 F.R.D. 410 (S.D. Ohio 1981).

85. *See id.* at 412.

86. *See id.* at 413–14.

87. Upjohn Co. v. United States, 449 U.S. 383, 395–96 (1981).

88. *See id.* at 396.

89. *See, e.g.,* Alaska R. Evid. 503 (a)(2) ("A representative of the client is one having authority to obtain professional legal services and to act on advice rendered pursuant thereto, on behalf of the client");

Nalian Truck Lines v. Nakano Warehouse & Transp. Corp., 8 Cal.Rptr.2d 467 (1992) (control group test maintained); Day v. Illinois Power Co., 199 N.E.2d 802, 806 (Ill. App. 1964) (employees' written reports to corporation's lawyer concerning investigation, repair or replacement of ruptured gas line not privileged because employees had no authority to determine corporate action based on lawyer's advice).

Sometimes, however, counsel may be working both for the corporation and for the employees as individual clients. In the absence of special circumstances, however, the default assumption is that only the corporation was the client. In *In re Grand Jury Subpoena (Newparent)*,[90] the court reviewed the precedent on the subject, and endorsed the position taken by *Matter of Bevill, Bresler & Schulman Asset Management Corp.*,[91] that corporate employees must establish five elements in order to assert a personal claim of attorney-client privilege:

> First, they must show they approached [counsel] for the purpose of seeking legal advice. Second, they must demonstrate that when they approached [counsel] they made it clear that they were seeking legal advice in their individual rather than in their representative capacities. Third, they must demonstrate that the [counsel] saw fit to communicate with them in their individual capacities, knowing that a possible conflict could arise. Fourth, they must prove that their conversations with [counsel] were confidential. And fifth, they must show that the substance of their conversations with [counsel] did not concern matters within the company or the general affairs of the company.[92]

The *Newparent* court added its own gloss to the fifth prong of the Belville test, stating that "if the communication between a corporate officer and corporate counsel specifically focuses upon the individual officer's personal rights and liabilities, then the fifth prong of *In Matter of Bevill* can be satisfied even though the general subject matter of the conversation pertains to matters within the general affairs of the company."[93] On the facts before it, however, the court held that employees had not made an adequate showing to take advantage of an individual attorney-client privilege separate from that of the corporation.[94]

The attorney-client privilege for government entities may be narrower than what the law provides for corporations, at least where information is sought by another government entity in a grand jury investigation.[95]

---

90. 274 F.3d 563 (1st Cir.2001).

91. 805 F.2d 120 (3d Cir.1986).

92. *Id.* at 123 (brackets in original).

93. 274 F.3d at 572.

94. *See also* United States v. Martin, 278 F.3d 988 (9th Cir.2002) (defendant, Curtis Martin, set up sham corporation in U.S. pretending to be subsidiary of real corporation in Hong Kong; lawyer hired by Martin to act as general counsel for sham corporation reported the fraud to government agents when he learned about it; held, attorney-client privilege did not apply; lawyer was not Martin's personal counsel and at any rate crime-fraud exception would apply).

95. *See* In re Witness Before Special Grand Jury 2000–2, 288 F.3d 289 (7th Cir. 2002) (held, though government agencies have attorney-client privilege, privilege did not apply to confidential communications made by former Illinois secretary of state to government counsel in case where former secretary was under bribery investigation and present secretary had waived department's attorney-client privilege); In re Lindsey, 158 F.3d 1263, 1282–83 (D.C. Cir. 1998) (where White House Counsel Bruce Lindsey refused to answer certain questions in grand jury testimony on grounds of attorney-client privilege, court held that privilege did not apply to communications between two federal officials (the President and White House Counsel) when information is sought by another federal official (the Independent Counsel) pursuant to grand jury subpoena); In re Grand Jury

The Limited Protection for a Lawyer's Work Product

When material in the hands of corporate counsel is sought during discovery, the claim of lawyer-client privilege is likely to be accompanied by a claim that the material is protected under the Federal Rules of Civil Procedure as the lawyer's "work product." Under Rule 26(b)(3) a party may obtain discovery of documents and tangible things prepared "in anticipation of litigation" by a lawyer or other agent of the opposing party only by showing "substantial need" and that it is unable, without undue hardship, to obtain the substantial equivalent from other sources. Moreover, even if the requisite showing of need is made, the court must protect against disclosure of "the mental impressions, conclusions, opinions, or legal theories of a lawyer or other representative of a party concerning the litigation."[96] However, under the Federal Rules of Civil Procedure, a party or a witness is entitled to obtain a copy of the party's own statement as a matter of course.[97]

On discovery, both the "work product" and the lawyer-client privilege rules protect material gathered for purposes of litigation. The two protections are distinct and there are several differences between them:

1.   Material that is covered by the lawyer-client privilege cannot be discovered even upon a showing of special need.[98] Material that is covered by work product protection can be discovered with such a showing, except for material that would reveal the mental impressions, etc., of the party's lawyer or other representative.[99]

2.   Only confidential communications between lawyer and client (or between the client and a representative of the lawyer) are covered

---

Subpoena Duces Tecum, 112 F.3d 910, 921 (8th Cir.1997) (in case involving Hillary Rodham Clinton, court agrees with Special Prosecutor Kenneth Starr that privilege does not cover consultation of public official with government attorney where information is sought by grand jury, stating that strong public interest in exposing wrongdoing by public officials would be "ill-served by recognition of a governmental attorney-client privilege applicable in criminal proceedings inquiring into the actions of public officials").

96. Rule 26(b)(3), in relevant part, reads as follows:

Subject to the provisions of subdivision (b)(4) of this rule [concerning trial preparation by experts], a party may obtain discovery of documents and tangible things otherwise discoverable under subdivision (b)(1) of this rule and prepared in anticipation of litigation or for trial by or for another party or by or for that other party's representative (including the other party's lawyer, consultant, surety, indemnitor, insurer, or agent)

only upon a showing that the party seeking discovery has substantial need of the materials in the preparation of the party's case and that the party is unable without undue hardship to obtain the substantial equivalent of the materials by other means. In ordering discovery of such materials when the required showing has been made, the court shall protect against disclosure of the mental impressions, conclusions, opinions or legal theories of a lawyer or other representative of a party concerning the litigation.

97. Rule 26 (b)(3) provides that "A party may obtain without the required showing a statement concerning the action or its subject matter previously made by that party. Upon request, a person not a party may obtain without the required showing a statement concerning the action or its subject matter previously made by that person."

98. See, e.g., Diversified Indus., Inc. v. Meredith, 572 F.2d 596, 602 (8th Cir. 1977) (privilege is absolute where it exists).

99. Fed. R. Civ. P. 26(b)(3).

by the lawyer-client privilege.[100] A much larger category of material is covered by the work product protection. A lawyer's memorandum about a statement to the lawyer from someone who is not a client, for example, falls within the work product privilege.[101] For that matter, a lawyer need not be involved at all for the work product protection to take effect. Information gathered by the party or the party's agent (such as a claim adjuster) is covered by the work product doctrine so long as the information is gathered in anticipation of litigation.[102]

3. The work product protection applies only to information gathered in "anticipation of litigation."[103] The lawyer-client privilege covers confidential communications to the lawyer seeking legal advice or services, whether or not litigation is expected.[104]

§ 8.10 The Lawyer–Client Privilege—The Crime–Fraud Exception to the Privilege

The crime-fraud exception removes the mantle of the privilege from communications between lawyer and client. If a client seeks advice or aid from a lawyer to facilitate a crime or fraud, the communications are not protected.[105] This exception to the lawyer-client privilege only applies to communications made in furtherance of a future or ongoing crime or fraud.[106] While the confidentiality of lawyer-client communications is

---

100. *See* § **8.05.**

101. *See, e.g.*, Upjohn Co. v. United States, 449 U.S. 383, 400 (1981) (purposes of Rule 26 included protection of memoranda based on oral statements of witnesses); Hickman v. Taylor, 329 U.S. 495, 507–14 (1947) (lawyer could not be forced to disclose memoranda on statements of witnesses).

102. *See,* Fed. R. Civ. P. 26(b)(3). Those protected materials include those produced by "party's lawyer, consultant, surety, indemnitor, insurer, or agent." *Id.*

103. *Id.*

104. *See* § **8.06.**

105. *See, e.g.*, Clark v. United States, 289 U.S. 1, 15 (1933) (privilege does not protect communications in furtherance of crime or fraud regardless of lawyer's guilt); In re Grand Jury Proceedings, 87 F.3d 377 (9th Cir. 1996)(client's intent to procure aid in crime or fraud is all that is needed to establish exception to privilege); In re Grand Jury Proceedings, 680 F.2d 1026, 1028–29 (5th Cir. 1982) (privilege does not protect identity of third party who hired lawyer in course of drug smuggling conspiracy to defend clients charged with transporting narcotics even though lawyer did not know of illegal purpose); In re Doe, 551 F.2d 899, 900–01 (2d Cir. 1977) (client's revelation to lawyer that he planned to

bribe juror not privileged); 1 McCormick on Evidence § 95 (5th ed. John W. Strong ed. 1999) (privilege does not apply where client seeks advice to further illegal or fraudulent scheme); 8 John H. Wigmore, Evidence in Trials at Common Law § 2298 (John T. McNaughton rev. 1961) (advice concerning criminal or fraudulent transaction is not privileged).

106. *See, e.g.*, In re John Doe Corp., 675 F.2d 482, 491 (2d Cir. 1982) (communication in furtherance of ongoing crime not privileged). *Cf.,* In re Grand Jury Subpoenas, 926 F.2d 847 (9th Cir. 1991). The government alleged that counsel aided in illegal export of goods to Iran, and the district court should not have examined in camera documents generated after the completion of the alleged crime. The court held that the crime-fraud exception does not cover communications about past or completed crimes where the government had not alleged an ongoing cover-up. *Id.* In the authors' opinion, the court's holding is dubious, because communications made after the completion of a crime might throw light upon whether earlier consultations with counsel were made for purposes of obtaining aid in planning the crime. *See also* Charles Wolfram, Modern Legal Ethics § 6.4 at 281 (1986) (exception applies to crimes ongoing at time of consultation).

important enough to our system of justice to protect a revelation to a lawyer of a past crime or fraud, there is no rationale for protecting communication to facilitate crime or fraud in the future.[107]

The crime-fraud exception, while easy to state, presents a ticklish problem of enforcement. A client seeking advice in aid of submitting a false insurance claim, laundering money, committing mail fraud, and the like is not entitled to the privilege. But how does a court determine whether the exception applies? Whether the communication was made in furtherance of crime or fraud cannot be known without knowing what was stated in the communication. Yet the communication may be privileged. Hence the apparent paradox: to determine whether the privilege applies, one must breach the privilege.

The United States Supreme Court reached a typical solution to this problem in *United States v. Zolin*.[108] Briefly put, the solution was to have the district court review the allegedly privileged materials in camera to determine whether the exception applied, but only after some kind of a preliminary showing of crime or fraud.[109]

In *Zolin*, the Church of Scientology sought to prevent the IRS from obtaining access to tape recordings of meetings between Church representatives and legal counsel. The IRS argued that the tapes fell within the crime-fraud exception to the lawyer-client privilege. It urged the District Court to listen to the tapes in camera to determine whether the exception applied. In support of its position, it submitted affidavits from an undercover agent who gave reasons for believing that the tapes were relevant, and who provided a partial transcript of the contents of the tapes.[110]

The Court held that while fishing expeditions were not to be permitted, a judge could, upon a proper showing, examine allegedly privileged materials alone in chambers and determine whether the crime-fraud exception applied. The requisite showing was that of "a factual basis adequate to support a good faith belief by a reasonable person."[111] Such a showing permits, but does not require a judge to review the materials in camera. Additional factors, such as the burden of reviewing voluminous materials, and the degree of need for the evidence in the litigation, should also be considered.[112] Further, the mere making of the showing does not mean that the privilege evaporates. It only means that the judge examines the materials alone, for the purpose of making a determination whether the protection of the privilege should be stripped away.

---

107. *See, e.g.*, In re Grand Jury Proceedings (Appeal of FMC Corp.), 604 F.2d 798, 803–04 (3d Cir. 1979) (communications privileged if crime completed before retention of counsel; 1 McCormick, *supra* note 105, § 95 (advice concerning past crimes or misconduct privileged as opposed to advice in furtherance of a crime or fraud which is not).

108. 491 U.S. 554 (1989).

109. *See id.* at 571–2.

110. *See id.* at 559.

111. *Id.* at 572 (quoting Caldwell v. District Court, 644 P.2d 26, 33 (Colo. 1982)).

112. *See id.*

Zolin also raised the issue of what materials could be used in making the preliminary showing. If an employee of the privileged party leaked privileged material to the opponent, or if an undercover agent acquired the material by participating in lawyer-client conferences, could that pilfered knowledge be used in making the preliminary showing? While purporting to recognize the dangers of abuse, the *Zolin* Court allowed that the showing could be made with knowledge acquired in an underhanded fashion, so long as the information had not previously been adjudged to be privileged and so long as the leaking or undercover work was not otherwise illegal.[113]

§ 8.11   The Lawyer–Client Privilege—Waiver of Privilege

Like other objections, the privilege can be waived at trial simply by failure to object. There are a number of other acts that can result in waiver of the privilege:

1.   Putting privileged material in issue. The privilege can be waived by putting privileged material in issue.[114] A client who claims to have believed a course of conduct to be legal, because of a lawyer's advice, waives the right to claim the privilege as to that advice.[115] This does not mean that the privilege is waived merely because the subject matter of communications between the lawyer and client is the same as the subject matter of litigation. The fact that lawyer and client discussed a contract, for example, does not mean the privilege is waived for those communications about the contract when the client later sues for its enforcement. Rather, the client must do something to put the lawyer-client confidential communications in issue in order to be deemed to have waived the privilege.[116]

2.   Intentional disclosure. Testimony about, or other disclosure of privileged material, can constitute waiver. The party cannot be allowed to selectively disclose, that is, to reveal in a self-serving way part of the privileged communications, while withholding the rest. Intentional partial disclosure of a communication will result, at least, in loss of the privilege with regard to the remainder of that communication.[117] The

---

113.   *See id.* at 574. In United States v. Chen 99 F.3d 1495 (9th Cir. 1996), the Ninth Circuit Court of Appeals, interpreting *Zolin*, held that a past corporate employee's affidavit disclosing privileged material could not be considered in conjunction with a motion invoking the crime-fraud exception, until after the court had determined that there was a good faith basis to believe that an in camera review would show a crime or fraud.

114.   *Zolin*, 491 U.S. at 574.

115.   *Miller*, 600 F.2d at 501–02.

116.   *See, e.g.*, Pitney–Bowes, Inc. v. Mestre, 86 F.R.D. 444, 447 (S.D. Fla. 1980) (although party did not waive privilege by seeking arbitration in contract dispute, it

did by placing intent of the parties in issue during subsequent litigation); Hearn v. Rhay, 68 F.R.D. 574, 581 (E.D. Wash. 1975) (a party waives privilege where: (1) assertion of privilege resulted from party's affirmative act; (2) party placed information in issue; and (3) application of privilege would deny opposing party information required to respond effectively).

117.   *See, e.g.*, Handgards, Inc. v. Johnson & Johnson, 413 F.Supp. 926, 929 (N.D. Cal. 1976) (voluntary partial disclosure of communication waives privilege as to remainder of communication concerning same subject matter); 8 John H. Wigmore, Evidence in Trials at Common Law § 2327 (John T. McNaughton rev. 1961) (offer of

better rule goes further: intentional partial disclosure results in loss of the privilege with regard to all communications on the same subject matter.[118]

3. *Disclosure by mistake.* Inadvertent revelation of privileged material, such as mistakenly turning over a privileged document during discovery, can result in waiver of the privilege.[119] If, however, the privileged party has taken reasonable precautions to protect the material, in fairness the waiver should not extend beyond the particular document. This result is suggested by the growing application of the privilege to conversations overheard by an eavesdropper. At common law, when an eavesdropper overhears an otherwise privileged conversation, the eavesdropper can testify about the contents of the conversation.[120] Recent authority suggests that the privilege is not waived and the testimony will not be allowed, if the client and lawyer have taken reasonable precautions to keep the conversation confidential.[121] This is particularly true when the eavesdropper's conduct involves some degree of invasion of privacy, or is actually illegal, as in the case of an illegal

---

testimony as to any part of communication waives privilege as to whole communication).

118. *See, e.g.,* In re Sealed Case (No. 81–1717), 676 F.2d 793, 824 (D.C. Cir. 1982) (company's submission of report to the Securities and Exchange Commission concerning bribes of foreign officials, waived privilege as to any document necessary to evaluate report); Chinnici v. Central Dupage Hosp. Ass'n., 136 F.R.D. 464, 465 (N.D. Ill. 1991) (condominium association's voluntary disclosure of meeting minutes summarizing attorney's advice waived attorney-client privilege with respect to all communications on the same subject); Haymes v. Smith, 73 F.R.D. 572, 576–77 (W.D.N.Y. 1976) (client's disclosure of letter waived privilege as to all communication involving same subject matter); Scott N. Stone & Ronald S. Liebman, Testimonial Privileges § 1.57 (1983) (where client reveals privileged communication concerning an issue or raises issue, privilege waived as to communications related to that issue). *See also* United States v. Thomas, 953 F.2d 107 (4th Cir. 1991) (trial judge violated confrontation clause by excluding client and client's present attorney from in camera hearing in which former attorney was examined to determine whether privilege had been waived).

119. *See, e.g.,* 8 Wigmore, *supra* note 117 § 2325, at 633 (privilege waived as to any information attorney reveals in litigation because attorney acts on implied authority of client). *But see* Hydraflow, Inc. v. Enidine Inc., 145 F.R.D. 626, 639 (W.D.N.Y. 1993) (inadvertent facsimile

transmittal of documents for patent application did not waive privilege for documents to which the privilege applied); Resolution Trust v. Dean, 813 F.Supp. 1426 (D. Ariz. 1993) (privilege not waived by publication of internal memo in unauthorized newspaper article); Martin v. Valley Nat'l Bank, 1992 WL 196798 (S.D.N.Y. 1992) (plaintiff did not waive attorney-client privilege with respect to five inadvertently disclosed documents, where plaintiff took reasonable measures to avoid disclosure; plaintiff's attorneys screened the 50,-000 pages of documents produced, and plaintiff requested return of inadvertently disclosed documents in timely manner); SCM Corp. v. Xerox Corp., 70 F.R.D. 508, 519 (D. Conn.1976) (client did not waive privilege by inadvertently disclosing privileged information in transfer of voluminous unscreened documents; client would have waived privilege, however, if it had individually screened documents).

120. *See, e.g.,* Schwartz v. Wenger, 124 N.W.2d 489, 493 (Minn. 1963) (conversation between lawyer and client overheard in the hallway of the courthouse admissible).

121. *See, e.g.,* In re Grand Jury Proceedings Involving Berkley & Co., 466 F.Supp. 863, 869 (D. Minn. 1979) (where employee retained documents without employer's consent and disclosed them, court held in camera hearing to determine if documents were privileged; modern trend preserves privilege when lawyer and client take reasonable precautions); Stone & Liebman, *supra* note 118 § 1.54, (privilege applies as long as reasonable precautions taken).

wiretap. The notion that the reasonable precautions taken by the lawyer and the client should limit the waiver of the privilege when material is disclosed by mistake has not had universal acceptance. There is authority that extends the waiver of the privilege not only to the mistakenly disclosed document or conversation, but also to the general subject matter covered by the mistaken disclosure.[122]

4. Refreshing memory with a privileged document. Showing a privileged document to a witness on the witness stand, even if the witness is a client or lawyer, will waive the privilege.[123] There is some authority for finding waiver when documents have been used before trial to refresh memory,[124] though the better view is that the privilege should ordinarily prevail.[125]

5. Disclosure during negotiations. Disclosure of privileged matter during negotiations ordinarily does not waive the privilege as to related matters not disclosed. The policy of promoting settlement militates in favor of the privilege and against treating this conduct as waiver.[126] There is authority, however, to the contrary.[127] If it is necessary to reveal privileged matter during settlement negotiations, precautions, such as obtaining a confidentiality agreement from the opponent, should be taken.[128] Reliance on Rule 408, which excludes statements by a lawyer during settlement negotiations, may not be sufficient to protect all privileged material. Rule 408 does not require the exclusion of evidence otherwise discoverable, merely because the existence or nature of the

122. *Id.* § 1.43 (unreasonable searches or seizures may warrant exclusion on Fourth Amendment grounds).

123. *See, e.g.,* Bailey v. Meister Brau, Inc., 57 F.R.D. 11, 13 (N.D. Ill. 1972) (client waived privilege by viewing documents to refresh memory; application of privilege would place unfair burden on cross-examiner). *See also* Fed. R. Evid. 612 (disclosure of document used to refresh memory while testifying required).

124. *See, e.g.,* People v. Scott, 193 N.E.2d 814, 821–22 (Ill. 1963) (prosecution must produce documents that police officer testified he used to refresh memory before trial); 1 McCormick on Evidence § 9 (5th ed. John W. Strong ed. 1999) (witness's consultation of document before testifying generally should constitute waiver of privilege). *See also* Fed. R. Evid. 612 (court has discretion to require disclosure of document used to refresh memory before testifying).

125. *See, e.g.,* Jos. Schlitz Brewing Co. v. Muller & Phipps (Hawaii), Ltd., 85 F.R.D. 118, 120 (W.D. Mo. 1980) (court should give privileged documents special discretionary safeguard against disclosure under Rule 612; Stone & Liebman, *supra* note 112 § 1.49 (although court has discretion under Rule 612 to compel disclosure of

privileged information, Congress intended that doubts be resolved against disclosure).

126. *See, e.g.,* Sylgab Steel & Wire Corp. v. Imoco–Gateway, 62 F.R.D. 454, 458 (N.D. Ill. 1974), *aff'd*, 534 F.2d 330 (7th Cir. 1976) (lawyer did not waive privilege by incorporating certain legal conclusions from an opinion letter to a client into letter sent to opposing party); International Business Mach. Corp. v. Sperry Rand Corp., 44 F.R.D. 10, 13 (D. Del. 1968) (disclosure during negotiations of privileged information concerning a specific subject did not waive privilege as to all related information); Stone & Liebman, *supra* note 118, § 1.51.

127. R. J. Hereley & Son Co. v. Stotler & Co., 87 F.R.D. 358, 359 (N.D. Ill. 1980) (partial disclosure of privileged memorandum from client to lawyer at settlement meeting waived privilege as to remainder of memorandum, and opponent is entitled to discovery of remainder of memorandum).

128. Stone & Liebman, *supra* note 118 § 1.51 (lawyer should avoid reference to confidential information in negotiations and when necessary, consider requesting opposing party to sign confidentiality agreement or moving for protective order).

evidence is revealed during compromise negotiations.[129] Pre-existing documents containing privileged information disclosed during a settlement conference, therefore, may not be protected, because the statements in them were made before, not during, the negotiations.

§ 8.12 The Lawyer–Client Privilege—Disputes Between Client and Lawyer

When a lawyer and client become involved in litigation against each other, the privilege disappears. The lawyer may reveal confidential information necessary to establish a claim or defense.[130] The lawyer may reveal client confidences, for example, when sued for malpractice,[131] or when necessary to establish the lawyer's right to be paid a fee by a recalcitrant client.[132]

This exception to the privilege, according to many courts, is not limited merely to litigation between the lawyer and client. It extends to certain other disputes involving third persons. There is authority, for example, for the position that when the client casts aspersions upon the lawyer's competence, even in a suit in which the lawyer is not a party, the lawyer may reveal confidences to defend the lawyer's reputation.[133]

§ 8.13 The Physician–Patient Privilege

The Federal Rules of Evidence do not create privileges, but rather, provide that privileges are governed by federal common law when a federal substantive rule provides the rule of decision and by state law when state substantive law provides the rule of decision.[134]

129. See §§ 5.45–5.51.

130. *See, e.g.,* United States v. Ballard, 779 F.2d 287, 292 (5th Cir.1986) (lawyer-client privilege does not apply in dispute between client and lawyer over fees or improper conduct); 8 John H. Wigmore, Evidence in Trials at Common Law §§ 2312(2), 2327(6) (John T. McNaughton rev. 1961) (privilege does not apply in dispute over fees or claim of negligence; client waives privilege by claiming breach of duty by lawyer); 1 McCormick on Evidence § 91 (5th ed. John W. Strong ed. 1999) (privilege does not apply in dispute between lawyer and client or when client attacks lawyer indirectly in litigation between third persons); Scott N. Stone & Ronald S. Liebman, Testimonial Privileges § 1.66 (1983) (privilege does not apply in dispute between client and lawyer or when client attacks lawyer in separate litigation).

131. *See, e.g.,* Kracht v. Perrin, Gartland & Doyle, 268 Cal.Rptr. 637, 641 n. 6 (App. 1990) (client may not sue former lawyer for malpractice and simultaneously claim privilege to obstruct lawyer's defense); Nave v. Baird, 12 Ind. 318, 320 (Ind.

1859) (lawyer present at confidential conference could testify as to communications between client and another lawyer when client sued the other lawyer for disobeying instructions and negligence).

132. *See, e.g.,* Sokol v. Mortimer, 225 N.E.2d 496, 501 (Ill. App. 1967) (lawyer could testify as to privileged and confidential communications with the client in suit against client for fees).

133. *See, e.g.,* United States v. Weger, 709 F.2d 1151, 1156–57 (7th Cir. 1983) (in criminal prosecution against former client for making false statements to secure a loan, law firm could rebut client's implication that it was involved in producing fraudulent title opinion by giving prosecutor confidential letter from former client written on her typewriter to demonstrate that client forged title opinion on firm's letterhead); Tasby v. United States, 504 F.2d 332, 336 (8th Cir. 1974) (lawyer permitted to testify when former client claimed ineffective assistance of counsel in habeas corpus proceeding, asserting that lawyer forced client to testify at trial).

134. Fed. R. Evid. 501.

The doctor-patient privilege was not recognized at common law.[135] A doctor was considered to be under a professional obligation to be discreet, but when called as a witness could be compelled to tell all that the doctor knew. Federal courts have generally declined to recognize the doctor-patient privilege as a matter of federal common law.[136]

Most state legislatures have sought to remedy this perceived defect in the common law and have passed privilege statutes,[137] usually at the behest of interest groups representing the medical profession.[138] The statutes, however, are diverse. Some states recognize a general physician-patient privilege.[139] Others restrict the privilege to therapists.[140] Some recognize other health professionals.[141]

The strongest argument for the privilege is simply that the patient has a privacy interest that outweighs the contribution that the medical information would make to the judicial process. Sometimes a utilitarian rationale similar to that advanced for the lawyer-client privilege is advanced for the doctor-patient privilege. The theory is that potential patients would be deterred from seeking medical advice if the privilege did not exist. The self-interest in getting sound medical advice and treatment, however, would seem to outweigh the danger that the information would at some later time be used detrimentally in court.[142]

Because of the great diversity among state statutes, it is difficult to generalize about medical privileges. The following features, however, are generally present:

1. A patient is the holder of a privilege if there is a professional relationship between physician and patient, if the patient is consulting the doctor for medical treatment. Thus, when a court-appointed psychiatrist examines a patient for purposes of determining the patient's mental condition, there is no privilege because no professional relationship exists.[143] The same holds true when the opposing side has a doctor

---

135. *See* Crow v. State, 230 S.W. 148 (Tex. Crim.App. 1921); 8 John H. Wigmore, Evidence in Trials at Common Law § 2380 (John T. McNaughton rev. 1961).

136. Scott N. Stone & Ronald S. Liebman, Testimonial Privileges § 7.01 (1983). *But see* Mann v. University of Cincinnati, 824 F.Supp. 1190, 1196–98 (S.D. Ohio 1993) (recognizing existence of general physician-patient privilege under federal common law).

137. 8 Wigmore, *supra* note 135 § 2380; Stone & Liebman, *supra* note 135 § 7.01.

138. 8 Wigmore, *supra* note 135 § 2380.

139. *See, e.g.,* Mich. Comp. Laws Ann. § 600.2157 (West 1980) (physicians); *Id.* at § 333.18237 (psychologists); Tex. Civ. Code Ann. art. 4459b § 508 (Vernon Supp. 1990) (physicians); *id.* at art. 5561h (professionals involved in treatment of "any mental or emotional condition or disorder").

140. *See, e.g.,* Fla. Stat. Ann. § 90.503 (West 1979) (psychotherapists); Md. Code Ann. [Cts. & Jud. Proc.] § 9–109 (West 1989) (psychiatrists and psychologists).

141. *See, e.g.,* Minn. Stat. § 595.02 (West 1988) (physicians, psychologists, chiropractors, dentists, registered nurses, and sexual assault counselors); 42 Pa. Cons. Stat. Ann. § 5929 (1982) (physicians); *id.* at § 5944 (psychologists); *id.* at § 5945 (school personnel); *id.* at § 5945.1 (sexual assault counselors).

142. 8 Wigmore, *supra* note 135 § 2380a; Zechariah Chafee, *Privileged Communications: Is Justice Served or Obstructed by Closing the Doctor's Mouth on the Witness Stand?*, 52 Yale L.J. 607, 609–10 (1943).

143. People v. Primmer, 444 N.E.2d 829, 834 (Ill. App. 1983) (state appointed psychiatrist's testimony is admissible over defendant's objection since state had defen-

examine an adverse party.[144] When a lawyer for the patient has a doctor examine the patient, not for treatment but for an expert opinion, the better view is that the doctor-patient privilege does not apply, but that the lawyer-client privilege applies because the doctor is acting as the lawyer's representative.[145] Note, however, that in most of these circumstances the privilege will be waived either by putting the patient's condition in issue or by offering the doctor's testimony.[146]

2. The privilege is not restricted to confidential communications, but covers other information acquired by the physician that is necessary to diagnosis or treatment. Even if the patient is in a coma when observed by the doctor, the facts learned by the doctor are covered by the privilege. In this respect, the doctor-patient privilege is broader than the lawyer-client privilege. In the latter case, observations of physical condition are not usually an integral part of the professional relationship, and so the latter privilege covers only confidential communications.[147] In the case of the doctor-patient relationship, the patient is entitled to have protection for information learned from examination and testing as well as information learned from patient communications.[148]

3. Statements to a physician that are not pertinent to diagnosis or treatment are not covered by the privilege. Thus, a patient's statement that the patient was wounded while trying to escape from police, or that the patient was hit by a car going through a red light, would not be covered.[149]

4. The privilege is riddled with exceptions. Some jurisdictions do not recognize it in criminal cases.[150] Others provide a more limited exception for treatment that is sought in furtherance of criminal activity,

---

dant examined to prepare for defendant's possible insanity defense); State v. Jensen, 174 N.W.2d 226, 230 (Minn. 1970) (defendant could not assert privilege to block psychiatrist's testimony about defendant's mental state because psychiatrist was appointed by court to judge defendant's competency to stand trial, not to offer diagnosis and treatment).

144. VanSickle v. McHugh, 430 N.W.2d 799, 801–2 (Mich. App. 1988) (in action for injuries in auto accident, plaintiff could not block testimony of physician employed by his no-fault insurance carrier since he lacked "reasonable expectation that the consultation [would be] cloaked with a veil of confidentiality" and examination was conducted by the insurance company which could be an adversary if plaintiff disputed his insurance award).

145. United States v. Alvarez, 519 F.2d 1036, 1046 (3d Cir. 1975) (in case where defense counsel retained psychiatrist to help prepare insanity defense, defendant's statements to psychiatrist are privileged because doctor was an agent offering expert assistance to counsel).

146. See § 8.13.

147. In situations in which something about the client's appearance, not obvious to the casual observer, is shown to the lawyer, the lawyer-client privilege probably would cover what the lawyer observes.

148. See, e.g., State v. Santeyan, 664 P.2d 652, 654 (Ariz. 1983) (results of defendant's urinalysis privileged when test was made in the course of his treatment for injuries sustained in a car accident and request for treatment was made by defendant, not by a law enforcement officer).

149. State v. Sweet, 453 A.2d 1131, 1133 (Vt. 1982) (where defendant told nurse he was too drunk to sign a consent-to-treatment form, that statement was not privileged because the nurse did not need defendant's statement in order to render treatment). See Stone & Liebman, supra note 136 § 7.12 (citations omitted).

150. See, e.g., Cal. Evid. Code § 998 (West 1966) (physician-patient privilege does not apply in criminal trials); 42 Pa. Cons. Stat. § 5929 (1982) (privilege exists only in civil cases).

such as patching a wound incurred in escape from prison, or plastic surgery designed to change a fugitive's appearance.[151] Many states impose reporting requirements when necessary for the public health or safety. Examples include mandatory reporting of sexually transmitted disease and child abuse.[152]

The privilege is waived easily. Most jurisdictions provide that once the party voluntarily places the party's mental or physical condition in controversy, the privilege is waived.[153] A party who brings a personal injury action, for example, has waived the privilege with regard to information relevant to evaluating the injury.[154] The privilege may also be waived in the same fashion as the lawyer-client privilege—for example, by selective disclosure,[155] or by calling the doctor to testify.[156]

§ 8.14   The Psychotherapist–Patient Privilege

The therapist-patient privilege is supported by stronger policy justifications than the doctor-patient privilege, which explains why some states and the federal courts have accepted only the former. The therapist is more likely to be the recipient of damaging, embarrassing and personal information than is the ordinary physician. Also, the deterrence hypothesis is stronger; some patients might not go to the therapist at all if there was a danger that their communications would become public.[157]

The Supreme Court of the United States, settling a split in the circuits, interpreted the principles of the common law "in the light of

151. People v. Traylor, 377 N.W.2d 371, 373 (Mich. App. 1985) (physician-patient privilege does not apply in case where physician testified in defendant's armed robbery trial about defendant's gunshot wound because Mich. Comp. Law § 750.411 requires that any wound inflicted by a deadly weapon be reported to the local authorities).

152. See, e.g., Cal. Penal Code § 11171(b) (West 1982) (imposes affirmative duty to report all suspected cases of child abuse on both physicians and psychotherapists; statute explicitly provides exception to physician-patient and psychotherapist-patient privileges).

153. Leslie v. Brames, 682 F.Supp. 608 (D. Me. 1988) (where plaintiff claimed he suffered head and back injuries in accident with defendant; that plaintiff put his physical condition in issue, thus waiving the physician-patient privilege).

154. See, e.g., Minn. R. Civ. P. 35.03.

155. See, e.g., In re: the Exxon Valdez, 270 F.3d 1215 (9th Cir.2001) (in celebrated case involving grounding of 900–foot oil tanker on reef, spilling 11 million gallons of oil, plaintiffs sought to prove failure to avoid danger was due to captain's own alcoholism; held, form sent by captain's doctor to company identifying captain as alcoholic was properly admitted; captain had provided Exxon form to doctor for purposes of excusing absence from work, and doctor's excuse sent to employer is not shielded by privilege); Jones v. Superior Court for County of Alameda, 174 Cal.Rptr. 148, 155 (App. 1981) (because plaintiff's mother testified she ingested DES, plaintiff's mother waived physician-patient privilege regarding that subject).

156. People v. Newbury, 290 N.E.2d 592, 596 (Ill. 1972) (defendant who voluntarily consults psychiatrist and offers psychiatrist's testimony waives the psychiatrist-patient privilege); Matthews v. Commonwealth, 709 S.W.2d 414 (Ky. 1985) (psychiatrist-patient privilege was not violated in case where defendant had psychiatrist testify he acted under extreme emotional disturbance and prosecution cross-examined psychiatrist on same subject but asked more detailed questions about defendant's communications with him).

157. Scott N. Stone & Ronald S. Liebman, Testimonial Privileges § 7.02 (1983).

reason and experience"[158] in *Jaffee v. Redmond*[159] and established the federal therapist-patient privilege. The "reason" was the need for the privilege to encourage effective therapy. The "experience" was that of the fifty states, each of which have a therapist-patient privilege of some kind.

The Court determined that the therapist-patient privilege would serve a "public good transcending the normally predominant principle of utilizing all rational means for ascertaining truth."[160] It followed the lead of many states in expanding the privilege to cover licensed social workers, observing that "drawing a distinction between the counseling provided by costly psychotherapists and the counseling provided by more readily accessible social workers serves no discernible public purpose."[161] Though it accepted most of the lower court's decision, the Court disagreed with the judgment that a balancing test to nullify the privilege in certain circumstances would be appropriate. In deciding not to allow a trial judge to determine that the need for testimony might be greater in a particular case than a patient's interest in privacy, the Court observed that such a balancing test would "eviscerate the effectiveness of the privilege."[162]

The Court did not detail the scope and operation of the privilege. The Court noted that the federal courts would probably recognize exceptions to the privilege as they developed its scope, and gave as an example the "dangerous patient" exception that applies in many states when the therapist reveals confidences to protect a person the patient threatens.[163] The Court also cited the Supreme Court Standard that had been originally submitted to Congress as Rule 504,[164] suggesting that the privilege as there detailed might be influential in determining the nature of the privilege as it is drawn by future decision. The standard applied to psychotherapists engaged in diagnosis or therapy,[165] took account of the need for confidentiality in situations where third parties, such as family members or group therapy members, are present,[166] and was expanded to

158. Fed. R. Evid. 501.

159. 518 U.S. 1 (1996).

160. *Id.* at 15.

161. *Id.* at 17.

162. *Id.*

163. For a post-*Jaffe* case discussing the dangerous patient exception, *see* United States v. Glass, 133 F.3d 1356 (10th Cir. 1998) (threat to president communicated to psychotherapist not automatically admissible; trial judge must make findings about seriousness of threat and whether revelation was necessary to avoid harm). *See also* United States v. Hayes, 227 F.3d 578, 586 (6th Cir.2000) (psychotherapist's testimony about patient's threats to kill postal supervisor inadmissible where patient asserted the psychotherapist-patient privilege; psychotherapist's professional and ethical duty to protect innocent third parties by disclos-

ing threats does not imply duty to testify against patient in criminal proceedings other than those related to patient's involuntary hospitalization); George C. Harris, *The Dangerous Patient Exception to the Psychotherapist–Patient Privilege: The* Tarasoff *Duty and the* Jaffe *Footnote*, 74 Wash. L. Rev. 33 (1999) (arguing that duty to warn potential victims should be broader than exception to privilege, so that therapist might have duty to warn but still not be obliged to testify against patient in court proceeding).

164. 518 U.S. at 8.

165. Fed. R. Evid. 504(a)(2) (Proposed draft 1972).

166. Fed. R. Evid. 504(a)(3) (Proposed draft 1972).

include treating a drug addiction.[167] It contained an exception for court ordered examinations, limited to the purpose of the examination,[168] and did not apply when the patient relied upon the condition as part of a claim or defense.[169] The Standard did not address issues of confidentiality for the name of the patient and permissible disclosure in the event of a dispute between therapist and patient. Although courts may be tempted to look at the lawyer-client privilege for guidance on these issues, disclosure of the identity of a person in therapy and the nature of communications during therapy may have more important privacy implications for the therapist's patients than for the lawyer's clients.

§ 8.15   The Marital Privileges

There are two spousal privileges. The first is the privilege against adverse spousal testimony. Designed to protect the peace and harmony of an existing marriage,[170] when successfully claimed, it prevents the spouse from taking the witness stand. Because exercise of the adverse spousal privilege renders the spouse incompetent to be a witness, it applies to all subject matter, not merely confidences and communications.[171] A wife, for example, could invoke the privilege to avoid testifying about her husband's reckless driving while she was a passenger. This would be so even though the driving is done for anyone to see and even if the marital partners said nothing to each other while the husband was driving. The second is the privilege for marital confidences. It applies only to confidences shared by marital partners.[172] It is often described as a privilege for confidential communications,[173] though some jurisdictions have extended it to acts that are performed in confidence before the spouse.[174]

Although the spousal privileges are not codified in the Federal Rules of Evidence, they have been recognized in the federal system.[175] Many states have passed statutes governing spousal privilege,[176] though some have created the privilege through case law.

---

167. *See* 42 U.S.C. § 290ee–3 (confidentiality of drug abuse program patient records).

168. Fed. R. Evid. 504(d)(2) (Proposed draft 1972).

169. Fed. R. Evid. 504(d)(3) (Proposed draft 1972).

170. United States v. Byrd, 750 F.2d 585, 590 (7th Cir. 1984) (privilege against adverse spousal testimony protects the marriage from the impact of negative testimony); In re Grand Jury Subpoena Koecher, 601 F.Supp. 385, 391 (S.D.N.Y. 1984) (the goal of privilege is "prevention of dissension between spouses which might result from testimony of one against the other").

171. *See* § 8.16.

172. United States v. Hamilton, 19 F.3d 350, 354 (7th Cir. 1994) (defendant's wife had not been divorced from previous husband, therefore no valid marriage and no privilege for marital confidences).

173. *See, e.g.,* 8 John H. Wigmore, Evidence in Trials at Common Law §§ 2332–2341 (John T. McNaughton rev. 1961); 1 McCormick on Evidence §§ 78–86 (5th ed. John W. Strong ed. 1999).

174. *See* § 8.17.

175. *See* §§ 8.16, 8.17.

176. *See, e.g.,* Conn. Gen. Stat. § 4–84a (West 1985); Minn. Stat. § 595.02(1)(a) (1985); N.C. Gen. Stat. § 8–57 (1986).

§ 8.16   The Marital Privileges—The Privilege Against Adverse Spousal Testimony

The marriage that ends in divorce or death needs no further protection. Similarly, when one spouse is ready and willing to testify against the other, the marriage is already in ruins and the adverse testimony will do little to damage it more. For that reason, the Supreme Court held in *Trammel v. United States*[177] that it is the witness spouse, not the party spouse, who holds the privilege. If the witness spouse chooses not to testify, the opponent cannot force the testimony. But if the witness spouse wishes to testify against the party spouse, then the party spouse cannot prevent it. Of course, it is possible that the witness spouse is willing to testify, not because the "peace and harmony" of the marriage has been destroyed, but because the government has threatened to prosecute the witness spouse on the underlying crime if the privilege is claimed. Government pressure, not the deterioration of the marriage, may well have been the situation in *Trammel*, but the possibility did not seem to bother the Supreme Court. Evidently the Court valued the testimony higher than what might be left of the marriage.

Not all states have followed the *Trammel* doctrine. Some make the party spouse the holder of the privilege.[178] Although some states allow the privilege in both civil and criminal cases,[179] in many jurisdictions it is limited to criminal cases.[180]

The adverse spousal testimony privilege protects the marriage against outsiders who seek to force testimony, but does not apply when the spouses are adversaries, such as a divorce action or an action in which one spouse is accused of a crime against the other.[181] It also does not apply in cases involving an alleged crime by one spouse against the children.[182] At least one state has created an exception for homicide cases

---

177. 445 U.S. 40 (1980).

178. *See, e.g.,* Ariz. Rev. Stat. Ann. § 13–4062(1) (1989) (criminal); *id.* § 12–2231 (1982) (civil); Minn. Stat. § 595.02(1)(a) (1988); Mont. Code Ann. § 26–1–802 (1989).

179. *See, e.g.,* Alaska R. Evid. (505)(a)(1) (1989); Minn. Stat. § 595.02(1)(a) (1988); Mont. Code Ann. § 26–1–802 (1989). The precedent on the question whether the adverse spousal testimony privilege applies in federal civil cases is scant and unclear. *See* United States v. Yerardi, 192 F.3d 14 (1st Cir.1999) (in the course of holding that the privilege applies in a criminal forfeiture case, court notes the absence of clear precedent on whether the privilege applies in pure civil cases). For analysis, *see* Katherine O. Eldred, Comment, *"Every Spouse's Evidence": Availability of the Adverse Spousal Testimonial Privilege in Federal Civil Trials*, 69 U. Chi. L. Rev. 1319 (2002).

180. *See, e.g.,* Conn. Gen. Stat. §§ 54–84a (West 1985); N.C. Gen. Stat. §§ 8–57 (1986); Or. Rev. Stat. § 40–255(3) (1988).

181. Brown v. Commonwealth, 292 S.E.2d 319, 323 (Va. 1982) (husband shot his wife and her grandmother and trial court severed cases for trial; wife may testify against defendant-husband in both trials); Hudson v. Commonwealth, 292 S.E.2d 317, 319 (Va. 1982) (spouse may testify against defendant husband regardless of whether the offense is committed against the spouse's person or her property). There is a division of authority on whether the adverse spousal testimony privilege is available to married couples who jointly participate in crimes against third persons. Compare United States v. Van Drunen, 501 F.2d 1393, 1396 (7th Cir.1974) (privilege not applicable) with Appeal of Malfitano, 633 F.2d 276 (3d Cir.1980) (privilege applicable).

182. United States v. Allery, 526 F.2d 1362, 1367 (8th Cir. 1975) (privilege does not apply when spouse commits crime

in which the marriage occurs after the crime. When the crime is homicide the societal interest in hearing the testimony outweighs the benefits of preserving the harmony of a new marriage that may have been consummated just to establish the privilege.[183]

As with other privileges, the adverse spousal testimony privilege can be waived. If a spouse testifies in favor of the other, or if the party spouse uses an out-of-court statement of the other as affirmative evidence, the privilege is waived, at least as to adverse testimony on the same subject matter.[184]

The adverse spousal privilege, though it is broader in subject matter coverage than the privilege for marital confidences, does not have the staying power of the marital communications privilege. Because the adverse spousal testimony privilege is based on the notion that the "peace and harmony" of the marriage should not be endangered by forcing one spouse to testify against another, the privilege does not survive the marriage.[185]

§ 8.17 The Marital Privileges—The Privilege for Marital Confidences

The privilege for marital confidences is rooted in the natural repugnance against the state's invasion of marital privacy. Although some jurists have suggested that the marital confidences privilege exists to

against child of either spouse, in case where wife testified against husband accused of attempting to rape their daughter).

183. Minn. Stat. § 595.02(a) (1988). For a similar result in a case not involving homicide, *see* United States v. Blair; 54 F.3d 639, 644–45 (10th Cir.1995) (not only did "sham" marriage not immunize defendant's wife from testifying against defendant regarding his involvement in illegal wagering, but it also resulted in a two-point sentence enhancement for obstruction of justice).

184. Donovan v. State 584 P.2d 708, 710 (Nev. 1978) (prosecution's use of wife's prior statement to impeach her testimony not improper since defendant-husband waived right to assert privilege by calling wife as witness). *Cf.*, State v. Walker, 403 A.2d 1, 4 (N.J. 1979) (defendant who testified he was with his wife at the time of the victim's rape, and wife was present during his testimony, "conveyed the impression" she supported the truth of his testimony; defendant thus made wife a "crucial" witness, and proper for prosecution to comment on defendant's failure to have his wife testify).

185. *See* United States v. Bolzer, 556 F.2d 948, 951 (9th Cir. 1977) (testimony of defendant's ex-wife admissible because the

privilege does not continue after marriage is legally ended). *See also* In re Witness Before Grand Jury, 791 F.2d 234, 238 (2d Cir. 1986) (woman unable to assert privilege because she had not lived with husband for eleven years and her husband lived with another woman); United States v. Snyder, 707 F.2d 139, 147 (5th Cir. 1983) (privilege can not be asserted when woman lived with defendant, but was not married to him); United States v. Cameron, 556 F.2d 752 (5th Cir. 1977) (policy reasons for privilege are "non-existent" when the couple's marriage is "moribund" with no chance for a possible reconciliation despite the fact the couple was still legally married; therefore, the privilege can not be asserted); Jurcoane v. Superior Court, 113 Cal.Rptr.2d 483 (Cal. App.2001) (held, wife could claim marital privilege so that she need not testify against husband charged with murder even though she had had no contact with husband for 17 years; magistrate erred in determining that marital privilege does not apply where a viable marital relationship no longer exists). *But see* United States v. Singleton, 260 F.3d 1295, 1300–01 (11th Cir.2001) (held, marital privilege does not apply when the couple was permanently separated without reasonable expectation of reconciliation; authors of this text query case, believing a bright-line rule is better than a particularistic inquiry into the health of each marriage).

encourage spouses to share confidences in the fashion of the lawyer-client privilege,[186] it seems doubtful that the existence of the privilege has much effect on marital intimacy, even in today's climate of ubiquitous law. Because it is limited in scope to communications during the marriage, but not limited in time to the existence of the marriage, the privilege for marital confidences is more complex than the privilege against adverse spousal testimony.

The privilege for marital confidences differs from jurisdiction to jurisdiction, but generally has the following features:

(1) The privilege is applicable only to confidences that were shared during the marriage. Confidential communications made after divorce are not covered. If the husband and wife are married but living separately, the applicability of the privilege is in doubt.[187] There is at least one case, however, extending the privilege to communications between separated spouses during an attempted reconciliation.[188]

(2) The privilege for confidences shared during the course of the marriage continues after the termination of the marriage.[189] This result may be based on the notion that the policy of the privilege is to encourage confidential communications during the marriage relationship, and allowing divorce to pierce the veil might conceivably discourage spouses from reposing confidences.[190] The former spouse has no legal obligation, however, to refrain from broadcasting marital confidences, so it is doubtful that the ordinary person takes the remote possibility of potential courtroom testimony into account in deciding whether to repose confidences in a spouse. The idea that the privilege survives marriage for pre-dissolution statements seems, nonetheless, to be well established.[191]

(3) In many jurisdictions, the privilege protects only confidences.[192] Express requests for secrecy, however, are uncommon in most marriages

---

186. *See, e.g.,* 8 John H. Wigmore, Evidence in Trials at Common Law § 2332 (John T. McNaughton rev. 1961); Scott N. Stone & Ronald S. Liebman, Testimonial Privileges § 5.09 (1983).

187. United States v. Porter, 986 F.2d 1014 (6th Cir. 1993) (privilege does not apply to statements made by one spouse to the other after the spouses have permanently separated; whether permanent separation had occurred prior to statement is to be determined by district court); United States v. Jackson, 939 F.2d 625, 627 (8th Cir. 1991) (not error to admit defendant's statement to wife made while the couple was permanently separated without any semblance of a marital relationship, even though the couple was not divorced; not protected by marital communication privilege); United States v. Fulk, 816 F.2d 1202 (7th Cir. 1987) (defendant could not assert communication privilege when communication was made at time when defendant-husband and wife were permanently sepa-

rated); In re Witness Before Grand Jury, 791 F.2d 234, 239 (2d Cir. 1986) (spouse could not claim marital communication privilege because she had lived apart from defendant-husband for four years when alleged communication occurred); Hazelwood v. State, 609 N.E.2d 10, 14–16 (Ind. App. 1993) (privilege does not extend to engaged couple weeks before their marriage). *See also* 8 Wigmore, *supra* note 186, § 2335.

188. People v. Oyola, 160 N.E.2d 494, 498, (N.Y. App. Div. 1959).

189. *See* 8 Wigmore, *supra* note 186 § 2341 (citations omitted).

190. *See id.* at § 2341.

191. *See, e.g.,* Cal. Evid. Code § 980 (West 1966); Mich. Comp. Laws Ann. § 600.2162 (West 1986); Minn. Stat. § 595.02(a) (1988); N.J. Stat. §§ Ann. § 2A:84A–22 (West 1976).

192. Cal. Evid. Code § 980 (West 1966); Fla. Stat. Ann. § 90.504 (West 1979). *See also* 8 Wigmore, *supra* note 186 § 2336.

and in many jurisdictions, marital communications are presumed to be confidential until the contrary appears.[193] The confidentiality requirement means that the presence of a third person during a communication between marital partners will destroy the privilege, as will the intention of the marital partner making the communication that it be relayed to a third person.[194] In jurisdictions that do not recognize a parent-child privilege, the presence of a child during the communication destroys confidentiality.[195]

(4) Although the privilege in most jurisdictions is limited to communications, some jurisdictions have extended it to testimony about conduct performed under circumstances suggesting reliance on the confidential nature of the marital relationship.[196] The act of hiding something in the presence of one's spouse, therefore, might be covered by the privilege for marital confidences in some jurisdictions.[197] One can argue in favor of this extension, on grounds that the security that the privilege is supposed to foster applies to conduct as well as words. The extension does not, however, cover all acts observed by the spouse. If a spouse sees the other start a fight on the subway, the privilege does not apply because there is nothing confidential about the fighter's public conduct.

(5) The spouse reposing the confidence is the holder of the privilege in many jurisdictions, on the theory that it is that spouse's communication or act that the privilege is designed to encourage.[198] The witness spouse, therefore, cannot testify to confidences reposed during the marriage, even if the witness spouse is eager to testify.[199] The wife who confides in her husband that she has committed a crime, therefore, is

193. *See, e.g.,* Cal. Evid. Code § 917 (West 1966); 8 Wigmore, *supra* note 186, § 2336.

194. *See* United States v. Madoch, 149 F.3d 596, 602 (7th Cir.1998) (spousal communication privilege does not apply to tape-recorded phone conversations made while husband was calling wife from jail; spouses should have known that inmate conversations are monitored); United States v. Pensinger, 549 F.2d 1150, 1152 (8th Cir. 1977) (communication privilege did not apply because husband's conversation with wife about details of his bank robbery in the presence of two other people destroyed the confidential nature of the communication); Resnover v. State, 372 N.E.2d 457, 459 (Ind. 1978) (information in husband's letter to wife was intended to be given to third parties and thus could not be protected by communication privilege).

195. People v. Sanders, 457 N.E.2d 1241, 1244 (Ill.1983) ("presence of children of spouses destroys confidentiality unless they are too young to understand what is being said").

196. Arnold v. State, 353 So.2d 524, 527 (Ala. 1977)(defendant-husband's act of driving by burned building with his wife is privileged communication because it was "performed with the confidence of the marriage in mind"); Commonwealth v. Byrd, 689 S.W.2d 618, 621 (Ky. App. 1985) (witness-spouse may not testify she saw her defendant-husband examine the contents of a stolen purse because husband did so in the marital home and would not have done so if they had not been married); Commonwealth v. Clark, 500 A.2d 440, 443 (Pa. Super. 1985) (defendant-husband could claim communication privilege in second degree murder case where wife witnessed husband washing and disposing the murder weapon).

197. 8 Wigmore, *supra* note 186 § 2337.

198. *See, e.g.,* Kan. Stat. Ann. § 60–428 (1983); 8 Wigmore, *supra* note 186, § 2340.

199. United States v. Neal, 532 F.Supp. 942, 947 (D. Colo. 1982), 8 Wigmore, *supra* note 186 § 2340.

able to invoke the privilege successfully, even if her husband wants to testify against her. Some jurisdictions require the consent of both spouses to waive the marital communications privilege.[200]

(6) If the holder of the privilege calls his or her spouse to testify about marital confidences, the privilege has been waived as to the subject matter.[201] In this respect, the privilege for marital confidences resembles the broader privilege against adverse spousal testimony. The privilege also can be waived by voluntary disclosure to a third person, as for example in a letter.[202] In this respect, the privilege for marital confidences is different than the privilege against adverse spousal testimony. The marital confidences privilege is based upon the confidentiality of the communication, so once the confidence is breached, there is no purpose to the marital confidences privilege.[203] The adverse spousal testimony privilege, however, is based upon the peace and harmony of the marriage, so even if the communication has been disclosed to another, there is reason to maintain the adverse spousal testimony privilege to avoid causing a rift in the marriage by the spouse's testimony.

(7) Accidental disclosure to persons outside the marriage can result in a waiver of the privilege. As in the case of the lawyer-client privilege, eavesdroppers, so long as they overhear legally, can testify to matters covered by the marital confidences privilege.[204] The same result occurs

---

200. *See e.g.,* Neb. Rev. Stat. § 27–505 (1984)

201. However, the fact that a party calls the party's spouse to the witness stand does not mean that the opponent can cross-examine the spouse about prior invocations of the privilege. *See* United States v. Morris, 988 F.2d 1335, 1339–40 (4th Cir. 1993) (reversible error for prosecutor to cross-examine defendant's wife and secretary of more than 20 years about her prior invocation of marital privilege during the grand jury investigation preceding trial). *See also* United States v. Hall, 989 F.2d 711, 715–16 (4th Cir. 1993) (reversible error for prosecutor during cross-examination of defendant to read from text of inculpatory statements made by defendant's wife when wife had invoked privilege after having made statements); Stone & Liebman, *supra* note 186, § 5.14.

202. *See, e.g.,* State v. Johnson, 643 P.2d 146, 152 (Kan. 1982) (common-law wife's daughter could testify about conversation she had with her mother that defendant-husband had shown his wife over $900 in cash because husband had shown both the testifying daughter and another daughter the money as well, in case where defendant-husband was on trial for first degree murder and aggravated robbery). *See also* Kan. Stat. Ann. § 60–437 (1983).

203. For a case that stretches the concept of waiver to the breaking point,*see* United States v. Smith, 33 M.J. 114, 117–18 (C.M.A. 1991). The majority of the court held that a wife waived the privilege for marital confidences with regard to a letter she wrote to her husband. In the letter, she urged him to testify that he had forced her to commit the crime with which she was currently charged, and to give other exculpatory testimony. *Id.* The court held that she waived the privilege by testifying at trial to conversations with the husband in which he placed her in fear. *Id.* She did not testify about the letter, but the court said that all the communications could properly be considered as one. *Id.* Hence the holding suggests that revealing one communication with a spouse waives any objection to other communications at different times that touch on the same general subject matter. The court avoided basing its decision on the theory that the letter was an invitation to commit perjury, apparently on grounds that it was doubtful that the Military Rules of Evidence contained a crime-fraud exception to the marital confidences privilege. *See also* 8 Wigmore, *supra* note 186 § 2340.

204. *See* State v. Summerlin, 675 P.2d 686, 695 (Ariz. 1983) (defendant-husband was told he could not have a private meeting with his wife, that defendant-husband

when a holder spouse accidentally discloses a writing, such as by losing a letter.[205] Bad faith disclosure by a turncoat spouse, however, does not destroy the privilege. If a husband gossips about his wife's secrets, for example, the privilege stops the recipient of the gossip from testifying against the wife, even if the court can find a way around the hearsay problem.[206] Of course, if it had been the wife, herself, who had disclosed her secret conversations with her husband, she would be precluded from objecting to the testimony.[207]

(8) The exceptions to the privilege for marital confidences are similar to the exceptions that apply to the privilege against adverse spousal testimony. The privilege, generally, does not apply in suits between husband and wife, including marriage dissolution, custody battles,[208] criminal charges of assault on the spouse,[209] crimes against a child of either spouse, or other matters involving the child, as where the state seeks to terminate parental rights.[210] In addition, a fraud exception to the application of the privilege has been recognized.[211]

§ 8.18   The Privilege Against Self-incrimination

The source of the privilege is the Fifth Amendment to the United States Constitution. It provides, in part, that "No person shall be . . . compelled in any criminal case to be a witness against himself. . . . " In 1964, the Supreme Court held that the Fifth Amendment was incorporated by the due process clause of the Fourteenth Amendment and therefore was applicable to states.[212] The protection of the Fifth Amendment is supplemented by various state constitutional provisions that are sometimes interpreted more broadly than the Fifth Amendment.[213]

It is impossible to state a simple and satisfying rationale for the privilege. The privilege seems to have evolved as a reaction to the

---

could not claim communication privilege because prison guard in room could possibly overhear the conversation); Sumlin v. State, 617 S.W.2d 372, 376 (Ark. 1981)(defendant-husband could not claim communication privilege because inmate overheard husband's conversation with his wife).

205. 8 Wigmore, *supra* note 186 § 2339.

206. United States v. Neal, 532 F.Supp. 942, 947 (D. Colo. 1982) (neither FBI agent or defendant's wife could testify about content of phone conversation between defendant and his wife because wife allowed FBI agent to monitored the call and defendant did not know call was monitored and expected his call to be confidential). *See also* 8 Wigmore, *supra* note 186 § 2339.

207. *See* State v. Johnson, 643 P.2d 146 (Kan. 1982).

208. Ariz. Rev. Stat. Ann. § 12–2232 (1982); Cal. Evid. Code § 984 (West 1966); Minn. Stat. § 595.02(a) (1988).

209. Cal. Evid. Code § 985 (West 1966); Minn. Stat. § 595.02 (1988).

210. Cal.Evid. Code § 985 (West 1966); Minn.Stat.§ 595.02 (1998).

211. *See* In re Donald Sheldon & Co, 191 B.R. 39, 48 (Bankr. S.D.N.Y. 1996) (privilege will not immunize spouse from disclosing marital communications where there was an effort to conceal assets from creditors; New York courts do not recognize the marital privilege when asserted to protect efforts to perpetrate fraud on third-party victims).

212. Malloy v. Hogan, 378 U.S. 1, 11 (1964).

213. *See, e.g.,* People v. Disbrow, 545 P.2d 272 (Cal. 1976); State v. Santiago, 492 P.2d 657 (Haw. 1971); Hansen v. Owens, 619 P.2d 315 (Utah 1980).

religious and political persecutions in England prior to the Restoration,[214] particularly the practice of examining suspects under oath to determine whether they held forbidden beliefs. When applied to crimes other than crimes of conscience, Bentham's charge that the privilege benefits only the guilty because the innocent will be eager to explain is hard to meet,[215] at least as it relates to gaining the "right" result in an individual case. The values it may have for the definition of a society and the importance of the individual may be a different matter.

Wigmore lists no fewer than a dozen policies that have been advanced in support of the privilege.[216] Perhaps the strongest are that the privilege serves as a prophylaxis against unreasonable interrogation methods, and that it is inherently inhumane to confront an individual with the trilemma of committing perjury, being held in contempt, or serving as the prosecution's witness.[217]

The privilege against self-incrimination is a personal privilege. It cannot be claimed on behalf of or used to protect another person, however unselfish one's motives may be.[218]

The privilege can be claimed only when there is a danger of incrimination, not merely of humiliation or degradation. It is not necessary, however, to show that prosecution is probable so long as some danger of incrimination exists.[219]

The privilege allows the witness to refuse to answer questions, if the answers would directly incriminate the witness. But it goes much further. It covers questions, the answers to which might provide an investigative lead for prosecution of the witness. For example, a witness is entitled to refuse to say whether the witness is acquainted with a certain person, if the information might provide the government with a lead.[220]

The privilege applies only to "testimonial" incrimination. So long as the government does not require a suspect to engage in communicative conduct that conveys factual assertions or information,[221] it can compel

214. 8 John H. Wigmore, Evidence in Trials at Common Law § 2250 (John T. McNaughton rev. 1961).

215. Jeremy Bentham, Rationale of Judicial Evidence (1827), (cited in 8 Wigmore, *supra* note 214 § 2251).

216. 8 Wigmore, *supra* note 214 § 2251.

217. *Id*. at § 2251. *See also* Murphy v. Waterfront Comm., 378 U.S. 52, 54 (1964):

[The privilege] reflects many of our fundamental values and most noble aspirations: our unwillingness to subject those suspected of crime to the cruel trilemma of self-accusation, perjury or contempt; our preference for an accusatorial rather than an inquisitorial system of criminal justice; our fear that self-incriminating statements will be elicited by inhumane treatment and abuses; our sense of fair

play which dictates a fair state-individual balance by requiring the government to leave the individual alone until good cause is shown for disturbing him and by requiring the government in its contest with the individual to shoulder the entire load.

218. Rogers v. United States, 340 U.S. 367 (1951).

219. Hoffman v. United States, 341 U.S. 479 (1951).

220. *See id.* at 486 (witness may refuse to state whether he knows an alleged criminal and where the alleged criminal is located if answers to those questions would "furnish a link in the chain of evidence needed to prosecute the claimant for a federal crime").

221. *See* Doe v. United States, 487 U.S. 201, 212 (1988).

the suspect to commit acts that aid an investigation, even if those acts help incriminate the suspect. An investigative target may be compelled, for example, to sign a form permitting the government to examine foreign bank records,[222] to furnish handwriting and voice exemplars,[223] to appear in a lineup,[224] or to give a blood sample.[225]

The privilege belongs only to human beings. A corporation or other organization cannot claim the benefit of the privilege.[226]

Although the Court, not the witness, decides whether the privilege applies,[227] a witness's assertion that an answer raises a danger of incrimination will usually stand up. The Supreme Court has indicated that the claim of privilege should be sustained unless it is "perfectly clear, from a careful consideration of all the circumstances in the case, that the witness is mistaken, and that the answer cannot possibly have [a] tendency to incriminate."[228] This statement appears to place the burden on the government to show that the answers could not possibly incriminate.

The privilege protects against incrimination, so a grant of immunity will abrogate the privilege, even if the answers may cause the witness embarrassment or disgrace. Early precedent suggested that the immunity had to be transactional, that is, the immunity had to protect the witness against prosecution for the entire transaction about which testimony was being compelled. It is now clear, however, that use immunity, prohibiting the compelled testimony to be used against the witness, is constitutionally sufficient.[229] If the government decides to prosecute the witness, the government has the burden of showing that the compelled testimony did not provide an investigatory lead helpful to the prosecution.[230]

The witness may also lose the right to invoke the privilege because the danger of incrimination has been removed through acquittal or conviction of the underlying charge. The constitutional prohibition against double jeopardy prevents a subsequent prosecution, so there is no longer any danger of incrimination. If, however, the questioning about the adjudicated crime could lead to prosecution for other crimes, the privilege may still be invoked.[231]

---

222. *Id.* at 218.

223. United States v. Dionisio, 410 U.S. 1, 7 (1973); Gilbert v. California, 388 U.S. 263, 266–7 (1967).

224. United States v. Wade, 388 U.S. 218, 221–2 (1967).

225. Schmerber v. California, 384 U.S. 757, 765 (1966).

226. Bellis v. United States, 417 U.S. 85, 101 (1974); Hale v. Henkel, 201 U.S. 43, 75 (1906).

227. Rogers v. United States, 340 U.S. 367 (1951).

228. Hoffman v. United States, 341 U.S. 479, 488 (1951).

229. Kastigar v. United States, 406 U.S. 441 (1972).

230. *Id.* at 460 ("This burden of proof ... imposes on the prosecution the affirmative duty to prove that the evidence it proposes to use is derived from a legitimate source wholly independent of the compelled testimony").

231. Malloy v. Hogan, 378 U.S. 1, 13 (1964).

The accused in a criminal case has a right not only to refuse to answer self-incriminating questions, but also to refuse to take the witness stand at all. Moreover, the prosecution may not allude to the defendant's failure to testify,[232] nor may it suggest in closing argument that the prosecution's evidence was uncontradicted, if the argument provides any implication that the defendant could have been the witness to provide the contradiction.[233] When a witness in a criminal case, other than the defendant, is likely to claim the privilege, especially if that witness is identified with the defendant, it is appropriate to make a motion in limine to prohibit the government from calling the witness. The jury may be confused or prejudiced against the defense by the spectacle of the witness who claims the privilege, and may not know how to interpret this conduct.[234]

Even though the privilege is against self-incrimination that could lead to criminal liability, witnesses in civil cases may exercise the privilege to refuse to answer on grounds of self-incrimination. They must, however, take the stand and claim the privilege. In civil cases, it is proper for the opposing party to ask the jury to draw an adverse inference from the witness's claim of the privilege.[235] If the person claiming the privilege is a litigant and not merely a witness, other adverse consequences may occur, including in some jurisdictions the dismissal of a plaintiff's case for withholding information.[236]

A witness may waive the right against self-incrimination. A witness who has testified about part of a transaction cannot claim the right to

---

232. Griffin v. California, 380 U.S. 609 (1965).

233. *Compare* Lent v. Wells, 861 F.2d 972 (6th Cir. 1988) (where defendant was the only one who could contradict), *with* Lindgren v. Lane, 925 F.2d 198 (7th Cir. 1991) (prosecutor argued that government witness was not contradicted because defense witness testifying on the same point was not believable).

234. *See, e.g.,* Namet v. United States, 373 U.S. 179 (1963) ("Error may be based upon a concept of prosecutorial misconduct, when the Government makes a conscious and flagrant attempt to build its case out of inferences arising from [the witness'] use of the testimonial privilege"); Foster v. State, 687 S.W.2d 829, 832 (Ark. 1985) (reversible error for prosecution to call wife of the deceased—whom the prosecution knew would invoke her privilege against self-incrimination—in defendant's murder trial because "there was an attempt by the prosecutor to build the state's case out of inferences arising from [the witness'] assertion of her fifth amendment privilege"). *See also* Commonwealth v. Brown, 619 S.W.2d 699, 703 (Ky. 1981) (prosecution could not call witnesses to stand because prosecution

knew the witnesses would claim the fifth amendment privilege).

235. Curtis v. M&S Petroleum, Inc., 174 F.3d 661, 673–75 (5th Cir.1999) (corporate president designated as representative by corporation took Fifth Amendment in individual capacity during deposition; held, trial judge should have given instruction that adverse inference could be drawn from assertion of the privilege); Brink's Inc. v. City of New York, 717 F.2d 700, 710 (2d Cir. 1983). *See also* Robert Heidt, *The Conjurer's Circle—The Fifth Amendment Privilege in Civil Cases*, 91 Yale L. J. 1062, 1107–8 (1982).

236. Lyons v. Johnson, 415 F.2d 540, 542 (9th Cir. 1969) (plaintiff's suit was properly dismissed because plaintiff refused to answer interrogatories, despite fact plaintiff refused on fifth amendment grounds); Penn Communications Specialities, Inc. v. Hess, 65 F.R.D. 510, 512 (E.D. Pa. 1975) (plaintiff's suit can be dismissed unless plaintiff answers defendant's interrogatories, despite fact plaintiff refused on fifth amendment grounds); Master v. Savannah Surety Associates, Inc., 252 S.E.2d 186, 187 (Ga. App. 1979) (dismissing suit).

self-incrimination when cross-examined about the remainder.[237] Testimony on a question of preliminary fact, however, such as testimony on a motion to suppress evidence resulting from an allegedly illegal search, does not waive a criminal defendant's right to assert the privilege.[238]

The right against self-incrimination applies to certain interrogations conducted by law enforcement officers before trial. In the celebrated case of *Miranda v. Arizona*, the Supreme Court ruled that statements made during custodial interrogation could not be used at trial, unless the person in custody had been given what have become known as the "Miranda warnings." The interrogation must be preceded by a warning that the suspect had a right to remain silent, that any statement made could be used in evidence, and that the suspect had a right to counsel, either retained or appointed.[239] If the warnings are not given of if the suspect does not waive the rights, any statement obtained through custodial interrogation is inadmissible. Such a statement may, however, be used to impeach a defendant who testifies.[240]

Silence, too, may be used to impeach a criminal defendant, even though the Constitution seems to guarantee the right of silence to a criminal defendant. A defendant who remains silent after receiving "Miranda warnings" and then testifies to an alibi or some other explanation may not be impeached with the previous silence in response to police interrogation. In *Doyle v. Ohio*, the Supreme Court recognized that the silence was likely to be in response to the *Miranda* warning's reminder of the right to remain silent.[241] A defendant who testifies during trial and who did not tell law enforcement about the gist of the testimony before trial may, however, be impeached by the silence, under certain circumstances. In *Jenkins v. Anderson*,[242] the government was allowed to impeach the defendant's testimony in pursuit of his self-defense claim by asking the defendant why he had initially remained silent about the homicide, not reporting it for two weeks. The defendant in *Fletcher v. Weir*,[243] who was arrested, not given the proper *Miranda* warnings, exercised his right to remain silent while in police custody, and exercised his right to testify at trial that the killing was in self-defense was impeached by his silence after arrest. The impeachment, which after *Doyle* would not have been allowed had the police officers followed the proper procedure and given the defendant *Miranda* warnings, was allowed precisely because the officers had not followed the proper procedure. The Court's reasoning—that the lack of a warning avoided the risk that the silence might be a response to the warning's caution—might have been better logic than law. Ignoring the purpose

237. Rogers v. United States, 340 U.S. 367, 372 (1951); United States v. Hearst, 563 F.2d 1331, 1341 (9th Cir. 1977).

238. Simmons v. United States, 390 U.S. 377, 394 (1968).

239. 384 U.S. 436, 467–73 (1966).

240. Harris v. New York, 401 U.S. 222, 226 (1971) (defendant's statement to authorities that was given without defendant having received a proper Miranda warning was admissible to impeach defendant's testimony even though the statement was inadmissible in prosecution's case in chief).

241. 426 U.S. 610 (1976).

242. 447 U.S. 231 (1980).

243. 455 U.S. 603 (1982).

and the spirit of *Miranda,* the *Weir* decision provides an incentive for police officers to forgo *Miranda* warnings after arrest as a way to ensure that a confused defendant cannot offer exculpatory testimony at trial.

§ 8.19 The Government's Privileges

Military and state secrets are protected from compelled disclosure.[244] The privilege covers information that might harm the national defense or international relations of the United States if disclosed. The trial judge may make a limited in camera review to determine whether the privilege applies.[245] If the privilege applies, it is absolute and cannot be overcome by a showing of necessity.[246]

In *United States v. Nixon*[247] the Supreme Court recognized an "executive privilege" for presidential communications made in confidence.[248] Unless military or state secrets are involved, however, the privilege is not absolute. It may be overcome by a showing of specific need for information that will be key evidence in a criminal trial.[249]

There are a variety of other privileges for governmental information. Often the privileges are governed by statute and protect information that individuals or corporations are required to provide to the government.[250] They cover matters ranging from grand jury proceedings[251] to census information.[252]

The informer's privilege is often asserted in criminal cases. It allows the government not to disclose the identities of informers, who for obvious reasons would rather not be known to those whom they have incriminated.[253] Where the identity of the informer is helpful to the defendant's case or is essential to a fair trial, the informer's identity must be revealed, or the case dismissed.[254] If, however, the informer was merely a supplier of probable cause to arrest or search, then the informer's identity need not be revealed.[255]

244. *See, e.g.,* United States v. Reynolds, 345 U.S. 1, 6–7 (1953) (Air Force accident report containing secret information that could not be disclosed without harming national security, privileged).

245. *Id.* at 9–10.

246. *Id.* at 10–11.

247. 418 U.S. 683 (1974).

248. *Id.* at 705–06.

249. *Id.* at 706–07.

250. *See* Scott N. Stone & Ronald S. Liebman, Testimonial Privileges § 9.23 (1983) (such privileges are collectively known as required reports or official information privileges).

251. *See, e.g.,* Fed. R. Crim. P. 6(e) (general rule imposing secrecy of grand jury proceedings).

252. *See, e.g.,* 13 U.S.C. §§ 8(b), 9(a) (1988) (access to and disclosure of census information limited to insure confidentiality).

253. *See, e.g.,* Roviaro v. United States, 353 U.S. 53, 59 (1957) (government not required to disclose communication that would reveal identity of person providing information concerning violation of law).

254. *See, e.g., id.* at 60–61 (identity of informer who witnessed crime not privileged because testimony might have been crucial to defense).

255. *See, e.g.,* McCray v. Illinois, 386 U.S. 300, 312 (1967) (identity of informant who told police defendant was dealing drugs, pointed defendant out to police, and then left, privileged).

§ 8.20   Other Privileges

Priest-penitent. A privilege for confidential communications between parishioners and clergy is widely recognized.[256] Though early versions of the privilege applied only to communications required by the discipline for the religion[257]—confessions made by Roman Catholics, for example—modern versions tend to include other communications made for spiritual guidance, comfort, or advice.[258]

Journalists. A privilege for journalists and other news gatherers has achieved recognition in several jurisdictions.[259] The United States Supreme Court has considered and rejected the argument that the First Amendment requires acceptance of a general privilege for journalists.[260] Some federal courts, nevertheless, recognize a qualified First Amendment journalists' privilege.[261]

The journalist's privilege is quite different from all of the other privileges insofar as it is not aimed at keeping communications confidential. On the contrary, the whole idea is that it will facilitate communication of information that might not otherwise be available. The privilege generally protects a reporter from being required to reveal the identity of a confidential source of information.[262] In some jurisdictions, it covers unpublished notes and materials prepared by the news gatherer. The statutory privileges are not absolute, and generally yield by application of some sort of balancing test. A statute might provide, for example, that the privilege must yield when there is a compelling reason for disclosure and no alternative means of getting the information.[263] Even where a statutory privilege purports to be absolute, an accused person's constitutional right to obtain witnesses may require that the privilege be pierced when the reporter seeks to conceal information crucial to the defense.[264] *In re Farber* grew out of a homicide prosecution of a physician for a

---

256. Scott N. Stone & Ronald S. Liebman, Testimonial Privileges §§ 6.02, 6.04, (1983) (privilege recognized by statute in nearly every state and recognized in federal courts as application of Fed. R. Evid. 501).

257. *See, e.g.*, People v. Gates, 13 Wend. 311, 323 (N.Y. Sup. Ct. 1835) (admission not pursuant to church discipline not privileged); 8 John H. Wigmore, Evidence in Trials at Common Law § 2395 (John T. McNaughton rev. 1961) (privilege applies to communications made in pursuance to church discipline).

258. *See,   e.g.,   Minn.   Stat.* § 595.02(1)(c) (1988) (privilege includes clergy's communications to "any person seeking religious or spiritual advice, aid, or comfort").

259. Stone & Liebman, *supra* note 256 § 8.08 (privilege recognized by statute in 26 states as of 1983).

260. Branzburg v. Hayes, 408 U.S. 665, 690 (1972).

261. *Id.*

262. *See, e.g.*, Ill. Comp. Stat. Ann. ch. 110 para. 8–901–09 (West 1990) (reporter generally cannot be compelled to disclose source of any information); Minn. Stat. §§ 595.021–595.024 (1988) (forced disclosure of confidential sources generally prohibited); N.J. Stat. Ann. §§ 2A:84A–21 (West Supp. 1990) (reporter has privilege to refuse to disclose source of information).

263. *See, e.g.*, Ill. Stat. Comp. Ann. ch. 110 para. 8–907 (West Supp. 1990) (exception to basic privilege); Minn. Stat. § 595.024(2) (1988).

264. *See* In re Farber (State v. Jascalevich), 394 A.2d 330, 337 (N.J.1978) (criminal defendant's right under New Jersey constitutional to compel attendance of witness and production of documents prevails over facially absolute language of statute).

death in a New Jersey hospital. Farber, a reporter for the New York Times, had been deeply involved in investigative reporting about the case, and may have been the driving force behind the prosecution. The trial judge held a hearing on the application of the privilege. At the hearing, the defendant showed that the main accuser had talked to Farber five times; that there was evidence suggesting that Farber might be in possession of a prior inconsistent statement of a witness; that another important witness, interviewed by Farber, would not talk to the defense; and that another witness interviewed by Farber had died.[265] The New Jersey Supreme Court upheld a criminal contempt conviction imposed upon Farber for refusing to turn over his materials for in camera inspection by the trial court.[266]

Parent-child. A few jurisdictions recognize a parent-child privilege.[267] This privilege allows a parent to refuse to reveal confidential communications from a child. It is subject to exceptions analogous to those applicable to the marital privileges. Communications involving crimes against the family, for example, are not covered.[268]

Accountant-client. A few states recognize an accountant-client privilege,[269] but there is no such privilege under Federal law.[270] In *United States v. Arthur Young & Co.*[271] the Supreme Court faced the issue whether an IRS subpoena for tax accrual work papers prepared by the corporation's independent CPA could be discovered pursuant to an IRS summons. The papers, prepared for a mandatory SEC filing, contained an evaluation of possible tax liability of the corporation, based on information including "opinions, speculations, and projections of man-

265. *Id.* at 340.

266. *Id.* at 341.

267. *See, e.g.,* Minn. Stat. § 595.02(1)(i) (1988) (communications made in confidence by minor to minor's parent privileged); In re Grand Jury Proceedings, Unemancipated Minor Child, 949 F.Supp. 1487, 1494–95 (E.D. Wash.1996) (because it is supported by policy reasons similar to spousal privilege, recognition of federal parent-child privilege comports with reason and experience; in instant case, however, grand jury subpoena to 17–year-old child would not be quashed because child failed to show either that confidential communications were sought or that testimony would be adverse to father's interests; court did not delineate precise contours of privilege); People v. Fitzgerald, 422 N.Y.S.2d 309, 312, 317 (N.Y. 1979) (parent-child privilege flows directly from United States and New York Constitutions; adult child's confidential communication with parent concerning hit and run accident privileged in criminal prosecution). *But see* In re Grand Jury, 103 F.3d 1140, 1140–47 (3d Cir.1997) (parent-child privilege rejected after thoughtful discussion and extensive examination of authority; courts suggests that

parent-child relationship unlikely to be influenced by privilege); In re Erato, 2 F.3d 11, 16 (2d Cir.1993) (refusing to recognize privilege in case where son residing in Netherlands was suspected of embezzling millions of dollars from United States citizens in fraudulent real estate scheme, and mother was allegedly benefiting from scheme; court suggested that privilege may not necessarily extend to protect adult child); United States v. Jones, 683 F.2d 817, 819 (4th Cir.1982) (privilege not recognized where adult child was ordered to give testimony against father).

268. *See, e.g.,* Minn. Stat. § 595.02(1)(j) (1988) (communications involving crimes against family members not privileged).

269. *See, e.g.,* Ill. Comp. Stat. Ann. ch. 111 para. 5533 (West 1990) (confidential communications with accountant privileged); Tex. Rev. Civ. Stat. Ann. art. 41a–1 (West 1982–83) (confidential communications with licensed accountant privileged).

270. *See, e.g.,* Couch v. United States, 409 U.S. 322, 335 (1973) (tax records in possession of her accountant not privileged).

271. 465 U.S. 805 (1984).

agement with regard to unclear, aggressive, or questionable tax positions that may have been taken on prior tax returns."[272] Despite the sensitive nature of the information, the Supreme Court held that it was not protected either by privilege or by the work product doctrine.[273]

272. *Id.* at 812.   **273.** *Id.* at 817–18.

Chapter 9

IMPEACHMENT AND
REHABILITATION
OF WITNESSES

Table of Sections

§ 9.01 Impeaching One's Own Witness; Objection to Calling Witness Solely to Impeach with Prior Inconsistent Statement [FRE 607]

A scholar or jurist who refers to the "common law rule" on a given subject is always engaging in a degree of simplification, even fictionalization. The common law of evidence was a growing, changing, fractious, and often contradictory body of precedents. Yet it is often useful to try to extract the common law attitude toward a topic even at the risk of oversimplification. If nothing else, it provides a useful background that helps explain the motives and goals of later codifiers who decided to depart from what they saw as the common law position. With those caveats, we will briefly sketch the broad outlines of the common law position on impeaching one's own witness, and then describe the Federal Rules position.

The common law rule prohibited impeaching one's own witness.[1] The prohibition applied whatever the method of impeachment—whether by character attack, showing of bias, impeachment by prior inconsistent statements, or by any other method.[2] In the case of impeachment by prior inconsistent statement, however, the common law developed a dispensing exception to aid the attorney whose witness has suddenly turned unfavorable. The exception had two requirements. First, the turncoat witness's testimony actually had to be harmful and not merely neutral.[3] In other words, it was not enough for the turncoat merely to testify "I don't know" or "I don't recall"; the witness's testimony had to be affirmatively harmful to allow impeachment. Second, the attorney had to be surprised by the witness's harmful testimony.[4] When the attorney knew beforehand that the witness was going to testify detrimentally, the attorney was supposed simply not to call the witness, rather than putting the witness on the stand and then impeaching the witness.

The historical roots and policy basis for the common law rule forbidding impeachment of one's own witness are unclear.[5] Wigmore thought the rule probably arose from an ancient form of trial known as "compurgation" in which a party's "witnesses" were called not for their personal knowledge of the facts of the case (in fact, they likely had no such knowledge), but rather for their belief in the party's truthfulness and general good character. Under such a system, it would be illogical to impeach one's own "oath-helper." Instead, the party was thought to "vouch" for the credibility of the witnesses the party called.[6] Another

---

1. In re San Miguel Gold Mining Co, 197 F. 126, 127 (W.D.Pa.1912) (party who called witness to institute bankruptcy proceeding vouched for the witness's credibility by putting him on the stand; therefore, he may not impeach his testimony); In re Calvi, 185 F. 642, 652 (N.D.N.Y.1911) ("when a party calls a witness, he represents him as worthy of credit, and cannot impeach him in any way"); 3A John H. Wigmore, Evidence in Trials at Common Law § 896 (James H. Chadbourn rev. 1970).

2. See 3A Wigmore, *supra* note 1 §§ 896–99.

3. Mitchell v. Swift & Co., 151 F.2d 770, 772 (5th Cir.1945) (plaintiff may not introduce ex parte statement of witness called by him solely because witness's testimony was not favorable to plaintiff's case); Arine v. United States, 10 F.2d 778, 780 (9th Cir.1926) (impeachment attempts by prosecutor improper in case where testimony is not harmful, but immaterial). See, e.g., State v. Perez, 594 N.E.2d 1041, 1045–46 (Ohio App. 1991) (trial court committed reversible error by declaring state's witness hostile and allowing impeachment by leading questions about prior inconsistent statement; Ohio R. Evid. R 607 allows impeach-

ment of own witness only on showing of "surprise and affirmative damage"; these elements are not shown in case at bar).

4. Bedell v. United States, 68 F.2d 776, 777 (D.C.Cir.1934) (prosecutor may impeach witness with prior written statement because he was genuinely surprised by witness's testimony, but prior statement may only be used for impeachment, not substantive purposes); Sullivan v. United States, 28 F.2d 147, 149 (9th Cir.1928) (held, in case where three convicts had signed a Joint statement implicating defendant, that failure of first witness to testify he saw defendant at robbery gave "fair warning" to government that other two convicts would very likely not testify against defendant; therefore government could not impeach latter two witnesses because it could not claim it was surprised by their statements).

5. See 27 Charles A. Wright & Victor J. Gold, Federal Practice and Procedure (Evidence) § 6092, at 489 (1990) ("The origins of the voucher rule are obscure").

6. Wigmore wrote that the voucher rule may have been based on "[t]he primitive notion, that a party is morally bound by the statements of his witnesses." 3A Wigmore, *supra* note 1 § 899.

prominent commentator believed this "voucher" rule probably did not arise from trial by compurgation, but rather was a consequence of the transition from inquisitorial to adversary systems of trial. Because under the inquisitorial system jurors decided the case based on their personal knowledge of the facts, there was simply no opportunity to call witnesses on one's own behalf. The author wrote, "Until there were witnesses in the modern sense, there could be no reason for the idea that a party was bound by his witness or that he could not impeach him."[7] The rationale that one vouches for one's witnesses ceased to have a sensible basis centuries ago, at least for occurrence witnesses as opposed to character and expert witnesses.[8] The common law litigant of modern times has had to take occurrence witnesses where they could be found, and had no control over the character and credibility of those who happened to have personal knowledge.

Another justification sometimes offered for the anti-impeachment rule is that allowing impeachment of one's own witness gave the proponent an opportunity for blackmail, because the proponent could put the witness on the stand under the threat of revealing dark secrets about the witness's past if the witness did not testify favorably to the proponent.[9] That might in a few cases be true, but it would pose an actual danger only in cases in which the proponent had character-smearing evidence that was not available to the opponent, because otherwise the witness would be subject to attack from either side. In any event, the theory does not explain why the anti-impeachment rule applied across the board, and not merely to prevent impeachment of a witness with evidence of the witness's bad character. Finally, the anti-impeachment rule may have served to prevent a proponent from calling an unfavorable witness solely for purposes of putting into evidence a prior inconsistent statement, in hopes that the jury would disregard instructions not to use the statement for the truth of what it asserts. This danger is real and worthy of consideration,[10] but it does not justify a broad rule prohibiting any impeachment of one's own witness.

Federal Rule of Evidence 607 provides, "The credibility of a witness may be attacked by any party, including the party calling the witness." These seventeen words abolish the hoary and troublesome common law rule. Primarily, abolition of the rule helps to secure the important goal of

---

7. Mason Ladd, *Impeachment of One's Own Witness—New Developments*, 4 U. Chi. L. Rev. 69, 72 (1936). For discussion of the Wigmore and Ladd views, *see* Don Johnsen, Note, *Impeachment With an Unsworn Prior Inconsistent Statement as Subterfuge*, 28 Wm. & Mary L. Rev. 295, 296 n.1 (1987).

8. Wigmore wrote that the "traditional notion of a witness, that of a person 'ex officio' a partisan pure and simple, persisted as a tradition long past the time when their function had ceased to be that of a

mere oath-taker and had become that of a testifier to facts." 3A Wigmore, *supra* note 1 § 896.

9. *See, e.g., id.* § 899.

10. *See, e.g.,* 1 Michael H. Graham, Handbook of Federal Evidence § 609.3, at 680–81 (4th ed. 1996); Randolph N. Jonakait, *The Supreme Court, Plain Meaning and the Changed Rules of Evidence*, 68 Tex. L. Rev. 745 (1990).

accurate factfinding by increasing the admissibility of relevant evidence, in this case, evidence concerning a witness's credibility.[11]

The new rule has caused little difficulty except in cases involving allegations that the proponent has called a witness *solely* to impeach the witness with evidence that is admissible only to impeach. The problem can be illustrated by the following hypothetical. Suppose a prosecutor wishes to put witness W on the stand to testify that he had been at D's house on January 19 and that D had shown W $100,000 in currency. W gave a police investigator a written statement about seeing the $100,000. Subsequently W recanted and now maintains that although present at D's house on the day in question, D did not show W any currency. Suppose the prosecutor knows to a certainty that the witness will testify that nothing happened at D's house—even that the defense counsel conducted a voir dire of the witness at this very trial and the witness testified that nothing happened at D's house. Nevertheless, the prosecutor seeks to put W on the stand before the jury. The prosecutor's aim is to have W testify that he saw no currency at D's house and to impeach W with W's prior statement to the investigator.

The prior statement to the investigator is not admissible for the truth of the matter asserted.[12] However, under a literal reading of Rule 607, one could argue that the prosecutor is permitted to impeach the prosecutor's own witness and that, when used only to impeach, the statement is not being offered to prove the truth of what it asserts.

What the prosecutor hopes, of course, is that the jury will disregard the instruction not to use the statement to prove the truth of what it asserts and that the jury will use the statement for exactly that purpose. Otherwise, there would be no reason to call the witness. The witness has no testimony that helps the prosecution, and merely showing an unhelpful witness to be a liar proves nothing.

In this type of situation, a number of courts have held that the prosecutor may not impeach its own witness.[13] To hold otherwise is to invite parties to call witnesses and offer evidence solely in hopes that the jurors will disregard the limiting instructions and use the evidence for an improper purpose.[14] As at common law, however, the party who

---

11. *See* 27 Wright & Gold, *supra* note 5 § 6092.

12. Had the statement been made under oath in a grand jury or other proceeding, it would have been admissible for the truth of what it asserts under Fed. R. Evid. 801(d)(2)(A). This statement, however, is admissible, if at all, only because it is not offered for the truth of what it asserts within the meaning of Fed. R. Evid. 801(c).

13. United States v. Hogan, 763 F.2d 697, 702 (5th Cir.1985), opinion withdrawn in part on other grounds, 771 F.2d 82 (5th Cir.1985) ("prosecution ... may not call a witness it knows to be hostile for the primary purpose of eliciting otherwise inad-

missible impeachment testimony, for such a scheme merely serves as a subterfuge to avoid the hearsay rule"); United States v. Crouch, 731 F.2d 621, 624 (9th Cir.1984) (improper for prosecution to call witness to testify in order to get her previous statement into evidence under the guise of impeachment, but not reversible error because defendant's guilt clearly demonstrated by admissible evidence).

14. United States v. Pollard, 38 M.J. 41, 50 (C.M.A. 1993) (held, trial court committed reversible error by allowing trial counsel to read, under guise of impeachment, the pretrial statements of 13–year-old alleged, sexual assault victim despite her

called the witness may still impeach if the witness's turnabout was a surprise.[15]

Although most cases involving the improper calling of a witness solely to impeach with otherwise inadmissible evidence involve prior inconsistent statements, not all arise in that context. In *United States v. Gomez–Gallardo*,[16] for example, defendant was charged with conspiracy to distribute cocaine. The government called as a witness one Gutierrez, who had previously pleaded guilty to participation in the conspiracy. Gutierrez testified that he had participated in one cocaine deal with another individual and that he knew defendant but had never participated in any drug transactions with him. He also testified that defendant was at the home of another alleged drug dealer, but only for innocent purposes. The government then called three witnesses to impeach Gutierrez by contradiction and by showing that he had a bad character. These witnesses contradicted Gutierrez by, among other things, describing other drug and illegal weapons transactions in which Gutierrez had participated, none of which involved defendant. In its closing argument, the government argued that there was no doubt of Gutierrez's guilt, and urged the jury to reject his testimony. The jury then found defendant guilty. On appeal, the court reversed. None of the contradiction evidence was properly admissible as substantive evidence of defendant's guilt, and the evidence suggesting Gutierrez's bad character was only admissible to impeach Gutierrez. Thus, the court held that "the government called Gutierrez for the primary purpose of impeaching Gutierrez's credibility to prove the substance of the charges against Gallardo."[17] This was impermissible.

subsequent recantation of those statements); Whitehurst v. Wright, 592 F.2d 834, 840 (5th Cir.1979) (proper for court to exclude use of witness's prior inconsistent statement for impeachment purposes when plaintiff knew witness would deny the facts asserted in previous statement during his testimony, because use of impeachment merely a ploy to "use hearsay evidence for substantive purposes").

There is some authority for the proposition that the judge should disregard the prosecutor's motive in deciding whether to exclude the evidence. *See* United States v. Logan, 121 F.3d 1172, 1175–76 (8th Cir. 1997) (government proffered prior inconsistent statements of government witness as impeachment evidence; court held that government's motive in calling witness was irrelevant, sole issue being whether evidence was prejudicial under Rule 403; here, where value of evidence for impeachment was minimal and danger of prejudice high, it was error to admit). In the authors' opinion, a test that completely disregards mo-

tive risks injustice, because the prosecution should be allowed to impeach an unexpected turncoat but not to impeach a witness called solely with the motive of offering otherwise inadmissible evidence. Consideration of motive has the beneficial effect of discouraging adversaries from offering unnecessary evidence in hopes of benefiting from prejudicial effect, while still safeguarding against the truth distortion that can occur when a party who is genuinely surprised by a change in testimony is deprived of the opportunity to put in the witness's inconsistent statements.

15. *See* United States v. Johnson, 977 F.2d 1360, 1381–82 (10th Cir.1992)(trial court may allow prosecutor to question federal marshal about prior, inconsistent statements made by government witness when prosecutor expected witness to testify that defendant fired on law enforcement officials with an automatic weapon, but witness testified he saw and recalled no weapons).

16. 915 F.2d 553 (9th Cir.1990).

17. *Id.* at 556.

§ 9.02   Methods of Impeachment—In General

A witness may be impeached in many different ways.[18] Among them are by a showing of bias or interest, by an attack on character for truthfulness, by contradiction through another witness, by a showing that the witness made a prior inconsistent statement, by showing defects in the witness's perception or ability to observe, or by showing a mental disease or defect of the witness.[19] Trial judges have leeway to regulate cross-examination on these subjects, and many allow fairly free-ranging cross-examination.[20] But when the impeacher is not satisfied with cross-examination of the witness being impeached, and wants also to bring in extrinsic evidence—evidence from a source other than the witness under attack—then the common law barred "collateral" evidence for certain categories of impeachment. It is to this set of rules about collateral evidence that we now turn.

In determining the propriety of offering any evidence to impeach a witness, it is crucial to identify not only that the evidence tends to impeach, but the precise *way or ways* by which it does so—the impeaching tools. This is because rules limiting certain forms of impeachment do not apply to all other forms. Thus, evidence that might be inadmissible if offered to impeach by one means might be admissible if offered to impeach on a different basis.

§ 9.03   Good Faith Cross–Examination of Witnesses

Trial courts have authority to prevent or curtail any impeachment or cross-examination that risks exposing the jury to potentially prejudicial innuendo. In particular, counsel conducting cross-examination is not permitted to conduct any inquiry in the absence of a good faith basis for the factual validity of any matters raised by the questions.[21] Though the

18. The authors of one treatise suggest five principal bases for attacking a witness's credibility: showing that the witness has made prior inconsistent statements, demonstrating the witness's bad character for truthfulness, showing that the witness is biased, contradicting the witness's testimony concerning a fact, and demonstrating the witness's impaired capacity to perceive, recall, or narrate facts. 27 Charles A. Wright & Victor J. Gold, Federal Practice and Procedure (Evidence) § 6094 (1990).

19. The credibility of a witness may also be attacked in other ways, such as by demonstrating the implausibility of the witness's story and by observing the demeanor of the witness while testifying. For a useful list of factors affecting the credibility of a witness, *see* Cal. Evid. Code § 780 (West 1966). These additional ways of attacking credibility are typically not subject to special evidentiary rules.

20. United States v. Phelps, 733 F.2d 1464, 1472 (11th Cir.1984) (trial court has discretion about scope and extent of cross-examination, and "presumption favors free ranging cross-examination on possible bias, motive, ability to perceive and remember, and general character for truthfulness").

21. *See* United States v. Sampol, 636 F.2d 621, 658 (D.C.Cir.1980) ("It is true, of course, that defense counsel need not proffer a factual foundation for all questions asked on cross-examination. A well reasoned suspicion that a circumstance is true is sufficient.... On the other hand, counsel must have a reasonable basis for asking questions on cross-examination which tend to incriminate or degrade the witness and thereby create an unfounded bias which subsequent testimony cannot fully dispel.... The general rule in such situations is that 'the questioner must be in possession of some facts which support a genuine belief that the witness committed the offense or the degrading act to which the questioning relates.'" Quoting United States v. Fowler, 465 F.2d 664, 666

application of this rule is highly situation-dependent, there are some guidelines. Counsel need not know the answer to every question before it is asked, nor need counsel demonstrate to the court a factual basis for every question asked of a witness. Courts have suggested that it is sufficient for counsel to possess a "well reasoned suspicion that a circumstance is true,"[22] that "although counsel may explore certain areas of inquiry in a criminal trial without full knowledge of the answer to anticipated questions, [counsel] must, when confronted with a demand for an offer of proof, provide some good faith basis for questioning that alleges adverse facts,"[23] and that when counsel will inquire about the witness's criminal or otherwise bad conduct, " 'the questioner must be in possession of some facts which support a genuine belief that the witness committed the offense or the degrading act to which the questioning relates.' "[24] Although these standards have special application in criminal cases (particularly in the government's cross-examination of defendant or defendant's witnesses), they also apply in civil cases. If it would be improper for the government to ask a criminal defendant's witness whether the witness was having an affair with the defendant in the absence of a good faith belief that the fact is true, it would be equally improper to ask the question of a party's witness in a civil case.

While the court must exercise control over improper cross-examination, the Supreme Court has made clear that trial courts must permit the parties to conduct probing cross-examination:

> Cross-examination is the principal means by which the believability of a witness and the truth of his testimony are tested. Subject always to the broad discretion of a trial judge to preclude repetitive and unduly harassing interrogation, the cross-examiner is not only permitted to delve into the witness' story to test the witness' perceptions and memory, but the cross-examiner has traditionally been allowed to impeach, i.e., discredit, the witness.[25]

The balance is therefore a delicate one. While courts may and indeed should curtail fishing expeditions that consume too much time and raise too great a danger of unfair prejudice, courts must also allow sufficient leeway for probing cross-examination of adverse or reluctant witnesses. The balance must be struck on a case-by-case basis, with the general standards as a guide.

§ 9.04   Impeachment by Contradiction

Impeachment by contradiction simply refers to impeachment by means of introducing contradictory testimony.[26] If witness X testifies

(D.C.Cir.1972).) *See also* United States v. Katsougrakis, 715 F.2d 769, 778–79 (2d Cir. 1983) ("Although counsel may explore certain areas of inquiry in a criminal trial without full knowledge of the answer to anticipated questions, he must, when confronted with a demand for an offer of proof, provide some good faith basis for questioning that alleges adverse facts").

22. United States v. Sampol, 636 F.2d 621, 658 (D.C.Cir.1980).

23. United States v. Katsougrakis, 715 F.2d 769, 779 (2d Cir.1983).

24. United States v. Lin, 101 F.3d 760, 768 (D.C.Cir.1996), quoting United States v. Fowler, 465 F.2d 664, 666 (D.C.Cir.1972).

25. Davis v. Alaska, 415 U.S. 308, 315 (1974).

26. See 27 Charles A. Wright & Victor J. Gold, Federal Practice and Procedure

that the light was red, and witness Y testifies that it was green, then witness X has been impeached by contradiction. This type of impeachment is to be distinguished from impeachment by prior inconsistent statement (self-contradiction). In one the witness is being attacked by contrary evidence about the underlying facts, in another the witness is being attacked by the witness's own prior inconsistent statement.

It has often been stated that a witness may not be impeached with collateral evidence that contradicts the witness through "extrinsic" evidence. An example of this type of forbidden impeachment is the evidence offered in *State v Oswalt*.[27] In *Oswalt*, the defendant was accused of robbing a house in Seattle. An alibi witness for the defendant testified that the defendant had been at the witness's restaurant in Portland on the day in question. On cross-examination, the witness also ventured that the defendant had been in the restaurant in Portland every day for a period of two months before the robbery. The prosecution then offered in evidence the testimony of a police officer that he had seen the defendant in Seattle on a date about a month before the robbery. One theory of admissibility was that this testimony impeached the alibi witness by contradiction. The alibi witness had testified that the defendant had been in a restaurant in Portland on that day; the police witness indirectly contradicted this testimony because it was unlikely that the defendant would be in the restaurant in Portland and also be in Seattle on the same day. The court held that the evidence should have been excluded at trial. In doing so, it endorsed an often-stated test: the contradicting evidence is inadmissible if it is "collateral." The court stated that the test for determining whether evidence is collateral is, "Could the fact, as to which error is predicated, have been shown in evidence for any purpose independently of the contradiction?"[28] Because the officer's testimony was only relevant to impeach the alibi witness by contradicting the witness's testimony about the defendant's whereabouts a month before the robbery, the evidence was collateral. And because the evidence was offered other than during cross-examination of the defendant's alibi witness, it was "extrinsic" evidence and thus inadmissible.[29]

(Evidence) § 6096, at 537 (1990) ("The credibility of a witness is attacked by contradiction when evidence is introduced suggesting that a fact to which the witness testified is not true").

27. 381 P.2d 617 (Wash.1963).

28. *Id*. at 619, quoting 3A John H. Wigmore, Evidence in Trials at Common Law § 1003 (James H. Chadbourn rev. 1970). This standard suggests a relevancy basis for determining whether evidence is "collateral." The principal is probably more complicated, however. *See* 27 Wright & Gold, *supra* note 26 § 6096, at 541–45 (sug-

gesting that the Wigmore test is underinclusive, encompassing only two of three types of non-collateral evidence that commentators have identified).

29. Of course, the trial judge retains the power to exclude the impeaching evidence even if offered during cross-examination. If, for example, the judge finds that the evidence is of infinitesimal probative value for impeachment purposes, and the time required to offer the evidence (even on cross-examination) would not justify its presentation, the judge may exclude it on Rule 403 grounds.

Examples

A witness shown by other evidence to have observed the accident in question testifies to seeing the accident while on the way home. Actually, the witness was on the way to a poker game. Extrinsic evidence that the witness lied when testifying to being on the way home is not admissible. The evidence has no relevance to the case except that of impeaching the witness by contradiction.

A witness for the plaintiff testifies to not having met the plaintiff before the litigation. Actually, the witness was involved in a business deal with the plaintiff. Extrinsic evidence of the prior relationship is admissible, because it not only impeaches the witness by contradiction; it also is relevant to the bias or interest of the witness. The business relationship between the plaintiff and the witness may bias the witness in the plaintiff's favor.

A witness for the plaintiff testifies to having been on the way home from a school meeting at the time of the accident. In fact, the witness had been drinking in a bar all night long. Extrinsic evidence of the drinking is admissible because it is relevant to the witness's perception, not merely to contradiction of the witness's testimony.

The second and third illustrations demonstrate why it is important to identify not only whether evidence is offered to impeach the witness, but the precise *means* by which it does so. In the second example, the testimony tends to impeach both by contradiction and by showing bias. Because bias impeachment is not limited in the same way as impeachment by contradiction,[30] the party is permitted to call the witness to offer the impeaching evidence. The same is true in the third illustration. While the evidence does tend to impeach by contradiction, it also impeaches by showing the possibility of impaired perception, a form of impeachment that is not limited by the collateral issue-extrinsic evidence rule.

The principal purpose of the rule prohibiting extrinsic evidence to impeach when the evidence concerns a collateral matter is to prevent confusion and waste of time.[31] It is wasteful to receive testimony on both sides about the collateral issue of whether the witness was going home or to a poker game, when the only relevance of the evidence would be on the question whether the witness gave inaccurate testimony about a matter irrelevant to the lawsuit. Showing an instance of an irrelevant matter has some probative value in demonstrating that a person is wrong about one fact and thus might be wrong about other, relevant facts, but it is not probative enough to justify the consumption of time with proof and counter-proof. The rule prohibiting extrinsic evidence of collateral matter is also supported by the danger that the jury may misuse the evidence when it involves information prejudicial to the

---

30. *See* § **9.10.**

31. *See* 27 Wright & Gold, *supra* note 26 § 6096, at 539 ("When the fact contradicted is not material, the trier of fact may become confused by the attention directed at an unimportant fact. As a result, the trier of fact may attach undue importance to extraneous matters").

witness or the party who called the witness.[32] This danger is particularly great when the witness is a party.

There is a question whether the rule against collateral impeachment has survived the adoption of the Federal Rules of Evidence, which make no explicit mention of the rule. The only provision of the Federal Rules that appears in any way related is Rule 608, but that rule on its face governs only impeachment of a witness by "character and conduct," not by contradicting the witness's testimony. Therefore, although Rule 608 does resemble the common law contradiction rules in that it contains limitations on the use of extrinsic evidence, it would be a mistake to assume without careful analysis that the subject of impeachment by contradiction is governed by that rule.

Some courts in Federal Rules jurisdictions have continued to follow the common-law collateral impeachment rule.[33] However, most other courts have held that the common-law rule is not embodied in Rule 608.[34] In addition, influential commentators[35] have maintained that a more flexible test should be used and that Federal Rule of Evidence 403 replaces the old rule.[36] The balancing test of Rule 403 makes no mention of any rule against collateral impeachment, nor do any of the other rules in the Federal Rules of Evidence. However, the traditional exclusion of

---

32. *See id.*

33. *See, e.g.,* United States v. Payne, 102 F.3d 289, 294 (7th Cir.1996) (evidence relevant only to impeach a witness's statement on cross-examination that his girlfriend did not know of his criminal activity inadmissible; collateral issue rule invoked); United States v. Edwards, 696 F.2d 1277, 1281 (11th Cir.1983) (extrinsic evidence that government witness was a drug dealer inadmissible to impeach by contradiction); United States v. Terebecki, 692 F.2d 1345, 1351 (11th Cir.1982) ("Since the statement did not concern a major issue in the case, impeachment would have been on a collateral issue and was properly excluded").

34. *See, e.g.,* United States v. Whiting, 28 F.3d 1296, 1301 (1st Cir.1994) (Rule 608(b) does not exclude evidence offered for non-character purpose); United States v. Fleming, 19 F.3d 1325, 1331 (10th Cir. 1994) (Rule 608(b) inapplicable when extrinsic evidence offered to show statement made by defendant on direct examination is untrue, even if statement concerns collateral issue); United States v. Chu, 5 F.3d 1244, 1249 (9th Cir.1993) (Rule 608(b) does not address whether extrinsic evidence is admissible to impeach by contradiction); Boutros v. Canton Regional Transit Authority, 997 F.2d 198, 205 (6th Cir.1993) (Rule 608(b) ban on extrinsic evidence not applicable to use of such evidence to contradict witness as to a material issue); Bufford v. Rowan Companies, Inc., 994 F.2d 155, 159–

60 (5th Cir.1993) (Rule 608(b) does not bar extrinsic evidence offered to contradict witness's testimony concerning material issue); United States v. Tarantino, 846 F.2d 1384, 1409 (D.C.Cir.1988) (Rule 608(b) inapplicable to impeachment by contradiction).

35. *See* 4 Weinstein's Federal Evidence § 609.06[3] (2d ed. Joseph M. McLaughlin ed. 1997).

36. *But see* 28 Charles A. Wright & Victor J. Gold, Federal Practice & Procedure (Evidence) § 6119 (1993). The authors recognize that the great weight of authority suggests that Rule 608 applies only to character impeachment evidence, and that this result is supported by the language of the rule, the Advisory Committee's Note, and United States v. Abel, 469 U.S. 45, 55–56 (1984), which held that the Rule 608(b) prohibition on extrinsic evidence does not apply to extrinsic evidence of bias. However, they note that impeachment by character and impeachment by contradiction are often "logically entwined," and that if a witness questioned about alleged misconduct probative of untruthfulness denies the misconduct, extrinsic evidence of the misconduct should not be admitted. The authors' reasoning is that if extrinsic evidence were admitted in this situation, Rule 608(b) would never keep the extrinsic evidence from the jury unless the witness admits the misconduct on cross-examination. This would defeat the purpose of Rule 608(b). *Id.*

collateral impeachment can be reconciled with the Federal Rules. The traditional rule can be regarded as just a rule of thumb that carries out the purposes of Rule 403 and is consistent with it. In other words, for ease of administration, one can argue that collateral evidence ought to be considered a waste of time, rather than inquiring in each case whether it is a waste of time. Exclusionary rules need not always be specifically stated in the Rules of Evidence so long as they are consistent with the general rules.[37]

An amendment to Federal Rule of Evidence 608(b), which took effect on December 1, 2003, partly resolves the question. The amendment replaces the word "credibility" with the phrase "character for truthfulness" in two places where the word appears. Most importantly for present purposes, the first sentence of Rule 608(b) now provides: "Specific instances of the conduct of the witness, for the purposes of attacking the witness's character for truthfulness, other than conviction of crime as provided in Rule 609, may not be proved by extrinsic evidence." The Advisory Committee explains that the purpose of the amendment is

> to clarify that the absolute prohibition on extrinsic evidence applies only when the sole reason for proffering that evidence is to attack or support the witness' character for truthfulness. . . . On occasion the Rule's use of the overbroad term "credibility" has been read "to bar extrinsic evidence for bias, competency and contradiction impeachment since they too deal with credibility." . . . The amendment conforms the language of the Rule to its original intent, which was to impose an absolute bar on extrinsic evidence only if the sole purpose for offering the evidence was to prove the witness' character for veracity. . . .

By limiting the application of the Rule to proof of a witness' character for truthfulness, the amendment leaves the admissibility of extrinsic evidence offered for other grounds of impeachment (such as contradiction, prior inconsistent statement, bias and mental capacity) to Rules 402 and 403.[38]

---

37. *See* **§ 6.07**. For example, rules against using hypnotically refreshed testimony have been endorsed in several jurisdictions, despite the lack of any specific provision against it. *See, e.g.,* State ex rel. Collins v. Superior Court, County of Maricopa, 644 P.2d 1266, 1294 (Ariz.1982) (hypnotically refreshed testimony is inadmissible, but witness may testify about facts recalled before hypnosis); People v. Gonzales, 329 N.W.2d 743, 748 (Mich.1982) (hypnotically refreshed testimony is "tainted" and must be excluded, but witness's prehypnotic statement may be retained with a deposition). The hypnotically refreshed testimony cases can be regarded as an elaboration either of Rule 403 or of the helpfulness requirement of Rule 702. Similarly, the collateral impeachment rule could be regarded as a useful elaboration of Rule 403. For a contrary view, see Edward J. Imwinkelreid, *Federal Rule of Evidence 402: The Second Revolution*, 6 Rev. of Litig. 129 (1987), arguing that "Rule 402 permits trial judges to exclude relevant evidence only on grounds recognized in the Constitution, by statute, or by court rule . . . Rule 402 impliedly abolishes all common-law evidentiary rules that have not been codified").

38. Advisory Committee's Note to proposed amendment to Fed. R. Evid. 608(b).

After the amendment, it is clear that the Federal Rules did not adopt the common law rule about impeachment by contradiction. At the same time, it is doubtful that the clarification will change the results of many cases. Most often, evidence that contradicts a witness concerning a collateral issue will be of only marginal value in denigrating the witness's credibility. That being true, it usually will not be worth the time to call another witness to provide the impeaching testimony. Thus, the court often should grant a Rule 403 motion to exclude the evidence. Of course, this will not always be true. If the case is very close, and will be decided largely on the basis of the jury's determination of the credibility of opposing witnesses, the court would be justified in permitting the opponent to call the impeaching witness.

§ 9.05   Impeachment by Prior Inconsistent Statement [FRE 613]

Witnesses are often impeached by showing that they made statements out of court that are inconsistent with their trial testimony. Showing that the witness said different things at different times throws doubt on credibility, whether the prior statements are believed or not.[39] Inconsistency as to one fact casts a shadow over the witness's reliability as to other facts.[40] Perhaps because of the popularity of this method of impeachment, a collage of rules have grown up around it. This section will deal with some of the common objections to attempts to impeach witnesses with prior inconsistent statements.

Objection—Prior Statement Is Consistent With Trial Testimony

Sometimes an objection to impeachment is based on the idea that what the witness said out of court is consistent with what the witness has asserted in the courtroom testimony. Suppose, for example, that the witness testifies in court that the witness has forgotten an event. A prior statement by the witness describes the event. Arguably, the two statements are consistent with each other. It is possible that the witness remembered the event soon after it occurred, but has now forgotten it.

In dealing with this sort of objection, the purpose of impeachment must be kept in mind. The cross-examiner is trying to throw doubt on credibility. The ultimate question is whether the prior statement actually throws light on the witness's believability. In this instance, it throws enough light to justify receiving it. It is true that the witness might have

---

39.   *See* 28 Charles A. Wright & Victor J. Gold, Federal Practice and Procedure (Evidence) § 6206, at 534 (1993) ("Evidence that a witness has told one story on the stand and a conflicting story at an earlier time suggests that the witness has lied or was mistaken when he made the prior statement or when he testified or both").

40.   The validity of this assumption has been challenged. *See id.* at 536 (challenging the assumption that evidence of a prior inconsistent statement carries much value for impeachment purposes, stating that "[i]t is simply not true to human nature to conclude that, because a person errs or even lies as to one matter, he is more likely to err or lie as to all other matters").

remembered before and forgotten now. It is also possible that the witness now remembers, and is not telling the truth. Which of these inferences is the correct one is a question for the jury to resolve. The test of admissibility is whether the statement really throws light on the witness's credibility, not whether it is inconsistent in some technical sense.[41]

A similar question arises when the witness testifies in detail about an event and adds testimony about a fact that the witness did not mention in the prior statement or report about the event. If the fact was one that would naturally have been mentioned in the report, then courts generally allow the report to be treated as a prior inconsistent statement.[42]

Objection—No Foundation for Extrinsic Evidence

Under the traditional common law rule, a foundation had to be laid with the witness being impeached before extrinsic evidence of the witness's prior inconsistent statement could be introduced. The impeaching attorney could freely ask the witness who made the statement about it without any foundation. But if the attorney wanted to bring in another witness to describe the statement—i.e., to use extrinsic evi-

---

41. United States v. Gajo, 290 F.3d 922 (7th Cir.2002) (when prosecution witness claims forgetfulness about facts that incriminate defendant, prosecution may present witness's prior grand jury testimony as substantive evidence under Rule 801(d)(1)(A); inconsistency does not mean logical incompatibility, but can consist of changes of position, silence, or evasive answers); United States v. Malik, 928 F.2d 17, 22–23 (1st Cir.1991) (not error to admit evidence of defendant's prior statements about heroin-smuggling after defendant's testimony, "We don't believe in heroin because we don't like it. And we don't do it"; contradiction need not be in "plain terms"); United States v. Stock, 948 F.2d 1299, 1300–01, (D.C.Cir.1991) (error, though harmless, to exclude evidence that officer's police, report omitted a statement allegedly made by defendant; police officer testified that defendant said "I don't have anything" as defendant pulled his hand out of dumpster in which drugs were later found); United States v. Causey, 834 F.2d 1277, 1283 (6th Cir.1987) (trial court did not abuse discretion in allowing prosecution to impeach witness with prior statement in case where witness testified she did not remember a conversation with her husband but had in fact called an FBI agent about the conversation previously); United States v. Jackson, 748 F.2d 1535 (11th Cir.1984) (defendant may be impeached with prior statement because testimony that he was supposed to receive football tickets and video

game passes was inconsistent with earlier statement that he did not know what was in the envelope he received, in case where defendant was charged with extortion involving approval of bank loans); United States v. Rogers, 549 F.2d 490, 496 (8th Cir.1976) ("A statement's inconsistency may be determined from the circumstances and is not limited to cases in which diametrically opposite assertions have been made. Thus inconsistencies may be found in changes in position; they may be implied through silence; and they may also be found in denial of recollection"). *Compare* United States v. Poindexter, 942 F.2d 354, 361 (6th Cir.1991) (testimony, in response to cross-examination questions, denying that drug use caused her to have memory loss, was not inconsistent with trial testimony that she was not using drugs; not error to exclude prior testimony); United States v. Devine, 934 F.2d 1325, 1344–45 (5th Cir.1991) (witness's prior conversation about defendant's role in conspiracy was not inconsistent with trial testimony that he could not remember conversation; not error to exclude prior statements).

42. *See, e.g.,* State v. Irving, 555 A.2d 575, 581 (N.J.1989) (held, in case where defendant testified his roommate was with him at the time of the alleged crime but did not name his roommate as a possible witness when he filed his original notice-of-alibi statement with the court, that the omission of his roommate's name was inconsistent with defendant's testimony).

dence—then a foundation had to be laid by giving the witness who made the statement the opportunity to explain or deny the statement on the witness stand. This was done by calling the witness's attention to the statement and the surrounding circumstance. A typical formulation of the requirement provided that "the [impeaching] statements must be related to him, with the circumstances of times, places, and persons present; and he shall be asked whether he has made such statements, and if so, allowed to explain them."[43]

The foundation requirement was designed to give the witness a fair chance to explain any circumstances, such as duress or influence, that might excuse the inconsistency; to reconcile the statements by explaining why they were not really inconsistent; or to deny having made the statement at all. The foundation requirement was also intended to require that the impeacher seek first to authenticate the inconsistent statement through the witness who made it. In many cases, this would obviate the need to call another witness to authenticate the statement.

The federal foundation requirement is more relaxed than its common law counterpart. Federal Rule of Evidence 613(b) provides that extrinsic evidence of a prior inconsistent statement is not admissible "unless the witness is afforded an opportunity to explain or deny the same and the opposite party is afforded an opportunity to interrogate the witness thereon, or the interests of justice otherwise require." This rule might at first glance seem to be the same as the common law requirement, but it is not. The advisory committee's note points out that the rule does not specify any particular time at which the witness must be given the opportunity to explain or deny. With this in mind, some courts have held that the rule is satisfied even if the witness is not asked about the prior statement on the stand, so long as the witness is still available.[44] The reasoning in support of this position is that the witness has the opportunity to explain or deny so long as the witness could be recalled for additional testimony. The federal liberalization has not been universally accepted, even by states that use the Federal Rules as a model.[45]

---

43. Coles v. Harsch, 276 P. 248, 250 (Or.1929) (quoting 1920 Or. Laws § 864).

44. Wammock v. Celotex Corp., 793 F.2d 1518, 1521–22 (11th Cir.1986) (Rule 613(b) does not require that witness be confronted with the inconsistent statement before extrinsic evidence is introduced, but the traditional method is still preferred especially if witness might be unavailable later); Theriot v. Bay Drilling Corp., 783 F.2d 527, 533 (5th Cir.1986) (Rule 613 only requires that a witness have the chance to deny or explain the inconsistent statement at some point in the proceedings, it does not require that the witness have that chance prior to the introduction of extrinsic evidence).

45. See, e.g., Alaska R. Evid. 613(b) ("before extrinsic evidence of a prior contradictory statement ... may be admitted, the examiner shall lay a foundation for impeachment by affording the witness an opportunity, while testifying, to explain or deny any prior statement"); Minn. R. Evid. 613(b) ("Extrinsic evidence of a prior inconsistent statement by a witness is not admissible unless the witness is afforded a prior opportunity to explain or deny the same"). See also State v. Martin, 964 S.W.2d 564, 568 (Tenn.1998) (though applying state rule identical to Fed. R. Evid. 613(b), court held that it was error, though harmless, to admit extrinsic evidence of prior inconsistent statement without requiring impeaching party to lay traditional foundation un-

The foundation requirement (whether under federal or common law) does not apply to statements of a party-opponent. These statements are admissible whether or not a foundation has been laid by asking the party-opponent about them.[46]

Objection—Document Should Be Shown to Witness Before Using It to Impeach

It is the fate of proceduralists to remember great cases for trivial rules. *Queen Caroline's Case* was known in its day as a spectacular contested divorce action in which George IV, King of England, accused his wife, Caroline, of adultery. The Queen resisted, and the case was dropped after a hearing in the House of Lords.[47]

The case is remembered today among evidence lecturers for the *Rule in the Queen's Case*, a rule about the foundation for prior inconsistent statements. Under that rule, announced by the Law Lords in response to a question from the House, a witness could not be cross-examined about a document written by the witness unless the document was first shown to the witness.[48]

The requirement that a document be shown to the witness first can sometimes be an impediment to cross-examination, especially when the cross-examiner is trying to destroy the witness rather than to get the witness to qualify unhelpful testimony. To illustrate how cross-examination could be hampered, suppose the theory of the cross-examiner is that the witness has taken an illicit payment. Cross-examination will be more effective if the cross-examiner conceals from the witness the fact that the cross-examiner has in hand a letter by the witness in which the witness describes receiving money from the person supposed to have given the illicit payment. If the witness denies ever having received money from that person, then the letter can be a bombshell. If the witness is allowed to view the letter first before being asked about transactions with the person, then the witness might come up with some relatively innocuous explanation, such as the explanation that the money was payment for legal services.[49] To prevent this blunting of cross-examination, the Feder-

---

der which witness being impeached is given prior opportunity to explain or deny statement).

46. *See* Fed. R. Evid. 613(b); 4 John H. Wigmore, Evidence in Trials at Common Law § 1051 (James H. Chadbourn rev. 1972).

47. Caroline had gone abroad after being excluded from court by her husband during his regency. When her husband ascended to the throne in 1820, she returned and claimed her rights as Queen. Her husband claimed that she had had an Italian lover while abroad. A bill was brought in the House of Lords seeking to deny the Queen all rights associated with her title and to grant the King a divorce, based on alleged adultery. After a hearing, the bill

was abandoned for lack of support even though it had passed by a slim margin on the third reading. Caroline lived out her few remaining days as titular Queen of England with an annuity of 50,000 pounds, though she never regained admission to court. For a vivid account of the facts of the case, see Richard H. Underwood, *Perjury: An Anthology*, 13 Ariz. J. Int'l & Comp. L. 307, 323–28 (1996). *See also* Encyclopedia Britannica 887 (1989).

48. The Queen's Case, 2 Br. & B. 284, 286–90, 129 Eng. Rep. 976, 11 Eng. R.C. 183 (1820); 4 Wigmore, *supra* note 46 §§ 1259–60.

49. Examples of crushing cross-examination in which the cross-examiner's knowledge was concealed from the witness

al Rules of Evidence abolish the Rule in the Queen's Case.[50] Rule 613(a) now provides that "when examining a witness concerning a prior statement made by the witness, whether written or not, the statement need not be shown nor its contents disclosed to the witness at that time, but on request the same shall be shown or disclosed to opposing counsel."

While the opportunity for devastating confrontation with a document that the witness has forgotten has been somewhat diminished in the modern era of discovery, the rule makers contemplated that it would sometimes arise, and that when it did, the witness's normal right under the rules of discovery to see the witness's own statement would be suspended temporarily until the end of cross-examination.[51]

Two things should be noted about Rule 613(a). First, when the cross-examiner is using a document that has not been placed in evidence, the rule expressly provides that the opposing counsel has the right to see the document. This rule is designed to prevent misquoting or misuse of the document. Second, if the cross-examiner purports to read from the document, some judges will require that it be shown to the witness despite the express language of Rule 613(a). This is arguably in the interest of fairness, since the cross-examiner may be distorting the document or reading it out of context. The witness might be able to prevent counsel from using the document in a misleading fashion. Were it not for Rule 613(a), there would be ample authority for this exercise of authority by the trial judge under the general power of Rule 611(a) to control the mode of interrogation of witnesses. Yet the plain language of 613(a) seems contrary to this exercise of authority.[52]

Objection—Collateral Impeachment

A prior inconsistent statement may not be proven with extrinsic evidence when the statement is being offered solely for collateral impeachment.[53] The impeachment is collateral when the statement is not independently relevant to some issue other than impeachment.[54]

---

are collected in 4 Wigmore, *supra* note 46 § 1260.

50. *See* 28 Wright & Gold, *supra* note 39 § 6202, at 506 (Federal Rule 613 "appears to abolish the requirement that the impeaching party reveal an inconsistent statement to the witness before proceeding with impeachment").

51. *See* Fed. R. Evid. 613(a) advisory committee's note.

52. The authors of one treatise argue that the policy justification for abandoning the common law rule is weak, and that in situations in which the justifications for the old rule are particularly strong, courts should have the power under Rule 611(a) to require the impeaching party to adhere to the common law rule by showing the statement to the witness before cross-examining the witness concerning it. 28 Wright & Gold, *supra* note 39 § 6203, at 510–11.

53. *Id.* § 6206, at 537 (noting a common law rule, generally followed by the federal courts, recognizing that when an inconsistency relates to a collateral matter, the inconsistency cannot be proven by extrinsic evidence. For a discussion of collateral impeachment in the context of impeachment by contradiction, *see* § **9.04**.

54. United States v. Roulette, 75 F.3d 418, 423 (8th Cir.1996) (endorsing independent relevance test and finding it satisfied under facts of case); United States v. Laughlin, 772 F.2d 1382, 1393–94 (7th Cir. 1985) (held, when witness testified her defendant-husband only used drugs if his friends brought drugs to his house, that extrinsic evidence that she previously told an FBI agent that her husband had a "source" for drugs was independently relevant, in case where defendant was charged

There is a distinction between collateral impeachment out of the witness's own mouth and collateral impeachment with extrinsic evidence. Trial judges have discretion to allow collateral impeachment by questioning of the witness being impeached. A collateral impeachment objection can still be made, but the trial judge has great leeway in deciding whether to sustain or overrule it. When collateral questioning is allowed, the questioner is bound by the witness's answer. The questioner may not bring in another witness to prove the making of the out-of-court statement. To do so would violate the rule against using extrinsic evidence for collateral impeachment.[55]

For example, suppose that in a sexual harassment case the witness denies that anything improper happened at the office picnic. On cross-examination the witness is questioned about the witness's prior inconsistent statements about (a) what food was served at the picnic and (b) whether the defendant tried to kiss the plaintiff. The trial judge would have discretion to allow cross-examination about both issues. The question about what food was served deals with a collateral matter of no importance, but so long as the cross-examiner is content merely to ask questions of the witness being impeached, not much time is wasted. The answers may reveal a confused or forgetful witness. However, if the witness denies making an inconsistent statement about what food was served, then the cross-examiner cannot bring in another witness (extrinsic evidence) to prove the making of the statement. That would be a waste of time. In contrast, if the prior inconsistent statement concerned something independently relevant—such as whether the defendant tried to kiss the plaintiff—then the extrinsic evidence would be admissible.

A prior inconsistent statement can be independently relevant because it goes to one of the substantive issues of the lawsuit, as in the example of the kiss at the picnic.[56] Or it can be independently relevant because it goes to bias (e.g., the witness denies making a prior statement that the witness was paid for testimony) or perception (the witness

---

55. *See, e.g.,* State v. Mangrum, 403 P.2d 925, 929 (Ariz.1965) (opponent could inquire on cross-examination about witness's alleged statement that witness had testified falsely in an unconnected case, but could not bring in extrinsic evidence about the alleged statement); 3A Wigmore, *supra* note 52 §§ 1020–23. *See also* United States v. Grooms, 978 F.2d 425, 428–29 (8th Cir. 1992) (in prosecution for child sex abuse, victims' mother denied stating that the victims' father coached their testimony; held, defendant may not call witness to testify that mother made the statement because issue was collateral; in authors' opinion, court's conclusion is questionable because the prior statement was relevant not only to the mother's credibility but also to bias of the child, witness).

with possession of cocaine with intent to distribute); United States v. Nace, 561 F.2d 763, 771 (9th Cir.1977) (held, in case where witness testified that he did not owe defendant any money but had listed the loan as a liability in his bankruptcy petition, that defendant could not impeach witness with his bankruptcy petition statement because the issue was whether defendant used extortion to get repayment of the alleged loan, not whether the witness had in fact borrowed money from the defendant); *cf.* United States v. Nazarenus, 983 F.2d 1480, 1485 (8th Cir.1993) (improper to impeach defendant, who told police officer who stopped him on night of alleged sex crime that he had sped only to test car's alignment, with evidence that he frequently drove fast); *see also* 3A John H. Wigmore, Evidence in Trials at Common Law § 1020 (James H. Chadbourn rev. 1970).

56. 3A Wigmore, *supra* note 54 § 1021.

denies having made a prior statement saying that the witness was drunk at the picnic).[57]

The requirement of independent relevance flirts with forbidden use of the inconsistent statement. The inconsistent statement is not admissible for the truth of the matter asserted.[58] To allow extrinsic evidence of a statement only when it is independently relevant is to say that such statements are more valuable than statements that go only to impeachment. The proposition that the statement is more valuable when relevant to something other than impeachment seems to rest on the assumption that the jury will in fact use it for something other than impeachment, i.e., for the truth of what it asserts—a forbidden use. On the other hand, perhaps the honest witness will be more careful to be truthful and accurate about an issue the witness knows to be important. If so, impeachment on a peripheral issue, such as whether steak or chicken was served at lunch, does not reveal as much about the witness's veracity as impeachment about an issue known to the witness to be central to the truth-finding process. By this reasoning one can observe the ban on using the statement for its truth while still retaining the independent relevance requirement.

The rule requiring independent relevance was arguably abolished by the Federal Rules of Evidence, which do not expressly require that inconsistent statements be independently relevant before they can be proven with extrinsic evidence. However, the requirement can be viewed as a useful rule of thumb that implements the general injunction in Rule 403 against wasting time. In any event, whether the rule is accepted in its particularized common law form or whether the exclusion of extrinsic evidence is viewed as a matter for the discretion of the trial judge, the result from fair-minded judges is likely to be the same: collateral impeachment by extrinsic proof of a prior inconsistent statement is not permissible.

§ 9.06 Showing Untruthful Character of Witness [FRE 608]

A witness may be impeached by showing that the witness has a bad character for truthfulness. This evidence comes in under an exception to the general rule prohibiting the use of character evidence to prove conduct.[59]

The impeachment may take one of three forms. First, the impeaching party can attack by offering generalities about character. It can do so by presenting testimony that the target witness has a bad reputation for truth or veracity. Under the Federal Rules of Evidence, it is also permissible to show that in the opinion of the impeaching witness the target witness has a bad character for truthfulness. Second, subject to

57. *Id.* § 1022.

58. This example assumes that the statement is admissible only to impeach. If the statement was made under oath at a proceeding, then the statement would be admissible without limit under Rule 801(d)(1)(A).

59. *See* § **5.05**.

the court's approval, the impeaching party may cross-examine the witness regarding specific misconduct of the witness that did not result in conviction and that reflects on truthfulness. Finally, the impeaching party may offer evidence of a prior criminal conviction of the witness, to show that the witness is untruthful.

Each of these methods of character attack is subject to fairly strict limits. It is worth noting at the outset, then, that the limits are only applicable when the attack is on the witness's character. If the witness is being impeached by some other method, such as a showing of bias or defects in perception or of mental health, then the attack is not an attack on character and the limits do not apply.[60] This is true even if the other evidence may reflect poorly on character, as would be the case if the evidence consisted of testimony that the witness took a bribe to testify falsely in the case. So long as the trier is being asked to follow a narrower inferential path than the path from testimony to general disposition to acts, the evidence is not character evidence and the restrictions on character evidence do not apply.

§ 9.07   Showing Untruthful Character of Witness [FRE 608]—Impeachment of Truthfulness of the Witness by Reputation and Opinion Testimony as to Character [FRE 608(a)]

The opponent of a witness may impeach the witness by calling another witness who testifies to reputation or, in jurisdictions following the Federal Rules of Evidence, opinion as to character.[61] The testimony must be restricted to the character trait of truthfulness. As with other reputation and opinion testimony, the testimony is supposed to be extremely general in form. An example of a minimalist examination of such a witness follows:

Q. Do you know Mr. X, the witness?

A. Yes.

Q. Do you know other persons in the community who know Mr. X?

A. Yes.

Q. Have you had occasion to hear Mr. X's reputation for truth and veracity discussed among those persons?

A. Yes, many times.

Q. Do you know Mr. X's reputation for truth and veracity?

A. Yes.

---

60. United States v. Abel, 469 U.S. 45, 49 (1984) (held, in case where witness and defendant were in a prison gang that required its members to commit perjury to help another gang member, that witness's membership in defendant's gang was probative of bias and admissible despite tendency of evidence to also show witness was a liar.

61. *See* Fed. R. Evid. 608(a). *See also* State v. Lewis, 847 P.2d 690, 690–94 (Kan. 1993) (in prosecution for attempted rape, reversible error for trial court to exclude four witnesses' testimony about victim's reputation for lack of veracity).

Q. What is that reputation?

A. It is very bad. He has the reputation of being a terrible liar.

Tradition allows the direct-examiner to add the following question:

Q. Based on that reputation, would you believe Mr. X when he testified under oath?[62]

A. No.

Note that although the reputation could come in, the specific acts of lying upon which it was based could not.

The Federal Rules go further, and permit the witness to be questioned about opinion, as well as about reputation. The stated reason for this addition is that much reputation testimony is actually opinion testimony in disguise, and that at any rate in a modern atomistic society a person who knows character may not know reputation for character.

The reception of opinion testimony leads to a danger of attempting to put testimony of specific acts in through the back door, by putting in facts about the witness's connection with the subject of the impeachment that will allow the jury to infer specific acts of dishonesty. Consider the following hypothetical examination:

Q. Do you know Mr. X?

A. Yes.

Q. How do you know him?

A. We work for the same company.

Q. What is your position with that company?

A. I am the comptroller.

Q. Do your duties as comptroller include the review of expense accounts?

A. Yes.

Q. Have you reviewed Mr. X's expense account?

A. Yes.

Q. Do you have an opinion about Mr. X's character for truthfulness?

A. Yes.

Q. What is that opinion?

A. He is extremely untruthful.

---

62. This is technically opinion and not reputation evidence. In theory, it would not be admissible at common law, where only reputation testimony was permitted. But custom sanctioned its reception even at common law. *See* 7 John H. Wigmore, Evidence in Trials at Common Law § 1982 (James H. Chadbourn rev. 1978). The Federal Rules do permit opinion testimony, though a technical objection could be made to the question in text on grounds that there is insufficient foundation to show a basis for a personal opinion of character. It is not clear how long or how well the testifying witness has known the witness whose character is being attacked.

The examination just described is a borderline case of putting in specific instances of conduct by extrinsic evidence, a form of impeachment prohibited by the Federal Rules and common law.[63] The examination carries with it the strong implication that the testifying witness examined Mr. X's expense account and found that it contained falsehoods. The examiner's conduct warrants an objection or, if foreseeable, a motion in limine.[64]

Another possible danger of abuse is testimony by police agents about the character of investigative targets. For example, in *United States v. Dotson*[65] the government called an FBI agent to the stand and elicited the following testimony:

Q. Have you had occasion to conduct an investigation into the activities of the defendant, Fred Dotson, and his associates?

A. Yes, sir, I have.

Q. As a result of this investigation and what you have learned and all that you have seen in this case, have you formed an opinion as to the truthfulness of the defendant, Frederick Leon Dotson?

A. Yes, sir, I have.

Q. Is that opinion of his truthfulness good or bad.

A. Bad.

Q. Would you believe Frederick Leon Dotson under oath?

A. No, sir, I would not.

The court held that the evidence should have been excluded. Its decision, however, was a limited one. It did not hold that government agents could not testify to an opinion about the character of defendant-witnesses that was formed during an investigation. It merely held that the foundation was insufficient in the case before it, because the agent had not described anything more than minimal contact with the defendants.[66]

---

63. Fed. R. Evid. 608(b); United States v. Perez–Perez, 72 F.3d 224, 227 (1st Cir., 1995) (held, complaints by other police officers about the witness's misconduct were properly excluded under rule 608(b); while certain prior good or bad acts of a witness may constitute character evidence bearing on veracity, they are not evidence of enough force to justify the detour of extrinsic proof). For the common law rule, see 3A John H. Wigmore, Evidence in Trials at Common Law § 979 (James H. Chadbourn rev. 1970), on how one cannot put in extrinsic evidence of bad acts not resulting in conviction.

64. For a case in which such testimony was approved, see United States v. Dotson, 799 F.2d 189, 193 (5th Cir.1986) (IRS agent's opinion about lack of financial truthfulness of witness, based on interviews, examination of tax returns, and study of witness's testimony before grand jury, noted approvingly in dictum as example of character opinion based on proper and sufficient foundation); *see also* People v. Bieri, 396 N.W.2d 506, 513 (Mich.App. 1986) (prison guard may testify about witness's reputation for untruthfulness because he had known the witness for five months and had discussed witness's reputation with other correctional officers).

65. 799 F.2d 189, 191 (5th Cir.1986).

66. *See also* United States v. Cortez, 935 F.2d 135, 139–40 (8th Cir.1991) (error, though harmless, to admit testimony of two law enforcement officers who spent less than one day each interviewing defendant about his conversations with a third person and who spoke only of their belief in a particular story rather than of defendant's general character for truthfulness); United States v. Williams, 822 F.2d 512, 516 (5th Cir.1987) (prosecution laid adequate foun-

Because of the potential dangers of character-based impeachment, the trial court has discretion to forbid or limit such impeachment.[67] The trial court may exclude such evidence when it finds that its value for impeachment purposes is substantially outweighed by any of the dangers listed in Rule 403, and the court may also place limits on the number of witnesses who may be called to attack the character of a witness. Where their testimony would all be the same, even a limit to one attacking witness has been upheld as a reasonable exercise of discretion to limit, pursuant to the authority granted by Rule 403, the introduction of cumulative evidence.[68]

§ 9.08 Showing Untruthful Character of Witness [FRE 608]—Impeachment of Truthfulness of the Witness with Evidence of Conduct That Did Not Lead to Conviction [FRE 608(b)]

The trial judge has discretion to permit a witness to be questioned about conduct that has not resulted in conviction, for purposes of supporting or attacking the truthfulness of the witness. The conduct must relate to truthfulness, not to some other character trait.[69] Thus, a witness may be questioned about the witness's dishonesty in falsifying an academic record on an employment application, but not about sexual misconduct.[70]

dation for opinion testimony by government agents about witness's character for truthfulness by showing both had learned about the witness through surveillance and by interviewing his acquaintances [note: court used the plain error standard to review the issue because defendant did not make proper objection during his trial]).

67. Rule 608 itself states only that such evidence "may" be admitted. *See* 27 Charles A. Wright & Victor J. Gold, Federal Practice and Procedure (Evidence) § 6114, at 51–52 (1990).

68. *See* United States v. Haynes, 554 F.2d 231 (5th Cir.1977).

69. *See* 28 Charles A. Wright & Victor J. Gold, Federal Practice and Procedure (Evidence) § 6115 (1993) (discussing the meaning of the phrase "character for truthfulness or untruthfulness" in Rule 608(a)); *id.* § 6118, at 102–09 (discussing meaning of phrase "if probative of truthfulness or untruthfulness" in Rule 608(b)).

70. United States v. McMillon, 14 F.3d 948, 955–56 (4th Cir.1994) (held, in conspiracy prosecution, defendant not entitled to cross-examine government's witness regarding witness's prior homosexual activities). *See also* United States v. Parker, 133 F.3d 322, 326–27 (5th Cir.1998) (held, not abuse of discretion to deny cross-examination of government witness in bribery case

about witness's alleged murder of witness's husband because acts of violence do not reflect on character for truthfulness); Ad-Vantage Tel. Directory Consultants, Inc. v. GTE Directories Corp., 37 F.3d 1460, 1464 (11th Cir.1994) (held, error to allow party's expert witness, a CPA and former lawyer, to be impeached. by cross-examination about his bankruptcy and his failure to pay debts; "seeking discharge in bankruptcy does not show a disregard for truth that would cast doubt on a witness' veracity"; remarkably, the court held it was also error to allow same witness to be cross-examined about forgery accusation that led to witness's resignation from the bar); Wood v. Alaska, 957 F.2d 1544 1550–51 (9th Cir. 1992) (evidence that alleged victim had modeled for pornographic magazines and movies was not admissible to impeach credibility in rape case); United States v. Blake, 941 F.2d 334, 339–41 (5th Cir.1991) (error, though harmless, to impeach narcotics defendant with questions about whether he had ever killed anyone and whether he had told police officer that he had killed 10 people); Mason v. Texaco, Inc., 948 F.2d 1546, 1555–56 (10th Cir.1991) (held, district court was within discretion in ruling that plaintiff's expert witnesses could not be cross-examined about allegedly biased study they prepared on subject unrelated to the instant suit; court states that such im-

If the witness denies the misconduct, then the cross-examiner must "take the answer."[71] This does not mean that the cross-examiner is prohibited from further efforts to get the witness to admit the misconduct,[72] but it does mean that extrinsic evidence of the misconduct is not admissible.[73] The main purpose of this ban on extrinsic evidence is to prevent the waste of time and confusion that would occur if mini-trials

peachment is barred on ground, among others, that the cross-examination would not have challenged character for truthfulness but merely objectivity on a particular study; in authors' opinion, court is in error in stating that evidence did not reflect on character, though its overall ruling that exclusion was within the district court's discretion is supportable); Wanke v. Lynn's Transp. Co., 836 F.Supp. 587, 597 (N.D.Ind. 1993) (in wrong full death action against trucking company, evidence of truck driver's prior arrests for disorderly conduct held, on motion in limine, not admissible under Rule 608(b) because not probative of veracity; evidence of alleged theft by truck driver also not admissible to impeach his testimony as witness, subject to reconsideration at trial should proponent be able to demonstrate that the conduct involved deception or "otherwise demonstrates lack of veracity"; fact that truck driver gave testimony at deposition, later corrected in deposition errata sheet, that he had no other arrests did not render evidence of arrest on theft charge admissible); Unmack v. Deaconess Medical Center, 967 P.2d 783, 785–86 (Mont.1998) (held, reversible error to allow impeachment of expert medical witness who was also a lawyer with evidence of improper solicitation of clients; bar discipline was not based on imputation of dishonesty); People v. Chaplin, 313 N.W.2d 899, 902 (Mich.1981) (reversible error to permit cross-examination suggesting witness was prostitute and defendant may have been her pimp); Heshelman v. Lombardi, 454 N.W.2d 603 (Mich.App.1990) (error to allow cross-examination of doctor about prior malpractice action).

For examples of cross-examination deemed permissible on grounds that it did not go to character for truthfulness, *see* Vichare v. AMBAC Inc. 106 F.3d 457, 468 (2d Cir.1996) (held, employment discrimination plaintiff could be impeached under Rule 608(b) by cross-examination about taking kickbacks; after-acquired evidence of misconduct can be used to impeach even though it does not automatically bar substantive recovery by providing grounds for discharge); United States v. Waldrip, .981

F.2d 799, 802–03 (5th Cir.1993) (under Rule 608(a), permissible for government to cross-exam defendant about incident in which defendant signed another's name to document without authorization, even though incident resembled crime charged). *Cf.* United States v. Smith, 80 F.3d 1188, 1193 (7th Cir.1996), where court held, in a case in which defendant was charged with cargo theft, that it was not plain error to allow him to be cross-examined about uncharged cargo thefts for purposes of impeachment under Rule 608(b), remarking that "[p]rior acts of theft or receipt of stolen property are, like acts of fraud or deceit, probative of a witness's truthfulness or untruthfulness under Rule 608(b)." The authors question whether any jury could be expected to use the fruits of such a cross-examination solely for the permitted purpose of impeaching credibility while ignoring its natural probative force in showing propensity to commit cargo theft.

71. *See, e.g.,* United States v. Perez–Perez, 72 F.3d 224, 227 (1st Cir.1995) (held, complaints by other police officers about the witness's misconduct were properly excluded under Rule 608(b); "while certain prior good or bad acts of a witness may constitute character evidence bearing on veracity, they are not evidence of enough force to justify the detour of extrinsic proof"); Lambert v. Commonwealth, 383 S.E.2d 752, 754 (Va.App.1989).

72. As one treatise states:

Courts often summarize the no-extrinsic-evidence rule by stating that "the examiner must take his or her answer." This phrase ... is misleading if it is taken to suggest that the cross-examiner cannot continue pressing for an admission—a procedure authorized by the second sentence of Rule 608(b).

4 Weinstein's Federal Evidence § 608.12[3], at 608–28 to 608–30 (2d ed. Joseph M. McLaughlin ed. 1997) (footnotes omitted).

73. Fed. R. Evid. 608(b) (forbidding use of extrinsic evidence).

were held about blemishes in each witness's past.[74] Confusion of issues and unfair surprise also underlie the rule.[75]

What constitutes extrinsic evidence? As the language of the rule itself makes clear, testimony from the mouth of the witness during cross-examination is not "extrinsic."[76] Just as clearly, testimony of another witness would be extrinsic.[77] Also, the rule would forbid the use of documents to impeach when it is necessary to call another witness to authenticate those documents.[78] Therefore, if on cross-examination, counsel asks the witness to admit that she once lied about her age in an effort to enter an adults-only bar, in its discretion the court could allow this question because it concerns conduct reflecting on the witness's truthfulness. If the witness refuses to admit that the event occurred, the opponent would not be permitted to call a friend to testify that she was with the witness when this event occurred, nor would the opponent be permitted to call an employee of the bar to authenticate a document reporting on the incident.

Suppose, however, that during cross-examination, the witness admits engaging in the conduct also evidenced by the document, or simply admits the authenticity of the document reporting the conduct? Would introduction of the document still violate the extrinsic evidence rule? The courts are divided on this question. Some courts hold that the document still constitutes extrinsic evidence.[79] Others, however, hold that the extrinsic evidence rule would not be violated by its admission.[80]

---

74. *See* United States v. Martz, 964 F.2d 787, 789 (8th Cir.1992) (the reason for barring extrinsic evidence "is to avoid holding mini-trials on peripherally related or irrelevant matters").

75. *See* Frederick C. Moss, *The Sweeping–Claims Exception and the Federal Rules of Evidence*, 1982 Duke L.J. 61, 70 ("The policy reasons for excluding extrinsic evidence are the avoidance of undue prolongation of the trial, confusion of the issues, and unfair surprise to the witness").

76. "Specific instances of the conduct of a witness, for the purpose of attacking or supporting the witness' credibility, . . . may, . . . in the discretion of the court, if probative of truthfulness or untruthfulness, be inquired into on cross-examination. . . ."

77. *See* United States v. McNeill, 887 F.2d 448, 453 (3d Cir.1989) ("Extrinsic evidence is evidence offered through other witnesses, rather than through cross-examination of the witness himself or herself"); Russell J. Davis, Annotation, *Construction and Application of Rule 608(b) of Federal Rules of Evidence, Dealing With Use of Specific Instances of Conduct to Attack or Support Credibility*, 36 A.L.R. Fed. 564, at §§ 3–6 (1978) (reviewing cases); 28 Wright & Gold, *supra* note 69 § 6117, at 88 (language of Rule 608(b) "invites the inference that the testimony of any other witness does constitute extrinsic evidence"). Wig-

more found this limitation to be entirely consistent with the underlying purposes of the rule forbidding extrinsic evidence. 3A John H. Wigmore, Evidence in Trials at Common Law § 979, at 826 (James H. Chadbourn rev. 1970).

78. *See* United States v. Lashmett, 965 F.2d 179, 181–82 (7th Cir.1992) (court filings in related civil action inadmissible under Rule 613, which contains same extrinsic evidence limitation); United States v. Peterson, 808 F.2d 969, 972–74 (2d Cir.1987) (where witness denied forging endorsement on check, party could not introduce check); Davis Annotation, *supra* note 77 §§ 7–10 (reviewing cases). *Cf.* United States v. Elliott, 89 F.3d 1360 (8th Cir.1996) (trial court did not err when it refused to allow defendant to use documentary exhibits during cross-examination of government witness in an effort to impeach witness by showing that she misrepresented her educational and work experience on her resume; though court based decision on Rule 608(b), defendant also appeared to have offered evidence substantively to prove a defense, for which purpose Rule 608(b) would not have applied).

79. *See, e.g.*, United States v. Whitehead, 618 F.2d 523, 529 (4th Cir.1980) (refusing to admit document even if the witness admits engaging in the conduct).

80. *See, e.g.*, Carter v. Hewitt, 617 F.2d 961, 969–70 (3d Cir.1980) (extrinsic evidence rule not violated when, during cross-

These latter courts appear to have the better argument. As one court stated, "[w]hen ... the extrinsic evidence is obtained from and through examination of the very witness whose credibility is under attack, ... [Rule 608(b)'s] core concerns are not implicated."[81] Because no other witness is involved, no extra time is spent inquiring into the credibility of yet another person.[82] The jury is less likely to be confused, and the witness is unlikely to be surprised by the document.[83]

Even if the witness denies the conduct or the authenticity of the document, the extrinsic evidence rule does not bar the attorney from using the document solely to attempt to refresh the witness's recollection.[84] Under those circumstances, any testimony still comes from the mouth of the witness; the document is not offered as evidence.[85]

---

examination of a witness, a letter that the witness admittedly had written and which evidenced his character for truthfulness was admitted into evidence). For a strict approach to the definition of extrinsic evidence, *see* United States v. Elliott, 89 F.3d 1360, 1368 (8th Cir.1996) (upholding trial court's decision to bar use of witness's allegedly false resume to attack her credibility on cross-examination; exact nature of attempted use unclear from opinion).

81. *Id.* at 970.

82. Of course, even asking additional questions of a witness consumes a small amount of time, and where the witness has actually admitted the conduct, the court may well exclude the document as cumulative and a waste of time. 28 Wright & Gold, *supra* note 69 § 6117, at 90. *See also* Carter v. Hewitt, 617 F.2d 961, 970–71 (3d Cir. 1980) (noting that where witness admits conduct, court may exclude evidence under Rule 403 as cumulative).

83. Most commentators have approved of the practice of allowing the use of a document on cross-examination where the witness admits the conduct or the authenticity of the document. As the authors of one treatise state:

> Where a witness admits to specific instances of conduct, admission of documentary evidence of the same instances cannot be unfair harassment in the sense described by Wigmore. The witness cannot complain of the unfairness of having to disprove conduct to which he admits. Similarly, because the witness so admits, there will be no confusion or delay generated by a protracted exchange of conflicting evidence pertinent to that conduct.

28 Wright & Gold, *supra* note 69 § 6117, at 90. *See also* Moss, *supra* note 75, at 70 (noting that in the context of the common-law rule governing impeachment by contradiction, which also contains an extrinsic evidence limitation, "[n]one of [the] policies [underlying the extrinsic evidence rule] is necessarily violated when a witness is confronted with nontestimonial evidence on cross-examination. If he is confronted with a document and admits its authenticity, the contradiction is completed, swiftly and clearly"). *But see* 3 Christopher B. Mueller and Laird C. Kirkpatrick, Federal Evidence § 267, at 183 (2d ed. 1994). The authors state that allowing the use of documents relating to or describing the conduct of witness violates the extrinsic evidence rule and can constitute reversible error in some cases. "Letting the attacking party offer documents is likely to sidetrack proceedings and invite further examination and explanation." However, where the witness has made a dishonest oral or written statement, the authors would approve the use of the document while questioning the witness. "Referring to the substance of the statement during questioning, and even making it obvious that the questioner has a writing that embodies the statement (or could produce a witness who heard it) should not run afoul of the restriction." *Id.* at 183–84.

Whether the reasoning described above approving the use of documents during cross-examination would support the use of self-authenticating documents in the face of the witness's refusal to admit the conduct or authenticate the document is not clear. Time is not of particular concern, as no additional witnesses need be called. However, issues of harassment and surprise might be implicated in some circumstances, counseling against admission.

84. *See* United States v. Chevalier, 1 F.3d 581, 584 n. 1 (7th Cir.1993) (in effort to convince defendant-witness to admit bank fraud, court properly allowed prosecution to use loan document to refresh recollection concerning statement defendant had made).

85. *See* § **7.15.**

Where the situation involves impeachment of a hearsay declarant under Rule 806,[86] it is not practicable to apply the precise limitations of Rule 608(b). If the declarant does not testify, there is no opportunity to cross-examine and it is necessary to call another witness or use other means to offer the impeaching evidence. If the declarant is available, the opponent presumably can call the declarant to the stand. The impeachment would then occur on direct examination rather than cross-examination, though without extrinsic evidence.[87]

One approach to avoiding the impact of the extrinsic evidence rule as applied to documents is to send the inculpating documentation to the witness and counsel before trial. While this will tip off the witness about the nature of the expected cross-examination, it will put the witness on notice before trial, so that the witness may feel obliged to tell the truth.[88]

The prohibition of extrinsic evidence applies only to extrinsic evidence that relates to the character of a witness.[89] Extrinsic evidence that impeaches the witness by showing bias is admissible.[90] Similarly, evidence that a witness engaged in a distinctively similar type of lying on different occasions may be received. It is admissible not as character evidence to impeach the witness, but as non-character evidence of a common scheme or plan. Thus, evidence that a witness has made prior false accusations of the same crime in the same circumstances is admissible.[91] Of course, if the evidence of a witness's bad acts tends indepen-

---

86. *See* § **7.62**.

87. Rule 806 appears to accommodate this reasoning. *See* Fed. R. Evid. 806 advisory committee's note; United States v. Friedman, 854 F.2d 535, 570 n. 8 (2d Cir.1988).

88. *See* B. House, Great Trials of Famous Lawyers 180–81 (1962) (describing counsel's preparation for cross-examination of witness who was a member of Congress; counsel sent witness letter asking witness to refresh memory on subjects so that witness would not claim to have forgotten facts surrounding prior falsifications).

89. An amendment to Fed. R. Evid. 608(b), which went effect on December 1, 2003, clarifies the rule by adding explicit language stating that its prohibition on the use of extrinsic evidence of specific instances of conduct applies to evidence offered to attack or support "character for truthfulness," not to all evidence offered to attack or support credibility. For discussion of this proposal, *see supra* § **9.04**.

90. *See* United States v. Abel, 469 U.S. 45 (1984) (extrinsic evidence that witness belonged to secret prison organization whose tenets required members to commit perjury, theft, and murder on each other's behalf admissible to show that witness was

biased in favor of another member of the organization). This result is consistent with the common law, though one must place a gloss on Rule 608(a) in order to reach it. The Rule provides that "specific instances of the conduct of a witness, for the purpose of attacking or supporting the witness' credibility, other than conviction of crime as provided in rule 609, may not be proven by extrinsic evidence." The rule should be read, after *Abel*, to refer only to attacking or supporting the witness's credibility with character evidence, not with other evidence. The Uniform Rules, *see* Unif. R. Evid. 616 (1986), were amended in 1986 to make explicit that extrinsic evidence attacking credibility with evidence of bias, prejudice, or interest is admissible. For an example of state adoption of this rule, *see* Minn. R. Evid. 616 (as amended Jan. 1, 1990).

91. *See* Fed. R. Evid. 404(b); United States v. Stamper, 766 F.Supp. 1396 (W.D.N.C.1991), *aff'd, In re* One Female Juvenile Victim, 959 F.2d 231 (4th Cir. 1992) (complainant's previous allegedly allegations of sexual abuse by, three other men admissible to motive of manipulating complainant's custodians) (table); People v. Mikula, 269 N.W.2d 195, 199 (Mich.App. 1978) defendant can prove by extrinsic evi-

dently to support a claim or defense regardless of whether it impeaches the witness, then the evidence is admissible.[92] This would be the case, for example, when the witness's prior acts included concealing from the defendant criminal activity of the type that the defendant is now alleged to have committed in concert with the witness. In these cases, even if the evidence is independently admissible for a non-impeachment purpose, the court should examine carefully whether the evidence should be excluded as unfairly prejudicial under Rule 403.[93]

The prohibition against use of extrinsic evidence to impeach the witness by showing bad character for truthfulness applies also to ban extrinsic evidence to support the witness by showing good character for truthfulness. For example, the government may not, in a criminal trial on the merits, support the credibility of its informer-witness by adducing testimony that the witness had previously given information that proved accurate and that resulted in arrests and convictions.[94]

Sometimes a witness, by voluntarily injecting an assertion about specific instances into testimony, will open the door to counter-attack that otherwise would not be permissible. For example, a witness who proclaims never to have been suspected of involvement with drugs opens the door to counter-evidence showing a prior drug arrest.[95] Of course, the information must be elicited on direct or volunteered in a non-responsive answer; the cross-examiner cannot force the witness into making the avowal for purposes of contradicting it.[96] The rule seems to be based on application of general principles of waiver. However, the objecting party has done nothing to waive the objection.

dence that complainant-witness made a previous allegation that a fourteen-year-old boy raped her, in case where complainant accused defendant of rape several months later). *See also* People v. Evans, 40 N.W. 473, 478 (Mich.1888) (defendant can show complainant had made several false accusations about sexual assault prior to her complaint against him, in case where defendant's daughter had previously accused her two brothers, among others, of raping her).

92. See United States v. Costa, 947 F.2d 919, 925–26 (11th Cir.1991) (while Rule 608(b) prohibits use of, extrinsic evidence of bad acts solely to impeach character, it does not prohibit extrinsic evidence that is independently relevant to defendant's defense that he was not involved in the drug ring which was the subject of the testimony of government witnesses).

93. *Cf.* United States v. Smith, 80 F.3d 1188, 1193 (7th Cir.1996), where the court held, in a case in which defendant was charged with cargo theft, that it was not plain error to allow him to be cross-examined about uncharged cargo thefts for pur-

poses of impeachment under Fed. R. Evid. 608(b), remarking that "Prior acts of theft or receipt of stolen property are, like acts of fraud or deceit, probative of a witness' truthfulness or untruthfulness under Rule 608(b)." *Query* whether any jury could be expected to use the fruits of such a cross-examination solely for the permitted purpose of impeaching credibility while ignoring its natural probative force in showing propensity to commit cargo theft.

94. *See* United States v. Taylor, 900 F.2d 779 (4th Cir.1990) and cases cited therein.

95. *See* United States v. Garcia, Camacho, 900 F.2d 571 (2d Cir.1990). *See also* State v. Syriani, 428 S.E.2d 118, 135 (N.C. 1993) (in prosecution for first-degree murder of defendant's wife, when defendant testified he was a "loving and supportive husband and father," trial court admitted evidence of prior threats and specific acts of violence by defendant against his wife and children).

96. *See* § 1.10.

§ 9.09 Impeachment of Witness with Evidence of Prior Convictions [FRE 609]

The ground rules for admitting prior convictions have been a source of continuous controversy. Some jurists have argued that only crimes of falsehood should be admitted to impeach, on grounds that crimes of violence are likely to prejudice the jury without throwing much light on credibility.[97] Others have argued that one who will maim or kill is enough of an outlaw to lie under oath, and that the jury should be trusted to handle the evidence.[98]

These viewpoints have led to a variety of approaches to prior convictions. Some states follow the *crimen falsi* approach, admitting only crimes of dishonesty or false statement.[99] Others have a more wide-open approach, either mandating or allowing judges to receive evidence of other crimes.[100]

After a checkered path through the legislative and rulemaking process, the federal rule makers arrived at a compromise position.[101] Convictions for crimes of dishonesty and false statement, regardless of the punishment, are admissible to impeach any witness without limit (except as set forth in subparts (b), (c), and (d) of the Rule). The trial judge has no authority to exclude.[102] Federal Rule of Evidence 403 does not apply and there is no weighing of probative value against prejudicial effect.[103] Crimes for which the sentence is one year or less (typically

97. *See, e.g.,* United States v. Fountain, 768 F.2d 790 (7th Cir.1985) (Posner, J.) ("Violent men are not necessarily liars, and indeed one class of violent men consists of those with an exaggerated sense of honor"); Mason Ladd, *Credibility Tests–Current Trends,* 89 U. Pa. L. Rev. 180–82 (1940) (quoting 7 Jeremy Bentham, Rationale of Judicial Evidence 407 (Bowrings ed. 1827)):

"Take homicide in the way of duelling. Two men quarrel; one of them calls the other a liar. So highly does he prize the reputation of veracity, that, rather than suffer a stain to remain upon it, he determines to risk his life, challenges his adversary to fight, and kills him. Jurisprudence, in its sapience, knowing no difference between homicide by consent, by which no other human being is put in fear-and homicide in pursuit of a scheme of highway robbery, of nocturnal housebreaking, by which every man who has a life is put in fear of it,—has made the one and the other murder, and consequently felony. The man prefers death to the imputation of a lie,—and the inference of the law is, that he cannot open his mouth but lies will issue from it. Such are the inconsistencies which are unavoidable in the application of any rule which takes improbity for a ground of exclusion."

98. *See* 3A John H. Wigmore, Evidence in Trials at Common Law § 982 (James H. Chadbourn rev. 1970) and cases cited therein.

99. Commonwealth v. Randall, 528 A.2d 1326, 1329 (Pa.1987); Alaska R. Evid. 609(a); Iowa R. Evid. 609(a).

100. *See* Cal. Evid. Code § 788 (West 1966); Idaho R. Evid. 609(a).

101. For a detailed examination of the legislative history of Rule 609, and of the compromise represented by the rule that emerged from the debates,*see* 28 Charles A. Wright & Victor J. Gold, Federal Practice and Procedure (Evidence) §§ 6131–6132 (1993). *See also* Victor J. Gold, *Impeachment by Conviction Evidence: Judicial Discretion and the Politics of Rule 609,* 15 Cardozo L. Rev. 2295 (1994).

102. *See* 28 Wright & Gold, *supra* note 101 § 6134, at 216 (if the crime involves dishonesty or false statement, "analysis under subdivision (a)(1) [of Rule 609] stops; the conviction will be admitted under subdivision (a)(2) and no weighing of probative value and prejudice need take place").

103. Fed. R. Evid. 609(a)(2); United States v. Wong, 703 F.2d 65, 68 (3d Cir. 1983). This absolute approach was not affected by the 1990 amendments to Rule 609.

misdemeanors) and that do not involve dishonesty or false statement are never admissible to impeach any witness. The admissibility of evidence of conviction for crimes punishable by death or imprisonment in excess of a year and which do not involve dishonesty or false statement depends on the witness being impeached, but in all cases, the court must consider the probative value of the evidence for impeachment purposes and the unfair prejudice the evidence might cause.[104]

Rule 609(a)(1) Crimes

Rule 609(a)(1) establishes two balancing tests; which one applies to a given situation depends on the witness being impeached. The Rule reads:

> [E]vidence that a witness other than an accused has been convicted of a crime shall be admitted, subject to Rule 403, if the crime was punishable by death or imprisonment in excess of one year under the law under which the witness was convicted, and evidence that an accused has been convicted of such a crime shall be admitted if the court determines that the probative value of admitting this evidence outweighs its prejudicial effect to the accused. . . .

Thus, if any witness other than a criminal accused has been convicted of a serious crime that is not one of dishonesty or false statement, the court may only exclude evidence of the conviction if Rule 403 so requires. This places the burden on the objecting party to demonstrate that the probative value of the evidence for impeachment purposes is substantially outweighed by the unfairly prejudicial effect (or other dangers listed in Rule 403), a showing that will be very difficult to make in most cases. If, on the other hand, the witness is the accused in a criminal case, then the court must affirmatively determine that the probative value of the evidence outweighs its prejudicial effect to the accused. This test provides greater protection for the accused than the normal Rule 403 balancing test, because it places the burden on the proponent to show probative value and because it does not require that prejudice "substantially outweigh" probative value.[105]

Neither the language of Rule 609 nor the commentary provide meaningful assistance in understanding the nature of the probative value/prejudicial impact balance the court must undertake.[106] In deciding whether a conviction is unduly prejudicial to the accused, a variety of factors should be taken into account. These include:

104. Fed. R. Evid. 609(a)(1).

105. Rule 403 provides that "evidence may be excluded if its probative value is substantially outweighed by the danger of unfair prejudice, confusion of the issues, or misleading the jury, or by considerations of undue delay, waste of time, or needless presentation of cumulative evidence." Rule 609(a)(1) provides that "evidence that an accused has been convicted of such a crime shall be admitted if the court determines that the probative value of admitting this evidence outweighs its prejudicial effect to the accused."

106. See 28 Wright & Gold, supra note 101 § 6134, at 230–45 (noting the lack of clarity in the rule and suggesting factors the courts should consider when conducting the balancing test).

1. The degree to which the crime reflects on credibility. For example, a sex crime may not reflect on credibility as much as a robbery conviction.[107]

2. The nearness or remoteness of the prior conviction. A person who has led a blameless life for years after a conviction is entitled to more consideration than one who was recently convicted. If the conviction is more than 10 years old, the Rule requires a strong showing of probative value after advance written notice, regardless of the nature of the crime.[108] Even for shorter periods, though, the time span is a significant factor.[109]

3. The similarity of the prior offense to the offense charged. This is a factor that weighs against admissibility when the only theory of admission is impeachment of the accused as a witness. The reason is that the jury may use the evidence not for its bearing upon the credibility of the witness, but for the inference that "because she did it before she probably did it again"—or, even worse, decide to re-punish the accused for the prior crime whether or not the current one was committed. Thus, a stronger case can be made for receiving a prior auto theft conviction in a bank robbery case than in an auto theft case.[110] Of course, if the

107. United States v. Larsen, 596 F.2d 347, 348 (9th Cir.1979) (error for trial court to admit defendant's two prior felony convictions for child molestation since crime "bears only nominally on credibility," but not reversible error because court "relied exclusively" on prosecution's case-in-chief in defendant's trial for uttering counterfeit government obligations). *See also* United States v. Lugo, 170 F.3d 996 (10th Cir. 1999) (held, in case in which defendant charged with drug offense disclaimed any involvement whatever with drugs, invoking anti-drug education by his father, could properly be impeached under Rule 609 with prior drug possession conviction) (authors' comment: the principle that a defendant who volunteers a sweeping claim of lifelong innocence has forfeited the right to object to evidence contradicting the claim might have been a better basis for the decision than Rule 609, because in the absence of such a claim, the probative value of a prior drug offense in impeaching veracity would have been outweighed by the danger that the jury would misuse it as evidence of a propensity to be involved with drugs); United States v. Walker, 613 F.2d 1349, 1354 (5th Cir.1980) (misdemeanor prostitution conviction is not admissible under Rule 609(a) because it does not involve dishonesty or false statement); *compare* United States v. Lipscomb, 702 F.2d 1049, 1072 (D.C.Cir.1983) (court did not abuse discretion in admitting witness's one-year-old robbery conviction into evidence, since

crime was recent and witness's credibility was central to the case because he corroborated defendant's testimony).

108. Fed. R. Evid. 609(b). If confinement is imposed, the ten-year period does not start running until release. *Id.* If a mistrial is offered and refused by the opponent, that refusal may be deemed a waiver of the objection to lack of notice. *See* Zinman v. Black & Decker (U.S.), Inc., 983 F.2d 431, 434–35 (2d Cir.1993) (in 1992 civil trial where 1975 conviction for Medicaid fraud admitted, plaintiff waived objection to sufficiency of notice by twice declining mistrial).

109. United States v. Rein, 848 F.2d 777, 782 (7th Cir.1988) (time of witness's prior conviction and her post-conviction behavior is factor to consider when evaluating probative value of conviction). *See also* People v. Allen, 420 N.W.2d 499, 522 (Mich. 1988) (when determining probative value of conviction, trial court must consider the recency of the conviction).

110. *See, e.g.*, People v. Barrick, 187 Cal.Rptr. 716, 722, 654 P.2d 1243, 1250 (Cal. 1982) (en banc) (error, under circumstances, to impeach defendant with prior conviction for an offense identical to the one charged). Though *Barrick* was not a Federal Rules case, it illustrates a principle that is equally applicable under the Federal Rules. For federal case examples,*see* United States v. Wallace, 848 F.2d 1464, 1473 (9th

two auto thefts were so similar that the first one was admissible under Rule 404(b) to show plan, intent, modus operandi, or the like, then the evidence should not be excluded on this ground.[111] But when the only basis for receiving it is to impeach credibility, similarity between the two crimes is a factor disfavoring admission.

4. The extent to which defendant's testimony is needed for fair adjudication of the trial. If defendant's testimony is crucial for his defense, this fact weighs against the admissibility of the prior convictions,[112] because if the evidence will be admissible, it is less likely the defendant will testify.

5. Whether the defendant's credibility is central to the case.[113]

Some courts will also consider whether the witness's credibility can be explored adequately without using evidence of the witness's prior conviction. If the witness can be impeached convincingly using other means (e.g., bias, prior inconsistent statement), the existence of such alternative impeachment methods is a factor weighing against allowing use of the prior conviction.[114]

Rule 609(a)(2) Crimes

Under Federal Rule 609(a)(2), crimes of dishonesty or false statement must be received. The judge has no discretion under this part of the Rule, and cannot balance probative value against prejudice or even exclude on grounds that the crime was a minor one. Only if the court makes the necessary findings under subparts (b), (c), and (d) of the Rule may the court exclude the evidence.[115]

Some crimes clearly fall in the category of crimes of dishonesty or false statement. The paradigm example is perjury. Other core examples include fraud and forgery.

In common usage, stealing is also a crime of dishonesty. However, there are good reasons to doubt that ordinary stealing should be consid-

Cir.1988) (error for trial court to admit defendant's prior conviction for heroin trafficking in defendant's trial for possession with intent to distribute heroin, especially since prosecution could also use his prior conviction for perjury for impeachment purposes); United States v. Field, 625 F.2d 862, 872 (9th Cir.1980) (defendant's prior conviction for receiving stolen property was sufficiently different from his alleged armed bank robbery that it was admissible for impeachment purposes).

111. *See* **Ch. 5**.

112. *See* United States v. Rein, 848 F.2d 777, 782 (7th Cir.1988).

113. United States v. DeVore, 839 F.2d 1330, 1333 (8th Cir.1988) (evidence of defendant's prior weapons conviction was properly admitted because his credibility was central to the jury's decision of his guilt/innocence, in case where defendant offered an alibi to his alleged robbery that was contradicted by other witnesses); United States v. Johnson, 720 F.2d 519, 522 (8th Cir.1983) (defendant's prior felony convictions were properly admitted in case where he testified he lacked intent to sell cocaine in his trial for cocaine distribution).

114. United States v. Reeves, 730 F.2d 1189, 1196 (8th Cir.1984) (evidence of witness's prior conviction for breaking and entering properly excluded since defendant offered several character witnesses and proof of witness's more recent conviction for selling controlled substances).

115. These subparts deal, respectively, with older convictions; the effect of pardon, annulment, or certificate of rehabilitation; and juvenile convictions.

ered "dishonest" within the meaning of Rule 609(a)(2). As the advisory committee's note to the 1990 Amendment states,

> Congress extensively debated the rule, and the Report of the House and Senate Conference Committee states that "[b]y the phrase 'dishonesty and false statement,' the Conference means crimes such as perjury, subornation of perjury, false statement, criminal fraud, embezzlement, or false pretense, or any other offense in the nature of *crimen falsi,* commission of which involves some element of deceit, untruthfulness, or falsification bearing on the accused's propensity to testify truthfully."

The 1990 advisory committee expressed disapproval of "some decisions that take an unduly broad view of 'dishonesty,' admitting convictions such as bank robbery or bank larceny." However, it did not recommend a clarification of the rule, stating that the legislative history gave sufficient guidance.[116]

Clarification would have been useful, since there are decisions under Rule 609(a) that use the ordinary meaning of "dishonesty" and not the special gloss offered by the Conference Committee and the Advisory Committee. For example, a panel of the First Circuit has held that armed robbery is a crime of dishonesty within the meaning of the Rule.[117] But there are also many cases that use "dishonesty" in the special sense intended by the Committee, holding that theft crimes are not crimes of dishonesty.[118] Others courts have looked beyond the definition of the crime to see whether under the particular facts the crime was carried out in a deceitful way,[119] an approach that raises dangers of collateral disputes and waste of time.

116. For discussion of the lack of clarity in the phrase "crimes involving dishonesty or false statement," and a discussion of approaches to interpreting the phrase,*see* 28 Wright & Gold, *supra* note 101 § 6135.

117. United States v. Del Toro Soto, 676 F.2d 13, 18 (1st Cir.1982) (grand larceny is a crime of dishonesty under Fed. R. Evid. 609(a)(2)). *See also* Wal–Mart Stores, Inc. v. Regions Bank Trust Dept., 69 S.W.3d 20 (Ark.2002) (held, "check-kiting" is a crime of dishonesty under state equivalent of Fed. R. Evid. 609(a)(2), even though definition of crime did not require intent to defraud). *But see* United States v. Brackeen, 969 F.2d 827, 827–31 (9th Cir.1992) (en banc) (bank robbery is not necessarily a crime of dishonesty under Rule 609(a)(2)); State v. Eugene, 536 N.W.2d 692, 694 (N.D. 1995) (possession of an imitation controlled substance with intent to deliver is not a crime of dishonesty, and therefore automatically admissible, since crime does not necessarily involve dishonest conduct or false statement; defendant's belief that the sub-

stance being delivered was actually a controlled substance, not an imitation, is no defense to the charge). Relying on legislative history, the court interpreted Rule 609 narrowly as applicable only to perjury, false statement, criminal fraud, embezzlement, false pretense, and the like. The court cited cases in accord from the Second, Fourth, Sixth, Seventh, Eighth, Tenth, and D.C. Circuits and a case in contradiction from the First Circuit.

118. *See, e.g.,* United States v. Yeo, 739 F.2d 385, 388 (8th Cir.1984) (theft is not a crime of dishonesty or false statement within the meaning of Fed. R. Evid. 609(a)(2)); United States v. Entrekin, 624 F.2d 597, 599 (5th Cir.1980) (shoplifting is not a crime of dishonesty or false statement under Fed. R. Evid. 609(a)(2)). *Cf.* United States v. Estes, 994 F.2d 147, 148–49 (5th Cir.1993) (misdemeanor conviction for impersonating a public official not admissible as a Rule 609(a)(2) conviction).

119. *See* Altobello v. Borden Confectionary Prods., Inc., 872 F.2d 215, 217 (7th

Summary of Admissibility of Convictions Under Rule 609(a)

The operation of Rule 609(a) can be presented in chart form. The horizontal axis represents the type of crime, and the vertical axis represents the type of witness being impeached. In all cases, the indicated result will occur unless other parts of Rule 609 require otherwise.[120] In addition, this chart only concerns admissibility for impeachment purposes.[121]

	CRIMINAL ACCUSED	ANY OTHER WITNESS
DISHONESTY/ FALSE STATEMENT	always admissible	always admissible
SERIOUS NON-DIS- HONESTY/FALSE STATEMENT	only admissible if probative value exceeds unfair prejudice	admissible unless probative value substantially outweighs by a 403 danger
MINOR NON-DISHONESTY/ FALSE STATEMENT	never admissible	never admissible

Extrinsic Evidence of Prior Convictions

When prior convictions qualify for admission under Rule 609, the proponent of the evidence may prove them with extrinsic evidence. The cross-examiner is not bound by the witness's denial of the prior conviction, but may prove its existence by public record. Often, the party supporting the witness, knowing that it will be admissible, will bring out the prior conviction on direct examination to blunt its impact.[122]

Eliciting the Details of Prior Convictions

Sometimes a party will want to go into the details of the prior conviction or present facts that are not on the face of the document constituting the certified conviction. The impeached witness may want to say that the guilty plea was entered to protect a loved one, or claim intoxication at the time of the crime. The impeacher may want to show that the crime was committed in a cruel and barbarous fashion or parade before the jury other details that show how deep and dirty is the gutter from which the witness has crawled. The courts have not settled on a single approach to the degree of detail that may be elicited.[123]

Cir.1989) (held, in case where plaintiff had previously been convicted for the misdemeanor offense of tampering with electric meters, that if the prior offense could possibly involve the use of deceit the trial court must discover if the method used to commit the crime was deceitful; if so, the prior conviction is admissible under Fed. R. Evid. 609(a)(2); government may impeach with prior conviction under Fed. R. Evid. 609(a)(2) if it can prove that the crime was committed using deceitful means, even if deceit is not an element of the crime).

120. This assumes the crime is not excludable under another part of Rule 609,

such as Rule 609(b), involving convictions over ten years old.

121. Thus, for example, it does not deal with any other use of conviction evidence, such as under Rule 404(b).

122. Former Fed. R. Evid. 609 spoke in terms only of bringing in the evidence during cross-examination. Fed. R. Evid. 609 (as amended effective Dec. 1, 1990) simply provides that qualifying convictions are admissible; it does not limit admission to situations in which the information is elicited on cross-examination.

123. See 28 Wright & Gold, *supra* note 101 § 6134, at 221–28.

Turning first to the impeacher, one finds cases which purport to set forth fairly strict limits. One formulation of these limits would restrict the impeacher to asking about (1) the existence of prior conviction(s); (2) the name of the crime(s); and (3) when the conviction(s) occurred.[124] Another common formulation would also allow inquiry into the length of the punishment imposed.[125] However, the impeaching party may go into details of the witness's conviction if the witness attempts to "explain away" the convictions.[126]

Certain tactics are also available to the party calling the witness who has been or will be impeached with prior convictions. For one thing, the party anticipating impeachment often will elicit the fact of the conviction during direct examination to blunt its effect on cross-examination.[127]

---

124. *See, e.g.,* United States v. Sampol, 636 F.2d 621, 670 (D.C.Cir.1980) (court properly prevented defendants from cross-examining witness about the length of his confinement in prison when the prosecution had already established his criminal record and the dates of his convictions); United States v. Tumblin, 551 F.2d 1001, 1004 (5th Cir.1977) (held, improper to inquire about matters such as length of time spent in prison and length of time between release from prison and arrest for current offense). *See also* United States v. Williams, 272 F.3d 845, 860 (7th Cir.2001) ("[o]rdinarily ... the details of the prior convictions should not be exposed to the jury. However, where a defendant attempts to explain away the prior conviction during direct examination by giving his own version of events, he has 'opened the door' "); Foulk v. Charrier, 262 F.3d 687 (8th Cir.2001) (held, trial court has discretion to exclude details of prior convictions if it determines convictions might inflame jury; here, trial judge acted within discretion in excluding fact that convictions were for sex crimes; trial judge did allow in evidence that plaintiff had been convicted of two felonies and sentenced to 20 years imprisonment); dicta in Shows v. M/V Red Eagle, 695 F.2d 114 (5th Cir.1983) (inquiry into witness's length of confinement for robbery conviction is impermissible even when impeachment is permissible under Fed. R. Evid. 609). *Cf.* United States v. Howell, 285 F.3d 1263, 1270 (10th Cir. 2002) (held, in case in which inmates testified against bank guard and were impeached with their prior convictions, it was an abuse of discretion for the trial judge to adopt blanket rule, without Fed. R. Evid. 403 balancing, that while prior felony convictions not involving fraud or dishonesty could be used to impeach, the nature of such convictions could not be revealed; "the judge made a blanket ruling that the fact and date of the witnesses' felony convictions could be admitted but nothing else

and implicitly determined that no Fed. R. 403 balancing was required. We hold that such a ruling was an abuse of discretion").

125. State v. Amburgey, 515 N.E.2d 925, 927 (Ohio 1987) ("a trial court has broad discretion to limit any questioning of a witness on cross-examination which asks more than the name of the crime, the time and place of conviction and the punishment imposed, when the conviction is admissible solely to impeach general credibility"); 1 McCormick on Evidence § 42, at 167 (5th ed. John W. Strong ed. 1999).

126. *See* United States v. Amahia, 825 F.2d 177, 181 (8th Cir.1987) (prosecution may cross-examine witness about details of prior conviction in case where defendant testified he only pleaded guilty to four felony counts because he was assured he would only receive probation and because of the strain of working and going to school); United States v. Wolf, 561 F.2d 1376, 1381 (10th Cir.1977) (defendant may be cross-examined about facts underlying his conviction for making false claims to the federal government in case where defendant claimed he agreed to plead guilty because he did not have the money to defend the charges).

127. *See, e.g.,* Michelson v. United States, 335 U.S. 469, 471 (1948) (in prosecution for bribing a federal revenue agent, defendant testified on direct examination concerning an old misdemeanor conviction dealing with trading in counterfeit watch dials); Gill v. Thomas, 83 F.3d 537 (1st Cir.1996) (in federal civil rights action, plaintiff, anticipating impeachment with several crimes, introduced them "preemptively to 'remove the sting' from [the] anticipated impeachment"). *See* United States v. Berry, 661 F.2d 618, 621 (7th Cir.1981) (noting that "defense counsel often uses this trial tactic to preclude the Government from first bringing out a defendant's prior criminal record").

Also, counsel expecting the opponent to impeach the witness with prior convictions may wish to elicit sufficient detail during direct examination to demonstrate that the convictions were minor, that the punishment was slight, or that other details of the convictions show that the convictions do not affect the witness's credibility.

If the party calling a witness chooses to elicit testimony concerning prior convictions of a witness, the cross-examiner still has the right to fill in details to the extent allowed by the governing law of the jurisdiction. For example, the cross-examiner could ask about when the conviction occurred and what the punishment was.[128] The fact that it is easy to step over the line, even in jurisdictions that give latitude to ask about punishment, is illustrated by *United States v. Harding*.[129] There, the appellate court considered it proper to impeach a defendant charged with a cocaine sale with evidence of a conviction for possession of marijuana with intent to sell. However, the prosecutor went beyond asking about the name of the crime, when it occurred, and the punishment. The prosecutor also asked questions that revealed that the crime involved 80 pounds of marijuana and that the marijuana was found in defendant's home, and another question that suggested that it might have been there at the time of the cocaine sale charged in the instant case.[130] The court reversed the conviction. It conceded that it was proper for the prosecutor to elicit information about the existence of the prior conviction and even about the fact that it involved 80 pounds of marijuana. These were facts that appeared on the written record of the conviction, and the court regarded the written record as an appropriate guideline in the case concerning what could be inquired about on cross-examination. However, the court thought that the prosecutor went too far in asking a question revealing that the marijuana was found at the defendant's home, and in suggesting that it might have been there at the time of the alleged cocaine transaction. The court regarded this as an emphasis on the similarity of the two offenses that "was plainly intended to convince the jury of appellant's guilt as opposed to his lack of veracity."[131] It would have been proper to use a marijuana conviction purely for the purpose of showing that the witness is a liar, but not to show that the witness has the character of being a drug dealer.[132]

Though limits on eliciting the details of prior convictions are sensible when the prior conviction goes only to impeachment, the impeacher may be able to find another theory under which the details of a crime can be ushered into evidence. That would be so if the witness being impeached were the criminal defendant, and the details revealed that the

---

128. This, of course, assumes that, as seems to be commonly the case, the jurisdiction allows questions about punishment. *See Amburgey*, 515 N.E.2d at 926–27.

129. 525 F.2d 84 (7th Cir.1975).

130. The discovery of the marijuana occurred after the alleged cocaine sale, but the marijuana conviction was obtained before the cocaine trial.

131. 525 F.2d at 90.

132. In the authors' opinion, the conviction should have been excluded completely. Its probative value on the issue of truth-telling ability is far overshadowed by the danger that the jury will use it to show that the defendant had the character of being a drug dealer.

defendant had used the same modus operandi in the prior crime as in the current one. Then, the prior crime is not being used only to impeach, but to show, under Rule 404(b), a common pattern.[133] Yet the similarity of the prior crime can cut both ways. When the prior crime is not quite similar enough to qualify under Rule 404(b), then one sometimes finds judges saying that similarity increases the prejudice of going into the details, because the jury is more likely to use the prior crime as evidence of propensity to commit the type of offense, rather than limiting its use purely to assessing credibility.[134]

Sometimes the details of a crime shed special light on credibility. For example, when the crime charged is larceny, the fact that the larceny was accomplished by a false statement bears on truthfulness. At least where the defendant is not the witness being impeached, this sort of limited inquiry might be helpful in assessing the witness. Yet there is authority upholding exclusion even in this situation.[135] Perhaps there is some justification for exclusion, since this type of inquiry could lead to a "mini-trial" of the witness, wasting time and distracting the jury.

Stale Convictions

The Federal Rules contain an express provision limiting the use of convictions when a period of more than 10 years has elapsed since conviction or release from confinement, whichever is later. The trial judge has authority to admit the conviction, but only upon a special showing and after notice and an opportunity to contest the use of the evidence.[136] The showing should not be confused with that required for exclusion under Rule 403. In fact, it is the opposite. The court must exclude evidence of the old conviction unless the *proponent* demonstrates that its "probative value ... supported by specific facts and circumstances substantially outweighs its prejudicial effect."

133. *See* United States v. Fountain, 768 F.2d 790, 796 (7th Cir.1985) (Posner, J.) (murder of prison guard; defendant's prior use of knife in stabbing other inmate 57 times admissible on grounds that it would illuminate intent and modus operandi under Rule 404(b); strong dissent by Swygert, J.).

134. *Cf.* United States v. Harding, 525 F.2d 84, 91 (7th Cir.1975) (described in text; held, improper to go into details of marijuana conviction in cocaine prosecution; similarity of crimes considered a factor weighing against going into details). Although it does not deal with receiving the details of the conviction, compare United States v. Wallace, 848 F.2d 1464, 1473 (9th Cir.1988), which suggests the duality of courts' attitudes toward similarity of crimes. There, the court said that an old conviction for heroin distribution should have been barred in a prosecution for the same crime, saying that similarity weighs against receiving the evidence, not in favor of receiving it. Had the crime been more similar—say, heroin distribution using the same highly unusual method then the prior conviction would have been admissible under 404(b).

135. *See* State v. Amburgey, 515 N.E.2d 925, 927 (Ohio 1987). The *Amburgey* court upheld, as not an abuse of discretion, a trial judge's refusal to allow the complaining witness in an attempted rape case to be questioned about the basis for a grand theft conviction. The question would apparently have revealed that the basis was welfare fraud, which would have made the crime one that more directly reflected on the witness's truthfulness than the general offense of grand theft.

136. *See* Fed. R. Evid. 609(b).

Pardons; Juvenile Adjudications

Crimes that have been pardoned and juvenile adjudications are generally not admissible. However, evidence of pardoned offenses may be received if the person was convicted of a subsequent crime and the pardon was grounded upon a basis other than a finding of innocence.[137] Juvenile convictions may be received if the convicted witness is someone other than the accused and the judge decides that justice requires the impeachment.[138]

§ 9.10   Impeachment with Evidence of Bias

Opponents may freely attack the credibility of a witness with evidence of bias or interest. For example, the following types of evidence are admissible:

1. That a witness is a friend or relative of a party;

2. That a witness bears a grudge against a party;

3. That a witness has a business relationship with a party;

4. That a witness testifying for the government has hopes of leniency in a criminal case pending against the witness;

5. That a witness's expenses (or expert fee) are being paid by a party;

6. That a witness has been coached by a party or the party's lawyer;[139] and

7. That the witness is a member of an organization that is interested in the lawsuit.[140]

---

137. *See* Fed. R. Evid. 609(c).

138. *See* Fed. R. Evid. 609(d). *Cf.* Davis v. Alaska, 415 U.S. 308 (1974) (unconstitutional to exclude juvenile record of witness under circumstances).

139. *See generally* 3A John H. Wigmore, Evidence in Trials at Common Law § 948–969. (James H. Chadbourn rev. 1970); *see also* State v. Sweeney, 443 So.2d 522, 529–30 (La.1983) (held, in case where government's two key witnesses had arrested one of defendant's proffered witnesses, that prosecution may cross-examine defense witness about his previous arrest by those officers to explore defendant's witness's bias towards the two officers).

140. Where the organization is faith-based, the value of bias impeachment will normally outweigh even the policies served by Fed. R. Evid. 610, which provides that beliefs about religion are not admissible for purposes of showing that "by reason of their nature the witness's credibility is impaired or enhanced." The purpose of the church membership evidence would not be to impeach by showing illogical or evil belief, but by showing bias due to loyalty to the institution, and the Advisory Committee's Note to Rule 610 states that "disclosure of affiliation with a church which is a party to the litigation would be allowable under the rule." Of course, care must be exercised to avoid receiving prejudicial evidence where its relevance to bias is remote. See Malek v. Federal Ins. Co., 994 F.2d 49, 54 (2d Cir.1993) (held, in properly owners' suit to recover proceeds from fire insurance policy, it was improper for district court to permit defendants to impeach plaintiffs' expert witness on cross-examination with evidence that plaintiffs were members of Hasidic Jewish community, that the witness was also Jewish, and that witness had other Hasidic clients; such impeachment violates Rule 610, which provides that "evidence of the beliefs or opinions of a witness on matters of religion is not admissible for the purpose of showing that by reason of their nature, the witness's credibility is impaired or enhanced"; dissent argued that evidence was properly admitted as evidence of bias because it demonstrated that witness depended in part on Hasidic community for his livelihood).

Evidence of bias and interest has never been subject to the rule against collateral proof. The cross-examiner is not obliged to "take the answer" of the witness. For example, if the witness is asked about fighting with the defendant, and the witness answers "no," the opponent is entitled to call another witness to introduce evidence that the fight took place.[141] The Supreme Court endorsed the view that extrinsic evidence of bias is admissible the case of *United States v. Abel*.[142] In that case, the government offered a witness who would testify that a defense witness belonged to the same prison gang as the defendant, and that the gang required its members to commit perjury, theft, and murder for each other. The Court upheld the admission of this evidence, noting that the common law of evidence permitted extrinsic evidence of bias while requiring the cross-examiner to "take the witness's answer" with regard to less favored forms of evidence. The Federal Rules of Evidence did not change this common law rule.

The Federal Rules of Evidence do not treat bias impeachment directly, though the Rules contain some language that could have been read to restrict the use of extrinsic evidence of bias. Originally, Rule 608(b) prohibited the use of extrinsic evidence about specific acts, except for evidence of prior convictions, for purposes of "attacking or supporting the witness' credibility." The quoted language was apparently intended to apply only to character attack, not to attack for bias, but read literally it could apply to both forms of attack. However, the *Abel* case settled the issue for the federal courts firmly in favor of admissibility of this type of evidence to demonstrate bias. (A recent amendment to Rule 608(b) makes clear that its limitations apply only to character impeachment.[143]) In addition, Uniform Rule 616 provides that "for the purpose of attacking the credibility of a witness, evidence of bias, prejudice, or interest of the witness for or against any party to the case is admissible."[144]

Extrinsic evidence of specific conduct is admissible to show bias, but not to attack character. When attacking a witness's character for truthfulness, the cross-examiner can ask about pertinent bad acts, but must "take the witness's answer" if the witness denies them. Extrinsic evidence is not admissible, unless it is evidence of an actual conviction.

Sometimes the border between bad acts that show character and bad acts that show bias is indistinct. For example, in a criminal case the defense might claim that uncharged misconduct by a prosecution witness

---

141. " 'Bias is never classified as a collateral matter which lies beyond the scope of inquiry, nor as a matter on which an examiner is required to take a witness' answer. Bias may be proved by extrinsic evidence even after a witness' disavowal of partiality' " United States v. Keys, 899 F.2d 983, 986 n. 2 (10th Cir.1990); United States v. Anderson, 881 F.2d 1128, 1139 (D.C.Cir. 1989); United States v. Robinson, 530 F.2d 1076, 1079 (D.C.Cir.1976). *See also* United States v. Harvey, 547 F.2d 720, 723 (2d Cir.1976) (reversible error to exclude ex-

trinsic evidence that witness had bias against defendant, consisting of witness's accusation charging defendant with fathering her child and refusing to take responsibility for it).

142. 469 U.S. 45, 52 (1984).

143. For discussion of the amendment, *see* § **9.04.**

144. Unif. R. Evid. 616 (1986); *see also* Minn. R. Evid. 616.

automatically goes to bias, because the witness is motivated by a desire not to be prosecuted by the government. However, the existence of this conceivable motive does not give defense counsel license to bring in evidence of every bad act of the witness. A foundation must be laid showing that there is a basis for believing that the witness is influenced by fear of prosecution. Some cases have required a showing of a deal between the government and the witness before the extrinsic evidence comes in.[145] For example, in *United States v. West*,[146] the Seventh Circuit described a fairly elaborate foundation requirement, stating that before the defense could question a prosecution witness about prior misconduct in order to establish bias and motive, a foundation had to be laid establishing (1) the bad act; (2) the government's knowledge of the act; (3) the lack of any prosecution; and (4) the existence of a promise not to prosecute.[147] These requirements ask too much, in view of the fact that the witness might well be influenced by fear of the government even in the absence of any explicit threat or promise. On the other hand, some foundation requirement is needed to keep the defense from bringing in witnesses to testify about collateral bad acts that would not be admissible against any nongovernment witness, and that serve only to destroy the character of a witness who may not be prepared to defend an entire lifetime of activity. A showing that the bad acts were known to the government under circumstances that would give rise to a reasonable fear of prosecution should be considered a sufficient foundation.

145. United States v. Capozzi, 883 F.2d 608, 616 (8th Cir.1989) (defendant claimed that government witness testified for the government to avoid prosecution for misconduct, and sought to put in extrinsic evidence of misconduct; court recognized that extrinsic evidence showing bias was admissible but upheld exclusion in this case because "[t]he record ... reveals no evidence of any arrangement or deal between the government and [the witness]"). *But see* United States v. Lankford, 955 F.2d 1545, 1548–49 (11th Cir.1992) (trial court violated defendant's Sixth Amendment right to cross-examine witnesses for possible bias by excluding evidence that two sons of prosecution's key witness were on probation for state court drug distribution convictions, even though witness had made no deal precluding federal investigation of his sons in exchange for the witness's testimony).

146. 670 F.2d 675, 683 (7th Cir.1982). For other cases on the foundation necessary for admission of evidence of prior crime to show bias of a prosecution witness, *see* United States v. Matthews, 168 F.3d 1234, 1243 (11th Cir.1999), opinion amended on denial of reh'g, 181 F.3d 1205 (11th Cir. 1999) (government witness allegedly had been arrested for vehicle theft, allegedly providing a motive for her to testify for the government; held, evidence of alleged arrest was properly excluded; theory that charges had been brought and dropped in exchange for cooperation were speculative and unsupported by evidence); United States v. Parker, 133 F.3d 322, 327 (5th Cir.1998) (trial judge in federal bribery case prevented defense from cross-examining witness about state charges pending against witness for murder of witness's husband; appellate opinion indicates that because defense failed to present evidence that federal prosecutors had agreed to help witness in state murder case, "any error that may have occurred was harmless"); United States v. Triplett, 104 F.3d 1074, 1079 (8th Cir.1997) (held, no error to exclude testimony that police search found a possible controlled substance in home of prosecution witness, despite possible bias due to witness's hope of leniency; court noted that "the confiscated substance was never tested or positively identified as a controlled substance" and that the witness was never charged).

147. *Cf.* United States v. Rovetuso, 768 F.2d 809, 817 (7th Cir.1985) (defendant-appellant may not offer evidence about witness's activities in Panama, based on theory that witness was afraid of being deported to Panama, on grounds that defendant had neither argued bias at trial nor laid a factual foundation).

Even when the evidence goes to bias, and not to character, the fact that extrinsic evidence is admissible does not give the impeaching party unlimited license. The trial judge has leeway under Rule 403 to exclude details that are cumulative, a waste of time, or prejudicial.[148]

One form of bias evidence consists of prior statements by the witness. For example, a witness might have made a statement about hating the defendant, or about intending to hurt the defendant. A plausible objection can be made if the cross-examiner fails to lay a foundation with the witness before extrinsic evidence of these statements becomes admissible. In addition, if (as in the example) the statement constitutes hearsay, the court must exclude it unless it is covered by an exception.

Must the witness being impeached be asked about the statement before extrinsic evidence becomes admissible? The point of such a requirement would be to give the witness being impeached a fair chance to explain or deny the bias-exhibiting statement. The Federal Rules of Evidence expressly impose a foundation requirement for prior inconsistent statements, but are silent about prior statements that exhibit bias.

---

148. *See* United States v. Williamson, 202 F.3d 974 (7th Cir.2000) (held, not abuse of discretion to restrict cross-examination of informant who was working for government in return for leniency; cross-examiner was allowed to ask question revealing witness was under investigation but was not allowed to extract exact nature of crimes of which witness was suspected); United States v. Phillips, 888 F.2d 38, 42 (6th Cir.1989) (defendant, in trial for unlawful cocaine distribution, cannot offer extrinsic evidence about government witnesses using drugs at a party, after witnesses denied the accusation because the only bias that could possibly exist were government witnesses lying about a "remote matter" in order to save their jobs; trial court acted within its discretion because the information "might be more damaging than probative"); United States v. Ferrell, 625 F.Supp. 41, 46–47 (E.D.Pa.1985) (held, in case where government witness testified he had not sold drugs in the past, that defendant could not offer extrinsic evidence that witness had sold drugs in the past because defendant could offer no theory on why evidence was probative of bias). *See also* Cummings v. Malone, 995 F.2d 817, 827 (8th Cir.1993) (in inmate's Eighth Amendment action for excessive force by prison officers, trial court property excluded testimony that two of the defendants testified in inmate's attempted rape prosecution, resulting in an additional 15 years of imprisonment, when record already contained indications of inmate's bias against defendants). *Compare* State v. McCall, 549 N.W.2d 418, 422 (Wis.1996) (held, not error to exclude evidence that the prosecutor had dismissed two pending charges against the alleged victim and sole prosecution witness in a prosecution growing out of a shooting in which the victim was rendered a quadriplegic; Justices Abramson and Bablitch dissented); United States v. Triplett, 104 F.3d 1074, 1079 (8th Cir.1997) (held, no error to exclude testimony that police search found a possible controlled substance in home of prosecution witness, despite possible bias due to witness's hope of leniency; court notes that "the confiscated substance was never tested or positively identified as a controlled substance" and that the witness was never charged); United States v. Morrison, 98 F.3d 619, 627–28 (D.C.Cir.1996) (held, no abuse of discretion for trial judge to cut off questioning of witness about whether she was testifying against defendant to get lower sentence and thus avoid losing children; question called for "speculative answer" by witness; *query* correctness of rationale since even a speculative belief of witness that cooperation would help her keep children would be probative of her motive to testify falsely); United States v. DiMarzo, 80 F.3d 656, 660 (1st Cir. 1996) (held, no error to refuse to allow drug defendant to put in evidence of harsh sentence that he faced in order to show motive of others to put the blame on him in order to escape prosecution themselves; "providing jurors sentencing information invites them to ponder matters that are not within their province, distracts them from their factfinding responsibilities, and creates a strong possibility of confusion").

Nonetheless, authority for requiring a foundation could be grounded on the trial judge's general authority to control the "mode and order of interrogating witnesses and presenting evidence" under Rule 611(a). There is a division of authority on the question whether a foundation is required.[149]

Even if the foundation is required, the requirement should not be treated as a rigid technical one. It is worth noting that even as to prior inconsistent statements, where the common law courts were fairly uniform in requiring a foundation, the Federal Rules of Evidence have liberalized foundational requirements. The relevant part of Federal Rule of Evidence 613(b) provides that "[e]xtrinsic evidence of a prior inconsistent statement by a witness is not admissible unless the witness is afforded an opportunity to explain or deny the same." Some courts have held that this provision means only that the witness must have an opportunity to come back and explain or deny the statement, not that the witness must be asked about it while originally on the witness stand.[150] In jurisdictions accepting this interpretation of Rule 613(b), it would be anomalous to impose a stricter foundation requirement on prior statements showing bias. Also, Rule 613(b) gives the trial judge authority to depart from the foundation requirement when the interests of justice require, and it would be doubly anomalous to say that this discretion did not exist when the ground for impeachment was bias, not inconsistency.

§ 9.11   Impeachment with Evidence of Defects in Perception, Memory, or Mental Health

One potentially powerful form of impeachment is to attack the witness's capacity to perceive, recollect, or narrate.[151] Defects in the witness's capacity may generally be shown on cross-examination or by the production of extrinsic testimony.[152] Much, however, depends on the nature of the particular defect and the attendant likelihood of prejudice.

149. *Compare* United States v. DiNapoli, 557 F.2d 962, 965 (2d Cir.1977) (extrinsic evidence of prior statement showing bias is inadmissible unless witness is allowed to explain or deny statement); United States v. Marzano, 537 F.2d 257, 265 (7th Cir.1976) (foundation is required when witness's prior statement is offered to prove bias) *with* State v. Kehn, 361 N.E.2d 1330, 1335 (Ohio 1977) (no foundation required before offering extrinsic evidence showing bias); State v. Carlson, 508 N.E.2d 999, 1002 (Ohio App. 1986) (held, in case where victim of assault had a civil suit filed against defendant, that evidence of victim/witness's suit was admissible to show bias even though witness was not given an opportunity to explain or deny the alleged bias). *See also* United States v. Hudson, 970 F.2d 948 (1st Cir.1992) (foundation for admission of prior inconsistent statement to show witness's bias requires only that wit-ness be available to be recalled to explain or deny the prior inconsistent statement; note that the trial court's exclusion of evidence of prior statement was reversed on other grounds; concurring opinion urged court to reconsider rule en banc at earliest opportunity and to join the majority of the circuits in requiring that witness first be given opportunity to explain or deny prior inconsistent statement).

150. *See* § 9.05.

151. *See* 27 Charles A. Wright & Victor J. Gold, Federal Practice and Procedure (Evidence) § 6097 (1990) (an attack on capacity "undermines credibility by showing that the witness lacks the perceptual, recall, or narrative abilities presupposed by his testimony").

152. *See, e.g.,* 1 McCormick on Evidence § 44 at 176 (5th ed. John W. Strong ed. 1999) (witness may be impeached by

Defects in the Five Senses

Such defects may freely be shown to cast doubt upon the witness's ability to perceive the events that were the subject of the witness's testimony.[153] Most commonly, the evidence concerns the witness's eyesight or hearing, although questioning about the sense of touch, smell, or taste would be permitted when relevant. Impeaching counsel may cross-examine on these subjects, but is not bound by the witness's answer; extrinsic evidence is freely admissible.[154]

Alcohol Intoxication and Alcoholism

Whether evidence of a witness's alcohol intoxication or alcoholism is admissible to impeach the witness is a complicated question. There is no doubt that counsel can show by evidence of drinking on the occasion in question that the witness's capacity to observe was impaired.[155] The difficult issues arise when the attempt is to attack credibility by showing chronic alcoholism or when evidence of chronic alcoholism is offered for the purpose of inviting the inference that the witness was intoxicated on the occasion in question. The traditional approach has been to exclude evidence of alcoholism as overly prejudicial.[156] If counsel is able to lay the

eliciting facts discrediting witness through cross-examination, or by proving facts discrediting witness through extrinsic evidence); 3A John H Wigmore, Evidence in Trials at Common Law § 931 at 758–59 (James H. Chadbourn rev. 1970) (extrinsic evidence admissible to prove defective power of observation, recollection, or communication).

153. *See, e.g.,* 1 McCormick on Evidence, *supra* note 152 § 45 at 176 (any deficiency of senses substantially lessening the witness's ability to perceive facts, to which witness testified is provable to attack that witness's credibility).

154. *See id,* (may prove defects in witness's sense by producing other witnesses); 3A Wigmore, *supra* note 152 § 931 at 758 (extrinsic evidence demonstrating defective power of observation of the events to which witness testifies admissible)

155. *See, e.g.,* United States v. Infelise, 1992 WL 7837 (N.D.Ill.1992) (prohibiting inquiry into witness's pattern of drinking during any particular period, but, allowing inquiry into whether he had had a drink on the particular day about which he testified); Rheaume v. Patterson, 289 F.2d 611, 614 (2d Cir.1961) (testimony that driver had been drinking before accident admissible to impeach credibility of driver's version of how accident happened); People v. McGuire, 163 N.E.2d 832, 833 (Ill.1960) (evidence indicating intoxication of witness at time of event to which witness testifies admissible); 4 Weinstein's Federal Evidence § 609.05[3], at 607–53 (2d ed. Joseph M.

McLaughlin ed. 1997) (general rule in most jurisdictions is that extrinsic evidence admissible to show witness intoxicated at time of events to which witness testifies or intoxicated when testifying). *See generally* C.C. Marvel, Annotation, *Impeachment of Witness with Respect to Intoxication,* 8 A.L.R.3d 749, 758 (1966) (widely recognized rule that intoxication of witness at time of the matter about which witness testifies is relevant to witness's credibility).

156. *See, e.g.,* United States v. DiPaolo, 804 F.2d 225, 229–30 (2d Cir.1986) (trial court properly refused to permit defendant to impeach prosecution witness on basis of drinking problem); Springer v. Reimers, 84 Cal.Rptr. 486, 494–95 (Cal.App.1970) (trial court erred in admitting evidence that witness had drinking problem where impeaching party did not show witness intoxicated when observing events about which he testified or when testifying); Smith v. State, 644 S.W.2d 500, 502 (Tex.App.1982) (trial court properly excluded evidence of general habit of intoxication to prove witnesses were drunk at time they observed events about which they testified); 4 Weinstein's Federal Evidence, *supra* note 155 § 609.05[3], at 607–53 to 607–54 (evidence of chronic alcoholism inadmissible to challenge general credibility); 3A Wigmore, *supra* note 152 § 933, at 767 (general habit of intemperance usually inadmissible because it reveals nothing about witness's testimonial capacity unless it indicates intoxication at time event observed or when testifying).

foundation for a more specific showing that the witness habitually became intoxicated on a certain occasion or at a certain place, however, then the evidence may be admissible.[157] Thus, if the witness invariably joined drinking buddies after work in a certain bar and drank excessively, the proponent of the impeachment evidence has a better chance of getting it admitted than if the evidence took the form of testimony that the witness had been drunk several times at different places and times.

Drug Use and Drug Addiction

Drug use and addiction often have been treated differently than alcohol intoxication and alcoholism. The witness who is a heavy drinker traditionally has been treated with more delicacy and regard than the witness who is a heavy, or even occasional, user of other drugs. Of course, evidence of drug use on the day that the witness made the observations reported in the witness's testimony is freely admitted[158]— just as in the case of alcohol use. Some courts have gone much further, and have been receptive to the idea that drug abuse on other occasions is admissible for impeachment purposes.[159] A broad-gauge acceptance of this approach is unjustified, in view of the different effects of different drugs and the prejudicial impact of evidence of use of forbidden psychoactive drugs. Accordingly, there appears to be a trend toward excluding evidence that the witness used drugs on occasions other than the one that was the subject of witness's testimony, unless there is evidence that habitual drug use has impaired the witness's ability remember and communicate observations.[160] One prominent treatise suggests that impeachment by evidence of drug abuse be allowed only if accompanied by expert testimony or proof from reliable scientific literature about the effects of the particular drug.[161]

157. *See* § **5.30**.

158. *See, e.g.,* United States v. Fowler, 465 F.2d 664, 665–66 (D.C.Cir.1972) (trial court erred in not allowing defendant to cross-examine prosecution witness as to whether he was using narcotics at the time he observed the defendant commit alleged offense).

159. *See, e.g.,* People v. Strother, 290 N.E.2d 201 (Ill.1972) (evidence of narcotics addiction admissible to impeach witness's general credibility because addicts are notorious liars); 3A Wigmore, *supra* note 152 § 934, at 763 (evidence of drug habit should be admissible).

160. *See, e.g.,* Gonzalez v. Van Zandt, 1992 WL 30616 (S.D.N.Y. 1992) (trial court did not violate defendant's Sixth Amendment confrontation right by limiting cross-examination of state's key witness about drug use history, where witness testified that he "felt all right" on the day in question and that his heroin habit hadn't "interfere[d] with anything" even though he had been without heroin for a few days);

United States v. Cameron, 814 F.2d 403, 405 (7th Cir.1987) (trial court properly excluded evidence of witness's drug use to attack general character; evidence of drug use admissible only when probative to witness's inability to recollect and relate); Lusher v. State, 390 N.E.2d 702, 704 (Ind. App.1979) (trial court erred in refusing to permit cross-examination of witness's use of different drugs causing problems with hallucinations; evidence of drug use admissible where it may have substantially affected witness's ability to perceive, remember, and testify).

161. 4 Weinstein's Federal Evidence, *supra* note 155 § 609.05[4][a] (counsel should furnish court with specific information about drugs, dosage, its probable effect on witness, when witness took drugs, and how frequently he used them on other occasions; counsel should also be prepared to substantiate claim by expert testimony or recognized literature). *Accord* People v. Balderas, 711 P.2d 480, 507 (Cal.1985) (trial court properly refused to permit inquiry

Mental Defect, Abnormality, or Disease

In considering evidence of mental defects and diseases, first note that many states have competency rules that prohibit testimony by witnesses whose mental state prevents them from accurately relating facts.[162] The present section deals with use of the evidence for impeachment of a witness, not its attempted use to prevent the witness from testifying altogether under the rules of competency.[163]

When offered for impeachment, evidence of low intelligence or mental retardation is admissible unless its value is substantially outweighed by considerations such as waste of time. Thus, evidence about how the witness did in school would ordinarily be excluded, though evidence of severe retardation would be admissible.[164]

Evidence of mental disease is admissible if relevant to the witness's ability to accurately perceive, recollect, or communicate information.[165] Its admissibility, however, is subject to standard Rule 403 considerations, such as prejudice or confusion of the issues.[166] Considerations of embarrassing the witness are not often mentioned, but undoubtedly are

into prosecution witness's use of narcotics on days other than the day to which he testified where defendant failed to offer expert testimony on probable effect of such use on general recall and perceptive abilities).

162. *See* § **6.02.** The Federal Rules of Evidence, however, have no such competency requirement. Fed. R. Evid. 601.

163. Although an attack on competency will not usually result in keeping the witness off the stand, it may provide a chance to acquire information about the witness's mental condition or get a mental exam, which, of course, can be used for impeachment purposes if the incompetency attack fails.

164. *Compare* Polson v. State, 207 N.E.2d 638 (Ind.1965) (trial court did abuse discretion in sustaining objection to defendant's question as to whether witness was "a little behind in school") *with* State v. Armstrong, 62 S.E.2d 50, 51 (N.C.1950) (trial court erred in refusing to permit physician and another witness to testify that prosecution witness was retarded, having the mind of a child 9 to 12 years old).

165. *See, e.g.,* United States v. Dieci-due, 603 F.2d 535, 551 (5th Cir.1979) (trial court did not err in refusing to admit witness's psychiatric records where witness's treatment had occurred 12 years before event to which he testified and were not probative of his ability to testify accurately); United States v. Partin, 493 F.2d 750, 763 (5th Cir.1974) (reversible error to refuse to admit evidence concerning witness's mental condition and treatment where wit-

ness entered hospital five months before events to which he testified occurred, complaining of auditory hallucinations and belief that he was some other person); People v. Cooks, 190 Cal.Rptr. 211, 268 (Cal.App. 1983) (trial court did not abuse discretion in refusing to allow defendant to cross-examine witness as to psychiatric treatment, where no evidence demonstrated that witness's mental condition impaired his ability to accurately perceive, recollect, or communicate); 3A Wigmore, *supra* note 152 § 932, at 759 (evidence of insanity admissible to discredit the witness, if the mental condition affected the witness at the time the event to which the witness testifies occurred, while the witness testifies, or in the meantime so as to impair the witness's ability to recollect). *Compare* United States v. Pryce, 938 F.2d 1343, 1345–50 (D.C.Cir. 1991) (trial court committed reversible error in refusing to allow cross-examination about witness's hallucinations, which occurred four months before events to which witness testified).

166. *See, e.g.,* United States v. Rivera–Santiago, 872 F.2d 1073, 1084–85 (1st Cir. 1989) (trial court properly refused to permit counsel to question witness as to court-ordered referral for psychiatric evaluation, because jury could improperly infer that witness needed psychiatric treatment; no other evidence supported such inference); United States v. Lopez, 611 F.2d 44, 45–46 (4th Cir.1979) (cross-examination concerning witness's mental condition subject to Rule 403 limitations; must not introduce collateral issue which would confuse jury).

also taken into consideration, as they should be.[167] Some conditions, such as schizophrenia, clearly have more probative value in showing that the witness's testimony may have been deluded than do others, such as depression in reaction to an exogenous event.[168]

If expert testimony is offered, an objection can sometimes be based on the expert's lack of opportunity to acquire information necessary for the diagnosis. If the expert did not do a clinical examination of the witness, some courts will exclude, or use the absence of the clinical examination as a factor in excluding.[169]

Expert testimony that the witness has an emotional condition that makes the witness a liar is often objectionable. Such evidence may be unhelpful to the jury in its special province of determining truthfulness; its scientific basis is often questionable; and it can amount to making a character attack under the guise of medical testimony.[170]

§ 9.12   Improper Rehabilitation of Witness

The general principle governing limits on rehabilitation of witnesses is simple. It is that there can be no support in absence of attack.[171] The

167. *Lopez*, 611 F.2d at 45 (trial court did not err in refusing to permit defendant to cross-examine prosecution witness as to psychiatric examination where examination had no relevance to witness's qualification and was merely an attempt to stigmatize witness).

168. *Compare* United States v. Lindstrom, 698 F.2d 1154, 1163 (11th Cir.1983) (trial court erred in refusing to permit defendant to cross-examine prosecution witness as to her mental condition, to support theory of vendetta against defendant, where witness's medical records suggested history of psychiatric disorders, including schizophrenia, manifesting themselves in violent threats and manipulative and destructive conduct) *with* United States v. Brumbaugh, 471 F.2d 1128, 1129 (6th Cir.1973) (trial court did not err in refusing to permit defendant to introduce hospital report concerning witness's treatment for depression into evidence to impeach witness).

169. *See, e.g.,* United States v. Riley, 657 F.2d 1377, 1387 (8th Cir. 1981) (trial court did not err in excluding expert testimony as to witness's mental condition and her capacity for telling the truth where expert's opinion was based only on court observations of witness); United States v. Daileda, 229 F.Supp. 148, 153–54 (M.D.Pa. 1964) (trial court properly excluded expert testimony concerning witness's capacity to tell the truth where expert did not treat or examine witness, but only observed witness testify).

170. *See, e.g.,* People v. Ainsworth, 755 P.2d 1017, 1033–34, 248 Cal.Rptr. 568, 583–85 (Cal. 1988) (dictum) (psychiatrist may not testify as to whether witness is telling truth on particular occasion where only purpose of testimony is to impeach witness's credibility); State v. Munro, 680 P.2d 708, 710 (Or.App.1984) (trial court properly excluded expert testimony concerning victim's emotional disturbance and effect on her perceptions and veracity; experts cannot testify as to veracity of particular witness). *Cf.* Westcott v. Crinklaw, 68 F.3d 1073, 1076–77 (8th Cir.1995) (in civil action alleging excessive force by a police officer, trial court erroneously admitted testimony of expert that police officer suffered from post-traumatic stress disorder to explain officer's incomplete and inaccurate statements after the shooting; expert testimony usurped the jury's role to determine credibility); United States v. Shay, 57 F.3d 126, 129–34 (1st Cir.1995) (held, abuse of discretion for trial judge to prevent defense from explaining defendant's self-incriminating statements with expert testimony by psychiatrist that defendant suffered from "pseudologia fantastica").

171. United States v. Binker, 795 F.2d 1218, 1223 (5th Cir.1986) (government on redirect may ask witness to testify that his plea agreement makes the promise that the witness will testify truthfully *after* defendant cross-examined witness for bias due to the plea agreement); United States v. Jackson, 588 F.2d 1046, 1055 (5th Cir.1979) (defendant who takes the stand to testify

witness who has not been attacked cannot be bolstered, whether by character evidence, prior consistent statements, or other support.

One specific instance of this rule is that rehabilitation with evidence of good character for truthfulness is not permitted unless the witness's character for truthfulness has been attacked.[172] When character for truthfulness has been attacked, in any fashion, the witness can be rehabilitated with reputation or opinion testimony about character for truthfulness.[173] Because impeachment by showing bias is not normally a character attack, the witness attacked with evidence of bias cannot be rehabilitated with testimony about character for truthfulness.[174] Other types of impeachment may be considered attacks on character. If the facts of the case show the impeachment to involve an attack on character for truthfulness (as may be the case when the witness is impeached by contradiction or with a prior inconsistent statement), evidence showing good character for truthfulness should be admissible.[175]

Rehabilitation with evidence of prior consistent statements is permitted in response to attack for fabrication or other improper influence.[176] Under the majority view, the consistent statement, to be admissi-

does not, as a matter of course, have the right to support his testimony; however, if his credibility is attacked defendant may introduce evidence of good character for truthfulness). *See also* 27 Charles A. Wright & Victor J. Gold, Federal Practice and Procedure (Evidence) § 6098 (1990) (describing the common law principle "that evidence supporting credibility is admissible only if credibility has been or certainly will be attacked") (footnotes omitted); 4 John H. Wigmore, Evidence in Trials at Common Law § 1104 (James H. Chadbourn rev. 1972) ("every witness may be assumed to be of normal moral character for veracity).

172. Fed. R. Evid. 608(a)(2); *see also* United States v. Dring, 930 F.2d 687, 690–95 (9th Cir.1991) (not error to exclude rehabilitative evidence of defendant's truthful character, where prosecution merely emphasized inconsistency between defendant's testimony and that of other witnesses and noted defendant's interest in outcome of case but did not offer evidence of defendant's general character for truthfulness); United States v. Jackson, 588 F.2d 1046, 1055 (5th Cir.1979) (mere fact prosecution pointed out defendant's version of facts was different than other witnesses was not an attack on defendant's credibility and defendant could not bolster his credibility by offering evidence of defendant's character for veracity).

Even where the defendant testifies, issues can arise about whether it is proper to admit consistent statements in anticipation of impeachment. *See* Ross v. Saint Augustine's College, 103 F.3d 338, 342 (4th Cir.

1996) (no error to allow plaintiff to put in her consistent statements prior to her testimony; evidence was linked up to later impeachment efforts by defendant when she did testify; court distinguished United States v. Bolick, 917 F.2d 135, 138–39 (4th Cir.1990), a case where the government pursued a deliberate strategy of attempting to minimize the unpalatability of its witnesses by putting in their statements through a federal agent first).

173. Beard v. Mitchell, 604 F.2d 485, 503 (7th Cir.1979) (defendant may offer proof of reputation for truthfulness after plaintiff introduced prior inconsistent statement by defendant in order to attack defendant's credibility); *see also* Fed. R. Evid. 608 (a)(2); 4 Wigmore, *supra* note 171, at § 1105.

174. Fed. R. Evid. 608 advisory committee's note.

175. *Id.* (recognizing that whether impeachment by contradiction constitutes a character attack must depend on circumstances); 1 McCormick on Evidence § 47, at 192 (5th ed. John W. Strong ed. 1999) (cautioning against categorical rules and stating that "in each case the judge should consider whether a particular impeachment for inconsistency or a conflict in testimony amounts in effect to an attack on character for truthfulness and accordingly exercise discretion to admit or exclude the character-support") (footnotes omitted).

176. United States v. Montague, 958 F.2d 1094, 1096 (D.C.Cir.1992) (trial court

ble, must have been made prior to the time the alleged motive for fabrication or improper influence arose.[177] Thus, if a prosecution witness is attacked for bias arising from a deal with the prosecution after the witness's arrest on a criminal charge, consistent statements by the witness made before the arrest would be admissible (the motive having not yet arisen), but statements made after the motive to cooperate with the prosecution arose would not. They simply do not bolster the witness. In *Tome v. United States*,[178] the Supreme Court approved this approach, holding that when a statement is offered under Rule 801(d)(1)(B) to rebut a charge of recent fabrication or improper influence or motive, the statement is admissible only when made before the charged recent fabrication or improper influence or motive.[179]

For the federal courts, the *Tome* case settled the question whether, when a statement is offered under Rule 801(d)(1)(B), the trial judge has discretion to admit pre-motive evidence to bolster the witness. The majority endorsed a per se rule that the statements must be excluded unless they were made before the motive to fabricate or improper influence arose.

Rehabilitation of a witness solely with character evidence is subject to the Rule 608(b) prohibition against extrinsic evidence of specific acts. Just as the party impeaching the witness may not offer extrinsic evidence of specific acts to show the target witness's bad character for

did not abuse discretion in allowing government to rehabilitate witness by introducing prior consistent statement, where defense's cross-examination of witness about terms of plea agreement was at least an "implied charge of improper motive"); United States v. Duncan, 693 F.2d 971, 980 (9th Cir.1982) (held, in case where customs agent testified that defendant made admission to him but did not include the admission in his notes from the interview, that government could introduce three prior consistent statements by agent to rebut defendant's claim that the agent fabricated the admission); United States v. Allen, 579 F.2d 531 (9th Cir.1978) (government may offer witness's prior consistent statement after defendant argued that witness's testimony was based on fear of being prosecuted herself); *see also* Fed. R. Evid. 801 (d)(1)(B); *compare to* Minn. R. Evid. 801 (d)(1)(B) (consistent statement may be admitted if it is helpful to the trier of fact in evaluating the witness's credibility; consistent statement admissible even if the witness is not charged with a recent fabrication).

In some jurisdictions; the statement in text would need to be qualified to be completely accurate. There is a division of authority about whether prior consistent statements (1) may be used only to rebut a charge of recent fabrication, undue influence, or improper motive, or (2) may in

special situations also be used to bolster credibility in other ways, for example by rebutting a charge that the witness's memory is faulty. *See* Norman M. Garland & Romy Schneider, *Prior Consistent Statements As Evidence in the United States and Canada*, 2 S.W.U. J.L. & Trade in the Americas 451 (1995). Though Tome v. United States, 513 U.S. 150 (1995), does not directly address this issue, some of the language in the case suggests that the Court assumed that Rule 801(d)(1)(B) was the only route through which evidence of a prior consistent statement could be received to counter impeachment of a witness.

177. 4 Wigmore, *supra* note 171 § 1128.

178. 513 U.S. 150 (1995). For further discussion of *Tome*, see § **7.05.**

179. *See also* United States v. Forrester, 60 F.3d 52 (2d Cir.1995) (government precluded from admitting prior consistent statement of witness, defendant's co-conspirator, including post-arrest interview notes, because motive to fabricate arose as soon as witness was arrested; government's purpose was to "bolster the credibility of a discredited witness whose motive to shade the truth existed before she drafted the contested statement" and statement is inadmissible under *Tome*).

truthfulness, the party rehabilitating the witness may not call other witnesses to tell stories about the target witness's honest deeds. This prohibition does not apply if the rehabilitation addresses a charge of bias as opposed to an attack on character, so evidence of bad deeds that show bias may be rebutted with extrinsic evidence.[180]

---

180. *See* United States v. Lindemann, 85 F.3d 1232, 1243 (7th Cir.1996) (Rule 608 does not limit rehabilitation of witness attacked for bias and hence extrinsic evidence is admissible for that purpose; government could show that prosecution witness had incriminated other persons who had pled guilty in order to meet defense contention that witness was fabricating case against defendant to save his own hide, the evidence showed that witness had many "bargaining chips," hence reducing his need to fabricate a case against the defendant).

Chapter 10

OPINION EVIDENCE & EXPERT TESTIMONY

Table of Sections

§ 10.01   The Common Law Rule Against Lay Opinion Testimony

Concern for trustworthiness of the evidentiary database has been the hallmark of the common law system of proof. Witnesses who have observed events are supposed to relate the observations to the jurors, whose task it is to interpret those observations, reach conclusions about what happened, and come to a decision between the contending presenters, in light of the law.

The common law's insistence on personal knowledge as the bedrock for testimony is codified in the Rule 602 admonition that "[a] witness may not testify to a matter unless evidence is introduced sufficient to support a finding that the witness has personal knowledge of the matter."

Rule 602 captures the essence of what Wigmore described as the British rule against opinion evidence. For centuries, the British courts have prohibited witnesses from speculating about subjects for which they had no personal knowledge base.[1] A witness' opinion, for example, that the queen dressed in purple on her birthday was not admissible if the witness had not seen the queen on her birthday.

Nineteenth century American courts did more than enforce the British rule against opinion testimony. They expanded upon it. Wigmore complained that in addition to prohibiting speculation about matters for

---

1. John H. Wigmore, Evidence in Trials at Common Law § 1917 (James H. Chadbourn rev. 1976) [hereinafter, Wigmore]. McCormick on Evidence § 11, (4th ed. John W. Strong ed. 1994) (quoting Coke's 1622 admonition from *Adams v. Canon*, Dyer 53b, "It is no satisfaction for a witness to say that he 'thinketh' or 'persuadeth himself.'").

which the witness had no personal knowledge, courts prohibited any inference or conclusion about matters for which the witness did have personal knowledge.[2]

The American opinion rule assumed a division between "fact" and "opinion." The orthodox American opinion rule was that witnesses testified to "facts," but the "opinion" about what those facts meant was for the jurors to decide. The witness, therefore, who did see the queen on her birthday could say that she wore purple, but only the jury could decide that she did not look good in purple. Under this approach, one could argue that a witness could testify that a person had bloodshot eyes, slurred speech, poor motor control, and breath that smelled of alcohol, but that it was for the jurors, not the witness, to conclude that the person was drunk.[3] The rule prohibiting a witness from testifying to inferences based upon perception, except in cases of "necessity," was the orthodox view in almost every American common law jurisdiction, though it may never have been enforced as often or as vigorously as it was articulated.

The dividing line between the "facts" of what a witness observes and the witness' "opinion" about those facts is rarely so clear as theory and the obvious examples suggest. More often than not—as in the case of the person who was red-eyed, foul smelling, word slurring, and could not walk a straight line—the "opinion," "conclusion," or "inference" that the person was drunk is only a more general articulation of the "facts" observed by the witness. Notice, for example, that the "fact" of "poor motor control" is really a "conclusion" about the comparative motor ability between the person observed and other persons the witness has observed. Similarly, "breath that smelled of alcohol" is not a "fact" about an odor, but rather is an "inference" about where on the person the smell came from and what it was that created the odor. Even in the halcyon days of the American opinion rule, courts were often better at articulating the distinction between "fact" and "opinion" than they were at identifying it and excluding "opinion."

§ 10.02 Lay Opinion Testimony Under the Federal Rules [FRE 701]

Wigmore's view that American courts should abolish their inference rule, because they had misapplied and unwisely added to the British opinion rule,[4] did not prevail entirely when the Federal Rules were drafted. Rule 701 allows inferential testimony under certain circumstances, but prefers more specific testimony to more general testimony. A lay witness may testify to "opinions or inferences" if they are "rationally based on the perception of the witness," "helpful to a clear understanding of the witness' testimony or the determination of a fact in

---

2. Wigmore, *supra* note 1, § 1917.

3. Even during the heyday of the orthodox rule, however, courts found it hard to resist common sense, and often admitted lay opinion about drunkenness. *See* Wig-more, *supra* note 1, § 1974 n. 1 (collecting authorities).

4. Wigmore, *supra* note 1, § 1929.

issue," and are "not based on scientific, technical or specialized knowledge within the scope of Rule 702."

The requirement that the inference be "based on the perception of the witness" is a restatement of the Rule 602 insistence on personal knowledge. Rule 701 prohibits lay opinion if it is speculation about events for which the witness has no personal knowledge. But the Rule permits the witness to testify to inferences from matters about which the witness has personal knowledge, if the inference will be "helpful" to the jurors.

The "helpful" test fits no formula. It signals that the trial judge will exercise discretion that is unlikely to be reversed on appeal. The judge's prior predilection about opinion evidence and the lawyer's ability to persuade the judge that a particular opinion is either not "rationally based" or will not be "helpful" to the jurors almost always will be determinative.

Inferences that are not logically connected to the underlying facts do not meet the Rule 701 requirement that the inference be "rationally based." A witness' opinion, for example, that a person walking unsteadily was drunk is arguably inadmissible, even though the inference is "based on the perception of the witness." The argument is that the inference of "drunk" is not "rationally based" on the perception of "walking unsteadily," because unsteady walking can be caused by too many phenomena. To allow the witness to speculate that drunkenness was the cause of the perceived unsteadiness ignores illness, concussion, ingestion of drugs, weariness, vertigo, or lameness, any of which is an equally likely cause.

"Drunk," however, is a conclusion that courts routinely allow lay witnesses to express when there are sufficient perceptions to make the inference "rationally based." The conclusion of drunkenness that is, arguably, not rational when based on a single ambiguous perception, may be "rationally based," if the witness smelled the odor of whiskey, or saw empty whiskey bottles, or heard slurred speech, or made some other observation consistent with drunkenness.

The idea that multiple perceptions will make a conclusion "rationally based" is sometimes called the collected facts doctrine. Even though the "rationally based" opinion the witness will give may be very general, the judge may consider it "helpful" to the jurors, because the underlying bundle of perceptions is universally understood. When the witness says "drunk," the jurors have no difficulty in picturing the collected facts the witness perceived. (If the judge is in doubt about whether the witness perceived the underlying bundle, Rule 104(a) allows the judge to require the proponent to demonstrate the witness' perception to the court before allowing the opinion.)

The collected facts doctrine is particularly helpful when a witness offers opinion testimony for which the collected facts are not as easily articulated as in the case of drunkenness. "I felt fine" or "he had an ominous look about him" are very general opinions that almost everyone would recognize and understand, but might be hard pressed to articulate specifically. "I was not coughing, not feverish, not debilitated, not crying, not sneezing, not taking medicine," and the like might begin to convey "fine", but it is hardly complete and does not convey the same idea as the opinion "I felt fine." "He had an ominous look about him" defies even an attempt at specification.

Whether a particular opinion is "helpful" to jurors is often contested from two diametrically opposing positions. The first is that the opinion is too general to be helpful to the jurors in understanding the underlying perceptions.[5] The second is that because of extensive testimony about the underlying perceptions the opinion is too obvious to be helpful to the jurors.[6]

A witness who perceives an accident and whose only testimony is that one of the drivers was "careless" arguably has said something too general to be helpful to the jurors. The problem is not that the witness has stated an inference or that the inference is not "rationally based on the perception of the witness." The problem is that the inference is not "helpful." The jurors have no idea whether the driver who was "careless" was not looking, was speeding, was swerving in and out of traffic, was talking on a cellular phone, or any number of other possibilities. Moreover, "careless" is an opinion capable of more specific description.

If, on the other hand, the witness describes in detail what happened at the intersection, any additional testimony that the driver was "careless" may, also, not be "helpful" to the jurors. The witness testifying that a driver was talking on a cellular phone, weaving in and out of traffic, traveling faster than other cars, and looking at the front seat passenger instead of the road, arguably adds nothing "helpful" to the jurors by testifying that the driver was being "careless."

The two reasons for not allowing a witness to testify that a driver was "careless" are examples of the law's preference for the more specific, rather than the more general. In the first instance, the testimony is too general to be helpful. In the second, it is superfluous. Superfluity, however, is not the whole story. There is another concern lingering behind the easy ruling that the inference of "careless" adds nothing.

Although the common law rule prohibiting witnesses from giving opinions on the ultimate question for the jury is specifically rejected in Rule 704,[7] some concern about the proposition seems to remain with those who speak the language of the courtroom. A judge is more likely to prohibit a witness from offering an opinion close to the question for the jury than to prohibit an opinion about something more remote. If the

---

5. United States v. Rea, 958 F.2d 1206 (2d Cir. 1992)(court found a witness' testimony too general to be helpful to the jurors, who needed to know what words were used and the context in which they were said).

6. *See* United States v. Skeet, 665 F.2d 983(9th Cir.1982) the court held, "If it is impossible or difficult to reproduce the data observed ... the witness may state ... opinions.... If the jury can be put into a position of equal vantage with the witness for drawing the opinion, then the witness may not give an opinion." *Id.* at 985.

7. *See infra* § **10.05**.

issue for the jury is whether the driver was careless, the witness' opinion that the driver was careless is unlikely to be received. If, on the other hand, the question is whether someone arrived at a particular destination at a particular time, a witness' testimony about seeing that someone driving carelessly on the way to the time and place in question is likely to be admitted. In each case, the opinion of carelessness is of such a general nature that a judge might, but need not, exclude the testimony, as not "helpful" to the jurors. The likely different results suggest that the less important the opinion, the more likely the judge will be tolerant of the opinion that is too general to be "helpful;" the more important the opinion, the more scrutiny the judge will give to whether the general opinion is "helpful."

The judge's discretion to allow or disallow lay opinion testimony will not be overturned on appeal absent a clear abuse of discretion.[8] Because the trial judge is effectively the court of last resort, the lawyer trying to exclude lay opinion testimony must be prepared to persuade the judge of the prejudice that will result if the inference rather than the underlying perceptions is communicated to the jury.

The lawyer contemplating an objection that the witness is about to offer an opinion should remember the admonition to "be careful what you ask for; you might get it." The witness who tells the jurors only that the person was "drunk" asks the jurors to accept the witness' opinion on faith. Nothing could be worse than the judge sustaining an objection that "drunk" is too general to be "helpful," followed by the witness explaining in detail that the person was stumbling, had red eyes and slurred speech, was disheveled, smelled of whiskey, and could not walk in a straight line.

The restriction that lay opinion be "not based on scientific, technical or specialized knowledge within the scope of Rule 702" was added in 2000 to ensure "that a party will not evade the expert witness disclosure requirements"[9] of the Federal Rules of Civil Procedure "to eliminate the risk that the reliability requirements" of Rule 702 could be "evaded through the simple expedient of proffering an expert in lay witness clothing."[10] For example, an undercover police officer might be qualified under Rule 702 to give an *expert* opinion concerning whether a defendant's conduct was consistent with that of a drug trafficker. But if the government cannot meet the reliability requirements of Rule 702, the government cannot call the officer to testify to having seen drug trafficking, having seen the conduct of the defendant, and then offer the lay opinion that they are the same.[11]

§ 10.03 Expert Testimony—A Brief History

Opinions from expert witnesses were not much more welcome in nineteenth and early twentieth century American courts than inferences

---

8. United States v. Hoffner, 777 F.2d 1423 (10th Cir.1985).

9. Fed. R. Evid. Advisory Committee Note, Rule 701.

10. *Id.*

11. *Id.* citing United States v. Figueroa–Lopez, 125 F.3d 1241, 1246 (9th Cir. 1997).

from lay witnesses. Until adoption of the Federal Rules, experts were relatively rare and their testimony comparatively limited. The distaste for expert opinion testimony led to rules that sharply curtailed the influence that an expert might have on the trial. For example, common law courts often required that the basis of expert testimony be specified, meaning that lawyers had to use hypothetical questions in examining experts. They often required that the basis for the expert testimony be put into evidence, meaning that the facts upon which the expert relied had to pass the test of rules such as the hearsay rule. Some courts also prohibited experts from testifying to the ultimate issue.[12]

Before enactment of the Federal Rules, the beginning inquiry for the judge in deciding whether expert testimony was appropriate was whether the testimony provided information beyond the ken of the average juror. There was little need to categorize expert testimony. Indeed, in the nineteenth and early twentieth centuries, courts did not look to the nature of the expertise, but rather, to whether the proposed witness qualified as an expert. If the witness was an expert, there must be an expertise around somewhere.[13] Medical testimony by doctors was among the earliest forms of expert testimony.[14] Doctors were respected and well educated about the magic of medicine, a subject about which jurors knew almost nothing.

The Frye Test

In 1923, William Marston, an attorney and research psychologist,[15] had conducted extensive psychological research and would have been, under normal circumstances, one of those experts who could bring to the trial something beyond the ken of the average juror. But Marston was called to testify to something that was not only beyond the ken of the jurors, but beyond the ken of almost everyone else in the world. He was proffered to testify that James Frye, a criminal defendant claiming innocence, had passed the "systolic blood pressure deception test," an early form of the lie detector. The trial judge would not permit Marston to testify, nor to conduct a test in the presence of the jury, because the subject matter was not proper.

> Just when a scientific principle or discovery crosses the line between the experimental and demonstrable stages is difficult to define. Somewhere in this twilight zone the evidential force of the principle must be recognized, and while courts will go a long way in admitting expert testimony deduced from a well-recognized scientific principle or discovery, the thing from which the deduction is made

---

12. *See* §§ **10.05**.

13. David Faigman, et al., Modern Scientific Evidence § 1–2.1 [hereinafter Scientific Evidence].

14. Stephan Landsman, *Of Witches, Madmen, and Products Liability: An Histor-*ical Survey of the Use of Expert Testimony, 13 Behav. Sci. & L. 131(1995).

15. Marston was, also, the creator of the comic book super heroine, Wonder Woman. *See* http://en2.wikipedia.org/wiki/Wonder_Woman.

must be sufficiently established to have gained general acceptance in the particular field in which it belongs.[16]

The *Frye* "general acceptance" test, devised by Associate Justice Van Orsdel to determine the admissibility of testimony about what he considered to be a "novel" scientific principle, became the dominant standard by which scientific expert testimony would be measured for more than half a century.

Scientific testimony is different in one sense from most other expert testimony, because it is more than merely an addition to the knowledge of the average juror. Science is way over the head of the average juror, not to mention the average judge, who "went to law school to avoid science or, for that matter, anything else that uses numbers other than to reference volumes and page numbers."[17] While fingerprint analysis, various chemical tests for the presence of controlled substance, radar speed-readings and the like are now so familiar in our courts that their foundations are a matter of judicial notice, it was not always so. Imagine a trial judge's reaction the first time a lawyer claimed to have a witness who would testify that some numbers appearing on the back of a black box held by a police officer constituted the exact speed of an approaching automobile. That judge, who probably never heard of the top secret World War II invention of radar, had to decide whether the numbers on the back of the box were science or hokum. It is not surprising that a standard that left the admissibility of new and mysterious material to the "general acceptance" of those educated people familiar with the scientific field at issue seemed reasonable to judges.

Enactment of the Federal Rules

Article VII of the Federal Rules, Opinions and Expert Testimony, codified a sea change in the American courts' approach to opinion evidence. The overall liberalizing influence of the Federal Rules has been nowhere more apparent than in its expansion of expert witness testimony in Rules 702 through 706. Testimony of once rare experts has become commonplace, if not overbearing,[18] in courts of every jurisdiction and the limitations on their testimony have been relaxed substantially. Expert testimony need no longer be necessary to provide information beyond the ken of the jurors to be admissible. It is enough if the testimony will "assist" the jurors. Experts now may be asked their opinions about the specific case, without resort to a hypothetical question. They may offer opinions about the ultimate issue for the jurors' consideration. They need not offer the bases for their opinions before offering their opinions.

---

16. Frye v. United States, 293 F. 1013, 1014 (D.C.Cir.1923).

17. G. Michael Fenner, *The Daubert Handbook*, 29 Creighton L. Rev. 939 (1996) [hereinafter *Daubert Handbook*]. Professor Fenner's observation is not limited to judges. While it may not be true for all of us who went to law school, there are not enough objectors to fill a telephone booth.

18. *See e.g.*, Barry J. Brett, *Expanded Use of Expert Witnesses Poses New Problems for Counsel*, Nat'l L.J., Dec. 31, 1979, p. 22; Walter Olson, *The Case Against Expert Witnesses*, Fortune, Sept. 15, 1989 at 133.

Their opinions may be based on material that is not and could never be admitted into evidence.[19]

Rule 702 allows "a witness qualified as an expert by knowledge, skill, experience, training, or education" to testify by opinion or otherwise to "scientific, technical, or other specialized knowledge" if it will "assist the trier of fact."

Jurors in all jurisdictions regularly hear dissertations and opinions from "experts" about everything from how drug deals work to how brakes work, to why airplanes crash, to what a dead person is worth. Some subjects, such as the permanence of injury, the value of lost opportunity, the operation of various criminal enterprises, and the results of various kinds of laboratory analysis have become staples of the system. The list of the possible areas for expert testimony is endless.

The influence of the adversary system of justice on expert testimony—each side hiring its own expert to fortify its own position—has long been compared unfavorably to other systems in which "neutral" experts present opinions untainted by the interest of one of the parties.[20] The description of the expert in an American courtroom as "the best expert that money can buy" has never been meant to be flattering, but the paid expert did not become an epidemic until enactment of the Federal Rules.[21]

The "liberal thrust" of the Federal Rules combined with the "general approach of relaxing the traditional barriers to 'opinion' testimony"[22] has changed the face of American litigation. Testimony of experts, be it generally descriptive or an opinion central to the resolution of the particular case, has become a staple of the common law trial.

The Daubert (Joiner–Kumho) Revolution

The *Frye* test, though not followed in all jurisdictions or supported by all commentators, dominated admission of and discussion about expert scientific testimony for half a century, including the first two decades of the Federal Rules. Those who opposed the "general acceptance" test argued that *Frye* created a lag period during which reliable evidence was excluded while the scientific community evaluated the novel technique.[23] At the same time, others decried what they considered the recognition by various courts of "junk science."[24]

---

19. *See infra* §§ 10.07–10.09.

20. Learned Hand, *Historical and Practical Considerations Regarding Expert Testimony*, 15 Harv. L. Rev. 40 (1901).

21. David Faigman et al., *Check Your Crystal Ball at the Courthouse Door, Please: Exploring the Past, Understanding the Present, and Worrying about the Future of Scientific Evidence*, 15 Cardozo L. Rev. 1799, 1808 (1994).

22. Beech Aircraft Corp. v. Rainey, 488 U.S. 153, 169 (1988).

23. *See, e.g.,* Paul C. Giannelli, *The Admissibility of Novel Scientific Evidence: Frye v. United States, a Half–Century Later*, 80 Colum. L. Rev. 1197 (1980).

24. *See e.g.,* Peter Huber, Galileo's Revenge: Junk Science in the Courtroom (1991); Kenneth J. Chesebro, *Galileo's Retort: Peter Huber's Junk Scholarship*, 42 Am. U. L. Rev. 1637 (1993).

The *Frye* objectors gained some allies, as the federal courts divided over the question of whether the "general acceptance" test survived enactment of Rule 702.[25] In 1993, the Supreme Court settled the issue, holding in *Daubert v. Merrell Dow Pharmaceuticals*[26] that the "austere standard" of *Frye*, that "made 'general acceptance' the exclusive test for admitting expert scientific testimony," was "incompatible with the Federal Rules and should not be applied in federal trials."[27]

Daubert was one of a number of cases in the federal system claiming that the drug Bendectin caused birth defects. The literature on Bendectin was substantial and consistent. It had been the subject of more than thirty published epidemiological studies, covering over a hundred thousand patients. None of the studies concluded that Bendectin was the cause of birth defects. Nevertheless, plaintiff's eight experts were prepared to testify—based on test tube and animal studies and on re-analysis of some of the prior epidemiological studies—that Bendectin was a teratogen (a substance causing fetal malformation) and that when ingested by the mothers during pregnancy caused the limb reduction defects suffered by the infant plaintiffs.[28]

The trial court ruled the plaintiffs' expert testimony was not "scientific knowledge" and, because that left plaintiffs with no causation evidence, granted defendant's motion for summary judgment:

> The federal courts have held that epidemiological studies are the most reliable evidence of causation in this area. Accordingly, expert opinion which is not based on epidemiological evidence is not admissible to establish causation because it lacks the sufficient foundation necessary under FRE 703.[29]

The Ninth Circuit Court of Appeals affirmed, citing *Frye*, and the importance of the "general acceptance" standard:

> We impose this requirement because such evidence 'create[s] a substantial danger of undue prejudice or of confusing the issues or of misleading the jury ... because of its aura of special reliability and trustworthiness.'[30]

In reversing the Ninth Circuit, the Supreme Court did not discuss the wisdom of the *Frye* standard, but made it clear that the *Frye* standard had not survived enactment of Rule 702:

> "General acceptance" is not a necessary precondition to the admissibility of scientific evidence under the Federal Rules of Evidence, but the Rules of Evidence—especially Rule 702—do assign to the trial

25. *Compare, e.g.,* United States v. Shorter, 809 F.2d 54 (D.C.Cir. 1987)(applying the "general acceptance" standard), *with,* DeLuca v. Merrell Dow Pharmaceuticals, Inc., 911 F.2d 941 (3d Cir. 1990)(rejecting the "general acceptance" standard).

26. 509 U.S. 579 (1993).

27. *Id.* at 589.

28. See the opinion below, Daubert v. Merrell Dow Pharmaceuticals, Inc., 727 F.Supp. 570 (S.D.Cal.1989).

29. *Id.* at 575.

30. Daubert v. Merrell Dow Pharmaceuticals, Inc., 951 F.2d 1128, 1129–30 (9th Cir.1991) (citations omitted).

judge the task of ensuring that an expert's testimony both rests on a reliable foundation and is relevant to the task at hand.[31]

The Court found in Rule 702 a requirement that the judge admit expert testimony only if it "rests on a reliable foundation and is relevant," but the Court provided little help for a scientifically challenged judiciary, suddenly denied the ability to rely entirely upon the scientific community to validate scientific knowledge. The Court admonished judges to focus "solely on principles and methodology, not on the conclusions that they generate."[32] It provided a non-exclusive list of five factors that might, but would not necessarily, be helpful in determining whether knowledge was "scientific." The judge might consider 1) whether a particular theory or technique can be and has been tested, 2) whether controls and standards were maintained, 3) whether the theory has been subject to peer review and publication, 4) whether there is a known error rate, and 5) whether the theory has acceptance within the scientific community.

At the time it was decided, *Daubert* may have left open more questions than it answered—does it apply to non-scientific expert testimony; do the criteria, criticized as "vague and abstract" by Chief Justice Rehnquist,[33] apply in every case; will more expert testimony come flooding in; what will be the standard of appellate review—but it left little doubt that the scientifically challenged judiciary could no longer rely on the opinion of the scientific community. After *Daubert*, the trial judges were the unquestioned gatekeepers of expert testimony, responsible for their own independent judgments about science and the reliability of expert witnesses. And it did not take long for many of the unanswered questions to be resolved.

In *General Electric Co. v. Joiner*,[34] decided four years after *Daubert*, it became clear that district judges were not only the responsible gatekeepers for the reliability of expert testimony, but virtually the last word. Joiner claimed that his small cell lung cancer was the result of exposure to PCBs while working for GE. The District Court ruled the testimony of Joiner's experts inadmissible and, as a result, granted summary judgment for GE. The Eleventh Circuit reversed, "[b]ecause the Federal Rules of Evidence governing expert testimony display a preference for admissibility, we apply a particularly stringent standard of review to the trial judge's exclusion of expert testimony."[35] The Supreme Court reversed, re-affirming that "abuse of discretion," the least stringent standard of review, was the proper standard of review for lower court decisions to admit or exclude expert testimony, and rejecting Joiner's contention that the review should be more stringent when the exclusion ruling was outcome determinative. Chief Justice Rehnquist

31. Daubert v. Merrell Dow Pharmaceuticals, Inc., 509 U.S. 579, 597 (1993).

32. *Id.* at 595.

33. Daubert v. Merrell Dow Pharmaceuticals, Inc., 509 U.S. 579, 599 (1993).

34. 522 U.S. 136 (1997).

35. *Id.* at 140, *citing*, 78 F.3d 524, at 529 (1996).

recognizing that the Federal Rules would "allow district courts to admit a somewhat broader range of scientific testimony than would have been admissible under *Frye*," reiterated *Daubert*'s command that the trial judge "must ensure that any and all scientific testimony or evidence admitted is not only relevant, but reliable," and held that a "court of appeals applying 'abuse-of-discretion' review to such rulings may not categorically distinguish between rulings allowing expert testimony and rulings disallowing it."[36]

Two years after *Joiner, Kumho Tire Co. v. Carmichael*[37] provided the long-awaited answer to the question of whether *Daubert* applied to non-scientific expert testimony—testimony based on technical or other specialized knowledge. The district court granted summary judgment for defendant tire company after excluding the testimony of the plaintiff's tire expert, who could not show through publications or otherwise, that other experts supported his views about detecting tire abuse. In holding that the exclusion was justified, the Supreme Court said that although the experts who base their testimony on specialized experience rather than formal scientific training need not meet the requirements that might be imposed on scientific testimony, they must nevertheless use a demonstrably valid methodology. The expert's theory in *Kumho* was that where two of four specified signs of owner abuse of the tire are missing, the cause of a tire's separation can be assigned to manufacturing defect. The Court agreed with the trial judge that the theory, in addition to having no demonstrable support from others in the field, did not have adequate data or other explanation to support it. Further, the Court would not credit the expert's implicit theory that his post-accident visual and tactile inspection of the tire could determine that the tire had not been abused despite the presence to some degree of the specified signs of abuse.

In addition to laying to rest those federal cases following *Daubert* that had drawn a sharp distinction between "specialized knowledge" and "scientific evidence,"[38] the *Kumho* opinion emphasized the flexibility to be exercised by a trial judge whose opinion would not be overturned without demonstrating an abuse of discretion:

> The conclusion, in our view, is that we can neither rule out, nor rule in, for all cases and for all time the applicability of the factors mentioned in *Daubert*, nor can we now do so for subsets of cases categorized by category of expert or by kind of evidence. Too much depends upon the particular circumstances of the particular case at issue.
>
> *Daubert* itself is not to the contrary. It made clear that its list of factors was meant to be helpful, not definitive. Indeed, those factors do not all necessarily apply even in every instance in which the reliability of scientific testimony is challenged. It might not be

---

36. *Id*. at 141.

37. 526 U.S. 137 (1999).

38. *See,* e.g., McKendall v. Crown Control Corp., 122 F.3d 803, 807 (9th Cir. 1997).

surprising in a particular case, for example, that a claim made by a scientific witness has never been the subject of peer review, for the particular application at issue may never previously have interested any scientist. Nor, on the other hand, does the presence of *Daubert's* general acceptance factor help show that an expert's testimony is reliable where the discipline itself lacks reliability, as, for example, do theories grounded in any so-called generally accepted principles of astrology or necromancy.[39]

The 2000 Amendments to FRE 701, 702, & 703

Rule 702, the core rule regarding the testimony of experts presents two FRE 104(a) "preliminary questions" for the judge to determine before admitting expert testimony: 1) Is the subject matter one appropriate for expert testimony?[40] 2) Is the person being proffered as an expert witness qualified?[41]

The original Rule 702 required the judge to decide whether the "knowledge will *assist the trier of fact* to understand the evidence or to determine a fact in issue" and whether the witness was *"qualified as an expert* by knowledge, skill, experience, training, or education:"[42] The 2000 amendment added three specific findings for the judge to make: "(1) the testimony is based upon sufficient facts or data, (2) the testimony is the product of reliable principles and methods, and (3) the witness has applied the principles and methods reliably to the facts of the case."

The Advisory Committee's note to Rule 702 states that the purpose of the amendment is to codify *Daubert* and *Kumho* and to provide "some general standards that the trial court must use to assess the reliability and helpfulness of proffered expert testimony." "An opinion from an expert who is not a scientist should receive the same degree of scrutiny for reliability as an opinion from an expert who purports to be a scientist."[43] Building on *Kumho*, the note waters down the *Daubert* statement that methodology, not conclusions, must be assessed, arguably increasing the trial judge's importance in the evaluating expert testimony: "Under the amendment, as under *Daubert*, when an expert purports to apply principles and methods in accordance with professional standards, and yet reaches a conclusion that other experts in the field would not reach, the trial court may fairly suspect that the principles and methods have not been faithfully applied." Emphasizing that *Daubert* factors were never intended to be mandatory or exclusive and that lower courts have added to the list, the Advisory Committee note acknowledges

---

39. 526 U.S. 137, 150–151 (1999).

40. *See* discussion at § 10:04.

41. *See* discussion at § 10:05.

42. Emphasis is the authors'.

43. Advisory Committee Note to 2000 Amendments to Rule 702, *citing* Watkins v.

Telsmith, Inc., 121 F.3d 984, 991 (5th Cir. 1997) (it "seems exactly backwards that experts who purport to rely on general engineering principles and practical experience might escape screening by the district court simply by stating that their conclusions were not reached by any particular method or technique").

and approves of some of these additional factors: whether the expertise was developed with the litigation in mind, whether the expert ruled out alternative explanations, and the degree of care used by the expert.[44]

In addition to the attempt to bring the Rules of Evidence in conformity with the *Daubert–Kumho* requirements, the 2000 amendments dealt with two related issues. Rule 701, lay opinion, was amended "to eliminate the risk that the reliability requirements" of Rule 702 could be "evaded through the simple expedient of proffering an expert in lay witness clothing,"[45] Rule 703, dealing with the bases for an experts opinion, was amended "to emphasize that when an expert reasonably relies on inadmissible information to form an opinion or inference, the underlying information is not admissible simply because the opinion or inference is admitted."[46]

44. The relevant text of the Advisory Committee Note to Rule 702 reads as follows:

Courts both before and after *Daubert* have found other factors relevant in determining whether expert testimony is sufficiently reliable to be considered by the trier of fact. These factors include:

(1) Whether experts are "proposing to testify about matters growing naturally and directly out of research they have conducted independent of the litigation, or whether they have developed their opinions expressly for purposes of testifying." *Daubert v. Merrell Dow Pharmaceuticals, Inc.*, 43 F.3d 1311, 1317 (9th Cir. 1995).

(2) Whether the expert has unjustifiably extrapolated from an accepted premise to an unfounded conclusion. *See General Elec. Co. v. Joiner*, 522 U.S. 136, 146 (1997) (noting that in some cases a trial court "may conclude that there is simply too great an analytical gap between the data and the opinion proffered").

(3) Whether the expert has adequately accounted for obvious alternative explanations. *See Claar v. Burlington N.R.R.*, 29 F.3d 499 (9th Cir. 1994) (testimony excluded where the expert failed to consider other obvious causes for the plaintiff's condition). *Compare Ambrosini v. Labarraque*, 101 F.3d 129 (D.C.Cir. 1996) (the possibility of some uneliminated causes presents a question of weight, so long as the most obvious causes have been considered and reasonably ruled out by the expert).

(4) Whether the expert "is being as careful as he would be in his regular professional work outside his paid litigation consulting." *Sheehan v. Daily Racing Form, Inc.*, 104 F.3d 940, 942 (7th Cir. 1997). *See Kumho Tire Co. v. Carmichael*, 119 S.Ct. 1167, 1176 (1999) (*Daubert* requires the trial court to assure itself that the expert "employs in the courtroom the same level of intellectual rigor that characterizes the practice of an expert in the relevant field").

(5) Whether the field of expertise claimed by the expert is known to reach reliable results for the type of opinion the expert would give. *See Kumho Tire Co. v. Carmichael*, 119 S.Ct. 1167, 1175 (1999) (*Daubert*'s general acceptance factor does not "help show that an expert's testimony is reliable where the discipline itself lacks reliability, as, for example, do theories grounded in any so-called generally accepted principles of astrology or necromancy."); *Moore v. Ashland Chemical Inc.*, 151 F.3d 269 (5th Cir. 1998) (en banc) (clinical doctor was properly precluded from testifying to the toxicological cause of the plaintiff's respiratory problem, where the opinion was not sufficiently grounded in scientific methodology); *Sterling v. Velsicol Chem. Corp.*, 855 F.2d 1188 (6th Cir. 1988) (rejecting testimony based on "clinical ecology" as unfounded and unreliable).

45. Fed. R. Evid. Advisory Committee Note, Rule 701. *See* § 10.01, *supra*.

46. Fed. R. Evid. Advisory Committee Note, Rule 703. *See* § 10.05, *infra*.

Which is Better—Daubert or Frye?

There are some points of agreement among supporters of the rival tests, *Daubert* and *Frye*. Everyone agrees that judges have some role in screening out "junk science," even if the expert is a qualified professional, for example a medical doctor or psychiatrist. The fact that an expert has strong credentials does not automatically mean that the expert can testify that watching television causes cancer or that people with long noses are congenital liars. But there is a difference of opinion on the degree to which judges should defer to an appropriate community of experts.

The *Frye* test seems based on a sound core of common sense. The idea behind it is that judges should defer to scientists. If scientists in the field believe that the principle is valid, then judges should admit the expert testimony. If scientists in the field reject the principle—if, for example, they believe that the polygraph test is not accurate—then judges should exclude the evidence. Judges shouldn't try to become amateur scientists. Experts are better qualified to make the judgment and it's a better use of time.

The *Frye* approach seems consistent with serious decision-making by sensible and informed people in making the major decisions of ordinary life. When deciding which airline to use, informed flyers ordinarily do not read the safety studies themselves nor do they bone up on aerodynamics. Deference to expert authority is the norm. The only way that the informed lay person knows that the earth goes around the sun is by trust of authority—the Copernican conclusion cannot be reached by lay observation or by lay evaluation of the raw data.[47]

Many jurisdictions do not accept the *Daubert* test. Even states that have copied the original[48] Federal Rules of Evidence need not adopt *Daubert*. Original Rule 702 merely provided that "If scientific, technical, or other specialized knowledge will assist the trier of fact to understand the evidence or to determine a fact in issue, a witness qualified as an expert by knowledge, skill, experience, training, or education, may testify thereto in the form of an opinion or otherwise." This rule hardly requires the adoption of the *Daubert* test. If *Frye* is better than *Daubert* on policy grounds, then it is a better way of deciding what will "assist" under the rule—and vice-versa.[49]

47. *See* Richard A. Posner, The Problems of Jurisprudence 79 (1990).

48. Though the original rules are susceptible to either a *Daubert* or a *Frye* interpretation, the December, 2000 amendments to the Federal Rules of Evidence do require a *Daubert*-like approach, allowing an expert to testify "if (1) the testimony is based upon sufficient facts or data, (2) the testimony is the product of reliable principles and methods, and (3) the witness has applied the principles and methods reliably to the facts of the case." Fed. R. Evid. 702 (as amended effective December 1, 2000).

49. In analyzing Rule 702, the Supreme Court merely observed that "[n]othing in the text of this Rule establishes 'general acceptance' as an absolute prerequisite to admissibility." Daubert v. Merrell Dow Pharmaceuticals, Inc., 509 U.S. 579, 588 (1993). That is a pretty weak reed on which to base a conclusion that the *Daubert* approach is required by the Federal Rules of Evidence. The fact that the rules don't say that judges can defer to legal authority in ruling on an expert testimony objection doesn't mean that a judge cannot do so, and similarly the fact that the rules don't specifically say that a judge can defer to scientific

The majority did not say anything of substance about what was wrong with *Frye*, so one must go outside the opinion to assess the policy issues. The voluminous literature about these issues has supplied some guidance:

1. Commentators have said that the *Frye* test is too vague because it is too hard to decide which field is the right field, or what "generally accepted" means.[50] But any test used to solve this problem will have an element of vagueness. If general acceptance (*Frye*) is vague, then general acceptance with other factors added will also be vague (*Daubert*).

2. Commentators have said that the *Frye* test is too slow, too unreceptive to new science.[51] Sometimes a new theory or technique might be useful for determining a fact, but there hasn't been enough time for the scientific community to evaluate it and decide whether to accept it. But there are more charlatans than Galileos operating beyond the pale of accepted science, and the legal system is not well equipped to distinguish the two. At any rate, if *Frye* is causing a problem with new science, the solution is to create an exception for new science. If the technique hasn't been around enough to be evaluated, let the party who wants to use it make a pre-trial motion showing special need and then let the court appoint a neutral expert or a special master to evaluate the theory.

3. A stronger argument for *Daubert* may be that it is healthy to have judges take a scientific perspective and to ask, "Can this be tested?" "Where's your data?"[52] Some fields, including ones whose disciples have traditionally been allowed to testify, do not have a strong tradition of data collection and impartial testing. This is true of many areas of forensic science, such as handwriting analysis and hair analysis.[53]

authority doesn't mean that the judge is powerless to do so. Deference to authority is one of the background assumptions of the legal system. The judge has to find some way to determine whether the evidence is helpful science that, in the language of original Rule 702, will "assist" the trier of fact, or whether it is junk science that will only do harm. The judge cannot become a true scientist—be a population geneticist one week and an epidemiologist the next—so some shortcut is necessary to implement the requirement that the testimony assist the trier of fact. *Frye* is one shortcut, *Daubert* another; the text of the rule provides no guidance about which to use beyond what one would get by deciding which is better as a matter of policy.

50. *See* Paul C. Giannelli, the Admissibility of Novel Scientific Evidence: Frye v. United States, a Half Century Later, 80 Colum. L. Rev. 1197, 1210–1211 (1980); 1 David L. Faigman et al., Modern Scientific

Evidence: The Law and Science of Expert Testimony § 1–2.4 (1997).

51. *See* Paul C. Giannelli, the Admissibility of Novel Scientific Evidence: Frye v. United States, a Half Century Later, 80 Colum. L. Rev. 1197, 1223–1224 (1980); 1 David L. Faigman et al., Modern Scientific Evidence: The Law and Science of Expert Testimony § 1–2.4 (1997).

52. David L. Faigman et al., Modern Scientific Evidence: The Law and Science of Expert Testimony § 1–2.4 at 9–10 (1997) (on the need to have independent look by judges rather than accepting standards of expert's field).

53. David L. Faigman et al., Modern Scientific Evidence: The Law and Science of Expert Testimony § 20.9.2.7 (handwriting identification vulnerable to attack on *Daubert* grounds), § 22 (extended discussion of validity of handwriting analysis, reaching unfavorable conclusions), § 20.9.2.3 (hair

Even if judges are capable of doing the job assigned by *Daubert*, a cost-benefit analysis might call for a less onerous approach. Is learning the basics of the scientific method the best use of judges' time? Study of the scientific method will come at the cost of the study of something else. Perhaps judges would be better off reading Holmes, Cardozo, or Wigmore, or merely studying with greater care the facts and law in the cases pending before them. But supporters of *Daubert* insist that scientific literacy is a necessity in contemporary life, and time may prove them right.

§ 10.04   Expert Testimony Subject Matter [FRE 702]

The extent and the shape of the *Daubert* Revolution are yet to be determined. A number of states, including the influential jurisdictions of California[54] and New York,[55] use the *Frye* test or some modification of it. Further, there is nothing in the text of the original Rule 702, a version of which has been adopted by a majority of states, that demands adopting a *Daubert* approach.[56]

In analyzing Rule 702, the *Daubert* Court merely observed that "[n]othing in the text of this Rule establishes 'general acceptance' as an absolute prerequisite to admissibility."[57] Had it been before them, they would have been compelled to say, "or any other particular test." The text of the rule provides no guidance about which test to use beyond what one would get by deciding which is better as a matter of policy. On the other hand, *Daubert* has become the label for an industry, spawning endless discussion about the general subject of expert testimony, well beyond the bounds of science or the issues before the *Daubert* Court.[58]

While the federal experience after *Daubert* presents some clues about the future shape of expert testimony in the federal system, much remains in doubt. *Daubert* both raises the bar for admission of expert testimony and lowers it. It is more permissive than *Frye* in admitting valid but novel science that might not have yet achieved general acceptance. At the same time, it raises higher barriers to scientifically questionable techniques that, while generally accepted by their practitioners, come up short if subjected to a searching and critical examination. As one astute commentator has written, "The single most important 'guide-

---

identification evidence vulnerable to attack on *Daubert* grounds).

54. People v. Kelly, 549 P.2d 1240 (Cal. 1976)

55. People v. Wesley, 611 N.Y.S.2d 97 (1994)

56. The original rule merely provided that "If scientific, technical, or other specialized knowledge will assist the trier of fact to understand the evidence or to determine a fact in issue, a witness qualified as an expert by knowledge, skill, experience,

training, or education, may testify thereto in the form of an opinion or otherwise."

57. 509 U.S. 579, 588 (1993)

58. In the four years following the decision, *Daubert* had been cited in 911 articles in legal periodicals and in more than 1000 cases—about once every day by some commentator and some judge, excluding, of course, the Sabbath and holidays. Following Kumho, the references to the two cases are beyond calculation.

post' contained in *Daubert* is the Court's directive to judges to actively evaluate scientific evidence."[59]

The Rule 104(a) preliminary question, "Is the subject matter one appropriate for expert testimony," focuses the trial judge's attention on the second of the three new requirements in Rule 702, whether the proposed "testimony is the product of reliable principles and methods" Rule 702 describes knowledge that might be the subject matter of expert testimony, as if there were three separate and readily identifiable categories: "scientific, technical, and other specialized." Although *Kumho* and the 2000 amendment to the Rule make it clear that *Daubert's* gatekeeper-reliability approach applies irrespective of the category, it is equally clear that the judge's task and the standards by which the judge determines whether the "testimony is the product of reliable principles and methods" will differ depending upon the category. But categorization is not always so obvious. Some enterprises are easy to categorize— the existence and structure of the atom is "scientific," the diagram for putting together a computer is "technical," and the best shape for a perfect apple might be considered "other specialized"—but not every example is so simple. Is how a cyclotron smashes atoms scientific or technical? Is how a computer processes information technical or scientific? What is psychology? Is it different from psychiatry? What do you call it when someone knows enough about racehorses to make a living handicapping races? What do you call it when someone knows enough about economics to predict how much someone might have earned had the person lived for twenty-five years?

Given *Kumho's* understanding that different categories of knowledge, as well as different areas of expertise within those categories, call for different benchmarks by which to gauge reliability, the courts over time will develop something for technical and specialized knowledge like the *Daubert* five factors for considering scientific knowledge. When those benchmarks have become familiar, the trial judge will first have to decide which category of knowledge—scientific, technical, or other specialized—is applicable to the particular expertise and then pick the benchmarks to use in deciding upon its reliability.

There was disagreement, following *Daubert*, whether the new articulation of how the law approaches scientific testimony would result in more, less, or different expert testimony than *Frye's* articulation. There is not yet sufficient experience with *Daubert* to be certain, but it appears that the predictions that abandoning the "general acceptance" standard would lead to a " 'free for all' in which befuddled juries are confounded by absurd and irrational pseudoscientific assertions"[60] have failed to materialize. And while it has not been clearly established that *Daubert's* judicial gatekeeper results in rejecting scientific evidence that *Frye's*

---

59. David L Faigman, Mapping the Labyrinth of Scientific Evidence, 46 Hastings L.J., 555 (1995).

60. Daubert v. Merrell Dow Pharmaceuticals, Inc., 509 U.S. 579, 595 (1993).

scientific community gatekeeper would allow,[61] there appears to be some movement in that direction.[62]

61. *See* Reforming the Civil Justice System (NYU Press Larry Kramer, Editor)(Samuel R. Gross, *Substance & Form in Scientific Evidence: What* Daubert *Didn't Do* p. 234 at 246).

62. *See, e.g.,* Black v. Food Lion, Inc., 171 F.3d 308 (5th Cir. 1999) (held, expert's opinion that fall in store caused fibromyalgia did not meet Daubert/Kumho standards; eliminating other possible causes without providing valid theory why a fall would have caused the condition is not sufficient); Moore v. Ashland Chemical Inc., 151 F.3d 269, 279 (5th Cir. 1998) (en banc) (trial court acted properly in preventing plaintiff's expert from testifying that plaintiff suffered from reactive airways dysfunction syndrome resulting from close contact with Toluene solution; though expert was highly qualified, he could not support his opinion by showing it was scientifically valid under principles of *Daubert*); Michigan Millers Mut. Ins. Corp. v. Benfield, 140 F.3d 915, 920–21 (11th Cir. 1998) (held, *Daubert* standard properly applied to expert who claimed to be expert on "science" of fire origins but who did no tests in course of determining, on basis of experience, that fire was incendiary because of inability to ascertain another cause of the fire); Smelser v. Norfolk Southern Ry. Co., 105 F.3d 299, 303–04 (6th Cir. 1997) (held, expert testimony of biomechanical engineer that shoulder belt had given way should have been excluded under *Daubert* for failure to use scientific method, including failure to test, verify, and consider alternative hypotheses); Peitzmeier v. Hennessy Industries, Inc., 97 F.3d 293, 297–98 (8th Cir. 1996) (engineer's testimony about how product's design could have been improved inadmissible under *Daubert* despite claim that it was based on accepted engineering principles and was not novel scientific evidence; engineer had not tested proposed safety devices, had only made a series of rough sketches, and had not submitted ideas for peer review); Cummins v. Lyle Industries, 93 F.3d 362, 367 (7th Cir. 1996) (held, proper to exclude testimony of engineer about his allegedly safer alternative designs for trim press that injured plaintiff; engineer should have tested alternative designs or based opinion on scientific studies of others); Watkins v. Telsmith, Inc., 121 F.3d 984, 990–91 (5th Cir. 1997) (*Daubert* factors of testing, peer review, and general acceptance are relevant to assessing engineering expert's testimony on product design; experts cannot escape scrutiny merely by claiming that expertise is based on experience); Allen v. Pennsylvania Eng'g

Corp., 102 F.3d 194, 195–96 (5th Cir. 1996) (no error to exclude plaintiff's expert testimony linking death from brain cancer to exposure to ethylene oxide; "Where, as here, no epidemiological study has found a statistically significant link between EtO exposure and human brain cancer; the results of animal studies are inconclusive at best; and there was no evidence of the level of Allen's occupational exposure to EtO, the expert testimony does not exhibit the level of reliability necessary to comport with Federal Rules of Evidence 702 and 703, the Supreme Court's *Daubert* decision, and this court's authorities"; fact that regulatory agencies had designated EtO as carcinogenic not controlling because their preventive perspective results in use of lower threshold of proof); Rosen v. Ciba–Geigy Corp., 78 F.3d 316, 318–19 (7th Cir. 1996) (Posner, C.J.) (held, not error to exclude cardiologist's opinion that nicotine patch contributed to heart attack; after *Daubert*, expert must supply more than bottom line).

But cf. Curtis v. M&S Petroleum, Inc., 174 F.3d 661 (5th Cir. 1999) (held, error to exclude opinion of plaintiff's expert about adverse health effect on workers of exposure to benzene; expert relied upon scientific studies and had adequate factual basis). Kennedy v. Collagen Corp., 161 F.3d 1226 (9th Cir. 1998), cert. denied, 526 U.S. 1099 (1999) (held, reversible error to exclude plaintiff's evidence that collagen injection caused lupus; expert relied upon published studies as well as clinical judgment; trial judges should be careful not to exclude expert testimony merely because they disagree with conclusions of expert); Compton v. Subaru of America, Inc., 82 F.3d 1513, 1519 (10th Cir. 1996) (engineer's testimony that design of car caused "excessive roof crush" on rollover not subject to *Daubert* because based on general engineering principles and 22 years of experience as automotive engineer; *Daubert* applicable only to cases involving "unique, untested, or controversial methodologies or techniques") (Author's note: the stated limit on *Daubert* is questionable in light of the Supreme Court's subsequent opinion in *Kumho, infra*); State v. Fukusaku, 946 P.2d 32, 42–43 (Haw. 1997) (held, prosecution expert's testimony that hair and fiber samples from crime scene were "consistent" with those connected to defendant was admissible, and was not subject to *Daubert* screening because comparisons of hair and fiber involves mere "technical knowledge"; court

If nothing else, the 2000 amendment to Rule 702 might provide better insight into why expert testimony is being admitted or excluded. "Assist the trier of fact" was the umbrella explanation for admitting or excluding expert testimony under the original rule. It was, generally, a liberalizing standard compared to the common law's requirement that placed the burden on the proponent to demonstrate that the testimony of the expert was "necessary" because it was about matters beyond the ken of the average juror.[63] The proponent's burden was usually so easily met that the onus was on the opponent to show that the testimony would not "assist the trier of fact." The liberalization, however, was not universal. This was particularly apparent for some of the "soft" sciences, such as forensic or social science. Courts differed markedly on whether a particular "expertise" would "assist the trier of fact"—the reliability of eyewitness testimony,[64] the modus operandi of drug dealers,[65] the identification of the individual depicted in a photograph or videotape,[66] the

goes on to opine, however, that the scientific principles underlying the comparisons are reliable); Cantrell v. GAF Corp., 999 F.2d 1007, 1014 (6th Cir. 1993) (held, in pre-*Kumho* decision, district court properly admitted, under *Daubert*, testimony of plaintiffs' medical expert witness, based on his own clinical experience, concerning relationship between asbestos exposure and laryngeal cancer; "[n]othing in Rules 702 and 703 or in *Daubert* prohibits an expert witness from testifying to confirmatory data, gained through his own clinical experience, on the origin of a disease or the consequences of exposure to certain conditions").

In a celebrated case, Judge Pollak first held that techniques of latent fingerprint comparisons did not meet the *Daubert* standards, so that fingerprint experts, though they could point out similarities and differences, could not declare a match. United States v. Llera Plaza, 179 F.Supp.2d 492, 57 Fed. R. Evid. Serv. 983 (E.D. Pa. 2002). On petition for reconsideration, he changed his ruling and held that the evidence was admissible. United States v. Llera Plaza, 188 F.Supp.2d 549 (E.D. Pa. 2002). Accord, United States v. Havvard, 260 F.3d 597, 56 Fed. R. Evid. Serv. 900 (7th Cir. 2001)(admitting latent print evidence). When attempting to prove that a place or thing is dangerous because a certain number of bad events have been associated with it, an elementary requirement of the scientific method is some sort of comparison with the rate of occurrence of the event elsewhere. For example, the fact that 100 people have contracted X disease after taking Y drug means nothing if the base rate for the disease is no higher among those who took Y drug than among the general population. On this principle, Judge Richard Posner upheld exclusion of the testimo-

ny of an expert criminologist in Boncher ex rel. Boncher v. Brown County, 272 F.3d 484, 58 Fed. R. Evid. Serv. 174 (7th Cir. 2001). The Boncher case arose out of a suit against the county by a prisoner who committed suicide in jail. The expert testified that there had been five suicides in the Brown County jail, and that this was an unusually high number. Judge Posner stated that the evidence was useless on two grounds (1) there had been no attempt to explicitly compare the rate in the Brown County jail with the rate elsewhere-neither the rate in the general population of Brown County or the rate in other jails, and (2) even if there had been, a statistical analysis would have been necessary in order to determine that the difference between the Brown County jail rate and the rate elsewhere was due to something other than normal variance (chance factors).

63. Bridger v. Union Ry., 355 F.2d 382, 387 (6th Cir. 1966).

64. *Compare* United States v. Moore, 786 F.2d 1308 (5th Cir. 1986)(approving expert testimony on the reliability of eyewitness identification) *with* United States v. Fosher, 590 F.2d 381 (1st Cir. 1979)(approving exclusion of expert testimony on the reliability of eyewitness identification).

65. *Compare* United States v. Chin, 981 F.2d 1275 (D.C.Cir.1992) *cert. denied*, 508 U.S. 923 (1993)(expert testimony on the modus operandi of drug dealers admissible under Rule 702) *with* United States v. Cruz, 981 F.2d 659 (2d Cir.1992)(expert testimony on the role of the broker in a drug operation not admissible under Rule 702).

66. *Compare* United States v. Snow, 552 F.2d 165 (6th Cir. 1977)(admitting ex-

future earnings of a deceased individual,[67] and the cause of an automobile accident[68] to mention only a few. Although "assist the trier of fact" is primarily a relevance judgment,[69] many of the exclusions of forensic and social science had overtones of a validity judgment—doubts about whether the testimony qualified as "scientific, technical, or other specialized" knowledge.[70] This expanded notion of relevance or "fit"[71] was sometimes articulated as a Rule 702 problem of not "assisting the trier of fact," or as a Rule 403 problem of being "confusing, misleading or prejudicial."[72] The 2000 amendments might make those previously hidden reasons for exclusion more transparent.

To be sure, some of the more intense speculation about the influence of *Daubert* has centered on forensic science—the application of the natural and physical sciences to the resolution of conflict in a legal setting—and on social science—the study of human behavior. Some applications of forensic science (e.g., latent print comparisons, handwriting identification), became so familiar to the courts that they were rarely challenged before *Daubert*. Social science has not had the same long acceptance in the courts. Although expert testimony about insanity, diminished capacity, and potential for violence have long histories in the courts, rape trauma, battered women, battered child, and other syndromes have only more recently become regular areas for expert testimony. Expert testimony about the unreliability of eyewitness identification, the accuracy of repressed memory, or the suggestiveness of interview techniques are among those mysteries that continue to be treated skeptically in many courts, but admitted in others.[73]

pert testimony comparing photographs) *with* United States v. Brown, 501 F.2d 146 (9th Cir.1974)(expert testimony comparing photographs not admissible).

67. *Compare* Hooks v. Washington Sheraton Corp., 578 F.2d 313 (D.C.Cir. 1977)(economist testimony about the future earnings of an eighteen year old admissible) *with* Barnes v. Smith, 305 F.2d 226 (10th Cir. 1962)(economist testimony about the future earnings of a seventeen year old not admissible).

68. *Compare* Seese v. Volkswagenwerk A.G., 648 F.2d 833, 844 (3d Cir.), *cert. denied* 454 U.S. 867 (1981)(admitting accident reconstructionist's testimony) *with* Dallas & Mavis Forwarding Co. v. Stegall, 659 F.2d 721, 722 (6th Cir.1981)(excluding accident reconstructionist's testimony

69. Daubert v. Merrell Dow Pharmaceuticals, Inc., 509 U.S. 579, 591 (1993).

70. "Rule 702's 'helpfulness' standard requires a valid scientific connection to the pertinent inquiry as a precondition to admissibility." *See id.,* at 591.

71. Coined by Judge Becker in United States v. Downing, 753 F.2d 1224, 1242 (3d Cir. 1985) and adopted by the Supreme Court in *Daubert*, "fit" may be another way to describe a failure to meet the reliability requirement of Rule 702, at least as related to the issues in the particular case.

72. *See, e.g.,* United States v. Curry, 977 F.2d 1042 (7th Cir.1992) (trial court non-specific exclusion of expert testimony regarding the reliability of eyewitness identification either because the testimony was something about which the jurors were "generally aware" or because it would be "confusing"). The court's ambivalence leaves room for the view that, despite a footnoted bow to the growing acceptability of the area, the court does not think much of the underlying "expertise."

73. *See, e.g.* United States v. Kime, 99 F.3d 870, 885 (8th Cir. 1996) (held, not abuse of discretion to determine defendant's proffer of testimony about fallibility of eyewitness identification did not satisfy *Daubert*); United States v. Norwood, 939 F.Supp. 1132, 1133, 1141 (D. N.J. 1996) (held, expert testimony on reliability of eyewitness identification admissible; case contains useful description of what this type of expertise could contribute); United States v. Rouse, 111 F.3d 561, 572 (8th Cir. 1997)

There are multi-volume treatises limited to scientific evidence that should be consulted for the student or lawyer who requires an exhaustive treatment of the subject or who is searching for the exotic application.[74] Here, we will merely sample six areas in which *Daubert* may have made a difference.

Handwriting Analysis

With Wigmore's enthusiastic endorsement, documents examiners (sometimes called forensic document analysts or questioned document examiners) have been permitted for many years to testify about whether documents were forged or authentic. In spectacular cases such as the trial of the alleged kidnapper of the Lindbergh baby and in more mundane cases, documents examiners have become a fixture in American courtrooms. The test of expertise was basically whether document examiners met the standards of the guild, that is, the standards established by other practitioners of their craft. There was no serious effort to test the underlying premises of documents examiners or the accuracy of their performance.

Debunkers of handwriting identification maintain that it has not been demonstrated that documents examiners can distinguish between forgeries and authentic documents by handwriting analysis. The expertise has been attacked both on grounds that its foundational assumptions are unproven and that the error rate as measured by proficiency testing is unacceptably high.[75] There are several ways in which the underlying premises and the performance of examiners could be tested: (1) The most fundamental premises of the field are that no two people write the same way, and that no one person writes the same way each time. Documents examiners assert, however, that inter-writer variations are greater than intra-writer (same writer) variations. The validity of that premise can be tested by having randomly chosen subjects submit several handwriting samples, and then having coders sort the samples by degree of similarity. Inter-writer variations could thus be compared with intra-writer variations. (2) Another basic premise is that forgeries are more likely to have blunt endings than genuine signatures. The validity of this premise could be tested by having subjects write their own signatures and then forge the signatures of others. Coders could then classify the signatures by whether they had blunt endings or not. (3) A third hypothesis is that slowly written handwriting is distinguishable from rapidly written handwriting. This premise could be tested by having subjects write rapidly and slowly, and then having documents examiners sort the samples into what they believe to have been rapidly

(on rehearing) (divided panel indicates that expert testimony about suggestiveness of pretrial treatment of child witnesses should have been admitted).

74. David L. Faigman et al., Modern Scientific Evidence Kaye.

75. See, e.g., D. Michael Risinger & Michael J. Saks, Science and Nonscience in the Courts: *Daubert* Meets Handwriting Identification Expertise, 82 Iowa L. Rev. 21 (1996).

written and slowly written categories. Practically no work of the kind suggested in this discussion has been done.

The proficiency of documents examiners could be tested by submitting mock "cases" to documents examiners to determine how successful they are at distinguishing authentic handwriting from forgeries. This has been done to some extent, but the results are discouraging. An influential pre-*Daubert* article, published in 1989, when handwriting identification expertise was being routinely admitted under *Frye*, undertook a comprehensive examination of proficiency studies available at that date. The authors concluded "[a] rather generous reading of the data would be that in 45% of the reports forensic document examiners reached the correct finding, in 36% they erred partially or completely, and in 19% they were unable to draw a conclusion."[76] In tests in which disguised handwriting was used—in which the exemplars contained some attempts to forge documents—the accuracy levels were even lower. Subsequent research has not done much to improve the error rate. A controversial study conducted for the FBI does indicate that document examiners do somewhat better than lay people,[77] though that result may be due merely to the greater motivation of document examiners to perform well in tests upon which their livelihood depends.

The weakness of the empirical data in substantiating the claims of documents examiners has probably made more difference under *Daubert* than under *Frye*. Many courts now limit the testimony of document examiners. Some courts have limited examiners to testimony about similarities between known samples and the questioned document, but do not allow examiners to state a conclusion about whether the samples were in fact written by the same person.[78] Some courts go further, excluding entirely the testimony of document examiners.[79] Still other courts continue to admit the testimony of document examiners with only a few restrictions, largely based on their faith in the ability of jurors to separate the wheat from the chaff.[80] One court has completely excluded the testimony of a document examiner.[81]

Polygraph Evidence

The differences between a *Daubert* approach and a *Frye* approach are aptly illustrated by the difference between *United States v. Piccinonna*,[82] and *State v. Porter*.[83] *Piccinonna* is a pre-*Daubert* case in which the

---

76. D. Michael Risinger et al.,. Exorcism of Ignorance as a Proxy for Rational Knowledge: The Lessons of Handwriting Identification "Expertise," 137 U. Pa. L. Rev. 731, 747 (1989).

77. Moshe Kam et al., Proficiency of Document Examiners in Writer Identification, 39 J. Forensic Sci. 5 (1994).

78. *See, e.g.,* United States v. Rutherford, 104 F.Supp.2d 1190, 1194 (D.Neb. 2000); United States v. Van Wyk, 83 F.Supp.2d 515, 524 (D. N.J. 2000); United

States v. Hines, 55 F.Supp.2d 62, 70–71 (D. Mass. 1999).

79. *See, e.g.,* United States v. Saelee, 162 F.Supp.2d 1097 (D. Alaska 2001).

80. *See, e.g.,* United States v. Starzecpyzel, 880 F.Supp. 1027 (S.D. N.Y. 1995).

81. *See* United States v. Saelee, 162 F.Supp.2d 1097 (D. Alaska 2001)(testimony of forensic documents examiner excluded in its entirety as failing meet *Daubert* test)

82. 885 F.2d 1529, 1536–37 (11th Cir. 1989).

83. 698 A.2d 739, 746 (Conn. 1997).

Eleventh Circuit held that properly conducted polygraph tests were admissible when both parties stipulate in advance to the circumstances of the test and the scope of its admissibility, or when used to impeach or corroborate witnesses. *State v. Porter* is a post-*Daubert* decision by the Connecticut Supreme Court. The *Porter* court decided to adopt *Daubert* as its state rule of decision. Applying *Daubert*, it held polygraph tests to be inadmissible.[84]

The *Piccinonna* case applied the broad holding of *Frye* (that the test is general acceptance) to undermine the narrow holding of *Frye* (that lie detector tests are not admissible). It cited works by polygraph enthusiasts for the general proposition that "tremendous advances have been made in polygraph instrumentation and technique," without going into the details.[85] It noted that the FBI, the Secret Service, military intelligence and law enforcement agencies use the polygraph[86] (without noting that using the polygraph to get investigatory leads or confessions is quite different from using it to find truth, or that the judicial system ought to be more concerned about avoiding false positives than agencies using the polygraph in intelligence work or for employment screening.) Noting these uses, it found that the "general acceptance" status of the polygraph had changed.[87] Its sole discussion of error rate or testing issues consisted of a footnote citing a legal hornbook, *McCormick on Evidence*, for the proposition that polygraph examiners claim accuracy rates of 92% and 100%, while others suggest figures in the range of 63–72%.[88]

In contrast, *State v. Porter* undertook a systematic review of the research on polygraph, including a review of the methodological problems of studying the polygraph, and a discussion of the dangers inherent in the use of the predominant "control question" test.[89] It notes the dubious scientific premise of the control question test, that innocent subjects will have a higher response to the control questions (questions that everyone is assumed to feel disturbed about) and that guilty ones will have an elevated response to the relevant questions (questions about the crime under investigation).[90] It describes the methodological problems of studying polygraph results in the laboratory, problems that make its generalization to real life situations questionable. For example, persons telling authorized lies do not have the same emotional stake as persons telling real lies, and the persons telling the truth about mock crimes do not have the same fear of being unjustly accused as real suspects in a criminal case.[91] The court also assessed the validity of field studies.[92] In such studies, the outcome measures are suspect because it is hard to know what the ground truth is, and the confession criterion used to determine whether the polygraph subject was guilty is not independent of the result reached by the polygraph operator. The court com-

---

84. *Id.* at 773.

85. Piccinonna, 885 F.2d at 1532.

86. *Id.*

87. *Id.*

88. *Id.* at 1533.

89. Porter, 698 A.2d at 760–61.

90. *Id.*

91. *Id.* at 765–66.

92. *Id.* at 766–67.

pared the error rates estimated by polygraph advocates with those estimated by critics, and offered reasons for discounting the laboratory studies used by advocates.[93] It also explained how the "predictive value" of the polygraph would not be the same as the error rate.[94] For example, if a test that has only a 10% false positive error rate is applied to a suspect population that is 95% innocent, then most of the subjects identified as guilty by the low-error-rate test will actually be innocent. Finally, the court notes the little-studied problem of countermeasures,[95] and discusses whether the data that does support the polygraph is questionable because it largely involved subjects not trained in countermeasures. In short, in *Piccinonna* we see a court taking a cursory look at the methodology and finding "general acceptance" in inapposite administrative applications of the polygraph, while in *State v. Porter* we see a court doing a sophisticated examination of polygraph theory, study methodology, and the results of testing. While the results might have been the same in the two cases even without the difference in rules— cursory opinions may be found under any rule—*Daubert* encourages courts to make a more thorough analysis of validity than *Frye* does, and hence it may encourage judges to write opinions like the one produced by the Connecticut court in *State v. Porter*.

An increasing number of courts have departed from *Frye*'s specific holding that polygraph evidence is inadmissible,[96] though others held to the position that it is not admissible, at least in the absence of stipulation by both parties.[97] Doubts about the methodology and general application of studies of validity seem likely to make the exclusionary position

93. *Id.*

94. *Id.*

95. An example of a "countermeasure" is biting one's tongue when asked a control question. *see Porter*, A.2d at 768. Instruction on countermeasures is given at the web site antipolygraph.org.

96. For example, the Fifth Circuit has declared that, in light of Daubert and scientific advances in polygraphy, polygraph evidence is no longer per se inadmissible. United States v. Posado, 57 F.3d 428, 433 (5th Cir. 1995). *See also* United States v. Crumby, 895 F.Supp. 1354, 1361 (D. Ariz. 1995); United States v. Piccinonna, 885 F.2d 1529 (11th Cir. 1989)(trial court has discretion to admit polygraph evidence if test properly conducted and notice given); United States v. Cordoba, 104 F.3d 225, 227 (9th Cir. 1997) (held, Daubert effectively overruled 9th Circuit per se rule excluding unstipulated polygraph evidence; vacated and remanded for particularized Daubert inquiry by district court). *See generally* James R. McCall, Misconceptions and Re-

evaluation—Polygraph Admissibility After Rock and Daubert, 1996 U. Ill. L. Rev. 363.

97. *See* Meyers v. Arcudi, 947 F.Supp. 581, 587 (D. Conn. 1996) (held, control question polygraph test did not meet *Daubert* standard; court alludes to problems of generalizing from lab studies to real-life litigation situations, and to difficulty of determining whether lying occurred in field tests; it reaches conclusion that technique has been tested but that testimony does not demonstrate scientific validity); United States v. Williams, 95 F.3d 723, 730 (8th Cir. 1996) (prosecution witness had failed polygraph examination administered by FBI agent during investigation and defense proffered evidence of exam results; held, not abuse of discretion to exclude exam results in absence of Daubert showing of validity of polygraph exam; testimony of polygrapher alone not sufficient to lay foundation if polygrapher not qualified to opine on Daubert factors). United States v. Lea, 249 F.3d 632, 640 (7th Cir. 2001) (polygraph test offered by the defendant was properly excluded; trial court need not do full Daubert analysis).

the dominant one for some time to come.[98] At any rate, it is now clear that the federal Constitution does not guarantee the accused the right to present exculpatory polygraph evidence. [99]

Social Science Evidence

Of course, *Daubert* applies to testimony of social scientists as it does to testimony of hard scientists, and courts have applied it, with divergent results, to testimony about subjects such as the testimony about the fallibility of eyewitness identification and the conditions that cause problems of identification,[100] about conditions that are likely to elicit false confessions,[101] about the effect of suggestive interviews on the

98. For a thoughtful opinion that extensively reviews the scientific evidence and decides to retain a per se rule against polygraph evidence, *see* State v. Porter, 698 A.2d 739 (Conn.1997).

99. *See* United States v. Scheffer, 523 U.S. 303 (1998), in which the Supreme Court reviewed a case in which a military trial judge excluded polygraph evidence offered by the accused in a court-martial. The accused claimed that Military Rule of Evidence 707, which makes polygraph evidence inadmissible, unconstitutionally abridged his right to present a defense. Reversing the United States Court of Appeals for the Armed Forces, the Supreme Court upheld Rule 707.

100. For examples of recent cases, *see* United States v. Kime, 99 F.3d 870, 885 (8th Cir. 1996) (not abuse of discretion to determine, under facts of case, that proffer by defendant seeking to introduce testimony about fallibility of eyewitness identification had not satisfied *Daubert* because it did not present enough information to determine scientific validity). United States v. Hicks, 103 F.3d 837 (9th Cir. 1996) (held, even if expert's proposed testimony about eyewitness identification satisfied *Daubert* criteria, district court had discretion to exclude it as unhelpful; district court gave a four-page jury instruction (not reproduced in the appellate opinion) telling jury what to consider in evaluating eyewitness testimony). United States v. Rincon, 28 F.3d 921 (9th Cir. 1994) (held, not abuse of discretion to exclude expert testimony on eyewitness identification where trial judge gave comprehensive instruction on eyewitness identification that addressed many of the factors about which the expert would have testified, including opportunity to observe, the length of time that had elapsed, the dangers of a showup versus a lineup, the danger of subsequent influence or suggestiveness, whether the eyewitness made inconsistent identifications, and whether the eyewitness was credible). (In the opinion of

the author, the instruction fell far short of giving the jury the information that an expert could have provided on topics such as subsequent influence.) United States v. Norwood, 939 F.Supp. 1132, 1133 (D.N.J. 1996) (held, expert testimony on reliability of eyewitness identification admissible in carjacking prosecution; case contains useful description of what this type of expertise could contribute). United States v. Smithers, 212 F.3d 306, 53 Fed. R. Evid. Serv. 1273, 2000 Fed.App. 0160P (6th Cir. 2000) (held, trial judge abused discretion by excluding eyewitness I.D. testimony without doing full *Daubert* analysis); United States v. Langan, 263 F.3d 613, 622–625, 57 Fed. R. Evid. Serv. 137 (6th Cir. 2001) (though expert testimony about eyewitness identification is not automatically inadmissible, in this case district court correctly concluded that it should be excluded on grounds that expert's testimony on "transference theory" described a theory that remained empirically unproven).

101. *See* United States v. Hall, 974 F.Supp. 1198 (C.D. Ill. 1997). There, the district court ruled on a pretrial motion to exclude the testimony of Dr. Richard Ofshe. Dr. Ofshe, a social psychologist, was offered as an expert on police interrogation techniques and false confessions. He was prepared to testify, based on extensive study, to various aspects of the phenomenon of false confessions, including the existence of "identifiable coercive police interrogation techniques which are likely to produce false confessions." At the first trial, the district court had excluded Dr. Ofshe's testimony, and on appeal the Seventh Circuit had remanded with instructions to conduct a full *Daubert* hearing. United States v. Hall, 93 F.3d 1337, 1344–45 (7th Cir. 1996). On remand, the district court wrote that though *Daubert* is applicable to the social sciences, the relevant screening criteria have to be tailored to the subject matter. Many social scientists rely primarily on

recollection of child witnesses,[102] the behavior of sexually abused children,[103] the impact of sexual harassment,[104] hedonic damages,[105] and many other topics.[106]

Police Experts

The testimony of police experts about matters such as the method of operation of criminal enterprises continues to be admissible. [107]Although,

"real-world experience rather than experimentation," 974 F.Supp. at 1202, and in assessing the testimony of social science experts the courts need not consider the same factors that they would consider in assessing "Newtonian" hard science. They should, however consider at a minimum the "longevity" of the expert's field, the amount of literature, the methods of peer review, the quantity of "observational or other studies," the "comparative similarity of observations obtained, the reasons why those studies are deemed valid and reliable, and the general consensus or debate as to what the raw data means." Id. at 1203. Applying these criteria on remand, the court held Dr. Ofshe's testimony to be admissible. Dr. Ofshe noted in his *Daubert* hearing testimony that controlled laboratory experiments were difficult to conduct for ethical reasons, and the research on which he relied was mostly field work in which actual confessions were examined. Researchers determined that certain confessions were false (often because the confessor's post-admission narrative description of crime facts did not match known facts), then examined the interrogation methods used to see which ones were associated with false confessions. Id. at 1204. The district judge, noting that Dr. Ofshe did not propose to state an opinion on the ultimate issue of whether Hall's confession was false held that he would be permitted to testify about the association of false confessions with certain police interrogation techniques. Id. at 1205.

102. *See* United States v. Rouse, 111 F.3d 561, 572 (8th Cir. 1997) (on rehearing) (affirming lower court in 3–way split, majority finds error in excluding defense expert testimony about suggestive nature of pretrial interviews of alleged child sex abuse victims, but only one member of panel considered error to be reversible).

103. *See* United States v. Bighead, 128 F.3d 1329 (9th Cir. 1997) (divided panel, over Judge Noonan's dissent, upholds admission of testimony of director of forensic services at Children's Advocacy Center; witness testified, based on experience with over 1,300 people who claimed to have been victims of child abuse, that delayed disclo-

sure was common; held, Daubert test did not apply to "specialized" as opposed to "scientific" knowledge; the latter conclusion is now dubious in light of the Supreme Court's opinion in Kumho, *supra*.).

104. *See* Jenson v. Eveleth Taconite Co., 130 F.3d 1287, 1296 (8th Cir. 1997) (Lay, J) (error to exclude plaintiffs' psychiatric evidence about impact of sexual harassment).

105. On the admissibility, after Daubert, of expert testimony about the value of the pleasure of life, *see* McGuire v. City of Santa Fe, 954 F.Supp. 230, 234, 46 Fed. R. Evid. Serv. (LCP) 942 (D.N.M. 1996) (Plaintiff in employment discrimination case offered expert testimony about hedonic damage; held, *Daubert* analysis applies to expert testimony about hedonic damage and testimony is inadmissible).

106. *See, e.g.,* United States v. Vallejo, 237 F.3d 1008, 1020, 55 Fed. R. Evid. Serv. 599 (9th Cir. 2001), opinion amended on other grounds on denial of reh'g, 246 F.3d 1150 (9th Cir. 2001)) (held, error to exclude defense expert's testimony on special problems that former special education students have when attempting to communicate in English in stressful situations, such as police interrogation; testimony was offered to explain discrepancies between recollection of defendant and of customs agent about statements allegedly made by defendant during interrogation).

107. In United States v. Vallejo, 237 F.3d 1008, 1020, 55 Fed. R. Evid. Serv. 599 (9th Cir. 2001), opinion amended on other grounds on denial of reh'g, 246 F.3d 1150 (9th Cir. 2001)) the appellate court found it to be an abuse of discretion to admit evidence about the characteristics of drug trafficking organizations in a case turning upon whether an alleged drug courier knew that the car he was driving contained hidden drugs. The police expert had testified that the drug smuggling business was compartmentalized, with specialized roles, and described the process of taking drugs from the marijuana grove to the market in the United States. On oral argument, the government said it introduced such testimony in

after *Kumho*, all expertise falls within the purview of *Daubert*, the expertise may be judged valid by use of criteria other than scientific testing, peer review and publication, or assessment of an error rate. The fact that all expertise must be screened, however, certainly indicates that it is appropriate for trial judges to ask police experts about the basis for their opinions and to exclude the opinions if they are not based on reliable data and methodology that is appropriate considering the subject matter and the practical alternatives.

Field Sobriety Tests

For several decades, it has been common for police officers to administer a series of "field sobriety tests" (FSTs) to drivers they suspect of being under the influence of alcohol. Developed for the National Highway Traffic Safety Administration (NHTSA) in the 1970s, there are three main tests.[108] The test that has the greatest claim to a scientific basis is the Horizontal Gaze Nystagmus Test (HGN). Nystagmus is the involuntary jerking of the eyes as a person gazes to the side. It is a natural phenomenon, but alcohol and certain other drugs are thought to magnify it. The officer administering the test looks for three "clues" to exaggerated nystagmus: the subject's inability to follow a

every drug smuggling case to rebut any inference jurors might draw from the absence of fingerprint evidence. One would not expect to find a courier's fingerprints on drug packages because they are typically packed by different members of the organization. After noting that no fingerprint issue was raised by the defense in this case, the court wrote:

> Although the Government claims it was not trying to show Vallejo was a key player in a drug cartel, it portrayed him as a member of an enormous international drug trafficking organization and implied that he knew of the drugs in his car because of his role in that organization. This expert testimony connected seemingly innocent conduct to a vast drug empire, and through this connection, it unfairly attributed knowledge—the sole issue in the case—Vallejo, a single individual, who was not alleged to be associated with a drug trafficking organization in even the most minor way. As a result, the introduction of this evidence created the same prejudice that has made drug courier profiles inadmissible.

Accord, United States v. McGowan, 274 F.3d 1251, 58 Fed. R. Evid. Serv. 890 (9th Cir. 2001) (citing and following Vallejo case in similar situation).

United States v. Gutierrez–Farias, 294 F.3d 657 (5th Cir. 2002) (testimony of police expert saying that drug rings do not recruit people of the street who have no knowledge,

but instead use people they can trust as couriers, inferentially was testimony that defendant knew that marijuana was concealed in tires of vehicle and hence a violation of Fed. R. Evid. 704(b)).

United States v. Castillo, 924 F.2d 1227, 1233–34, 32 Fed. R. Evid. Serv. 59 (2d Cir. 1991) (held, reversible error to allow expert to testify about practices of drug dealers in using scales, plastic bags, tinfoil, and guns; "we are not convinced that New York jurors in today's climate, flush with daily news of latest drug bust, need an expert to enlighten them as to such elementary issues as the function of a scale or an index card in a drug deal," such expertise was unnecessary where the jurors had testimony by police agent who had witnessed these defendants making use of such items; admitting expert testimony that drug dealers use guns to intimidate purchasers into snorting cocaine in order to flush out undercover agents was prejudicial because it was being used to corroborate police agent's testimony that he saw protruding gun and was asked to snort cocaine; syllogism that drug dealers use guns to force snorting, these defendants were drug dealers, ergo they used guns to force agent to snort was "an improper guilt by alleged association argument" using conduct of others to convict the defendants).

108. For a detailed discussion of the various tests, *see* United States v. Horn, 185 F.Supp.2d 530, 535–38 (D. Md. 2002).

slowly moving stimulus smoothly; a more distinct nystagmus when the subject has moved the eyes as far as possible to the left or right and held them in that position for several seconds; and the presence of nystagmus before the eyes have moved 45 degrees to the left or right. NHTSA publications, which are cited repeatedly in judicial opinions, take the position that if a subject exhibits nystagmus before moving the eyes 45 degrees to the right or left, the subject normally has a blood alcohol content (BAC) above 0.10, which is above the legal limit in many states. Because the HGN test requires the administering officer to make visual measurements based on these "clues,"[109] the validity of the test depends on the officer's accuracy.

The other FSTs are considerably more subjective and based less on scientifically observed phenomena. The "Walk and Turn" test (WAT) requires the subject to walk a straight line in the heel-to-toe position for a set number of paces, and then to turn and walk back in the same manner, all the while holding his hands to the side, watching his feet, and counting his steps out loud. As with the HGN test, NHSTA publications assert that the officer should watch for certain "clues," and that the subject's performance can indicate a BAC above 0.10.[110] The One Leg Stand (OLS) is much as its name suggests. Again, the officer monitors the subject's performance using certain "clues," and is purported to be able to make a judgment with reasonable accuracy that a given subject has a BAC of over 0.10. Other tests include a "finger-count" test, and a test in which the subject is asked to write the letters of the alphabet.

Prosecutors in drunk driving cases have offered FST evidence for two principal purposes: (2) to demonstrate the existence of probable cause to charge a driver with driving under the influence of alcohol; and (2) to prove a subject's actual BAC.

Beginning in the 1980s, state courts began to evaluate the admissibility of FST evidence.[111] Many courts distinguish the HGN test from the other, less "scientific" FSTs. These courts have generally evaluated the HGN test under the applicable standard for scientific evidence, while viewing the other tests as involving the kinds of common sense observations within the general knowledge of laypersons, and thus not requiring expert testimony.[112] Often, courts admit this evidence simply as the lay

---

109. There are, in fact, six "clues" because the officer must apply the three clues to each of the subject's eyes. *Id.*

110. The NHTSA asserts that when the results of the HGN and WAT tests are combined, the officer can achieve 80 percent accuracy in judging that the subject's BAC exceeds 0.10.

111. Apparently the first reported opinion is that of the Arizona Supreme Court in State v. Superior Court, 718 P.2d 171 (Ariz. 1986), where the court held the results of the HGN test sufficiently trustworthy to establish probable cause for arrest. The court also held that the HGN test

had achieved general acceptance among behavioral psychologists, highway safety experts, neurologists, and law enforcement agencies.

112. *See, e.g.*, State v. Cissne, 865 P.2d 564, 568 (Wash. App. 1994) ("The HGN test is a different type of test from balancing on one leg or walking a straight line because it rests almost entirely upon an assertion of scientific legitimacy rather than a basis of common knowledge"); State v. Witte, 836 P.2d 1110, 1111 (Kan. 1992) ("The horizontal gaze nystagmus test is distinguished from other field sobriety tests in that science, rather than common knowl-

observation of the police officer that can be helpful in determining whether the subject was intoxicated.[113]

Courts have usually held that the HGN test satisfies the *Frye* standard.[114] Unfortunately, many courts have admitted the evidence with little effort to analyze whether it actually satisfied established legal standards.[115] Some, in fact, have taken judicial notice of the reliability of the test.[116] A few courts have held that the test does not meet the *Frye* standard because the test is not generally accepted in the relevant scientific community.[117] At the same time, most courts have allowed the evidence only as circumstantial evidence of intoxication or impairment, and not as proof of defendant's specific BAC.[118]

FSTs, and particularly the HGN test, require somewhat greater scrutiny under the standards set forth in *Daubert, Kumho Tire*, and Rule 702. FSTs might be viewed as based on "scientific" knowledge, though it is also possible to characterize them as based on technical expert knowledge to which Rule 702 (as amended) applies.[119] Though research appears to support the validity of the assumptions underlying the HGN test (that an intoxicated person exhibits exaggerated nystagmus), neither that test nor any of the more subjective FSTs are likely to be sufficiently

edge, provides the legitimacy for horizontal gaze nystagmus testing"). *But see* State v. Bresson, 554 N.E.2d 1330 (Ohio 1990) (HGN test is no different from any other FST).

113. *See, e.g.,* State v. Meador, 674 So.2d 826, 832 (Fla. App. 1996) (holding the "psychomotor FSTs" admissible to show intoxication, but holding that officer should avoid referring to the observations as "tests" or suggesting that the subject "failed" or received a certain number of "points").

114. *See, e.g.,* Williams v. State, 710 So.2d 24 (Fla. App. 1998) (HGN test is "quasi-scientific" and is generally accepted, thus satisfying Frye standard; no need for trial courts to reapply Frye test in every case); Hawkins v. State, 476 S.E.2d 803 (Ga. App. 1996) (HGN is generally accepted and thus satisfies Frye test); People v. Buening, 592 N.E.2d 1222 (Ill. App. 1992) (HGN test satisfies Frye standard).

115. One court has stated that in upholding the admissibility of FSTs, state courts "more often than not expressed their holdings in passing and without analysis." United States v. Horn, 185 F.Supp.2d 530, 557 (D. Md. 2002). The courts frequently rely on the same few studies, all commissioned by the NHTSA in the 1970s. Id. at 535–36. In addition, many courts simply rely on other courts' conclusions. Id. One writer asserts that *Horn* "signal[s] federal courts to re-examine admissibility issues in light of Daubert, Kumho Tire and amended

Rule 702 . . . and challenges state courts to abandon the lax standards used for nearly two decades to admit SFST evidence, and to re-examine SFST admissibility by adopting the more conservative and objective approach for admission of scientific, technical or specialized evidence dictated by . . . *Frye* and Kumho Tire." Bruce Kapsack, DWI, 26 Champ 57, 58–59 (Nov. 2002).

116. *See, e.g.,* Schultz v. State, 664 A.2d 60, 69–74 (Md. App. 1995). (after evaluating other cases and published literature on HGN test, court holds that test is trustworthy and meets *Frye* general acceptance test).

117. *See, e.g.,* Young v. City of Brookhaven, 693 So.2d 1355 (Miss. 1997) (HGN is a scientific test but is not generally accepted; it is not admissible before a jury, but may be used to show probable cause at a probable cause hearing); Commonwealth v. Apollo, 603 A.2d 1023 (Pa. Super. 1992) (affirming trial court's decision to exclude HGN evidence on ground *Frye* standard had not been met).

118. *See, e.g.,* Ballard v. State, 955 P.2d 931 (Alaska App. 1998); State v. Superior Court, 718 P.2d 171 (Ariz. 1986); State v. Taylor, 694 A.2d 907 (Me. 1997); State v. Baue, 607 N.W.2d 191 (Neb. 2000).

119. *See* David L. Faigman et al., Science in the Law—Forensic Science Issues § 8–1.2.6, at 407 (2002) (noting that this is one possible approach).

trustworthy to justify an estimate of a subject's actual BAC. In fact, the data supporting FSTs is rather thin, and the error rates are relatively high. Thus, courts applying the standards are more likely to place significant restrictions on FST testimony.

The most searching judicial analysis to date of the admissibility of FST evidence under the federal standard was conducted by the district court in *United States v. Horn*,[120] which held a two-day hearing on the admissibility of FSTs. The court considered the affidavits of four defense experts as well as the arresting officer. The government also introduced a number of "validation studies." The defense experts criticized these studies on many grounds. Among the more important criticisms were that some studies were conducted under laboratory conditions that facilitated observation of would not be duplicated in the field; that the officers who submitted to some tests were self-selected and might not have been representative; that some estimates of accuracy were artificially inflated by the test methodology, that some data was described incompletely or in a manner that cannot be evaluated adequately; that certain studies reported misleadingly high accuracy rates; and that the results of the studies were not published in peer reviewed journals.[121] The court ultimately concluded that the results of the tests would only be admissible to determine whether probable cause exists to charge a driver with driving while intoxicated, that the test results, whether taken individually or combined, are not admissible to prove the specific BAC of a subject, and that while a police officer trained in FSTs may testify about her observations of a subject's performance on properly administered tests, the officer may not use "value-added descriptive language to characterize the subject's performance." In addition, the court held that although the officer may offer an opinion as a lay witness that the defendant was driving while intoxicated, she may not bolster that opinion by referring to any scientific, technical, or specialized information gleaned from law enforcement instruction.[122]

Though some courts applying the *Daubert/Kumho Tire*/Rule 702 standards have been more generous toward admission of FST evidence,[123] the direction suggested by the *Horn* court seems most appropriate under those standards.

Clinical Experience of Physicians

Now that *Kumho* has held that all expertise must be assessed for reliability under the *Daubert* standards, one may expect enhanced attacks upon the validity of experts who assess such subjects as medical causation by reference to clinical experience rather than systematic scientific studies. In assessing the admissibility of such evidence, it is appropriate to consider whether scientific assessment is feasible under

---

120. 185 F.Supp.2d 530 (D. Md. 2002).

121. *Id.* at 539–46.

122. *Id.* at 532–34.

123. *See, e.g.*, Volk v. United States, 57 F.Supp.2d 888 (N.D. Cal. 1999) (holding that the Kumho Tire standard applies, and that courts have broad discretion within that standard).

the circumstances, the opinions of authorities who have done a more systematic evaluation of the subject, whether the opinion was developed in anticipation of litigation, whether the expert has considered and ruled out alternative causal explanations, and other factors bearing on the appropriateness of accepting a clinical opinion. [124]

§ 10.05 Expert Testimony—Presentation [FRE 703–705]

Anyone qualified by "knowledge, skill, experience, training, or education"[125] might provide expert testimony. Though witnesses with extensive education and many degrees are common as expert witnesses, an expert need not have acquired expert knowledge through formal education. A carpenter or other skilled worker without a day of formal education might qualify as an expert, if the person's experience provides specialized knowledge.[126]

Before *Daubert*, a party wishing to qualify an expert had only to show that the expert was qualified to testify to the particular knowledge to be offered. This showing was normally made by direct examination of the proffered expert. After the witness' qualifications had been presented on direct examination and before the witness gave an opinion on the substantive issues of the case, a party objecting could cross-examine the

---

124. Cooper v. Smith & Nephew, Inc., 259 F.3d 194, 203, 56 Fed. R. Evid. Serv. 1001 (4th Cir. 2001) (held, though reliable differential diagnosis is admissible, in this case it was not because it amounted to a wholly conclusory finding based upon subjective beliefs rather than science, one which utterly failed to consider alternative causes); Domingo ex rel. Domingo v. T.K., M.D., 276 F.3d 1083, 1089, 58 Fed. R. Evid. Serv. 80 (9th Cir. 2002), opinion amended on other grounds and superseded, 289 F.3d 600 (9th Cir. 2002) (held, plaintiff's expert testimony on medical causation properly excluded on grounds, inter alia, that conclusion that lengthy malleting during hip surgery was atypical did not support conclusion that overlong malleting was cause of fat embolism syndrome; "FES is a known risk of hip replacement surgery. There is nothing in the research cited that suggests that FES is a greater risk when something atypical or substandard occurs during the surgery"); Turner v. Iowa Fire Equipment Co., 229 F.3d 1202, 1208 (8th Cir. 2000) (held, proper to exclude treating physician's testimony about cause of respiratory illness where physician did not systematically rule out other causes).

125. Fed. R. Evid. 702

126. *See, e.g.,* Fed. R.Evid. 702 advisory committee's note. *Compare,* Scott v. Yates, 643 N.E.2d 105 (Ohio 1994)(abuse of discretion to allow officer with no accident reconstruction training to testify about

cause of accident); Peavey Co. v. M/V ANPA, 971 F.2d 1168, 1174 (5th Cir.1992) (affirming trial court's determination that insurer-defendant's claims manager was unqualified to testify as to whether insured-plaintiff's failure to retain a "qualified" electrical engineering expert to inspect damages prejudiced defendant), *with* Sullivan v. Rowan Cos., 952 F.2d 141 (5th Cir. 1992) (trial judge did not abuse discretion by ruling that expert who had Ph.D in geology, but who was not an engineer and whose only formal study in metallurgy was a three-day seminar, was not qualified to testify about metal failure despite fact that expert had been employed for more than 10 years in private laboratories performing metal failure analyses using scanning electron microscopes; query whether district judge might have given too much weight to lack of formal education in particular field); United States v. Welch, 945 F.2d 1378 (7th Cir.1991) (court held that there was error in holding that defense witness, a chief production engineer and professor, was not qualified as expert, where witness lacked sufficient training or experience in forensic tape analysis and where witness was unfamiliar with the use of technological instruments used to detect alterations in taped conversations;), *cert. denied,* 502 U.S. 1118 (1992); *c.f.,* Asplundh Mfg. Div. v. Benton Harbor Eng'g, 57 F.3d 1190, 1192 (3d Cir. 1995)(lay witness could not testify about metal fatigue in absence of showing of sufficient special knowledge or experience).

witness to expose defects in training and experience. The trial judge had discretion to require that the parties conduct this examination beyond the hearing of the jury.[127] If the trial judge determined the witness was qualified, the party offering the testimony then continued the examination of the witness to elicit the witness's expert testimony. Afterward, the opposing party had another opportunity to cross-examine for purposes of exposing defects in the opinion, obtaining concessions, or impeaching the witness.

In cases involving medical experts, controversies often arose about whether the testimony of a specialist was required. The general tendency of courts had been to admit the testimony of general practitioners, even where a specialist might be more knowledgeable. Even if the general practitioner had no special training, medical school training and general experience qualified the general practitioner to testify about a variety of matters that are often referred to specialists. For example, a general practitioner could testify to the psychological damage caused by an injury.[128]

Most of the procedure remains after the 2000 amendment to Rule 702, but, in addition, what is now known as a *Daubert* hearing has become a part of almost every trial involving experts. Indeed, failure to do an adequate *Daubert* scrutiny can itself be grounds for appeal. Some courts applying *Daubert* have reversed trial court rulings on expert testimony, not because the district judge made a demonstrable mistake in assessing the scientific validity of a theory or application, but because the district court did not make a *Daubert* inquiry at all.[129]

---

127. *See,* United States v. Bartley, 855 F.2d 547, 552 (8th Cir.1988) (no requirement that court determine in presence of the jury that witness is qualified to testify as expert); Hall v. General Motors Corp., 647 F.2d 175, 182–183 (D.C.Cir.1980) (trial judge did not abuse her discretion when refusing to permit cross-examination as substitute for voir dire inquiry concerning witness' expertise). Weinstein's Federal Evidence, § 702.02[1] (2nd ed. Joseph M. McLaughlin 1997).

128. *See, e.g.,* Holbrook v. Lykes Bros. S.S. Co., 80 F.3d 777, 782 (3d Cir. 1996) (trial court committed reversible error in excluding testimony by nonspecialist treating physician diagnosing patient's cancer as mesothelioma); Nunley v. Kloehn, 888 F.Supp. 1483,1487–88 (E.D.Wis.1995) (dermatologist who had performed lip augmentations could testify about standard of care of plastic surgeons performing the same procedure with different substances). But c.f., Fortney v. Al-Hajj, 425 S.E.2d 264, 269–71 (W.Va.1992) (though West Virginia Code requires that malpractice expert be engaged or qualified in a substantially simi-

lar field as the defendant health care provider, this requirement does not mean that witness's board certification must be in the same field). Fed. R. Evid. 702

129. Tyus v. Urban Search Management, 102 F.3d 256, 263–64 (7th Cir. 1996) (held, in housing discrimination action, district court erred in excluding, without applying Daubert, testimony of well-qualified expert in marketing communication about how advertising sends a message to its target market and how an all-white advertising campaign affects African–Americans; Daubert framework applies to social science experts just as it applies to experts in hard sciences; remanded for reconsideration of proffer and application of Daubert criteria); United States v. Hall, 93 F.3d 1337, 1345 (7th Cir. 1996) (held, reversible error to fail to make full Daubert inquiry before excluding crucial testimony (1) by defense psychiatrist that defendant confessed because he had a personality disorder making him abnormally suggestible and eager to please and (2) testimony of another defense expert about conditions under which false confessions are made).

The judge, in addition to determining whether the witness is an expert—a person who knows more about the subject matter than the average duck—must make some inquiry to determine whether the expert's testimony is reliable—whether there are sufficient facts and data and whether the expert has properly applied the principles and methods to the facts of the case. Some judges have used court-appointed experts to help them,[130] a practice encouraged by Justice Breyer in his *Joiner* concurrence.[131] Commentators generally agree that it is now for the judge, not the jury, to screen for validity.

In the case of a highly qualified expert, the party opposing the expert may offer to stipulate that the witness is qualified as an expert, hoping thereby to avoid having the expert's impressive credentials paraded before the jury. That party may then make an objection to testimony about the witness' background, education, and achievements on grounds that it is irrelevant or immaterial, since the witness' competence to testify as an expert is not in dispute. The objection should be overruled.[132] The testimony is relevant and material because the jurors must still assess the credibility of the expert. The jurors are entitled to know the witness' background and achievements in order to assess credibility. Nonetheless, the lawyer making this objection may succeed in limiting the duration of the direct examination, since extended and detailed review of qualifications may be a waste of time when the witness' competence to testify as an expert is not in dispute.

It should be noted that the stipulation that the expert is competent to testify is only a stipulation that the expert's testimony is admissible; not that it is accurate or correct.

The Form of the Question

The manner of examination of an expert witness was of critical importance under the common law. It was formalistic. Failure to follow the formula with precision could result in exclusion of the expert's opinion.

An expert was not allowed to offer an opinion unless it was based upon personal knowledge of the underlying information (a relatively rare

130. *See* Hall v. Baxter Healthcare Corp., 947 F.Supp. 1387, 1413 (D. Or. 1996) (court appointed four "technical advisors" to assist in four-day Rule 104(a) hearing in consolidated breast implant cases; "technical advisors" participated in questioning of parties' experts and issued reports; court determined that plaintiffs' theory that silicon implants cause systemic illness or syndrome did not meet *Daubert* standards but deferred effective date of opinion pending decision of "national panel" appointed by Judge Pointer in another case).

For accounts of the background of the Hall case and of Judge Pointer's "national Rule 706 panel", *see* Michael Hoenig, Court—Appointed Experts, 217 New York Law Journal 3 (1/13/97); Kathryn Ericson, "Scientific Panel Ordered for Breast Implant Litigation," 6–5–96 West's Legal News 5277, 1996 WL 294522.

131. General Electric Co. v. Joiner, 522 U.S. 136, 149–150 (1997)(concurring opinion).

132. Murphy v. National R.R. Passenger Corp., 547 F.2d 816, 817 (4th Cir.1977). Despite stipulation of the witness' expertise, "a jury can better assess the weight to be accorded an expert's opinion if the witness is permitted to explain his qualifications." *Id.*

occurrence) or upon facts that had already been admitted into evidence.[133] Moreover, the nature of the facts relied upon had to be made specific, so that the trier of fact could reject the opinion if it rejected its factual basis. The rule of examination, therefore, was that no opinion could be elicited from an expert without first identifying the underlying facts or data the expert relied upon in forming the opinion.

The following example, though maybe not wise, is allowable under Rule 705, "unless the court requires otherwise."

Lawyer:	[After first qualifying the witness.] Do you have an opinion, to a reasonable medical certainty, about the cause of Billy Johnson's death?
Witness:	Yes.
Lawyer:	What is your opinion?
Witness:	The removal of his spleen during surgery caused him to lose his resistance to infection, and as a result he contracted an overwhelming infection that led to his death.
Lawyer:	In your opinion, was it sound medical practice to remove Billy's spleen?
Witness:	No.
Lawyer:	In making his decision to remove Billy's spleen, did Dr. Smith exercise the professional care and skill ordinarily possessed by others in his profession in this community?
Witness:	No, he did not.

The common law would not tolerate the foregoing examination. To make sure the underlying facts and data were before the witness and the jury, the common law developed the hypothetical question as the universally accepted device for eliciting expert testimony. The examining lawyer would ask the expert to assume the existence of certain specified facts and then to give an opinion based upon those facts—hence the term "hypothetical." If the expert had been in the courtroom and heard previous testimony, the examining lawyer could ask the expert to assume the truthfulness of specified testimony and to give an opinion based upon the facts from the testimony. Often the examining lawyer would ask a hypothetical that combined the two approaches.[134]

If, in the above splenectomy example, the treating doctor (defendant) had testified as an adverse witness and Billy's hospital records had

---

133. *See, e.g.,* Stanley Co. of Am. v. Hercules Powder Co., 108 A.2d 616, 621 (N.J.1954). "The opinions of experts must be based either upon facts within their own knowledge which they detail to the jury or upon hypothetical questions embracing facts supported by the evidence upon which the expert opinion is sought." *Id.* at 621.

134. Wigmore, *supra* note 1, §§ 672–84 .

been admitted, Billy's lawyer might next call a non-treating expert to offer the opinion that Billy's treatment had not been proper. If the expert had not heard the testimony, the hypothetical would recount the information:

> "Doctor, suppose that a twelve year old boy suffered a fall that resulted in a two-centimeter laceration of the spleen, [and every other fact in evidence the lawyer wants the jury to remember], would it be sound medical practice to remove the spleen?"

If the expert had been in the courtroom, heard the testimony, and seen the exhibits, the hypothetical might avoid recitation of the facts:

> "Doctor, you heard the testimony of Dr. Smith. Assume it to be true. You have seen the hospital records admitted into evidence. Assume them to be correct. Based on the facts stated by Dr. Smith and the information in the hospital records, do you have an opinion about whether it was sound medical practice to remove Billy's spleen?"[135]

The hypothetical question form, though a logical outgrowth of the desire to show the trier of fact the basis for the expert's opinion, was repeatedly criticized by scholars and reformers who objected to lawyers using extended hypothetical questions as vehicles for arguing their cases to juries.[136]

The Federal Rules of Evidence take a more liberal and flexible approach to expert testimony than did the common law. One of the consequences was to diminish the importance of the manner of examination. The Federal Rules do not require the use of hypothetical questions, nor do they prohibit them. Some lawyers in Federal Rules jurisdictions continue to use the hypothetical, believing that the form provides an opportunity to control and focus the expert and to sum up damaging testimony in the middle of trial.

Some federal courts, despite the permissive language of the Federal Rules continue to require the use of hypothetical questions in some criminal cases involving testimony by police experts. A prosecutor offering a police investigator/expert with an opinion about whether the defendant possessed drugs for distribution or for personal use might have to use hypothetical questions, asking the witness to assume the presence of a certain quantity of drugs and certain paraphernalia, as opposed to testifying that on the basis of his investigation he believes that this defendant possessed drugs for distribution.[137] The concern is

---

135. *See,* Treffinger v. Sterling, 305 A.2d 829, 831(Md.1973) (question asking witness to assume truth of testimony a proper substitute for hypothetical question setting forth specific facts); Annotations, *Modern Status of Rules Regarding Use of Hypothetical Questions in Eliciting Opinion of Expert Witness,* 56 A.L.R.3d 300, 312–315 (1974).

136. "Its abuses have become so obstructive and nauseous that no remedy

short of extirpation will suffice." Wigmore, *supra* note 1, § 686. "[A] failure in practice and an obstruction to the administration of justice." McCormick, *supra* note 2, § 16.

137. *See* State v. Odom, 560 A.2d 1198 (N.J. 1989)(held, in Federal Rules state, police offer testifying about whether defendant possessed crack for his own use or with intent to distribute must testify in response to hypothetical questions that do not use defendant's name and that are

that a police expert might base an opinion on facts that are not and never could be admitted, such as facts discovered in an illegal search or learned through third-hand hearsay and gossip among law enforcement officers and informants. Even if the police expert based an opinion solely on evidence produced in court, in the absence of a hypothetical specifying the exact basis for the opinion the jury might think that the police expert had confidential information about the particular defendant that had not been put into evidence.[138] Allowing the testimony with reference to the particular defendant, rather than by hypothetical, runs the risk of undermining basic constitutional safeguards such as the protections against illegal searches and confessions and the right to confront and cross-examine witnesses. Although the courts have not explained the inconsistency between requiring hypothetical questions in these situations and the Rules' failure to include the common law requirement, it is perhaps a matter of the court's discretion under Rule 705 or the Rule 702 general requirement of helpfulness combined with the Rule 403 admonition against unfair prejudice.

Hypothetical questions present a particular challenge to the examiner and the opponent because they usually involve an extended recitation of facts upon which the expert is expected to base an opinion. If the hypothetical omits material undisputed facts, misstates facts, or includes prejudicial facts it may be misleading, confusing, or prejudicial and, thereby, improper under Rule 403. In order to preserve rights on appeal, the objecting party should be careful to specify omitted, misstated, or prejudicial facts that make the hypothetical objectionable.[139]

Although a hypothetical question may be deemed misleading for a mishandling of the facts, it is not misleading if it merely fails to include the opponent's version of disputed facts. When material facts are in dispute, the examiner may include the client's version of the dispute and exclude the opponent's without running the risk of having an objection sustained on grounds that the question is misleading. If, for example, one witness testifies that plaintiff was exposed to a toxic chemical and others testify that plaintiff was not exposed, it is permissible to ask the expert to assume the plaintiff was exposed to the chemical, and to base an opinion on that assumption.[140] This slanting of the hypothetical is not objectionable, because the opponent is free, on cross-examination, to ask

---

based on facts admitted in evidence); United States v. Scop, 846 F.2d 135, 140 (2d Cir. 1988)(hypothetical questions needed in case of expert testifying about how securities fraud scheme worked). But cf. People v. Gardeley, 59 Cal.Rptr.2d 356, 927 P.2d 713, 721 (1996)(under provision similar to Federal Rules, expert allowed to base testimony about criminal gang activity on interviews with gang members, not strictly on facts in evidence that were incorporated into hypothetical questions.)

138. *Cf.* Note, The Admissibility of Ultimate Issue Expert Testimony by Law Enforcement Officers in Criminal Trials, 93 Colum. L. Rev. 231 (1993).

139. First Nat'l Bank of Dunmore v. WCAB, 532 A.2d 526, 528 (Pa. Commw.1987); Serafin v. Workmen's Compensation Appeal Bd., 436 A.2d 1239, 1241–42 (Pa.Commw.1981).

140. *See, e.g.,* Taylor v. Reo Motors, 275 F.2d 699 (10th Cir.1960).

the expert what the opinion would be if the cross-examiner's version of the disputed fact were true.[141]

Three common ways in which facts are mishandled in a hypothetical will make the question objectionable: omission of a material undisputed fact, addition of a fact either by misstatement or invention, or inclusion of a prejudicial fact.

Stumpf v. State Farm Mutual,[142] is an example of omitted material facts that were not in dispute. The issue in the case was whether the insured had made an intentionally false statement on an automobile insurance application when he stated that he did not have a mental or physical disability. The insured had been suffering from epilepsy for several years, but contended that it did not constitute a disability. His lawyer asked the following question to a specialist in internal medicine who had been called as an expert witness:

> Doctor, assuming that you have a patient who is gainfully employed and has a history of infrequent epileptic seizures of the grand mal type over a period of years, takes regular oral medication for his epileptic condition three times daily, assume further that the patient, before suffering an epileptic seizure gets warning of the impending seizure sufficient to allow him to sit down and make adjustments, do you have an opinion, based on reasonable medical probability, whether that patient has a mental or physical disability?[143]

State Farm's objection that the question omitted several material facts was sustained by the trial court and affirmed on appeal. The question omitted that the insured had also suffered petit mal seizures (which, unlike grand mal seizures, came upon him without warning) and that he had been discharged from the Marine Corps with a 30% disability because of epilepsy.[144] The Court of Appeals said that the omissions caused the question to fall short of the standard that a hypothetical question "should contain a fair summary of the material facts in evidence essential to the formulation of a rational opinion concerning the matter to which it relates."[145]

Courts have displayed various degrees of liberality in allowing the omission of undisputed facts from hypothetical questions, depending mostly upon the importance of the fact. A certain amount of leeway is given when the omission is not materially misleading and may be subject to correction by an alert cross-examiner.[146] When, however, the omission of undisputed fact reduces the value of the resulting opinion to a point

141. Johns–Manville Products Corp. v. Industrial Comm., 399 N.E.2d 606, 611 (Ill. 1979). On the other hand, if certain facts are not in dispute, they must be incorporated in the hypothetical question if the question would be misleading without them. *See, e.g.,* De Donato v. Wells, 41 S.W.2d 184 (Mo.1931).

142. 251 A.2d 362 (Md.1969).

143. 251 A.2d at 372 (1969).

144. *Id.* at 372–73.

145. *Id.* at 372, (quoting Wolfinger v. Frey, 162 A.2d 745, 749 (Md.1960)).

146. *See* Wigmore, *supra* note 1, § 682.

where its probative value is outweighed by dangers of prejudice or of misleading the trier of fact, the question will not be allowed.[147]

Stanley Co. of America v. Hercules Powder Co.[148], is an example of adding a fact either by misstatement or invention.[149] Plaintiff claimed that an explosion in defendant's plant caused structural damage to plaintiff's theater. Plaintiff's expert on the cause of damage was asked to assume that there had been one explosion of 30,000 tons of nitroglycerin. The only evidence on the point indicated that there had been three separate smaller explosions adding up to 30,000 tons. The court reversed on grounds that the hypothetical question was improper because it misstated a material fact.

The line between a misstated fact and a fact that is slanted toward the proponent's perspective can be sufficiently indistinct so that it is unlikely the trial court's view will be reversed on appeal. In *Cortrim Mfg. Co. v. Smith*,[150] for example, an expert was asked whether an employee's exertion while "setting up"[151] a large machine could have contributed to the employee's fatal heart attack. "Setting up" was characterized by the question as requiring a "tremendous amount[152]" of stretching, bending and reaching down. The evidence showed that the employee had been engaged in adjusting the machine, not setting it up. "Tremendous amount" exaggerated the exertion involved.[153] The trial court permitted the question and the appellate court affirmed, noting that the record indicated that the work did require somewhat strenuous effort and that the defendant had the opportunity to restate the question on cross-examination.

A constant pre-rules criticism of the hypothetical was centered around the use lawyers made of the question to inject or unduly emphasize case facts unrelated to anything the expert needed as a basis for an opinion. In the hands of a skilled practitioner, the hypothetical question was transformed into a final argument. *Ingram v. McCuiston*[154] is an example—and not as atypical as the length of the hypothetical might suggest. The plaintiff's lawyer asked the expert a twenty-three-

---

147. *See, e.g.,* Podedworny v. Harris, 745 F.2d 210, 218–19 (3d Cir. 1984) (hypothetical question about whether claimant's disability was defective because it failed to mention claimant's dizziness and blurred vision); Baugus v. Secretary of Health & Human Services, 717 F.2d 443, 447 (8th Cir.1983)(similar).

148. 108 A.2d 616 (N.J.1954).

149. *See also,* Raugust v. Diamond Int'l Corp., 692 P.2d 368, 369–70 (Idaho 1984) (hypothetical question assuming that victim had suffered neck injury in accident improper when evidence showed no injury to neck); Rosenberg v. Pritchard Serv., Inc., 774 F.2d 293, 295–97 (8th Cir.1985) (hypothetical question and answer properly stricken when question assumed that defendant's servant always emptied ashtrays directly into trashbags, when evidence, construed most favorably to plaintiff, showed only that she sometimes did so); Johnson v. Toscano, 136 A.2d 341 (Conn. 1957) (hypothetical question properly excluded, both because it omitted material facts and because it referred to inadmissible facts).

150. 570 S.W.2d 854 (Tenn.1978); *see also,* Coleman v. De Minico, 730 F.2d 42, 46 (1st Cir.1984).

151. 570 S.W.2d at 855.

152. *Id.*

153. *See id.*

154. 134 S.E.2d 705 (1964).

paragraph question, purportedly to elicit the expert's opinion as to whether the plaintiff had been disabled by her injury. The question was replete with facts relevant to liability, but not to damages. The lawyer included in the question, for example, that the plaintiff had been hit from behind while stopped "in obedience to a traffic control device."[155] The lawyer included in the question the assertion that the plaintiff had slowed down because "she saw, and anyone who was properly observant could and should have seen"[156] that the traffic ahead was slowing down. In holding that the hypothetical question was improperly prejudicial because it was "slanted and argumentative," the court said: "it was no part of the legitimate purpose of the hypothetical question under consideration to establish defendants' negligence."[157]

The Bases for the Expert Witness' Opinion

The Federal Rules changed much more than the form of the question posed to an expert. They changed the permissible base upon which the opinion might rest. The combination of Rule 703—allowing the expert to base the opinion on information from others (even inadmissible information) and Rule 705—permitting an expert to give an opinion without prior disclosure of the underlying facts (unless the court directs otherwise) provided before or during the hearing—was a revolution. It not only unseated the hypothetical as the dominant form for questioning an expert, it overthrew the notion that the expert's opinion must be based on facts available to the jurors.

Rule 703 reverses the common law rule that the expert must base an opinion upon facts already presented to the jurors. It not only permits the expert to base the opinion upon matters not presented to the jury, it allows the expert to base the opinion upon matters that would not be admissible in evidence in the normal course—usually hearsay and the opinions of others. So long as the information is "of a type reasonably relied upon by experts in the particular field in forming opinions or inferences upon the subject,"[158] the expert may use it to form an opinion.

"The rule is designed to broaden the basis for expert opinions ... to bring judicial practice into line with the practice of the experts themselves when not in court."[159] The Advisory Committee Note focuses on the circumstances of the medical expert, noting that physicians rely upon "statements by patients and relatives, reports and opinions from nurses, technicians, and other doctors, hospital records and x-rays" to make "life-and-death decisions" the Committee argues that those opinions and hearsay "ought to suffice for judicial purposes." Despite the "life-and-death" rationale, the Rule is not so restricted. Experts testifying about everything from product liability[160] to land value[161] to chemical composi-

---

155. *Id.* at 708
156. *Id.*
157. *Id.* at 712.
158. Fed. R. Evid. 703.
159. Advisory Committee Note, Fed. R. Evid 703

160. *See, e.g.,* Lewis v. Rego Co., 757 F.2d 66 (3d Cir. 1985).

161. *See, e.g.,* United States v. 1,014.16 Acres, 558 F.Supp. 1238 (W.D.Mo.1983).

tion[162] have relied upon hearsay and the opinions of others in presenting their testimony. There have, however, been some exceptions to the wholesale acceptance of expert opinions based upon inadmissible hearsay.

In re Agent Orange Product Liability Litigation,[163] provides an example of the kind of hearsay not considered to be the type of information on which an expert could reasonably rely under Rule 703. The plaintiff's decedent had allegedly contracted cancer as a result of contact with Agent Orange in Vietnam. On a motion for summary judgment, defendants claimed there was insufficient evidence of cause to create a genuine issue of material fact. Plaintiff, in response, produced the affidavit of a qualified medical expert who concluded that the decedent's illness and death had been caused by contact with Agent Orange. The expert had based his opinion partly upon conversations with family members, whose information in turn came mainly from the decedent. They reported to the expert that decedent had been in contact with Agent Orange and not with other chemicals. Judge Weinstein noted that the expert's opinion would not be admissible at trial and, therefore, granted the motion for summary judgment. The expert's facts about the decedent's symptoms, habits, and background were based almost exclusively on hearsay that was not the type of hearsay on which physicians customarily rely in diagnosing illness. The wife's statements to the expert, for example, were not "the kind of reliable statements about direct observation of actions, contemporaneous statements and symptoms usually related by a spouse."[164] She had "little or no contact with her husband for long periods of time and made no direct observations about his work or its effects upon him."[165] Indicating that in some cases statements by a spouse might properly be considered by a medical expert in forming an opinion, as hypothesized in the Advisory Committee Note, Judge Weinstein found that the spouse's reports here—confused and based on hearsay—were simply not sufficiently reliable.[166]

---

162. *See e.g.,* United States v. Smith, 964 F.2d 885 (D.C. Cir. 1992).

163. In re Agent Orange Product Liability Litigation, 611 F.Supp. 1267 (E.D.N.Y. 1985), decision affd., 818 F.2d 187 (2d Cir. 1987) (Weinstein, J.).

164. In re Agent Orange Product Liability Litigation, 611 F.Supp. 1267, 1280–1281 (E.D.N.Y. 1985), decision affd, 818 F.2d 187 (2d Cir. 1987).

165. In re Agent Orange Product Liability Litigation, 611 F.Supp. 1267, 1281 (E.D.N.Y. 1985), decision affd, 818 F.2d 187 (2d Cir. 1987).

166. For other cases excluding testimony about opinions on grounds that they were based on unreliable hearsay, *see* In re Air Crash Disaster, 86 F.3d 498, 537, 34 Fed. R. Serv. 3d 1067 (6th Cir. 1996) (in forming opinion, expert could not reasonably rely upon second-hand report about criticism of airline crew by expert employee of opposing party); In re Agent Orange Product Liability Litigation, 611 F.Supp. 1223, 1246–1247 (E.D.N.Y. 1985) (Weinstein, J.), decision affd, 818 F.2d 187 (2d Cir. 1987) (exclusion of expert testimony because hearsay checklists concerning health conditions completed for litigation by litigants is not the type of information relied upon by reputable physicians); In re Agent Orange Product Liability Litigation, 611 F.Supp. 1223, 1247–1248 (E.D.N.Y. 1985), decision affd, 818 F.2d 187 (2d Cir. 1987) (exclusion of expert testimony relying on self-serving unsupported hearsay statements indicating exposure to Agent Orange by plaintiffs); Dallas & Mavis Forwarding Co., Inc. v. Stegall, 659 F.2d 721 (6th Cir. 1981). For cases admitting opinions based at least partly upon hearsay reports of others, *see* First Nat. Bank of Louisville v. Lustig, 96 F.3d 1554, 1575 (5th Cir. 1996)

The most difficult question under Rule 703 has been what to do about the inadmissible hearsay or opinion base when the expert has "reasonably relied" on it and the expert's opinion is admissible. The Advisory Committee recognized, in its note to Rule 703, the fear amongst lawyers, judges and commentators "that enlargement of permissible data may tend to break down the rules of exclusion unduly" and attempted to dispel it by calling attention to the requirement that the hearsay or opinion upon which the expert might base an opinion must be of the "type reasonably relied upon by experts in the particular field." In sharp contrast to the suggestion that the Rule would not open the floodgates to inadmissible hearsay, at least one court said, "expert witness testimony is a well recognized exception to the rule against hearsay testimony."[167]

Commentators disagreed about the wisdom of the Rule[168] and the courts disagreed about how to deal with inadmissible hearsay or opinion that was "reasonably relied" upon in arriving at the expert's opinion. Some courts accepted that the otherwise inadmissible hearsay became admissible in the mouth of the expert. They were quite permissive in allowing the expert to relate to the jury the content of the hearsay statements or opinions the expert "reasonably relied" upon.[169] Many

(court allows "expert in civil fraud detection and investigation" to testify for bank that bank relied on loan officer's misrepresentations in approving loans even though witness had no personal knowledge of this fact; "experts may rely on hearsay evidence in forming their opinions."); United States v. Lundy, 809 F.2d 392, 395 (7th Cir. 1987)(expert's testimony based partially upon hearsay and third-party observations was properly admitted); Nachtsheim v. Beech Aircraft Corp., 847 F.2d 1261, 1270 (7th Cir. 1988) (expert opinion relying on hearsay held admissible); United States v. Rollins, 862 F.2d 1282, 1293 (7th Cir. 1988) (expert testimony properly admitted even though based partially on word meanings supplied by informant); United States v. Posey, 647 F.2d 1048 (10th Cir. 1981).

167. United States v. Williams, 447 F.2d 1285, 1290 (5th Cir.1971).

168. *Compare*, S. Saltzburg & K. Redden, Federal Rules of Evidence Manual 671 (4th ed 1986)(taking a broad view of the expert's freedom to show the basis for the opinion) with Carlson, Policing the Bases of Modern Expert Testimony, 39 Vand. L. Rev 577 (1986)(suggesting a more limited approach of allowing the expert to identify the sources of the underlying data, and to give a description of the general subjects discussed in underlying reports) with Paul R. Rice, Inadmissible Evidence as a Basis for Expert Testimony: A Response to Professor Carlson, 40 Vand.L.Rev. 583 (1987) (favoring free admissibility to explain basis, on grounds that otherwise jury must blindly

defer to or reject expert's testimony.) *See also*, Paul Rice, *Expert Testimony: A Debate Between Logic or Tradition Rather than Between Deference or Education*, 87 Nw. U.L. Rev. 1166(1993); Richard Lempert, *Experts, Stories, and Information*, 87 Nw. U.L. Rev. 1169 (1993); Edward J. Imwinkelried, *The Educational Significance of the Syllogistic Structure of Expert Testimony*, 87 Nw. U.L. Rev. 1148 (1993); Ronald L. Carlson, *In Defense of a Constitutional Theory of Experts*, 87 Nw. U. L. Rev. 1182 (1993).

169. *See* Brunner v. Brown, 480 N.W.2d 33 (Iowa 1992) (in Federal Rules state, psychiatrist testifying as expert on testator's capacity should have been allowed to describe contents of interviews he had with testator's acquaintances and doctor, but refusal to admit description not reversible error); United States v. Smith, 964 F.2d 1221 (D.C. Cir. 1992) (trial court properly allowed forensic chemist's supervisor to testify about contents of drug analysis report prepared by the chemist as part of more general expert testimony); Ramsey County v. Miller, 316 N.W.2d 917 (Minn. 1982) (in condemnation case, under original Rule 703, experts may give unfettered testimony about matters relating to value, including underlying hearsay data about comparable sales, alternative land use, and projected development cost). For an example of case exemplifying a very permissive attitude toward use of hearsay by a prosecution expert in a criminal case, *see* People v. Gardeley, 59 Cal.Rptr.2d 356, 927 P.2d 713, 721 (1996), as modified on denial of

courts, however, did not allow the expert to relate the underlying hearsay.[170]

In *Rose Hall, Ltd. v. Chase Manhattan Overseas Banking Corp.*,[171] the expert testified about the value of 3000 acres of land. He relied partly on a surveyor's report and on information received by telephone about how much was sand beach and how much was swamp. The court admitted his opinion about value, but excluded evidence about the telephone conversation. It stated that "[w]hile an expert witness may base his opinion on such evidence, this does not magically render the hearsay evidence admissible."[172]

In *State v. Towne*,[173] the hearsay in question was the opinion of another expert—one who did not testify at trial. Although Rule 703 does away with suggestions under the common law that an expert's opinion could not be based upon the opinion of another, it does not follow that all opinions can form the basis for the expert's opinion. In *Towne*, a psychiatrist testifying for the state on the insanity defense gave his opinion about the defendant's mental state, and then testified that he had called his friend Dr. Dick Rada to talk about the case. The expert testified that Dr. Rada was the leading expert in the country on the subject, and that Dr. Rada agreed with the diagnosis. The Vermont Supreme Court decided that the witness' description of Dr. Rada's opinion should have been excluded.[174]

reh'g, (Feb. 19, 1997) (under state rule similar to Rule 703, expert on criminal gang activity should be allowed to testify to results of interview he had with nonparty nontestifying gang member, since experts may rely on hearsay in forming opinions). Cf. Ratliff v. Schiber Truck Co., Inc., 150 F.3d 949, 955 (8th Cir. 1998) (where plaintiff's accident reconstruction expert testified that accident was fault of defendant truck driver, not error to ask expert whether he was aware of police investigator's conclusion that, had plaintiff's decedent kept to speed limit, she could have avoided the accident).

170. *See, e.g.*, United States v. Tran Trong Cuong, 18 F.3d 1132 (4th Cir. 1994) (reversible error to allow physician-witness to testify that another physician's conclusion was "essentially the same" as his own); Hutchinson v. Groskin, 927 F.2d 722, 724–726 (2d Cir. 1991) (reversible violation of hearsay rule to allow defendant's expert witness to identify letters expressing medical opinions, testify regarding qualifications of physician authors, then express his expert opinion and testify that his opinion was consistent with those expressed in letters). For an example of a prosecutor's attempt to use Rule 703 in an astoundingly broad fashion, *see* United States v. Cantu, 167 F.3d 198, 205–206 (5th Cir. 1999), cert. denied, 528 U.S. 818 (1999). There, an investigating agent testified on the basis of hearsay evidence that the reason a search had not turned up much incriminating evidence was that defendant was aware of government scrutiny. The government made no attempt to qualify the expert as an expert at trial, but argued on appeal that he was in fact an expert. Holding that the government could not present just any officer involved in an investigation as an expert as a way of getting in hearsay-based testimony, the appellate court rejected this argument, but held admission of the evidence to be harmless error.

171. 576 F.Supp. 107 (D. Del. 1983), judgment affd, 740 F.2d 956 (3d Cir. 1984)

172. 576 F.Supp. at 158.

173. 453 A.2d 1133 (Vt.1982)

174. *Accord*, Bunyak v. Clyde J. Yancey and Sons Dairy, Inc., 438 So.2d 891, 893 (Fla. Dist. Ct. App. 2d Dist. 1983)(expert witness may not testify to an expert opinion given to him by another expert); O'Kelly v. State, 94 N.M. 74, 607 P.2d 612, 615 (1980) (error for medical expert to testify about content of opinion of nontestifying expert).

While few courts would allow a testifying expert to merely parrot the opinion of another[175] or to bolster an opinion by claiming that another expert, not subject to cross-examination, agrees with it, the question of putting before the jury the other inadmissible hearsay upon which the testifying expert relied proved continuingly vexatious. Consider the earlier splenectomy example and assume the expert reasonably relied upon reports and opinions from others, the court would allowed the opinion, but would not allow the doctor to testify about the substance of the underlying reports and opinions. The cursory examination would be allowable under Rule 705, but it would hardly be satisfactory. Begging the question, what is that opinion based on, it poses a difficult problem for both the direct and the cross-examiner. For the direct examiner, the jurors have no idea how the expert arrived at the opinion and might not, therefore, give it much credit. The cross-examiner is in a double bind. To attack the opinion, the cross-examiner will elicit the underlying inadmissible material; to not attack runs the risk that the jury will accept the opinion because the expert is either renowned or persuasive in presentation, or both. On the other hand, if the cross-examiner brings out the underlying facts in a way that makes it seem as if the expert had been hiding something on direct examination, the inability to offer the underlying data on direct has unfairly disadvantaged the proponent of the opinion.

Some courts responded to the problem by allowing some, but not all of the underlying hearsay or opinion. In *United States v. McCollum*,[176] for example, the defense presented expert testimony that the defendant acted under hypnosis—an opinion based in part on inadmissible hearsay. The court did not exclude the underlying hearsay, but limited the method by which it was presented. The testimony of the expert, Dr. Jorgensen, was based upon interviews with the defendant while the defendant was under hypnosis. The trial judge ruled that the defense could introduce an edited segment of the videotape of the interviews and of Jorgensen purporting to hypnotize the defendant for the purpose of demonstrating the basis for Jorgensen's opinion. It would not admit the part of the videotape in which the defendant recited his "enhanced memory" version of events on the day in question, but did allow Jorgensen to present the information concerning the basis for his opinion through his own testimony. Other courts tried to reduce the damage from allowing otherwise inadmissible evidence in through the expert by instructing the jurors about the limited use of the information. When the inadmissible information is communicated to the jurors for explanatory purposes, the opposing party is entitled to a limiting instruction to the jury that the evidence may be considered "solely as a basis for the expert opinion and not as substantive evidence."[177] Still other courts, recognizing the difficulty of persuading jurors that they might accept that the

175. An opinion prepared for litigation, even if it is of the kind upon which a testifying expert might have "reasonably relied" had it been available at the time the expert would have exercised professional judgment, cannot provide the basis for the expert testimony. United States v. Tran Trong Cuong, 18 F.3d 1132 (4th Cir. 1994).

176. 732 F.2d 1419, 1422–23 (9th Cir. 1984), *cert. denied*, 469 U.S. 920 (1984).

177. 745 F.2d at 1262.

expert reasonably relied upon certain facts, but not accept those facts as proof of what they assert did not allow the underlying data to be presented to the jurors, usually relying on Rule 403 for the exclusion.[178]

The 2000 amendments to Rule 703, invoking a kind of reverse Rule 403 balance, tried to solve the problem of what to do with the inadmissible base for the expert's opinion by adding: "Facts or data that are otherwise inadmissible shall not be disclosed to the jury by the proponent of the opinion or inference unless the court determines that their probative value in assisting the jury to evaluate the expert's opinion substantially outweighs their prejudicial effect."

It is too early to determine whether the amendment will be effective in resolving the problem. The authors express some doubt, given the inevitability of most presentations and cross-examinations. The Advisory Committee note, recognizing that the direct examiner might wish to " 'remove the sting' from the opponent's anticipated attack and thereby prevent the jury from drawing an unfair negative inference" tells the judge to consider that possibility as a factor in determining whether to allow the direct examiner to present the underlying basis. In most cases where the issue will matter, the court will anticipate a vigorous cross-examination and will likely allow the information to be brought out on direct examination, since it is going to come out anyway. If that happens, the Advisory Committee falls back on the limiting instruction to cure the problem: "If the otherwise inadmissible information is admitted under this balancing test, the trial judge must give a limiting instruction upon request." As Professor Park has noted elsewhere, "the instruction can never be 'effective.' "[179]

Opinions About the Ultimate Issue and Opinions About the Law

Until about the middle of the twentieth century, many jurisdictions had prohibitions against asking experts to express an opinion about the ultimate issue.[180] A psychiatrist testifying in an insanity defense case, for example, might be precluded from testifying that the defendant could not distinguish right from wrong, on grounds that it is the ultimate issue to be decided by the jurors. Exclusion of such testimony was justified on

---

178. *See, e.g.,* Nachtsheim v. Beech Aircraft Corp., 847 F.2d 1261, 1270–71 (7th Cir.1988).

179. Roger C. Park, Trial Objections Handbook 2d § 8:26. The instruction tells the jury to decide on the accuracy of the opinion without making any judgment about the accuracy of the data upon which the opinion is based. Although one can imagine mental gymnastics by which this feat is accomplished by using the evidence only to check on the expert's diligence and reasoning apart from the accuracy of the underlying information, the trick is beyond the talents of ordinary mortals. The author

thinks this proposition about the ineffectiveness of the instruction is virtually self-evident. However, the proposition also finds support in the empirical literature on jury instructions, including one study that looks specifically at the mock jurors' ability to apply a limiting instruction governing the use of hearsay evidence presented through an expert. *See* Regina A. Schuller, The Influence of "Secondhand" Information on Jurors' Decisions, 19 Law & Hum. Behav. 501 (1998)(finding instruction ineffective).

180. McCormick , *supra,* note 2, § 12.

grounds that the testimony concerned the "very issue before the jury"[181] and that by giving it the expert would be "usurping the function of the jury."[182] Critics of the rule argued that it placed an undue restriction on expert testimony and created unnecessary litigation about whether questions concerned ultimate facts or not—an illusory dichotomy. The charge that the expert would be "usurping the function of the jury" was rebutted with the observation that the jury could always reject the expert's testimony.[183]

When the Federal Rules of Evidence were originally enacted in 1975, Rule 704 abolished the ultimate issue objection completely. In the wake of controversy over expert testimony in insanity defense cases that followed the shooting of a President, however, Congress partially resurrected the prohibition. It carved out an exception to the rule allowing expert testimony on the ultimate issue, prohibiting expert testimony about whether a criminal defendant possessed a mental state or condition at issue in the case.

Rule 704 Opinion on Ultimate Issue

(a) Except as provided in subdivision (b), testimony in the form of an opinion or inference otherwise admissible is not objectionable because it embraces an ultimate issue to be decided by the trier of fact.

(b) No expert witness testifying with respect to the mental state or condition of a defendant in a criminal case may state an opinion or inference as to whether the defendant did or did not have the mental state or condition constituting an element of the crime charged or of a defense thereto. Such ultimate issues are matters for the trier of fact alone.

Although Rule 704 appears to maintain the common law rule prohibiting a witness from offering an opinion on the ultimate issue for the jury, only in criminal cases when the opinion is "whether the defendant did or did not have the mental state or condition constituting an element of the crime charged;" and reverse it in all other situations, neither the maintenance nor the reversal is as clear as the language of the rule suggests.

Despite the language of the Rule and its intent to prohibit opinion testimony about a criminal defendant's mental state, experts have been allowed to testify that the defendant's mental illness "could" have affected his ability to appreciate his acts (when the ability to appreciate one's acts is an ultimate issue), or even that it "would" have affected that ability.[184] The courts also generally have been receptive to expert

---

181. Wigmore, *supra* note 1, § 1921.

182. Wigmore, *supra* note 1, § 1920.

183. Wigmore, *supra* note 1, § 1920–1921. *See* Stoebuck, *Opinions on Ultimate Facts: Status, Trends, and a Note of Caution*, 41 Den. L. C. J. 226 (1964).

184. *See* United States v. Kristiansen, 901 F.2d 1463, 1466 (8th Cir. 1990). *Cf.* United States v. Reno, 992 F.2d 739, 743 (7th Cir. 1993) (held, psychiatrist's testimony as to effect of paranoid schizophrenic's delusions on ability to appreciate wrongfulness of his acts did not violate Rule 704

testimony that virtually tells the jury that the defendant intended to distribute a controlled substance, even though intent to distribute is an ultimate issue.[185]

Just as maintenance of the common law rule has not been absolute regarding a defendant's mental state, the reversal of the rule generally, and the notion that opinion on the ultimate issue is admissible per se in civil cases, is not absolute. The Advisory Committee Note to Rule 704 explains that some of the testimony previously objectionable in civil cases as going to the ultimate issue, while not prohibited by Rule 704, is still objectionable on other grounds that sound pretty similar:

because testimony aided jury by describing presence of mental disorder and its behavioral characteristics); United States v. Blumberg, 961 F.2d 787 (8th Cir. 1992) (exclusion of defense expert's ultimate opinion about whether defendant appreciated the nature and wrongfulness of his acts was appropriate under Rule 704(b) and did not violate defendant's due process right to present relevant evidence; Rule 704(b) gives defense ample opportunity to present evidence about mental condition, so long as expert does not testify to ultimate issue); United States v. DiDomenico, 985 F.2d 1159, 1163–65 (2d Cir. 1993) (broad interpretation of Rule 704(b), holding that trial court within discretion to exclude testimony about defendant's alleged dependent personality disorder as ultimate issue testimony in case where defense offered the evidence to support inference that defendant had been fooled by dominant boyfriend into innocently participating in the sale of stolen goods). On the ultimate issue rule generally, see United States v. Sheffey, 57 F.3d 1419, 1426 (6th Cir. 1995) (permissible to ask witnesses whether defendant drove "recklessly and in extreme disregard of human life" even though that was the ultimate issue); United States v. Boney, 977 F.2d 624, 628–30 (D.C. Cir. 1992) (held, expert permitted to give opinion, in narcotics case, that defendants' conduct was a common pattern in cocaine sales, and that one person was a "runner," another was a "holder," and a third was the one "who was going to actually make the sale"); Dixon v. CSX Transp., Inc., 990 F.2d 1440, 1452 (4th Cir. 1993) (in personal injury action, reversible error for trial court to allow plaintiff's "human factors expert" to testify that, in his independent study of location of the accident, 96% of motorists did not stop and 64% did not look in both directions, from which plaintiff's counsel concluded plaintiff was not contributorily negligent; held, evidence not relevant to case at hand and improperly went to ultimate question). Cf. United States v. Abou-Kassem, 78 F.3d 161, 166 (5th Cir. 1996)

(held, trial court's exclusion of expert opinion on whether defendant was "legally insane" did not violate due process or equal protection); United States v. Scop, 846 F.2d 135, 140 (2d Cir. 1988) (held, error to admit testimony by an securities trading expert that defendant committed securities fraud, since testimony embodied legal conclusions and used language from statute). See generally Note: The Admissibility of Ultimate Issue Expert Testimony by Law Enforcement Officers in Criminal Trials, 93 Colum. L. Rev. 231 (1993).

185. See United States v. Valle, 72 F.3d 210, 214–16 (1st Cir 1995) (held, permissible for police expert to testify that "street value" of the cocaine was $1500 and that large amounts such as the one found with defendant are consistent with distribution and not personal use); State v. Odom, 560 A.2d 1198, 1205, 83 A.L.R.4th 611 (N.J. 1989) (held, a police officer qualified as an expert on narcotics distribution was allowed to opine that defendant possessed cocaine with intent to distribute as opposed to possessing it for personal use; state had not, however, adopted Rule 704(b)). But see United States v. Mitchell, 996 F.2d 419 (D.C. Cir. 1993) (admission of prosecution expert's testimony that zip-lock bag packaging of cocaine found on defendant's person indicated "intent" to distribute was impermissible under Rule 704(b); however, reversal is not warranted since defendant failed to object at trial and admission of testimony by itself was not plain error). See also Note, The Admissibility of Ultimate Issue Expert Testimony by Law Enforcement Officers in Criminal Trials, 93 Colum. L. Rev. 231 (1993). United States v. Gutierrez–Farias, 294 F.3d 657 (5th Cir. 2002) (testimony of police expert saying that drug rings do not recruit people of the street who have no knowledge, but instead use people they can trust as couriers, inferentially was testimony that defendant knew that marijuana was concealed in tires of vehicle and hence a violation of Fed. R. Evid. 704(b)).

The abolition of the ultimate issue rule does not lower the bars so as to admit all opinions. Under Rules 701 and 702, opinions must be helpful to the trier of fact. Rule 403 provides for exclusion of evidence that wastes time. These provisions afford ample assurances against the admission of opinion that would merely tell the jury what result to reach somewhat in the manner of the oath-helpers of an earlier day. They also stand ready to exclude opinions phrased in terms of inadequately explored legal criteria.

Closely related to the common law rule against opinions on the ultimate issue was the common law rule prohibiting expert testimony concerning domestic law.[186] A witness could not, for example, testify that the conduct of the parties resulted in the formation of a legally enforceable contract. In jury trials, conflicting opinions could confuse the jury and undermine the authority of the judge. In bench trials, the judge's specialized knowledge made the testimony superfluous.[187]

There is some question as to whether the common law rule against opinion testimony about domestic law survived enactment of Rule 704. McCormick states flatly that the exclusionary rule still applies.[188] The Federal Rules, however, contain no express prohibition of expert testimony about the law.[189] Some have argued, therefore, that the admissibility of expert testimony about the law should be judged by the general criteria of helpfulness set forth in Rule 702.[190]

Jury trials and bench trials present different issues. If a judge conducting a bench trial believes that he or she will benefit from expert testimony about law, as opposed to having a legal expert brief or argue the issue, then there seems to be little potential for harm in allowing the

186. *See,* Adalman v. Baker, Watts & Co., 807 F.2d 359, 366 (4th Cir.1986), *rev'd in part on other grounds,* Baker, Watts & Co. v. Miles & Stockbridge, 876 F.2d 1101 (4th Cir.1989); Specht v. Jensen, 853 F.2d 805, 808 (10th Cir.1988), *cert. denied,* 488 U.S. 1008 (1989) (expert testimony of lawyer in § 1983 case as to whether search occurred and whether plaintiffs consented was improperly admitted. Testimony concerned broad array of legal conclusions, not ultimate issue of fact.); Wigmore, *supra* note 1, § 1952; McCormick, *supra* note 2, § 12.

187. *See* Wigmore, *supra* note 1 at § 1952.

188. McCormick on Evidence (3d ed.) § 31, relying upon Marx & Co., Inc. v. Diners" Club Inc., 550 F.2d 505, 510 (2d Cir. 1977).

189. *See* Fed. R. Evid. 701–705. The Fed. R. Evid. Advisory Committee Note, Rule 704, which permits expert testimony to embrace the ultimate issue, suggests that ultimate issue testimony involving the ap-plication of law to fact, while not per se inadmissible, should be excluded when it might be misleading. The note states that under Rule 702, which requires that opinions must be helpful to the trier of fact, and Rule 403, which provides for exclusion of evidence which wastes time, the trial court could exclude "opinions phrased in terms of inadequately explored legal criteria." Thus, in the advisory committee's view, an objection to the question, "Did T have capacity to make a will?" should be sustained, while the question, "Did T have sufficient mental capacity to know the nature and extent of his property and the natural objects of his bounty and to formulate a rationale scheme of distribution?" should be permitted.

190. *See* Note, Expert Legal Testimony, 97 Harv. L. Rev. 797 (1984). For other useful commentary, *see* Thomas E. Baker, The Impropriety of Expert Witness Testimony on the Law, 10 Kan. L. Rev. 325 (1992), and Howard G. Pollack, The Admissibility and Utility of Expert Legal Testimony in Patent Litigation, 32 Idea 361–381 (1992).

testimony.[191] In a jury trial, there is a danger that the jury might become confused or that it might follow the expert's view of the law instead of the judge's view. Nonetheless, there are circumstances where such testimony can be helpful even in jury trials, as, for example, where the expert possesses highly specialized knowledge not readily accessible to the judge and where the expert is presenting a mixture of specialized knowledge about the law, legal environment, and law practice.[192]

191. *See* Knisley v. United States, 817 F.Supp. 680, 690 (S.D. Ohio 1993) (in bench trial, expert legal testimony admissible in legal malpractice action; judge might "frequently find help in expert legal opinion orally delivered, as opposed to being found in books"). *Compare* Willette v. Finn, 778 F.Supp. 10 (E.D. La. 1991) (expert testimony on law of informed consent to medical procedures is inadmissible, at least in jury trial).

192. For a useful discussion, *see* Judge Sandra L. Lynch's opinion in Nieves–Villanueva v. Soto–Rivera, 133 F.3d 92 (1st Cir. 1997). Judge Lynch wrote that Rule 704(a) did not abolish the traditional rule against expert opinion on questions of domestic law, though she could imagine that in rare cases involving "highly complex and technical matters" a trial judge might utilize "limited and controlled mechanisms" to permit some testimony "seemingly in variance with the general rule." *Id.* at 101. However, in the case at bar, an employment discrimination case in which a defense witness testified about holdings of cases (and then in a misleading fashion), the rule against expert opinions on law was clearly violated. For other cases excluding testimony about legal conclusions, *see* United States v. Wilson, 133 F.3d 251 (4th Cir. 1997) (Prosecution for violation of Clean Water Act; held, though government witnesses administering complex regulations understandably refer to those regulations in describing their actions and motives, their testimony should have been limited to "facts of history, practices and procedures followed by them in their work" and to matters in which they had "demonstrated expertise"; district court should not have permitted experts to "give opinions on what the law means or how it is to be interpreted"; the role of instructing the jury on the law belongs exclusively to the judge); CMI–Trading, Inc. v. Quantum Air, Inc., 98 F.3d 887, 890 (6th Cir. 1996) (held, opinion of expert who was specialist in private equity transactions that transaction was intended as joint venture, not as a loan, was inadmissible as trenching on jury's territory to the extent it unhelpfully drew conclusions on intent, and on court's territory to the extent that it defined legal concepts); State of

Ohio ex rel. Montgomery v. Louis Trauth Dairy, Inc., 925 F.Supp. 1247, 1254 (S.D. Ohio 1996) (held, in antitrust case, expert could testify about defendant's business activities using statistical analysis, but could not testify as to legal issue concerning existence of price fixing conspiracy); Estes v. Moore, 993 F.2d 161, 163 (8th Cir. 1993) (in action for deprivation of civil rights, trial court properly excluded testimony from plaintiff's expert as to whether police officer had probable cause to arrest plaintiff; although probable cause involves both legal and factual issues, the "ultimate concern is a question of law"); Hermitage Industries v. Schwerman Trucking Co., 814 F.Supp. 484, 487 (D.S.C. 1993) (excluding testimony from defense expert that plaintiff was "negligent" and was the "direct, proximate and efficient cause" of the accident; both phrases have "a clear legal meaning which is distinct from the common vernacular"); Davidson v. Prince, 813 P.2d 1225, 1230–31 (Utah Ct. App. 1991) (in action for negligence, trial court properly prevented plaintiff's accident reconstruction expert to state opinion on whether defendant was "negligent" because such opinion would be "legal conclusion"; although state has adopted its own version of Rule 704, ultimate issue testimony in form of legal conclusion is still not admissible); Marx & Co. v. Diners™ Club, Inc., 550 F.2d 505 (2d Cir. 1977)(lawyer should not have been permitted to testify about legal obligations under contract or about nature of "best efforts" required under contract). *Compare*, United States v. Barile, 286 F.3d 749 (4th Cir. 2002) (Williams, J.) ("To determine when a question posed to an expert witness calls for an improper legal conclusion, the district court should consider first whether the question tracks the language of the [doctrine or statute] and second, whether any terms employed have specialized legal meaning"; here, defense expert's testimony that defendant's FDA submission had combined data in a way that was "unclear but not unreasonable" would assist the trier of fact in a case in which plaintiff alleged that the FDA submission was misleading; hence, absent any other basis for exclusion, the opinion should be admitted on retrial).

In an important sense, the "legal opinion/ultimate issue" problem is more a problem of artful examination for the lawyer than it is a problem about the exclusion of ideas. The Advisory Committee Note provides an example. "Did the testator have the capacity to make a will?" is about the ultimate issue, but it is excludable because it asks for an opinion about "inadequately explored legal criteria." "Did the testator have sufficient mental capacity to know the nature and extent of his property and the natural objects of his bounty and to formulate a rational scheme of distribution?" is about the same ultimate issue, but it would be allowed because the legal criteria are spelled out.

Whether a lawyer is trying to put before the jury expert testimony about the ultimate issue of mental state in a criminal case or about an opinion on the law, the goals are likely to be achieved, despite the rules prohibiting them, if the lawyer and the witness avoid legal terms. The discussion by the court in *United States v. Kristiansen*[193] is instructive.

> We have interpreted rule 704(b) to exclude testimony that "specifically comments on the presence or absence of an element of the crime charged, . . . too conclusory to be helpful to the jury." We concluded that the trial court in Gipson properly excluded the question, " 'did [Gipson] have the requisite mental state to have willfully or intentionally attempted to escape,' " because it asked "for a mere legal conclusion." We approved asking the expert whether the defendant was suffering from a mental disease or defect at the time the crime was committed. Similarly, in United States v. Dubray, 854 F.2d 1099 (8th Cir.1988), we permitted a doctor to testify that the defendant was not suffering from psychosis at the time of the offense. We reasoned that this testimony related to the defendant's mental state which "has definite implications for the determination of Dubray's legal sanity," but that it did not state a legal conclusion "and did not state an opinion whether Dubray was able to appreciate the wrongfulness of his actions."

For cases admitting evidence despite an objection that it was testimony about legal conclusions, *see* Allison v. Ticor Title Ins. Co., 979 F.2d 1187, 1196 (7th Cir. 1992) (in action by unitholders to recover interest against insurance policies from leases lost in bankruptcy, trial court acted within its discretion in admitting testimony from unitholders' bankruptcy attorney that unitholders must "sign off" of purchase agreement in order to transfer their interest; testimony was a factual determination, not a legal conclusion about contractual rights). Okland Oil Co. v. Conoco Inc., 144 F.3d 1308, 1328, (10th Cir. 1998) (plaintiff's expert properly testified on issue of contract deceit; expert did not offer bare conclusion of fraudulent conduct but explained the basis of testimony in sufficient detail to permit the jury to arrive at independent decision); United States v. Izydore, 167 F.3d 213, 218 (5th Cir. 1999) (held, no violation of ultimate issue rule when bankruptcy trustee, testifying as non-expert, testified that certain money taken by defendants from business was "not legally taken"; opinion did not express conclusion about ultimate issue of whether defendants were guilty of criminal fraud, but rather was trustee's opinion about whether the money belonged to them). *Cf.* Sharp v. Coopers & Lybrand, 457 F.Supp. 879, 883 (E.D. Pa. 1978) *affd in part*, 649 F.2d 175 (3d Cir. 1981), *cert. denied*, 455 U.S. 938 (1982) (trial judge permitted, apparently without objection, testimony by Professor Bernard Wolfman on issue of whether defendant's opinion letter recklessly misdescribed characteristics of a tax shelter).

193.   901 F.2d 1463 (8th Cir.1990).

Under Gipson and Dubray, the defense clearly could ask whether Kristiansen was suffering from a mental disease or defect at the time of the offense. Just as clearly, the defense could not ask whether Kristiansen was unable to appreciate the nature and quality of his actions.... The more difficult question is whether the court erred in not permitting the defense to ask whether the mental disease or defect of the type that Kristiansen allegedly had *would* affect a person's ability to appreciate their actions.

We conclude that the defense should have been permitted to ask this question because it relates to the symptoms and qualities of the disease itself and does not call for an answer that describes Kristiansen's culpability at the time of the crime. Rule 704(b) was not meant to prohibit testimony that describes the qualities of a mental disease. "Under this proposal, expert psychiatric testimony would be limited to presenting and explaining their diagnoses, such as whether the defendant had a severe mental disease or defect and what the characteristics of such a disease or defect, if any, may have been."[194]

The choice of the language used to communicate the expert opinion has been determinative as to the admissibility of legal opinion in a variety of circumstances, from an attorney's fraudulent intent,[195] to whether lease unitholders must "sign off" of purchase agreements to transfer their interests,[196] to whether facts suggested that a criminal defendant had the requisite "intent" to distribute drugs.[197]

---

194. 901 F.2d 1463, 1465–1466 (citations omitted) (emphasis added).

195. United States v. Cavin, 39 F.3d 1299(5th Cir.1994).

196. Allison v. Ticor Title Ins. Co., 979 F.2d 1187 (7th Cir.1992).

197. United States v. Mitchell, 996 F.2d 419 (D.C.Cir.1993). *See generally,* Deon J. Nossel, *The Admissibility of Ultimate Issue Expert Testimony by law Enforcement Officers in Criminal Trials*, 93 Colum. L. Rev. 231 (1993).

Chapter 11

AUTHENTICATION, IDENTIFICATION, AND EXHIBITS

Table of Sections

§ 11.01 Authentication and Identification Under the Rules [FRE 901, 902]

Any tangible item that a lawyer intends to offer into evidence must first be authenticated. Rule 901(a) requires the lawyer to present evidence "sufficient to support a finding that the matter in question is what its proponent claims." Is the computer offered into evidence the very computer that was stolen from the victim? Is the white powder being offered into evidence the same powder that was found when the police searched the defendant? Is the letter containing an offer to sell corn one that was sent by the person alleged to be the offeror? Each of the foregoing is a question of authentication. Rule 901 applies, also, to some *viva voce* evidence. A party to a telephone conversation, for example, may not testify to the contents of that conversation or even establish the existence of the call without sufficient identification of the party on the other end of the line.[1]

Some items are self-authenticating. Rule 902 lists twelve items that will be admitted into evidence without any extrinsic evidence of authen-

---

1. Fed. R. Evid. 901(b)(5) & (6).

ticity, including various official, public, or acknowledged documents,[2] newspapers,[3] trade inscriptions,[4] commercial paper,[5] and certified "business" records.[6]

Most items require extrinsic evidence of authenticity. Rule 901(b) contains ten illustrations (the list is not exclusive) of the kind of extrinsic evidence that meets the rule's authentication and identification requirements. Opinion about the similarity of handwriting or other specimens,[7] distinctive characteristics of items,[8] and demonstration that various processes produce accurate results[9] are exemplary.

The authentication required before an item may be admitted into evidence is not the same as a determination that the item is authentic. The difference between the process of "authentication" for an item to be admitted into evidence and a finding that the item is "authentic" has to do with who decides and how much proof is needed.

The division of labor contemplated by Rule 104(a) and (b) applies to authentication. The judge decides whether the "authentication" is sufficient for an item to be admitted into evidence.[10] The jury decides whether the evidence is sufficient to decide that the item is, in fact, "authentic."[11]

"Authentication"—the judge's call—requires only enough extrinsic evidence to establish a *prima facie* case that the item is what it purports to be.[12] If the evidence persuades the judge that a reasonable jury could find the item to be what the proponent claims it to be, that is enough, even if the judge personally believes that, on balance, the item is not what it purports to be.[13] As a practical matter, the judge looks only to the

---

2. Fed. R. Evid. 902(1),(2)(3),(4),(5),(8), & (10).

3. Fed. R. Evid. 902(6).

4. Fed. R. Evid. 902(7)

5. Fed. R. Evid. 902(9).

6. Fed. R. Evid. 902 (11) & (12).

7. Fed. R. Evid. 901(b)(2) & (3).

8. Fed. R. Evid. 901(b)(4).

9. Fed. R. Evid. 901(b)(9).

10. *See* Fed. R. Evid. 901 advisory committee's note. This requirement of showing authenticity or identity falls in the category of relevancy dependent upon fulfillment of a condition of fact and is governed by the procedure set forth in Rule 104(b). *Id. See also* 2 McCormick on Evidence § 227 (5th ed. 2001). The judge's ruling on an authentication question can only be reversed on the basis of an abuse of discretion. *See e.g.,* United States v. Mirelez, 59 Fed.Appx. 286, 287 (10th Cir. 2003); United States v. Hemphill, 40 Fed.Appx. 809 (4th Cir. 2002); United States v. Thomas, 294 F.3d 899, 904 (7th Cir. 2002).

11. Reeves v. Sanderson Plumbing Prods., Inc., 530 U.S. 133, 153 (2000);

United States v. Beidler, 110 F.3d 1064, 1067 (4th Cir. 1997) ("The jury, not the reviewing court, weighs the credibility of the evidence and resolves any conflicts in the evidence presented." (internal quotes omitted)).

12. *See* Fed. R. Evid. 901(a); United States v. Thomas, 294 F.3d 899, 904 (7th Cir. 2002); United States v. Tropeano, 252 F.3d 653, 661 (2d Cir. 2001) ("The burden of authentication does not require the proponent of the evidence to rule out all possibilities inconsistent with authenticity, or to prove beyond any doubt that the evidence is what it purports to be. Rather, the standard for authentication, and hence for admissibility, is one of reasonable likelihood.")

13. *See* United States v. Alicea–Cardoza, 132 F.3d 1, 4 (1st Cir. 1997) ("Generally, if the district court is satisfied that the evidence is sufficient to allow a reasonable person to believe the evidence is what it purports to be, Rule 901(a) is satisfied and the jury may decide what weight it will give the evidence."). 5 Weinstein, *supra* note 11, at § 901.02[2] ("The rule requires only that the court admit evidence if sufficient proof

proponent's evidence. Assume that a witness testifies to familiarity with the defendant's handwriting and that the handwriting on a letter being offered into evidence is the defendant's. The judge must find the letter has been authenticated, even though the defendant has an expert to testify the handwriting is not the defendant's, the defendant will testify that the letter is a forgery, and the judge believes the defendant's evidence is more persuasive.[14]

"Authentic"—the jury's call—is about the comparative persuasive power of defendant's expert handwriting testimony and the defendant's testimony that the letter is a forgery as opposed to the plaintiff's opinion that the handwriting is the defendant's.[15]

§ 11.02   Handling Exhibits in the Courtroom

Exhibits present unique visual opportunities in an otherwise heavily oral environment, so most lawyers work very hard to achieve maximum persuasive advantage from the process of authenticating and offering an exhibit. But no matter the nature of the exhibit—document, photograph, diagram, model, etc.—or the particular persuasive approach employed, a lawyer offering an exhibit follows a basic procedural pattern.[16] The pattern may vary a bit from courtroom to courtroom, but the basic requirements remain. Pre-trial marking of exhibits or informality of practice will sometimes allow exhibits to be offered and received into evidence, without going through each of the steps of proper exhibit handling. A lawyer must understand the process, nevertheless, for those times when an exhibit must be marked and offered in a courtroom in which the judge expects exhibits to be handled in the formal fashion.

1.   *Ask the court's permission to have the clerk, the court reporter, or the bailiff (whoever marks exhibits in the particular courtroom) mark the exhibit for identification.*

Exhibits are numbered or lettered in sequence. In many jurisdictions the plaintiff's or prosecution's exhibits are numbered and the defendant's exhibits are lettered.

2.   *Show the exhibit to the opposing lawyer.*

has been introduced so that a reasonable juror could find in favor of authentication or identification").

14. Weinstein's, *supra* note 11, at § 901.02[2]:

> Thus, if the question is whether one of the parties signed the contract being offered, it will be admitted if a witness testifies that he is familiar with the signature and identifies it, regardless of what other evidence may subsequently be introduced to rebut that testimony. *Id.*

15. *See e.g.,* United States v. Blankenship, 69 Fed.Appx. 114, 115 (4th Cir. 2003) ("Under Fed. R. Evid. 901, the admission of an exhibit must be preceded by 'evidence sufficient to support a finding that the matter in question is what its proponent claims.' This showing is satisfied by 'sufficient proof that the evidence is what it purports to be and has not been altered in any material respect,' and is not intended as an iron-clad rule that requires exclusion of real evidence based on a missing link in its custody."); United States v. Alicea–Cardoza, 132 F.3d 1, 4 (1st Cir. 1997); Weinstein's, *supra* note 11, at § 901.02[2].

16. *See* Steven H. Goldberg, The First Trial (Where Do I Sit? What Do I Say?) 26 (Presenting Exhibits "By the Numbers") (1982).

More often than not, the lawyer will have seen the item during discovery, but it is important to show the exhibit, nevertheless. The lawyer who is being shown the prospective exhibit and has seen it during discovery is well advised to make sure that the exhibit is in the same shape and represents the same information at trial that it did during discovery.

While walking around the courtroom with an exhibit that can be identified easily upon sight, such as a photograph or a gun, it is important to ensure that jurors do not see the exhibit before it is admitted into evidence. If the exhibit is one that ultimately will not be received, exhibition of it to the jurors could result in sanctions against the lawyer and, if the prejudice is sufficiently serious, a mistrial.

Some items may be difficult to handle without exposing them to the jurors during the authentication process. If the exhibit is not seriously contested, or if the item is one that will not cause much prejudice if the jurors see it during the process, opposing counsel may agree or the court may allow it to be within the jurors' view before it has been received in evidence.

3. Ask the court's permission to approach the witness. Hand the exhibit to the witness and ask whether the witness can identify the exhibit.

It is important for the lawyer to refer to the item by its identification number so that the record is clear, in the event an appellate court is asked to review it.

Proponent:	I hand you what has been marked Plaintiff's Exhibit No. 1 for identification. Do you recognize it?
Witness:	Yes.
Proponent:	What is it?

The same care must be taken with the question to the witness about the nature of the exhibit as must be taken in concealing certain exhibits from the jurors before they are received in evidence. The lawyer must ensure that neither the question nor the answer tells the jurors about the contents or the nature of the exhibit—information that is appropriate only after the exhibit has been received. A questions such as, "Mr. Smith, would you examine the shrunken head that has been marked as State's Exhibit No. 1 for identification?" is likely to provoke an objection and could provide the basis for a mistrial.[17]

4. Ask the witness the questions needed to lay the foundation for the admission of the exhibit into evidence.

The particular authenticating questions will vary from exhibit to exhibit, but all authentication testimony involves the witness explaining

---

17. *See* Mayer v. Angelica, 790 F.2d 1315, 1338–41 (7th Cir. 1986)(admission of unauthenticated letters was prejudicial, thus requiring new trial)

to the jury why the exhibit is what it purports to be. In preparing a witness to lay the foundation for an exhibit, the lawyer should remember that the testimony serves two purposes. It provides the authentication so the judge will admit the evidence, but more importantly, it provides the information that will persuade the jurors that the exhibit is authentic, or that it is one from which they should draw inferences important to the lawyer offering the exhibit.

5. *Offer the exhibit into evidence: "Your honor, I offer (whatever the item is) that has been marked as Plaintiff's exhibit number one for identification into evidence as Plaintiff's exhibit number one."*

In some jurisdictions, an item is marked originally with a number or letter, without the "for identification" limitation. In such a jurisdiction, the lawyer need not refer to the marked item as an exhibit "for identification" and might offer the exhibit by saying, "Your honor, I offer plaintiff's exhibit number one (whatever the item is) into evidence."

In jurisdictions in which the original marking is "for identification," the judge will have the court personnel who marked the exhibit strike the "for identification" limitation when the exhibit is received in evidence.

6. *Make sure that the contents or the nature of the exhibit is apparent to the jurors.*

The most important part of having an exhibit admitted into evidence is its influence on the jurors in deciding the case. The lawyer should make sure that the full force of the exhibit is brought to bear when it is accepted into evidence. If it is a document, the lawyer should ask the court's permission to have the witness read the contents to the jurors. Providing copies of a document for distribution to each juror is another way to bring the contents of the document to the jurors' attention. Copies of a diagram might be distributed, as well, but more often displaying a blown up version of the diagram on an easel is more effective, and allows the witness to use the exhibit to make the testimony memorable. Photographs, as well, might be blown up and displayed to the jurors or passed among the jurors. Objects are often passed among the jurors for closer inspection.

Whatever method the lawyer chooses for bringing the exhibit to the attention of the jurors, the lawyer should be sure to receive the court's permission. "Your honor, may I distribute copies of plaintiff's exhibit number one to the jurors?" "Your honor, may the witness read plaintiff's exhibit number one to the jurors?" "Your honor, I have a blow up of the photograph that has been received as plaintiff's exhibit number one. May it be displayed to the jurors?"

§ 11.03   "Laying a foundation" for a Variety of Exhibits

The presentation of the extrinsic evidence to authenticate an exhibit is usually called "laying the foundation." The foundation can be laid either by direct evidence or by circumstantial evidence. Sometimes one witness is sufficient; in other cases, more than one is necessary.

In determining what evidence must be offered to lay the foundation for a particular exhibit, the lawyer must determine what it is the exhibit is offered to prove. A diagram of an intersection, for example, may be used to assist a witness in describing what the witness saw, but it might prove, also, exactly where items of importance were located. For the first purpose, the witness can lay the foundation merely by testifying to three simple matters. 1) The witness is familiar with the intersection. 2) The diagram is a fair and accurate representation of the way the intersection looked on the day of the collision. 3) The diagram would be helpful to the witness in explaining to the jurors what happened. For the second purpose, to show the exact position of cars, skid-marks, glass fragments, etc., a more detailed foundation is required from one or more witnesses. 1) How the diagram was drawn to scale and the scale used. 2) How the measurements of the location of items shown on the diagram were taken at the scene. 3) The measurements taken at the scene were converted in accord with the scale to which the diagram was drawn.

All foundations for exhibits fall into one of three general categories: foundations for real evidence, demonstrative evidence that is illustrative of other evidence, and demonstrative evidence that carries its own substantive value.

§ 11.04   "Real" Evidence—"The Chain of Custody"

Items that were actually involved in the transaction or occurrence that gave rise to the litigation are called "real evidence."[18] The stolen goods in a burglary case, the signed agreement in a contract case, and headlight glass fragments found on the road in a personal injury case are common examples. Real evidence is authenticated by showing that the exhibit in court is the actual item from the transaction or event and that it has not undergone any significant change.[19] The requirement that the exhibit be in the same condition as it was at the time of the transaction or event applies only if the condition that has been changed matters in the litigation. If the changes can be explained or understood by the jurors, the change is not a bar to admission. In a counterfeiting trial, therefore, the seized counterfeit money could be authenticated as the "real" counterfeit despite a change in the color of the money to blue during government fingerprint analysis of the bills. The identification of the counterfeit money and its relevance to the litigation did not depend upon the color.[20]

18. 4 John H. Wigmore, Evidence in Trials at Common Law § 1150 (James H. Chadbourn rev. 1972).

19. United States v. Jones, 56 Fed. Appx. 416, 419 (9th Cir. 2003); United States v. Bokshoven, 258 F.Supp.2d 397, 400 (E.D.Pa. 2003).

20. United States v. Skelley, 501 F.2d 447, 451 (7th Cir. 1974) (counterfeit bills were admissible to prove defendant's knowledge that they were counterfeit because they had identical serial numbers and were found on defendant).

"Real evidence" is frequently authenticated in the manner of 901(b)(4) by reference to its distinctive characteristics. If the condition of the item is not important or if the item is distinctive, real evidence often can be authenticated by simple identification. Documents, for example, are probably the most common "real evidence" and they are usually authenticated in the fashion of 901(b)(2) or (3), by identification of the handwriting.[21] Real evidence that is non-documentary is often authenticated in the fashion of 901(b)(4), by distinctive characteristics or circumstances. A police officer, who initialed a weapon upon seizing it from a suspect, might authenticate the weapon by recognizing the initials and testifying about circumstances of the seizure and marking. Money, televisions sets, automobiles, etc. may be authenticated by showing that the witness recorded the item's serial number at the time of the seizure and that the serial number of the proposed exhibit matches.

When the item of real evidence is not distinctive, or when its condition at the time of testing or trial is critical, a chain of custody is the most effective way to authenticate the exhibit. A perfect demonstration of the chain of custody would include testimony about every link in the chain, from the moment the item was picked up at the scene of the event to the time it is offered into evidence. Each person who touched the exhibit would describe how and from whom it was received, where it was and what happened to it while in the witness' possession, the condition in which it was received and the condition in which it was delivered to the next link in the chain. The witnesses would describe the precautions taken to ensure there was no change in the condition of the exhibit and no opportunity for someone not in the chain to have possession of the item.

Testimony about the perfect chain is almost impossible and has never been the standard. Before adoption of the Federal Rules, a chain of custody could be established only if there was reasonable certainty that all the links in the chain were firmly connected. The Rules may have made the required showing less onerous. The authentication standard in Rule 901(a) requires only enough evidence to support a finding that the item is what it purports to be. Some courts in Federal Rules jurisdictions have taken the new standard literally and have allowed greater gaps between the links in a chain of custody.[22] Other courts have remained

---

21. *See* § **11.10** *infra* for examples of document foundations. *See also* Edward J. Imwinkleried, Evidentiary Foundations (2002).

22. *See, e.g.,* United States v. Smith, 70 Fed.Appx. 359 (7th Cir. 2003) ("evidence kept in official custody is presumed to be authentic absent specific evidence of tampering."); United States v. McGraw, 62 Fed. Appx. 679, 681 (7th Cir. 2003) ("Fed. R. Evid. 901(a) advisory committee notes state that the requirement of proving authenticity falls in the category of relevancy dependent upon fulfillment of a condition of fact

and is governed by the procedure set forth in Fed. R. Evid. 104(b). In determining whether there is sufficient evidence to meet the requirements of Rule 104(b), the court neither weighs credibility nor makes a finding that the government has proved the conditional fact by a preponderance of the evidence. The court's role is to examine the evidence to determine whether the jury could reasonably find the conditional fact by a preponderance of the evidence."); Weighing the evidence is traditionally a jury function and United States v. Jones, 56 Fed.Appx. 416 (9th Cir. 2003), held that "[a]ny defect in the chain of custody goes to

strict and have repeated the reasonable certainty standard of the pre-Rules era.[23]

Custody chains are commonly used to demonstrate that a substance seized in one place is the same substance and in the same condition as the substance tested in another place and then returned for use in court. The exhibit will have passed through many hands from its point of origin to the laboratory to the courtroom, and it also will have been processed or analyzed. The exhibit and the laboratory analysis will not be admissible unless the proponent can show the chain of custody of the exhibit from the time it was seized to the time it arrives in court.[24] Urine samples, bloody gloves, trace elements of hair, are exemplary of the myriad of objects that might require the showing of a custody chain, but drugs seized in a drug bust are the most common example.

In the typical drug case, someone associated with the government secures the drugs. Often it is an undercover officer or an informer who made the buy. The drugs are often transferred to at least one other law enforcement officer. The drugs are then stored in an evidence locker; sent via some delivery service to a laboratory for testing; stored, handled, and tested in the laboratory by at least one technician; and sent via some delivery service back to the law enforcement officer. If at any of these links there is tampering, inadvertent alteration, or substitution of white powder from some other case in which similar evidence was seized, the test results may be wrong and the exhibit offered in court may not be

the weight, not the admissibility, of the evidence introduced." *Id.* at 419; United States v. Watts, 78 Fed.Appx. 350, 2003 WL 22351968, *1 (5th Cir. 2003) ("The determination of the authenticity of heroin is within the province of the jury."); United States v. Myers, 294 F.3d 203 (1st Cir. 2002) ("The links in a chain of custody need not be welded to one another, but, rather, may be more loosely connected. '[T]he prosecution's chain-of-custody evidence must be adequate—not infallible.' To the extent that there were any weak links in the instant chain—notably, the time between the end of the chase and the time when the guns were found—their effect on the authenticity of the evidence was a matter within the exclusive province of the jury.") (internal citations omitted).

23. *See, e.g.,* United States v. Chapman, 345 F.3d 630, 637 (8th Cir. 2003) ("A district court may admit physical evidence if the court believes a reasonable probability exists that the evidence has not been changed or altered. In making this determination, absent a showing of bad faith, ill will, or proof of tampering, the court operates under a presumption of integrity for the physical evidence."); United States v.

Diaz–Villasenor, 68 Fed.Appx. 791, 792 (9th Cir. 2003) ("A district court's ruling on the chain of custody is reviewed for abuse of discretion. The prosecution may establish chain of custody to lay a proper foundation for admission of physical evidence if it is able to prove that a reasonable juror could find that the evidence is in substantially the same condition as when it was seized and if there is a reasonable probability the evidence has not been changed in important respects.")

24. Paul C. Gianelli, *Chain of Custody and the Handling of Real Evidence*, 20 Am. Crim. L. Rev. 527, 538 (1983); An example of acceptable chain of custody shown by government is discussed in United States v. Jackson, 345 F.3d 59 (2d Cir. 2003) "The government established a chain of custody consisting of (i) a videotape that showed Mazyck giving the substance to Redman; (ii) a DEA agent's testimony regarding the government's surveillance of Redman for most of the time before, during, and after the videotaped transaction; (iii) an agent's testimony regarding the DEA's field-testing and storage of the drugs; and (iv) the testimony of the forensic chemist who subjected the substance to laboratory testing." *Id.* at 65.

that originally seized or procured by the first law enforcement personnel to handle the drugs.

The chain of custody can be established without testimony from everyone who handled the drugs. The habit rule, the business record exception and the public record exception to the hearsay rule make it possible for documentary evidence to be used to establish some of the links in the chain.[25] Moreover, imperfect chains and minor gaps are often accepted for purpose of authentication, the issue of the weight to be given to the testimony left to the jury.[26] Despite the flexibility shown when there are minor gaps in the chain, courts will not admit exhibits if the defect in the chain might reasonably affect the authenticity of the exhibit.[27]

In *Graham v. State*,[28] an informer made a supervised purchase of a substance that was later analyzed as heroin. The break in the chain of custody occurred after the exhibit was deposited in the police property room. The property room records showed that before the exhibit was analyzed, one officer removed the exhibit from the property room and six days later, another officer returned the exhibit to the property room. Neither officer testified at trial. There was no evidence of where the exhibit was, or in whose possession, during the six days that it was not in the police property room. The trial judge admitted the evidence. In holding that it was error to admit the exhibit with the break in the chain of custody, the appellate court emphasized the special nature of substances such as narcotics. It said that "the danger of tampering, loss, or

---

25. *See e.g.*, United States v. Lauersen, 348 F.3d 329 (2d Cir. 2003); Hulmes v. Honda Motor Co., 960 F.Supp. 844 (D.N.J); Judd v. State, Department of Transp. & Dev., 663 So.2d 690 (La. 1995).

26. *See, e.g.,* United States v. Pressley, 978 F.2d 1026, 1028–29 (8th Cir. 1992) (trial court properly admitted substance in package marked by an officer at the scene of the crime, when chemist testified she tested substance in same package; held, "[t]he government is not required to maintain an eternal vigilance over all evidence in its custody"); United States v. Turpin, 65 F.3d 1207 (4th Cir. 1995); United States v. Diaz–Villasenor, 68 Fed.Appx. 791, 792–93 (9th Cir. 2003) ("Merely raising the possibility of tampering, however, is not enough to render evidence inadmissible. Furthermore, a defect in the chain of custody goes to the weight, not the admissibility, of the evidence introduced."); Lee v. State, 689 N.E.2d 435, 439 (Ind. 1997) ("[T]he State need not negate every remote possibility of tampering. It is sufficient if the State presents evidence which strongly suggests the exact whereabouts of the evidence at all times. Once the State has presented such evidence, any gaps in the chain of custody would go to the weight of the evidence and

not to the admissibility of the evidence.") (internal quotations and citations omitted); Nimmons v. State, 814 So.2d 1153 (Fla. App. 2002) ("In order to bar the introduction of relevant evidence due to a gap in the chain of custody, the defendant must show that there was a probability of tampering with the evidence, and a mere possibility of tampering is insufficient."); ("It is worthy to note that even if Arriola had pointed to a specific gap within the chain of custody between the SmithKline Patient Servicing Center and the actual testing laboratory, our review of the jurisprudence indicates that courts have treated gaps within the chain of custody as a question involving the weight of the evidence, rather than its admissibility.").

27. Rabovsky v. Commonwealth, 973 S.W.2d 6 (Ky. 1998) ("Blood test results were not admissible in a murder trial simply because the results had been placed into the hospital records where the state had failed to show a chain of custody sufficient to indicate a lack of material tampering."); Crisco v. State, 328 Ark. 388, 943 S.W.2d 582 (Ark. 1997) (Methamphetamine tested by the State was excluded due to serious defect in chain of custody)

28.   255 N.E.2d 652, 655 (Ind. 1970).

mistake with respect to an exhibit is greatest where the exhibit is small and is one which has physical characteristics fungible in nature and similar in form to substances familiar to people in their daily lives."[29] It noted the white powder seized could have been heroin, or it could have been sugar or baking powder. It stated the chain of custody rule for substances such as narcotics as follows:

> Unless the state can show by producing records or testimony, the continuous whereabouts of the exhibit at least between the time it came into their possession until it was laboratory tested to determine its composition, testimony of the state as to the laboratory's findings is inadmissible.[30]

Robinson v. Commonwealth,[31] is a case in which the authentication did not match the purpose for which the exhibit was offered. The victim of a rape identified her panties and blouse in court, which had been handed over to the investigating officer shortly after the incident. The evidence would have been sufficient to authenticate the clothing as that she was wearing when she was attacked. The clothing items were offered, however, as the base for the opinion of an FBI expert. The expert testified about the semen stains, bloodstains, and wool fibers found on the clothing—evidence that linked the defendant to the crime. The prosecution did not offer any evidence as to who had handled or what happened to the items of clothing from the time they were taken from the victim to the time they were given to the local police for storage—the time during which the FBI analysis took place. In reversing the conviction because the chain of custody was inadequate to authenticate the items, the court said:

> It is true that the blouse and panties were identified at the trial by the victim as a part of the clothes she was wearing when attacked. The Commonwealth contends that they were properly admitted because the victim identified them. If they had been admitted only to establish what the victim was wearing when attacked, then we would agree with the Commonwealth's position. But the blouse and the panties were also admitted to supply a basis for the opinion testimony of the FBI agents. The mere fact the blouse and the panties were identified did not prove the chain of possession necessary to validate the FBI analysis of them.[32]

§ 11.05 Demonstrative Exhibits That Are Illustrative of Other Testimony

Demonstrative evidence that illustrates, clarifies, and amplifies *viva voce* testimony brings life to a lawsuit. Trial lawyers are constantly in search of visual aids that will assist them in persuading jurors. They use diagrams, models, similar objects, photographs, and drawings to illustrate the ideas to which witnesses testify. The simplest and most

---

29. *Graham*, 255 N.E.2d at 655.

30. *Id.*

31. 183 S.E.2d 179 (Va. 1971).

32. *Id.* at 181.

common example is the intersection diagram on which a witness illustrates the many simultaneous movements that make up the average intersection collision.

The foundation for demonstrative evidence that is offered only to illustrate other testimony is deceptively simple. The witness must demonstrate familiarity with whatever it is that is depicted, must testify that the exhibit fairly and accurately represents what is depicted, and, in some courts, that the exhibit will assist the witness in explaining the testimony to the jurors. It does not matter whether it is a photograph or a diagram, or a duplicate object, for that matter. The foundation that the exhibit is a fair and accurate representation can be laid by anyone who knows what the thing depicted looks like. So the testimony of the photographer or the diagram maker, for example, is not required.

The foundation for most demonstrative evidence offered for illustrative purposes, fits the pattern that follows for a diagram.

Example

Direct examiner:	Are you familiar with the intersection of First Avenue and Maple?
Witness:	Yes.
Direct examiner:	How are you familiar with that intersection?
Witness:	I drive through it regularly—at least three times a week.
Direct examiner:	I show you what has been marked Plaintiff's exhibit number one for identification. Do you recognize it?
Witness:	Yes, I do.
Direct examiner:	What is it?
Witness:	Looks like the intersection of First Avenue and Maple.
Direct examiner:	Does Plaintiff's exhibit number one for identification fairly and accurately represent the way the intersection of First Avenue and Maple appeared on (the date of incident?)
Witness:	Yes, it does.
Direct examiner:	Would the diagram assist you in explaining to the jurors what you saw?
Witness:	Yes.

Direct examiner:	Your honor, I offer the diagram of First Avenue and Maple into evidence as Plaintiff's exhibit number one.
Opposing attorney:	Your honor, I request a limiting instruction be given informing the jurors that the diagram is not drawn to scale.
Judge:	Members of the jury. The diagram that has just been received in evidence as Plaintiff's exhibit number one is not drawn to scale. While it is basically accurate as to the intersection of First Avenue and Maple, the distances shown are approximate, and should not be taken by you to necessarily represent the distance relationships on the intersection.

The foundation—that the exhibit fairly and accurately represents whatever it is it represents and that it would assist the witness in testifying—is as sufficient for a complex model or for a hologram as it is for a simple diagram.

Demonstrative evidence used for illustrative purposes is handled differently from jurisdiction to jurisdiction and sometimes from courtroom to courtroom. Trial courts have great discretion in the handling of demonstrative evidence offered for illustrative purposes.[33] Demonstrative exhibits that are used for illustrative purposes are not even marked in some courtrooms, though a lawyer who insists upon having such an exhibit marked to make the record understandable for an appellate court should prevail. Some courts allow the use of demonstrative evidence for illustrative purposes, but do not allow the exhibits to be admitted into evidence.[34] In other courts, demonstrative evidence used for illustrative purposes is received in evidence, but the jurors are given an instruction that the exhibit is for illustrative purposes only. In some instances, such as when a replica of a gun used in a robbery is admitted for illustrative purposes, it may be error not to give an instruction reminding the jury that the gun is not the actual gun.[35] At one time demonstrative exhibits

---

33. Carson v. Polley, 689 F.2d 562 (5th Cir. 1982); State v. Finch, 975 P.2d 967 (Wash. 1999); Ware v. State, 702 A.2d 699 (Md. 1997); *but see* People v. Blue, 724 N.E.2d 920 (Ill.2000) (Appellate court held that trial court erred in allowing the State's demonstrative evidence into the jury room where that evidence was a blood and brain matter splattered police officer's uniform worn by a life size mannequin and where that mannequin was accompanied with rubber gloves, inviting the jury to interact with it.)

34. *See, e.g.,* United States v. Walt, 117 F.3d 1427 (9th Cir. 1997); Standard Jury Instructions—Civil Cases (99–1), 778 So.2d 264 (Fla. 2000) (provides an example of jury instruction regarding demonstrative evidence: "This witness will be using (identify demonstrative or visual aid(s)) to assist in explaining or illustrating [his] [her] testimony. The testimony of the witness is evidence; however, [this] [these] (identify demonstrative or visual aid(s)) [is] [are] not to be considered as evidence in the case unless received in evidence, and should not be used as a substitute for evidence. Only items received in evidence will be available to you for consideration during your deliberations."); Pickren v. State, 500 S.E.2d 566 (Ga.1998).

35. United States v. Cox, 633 F.2d 871, 874 (9th Cir. 1980); Robinson v. Missouri Pac. R.R., 16 F.3d 1083 (10th Cir. 1994);

were routinely excluded from the jury room during deliberations. The modern tendency is to allow most exhibits to be taken into the jury room,[36] unless it is impractical (bulky items or contraband) or, in some cases, when the evidence is merely testimonial evidence in written form.[37]

The most common objection to demonstrative evidence used for an illustrative purpose is that it is misleading. Diagrams that appear to be to scale but are not can mislead the jurors into forgetting that the distances shown are approximate. A photograph taken under different lighting conditions can mislead the jurors into thinking that the lighting shown in the photograph reflects what someone on the scene could see at the time. Sometimes the problem is handled by an instruction, but if the evidence is sufficiently misleading, the judge may exclude it under Rule 403.

§ 11.06   Demonstrative Exhibits That Are Illustrative of Other Testimony—Diagrams and Models

Diagrams and models used to illustrate testimony are used in many cases and are a staple in tort cases. Many diagrams are offered with the first occurrence witness and remain in front of the jury throughout the trial, often referred to or marked on by more than one witness. Courts have different preferences about how diagrams are handled. If the diagram is one that a witness or a number of witnesses will mark on, some judges will not admit the diagram until all of the marking has been completed. Others will allow the diagram to be admitted and then amended as others mark on it. In some courts, diagrams are considered entirely illustrative and are neither admitted in evidence nor allowed in the jury room during deliberations.

Marking on diagrams is one way to make sure that the jurors understand what happened and that the appellate court can figure it out as well. While the jurors know what a witness means by pointing to a spot on a diagram and saying, "I was standing right here," they may not remember it when they arrive in the jury room. The appellate court will never know what "here" meant. If the witness marks clearly on the diagram, the jurors will remember when they take the diagram into the jury room and the appellate court will be able to understand by looking at the diagram.

Garrison v. State, 893 S.W.2d 763 (Ark. 1995); Dunlap v. State, 761 N.E.2d 837 (Ind. 2002).

36. McCormick on Evidence § 217 (5th ed. John W. Strong ed. 1999). United States v. Salerno, 108 F.3d 730, 744 (7th Cir. 1997)("As long as the district court is even-handed in its evidentiary rulings, it has wide discretion in determining whether an exhibit will be allowed to go into the jury deliberation room."); People v. Blue, 724 N.E.2d 920 (Ill.2000).

37. State v. Crimi, 665 N.E.2d 230 (Ohio App.1995) (jurors are generally entitled to see exhibits received in evidence but testimonial evidence presents a "speaking continuous witness" problem); State v. Monroe, 27 P.3d 1249 (Wash. Ct. App. 2001)(same).

While the foundation for most diagrams is the one set out in § 11.05, if the diagram is drawn to scale and is offered to illustrate testimony about precise measurements the witness must lay a much more complete foundation. Moreover, the witness must be one who can testify from first hand knowledge about the creation of the diagram. The witness must be able to explain how the measurements were obtained, how they were converted to the diagram, and the scale used.

Example

Direct examiner:	Are you familiar with the intersection of First Avenue and Maple?
Witness:	Yes.
Direct examiner:	How are you familiar with that intersection?
Witness:	I have driven through it, have gone over the construction plans for the intersection in the city engineer's office, and have taken measurements on the intersection itself.
Direct examiner:	I show you what has been marked Plaintiff's exhibit number one for identification. Do you recognize it?
Witness:	Yes, I do.
Direct examiner:	What is it?
Witness:	It is a diagram of the intersection of First Avenue and Maple.
Direct examiner:	Do you know how it was constructed?
Witness:	Yes, I do.
Direct examiner:	How was it constructed?
Witness:	I drew it to scale, based on information about its dimensions gained from the current plans in the city engineer's office and from measurements made on (the date of the incident) by the investigating police officer as to the position of various objects and marks.
Direct examiner:	How did you draw it to scale?
Witness:	I used a scale of five feet—sixty inches—to one inch. By using a standard ruler, I re-created the intersection and the objects on the diagram from the measurements I had. Every five feet or sixty

	inches of distance on the intersection is represented by one inch on the diagram.
Direct examiner:	How were you able to locate the various objects in the intersection?
Witness:	I had the measurements for every object that the investigating officer identified in his report and four measurements—one from each direction, N, S, E & W—from identified landmarks or points on the intersection to each object.
Direct examiner:	Your honor, I offer the scale diagram of First Avenue and Maple—drawn to a scale of 60 to 1 into evidence as Plaintiff's exhibit number one.

Once a diagram is accepted into evidence as a scale diagram, non-scale marks added to the diagram may destroy the foundation and the exhibit. Markings that show directions, etc. might be added, because they do not purport to represent distances, but any other marking that reflects a distance must be made to scale with a ruler or placed on an overlay that can be separated from the scale diagram.

When more than one witness will mark on a diagram, a number of different methods might be employed to ensure that the diagram is an aid to testimony, rather than something that makes matters more confusing. Using a different colored pen for each witness, and creating a legend on the bottom of the diagram, so the jurors can remember which witness used which colored pen is one method. Using a different clear acetate overlay for each witness—making sure that the acetates are individually marked—is another method that provides the lawyer with flexibility.

Models used for illustrative purposes are merely three-dimensional diagrams. Courts are occasionally less careful about the marking and offering of models used to illustrate testimony than they are about diagrams. A skeleton used by an orthopedic surgeon, for example, to show the jurors where the various bones the doctor is talking about are located may often be used without being either marked or admitted. The better practice, however, is to have the model marked and offered. Among other things, it is more likely to be allowed into the jury room if admitted.

A model with working parts requires greater foundational detail to ensure that the working parts on the model do not work in a different fashion than the parts represented. "Misleading" remains the condition that will persuade the court to exclude demonstrative evidence used for illustrative purposes.

§ 11.07   Demonstrative Exhibits That Are Substantive

Demonstrative evidence that is not real evidence can, nevertheless, often have substantive value, independent of any testimony to which it might relate. Photography, sound recordings, and documents are the three major areas in which demonstrative evidence might have independent substantive value. A photograph, properly authenticated, may be received as independent evidence of what it shows. A tape recording might be admitted as independent evidence of the conversation. While a written contract constitutes real evidence, if the contract is ambiguous, one party's memorandum about the contract may be admissible as independent substantive evidence of whether there was a meeting of the minds. If these pieces of demonstrative evidence are to have independent evidentiary value, the foundation requires something more than a witness who will testify that the exhibit is a "fair and accurate representation" of what it depicts. The foundation must demonstrate the reason that the exhibit should be considered authentic. A determination that the photograph, document, or recording is authentic does not, however, end the question of admissibility. The exhibit must still pass the hearsay and best evidence hurdles.[38] Authentication is a cumulative requirement.

§ 11.08 Demonstrative Exhibits That Are Substantive— Photography

Photography, whether it is in the form of a still photo, film, or videotape has a history of being viewed first with suspicion by the courts and then being viewed as common. Each succeeding technology has had to travel the authentication trail from a detailed explanation of the entire technology to acceptance by the court based upon the affirmation from any witness with knowledge that the picture is a fair and accurate representation of what it shows. In discussing the journey for still photographs, the Court in *United States v. Hobbs*[39] described the journey that each of the photographic technologies has taken:

> When photographs first began finding their way into judicial trials they were viewed with suspicion and received with caution. It was not uncommon to place upon the offering party the burden of producing the negative as well as the photograph itself, and of proving that neither retouching or other manual or chemical intervention was reflected in the proffered print. That burden has now shifted, and the proponent of a proffered photograph has established a prima facie case for its admissibility when he has shown it to be an accurate representation of the scene in question. The opposing party should then be afforded an opportunity for voir dire to show that the picture is not in fact an accurate representation.[40]

Today, most courts will accept pictures—stills, film, videotapes—into evidence upon a showing that in accord with 901(b)(1) a witness with

---

38. *See* Fed. R. Evid. 901(b) advisory committee's note ("It should be observed that compliance with requirements of authentication or identification by no means assures admission of an item into evidence, as other bars, hearsay for example, may remain"). *See also* Orr v. Bank of Am., NT & SA, 285 F.3d 764, 778 (9th Cir. 2002); United States v. Wadena, 152 F.3d 831 (8th Cir. 1998).

39. 403 F.2d 977 (6th Cir. 1968).

40. *Id.* at 978.

knowledge has testified that the picture "fairly and accurately" represents what the witness saw.

Example

[Witness has been identified and the photograph has been marked and shown to opposing counsel.]

Direct examiner: Where were you at 3:00 p.m. on November 1, 1997?

Witness: On the southeast corner of First Avenue and Maple.

Direct examiner: What happened while you were on the corner?

Witness: There was a collision between a Ford and a Chevrolet.

Direct examiner: I show you what has been marked Plaintiff's exhibit number one for identification. Do you recognize it?

Witness: Yes.

Direct examiner: What is it?

Witness: It is a picture of the intersection of First Avenue and Maple shortly after the collision.

Direct examiner: Does Plaintiff's exhibit number one fairly and accurately represent the scene at the intersection of First Avenue and Maple on November 1, 1997 as you saw it shortly following the collision between the Ford and the Chevrolet?

Witness: Yes it does.

Direct examiner: Are there any differences between plaintiff's exhibit number one for identification and the scene at the intersection of First Avenue and Maple as you saw it immediately following the collision?

Witness: Only one that I can see.

Direct examiner: What is that difference?

Witness: The photograph includes a police car parked off to the side that was not there right after the collision. The police officer arrived about five minutes later.

Direct examiner: Other than the police car, is there anything different?

Witness: No.

Direct examiner: Your honor, I offer the picture of the intersection of First Avenue and Maple following the collision into evidence as Plaintiff's exhibit number one.

As a persuasive matter, the lawyer might expand the examination about what the witness saw. If the witness saw the photographer take the picture, that, too, might be the subject of examination. But neither is necessary to lay the foundation for the photograph.[41]

Although earlier twentieth century courts treated photographs of the kind now authenticated under 901(b)(1) as "pictorial testimony," merely illustrative of other testimony,[42] the modern trend is to accept that photographs inevitably carry their own independent evidentiary value.[43] Many of the details in the photograph will not have been the subjects of the witness' testimony, but the photograph constitutes evidence of everything that it shows, based on judicial notice of the general reliability of the photographic process.[44] Photographs and the purposes for which they are admitted are uniquely within the trial court's discretion, which will not be overturned unless there is an apparent abuse of discretion.[45]

While the trend is to allow photographs into evidence for whatever they show, so long as there is sufficient foundation,[46] the sufficient foundation varies with the purpose. When something more, or instead of, a witness' affirmation that the picture "fairly and accurately represents" what the witness saw is needed, authentication is often demonstrated by showing a Rule 901(b)(9) process that produces accurate results.

41. Bryant v. State, 810 So.2d 532 (Fla. App. 2002)(witness qualifying a photograph need not be the photographer or see the picture taken); Pless v. State, 545 S.E.2d 340 (Ga. App. 2001); United States v. Stephens, 202 F.Supp.2d 1361 (D.Ga. 2002).

42. *See generally*, Diane M. Allen, Annotation, *Admissibility of Visual Recording of Event or Matter Giving Rise to Litigation or Prosecution*, 41 A.L.R.4th 812 (1985)(Supp. 2000)); R. B. Kaman, Annotation, *Admissibility of Posed Photograph Based on Recollection of Position of Persons or Movable Objects*, 19 A.L.R.2d 877 (1951) (admissibility of photographs of reenactment of crime or accident scenes).

43. *See e.g.*, Bryant v. State, 810 So.2d 532, 536 (Fla. App. 2002) ("Only if a picture is verified as a true representation of the subject about which testimony is offered, is

it admissible in evidence."); United States v. Holmquist, 36 F.3d 154 (1st Cir. 1994).

44. 1 Charles Calvin Scott, Photographic Evidence 351–52 (1969); United States v. Rembert, 863 F.2d 1023 (D.C. Cir. 1988); United States v. Smith, 27 Fed.Appx. 577 (6th Cir. 2001); United States v. Stephens, 202 F.Supp.2d 1361 (N.D.Ga. 2002).

45. *See e.g.*, McCrary–El v. Shaw, 992 F.2d 809, 811, 813 (8th Cir. 1993); State v. Vang, 353 S.C. 78 (S.C. App. 2003); ACTONet, Ltd. v. Allou Health & Beauty Care, 219 F.3d 836 (8th Cir. 2000).

46. *See, e.g.*, United States v. Stearns, 550 F.2d 1167, 1171 (9th Cir. 1977); United States v. Tropeano, 252 F.3d 653 (2d Cir. 2001); United States v. Patterson, 277 F.3d 709 (4th Cir. 2002).

"Silent Witness" Photographs

The idea of the "silent witness" first appeared in the discussion of whether a photograph was merely illustrative or had independent evidentiary value.[47] Today, however, when most jurisdictions consider all photographs to have some independent evidentiary value,[48] the term is used for those photographs for which there is no witness and no photographer. The picture with no witness and no photographer has become common with the proliferation of security cameras in apartment buildings, banks, and many other places. Despite the lack of a witness to or a photographer of the scene, pictures of intruders and robbers taken by these silent sentinels have been received in evidence, under the "silent witness" theory of authentication, when the proper foundation has been laid.[49] While there are a myriad of circumstances that might in a particular case authenticate a picture when there is no witness or photographer, a common approach is for the proponent to show the process by which the camera is activated, the scene is recorded, and the film is processed.

The courts' relatively recent comfort with the "silent witness" theory, upon which pictures are accepted as evidence of what they show, even though no live witness is available, may be short lived. The risk of alteration of a picture has been considered reasonable because, among other things, alterations were detectable. Detection is no longer possible if the alteration is done through the now widespread use of digital technology. Whether the new world of digital creation and re-creation will also provide a kind of electronic fail-safe remains to be seen. In considering the possibility of federal guidelines related to various criminal law issues raised by the burgeoning computer technology, The Computer Search and Seizure Working Group, made up of members of various federal agencies, hypothesized the following evidentiary horror story:

> Agents and prosecutors were shown a photograph of a body—twisted on the floor, a gaping wound in the chest. Across the room on the floor was a large pistol. On the white wall above the victim's body, scrawled in the victim's own blood, were the words, "I'll kill again. You'll never catch me."
>
> ... [T]his picture was not created with film, but with a digital camera ... law enforcement agents, using commercially available

---

47. *See e.g.*, United States v. Bynum, 567 F.2d 1167 (1st Cir. 1978); Fisher v. State, 643 S.W.2d 571 (Ark. App. 1982) (citing all the cases); United States v. Goslee, 389 F.Supp. 490, 493 (W.D.Pa. 1975) ("Under the 'silent witness' theory, when an adequate foundation is provided to assure the accuracy of the process producing a photograph, the photograph can be admitted to speak for itself, even though no witness has vouched for its accuracy."); Department of Pub. Safety & Correctional Servs. v. Cole, 672 A.2d 1115 (Md. 1996);

United States v. Harris, 53 M.J. 514 (N–MC C.C.A. 2000).

48. 3 John H. Wigmore, Evidence in Trials at Common Law § 792 (James H. Chadbourn rev. 1972).

49. *See, e.g.*, John W. Strong, McCormick on Evidence § 214 vol. 2 (5th ed. 1999); United States v. Harris, 55 M.J. 433 (C.A.A.F 2001); Wagner v. State, 707 So.2d 827, (Fla. App. 1998).

software, started rearranging the digits. They "cleaned" the wall . . . closed the chest wound, choosing instead to have blood trickling from the victim's temple . . . moved the gun into the victim's hand. The case was now solved: the report would claim, and the photograph would "prove," the victim committed suicide.[50]

Various Medical Imaging Machines

The authentication of x-rays, MRIs and CAT scans is similar to that developed in the "silent witness" approach to the authentication of photographs and videotapes, in that authentication depends upon proof that the process produces an accurate result. This Rule 901(b)(9) method of authentication is in many respects similar to the showing that is a pre-condition to admission of expert scientific opinion testimony.

X-rays have been around for sufficient time to realize the Advisory Committee's assumption that courts may well take judicial notice of the accuracy of the x-ray process.[51] The MRI and CAT scan may well be sufficiently familiar to have courts take judicial notice of the accuracy of their processes. In a court taking judicial notice of the validity of the scientific process by which the device produces a picture of internal portions of the human body not visible to any witness, the foundation focuses on the normal operation of the process and of the proper matching of picture to person.

Some courts admit x-rays and other medical imaging pictures as the hospital business records, accepting the x-ray custodian's testimony that the proper x-ray record was located and brought to court. Many hospitals

---

50. 56 Cr. L. 2023, 2053 (December 21,1994). United States v. Harris, 53 M.J. 514, 519 (N–MC C.C.A. 2000)("Courts have traditionally taken a strict view towards the admissibility of recordings, recognizing that tapes could be tampered with or distorted. Under the traditional approach, the proponent of the tape was required to account for the custody of the tape. However, with the development of technological means to detect whether a tape has been altered, the foundational standards have been relaxed. If the integrity of the tape is challenged, an expert witness can be called upon to examine the tape. Furthermore, protection against falsification or misrepresentation lies in the requirement of preliminary proof that the picture is an accurate reproduction of the event which it depicts and in the opportunity for cross examination of the witness making such proof."); Bryant v. State, 810 So.2d 532, 536 (Fla. App. 2002)("If no witness who is available has seen what videotape or a photograph depicts, proof of surrounding circumstances may nevertheless be sufficient for the court to find that the photograph is a fair and accurate representation of a material fact. This approach reflects resort to the so-called 'silent witness' theory which entails

proof of foundational facts establishing the reliability of the process that yielded the photographic images, taking into account the following factors: (1) evidence establishing the time and date of the photographic evidence; (2) any evidence of editing or tampering; (3) the operating condition and capability of the equipment producing the photographic evidence as it relates to the accuracy and reliability of the photographic product; (4) the procedure employed as it relates to the preparation, testing, operation, and security of the equipment used to produce the photographic product, including the security of the product itself; and (5) testimony identifying the relevant participants depicted in the photographic evidence.")

51. The advisory committee's note to Rule 901(b)(9) lists the x-ray as a "familiar instance" and states specifically that example 9 "does not foreclose taking judicial notice of the accuracy of the process or system." In addition, some states have passed statutes and rules providing for the easy admission of properly identified x-rays, for example, N.Y. C.P.L.R. 4532–a.

avoid even this authentication by using a lead identification number with each x-ray assembly, making each x-ray picture a separately identifiable item. The normal foundation, absent stipulation or statutory shortcut involves the testimony of a qualified x-ray technician who can testify:

1.   that particular parts of a particular person's body were x-rayed at a particular time,

2.   that well maintained and working x-ray equipment was used, and

3.   that the operator used the proper procedures in identifying and taking the x-ray.

In addition, the witness should testify to the process for handling and storing the x-ray in the hospital.

Motion Pictures and Videotape

There is nothing about authentication of film or videotape that is analytically any different from still photographs. Because the technology was not as familiar, courts treated film and videotape differently for many years, requiring more elaborate foundations that described in detail the qualifications of the camera operator and the detail of the film process.[52] Most modern courts accept motion pictures and videotape on a lesser showing.[53]

The authentication problems that arise from the introduction of film or videotape are related more to the subject matter than to the technical process. When a tape or film purports to show conditions as they existed at the time of an accident or crime, then of course an objection can be interposed on grounds that conditions may have changed between the event and the recording.[54] When the tape or film reenacts a crime or

52.   *See, e.g.,* United States v. Gross, 917 F.2d 23 (4th Cir. 1990)(Adequate foundation was laid where the Agent testified that he had reviewed the tape and that it fairly and accurately depicted the events he had described); United States v. Roach, 28 F.3d 729, 733 (8th Cir. 1994) (There are "seven foundational guidelines for the admission of electronic tape recordings, these guidelines consisting of a showing by the government that: (1) the recording device was capable of recording the events offered in evidence; (2) the operator was competent to operate the device; (3) the recording is authentic and correct; (4) changes, additions, or deletions have not been made in the recording; (5) the recording has been preserved in a manner that is shown to the court; (6) the speakers on the tape are identified; and (7) the conversation elicited was made voluntarily and in good faith, without any kind of inducement [to counter a claim of entrapment].").

53.   *See, e.g.,* Jones v. City of Los Angeles, 20 Cal.App.4th 436 (Cal. App. 1993); (authentication standard applicable to photographs also applicable to motion pictures, film or videotape); Carter v. State, 1995 WL 755918, *1 (Tex. App. 1995)("The predicate for motion pictures is the same as that for still photographs. Like still photographs, motion pictures may be admitted into evidence where they are properly authenticated, relevant to the issues, and not violative of the rules established for the admissibility of photographs").

54.   *See, e.g.,* People v. Mayfield, 14 Cal.4th 668 (Cal. 1997)(Videotape properly admitted even though taken during the day and 18 months following the crime where the lighting and date of recording were irrelevant to show the position of fences and walls, which had not changed); State v. Wilson, 637 A.2d 1237 (N.J. 1994); Truesdell v. Rite Aid, 644 N.Y.S.2d 428, 429 (A.D. 3d Dept. 1996)(Excluded photographs taken

accident, questions about whether the reenactment is slanted, misleading, or prejudicial are often raised.[55] Hearsay objections may also be interposed, on grounds that the reenactment is an assertion by an out-of-court declarant about how something happened, offered to show the truth of the assertion.[56] A voice narration accompanying the reenactment may also be the legitimate target of a hearsay objection, and the objecting party may succeed at least in having the tape or film played without its narrative. The tape or film of an experiment, if the conditions of the experiment are not similar to those pertaining at the time of the event, can cause a film or tape to be excluded on the basis that the experiment is unfair or misleading.[57]

One of the common uses of videotape is the video diary of the "day in the life" of a personal injury plaintiff. It is used to show the pain and difficulties the plaintiff suffers as a result of the injury by focusing on the difficulty of things as mundane as moving around the home, performing daily tasks, and interacting with other members of the household. Authentication should not be particularly difficult in theory. The

six weeks after plaintiff's fall for which there was no evidence in the record to establish that the condition at the time of plaintiff's fall was substantially as shown in the photographs).

55. *See, e.g.,* Harris v. State, 13 P.3d 489, 495–96 (Okla. Crim. App. 2000)("In order for a video or computer crime scene reenactment to be seen by a jury, as an aid to illustrate an experts witness's testimony, the court should require (1) that it be authenticated—the trial court should determine that it is a correct representation of the object portrayed, or that it is a fair and accurate representation of the evidence to which it relates, (2) that it is relevant, and (3) that its probative value is not substantially outweighed by the danger of unfair prejudice, confusion of the issues, misleading the jury, undue delay, needless presentation of cumulative evidence, or unfair and harmful surprise." Okla. Stat. tit. 12, §§ 2401–2403, 2901 (1991). In addition, "[t]he court should give an instruction, contemporaneous with the time the video reenactment evidence is presented, that the exhibition represents only a re-creation of the proponent's version of the event; that it should in no way be viewed as an actual recreation of the crime, and like all evidence, it may be accepted or rejected in whole or in part. The court must also ensure that the other party has prior opportunity to examine the reenactment and underlying data. The trial court should also mark the video reenactment as a court's exhibit so that the record may be preserved."); Wallace v. GMC, 1997 WL 269498 (E.D.La. 1997) (Motion in limine to exclude evidence of video of left angle barri-

er tests was granted because the video action depicted was not substantially similar to the accident in question and because the events depicted would tend to confuse the jury and any probative value was outweighed by the prejudice.); Gorman v. Hunt, 19 S.W.3d 662 (Ky. 2000) (posed photos admissible if authenticated). Gregory P. Joseph, *Videotape Evidence in the Courts*, 1985 A.B.A. Sec. Subcomm. Evid. (courts carefully scrutinize reenactments, because they afford opportunity for confusion, misconception, and manipulation).

56. *See e.g.,* Nicholas v. Wal–Mart Stores, Inc., 33 Fed.Appx. 61 (4th Cir. 2002) (action caught on tape was not assertive conduct and hearsay objection overruled); Marino v. State, 934 P.2d 1321 (part of videotape of defendant's interview with police was admitted over hearsay objections as non-assertive conduct but defendant was barred from using those portions where defendant protests his innocence because the "verbal conduct" was not non-assertive.); People v. Taylor, 732 N.E.2d 120 (Ill. App. 2000) (Conduct observed on videotape was not hearsay).

57. *See, e.g.,* Fields v. Commonwealth, 12 S.W.3d 275 (Ky. 2000)(audio narrative on videotape does not fall within any hearsay exception) State v. Coleman, 756 So.2d 1218 (La. App. 2000) (audio narrative on videotape was hearsay but admission was harmless error); Emerson Electric Co. v. Superior Court, 946 P.2d 841 (Cal. 1997)(Even if video recreation admitted, narrative on videotape might still be excluded based on hearsay, authenticity or other objection).

plaintiff, the plaintiff's family, or the filmmaker are all potential witnesses to testify that the film "fairly and accurately represents" an average day in the plaintiff's life. Some courts, however, have taken a very restrictive approach to admission of "day in the life" films.

In *Bolstridge v. Central Maine Power Co.*,[58] the defendant made various claims that the film was unrealistic or slanted. According to defendant, the film was unfair in depicting experiences that plaintiff would only perform very rarely, such as ordering a wheelchair, and in emphasizing difficulties instead of giving a true slice of a day's activities.[59] Without making a specific finding that the film was slanted in this fashion, the court excluded the film. It said the plaintiff could depict the same difficulties in the courtroom, and that physicians and relatives could testify about her handicap. It expressed concern about the dangers of slanted presentation and the impossibility of cross-examining a videotape. A "day in the life" film, in the court's view, should be admissible only when the plaintiff could give a specific reason why in-court testimony would not be sufficient to convey the information, and that such a showing had not been made in the case before it.[60]

Bannister v. Town of Noble,[61] is representative of those courts that have admitted "day in the life" films.[62] In an opinion that recognized the benefits as well as the dangers of such evidence, the court noted that the tape could illustrate, better than words, the impact of the injury.[63] The trial judge had viewed the film before it was shown to the jury and was persuaded the film fairly represented the impact of the injury on the plaintiff's day-to-day activities. It was not full of exaggerated difficulties or heart-wrenching staged episodes. Moreover, the participants in the film were present and available for cross-examination about the accuracy of the film.

In jurisdictions that recognize the "day in the life" film, the objecting party cannot merely rest upon an assertion that in-court testimony would be adequate to depict injuries. Counsel should be prepared to show, with as much specificity as possible, what is wrong with the film. Perhaps the film does not show a typical slice of a day, exaggerates difficulties, or depicts rarely encountered obstacles. Perhaps the film makes an undue appeal to sympathy, for example by showing tearful

---

58.   621 F.Supp. 1202 (D. Me. 1985).

59.   *Id.* at 1203 & n 1.

60.   *Id.* at 1204.

61.   812 F.2d 1265 (10th Cir. 1987).

62.   *See, e.g.,* Regalado v. City of Chicago, 1998 WL 919712 (N.D.Ill. 1998) (case law does not categorically bar a-day-in-the-life videos without a showing of unfair prejudice); Eckman v. Moore, 2003 WL 22411078 (Miss. 2003); Wal–Mart Stores, Inc. v. Hoke, 2001 WL 931658 (Tex. App. 2001); Burke v. 12 Rothschild's Liquor Mart, Inc., 568 N.E.2d 80, 84 (Ill. App. 1991) (not error to admit day-in-the-life

film, despite opposing counsel's lack of advance notice and opportunity to be present at filming, as long as probative value of film outweighs potential prejudice and there are no demonstrated improprieties in content or production); Wagner v. York Hosp., 608 A.2d 496, 499–501 (Pa. Super. 1992) (day-in-the-life film properly admitted over objection that it inaccurately depicted reflexive sounds and movements as voluntary and conscious; not misleading because victim's consciousness of surroundings was disputed).

63.   *Bannister*, 812 F.2d at 1269.

scenes or the emotional reaction of the family to the plaintiff's injuries. Perhaps it has been edited in a misleading way, for example by including "reaction shots" that were not filmed at the same time as the rest of the film. Defects of this nature can support a Rule 403 objection that the film is prejudicial, misleading, or a waste of time.[64] As a matter of tactics, defense counsel may ask to be present at plaintiff's filming of a "day in the life" film. If the court grants a formal request, counsel will be in a position to know if something was left out of the final edited film, redone, or was in some other way at variance with the experience of the day. Even if the court does not grant a formal request to observe,[65] counsel may be able to argue the unfairness of the process to the jury. Correspondingly, if plaintiff has a strong case on damages, plaintiff may want to invite defense counsel to be present at the filming, either to promote settlement or to demonstrate fairness to the tribunal. Any "day in the life" film that has a voiceover narration or other verbal component is also potentially subject to a hearsay objection, on grounds that the film contains statements by an out-of-court declarant offered to prove the truth of what they assert. Moreover, if the film depicts assertive conduct that is the equivalent of a statement by the plaintiff about the nature of a disability, then a hearsay objection can also be interposed.[66]

Photographs Used to Prove "Actual" Conditions

What if a witness' ability to see under the existing lighting at the scene is at issue? Can a lawyer prove what the witness could (or could not) see by showing the witness a picture taken at the same place and hour and asking whether it "fairly and accurately" represents the light level at the time of the incident and the objects the witness could see?

[handwritten marginalia: "Fairly & accurately / not good enough / it must be precisely / authenticated"]

64. *See generally,* Joseph M. Herlihy, *Beyond Words: The Evidentiary Status of "Day in the Life" Films,* 66 B.U. L. Rev. 133, 136–41 (1986) (common objections to "day-in-the-life" films based on unfair prejudice and cumulative evidence). *See also* Hahn v. Tri–Line Farmers Co-op, 478 N.W.2d 515, 524–25 (Minn. App. 1991) (under Minn. R. Evid. 403, not error to admit film segments in which paraplegic withdraws small amount of money from bank and bends over to pick up newspaper from floor, over objection that segment prejudicially suggested financial hardship and was cumulative and inflammatory; even though injured party, his family, doctors, and vocational experts testified about his rehabilitation); Cisarik v. Palos Community Hosp., 579 N.E.2d 873, 874 (Ill. 1991) ("Because a day-in-the-life film is a form of motion picture it is admissible evidence on the same basis as photographs. Consequently, before a "day-in-the-life" film can become evidence at trial it must first pass a two-prong test. First, someone having personal knowledge of the filmed object must lay a foundation,, that the film is an accurate portrayal of what it purports to show. Second, the film is only admissible if its probative value is not substantially outweighed by the dan-

ger of unfair prejudice." Holding "opposing counsel has no right to intrude into the production of this demonstrative evidence") Id. at 875.

65. Cisarik v. Palos Community Hosp., 579 N.E.2d 873, 874–75 (Ill. 1991) (reversing protective order that would have allowed opposing counsel to be present during day-in-the-life film, to have edited-out footage, and to have copy of completed film); Southern Scrap Material Co. v. Fleming, 2003 WL 22415995 (E.D.La. 2003) (Surveillance video of plaintiff taken to discredit plaintiff's version of her injuries was considered work product); Martin v. Intex Recreational Corp., 1994 WL 665742 (D.Kan. 1994) (video made of expert's reenactment was not work product but discoverable expert opinion).

66. *See e.g.,* Marino v. State, 934 P.2d 1321 (Alaska App.1997) (part of videotape of defendant's interview with police was admitted over hearsay objections as nonassertive conduct but defendant was barred from using those portions where defendant protests his innocence because the "verbal conduct" was assertive.); People v. Taylor, 732 N.E.2d 120 (Ill. App. 2000) (Conduct observed on videotape was not hearsay).

Such an offer should provoke a Rule 403 objection that the photograph is misleading as to the purpose for which it is offered. While the judge might admit such a photograph without hesitation, if it were offered to show merely what was at the scene, the greater purpose should require a more precise authentication. Just as the 901((b)(1) showing that something is "what it is claimed to be" requires a scale diagram to be authenticated as an "exact" rather than a "fair and accurate" representation, so too with a photograph or videotape that purports to be exact in some respect.[67] The misleading issue is based upon the potential for distortion. The more the authentication can demonstrate that conditions are similar, the more likely the picture will be admissible. A picture taken simultaneously with the time the witness is observing is superior to one taken on a different day at a time calculated to show the same light level. Similarly, the camera settings, lenses, filters, etc. used when the picture was made will be important. Whether the problem is that the picture shows a re-creation of events or circumstances, or is that the picture shows the actual events under technical circumstances that might be distorting, the lawyer's task is to lay a foundation that demonstrates a lack of disparity. The judge's decision under Rule 403 will be based upon how serious the judge views the disparity between the authentication and the reality of the event.

Authentication as something more than "fair and accurate," be it termed "exact" or "actual," does not guarantee that a picture will be admitted. No matter how strong the authentication or how close to reality the picture may be, Rule 403 may provide a further basis for objection. Courts have been quite liberal in admitting revolting or repulsive pictures even when their probative value on disputed issues is meager,[68] but the Rule remains a vehicle by which the judge may exclude such evidence, irrespective of its authenticity.[69]

67. See, e.g., Gregg v. Weeks Marine, Inc., 2000 WL 798493 (E.D.La. 2000) ("Video reenactments may be properly admitted only if they were filmed under conditions substantially similar to those of the actual accident. The conditions do not have to be identical but should be nearly the same in substantial particulars as to afford a fair comparison in respect to the particular issue to which the test is directed. The purpose behind the substantially similar requirement is to avoid the risk of misleading members of the jury who may attach exaggerated significance to the evidence.") (internal citations and quotations omitted); United States v. Beeler, 62 F.Supp.2d 136 (D.Me. 1999) (time lapse video admitted over objection); State v. Terry, 130 Ohio App.3d 253 (Ohio App. 1998).

68. See, e.g., Government of the V.I. v. Albert, 241 F.3d 344, 346 (3d Cir. 2001)(Court held that a "videotape of the crime scene which included a detailed look at [victim's] partially naked body tied to the bed with the neck wound revealed" was properly admitted despite it's gruesome depiction); Taylor v. Lafler, 2003 WL 22284561, *5 (E.D.Mich. 2003)("Petitioner has no right to the writ of habeas corpus on the basis of this claim, because the erroneous admission of gruesome photographs fails to state a constitutional claim."); Simmons v. State, 797 So.2d 1134 (Ala. Crim. App. 2000) (Court held that it was not error to admit pictures of the crime scene including one showing pieces of the victim's intestines in the toilet.); Newman v. State, 106 S.W.3d 438 (Ark. 2003) (gruesome photos properly admitted as more probative than prejudicial); Harris v. State, 843 So.2d 856 (Fla. 2003)(photos of victim showing maggots around head wounds, and short video of body at crime scene were properly admitted even where they were admittedly gruesome and showed the body in a clear state of decomposition). See generally, Andre A. Moenssens, et al., Scientific Evidence in Criminal Cases § 2.14 (4th ed. 1995).

69. See, e.g., Spears v. Mullin, 343 F.3d 1215, 1227 (10th Cir. 2003)(admission of

§ 11.09 Demonstrative Exhibits That Are Substantive— Sound Recordings and Other Conversations

Authentication of sound recordings, like that of "silent witness" photographs and videotapes, is in significant part about proof of process in the fashion of 901(b)(9), as discussed above in § 11.08. Authentication of sound recordings, like that of documents, is often as much about the "best evidence" rule as discussed in § 11.11, as it is about identification.

Authentication of sound recordings and other conversations, be they telephonic or in person, always begins with identifying the participants by identifying the voices in the fashion of 901(b)(5) & (6). Motivated perhaps by the imperative of criminal law, courts have been less than rigorous in the familiarity required for a witness to identify a voice as belonging to a particular individual. A witness' testimony that a voice heard on the phone is the same as one heard a month later in person has been deemed sufficient for identification, even when there were no other instances of hearing or identifying the voice.[70] Although experts differ on the validity of voiceprints, some courts have ruled that sound spectrography may be used to identify unidentified voices in conversations.[71]

Someone who has not previously heard a person's voice may, nevertheless, authenticate a telephone conversation with a person. Rule 901(b)(6) provides for authentication of a telephone call by evidence that "a call was made to the number assigned . . . to a particular person" and "circumstances, including self-identification, show the person answering to be the one called." In the case of a business, a call placed to a number assigned to the business can be authenticated, if "the conversation related to business reasonably transacted over the telephone." Although there is no similar authentication illustration for incoming calls, because of the ease of fabrication on the part of the caller,[72] the advent of the

photographs depicting numerous post-mortem stab wounds, large gash wounds, exposed intestines, swollen face, and black eye rendered trial fundamentally unfair); Turben v. State, 726 N.E.2d 1245 (Ind. 2000)(Admission of autopsy photo was improper but harmless error); United States ex rel. Gonzalez v. DeTella, 918 F.Supp. 1214 (D.Ill. 1996)(close up photos of deceased improperly admitted but admission not harmful error).

70. See e.g., United States v. Hull, 74 Fed.Appx. 615 (7th Cir. 2003).

71. *See,* Edward J. Imwinkelried, Evidentiary Foundations § 4.05[4] (5th ed. 2002) and cases cited therein; United States v. Capanelli, 257 F.Supp.2d 678 (S.D.N.Y. 2003)(voice identification); United States v.

Drones, 218 F.3d 496 (5th Cir.2000) (voiceprints under *Daubert* and pre *Daubert*); State v. Jackson, 54 P.3d 739 (Wash. App. 2002); Carter v. State, 1997 WL 663310 (Tex. App. 1997)(regarding audio tape).

72. *See, e.g.,* State v. Valentine, 762 A.2d 1278 (Conn. 2000) (call from one who self-identifies cannot be authenticated by the self-identification, without more); Kalola v. Eisenberg, 344 N.J.Super. 198, 781 A.2d 77 (N.J. Super. 2001) (Self identification combined with "other reliable circumstantial evidence" is sufficient even absent authentication of the voice by the witness taking the call); State v. Hill, 630 N.W.2d 276 (Wis. App. 2001) (A person who has heard the voice on the tape only once at any time may authenticate it for purposes of admissibility).

technology by which the receiving telephone instrument records the number from which a call is placed may provide a different result.

Reference to other events or conversations that identify the speaker are common circumstantial methods of identifying a voice sufficiently to authenticate a conversation.

Sound recordings are commonly used in the prosecution of organized crime cases in which wiretaps and bugs are *de rigueur.* A tape recording may occasionally be authenticated by someone hearing the conversation and testifying that the recording is an accurate rendition,[73] but often the recording is the result of surreptitious recording to which there is no willing witness. When the "silent witness" approach is required, someone must provide the 901(b)(9) testimony about the process that produces an accurate result, in the same fashion as is required for videotape from a surveillance camera.[74]

§ 11.10   Demonstrative Exhibits That Are Substantive—Documents

Documents are the most common of trial exhibits. There are three hurdles to admission of a document: hearsay, best evidence, and authentication.

The authentication of a document depends upon the purpose for which it is offered. A document's appearance, contents, substance, internal patterns, or other distinctive characteristics, taken in conjunction with circumstances can provide sufficient indicia of reliability to permit a finding that it is authentic.[75] Direct testimony, however, of a person with first hand knowledge that the document is what it purports to be (901(b)(1)) or of someone who can identify handwriting (901(b)(2) & (3)) is the common method for authenticating documents.

---

73. *See, e.g.,* State v. Anderson, 119 Wash.App. 1051 (2003) (Informant equipped with recorder who was witness to actual conversation testified to the identity of the person on the tape); United States v. Polk, 56 F.3d 613 (5th Cir. 1995)(Officer who wired informant and recorded conversation while simultaneously recording it and watching defendant and informant speaking properly authenticated the tape and the voices on it).

74. *See, e.g.,* United States v. Stephens, 202 F.Supp.2d 1361, 1367 (D.Ga. 2002) ("To determine whether the proponent of electronic surveillance evidence has introduced evidence of its genuineness sufficient to support a finding of authenticity by the jury, within the meaning of Fed. R. Evid. 901(a) and Fed. R. Evid. 104(b), the United States Court of Appeals for the Eleventh Circuit adopts a flexible inquiry.

The standard requires the proponent to show, in a criminal case: (1) the competency of the operator of the recording equipment; (2) the fidelity of the recording equipment; (3) the absence of material deletions, additions, or alterations in the relevant part of the tape; and (4) the identification of the relevant speakers."); United States v. Tropeano, 252 F.3d 653, 661 (2d Cir. 2001) ("The government is not required to call as a witness a participant in a recorded conversation in order to authenticate the recording; it may lay the foundation for the recording through the testimony of the technician who actually made it."). *See also* Imwinkelried, *supra* note 69.

75. United States v. Paulino, 13 F.3d 20, 23 (1st Cir. 1994); United States v. Grimmer, 199 F.3d 1324 (2d Cir. 1999)("Authenticity of a document may be inferred from circumstantial evidence.")

901(b)(1) Example

[Witness has been identified and the document has been marked and shown to opposing counsel.]

Direct examiner: I hand you what has been marked as Plaintiff's exhibit number two. Do you recognize it?

Witness: Yes.

Direct examiner: What is it?

Witness: A letter.

Direct examiner: Have you seen plaintiff's exhibit number two before?

Witness: Yes.

Direct examiner: Please describe the circumstances?

Witness: I was at Mr. Writer's office about a week ago when he was sending out a series of letters to potential investors. He handed me the pile so that I could see who it was that he hoped would invest in the enterprise.

Direct examiner: Do you recognize plaintiff's exhibit number two?

Witness: Yes.

Direct examiner: How do you recognize it?

Witness: Well, I went through the letters to check the list and the amounts that the various potential investors were asked for. I remember this letter by the name of the person to whom it was sent and the suggested investment amount.

Direct examiner: Your honor, I offer plaintiff's exhibit number two for identification into evidence as plaintiff's exhibit number two.

901 (b)(20) Example

[Witness has been identified and the document has been marked and shown to opposing counsel.]

Direct examiner: I hand you what has been marked as Plaintiff's exhibit number two. Do you recognize it?

Witness: Yes.

Direct examiner: What is it?

Witness:	A letter I received on November 5th of this year.
Direct examiner:	Is it signed?
Witness:	Yes.
Direct examiner:	Do you recognize the signature?
Witness:	Yes, I do.
Direct examiner:	How do you recognize it?
Witness:	It is a signature that I have seen many times on letters and occasionally on a check.
Direct examiner:	Who signed plaintiff's exhibit number two for identification?
Witness:	Walter Writer.
Direct examiner:	Your honor, I offer the letter from Walter Writer to Willie Witness into evidence as plaintiff's exhibit number two.

Rule 901(b)(3) contemplates authentication of a writing by either expert or juror handwriting comparison of the document in question to a known, authenticated exemplar. Courts have allowed this kind of expert authentication, despite the growing concern that forensic document examination may not be scientifically valid.[76]

Indeed, if the trial judge believes that the handwriting on a document in question is sufficiently similar to the handwriting on a known exemplar so that a reasonable jury could find them to be written by the same person, the judge may admit the document and leave it to the jurors to decide its authenticity.[77]

Documents can be authenticated by circumstantial evidence. The content of a reply letter is an example of the kind of circumstantial evidence that can, on its own, authenticate a letter. The Advisory Committee note to 901(b)(4) incorporates the common law reply letter doctrine. If one party sends a letter to another, and then receives a letter

76. *See, e.g.,* United States v. Blackwood, 878 F.2d 1200, 1202 (9th Cir. 1989) (approving expert testimony authentication; United States v. Saelee, 162 F.Supp.2d 1097, 1106 (D. Alaska 2001) ("Rule 901(b)(3) contemplates testimony by an expert—but before an expert's testimony can be admitted, it must past through the gates of Rule 702."); United States v. Gricco, 2002 WL 31689241 (E.D.Pa. 2002) (Qualified handwriting expert testimony comparing handwriting admitted after passing muster under *Daubert*). *Cf.,* § **10.04** (discussion of the growing controversy over forensic document examination).

77. United States v. Wylie, 919 F.2d 969, 978 (5th Cir. 1990).

purporting to be from that person with contents suggesting it is in reply to the first letter, that is sufficient to authenticate the second letter.[78]

Rules 901 and 902 (self-authentication) provide relatively simple and straightforward methods for authenticating ancient documents, business documents, and public documents.

The increasing popularity of e-mail as a common method of communication creates potential authentication problems that have long been resolved for mail that is signed and sent. While authentication by circumstantial evidence, such as the reply letter, the content of the message, or action consistent with the message, might suffice in most cases, there may be instances in which the potential of computers and the Internet to mask identity create unique authentication problems. Cryptography, digital signatures, and other electronic identifying equivalents to the written signature might eliminate some of those problems, but those cases have yet to arise.[79]

§ 11.11 The Special Problems of Computer Generated Exhibits

The computer, which has had a major influence on society, has also had an enormous influence on the courtroom. Some of that influence has been on the generation of evidence. Computers generate demonstrative evidence that is illustrative of other testimony as well as demonstrative evidence that carries its own independent evidentiary value.

Business records are the most common example. The computer is on its way to becoming the universal record keeper in businesses. The use of a computer to generate business records does not change the necessary foundation under Rule 803(6), but it can require additional proof of the underlying operating theory and reliability of the computer. To the extent that computer output is a product of a process that relies upon certain assumptions that are not immediately apparent to those outside the field, it may be seen as a type of scientific evidence. Some courts require almost nothing in addition to the normal business record foundation other than an affirmation that the business has successfully used the computer. They take judicial notice of the operating theory and reliability of computer generated information in the same fashion as they take judicial notice of the validity of radar.[80] Some courts have required an affirmation or demonstration that the particular computer or software is reliable,[81] but the affirmation could be made without the witness

---

78. United States v. Weinstein, 762 F.2d 1522, 1533 (11th Cir. 1985); Fed. R. Evid. 901 Advisory Committee Notes.

79. For a complete discussion of the potential problems, solutions, and proposed foundational examinations, *see* Edward J. Imwinkelried, Evidentiary Foundations § 4.03[4] (LexisNexis 5th Edition)

80. *See, e.g.,* United States v. Moore, 923 F.2d 910, 915 (1st Cir. 1991) (nothing special needed for computer generated busi-

ness record, citing cases); In re D. W., 2002 Ohio 5322 (Oh. Ct. App. 2002); United States v. Salgado, 250 F.3d 438 (6th Cir. 2001); People v. Huehn, 53 P.3d 733 (Colo. App. 2002).

81. *See, e.g.,* Burleson v. State, 802 S.W.2d 429, 441 (Tex. App. 1991); People v. Huehn, 53 P.3d 733 (Colo. App. 2002)("While presentation of scientific evidence usually requires proof of the validity of the underlying theory and the reliability of the instrument, computers are so widely

having any particular knowledge of the workings of the hardware or software.[82]

There have been some calls by commentators for a more rigorous foundation for computer generated business records,[83] but few courts have responded. When computer generated business records have not been received in evidence, the failure has almost always been related to the failure of the normal business record foundation as it relates to computers.[84]

A person who can identify the computer system used, testify to the method by which information is gathered and put into the computer, and can relate the procedures by which the particular record offered in court is produced will almost always be a "qualified person" as required by Rule 803(6).[85] There is little reason to believe that courts that have been willing to accept that foundation would balk at considering business records to be self-authenticating under Fed. R. Evid. 902(11) so long as

accepted and used that the proponent of computer evidence need not prove those two elements of the foundation."); *but see* FDIC v. Carabetta, 739 A.2d 301, 307 (Conn. App. 1999) ("When computer records are offered as evidence, the proponent must satisfy a two part test. In addition to meeting the three requirements of the business records exception to the hearsay rule, the proponent also must establish that the basic elements of the computer system are reliable.").

82. *See, e.g.,* United States v. Linn, 880 F.2d 209, 216 (9th Cir. 1989); Midfirst Bank v. C.W. Haynes & Co., 893 F.Supp. 1304, 1311 (D.S.C. 1994) ("Computer records are admissible so long as the requirements of Rule 803(6) are met, and no more is required."); Garden State Bank v. Graef, 775 A.2d 189, 192 (N.J. Super. 2001) ("[C]omputers are universally used and accepted, have become part of everyday life and work and are presumed reliable. There is no reason to believe that a computerized business record is not trustworthy unless the opposing party comes forward with some evidence to question its reliability.") (internal citations and quotations omitted); *but see* FDIC v. Carabetta, 739 A.2d 301, 307 (Conn. App. 1999).

83. *See, e.g.,* Rudolph J. Peritz, *Computer Data Reliability: A Call for Authentication of Business Records Under the Federal Rules of Evidence*, 80 Nw. U.L. Rev. 956 (1986); James E. Carbine and Lynn McLain, *Proposed Model Rules Governing The Admissibility Of Computer–Generated Evidence*, 15 Santa Clara Computer & High Tech. L.J. 1 (January 1999); *but see* Fred Galves, *Where the Not–So–Wild Things Are:*

Computers in the Courtroom, the Federal Rules of Evidence, and the Need for Institutional Reform and More Judicial Acceptance, 13 Harv. J. Law & Tec. 161 (Winter 2000).

84. *See, e.g.,* Baber v. Commonwealth, 2003 WL 1810510 (Va. App. 2003) (computer records improperly admitted under business records exception where print outs of information not provided and foundation therefore not properly laid); United States v. Jackson, 208 F.3d 633 (7th Cir. 2000); United States v. Diaz, 176 F.3d 52 (2d Cir. 1999) (foundation problem, witness unable to testify that computer generated photo was a "fair and accurate representation".); United States v. Cestnik, 36 F.3d 904, 910 (10th Cir. 1994) ("A computer printout is admissible under Fed. R. Evid. 803(6), as with any other form of business record, if the offeror establishes a sufficient foundation in the record for its introduction. Computer business records are admissible if (1) they are kept pursuant to a routine procedure designed to assure their accuracy, (2) they are created for motives that tend to assure accuracy, for example, not including those prepared for litigation, and (3) they are not themselves mere accumulations of hearsay.")

85. *See, e.g.,* Dyno Constr. Co. v. McWane, Inc., 198 F.3d 567 (6th Cir. 1999) (Fed Ex operations manager); State v. Pannier, 1999 WL 1216327 (Minn. App. 1999) (quality insurance regulatory affairs manager); State v. Hall, 2003 Ohio 2824 (Ohio App. 2003) (retail help desk specialist); Fed. R. Evid. 803(6) requires testimony concerning business records by the custodian or some other "qualified fitness".

the affirmation of "regularly conducted activity as a regular practice"[86] includes the same information.

Computer simulations and animations may create both easier and more difficult authentication issues than those presented by computer generated business records. As a matter of consistent theory regarding demonstrative evidence offered for illustrative purposes, computer animation is no different from any other diagram or picture offered for the same purpose—it must be a "fair and accurate" representation of what someone saw or of the oral testimony that it illustrates.[87] But the fact is that a computer animation or simulation is not just another diagram. The impact on a jury of a filmed re-creation generated by data in a computer is tremendous and there is a suspicion in the courts that no instruction minimizing the evidentiary status of the computer simulation can be effective. As a result, many courts require a more complex foundation for computer animations and simulations.[88]

Computer simulations are most common in airline disaster cases[89] and in automobile accident re-constructions.[90] They usually reflect or are the basis for expert testimony. To lay the foundation for the simulation, the expert must lay the same foundation as would be necessary for the expert's testimony,[91] plus an explanation of how the computer either

86. Fed. R. Evid. 902(11)(C)

87. *See, e.g.,* Pierce v. State, 671 So.2d 186, 190 (Fla. App. 1996) (computer animation must be a fair and accurate depiction of that which it purports to be, the same foundation that must be established to admit any pictorial representation); People v. McHugh, 476 N.Y.S.2d 721, 722, 723 (1984) ("fairly and accurately" reflect the oral testimony); People v. Cauley, 32 P.3d 602 (Colo. App. 2001)(Computer animation is demonstrative evidence and proponent must testify that it fairly and accurately represents the testimony it relates to. Computer simulation is considered scientific evidence and is subject to the additional strictures regarding admission of scientific proof)

88. *See, e.g.,* Bray v. Bi–State Development Corp., 949 S.W.2d 93 (Mo.App. E.D. 1997) (collecting and discussing the cases from various jurisdictions); *see also* Note, Carole E. Powell, *Computer Generated Visual Evidence: Does* Daubert *Make a Difference?* 12 Ga. St. U.L. Rev. 577 (1996); State v. Tollardo, 2003 NMCA 122, *12, 77 P.3d 1023, 1027–28 (N.M.App.2003) ("Some courts divide computer-generated exhibits into two categories: computer animations and computer simulations. An 'animation' is a computer-generated exhibit that is used as a visual aid to illustrate an opinion that has been developed without using the computer. On the other hand, a 'simulation' is a computer-generated exhibit created when

information is fed into a computer that is programmed to analyze the data and draw a conclusion from it. When the image is used as a visual aid, the courts do not require a showing that the exhibit was produced by a scientifically or technologically valid method. On the other hand, before admitting a simulation, in which the computer has been used to analyze data, the courts require proof of the validity of the scientific principles and data. At least one commentator has noted, however, that courts are not always consistent in applying these labels to the particular exhibit at issue.")

89. *See* Paul Marcotte, *Animated Evidence: Delta 191 Crash Re–Created Through Computer Simulations at Trial,* A.B.A. J., Dec. 1989 at p. 52 for a description of competing uses of computer simulations accepted by court as substantive evidence in In re Air Crash at Dallas/Fort Worth Airport on August 2, 1985; Kathleen Connors, et al. v. United States, 720 F.Supp. 1258 (N.D. Tex. 1989); Carlo D'Angelo, *The Snoop Doggy Dogg Trial: A Look at How Computer Animation Will Impact Litigation in the Next Century,* 32 U. San. Fran. L. Rev. 561 (Spring 1998).

90. *See, e.g.,* Kudlacek v. Fiat S.p.A., 509 N.W.2d 603 (Neb. 1994); National Union Fire Ins. Co. v. Dowd & Dowd, P.C., 191 F.R.D. 566 (E.D.Ill. 1999); Smith v. BMW N. Am., Inc., 308 F.3d 913 (8th Cir. 2002).

91. *See* **Ch. 10** *infra.*

contributed to or reflects the opinion. Although there is little case law in a rapidly developing area, the foundation described in *Commercial Union v. Boston Edison*,[92] decided in a *Frye* jurisdiction, has been quoted with approval in many jurisdictions. The *Commonwealth Union* court required a showing that (1) the computer was functioning properly, (2) the input and underlying equations were sufficiently complete and accurate (and disclosed to the opposing party so they might be challenged), and (3) the software used is generally accepted in the appropriate community of scientists.[93] Although it would be fair to assume that a more detailed foundation might be required under *Daubert* the cases have to date offered little guidance.[94]

Unlike the expert testimony that a computer simulation may illustrate, the computer cannot be cross-examined. Some of the expert's assumptions are built into the computer software. This requires the cross-examiner to cross-examine the expert on how the computer is programmed to "decide" what happened as well as to conduct the normal cross-examination concerning the bases and scientific assumptions that may be involved in the expert's testimony.

The use of computer animations, simulations, and conclusions will continue to grow. The more the computer generates the information or conclusion, the more rigorous the courts will be in requiring a complete scientific evidence foundation.

§ 11.12   The "Best Evidence" of the Contents of Writings, Recordings and Photographs [FRE 1001–1006]

Every time a lawyer wants to prove the contents of a document, photograph, or recording, the lawyer must take account of the "best evidence" rule—more commonly referred to under the Federal Rules as the "original document" rule—though it applies to recordings and photographs as well as to writings. As a general matter, the rule requires use of the original or a mechanically reproduced duplicate to prove the contents of a photograph, recording or writing, unless the proponent can show that the original is unavailable.[95] Proof of compliance with the original documents rule usually comes from the same source as, and is usually presented as an integral part of, the foundation testimony for the exhibit. The common law "best evidence" rule applied only to documents,[96] but the Federal Evidence Rule applies to writings, recordings, and photographs.[97]

---

92. 591 N.E.2d 165 (Mass. 1992).

93. *Id.*

94. Edward J. Imwinkelried, Evidentiary Foundations § 4.09[4][c](5th ed. 2002)contains a sample foundation that is likely to be sufficient in courts applying *Daubert* reliability requirements to computer simulations.

95. Fed. R. Evid. 1002.

96. *Cf.,* Burney v. United States, 339 F.2d 91 (5th Cir. 1964)(best evidence rule applies only to writings); In re Reed's Estate, 672 P.2d 829, 834 (Wyo. 1983) (quoting 5 David W. Louisell & Christopher B. Mueller, Federal Evidence § 549 (1981) as stating that best evidence rule "expand[s] to some extent the common law tradition, which had sometimes insisted that the doctrine applied only to writings").

97. Fed. R. Evid. 1002.

Example

Direct examiner:	Did your wife communicate with you after that?
Witness:	Yes.
Direct examiner:	In what way?
Witness:	I got a letter from her in the mail.
Direct examiner:	When did you receive the letter?
Witness:	On July 13, 1998.
Direct examiner:	What did the letter say?
Opponent:	Objection!

There are three bases upon which to object to "What did the letter say?"

1. Hearsay. A document is an out-of-court statement, and if offered to prove the truth of the matter asserted, is hearsay, unless it falls within one of the Rule 801(d) categories. If the lawsuit is between the husband and wife, the letter is an admission of a party opponent.[98]

2. Authentication. The witness has not laid the foundation for authentication or identification of the letter. Even though the letter itself is not being offered, no evidence of its contents can be admitted until the letter is authenticated. The husband can satisfy the authentication objection by testifying that he recognized his wife's handwriting.[99]

3. Best evidence. If the hearsay and authentication objections are satisfied, the question "What did the letter say?" is still objectionable. The question asks about the contents of the letter, which is not admissible unless the proponent of the testimony can (a) produce the original of the letter, (b) produce a mechanically created "duplicate," or (c) demonstrate that the letter was lost, destroyed, otherwise unavailable, or concerned with a collateral matter.[100]

The drafters of the Federal Rules avoided applying the term "best evidence" to Article X (Contents of Writings, Recordings, and Photographs) because "best evidence" is a misnomer at best, and a vestige of a different and inapplicable principle at worst. The heart of the Federal Rule is that "to prove the content of a writing recording, or photograph, the original writing, recording, or photograph is required."[101]

---

98. Fed. R. Evid. 801(d)(2)(A).

99. Fed. R. Evid. 901(a)(2).

100. *See* Fed. R. Evid. 1002 (general rule that evidence of contents not admissible unless original produced); Fed. R. Evid. 1004 (excuses for not producing the original).

101. Fed. R. Evid. 1002.

At least some common law courts were confused about whether there was a general rule that an advocate must use the best evidence in presenting a case. Most courts held there was no such rule,[102] although every once in a while a case such as *State v. Price*,[103] would occur in which the court would get it wrong. The *Price* court allowed the use of the branded hide of a dead calf instead of the deteriorating carcass to prove the loss of the heifer only because the hide was the best available evidence. The court stated that the best evidence rule, as it understood it, "requires that the highest degree of proof of which a case is susceptible must be produced, if such proof is accessible."[104]

The *Price* court was almost assuredly wrong under the common law, but whatever the circumstance, the Federal Rules contain no "best evidence" requirement. A lawyer might try to offer the most persuasive evidence possible as a matter of strategy, but not because evidence law has any general hierarchy of evidence. Live testimony, for example, need not be presented in lieu of hearsay that is admissible because it fits one of the many exceptions to the rule excluding hearsay. Similarly oral testimony about an object central to the event in question is admissible even if the item is not offered, in spite of it being available, and capable of authentication.[105] So, if Carrie Nation—the famous late 19th century temperance agitator who prayed in saloons before busting them up—is charged with breaking a saloonkeeper's mirror, there is no "best evidence" rule that requires production of the mirror shards in court or an explanation of why they are not produced. The saloonkeeper's oral testimony about breaking the mirror is fully admissible and legally sufficient to prove the mirror was broken.[106]

There was, for a brief time, concern about what a lawyer was to do when attempting to prove the "content" of an inscribed item. Commentators were concerned about whether a tombstone, a branded cow, an automobile with a VIN number, and the like constituted very big writings to which the original documents rule might apply. The commentators favored a balancing approach toward inscribed chattels, taking into account the need for the evidence and the ease or difficulty of production.[107] The problem with the approach, of course, is that there is no express basis in the rules for balancing the difficulty of obtaining the original against the need for it.[108] Courts that have been forced to deal with this weighty problem have taken slightly different approaches. The

102. McCormick on Evidence § 229 5th ed. 1999).

103. 265 P.2d 444 (Ariz. 1954).

104. *Id.* at 446.

105. *See* Weinstein's Federal Evidence § 1001.03[2] (2d ed. 2003); *cf.,* United States v. Yamin, 868 F.2d 130, 134 (5th Cir. 1989) (best evidence rule does not apply to chattels); Byrd v. Bentley, 850 So.2d 232 (Ala. 2002) (Alabama's best evidence rule continues to be applicable only to writings).

106. *Cf.,* People v. Ojeda, 758 F.2d 403, 407 (9th Cir. 1985) (in burglary case, it is not necessary to produce stolen jewelry or excuse for non-production).

107. *See* 2 McCormick, *supra* note 97, § 232; 4 John H. Wigmore, Evidence in Trials at Common Law § 1182 (James H. Chadbourn rev. 1972).

108. Rule 1004 lists various excuses for not producing the original of a writing, but the physical difficulty of producing an inscribed chattel is not one of the listed excuses.

Alabama court, in *Drummond v. State*,[109] avoided the potential danger of cow dung in the courtroom (at least on the floor) by fiat: "We conclude it was competent for the witness to testify as to the markings he saw on the cow without producing her in court." The federal courts have engaged in a more sophisticated analysis, interpreting Rule 1002 not to apply to chattels.[110] The result has been the same. There is little need for wranglers in federal courtrooms.

The only hierarchy of evidence in the Federal Rules applies to writings, recordings, and photographs, and only if their contents are to be proved. In a prosecution for exhibition of an obscene movie, therefore, where the contents of the film must be proved to make the case, the prosecutor must produce the original film or an acceptable excuse for not having it.[111] Similarly, a plaintiff seeking to enforce a written contract with a defendant must produce the contract or an acceptable excuse for not having it.

It is important to remember that the rule does not require producing the writing, recording, or photograph, merely because it exists. If a witness is giving testimony about the underlying event based on knowledge from a source other than the writing, recording, or photograph, there is no requirement that the writing, recording, or photograph be produced. Consider the following examples.

If the court reporter who transcribed an earlier hearing at which Walter testified is asked, "What did Walter say at the hearing you transcribed?" the witness may answer. The testimony is about what the witness heard, not what is in the transcript.[112] If the witness is asked, "What does your transcript say Walter said at the hearing you transcribed?" the witness may not answer. That testimony would be about the contents of the transcript and is inadmissible, unless the original is produced.

If a witness to an accident that was videotaped is asked, "Which car entered the intersection first?" the witness may answer. The testimony is about what the witness saw, not what is on the videotape. If the witness is asked, "Which car does the videotape show entering the

---

109. 67 So.2d 280, 282 (Ala. App. 1953).

110. *See* United States v. Yamin, 868 F.2d 130, 134 (5th Cir. 1989) (in case involving counterfeiting of watches, court notes that, at least in part, the writing (trademark) on the watch makes it counterfeit; however court states that "an object bearing a mark is both a chattel and a writing, and the trial judge has discretion to treat it as a chattel, to which the best evidence rule does not apply") (*citing* United States v. Duffy, 454 F.2d 809, 812 (5th Cir. 1972)).

111. *See* People v. Enskat, 98 Cal.Rptr. 646 (Cal. App. Dept., Super. Ct. 1971); Wagman v. Bradshaw, 739 N.Y.S.2d 421 (A.D.2d Dept)(where the contents of an X-ray film

or MRI are to be proven, the original x-ray or MRI must be produced unless unavailability is adequately described and any secondary evidence offered accurately portrays and describes the films.)

112. *See* Texas Health Enters. v. Lytle Nursing Home, 72 Fed.Appx. 122 (5th Cir. 2003) (Court did not err in allowing testimony about a letter sent when the testimony was used to prove that *a* letter was sent and not what the content of that letter was.); United States v. Parkins, 7 Fed.Appx. 287, 289 (4th Cir. 2001) ("The best evidence rule does not apply where testimony of detectives is offered to prove the content of the conversations rather than the content of the tapes.").

intersection first?" the witness may not answer. The testimony would be about the contents of the videotape and is inadmissible, unless the original is produced.[113]

In a child custody proceeding, one spouse seeks to show that the other is unfit by producing evidence that the other spouse engaged in group sex, which was captured in a photograph. If the witness is one of the participants and is asked, "Did the spouse engage in group sex?" the witness may answer. But if the witness is someone who was not present, but to whom the photograph was shown, the witness may not answer the question, "Did the spouse engage in group sex?" The witness has no first hand knowledge, so must be reciting the contents of the photograph the witness saw. The proponent must produce the photograph or an excuse for not having it.[114]

The principal concern of the best evidence rule is the danger of mistakes in the oral reporting (or human copying) of the contents of documents, photographs, and recordings. Mechanically produced copies are considered accurate and are admissible, therefore, in lieu of originals, without any need to explain the absence of the original. The duplication can take the form of a copy machine or photographic copy of a document,[115] a re-recording of a tape recording,[116] or equivalent techniques that accurately reproduce the original.[117] These "duplicates" are admissible "to the same extent as an original" under Rule 1003, "unless (1) a genuine question is raised as to the authenticity of the original or (2) in the circumstances it would be unfair to admit the duplicate in lieu of the original." The mere assertion, without supporting evidence, that a duplicate is an inaccurate reproduction is not enough to raise a genuine question.[118]

Non-Production Allowed

The prohibition against proving the contents of a writing, recording, or photograph without the original does not apply when the "the writing, recording, or photograph is not closely related to a controlling issue."

113. See Weinstein's, *supra* note 11, at § 1001.04[1].

114. See Heinz v. Heinz, 165 P.2d 967, 971 (Cal. App. 1946) (court recognizes applicability of best evidence rule to testimony about contents of nude photos, but admits testimony because original photos beyond reach of subpoena power); United States v. Nelson, 38 Fed.Appx. 386 (9th Cir. 2002)(original photo required to prove content of photo unless the original has been destroyed or otherwise fits within an exception to the rule, in which case secondary evidence of content may be admissible).

115. See Communities for Equity v. Michigan High Sch. Ath. Ass'n, 137 F.Supp.2d 910 (W.D.Mich. 2001) (photocopy just as good as original and it is up to opponent to object on the ground that the photocopy is inaccurate); State v. Brown, 743 A.2d 262; (Md. App. 1999) (photocopy of warrant introduced where there was no question of its authenticity).

116. United States v. Capanelli, 257 F.Supp.2d 678 (S.D.N.Y. 2003); State v. Fujimoto, 36 P.3d 813 (Haw. 2001); Bryant v. State, 810 So.2d 532 (Fla. App. 2002).

117. Fed. R. Evid. 1001(4).

118. Fed. R. Evid. 1001(4).

Example

Direct examiner:	Where were you going?
Witness:	I continued down Kirby Avenue.
Direct examiner:	You didn't stop?
Witness:	No. I was late for an appointment.
Direct examiner:	Did you later report that you had seen the accident?
Witness:	Yes.
Direct examiner:	When?
Witness:	The next day.
Direct examiner:	Why did you report it the next day?
Witness:	I read in the newspaper someone had been killed in the accident and I did not agree with the description of how it all took place.

If the testimony is offered solely for the purpose of explaining why the witness called the police the next day, the contents of the newspaper are collateral and the newspaper itself need not be produced.[119]

Even when the matter is not collateral, the best evidence rule should rarely prevent a diligent lawyer from introducing testimony about the contents of a writing. If neither an original nor a duplicate is available, the lawyer should be able to have a witness lay the foundation for oral testimony about the contents of a document by establishing the writing was

1. lost or stolen; or

2. destroyed (in good faith); or

3. in someone else's hands, and not obtainable by judicial process; or

4. in the possession of the opponent, and the opponent had notice to produce it, by the pleadings or otherwise.[120]

If the lawyers properly prepare their cases, the only circumstance in which the best evidence rule should actually exclude evidence is when the client has destroyed it in bad faith.

---

119. *See, e.g.,* People v. Hamilton, 757 N.Y.S.2d 739 (A.D. 1st Dept. 2003)(collateral writings are exempt from the best evidence rule); Bickley v. FMC Techs., Inc., 84 Empl. Prac. Dec. (CCH) P41,437 (N.D. Ohio 2003)(same); Farr v. Zoning Board of Appeals of Town of Manchester, 95 A.2d 792, 794 (Conn. 1953)(issue of land ownership relates only to standing to appeal, not to substance of the dispute, and is, therefore, collateral, allowing oral testimony.).

120. *See* Fed. R. Evid. 1004.

Any Secondary Evidence Will Do

There are no degrees of secondary evidence under Rules 1001–1006. If the proponent satisfies the judge that the original is missing or that there is some other valid excuse for not producing the original, the proponent can prove the contents of the original either by oral testimony or by producing a copy. There is no "second best evidence" rule requiring the proponent to produce the best that is available.[121] If, for example, the original of a hospital record is not available because it is not subject to subpoena, oral testimony about its contents is permitted, even though a machine copy might be obtained easily and offered.

Strict logic might call for extending the principle of preference beyond simply preferring the original, but the drafters believed that creating a hierarchy of preferences and a procedure for making it effective involved unwarranted complexities.[122] Most, if not all, that would be accomplished by an extended scheme of preferences will be achieved through the normal motivation of a party to present the most convincing evidence possible and the arguments and procedures available to the opponent in the absence of the more persuasive evidence.

Official records are the single exception to the rule that there is no hierarchy of secondary evidence. Rule 1005 states a clear preference for copies that are certified or that are presented through the testimony of a witness who has compared the copy with the original. Other evidence of the contents of an official record is admissible only if the certified or compared copy cannot be obtained by the exercise of due diligence.[123]

Summaries

Rule 1006 allows into evidence charts, summaries, or calculations to prove the content of voluminous writings, recordings, or photographs. This exception to the requirement of the original to prove the contents of a document, recording or photograph is intended to make it more convenient for the trier of fact to assimilate the information.[124] The Rule requires the originals to be so "voluminous" that they "cannot conveniently be examined in court" and requires that the originals be made available for other parties to examine at a "reasonable time and place."

Charts have been admitted under the Rule to summarize as few as 20 drug transactions when inspection of various underlying hotel receipts and phone bills would be inconvenient.[125] The need for a summary

---

121. Advisory committee's note to Rule 1004 ("The rule recognizes no 'degrees' of secondary evidence").

122. *Id.*

123. Compliance with Rule 1005 will satisfy both the authentication requirement—showing the copy to be what it purports to be—and the best evidence rule. In order for the record to be admissible under the public records exception to the rule against hearsay, it must also satisfy the requirements of Rule 803(8). A public record that does not describe any of the matters set forth in rule 803(8) is not admissible merely because it satisfies Rule 1005.

124. Fed. R. Evid. 1006 advisory committee's note.

125. United States v. Possick, 849 F.2d 332, 339 (8th Cir. 1988); Martin v. Funtime, Inc., 963 F.2d 110 (6th Cir. 1992); FTC v. Kuykendall, 312 F.3d 1329 (10th Cir. 2002).

of voluminous material increases when the material involves hard-to-understand technical data,[126] or when it clarifies a confusing sequence of events.[127]

The chart or summary that is admitted under Rule 1006 is evidence and not merely an illustration to aid the trier in understanding other admitted evidence.[128]

Admission of summaries under Rule 1006 is committed to the discretion of the courts.[129] Discretion should be guided by whether the summary will be helpful under the circumstances. In the circumstances of a given case the court may feel that the jury ought to consider the source documents in resolving a fact issue and that, on balance, a summarization of such evidence would detract from the proper weight or emphasis to be given it.[130]

The proponent of a Rule 1006 chart or summary must show that the materials on which it is based are admissible in evidence.[131] Any part of a Rule 1006 summary that is based on inadmissible evidence is itself inadmissible,[132] and the entire chart or summary is inadmissible, unless the admissible portion can be segregated and identified.[133]

The source documents must be available to the opposing party prior to introduction of the summary,[134] although the summary, itself, need not be.[135] This requirement is met when the trial judge determines that

126. *See* United States v. Campbell, 845 F.2d 1374, 1381 (6th Cir. 1988) (summary chart admitted in evidence when "... without the chart, the jury would have been forced to review hundreds of pages of technical information which may not have been readily understandable to the lay reader"); United States v. DeBoer, 966 F.2d 1066 (6th Cir. 1992); *but see* United States v. Taylor, 210 F.3d 311 (5th Cir. 2000). ("Admission of organizational chart in drug conspiracy prosecution was erroneous where it did not accurately reflect underlying testimony; lines of chart showed that defendant supplied drugs to two persons who testified that they never received drugs from defendant.").

127. *See* United States v. Meyers, 847 F.2d 1408, 1412 (9th Cir. 1988) (summary chart admitted where underlying FBI surveillance logs for the day in question were admissible and available, but the sequence of events was confusing).

128. United States v. Smyth, 556 F.2d 1179 (5th Cir. 1977);United States v. Pharis, 2000 WL 1469330 (E.D.Pa. 2000);*but see* United States v. Buck, 324 F.3d 786, (5th Cir.2003) (summaries used illustratively to clarify or enhance testimony should not be admitted in evidence).

129. *See, e.g.,* James v. Nico Energy Corp., 838 F.2d 1365, 1373 (5th Cir. 1988); Gomez v. Great Lakes Steel Div., 803 F.2d 250, 257 (6th Cir. 1986); Martin v. Funtime, Inc., 963 F.2d 110 (6th Cir. 1992).

130. *Smyth*, 556 F.2d at 1184 n. 11.

131. See, e.g., State Office Systems v. Olivetti Corp., 762 F.2d 843, 845 (10th Cir. 1985); Paddack v. Dave Christensen, Inc., 745 F.2d 1254, 1260 (9th Cir. 1984); Sotavento Corp. v. Morningside, 2001 WL 951329 (Conn. Super. 2001); United States v. Hazlewood, 40 Fed.Appx. 347 (9th Cir. 2002).

132. *See* Bergstein v. Jordache Enters., 1996 WL 271910 (S.D.N.Y. 1996); SEC v. Price Waterhouse, 797 F.Supp. 1217 (S.D.N.Y. 1992).

133. Paddack v. Dave Christensen, Inc., 745 F.2d 1254, 1260–61 (9th Cir. 1984) (audit report based in part on inadmissible hearsay excluded).

134. *Hackett*, 750 F.2d at 1312 (summary inadmissible under Rule 1006 because proponent party failed to produce underlying documents). *Cf.,* United States v. Miller, 771 F.2d 1219, 1238 (9th Cir. 1985); United States v. Modena, 302 F.3d 626 (6th Cir. 2002).

135. Coates v. Johnson & Johnson, 756 F.2d 524, 550 (7th Cir. 1985); People v. McDonald, 15 P.3d 788 (Colo. App. 2000); United States v. Stoecker, 215 F.3d 788 (7th Cir. 2000).

the underlying documents were made available at a reasonable time and place[136] even if opposing counsel fails to make use of the opportunity to review the documents.[137]

Although Rule 1006 is designed to provide an alternative to admitting voluminous records, admission of the underlying records does not prohibit the use of a Rule 1006 chart or summary. If despite their admission into evidence, the records are too voluminous to "conveniently be examined in court," a Rule 1006 chart or summary is admissible.[138]

The question that has caused confusion in the courts is whether a judge has the discretion to allow the use of a chart or summary when the underlying material is admitted into evidence and has been examined in court. The courts have universally agreed that the judge has authority to allow the use of the summary, but have disagreed about the status and use of the summary. Although some courts talk about Rule 1006 in this circumstance, the language of the rule says that a Rule 1006 summary is conditioned upon the notion that the underlying information "cannot conveniently be examined in court." The better analysis is that admission of the summary is within the court's discretion under Rule 611(a)—Mode and Order of Interrogation and Presentation.[139]

The difference between admission under Rule 1006 and Rule 611 is the difference between demonstrative evidence that has its own independent value and demonstrative evidence that is merely illustrative. The courts have called the summaries of the second kind, "pedagogic." One court has suggested that the difference is important in determining whether the summary or chart should go back to the jury room during deliberations—allowing the Rule 1006 summary into the jury room, but not the pedagogic summary.[140] Another court has not seemed so concerned about whether the summary goes to the jury room as that the court gives the jury the proper instructions about the lack of evidentiary value in the summary.[141]

There is a growing danger in the courts' willingness to admit summaries of already examined evidence under Rule 611(a) that the

---

136. *See* Davis & Cox v. Summa Corp., 751 F.2d 1507, 1516 (9th Cir. 1985) (summaries inadmissible where underlying documents not made available to party opponent until just before trial); Air Safety, Inc. v. Roman Catholic Archbishop of Boston, 94 F.3d 1 (1st Cir. 1996); Fed. R. Evid. 1006 Advisory Notes.

137. Frank Music Corp. v. Metro-Goldwyn–Mayer, 772 F.2d 505, 515 n. 9 (9th Cir. 1985).

138. Heinzerling v. Goldfarb, 818 A.2d 345 (N.J. Super. 2002); United States v. Taylor, 210 F.3d 311 (5th Cir. 2000).

139. *See, e.g.,*; United States v. Pinto, 850 F.2d 927, 935–36 (2d Cir. 1988); United States v. Scales, 594 F.2d 558, 563–64 (6th Cir. 1979) (alternative holding). *See also* Weinstein's, *supra* note 11, at

§ 1006.08[4] (a summary chart "prepared by a witness from his own knowledge to assist the jury in understanding or remembering a mass of details . . . is admissible, not under an exception to the best evidence rule, but under such general principles of good sense embodied in a court's duty to control the presentation of evidence"). The decision whether to admit such summary evidence pursuant to Rule 611(a) is left to the sound discretion of the district court. *Pinto*, 850 F.2d at 935–36; United States v. Johnson, 54 F.3d 1150 (4th Cir. 1995).

140. United States v. Buck, 324 F.3d 786 (5th Cir. 2003); Heinzerling v. Goldfarb, 818 A.2d 345 (N.J. Super. 2002).

141. United States v. Pena, 213 F.3d 634 (4th Cir. 2000).

summary will become a vehicle for prematurely and unfairly arguing the case to the jury. It happens mostly in criminal cases and almost always to the advantage of the government. In *United States v. Scales*,[142] the court found that a chart was admissible under Rule 1006, because the underlying material, though admitted, could not "conveniently be examined in court." The court allowed, also, that if the summary had not been admissible under Rule 1006, it would have been under Rule 611(a). It warned, however, that conclusory summaries, or those that presented the evidence from the government's perspective, ought not be allowed.[143] In *United States v. Johnson*,[144] the Fourth Circuit refused to reverse a conviction where the government offered a summary that not only reiterated objective information that was before the jury, but that commented on the credibility of witnesses and summarized the evidence in a manner most favorable to the government. The summary was not only admitted into evidence, but was allowed into the jury room. The appellate court held that the procedure was within the discretion of the court, since it instructed the jury that the summary was not evidence.[145]

142. 594 F.2d 558 (6th Cir. 1979).

143. *Id.* at 564.

144. 54 F.3d 1150 (4th Cir. 1995)

145. *Id.* at 1159. For sharp criticism of the result as giving the government an extra final argument, *See* Emilia A. Quesada, *Summarizing Prior Witness Testimony: Admissible Evidence, Pedagogical Device, or Violation of the Federal Rules of Evidence?* 24 Fla. St. U. L. Rev. 151(1996).

Chapter 12

APPELLATE REVIEW OF RULINGS
ON OBJECTIONS

Table of Sections

§ 12.01 Meaning of Error in Evidentiary Context

A trial is much like a living organism. It is dynamic, changing from moment to moment; its appearance and character are affected not only by the parties that brought it about, but its own history since its creation. Though all are governed by a set of general rules and principles, those rules and principles must be adapted to each case. Like living things, no two are truly identical in both heredity and environment.

As a result, trial judges must have a good deal of leeway in applying evidentiary rules if they are to help maximize the chances that the trial will achieve its principal goal of truth-determination.[1] It is primarily for this reason that the Federal Rules of Evidence contain a great deal of flexibility.[2] Most of its provisions are not categorical in nature, but instead grant the trial court the authority—guided by the terms of the rules themselves—to reach a result appropriate to the particular trial. The most obvious example is Rule 403, which allows the trial court to

---

1. For discussion of the many goals of the trial, *see* 1A John H. Wigmore, Evidence in Trials at Common Law § 37.1, at 1018 (Peter Tillers rev. 1983); Milner S. Ball, *The Play's the Thing: An Unscientific Reflection on Courts Under the Rubric of Theater*, 28 Stan. L. Rev. 81, 83 (1975); David P. Leonard, *The Use of Character to Prove Conduct: Rationality and Catharsis in the Law of Evidence*, 58 U. Colo. L. Rev. 1 (1987); Charles R. Nesson, *The Evidence or the Event? On Judicial Proof and the Acceptability of Verdicts*, 98 Harv. L. Rev. 1357, 1360 (1985); Laurence H. Tribe, *Trial by Mathematics: Precision and Ritual in the Legal Process*, 84 Harv. L. Rev. 1329, 1376 (1971).

2. For discussion of the flexibility of the Federal Rules and the authority this gives to trial judges, *see* David P. Leonard, *Power and Responsibility in Evidence Law*, 63 S. Cal. L. Rev. 937 (1990); Thomas R. Mengler, *The Theory of Discretion in the Federal Rules of Evidence*, 74 Iowa L. Rev. 413 (1989); Jon R. Waltz, *Judicial Discretion in the Admission of Evidence Under the Federal Rules of Evidence*, 79 Nw. U.L. Rev. 1097 (1984).

exclude otherwise admissible evidence when the court finds that its probative value is substantially outweighed by certain specified dangers.[3] Guided by the terms of the Rule itself, as well as certain general provisions of the Federal Rules,[4] the court must make its 403 rulings in the specific context of the trial. Many other provisions of the Federal Rules are similar; in whole or in part, they contain standards rather than categorical admission or exclusion rules.[5]

When an evidence rule gives "discretion" to the trial court, the appellate court is rarely in as good a position as the trial court to determine the most appropriate ruling. The appellate court, after all, is faced with the cold, written record, and cannot observe the demeanor of witnesses, the effect certain evidence appears to have on the jury, and other factors one would have to "be there" to observe. Thus, it is said that the appellate court should only reverse the trial court's application of such rules if the trial court "abused its discretion," a standard rarely satisfied in actual practice.[6] Whether this is justified can be debated, but the fact remains that trial courts are granted a virtual shield from reversal based on error in applying discretionary rules.

Nevertheless, not all evidentiary rules are alike in terms of the authority granted to trial judges. As already pointed out, some rules are categorical. The court has no authority, for example, to allow the prosecution to offer evidence of the defendant's character to prove circumstantially that the defendant committed the crime, unless the defendant has opened the door to such evidence by offering character to prove innocence.[7] Conversely, most courts hold that the trial court has no discretion to *exclude* evidence that a witness committed a crime involving dishonesty or false statement, when that evidence is offered to

---

3. *See* § **5.04.**

4. *See, e.g.*, Fed. R. Evid. 102 (requiring the court to construe the rules in such a way as "to secure fairness in administration, elimination of unjustifiable expense and delay, and promotion of the growth and development of the law of evidence to the end that the truth may be ascertained and proceedings justly determined"); Fed. R. Evid. 611(a) (requiring the court to "exercise reasonable control over the mode and order of interrogating witnesses and presenting evidence so as to (1) make the interrogation and presentation effective for the ascertainment of the truth, (2) avoid needless consumption of time, and (3) protect witnesses from harassment or undue embarrassment").

5. A key example of a hybrid rule is Fed. R. Evid. 608(b), which absolutely forbids the use of extrinsic evidence of other misconduct of a witness to impeach the witness's credibility, but allows inquiry into such misconduct on cross-examination "in

the discretion of the court, if probative of truthfulness or untruthfulness." The Rule thus has both categorical and "discretionary" aspects.

6. *See* Margaret A. Berger, *When, If Ever, Does Evidentiary Error Constitute Reversible Error?*, 25 Loy. L.A. L. Rev. 893, 894 (1992) (finding only 30 officially reported decisions out of over 20,000 tried federal cases during 1990 in which a federal appellate court reversed a trial court for evidentiary error); David P. Leonard, *Appellate Review of Evidentiary Rulings*, 70 N. Caro. L. Rev. 1155, 1212–29 (1992) (finding virtually no reversals for error in applying Rules 608(b) and 611 for a ten-year period). While the measure of actual reversals does not correlate perfectly with the number of instances of "harmless" error, courts rarely even find harmless error in reviewing trial court discretionary rulings.

7. *See* Fed. R. Evid. 404(a). *See* §§ **5.07–5.08.** Rules 413–415 provide exceptions.

impeach the witness's credibility.[8] If the rule applied by the trial court did not confer discretion on the judge, the appellate court's standard of review should not be abuse of discretion, but a more searching standard such as "error of law."[9] For example, if in a murder prosecution, the trial court allowed the government to call a witness during its case in chief to testify to defendant's prior acts of murder, for the purpose of showing a character-based propensity to commit such crimes,[10] the appellate court should not review the trial court's ruling for "abuse of discretion," for the trial court had no discretion to allow the government to offer such evidence. Rather, the appellate court should simply find that the trial court erred as a matter of law.[11]

Unfortunately, appellate courts all too often fail to recognize that trial courts do not always have discretion in applying evidence rules. It is not uncommon for courts to state simply, and generally, that they review evidentiary rulings for abuse of discretion.[12] In *General Elec. Co. v. Joiner*,[13] the Supreme Court approved this view, holding that the "abuse of discretion" standard applies even to the trial court's *Daubert* rulings. As a result of the Court's decision in *Joiner*, it is more apparent than ever that appellate oversight of trial court evidence rulings is quite limited. Applied to the *Daubert* context, one consequence will be that a type of forensic test found admissible in one courtroom will be found inadmissible in another. Holding that evidentiary rulings are reviewed on the basis of abuse of discretion virtually ensures that the trial court's rulings will not be disturbed on appeal.[14]

---

8. *See* Fed. R. Evid. 609(a)(2). *See* § **9.09**.

9. *Cf.* United States v. McConney, 728 F.2d 1195 (9th Cir.1984) (en banc) (reviewing possible standards of review of trial court's ruling on constitutionality of federal agents' entry into defendant's home with a search warrant, and distinguishing situations in which review should be based on "clearly erroneous" standard and those in which appellate court should review for "error of law").

10. We are assuming, for purposes of this example, that the prosecution does not argue that the prior murders are admissible for some other purpose, such as to show motive for the charged offense. *See* Fed. R. Evid. 404(b), discussed in **Ch. 5**.

11. The trial court's ruling would have constituted error for two reasons. First, the government would not be entitled to offer character evidence under these circumstances. *See* Fed. R. Evid. 404(a). Second, even were character evidence admissible, it could not be offered in the form of specific instances of conduct during direct examination. *See* Fed. R. Evid. 405(a).

12. *See, e.g.,* Holmes v. Elgin, Joliet & E. Ry., 18 F.3d 1393, 1397 (7th Cir.1994) ("We review the trial court's admission of evidence under the abuse of discretion standard, inquiring not whether we would have ruled the same way but rather whether any reasonable person would have agreed with the trial court"); United States v. Kristiansen, 901 F.2d 1463, 1465 (8th Cir.1990) ("We review evidentiary rulings under the abuse of discretion standard").

13. 522 U.S. 136 (1997).

14. Some federal courts have acknowledged that even in situations in which the trial court has discretion in evidentiary rulings, a more searching review is sometimes called for. In In re Paoli Railroad Yard PCB Litigation, 35 F.3d 717 (3d Cir.1994), the question concerned the admissibility of expert scientific testimony. While recognizing that the *Daubert* standard confers discretion on the trial court in assessing the reliability of scientific methodologies and data, the court was nevertheless concerned that the trial court might set the admissibility threshold too high and effectively force plaintiffs to prove their case twice (once to the court, and once to the jury). *Id.* at 749–50. To avoid this problem, the court wrote:

We acknowledge that there is arguably a tension between the substantial defer-

When arguing evidentiary issues on appeal, counsel should review carefully the nature of the rule in dispute and be prepared to argue for the appropriate standard of review. Though a finding that the trial court erred is only the first hurdle in winning reversal (such error must also be found prejudicial[15]), the first hurdle must be overcome to have even a chance of reversal.

§ 12.02 Preserving Error for Appeal—In General

To preserve an error for appeal, counsel generally must make a timely and specific objection, obtain a ruling from the court, and make certain that the objection and ruling appear in the record.[16] The path to a properly preserved error, however, is fraught with dangers of forfeiture at many points in the lower court proceeding. Failure to make motions, to strike or move for a mistrial,[17] or to request a limiting instruction[18] may result in forfeiture of the right to pursue an otherwise properly made objection. When an objection which is sustained results in the exclusion of evidence, opposing counsel's failure to make an offer of proof may also result in the forfeiture of the right to claim error.[19]

Counsel, in addition, must navigate successfully the narrows of post-trial procedure in order to have an error reviewed. Failure to make post-trial motions for a new trial or for judgment n.o.v. may lead to forfeiture of claims of error otherwise properly preserved.[20] Error properly preserved at trial but not raised on appeal is generally considered forfeited,[21] as is error from which appeal is not timely filed.[22] The right to raise

ence normally accorded to rulings where the trial court has a superior vantage point and the preference for admissibility of the Federal Rules of Evidence. We resolve any such tension by holding that when the district court's exclusionary evidentiary rulings with respect to scientific opinion testimony will result in a summary or directed judgment, we will give them a "hard look" (more stringent review, ...) to determine if a district court has abused its discretion in excluding evidence as unreliable.

Id. at 750 (Becker, J.). *See also* United States v. Criden, 648 F.2d 814, 817 (3d Cir.1981) ("the justifications for committing decisions to the discretion of the court are not uniform, and may vary with the specific type of decisions. Although the standards of review in such instances is generally framed as 'abuse of discretion,' in fact the scope of review will be directly related to the reason why that category or type of decision is committed to the trial court's discretion in the first instance"); Brody v. Spang, 957 F.2d 1108, 1115 (3d Cir.1992) ("We review a denial of a motion to intervene as of right for abuse of discretion, although this review is 'more stringent' than the abuse of discretion review we

apply to a denial of a motion for permissive intervention"). *Cf.* Hancock v. Dodson, 958 F.2d 1367 (6th Cir.1992) (held, district court's "evidentiary determinations" are reviewed for abuse of discretion, but "conclusions of law, such as whether proffered evidence constitutes hearsay" are reviewed de novo).

15. *See* § **12.03.**

16. *See* **Ch. 2.**

17. *See id.*

18. *See id.*

19. *See id*; Wright v. Hartford Accident & Indemnity Co., 580 F.2d 809, 810 (5th Cir.1978); Yost v. A.O. Smith Corp., 562 F.2d 592, 595 (8th Cir.1977).

20. Barry Sullivan, Barry Levenstam & David von Ebers, *Preserving Error in Civil Cases: Some Fundamental Principles*, 32 Trial Law. Guide 1, 13–15 (1988).

21. *See, e.g.,* McClure v. State, 648 S.W.2d 667, 677 (Tex.Crim.App.1982); *see also* 5 Am. Jur. 2d *Appeal & Error* §§ 654–55 (1962).

22. *See* 5 Am. Jur. 2d *Appeal & Error* § 665 (1962).

constitutional errors in a collateral proceeding such as habeas corpus may be forfeited by "procedural default," thus preventing the review of a federal constitutional claim by a federal court.[23]

§ 12.03 Prejudicial Error and Harmless Error

Introduction

Generally speaking, an appellate court will reverse because of an erroneous ruling on an objection if the error was serious and prejudiced one of the parties. If, however, the reviewing court finds that the error was "harmless"—that is, the error did not affect substantial rights of a party or did not significantly affect the outcome of the case—the error will not justify a reversal. Most types of errors are subject to this harmless error analysis, including most constitutional errors.[24] The harmless error doctrine is codified in federal and state rules.[25]

Although errors which were not properly preserved below are generally deemed waived, federal and many state courts also have discretion to find "plain error" if failure to address an unpreserved error would result in a miscarriage of justice. The plain error doctrine[26] is applied most often in criminal cases, but some jurisdictions also find plain error in civil cases.

Judicial Standards for Prejudicial and Harmless Error

The Federal Rules of Evidence,[27] Federal Rules of Civil Procedure,[28] and Federal Rules of Criminal Procedure[29] all mandate that courts disregard errors that do not "affect the substantial rights of the parties."[30] Thus, reversible or prejudicial errors are those which affect the substantial rights of parties. The party challenging a nonconstitutional error has the burden of proving that the error was substantial.[31] The definition of substantial rights is vague and courts review the entire record in making the determination of prejudice.[32] Therefore, prejudice is determined on a case-by-case basis. Some generalizations emerge, however, from the case law, rules, and commentators. On the one hand, purely technical errors that do not go to the merits of the case are never prejudicial.[33] On the other hand, "[i]f the evidence is insufficient to support the verdict without the erroneously admitted evidence, the error

23. Procedural default occurs when a defendant waives the right to state court review by procedural error. *See* United States v. Frady, 456 U.S. 152, 167–69 (1982) (collateral attacks are reviewed under cause-and-prejudice test of Wainwright v. Sykes, 433 U.S. 72, 87 (1977); § **12.04.**

24. Some constitutional errors are always grounds for reversal. *See* § **12.05**.

25. *See, e.g.,* Fed. R. Evid. 103(a); Fed. R. Civ. Proc. 61; Fed. R. Crim. Proc. 52(a).

26. The doctrine is called fundamental error in some states. *See, e.g.,* State v. Flores, 682 P.2d 1136, 1141 (Ariz.App.

1984); State v. Rutherford, 693 P.2d 1112, 1117 (Idaho App.1985).

27. *See* Fed. R. Evid. 103(a).

28. *See* Fed. R. Civ. Proc. 61.

29. *See* Fed. R. Crim. Proc. 52(a).

30. *See id.*

31. United States v. Montoya, 827 F.2d 143, 154 (7th Cir.1987).

32. *See* United States v. Young, 470 U.S. 1, 12 (1985).

33. *See* Kotteakos v. United States, 328 U.S. 750, 760 (1946); 1 Weinstein's Federal Evidence § 103.41, at 103–48 (2d

must be held prejudicial."[34] In between these two extremes, courts look at the entire case to determine prejudice. No presumptions guide the court in this determination of whether the trial was unfairly tainted by an error.[35]

The Supreme Court has held that substantial rights are affected if the error "substantially swayed" the jury's verdict[36] or "materially affected the deliberations of the jury."[37] Thus, if the error did not affect the jury deliberations or the outcome of the case, it will be harmless error, not prejudicial error. Courts differ on what degree of certainty that the error did not affect the outcome is required to find an error harmless. The standard employed by courts ranges from "beyond a reasonable doubt"[38] to "more probable than not."[39]

The purposes of the prejudicial error/harmless error doctrine are to avoid clogging the appellate courts with appeals from technical violations and to avoid unnecessary reversals where no real injustice was done.[40] The leading Supreme Court case articulating the harmless error doctrine is *Kotteakos v. United States*.[41] In *Kotteakos*, the Court was interpreting § 269 of the Judicial Code of 1911, an early formulation of the harmless error rule, but the Court has cited the holding in recent harmless error cases,[42] as have the lower courts.[43]

In *Kotteakos* the Court stated:

> It comes down ... to a very plain admonition: "Do not be technical, where technicality does not really hurt the party whose rights in the trial and in its outcome the technicality affects." ...

ed. Joseph M. McLaughlin ed. 1997) ("Determining whether a substantial right has been affected is not susceptible to a mechanical analysis. the facts of each case are crucial....").

34. 11 Charles A. Wright, Arthur R. Miller & Mary Kay Kane, Federal Practice and Procedure § 2885, at 466 (2d ed. 1995); *see also* United States v. Silverman, 861 F.2d 571, 580 (9th Cir.1988) (finding error prejudicial because it was "undoubtedly the bas[i]s for the jury's conclusion").

35. *See* 5 Am. Jur. 2d *Appeal & Error* § 780 (1962).

36. *See* Kotteakos v. United States, 328 U.S. 750, 765 (1946); *see also* United States v. Lane, 474 U.S. 438, 449 (1986); United States v. Donahue, 948 F.2d 438, 442 (8th Cir.1991) (error based on constitutional hearsay grounds is not harmful unless it may have "substantially swayed" the jury).

37. *See* Holloway v. Arkansas, 435 U.S. 475, 490 (1978).

38. *See* Chapman v. California, 386 U.S. 18, 24 (1967) (the standard for evaluating whether an error is harmless is whether it was "harmless beyond a reason-

able doubt"); State v. VanWagner, 504 N.W.2d 746, 750 (Minn.1993) (prosecutor's pointed and persistent references to police interview with witness which led them to charge defendant with drunk driving improperly alluded to excluded hearsay statements, and, although misconduct was probably harmless beyond a reasonable doubt, court reversed for "prophylactic reasons" and to protect the "integrity of the factfinding process").

39. *See* United States v. Valle–Valdez, 554 F.2d 911, 914–15 (9th Cir.1977).

40. Historically, any error was ground for reversal and, as a result, counsel began sowing error in the record to create an escape hatch from an unfavorable verdict. To stem this tide, the courts developed the harmless error doctrine. *See* 11 Wright, Miller & Kane, *supra* note 34 § 2881.

41. 328 U.S. 750 (1946).

42. *See* United States v. Lane, 474 U.S. 438, 446 (1986); Brecht v. Abrahamson, 507 U.S. 619 (1993). *See also* 11 Wright, Miller & Kane, *supra* note 33 § 2881, at 272 n.4.

43. *See, e.g.*, United States v. Pirovolos, 844 F.2d 415, 425 (7th Cir.1988).

If, when all is said and done, the conviction is sure that the error did not influence the jury, or had but very slight effect, the verdict and the judgment should stand, except perhaps where the departure is from a constitutional norm or a specific command of Congress.... *But if one cannot say, with fair assurance, after pondering all that happened without stripping the erroneous action from the whole, that the judgment was not substantially swayed by the error, it is impossible to conclude that substantial rights were not affected.* The inquiry cannot be merely whether there was enough to support the result, apart from the phase affected by the error. It is rather, even so, whether the error itself had substantial influence. If so, or if one is left in grave doubt, the conviction cannot stand.[44]

A finding of harmlessness should be based on the probable effect of the error on the jury's deliberation.[45] When the evidence of guilt is overwhelming, however, some courts disregard the effect of the error on the jury and find the error harmless, because the court below reached the "right" result.[46] While the *Kotteakos* Court noted that the quantity of evidence cannot be ignored in evaluating whether the jury's determination was affected by an error, it placed primary emphasis on the effect of the error on the jury's determination, not on the correctness of the result.[47] Despite the continuing vitality of *Kotteakos*, in several recent cases, the Supreme Court has emphasized the existence of overwhelming guilt in its findings of harmless error.[48]

In reviewing the entire record to determine whether an error is harmless or prejudicial, courts consider several factors,[49] including: the

44. *Kotteakos*, 328 U.S. at 764–65 (citations omitted; emphasis added).

45. *See* 1 John H. Wigmore, Evidence in Trials at Common Law § 21, at 933 (Peter Tillers rev. 1983).

46. *Id*. at 930–31. *See* United States v. Fortna, 796 F.2d 724, 735 (5th Cir.1986) (finding error in admitting testimony was harmless because the witness was not a significant one and the evidence of guilt was overwhelming).

47. *Kotteakos*, 328 U.S. at 761, 764–65).

48. *See* Darden v. Wainwright, 477 U.S. 168, 182 (1986); United States v. Young, 470 U.S. 1, 19 (1985). *See also* United States v. Simon, 995 F.2d 1236 (3d Cir. 1993) (held, trial court's "otherwise reversible error" in failing to give burden of proof jury instruction was harmless where government presented overwhelming evidence of defendant's guilt); United States v. Pirovolos, 844 F.2d 415, 427 (7th Cir.1988) (noting that "evidence of Pirovolos's guilt was truly overwhelming" and finding the error harmless); United States v. Montoya, 827 F.2d 143, 152 (7th Cir.1987) (citing over-

whelming evidence of guilt); United States v. Fortna, 796 F.2d 724, 735 (5th Cir.1986) (noting that evidence of guilt was overwhelming).

In objecting to this use of overwhelming evidence as the test for harmless error, Judge Clark of the Fifth Circuit wrote: "Unnecessary language seems to invite review of the sufficiency of the non-objectionable evidence *alone*, even though our attention over and over again is *properly* called to the prejudicial impact of the objectionable evidence." Harryman v. Estelle, 616 F.2d 870, 885 (5th Cir.1980) (Clark, J., concurring in part and dissenting in part); *see also* Fahy v. Connecticut, 375 U.S. 85, 86–87 (1963) ("The question is whether there is a reasonable possibility that the evidence complained of might have contributed to the conviction"); United States v. Ruffin, 575 F.2d 346, 359–60 (2d Cir.1978) (noting that error may be prejudicial even though "there was sufficient other evidence to sustain the conviction. The crucial question is whether the error influenced the jury's verdict").

49. *See* 1 Weinstein's Federal Evidence, *supra* note 33 § 103.41[5].

number of errors in relation to the length of the trial, the closeness of factual disputes, whether the evidence related to a material consequential fact, the prejudicial effect of the evidence, the instructions given, whether the evidence was important corroboration of other testimony, whether the evidence was cumulative,[50] and the amount of reliance counsel placed on the tainted evidence in their arguments.[51]

Courts using the effect-on-the-jury analysis for harmlessness differ on how small the likelihood of the error affecting the jury deliberation must be to justify a finding of harmlessness.[52] For example, the Ninth Circuit uses a "more probably harmless than not" test for nonconstitutional errors.[53] The Third Circuit standard is more onerous, requiring reversal unless it is "highly probable" that the verdict would have been the same if the error had not occurred.[54] In the Fifth Circuit, reversal is required unless the court is "sure that the error did not influence the jury, or had but slight effect."[55] In the case of constitutional errors, the Supreme Court has held that the prosecution has the burden of proving that the error was harmless beyond a reasonable doubt.[56]

Courts generally apply the same standard for harmless error in civil cases as in criminal cases,[57] although some cases argue that the standards should differ in accordance with the differing standards of proof applicable to civil and criminal cases.[58] State court standards for determining harmless error are similar to federal court standards.[59] In diversi-

50. *See* United States v. Austin, 823 F.2d 257, 260 (8th Cir.1987).

51. *See* 1 Weinstein's Federal Evidence, *supra* note 33 § 103.41[5][f].

52. *See* United States v. Valle–Valdez, 554 F.2d 911, 914–15 (9th Cir.1977) (noting that "standards guiding appellate determination of harmless error are variable, often confusing and frequently left unarticulated . . . , however, those standards are statements of the degree of certainty an appellate court must achieve regarding the effect of error on the verdict").

53. *See* United States v. Gwaltney, 790 F.2d 1378, 1383 (9th Cir.1986); *see also* U.S. Indus., Inc. v. Touche Ross & Co., 854 F.2d 1223, 1252–53 (10th Cir.1988) (applying the more probably harmless than not standard in civil case).

54. *See* United States v. Grayson, 795 F.2d 278, 290 (3d Cir. 1986) (court must have " 'sure conviction that the error did not prejudice the defendant,' but need not disprove every 'reasonable possibility' of prejudice"); McQueeney v. Wilmington Trust Co., 779 F.2d 916, 924 (3d Cir.1985); *see also* United States v. Thompson, 716 F.2d 248, 251 (4th Cir.1983), *vacated by* 728 F.2d 654 (4th Cir.1984) (stating that a "fair assurance" that verdict was not affected by error is the standard).

55. United States v. Arias–Diaz, 497 F.2d 165, 171, 172 (5th Cir.1974) (citing *Kotteakos*); *see also* McKinnon v. Skil Corp., 638 F.2d 270, 276 (1st Cir.1981) (finding error harmless because it did not affect substantial rights). This standard is similar to the requirement that constitutional errors are prejudicial unless proven harmless "beyond a reasonable doubt." *See* Chapman v. California, 386 U.S. 18, 23 (1967).

For a discussion of the possible standards for determining whether an error is prejudicial, *see* Roger Traynor, The Riddle of Harmless Error 35 (1970).

56. *See* Chapman v. California, 386 U.S. 18, 23 (1967); *see* § **12.05**.

57. *Cf.* McDonough Power Equip., Inc. v. Greenwood, 464 U.S. 548, 553–54 (1984).

58. *See* U.S. Indus., Inc. v. Touche Ross & Co., 854 F.2d 1223, 1252 n. 39 (10th Cir.1988) (noting that "it seems reasonable, absent some countervailing policy, that the harmless error standard should mirror the standard applied at trial"); *see also* Stephen A. Saltzburg, *The Harm of Harmless Error*, 59 Va. L. Rev. 988, 988 (1973).

59. *See, e.g.,* State v. Naoum, 548 A.2d 120, 124 (Me.1988) (using "highly probable" standard); People v. Stubl, 385 N.W.2d 719, 721 (Mich.App.1986) (holding erroneous admission of hearsay was harmless

ty cases, however, a federal court applies its own harmless error standard, rather than the state court standard.[60]

§ 12.04   Plain Error

If the party opposing the admission of evidence did not object, objected on the wrong ground, or failed to specify a ground, the appellate court will reverse only if the trial judge's ruling admitting the evidence was "plain error."[61] Similarly, if trial counsel failed to object to an improper closing argument, or objected to it on the wrong ground, the appellate court will reverse only upon a finding of plain error.

"Plain error" differs from "prejudicial error." Even if trial counsel objected on proper grounds and the trial judge erroneously admitted the evidence over the objection, the appellate court may still refuse to reverse if it finds that the error was harmless—that is, if the error is deemed not to be prejudicial. Prejudicial error analysis focuses on the probable impact of the error in influencing the decision of the trier of fact. Plain error analysis takes the impact of the error into account, but it considers an additional factor as well—whether the error was obvious.[62] Trial counsel who fails to make a proper objection calling the point to the trial judge's attention must suffer the consequences, unless the error was so obvious that the appellate court is willing to reverse because the trial court failed to recognize the error on its own initiative.

Note that error in rulings on evidence can be prejudicial but not plain. Suppose, for example, that in response to an objection wrongly based on relevancy grounds, the trial judge admits devastating evidence that should have been excluded on hearsay grounds. This error would be prejudicial (because the jury heard very damaging evidence it should not have heard), but if the hearsay question was actually close, it would not likely be "plain." Reversal in such a case is highly unlikely. Similarly, it is also possible to have plain error that is not prejudicial. For example, if the trial judge erroneously excluded a lay opinion that the plaintiff was intoxicated, but admitted evidence of the person's specific behavior and

---

based on "beyond a reasonable doubt" standard); State v. Davis, 401 N.W.2d 721, 725 (S.D.1987) (holding errors are prejudicial when "jury might and probably would have returned a different verdict if the alleged error hadn't occurred") (emphasis omitted)); State v. Dyess, 370 N.W.2d 222, 231–32 (Wis.1985) (stating that "no reasonable possibility" standard applies to nonconstitutional and constitutional errors). *But cf.* State v. VanWagner, 504 N.W.2d 746, 750 (Minn.1993) (harmless error rising from deliberate prosecutorial misconduct is still grounds for reversal as a prophylactic measure against future prosecutorial misconduct).

60. *See* 11 Wright, Miller, & Kane, *supra* note 34 § 2883, at 450.

61. *See* Fed. R. Evid. 103(a)(1) (proper objection required) and 103(d) (plain error rule).

62. *See* Permian Petroleum Co. v. Petroleos Mexicanos, 934 F.2d 635, 648 (5th Cir.1991) (trial counsel did not object to admission of worksheet the admission of which was questioned on appeal, but did object to a witness's description of part of the worksheet; court stated that "[w]hen a party fails to object to the admission of evidence, we review for plain error.... Plain error is error which ... is so obvious and substantial that failure to notice and correct it would affect the fairness, integrity, or public reputation of judicial proceedings").

symptoms of intoxication, the error might be "plain" (because the opinion should have been permitted), but harmless (because the testimony admitted by the court was most likely a reasonable substitute for the evidence wrongly excluded). In such a case, the appellate court will not reverse.

Courts enforce the procedural requirements for preserving error for three reasons: (1) judicial economy, (2) to encourage lower courts to correct errors at the time they occur, and (3) to avoid unfairness to a prevailing party.[63] At the same time, federal courts and many state courts recognize that enforcing the rights of the parties should be of greater concern than enforcing legal technicalities.[64] Because trials are stressful and often fast-paced, even the most competent attorney[65] may fail to object to improper evidence, comment, or argument, or may omit one technical step in the procedure for properly preserving error. The plain error doctrine embodies this overriding concern for preserving important rights.[66] The rule is set out in the Federal Rules of Evidence,[67] the Federal rules of Criminal Procedure,[68] and analogous state court rules.[69]

Plain error is found most often in criminal cases, where the defendant appeals from a conviction that takes away some form of liberty. Under Rule 52(b) of the Federal Rules of Criminal Procedure, plain error applies to direct appeals and petitions for certiorari of criminal cases. It does not apply, however, to habeas petitions by federal or state prisoners; those prisoners are required to meet the cause-and-prejudice test of

63. Barry Sullivan, Barry Levenstam & David von Ebers, *Preserving Error in Civil Cases: Some Fundamental Principles*, 32 Trial Law. Guide 1, 2 (1988).

64. *See* Hormel v. Helvering, 312 U.S. 552, 557 (1941); *see generally* 1 Weinstein's Federal Evidence § 103.42[3], at 103–67 to 103–68 (2d ed. Joseph M. McLaughlin ed. 1997) ("the doctrine should be applied only when the error is so obvious that a failure to notice it would seriously affect the fairness, integrity, and public reputation of the judicial proceeding"); John E. Theuman, Annotation, *Supreme Court's views as to what constitute harmless errors or plain errors, under Rule 52 of Federal Rules of Criminal Procedure*, 84 L.Ed.2d 876, 878 (1987).

65. It has been pointed out that the need for the plain error doctrine is especially great in the cases of children and of criminal defendants who have court-appointed counsel. *See* Government of the Canal Zone v. P. (Pinto), 590 F.2d 1344, 1353 (5th Cir.1979) (defendant had a series of court-appointed attorneys).

66. *See* United States v. Atkinson, 297 U.S. 157, 160 (1936) (describing plain error).

67. Fed. R. Evid. 103(d) states: "Nothing in this rule precludes taking notice of plain error affecting substantial rights although they were not brought to the attention of the court."

68. Fed. R. Crim. Proc. 52(b) states: "Plain errors or defects affecting substantial rights may be noticed although they were not brought to the attention of the court." The notes of the advisory committee on rules state that this rule is a restatement of existing case law.

See also Sup. Ct. R. 34.1(a) ("At its option, however, the Court may consider a plain error not among the questions presented, but evident from the record and otherwise within its jurisdiction"). For a discussion of Supreme Court review of errors not raised in briefs, *see* Girardeau A. Spann, *Functional Analysis of the Plain Error Rule*, 71 Geo. L.J. 945, 946–47 (1983).

69. *See, e.g.*, Minn. R. Crim. Proc. 31.02: "Plain errors or defects affecting substantial rights may be considered by the court upon motions for new trial, post-trial motions, and on appeal although they were not brought to the attention of the trial court."

Wainwright v. Sykes[70] before a waived or "defaulted" error will be reviewed by the federal courts.[71]

Federal courts and some state courts also apply the plain error doctrine in civil cases.[72] While there is no plain error rule in the Federal Rules of Civil Procedure, the rule is embodied in Federal Rule of Evidence 103(d),[73] and the circuit courts have recognized the doctrine as necessary for fairness and justice in some cases.[74]

Plain error is not easily defined and allows for substantial judicial discretion. Courts employing the doctrine have found plain error when "substantial rights" are involved, the error was "particularly egregious,"[75] a "miscarriage of justice"[76] resulted from the error, or the error deprived the defendant of a fair trial.[77] The facts of the case, the gravity of the offense, and the probable effect of the error are factors considered by the court in determining whether substantial rights have been violated.[78] Some courts require that the error be obvious in the record.[79]

70. 433 U.S. 72, 84–86 (1977). The test, based on Fed. R. Crim. Proc. 12(b)(2), requires the petitioner to demonstrate both cause for noncompliance and actual prejudice resulting from the alleged violation.

71. 8 Moore's Federal Practice § 52 (2d ed. 1988); *see also* United States v. Frady, 456 U.S. 152, 167–69 (1982).

72. *See* 1 Weinstein's Federal Evidence, *supra* note 64 § 103.42[3]; *see, e.g.,* Bannister v. Town of Noble, 812 F.2d 1265, 1271 (10th Cir.1987); Jackson v. Firestone Tire & Rubber Co., 788 F.2d 1070, 1075 (5th Cir.1986); Teen–Ed, Inc. v. Kimball Intl., Inc., 620 F.2d 399, 401–02 (3d Cir. 1980); Liner v. J.B. Talley & Co., 618 F.2d 327, 329 (5th Cir.1980); Edwards v. Sears, Roebuck & Co., 512 F.2d 276, 286 (5th Cir.1975); Alger v. Hayes, 452 F.2d 841, 845 (8th Cir.1972).

73. Rule 103(d) provides: "Nothing in this rule precludes taking notice of plain errors affecting substantial rights although they were not brought to the attention of the court."

74. *See Teen–Ed, Inc.*, 620 F.2d at 401–02. The rationale underlying the plain error doctrine in criminal cases—protecting those whose liberty is at risk from the inadequacies of counsel—does not apply in civil cases.

In addition to finding plain error in civil trial court rulings on evidentiary matters and arguments of counsel, appellate courts occasionally find plain error in trial court decisions on matters of law, such as rulings on motions for directed verdict or summary judgment. In this regard one state court has explained that plain error "is reserved for situations where it is necessary to preserve confidence in the fairness and integrity of the adjudicative process, or where the issue is important to the development of the law." Daley v. Gaitor, 547 A.2d 1375, 1378 (Conn.App.1988) (finding plain error in trial court's granting of directed verdict); *see also* Harper v. Landers, 348 S.E.2d 698, 701 (Ga.App.1986) (finding plain error in grant of motion to dismiss in custody action).

75. *See* United States v. Gwaltney, 790 F.2d 1378, 1383–84 (9th Cir.1986).

76. *See* United States v. Frady, 456 U.S. 152, 163 (1982); United States v. Griffin, 818 F.2d 97, 99 (1st Cir.1987).

77. *See* State v. Smith, 561 P.2d 739, 744 (Ariz.1977). *See also* State v. Salitros, 499 N.W.2d 815, 819–20 (Minn.1993) (ordering new trial "in the interests of justice" when defense counsel failed to object to prosecutor's improper statements in closing arguments that constitutional guarantees "are designed to protect the innocent ... [t]hey have never been designed to serve as a shield for the guilty to hide behind" and his urging the jury to "pull this defendant out from behind that shield and hold him accountable for the crimes that he was involved in committing").

78. *See* 1 Weinstein's Federal Evidence, *supra* note 64 § 103.42[a]; *see also* United States v. Young, 470 U.S. 1, 12 (1985); United States v. Santana–Camacho, 833 F.2d 371, 374 (1st Cir.1987) (plain error in mischaracterizing defendant as "illegal" alien); United States v. Roenigk, 810 F.2d 809, 816 (8th Cir.1987); Rojas v. Richardson, 703 F.2d 186, 190–92 (5th Cir. 1983); United States v. Grunberger, 431 F.2d 1062, 1069 (2d Cir.1970); United States v. Segna, 555 F.2d 226, 231 (9th Cir.1977).

79. *See* Lowery v. State, 762 P.2d 457, 459 n. 1 (Alaska App.1988).

Subsumed in the plain error determination is consideration of whether the alleged error was prejudicial to the rights of the appealing party.[80] Thus a finding of plain error has the identical effect on a proceeding as a finding of prejudicial error—the lower court's decision will be reversed, and, in most situations, the case will be remanded.

In an interpretation of language in the Federal Rules of Criminal Procedure that is similar to language in Federal Rule of Evidence 103, the Supreme Court clarified the scope of review for plain error. In *United States v. Olano*,[81] the Court first held that the doctrine applies only to "forfeited" rights (rights lost by failure to assert them in a timely fashion), and not to "waived" rights (rights intentionally relinquished).[82] Second, the error must be "plain" in that it was clear under current law.[83] Third, the error must affect substantial rights.[84] The defendant bears the burden of persuasion that the error was prejudicial and must demonstrate that the error affected the outcome of the trial proceedings; normally, the defendant must make a specific showing of prejudice.[85] If the forfeited error is plain and affects substantial rights, the appellate court may but is not required to exercise its discretion to remedy the error.[86] The appellate court should exercise discretion when the error " 'seriously affect[s] the fairness, integrity or public reputation of judicial proceedings.' "[87]

The Ninth Circuit has employed this analysis to hold that it was not plain error to admit a witness's prior inconsistent out-of-court statement, which was not made under oath, without an instruction limiting the jury's use of the statement for purposes of impeachment only.[88]

Reversal for plain error is relatively rare.[89] Therefore counsel should never rely on the discretion of appellate courts to find plain error. It is

80. *See* § 12.03 (discussing prejudicial error).

81. 507 U.S. 725 (1993).

82. *Id*. at 731–34.

83. *Id*. at 734.

84. *Id*. at 734–35.

85. *Id*. at 735.

86. *Id*.

87. *Id*. at 736 (quoting United States v. Atkinson, 297 U.S. 157, 160 (1936)). *See also* Johnson v. United States, 520 U.S. 461 (1997) (held, even if judge's error was obvious in sense of being departure from well-settled law, and hence was plain error, it was not "reversible" unless it seriously affected fairness, integrity, or public reputation of proceedings; trial judge's erroneous decision not to instruct jury on element of "materiality" in perjury prosecution hence was not plain error because no plausible argument could be made that defendant's false testimony was not material).

In the authors' opinion, the concepts of "plain error" and "prejudicial error" would be easier to understand and analyze if courts clearly distinguished between the two. For example, "plain error" could be defined as obvious error—error that any competent judge should be able to avoid without needing the help of an objection from the parties. By contrast, the concept of "prejudicial error" (error that is not harmless) could be defined in terms of its likely impact on the fact-finder. Under this analysis, plain error would not be prejudicial error if it would not have changed the result because the evidence was overwhelming. Unfortunately, cases like *Johnson* pass over the simplicity and clarity of such a distinction and confound the two concepts.

88. *See* United States v. Armijo, 5 F.3d 1229, 1233–34 (9th Cir.1993).

89. *See* United States v. Robinson, 485 U.S. 25, 35 (1988) (Blackmun, J., concurring in part and dissenting in part); United States v. Young, 470 U.S. 1, 15 (1985) (noting that plain error exception to the con-

counsel's duty to effectively present the client's case and protect the client's rights by avoiding error and preserving error made by opposing counsel or the court.[90] This principle applies both to the erroneous admission and erroneous exclusion of evidence. Thus, if counsel believes the court has improperly admitted evidence, it is counsel's responsibility to place on the record the reasons for the claimed error. If counsel believes the court has erroneously excluded evidence, counsel must make a record of precisely what the excluded evidence was in order to provide the appellate court with a basis both for holding both that the trial court erred and that the error was prejudicial. Without a complete record, it is often very difficult for the appellate court to make the desired findings.

When litigating under state law, counsel must research the case law and statutes to determine whether plain error will be applied in the courts of the state. Some states do not accept the plain error doctrine, holding instead that failure to object is an absolute forfeiture of the right to appeal.[91] Some states will find plain error when the court errs on issues of law such as instructions to the jury or rulings on motions to dismiss or for summary judgment, but may not find plain error in relation to unpreserved errors in evidentiary rulings.[92]

§ 12.05   Constitutional Error

Issues of constitutional error arise most frequently in criminal cases. These errors include violations of the fourth amendment, the fifth amendment, self-incrimination clause, due process rights under the fifth and fourteenth amendments, sixth amendment rights to counsel, to an impartial tribunal and to confrontation, and eighth amendment protections against excessive punishment. Counsel should be aware that in criminal cases, constitutional error is not limited to cases in which the trial court erroneously admits evidence offered by the prosecution. Trial courts may also commit constitutional err by excluding evidence offered by the defense. Potential constitutional issues arise in a variety of situations in which the trial court employs evidence rules to exclude crucial exculpatory evidence offered by the defendant.[93] These types of

temporaneous objection rule is to be "used sparingly" (quoting United States v. Frady, 456 U.S. 152, 163 n. 14 (1982)).

90. *See* § 2.10; Sykes v. United States, 373 F.2d 607, 613 (5th Cir.1966) ("Whether or not there was error was not visible because all of the circumstances of the arrest were not before the court. That which is not visible cannot be 'plain.' We are not equipped for divination").

91. *See, e.g.*, Calhoun v. State, 530 So.2d 259, 262 (Ala.Crim.App.1988) ("plain error doctrine applies only to death cases"); Barker v. State, 453 S.W.2d 413, 416–17 (Ark.1970); Jones v. State, 453 S.W.2d 403, 404 (Ark.1970); State v. Miles, 344 N.W.2d 231, 233 (Iowa 1984).

92. *Compare* State v. Patterson, 755 P.2d 551, 556 (Kan.1988) (reviewing jury instruction for plain error) *with* State v. Bird, 708 P.2d 946, 961–62 (Kan.1985) (stating that "failure to comply with the contemporaneous objection rule bars a challenge to the [prosecutor's argument] in a state court"). For further discussion of plain error in the context of jury instructions, *see* 9A Charles A. Wright, Arthur R. Miller & Mary Kay Kane, Federal Practice and Procedure § 2558 (2d ed. 1995).

93. *See, e.g.*, Chambers v. Mississippi, 410 U.S. 284 (1973), in which the Supreme Court held that the state court's application of hearsay doctrine and the "voucher rule" to exclude evidence strongly suggesting de-

cases have spawned a body of law setting forth parameters for those situations in which exclusionary rules of evidence must give way to the defendant's constitutional rights, primarily under the due process clauses of the sixth and fourteenth amendments and the right to present a defense created by the sixth amendment.[94]

Prior to the Supreme Court's decision in *Chapman v. California,*[95] it was thought that constitutional errors were always grounds for reversal.[96] *Chapman* held, however, that the harmless error doctrine applies to most[97] constitutional errors.[98] Thus a constitutional error that did not contribute to a criminal conviction may be deemed harmless. However, "before a federal constitutional error can be held harmless, the court must be able to declare a belief that it was harmless *beyond a reasonable doubt.*"[99] This is a higher standard than the one applied to nonconstitutional errors.[100] A court, for example, will reverse for improperly obtained evidence if the jury's decision was influenced beyond a reasonable doubt by the improper evidence.[101] If, however, the improper evidence is merely cumulative of other, properly admitted evidence, the error may be found harmless because the jury's judgment was not affected.[102]

The burden of proving that a constitutional error was harmless is on the prosecution.[103] Courts consider the entire record in deciding whether a constitutional error was harmless[104] and the factors considered are the same as in nonconstitutional errors.[105] The plain error doctrine also applies to constitutional errors.[106]

Although *Chapman* required "courts to focus on the possible impact of the erroneously admitted or excluded evidence on the jurors' minds,[107] subsequent Supreme Court decisions have found constitutional errors harmless because the evidence of guilt was "overwhelming."[108] Commentators have criticized the *Chapman* harmless error rule as having no

---

fendant's innocence violated defendant's due process rights.

94. For a detailed examination of the right to present exculpatory evidence, *see* Edward J. Imwinkelried & Norman M. Garland, Exculpatory Evidence (2d ed.1996).

95. 386 U.S. 18 (1967).

96. *See* 1 John H. Wigmore, Evidence in Trials at Common Law § 21, at 937 (Peter Tillers rev. 1983).

97. A few constitutional errors are not subject to harmless error analysis. *See infra* notes 111–116 and accompanying text.

98. *Chapman,* 386 U.S. at 23.

99. *Id.*

100. *See* § 12.02.

101. *See, e.g.,* Holland v. Attorney General, 777 F.2d 150, 159 (3d Cir.1985) (reversing for *Bruton* error); United States v. McKinney, 707 F.2d 381, 385 (9th Cir.

1983) (reversing for confrontation clause error).

102. *See, e.g.,* Brown v. United States, 411 U.S. 223, 231 (1973) (Burns v. Clusen, 798 F.2d 931, 943–44 (7th Cir.1986).

103. Schneble v. Florida, 405 U.S. 427, 428 (1972).

104. *See* United States v. Hasting, 461 U.S. 499, 509 (1983).

105. *See* § 12.03.

106. *See, e.g.,* United States v. Mouzin, 785 F.2d 682, 693 (9th Cir.1986).

107. 1 Weinstein's Federal Evidence § 103.43[3][b] (2d ed. Joseph M. McLaughlin ed. 1997); United States v. Berkery, 865 F.2d 587, 590, *vacated on other grounds and reh'g.,* 889 F.2d 1281 (3d Cir.1989) (citing *Chapman,* 386 U.S. at 24).

108. *See* Milton v. Wainwright, 407 U.S. 371, 377 (1972); *cf.* United States v. Pirovolos, 844 F.2d 415, 427 (7th Cir.1988).

substantive doctrinal base,[109] and as outcome-oriented.[110] They note that the current Supreme Court is most concerned about the accuracy of the guilt/innocence determination[111]—"reaching the right result"—rather than the protection of an individual's constitutional rights.[112]

Some constitutional errors continue to be prejudicial per se because the rights affected are "so basic to a fair trial that their infraction can never be treated as harmless error."[113] These errors include right to counsel violations,[114] absence of an impartial tribunal,[115] and complete denial of the opportunity to cross-examine.[116] At one time, the Court considered the use of coerced confessions never to be harmless,[117] but in 1991, the Court reversed course on its treatment of coerced confessions, holding that harmless error analysis applies even to cases involving illegally coerced confessions.[118] Similarly, receiving out-of-court statements as evidence in violation of the defendant's Sixth Amendment right to confrontation is not a ground for reversal if the error was harmless.[119] Some constitutional errors, while not prejudicial per se, mandate rever-

---

109. *See* Steven H. Goldberg, *Harmless Error: Constitutional Sneak Thief*, 71 J. Crim. L. & Criminology 421, 427 (1980).

110. *See* Tom Stacy & Kim Dayton, *Rethinking Harmless Constitutional Error*, 88 Colum. L. Rev. 79, 84 (1988).

111. Delaware v. Van Arsdall, 475 U.S. 673, 677–78 (1986) (stating that "the central purpose of a criminal trial is to decide the factual question of the defendant's guilt or innocence").

112. Stacy & Dayton, *supra* note 110, at 143.

113. *Chapman*, 386 U.S. at 23; *see also* Sullivan v. Louisiana, 508 U.S. 275 (1993) (reversing conviction because trial court's incorrect definition of reasonable doubt in jury instructions deprived defendant of right to trial by jury; due to trial court's error, jury could not render a verdict of guilty beyond a reasonable doubt); Stacy & Dayton, *supra* note 110, at 80 (quoting Rose v. Clark, 478 U.S. 570, 577–78 (1986), in which the Court stated these rights are so fundamental that in their absence "a criminal trial cannot reliably serve its function as a vehicle for determination of guilt or innocence . . . and no criminal punishment may be regarded as fundamentally fair"). *But see* California v. Roy, 519 U.S. 2, 4–5 (1996), in which a state trial judge gave an erroneous aiding and abetting instruction that misdescribed the crime so that it failed to expressly require that the accused intend to encourage or facilitate the principal's offense. On habeas review, the Ninth Circuit reversed the conviction, applying a special harmless error rule under which an omission of an element from an instruction is harmless only if review of the facts found by the jury establishes that the jury neces-

sarily found the omitted element. The Supreme Court disagreed, holding that this was not the sort of "structural error" that defies ordinary harmless error analysis. Citing Brecht v. Abrahamson, 507 U.S. 619 (1993), the Court held that the standard was "whether the error had substantial and injurious effect or influence in determining the jury's verdict." (Interior quotation marks omitted.)

114. Gideon v. Wainwright, 372 U.S. 335, 343 (1963).

115. Tumey v. Ohio, 273 U.S. 510, 535 (1927).

116. Davis v. Alaska, 415 U.S. 308, 318 (1974) (complete denial of cross-examination held constitutional error); *cf.* United States v. Owens, 484 U.S. 554, 560 (1988) (finding no confrontation clause violation where witness could not be thoroughly cross-examined about a prior statement of which he had no memory due to brain damage); Delaware v. Van Arsdall, 475 U.S. 673, 684 (1986) (unconstitutional restriction on defendant's right to cross-examine a witness subject to harmless error analysis).

117. *See* Payne v. Arkansas, 356 U.S. 560, 568 (1958).

118. Arizona v. Fulminante, 499 U.S. 279 (1991) (a 5–4 decision). For criticism of that decision, *see* Charles J. Ogletree, *Arizona v. Fulminate: The Harm of Applying Harmless Error to Coerced Confessions*, 105 Harv. L. Rev. 152 (1991).

119. Lilly v. Virginia, 527 U.S. 116 (1999) (after finding violation of Confrontation Clause, Court remanded for harmless error determination).

sal unless the defendant can make a relatively low threshold showing. For example, the prosecution's failure to disclose material exculpatory evidence requires reversal if the defendant can demonstrate a "reasonable probability that, had the evidence been disclosed to the defense, the result of the proceeding would have been different."[120]

The *Chapman* standard does not apply to collateral attacks on constitutional error. In *Brecht v. Abrahamson*,[121] the Supreme Court reviewed a habeas case arising from a trial in which the prosecutor was erroneously allowed to refer to the defendant's post-*Miranda* silence. The Court rejected the argument that the *Chapman* "harmless-beyond-reasonable-doubt standard" had to be satisfied in order to uphold the conviction. Instead, it held that when a conviction is collaterally attacked for constitutional error, the more lenient *Kotteakos* standard applies, so that the judgment will be upheld unless it is shown that the error "had substantial and injurious effect or influence in determining the jury's verdict."[122] However, the Supreme Court has cautioned that a constitutional error cannot be considered harmless where the trial judge has a "grave doubt" or is uncertain about the injurious effect of the error.[123]

In response to *Brecht*, the Eighth Circuit has held that *Chapman* is the proper standard for collateral review of constitutional error when the state courts did not already apply the *Chapman* test to the contested error.[124]

Whether an error in a criminal trial rises to the level of constitutional error depends on the rights allegedly violated. If the error involves violation of a specific provision of the Bill of Rights (e.g., the right to counsel or the fifth amendment privilege against self-incrimination), it will be deemed a constitutional error.[125] Because of the liberty interests at stake in a criminal trial, however, many errors that would affect the outcome of the case, and therefore are prejudicial, but are not violations of a specific provision of the Bill of Rights, may be raised on appeal as due process violations under the fifth or fourteenth amendments. Errors in the prosecutor's closing argument often fall into this category. In these due process cases, the Supreme Court evaluates whether the error "so infected the trial with unfairness as to make the resulting conviction a denial of due process."[126] Because the entire proceeding is examined for unfairness, error that does not implicate a specific right will rarely be found to be constitutional error.[127] Even if a specific right is implicated,

---

120. Kyles v. Whitley, 514 U.S. 419, 433 (1995), quoting United States v. Bagley, 473 U.S. 667, 682 (1985).

121. 507 U.S. 619 (1993).

122. *Accord*, California v. Roy, 519 U.S. 2 (1996) (*Kotteakos* "harmless error" standard applies where trial court failed to instruct jury that in order to find defendant guilty of murder committed by a confederate, it must find that defendant had knowledge and intent or purpose of committing, encouraging, or facilitating the killing; error was "trial error" rather than "structural error").

123. O'Neal v. McAninch, 513 U.S. 432, 436–43 (1995).

124. Orndorff v. Lockhart, 998 F.2d 1426, 1429 (8th Cir.1993).

125. *See* Donnelly v. DeChristoforo, 416 U.S. 637, 643 (1974).

126. *Id.*

127. *See, e.g.,* Darden v. Wainwright, 477 U.S. 168, 182 (1986). *But see* Wain-

for instance, the right against self-incrimination, the Court may find that no constitutional error occurred based on the whole record.[128] In the case of closing arguments, the Court often invokes the invited response doctrine[129] in concluding that no constitutional violation occurred.[130] Counsel appealing due process errors, therefore, should also challenge the error on non-constitutional grounds.

wright v. Greenfield, 474 U.S. 284, 295 (1986) (holding that use of *Miranda* silence as evidence of sanity rendered trial fundamentally unfair).

Despite constitutional guarantees of due process, errors in criminal trial that do not involve violations of specific provisions of the Bill of Rights generally are not considered constitutional, because the "interests involved are not sufficiently important to merit explicit constitutional protection." United States v. Valle–Valdez, 554 F.2d 911, 916 (9th Cir.1977).

128. *See* United States v. Robinson, 485 U.S. 25, 32–33 (1988).

129. *See* § **1.10.**

130. *See Robinson* at 33–34; Darden v. Wainwright, 477 U.S. 168, 182 (1986).

*

Appendix A

FEDERAL RULES OF EVIDENCE FOR UNITED STATES COURTS

As amended to Dec. 1, 2003

Table of Rules

ARTICLE I. GENERAL PROVISIONS

ARTICLE II. JUDICIAL NOTICE

ARTICLE III. PRESUMPTIONS IN CIVIL ACTIONS AND PROCEEDINGS

ARTICLE IV. RELEVANCY AND ITS LIMITS

619

ARTICLE I.   GENERAL PROVISIONS

Rule 101.   Scope

These rules govern proceedings in the courts of the United States and before the United States bankruptcy judges and United States magistrate judges, to the extent and with the exceptions stated in rule 1101.

Rule 102.   Purpose and Construction

These rules shall be construed to secure fairness in administration, elimination of unjustifiable expense and delay, and promotion of growth and development of the law of evidence to the end that the truth may be ascertained and proceedings justly determined.

Rule 103.   Rulings on Evidence

(a) Effect of erroneous ruling.   Error may not be predicated upon a ruling which admits or excludes evidence unless a substantial right of the party is affected, and

(1) Objection. In case the ruling is one admitting evidence, a timely objection or motion to strike appears of record, stating the specific ground of objection, if the specific ground was not apparent from the context; or

(2) Offer of proof. In case the ruling is one excluding evidence, the substance of the evidence was made known to the court by offer or was apparent from the context within which questions were asked.

Once the court makes a definitive ruling on the record admitting or excluding evidence, either at or before trial, a party need not renew an objection or offer of proof to preserve a claim of error for appeal.

(b) Record of offer and ruling. The court may add any other or further statement which shows the character of the evidence, the form in which it was offered, the objection made, and the ruling thereon. It may direct the making of an offer in question and answer form.

(c) Hearing of jury. In jury cases, proceedings shall be conducted, to the extent practicable, so as to prevent inadmissible evidence from being suggested to the jury by any means, such as making statements or offers of proof or asking questions in the hearing of the jury.

(d) Plain error. Nothing in this rule precludes taking notice of plain errors affecting substantial rights although they were not brought to the attention of the court.

Rule 104. Preliminary Questions

(a) Questions of admissibility generally. Preliminary questions concerning the qualification of a person to be a witness, the existence of a privilege, or the admissibility of evidence shall be determined by the court, subject to the provisions of subdivision (b). In making its determination it is not bound by the rules of evidence except those with respect to privileges.

(b) Relevancy conditioned on fact. When the relevancy of evidence depends upon the fulfillment of a condition of fact, the court shall admit it upon, or subject to, the introduction of evidence sufficient to support a finding of the fulfillment of the condition.

(c) Hearing of jury. Hearings on the admissibility of confessions shall in all cases be conducted out of the hearing of the jury. Hearings on other preliminary matters shall be so conducted when the interests of justice require, or when an accused is a witness and so requests.

(d) Testimony by accused. The accused does not, by testifying upon a preliminary matter, become subject to cross-examination as to other issues in the case.

(e) Weight and credibility. This rule does not limit the right of a party to introduce before the jury evidence relevant to weight or credibility.

Rule 105. Limited Admissibility

When evidence which is admissible as to one party or for one purpose but not admissible as to another party or for another purpose is admitted, the court, upon request, shall restrict the evidence to its proper scope and instruct the jury accordingly.

Rule 106. Remainder of or Related Writings or Recorded Statements

When a writing or recorded statement or part thereof is introduced by a party, an adverse party may require the introduction at that time of any other part or any other writing or recorded statement which ought in fairness to be considered contemporaneously with it.

ARTICLE II. JUDICIAL NOTICE

Rule 201. Judicial Notice of Adjudicative Facts

(a) Scope of rule. This rule governs only judicial notice of adjudicative facts.

(b) Kinds of facts. A judicially noticed fact must be one not subject to reasonable dispute in that it is either (1) generally known within the territorial jurisdiction of the trial court or (2) capable of accurate and ready determination by resort to sources whose accuracy cannot reasonably be questioned.

(c) When discretionary. A court may take judicial notice, whether requested or not.

(d) When mandatory. A court shall take judicial notice if requested by a party and supplied with the necessary information.

(e) Opportunity to be heard. A party is entitled upon timely request to an opportunity to be heard as to the propriety of taking judicial notice and the tenor of the matter noticed. In the absence of prior notification, the request may be made after judicial notice has been taken.

(f) Time of taking notice. Judicial notice may be taken at any stage of the proceeding.

(g) Instructing jury. In a civil action or proceeding, the court shall instruct the jury to accept as conclusive any fact judicially noticed. In a criminal case, the court shall instruct the jury that it may, but is not required to, accept as conclusive any fact judicially noticed.

ARTICLE III. PRESUMPTIONS IN CIVIL ACTIONS AND PROCEEDINGS

Rule 301. Presumptions in General in Civil Actions and Proceedings

In all civil actions and proceedings not otherwise provided for by Act of Congress or by these rules, a presumption imposes on the party against whom it is directed the burden of going forward with evidence to rebut or meet the presumption, but does not shift to such party the burden of proof in the sense of the risk of nonpersuasion, which remains throughout the trial upon the party on whom it was originally cast.

Rule 302. Applicability of State Law in Civil Actions and Proceedings

In civil actions and proceedings, the effect of a presumption respecting a fact which is an element of a claim or defense as to which State law supplies the rule of decision is determined in accordance with State law.

ARTICLE IV. RELEVANCY AND ITS LIMITS

Rule 401. Definition of "Relevant Evidence"

"Relevant evidence" means evidence having any tendency to make the existence of any fact that is of consequence to the determination of the action more probable or less probable than it would be without the evidence.

Rule 402. Relevant Evidence Generally Admissible; Irrelevant Evidence Inadmissible

All relevant evidence is admissible, except as otherwise provided by the Constitution of the United States, by Act of Congress, by these rules, or by other rules prescribed by the Supreme Court pursuant to statutory authority. Evidence which is not relevant is not admissible.

Rule 403. Exclusion of Relevant Evidence on Grounds of Prejudice, Confusion, or Waste of Time

Although relevant, evidence may be excluded if its probative value is substantially outweighed by the danger of unfair prejudice, confusion of the issues, or misleading the jury, or by considerations of undue delay, waste of time, or needless presentation of cumulative evidence.

Rule 404. Character Evidence Not Admissible to Prove Conduct; Exceptions; Other Crimes

(a) Character evidence generally. Evidence of a person's character or a trait of character is not admissible for the purpose of proving action in conformity therewith on a particular occasion, except:

(1) Character of accused. Evidence of a pertinent trait of character offered by an accused, or by the prosecution to rebut the same, or if evidence of a trait of character of the alleged victim of the crime is offered by an accused and admitted under Rule 404 (a) (2), evidence of the same trait of character of the accused offered by the prosecution;

(2) Character of alleged victim. Evidence of a pertinent trait of character of the alleged victim of the crime offered by an accused, or by the prosecution to rebut the same, or evidence of a character trait of peacefulness of the alleged victim offered by the prosecution in a homicide case to rebut evidence that the alleged victim was the first aggressor;

(3) **Character of witness.** Evidence of the character of a witness, as provided in rules 607, 608, and 609.

(b) **Other crimes, wrongs, or acts.** Evidence of other crimes, wrongs, or acts is not admissible to prove the character of a person in order to show action in conformity therewith. It may, however, be admissible for other purposes, such as proof of motive, opportunity, intent, preparation, plan, knowledge, identity, or absence of mistake or accident, provided that upon request by the accused, the prosecution in a criminal case shall provide reasonable notice in advance of trial, or during trial if the court excuses pretrial notice on good cause shown, of the general nature of any such evidence it intends to introduce at trial.

Rule 405. Methods of Proving Character

(a) **Reputation or opinion.** In all cases in which evidence of character or a trait of character of a person is admissible, proof may be made by testimony as to reputation or by testimony in the form of an opinion. On cross-examination, inquiry is allowable into relevant specific instances of conduct.

(b) **Specific instances of conduct.** In cases in which character or a trait of character of a person is an essential element of a charge, claim, or defense, proof may also be made of specific instances of that person's conduct.

Rule 406. Habit; Routine Practice

Evidence of the habit of a person or of the routine practice of an organization, whether corroborated or not and regardless of the presence of eyewitnesses, is relevant to prove that the conduct of the person or organization on a particular occasion was in conformity with the habit or routine practice.

Rule 407. Subsequent Remedial Measures

When, after an injury or harm allegedly caused by an event, measures are taken that, if taken previously, would have made the injury or harm less likely to occur, evidence of the subsequent measures is not admissible to prove negligence, culpable conduct, a defect in a product, a defect in a product's design, or a need for a warning or instruction. This rule does not require the exclusion of evidence of subsequent measures when offered for another purpose, such as proving ownership, control, or feasibility of precautionary measures, if controverted, or impeachment.

Rule 408. Compromise and Offers to Compromise

Evidence of (1) furnishing or offering or promising to furnish, or (2) accepting or offering or promising to accept, a valuable consideration in compromising or attempting to compromise a claim which was disputed as to either validity or amount, is not admissible to prove liability for or invalidity of the claim or its amount. Evidence of conduct or statements made in compromise negotiations is likewise not admissible. This rule does not require the exclusion of any evidence otherwise discoverable merely because it is presented in the course of compromise negotiations. This rule also does not require exclusion when the evidence is offered for another purpose, such as proving bias or prejudice of a witness, negativing a contention of undue delay, or proving an effort to obstruct a criminal investigation or prosecution.

Rule 409. Payment of Medical and Similar Expenses

Evidence of furnishing or offering or promising to pay medical, hospital, or similar expenses occasioned by an injury is not admissible to prove liability for the injury.

Rule 410. Inadmissibility of Pleas, Plea Discussions, and Related Statements

Except as otherwise provided in this rule, evidence of the following is not, in any civil or criminal proceeding, admissible against the defendant who made the plea or was a participant in the plea discussions:

(1) a plea of guilty which was later withdrawn;

(2) a plea of nolo contendere;

(3) any statement made in the course of any proceedings under Rule 11 of the Federal Rules of Criminal Procedure or comparable state procedure regarding either of the foregoing pleas; or

(4) any statement made in the course of plea discussions with an attorney for the prosecuting authority which do not result in a plea of guilty or which result in a plea of guilty later withdrawn.

However, such a statement is admissible (i) in any proceeding wherein another statement made in the course of the same plea or plea discussions has been introduced and the statement ought in fairness be considered contemporaneously with it, or (ii) in a criminal proceeding for perjury or false statement if the statement was made by the defendant under oath, on the record and in the presence of counsel.

Rule 411. Liability Insurance

Evidence that a person was or was not insured against liability is not admissible upon the issue whether the person acted negligently or otherwise wrongfully. This rule does not require the exclusion of evidence of insurance against liability when offered for another purpose, such as proof of agency, ownership, or control, or bias or prejudice of a witness.

Rule 412. Sex Offense Cases; Relevance of Alleged Victim's Past Sexual Behavior or Alleged Sexual Predisposition

(a) **Evidence generally inadmissible.** The following evidence is not admissible in any civil or criminal proceeding involving alleged sexual misconduct except as provided in subdivisions (b) and (c):

(1) Evidence offered to prove that any alleged victim engaged in other sexual behavior.

(2) Evidence offered to prove any alleged victim's sexual predisposition.

(b) Exceptions.

(1) In a criminal case, the following evidence is admissible, if otherwise admissible under these rules:

> **(A)** evidence of specific instances of sexual behavior by the alleged victim offered to prove that a person other than the accused was the source of semen, injury or other physical evidence;

> **(B)** evidence of specific instances of sexual behavior by the alleged victim with respect to the person accused of the sexual misconduct offered by the accused to prove consent or by the prosecution; and

> **(C)** evidence the exclusion of which would violate the constitutional rights of the defendant.

(2) In a civil case, evidence offered to prove the sexual behavior or sexual predisposition of any alleged victim is admissible if it is otherwise admissible under these rules and its probative value substantially outweighs the danger of harm to any victim and of unfair prejudice to any party. Evidence of an alleged victim's reputation is admissible only if it has been placed in controversy by the alleged victim.

(c) Procedure to determine admissibility.

(1) A party intending to offer evidence under subdivision (b) must:

> **(A)** file a written motion at least 14 days before trial specifically describing the evidence and stating the purpose for which it is offered unless the court, for good cause requires a different time for filing or permits filing during trial; and

> **(B)** serve the motion on all parties and notify the alleged victim or, when appropriate, the alleged victim's guardian or representative.

(2) Before admitting evidence under this rule the court must conduct a hearing in camera and afford the victim and parties a right to attend and be heard. The motion, related papers, and the record of the hearing must be sealed and remain under seal unless the court orders otherwise.

Rule 413. Evidence of Similar Crimes in Sexual Assault Cases

(a) In a criminal case in which the defendant is accused of an offense of sexual assault, evidence of the defendant's commission of another offense or offenses of sexual assault is admissible, and may be considered for its bearing on any matter to which it is relevant.

(b) In a case in which the Government intends to offer evidence under this rule, the attorney for the Government shall disclose the evidence to the defendant, including statements of witnesses or a summary of the substance of any testimony that is expected to be offered, at least fifteen days before the scheduled date of trial or at such later time as the court may allow for good cause.

(c) This rule shall not be construed to limit the admission or consideration of evidence under any other rule.

(d) For purposes of this rule and Rule 415, "offense of sexual assault" means a crime under Federal law or the law of a State (as defined in section 513 of title 18, United States Code) that involved—

(1) any conduct proscribed by chapter 109A of title 18, United States Code;

(2) contact, without consent, between any part of the defendant's body or an object and the genitals or anus of another person;

(3) contact, without consent, between the genitals or anus of the defendant and any part of another person's body;

(4) deriving sexual pleasure or gratification from the infliction of death, bodily injury, or physical pain on another person; or

(5) an attempt or conspiracy to engage in conduct described in paragraphs (1)–(4).

Rule 414. Evidence of Similar Crimes in Child Molestation Cases

(a) In a criminal case in which the defendant is accused of an offense of child molestation, evidence of the defendant's commission of another offense or offenses of child molestation is admissible, and may be considered for its bearing on any matter to which it is relevant.

(b) In a case in which the Government intends to offer evidence under this rule, the attorney for the Government shall disclose the evidence to the defendant, including statements of witnesses or a summary of the substance of any testimony that is expected to be offered, at least fifteen days before the scheduled date of trial or at such later time as the court may allow for good cause.

(c) This rule shall not be construed to limit the admission or consideration of evidence under any other rule.

(d) For purposes of this rule and Rule 415, "child" means a person below the age of fourteen, and "offense of child molestation" means a crime under Federal law or the law of a State (as defined in section 513 of title 18, United States Code) that involved—

(1) any conduct proscribed by chapter 109A of title 18, United States Code, that was committed in relation to a child;

(2) any conduct proscribed by chapter 110 of title 18, United States Code;

(3) contact between any part of the defendant's body or an object and the genitals or anus of a child;

(4) contact between the genitals or anus of the defendant and any part of the body of a child;

(5) deriving sexual pleasure or gratification from the infliction of death, bodily injury, or physical pain on a child; or

(6) an attempt or conspiracy to engage in conduct described in paragraphs (1)–(5).

Rule 415.　Evidence of Similar Acts in Civil Cases Concerning Sexual Assault or Child Molestation

(a) In a civil case in which a claim for damages or other relief is predicated on a party's alleged commission of conduct constituting an offense of sexual assault or child molestation, evidence of that party's commission of another offense or offenses of sexual assault or child molestation is admissible and may be considered as provided in Rule 413 and Rule 414 of these rules.

(b) A party who intends to offer evidence under this Rule shall disclose the evidence to the party against whom it will be offered, including statements of witnesses or a summary of the substance of any testimony that is expected to be offered, at least fifteen days before the scheduled date of trial or at such later time as the court may allow for good cause.

(c) This rule shall not be construed to limit the admission or consideration of evidence under any other rule.

ARTICLE V.　PRIVILEGES

Rule 501.　General Rule

Except as otherwise required by the Constitution of the United States or provided by Act of Congress or in rules prescribed by the Supreme Court pursuant to statutory authority, the privilege of a witness, person, government, State, or political subdivision thereof shall be governed by the principles of the common law as they may be interpreted by the courts of the United States in the light of reason and experience.　However, in civil actions and proceedings, with respect to an element of a claim or defense as to which State law supplies the rule of decision, the privilege of a witness, person, government, State, or political subdivision thereof shall be determined in accordance with State law.

ARTICLE VI.　WITNESSES

Rule 601.　General Rule of Competency

Every person is competent to be a witness except as otherwise provided in these rules.　However, in civil actions and proceedings, with respect to an element of a claim or defense as to which State law supplies the rule of decision, the competency of a witness shall be determined in accordance with State law.

Rule 602. Lack of Personal Knowledge

A witness may not testify to a matter unless evidence is introduced sufficient to support a finding that the witness has personal knowledge of the matter. Evidence to prove personal knowledge may, but need not, consist of the witness' own testimony. This rule is subject to the provisions of rule 703, relating to opinion testimony by expert witnesses.

Rule 603. Oath or Affirmation

Before testifying, every witness shall be required to declare that the witness will testify truthfully, by oath or affirmation administered in a form calculated to awaken the witness' conscience and impress the witness' mind with the duty to do so.

Rule 604. Interpreters

An interpreter is subject to the provisions of these rules relating to qualification as an expert and the administration of an oath or affirmation to make a true translation.

Rule 605. Competency of Judge as Witness

The judge presiding at the trial may not testify in that trial as a witness. No objection need be made in order to preserve the point.

Rule 606. Competency of Juror as Witness

(a) At the trial. A member of the jury may not testify as a witness before that jury in the trial of the case in which the juror is sitting. If the juror is called so to testify, the opposing party shall be afforded an opportunity to object out of the presence of the jury.

(b) Inquiry into validity of verdict or indictment. Upon an inquiry into the validity of a verdict or indictment, a juror may not testify as to any matter or statement occurring during the course of the jury's deliberations or to the effect of anything upon that or any other juror's mind or emotions as influencing the juror to assent to or dissent from the verdict or indictment or concerning the juror's mental processes in connection therewith, except that a juror may testify on the question whether extraneous prejudicial information was improperly brought to the jury's attention or whether any outside influence was improperly brought to bear upon any juror. Nor may a juror's affidavit or evidence of any statement by the juror concerning a matter about which the juror would be precluded from testifying be received for these purposes.

Rule 607. Who May Impeach

The credibility of a witness may be attacked by any party, including the party calling the witness.

Rule 608. Evidence of Character and Conduct of Witness

(a) Opinion and reputation evidence of character. The credibility of a witness may be attacked or supported by evidence in the form of opinion or reputation, but subject to these limitations: (1) the evidence may refer only to character for truthfulness or untruthfulness, and (2) evidence of truthful character is admissible only after the character of the witness for truthfulness has been attacked by opinion or reputation evidence or otherwise.

(b) Specific instances of conduct. Specific instances of the conduct of a witness, for the purpose of attacking or supporting the witness' character for truthfulness, other than conviction of crime as provided in rule 609, may not be proved by extrinsic evidence. They may, however, in the discretion of the court, if probative of truthfulness or untruthfulness, be inquired into on cross-examination of the witness (1) concerning the witness' character for truthfulness or untruthfulness, or (2) concerning the character for truthfulness or untruthfulness of another witness as to which character the witness being cross-examined has testified.

The giving of testimony, whether by an accused or by any other witness, does not operate as a waiver of the accused's or the witness' privilege against self-incrimination when examined with respect to matters that relate only to character for truthfulness.

Rule 609. Impeachment by Evidence of Conviction of Crime

(a) General rule. For the purpose of attacking the credibility of a witness,

> **(1)** evidence that a witness other than an accused has been convicted of a crime shall be admitted, subject to Rule 403, if the crime was punishable by death or imprisonment in excess of one year under the law under which the witness was convicted, and evidence that an accused has been convicted of such a crime shall be admitted if the court determines that the probative value of admitting this evidence outweighs its prejudicial effect to the accused; and

> **(2)** evidence that any witness has been convicted of a crime shall be admitted if it involved dishonesty or false statement, regardless of the punishment.

(b) Time limit. Evidence of a conviction under this rule is not admissible if a period of more than ten years has elapsed since the date of the conviction or of the release of the witness from the confinement imposed for that conviction, whichever is the later date, unless the court determines, in the interests of justice, that the probative value of the conviction supported by specific facts and circumstances substantially outweighs its prejudicial effect. However, evidence of a conviction more than 10 years old as calculated herein, is not admissible unless the proponent gives to the adverse party sufficient advance written notice of intent to use such evidence to provide the adverse party with a fair opportunity to contest the use of such evidence.

(c) Effect of pardon, annulment, or certificate of rehabilitation. Evidence of a conviction is not admissible under this rule if (1) the conviction has been the subject of a pardon, annulment, certificate of rehabilitation, or other equivalent procedure based on a finding of the rehabilitation of the person convicted, and that person has not been convicted of a subsequent crime which was punishable by death or imprisonment in excess of one year, or (2) the conviction has been the subject of a pardon, annulment, or other equivalent procedure based on a finding of innocence.

(d) Juvenile adjudications. Evidence of juvenile adjudications is generally not admissible under this rule. The court may, however, in a criminal case allow evidence of a juvenile adjudication of a witness other than the accused if conviction of the offense would be admissible to attack the credibility of an adult and the court is satisfied that admission in evidence is necessary for a fair determination of the issue of guilt or innocence.

(e) Pendency of appeal. The pendency of an appeal therefrom does not render evidence of a conviction inadmissible. Evidence of the pendency of an appeal is admissible.

Rule 610. Religious Beliefs or Opinions

Evidence of the beliefs or opinions of a witness on matters of religion is not admissible for the purpose of showing that by reason of their nature the witness' credibility is impaired or enhanced.

Rule 611. Mode and Order of Interrogation and Presentation

(a) Control by court. The court shall exercise reasonable control over the mode and order of interrogating witnesses and presenting evidence so as to (1) make the interrogation and presentation effective for the ascertainment of the truth, (2) avoid needless consumption of time, and (3) protect witnesses from harassment or undue embarrassment.

(b) Scope of cross-examination. Cross-examination should be limited to the subject matter of the direct examination and matters affecting the credibility of the witness. The court may, in the exercise of discretion, permit inquiry into additional matters as if on direct examination.

(c) Leading questions. Leading questions should not be used on the direct examination of a witness except as may be necessary to develop the witness' testimony. Ordinarily leading questions should be permitted on cross-examination. When a party calls a hostile witness, an adverse party, or a witness identified with an adverse party, interrogation may be by leading questions.

Rule 612. Writing Used to Refresh Memory

Except as otherwise provided in criminal proceedings by section 3500 of title 18, United States Code, if a witness uses a writing to refresh memory for the purpose of testifying, either—

(1) while testifying, or

(2) before testifying, if the court in its discretion determines it is necessary in the interests of justice,

an adverse party is entitled to have the writing produced at the hearing, to inspect it, to cross-examine the witness thereon, and to introduce in evidence those portions which relate to the testimony of the witness. If it is claimed that the writing contains matters not related to the subject matter of the testimony the court shall examine the writing in camera, excise any portions not so related, and order delivery of the remainder to the party entitled thereto. Any portion withheld over objections shall be preserved and made available to the appellate court in the event of an appeal. If a writing is not produced or delivered pursuant to order under this rule, the court shall make any order justice requires, except that in criminal cases when the prosecution elects not to comply, the order shall be one striking the testimony or, if the court in its discretion determines that the interests of justice so require, declaring a mistrial.

Rule 613. Prior Statements of Witnesses

(a) Examining witness concerning prior statement. In examining a witness concerning a prior statement made by the witness, whether written or not, the statement need not be shown nor its contents disclosed to the witness at that time, but on request the same shall be shown or disclosed to opposing counsel.

(b) Extrinsic evidence of prior inconsistent statement of witness. Extrinsic evidence of a prior inconsistent statement by a witness is not admissible unless the witness is afforded an opportunity to explain or deny the same and the opposite party is afforded an opportunity to interrogate the witness thereon, or the interests of justice otherwise require. This provision does not apply to admissions of a party-opponent as defined in rule 801(d)(2).

Rule 614. Calling and Interrogation of Witnesses by Court

(a) Calling by court. The court may, on its own motion or at the suggestion of a party, call witnesses, and all parties are entitled to cross-examine witnesses thus called.

(b) Interrogation by court. The court may interrogate witnesses, whether called by itself or by a party.

(c) Objections. Objections to the calling of witnesses by the court or to interrogation by it may be made at the time or at the next available opportunity when the jury is not present.

Rule 615.   Exclusion of Witnesses

At the request of a party the court shall order witnesses excluded so that they cannot hear the testimony of other witnesses, and it may make the order of its own motion.   This rule does not authorize exclusion of (1) a party who is a natural person, or (2) an officer or employee of a party which is not a natural person designated as its representative by its attorney, or (3) a person whose presence is shown by a party to be essential to the presentation of the party's cause, or (4) a person authorized by statute to be present.

ARTICLE VII.   OPINIONS AND EXPERT TESTIMONY

Rule 701.   Opinion Testimony by Lay Witnesses

If the witness is not testifying as an expert, the witness' testimony in the form of opinions or inferences is limited to those opinions or inferences which are (a) rationally based on the perception of the witness, and (b) helpful to a clear understanding of the witness' testimony or the determination of a fact in issue, and (c) not based on scientific, technical, or other specialized knowledge within the scope of Rule 702.

Rule 702.   Testimony by Experts

If scientific, technical, or other specialized knowledge will assist the trier of fact to understand the evidence or to determine a fact in issue, a witness qualified as an expert by knowledge, skill, experience, training, or education, may testify thereto in the form of an opinion or otherwise, if (1) the testimony is based upon sufficient facts or data, (2) the testimony is the product of reliable principles and methods, and (3) the witness has applied the principles and methods reliably to the facts of the case.

Rule 703.   Bases of Opinion Testimony by Experts

The facts or data in the particular case upon which an expert bases an opinion or inference may be those perceived by or made known to the expert at or before the hearing. If of a type reasonably relied upon by experts in the particular field in forming opinions or inferences upon the subject, the facts or data need not be admissible in evidence in order for the opinion or inference to be admitted. Facts or data that are otherwise inadmissible shall not be disclosed to the jury by the proponent of the opinion or inference unless the court determines that their probative value in assisting the jury to evaluate the expert's opinion substantially outweighs their prejudicial effect.

Rule 704. Opinion on Ultimate Issue

(a) Except as provided in subdivision (b), testimony in the form of an opinion or inference otherwise admissible is not objectionable because it embraces an ultimate issue to be decided by the trier of fact.

(b) No expert witness testifying with respect to the mental state or condition of a defendant in a criminal case may state an opinion or inference as to whether the defendant did or did not have the mental state or condition constituting an element of the crime charged or of a defense thereto. Such ultimate issues are matters for the trier of fact alone.

Rule 705. Disclosure of Facts or Data Underlying Expert Opinion

The expert may testify in terms of opinion or inference and give reasons therefor without first testifying to the underlying facts or data, unless the court requires otherwise. The expert may in any event be required to disclose the underlying facts or data on cross-examination.

Rule 706. Court Appointed Experts

(a) Appointment. The court may on its own motion or on the motion of any party enter an order to show cause why expert witnesses should not be appointed, and may request the parties to submit nominations. The court may appoint any expert witnesses agreed upon by the parties, and may appoint expert witnesses of its own selection. An expert witness shall not be appointed by the court unless the witness consents to act. A witness so appointed shall be informed of the witness' duties by the court in writing, a copy of which shall be filed with the clerk, or at a conference in which the parties shall have opportunity to participate. A witness so appointed shall advise the parties of the witness' findings, if any; the witness' deposition may be taken by any party; and the witness may be called to testify by the court or any party. The witness shall be subject to cross-examination by each party, including a party calling the witness.

(b) Compensation. Expert witnesses so appointed are entitled to reasonable compensation in whatever sum the court may allow. The compensation thus fixed is payable from funds which may be provided by law in criminal cases and civil actions and proceedings involving just compensation under the fifth amendment. In other civil actions and proceedings the compensation shall be paid by the parties in such proportion and at such time as the court directs, and thereafter charged in like manner as other costs.

(c) Disclosure of appointment. In the exercise of its discretion, the court may authorize disclosure to the jury of the fact that the court appointed the expert witness.

(d) Parties' experts of own selection. Nothing in this rule limits the parties in calling expert witnesses of their own selection.

ARTICLE VIII. HEARSAY

Rule 801. Definitions

The following definitions apply under this article:

(a) Statement. A "statement" is (1) an oral or written assertion or (2) nonverbal conduct of a person, if it is intended by the person as an assertion.

(b) Declarant. A "declarant" is a person who makes a statement.

(c) Hearsay. "Hearsay" is a statement, other than one made by the declarant while testifying at the trial or hearing, offered in evidence to prove the truth of the matter asserted.

(d) Statements which are not hearsay. A statement is not hearsay if—

(1) Prior statement by witness. The declarant testifies at the trial or hearing and is subject to cross-examination concerning the statement, and the statement is (A) inconsistent with the declarant's testimony, and was given under oath subject to the penalty of perjury at a trial, hearing, or other proceeding, or in a deposition, or (B) consistent with the declarant's testimony and is offered to rebut an express or implied charge against the declarant of recent fabrication or improper influence or motive, or (C) one of identification of a person made after perceiving the person; or

(2) Admission by party-opponent. The statement is offered against a party and is (A) the party's own statement, in either an individual or a representative capacity or (B) a statement of which the party has manifested an adoption or belief in its truth, or (C) a statement by a person authorized by the party to make a statement concerning the subject, or (D) a statement by the party's agent or servant concerning a matter within the scope of the agency or employment, made during the existence of the relationship, or (E) a statement by a coconspirator of a party during the course and in furtherance of the conspiracy. The contents of the statement shall be considered but are not alone sufficient to establish the declarant's authority under subdivision (C), the agency or employment relationship and scope thereof under subdivision (D), or the existence of the conspiracy and the participation therein of the declarant and the party against whom the statement is offered under subdivision (E).

Rule 802. Hearsay Rule

Hearsay is not admissible except as provided by these rules or by other rules prescribed by the Supreme Court pursuant to statutory authority or by Act of Congress.

Rule 803. Hearsay Exceptions; Availability of Declarant Immaterial

The following are not excluded by the hearsay rule, even though the declarant is available as a witness:

(1) **Present sense impression.** A statement describing or explaining an event or condition made while the declarant was perceiving the event or condition, or immediately thereafter.

(2) **Excited utterance.** A statement relating to a startling event or condition made while the declarant was under the stress of excitement caused by the event or condition.

(3) **Then existing mental, emotional, or physical condition.** A statement of the declarant's then existing state of mind, emotion, sensation, or physical condition (such as intent, plan, motive, design, mental feeling, pain, and bodily health), but not including a statement of memory or belief to prove the fact remembered or believed unless it relates to the execution, revocation, identification, or terms of declarant's will.

(4) **Statements for purposes of medical diagnosis or treatment.** Statements made for purposes of medical diagnosis or treatment and describing medical history, or past or present symptoms, pain, or sensations, or the inception or general character of the cause or external source thereof insofar as reasonably pertinent to diagnosis or treatment.

(5) **Recorded recollection.** A memorandum or record concerning a matter about which a witness once had knowledge but now has insufficient recollection to enable the witness to testify fully and accurately, shown to have been made or adopted by the witness when the matter was fresh in the witness' memory and to reflect that knowledge correctly. If admitted, the memorandum or record may be read into evidence but may not itself be received as an exhibit unless offered by an adverse party.

(6) **Records of regularly conducted activity.** A memorandum, report, record, or data compilation, in any form, of acts, events, conditions, opinions, or diagnoses, made at or near the time by, or from information transmitted by, a person with knowledge, if kept in the course of a regularly conducted business activity, and if it was the regular practice of that business activity to make the memorandum, report, record, or data compilation, all as shown by the testimony of the custodian or other qualified witness, or by certification that complies with Rule 902(11), Rule 902(12), or a statute permitting certification, unless the source of information or the method or circumstances of preparation indicate lack of trustworthiness. The term "business" as used in this paragraph includes business, institution, association, profession, occupation, and calling of every kind, whether or not conducted for profit.

(7) **Absence of entry in records kept in accordance with the provisions of paragraph (6).** Evidence that a matter is not included in the memoranda, reports, records, or data compilations, in any form, kept in accordance with the provisions of paragraph (6), to prove the nonoccurrence or nonexistence of the matter, if the matter was of a kind of which a memorandum, report, record, or data compilation was regu-

larly made and preserved, unless the sources of information or other circumstances indicate lack of trustworthiness.

(8) Public records and reports. Records, reports, statements, or data compilations, in any form, of public offices or agencies, setting forth (A) the activities of the office or agency, or (B) matters observed pursuant to duty imposed by law as to which matters there was a duty to report, excluding, however, in criminal cases matters observed by police officers and other law enforcement personnel, or (C) in civil actions and proceedings and against the Government in criminal cases, factual findings resulting from an investigation made pursuant to authority granted by law, unless the sources of information or other circumstances indicate lack of trustworthiness.

(9) Records of vital statistics. Records or data compilations, in any form, of births, fetal deaths, deaths, or marriages, if the report thereof was made to a public office pursuant to requirements of law.

(10) Absence of public record or entry. To prove the absence of a record, report, statement, or data compilation, in any form, or the nonoccurrence or nonexistence of a matter of which a record, report, statement, or data compilation, in any form, was regularly made and preserved by a public office or agency, evidence in the form of a certification in accordance with rule 902, or testimony, that diligent search failed to disclose the record, report, statement, or data compilation, or entry.

(11) Records of religious organizations. Statements of births, marriages, divorces, deaths, legitimacy, ancestry, relationship by blood or marriage, or other similar facts of personal or family history, contained in a regularly kept record of a religious organization.

(12) Marriage, baptismal, and similar certificates. Statements of fact contained in a certificate that the maker performed a marriage or other ceremony or administered a sacrament, made by a clergyman, public official, or other person authorized by the rules or practices of a religious organization or by law to perform the act certified, and purporting to have been issued at the time of the act or within a reasonable time thereafter.

(13) Family records. Statements of fact concerning personal or family history contained in family Bibles, genealogies, charts, engravings on rings, inscriptions on family portraits, engravings on urns, crypts, or tombstones, or the like.

(14) Records of documents affecting an interest in property. The record of a document purporting to establish or affect an interest in property, as proof of the content of the original recorded document and its execution and delivery by each person by whom it purports to have been executed, if the record is a record of a public office and an applicable statute authorizes the recording of documents of that kind in that office.

(15) Statements in documents affecting an interest in property. A statement contained in a document purporting to establish or affect an interest in property if the matter stated was relevant to the purpose of the document, unless dealings with the property since the document was made have been inconsistent with the truth of the statement or the purport of the document.

(16) Statements in ancient documents. Statements in a document in existence twenty years or more the authenticity of which is established.

(17) Market reports, commercial publications. Market quotations, tabulations, lists, directories, or other published compilations, generally used and relied upon by the public or by persons in particular occupations.

(18) Learned treatises. To the extent called to the attention of an expert witness upon cross-examination or relied upon by the expert witness in direct examination, statements contained in published treatises, periodicals, or pamphlets on a subject of history, medicine, or other science or art, established as a reliable authority by the testimony or admission of the witness or by other expert testimony or by judicial notice. If admitted, the statements may be read into evidence but may not be received as exhibits.

(19) Reputation concerning personal or family history. Reputation among members of a person's family by blood, adoption, or marriage, or among a person's associates, or in the community, concerning a person's birth, adoption, marriage, divorce, death, legitimacy, relationship by blood, adoption, or marriage, ancestry, or other similar fact of his personal or family history.

(20) Reputation concerning boundaries or general history. Reputation in a community, arising before the controversy, as to boundaries of or customs affecting lands in the community, and reputation as to events of general history important to the community or State or nation in which located.

(21) Reputation as to character. Reputation of a person's character among associates or in the community.

(22) Judgment of previous conviction. Evidence of a final judgment, entered after a trial or upon a plea of guilty (but not upon a plea of nolo contendere), adjudging a person guilty of a crime punishable by death or imprisonment in excess of one year, to prove any fact essential to sustain the judgment, but not including, when offered by the Government in a criminal prosecution for purposes other than impeachment, judgments against persons other than the accused. The pendency of an appeal may be shown but does not affect admissibility.

(23) Judgment as to personal, family, or general history, or boundaries. Judgments as proof of matters of personal, family or general history, or boundaries, essential to the judgment, if the same would be provable by evidence of reputation.

(24) [Transferred to Rule 807]

Rule 804. Hearsay Exceptions; Declarant Unavailable

(a) Definition of unavailability. "Unavailability as a witness" includes situations in which the declarant—

(1) is exempted by ruling of the court on the ground of privilege from testifying concerning the subject matter of the declarant's statement; or

(2) persists in refusing to testify concerning the subject matter of the declarant's statement despite an order of the court to do so; or

(3) testifies to a lack of memory of the subject matter of the declarant's statement; or

(4) is unable to be present or to testify at the hearing because of death or then existing physical or mental illness or infirmity; or

(5) is absent from the hearing and the proponent of statement has been unable to procure the declarant's attendance (or in the case of a hearsay exception under subdivision (b)(2), (3), or (4), the declarant's attendance or testimony) by process or other reasonable means.

A declarant is not unavailable as a witness if exemption, refusal, claim of lack of memory, inability, or absence is due to the procurement or wrongdoing of the proponent of a statement for the purpose of preventing the witness from attending or testifying.

(b) Hearsay exceptions. The following are not excluded by the hearsay rule if the declarant is unavailable as a witness:

(1) Former testimony. Testimony given as a witness at another hearing of the same or a different proceeding, or in a deposition taken in compliance with law in the course of the same or another proceeding, if the party against whom the testimony is now offered, or, in a civil action or proceeding, a predecessor in interest, had an opportunity and similar motive to develop the testimony by direct, cross, or redirect examination.

(2) Statement under belief of impending death. In a prosecution for homicide or in a civil action or proceeding, a statement made by a declarant while believing that the declarant's death was imminent, concerning the cause or circumstances of what the declarant believed to be impending death.

(3) Statement against interest. A statement which was at the time of its making so far contrary to the declarant's pecuniary or proprietary interest, or so far tended to subject the declarant to civil or criminal liability, or to render invalid a claim by the declarant against another, that a reasonable person in the declarant's position would not have made the statement unless believing it to be true. A statement tending to expose the declarant to criminal liability and offered to exculpate the accused is not admissible unless corroborating circumstances clearly indicate the trustworthiness of the statement.

(4) Statement of personal or family history. (A) A statement concerning the declarant's own birth, adoption, marriage, divorce, legitimacy, relationship by blood, adoption, or marriage, ancestry, or other similar fact of personal or family history, even though declarant had no means of acquiring personal knowledge of the matter stated; or (B) a statement concerning the foregoing matters, and death also, of another person, if the declarant was related to the other by blood, adoption, or marriage or was so intimately associated with the other's family as to be likely to have accurate information concerning the matter declared.

(5) [Transferred to Rule 807]

(6) Forfeiture by wrongdoing. A statement offered against a party that has engaged or acquiesced in wrongdoing that was intended to, and did, procure the unavailability of the declarant as a witness.

Rule 805.   Hearsay Within Hearsay

Hearsay included within hearsay is not excluded under the hearsay rule if each part of the combined statements conforms with an exception to the hearsay rule provided in these rules.

Rule 806.   Attacking and Supporting Credibility of Declarant

When a hearsay statement, or a statement defined in Rule 801(d)(2)(C), (D), or (E), has been admitted in evidence, the credibility of the declarant may be attacked, and if attacked may be supported, by any evidence which would be admissible for those purposes if declarant had testified as a witness. Evidence of a statement or conduct by the declarant at any time, inconsistent with the declarant's hearsay statement, is not subject to any requirement that the declarant may have been afforded an opportunity to deny or explain. If the party against whom a hearsay statement has been admitted calls the declarant as a witness, the party is entitled to examine the declarant on the statement as if under cross-examination.

Rule 807.   Residual Exception

A statement not specifically covered by Rule 803 or 804 but having equivalent circumstantial guarantees of trustworthiness, is not excluded by the hearsay rule, if the court determines that (A) the statement is offered as evidence of a material fact; (B) the statement is more probative on the point for which it is offered than any other evidence which the proponent can procure through reasonable efforts; and (C) the general purposes of these rules and the interests of justice will best be served by admission of the statement into evidence. However, a statement may not be admitted under this exception unless the proponent of it makes known to the adverse party sufficiently in advance of the trial or hearing to provide the adverse party with a fair opportunity to prepare to meet it, the proponent's intention to offer the statement and the particulars of it, including the name and address of the declarant.

ARTICLE IX. AUTHENTICATION AND IDENTIFICATION

Rule 901. Requirement of Authentication or Identification

(a) General provision. The requirement of authentication or identification as a condition precedent to admissibility is satisfied by evidence sufficient to support a finding that the matter in question is what its proponent claims.

(b) Illustrations. By way of illustration only, and not by way of limitation, the following are examples of authentication or identification conforming with the requirements of this rule:

(1) Testimony of witness with knowledge. Testimony that a matter is what it is claimed to be.

(2) Nonexpert opinion on handwriting. Nonexpert opinion as to the genuineness of handwriting, based upon familiarity not acquired for purposes of the litigation.

(3) Comparison by trier or expert witness. Comparison by the trier of fact or by expert witnesses with specimens which have been authenticated.

(4) Distinctive characteristics and the like. Appearance, contents, substance, internal patterns, or other distinctive characteristics, taken in conjunction with circumstances.

(5) Voice identification. Identification of a voice, whether heard firsthand or through mechanical or electronic transmission or recording, by opinion based upon hearing the voice at any time under circumstances connecting it with the alleged speaker.

(6) Telephone conversations. Telephone conversations, by evidence that a call was made to the number assigned at the time by the telephone company to a particular person or business, if (A) in the case of a person, circumstances, including self-identification, show the person answering to be the one called, or (B) in the case of a business, the call was made to a place of business and the conversation related to business reasonably transacted over the telephone.

(7) Public records or reports. Evidence that a writing authorized by law to be recorded or filed and in fact recorded or filed in a public office, or a purported public record, report, statement, or data compilation, in any form, is from the public office where items of this nature are kept.

(8) Ancient documents or data compilation. Evidence that a document or data compilation, in any form, (A) is in such condition as to create no suspicion concerning its authenticity, (B) was in a place where it, if authentic, would likely be, and (C) has been in existence 20 years or more at the time it is offered.

(9) Process or system. Evidence describing a process or system used to produce a result and showing that the process or system produces an accurate result.

(10) Methods provided by statute or rule. Any method of authentication or identification provided by Act of Congress or by other rules prescribed by the Supreme Court pursuant to statutory authority.

Rule 902. Self–Authentication

Extrinsic evidence of authenticity as a condition precedent to admissibility is not required with respect to the following:

(1) Domestic public documents under seal. A document bearing a seal purporting to be that of the United States, or of any State, district, Commonwealth, territory, or insular possession thereof, or the Panama Canal Zone, or the Trust Territory of the Pacific Islands, or of a political subdivision, department, officer, or agency thereof, and a signature purporting to be an attestation or execution.

(2) Domestic public documents not under seal. A document purporting to bear the signature in the official capacity of an officer or employee of any entity included in paragraph (1) hereof, having no seal, if a public officer having a seal and having official duties in the district or political subdivision of the officer or employee certifies under seal that the signer has the official capacity and that the signature is genuine.

(3) Foreign public documents. A document purporting to be executed or attested in an official capacity by a person authorized by the laws of a foreign country to make the execution or attestation, and accompanied by a final certification as to the genuineness of the signature and official position (A) of the executing or attesting person, or (B) of any foreign official whose certificate of genuineness of signature and official position relates to the execution or attestation or is in a chain of certificates of genuineness of signature and official position relating to the execution or attestation. A final certification may be made by a secretary of embassy or legation, consul general, consul, vice consul, or consular agent of the United States, or a diplomatic or consular official of the foreign country assigned or accredited to the United States. If reasonable opportunity has been given to all parties to investigate the authenticity and accuracy of official documents, the court may, for good cause shown, order that they be treated as presumptively authentic without final certification or permit them to be evidenced by an attested summary with or without final certification.

(4) Certified copies of public records. A copy of an official record or report or entry therein, or of a document authorized by law to be recorded or filed and actually recorded or filed in a public office, including data compilations in any form, certified as correct by the custodian or other person authorized to make the certification, by certificate complying with paragraph (1), (2), or (3) of this rule or complying with any Act of Congress or rule prescribed by the Supreme Court pursuant to statutory authority.

(5) Official publications. Books, pamphlets, or other publications purporting to be issued by public authority.

(6) Newspapers and periodicals. Printed materials purporting to be newspapers or periodicals.

(7) Trade inscriptions and the like. Inscriptions, signs, tags, or labels purporting to have been affixed in the course of business and indicating ownership, control, or origin.

(8) Acknowledged documents. Documents accompanied by a certificate of acknowledgment executed in the manner provided by law by a notary public or other officer authorized by law to take acknowledgments.

(9) Commercial paper and related documents. Commercial paper, signatures thereon, and documents relating thereto to the extent provided by general commercial law.

(10) Presumptions under Acts of Congress. Any signature, document, or other matter declared by Act of Congress to be presumptively or prima facie genuine or authentic.

(11) Certified domestic records of regularly conducted activity. The original or a duplicate of a domestic record of regularly conducted activity that would be admissible under Rule 803(6) if accompanied by a written declaration of its custodian or other qualified person, in a manner complying with any Act of Congress or rule prescribed by the Supreme Court pursuant to statutory authority, certifying that the record—

(A) was made at or near the time of the occurrence of the matters set forth by, or from information transmitted by, a person with knowledge of those matters;

(B) was kept in the course of the regularly conducted activity; and

(C) was made by the regularly conducted activity as a regular practice.

A party intending to offer a record into evidence under this paragraph must provide written notice of that intention to all adverse parties, and must make the record and declaration available for inspection sufficiently in advance of their offer into evidence to provide an adverse party with a fair opportunity to challenge them.

(12) Certified foreign records of regularly conducted activity. In a civil case, the original or a duplicate of a foreign record of regularly conducted activity that would be admissible under Rule 803(6) if accompanied by a written declaration by its custodian or other qualified person certifying that the record—

(A) was made at or near the time of the occurrence of the matters set forth by, or from information transmitted by, a person with knowledge of those matters;

(B) was kept in the course of the regularly conducted activity; and

(C) was made by the regularly conducted activity as a regular practice.

The declaration must be signed in a manner that, if falsely made, would subject the maker to criminal penalty under the laws of the country where the declaration is signed. A party intending to offer a record into evidence under this paragraph must provide written notice of that intention to all adverse parties, and must make the record and declaration available for inspection sufficiently in advance of their offer into evidence to provide an adverse party with a fair opportunity to challenge them.

Rule 903.   Subscribing Witness' Testimony Unnecessary

The testimony of a subscribing witness is not necessary to authenticate a writing unless required by the laws of the jurisdiction whose laws govern the validity of the writing.

ARTICLE X.   CONTENTS OF WRITINGS, RECORDINGS, AND PHOTOGRAPHS

Rule 1001.   Definitions

For purposes of this article the following definitions are applicable:

(1) Writings and recordings. "Writings" and "recordings" consist of letters, words, or numbers, or their equivalent, set down by handwriting, typewriting, printing, photostating, photographing, magnetic impulse, mechanical or electronic recording, or other form of data compilation.

(2) Photographs. "Photographs" include still photographs, X-ray films, video tapes, and motion pictures.

(3) Original. An "original" of a writing or recording is the writing or recording itself or any counterpart intended to have the same effect by a person executing or issuing it. An "original" of a photograph includes the negative or any print therefrom. If data are stored in a computer or similar device, any printout or other output readable by sight, shown to reflect the data accurately, is an "original".

(4) Duplicate. A "duplicate" is a counterpart produced by the same impression as the original, or from the same matrix, or by means of photography, including enlargements and miniatures, or by mechanical or electronic re-recording, or by chemical reproduction, or by other equivalent technique which accurately reproduces the original.

Rule 1002.   Requirement of Original

To prove the content of a writing, recording, or photograph, the original writing, recording, or photograph is required, except as otherwise provided in these rules or by Act of Congress.

Rule 1003. Admissibility of Duplicates

A duplicate is admissible to the same extent as an original unless (1) a genuine question is raised as to the authenticity of the original or (2) in the circumstances it would be unfair to admit the duplicate in lieu of the original.

Rule 1004. Admissibility of Other Evidence of Contents

The original is not required, and other evidence of the contents of a writing, recording, or photograph is admissible if—

(1) Originals lost or destroyed. All originals are lost or have been destroyed, unless the proponent lost or destroyed them in bad faith; or

(2) Original not obtainable. No original can be obtained by any available judicial process or procedure; or

(3) Original in possession of opponent. At a time when an original was under the control of the party against whom offered, that party was put on notice, by the pleadings or otherwise, that the contents would be a subject of proof at the hearing, and that party does not produce the original at the hearing; or

(4) Collateral matters. The writing, recording, or photograph is not closely related to a controlling issue.

Rule 1005. Public Records

The contents of an official record, or of a document authorized to be recorded or filed and actually recorded or filed, including data compilations in any form, if otherwise admissible, may be proved by copy, certified as correct in accordance with rule 902 or testified to be correct by a witness who has compared it with the original. If a copy which complies with the foregoing cannot be obtained by the exercise of reasonable diligence, then other evidence of the contents may be given.

Rule 1006. Summaries

The contents of voluminous writings, recordings, or photographs which cannot conveniently be examined in court may be presented in the form of a chart, summary, or calculation. The originals, or duplicates, shall be made available for examination or copying, or both, by other parties at reasonable time and place. The court may order that they be produced in court.

Rule 1007. Testimony or Written Admission of Party

Contents of writings, recordings, or photographs may be proved by the testimony or deposition of the party against whom offered or by that party's written admission, without accounting for the nonproduction of the original.

Rule 1008. Functions of Court and Jury

When the admissibility of other evidence of contents of writings, recordings, or photographs under these rules depends upon the fulfillment of a condition of fact, the question whether the condition has been fulfilled is ordinarily for the court to determine in accordance with the provisions of rule 104. However, when an issue is raised (a) whether the asserted writing ever existed, or (b) whether another writing, recording, or photograph produced at the trial is the original, or (c) whether other evidence of contents correctly reflects the contents, the issue is for the trier of fact to determine as in the case of other issues of fact.

ARTICLE XI. MISCELLANEOUS RULES

Rule 1101. Applicability of Rules

(a) Courts and judges. These rules apply to the United States district courts, the District Court of Guam, the District Court of the Virgin Islands, the District Court for the Northern Mariana Islands, the United States courts of appeals, the United States Claims Court, and to United States bankruptcy judges and United States magistrate judges, in the actions, cases, and proceedings and to the extent hereinafter set forth. The terms "judge" and "court" in these rules include United States bankruptcy judges and United States magistrate judges.

(b) Proceedings generally. These rules apply generally to civil actions and proceedings, including admiralty and maritime cases, to criminal cases and proceedings, to contempt proceedings except those in which the court may act summarily, and to proceedings and cases under title 11, United States Code.

(c) Rule of privilege. The rule with respect to privileges applies at all stages of all actions, cases, and proceedings.

(d) Rules inapplicable. The rules (other than with respect to privileges) do not apply in the following situations:

(1) Preliminary questions of fact. The determination of questions of fact preliminary to admissibility of evidence when the issue is to be determined by the court under rule 104.

(2) Grand jury. Proceedings before grand juries.

(3) Miscellaneous proceedings. Proceedings for extradition or rendition; preliminary examinations in criminal cases; sentencing, or granting or revoking probation; issuance of warrants for arrest, criminal summonses, and search warrants; and proceedings with respect to release on bail or otherwise.

(e) Rules applicable in part. In the following proceedings these rules apply to the extent that matters of evidence are not provided for in the statutes which govern procedure therein or in other rules prescribed by the Supreme Court pursuant to statutory authority: the trial of minor and petty offenses by United States magistrates; review of agency actions when the facts are subject to trial de novo under section 706(2)(F) of title 5, United States Code; review of orders of the Secretary of Agriculture under section 2 of the Act entitled "An Act to authorize association of producers of agricultural products" approved February 18, 1922 (7 U.S.C. 292), and under sections 6 and 7(c) of the Perishable Agricultural Commodities Act, 1930 (7 U.S.C. 499f, 499g(c)); naturalization and revocation of naturalization under sections 310–318 of the Immigration and Nationality Act (8 U.S.C. 1421–1429); prize proceedings in admiralty under sections 7651–7681 of title 10, United States Code; review of orders of the Secretary of the Interior under section 2 of the Act entitled "An Act authorizing associations of producers of aquatic products" approved June 25, 1934 (15 U.S.C. 522); review of orders of petroleum control boards under section 5 of the Act entitled "An Act to regulate interstate and foreign commerce in petroleum and its products by prohibiting the shipment in such commerce of petroleum and its products produced in violation of State law, and for other purposes", approved February 22, 1935 (15 U.S.C. 715d); actions for fines, penalties, or forfeitures under part V of title IV of the Tariff Act of 1930 (19 U.S.C. 1581–1624), or under the Anti-Smuggling Act (19 U.S.C. 1701–1711); criminal libel for condemnation, exclusion of imports, or other proceedings under the Federal Food, Drug, and Cosmetic Act (21 U.S.C. 301–392); disputes between seamen under sections 4079, 4080, and 4081 of the Revised Statutes (22 U.S.C. 256–258); habeas corpus under sections 2241–2254 of title 28, United States Code; motions to vacate, set aside or correct sentence under section 2255 of title 28, United States Code; actions for penalties for refusal to transport destitute seamen under section 4578 of the Revised Statutes (46 U.S.C. 679); actions against the United States under the Act entitled "An Act authorizing suits against the United States in admiralty for damage caused by and salvage service rendered to public vessels belonging to the United States, and for other purposes", approved March 3, 1925 (46 U.S.C. 781–790), as implemented by section 7730 of title 10, United States Code.

Rule 1102.   Amendments

Amendments to the Federal Rules of Evidence may be made as provided in section 2072 of title 28 of the United States Code.

Rule 1103.   Title

These rules may be known and cited as the Federal Rules of Evidence.

*

Appendix B

RESEARCHING EVIDENCE LAW

Analysis

Section 1. Introduction

Evidence Law, A Student's Guide to the Law of Evidence as Applied in American Trials provides a strong base for analyzing even the most complex problem involving the law of evidence. Whether your research requires examination of rules, statutes, case law, expert commentary, or other materials, West books and Westlaw are excellent sources of information.

To keep you informed of current developments, Westlaw provides frequently updated databases. With Westlaw, you have unparalleled legal research resources at your fingertips.

Additional Resources

If you have not previously used Westlaw or if you have questions not covered in this appendix, call the West Reference Attorneys at 1–800–REF–ATTY (1–800–733–2889). The West Reference Attorneys are trained, licensed attorneys, available 24 hours a day to assist you with your Westlaw search questions. To subscribe to Westlaw, call 1–800–344–5008 or visit westlaw.com at **www.westlaw.com**.

Section 2.   Westlaw Databases

Each database on Westlaw is assigned an abbreviation called an *identifier*, which you can use to access the database. You can find identifiers for Westlaw databases in the online Westlaw Directory and in the printed *Westlaw Database Directory*. When you need to know more detailed information about a database, use Scope. Scope contains coverage information, lists of related databases, and valuable search tips.

The following chart lists selected Westlaw databases that contain information pertaining to evidence law. For a complete list of evidence law databases, see the online Westlaw Directory or the printed *Westlaw Database Directory*. Because new information is continually being added to Westlaw, you should also check the tabbed Westlaw page and the online Westlaw Directory for new database information.

Selected Evidence Law Databases on Westlaw

Database	Identifier	Coverage
Federal Statutes and Regulations		
United States Code Annotated®	USCA	Current data
United States Public Laws	US–PL	Current data
Code of Federal Regulations	CFR	Current data
Federal Register	FR	Begins with July 1980
Legislative History–U.S. Code, 1948 to Present	LH	Begins with 1948
Federal Rules and Orders		
Federal Rules	US–RULES	Current data
Federal Orders	US–ORDERS	Current data
Federal Rules Decisions Rules	FRD–RULES	Begins with 1938
Federal Rules of Practice and Procedure Advisory Committee Minutes	US–RULESCOMM	Varies by committee

Database	Identifier	Coverage
Federal and State Case Law Combined		
Federal and State Case Law	ALLCASES	Begins with 1945
Federal and State Case Law–Before 1945	ALLCASES–OLD	1789–1944
Federal Case Law		
Federal Case Law	ALLFEDS	Begins with 1945
Federal Case Law–Before 1945	ALLFEDS–OLD	1789–1944
U.S. Supreme Court Cases	SCT	Begins with 1945
U.S. Supreme Court Cases–Before 1945	SCT–OLD	1790–1944
U.S. Courts of Appeals Cases	CTA	Begins with 1945
U.S. Courts of Appeals Cases–Before 1945	CTA–OLD	1891–1944
U.S. District Courts Cases	DCT	Begins with 1945
U.S. District Courts Cases–Before 1945	DCT–OLD	1789–1944
State Statutes and Regulations		
State Statutes–Annotated	ST–ANN–ALL	Varies by state
Individual State Statutes–Annotated	XX–ST–ANN (where XX is a state's two-letter postal abbreviation)	Varies by state
State Administrative Code Multibase	ADC–ALL	Varies by state
Individual State Administrative Code	XX–ADC (where XX is a state's two-letter postal abbreviation)	Varies by state
State Rules and Orders		
State Court Rules	RULES–ALL	Varies by state
Individual State Court Rules	XX–RULES (where XX is a state's two-letter postal abbreviation)	Varies by state

Database	Identifier	Coverage
State Court Orders	ORDERS–ALL	Varies by state
Individual State Court Orders	XX–ORDERS (where XX is a state's two-letter postal abbreviation)	Varies by state

State Case Law

State Case Law	ALLSTATES	Begins with 1945
State Case Law Before 1945	ALLSTATES–OLD	1821–1944
Individual State Cases	XX–CS (where XX is a state's two-letter postal abbreviation)	Varies by state

Journals and Law Reviews

Texts and Periodicals–All Law Reviews, Texts, and Bar Journals	TP–ALL	Varies by publication
Litigation–Law Reviews, Texts, and Bar Journals	LTG–TP	Varies by publication
American Journal of Trial Advocacy	AMJTA	Selected coverage begins with 1982 (vol. 6); full coverage begins with 1993 (vol. 17)
Federal Courts Law Review	FEDCTLR	Full coverage begins with 1998 (vol. 1998)
Federal Rules Decisions Articles	FRD–ART	Begins with 1938
Journal of Appellate Practice and Process	JAPPPR	Full coverage begins with 1999 (vol. 1)
Journal of Forensic Document Examination	JFDE	Full coverage begins with 1993 (vol. 6)
Suffolk Journal of Trial and Appellate Advocacy	SFKJTAA	Full coverage begins with 1995 (vol. 1)
Trial	JTLATRIAL	Selected coverage begins with 1997 (vol. 33, no. 11)
Trial Magazine	TRIAL–MAG	Begins with January 1995

Legal Texts and Practice Materials

Texts and Periodicals–All Law Reviews, Texts, and Bar Journals	TP–ALL	Varies by publication
Litigation–Law Reviews, Texts, and Bar Journals	LTG–TP	Varies by publication

Database	Identifier	Coverage
Admissibility of Evidence: A Manual for Pennsylvania Trial Lawyers	PAAOE	Second edition
Admissibility of Evidence in North Carolina	NCPRAC–EVD	Current data
Agnor's Georgia Evidence	GAEVIDENCE	Third edition
Alabama Evidence	ALEVID	Third edition
Andrews Expert and Scientific Evidence Litigation Reporter	ANESELR	Begins with December 2003
Baldwin's Ohio Practice–Evidence	OHPRAC–EVID	Current data
Bankruptcy Evidence Manual	BKRMANUAL	2003 edition
California Evidence	WITEVID	Fourth edition
Courtroom Handbook on Federal Evidence	CTHB–FEDEVID	2003 edition
Courtroom Handbook on Georgia Evidence	GAHANDEVID	2003 edition
Daniel's Georgia Handbook on Criminal Evidence	GACRIMEVID	2003 edition
Daubert Citator	DAUBERT	July 1993–December 2000
Evidence in Negligence Cases	PLIREF–NEGEVD	10th edition
Eyewitness Identification: Legal and Practical Problems	EYEWITN	Current data
Federal Evidence (Mueller and Kirkpatrick)	FEDEV	Second edition
Federal Rules of Evidence	FEDRLSEV	Third edition
Federal Rules of Evidence with Trial Objections	FEDEVID–OBJ	Current data
Federal Testimonial Privileges	FEDPRIV	Second edition
Georgia Rules of Evidence	GARULEEVID	Second edition
Gibson: Criminal Law Evidence, Practice and Procedure	CRLEVIDPP	Current data
Green Georgia Law of Evidence	GALAWEVID	Fifth edition
Handbook of Federal Evidence	FEDEVID	Fifth edition
Hearsay Handbook 4th	HEARSAY	Current data

Database	Identifier	Coverage
Herman and McLaughlin Admissibility of Evidence in Civil Cases: A Manual for Georgia Trial Lawyers	GAEVIDCIVL	Current data
Indiana Practice Series: Courtroom Handbook on Indiana Evidence	INPRAC–CHIE	Current data
Indiana Practice Series: Evidence	INPRAC–EVID	Current data
Louisiana Civil Law Treatise–Evidence and Proof	LACIVL–EVID	Current data
Louisiana Evidence	LA–EVID	Fourth edition
Massachusetts Practice Series: Evidence	MAPRAC–EVID	Current data
McCormick on Evidence	MCMK–EVID	Fifth edition
Michigan Court Rules Practice–Evidence	MICRP–EVID	Current data
Military Criminal Law Evidence	MCLE	July 15, 1987
Minnesota Practice Series: Courtroom Handbook of Minnesota Evidence	MNPRAC–CHME	Current data
Minnesota Practice Series: Evidence	MNPRAC–EVID	Current data
Missouri Practice Series: Courtroom Handbook on Missouri Evidence	MOPRAC–CHME	Current data
Missouri Practice Series: Missouri Evidence	MOPRAC–ME	Current data
Modern Scientific Evidence: The Law and Science of Expert Testimony	MODSCIEVID	Current data
New Jersey Practice Series: Evidence Rules Annotated	NJPRAC–ERA	Current data
Oklahoma Practice Series: Courtroom Guide to the Oklahoma Evidence Code	OKPRAC–CG	Current data
Oklahoma Practice Series: Evidence, Commentary on the Law of Evidence	OKPRAC–ECLE	Current data
Overly on Electronic Evidence in California	CAELECEVID	2003 edition
Reference Manual on Scientific Evidence	RMSCIEVID	Second edition

Database	Identifier	Coverage
Simons on California Evidence	SIMCAEVID	Current data
Texas Practice Guide: Evidence	TXPG–EVID	2003 edition
Texas Practice Series: Handbook on Texas Evidence	TX–PRACHE	Current data
Texas Practice Series: Rules of Evidence	TX–PRACRE	Current data
The Rutter Group–California Practice Guide: Civil Trials and Evidence	TRG–CACIVEV	2002 edition
The Rutter Group–California Practice Guide: Federal Civil Trials and Evidence	TRG–FEDCIVEV	2003 edition
Washington Practice Series: Evidence Law and Practice	WAPRAC–ELP	Current data
Washington Practice Series: Handbook on Washington Evidence	WAPRAC–HWE	Current data
Watt's Manual of Criminal Evidence	WATTCRIMEV	Current data
West's Florida Practice Series: Ehrhardt's Florida Evidence	FLPRAC–EVID	Current data
Wharton's Criminal Evidence	CRIMEVID	Current data
Wisconsin Practice Series–Wisconsin Evidence	WIPRAC–WE	Current data
Young's Federal Rules of Evidence	YFREVID	Current data

Legal Newsletters, Current Awareness Materials, and Directories

Andrews Expert and Scientific Evidence Litigation Reporter	ANESELR	Begins with December 2003
Westlaw Topical Highlights–Litigation	WTH–LTG	Current data
West Legal Directory®–Litigation	WLD–LIT	Current data

Section 3.   Retrieving a Document with a Citation: Find and Hypertext Links

3.1   Find

Find is a Westlaw service that allows you to retrieve a document by entering its citation. Find allows you to retrieve documents from any page in westlaw.com without accessing or changing databases. Find is available for many documents, including case law (state and federal), the *United States Code Annotated*, state statutes, administrative materials, and texts and periodicals.

To use Find, simply type the citation in the *Find this document by citation* text box on the tabbed Westlaw page and click **GO**. The following list provides some examples:

To retrieve this document:	Access Find and type:
Fed. R. Evid. 901	**fre 901**
Cal. Evid. Code § 795	**ca evid s 795**
U.S. v. Owens 108 S. Ct. 838 (1988)	**108 sct 838**
Kelley v. American Heyer–Schulte Corp. 957 F. Supp. 873 (W.D. Tex. 1997)	**957 fsupp 873**

For a complete list of publications that can be retrieved with Find and their abbreviations, click **Find** on the toolbar and then click **Publications List**.

3.2 Hypertext Links

Use hypertext links to move from one location to another on Westlaw. For example, use hypertext links to go directly from the statute, case, or law review article you are viewing to a cited statute, case, or article; from a headnote to the corresponding text in the opinion; or from an entry in a statutes index to the full text of the statute.

Section 4.   Searching with Natural Language

Overview: With Natural Language, you can retrieve documents by simply describing your issue in plain English. If you are a relatively new Westlaw user, Natural Language searching can make it easier for you to retrieve cases that are on point. If you are an experienced Westlaw user, Natural Language gives you a valuable alternative search method to the Terms and Connectors search method described in Section 5.

When you enter a Natural Language description, Westlaw automatically identifies legal phrases, removes common words, and generates variations of terms in your description. Westlaw then searches for the concepts in your description. Concepts may include significant terms, phrases, legal citations, or topic and key numbers. Westlaw retrieves the documents that most closely match the concepts in your description, beginning with the document most likely to match.

4.1 Natural Language Search

Access a database, such as the U.S. Courts of Appeals Cases database (CTA). Click **Natural Language** and type the following description in the text box:

dismissal of case as sanction for spoliation of evidence

4.2 Browsing Search Results

Citations List: The citations list lists the documents retrieved by the search. Click a document's title to display the full text of the document in the right frame.

Best Mode: To display the best portion (the portion that most closely matches your description) of each document in a Natural Language search result, click the **Best** arrows at the bottom of the right frame.

Term Mode: Click the **Term** arrows at the bottom of the right frame to display portions of the document that contain your search terms.

Previous/Next Document: Click the left or right **Doc** arrow at the bottom of the right frame to view the previous or next document in the search result.

4.3 Next 20 Documents

Westlaw displays the 20 documents that most closely match the concepts in your Natural Language description, beginning with the document most likely to match. If you want to view an additional 20 documents, click the right arrow at the bottom of the Result List tab in the left frame.

Section 5. Searching with Terms and Connectors

Overview: With Terms and Connectors searching, you enter a query consisting of key terms from your issue and connectors specifying the relationship between these terms.

Terms and Connectors searching is useful when you want to retrieve a document for which you know specific details, such as the title or the fact situation. Terms and Connectors searching is also useful when you want to retrieve all documents containing specific terms.

5.1 Terms

Plurals and Possessives: Plurals are automatically retrieved when you enter the singular form of a term. This is true for both regular and irregular plurals (e.g., **child** retrieves *children*). If you enter the plural form of a term, you will not retrieve the singular form.

If you enter the nonpossessive form of a term, Westlaw automatically retrieves the possessive form as well. However, if you enter the possessive form, only the possessive form is retrieved.

Compound Words and Abbreviations: When a compound word is one of your search terms, use a hyphen to retrieve all forms of the word. For example, the term **non-hearsay** retrieves *non-hearsay, nonhearsay,* and *non hearsay.*

When using an abbreviation as a search term, place a period after each of the letters to retrieve any of its forms. For example, the term **f.r.e.** retrieves *fre, f.r.e., f r e,* and *f. r. e.* The abbreviation does not retrieve the phrase *federal rules of evidence*, so remember to add additional alternative terms such as **"federal rule of evidence"** to your query.

The Root Expander and the Universal Character: When you use the Terms and Connectors search method, placing the root expander (!) at the end of a root term generates all other terms with that root. For example, adding the ! to the root *testi* in the query

expert /s testi!

instructs Westlaw to retrieve such terms as *testify*, *testified*, *testifying*, and *testimony*.

The universal character (*) stands for one character and can be inserted in the middle or at the end of a term. For example, the term

withdr*w

will retrieve *withdraw* and *withdrew*. Adding three asterisks to the root *elect*

elect* * *

instructs Westlaw to retrieve all forms of the root with up to three additional characters. Terms such as *elected* or *election* are retrieved by this query. However, terms with more than three letters following the root, such as *electronic,* are not retrieved. Plurals are always retrieved, even if the plural form of the term has more than three letters following the root.

Phrase Searching: To search for an exact phrase, place it within quotation marks. For example, to search for references to *judicial notice*, type **"judicial notice"**. When you are using the Terms and Connectors search method, you should use phrase searching only if you are certain that the terms in the phrase will not appear in any other order.

5.2 Alternative Terms

After selecting the terms for your query, consider which alternative terms are necessary. For example, if you are searching for the term *admissible*, you might also want to search for the term *inadmissible*. You should consider both synonyms and antonyms as alternative terms. You can also use the Westlaw thesaurus to add alternative terms to your query.

5.3 Connectors

After selecting terms and alternative terms for your query, use connectors to specify the relationship that must exist between search terms in your retrieved documents. The connectors are described below:

Type:	To retrieve documents with:	Example:
& (and)	both search terms	**expert & opinion**
or (space)	either search term or both search terms	**relevan! irrelevant!**

/p	search terms in the same paragraph	**hearsay /p exception**
/s	search terms in the same sentence	**character /s witness**
+s	the first search term preceding the second within the same sentence	**burden +s prov! proof**
/n	search terms within *n* terms of each other (where *n* is a number)	**refresh! /5 memory**
+n	the first search term preceding the second by *n* terms (where *n* is a number)	**excited +3 utterance**
" "	search terms appearing in the same order as in the quotation marks	**"subsequent remedial measure"**

Type:	**To exclude documents with:**	**Example:**
% (but not)	search terms following the % symbol	**d.n.a. "deoxyribonucleic acid" % criminal**

5.4 Field Restrictions

Overview: Documents in each Westlaw database consist of several segments, or *fields*. One field may contain the citation, another the title, another the synopsis, and so forth. Not all databases contain the same fields. Also depending on the database, fields with the same name may contain different types of information.

To view a list of fields and their contents for a specific database, see Scope for that database. Note that in some databases not every field is available for every document.

To retrieve only those documents containing your search terms in a specific field, restrict your search to that field. To restrict your search to a specific field, type the field name or abbreviation followed by your search terms enclosed in parentheses. For example, to retrieve a U.S. Supreme Court case titled *Daubert v. Merrell Dow Pharmaceuticals, Inc.*, access the U.S. Supreme Court Cases database (SCT) and search for your terms in the title field (ti):

ti(daubert & "merrell dow")

The fields discussed below are available in Westlaw case law databases you might use for researching issues related to evidence.

Digest and Synopsis Fields: The digest (di) and synopsis (sy) fields summarize the main points of a case. The synopsis field contains a brief description of a case. The digest field contains the topic and headnote fields and includes the complete hierarchy of concepts used by West editors to classify the headnotes to specific West digest topic and key numbers. Restricting your search to the synopsis and digest fields limits your result to cases in which your terms are related to a major issue in the case.

Consider restricting your search to one or both of these fields if

- you are searching for common terms or terms with more than one meaning, and you need to narrow your search; or

- you cannot narrow your search by using a smaller database.

For example, to retrieve New York cases that discuss the present sense impression exception to the hearsay rule, access the New York Cases database (NY–CS) and type the following query:

sy,di(hearsay /p "present sense impression")

Headnote Field: The headnote field (he) is part of the digest field but does not contain topic numbers, hierarchical classification information, or key numbers. The headnote field contains a one-sentence summary for each point of law in a case and any supporting citations given by the author of the opinion. A headnote field restriction is useful when you are searching for specific statutory sections or rule numbers. For example, to retrieve headnotes from federal district court cases that cite Fed. R. Evid. 613(b), access the U.S. District Courts Cases database (DCT) and type the following query:

he(613(b))

Topic Field: The topic field (to) is also part of the digest field. It contains hierarchical classification information, including the West digest topic names and numbers and the key numbers. You should restrict your search to the topic field in a case law database if

- a digest field search retrieves too many documents; or

- you want to retrieve cases with digest paragraphs classified under more than one topic.

For example, the topic Evidence has the topic number 157. To retrieve state cases that discuss dying declarations, access the State Case Law database (ALLSTATES) and type a query like the following:

to(157) /p "dying declaration"

To retrieve cases classified under more than one topic and key number, search for your terms in the topic field. For example, to retrieve recent federal cases discussing evidence in criminal proceedings, which may be classified to Constitutional Law (92), Criminal Law (110), Double Jeopardy (135H), Evidence (157), Grand Jury (193), Weapons (406), or Witnesses (410), among other topics, access the Federal Case Law database (ALLFEDS) and type a query like the following:

to(eviden! /p crim!) & da(aft 2003)

For a complete list of West digest topics and their corresponding topic numbers, access the Custom Digest by choosing **Key Numbers and Digest** from the *More* drop-down list on the toolbar.

> *Note*: Slip opinions and cases from topical services do not contain the West digest, headnote, and topic fields.

Prelim and Caption Fields: When searching in a database containing statutes, rules, or regulations, restrict your search to the prelim (pr) and caption (ca) fields to retrieve documents in which your terms are important enough to appear in a section name or heading. For example, to retrieve federal rules regarding hearsay, access the Federal Rules database (US–RULES) and type the following:

pr,ca(hearsay)

5.5 Date Restrictions

You can use Westlaw to retrieve documents *decided* or *issued* before, after, or on a specified date, as well as within a range of dates. The following sample queries contain date restrictions:

da(2003) & "work product"

da(aft 1998) & presumed /3 fact

da(12/20/1995) & prior /s conviction

You can also search for documents *added to a database* on or after a specified date, as well as within a range of dates, which is useful for updating your research. The following sample queries contain added-date restrictions:

ad(aft 1999) & "harmless error"

ad(aft 11/9/2001 & bef 6/23/2002) & impeach! /s witness

Section 6. Searching with Topic and Key Numbers

To retrieve cases that address a specific point of law, use topic and key numbers as your search terms. If you have an on-point case, run a search using the topic and key number from the relevant headnote in an appropriate database to find other cases containing headnotes classified to that topic and key number. For example, to search for federal courts of appeals cases containing headnotes classified under topic 157 (Evidence) and key number 146 (Tendency to Mislead or Confuse), access the U.S. Courts of Appeals Cases database (CTA) and enter the following query:

157k146

For a complete list of West digest topics and their corresponding topic numbers, access the Custom Digest by choosing **Key Numbers and Digest** from the *More* drop-down list on the toolbar.

> *Note*: Slip opinions and cases from topical services do not contain the West topic and key numbers.

6.1 Custom Digest

The Custom Digest contains the complete topic and key number outline used by West editors to classify headnotes. You can use the Custom Digest to obtain a single document containing all case law headnotes from a specific jurisdiction that are classified under a particular topic and key number.

Access the Custom Digest by choosing **Key Numbers and Digest** from the *More* drop-down list on the toolbar. Select up to 10 topics and key numbers from the easy-to-browse outline and click **Search**. Then follow the displayed instructions.

For example, to research issues involving evidence, scroll down the Custom Digest page until topic 157, *Evidence*, is displayed. Click the plus symbols (+) to display key number information. Select the check box next to each key number you want to include in your search, then click **Search**. Select the jurisdiction from which you want to retrieve head-notes and, if desired, type additional search terms and select a date restriction. Click **Search**.

6.2 KeySearch

KeySearch is a research tool that helps you find cases and secondary sources in a specific area of the law. KeySearch guides you through the selection of terms from a classification system based on the West Key Number System® and then uses the key numbers and their underlying concepts to automatically formulate a query for you.

To access KeySearch, click **KeySearch** on the toolbar. Then browse the list of topics and subtopics and select a topic or subtopic to search by clicking the hypertext links. For example, to search for sources that discuss the best evidence rule, click **Evidence and Witnesses** below *Civil Procedure* at the first KeySearch page. Then click **Best Evidence Rule** on the next page. Select the source from which you want to retrieve documents and, if desired, type additional search terms. Click **Search**.

Section 7.   Verifying Your Research with Citation Research Services

Overview: A citation research service, such as KeyCite, is a tool that helps you ensure that your cases, statutes, regulations, and administrative decisions are good law; helps you retrieve cases, legislation, articles, or other documents that cite them; and helps you verify the spelling and format of your citations.

7.1 KeyCite for Cases

KeyCite for cases covers case law on Westlaw, including unpublished opinions. KeyCite for cases provides the following:

- direct appellate history of a case, including related references, which are opinions involving the same parties and facts but resolving different issues

- negative indirect history of a case, which consists of cases outside the direct appellate line that may have a negative impact on its precedential value

- the title, parallel citations, court of decision, docket number, and filing date of a case

- citations to cases, administrative decisions, secondary sources, and briefs on Westlaw that have cited a case

- complete integration with the West Key Number System so you can track legal issues discussed in a case

7.2 KeyCite for Statutes and Regulations

KeyCite for statutes and regulations covers the *United States Code Annotated* (USCA®), the *Code of Federal Regulations* (CFR), statutes from all 50 states, and regulations from selected states. KeyCite for statutes and regulations provides the following:

- links to session laws or rules amending or repealing a statute or regulation

- statutory credits and historical notes

- citations to pending legislation affecting a federal statute or a statute from selected states

- citations to cases, administrative decisions, secondary sources, and briefs that have cited a statute or regulation

7.3 KeyCite for Administrative Decisions

KeyCite for administrative decisions includes the following:

- National Labor Relations Board decisions beginning with 1935

- Board of Contract Appeals decisions (varies by agency)

- Board of Immigration Appeals decisions beginning with 1940

- Comptroller General decisions beginning with 1921

- Environmental Protection Agency decisions beginning with 1974

- Federal Communications Commission decisions beginning with 1960

- Federal Energy Regulatory Commission (Federal Power Commission) decisions beginning with 1931

- Internal Revenue Service revenue rulings beginning with 1954

- Internal Revenue Service revenue procedures beginning with 1954

- Internal Revenue Service private letter rulings beginning with 1954

- Internal Revenue Service technical advice memoranda beginning with 1954

- Public Utilities Reports beginning with 1966

- U.S. Merit Systems Protection Board decisions beginning with 1979

- U.S. Patent and Trademark Office decisions beginning with 1984

- U.S. Tax Court (Board of Tax Appeals) decisions beginning with 1924

- U.S. patents beginning with 1976

7.4 KeyCite Alert

KeyCite Alert monitors the status of your cases, statutes, regulations, and administrative decisions and automatically sends you updates at the frequency you specify when their KeyCite information changes. To access KeyCite Alert, choose **KeyCite Alert** from the *More* drop-down list on the toolbar.

Section 8.   Researching with Westlaw: Examples

8.1   Retrieving Law Review Articles

Law review articles are often a good place to begin researching a legal issue. Law review articles serve as an excellent introduction to a new topic or review for an old one, providing terminology to help you formulate a query; as a finding tool for pertinent primary authority, such as rules, statutes, and cases; and in some instances, as persuasive secondary authority.

Suppose you need to gain background information on the admissibility of subsequent remedial measures.

Solution

- To retrieve law review articles relevant to your issue, access the Texts and Periodicals–All Law Reviews, Texts, and Bar Journals database (TP–ALL). Using the Natural Language search method, enter a description like the following:

subsequent remedial measure

- If you have a citation to an article in a specific publication, use Find to retrieve it. For more information on Find, see Section 3.1 of this appendix. For example, to retrieve the article found at 70 Defense Counsel Journal 240, access Find and type the following:

70 def couns j 240

If you know the title of an article but not the journal in which it was published, access TP–ALL and search for key terms in the title field. For example, to retrieve the article "Subsequent Remedial Measures 2000 and Beyond," type the following Terms and Connectors query:

ti(subsequent & remedial & 2000)

8.2 Retrieving Rules

Suppose you need to retrieve federal rules dealing with expert opinion.

Solution

- Access the Federal Rules database (US–RULES). Search for your terms in the prelim and caption fields using the Terms and Connectors search method:

pr,ca(expert & opinion testi!)

- When you know the citation for a specific rule, use Find to retrieve it. For example, to retrieve Fed. R. Evid. 404, access Find and type the following:

fre 404

- To look at surrounding rules, use the Table of Contents service. Click **Table of Contents** on the Links tab in the left frame. To display a rule listed in the Table of Contents, click its hypertext link. You can also use Documents in Sequence to retrieve the rule following Fed. R. Evid. 404 even if that subsequent rule was not retrieved with your search or Find request. Choose **Documents in Sequence** from the *Tools* menu at the bottom of the right frame.

8.3 Retrieving Case Law

Suppose you need to retrieve Florida case law dealing with the physician-patient privilege.

Solution

- Access the Florida Cases database (FL–CS). Type a Terms and Connectors query such as the following:

doctor physician /5 patient /s privilege

- When you know the citation for a specific case, use Find to retrieve it. For more information on Find, see Section 3.1 of this appendix. For example, to retrieve *Acosta v. Richter*, 671 So.2d 149 (Fla. 1996), access Find and type the following:

671 so2d 149

- If you find a topic and key number that is on point, run a search using that topic and key number to retrieve additional cases discussing that point of law. For example, to retrieve cases from other states containing headnotes classified under topic 410 (Witnesses) and key number 209 (Relation of Physician and Patient), access ALLSTATES and type the following query:

410k209

- To retrieve cases written by a particular judge, add a judge field (ju) restriction to your query. For example, to retrieve opinions written by Justice Anstead of the Florida Supreme Court that contain headnotes classified under topic 410 (Witnesses), access the Florida Cases database (FL–CS) and type the following query:

ju(anstead) & to(410)

- You can also use KeySearch and the Custom Digest to retrieve cases and headnotes that discuss the issue you are researching.

8.4   Using KeyCite

Suppose one of the cases you retrieve in your case law research is *Daubert v. Merrell Dow Pharmaceuticals, Inc.*, 113 S. Ct. 2786 (1993). You want to determine whether this case is good law and to find other cases or sources that have cited this case.

Solution

- Use KeyCite to retrieve direct and negative indirect history for *Daubert*. Access KeyCite and type **113 sct 2786**.

- Use KeyCite to display citing references for *Daubert*. Click **Citing References** on the Links tab in the left frame.

8.5   Following Recent Developments

If you are researching issues related to evidence law, it is important to keep up with recent developments. How can you do this efficiently?

Solution

One of the easiest ways to follow recent developments in evidence and litigation is to access the Westlaw Topical Highlights–Litigation database (WTH–LTG). The WTH–LTG database contains summaries of recent legal developments, including court decisions, legislation, and materials released by administrative agencies. When you access WTH–LTG, you automatically retrieve a list of documents added to the database in the last two weeks.

You can also use the WestClip® clipping service to stay informed of recent developments of interest to you. WestClip will run your Terms and Connectors queries on a regular basis and deliver the results to you automatically. You can run WestClip queries in legal and news and information databases.

Table of Cases

A

B

E

G

I

J

U

V

W

*

Table of Statutes and Rules

UNITED STATES

UNITED STATES CONSTITUTION

Amend.	This Work Sec.	Note
1	8.20	
4	12.05	
5	8.18	
5	8.18	235
5	8.18	236
5	12.05	
6	7.15	179
6	7.51	436
6	7.54	
6	9.11	160
6	12.05	
8	9.10	148
8	12.05	
14	8.18	
14	12.05	

UNITED STATES CODE ANNOTATED

13 U.S.C.A.—Census

Sec.	This Work Sec.	Note
8(b)	8.19	252
9(a)	8.19	252

28 U.S.C.A.—Judiciary and Judicial Procedure

Sec.	This Work Sec.	Note
2671	5.58	394

42 U.S.C.A.—The Public Health and Welfare

Sec.	This Work Sec.	Note
290ee–3	8.14	167
1983	7.27	242
1983	10.05	186

POPULAR NAME ACTS

CIVIL RIGHTS ACT OF 1964

Sec.	This Work Sec.	Note
Tit. VII	4.08	57
Tit. VII	5.10	104

STATE STATUTES

ALABAMA CODE

Sec.	This Work Sec.	Note
12–21–45	5.58	393
12–21–165	6.02	14

ALASKA RULES OF EVIDENCE

Rule	This Work Sec.	Note
404	5.32	251
503(a)(2)	8.09	89
505(a)(1)	8.16	179
609(a)	9.09	99
613(b)	9.05	45

ARIZONA REVISED STATUTES

Sec.	This Work Sec.	Note
8.16	8.16	178
12–2232	8.17	208
13–4062(1)	8.16	178

WEST'S ANNOTATED CALIFORNIA CIVIL CODE

Sec.	This Work Sec.	Note
3294	4.04	16

WEST'S ANNOTATED CALIFORNIA EVIDENCE CODE

Sec.	This Work Sec.	Note
110	4.06	27
115	4.03	3
210	5.03	14
240(a)(3)	7.57	540
240(c)	7.57	540
500	4.05	20
550	4.06	28
600(a)	4.08	51

WEST'S ANNOTATED CALIFORNIA EVIDENCE CODE

WEST'S ANNOTATED CALIFORNIA FAMILY CODE

WEST'S ANNOTATED CALIFORNIA PENAL CODE

CONNECTICUT GENERAL STATUTES ANNOTATED

WEST'S FLORIDA STATUTES ANNOTATED

OFFICIAL CODE OF GEORGIA ANNOTATED

HAWAII RULES OF EVIDENCE

IDAHO RULES OF EVIDENCE

ILLINOIS COMPILED STATUTES

WEST'S ANNOTATED INDIANA CODE

IOWA RULES OF EVIDENCE

KANSAS STATUTES ANNOTATED

MAINE RULES OF EVIDENCE

Rule	This Work Sec.	Note
403	5.59	403

MARYLAND ANNOTATED CODE

Art.	This Work Sec.	Note
27, § 461A	5.09	87

MARYLAND CODE, COURTS AND JUDICIAL PROCEEDINGS

Sec.	This Work Sec.	Note
9–109	8.13	140

MASSACHUSETTS GENERAL LAWS ANNOTATED

Ch.	This Work Sec.	Note
233, § 21B	5.09	85
233, § 23D	5.55	351
233, § 65	7.57	534

MICHIGAN COMPILED LAWS ANNOTATED

Sec.	This Work Sec.	Note
333.18237	8.13	139
600.2157	8.13	139
600.2162	8.17	191
750.411	8.13	151
750.520j	5.09	85

MICHIGAN RULES OF EVIDENCE

Rule	This Work Sec.	Note
601	6.02	14
601	6.02	15

MINNESOTA STATUTES ANNOTATED

Sec.	This Work Sec.	Note
595.02	8.13	141
595.02	8.17	209
595.02	8.17	210
595.02(1)(a)	8.15	176
595.02(1)(a)	8.16	178
595.02(1)(a)	8.16	179
595.02(1)(c)	8.20	258
595.02(1)(f)	6.02	15
595.02(1)(i)	8.20	267
595.02(1)(j)	8.20	268
595.02(1)(*l*)	6.03	20
595.02(3)	7.57	539
595.02(a)	8.16	183
595.02(a)	8.17	191

MINNESOTA STATUTES ANNOTATED

Sec.	This Work Sec.	Note
595.02(a)	8.17	208
595.021—595.024	8.20	262
595.024(2)	8.20	263

MINNESOTA RULES OF CIVIL PROCEDURE

Rule	This Work Sec.	Note
35.03	8.13	154

MINNESOTA RULES OF CRIMINAL PROCEDURE

Rule	This Work Sec.	Note
7.05	5.32	250
31.02	12.04	69

MINNESOTA RULES OF EVIDENCE

Rule	This Work Sec.	Note
403	5.04	38
403	11.08	64
404(c)	5.09	85
404(c)	5.09	88
613(b)	9.05	45
616	9.08	90
616	9.10	144
801(d)(1)(B)	7.05	45
801(d)(1)(B)	9.12	176

REVISED STATUTES OF MISSOURI

Sec.	This Work Sec.	Note
566.025	5.10	107

MONTANA CODE ANNOTATED

Sec.	This Work Sec.	Note
26–1–802	8.16	178
26–1–802	8.16	179

NEBRASKA REVISED STATUTES

Sec.	This Work Sec.	Note
27–505	8.17	200

NEW JERSEY STATUTES ANNOTATED

Sec.	This Work Sec.	Note
2A:84A–21	8.20	262
2A:84A–22	8.17	191

NEW YORK, MCKINNEY'S STATUTES

Sec.	This Work Sec.	Note
Pt. 3, c. 7, tit. 3, art. 8, § 73	8.01	3

NEW YORK, MCKINNEY'S CIVIL PRACTICE LAW AND RULES

Sec.	This Work Sec.	Note
4532–a	11.08	51

NEW YORK, MCKINNEY'S JUDICIARY LAW

Sec.	This Work Sec.	Note
269	12.03	

NORTH CAROLINA GENERAL STATUTES

Sec.	This Work Sec.	Note
8–57	8.15	176
8–57	8.16	180
8–85	7.47	410

NORTH CAROLINA RULES OF EVIDENCE

Rule	This Work Sec.	Note
601(b)	6.02	15

OHIO RULES OF EVIDENCE

Rule	This Work Sec.	Note
601(A)	6.02	14
601(A)	6.03	18
607	9.01	3

OREGON REVISED STATUTES

Sec.	This Work Sec.	Note
40–255(3)	8.16	180

OREGON LAWS

Year	This Work Sec.	Note
1920, § 864	9.05	43

PENNSYLVANIA CONSOLIDATED STATUTES ANNOTATED

Sec.	This Work Sec.	Note
42, § 5929	8.13	141
42, § 5929	8.13	150

PENNSYLVANIA CONSOLIDATED STATUTES ANNOTATED

Sec.	This Work Sec.	Note
42, § 5944	8.13	141
42, § 5945	8.13	141
42, § 5945.1	8.13	141

RHODE ISLAND GENERAL LAWS

Sec.	This Work Sec.	Note
11–37–13	5.09	90

VERNON'S ANNOTATED TEXAS CIVIL STATUTES

Art.	This Work Sec.	Note
41a–1	8.20	269
4459b, § 508	8.13	139
5561h	8.13	139

V.T.C.A., CIVIL PRACTICE AND REMEDIES CODE

Sec.	This Work Sec.	Note
18.061	5.55	351

TEXAS RULES OF EVIDENCE

Rule	This Work Sec.	Note
601(a)(1)	6.02	14

VERMONT RULES OF CRIMINAL PROCEDURE

Rule	This Work Sec.	Note
26(c)	5.32	251

WEST VIRGINIA RULES OF EVIDENCE

Rule	This Work Sec.	Note
806	7.63	599

FEDERAL RULES OF CIVIL PROCEDURE

Rule	This Work Sec.	Note
25	7.47	414
26(b)(3)	8.09	
26(b)(3)	8.09	96
26(b)(3)	8.09	97
26(b)(3)	8.09	99
26(b)(3)	8.09	102
32	7.47	
32(a)	7.47	414
32(a)(3)	7.47	

*

Index

References are to sections

†

0–314–14401–3

90000

9 780314 144010